# COMPUTER GRAPHICS

## PROCEEDINGS

Annual Conference Series    1994

SIGGRAPH 94
Conference Proceedings
July 24–29, 1994
Papers Chair Andrew S. Glassner
Panels Chair Mike Keeler

A publication of ACM SIGGRAPH
Production Editor Steve Cunningham

*Sponsored by the Association for
Computing Machinery's Special
Interest Group on Computer Graphics*

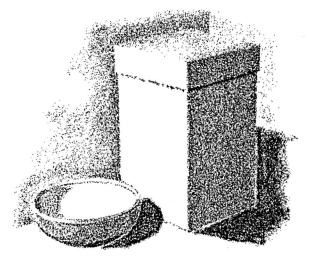

**The Association for Computing Machinery, Inc.**
1515 Broadway, 17th Floor
New York, NY 10036

Sample Citation Information:
...Proceedings of SIGGRAPH 94 (Orlando, Florida, July 24–29, 1994). In *Computer Graphics* Proceedings, Annual Conference Series, 1994, ACM SIGGRAPH, pp. xx–yy.

## ORDERING INFORMATION

**Orders from nonmembers of ACM placed within the United States should be directed to:**

Addison-Wesley Publishing Company
Order Department
Jacob Way
Reading, MA 01867
Tel: 1-800-447-2226

Addison-Wesley will pay postage and handling on orders accompanied by check. Credit card orders may be placed by mail or by calling the Addison-Wesley Order Department at the number above. Follow-up inquiries should be directed to the Customer Service Department at the same number. Please include the Addison-Wesley ISBN number with your order:
A-W Softcover Proceedings and
CD-ROM Package ISBN: 0-201-60795-6

**Orders from nonmembers of ACM placed from outside the United States should be addressed as noted below.**

**Europe/Middle East:**
Addison-Wesley Publishing Group
Concertgebouwplein 25
1071 LM Amsterdam
The Netherlands
Tel: +31 20 6717296
Fax: +31 20 6645334

**Germany/Austria/Switzerland:**
Addison-Wesley Verlag Deutschland GmbH
Hildachstraße 15d
Wachsbleiche 7-12
53111 Bonn
Germany
Tel: +49 228 98 515 0
Fax: +49 228 98 515 99

**United Kingdom/Africa:**
Addison-Wesley Publishers Ltd.
Finchampstead Road
Wokingham, Berkshire RG11 2NZ
United Kingdom
Tel: +44 734 794000
Fax: +44 734 794035

**Asia:**
Addison-Wesley Singapore Pte. Ltd.
15 Beach Road
#05-02/09/10 Beach Centre
Singapore 0718
Tel: +65 339 7503
Fax: +65 339 9709

**Japan:**
Addison-Wesley Publishers Japan Ltd.
Nichibo Building
1-2-2 Sarugakucho
Chiyoda-ku, Tokyo 101
Japan
Tel: +81 33 2914581
Fax: +81 33 2914592

**Australia/New Zealand:**
Addison-Wesley Publishers Pty. Ltd.
6 Byfield Street
North Ryde, N.S.W. 2113
Australia
Tel: +61 2 878 5411
Fax: +61 2 878 5830

**Latin America:**
Addison Wesley Iberoamericana S.A.
Boulevard de las Cataratas #3
Colonia Jardines del Pedregal
Delegacion Alvaro Obregon
01900 Mexico D.F.
Tel: +52 5 660 2695
Fax: +52 5 660 4930

**Canada:**
Addison-Wesley Publishing (Canada) Ltd.
26 Prince Andrew Place
Don Mills, Ontario M3C 2T8 Canada
Tel: 416-447-5101
Fax: 416-443-0948

**Orders from ACM Members:**

A limited number of copies are available at the ACM member discount. Send order with payment in U.S. dollars to:

ACM Order Department
P.O. Box 12114
Church Street Station
New York, NY 10257

OR, for information on accepted European currencies and exchange rates, contact:

ACM European Service Center
Avenue Marcel Thiry 204
1200 Brussels
Belgium
Tel: +32 2 774 9602
Fax: +32 2 774 9690
Email: acm_europe@acm.org

Credit card orders from U.S. and Canada:
1-800-342-6626
Credit card orders may also be placed by mail.

Credit card orders from the New York metropolitan area and outside the U.S.:
+1 212-626-0500

Single-copy orders placed by fax:
+1 212-944-1318

Electronic mail inquiries may be directed to acmhelp@acm.org.

**Please include your ACM member number and the ACM order number with your order.**

ACM Order Number: 428940

ACM ISBN: 0-89791-667-0

ISSN: 1069-529X

# Contents

## Papers Sessions, Thursday, July 28, 1994

## Papers Sessions, Friday, July 29, 1994

## Panel Sessions, Wednesday, July 27, 1994

## Panel Sessions, Thursday, July 28, 1994

# Panel Sessions, Friday, July 29, 1994

# Preface

This book contains the permanent record of the technical papers program from SIGGRAPH 94, held in late July in Orlando, Florida. It is an amazing work. I would like to share with you a look back on the the sheer amount of effort that went into the creation of the submitted papers, and the review process that selected the 57 between these covers.

This year, 242 papers (more than ever before) were submitted to the conference. These papers represented the refined and concentrated creative work of hundreds of researchers across the world. Almost 200 of those papers arrived at my office in Xerox PARC in California via courier on the day of the deadline! The intellectual and emotional energy that went into these papers is staggering; standing amidst the boxes and envelopes I felt as I do when seeing trees start to bud in spring: you know that large and highly focused forces are coming together at that moment to create something new and wonderful.

Five volunteers from Stanford University came over the next day, and we spent an intense eighteen hours opening, checking, and numbering each paper before entering it into a database. My thanks go to Maneesh Agrawala, Chase Garfinkle, Harry Sun, Greg Turk, and Eric Veach for their cheerful and dedicated help during that long day.

Chase and I spent the next two days checking everything for correctness, and then Rob Cook (the 95 papers chair) drove down, and together we sorted the papers. I invited a committee of twenty-four people, nine of whom had never served before. Rob and I had to consider each paper and determine which committee member was best qualified to be the senior reviewer, responsible for both reading and reviewing the paper, and finding at least three additional people (not on the committee) to read and review it. Additionally, we had to find a second committee member to read and review each paper, to better insure that any unintentional biases would be avoided. The job took three days to do right; we looked at each paper carefully, and did our best to make sure that the best balance was achieved. I think we did a good job, and I thank Rob for his invaluable help in making it so.

Chase and I then bundled up twenty-four boxes and got them ready for distribution to the committee members. Part of this process involved preparing the papers for blind reviewing, by removing the title sheet from each one. With this action, the only mention of the author's name and institution was removed from the paper. And since I had asked authors to try to hide their identities (e.g. by avoiding the first person when referring to previous work, not using models or images strongly associated with a certain person or group, and leaving off acknowledgements), there was usually no explicit information to tell a reviewer who wrote the paper.

I instituted blind reviewing into the review process this year because I have always wished SIGGRAPH would do it, and now I had my chance to try it out. The secrecy started just below the committee level; I felt it was appropriate for the committee to know the author's identities when deliberating on the final judgement for a paper.

My motivation in instituting a blind reviewing process was basically to make the process more fair. The basic thinking is that if a reviewer doesn't know who wrote a paper, then they are less likely to be biased in their review. I know from my personal experience that I have been influenced by an author's reputation when reviewing a paper. I think it's inevitable and very difficult to suppress. The arguments against blind reviewing are important and need to be addressed. They boil down to two: it is an increase in the amount of work for the committee, and some reviewers will guess the identity of some authors.

The first argument is perfectly accurate: I estimate that when all was said and done, this procedure added about 20% to the time required by myself and the committee to handle the entire process. I decided that the benefits were worth the cost.

The validity of the latter argument varies greatly, depending on how forcefully it is put. Some people feel that if a reviewer cannot guess the identity of the author, than that person is not qualified to review the paper. I disagree; although it is important that a reviewer be current with the field, that person does not need to have a personal or social connection with everyone else in order to be an effective judge of technical results. This leads to a weaker form of the argument, which is that most reviewers will guess most authors. I think that again this is too strong, and is a result of the fact that some people publish more often than others, and have developed a recognizable style. This is true for some authors, but by no means all. I am happy to report that most of the papers submitted this year came from authors whose work has rarely (or never) appeared in SIGGRAPH before, and whose style is therefore unfamiliar. We are left with the argument that some reviewers will guess some authors, and this I agree with. I see no way around it, but I don't see it as a major problem. My goal was not to trick reviewers, make a game of guessing authors, or damage the quality of papers by imposing overly-strong stylistic constraints. I realized some people would correctly guess some authors, but others wouldn't, and in any case few would know for sure. I felt that this was a reasonable place to draw the line.

When the papers came back to the senior reviewers, the final scores were collated and final reports written. The entire committee then met for two days to assemble the papers program.

An opportunity was available to us for the first time in over a decade: parallel papers sessions at the conference. In previous years this was disallowed by SIGGRAPH rules, or else prohibited by the cost of producing and printing larger proceedings. The formal prohibition had been lifted some years before, so that hurdle was gone. Just as significant was the decision by the SIGGRAPH 94 chair, Dino Schweitzer, to allow parallel paper sessions in the conference, and to support the publication of all the papers we selected. This was a difficult and brave decision, and I thank Dino for unlocking that door for us.

There was no intention, going into the meeting, that we would certainly have parallel papers sessions. Personally, I didn't like the idea very much: I enjoy the papers presentations, and regularly found myself torn between the many parallel tracks SIGGRAPH already supported in papers, panels, art show, animation screening room, exhibition, and so on. But I decided that the proceedings offered a permanent and detailed record of the research work, and that our job was to assemble the best collection of innovative, stimulating, and imaginative work we could. In the final analysis, if one felt torn between presentations, one could read the missed paper in the proceedings.

With this in mind, I started our committee meeting by encouraging everyone to simply select the best papers for the conference, and we would somehow create a schedule when we were done. I didn't care if we accepted 20 papers or 80, as long as we accepted the best ones for our community. When we finished two days later, we had selected 57 papers — a new record. Several volunteers stayed after the meeting to organize the papers into thematically-related sessions. The rest was sheer arithmetic: we had eleven time slots and thirteen sessions, so two sessions were doubled up and parallel papers appeared. I am sad that we have introduced this extra parallelism, but I am happy that we found so many papers of such quality that they had to be included. I feel strongly that this was the right result for our community.

The committee meeting itself was exhilarating. It's rare in my life that I have been surrounded by two dozen highly intelligent, informed, opinionated, and articulate people speaking their minds openly and directly; there simply wasn't time for extended diplomacy and subtlety. Because anyone related to a paper under discussion had to leave the room, papers authored by committee members were judged by the same standards (or perhaps even a slightly higher standard) as all the others. I feel that everyone on the committee worked hard to be as fair as they could be, and I am impressed by the integrity and honesty of each member. It was an honor to serve with them, and I thank them each for their contributions.

Computer graphics is an exciting field in which to work. It combines abstract thought with pragmatic implementation, mathematical elegance with visual pleasure. We are creating a new medium for expression, and as social theorists from McLuhan to Postman have observed, new media let us say new things about ourselves and our world. It's rewarding to work in a field that integrates our intellectual and artistic instincts so deeply. To create meaningful images and animations we need to combine all the tools of cinematography, computer science, psychology, visual art, movement, fiction, physiology, mathematics, and other fields. The promise of computer graphics is that it offers us another way to communicate with our hearts and minds, to say things that we need to say, and hear things that we need to hear. By pressing against the limits and grasping for new possibilities in the medium, we create the chance to find new ways to express important truths about ourselves and our relationships with each other and the world. At its best, computer graphics transcends both the computer and the graphics to become something new, and that is what we are all striving to discover and explore.

Acting as the papers chair has been a difficult but thrilling experience. It has pushed me intellectually, physically, spiritually, and emotionally. I have been greatly helped and supported by my employer, Xerox PARC, and I've received encouragement and advice from many members of the computer graphics community around the world. To all that have helped me, I thank you. I must also single out my assistant, Chase Garfinkle, for his untold hours of labor doing everything from programming databases to addressing envelopes; I could not have done this job alone. Thanks, Chase.

This year I have created a new venue at the conference itself. Called "Technical Sketches", this is an opportunity for researchers to present their work in an informal setting. There is no published record from the Technical Sketches program except for a 30-word abstract of each paper in the final program. This way nobody risks being turned down by a journal who might otherwise consider this a prior publication, yet by handing out a technical report or similar document they can clearly and publicly establish priority on the idea and work. The spirit of Technical Sketches is something like an oral poster session. Speakers will be encouraged to present new and exciting ideas that are not yet mature enough for the technical program, and can benefit from conversations and discussions with the community at large. I hope this will provide an opportunity for people to meet each other and have stimulating conversations.

The work of the committee and hundreds of reviewers is done, and you hold in your hands the distilled essence of the best efforts we have seen. May you find tools, and inspiration.

— Andrew Glassner

## 1994 ACM SIGGRAPH Awards

# Computer Graphics Achievement Award

# Kenneth E. Torrance

The SIGGRAPH Achievement Award is presented to Dr. Kenneth E. Torrance in recognition of his contributions in the fields of radiosity and physically-based reflectance models. These contributions are the underpinnings of the majority of computer graphics images produced during the past fifteen years.

Kenneth Torrance received his Bachelor's (1961), Master's (1962) and doctoral (1966) degrees in Mechanical Engineering from the University of Minnesota, where Ephraim Sparrow served as his graduate advisor. He was a visitor at the National Institute for Standards and Technology in Washington, DC, and the National Center for Atmospheric Research in Boulder, Colorado. Dr. Torrance is Professor of Mechanical and Aerospace Engineering at Cornell University, Ithaca, New York where he has also served as Associate Dean of the College of Engineering. A Fellow of the American Association of Mechanical Engineers, he has nearly ninety publications in the fields of combustion, heat transfer, experimental and computational methods, and realistic image synthesis in computer graphics. His work has included interdisciplinary studies in such fields as destructive fires, environmental and geophysical fluid motions, and industrial thermal management.

Dr. Torrance was known to the computer graphics community before the computer graphics community was known to him. Jim Blinn initially employed the Torrance-Sparrow model as the first application of a physically-based reflectance model in 1977. Dr. Torrance subsequently collaborated with Rob Cook in 1980 to apply a more complete version of this model.[1] In 1991, with Sheldon He and others, Torrance improved the model and compared and verified the results with experimental values.

These contributions became even more significant when, over a period of several years, he and and Don Greenberg collaborated to guide many students who developed and expanded the radiosity approach to rendering. Radiosity represented a new and important basic paradigm for rendering. It is based on a global model of the interaction of light and surfaces. The complexity of these interactions of light with many surfaces was previously considered intractable. Torrance provided the guiding light and scientific leadership over more than a decade of critical development of this new paradigm.

Torrance's seminal work inspired other computer graphics researchers at several institutions to explore this new approach.

---

[1] Both Blinn and Cook received SIGGRAPH Achievement Awards based, in part, on this important contribution.

Indeed, we might well say that Torrance is the father of radiosity in computer graphics.

### References

Torrance, K.E. and E.M. Sparrow, "Theory for Off-Specular Reflection from Roughened Surfaces," *J. Opt. Soc. Am.*, 57(9), September 1967, 1105-1114.

Cook, Robert L., and Torrance, Kenneth E., "A Reflectance Model for Computer Graphics," *Computer Graphics* (SIGGRAPH '81 Proceedings) vol 15, August 1981, 307-316. Republished by request in *ACM Transactions on Graphics*, vol. 1, no. 1, January 1982, 7-24. Republished by request in *Computer Graphics: Image Synthesis*, ed. K. Joy, C.W. Grant, N.L. Max and L. Hatfield, Computer Society of IEEE Press, Washington, DC, 1988, 244-253.

Goral, Cindy M., Torrance, Kenneth E., Greenberg, Donald P., and Battaile, Bennett, "Modeling the Interaction of Light Between Diffuse Surfaces," *Computer Graphics* (SIGGRAPH '84 Proceedings), vol. 18, no. 3, July 1984, 213-222.

Meyer, G.W., H.E. Rushmeier, M. F. Cohen, D. P. Greenberg and K. E. Torrance, "An Experimental Assessment of Computer Graphics Images," *ACM Transactions on Graphics*, vol 5, January 1986, 30-50.

Greenberg, D.P., M.F. Cohen and K.E. Torrance, "Radiosity: A Method for Computing Global Illumination," *The Visual Computer*, vol 2, 1986, pp. 291-297.

Rushmeier, Holly E. and Torrance, Kenneth E., "The Zonal Method for Calculating Light Intensities in the Presence of a Participating Medium", *Computer Graphics* (SIGGRAPH '87 Proceedings), vol. 21, no. 4, July 1987, 293-302.

Rushmeier, H.E. and K.E. Torrance, "Extending the Radiosity Method to Include Specularly Reflecting and Transmitting Materials," *ACM Transactions on Graphics*, vol 9, January 1990, 1-27.

He, Xiao D., Torrance, Kenneth E., Sillion, François X., and Greenberg, Donald P., "A Comprehensive Physical Model for Light Reflection," *Computer Graphics* (SIGGRAPH '91 Proceedings), vol. 25, no. 4, July 1991, 175-186.

He, Xiao D., Heynen, Patrick O., Phillips, Richard L., Torrance, Kenneth E., Salesin, David H. and Greenberg, Donald P., "A Fast and Accurate Light Reflection Model," *Computer Graphics* (SIGGRAPH '92 Proceedings), vol. 26, no. 2, July 1992, 253-254.

Westin, Stephen H., Arvo, James R., and Torrance, Kenneth E., "Predicting Reflectance Functions from Complex Surfaces," *Computer Graphics* (SIGGRAPH '92 Proceedings), vol. 26, no. 2, July 1992, 255-264.

Arvo, James, Kenneth Torrance, and Brian Smits, "A Framework for the Analysis of Error in Global Illumination Algorithms," *Computer Graphics* (SIGGRAPH '94 Proceedings), Annual Conference Series, 1994, 75-84.

**Previous award winners**

| | |
|---|---|
| 1993 | Pat Hanrahan |
| 1992 | Henry Fuchs |
| 1991 | James T. Kajiya |
| 1990 | Richard Shoup and Alvy Ray Smith |
| 1989 | John Warnock |
| 1988 | Alan H. Barr |
| 1987 | Robert Cook |
| 1986 | Turner Whitted |
| 1985 | Loren Carpenter |
| 1984 | James H. Clark |
| 1983 | James F. Blinn |

# Evolving Virtual Creatures

## Karl Sims

Thinking Machines Corporation
245 First Street, Cambridge, MA 02142

## Abstract

This paper describes a novel system for creating virtual creatures that move and behave in simulated three-dimensional physical worlds. The morphologies of creatures and the neural systems for controlling their muscle forces are both generated automatically using genetic algorithms. Different fitness evaluation functions are used to direct simulated evolutions towards specific behaviors such as swimming, walking, jumping, and following.

A genetic language is presented that uses nodes and connections as its primitive elements to represent directed graphs, which are used to describe both the morphology and the neural circuitry of these creatures. This genetic language defines a hyperspace containing an indefinite number of possible creatures with behaviors, and when it is searched using optimization techniques, a variety of successful and interesting locomotion strategies emerge, some of which would be difficult to invent or build by design.

## 1 Introduction

A classic trade-off in the field of computer graphics and animation is that of complexity vs. control. It is often difficult to build interesting or realistic virtual entities and still maintain control over them. Sometimes it is difficult to build a complex virtual world at all, if it is necessary to conceive, design, and assemble each component. An example of this trade-off is that of kinematic control vs. dynamic simulation. If we directly provide the positions and angles for moving objects, we can control each detail of their behavior, but it might be difficult to achieve physically plausible motions. If we instead provide forces and torques and simulate the resulting dynamics, the result will probably look correct, but then it can be very difficult to achieve the desired behavior, especially as the objects we want to control become more complex. Methods have been developed for dynamically controlling specific objects to successfully crawl, walk, or even run [11,12,16], but a new control algorithm must be carefully designed each time a new behavior or morphology is desired.

Optimization techniques offer possibilities for the automatic generation of complexity. The genetic algorithm is a form of artificial evolution, and is a commonly used method for optimization. A Darwinian "survival of the fittest" approach is employed to search for optima in large multidimensional spaces [5,7]. Genetic algorithms permit virtual entities to be created without requiring an understanding of the procedures or parameters used to generate them. The measure of success, or *fitness*, of each individual can be

calculated automatically, or it can instead be provided interactively by a user. Interactive evolution allows procedurally generated results to be explored by simply choosing those that are the most aesthetically desirable for each generation [2,18,19,21].

The user sacrifices some control when using these methods, especially when the fitness is procedurally defined. However, the potential gain in automating the creation of complexity can often compensate for this loss of control, and a higher level of user influence is still maintained by the fitness criteria specification.

In several cases, optimization has been used to automatically generate dynamic control systems for given articulated structures: de Garis has evolved weight values for neural networks [4], Ngo and Marks have performed genetic algorithms on stimulus-response pairs [14], and van de Panne and Fiume have optimized sensor-actuator networks [15]. Each of these methods has resulted in successful locomotion of two-dimensional stick figures.

The work presented here is related to these projects, but differs in several respects. In previous work, control systems were generated for fixed structures that were user-designed, but here entire creatures are evolved: the optimization determines the creature morphologies as well as their control systems. Also, here the creatures' bodies are three-dimensional and fully physically based. The three-dimensional physical structure of a creature can adapt to its control system, and vice versa, as they evolve together. The "nervous systems" of creatures are also completely determined by the optimization: the number of internal nodes, the connectivity, and the type of function each neural node performs are included in the genetic description of each creature, and can grow in complexity as an evolution proceeds. Together, these remove the necessity for a user to provide any specific creature information such as shape, size, joint constraints, sensors, actuators, or internal neural parameters. Finally, here a developmental process is used to generate the creatures and their control systems, and allows similar components including their local neural circuitry to be defined once and then replicated, instead of requiring each to be separately specified. This approach is related to L-systems, graftal grammars, and object instancing techniques [6,8,10,13,20].

It is convenient to use the biological terms *genotype* and *phenotype* when discussing artificial evolution. A *genotype* is a coded representation of a possible individual or problem solution. In biological systems, a genotype is usually composed of DNA and contains the instructions for the development of an organism. Genetic algorithms typically use populations of genotypes consisting of strings of binary digits or parameters. These are read to produce *phenotypes* which are then evaluated according to some fitness criteria and selectively reproduced. New genotypes are generated by copying, mutating, and/or combining the genotypes of the most fit individuals, and as the cycle repeats the population should ascend to higher and higher levels of fitness.

Variable length genotypes such as hierarchical Lisp expressions or other computer programs can be useful in expanding the set of possible results beyond a predefined genetic space of fixed dimensions. Genetic languages such as these allow new parameters and new dimensions to be added to the genetic space as an evolution proceeds, and therefore define rather a *hyperspace* of possible results. This approach has been used to genetically program solutions to a variety of problems [1,9], as well as to explore procedurally generated images and dynamical systems [18,19].

In the spirit of unbounded genetic languages, directed graphs are presented here as an appropriate basis for a grammar that can be used to describe both the morphology and nervous systems of virtual creatures. New features and functions can be added to creatures, or existing ones removed, so the levels of complexity can also evolve.

The next two sections explain how virtual creatures can be represented by directed graphs. The system used for physical simulation is summarized in section 4, and section 5 describes how specific behaviors can be selected. Section 6 explains how evolutions are performed with directed graph genotypes, and finally a range of resulting creatures is shown.

## 2 Creature Morphology

In this work, the phenotype embodiment of a virtual creature is a hierarchy of articulated three-dimensional rigid parts. The genetic representation of this morphology is a directed graph of nodes and connections. Each graph contains the developmental instructions for growing a creature, and provides a way of reusing instructions to make similar or recursive components within the creature. A phenotype hierarchy of parts is made from a graph by starting at a

defined *root-node* and synthesizing parts from the node information while tracing through the connections of the graph. The graph can be recurrent. Nodes can connect to themselves or in cycles to form recursive or fractal like structures. They can also connect to the same child multiple times to make duplicate instances of the same appendage.

Each node in the graph contains information describing a rigid part. The *dimensions* determine the physical shape of the part. A *joint-type* determines the constraints on the relative motion between this part and its parent by defining the number of degrees of freedom of the joint and the movement allowed for each degree of freedom. The different joint-types allowed are: *rigid, revolute, twist, universal, bend-twist, twist-bend,* or *spherical. Joint-limits* determine the point beyond which restoring spring forces will be exerted for each degree of freedom. A *recursive-limit* parameter determines how many times this node should generate a phenotype part when in a recursive cycle. A set of local *neurons* is also included in each node, and will be explained further in the next section. Finally, a node contains a set of *connections* to other nodes.

Each connection also contains information. The placement of a child part relative to its parent is decomposed into *position, orientation, scale,* and *reflection,* so each can be mutated independently. The position of attachment is constrained to be on the surface of the parent part. Reflections cause negative scaling, and allow similar but symmetrical sub-trees to be described. A *terminal-only* flag can cause a connection to be applied only when the recursive limit is reached, and permits tail or hand-like components to occur at the end of chains or repeating units.

Figure 1 shows some simple hand-designed graph topologies and resulting phenotype morphologies. Note that the parameters in the nodes and connections such as *recursive-limit* are not shown for the genotype even though they affect the morphology of the phenotype. The nodes are anthropomorphically labeled as "body," "leg," etc. but the genetic descriptions actually have no concept of specific categories of functional components.

## 3 Creature Control

A virtual "brain" determines the behavior of a creature. The brain is a dynamical system that accepts input sensor values and provides output effector values. The output values are applied as forces or torques at the degrees of freedom of the body's joints. This cycle of effects is shown in Figure 2.

Sensor, effector, and internal neuron signals are represented here by continuously variable scalars that may be positive or negative. Allowing negative values permits the implementation of single effectors that can both push and pull. Although this may not be biologically realistic, it simplifies the more natural development of muscle pairs.

**Genotype**: directed graph.    **Phenotype**: hierarchy of 3D parts.

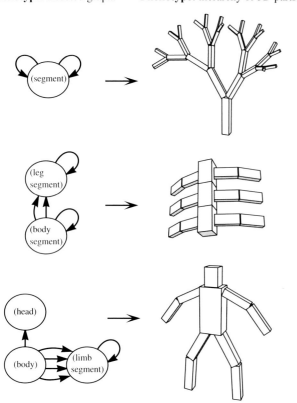

**Figure 1**: Designed examples of genotype graphs and corresponding creature morphologies.

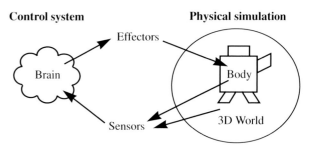

**Figure 2**: The cycle of effects between brain, body and world.

## 3.1 Sensors

Each sensor is contained within a specific part of the body, and measures either aspects of that part or aspects of the world relative to that part. Three different types of sensors were used for these experiments:

1. *Joint angle sensors* give the current value for each degree of freedom of each joint.

2. *Contact sensors* activate (1.0) if a contact is made, and negatively activate (-1.0) if not. Each contact sensor has a sensitive region within a part's shape and activates when any contacts occur in that area. In this work, contact sensors are made available for each face of each part. No distinction is made between self-contact and environmental contact.

3. *Photosensors* react to a global light source position. Three photosensor signals provide the coordinates of the normalized light source direction relative to the orientation of the part. This is the same as having pairs of opposing photosensitive surfaces in which the left side negates its response and adds it to the right side for the total response.

Other types of sensors, such as accelerometers, additional proprioceptors, or even sound or smell detectors could also be implemented, but these basic three are enough to allow interesting and adaptive behaviors to occur. The inclusion of the different types of sensors in an evolving virtual brain can be enabled or disabled as appropriate depending on the physical environment and behavior goals. For example, contact sensors are enabled for land environments, and photosensors are enabled for following behaviors.

## 3.2 Neurons

Internal neural nodes are used to give virtual creatures the possibility of arbitrary behavior. Ideally a creature should be able to have an internal state beyond its sensor values, or be affected by its history.

In this work, different neural nodes can perform diverse functions on their inputs to generate their output signals. Because of this, a creature's brain might resemble a dataflow computer program more than a typical neural network. This approach is probably less biologically realistic than just using sum and threshold functions, but it is hoped that it makes the evolution of interesting behaviors more likely. The set of functions that neural nodes can have is: *sum, product, divide, sum-threshold, greater-than, sign-of, min, max, abs, if, interpolate, sin, cos, atan, log, expt, sigmoid, integrate, differentiate, smooth, memory, oscillate-wave, and oscillate-saw.*

Some functions compute an output directly from their inputs, while others such as the oscillators retain some state and can give time varying outputs even when their inputs are constant. The number of inputs to a neuron depends on its function, and here is at most three. Each input contains a connection to another neuron or a sensor from which to receive a value. Alternatively, an input can simply receive a constant value. The input values are first scaled by weights before being operated on.

For each simulated time interval, every neuron computes its output value from its inputs. In this work, two brain time steps are performed for each dynamic simulation time step so signals can propagate through multiple neurons with less delay.

## 3.3 Effectors

Each effector simply contains a connection to a neuron or a sensor from which to receive a value. This input value is scaled by a constant weight, and then exerted as a joint force which affects the dynamic simulation and the resulting behavior of the creature. Different types of effectors, such as sound or scent emitters, might also be interesting, but only effectors that exert simulated muscle forces are used here.

Each effector controls a degree of freedom of a joint. The effectors for a given joint connecting two parts, are contained in the part further out in the hierarchy, so that each non-root part operates only a single joint connecting it to its parent. The angle sensors for that joint are also contained in this part.

Each effector is given a *maximum-strength* proportional to the maximum cross sectional area of the two parts it joins. Effector forces are scaled by these strengths and not permitted to exceed them. Since strength scales with area, but mass scales with volume, as in nature, behavior does not always scale uniformly.

## 3.4 Combining Morphology and Control

The genotype descriptions of virtual brains and the actual phenotype brains are both directed graphs of nodes and connections. The nodes contain the sensors, neurons, and effectors, and the connections define the flow of signals between these nodes. These graphs can also be recurrent, and as a result the final control system can have feedback loops and cycles.

However, most of these neural elements exist within a specific part of the creature. Thus the genotype for the nervous system is a nested graph: the morphological nodes each contain graphs of the neural nodes and connections. Figure 3 shows an example of an evolved nested graph.

When a creature is synthesized from its genetic description, the neural components described within each part are generated along with the morphological structure. This causes blocks of neural control circuitry to be replicated along with each instanced part, so each duplicated segment or appendage of a creature can have a similar but independent local control system.

These local control systems can be connected to enable the possibility of coordinated control. Connections are allowed between adjacent parts in the hierarchy: the neurons and effectors within a part can receive signals from sensors or neurons in their parent part or in their child parts.

Creatures are also given a set of neurons that are not associated

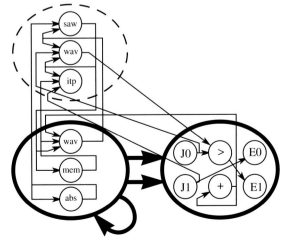

**Figure 3**: Example evolved nested graph genotype. The outer graph in bold describes a creature's morphology. The inner graph describes its neural circuitry. J0 and J1 are joint angle sensors, and E0 and E1 are effector outputs. The dashed node contains centralized neurons that are not associated with any part.

with a specific part, and are copied only once into the phenotype. This gives the opportunity for the development of global synchronization or centralized control. These neurons can receive signals from each other or from sensors or neurons in specific instances of any of the creature's parts, and the neurons and effectors within the parts can optionally receive signals from these unassociated-neuron outputs.

In this way the genetic language for morphology and control is merged. A local control system is described for each type of part, and these are copied and connected into the hierarchy of the crea-

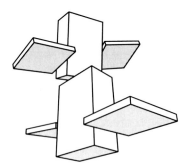

**Figure 4a**: The phenotype morphology generated from the evolved genotype shown in figure 3.

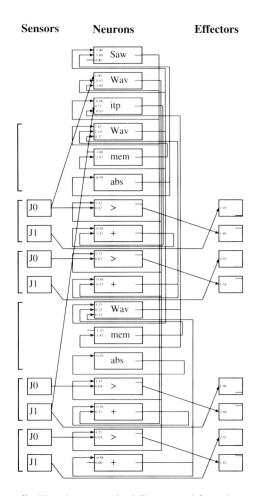

**Figure 4b**: The phenotype "brain" generated from the evolved genotype shown in figure 3. The effector outputs of this control system cause paddling motions in the four flippers of the morphology above.

ture's body to make a complete distributed nervous system. Figure 4a shows the creature morphology resulting from the genotype in figure 3. Again, parameters describing shapes, recursive-limits, and weights are not shown for the genotype even though they affect the phenotype. Figure 4b shows the corresponding brain of this creature. The brackets on the left side of figure 4b group the neural components of each part. Some groups have similar neural systems because they are copies from the same genetic description. This creature can swim by making cyclic paddling motions with four similar flippers. Note that it can be difficult to analyze exactly how a control system such as this works, and some components may not actually be used at all. Fortunately, a primary benefit of using artificial evolution is that understanding these representations is not necessary.

## 4 Physical Simulation

Dynamics simulation is used to calculate the movement of creatures resulting from their interaction with a virtual three-dimensional world. There are several components of the physical simulation used in this work: articulated body dynamics, numerical integration, collision detection, collision response, friction, and an optional viscous fluid effect. These are only briefly summarized here, since physical simulation is not the emphasis of this paper.

Featherstone's recursive O(N) articulated body method is used to calculate the accelerations from the velocities and external forces of each hierarchy of connected rigid parts [3]. Integration determines the resulting motions from these accelerations and is performed by a Runge-Kutta-Fehlberg method which is a fourth order Runge-Kutta with an additional evaluation to estimate the error and adapt the step size. Typically between 1 and 5 integration time steps are performed for each frame of 1/30 second.

The shapes of parts are represented here by simple rectangular solids. Bounding box hierarchies are used to reduce the number of collision tests between parts from $O(N^2)$. Pairs whose world-space bounding boxes intersect are tested for penetrations, and collisions with a ground plane are also tested if one exists. If necessary, the previous time-step is reduced to keep any new penetrations below a certain tolerance. Connected parts are permitted to interpenetrate but not rotate completely through each other. This is achieved by using adjusted shapes when testing for collisions between connected parts. The shape of the smaller part is clipped halfway back from its point of attachment so it can swing freely until its remote end makes contact.

Collision response is accomplished by a hybrid model using both impulses and penalty spring forces. At high velocities, instantaneous impulse forces are used, and at low velocities springs are used, to simulate collisions and contacts with arbitrary elasticity and friction parameters.

A viscosity effect is used for the simulations in underwater environments. For each exposed moving surface, a viscous force resists the normal component of its velocity, proportional to its surface area and normal velocity magnitude. This is a simple approximation that does not include the motion of the fluid itself, but is still sufficient for simulating realistic looking swimming and paddling dynamics.

It is important that the physical simulation be reasonably accurate when optimizing for creatures that can move within it. Any bugs that allow energy leaks from non-conservation, or even round-off errors, will inevitably be discovered and exploited by the evolving creatures. Although this can be a lazy and often amusing approach for debugging a physical modeling system, it is not necessarily the most practical.

# 5 Behavior Selection

In this work, virtual creatures are evolved by optimizing for a specific task or behavior. A creature is grown from its genetic description as previously explained, and then it is placed in a dynamically simulated virtual world. The brain provides effector forces which move parts of the creature, the sensors report aspects of the world and the creature's body back to the brain, and the resulting physical behavior of the creature is evaluated. After a certain duration of virtual time (perhaps 10 seconds), a *fitness* value is assigned that corresponds to the success level of that behavior. If a creature has a high fitness relative to the rest of the population, it will be selected for survival and reproduction as described in the next section.

Before creatures are simulated for fitness evaluation, some simple viability checks are performed, and inappropriate creatures are removed from the population by giving them zero fitness values. Those that have more than a specified number of parts are removed. A subset of genotypes will generate creatures whose parts initially interpenetrate. A short simulation with collision detection and response attempts to repel any intersecting parts, but those creatures with persistent interpenetrations are also discarded.

Computation can be conserved for most fitness methods by discontinuing the simulations of individuals that are predicted to be unlikely to survive the next generation. The fitness is periodically estimated for each simulation as it proceeds. Those are stopped that are either not moving at all or are doing somewhat worse than the minimum fitness of the previously surviving individuals.

Many different types of fitness measures can be used to perform evolutions of virtual creatures. Four examples of fitness methods are described here.

## 5.1 Swimming

Physical simulation of a water environment is achieved by turning off gravity and adding the viscous water resistance effect as described. Swimming speed is used as the fitness value and is measured by the distance traveled by the creature's center of mass per unit time. Straight swimming is rewarded over circling by using the maximum distance from the initial center of mass. Continuing movement is rewarded over that from a single initial push, by giving the velocities during the final phase of the test period a stronger relative weight in the total fitness value.

## 5.2 Walking

The term *walking* is used loosely here to indicate any form of land locomotion. A land environment is simulated by including gravity, turning off the viscous water effect, and adding a static ground plane with friction. Additional inanimate objects can be placed in the world for more complex environments. Again, speed is used as the selection criteria, but the vertical component of velocity is ignored.

For land environments, it can be necessary to prevent creatures from generating high velocities by simply falling over. This is accomplished by first running the simulation with no friction and no effector forces until the height of the center of mass reaches a stable minimum.

## 5.3 Jumping

Jumping behavior can be selected for by measuring the maximum height above the ground of the lowest part of the creature. An alternative method is to use the average height of the lowest part of the creature during the duration of simulation.

## 5.4 Following

Another evaluation method is used to select for creatures that can adaptively follow a light source. Photosensors are enabled, so the effector output forces and resulting behavior can depend on the relative direction of a light source to the creature. Several trials are run with the light source in different locations, and the speeds at which a creature moves toward it are averaged for the fitness value. Following behaviors can be evolved for both water and land environments.

Fleeing creatures can also be generated in a similar manner, or following behavior can be transformed into fleeing behavior by simply negating a creature's photo sensor signals.

Once creatures are found that exhibit successful following behaviors, they can be led around in arbitrary paths by movement of the light sources.

# 6 Creature Evolution

An evolution of virtual creatures is begun by first creating an initial population of genotypes. These initial genotypes can come from several possible sources: new genotypes can be synthesized "from scratch" by random generation of sets of nodes and connections, an existing genotype from a previous evolution can be used to seed the initial population of a new evolution, or a seed genotype can be designed by hand. However, no hand-designed seed genotypes were used in the examples shown here.

A *survival-ratio* determines the percentage of the population that will survive each generation. In this work, population sizes were typically 300, and the survival ratio was 1/5. If the initially generated population has fewer individuals with positive fitness than the number that should survive, another round of seed genotypes is generated to replace those with zero fitness.

For each generation, creatures are grown from their genetic descriptions, and their fitness values are measured by a method such as those described in the previous section. The individuals whose fitnesses fall within the survival percentile are then reproduced, and their offspring fill the slots of those individuals that did not survive. The survivors are kept in the population for the next generation, and the total size of the population is maintained. The number of offspring that each surviving individual generates is proportional to its fitness – the most successful creatures make the most children.

Offspring are generated from the surviving creatures by copying and combining their directed graph genotypes. When these graphs are reproduced they are subjected to probabilistic variation or mutation, so the corresponding phenotypes are similar to their parents but have been altered or adjusted in random ways.

## 6.1 Mutating Directed Graphs

A directed graph is mutated by the following sequence of steps:

1. The internal parameters of each node are subjected to possible alterations. A mutation frequency for each parameter type determines the probability that a mutation will be applied to it at all. Boolean values are mutated by simply flipping their state. Scalar values are mutated by adding several random numbers to them for a Gaussian-like distribution so small adjustments are more likely than drastic ones. The scale of an adjustment is relative to the original value, so large quantities can be varied more easily and small ones can be carefully tuned. A scalar can also be negated. After a mutation occurs, values are clamped to their legal bounds. Some parameters that only have a limited number of legal values are mutated by simply picking a new value at random from the set

of possibilities.

2. A new random node is added to the graph. A new node normally has no effect on the phenotype unless a connection also mutates a pointer to it. Therefore a new node is always initially added, but then garbage collected later (in step 5) if it does not become connected. This type of mutation allows the complexity of the graph to grow as an evolution proceeds.

3. The parameters of each connection are subjected to possible mutations, in the same way the node parameters were in step 1. With some frequency the connection pointer is moved to point to a different node which is chosen at random.

4. New random connections are added and existing ones are removed. In the case of the neural graphs these operations are not performed because the number of inputs for each element is fixed, but the morphological graphs can have a variable number of connections per node. Each existing node is subject to having a new random connection added to it, and each existing connection is subject to possible removal.

5. Unconnected elements are garbage collected. Connectedness is propagated outwards through the connections of the graph, starting from the root node of the morphology, or from the effector nodes of neural graphs. Although leaving the disconnected nodes for possible reconnection might be advantageous, and is probably biologically analogous, at least the unconnected newly added ones are removed to prevent unnecessary growth in graph size.

Since mutations are performed on a per element basis, genotypes with only a few elements might not receive any mutations, where genotypes with many elements would receive enough mutations that they rarely resemble their parents. This is compensated for by temporarily scaling the mutation frequencies by an amount inversely proportional to the size of the current graph being mutated, such that on the average, at least one mutation occurs in the entire graph.

Mutation of nested directed graphs, as are used here to represent creatures, is performed by first mutating the outer graph and then mutating the inner layer of graphs. The inner graphs are mutated last because legal values for some of their parameters (inter-node neural input sources) can depend on the topology of the outer graph.

## 6.2  Mating Directed Graphs

Sexual reproduction allows components from more than one parent to be combined into new offspring. This permits features to evolve independently and later be merged into a single individual. Two different methods for mating directed graphs are presented.

The first is a *crossover* operation (see figure 5a). The nodes of two parents are each aligned in a row as they are stored, and the nodes of the first parent are copied to make the child, but one or more crossover points determine when the copying source should switch to the other parent. The connections of a node are copied with it and simply point to the same relative node locations as before. If the copied connections now point out of bounds because of varying node numbers they are randomly reassigned.

A second mating method *grafts* two genotypes together by connecting a node of one parent to a node of another (see figure 5b). The first parent is copied, and one of its connections is chosen at random and adjusted to point to a random node in the second parent. Newly unconnected nodes of the first parent are removed and the newly connected node of the second parent and any of its descendants are appended to the new graph.

A new directed graph can be produced by either of these two mating methods, or asexually by using only mutations. Offspring

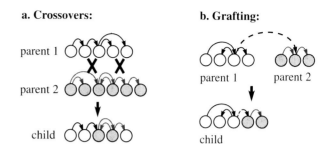

**Figure 5**: Two methods for mating directed graphs.

from matings are sometimes subjected to mutations afterwards, but with reduced mutation frequencies. In this work a reproduction method is chosen at random for each child to be produced by the surviving individuals using the ratios: 40% asexual, 30% crossovers, and 30% grafting. A second parent is chosen from the survivors if necessary, and a new genotype is produced from the parent or parents.

After a new generation of genotypes is created, a phenotype creature is generated from each, and again their fitness levels are evaluated. As this cycle of variation and selection continues, the population is directed towards creatures with higher and higher fitness.

## 6.3  Parallel Implementation

This genetic algorithm has been implemented to run in parallel on a Connection Machine® CM-5 in a master/slave message passing model. A single processing node performs the genetic algorithm. It farms out genotypes to the other nodes to be fitness tested, and gathers back the fitness values after they have been determined. The fitness tests each include a dynamics simulation and although most can execute in nearly real-time, they are still the dominant computational requirement of the system. Performing a fitness test per processor is a simple but effective way to parallelize this genetic algorithm, and the overall performance scales quite linearly with the number of processors, as long as the population size is somewhat larger than the number of processors.

Each fitness test takes a different amount of time to compute depending on the complexity of the creature and how it attempts to move. To prevent idle processors from just waiting for others to finish, new generations are started before the fitness tests have been completed for all individuals. Those slower simulations are simply skipped during that reproductive cycle, so all processors remain active. With this approach, an evolution with population size 300, run for 100 generations, might take around three hours to complete on a 32 processor CM-5.

## 7  Results

Evolutions were performed for each of the behavior selection methods described in section 5. A population of interbreeding creatures often converges toward homogeneity, but each separately run evolution can produce completely different locomotion strategies that satisfy the requested behavior. For this reason, many separate evolutions were performed, each for 50 to 100 generations, and the most successful creatures of each evolution were inspected. A selection of these is shown in figures 6-9. In a few cases, genotypes resulting from one evolution were used as seed genotypes for a second evolution.

The swimming fitness measure produced a large number of

simple paddling and tail wagging creatures. A variety of more complex strategies also emerged from some evolutions. A few creatures pulled themselves through the water with specialized sculling appendages. Some used two symmetrical flippers or even large numbers of similar flippers to propel themselves, and several multi-segmented watersnake creatures evolved that wind through the water with sinusoidal motions.

The walking fitness measure also produced a surprising number of simple creatures that could shuffle or hobble along at fairly high speeds. Some walk with lizard-like gaits using the corners of their parts. Some simply wag an appendage in the air to rock back and forth in just the right manner to move forward. A number of more complex creatures emerged that push or pull themselves along, inchworm style. Others use one or more leg-like appendages to successfully crawl or walk. Some hopping creatures even emerged that raise and lower arm-like structures to bound along at fairly high speeds.

The jumping fitness measure did not seem to produce as many different strategies as the swimming and walking optimizations, but a number of simple jumping creatures did emerge.

The light-following fitness measure was used in both water and land environments, and produced a wide variety of creatures that can swim or walk towards a light source. Some consistently and successfully follow the light source at different locations. Others can follow it some of the time, but then at certain relative locations fail to turn towards it. In the water environment, some developed steering fins that turn them towards the light using photosensor inputs. Others adjust the angle of their paddles appropriately as they oscillate along.

Sometimes a user may want to exert more control on the results of this process instead of simply letting creatures evolve entirely automatically. Aesthetic selection is a possible way to achieve this,

**Figure 7**: Creatures evolved for walking.

**Figure 8**: Creatures evolved for jumping.

but observation of the trial simulations of every creature and providing every fitness value interactively would require too much patience on the part of the user. A convenient way of mixing automatic selection with aesthetic selection, is to observe the final successful results of a number of evolutions, and then start new evolutions with those that are aesthetically preferred. Although the control may be limited, this gives the user some influence on the creatures that are developed.

Another method of evolving creatures is to interactively evolve a morphology based on looks only, or alternatively hand design the morphology, and then automatically evolve a brain for that morphology that results in a desirable behavior.

Creatures that evolved in one physical world can be placed in another and evolved further. An evolved watersnake, for example, was placed on land and then evolved to crawl instead of swim.

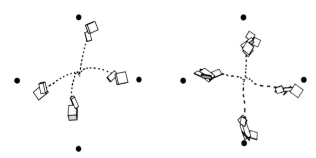

**Figure 9**: Following behavior. For each creature, four separate trials are shown from the same starting point toward different light source goal locations.

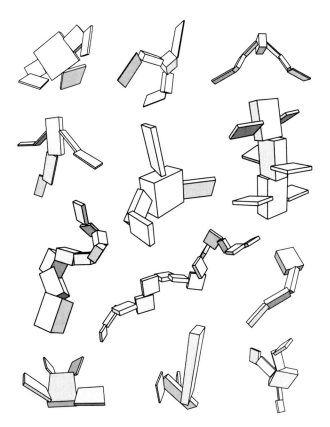

**Figure 6**: Creatures evolved for swimming.

## 8 Future Work

One direction of future work would be to experiment with additional types of fitness evaluation methods. More complex behaviors might be evolved by defining fitness functions that could measure the level of success at performing more difficult tasks, or even multiple tasks. Fitness could also include the efficiency at which a behavior was achieved. For example, a fitness measure might be the distance traveled divided by the amount of energy consumed to move that distance.

Alternatively, fitness could be defined in a more biologically realistic way by allowing populations of virtual creatures to compete against each other within a physically simulated changing world. Competition has been shown to facilitate complexity, specialization, or even social interactions [17,22]. It becomes difficult to define explicit evaluations that can select for "interesting" behavior, but perhaps systems like these could help produce such results.

Another direction of future work might be to adjust the genetic language of possible creatures to describe only those that could actually be built as real robots. The virtual robots that can best perform a given task in simulation would then be assembled, and would hopefully also perform well in reality.

Much work could be done to dress up these virtual creatures to give them different shapes and improved rendered looks. Flexible skin could surround or be controlled by the rigid components. Various materials could be added such as scales, hair, fur, eyes, or tentacles, and they might flow or bounce using simple local dynamic simulations, even if they did not influence the overall dynamics. The shape details and external materials could also be included in the creatures' genetic descriptions and be determined by artificial evolution.

## 9 Conclusion

In summary, a system has been described that can generate autonomous three-dimensional virtual creatures without requiring cumbersome user specifications, design efforts, or knowledge of algorithmic details. A genetic language for representing virtual creatures with directed graphs of nodes and connections allows an unlimited hyperspace of possible creatures to be explored. It is believed that these methods have potential as a powerful tool for the creation of desirable complexity for use in virtual worlds and computer animation.

As computers become more powerful, the creation of virtual actors, whether animal, human, or completely unearthly, may be limited mainly by our ability to design them, rather than our ability to satisfy their computational requirements. A control system that someday actually generates "intelligent" behavior might tend to be a complex mess beyond our understanding. Artificial evolution permits the generation of complicated virtual systems without requiring design, and the use of unbounded genetic languages allows evolving systems to increase in complexity beyond our understanding. Perhaps methods such as those presented here will provide a practical pathway toward the creation of intelligent behavior.

## Acknowledgments

Thanks to Gary Oberbrunner and Matt Fitzgibbon for Connection Machine and software help. Thanks to Lew Tucker and Thinking Machines Corporation for supporting this research. Thanks to Bruce Blumberg and Peter Schröder for dynamic simulation help and suggestions. And special thanks to Pattie Maes.

## References

1. Cramer, N.L., "A Representation for the Adaptive Generation of Simple Sequential Programs," *Proceedings of the First International Conference on Genetic Algorithms*, ed. by J. Grefenstette, 1985, pp.183-187.

2. Dawkins, R., *The Blind Watchmaker*, Harlow Longman, 1986.

3. Featherstone, R., *Robot Dynamics Algorithms*, Kluwer Academic Publishers, Norwell, MA, 1987.

4. de Garis, H., "Genetic Programming: Building Artificial Nervous Systems Using Genetically Programmed Neural Network Modules," *Proceedings of the 7th International Conference on Machine Learning*, 1990, pp.132-139.

5. Goldberg, D.E., *Genetic Algorithms in Search, Optimization, and Machine Learning*, Addison-Wesley, 1989.

6. Hart, J., "The Object Instancing Paradigm for Linear Fractal Modeling," *Graphics Interface*, 1992, pp.224-231.

7. Holland, J.H., *Adaptation in Natural and Artificial Systems*, Ann Arbor, University of Michigan Press, 1975.

8. Kitano, H., "Designing neural networks using genetic algorithms with graph generation system," *Complex Systems*, Vol.4, pp.461-476, 1990.

9. Koza, J., *Genetic Programming: on the Programming of Computers by Means of Natural Selection*, MIT Press, 1992.

10. Lindenmayer, A., "Mathematical Models for Cellular Interactions in Development, Parts I and II," *Journal of Theoretical Biology*, Vol.18, 1968, pp.280-315.

11. McKenna, M., and Zeltzer, D., "Dynamic Simulation of Autonomous Legged Locomotion," *Computer Graphics*, Vol.24, No.4, July 1990, pp.29-38.

12. Miller, G., "The Motion Dynamics of Snakes and Worms," *Computer Graphics*, Vol.22, No.4, July 1988, pp.169-178.

13. Mjolsness, E., Sharp, D., and Alpert, B., "Scaling, Machine Learning, and Genetic Neural Nets," *Advances in Applied Mathematics*, Vol.10, pp.137-163, 1989.

14. Ngo, J.T., and Marks, J., "Spacetime Constraints Revisited," *Computer Graphics*, Annual Conference Series, 1993, pp.343-350.

15. van de Panne, M., and Fiume, E., "Sensor-Actuator Networks," *Computer Graphics*, Annual Conference Series, 1993, pp.335-342.

16. Raibert, M., and Hodgins, J.K., "Animation of Dynamic Legged Locomotion," *Computer Graphics*, Vol.25, No.4, July 1991, pp.349-358.

17. Ray, T., "An Approach to the Synthesis of Life," *Artificial Life II*, ed. by Langton, Taylor, Farmer, & Rasmussen, Addison-Wesley, 1991, pp.371-408.

18. Sims, K., "Artificial Evolution for Computer Graphics," *Computer Graphics*, Vol.25, No.4, July 1991, pp.319-328.

19. Sims, K., "Interactive Evolution of Dynamical Systems," *Toward a Practice of Autonomous Systems: Proceedings of the First European Conference on Artificial Life*, ed. by Varela, Francisco, & Bourgine, MIT Press, 1992, pp.171-178.

20. Smith, A.R., "Plants, Fractals, and Formal Languages," *Computer Graphics*, Vol.18, No.3, July 1984, pp.1-10.

21. Todd, S., and Latham, W., *Evolutionary Art and Computers*, London, Academic Press, 1992.

22. Yaeger, L., "Computational Genetics, Physiology, Metabolism, Neural Systems, Learning, Vision, and Behavior or Poly-World: Life in a New Context," *Artificial Life III*, ed. by C. Langton, Santa Fe Institute Studies in the Sciences of Complexity, Proceedings Vol. XVII, Addison-Wesley, 1994, pp.263-298.

# Fast Contact Force Computation for Nonpenetrating Rigid Bodies

*David Baraff*

Robotics Institute
Carnegie Mellon University
Pittsburgh, PA 15213

## Abstract

A new algorithm for computing contact forces between solid objects with friction is presented. The algorithm allows a mix of contact points with static and dynamic friction. In contrast to previous approaches, the problem of computing contact forces is not transformed into an optimization problem. Because of this, the need for sophisticated optimization software packages is eliminated. For both systems with and without friction, the algorithm has proven to be considerably faster, simpler, and more reliable than previous approaches to the problem. In particular, implementation of the algorithm by nonspecialists in numerical programming is quite feasible.

## 1. Introduction

In recent work, we have established the viability of using analytical methods to simulate rigid body motion with contact[1,2,3]. In situations involving only bilateral constraints (commonly referred to as "equality constraints"), analytical methods require solving systems of simultaneous linear equations. Bilateral constraints typically arise in representing idealized geometric connections such as universal joints, point-to-surface constraints etc. For systems with contact, unilateral (or "inequality") constraints are required to prevent adjoining bodies from interpenetrating. In turn, the simultaenous linear equations arising from a system of only bilateral constraints must be augmented to reflect the unilateral constraints; the result is in general an inequality-constrained nonlinear minimization problem.

However, analytical techniques for systems with contact have yet to really catch on in the graphics/simulation community. We believe that this is because of the perceived practical and theoretical complexities of using analytical techniques in systems with contact. This paper has two goals, one of which is to address these concerns: in particular, we present analytical methods for systems with contact that can be practically implemented by those of us (such as the author) who *are not specialists in numerical analysis or optimization*. These methods are simpler, reliable, and faster than previous methods used for either systems with friction, or systems without friction.

Our other goal is to extend and improve previous algorithms for computing contact forces with friction[3]. We present a simple, fast algorithm for computing contact forces with friction. The restriction of our algorithm to the frictionless case is equivalent to an algorithm described in Cottle and Dantzig[4] (but attributed to Dantzig) for

solving linear complementarity problems. It is not our intention to reinvent the wheel; however, it is necessary to first understand Dantzig's algorithm and why it works for our frictionless sytems before going on to consider the more general solution algorithm we propose to deal with friction. We give a physical motivation for Dantzig's algorithm and discuss its properties and implementation in section 4. For frictionless systems, our implementation of Dantzig's algorithm compares very favorably with the use of large-scale, sophisticated numerical optimization packages cited by previous systems[11,7,8,6]. In particular, for a system with $n$ unilateral constraints, our implementation tends to require approximately three times the work required to solve a square linear system of size $n$ using Gaussian elimination. Most importantly, Dantzig's algorithm, and our extensions to it for systems with friction, are sufficiently simple that nonspecialists in numerical programming can implement them on their own; this is most assuredly *not* true of the previously cited large-scale optimization packages.

Interactive systems with bilateral constraints are common, and there is no reason that moderately complicated interactive simulation with collision and contact cannot be achieved as well. We strongly believe that using our algorithms, interactive simulations with contact and friction are practical. We support this claim by demonstrating the first known system for interactive simulations involving contact and a correct model of Coulomb friction.

## 2. Background and Motivation

Lötstedt[10] represents the first attempt to compute friction forces in an analytical setting, by using quadratic programming to compute friction forces based on a simplification of the Coulomb friction model. Baraff[3] also proposed analytical methods for dealing with friction forces and presents algorithms that deal with dynamic friction (also known as sliding friction) and static friction (also known as dry friction). The results for dynamic friction were the more comprehensive of the two, and the paper readily acknowledges that the method presented for computing contact forces with static friction (a Gauss-Seidel-like iterative procedure) was not very reliable. The method also required an approximation for three-dimensional systems (but not for planar systems) that resulted in anisotropic friction. Finally, the results presented did not fully exploit earlier discoveries concerning systems with only dynamic friction, and no static friction.

In this paper, we present a method for computing contact forces with both dynamic and static friction that is considerably more robust than previous methods. Our method requires no approximations for three-dimensional systems, and is much simpler and faster than previous methods. We were extremely surprised to find that our implementation of the method, applied to frictionless systems, was a large improvement compared with the use of large-scale optimization software packages, both in terms of speed and, especially, simplicity.[1] Previous simulation systems for frictionless contact that we know of have used either heuristic solution methods based on linear programming[11], quadratic programming algorithms[7], or constrained linear least-squares algorithms[6]. In all cases the numerical software required is sufficiently complicated that either public-domain or commercially available software packages are required. The problems with this are:

- Serious implementations of linear programming codes are much less common than serious implementations for solving linear systems. Serious implementations for quadratic programming are even rarer.

- A fair amount of mathematical and coding sophistication is required to interface the numerical software package with the simulation software. In some cases, the effort required for an efficient interface was prohibitively high[12].

- The packages obtained contained a large number of adjustable parameters such as numerical tolerances, iteration limits, etc. It is not uncommon for certain contact-force computations to fail with one set of parameters, while succeeding with another, or for a problem to be solvable using one software package, but unsolvable using a different package. In our past work in offline motion simulation, reliability has been a vexing, but tolerable issue: if a given simulation fails to run, one can either alter the initial conditions slightly, hoping to avoid the specific configuration which caused the difficulty, or modify the software itself prior to rerunning the simulation. This approach is clearly not practical in an interactive setting.

- Along the same lines, it is difficult to isolate numerical problems during simulation, because of the complexity of the software packages. Unless great effort is put into understanding the internals of the code, the user is faced with a "black box." This is desirable for black-box code that is bullet-proof, but a serious impediment when the code is not.

Given these hurdles, it is not surprising that analytical methods for systems with contact have not caught on yet. Our recent work has taught us that the difficulties encountered are, in a sense, self-created. In computing contact forces via numerical optimization, we translate a very specific problem (contact-force computation) into a much more general problem (numerical optimization). The translation loses some of the specific structure of the original problem, making the solution task more difficult. The approach we take in this paper is to avoid (as much as possible) abstracting our specific problem into a more general problem. The result is an algorithm that solves a narrower range of problems than general purpose optimization software, but is faster, more reliable, and considerably easier to implement.

## 3. Contact Model

In this section we will define the structure of the simplest problem we deal with: a system of frictionless bodies contacting at $n$ distinct points. For each contact point $\mathbf{p}_i$ between two bodies, let the scalar $a_i$ denote the relative acceleration between the bodies normal to the contact surface at $\mathbf{p}_i$. (We will not consider the question of impact in this paper; thus, we assume that the relative normal *velocity* of bodies at each contact is zero.) We adopt the convention that a positive acceleration $a_i$ indicates that the two bodies are breaking contact at $\mathbf{p}_i$. Correspondingly, $a_i < 0$ indicates that the bodies are accelerating so as to interpenetrate. An acceleration of $a_i = 0$ indicates that the bodies have zero normal acceleration at $\mathbf{p}_i$ and

remain in contact (although the relative tangential acceleration may be nonzero). To prevent interpenetration we require $a_i \geq 0$ for each contact point.

For frictionless systems, the force acting between two bodies at a contact point is normal to the contact surface. We denote the magnitude of the normal force between the bodies at $\mathbf{p}_i$ by the scalar $f_i$. A positive $f_i$ indicates a repulsive force between the bodies at $\mathbf{p}_i$, while a negative $f_i$ indicates an attractive force. Since contact forces must be repulsive, a necessary condition on $f_i$ is $f_i \geq 0$. Also, since frictionless contact forces are conservative, we must add the condition $f_i a_i = 0$ for each contact point. This condition requires that at least one of $f_i$ and $a_i$ be zero for each contact: either $a_i = 0$ and contact remains, or $a_i > 0$, contact is broken, and $f_i$ is zero.

We will denote the $n$-vector collection of $a_i$'s as $\mathbf{a}$; the $i$th element of $\mathbf{a}$ is $a_i$. The vector $\mathbf{f}$ is the collection of the $f_i$'s. (In general, boldface type denotes matrices and vectors; the $i$th element of a vector $\mathbf{b}$ is the scalar $b_i$, written in regular type. The symbol $\mathbf{0}$ denotes on appropriately sized vector or matrix of zeros.) The vectors $\mathbf{a}$ and $\mathbf{f}$ are linearly related; we can write

$$\mathbf{a} = \mathbf{A}\mathbf{f} + \mathbf{b} \tag{1}$$

where $\mathbf{A} \in \mathbf{R}^{n \times n}$ is symmetric and positive semidefinite (PSD), and $\mathbf{b} \in \mathbf{R}^n$ is a vector in the column space of $\mathbf{A}$ (that is, $\mathbf{b} = \mathbf{A}\mathbf{x}$ for some vector $\mathbf{x}$). The matrix $\mathbf{A}$ reflects the masses and contact geometries of the bodies, while $\mathbf{b}$ reflects the external and inertial forces in the system. At any instant of time, $\mathbf{A}$ and $\mathbf{b}$ are known quantities while $\mathbf{f}$ is the unknown we are interested in solving for.

The problem of determining contact forces is therefore the problem of computing a vector $\mathbf{f}$ satisfying the conditions

$$a_i \geq 0, \quad f_i \geq 0 \quad \text{and} \quad f_i a_i = 0 \tag{2}$$

for each contact point. We will call equation (2) the *normal force conditions*. Using equation (1), we can phrase the problem of determining a suitable $\mathbf{f}$ in several forms. First, since $f_i$ and $a_i$ are constrained to be nonnegative, the requirement that $f_i a_i = 0$ for each $i$ is equivalent to requiring that

$$\sum_{i=1}^{n} f_i a_i = \mathbf{f}^T \mathbf{a} = 0 \tag{3}$$

since no cancellation can occur. Using equation (1), we can say that $\mathbf{f}$ must satisfy the conditions

$$\mathbf{A}\mathbf{f} + \mathbf{b} \geq \mathbf{0}, \quad \mathbf{f} \geq \mathbf{0} \quad \text{and} \quad \mathbf{f}^T(\mathbf{A}\mathbf{f} + \mathbf{b}) = 0. \tag{4}$$

Equation (4) defines what is known as a linear complementarity problem (LCP). Thus one solution method for computing contact forces is to formulate and solve the LCP of equation (4). We can also compute contact forces by considering the conditions of equation (2) as a quadratic program (QP): we can equivalently say that a vector $\mathbf{f}$ satisfying equation (4) is a solution to the quadratic program

$$\min_{\mathbf{f}} \mathbf{f}^T(\mathbf{A}\mathbf{f} + \mathbf{b}) \quad \text{subject to} \quad \left\{ \begin{array}{c} \mathbf{A}\mathbf{f} + \mathbf{b} \geq \mathbf{0} \\ \mathbf{f} \geq \mathbf{0} \end{array} \right\}. \tag{5}$$

Phrasing the computation of $\mathbf{f}$ as a QP is a natural choice. (The problem of solving QP's has received more attention than the problem of solving LCP's. Both problems are *NP*-hard in general but can be practically solved when $\mathbf{A}$ is PSD.) Having transformed the problem of computing contact forces into a QP, we have a variety of techniques available for solving the QP. Unfortunately, by moving to an optimization problem—minimize $\mathbf{f}^T(\mathbf{A}\mathbf{f} + \mathbf{b})$—we necessarily lose sight of the original condition $f_i a_i = 0$ for each contact point. Because of this, we are solving a more general, and thus harder,

---

[1] Actually, not being numerical specialists, any working numerical software we were capable of creating would have to be simpler. We automatically assumed however that such software would be slower than the more comprehensive packages written by experts in the field.

problem than we really need to. In developing an algorithm, we prefer to regard the relationship between $f$ and $\mathbf{a}$ in terms of the $n$ separate conditions $f_i a_i = 0$ in equation (2) rather than the single constraint $f^T \mathbf{a} = 0$ in equation (4) or the minimization of $f^T \mathbf{a}$ in equation (5). In the next section, we describe a physically-motivated method for solving equation (2), along with a practical implementation. Following this, we consider friction in section 5.

## 4. Frictionless Systems

In this section we present a restriction of our algorithm for computing contact forces with friction to the frictionless case. We also sketch a proof of correctness. We extend the algorithm in section 5 to handle static friction, and dynamic friction in section 6. A description of Dantzig's algorithm for solving LCP's, and an excellent treatment of LCP's in general can be found in Cottle *et al.*[5].

### 4.1 Algorithm Outline

Dantzig's algorithm for solving LCP's is related to pivoting methods used to solve linear and quadratic programs. The major difference is that all linear and most quadratic programming algorithms begin by first finding a solution that satisfies the constraints of the problem (for us, $\mathbf{A}f + \mathbf{b} \geq \mathbf{0}$ and $f \geq \mathbf{0}$) and then trying to minimize the objective function (for us, $f^T \mathbf{A}f + f^T \mathbf{b}$).

In contrast, Dantzig's algorithm, as applied to the problem of computing contact forces, works as follows. Initially, all contact points but the first are ignored, and $f_i$ is set to zero for all $i$. The algorithm begins by computing a value for $f_1$ that satisfies the normal force conditions—equation (2)—for $i = 1$, without worrying about those conditions holding for any other $i$. Next, the algorithm computes a value for $f_2$ that satisfies the normal force conditions for $i = 2$ while maintaining the conditions for $i = 1$. This may require modification of $f_1$. The algorithm continues in this fashion: at any point, the conditions at contact points $1 \leq i \leq k - 1$ are satisfied for some $k$ and $f_i = 0$ for $i > k$, and the algorithm determines $f_k$, possibly altering some of the $f_i$'s for $i < k$, so that the conditions now hold for all $i \leq k$. When the conditions hold for all $n$ contact points, the algorithm terminates.

To make this concrete, imagine that we have so far computed values $f_1$ through $f_{n-1}$ so that the normal force conditions hold everywhere except possibly at the $n$th contact point. Suppose that with $f_n$ still set to zero we have $a_n \geq 0$. If so, we immediately have a solution $f$ that satisfies the normal conditions at all $n$ contact points.

Suppose however that for $f_n = 0$ we have $a_n < 0$. Our physical intuition tells us that since we currently have $f_n = 0$, the problem is that the $n$th contact force is not doing its fair share. We must increase $f_n$ until we reach the point that $a_n$ is zero, and we must do so without violating the normal force conditions at any of the first $n - 1$ contact points. Since increasing $f_n$ may change some of the $a_i$'s, we will generally need to modify the other $f_i$ variables as we increase $f_n$. Our goal is to seek a strength for $f_n$ that is just sufficient to cause $a_n$ to be zero. (We emphasize that this is not a process which takes place over some time interval $t_0$ to $t_1$ during a simulation; rather, we are considering the proper value that $f$ should assume at a specific instant in time.)

The adjustments we need to make to $f_1$ through $f_{n-1}$ as we increase $f_n$ are simple to calculate. Since the order in which contacts are numbered is arbitrary, let us imagine that for the current values of the $f_i$'s we have $a_1 = a_2 = ... = a_k = 0$ for some value $0 \leq k \leq n - 1$, and for all $k + 1 \leq i \leq n - 1$, we have $a_i > 0$. Remember that $a_n < 0$. To simplify bookkeeping, we will employ two disjoint index sets $C$ and $NC$. At this point in the algorithm, let $C = \{1, 2, ..., k\}$; thus, $a_i = 0$ for all $i \in C$. Similarly, let $NC = \{k + 1, k + 2, ..., n - 1\}$; since $a_i > 0$ for all $i \in NC$, and we have assumed that $f_i a_i = 0$ for $i \leq n - 1$, it must be that

$f_i = 0$ for all $i \in NC$. Throughout the algorithm, we will attempt to maintain $a_i = 0$ whenever $i \in C$. Similarly, we will try to maintain $f_i = 0$ whenever $i \in NC$. When $i \in C$, we say that the $i$th contact point is "clamped," and when $i \in NC$ we say the $i$th contact point is "unclamped." (If $i$ is in neither, the $i$th contact point is currently being ignored.)

For a unit increase of $f_n$ (that is, if we increase $f_n$ to $f_n + 1$) we must adjust each $f_i$ by some amount $\Delta f_i$. Let $\Delta f_n = 1$, and let us set $\Delta f_i = 0$ for all $i \in NC$, since we wish to maintain $f_i = 0$ for $i \in NC$. We wish to choose the remaining $\Delta f_i$'s for $i \in C$ such that $\Delta a_i = 0$ for $i \in C$. The collection $\Delta \mathbf{a}$ of the $\Delta a_i$'s is defined by

$$\Delta \mathbf{a} = \mathbf{A}(f + \Delta f) + \mathbf{b} - (\mathbf{A}f + \mathbf{b}) = \mathbf{A}\Delta f \qquad (6)$$

where $\Delta f$ denotes the collection of the $\Delta f_i$'s.

Intuitively, we picture the force $f_i$ at a clamped contact point undergoing some variation in order to maintain $a_i = 0$, while the force at an unclamped contact remains zero. Modifications of this sort will maintain the invariant that $f_i a_i = 0$ for all $1 \leq i \leq n - 1$. Since $C$ currently has $k$ elements, computing the unspecified $\Delta f_i$'s requires solving $k$ linear equations in $k$ unknowns. (In general, $C$ will vary in size during the course of the algorithm. At any point in the algorithm when we are establishing the conditions at the $r$th contact, $C$ will contain $r - 1$ or fewer elements.)

However, we also need to maintain the conditions $f_i \geq 0$ and $a_i \geq 0$. Thus, as we increase $f_n$, we may find that for some $i \in C$, $f_i$ has decreased to zero. At this point, it may be necessary to unclamp this contact by removing $i$ from $C$ and adding it to $NC$, so that we do not cause $f_i$ to decrease any further. Conversely, we may find that for some $i \in NC$, $a_i$ has decreased to a value of zero. In this case, we will wish to clamp the contact by moving $i$ from $NC$ into $C$, preventing $a_i$ from decreasing any further and becoming negative. The process of moving the various indices between $C$ and $NC$ is exactly the numerical process known as pivoting. Given that we start with suitable values for $f_1$ through $f_{n-1}$, computing $f_n$ is straightforward. We set $\Delta f_n = 1$ and $\Delta f_i = 0$ for $i \in NC$, and solve for the $\Delta f_i$'s for $i \in C$ so that $\Delta a_i = 0$ for all $i \in C$. Next, we choose the smallest scalar $s > 0$ such that increasing $f$ by $s\Delta f$ causes either $a_n$ to reach zero, or some index $i$ to move between $C$ and $NC$. If $a_n$ has reached zero, we are done; otherwise, we change the index sets $C$ and $NC$, and loop back to continue increasing $f_n$.

We now describe the process of computing $\Delta f$ along with the step size $s$. After this, we present the complete algorithm and discuss its properties.

### 4.2 The Pivot Step

The relation between the vectors $\mathbf{a}$ and $f$ is given by $\mathbf{a} = \mathbf{A}f + \mathbf{b}$. Let us continue with our example in which $C = \{1, 2, ..., k\}$ and $NC = \{k + 1, k + 2, ..., n - 1\}$. We need to compute $\Delta f$ and then determine how large a multiple of $\Delta f$ we can add to $f$. Currently, we have $a_n < 0$. Let us partition $\mathbf{A}$ and $\Delta f$ by writing

$$\mathbf{A} = \begin{pmatrix} \mathbf{A}_{11} & \mathbf{A}_{12} & \mathbf{v}_1 \\ \mathbf{A}_{12}^T & \mathbf{A}_{22} & \mathbf{v}_2 \\ \mathbf{v}_1^T & \mathbf{v}_2^T & \alpha \end{pmatrix} \quad \text{and} \quad \Delta f = \begin{pmatrix} \mathbf{x} \\ \mathbf{0} \\ 1 \end{pmatrix} \qquad (7)$$

where $\mathbf{A}_{11}$ and $\mathbf{A}_{22}$ are square symmetric matrices, $\mathbf{v}_1 \in \mathbf{R}^k$, $\mathbf{v}_2 \in \mathbf{R}^{(n-1)-k}$, $\alpha$ is a scalar, and $\mathbf{x} \in \mathbf{R}^k$ is what we will need to compute. The linear system $\Delta \mathbf{a} = \mathbf{A}\Delta f$ has the form

$$\Delta \mathbf{a} = \mathbf{A}\Delta f = \mathbf{A} \begin{pmatrix} \mathbf{x} \\ \mathbf{0} \\ 1 \end{pmatrix} = \begin{pmatrix} \mathbf{A}_{11}\mathbf{x} + \mathbf{v}_1 \\ \mathbf{A}_{12}^T\mathbf{x} + \mathbf{v}_2 \\ \mathbf{v}_1^T\mathbf{x} + \alpha \end{pmatrix}. \qquad (8)$$

Since the first $k$ components of $\Delta \mathbf{a}$ need to be zero, we require $\mathbf{A}_{11}\mathbf{x} + \mathbf{v}_1 = \mathbf{0}$; equivalently, we must solve

$$\mathbf{A}_{11}\mathbf{x} = -\mathbf{v}_1.$$

After solving equation (9), we compute $\Delta\mathbf{a} = \mathbf{A}\Delta\mathbf{f}$, and are ready to find the maximum step size parameter $s$ we can scale $\Delta\mathbf{f}$ by. For each $i \in C$, if $\Delta f_i < 0$, then the force at the $i$th contact point is decreasing. The maximum step $s$ we can take without forcing $f_i$ negative is

$$s \leq \frac{f_i}{-\Delta f_i}. \tag{10}$$

Similarly, for each $i \in NC$, if $\Delta a_i < 0$ then the acceleration $a_i$ is decreasing; the maximum step is limited by

$$s \leq \frac{a_i}{-\Delta a_i}. \tag{11}$$

Since we do not wish $a_n$ to exceed zero, if $\Delta a_n > 0$, the maximum step is limited by

$$s \leq \frac{-a_n}{\Delta a_n}. \tag{12}$$

Once we determine $s$, we increase $\mathbf{f}$ by $s\Delta\mathbf{f}$, which causes $\mathbf{a}$ to increase by $\mathbf{A}(s\Delta\mathbf{f}) = s\Delta\mathbf{a}$. If this causes a change in the index sets $C$ and $NC$, we make the required change and continue to increase $f_n$. Otherwise, $a_n$ has achieved zero.

### 4.3 A Pseudo-code Implementation

The entire algorithm is described below in pseudo-code. The main loop of the algorithm is simply:

> **function** *compute-forces*
>     $\mathbf{f} = 0$
>     $\mathbf{a} = \mathbf{b}$
>     $C = NC = \emptyset$
>     **while** $\exists d$ such that $a_d < 0$
>         *drive-to-zero*$(d)$

The function *drive-to-zero* increases $f_d$ until $a_d$ is zero. The direction of change for the force, $\Delta\mathbf{f}$, is computed by *fdirection*. The function *maxstep* determines the maximum step size $s$, and the constraint $j$ responsible for limiting $s$. If $j$ is in $C$ or $NC$, $j$ is moved from one to the other; otherwise, $j = d$, meaning $a_d$ has been driven to zero, and *drive-to-zero* returns:

> **function** *drive-to-zero*$(d)$
>   $L_1$:
>     $\Delta\mathbf{f} = \textit{fdirection}(d)$
>     $\Delta\mathbf{a} = \mathbf{A}\Delta\mathbf{f}$
>     $(s,j) = \textit{maxstep}(\mathbf{f}, \mathbf{a}, \Delta\mathbf{f}, \Delta\mathbf{a}, d)$
>     $\mathbf{f} = \mathbf{f} + s\Delta\mathbf{f}$
>     $\mathbf{a} = \mathbf{a} + s\Delta\mathbf{a}$
>     **if** $j \in C$
>         $C = C - \{j\}$
>         $NC = NC \cup \{j\}$
>         **goto** $L_1$
>     **else if** $j \in NC$
>         $NC = NC - \{j\}$
>         $C = C \cup \{j\}$
>         **goto** $L_1$
>     **else**        *j must be d, implying* $a_d = 0$
>         $C = C \cup \{j\}$
>     **return**

The function *fdirection* computes $\Delta\mathbf{f}$. We write $\mathbf{A}_{CC}$ to denote the submatrix of $\mathbf{A}$ obtained by deleting the $j$th row and column of $\mathbf{A}$ for all $j \notin C$. Similarly, $\mathbf{A}_{Cd}$ denotes the $d$th column of $\mathbf{A}$ with element $j$ deleted for all $j \notin C$. The vector $\mathbf{x}$ represents the change in contact force magnitudes at the clamped contacts. The transfer of $\mathbf{x}$ into $\Delta\mathbf{f}$ is the reverse of the process by which elements are removed from the $d$th column of $\mathbf{A}$ to form $\mathbf{A}_{Cd}$. (That is, for all

$i \in C$, we assign to $\Delta f_i$ the element of $\mathbf{x}$ corresponding to the $i$th contact.)

> **function** *fdirection*$(d)$
>     $\Delta\mathbf{f} = 0$         *set all* $\Delta f_i$ *to zero*
>     $\Delta f_d = 1$
>     **let** $\mathbf{A}_{11} = \mathbf{A}_{CC}$
>     **let** $\mathbf{v}_1 = \mathbf{A}_{Cd}$
>     **solve** $\mathbf{A}_{11}\mathbf{x} = -\mathbf{v}_1$
>     **transfer x into** $\Delta\mathbf{f}$
>     **return** $\Delta\mathbf{f}$

Last, the function *maxstep* returns a pair $(s, j)$ with $s$ the maximum step size that can be taken in the direction $\Delta\mathbf{f}$ and $j$ the index of the contact point limiting the step size $s$:

> **function** *maxstep*$(\mathbf{f}, \mathbf{a}, \Delta\mathbf{f}, \Delta\mathbf{a}, d)$
>     $s = \infty$
>     $j = -1$
>     **if** $\Delta a_d > 0$
>         $j = d$
>         $s = -a_d/\Delta a_d$
>     **for** $i \in C$
>         **if** $\Delta f_i < 0$
>             $s' = -f_i/\Delta f_i$
>             **if** $s' < s$
>                 $s = s'$
>                 $j = i$
>     **for** $i \in NC$
>         **if** $\Delta a_i < 0$
>             $s' = -a_i/\Delta a_i$
>             **if** $s' < s$
>                 $s = s'$
>                 $j = i$
>     **return** $(s, j)$

It is clear that if the algorithm terminates, the solution $\mathbf{f}$ will yield $a_i \geq 0$ for all $i$. Since each $f_i$ is initially zero and is prevented from decreasing below zero by *maxstep*, at termination $f_i \geq 0$ for all $i$. Last, at termination, $f_i a_i = 0$ for all $i$ since either $i \in C$ and $a_i = 0$, or $i \notin C$ and $f_i = 0$.

The only step of the algorithm requiring substantial coding is *fdirection*, which requires forming and solving a square linear system. Remarkably, even if $\mathbf{A}$ is singular (and $\mathbf{A}$ is often extremely rank-deficient in our simulations), the submatrices $\mathbf{A}_{11}$ encountered in the frictionless case are never singular. This is a consequence of $\mathbf{b}$ being in the column space of $\mathbf{A}$.

### 4.4 Termination of the Algorithm

We will quickly sketch why the algorithm we have described must always terminate, with details supplied in appendix A. Examining the algorithm, the two critical steps are solving $\mathbf{A}_{11}\mathbf{x} = -\mathbf{v}_1$ and computing the step size $s$. First off, could the algorithm fail because it could not compute $\mathbf{x}$? Since $\mathbf{A}$ is symmetric PSD, if $\mathbf{A}$ is nonsingular then $\mathbf{A}_{11}$ is nonsingular and $\mathbf{x}$ exists. Even if $\mathbf{A}$ is singular, the submatrices $\mathbf{A}_{11}$ considered by the algorithm are never singular, as long as $\mathbf{b}$ lies in the column space of $\mathbf{A}$.[2] As a result, the system $\mathbf{A}_{11}\mathbf{x} = -\mathbf{v}_1$ can always be solved. This is however a theoretical result. In actual practice, when $\mathbf{A}$ is singular it is possible

---

[2] A complete proof of this is somewhat involved. The central idea is that if the $j$th contact point has not yet been considered and represents a "redundant constraint" (that is, adding $j$ into $C$ makes $\mathbf{A}_{11}$ singular) then $a_j$ will not be negative, so there will be no need to call *drive-to-zero* on $j$. Similarly, if $j \in NC$ and moving $j$ to $C$ would make $\mathbf{A}_{11}$ singular, it will not be the case that $a_j$ tries to decrease below zero, requiring $j$ to be placed in $C$. Essentially, the nonzero $f_i$'s will do the work of keeping $a_j$ from becoming negative, without $f_j$ having to become positive, allowing $j$ to remain outside of $C$.

that roundoff errors in the algorithm may cause an index $j$ to enter $C$ so that the resulting matrix $\mathbf{A}_{11}$ is singular. This is a very rare occurrence, but even so, it does not present a practical problem. Appendix A establishes that the vector $\mathbf{v}_1$ is always in the column space of the submatrix $\mathbf{A}_{11}$ arising from *any* index set $C$. Thus, even if $\mathbf{A}_{11}$ is singular, the equation $\mathbf{A}_{11}\mathbf{x} = -\mathbf{v}_1$ is well-conditioned, and is easily solved by standard factorization methods.[3] In essence, we assert that "$\mathbf{A}_{11}$ is never singular, and even if it is, $\mathbf{A}_{11}\mathbf{x} = -\mathbf{v}_1$ is still easily solved."

Since it is always possible to solve $\mathbf{A}_{11}\mathbf{x} = -\mathbf{v}_1$ and obtain $\Delta\mathbf{f}$, the real question of termination must depend on each call to *drive-to-zero* being able to force $a_d$ to zero. To avoid being bogged down in details, let us assume that $\mathbf{A}$ is nonsingular, with specific proofs deferred to appendix A; additionally, appendix A discusses the necessary extensions to cover the case when $\mathbf{A}$ is singular. Although the singular versus the nonsingular cases require slightly different proofs, we emphasize that *the algorithm itself* remains unchanged; that is, the algorithm we have just described works for both positive definite and positive semidefinite $\mathbf{A}$.

The most important question to consider is whether increasing $\mathbf{f}$ by an amount $s\Delta\mathbf{f}$ actually increases $a_d$. Given a change $s\Delta\mathbf{f}$ in $\mathbf{f}$, from equation (8) the increase in $a_d$ is

$$s(\mathbf{v}_1^T\mathbf{x} + \alpha) = s\Delta a_d. \tag{13}$$

Theorem 2 shows that if $\mathbf{A}$ is positive definite, $\mathbf{v}_1^T\mathbf{x} + \alpha$ is always positive. Thus, $a_d$ will increase as long as $s$ is always positive. Since $\mathbf{v}_1^T + \alpha = \Delta a_d > 0$, this shows that *maxstep* never returns with $s = \infty$ and $j = -1$.

Can the algorithm take steps of size zero? In order for *maxstep* to return $s = 0$, it would have to the case that either $f_i = 0$ and $\Delta f_i < 0$ for some $i \in C$ or $a_i = 0$ and $\Delta a_i < 0$ for some $i \in NC$. Theorems 4 and 5 shows that this cannot happen. Thus, $s$ is always positive. Therefore, the only way for $a_d$ to not reach zero is if *drive-to-zero* takes an infinite number of steps $s\Delta\mathbf{f}$ that result in in $a_d$ converging to some limit less than or equal to zero. This possibility is also ruled out, since theorem 3 in appendix A shows that the set $C$ of clamped contact points is never repeated during a given call to *drive-to-zero*. Thus, *drive-to-zero* can iterate only a finite number of times before $a_d$ reaches zero.

### 4.5 Implementation Details

The algorithm just described is very simple to implement and requires relatively little code. The most complicated part involves forming and solving the linear system $\mathbf{A}_{11}\mathbf{x} = -\mathbf{v}_1$. This involves some straightforward bookkeeping of the indices in $C$ and $NC$ to correctly form $\mathbf{A}_{11}$ and then distribute the components of $\mathbf{x}$ into $\Delta\mathbf{f}$. It is important to note that each call to *fdirection* will involve an index set $C$ that differs from the previous index set $C$ by only a single element. This means that each linear system $\mathbf{A}_{11}\mathbf{x} = -\mathbf{v}_1$ will differ from the previous system only by a single row and column. Although each such system can be solved independently (for example, using Cholesky decomposition), for large problems it is more efficient to use an incremental approach.

In keeping with our assertion that nonspecialists can easily implement the algorithm we describe, we note that our initial implementation simply used Gaussian elimination, which we found to be completely satisfactory. (Anticipating the developments of the next section when $\mathbf{A}_{11}$ is nonsymmetrical, we did not bother to use a Cholesky factorization, although this would have performed significantly faster.)

Gill *et al.*[9] describe a package called LUSOL that incrementally factors a sparse matrix $\mathbf{A}$ into the form $\mathbf{A} = \mathbf{LU}$ where $\mathbf{L}$ is lower

triangular and $\mathbf{U}$ is upper triangle. Given such a factorization, if $\mathbf{A}$ has dimension $n$ and a new row and column are added to $\mathbf{A}$, or a row and column are eliminated from $\mathbf{A}$, a factorization of the new matrix can be recomputed quickly. Unfortunately, the coding effort for LUSOL is large. One of the authors of the LUSOL package was kind enough to provide us with a modified version of the software[13] that treats $\mathbf{A}$ as a dense matrix and computes a factorization $\mathbf{LA} = \mathbf{U}$ (where $\mathbf{L}$ is no longer triangular). In the dense case, an updated factorization is obtained in $O(n^2)$ time when $\mathbf{A}$ is altered. The modified version contains a reasonably small amount of code. For a serious implementation we highly recommend the use of an incremental factorization routine.

In addition, it is trivial to make the algorithm handle standard bilateral constraints. For a bilateral constraint, we introduce a pair $f_i$ and $a_i$, and we constrain $a_i$ to always be zero while letting $f_i$ be either positive or negative. Given $k$ such constraints, we initially solve a square linear system of size $k$ to compute compute initial values for all the bilateral $f_i$'s so that all the corresponding $a_i$'s are zero. Each such $i$ is placed into $C$ at the beginning of the algorithm. In *maxstep*, we ignore each index $i$ that is a bilateral constraint, since we do not care if that $f_i$ becomes negative. As a result, the bilateral $i$'s always stay in $C$ and the bilateral $a_i$'s are always zero. Exactly the same modification can be made in the algorithm presented in the next section.

### 5. Static Friction

The algorithm of the previous section can be considered a constructive proof that there exists a solution $\mathbf{f}$ satisfying the normal force conditions for any frictionless system. The algorithm presented in this section grew out of an attempt to prove the conjecture that all systems with static friction, but no dynamic friction, also possess solutions. (The conjecture is false for systems with dynamic friction.) The conjecture currently remains unproven. We cannot prove that the algorithm we present for computing static friction forces will always terminate; if we could, that in itself would constitute a proof of the conjecture. On the other hand, we have not yet seen the algorithm fail, so that the algorithm is at least practical (for the range of simulations we have attempted so far).

Let us consider the situation when there is friction at a contact point. The friction force at a point acts tangential to the contact surface. We will denote the magnitude of the friction force at the $i$th contact by $f_{F_i}$, and the magnitude of the relative acceleration in the tangent plane as $a_{F_i}$. We will also denote the magnitude of the normal force as $f_{N_i}$, rather than $f_i$, and the magnitude of the normal acceleration as $a_{N_i}$ rather than $a_i$. To specify the tangential acceleration and friction force completely in a three-dimensional system, we would also need to specify the *direction* of the acceleration and friction force in the tangent plane. For simplicity, we will begin by dealing with two-dimensional systems. At each contact point, let $\mathbf{t}_i$ be a unit vector tangent to the contact surface; $\mathbf{t}_i$ is unique except for a choice of sign. In a two dimensional system, we will treat $f_{F_i}$ and $a_{F_i}$ as signed quantities. A friction force magnitude of $f_{F_i}$ denotes a friction force of $f_{F_i}\mathbf{t}_i$, and an acceleration magnitude $a_{F_i}$ denotes an acceleration of $a_{F_i}\mathbf{t}_i$. Thus, if $a_{F_i}$ and $f_{F_i}$ have the same sign, then the friction force and tangential acceleration point in the same direction.

Static friction occurs when the relative tangential velocity at a contact point is zero; otherwise, the friction is called dynamic friction. In this section, we will consider only static friction. Any configuration of objects that is initially at rest will have static friction, but no dynamic friction. Additionally, a "first-order" (or quasistatic) simulation world where force and *velocity* are related by $f = mv$ also has static friction but never any dynamic friction

---

[3]Since $\mathbf{A}_{11}$ is both symmetric and PSD, $\mathbf{A}_{11}$ will still have a Cholesky factorization $\mathbf{A}_{11} = \mathbf{LL}^T$, although $\mathbf{L}$ is singular. Since $\mathbf{L}$ can be simply and reliably computed, this is one possible way of solving for $\mathbf{x}$.

## 5.1 Static Friction Conditions

At a contact point with static friction, the magnitude $v_{Fi}$ of the relative tangential velocity is zero. If the effect of all the forces in the system produces $a_{Fi} = 0$, meaning that the condition $v_{Fi} = 0$ is being maintained, then $f_{Fi}$ need satisfy only

$$- \mu f_{Ni} \leq f_{Fi} \leq \mu f_{Ni} \qquad (14)$$

where the scalar $\mu$ denotes the coefficient of friction at the contact point. (We will not bother to index $\mu$ over the contact points, although this is easily done.) If the tangential acceleration is not zero, then the conditions on $f_{Fi}$ are more demanding: $|f_{Fi}|$ must be equal to $\mu f_{Ni}$ and $f_{Fi}$ must have sign opposite that of $a_{Fi}$.

Following the pattern of section 4, we write that $f_{Ni}$, $a_{Ni}$, $f_{Fi}$ and $a_{Fi}$ must satisfy the normal force conditions

$$f_{Ni} \geq 0, \quad a_{Ni} \geq 0 \quad \text{and} \quad f_{Ni}a_{Ni} = 0, \qquad (15)$$

as well as

$$|f_{Fi}| \leq \mu f_{Ni}, \; a_{Fi}f_{Fi} \leq 0 \; \text{ and } \; a_{Fi}(\mu f_{Ni} - |f_{Fi}|) = 0. \qquad (16)$$

The condition $a_{Fi}(\mu f_{Ni} - |f_{Fi}|) = 0$ forces $f_{Fi}$ to have magnitude $\mu f_{Ni}$ if $a_{Fi}$ is nonzero. The condition $a_{Fi}f_{Fi} \leq 0$ forces $a_{Fi}$ and $f_{Fi}$ to have opposite sign, which means that the friction force opposes the tangential acceleration. We will call the conditions of equation (16) the *static friction conditions*; unless specifically noted, a contact point said to satisfy the static friction conditions implies satisfaction of the normal force conditions as well.

The approach taken by previous attempts[10,3] at modeling static friction has been to form an optimization problem. If we define the quantity scalar $z$ by

$$z = \sum_i \left( |a_{Fi}|(\mu f_{Ni} - |f_{Fi}|) + f_{Ni}a_{Ni} \right) \qquad (17)$$

then the problem becomes

$$\min_{f_{Ni}, f_{Fi}} z \text{ subject to } \begin{Bmatrix} f_{Ni} \geq 0 \\ a_{Ni} \geq 0 \end{Bmatrix} \text{ and } \begin{Bmatrix} a_{Fi}f_{Fi} \leq 0 \\ |f_{Fi}| \leq \mu f_{Ni} \end{Bmatrix}.$$

Computing contact forces in this manner does not appear to be practical.

## 5.2 Algorithm Outline

We believe it is better to deal with the problem as we did in the frictionless case: as a number of separate conditions. Let us consider the static friction condition with that perspective. We can state the conditions on $a_{Fi}$ and $f_{Fi}$ by considering that the "goal" of the friction force is to keep the tangential acceleration as small as possible, under the restriction $|f_{Fi}| \leq \mu f_{Ni}$. Accordingly, whenever $a_{Fi}$ is nonzero we insist that the friction force do its utmost to "make" $a_{Fi}$ be zero by requiring that the friction force push as hard as possible opposite the tangential acceleration. The reason that we find this a useful characterization is that it is *essentially the same characterization* we employed in section 4 to motivate the development of Dantzig's algorithm.

In section 4.1, we assumed that the normal force conditions were initially met for contacts 1 through $n - 1$ and began with $f_{Nn} = 0$. If this resulted in $a_{Nn}$ being nonnegative, then we immediately had a solution. Otherwise, it was in a sense $f_{Nn}$'s "fault" that $a_{Nn}$ was negative, and we increased $f_{Nn}$ to remedy the situation. We can do *exactly* the same thing to compute static friction forces! Suppose that the first $n-1$ contacts of our system satisfy all the conditions for static friction and that the normal force condition holds for the $n$th contact point. We set $f_{Fn} = 0$ and consider $a_{Nn}$. If $n \in NC$, or $n \in C$ but $f_{Nn} = 0$, then the static force condition is trivially met since

$|f_{Fn}| = 0 = \mu f_{Nn}$. If not, but it happens that $a_{Fn} = 0$, again, we have satisfied the static friction conditions, since $|f_{Fn}| = 0 < \mu f_{Nn}$. Otherwise, $a_{Fn}$ is nonzero and following our characterization of static friction we must increase the magnitude of the friction force to oppose the tangential acceleration as much as possible.

The procedure to do this is essentially the same as in the frictionless case. Without loss of generality, assume that at the $n$th contact point $a_{Fn} < 0$. We will gradually increase $f_{Fn}$ while maintaining the static friction and normal conditions at all the other $n - 1$ contact points and the normal condition at the $n$th contact point. As we increase $f_{Fn}$, at some point, one of two things must happen: either we will reach a point where $f_{Fn} = \mu f_{Nn}$, or we will reach a point where $a_{Fn} = 0$. In either case, the static friction conditions will then be met.

## 5.3 Maintaining the Static Friction Conditions

Once we have established the static friction conditions at a contact point, we need to maintain them. As before, we maintain the conditions $f_{Ni} \geq 0$, $a_{Ni} \geq 0$ and $f_{Ni}a_{Ni} = 0$ using the index sets $C$ and $NC$. To maintain the conditions on the $f_{Fi}$ and $a_{Fi}$ variables, we introduce the sets $C_F$, $NC^-$ and $NC^+$. The set $C_F$ is analogous to $C$; whenever $i \in C_F$, we manipulate $f_{Fi}$ to maintain $a_{Fi} = 0$. (We can have $i \in C_F$ and $i \in C$. The fact that $i \in C_F$ means we are maintaining $a_{Fi} = 0$, while the fact that $i \in C$ means we are maintaining $a_{Ni} = 0$.) In contrast to $C_F$, if $i \in NC^+$, then we have $a_{Fi} < 0$ and $f_{Fi} = \mu f_{Ni}$. As long as $i \in NC^+$, we vary $f_{Fi}$ so that it is always equal to $\mu f_{Ni}$. If $a_{Fi}$ becomes zero, we move $i$ from $NC^+$ into $C_F$. Thus, $NC^+$ denotes the set of contacts that have $f_{Fi}$ positive and at the upper bound of $\mu f_{Ni}$. Conversely, if $i \in NC^-$, then we have $a_{Fi} > 0$ and $f_{Fi} = -\mu f_{Ni}$. Again, as long as $i \in NC^-$ we will maintain the condition $f_{Fi} = -\mu f_{Ni}$, and move $i$ into $C_F$ if $a_{Ni}$ becomes zero. Whenever we are increasing some $f_{Nd}$ or increasing or decreasing some $f_{Fd}$, computing the corresponding changes in the other $f_{Fi}$ and $f_{Ni}$ variables, along with the maximum possible step size, is exactly the same as in the previous section.

In the frictionless case, when we managed to drive $a_{Nd}$ to zero, we added $d$ into $C$. For static friction, if the driving process stops because $a_{Fd}$ has reached zero, we insert $d$ into $C_F$. Otherwise, the process stopped because $|f_{Fd}| = \mu f_{Nd}$ and we add $d$ into $NC^-$ or $NC^+$ as appropriate. Before we present our algorithm for computing static friction forces in two dimensions, we discuss why the algorithm we present is not guaranteed to terminate.

## 5.4 Algorithm Correctness

In section 4, we showed that as we increased $f_d$, the acceleration $a_d$ always increased in response, guaranteeing that a sufficiently large increase of $f_d$ would achieve $a_d = 0$. We also showed that the index set $C$ would never repeat while forcing a particular $a_d$ to zero, guaranteeing we would not converge to some negative value. Finally, we showed that steps of size zero would not occur, guaranteeing that we would always make progress towards $a_d = 0$. For static friction, we can show all these properties except for the last.

First, let us show that if we start with $a_{Fd} < 0$, as we increase $f_{Fd}$, either we will reach a point where $f_{Fd} = \mu f_{Nd}$, or we will reach a point where $a_{Fd} = 0$. This is not obvious. Since $f_{Nd}$ is nonzero (otherwise $f_{Fd} = 0$ would satisfy the static friction conditions), we must have $d \in C$. This means that as we increase $f_{Fd}$, we may also be requiring that $f_{Nd}$ change as well. If $\mu f_{Nd}$ increases faster than $f_{Fd}$ does, then $f_{Fd}$ will never reach a value of $\mu f_{Nd}$.

Similarly, it is not necessarily the case that increasing $f_{Fd}$ will cause $a_{Fd}$ to increase. The reason for this is the following: the relation between the acceleration variables and force variables is still linear, and we can write

$$\mathbf{a} = \begin{pmatrix} a_{N1} \\ a_{F1} \\ \vdots \\ a_{Nn} \\ a_{Fn} \end{pmatrix} = \mathbf{A} \begin{pmatrix} f_{N1} \\ f_{F1} \\ \vdots \\ f_{Nn} \\ f_{Fn} \end{pmatrix} + \mathbf{b} = \mathbf{A}f + \mathbf{b} \qquad (18)$$

where $\mathbf{A} \in \mathbf{R}^{2n \times 2n}$ and $\mathbf{b} \in \mathbf{R}^{2n}$ and $f$ and $\mathbf{a}$ are the collection of the $f$ and $a$ variables. As long as we have no dynamic friction, it is still the case that $\mathbf{A}$ is symmetric and PSD. For a unit increase in $f_{F_d}$, we solve for $\Delta f_{N_i}$ and $\Delta f_{F_i}$ exactly as we did in section 4. That is, for $i \in C$, we require $\Delta a_{N_i} = 0$, and for all other $i$, we have $\Delta f_{N_i} = 0$. For the friction forces, almost the same holds: for $i \in C_F$ we require $\Delta a_{F_i} = 0$. However, for $i \in NC^-$, instead of setting $\Delta f_{F_i} = 0$, we require $\Delta f_{F_i} = -\mu \Delta f_{N_i}$, to maintain $f_{F_i} = -\mu f_{N_i}$. Similarly, for $i \in NC^+$ we require $\Delta f_{F_i} = \mu \Delta f_{N_i}$ to maintain $f_{F_i} = \mu f_{N_i}$. The side conditions $\Delta f_{F_i} = \pm \mu \Delta f_{N_i}$ prevent us from applying theorem 2 as we did in section 4 and claiming that $a_{F_d}$ increases as $f_{F_d}$ increases. In fact, in some situations, increasing $f_{F_d}$ will cause $a_{F_d}$ to *decrease*. The same holds for $f_{N_d}$ as well; prior to working on $f_{F_d}$ we may find that increasing $f_{N_d}$ to establish the normal force conditions may cause causes $a_{N_d}$ to decrease.

Is it possible then that we can drive some $f_{F_d}$ or $f_{N_d}$ infinitely far without reaching a stopping point? Fortunately, it is not. Theorem 3 of appendix A states that for frictionless systems, as we increase $f_{N_i}$ the index set $C$ never repeats. Exactly the same theorem is trivially extended to cover static friction. Thus, we will never encounter exactly the same sets $C$, $NC$, $C_F$, $NC^-$ and $NC^+$ while driving a given $f_{N_n}$ or $f_{F_n}$ variable. We can use this to show that increasing $f_{N_d}$ will eventually cause $a_{N_d}$ to increase. Exactly the same argument shows that increasing $f_{F_d}$ eventually causes $a_{F_d}$ to increase.

**THEOREM 1** *In a problem with static friction only, if $a_{N_d} < 0$ and $f_{N_d} = 0$ hold initially, a large enough increase in $f_{N_d}$ will eventually force $a_{N_d}$ to increase.*

**PROOF.** Suppose that we could arbitrarily increase $f_{N_d}$ without causing $a_{N_d}$ to increase. Since $\mathbf{A}$ is positive definite, in light of theorem 2 this can only happen if one or more of the side conditions $\Delta f_{F_i} = \pm \mu \Delta f_{N_i}$ hold, implying that $NC^- \cup NC^+ \neq \emptyset$. Since the index sets $C$, $NC$, $C_F$, $NC^-$ and $NC^+$ never repeat, there are only finitely many combinations of those sets that can be encountered while increasing $f_{N_d}$. That means that we can only undergo finitely many changes of the sets while increasing $f_{N_d}$. Eventually, we settle into a state where we can increase $f_{N_d}$ without $a_{N_d}$ increasing and without any change occurring in the index sets.

However, this cannot be, because of the definition of the index sets. For $i \in C$, to avoid a change in index sets, we must have $\Delta f_{N_i} \geq 0$; otherwise, a sufficiently large step will move $i$ into $NC$. The same logic requires that for $i \in NC$ we must have $\Delta a_{N_i} \geq 0$, otherwise $a_{N_i}$ will fall to zero. This yields $\Delta f_{N_i} \Delta a_{N_i} = 0$ for all $i$. For the friction forces, if $i \in C_F$, then $\Delta a_{F_i} = 0$ so $\Delta a_{F_i} \Delta f_{F_i} = 0$. For $i \in NC^+$, we have $a_{F_i} < 0$, requiring $\Delta a_{F_i} \leq 0$ to avoid having to move $i$ from $NC^+$ to $C_F$. Since $\Delta f_{N_i} \geq 0$ for all $i$ and $\Delta f_{F_i} = \mu \Delta f_{N_i}$, we have $\Delta f_{F_i} \geq 0$. This yields $\Delta a_{F_i} \Delta f_{F_i} \leq 0$ for all $i \in NC^+$. A symmetric argument holds, yielding $\Delta a_{F_i} \Delta f_{F_i} \leq 0$ for all $i \in NC^-$.

Additionally, for at least one $i$ in $NC^-$ or $NC^+$, both $\Delta a_{F_i}$ and $\Delta f_{F_i}$ are nonzero; otherwise, we could remove each side condition $\Delta f_{F_i} = \pm \mu \Delta f_{N_i}$ and add the conditions $\Delta f_{F_i} = 0$ and $\Delta a_{F_i} = 0$ without altering any other $\Delta f_{N_i}$ or $\Delta f_{F_i}$. If we did so however, we would then be entitled to apply theorem 2, contradicting our assumption that $a_{N_d}$ is nonincreasing. Thus, for at least one $i$ we

have $\Delta a_{F_i} \Delta f_{F_i}$ strictly less than zero. Combining that with the fact that $\Delta a_{N_i} \Delta f_{N_i} \leq 0$ and $\Delta a_{F_i} \Delta f_{F_i} \leq 0$ for all $i$ we obtain

$$\sum_i^n \Delta a_{N_i} \Delta f_{N_i} + \sum_i^n \Delta a_{F_i} \Delta f_{F_i} = \Delta \mathbf{a}^T \Delta f < 0. \qquad (19)$$

Since $\Delta \mathbf{a} = \mathbf{A} \Delta f$, this gives us

$$\Delta \mathbf{a}^T \Delta f = \Delta f^T \mathbf{A} \Delta f < 0. \qquad (20)$$

Since $\Delta f$ is nonzero and $\mathbf{A}$ is PSD, this is a contradiction (even if $\mathbf{A}$ is singular). Thus, $f_{N_d}$ cannot be increased without bound without eventually causing $a_{N_d}$ to increase. □

However, there is still the possibility of taking steps of size zero, and this is something that can and does occur when running the algorithm. Theorems 4 and 5 may fail to hold because of the side conditions $\Delta f_{F_i} = \pm \mu \Delta f_{N_i}$. The following scenario is possible: for some $i \in C$, $f_{N_i}$ decreases to zero. Accordingly, $i$ is moved from $C$ to $NC$. Upon computing $\Delta f$ with the new index set, we may find that $\Delta a_{N_i} < 0$ (which is ruled out in the frictionless case by theorem 4). As a result, a step of size zero is taken, and $i$ is moved *back* into $C$. Clearly, the algorithm settles into a loop, alternately moving $i$ between $C$ and $NC$ by taking a step of size zero each time. We cannot rule this behavior out in our algorithm for static friction. (This is also our current sticking point in trying to prove the conjecture that all systems with only static friction have solutions.) Fortunately, we have found a practical remedy for the problem.

While attempting to establish the normal force or static friction conditions at some point $k$, if we observe that a variable $i$ is alternating between $C$ and $NC$ (or between $NC^-$ and $C_F$ or $NC^+$ and $C_F$), we remove $i$ from *both* $C$ and $NC$ (or from $C_F$ and $NC^-$ or $NC^+$). Temporarily, we will "give up" trying to maintain the normal or static friction conditions at the $i$th contact point. We do so at the expense of making "negative progress," in the sense that although we will have achieved our immediate goal (establishing normal or friction conditions at a particular contact point), we will have done so by sacrificing normal and/or static friction conditions previously achieved at other contacts. The algorithm will be forced to reestablish the conditions at the points we have given up on at some later time. Since contact points no long necessarily keep their static friction or normal force conditions once established, we cannot prove (as yet) that this process will ever terminate.

We have however used this algorithm on a large variety of problems, and we have never yet encountered any situation for which our algorithm went into an infinite loop. We speculate that either no such situation is possible, meaning that all systems with static friction have solutions, or it requires an extremely carefully constructed problem to cause our algorithm to loop (although the latter possibility does not necessarily imply that there is in fact no solution $f$). A third possibility of course is that we simply have not sufficiently exercised our simulation system.

### 5.5 Algorithm for Computing Static Friction Forces

We now describe the necessary modifications to Dantzig's algorithm to handle static friction forces. The modifications increase the complexity of the "logical" portion of the algorithm, but the heart of the numerical code, computing $\Delta f$, remains the same. We give a description of the necessary modifications of each procedure of the algorithm.

### Modifications to *compute-frictionless-forces*

The sets $C$, $NC$, $C_F$, $NC^+$, and $NC^-$ are all initially empty. The main loop continually scans for a contact point at which the normal or static friction conditions are not met. If no such points exist, the algorithm terminates, otherwise, *drive-to-zero* is called to establish the conditions. Note that one must first establish the normal force conditions at a given point before establishing the static friction conditions there. In the event that the algorithm gives up on a contact point $i$ which has the normal conditions established, it will do so because $f_{N_i}$ is oscillating between $C$ and $NC$. At this point $f_{N_i} = 0$, and the normal conditions can be reestablished later.

If however we give up on the static friction conditions at the $i$th contact point, $f_{F_i}$ may be nonzero. (We cannot discontinuously set $f_{F_i}$ to zero as this might break the conditions at *all* the other contact points.) Later, when the algorithm attempts to reestablish the static friction conditions at $i$, we first drive $f_{F_i}$ to zero (simply by instructing *drive-to-zero* to increase or decrease $f_{F_i}$ until $f_{F_i} = 0$).

### Modifications to *drive-to-zero*

This function is the same, except that there are more ways for the index sets to change. If the limiting constraint $j$ returned by *maxstep* is the index of the force being driven, $j$ is moved into $C$ if it represents a normal force, and otherwise into $C_F$, $NC^-$, or $NC^+$ as appropriate; the procedure then returns. Otherwise, $j$ is moved between $C$ and $NC$ if it represents a normal force, and otherwise between $C_F$ and $NC^-$ or $NC^+$ as appropriate. If $j$ attempts to move into a set it just came from, and the previous step size was zero, $j$ is removed from whatever index set it was in. This is the point at which the algorithm temporarily gives up on maintaining the conditions at the $j$th contact point.

### Modifications to *fdirection*

The modifications are minor. First, if we are driving a normal force, we set $\Delta f_{N_d} = 1$, otherwise we set $\Delta f_{F_d} = \pm 1$, depending which way we want to drive the force. The index sets establish the set of equations to solve: for $i \in NC$, we set $\Delta f_{N_i} = 0$; for $i \in C$ we require $\Delta a_{N_i} = 0$; for $i \in C_F$ we require $\Delta a_{F_i} = 0$; and for $i \in NC^+ \cup NC^-$ we require $\Delta f_{F_i} = \pm \Delta f_{N_i}$.

### Modifications to *maxstep*

The modifications here are obvious. For each member $j$ in an index set, we compute the minimum step size $s$ that causes $j$ to need to change to another set. For the driving index $d$, we compute the step size that causes us to reach $a_{N_d} = 0$ for a normal force, and $a_{F_d} = 0$ or $f_{F_d} = \pm \mu f_{N_d}$ for a friction force. The minimum step $s$ that can be taken, along with the constraint $j$ responsible for that limit, is returned.

### 5.6 Three-dimensional Systems

We have been assuming that our system is two-dimensional. The extension to three dimensions is straightforward. At each contact point, let us denote vectors $\mathbf{u} \in \mathbf{R}^3$ tangent to the contact surface as pairs $(x, y)$ by choosing a local coordinate system such that $(1, 0)$ and $(0, 1)$ denote an orthonormal pair of tangent vectors. Let $(a_{x_i}, a_{y_i})$ and $(f_{x_i}, f_{y_i})$ denote the relative tangential acceleration and friction force, respectively, at the $i$th contact point. In three dimensions, the Coulomb friction law requires that the friction force be at least partially opposed to the tangential acceleration; that is,

$$(f_{x_i}, f_{y_i}) \cdot (a_{x_i}, a_{y_i}) = f_{x_i} a_{x_i} + f_{y_i} a_{y_i} \le 0. \quad (21)$$

The optimization approach taken in previous work[10,3] makes enforcing $|f_{F_i}| \le \mu f_{N_i}$ difficult, because

$$|f_{F_i}| = (f_{x_i}^2 + f_{y_i}^2)^{\frac{1}{2}} \le \mu f_{N_i} \quad (22)$$

is a nonlinear constraint. However, this constraint is easily dealt with by our algorithm. In place of the two sets $NC^-$ and $NC^+$, for three-dimensional systems, we use a single set $NC_F$. In two

dimensions, given $\Delta f_{N_i}$ and $\Delta f_{F_i}$, determining the step size $s$ so that $f_{F_i} + s\Delta f_{F_i} = \mu(f_{N_i} + s\Delta f_{N_i})$ is trivial. In three dimensions, computing $s > 0$ so that

$$(f_{x_i} + s\Delta f_{x_i})^2 + (f_{y_i} + s\Delta f_{y_i})^2 = (\mu(f_{N_i} + s\Delta f_{N_i}))^2 \quad (23)$$

is also trivial. As a result, it is easy to augment *maxstep* to move $i$ into $NC_F$ when $f_{x_i}^2 + f_{y_y}^2 = (\mu f_{N_i})^2$ and also easy to detect when to move $i$ back into $C_F$. When $i$ moves into $NC_F$, we record the direction that the friction force is pointing in. As long as $i$ remains in $NC_F$, we require the friction force $(f_{x_i}, f_{y_i})$ to maintain the same direction it had when $i$ most recently entered $NC_F$. Once $i$ moves back into $C_F$, the pair $(f_{x_i}, f_{y_i})$ may point in any direction.

To initially establish the static friction conditions for $f_{x_i}$ and $f_{y_i}$, we first increase $f_{x_i}$ (assuming $a_{x_i} < 0$) until either $i$ moves into $NC_F$, or $a_{x_i}$ reaches zero. If $i$ is in $NC_F$, we are done, otherwise, we now adjust $f_{y_i}$ so that either $a_{y_i}$ reaches zero, or $i$ moves into $NC_F$. Reversing the order with which one considers $x$ and $y$, or rotating the local coordinate system in the tangent plane may give rise to different solutions of $f$ with this method. This is a consequence of the condition of equation (21), which does not completely specify the direction of friction when the tangential acceleration is nonzero at a contact point.

### 6. Dynamic Friction

If the relative tangential velocity at a contact point is nonzero, then dynamic friction occurs, as opposed to static friction. Regardless of the resulting tangential acceleration, the strength of the friction force satisfies

$$|f_{F_i}| = \mu f_{N_i}, \quad (24)$$

with the direction of the force exactly opposite the relative tangential velocity. Since $f_{F_i}$ is no longer an independent variable, when we formulate equation (18), we can replace all occurences of $f_{F_i}$ with $\pm \mu f_{N_i}$. This replacement results in a matrix $\mathbf{A}$ which is unsymmetric and possibly indefinite as well. Because of this, systems with dynamic friction can fail to have solutions for the contact force magnitudes, requiring the application of an impulsive force. Another consequence of $\mathbf{A}$ losing symmetry and definiteness is that all the theorems in this paper which require $\mathbf{A}$ to be symmetric and PSD fail to hold. Remarkably, this turns out to be a fortunate development.

Previously, Baraff[3] presented an algorithm for computing friction forces and impulses for systems with dynamic friction but no static friction; the intent was to treat the problem of nonexistence of a solution $f$. Baraff's method for computing either regular or impulsive forces for systems with dynamic friction involved using Lemke's algorithm[5] for solving LCP's. It is noted that Lemke's algorithm can terminate by encountering an "unbounded ray." The algorithm we have just presented for static friction requires absolutely no modifications to handle dynamic friction in this manner. An unbounded ray corresponds to finding a state in which one can drive a variable $f_{N_i}$ or $f_{F_i}$ to infinity without forcing $a_{N_i}$ or $a_{F_i}$ to zero, or inducing a change in the index sets $C$, $NC$, $C_F$, $NC^+$ or $NC^-$. When this occurs, it is easily detected, in that *maxstep* returns a step size of $s = \infty$. Note that theorem 2 tells us that an infinite step cannot occur if $\mathbf{A}$ is symmetric and PSD. which means that infinite steps are possible only if there is dynamic friction in the system. Either our algorithm finds a solution $f$, or at some point $s = \infty$, and the current force direction $\Delta f$ matches the definition proposed by Baraff for suitably applying impulsive forces to systems with dynamic friction. As a result, we can unify our treatment of both dynamic and static friction in a single algorithm. We note in closing that we feel that this is mostly a theoretical, and not a practical concern, because we have encountered this infinite driving mostly in situations where $\mu$ has been made unrealistically large.

## 7. Results

Our method for computing contact and friction forces is both reliable and fast. Like most pivoting algorithms (for example, the simplex algorithm for linear programming), worst-case problems resulting in exponential running times can be constructed. Empirically however, the algorithm appears to require about $O(n)$ calls to *drive-to-zero* for systems with and without friction. Our real interest however is the performance of the algorithm in actual practice.

We have implemented the two-dimensional algorithm for static friction in an interactive setting and the three-dimensional algorithm in an offline simulation system. For frictionless systems, our solution algorithm compares favorably to Gaussian elimination with partial pivoting. Given a matrix $\mathbf{A}$ and vector $\mathbf{b}$, the algorithm of section 4 takes *only* two to three times longer to compute the contact forces than it would take to solve the linear system $\mathbf{Ax} = \mathbf{b}$, using Gaussian elimination. Compared with the best QP methods we know of, our algorithm runs five to ten times faster, on problems up to size $n = 150$. For systems with friction, there is no comparable solution algorithm we can compare our algorithm to.

Interactive simulations of $2\frac{1}{2}$D mechanisms are shown in figures 1 and 2. Fixed objects are colored in black. Objects in different "levels" are different colors (orange, purple, and green) and have no collision interaction. White circles indicate a bilateral point-to-point constraint. In figure 2, the green circles indicate contact points. Both systems can be simulated robustly at a consistent framerate of 20–30Hz on an SGI R4400 workstation.

## Acknowledgements

This research was funded in part by an NSF Research Initiation Award and an AT&T Foundation Equipment Grant. We would like to sincerely thank Michael Saunders and Richard Cottle for supplying us with a dense version of the LUSOL package and for clarifying several technical and historical points about LCP's.

## Appendix A: Theorems

In this appendix, we prove some theorems necessary to show that the algorithm for frictionless contact forces in section 4 terminates. For simplicity, we consider only the case when $\mathbf{A}$ is nonsingular and sketch the modifications necessary if $\mathbf{A}$ is singular.

**THEOREM 2** *Let the symmetric positive definite matrix $\mathbf{A}$ be partitioned as in equation (7). If $\mathbf{x}$ satisfies $\mathbf{A}_{11}\mathbf{x} = -\mathbf{v}_1$, then the quantity $\mathbf{v}_1^T\mathbf{x} + \alpha$ is always positive.*

**PROOF.** Principal submatrices of $\mathbf{A}$ are positive definite, so $\alpha > 0$, $\mathbf{A}_{11}$ is positive definite and the submatrix

$$\begin{pmatrix} \mathbf{A}_{11} & \mathbf{v}_1 \\ \mathbf{v}_1^T & \alpha \end{pmatrix}$$

is positive definite. Applying a Cholesky factorization, we can write

$$\begin{pmatrix} \mathbf{A}_{11} & \mathbf{v}_1 \\ \mathbf{v}_1^T & \alpha \end{pmatrix} = \begin{pmatrix} \mathbf{L}_{11} & \mathbf{0} \\ \mathbf{L}_{12}^T & \mathbf{L}_{22} \end{pmatrix} \begin{pmatrix} \mathbf{L}_{11}^T & \mathbf{L}_{12} \\ \mathbf{0} & \mathbf{L}_{22} \end{pmatrix} \quad (25)$$

where $\mathbf{L}_{11}$ and $\mathbf{L}_{12}$ have the same dimensions as $\mathbf{A}_{11}$ and $\mathbf{v}_1$ respectively, and $\mathbf{L}_{22}$ is a positive scalar. Note that since $\mathbf{A}_{11} = \mathbf{L}_{11}\mathbf{L}_{11}^T$ is invertible, $\mathbf{L}_{11}$ is also invertible and $\mathbf{A}_{11}^{-1} = \mathbf{L}_{11}^{-T}\mathbf{L}_{11}^{-1}$. From equation (25), we have $\mathbf{v}_1 = \mathbf{L}_{11}\mathbf{L}_{12}$. Since $\mathbf{A}_{11}\mathbf{x} = -\mathbf{v}_1$, we also have $\mathbf{x} = -\mathbf{A}_{11}^{-1}\mathbf{v}_1$. Then

$$\begin{aligned} \mathbf{v}_1^T\mathbf{x} + \alpha &= \alpha - \mathbf{v}_1^T\mathbf{A}_{11}^{-1}\mathbf{v}_1 \\ &= \alpha - (\mathbf{L}_{12}^T\mathbf{L}_{11}^T)\mathbf{A}_{11}^{-1}(\mathbf{L}_{11}\mathbf{L}_{12}) \end{aligned}$$

$$\begin{aligned} &= \alpha - \mathbf{L}_{12}^T\mathbf{L}_{11}^T\mathbf{L}_{11}^{-T}\mathbf{L}_{11}^{-1}\mathbf{L}_{11}\mathbf{L}_{12} \\ &= \alpha - \mathbf{L}_{12}^T\mathbf{L}_{12}. \end{aligned}$$

From equation (25) we have $\alpha = \mathbf{L}_{12}^T\mathbf{L}_{12} + \mathbf{L}_{22}^2$; thus

$$\mathbf{v}_1^T\mathbf{x} + \alpha = \alpha - \mathbf{L}_{12}^T\mathbf{L}_{12} = \mathbf{L}_{22}^2. \quad (26)$$

Since $\mathbf{L}_{22}$ is positive, $\mathbf{v}_1^T\mathbf{x} + \alpha$ is positive. $\square$

Almost the same result applies when $\mathbf{A}$ is not invertible. In this case, $\mathbf{A}_{11}$ may be singular; note however that a Cholesky factorization can still be obtained although $\mathbf{L}_{11}$ may now be singular. Since it is still the case that $\mathbf{A}_{11} = \mathbf{L}_{11}\mathbf{L}_{11}^T$, and $\mathbf{L}_{11}$ and $\mathbf{L}_{11}\mathbf{L}_{11}^T$ have exactly the same column space, the fact that $\mathbf{v}_1 = \mathbf{L}_{11}\mathbf{L}_{12}$ implies that $\mathbf{v}_1$ is in the column space of $\mathbf{A}_{11}$. Thus, the equation $\mathbf{A}_{11}\mathbf{x} = -\mathbf{v}_1$ will always have a solution. Using basic continuity principles[4] it can be shown that in the singular case, $\mathbf{v}_1^T\mathbf{x} + \alpha \geq 0$.

**THEOREM 3** *During a given call to drive-to-zero, the same index set $C$ is never repeated.*

**PROOF.** Suppose some index set $C$ was repeated during a call to *drive-to-zero*. Since $C \cup NC$ remains constant during a given invocation of *drive-to-zero* (except at the last step, where the driving index $d$ is added to $C$), whenever $C$ is repeated, $NC$ is repeated as well. Let the values of $\boldsymbol{f}$ the first time and second time $C$ is encountered be denoted $\boldsymbol{f}^{(1)}$ and $\boldsymbol{f}^{(2)}$ respectively. Let $\mathbf{a}^{(1)} = \mathbf{A}\boldsymbol{f}^{(1)} + \mathbf{b}$ and $\mathbf{a}^{(2)} = \mathbf{A}\boldsymbol{f}^{(2)} + \mathbf{b}$. The intuition of the proof is simple: if the algorithm could have increased $\boldsymbol{f}$ along a straight line from $\boldsymbol{f}^{(1)}$ to $\boldsymbol{f}^{(2)}$, it would have done so. The fact that it did not means that increasing from $\boldsymbol{f}^{(1)}$ to $\boldsymbol{f}^{(2)}$ must have required a change between $C$ and $NC$. We show that this cannot happen because of the inherent convexity involved, contradicting the fact that $C$ was repeated.

Specifically, we have $a_i^{(1)} = a_i^{(2)} = 0$ for all $i \in C$ and $a_i^{(1)} \geq 0$ and $a_i^{(2)} \geq 0$ for all $i \in NC$. Given $C$ and $NC$, the vector $\boldsymbol{f}$ is increased in the direction $\Delta\boldsymbol{f}$ where $\Delta f_i = 0$ for $i \in NC$, $\Delta f_d = 1$ and $\Delta a_i = 0$ for $i \in C$. However, the vector

$$\mathbf{y} = \frac{\boldsymbol{f}^{(2)} - \boldsymbol{f}^{(1)}}{f_d^{(2)} - f_d^{(1)}} \quad (27)$$

fulfills all the conditions for $\Delta\boldsymbol{f}$, since $y_d = 1$, $y_i = 0$ for $i \in NC$, and the vector

$$\mathbf{Ay} = \frac{\mathbf{A}(\boldsymbol{f}^{(2)} - \boldsymbol{f}^{(1)})}{f_d^{(2)} - f_d^{(1)}} = \frac{\mathbf{a}^{(2)} - \mathbf{a}^{(1)}}{f_d^{(2)} - f_d^{(1)}} \quad (28)$$

has its $i$th component equal to zero for all $i \in C$. Thus, when $C$ was first encountered, $\Delta\boldsymbol{f} = \mathbf{y}$ was chosen. If $a_d = 0$ could have been achieved by increasing $\boldsymbol{f}$ in this direction, *drive-to-zero* would have terminated, and $C$ would not have been repeated. This means that in increasing from $\boldsymbol{f}^{(1)}$ in the direction $\Delta\boldsymbol{f} = \mathbf{y}$, it was necessary to change $C$ and $NC$ prior to reaching $\boldsymbol{f}^{(2)}$; that is for some value $t$ in the range $0 < t < 1$, either

$$\left(\mathbf{A}(\boldsymbol{f}^{(1)} + t(\boldsymbol{f}^{(2)} - \boldsymbol{f}^{(1)})) + \mathbf{b}\right)_j < 0 \quad (29)$$

for some $j \in NC$ or

$$\left(\boldsymbol{f}^{(1)} + t(\boldsymbol{f}^{(2)} - \boldsymbol{f}^{(1)})\right)_j < 0 \quad (30)$$

for some $j \in C$. However, since neither of the above two equations are satisfied when $t = 0$ or $t = 1$, and the equations involve only

---

[4] If $\mathbf{A}$ is a symmetric PSD singular matrix, then there exist arbitrarily small perturbation matrices $\epsilon$ such that $\mathbf{A} + \epsilon$ is symmetric positive definite (and hence nonsingular).

linear relations and inequalities, by convexity, neither of the two above equations are satisfied for any value $0 < t < 1$. This contradicts the assumption that the same set $C$ was encountered twice during a call of *drive-to-zero*. □

This theorem also extends to the algorithm for static friction in section 5. Namely, we claim that the index sets $C$, $NC$, $C_F$, $NC^-$ and $NC^+$ are never repeated while driving a given force variable $f_{N_d}$ or $f_{F_d}$. The proof is exactly the same, the only difference being that extra conditions of the form $\Delta f_{F_i} = \pm\mu\Delta f_{N_i}$ may be present. However, given that $f^{(1)}$ and $f^{(2)}$ satisfy these extra conditions, any vector $f^{(1)} + t(f^{(2)} - f^{(1)})$ for $0 < t < 1$ will satisfy these properties as well. Again, this means that the algorithm should have gone directly from $f^{(1)}$ to $f^{(2)}$, contradicting the fact that the index sets were repeated.

The last two theorems guarantee that the frictionless algorithm never takes steps of size zero, as long as the system is not degenerate. A *degenerate problem* (not to be confused with $\mathbf{A}$ being singular) is one that would require the algorithm to to make two or more changes in the index sets $C$ and $NC$ at exactly the same time (for example, if two normal forces decreased to zero simultaneously). When degeneracy occurs, it is possible that some number of size zero steps are taken. Cottle[5, section 4.2, pages 248–251] proves that the frictionless algorithm cannot loop due to degeneracy.

Proving that a nondegenerate problem never takes steps of size zero is relatively straightforward. We need to show that whenever $i \in C$ moves to $NC$, $a_i$ immediately increases. As a result, $i$ cannot immediately move back to $C$ without taking a step of nonzero size. Similarly, we need to show that whenever $i \in NC$ moves to $C$, $f_i$ immediately increases.

**THEOREM 4** *In a nondegenerate problem, when an index $i$ moves from $C$ to $NC$, $a_i$ immediately increases.*

**PROOF.** Without loss of generality, let $C = \{1, 2, ..., k - 1\}$ and let us assume that the $k$th contact has just moved from $C$ to $NC$. When $k$ was still in $C$, we computed $\Delta f_i$ by solving the system $\mathbf{A}_{11}\mathbf{x} = -\mathbf{v}_1$ and setting $\Delta f_i = x_i$. Let $\mathbf{A}_{11}$ and $\mathbf{x}$ be partitioned by

$$\mathbf{A}_{11}\mathbf{x} = \begin{pmatrix} \mathbf{B} & \mathbf{w} \\ \mathbf{w}^T & \beta \end{pmatrix}\begin{pmatrix} \mathbf{u} \\ y \end{pmatrix} = \begin{pmatrix} \mathbf{z} \\ c \end{pmatrix} = -\mathbf{v}_1 \quad (31)$$

where $\mathbf{B} \in \mathbf{R}^{(k-1)\times(k-1)}$, $\mathbf{u}, \mathbf{w}, \mathbf{z} \in \mathbf{R}^k$ and $y$, $\beta$, and $c$ are scalars. This yields

$$\mathbf{u} = \mathbf{B}^{-1}(\mathbf{z} - \mathbf{w}y) \quad \text{and} \quad \mathbf{w}^T\mathbf{u} = c - \beta y \quad (32)$$

or

$$\mathbf{w}^T\mathbf{B}^{-1}(\mathbf{z} - \mathbf{w}y) = c - \beta y. \quad (33)$$

Since this $\Delta f$ caused $f_k$ to decrease to zero, $\Delta f_k = y$ must have been negative.

Once $k$ moves into $NC$ and we recompute $\Delta f$, we need to show the new $\Delta a_k$ will be positive. Let $\tilde{\mathbf{u}}$ and $\tilde{y}$ denote the new values computed for $\mathbf{u}$ and $y$ when we resolve for $\Delta f$. Since $k$ is now in $NC$, we set $\Delta f_k = \tilde{y} = 0$, and solve

$$\mathbf{B}\tilde{\mathbf{u}} + \mathbf{w}\tilde{y} = \mathbf{z} \quad (34)$$

to obtain

$$\tilde{\mathbf{u}} = \mathbf{B}^{-1}\mathbf{z}. \quad (35)$$

From equations (8) and (31), the new $\Delta a_k$ is

$$\Delta a_k = \mathbf{w}^T\tilde{\mathbf{u}} + \beta\tilde{y} - c = \mathbf{w}^T\tilde{\mathbf{u}} - c. \quad (36)$$

Substituting from equations (35) and (33), we have

$$\begin{aligned} \Delta a_k &= \mathbf{w}^T\mathbf{B}^{-1}\mathbf{z} - c \\ &= -\mathbf{w}^T\mathbf{B}^{-1}\mathbf{w}y - \beta y \quad (37) \\ &= -y(\mathbf{w}^T\mathbf{B}^{-1}\mathbf{w} + \beta). \end{aligned}$$

Since $\mathbf{A}_{11}$ is positive definite, $\mathbf{B}^{-1}$ is positive definite, and $\beta$ is positive, so $\mathbf{w}^T\mathbf{B}^{-1}\mathbf{w} + \beta$ must be positive. Since $y$ is negative, $-y$ is positive, and we conclude that $\Delta a_k > 0$. □

This theorem extends immediately to the case when $\mathbf{A}$ is singular, because the index sets $C$ encountered never produce a singular submatrix $\mathbf{A}_{11}$.

**THEOREM 5** *In a nondegenerate problem, when an index $i$ moves from $NC$ to $C$, $f_i$ immediately increases.*

**PROOF.** The proof is constructed in the same way as the proof of the previous theorem. □

## References

[1] D. Baraff. Analytical methods for dynamic simulation of non-penetrating rigid bodies. In *Computer Graphics (Proc. SIGGRAPH)*, volume 23, pages 223–232. ACM, July 1989.

[2] D. Baraff. Curved surfaces and coherence for non-penetrating rigid body simulation. In *Computer Graphics (Proc. SIGGRAPH)*, volume 24, pages 19–28. ACM, August 1990.

[3] D. Baraff. Issues in computing contact forces for non-penetrating rigid bodies. *Algorithmica*, 10:292–352, 1993.

[4] R.W. Cottle and G.B. Dantzig. Complementary pivot theory of mathematical programming. *Linear Algebra and its Applications*, 1:103–125, 1968.

[5] R.W. Cottle, J.S. Pang, and R.E. Stone. *The Linear Complementarity Problem*. Academic-Press, Inc., 1992.

[6] P. Gill, S. Hammarling, W. Murray, M. Saunders, and M. Wright. User's guide for LSSOL: A Fortran package for constrained linear least-squares and convex quadratic programming. Technical Report Sol 86-1, Systems Optimization Laboratory, Department of Operations Research, Stanford University, 1986.

[7] P. Gill, W. Murray, M. Saunders, and M. Wright. User's guide for QPSOL: A Fortran package for quadratic programming. Technical Report Sol 84-6, Systems Optimization Laboratory, Department of Operations Research, Stanford University, 1984.

[8] P. Gill, W. Murray, M. Saunders, and M. Wright. User's guide for NPSOL: A Fortran package for nonlinear programming. Technical Report Sol 86-2, Systems Optimization Laboratory, Department of Operations Research, Stanford University, 1986.

[9] P.E. Gill, W. Murray, M.A. Saunders, and H.W. Wright. Maintaining LU factors of a general sparse matrix. *Linear Algebra and its Applications*, 88/89:239–270, 1987.

[10] P. Lötstedt. Numerical simulation of time-dependent contact friction problems in rigid body mechanics. *SIAM Journal of Scientific Statistical Computing*, 5(2):370–393, 1984.

[11] R.E. Marsten. The design of the XMP linear programming library. *ACM Transactions on Mathematical Software*, 7(4):481–497, 1981.

[12] B. Murtagh and M. Saunders. MINOS 5.1 User's guide. Technical Report Sol 83-20R, Systems Optimization Laboratory, Department of Operations Research, Stanford University, 1987.

[13] M. Saunders. Personal communication. September 1993.

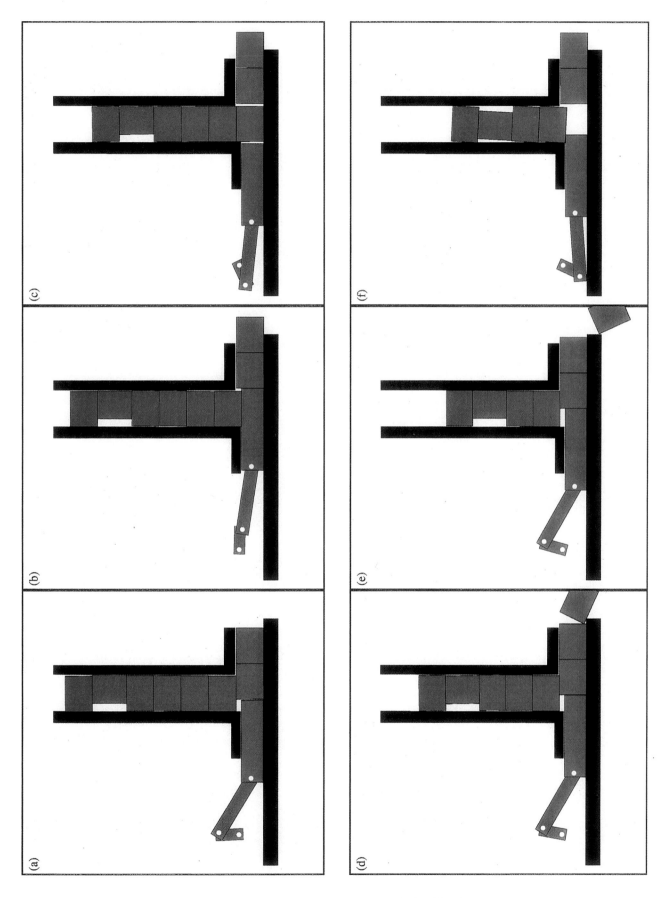

**Figure 1: Time-lapse simulation sequence of a blockfeeder.**

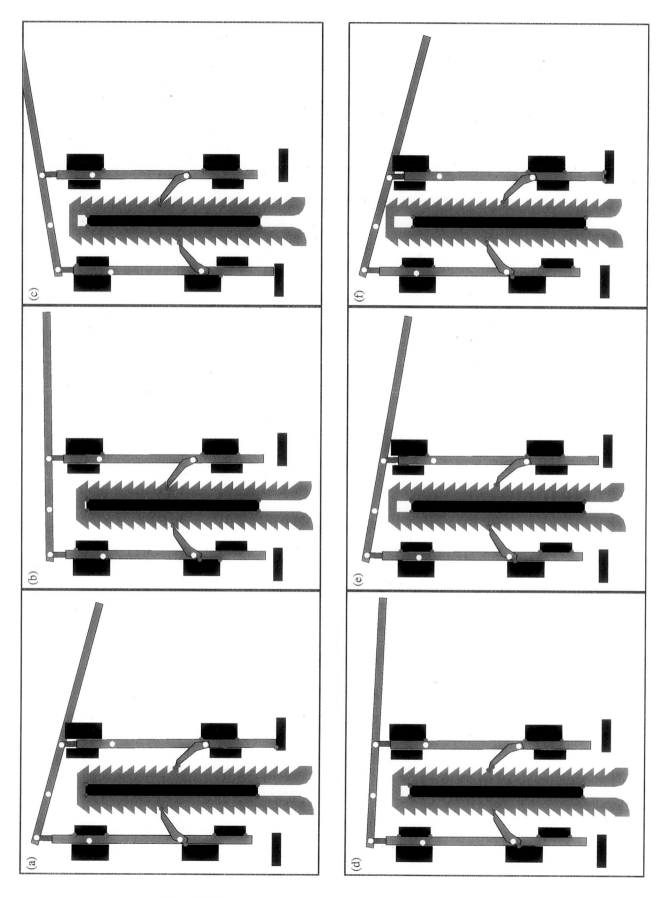

**Figure 2: Time-lapse simulation sequence of a double-action jack.**

# Hierarchical Spacetime Control

Zicheng Liu
zl@cs.princeton.edu

Steven J. Gortler
sjg@cs.princeton.edu

Michael F. Cohen
mfc@cs.princeton.edu

Department of Computer Science
Princeton University

## Abstract

Specifying the motion of an animated linked figure such that it achieves given tasks (e.g., throwing a ball into a basket) and performs the tasks in a realistic fashion (e.g., gracefully, and following physical laws such as gravity) has been an elusive goal for computer animators. The *spacetime constraints* paradigm has been shown to be a valuable approach to this problem, but it suffers from computational complexity growth as creatures and tasks approach those one would like to animate. The complexity is shown to be, in part, due to the choice of finite basis with which to represent the trajectories of the generalized degrees of freedom. This paper describes new features to the spacetime constraints paradigm to address this problem.

The functions through time of the generalized degrees of freedom are reformulated in a hierarchical wavelet representation. This provides a means to automatically add detailed motion only where it is required, thus minimizing the number of discrete variables. In addition the wavelet basis is shown to lead to better conditioned systems of equations and thus faster convergence.

**CR Categories and Subject Descriptors:** I.3.7 [Computer-Graphics]: *Three Dimensional Graphics and Realism* ; I.6.3 [Simulation and Modeling]: *Applications* ; G.1.6 [Constrained Optimization]

**Additional Key Words and Phrases: Animation, Spacetime, Wavelets.**

## 1 Introduction

The spacetime constraint method, proposed in 1988 by Witkin and Kass [18], and extended by Cohen [5], has been shown to be a useful technique for creating physically based and goal directed motion of linked figures. The basic idea of this approach can be illustrated with a three-link arm and a ball (see Figure 1). The problem statement begins with specifying *constraints*, examples being specifying the position of the arm at a given time, requiring the ball to be in the hand (end effector) at time $t_0$, and that the arm is to throw the ball at time $t_1$ to land in a basket at time $t_2$. In addition, the animator must specify an *objective* function, such as to perform the tasks specified by the constraints with minimum energy or some other style consideration. The solution to such a series of specifications is a set of functions through time (or *trajectories*) of each degree of freedom (DOF), which in this case are the joint angles of the arm. Thus the unknowns span both space (the joint angles) and time, and have led to the term *spacetime constraints*.

Related approaches to the spacetime constraint paradigm are reported in [17, 12]. In each of these papers, feedback control

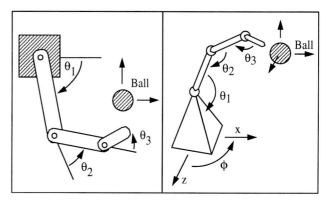

**Figure 1**: A planar three-link arm and a 6 DOF basketball player.

strategies are the fundamental unknown functions rather than DOF trajectories. The goal is set, for example, for the creature to move in some direction as far as possible in 10 seconds, and a *score* for a particular motion is defined as the distance traveled. An initial control strategy is selected, a dynamic simulation is run and the results are scored. Iterations change the control strategy, as opposed the motion curves, producing a simulation that, hopefully, has a higher score. The results of these studies are encouraging, however, they are distinctly different from that in the previous spacetime constraint work (and the work described in this paper) in which the aim is to provide the animator with the overall control of the motion.

The spacetime constraint formulation leads to a non-linear constrained variational problem, that in general, has no closed form solution. In practice, the solution is carried out by reducing the space of possible trajectories to those representable by a linear combination of basis functions such as cubic B-splines. Finding the finite number of coefficients for the B-splines involves solving the related constrained optimization problem, (i.e., finding the coefficients to create motion curves for the DOF that minimize the objective while satisfying the constraints). Unfortunately, general solutions to such a non-linear optimization problem are also unknown.

Based on this observation, Cohen developed an interactive spacetime control system using hybrid symbolic and numeric processing techniques [5]. In this system, the user can interact with the iterative numerical optimization and can *guide* the optimization process to converge to an acceptable solution. One can also focus attention on subsets or *windows* in spacetime. This system produces physically based and goal directed motions, but it still suffers from a number of computational difficulties, most notably as the complexity of the creature or animation increases. Addressing this problem is the central focus of this paper.

One problem that arises is the symbolic processing of the constraints and objective, and the subsequent evaluation of expressions. Constraints and objectives are entered into the system by the user and/or by automatic construction of the equations of motion from the linkage description. These may be any second order

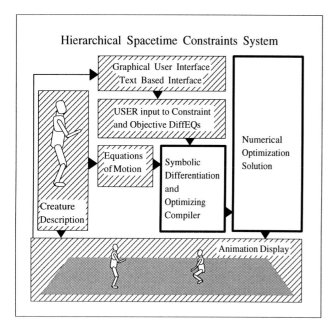

**Figure 2**: The Hierarchical Spacetime Constraints System. This paper focuses on the Symbolic Differentiation and Optimizing Equation Compiler, and the Numerical Optimization System

differential equation of the linkage DOF. The symbolic processing stage is responsible for deriving the first (and possibly second) derivatives of each constraint expression and the objective with respect to each DOF. The result is the construction of evaluation trees to evaluate each expression and its derivatives. Unfortunately, even a planar three-link arm can result in evaluation trees containing over 145,000 nodes, that must be evaluated multiple times during the optimization process. The process described above is closely related to that of compiler design and optimization [1]. In particular, the compiler optimization technique of *common subexpression elimination* has been shown to be of great value in reducing the size of the evaluation trees and thus greatly speeds up the symbolic computation of the derivative expressions and the subsequent numerical evaluations [11]. In our experiments, common subexpression elimination resulted in one to two orders of magnitude of reduction in evaluation of the resulting expressions.

A more important difficulty in the spacetime system is that the user is required to choose the discretization of the B-spline curves. If not enough control points are selected, there may be no feasible solution (i.e., one that meets all constraints), or the restriction to the curve is so severe, that the resulting motion curves have a much higher objective cost than necessary. If too many control points are selected, then the computational complexity is increased unnecessarily due to the larger number of unknowns as well as the resulting ill-conditioning of the linear subproblems that arise in the solution [16]. This complexity issue is addressed by reformulating the DOF functions in a *hierarchical* basis, in particular, in a B-spline wavelet (B-wavelet) basis. Wavelets provide a natural and elegant means to include the proper amount of local detail in regions of spacetime that require the extra subdivision without overburdening the computation as a whole.

## 2 System overview

The interactive spacetime control system is shown in Figure 2. Input to the system includes user defined constraints and objectives and a creature description from which the symbolic equations of motion are generated automatically. The equations of motion

define the torque at each joint as a function of the position and velocity of all joints as well as physical properties such as mass and length of the links. These expressions for torque are central to the definition of a minimum energy objective. The expressions are next symbolically differentiated and compiled to create concise evaluation trees.

The main focus of this paper is on the next section, the numerical process that solves for the coefficients of the chosen B-spline or hierarchical wavelet basis. Finally, the intermediate and final animations are displayed graphically. The animator can simply watch the progress of the optimization procedure or can interact directly with the optimization by creating starting motion curves for the DOF and/or by modifying intermediate solutions.

### 2.1 Symbolic Constraints and Objectives

An important feature of the interactive spacetime constraints system is the ability to specify and modify constraints and the objective at run-time. This requires a high level graphical and/or textual interface to communicate the animator's intentions. The constraints and/or objective may be any second order integro-differential expression. A simple language interface has been developed for this specification with a syntax much like general mathematical expressions. In most cases, a constraint is a simple differential expression such as that a particular joint, at a particular point in time must have a given value, or that its velocity must be zero or some other value. The expressions arising from the equations of motion are much longer and include many transcendental functions. In addition, these expressions form the terms of the integrand of the minimum energy objective defined by integrating the square of the joint torques over time. For example, for the three link arm

$$f(\Theta) = \int_{t_0}^{t_f} \tau_1^2 + \tau_2^2 + \tau_3^2 \, dt \qquad (1)$$

where $\Theta$ are the generalized DOF (i.e., the joint angles), and $\tau_i$ is the torque about joint $i$. Numerical quadrature of such expressions can then be carried out by evaluating the expression at multiple values of $T$.

### 2.2 Expression Differentiation and Compilation

The symbolic expressions for constraints and objectives are then *compiled* for evaluation during the numerical optimization process. Compiler designers are faced with similar problems and thus many techniques from the compiler optimization literature [1] are applicable here. Related work is also found in the literature on automatic differentiation [15], and similar work to the current application is described in the CONDOR system by Kass [11].

The compiler developed in the spacetime problem begins with a bottom up parser that produces an evaluation tree for each expression. The expression can then be evaluated by inserting the DOF values in the leaves of the tree and recursively evaluating nodes upward until the value of the expression is contained at the topmost node. The expressions arising in this context, however, often contain many common subexpressions. The problems in building and evaluating the expressions is exacerbated by the fact that the optimization routines require gradients (Jacobians) and possibly Hessians of the constraints and objective.

To avoid extra evaluation, common subexpressions are extracted by recursively moving from the leaves to the top node, making a list of unique nodes and checking each new node against the list. In the case of leaf nodes that are always variable ID's, this is simple, for internal function nodes their children must be checked, and in the case of commutative operations both orderings must be checked.

As an example of the power of the common subexpression elimination (CSE), the expression trees for the three link arm without CSE contained 145,584 nodes, compared to 2,932 nodes after CSE[1]!

Once the reduced expression trees are built, each expression is evaluated one or more times per optimization iteration. The greatest savings occur in the evaluation of the integrals that comprise the objective since the numerical quadratures request multiple evaluations of the compiled expressions with different values of $T$. The change in $T$ directly affects only the values inserted at the leaves of the trees, and thus a single compilation may be used hundreds or thousands of times.

## 3  Hierarchical B-splines

In the most general setting, the trajectory of a DOF, $\theta(t)$, can be any function in $L^2$. In practice, however, solving the spacetime constraint problem requires restricting the solution to some finite dimensional function space, leading to a finite number of scalar unknowns. The possible trajectories a particular DOF can take are thus restricted to be a linear combination of basis functions chosen to represent the DOF motion curve. In other words, given $n$ basis functions,

$$\theta(t) = \sum_{i=1}^{n} c_i \, \phi_i(t) \qquad (2)$$

where the coefficients $c_i$ scale the basis functions $\phi_i(t)$. In the spacetime constraint systems to date, Witkin and Kass [18] used discretized functions consisting of evenly spaced points in time from which derivatives were approximated by finite differencing. Cohen represented the DOF functions as uniform cubic B-spline curves, with some provision to change the resolution of the B-splines within specified regions of the curve.

The more basis functions and corresponding coefficients that are used, the larger the space of possible solutions. Unfortunately, for two reasons, one pays a high cost in terms of computational resources for this extra freedom. The extra unknown coefficients translate into larger subproblems at each iteration of the solution. In addition, discretizations of this type also lead to ill-conditioned systems requiring more iterations to solve [16].

Ideally, one would like to select a function space with just enough freedom to allow an almost optimal answer. In smooth portions of the trajectories, basis functions can be wider and in regions where the trajectory varies quickly, there should be more, narrower bases. Unfortunately, the optimal trajectories are not known in advance and thus a more flexible basis must be developed that can *adapt* to the local detail in the trajectories as the iterative solution proceeds.

*Hierarchical* systems of basis functions offer just this type of adaptivity. Hierarchical B-splines have been used in the context of shape design [8] to allow modification of curves and surfaces at levels of detail selected by the user. The hierarchical B-spline basis consists of a pyramid of translations and dilations of B-splines (the rows labeled $V$ in Figure 3) ranging from very wide B-splines at the top to finer scaled basis functions below.

Each level going down contains twice as many basis functions per unit length. This hierarchical basis has attractive properties for use in describing the trajectories in the current application. However, this is a *redundant* basis, since any function realizable at one level can also be created from the finer basis functions below. In addition, how to achieve the desired adaptivity is not immediately apparent.

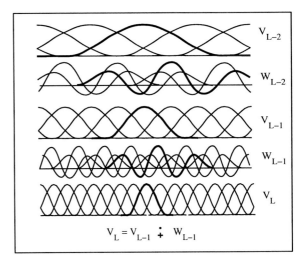

$$V_L = V_{L-1} \; \dotplus \; W_{L-1}$$

**Figure 3**: Hierarchy of B-spline and Wavelet Bases.

## 4  Wavelets

A more elegant and concise hierarchical basis, and one that leads naturally to an adaptive basis, is offered by a *wavelet* construction. This section concentrates on the advantages of wavelets and wavelet formulations in the spacetime animation problem.

The primary difference between wavelets and hierarchical B-splines is that the wavelet coefficients at each level represent *differences* from the levels above as opposed to directly representing the local function value. Also, unlike hierarchical B-splines, each new layer is not redundant with those above but rather adds only *local detail* in the result at some resolution.

### 4.1  Advantages of Wavelets to Spacetime Animation

The wavelet construction results in a non-redundant basis that provides the means to begin with a low resolution basis and then *adaptively refine* the representation layer by layer when necessary without changing the representation above. If refinements are required in only part of the interval, then only those coefficients whose bases have support in this region need to be added.

Since the wavelet coefficients encode differences, in smooth portions of the trajectory the coefficients encoding finer scale detail will be zero. Thus, only those basis functions with resulting coefficients greater than some $\epsilon$ will have a significant influence on the curve and the rest can be ignored. In other words, given an *oracle* function [10, 9], (discussed later) that can predict which coefficients will be above a threshold, only the corresponding subset of wavelets needs to be included.

Solutions to the non-linear spacetime problem, as discused in more detail below, involve a series of quadratic subproblems for which the computational complexity depends on the number of unknown coefficients. The smaller number of significant unknown coefficients in the wavelet basis provide faster iterations. In addition, the wavelet basis provides a better conditioned system of equations than the uniform B-spline basis, and thus requires less iterations. The intuition for this lies in the fact that there is no single basis in the original B-spline basis that provides a global estimate of the final trajectory (i.e., the locality of the B-spline basis is, in this case, a detriment). Thus, if the constraints and objective do not cause interactions across points in time, then information about changes in one coefficient travels very slowly (in $O(n)$ iterations) to other parts of the trajectory. In contrast, the hierarchical wavelet basis provides a shorter ($O(\log(n))$) "communication" distance between any two basis functions. This is the

---

[1] It should be noted that further reductions in the DAGs could be made through the use of trigonometric identities, however, this has not been done in the current implementation.

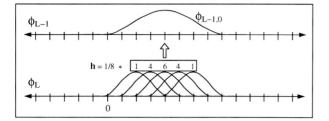

**Figure 4**: Five B-splines $\phi_{L,j}$ may be combined using the weights $h$ to construct the double width B-spline $\phi_{L-1,0}$

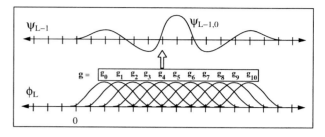

**Figure 5**: Eleven B-splines $\phi_{L,j}$ may be combined using the weights $g$ to construct the wavelet function $\psi_{L-1,0}$

basic insight leading to *multigrid* methods [16], and the related hierarchical methods discussed here.

An additional benefit involves the integration of the objective. Since a lower resolution results, by definition, in a smoother trajectory, less samples must be taken during the numerical quadrature. As wavelets are added in particular regions, the sampling density only needs to be increased in these areas.

Finally, the wavelet representation allows the user to easily lock in the coarser level solution and only work on details simply by removing the coarser level basis functions from the optimization. This provides the means to create small systems that solve very rapidly to develop the finest details in the trajectories.

### 4.2 Wavelet Construction: Two-Part Basis

To explain the complete wavelet construction, a first step will be to create a new basis for the same space of functions defined by the B-splines, but consisting of two distinct types of basis functions. To understand the two-part basis, begin with the familiar cubic B-spline basis made up of translated copies of the B-spline blending function $\phi(t)$. Let us denote the basis functions as

$$\phi_{L,j}(t) = \phi(t - j) \qquad (3)$$

(the index $j$ represents the translation of a specific basis function from the canonical B-spline basis function left justified at zero [2], and $L$ is the *level* or resolution of the basis). The space (or family) of functions spanned by all linear combinations of these basis functions will be denoted $V_L$. $V_L$ contains all functions that are piecewise cubic between adjacent integers, and are $C^2$ (have simple knots at the integers).

Wavelets offer an alternative basis for the same space $V_L$, in particular, a hierarchical basis. But let us begin by building a two-part basis at level $L - 1$ of the hierarchy (i.e., at half the resolution). The two-part basis begins with the basis functions

$$\phi_{L-1,j}(t) = \phi(2^{-1}t - j) \qquad (4)$$

These basis functions are twice as wide as the original B-spline basis functions, and hence the space they span contains piecewise cubic functions with simple knots at all *even* integers. This space will be referred to as $V_{L-1}$. According to the well known B-spline knot insertion algorithm [2, 4] there is the following relationship

$$\phi_{L-1,j} = \sum_k h_{k-2j} \, \phi_{L,k} \qquad (5)$$

where the sequence $h$ is given in the appendix. See Figure 4.

Clearly $V_{L-1}$ is a proper subset of $V_L$ and thus, it is not as rich as the space $V_L$. Therefore, to find a new basis for $V_L$, more basis functions are needed than just those that span $V_{L-1}$. In the wavelet methodology, this is accomplished by introducing into the basis, translated copies of a special wavelet shape $\psi$. Just as with the B-splines, the relationship between the wavelet basis functions and the model wavelet shape is notated $\psi_{L-1,j}(t) = \psi(2^{-1}t - j)$. These new basis functions are defined as:

$$\psi_{L-1,j} = \sum_k g_{k-2j} \, \phi_{L,k} \qquad (6)$$

where the sequence $g$ is given in the appendix. See Figure 5. There is some degree of freedom in choosing the sequence $g$, as long as the new basis functions "fill in" the missing space between $V_L$ and $V_{L-1}$. In other words the $\psi_{L-1,j}$ must span a function space $W_{L-1}$ such that $V_{L-1} \dot{+} W_{L-1} = V_L$ (direct sum). See Figure 3.

The sequence used here was chosen so that the basis functions $\psi_{L-1,j}$ are orthogonal to the basis functions $\phi_{L-1,j}$ with respect to the $L_2$ inner product, defined for general functions $f$ and $g$ as

$$\langle f(t), g(t) \rangle = \int_{-\infty}^{+\infty} f(t)g(t) \, dt \qquad (7)$$

This type of construction is called *semi-orthogonal*. (In an orthogonal construction *all* of the basis functions are orthogonal to each other.) Other advantages to this particular choice of $g$ include compactness and symmetry.

With this construction, we now have two alternate bases for $V_L$, the B-spline basis

$$\{\phi_{L,j}\} \qquad (8)$$

and the *two-part* basis

$$\{\phi_{L-1,j}, \psi_{L-1,j}\} \qquad (9)$$

Just as the two-part basis functions can be expressed as a combination of the B-splines basis functions (Equations (5) and (6)), so too, the B-spline basis functions can theoretically be expressed as combinations of the two-part basis functions. This is given by

$$\phi_{L,j} = \sum_k \tilde{h}_{j-2k} \, \phi_{L-1,k} + \sum_k \tilde{g}_{j-2k} \, \psi_{L-1,k} \qquad (10)$$

The sequences $\tilde{h}$ and $\tilde{g}$ which are described in [4] have infinite length but decay quickly from their centers. In the literature, there are many wavelet constructions, each with its own particular functions $\phi$ an $\psi$, and sequences $h$, $g$, $\tilde{h}$, and $\tilde{g}$, with varying degrees of orthogonality, compactness, and smoothness. The sequences and the particular wavelet construction described in this paper are derived in [4], and were chosen because of the semi-orthogonality of the basis, the associated $\phi$ is a cubic B-spline (i.e., $C^2$), and the wavelet function $\psi$ is symmetric with compact support.

Suppose some DOF function $\theta(t)$ in $V_L$ has been expressed as a linear combination of the B-spline basis functions

$$\theta(t) = \sum_j c_{\phi_{L,j}} \, \phi_{L,j} \qquad (11)$$

where the $c$ are scalar coefficients. The coefficients needed to express the function in the two-part basis can be found using the following formula

$$c_{\phi_{L-1,j}} = \sum_k \tilde{h}_{k-2j} \, c_{\phi_{L,k}}$$

$$c_{\psi_{L-1,j}} = \sum_k \tilde{g}_{k-2j} \, c_{\phi_{L,k}} \qquad (12)$$

and now

$$\theta(t) = \sum_j c_{\phi L-1,j} \; \phi_{L-1,j}(t) + \sum_j c_{\psi L-1,j} \; \psi_{L-1,j}(t) \quad (13)$$

(This process is similar to the one illustrated in Figures (4-5) except that $h$ and $g$ and are interchanged with $\tilde{h}$ and $\tilde{g}$). Intuitively speaking, the $c_{\phi L-1,j}$ encode the smooth (low frequency) information about the function $\theta(t)$, and the $c_{\psi L-1,j}$ encode the detail (higher frequency) information. In a semi-orthogonal construction (as well as a fully orthogonal one), the smooth component $s(t) = \sum_j c_{\phi L-1,j} \, \phi_{L-1,j}(t)$ is the orthogonal projection of $\theta(t)$ into $V_{L-1}$. Thus, it is the best approximation of $\theta(t)$ in the space $V_{L-1}$ where the error is measured by

$$\| e(t) \| = \langle e, e \rangle^{1/2} \quad (14)$$

Alternatively if $\theta(t)$ has been represented with respect to the two-part basis, the representation with respect to the B-spline basis can be found with

$$c_{\phi L,j} = \sum_k h_{j-2k} \; c_{\phi L-1,k} + \sum_k g_{j-2k} \; c_{\psi L-1,k} \quad (15)$$

## 4.3   Wavelets on the Interval

In a classical wavelet construction, the index $j$ goes from $-\infty \ldots \infty$, and $V_L$ includes functions of unbounded support. In an animation context, only functions over some fixed finite interval of time need to be expressed, and it is important to only deal with a finite number of basis functions. Therefore, the space $V_L$ used here will be the space of all $C^2$ functions defined over the interval $[0 \ldots 2^L]$ that are piecewise cubic between adjacent integers (simple knots at the inner integers and quadruple knots at the boundaries). A basis for $V_L$ is made up of *inner* basis functions, which are just those translational basis functions $\phi_{L,j}$ from Section 4.2 whose support lies completely within the interval, as well as three special *boundary* B-spline basis functions at each end of the interval. For the boundary basis functions, one may either choose to include the translational basis functions $\phi_{L,j}$ themselves from Section 4.2 whose support intersects the boundaries by just truncating those basis functions at the boundary, or else one may use the special boundary basis functions that arise from placing quadruple knots at the boundaries [2]. This complete set of basis functions will be denoted $\phi_{L,j}$ with $j$ in $\{-3 \ldots 2^L - 1\}$, where it is understood that the first and last three basis functions are the special boundary B-spline basis functions.

The two-part basis for $V_L$ begins with the wider B-spline functions $\phi_{L,j}$ with $j$ in $\{-3 \ldots 2^{L-1} - 1\}$ where again the first and last three basis functions are scaled versions of the special boundary B-splines functions. The two-part basis is completed with the wavelet functions $\psi_{L-1,j}$ with $j$ in $\{-3 \ldots 2^{L-1} - 4\}$. Here too, the *inner* wavelet basis functions are just those translational functions $\psi_{L-1,j}$ from Section 4.2 that do not intersect the boundaries, while the first three and the last three interval wavelet basis functions must be specially designed to fit in the interval and still be orthogonal to the $\phi_{L-1,j}$. A full description of this construction is given in [3, 14].

This interval construction, which on the real line corresponds to Equations (5) and (6), is described by the linear time procedure **basis_xform_up** that is given in the appendix. As this procedure is equivalent to multiplication with a banded matrix, the inverse procedure **basis_xform_down** which describes the interval version of Equation (10) can be implemented by solving the banded linear system. This too can be done in linear time.

The interval version of Equation (15) can be implemented with the procedure **coef_xform_down**. And the inverse transformation, which is the interval equivalent of Equation (12) may be implemented by the procedure **coef_xform_up**.

## 4.4   Complete Wavelet Basis

The reasoning that was used to construct the two-part basis can now be applied recursively $L - 3$ times to construct a multilevel *wavelet basis*. Thus far, a two-part basis $\{\phi_{L-1,j}, \psi_{L-1,j}\}$ has been discussed as an alternative for the B-spline basis $\{\phi_{L,j}\}$.

Note that roughly half of the basis functions in the two-part basis are themselves B-spline basis functions (only twice as wide). To continue the wavelet construction, keep the basis functions $\psi_{L-1,j}$ and re-apply the reasoning of section 4.2 to replace the $\phi_{L-1,j}$ with $\{\phi_{L-2,j}, \psi_{L-2,j}\}$ This results in the new basis $\{\phi_{L-2,j}, \psi_{L-2,j}, \psi_{L-1,j}\}$.

Each time this reasoning is applied, the number of B-spline functions in the hierarchical basis is cut in half (roughly), and the new basis functions become twice as wide. After $L - 3$ applications [2], the wavelet basis

$$\{\phi_{3,k}, \psi_{i,j}\} \quad (16)$$

is obtained, with $i$ in $\{3 \ldots L - 1\}$, $k$ in $\{-3 \ldots 7\}$ and $j$ in $\{-3 \ldots 2^i - 4\}$, where the inner basis functions are defined by

$$\begin{aligned} \phi_{i,j}(t) &= \phi(2^{(i-L)}t - j) \\ \psi_{i,j}(t) &= \psi(2^{(i-L)}t - j) \end{aligned} \quad (17)$$

This basis is made up of eleven wide B-splines, and translations (index $j$) and scales (index $i$) of the wavelet shape (as well as scales of the boundary wavelet basis functions).

The coefficients representing some function in the B-spline basis can be transformed to the full wavelet basis using the procedure **coef_pyrm_up**, that makes $L - 3$ calls to **coef_xform_up** each time with an input vector of $1/2$ the length. (Note since this transforms an n-vector to an n-vector, it can be implemented with proper indexing using linear storage).

```
coef_pyrm_up( b_in[], b_out[], w_out[][], L )
   b_temp[L][] = b_in[] ;
   for( i = L; i ≥ 4; i-- )
      coef_xform_up( b_temp[i][], b_temp[i-1][],
                     w_out[i-1][], i ) ;
   b_out[] = b_temp[3][] ;
```

The inverse transformation is

```
coef_pyrm_down( b_in[], w_in[][] , b_out[], L )
   b_temp[3][] = b_in[] ;
   for( i = 4; i ≤ L; i++ )
      coef_xform_down( b_temp[i-1][], w_in[i-1][],
                       b_temp[i][], i ) ;
   b_out[] = b_temp[L][] ;
```

Finally, the basis transformations **basis_pyrm_up** and **basis_pyrm_down** are identical to the above procedures, with the exception of replacing the procedures **coef_xform_up** and **coef_xform_down** with **basis_xform_up** and **basis_xform_down**.

The running time of these pyramid procedures is governed by the geometric series $(n + \frac{n}{2} + \frac{n}{4} + \ldots + 1) = O(n)$, and hence they run in linear time. Each one of these four procedures transforms one $n$-vector, to another, and thus can be represented as a matrix. If $M$ is the matrix of the linear transformation performed by the procedure **coef_pyrm_up**, then $M^{-1}$ is the matrix of

---

[2] This process is stopped after $L - 3$ applications so that the three left boundary basis functions don't intersect the right boundary and vice versa

**coef_pyrm_down**, $M^{-T}$ is the matrix of **basis_pyrm_up** and $M^T$ is the matrix of **basis_pyrm_down**.

The wavelet basis is an alternate basis for $V_L$, but unlike the B-spline basis, it is an $L - 3$ level hierarchical basis. At level 3 there are eleven broad B-splines, and eight broad wavelets. These basis functions give the coarse description of the function. At each subsequent level going from level 3 to $L - 1$, the basis includes twice as many wavelets, and these wavelets are twice as narrow as the ones on the previous level. Each level successively adds more degrees of detail to the function.

Since each wavelet coefficients represents the amount of local detail of a particular scale, *if the function is sufficiently smooth in some region, then very few non-zero wavelet coefficients will be required in that region*[3].

### 4.5 Scaling

One final issue is the scaling ratio between the basis functions. Traditionally [4] the wavelet functions are defined with the following scaling:

$$\begin{aligned} \phi_{i,j}(t) &= 2^{(i-L)/2} \, \phi(2^{(i-L)}t - j) \\ \psi_{i,j}(t) &= 2^{(i-L)/2} \, \psi(2^{(i-L)}t - j) \end{aligned} \tag{18}$$

This means that at each level up, the basis functions become twice as wide, and are scaled $\frac{1}{\sqrt{2}}$ times as tall. While in many contexts this normalizing may be desirable, for optimization purposes it is counter productive. For the optimization procedure to be well conditioned [6] it is advantageous to emphasize the coarser levels and hence use the scaling defined by

$$\begin{aligned} \phi_{i,j}(t) &= 2^{L-i} \, \phi(2^{(i-L)}t - j) \\ \psi_{i,j}(t) &= 2^{L-i} \, \psi(2^{(i-L)}t - j) \end{aligned} \tag{19}$$

where the wider functions are also taller. In the pyramid code, this is achieved by multiplying all of the $h$ and $g$ entries by 2.

## 5 Implementation

The input to the wavelet spacetime problem includes the creature description, the objective function (i.e., symbolic expressions of joint torques generated from the creature description), and user defined constraints specifying desired actions (throw, catch, etc.), and inequality constraints such as joint limits on the elbow. As discussed in section 2.1, these symbolic expressions are differentiated and *compiled* into DAGs.

At this point, a constrained variational problem is defined

$$\begin{aligned} \text{minimize} \quad & f(\Theta, \dot{\Theta}, \ddot{\Theta}) \\ \text{subject to} \quad & C_i(\Theta, \dot{\Theta}, \ddot{\Theta}) = 0, \, i \in n_{eq} \\ & C_i(\Theta, \dot{\Theta}, \ddot{\Theta}) \geq 0, \, i \in n_{ineq} \end{aligned} \tag{20}$$

where $\Theta$ is the vector of trajectories of the degrees of freedom of the creature.

Each trajectory, $\theta(t)$, is represented in the uniform cubic B-spline basis. The unknowns are then the B-spline coefficients, **b**, or the equivalent wavelet coefficients, **c**, scaling the individual basis functions. This finite set of coefficients provide the information to evaluate the $\theta(t)$, $\dot{\theta}(t)$, and $\ddot{\theta}(t)$ at any time $t$, that comprise the leaves of the DAGs. This finite representation transforms the variational problem into a constrained non-linear optimization problem.

Non-linear optimization methods, in general, require a step that transforms the constrained problem into an unconstrained one.

Possibilities include constructing a system of Lagrange multipliers as was used in [5] or using penalty functions for the constraints [13]. In the case of penalty functions a unified *cost function* to minimize is derived as

$$F(\Theta) = f(\Theta) + \sum_{i \in n_{eq}} w_i * C_i(\Theta)^2 + \sum_{i \in n_{ineq}} w_i * (\min(C_i(\Theta), 0))^2 \tag{21}$$

where the $w_i$ weight the individual constraints.

Solution methods then may consist of a sequence of quadratic subproblems (SQP) making a series of Newton steps towards a solution (as described in [5]). Alternatively, quasi-Newton methods such the Broyden-Fletcher-Goldfarb-Shanno (BFGS) can be used to solve the unconstrained problem [7, 13]. Quasi-Newton methods are similar to Newton's method except that the inverse of the Hessian at each iteration is approximated by a symmetric positive definite matrix, that is corrected or updated from iteration to iteration.

BFGS iterations begin with a user provided initial guess of wavelet coefficients $\mathbf{c}_0$ (that can be derived from B-spline coefficients using **coef_pyrm_up**) and a guess $\mathbf{H}_0$ of the inverse of the Hessian (usually an identity matrix leading to the first iteration being a simple gradient descent).

At each iteration, if the current solution is $\mathbf{c}_k$ and the current guess of the inverse of the Hessian is $\mathbf{H}_k$, then the descent direction is $\Delta \mathbf{c}_k = -\mathbf{H}_k * \mathbf{c}_k$ and a line search finds the $\lambda_k > 0$ minimizing $F(\mathbf{c}_k + \lambda_k * \Delta \mathbf{c}_k)$. A (hopefully) better solution $\mathbf{c}_{k+1}$ is found as $\mathbf{c}_{k+1} = X_k + \lambda_k * \Delta \mathbf{c}_k$. If using the quasi-Newton method $\mathbf{H}_{k+1}$ is updated correspondingly by using BFGS correction formula [7]

$$\mathbf{H}_{k+1} = \mathbf{H}_k + \left(1 + \frac{\gamma^T \mathbf{H}_k \gamma}{\delta^T \gamma}\right) \frac{\delta \delta^T}{\delta^T \gamma} - \left(\frac{\delta \gamma^T \mathbf{H}_k + \mathbf{H}_k \gamma \delta^T}{\delta^T \gamma}\right) \tag{22}$$

where $\gamma = \nabla F_{k+1} - \nabla F_k$ (the change in the gradient of the cost function) and $\delta = \mathbf{c}_{k+1} - \mathbf{c}_k$ (the change in the coefficients, both B-spline and wavelet).

The newly obtained solution $\mathbf{c}_{k+1}$ is then transformed into B-spline coefficients $\mathbf{b}_{k+1}$ with **coef_pyrm_down**, and $\mathbf{b}_{k+1}$ is sent to the graphical user interface for display.

If the initial function space is restricted to a coarse representation consisting of the broad B-splines and a single level of wavelets, after each iteration a simple *oracle* function adds wavelets at finer levels only when the wavelet coefficient above exceeds some tolerance. This procedure quickly approximates the optimal trajectory and smoothly converges to a final answer with sufficient detail in those regions that require it.

An important feature of the system discussed in [5] is also available in the current implementation. The user can directly modify the current solution with a simple key frame system to help *guide* the numerical process. This is critical to allow the user, for example, to move the solution from an underhand to an overhand throw, both of which represent local minima in the same optimization problem. The next iteration then begins with these new trajectories as the current guess.

## 6 Results

A set of experiments was run on the problem of a three-link arm and a ball (see Figure 1). The goal of the arm is to begin and end in a rest position hanging straight down, and to throw the ball into a basket. The objective function is to minimize energy, where energy is defined as the integral of the sum of the squares of the joint torques. Gravity is active.

The four graphs in Figure 6 show the convergence of five different test runs of the arm and ball example. Each plot differs only

---

[3]In this case, non-zero can be defined to be having an absolute value greater than some epsilon without incurring significant error in the representation.

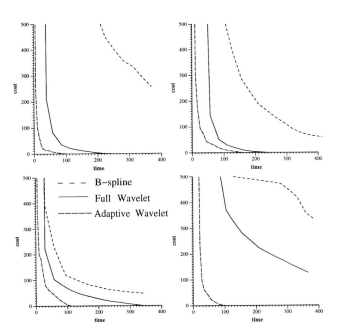

**Figure 7**: Scene from a basketball game.

**Figure 6**: Convergence of Arm and Ball example for 4 different starting trajectories. The first and fourth examples resulted in underhand throws, and the rest overhand. Time is in seconds, and the cost is a weighted sum of constraint violations and energy above the local minimum.

in the starting trajectories of the arm DOF. Each run converged to either an underhand or overhand throw into the basket. The full B-spline basis contained 67 basis functions for each of the three DOF, thus there were 201 unknown coefficients to solve for. Iterations took approximately 7 seconds each on an SGI workstation with an R4000 processor. Convergence was achieved on each, but only after many iterations due to the ill-conditioning of the B-spline formulation.

The full wavelet basis also contained 67 basis function per DOF (11 B-splines at the top level and 56 wavelets below), thus iterations also took approximately the same 7 seconds. Figure 6 clearly shows the improved convergence rates of the wavelet formulations over the B-spline basis, due to better conditioned linear systems. The adaptive wavelet method with the oracle was the fastest since the number of unknowns was small in early iterations, leading to a very fast approximation of the final trajectories, in addition to the better conditioning provided by the hierarchical basis. The final few iterations involved more wavelets inserted by the oracle to complete the process. Note that in each case, a good approximation to the complete animation was achieved in less than a minute of computation.

A short sequence involving two basketball players with six degrees of freedom each (see Figures 1,7) was animated. The task was a "give and go" play. Player A passes the ball to player B, then moves towards the basket. Player B passes it pack to A who makes the shot. This animation was created in stages: first player A throws the ball to a location set by the user, then player B's actions are animated to catch the ball, then player B's throw is animated followed by player A catching this throw and making the basket. Each stage of the animation took between 10 and 25 iterations of approximately 6-10 seconds each. The longer iteration times are due to the 6 DOF of each creature leading to twice the number of unknowns.

## 7 Conclusion

The spacetime constraint system first suggested by Witkin and Kass [18] for animating linked figures has been shown to be an effective means of generating goal based motion. Cohen enhanced this work by demonstrating how to focus the optimization step on *windows* of spacetime and methodologies to keep the user in the optimization loop. This paper has extended this paradigm by removing two major difficulties.

The first improvement is in the runtime symbolic differentiation and subsequent *compilation* of constraints and objectives. By utilizing common subexpression elimination, a technique adopted from compiler optimization and automatic differentiation, the size and evaluation of the resulting expression trees is reduced by two orders of magnitude.

Perhaps the more important improvement lies in the representation of the trajectories of the DOF in a wavelet basis. This resulted in faster optimization iterations due to less unknown coefficients needed in smooth regions of the trajectory. In addition, even with the same number of coefficients, the systems become better conditioned and thus less iterations are required to settle to a local minimum. Results are shown for a planar three-link arm and two six DOF "basketball players".

The paper has not discussed details of the user interface to the new spacetime system. Important aspects of the system are the ability to construct creature descriptions, specify and modify constraints and objectives and modify trajectories between optimization iterations. This requires integration of other technologies such as inverse kinematic specification, and could take advantage of high level language interfaces. These aspects of the total system are currently being investigated. The underlying mathematical framework described in this paper should now provide an excellent platform for these endeavors.

## Appendix

This appendix provides pseudo code for the procedures discussed in Section 4.3. The sequence $h$ and the sequence $g$ are the convolution sequences used to construct the inner basis functions [4], while the vectors $\underline{h}_j$ and the vectors $\underline{g}_j$ are used to construct the boundary basis functions [3, 14]. Only the vectors for the left boundary are given, the vectors for the right boundaries are the mirror images of these vectors. It is assumed that the boundary B-spline basis functions are those that arise by placing quadruple knots at the boundaries.

$$h[0..4] = \frac{1}{8} * \{1, 4, 6, 4, 1\}$$
$$g[0..10] = \frac{1}{8!} * \{-1, 124, -1677, 7904, -18482, 24264, -18482,$$
$$7904, -1677, 124, -1\}$$
$$\underline{h}_{-3} = \frac{1}{16} * \{16, 8, 0, 0, 0, \ldots\}$$
$$\underline{h}_{-2} = \frac{1}{16} * \{0, 8, 12, 3, 0, 0, \ldots\}$$
$$\underline{h}_{-1} = \frac{1}{16} * \{0, 0, 4, 11, 8, 2, 0, \ldots\}$$

$$\frac{1}{8!} * \begin{pmatrix} \underline{g}_{-3} & \underline{g}_{-2} & \underline{g}_{-1} \\ \frac{1136914560}{27877} & -\frac{2387315040}{195139} & \frac{123066720}{1365937} \\ -\frac{1655323200}{27877} & \frac{2141121840}{195139} & -\frac{2226000}{1365937} \\ \frac{1321223960}{27877} & \frac{878161880}{195139} & \frac{188417600}{1365937} \\ -\frac{633094403}{27877} & -\frac{498772701}{27877} & -\frac{2293862247}{1365937} \\ \frac{229000092}{27877} & \frac{4726413628}{195139} & \frac{10796596516}{1365937} \\ -\frac{46819570}{27877} & -\frac{3606490941}{195139} & -\frac{25245248833}{1365937} \\ 124 & 7904 & 24264 \\ -1 & -1677 & -18482 \\ 0 & 124 & 7904 \\ . & -1 & -1677 \\ . & 0 & 124 \\ . & . & -1 \\ . & . & 0 \\ . & . & . \end{pmatrix}$$

The following procedure describes how the two-part basis functions are constructed by linearly combining the B-spline basis functions. (see Equations 5 and 6).

```
basis_xform_up( b_in[], b_out[], w_out[], L )
    b_out = w_out = 0 ; /* zero vectors */
    for (j = 0; j ≤ 2^{L-1}-4; j++)
        for (k = 2j; k ≤ (2j+4); k++)
            b_out[j] += h[k-2j] * b_in[k] ;
    for (j = 0; j ≤ 2^{L-1}-7; j++)
        for (k = 2j; k ≤ (2j+10); k++)
            w_out[j] += g[k-2j] * b_in[k] ;
    for (j in [-3,-2,-1,2^{L-1}-3,2^{L-1}-2,2^{L-1}-1] )
        b_out[j] = h_j · b_in ; /*dot product*/
    for (j in [-3,-2,-1,2^{L-1}-4,2^{L-1}-5,2^{L-1}-6] )
        w_out[j] = g_j · b_in ;
```

This procedure can be expressed as multiplication by a banded matrix, and so the inverse procedure
`basis_xform_down( b_in[], w_in[], b_out[], L )`
can be obtained by solving this banded linear system.

The following procedure can be used to obtain B-spline coefficients given two-part coefficients.

```
coef_xform_down( b_in[], w_in[], b_out[], L )
    b_out = 0 ; /* zero vector */
    for(k = 0; k ≤ 2^{L-1}-4; k++)
        for(j = 2k; j ≤ (2k+4); j++)
            b_out[j] += h[j-2k] * b_in[k] ;
    for(k = 0; k ≤ 2^{L-1}-7; k++)
        for(j = 2k; j ≤ (2k+10); j++)
```

```
            b_out[j] += g[j-2k] * w_in[k] ;
    for(k in [-3,-2,-1,2^{L-1}-3,2^{L-1}-2,2^{L-1}-1] )
        b_out += h_k * b_in[k] ; /*vector addition*/
    for(k in [-3,-2,-1,2^{L-1}-4,2^{L-1}-5,2^{L-1}-6] )
        b_out += g_k * w_in[k] ;
```

This procedure can be expressed as multiplication by a banded matrix, and so the inverse procedure
`coef_xform_up( b_in[], b_out[], w_out[], L )`
can be obtained by solving this banded linear system.

## Acknowledgements

The authors owe a debt to Charles Rose who implemented the user interface for this work. This research was supported in part by the National Science Foundation, Grant CCR-9296146.

## References

[1] AHO, A. V., SETHI, R., AND ULLMAN, J. D. *Compilers: Priciples, Techniques and Tools.* Addison Wesley, 1986.

[2] BARTELS, R., BEATTY, J., AND BARSKY, B. *An Introduction to Splines for Use in Computer Graphics and Modeling.* Morgan Kaufmann, 1987.

[3] CHUI, C., AND QUAK, E. Wavelets on a bounded interval. *Numerical Methods of Approximation Theory 9* (1992), 53–75.

[4] CHUI, C. K. *An Introduction to Wavelets*, vol. 1 of *Wavelet Analysis and its Applications.* Academic Press Inc., 1992.

[5] COHEN, M. F. Interactive spacetime control for animation. *Computer Graphics 26*, 2 (July 1992), 293–302.

[6] DAHMEN, W., AND KUNOTH, A. Multilevel preconditioning. *Numerische Mathematik 63* (1992), 315–344.

[7] FLETCHER, R. *Practical Methods of Optimization*, vol. 1. John Wiley and Sons, 1980.

[8] FORSEY, D., AND BARTELS, R. Hierarchical b-spline refinement. *Computer Graphics 22*, 4 (August 1988), 205–212.

[9] GORTLER, S., AND COHEN, M. F. Variational modeling with wavelets. Tech. Rep. CS-TR-456-94, Department of Computer Science, Princeton University, 1994.

[10] GORTLER, S., SCHRÖDER, P., COHEN, M., AND HANRAHAN, P. Wavelet radiosity. In *Computer Graphics, Annual Conference Series, 1993* (August 1993), Siggraph, pp. 221–230.

[11] KASS, M. Condor: Constraint based dataflow. *Computer Graphics 26*, 2 (July 1992), 321–330.

[12] NGO, J. T., AND MARKS, J. Spacetime constraints revisited. In *Computer Graphics, Annual Conference Series, 1993* (August 1993), Siggraph, pp. 343–350.

[13] PAPALAMBROS, P. Y., AND WILDE, D. J. *Principles of Optimal Design.* Cambridge University Press, Cambridge, England, 1988.

[14] QUAK, E., AND WEYRICH, N. Decomposition and reconstruction algorithms for spline wavelets on a bounded interval. Tech. Rep. 294, Center for Approximation Theory, Texas A&M, 1993.

[15] RALL, L. B. *Automatic Differentiation: Techniques and Applications.* Springer-Verlag, 1981.

[16] TERZOPOULOS, D. Image analysis using multigrid relaxation methods. *IEEE PAMI 8*, 2 (March 1986), 129–139.

[17] VAN DE PANNE, M., AND FIUME, E. Sensor-actuator networks. In *Computer Graphics, Annual Conference Series, 1993* (August 1993), Siggraph, pp. 335–342.

[18] WITKIN, A., AND KASS, M. Spacetime constraints. *Computer Graphics 22*, 4 (August 1988), 159–168.

# Artificial Fishes:
# Physics, Locomotion, Perception, Behavior

Xiaoyuan Tu and Demetri Terzopoulos

Department of Computer Science, University of Toronto

**Keywords:** *behavioral animation, artificial life, autonomous agents, animate vision, locomotion control, physics-based modeling*

**Abstract:** *This paper proposes a framework for animation that can achieve the intricacy of motion evident in certain natural ecosystems with minimal input from the animator. The realistic appearance, movement, and behavior of individual animals, as well as the patterns of behavior evident in groups of animals fall within the scope of the framework. Our approach to emulating this level of natural complexity is to model each animal holistically as an autonomous agent situated in its physical world. To demonstrate the approach, we develop a physics-based, virtual marine world. The world is inhabited by artificial fishes that can swim hydrodynamically in simulated water through the motor control of internal muscles that motivate fins. Their repertoire of behaviors relies on their perception of the dynamic environment. As in nature, the detailed motions of artificial fishes in their virtual habitat are not entirely predictable because they are not scripted.*

## 1 Introduction

Imagine a virtual marine world inhabited by a variety of realistic fishes. In the presence of underwater currents, the fishes employ their muscles and fins to gracefully swim around immobile obstacles and among moving aquatic plants and other fishes. They autonomously explore their dynamic world in search of food. Large, hungry predator fishes hunt for smaller prey fishes. Prey fishes swim around happily until they see a predator, at which point they take evasive action. When a predator appears in the distance, similar species of prey form schools to improve their chances of escape. When a predator approaches a school, the fishes scatter in terror. A chase ensues in which the predator selects victims and consumes them until satiated. Some species of fishes seem untroubled by predators. They find comfortable niches and forage on floating plankton when they are hungry. When compelled by their libidos, they engage in elaborate courtship rituals to secure mates.

The animation of such scenarios with visually convincing results has been elusive. In this paper, we develop an animation framework within whose scope fall all of the above complex patterns of action, and many more, without any keyframing. The key to achieving this level of complexity, and beyond, with minimal intervention by the animator, is to create fully functional artificial animals—in this instance, artificial fishes. Artificial fishes are autonomous agents whose

---

[1] 10 King's College Road, Toronto, Ontario, Canada, M5S 1A4
E-mail: {tu|dt}@cs.toronto.edu

appearance and complicated group interactions are as faithful as possible to nature's own. To this end, we pursue a bottom-up, compositional approach in which we model not just form and superficial appearance, but also the basic physics of the animal and its environment, its means of locomotion, its perception of its world, and last but not least, its behavior. The holistic nature of our approach to synthesizing artificial fishes is crucial to achieving realism. Partial solutions that do not adequately model physics, locomotion, perception, and behavior, and do not combine these models intimately within the agent will not produce convincing results.

An early result of our research is the computer animation "Go Fish!" [18]. The final sequence of this animation shows a colorful variety of artificial fishes feeding in translucent water (see Plate 1). Dynamic aquatic plants grow from the seabed. A sharp hook on a line descends towards the hungry fishes and attracts them (Plate 1(a)). A hapless fish, the first to bite the bait, is caught and dragged to the surface (Plate 1(b)). Only the camera and the fishing line were scripted in the animation. The beauty of the animation is enhanced by the detailed motions of the artificial fishes which emulate the complexity and unpredictability of movement of their natural counterparts.

### 1.1 Background

At its lowest level of abstraction, our work is an instance of physics-based graphics modeling. The physics-based artificial fish model that we develop is inspired by the surprisingly effective model of snake and worm dynamics proposed by Miller [9] and the facial model proposed by Terzopoulos and Waters [14]. Our fish model is also an animate spring-mass system with internal contractile muscles that are activated to produce the desired motions. Unlike these previous models, however, we simulate the spring-mass system using a more sophisticated implicit Euler method which maintains the stability of the simulation over the large dynamic range of forces produced in our simulated aquatic world. Using spring-mass systems, we also model the dynamic plants found in the artificial fish habitat.

The control of physics-based animate models has attracted significant attention, especially the control of articulated models to animate legged locomotion [2, 11]. Fish animation poses control challenges particular to highly deformable, muscular bodies not unlike those of snakes [9]. We have devised a motor control subsystem that achieves muscle-based, hydrodynamic locomotion by simulating the forces of interaction of a deformable body in an aquatic medium. The motor controller harnesses the hydrodynamic forces produced by fins to achieve forward locomotion over a range of speeds, execute turns, and alter body roll, pitch, and yaw so that the fish can move at will within its 3D virtual world.

At a higher level of abstraction, our research may be categorized as advanced behavioral animation. Several researchers have endeavored to develop behavioral models for computer animation. Simpler behavioral approaches than ours have been proposed to cope with the complexity of animating anthropomorphic figures [22], animating the synchro-

---

nized motions of flocks, schools, or herds [13], and interactive animation control [20] (see, also, the papers by Badler, Calvert, Girard, Green, Miller, Wilhelms, and Zeltzer in [2]). Artificial fishes are "self-animating" in the sense of Reynolds' pioneering work [13], but unlike his procedural "boid" actors, they are fairly elaborate physical models.

To achieve a level of behavioral realism consistent with the locomotive abilities of artificial fishes, it is prudent to consult the ethology literature [16, 5, 7, 1]. Tinbergen's landmark studies of the three-spined stikleback highlight the great diversity of piscatorial behavior, even within a single species. We achieve the nontrivial patterns of behavior outlined in the introductory paragraph of this paper, including schooling behaviors as convincing as those demonstrated by Reynolds, in stages. First, we implement primitive reflexive behaviors, such as obstacle avoidance, that tightly couple perception to action [3]. Then we combine the primitive behaviors into motivational behaviors whose activation depends also on the artificial fish's mental state, including hunger, libido, etc.

Behavior is supported by perception as much as it is by action. Evolution has developed in most animals, including fishes, acute perceptual modalities to increase their chances of survival in an unpredictable and often hostile world. Reynolds' "boids" maintained flock formations through simple perception of other nearby actors [13]. The roach actor described in [8] retreated when it sensed danger from a virtual hand. Renault *et al.* [12] advocate a more extensive form of synthetic vision for behavioral actors, including the automatic computation of internal spatial maps of the world. Our artificial fishes are currently able to sense their world through simulated visual perception within a deliberately limited field of view. Subject to the natural limitations of occlusion, they can sense lighting patterns, determine distances to objects, and identify objects. Furthermore, they are equipped with secondary nonvisual modalities, such as the ability to sense the local water temperature.

The confluence of behavior, perception, and motor systems makes the artificial fish an autonomous agent. In this regard, our design of virtual agents is compatible with recent work in robotics aimed at the implementation of physical agents (see, e.g., the compilation [6]). Interestingly, as our holistic computational model exceeds a certain level of physical, motor, perceptual, and behavioral sophistication, the agent's range of functionality broadens due to emergent behaviors, not explicitly programmed, but nonetheless manifest as the artificial fish interacts with a complex dynamic world populated by other artificial fishes. We aim to emulate convincingly the appearance of the animal as well, so that our computational model will be useful for the purposes of animation.

## 1.2 Overview

Fig. 1 shows an overview of an artificial fish situated in its world, illustrating the motor, perception, and behavior subsystems.

The motor system comprises the dynamic model of the fish, the actuators, and a set of motor controllers (MCs). Since our goal is to animate an animal realistically and at reasonable computational cost, we have crafted a mechanical model that represents a good compromise between anatomical consistency, hence realism, and computational efficiency. Our model is rich enough so that we can build MCs by gleaning information from the animal biomechanics literature. The MCs are parameterized procedures. Each is dedicated to carrying out a specific motor function, such as "swim forward" or "turn left". They translate natural control parameters such as the forward speed or angle of the turn into detailed muscle actions.

The perception system employs a set of virtual on-board

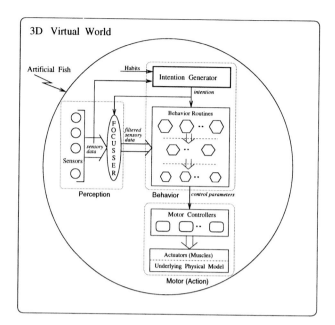

Figure 1: Control and information flow in artificial fish.

sensors to provide all the sensory information about the dynamic environment. The system includes a perceptual attention mechanism which allows the artificial fish to train its sensors at the world in a task-specific way, filtering out undesired sensory information according to the needs of the behavior routines.

The behavior system of the artificial fish mediates between its perception system and its motor system. An intention generator, the fish's "cognitive" center, harnesses the dynamics of the perception-action cycle. The animator establishes the innate character of the fish through a set of habit parameters that determine whether or not it likes darkness or is a male/female, etc. The intention generator combines the habits with the incoming stream of sensory information to generate dynamic goals for the fish, such as to hunt and feed on prey. It ensures that goals have some persistence by exploiting a single-item memory. The intention generator also controls the perceptual attention mechanism to filter out sensory information unnecessary to accomplishing the goal at hand. For example, if the intention is to eat food, then the artificial fish attends to sensory information related to nearby food sources. At every simulation time step, the intention generator activates behavior routines that input the filtered sensory information and compute the appropriate motor control parameters to carry the fish one step closer to fulfilling the current intention. Primitive behavior routines, such as obstacle avoidance, and more sophisticated motivational behavior routines, such as mating, implement the artificial fish's repertoire of behaviors.

## 2   Physics-Based Fish Model and Locomotion

Studies into the dynamics of fish locomotion show that most fishes use their caudal fin as the primary motivator [19]. Caudal swimming normally uses posterior muscles on either side of the body, while turning normally uses anterior muscles. To synthesize realistic fish locomotion we have designed a dynamic fish model consisting of 23 nodal point masses and 91 springs. The spring arrangement maintains the structural stability of the body while allowing it to flex. Twelve of the springs running the length of the body also serve as simple muscles (Fig. 2).

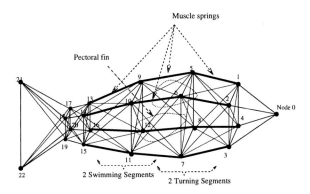

Figure 2: The spring-mass dynamic fish model. Springs are at their rest lengths.

## 2.1 Mechanics

The mechanics of the spring-mass model are specified as follows: Let node $i$ have mass $m_i$, position $\mathbf{x}_i(t) = [x_i(t), y_i(t), z_i(t)]$, velocity $\mathbf{v}_i(t) = d\mathbf{x}_i/dt$, and acceleration $\mathbf{a}_i(t) = d^2\mathbf{x}_i/dt^2$. Let spring $S_{ij}$ connect node $i$ to node $j$. Denote its spring constant as $c_{ij}$ and natural, rest length as $l_{ij}$. Its deformation is $e_{ij}(t) = ||\mathbf{r}_{ij}|| - l_{ij}$, where $\mathbf{r}_{ij} = \mathbf{x}_j(t) - \mathbf{x}_i(t)$. The force $S_{ij}$ exerts on node $i$ is $\mathbf{f}_{ij}^s = c_{ij} e_{ij}(t)\mathbf{r}_{ij}/||\mathbf{r}_{ij}||$ (and it exerts the force $-\mathbf{f}_{ij}^s$ on node $j$). The Lagrange equations of motion of the dynamic fish are:

$$m_i \frac{d^2\mathbf{x}_i}{dt^2} + \varrho_i \frac{d\mathbf{x}_i}{dt} - \mathbf{w}_i = \mathbf{f}_i^w; \qquad i = 0, ..., 22, \qquad (1)$$

where $\varrho_i$ is the damping factor, $\mathbf{w}_i(t) = \sum_{j \in N_i} \mathbf{f}_{ij}^s(t)$ is the net internal force on node $i$ due to springs connecting it to nodes $j \in N_i$, where $N_i$ is the index set of neighboring nodes. Finally, $\mathbf{f}_i^w$ is the external (hydrodynamic) force on node $i$.

To integrate the differential equations of motion, we employ a numerically stable, implicit Euler method [10]. The method assembles the sparse stiffness matrix for the spring-mass system in "skyline" storage format. The matrix is factorized once at the start of the simulation and then resolved at each time step.[1]

## 2.2 Swimming Using Muscles and Hydrodynamics

The artificial fish moves as a real fish does, by contracting its muscles. If $S_{ij}$ is a muscle spring, it is contracted by decreasing the rest length $l_{ij}$. For convenience, we assign a minimum contraction length $l_{ij}^{min}$ to the muscle spring and express the contraction factor as a number in the range $[0, 1]$. The characteristic swinging of the fish's tail can be achieved by periodically contracting the swimming segment springs on one side of the body while relaxing their counterparts on the other side.

When the fish's tail swings, it sets in motion a volume of water. The inertia of the displaced water produces a reaction force normal to the fish's body and proportional to the volume of water displaced per unit time, which propels the fish forward (Fig. 3(a)). Under certain assumptions, the instantaneous force on the surface $S$ of a body due to a viscous fluid is approximately proportional to $- \int_S (\mathbf{n} \cdot \mathbf{v}) \mathbf{n}\, dS$, where $\mathbf{n}$ is the unit outward normal function over the surface and $\mathbf{v}$ is the relative velocity function between the surface and

the fluid. For efficiency, we triangulate the surface of the fish model between the nodes and approximate the force on each planar triangle as $\mathbf{f} = \min[0, -A(\mathbf{n} \cdot \mathbf{v})\mathbf{n}]$, where $A$ is the area of the triangle and $\mathbf{v}$ is its velocity relative to the water. The $\mathbf{f}_i^w$ variables at each of the three nodes defining the triangle are incremented by $\mathbf{f}/3$.

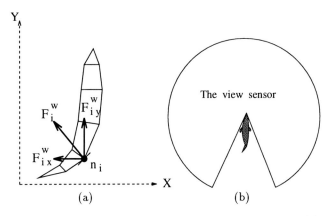

Figure 3: Hydrodynamic locomotion and vision sensor. (a) With tail swinging towards positive $X$ axis, reaction force $\mathbf{F}_i^w$ at point $n_i$ acts along the inward normal. Component $\mathbf{F}_{ix}^w$ resists the lateral movement, while $\mathbf{F}_{iy}^w$ is forward thrust. Aggregate thrust propels fish towards positive $Y$ axis. (b) Visual perception limited to 300 degree solid angle.

## 2.3 Motor Controllers

Currently the artificial fish has three MCs. The swim-MC produces straight swimming, while the left-turn-MC and right-turn-MC execute turns. The MCs prescribe muscle contractions to the mechanical model. The swimming MC controls the swimming segment muscles (see Fig. 2), while the turning MCs control the turning segment muscles.

According to [19], the swimming speed of most fishes is roughly proportional to the amplitude and frequency of the periodic lateral oscillation of the tail, below certain threshold values. Our experiments with the mechanical model agree well with these observations. Both the swimming speed and the turn angle of the fish model are approximately proportional to the contraction amplitudes and frequencies/rates of the muscle springs.

The swim-MC (swim-MC(speed) $\mapsto \{r_1, s_1, r_2, s_2\}$) converts a swim speed parameter into contraction amplitude and frequency control parameters for the anterior $(r_1, s_1)$ and posterior $(r_2, s_2)$ swim segments. One pair of parameters suffice to control each of the two swim segments because of symmetry—the four muscle springs have identical rest lengths and minimum contraction lengths, identical spring constants, and the contractions of the muscle spring pairs on opposite sides are exactly out of phase. Moreover, the swim-MC produces periodic muscle contractions in the posterior swim segment which lag 180 degrees behind those of the anterior swim segment; hence the mechanical models displays a sinusoidal body shape as the fish swims (see [19]).

By experimenting, we have found a set of four maximal parameters, $\hat{r}_1, \hat{s}_1, \hat{r}_2$ and $\hat{s}_2$, which produce the fastest swimming speed. The swim-MC generates slower swim speeds by specifying parameters that have values between 0 and the maximal parameters. For example, $\{0.8\hat{r}_1, \hat{s}_1, 0.7\hat{r}_2, \hat{s}_2\}$ results in a slower-swimming fish.

As mentioned earlier, most fishes use their anterior muscles for turning, and the turn angle is approximately proportional to the degree and speed of the anterior bend, up to the limit of the fish's physical strength [19]. The artificial

---

[1]In our simulation: $m_i = 1.1$ for $i = 0$ and $13 \le i \le 19$; $m_i = 6.6$ for $1 \le i \le 4$ and $9 \le i \le 12$; $m_i = 11.0$ for $5 \le i \le 8$, and $m_i = \overline{0.165}$ for $i = 21, \overline{22}$. The cross springs (e.g., $c_{27}$) which resist shearing have spring constants $c_{ij} = 38.0$. The muscle springs (e.g., $c_{26}$) have spring constants $c_{ij} = 28.0$, and $c_{ij} = 30$ for the remaining springs. The damping factor $\varrho_i = 0.05$ in (1) and the time step used in the Euler time-integration procedure is 0.055.

fish turns by contracting and expanding the springs of the turning segments (Fig. 2) in similar fashion. For example, a left turn is achieved by quickly contracting the left side springs of the segments and relaxing those on the right side. This effectively deflects the fish's momentum and brings it into the desired orientation. Then the contracted springs are restored to their rest lengths at a slower rate, so that the fish regains its original shape with minimal further change in orientation.

Similarly, the left and right turn MCs (turn-MC(angle) $\mapsto$ $\{r_0, s_0, r_1, s_1\}$) convert a turn angle to control parameters for the anterior and posterior turning segments to execute the turn (note that the posterior turning segment also serves as the anterior swim segment). Through experimentation, we established 4 sets of parameter values $P_i = \{r_0^i, s_0^i, r_1^i, s_1^i\}$ which enable the fish to execute natural looking turns of approximately 30, 45, 60, and 90 degrees. By interpolating the key parameters, we define a steering map that allows the fish to generate turns of approximately any angle up to 90 degrees. Turns greater than 90 degrees are composed as sequential turns of lesser angles.

## 2.4 Pectoral Fins

On most fishes, the pectoral fins control pitching (the up-and-down motion of the body) and yawing (the side-to-side motion). The pectorals can be held close to the body to increase speed by reducing drag or they can be extended to serve as a brake by increasing drag [21]. Many reef fishes use a pectoral swimming style to achieve very fine motion control when foraging, including backwards motions, by keeping their bodies still and using their pectorals like oars.

The artificial fish has a pair of pectoral fins which enable it to navigate freely in its 3D world. The pectoral fins function in a similar, albeit simplified, manner to those on real fishes. Instead of creating a detailed physics-based model of the pectoral fins, we are content to simulate only their dynamic effect on the locomotion of the fish. This is because for our purposes the detailed movement of the pectoral fins is of lesser interest than the movement of the fish body. Furthermore, we wish to simplify the fish model and its numerical solution.

The pectoral fins (Fig. 4) work by applying reaction forces to nodes in the midsection, i.e. nodes $1 \leq i \leq 12$ (see Fig. 2).

Figure 4: The pectoral fins

The pectoral fins are analogous to the wings of an airplane. Pitch, yaw, and roll control stems from changing their orientations relative to the body; i.e., the angle $\pi/4 \leq \gamma \leq \pi$. Assuming that a fin has an area $A$, surface normal $\mathbf{n}$ and the fish has a velocity $\mathbf{v}$ relative to the water (Fig. 4), the fin force is $F_f = -A(\mathbf{n} \cdot \mathbf{v})\mathbf{n} = -A(\|\mathbf{v}\| \cos \gamma)\mathbf{n}$ which is distributed equally to the 12 midsection nodes. When the leading edge of a fin is elevated, a lift force is imparted on the body and the fish ascends, and when it is depressed a downward force is exerted and the fish descends. When the fin angles differ the fish yaws and rolls. The artificial fish can produce a braking effect by angling its fins to decrease its forward speed (i.e. $\gamma = \pi$). This motion control is useful, for instance, in maintaining schooling patterns.

## 3 Sensory Perception

The artificial fish currently has two on-board sensors with which to perceive its environment and govern its actions—a vision sensor and a temperature sensor.

The temperature sensor samples the ambient water temperature at the center of the artificial fish's body. The vision sensor is more complicated. We do not attempt to emulate the highly evolved vision system of a real fish. Instead, the vision sensor extracts from the 3D virtual world only some of the most useful information that fish vision can provide real fishes about their world, such as the colors, sizes, distances, and identities of objects.

The artificial fish's vision sensor has access to the geometry, material property, and illumination information that is available to the graphics pipeline for rendering purposes. In addition, the vision sensor can interrogate the object database to identify nearby objects and interrogate the physical simulation to obtain information such as the instantaneous velocities of objects of interest.

Currently, the artificial fish's vision is cyclopean, and it covers a 300 degree spherical angle extending to an effective radius that is appropriate for the assigned visibility of the translucent water (Fig. 3(b)). An object is "seen" if any part of it enters this view volume and is not fully occluded by another object.

A more realistic emulation of piscatorial visual processes would involve the application of computer vision algorithms to extract information from images (and associated z-buffers) of the 3D world rendered from the vantage point of the artificial fish's (binocular) vision sensor. At present the artificial fish can average the image to determine the overall light.

For further details about perceptual modeling in artificial fishes see [17].

## 4 Behavioral Modeling and Animation

The artificial fish's behavior system runs continuously within the simulation loop. At each time step the intention generator issues an intention based on the fish's habits, mental state, and incoming sensory information. It then chooses and executes a behavior routine which in turn runs the appropriate motor controllers. It is important to note that the behavior routines are incremental by design. Their job is to get the artificial fish one step closer to fulfilling the intention during the current time step. The intention generator employs a memory mechanism to avoid dithering.

### 4.1 Habits

Using a simple user interface, the animator establishes the innate character of the fish through a set of habit parameters that determine whether it likes brightness, darkness, cold, warmth, schooling, is male or female, etc.

### 4.2 Mental State

The artificial fish has three mental state variables, hunger $H$, libido $L$, and fear $F$. The range of each variable is $[0, 1]$, with higher values indicating a stronger urge to eat, mate and avoid danger, respectively. The variables are calculated as follows:

$$
\begin{aligned}
H(t) &= \min[1 - n^e(t)R(\Delta t^H)/\alpha, 1], \\
L(t) &= \min[s(\Delta t^L)(1 - H(t)), 1], \\
F(t) &= \min\left[\sum F^i, 1\right], \text{ where } F^i = \min[D_0/d^i(t), 1];
\end{aligned}
$$

where $t$ is time, $n^e(t)$ is the amount of food consumed as measured by the number of food particles or prey fishes eaten, $R(x) = 1 - p_0 x$ with constant $p_0$ is the digestion rate, $\Delta t^H$ is the time since the last meal, $\alpha$ is a constant that dictates the appetite of the fish (bigger fishes have a larger $\alpha$), $s(x) = p_1 x$ with constant $p_1$ is the libido function, $\Delta t^L$ is the time since the last mating, $D_0 = 100$ is a constant, and $F^i$ and $d^i$ are, respectively, the fear of and distance to sighted predator $i$. Nominal constants are $p_0 = 0.00067$ and $p_1 = 0.0025$. Certain choices can result in ravenous fishes (e.g, $p_0 = 0.005$) or sexual mania (e.g., $p_1 = 0.01$).

## 5 Intention Generator

Fig. 5 illustrates the generic intention generator which is responsible for the goal-directed behavior of the artificial fish in its dynamic world.

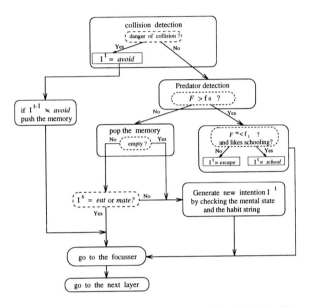

Figure 5: Generic intention generator (simplified). Set of intentions: { *avoid, escape, school, eat, mate, leave, wander* }. $f_0$ and $f_1$ are thresholds with $f_0 < f_1$.

The intention generator first checks the sensory information stream to see if there is any immediate danger of collision. If any object penetrates the fish's collision sensitivity region (a bounding box around the fish body) then the intention $I$ generated is to *avoid* collision. A large sensitivity region results in a 'timid' fish that takes evasive action to avoid a potential collision well in advance, while a tight sensitivity region yields a 'courageous' fish that takes evasive action only at the last second.

If there is no immediate danger of collision, the neighborhood is searched for predators, the fear state variable $F$ and the most dangerous predator $m$ for which $F^m \geq F^i$ are calculated. If the total fear $F > f_0$ (where $0.1 \leq f_0 \leq 0.5$ is a threshold value) evasive action is to be taken. If the most dangerous predator is not too threatening (i.e. $F^m < f_1$ where $f_1 > f_0$) and the fish has a schooling habit, then the *school* intention is generated, otherwise the *escape* intention is generated.

If fear is below threshold, the hunger and libido mental state variables $H$ and $L$ are calculated. If the greater of the two exceeds a threshold $0 < r < 0.5$, the intention generated will be to *eat* or *mate* accordingly.

If the above test fails, the intention generator accesses the ambient light and temperature information from the perception system. If the fish's habits dictate contentment with the ambient conditions, the intention generated will be to *wander* about, otherwise it will be to *leave* the vicinity.

Note that after the intention generator chooses an intention, it invokes the perceptual focus mechanism. For example, when the *avoid* intention is generated, the perception focusser is activated to locate the positions of the obstacles, paying special attention to the most dangerous one, generally the closest. Then the focusser computes qualitative constraints, such as *obstacle to the left* $\Rightarrow$ *no left turn*. The focusser passes only the position of the most dangerous obstacle along with these constraints to the behavior routines. When the intention of a male fish is to *mate*, the focusser targets the most desirable female fish; when the intention is to *escape* from predators, only the information about the most threatening predator is passed to the next layer; etc.

In a complex dynamic world, the artificial fish should have some persistence in its intentions, otherwise it will tend to dither, perpetually switching goals. If the current behavior is interrupted by a high priority event, the intention generator is able to store, in a single-item short term memory, the current intention and some associated information that may be used to resume the interrupted behavior. Such persistence serves primarily to make longer duration behaviors such as feeding and mating more robust. Suppose for example that the current behavior is mating and an imminent collision is detected. This causes an *avoid* intention and the storage of the *mate* intention (we refer to the stored intention as $I^s$) along with the identity of the mating partner. After the obstacle is cleared, the intention generator commands the focusser to generate up-to-date heading and range information about the mating partner, assuming it is still in viewing range. A similar scenario may occur during feeding.

Our design of the intention generator and focusser simplifies the modification of existing personalities and behaviors and the addition of new ones. For example, we can create artificial fishes with different persistences by augmenting the focusser with a new positive threshold. Suppose the current intention of a predator fish is to *eat* and let the distance to some currently targeted prey be $l_c$ and the distance to some other prey be $l_n$. If $l_c - l_n$ is greater than the threshold, the fish will target the new prey. Varying the threshold will vary the fish's level of persistence. The same heuristic can be applied to mates when the fish is trying to *mate*. One can make the fish 'fickle' by setting the value of the threshold close to zero or make it 'devoted' by setting a large value.

### 5.1 Behavior Routines

Once the intention generator selects an intention it attempts to satisfy the intention by passing control to a behavior routine along with the data from the perception focusser. The artificial fish currently includes eight behavior routines: *avoiding-static-obstacle, avoiding-fish, eating-food, mating, leaving, wandering, escaping,* and *schooling* which serve the obvious purposes. The behavior routine uses the focused perceptual data to select an MC and provide it with the proper motor control parameters. We now briefly describe the function of the routines.

The *avoiding-static-obstacle* and *avoiding-fish* routines operate in similar fashion. Given the relative position of the obstacle, an appropriate MC (e.g. *left-turn-MC*) is chosen and the proper control parameters are calculated subject to the constraints imposed by other surrounding obstacles. For efficiency the *avoid-fish* routine treats the dynamic obstacle as a rectangular bounding box moving in a certain direction. Although collisions between fishes cannot always be avoided, bounding boxes can be easily adjusted such that they almost always are, and the method is very efficient. An enhancement would be to add collision resolution.

The *eating-food* routine tests the distance $d$ from the fish's mouth to the food (see Fig. 4). If $d$ is greater than some threshold value, the subroutine *chasing-target* is invoked.[2] When $d$ is less than the threshold value the subroutine *suck-in* is activated where a "vacuum" force (to be explained in section 6.1) is calculated and then exerted on the food.

The *mating* routine invokes four subroutines: *looping, circling, ascending* and *nuzzling* (see Section 6.3 for details). The *wandering-about* routine sets the fish swimming at a certain speed by invoking the swim-MC, while sending random turn angles to the turn-MCs. The *leaving* routine is similar to the *wandering-about* routine. The *escaping* routine chooses a suitable MC according to the relative position, orientation of the predator to the fish. The *schooling* routine will be discussed in Section 6.2.

# 6 Artificial Fish Types

The introductory paragraph of the paper described the behavior of three types of artificial fishes—predators, prey, and pacifists. This section presents their implementation details.

## 6.1 Predators

Fig. 6 is a schematic of the intention generator of a predator, which is a specialized version of Fig. 5. To simplify matters, predators currently do not prey upon by other predators, so they perform no predator detection, and *escape, school*, and *mate* intentions are disabled ($F = 0, L = 0$). Since predators cruise perpetually, the *leave* intention is also disabled.

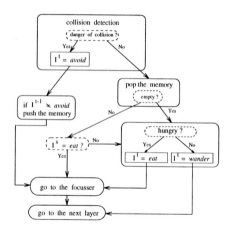

Figure 6: The intention generator of a Predator

Generally prey is in less danger of being hunted when it is far away from the predator, or is in a school, or is behind the predator. A predator chases prey $k$ if the cost $C_k = d_k(1 + \beta_1 S_k + \beta_2 E_k/\pi)$ of reaching it is minimal. Here, $d_k$ is the distance between the mouth of the predator and the center of prey $k$'s body, $S_k = 1$ if prey $k$ is in a school of fishes, otherwise $S_k = 0$, and the angle $E_k \in [0, \pi)$ (Fig. 4) measures the turning cost. $\beta_1$ and $\beta_2$ are parameters that tune the contributions of $S_k$ and $E_k$. We use $\beta_1 = 0.5$ and $\beta_2 = 0.2$ in our implementation of the focusser. Plate 2(a) shows a (green) predator stalking prey.

Most teleost fishes do not bite on their victims like sharks do. When a fish is about to eat it swims close to the victim and extends its protrusile jaw, thus creating a hollow space within the mouth. The pressure difference between the inside and the outside of the mouth produces a vacuum force that sucks into the mouth the victim and anything else in the nearby water. The predator closes its mouth, expels the water through the gills, and grinds the food with pharyngeal

jaws [21]. We simulate this process by enabling the artificial fish to open and close its mouth kinematically. To suck in prey, it opens its mouth and, while the mouth is open, exerts vacuum forces on fishes (the forces are added to external nodal forces $\mathbf{f}_i$ in equation (1) and other dynamic particles in the vicinity of the open mouth, drawing them in (see Plate 2(b)).

## 6.2 Prey

The intention generator of a prey fish is a specialization of the generic intention generator of Fig. 5 as follows:

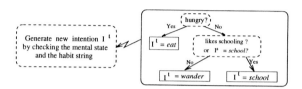

Figure 7: Portion of intention generator of prey.

Schooling and evading predators are two distinct behaviors of prey. Because of space constraints, we briefly describe the implementation of only the *schooling* behavior. Schooling is a complex behavior where all the fishes swim in generally the same direction (see Plate 3(a)). Each fish constantly adjusts its speed and direction to match those of other members of the school. They establish a certain distance from one another, roughly one body length from neighbors, on average [21]. As in [13], each member of a school of artificial fish acts autonomously, and the schooling behavior is achieved through sensory perception and locomotion. An inceptive school forms when a few fish swim towards a lead fish. Once a fish is in some proximity to some other schooling fish, the *schooling* behavior routine outlined in Fig. 8 is invoked.

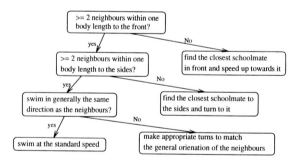

Figure 8: Schooling behavior routine.

The intention generator prevents schooling fish from getting too close together, because the *avoid* collision intention has highest precedence. To create more compact schools, the collision sensitivity region of a schooling fish is decreased, once it gets into formation. When a large school encounters an obstacle, the autonomous obstacle avoidance behavior of individual fishes may cause the school to split into two groups and rejoin once the obstacle is cleared and the *schooling* behavior routine regains control (Plate 3(b)).

## 6.3 Pacifists

The intention generator of a pacifist differs from that of prey in that intention *mate* is activated and *escape* and *school* are deactivated.

Piscatorial mating behaviors show great interspecies and intraspecies diversity [15]. However, two behaviors are prevalent: (i) nuzzling, where typically the male approaches the

---

[2] The *chasing-target* subroutine guides a fish as it swims towards a goal. It plays a crucial role in several behavior routines. We describe it in more detail elsewhere [17].

female from underneath and nudges her abdomen repeatedly until she is ready to spawn, and (ii) spawning ascent, where in its simplest form, the female rapidly swims towards the surface pursued by the male and releases gametes at the peak of her ascent. Moreover, courtship dancing is common in many species, albeit with substantial variation. Two frequently observed patterns are looping, in which the male swims vigorously up and down in a loop slightly above and in front of the female, and circling, in which the male and female circle, seemingly chase each other's tail.

We have implemented an elaborate *mating* behavior routine which simulates courtship competition (Plate 4(a)), looping, circling, spawning ascent, and nuzzling (Plate 4(b)) behavior patterns in sequence. A male fish selects a mate based on the following criteria: a female of the same species is more attractive than one of different species, and closer females are more attractive than ones further away. A female selects a mate similarly, but shows preference to male fish size (stronger, more protective) rather than proximity.

Once fish $i$ has selected a potential partner $j$ based on the above criteria, it sends a signal to fish $j$, and there are three possibilities: *Case 1*: If fish $j$'s intention is not to *mate*, fish $i$ approaches $j$ and follows it around using *chasing-target* with the center of $j$'s body as target. *Case 2*: If fish $j$'s intention is to *mate* but its intended partner is not fish $i$. In this case if $i$ is male it will perform a *looping* behavior in front of $j$ for a certain amount of time. If $j$ is impressed and selects $i$ during this time limit, then the courtship sequence continues, otherwise $i$ will discontinue *looping* and leave $j$ to find a new potential partner. Otherwise, if $i$ is female it will choose another potential male. *Case 3*: If fish $j$'s intention is to *mate* and its intended partner is fish $i$, the *courtship* behavior starts with the male looping in front of the female while she hovers and bobs her head. Looping is simulated by invoking *chasing-target* at a point in front of the female's head which moves up and down at a certain frequency. The female's hovering and head bobbing is accomplished through motor control of her pectoral fins (i.e., parameter $\gamma$)

The male counts the number of times his mouth reaches the vicinity of the moving point, and when the count exceeds a set threshold (currently 6) he makes a transition from *looping* to *circling* behavior. Although the threshold count is fixed, the actual motions and duration of looping is highly unpredictable for any number of reasons, including the fact that looping may be temporarily interrupted to handle high priority items such as potential collisions between the pair or with other fishes that may pass by.

Before the transition to *circling*, the female fish may reject her initial partner and turn to a new larger male fish if the latter joins in the *looping* display. At this point the initially engaged male turns away as in case 2 above. *Circling* is achieved when the fishes invoke *chasing-target* to chase each other's tail.

The *circling* routine ends and the spawning *ascending* routine begins after the female has made a fixed number of turns during circling. The female fish ascends quickly through fast swimming followed by hovering. The male fish invokes *chasing-target* to follow the abdomen of the female. The *nuzzling* routine requires the male to approach her abdomen from below. Once his mouth touches her abdomen, the male backs off for a number of time steps. This procedure repeats, until the male successfully touches the female 3 times. To permit the mating pair to come close together, the regions of sensitivity are set very tightly to their bodies. It is intriguing to watch some of the male artificial fish's attempts fail because of an inappropriate approach angle which triggers the *avoiding-fish* response. The male turns away to avoid the collision and tries again.

## 7 Conclusion

We have demonstrated a framework for behavioral animation featuring an artificial fish model with some astonishing behaviors. These behaviors yield realistic individual and collective motions with minimal intervention from the animator. The easy extensibility of our framework is made most evident by the complex patterns of mating behavior that we have been able to implement to date. Our implementation can run a simulation of 10 fishes, 15 food particles, and 5 static obstacles at about 4 frames/sec (including wireframe rendering time) on a Silicon Graphics R4400 Indigo2. One of the many exciting directions for future research is to further increase the relevance of our work to the burgeoning field of artificial life [4]. We may be within reach of computational models that imitate the spawning behavior of the female (release of gametes) and the male (fertilization), hence the evolution of new varieties of artificial fishes through simulated sexual reproduction.

## References

[1] H. E. Adler. *Fish Behavior: Why Fishes do What They Do*. T.F.H Publications, Neptune City, NJ, 1975.

[2] N. Badler, B. Barsky, and D. Zeltzer, editors. *Making Them Move*. Morgan Kaufmann, San Mateo, CA, 1991.

[3] V. Braitenberg. *Vehicles, Experiments in Synthetic Psychology*. The MIT Press, Cambridge, MA, 1984.

[4] S. Levy. *Artificial Life*. Vintage Books, NY, 1992.

[5] K. Lorenz. *Foundations of Ethology*. Springer-Verlag, New York, 1973.

[6] P. Maes, editor. *Designing Autonomous Agents*. The MIT Press, Cambridge, MA, 1991.

[7] D. Mcfarland. *Animal Behaviour*. Pitman, 1985.

[8] M. McKenna, S. Pieper, and D. Zeltzer. Control of a virtual actor: The roach. *ACM SIGGRAPH 1990 Symposium on Interactive 3D Graphics*, 24(2):165–174, 1990.

[9] G. S. P. Miller. The motion dynamics of snakes and worms. *Computer Graphics*, 22(4):169–177, 1988.

[10] W. Press, B. Flannery, S. Teukolsky, and W. Vetterling. *Numerical Recipes: The Art of Scientific Computing*. Cambridge University Press, Cambridge, England, 1986.

[11] M. H. Raibert and J. K. Hodgins. Animation of dynamic legged locomotion. *Computer Graphics*, 25(4):349–358, 1991.

[12] O. Renault, N. Magnenat-Thalmann, and D. Thalmann. A vision-based approach to behavioural animation. *Visualization and Computer Animation*, 1:18–21, 1990.

[13] C. W. Reynolds. Flocks, herds, and schools: A distributed behavioral model. *Computer Graphics*, 21(4):25–34, 1987.

[14] D. Terzopoulos and K Waters. Physically-based facial modelling, analysis, and animation. *Visulization and Computer Animation*, 1:73–80, 1990.

[15] R. E. Thresher. *Reproduction in Reef Fishes*. T.F.H. Publications, Neptune City, NJ, 1984.

[16] N. Tinbergen. *The Study of Instinct*. Clarendon Press, Oxford, England, 1950.

[17] X. Tu and D. Terzopoulos. Perceptual modeling for behavioral animation of fishes. In *Proc. 2nd Pacific Conf. on Computer Graphics*, Beijing, China, 1994.

[18] X. Tu, D. Terzopoulos, and E. Fiume. Go Fish! ACM SIGGRAPH Video Review Issue 91: SIGGRAPH'93 Electronic Theater, 1993.

[19] P. W. Webb. Form and function in fish swimming. *Scientific American*, 251(1), 1989.

[20] J. Wilhelms and R. Skinner. A "notion" for interactive behavioral animation control. *IEEE Computer Graphics and Applications*, 10(3):14–22, 1990.

[21] R. Wilson and J. Q. Wilson. *Watching Fishes*. Harper and Row, New York, 1985.

[22] D. Zeltzer. Motor control techniques for figure animation. *IEEE Computer Graphics and Application*, 2(9):53–59, 1982.

(a)

(b)

Plate 1: Hook sequence from "Go Fish!"

Plate 3: Schooling behaviors.

(a)

(b)

Plate 2: Predator stalking and eating prey.

Plate 4: Mating behaviors.

# Textures and Radiosity:
## Controlling Emission and Reflection with Texture Maps

Reid Gershbein        Peter Schröder        Pat Hanrahan

Department of Computer Science
Princeton University

## Abstract

In this paper we discuss the efficient and accurate incorporation of texture maps into a hierarchical Galerkin radiosity algorithm. This extension of the standard algorithm allows the use of textures to describe complex reflectance and emittance patterns over surfaces, increasing the realism and complexity of radiosity images. Previous approaches to the inclusion of textures have either averaged the texture to yield a single color for the radiosity computations, or exhaustively generated detail elements—possibly as many as one per texture pixel. The former does not capture important lighting effects due to textures, while the latter is too expensive computationally to be practical.

To handle texture maps requires a detailed analysis of the underlying operator equation. In particular we decompose the radiosity equation into two steps: (i) the computation of irradiance on a surface from the radiosities on other surfaces, and (ii) the application of the reflectance operator $\rho$ to compute radiosities from irradiances. We then describe an algorithm that maintains hierarchical representations of both radiosities and textures. The numerical error involved in using these approximations is quantifiable and a time/error tradeoff is possible. The resulting algorithm allows texture maps to be used in radiosity computations with very little overhead.

**CR Categories and Subject Descriptors:** I.3.7 [Computer Graphics]: *Three-Dimensional Graphics and Realism – Radiosity*; G.1.9 [Numerical Analysis]: *Integral Equations – Fredholm equations*; J.2 [Physical Sciences and Engineering]: *Engineering*.

**Additional Key Words and Phrases:** global illumination, wavelets, hierarchical radiosity, texture mapping.

## 1 Introduction

Radiosity methods compute the illumination, both direct and indirect, from environments consisting of perfectly diffuse (Lambertian) reflecting and emitting surfaces [10, 15, 6, 5]. The resulting pictures contain subtle but important lighting effects, such as soft shadows and color bleeding, that enhance their realism. However, radiosity algorithms are still complex and far from general. For example, most computer graphics radiosity algorithms are limited to environments consisting of polygonal elements whose radiosities and reflectances are constant. Naturally such assumptions limit both the realism of the resulting pictures, and the utilization of the radiosity method in many applications. This immediately leads to the question of what additional rendering and modeling techniques can be combined with the radiosity method to further enhance the realism of the final imagery.

**Figure 1**: *A complex scene illustrating the lighting effects due to texture maps. The window and surrounding wall are a single polygon with emittance and reflectance textures (see Figure 9).*

One of the oldest rendering techniques is the use of texture maps to modulate surface color [3]. In the case of radiosity, texture maps may be used to spatially modulate the emittance and reflectance of the surface. The advantage of texture maps is that the apparent surface complexity increases without the increase in geometric complexity that arises if the surface were to be subdivided into many small surface polygons. This last distinction is particularly important in the case of radiosity, since the computational cost of a radiosity simulation may grow quadratically with the number of primitives in the scene.

These difficulties notwithstanding earlier researchers have incorporated emissive as well as reflective textures into radiosity systems to increase the realism of the generated images. Cohen *et al.* [5] incorporated textures as a post process. During the radiosity computations a texture mapped polygon would have a constant reflectance equal to the average texture map reflectance. For final renderings the textures were incorporated at the resolution of the original texture. This was done by dividing the computed radiosities by the average reflectance and then multiplying them by the true reflectance. This yields visually complex images, but does not accurately account for lighting effects because the spatially varying emission and reflection across a surface is not considered during the radiosity calculation. Dorsey *et al.* [8] also incorporated texture maps. They were motivated by the need to simulate lighting effects for opera lighting design. Consequently the simple average/post-process technique was not applicable. Instead they created many small polygons to get a reasonable approximation of the original texture. As mentioned above this quickly leads to excessive computation times, but does lead to extraordinary pictures.

To summarize, the averaging technique does not compute the correct illumination effects, and the exhaustive approach is expensive in both time and storage. An approach that captures the indirect illumination effects due to texture maps to within some accuracy while having low computational cost is clearly desirable, and is the motivation behind this paper.

Two developments in recent radiosity research are relevant for our present discussion, hierarchical radiosity, and higher order Galerkin methods. A two level hierarchy was first proposed by Cohen *et al.* [7] as substructuring. They allowed coarse subdivision of sources while requiring a finer subdivision of receivers. Hanrahan *et al.* [12] introduced a multi level hierarchy. In their algorithm objects are allowed to exchange energy at many different levels of detail. This is based on the observation that interactions between relatively far away primitives can be approximated with a coarse subdivision, while only close interactions require a fine subdivision. The level of detail at which two objects (or parts of objects) interact is determined by their ability to capture an interaction correctly within a specified error criterion. An asymptotically faster radiosity algorithm results.

Galerkin approaches, first introduced by Heckbert [13] and consequently elaborated by Zatz [20], and Troutman and Max [18], use classical finite element techniques to solve the underlying radiosity integral equation. The main goal is to compute smoother answers than classical radiosity. The higher order basis functions also reduce the need for subdivision and accelerate convergence overall. In any Galerkin approach all functions (emittance, reflectance, and the geometric kernel) are written out with respect to some set of basis functions. It has been pointed out by Zatz that this trivially allows for emittances which vary in some complex way over a surface so long as this variance can be described with the chosen set of basis functions.

The benefits of hierarchical radiosity and Galerkin methods have recently been unified under the framework of *wavelets* by Gortler *et al.* [11] and Schröder *et al.* [16].

Starting with a wavelet radiosity system we extend it to handle both emission and reflection textures. The theory and the resulting algorithm is the subject of this paper. We first carefully examine the structure of the underlying operator equation. In particular we show that the usual computation of radiosity as the product of reflectance and irradiance (and possibly active emission) is complicated by the hierarchical framework, which aims to preserve the computational advantage afforded by multi level descriptions. In fact, we formally and algorithmically separate the computation of irradiance from that of radiosity. This allows us to exploit economies in each of the computational steps which would be hard to take advantage of in the usual combined framework. In the resulting algorithm, the cost of performing a radiosity computation with texture maps is very similar to the cost without texturing.

## 2 Theory

### 2.1 The radiosity equation

The radiosity equation can be written as a simplification of the rendering equation [14] by assuming that all participating surfaces are perfectly diffuse (Lambertian), giving rise to the classical radiosity integral equation

$$B(x) = B^e(x) + B^r(x) = B^e(x) + \rho(x)E(x) \quad (1)$$
$$= B^e(x) + \rho(x) \int dA_{x'} G(x, x') \pi^{-1} B(x')$$

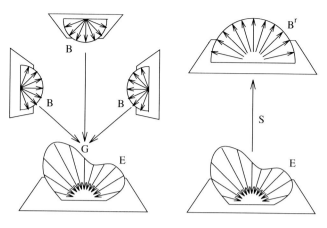

**Figure 2**: *Reflected radiosity,$B^r$, is computed in two steps. First the computation of irradiance, denoted by G, second the computation of the scattered irradiance, denoted by S.*

where $B(x)$ is the radiosity at point $x$, consisting of emitted and reflected radiosity, $\rho(x)$ the reflectance, and $G(x, x') = \frac{\cos\theta_x \cos\theta_{x'}}{\|x - x'\|^2} V(x, x')$ characterizes the radiant coupling between points $x$ and $x'$. $G$ accounts for relative surface orientations, distance, and visibility, $V = 1$ or $V = 0$, depending on whether $x$ can or cannot see $x'$. The integral is taken over the hemisphere about $x$ and represents the amount of energy per unit area received from other surfaces. This is the irradiance $E(x)$, which contributes to radiosity after multiplication by $\rho(x)$.

### 2.2 The radiosity operator

The radiosity equation may be decomposed into two steps as shown in Figure 2:

1. *Compute irradiance from scene radiosities.*

   Define the operator $\mathcal{G}$ for a general function $f$

   $$\mathcal{G}(f)(x) = \int dA_{x'} G(x, x') \pi^{-1} f(x')$$

   then $E(x) = \mathcal{G}(B)(x)$. Note that $\mathcal{G}$ is a geometric operator that takes into account the radiant exchange between a receiver surface and all other source surfaces in the scene.

   $\mathcal{G}$ is dense and non-local, but it is smooth (in the absence of shadows). It is dense since $\mathcal{G}$ may potentially couple any part of the environment to any other part. It is smooth because $\mathcal{G}$ varies slowly as a function of position on the source and receiver. In the parlance of integral equations we say that $\mathcal{G}$ has a smooth kernel [2].

2. *Compute radiosities from irradiances and reflectivities.*

   Define the scattering operator $\mathcal{S}$

   $$\mathcal{S}(f)(x) = \rho(x)f(x)$$

   yielding $B^r(x) = \mathcal{S}(E)(x)$. Note that $\mathcal{S}$ is completely determined by surface properties and as such does not depend on the environment.

   In contrast to $\mathcal{G}$, $\mathcal{S}$ is a local operator but not always smooth. This is because the texture map representing the reflectance may contain high frequencies. Since it is a local operator it does however have efficient representations as a diagonal, sparse operator in the proper basis.

Using this operator notation we can rewrite Equation 1 as

$$B(x) = B^e(x) + \mathcal{K}(B)(x) = B^e(x) + \mathcal{S} \circ \mathcal{G}(B)(x)$$

where $\circ$ denotes concatenation. The separation into $\mathcal{G}$ and $\mathcal{S}$ allows us to pursue different strategies to efficiently represent each operator individually. Sparse operators such as $\mathcal{S}$ are easy to represent efficiently. In contrast, dense operators such as $\mathcal{G}$ are normally difficult to represent efficiently. However, methods exist to efficiently approximate dense, smooth integral operators [2]. In particular, hierarchical or wavelet radiosity algorithms provide an efficient method for representing $\mathcal{G}$ [12, 11, 16]. They work because the smoothness of $\mathcal{G}$ allows it to be approximated efficiently using a hierarchy of levels of detail. Unfortunately, combining $\mathcal{S}$ with $\mathcal{G}$ creates an operator which is dense, but no longer smooth, causing difficulties for the hierarchical methods.

## 2.3 Projection methods

In order to make a radiosity system tractable it must be approximated by using a finite dimensional function space. This is done by projecting the radiosity, emittance, and reflectance functions onto a finite set of basis functions $\{N_i\}_{i=1,\ldots,n}$ (for some arbitrary but fixed $n$). For example, these basis functions might be piecewise constant, as in classical radiosity, they might be higher order polynomials as proposed by Zatz [20] for Galerkin radiosity, or wavelets [11]. The level of resolution in the reflectance is typically limited by the solution of the input geometry. We treat the case of incorporating reflectance functions which have potentially much finer resolution than the element subdivision induced by the radiosity solver. The term *nodal basis* will be used to describe a basis consisting of functions at some finest level. For example, a piecewise constant or linear basis over small elements. This is in contrast to hierarchical bases which contain functions at many levels of resolution and often overlapping support. The projection results in approximations $B(x) \approx \hat{B}(x) = \sum_{i=1}^{n} B_i N_i(x)$, $\rho(x) \approx \hat{\rho}(x) = \sum_{l=1}^{n} \rho_l N_l(x)$. Limiting everything to these basis functions, the solution to the original radiosity integral equation can be approximated by solving the following linear system[1]

$$\forall i : B_i = B_i^e + \sum_{j=1}^{n} K_{ij} B_j$$

$$K_{ij} = \int dx \, \hat{\rho}(x) \int dA_{x'} \, G(x,x') \pi^{-1} N_j(x') N_i(x)$$

Writing it in this conventional form (e.g. for constant radiosity $K_{ij} = \rho_i F_{ij}$) we have approximated the *compound* action of $\mathcal{S} \circ \mathcal{G}$ by a single set of coefficients $K_{ij}$.

Instead let us consider each step separately. First irradiance is computed with respect to the chosen basis. This step is not fundamentally different from the compound step if $\rho$ is assumed constant across the support of the given basis function. In this case one typically finds a computation step of the form $E_i = \sum_{j=1}^{n} F_{ij} B_j$. However, if $\rho(x)$ is allowed to vary, the second step, multiplication with $\rho(x)$, changes in a significant way. Since $\rho(x)$ is given in some basis (typically the same as that used for $E$), we get

$$B^r(x) = \hat{\rho}(x) E(x) = \left( \sum_{l=1}^{n} \rho_l N_l(x) \right) \left( \sum_{i=1}^{n} E_i N_i(x) \right) \quad (2)$$

Finally the emitted radiosity is added. This is straightforward and we will therefore focus on the scattering operator in the remaining discussion.

## 2.4 Representation of $\mathcal{S}$

If our chosen basis is a piecewise constant nodal basis, as is typically used in classical radiosity, the application of $\mathcal{S}$ is straightforward. For such a basis the supports of two basis functions with

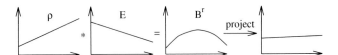

**Figure 3**: *Multiplying an irradiance and reflectance, both representable by a given basis (e.g. piecewise linear), can yield a reflected radiosity (e.g. piecewise quadratic) not representable in the same basis, requiring a reprojection step.*

different index do not intersect. Therefore the application of the operator reduces to a simple multiplication of $E_i$'s and $\rho_i$'s. In this basis $\mathcal{S}$ is a diagonal, sparse operator. Suppose instead that our basis was a piecewise polynomial basis of some higher order, but still with local support. In this case the matrix corresponding to $\mathcal{S}$ would be block diagonal. Each block couples the basis functions with overlapping support. Once again the resulting operator is sparse since only a small constant number of functions overlap.

The important observation is that the local support property of a given basis results in a (block-) diagonal scattering operator $\mathcal{S}$, which can be executed efficiently due to its sparse nature.

When multiplying basis functions a difficulty arises. Consider the use of a piecewise linear basis set and the case depicted in Figure 3. A linearly varying irradiance is multiplied with a linearly varying reflectance resulting in a quadratically varying radiosity. The latter cannot be represented in the chosen basis. The radiosity is of higher polynomial order than the individual component functions. This difficulty can be addressed by following up the multiplication with a reprojection step (see the rightmost step in Figure 3). The error incurred by the reprojection will be analyzed below in the context of the proper level of representation for irradiance and radiosity.

The above operator decomposition can be turned into a straightforward algorithm. Whichever basis is used, the application of $\mathcal{S}$ leads to the following four step algorithm:

### Algorithm 1

1. Transform irradiance from its preferred basis to a nodal basis
2. Apply (block-) diagonal $\mathcal{S}$
3. Reproject onto the nodal basis
4. Transform back to preferred basis for radiosity

This algorithm has the advantage that $\mathcal{S}$ is represented efficiently. However, it has the disadvantage that it requires an intermediate transformation between the preferred basis and the nodal basis. In general, this transformation may require $n^2$ operations. Fortunately, if the preferred basis is the wavelet basis, the transformation to and from the nodal basis requires only a linear number of operations.

At this point the two step decomposition of $\mathcal{G}$ and $\mathcal{S}$ has already resulted in a very efficient algorithm. The first step proceeds as usual, but by separating out the second step we avoid forcing unnecessary subdivision on all surfaces due to the presence of textures. The second step is linear in the complexity of the texture because of the diagonal, sparse nature of $\mathcal{S}$. However, we can do even better since much of the detail computed in going to the finest level will not be needed for the next iteration step.

An obvious improvement would be to express $\mathcal{S}$ directly in the wavelet basis. Unfortunately, the multiplication of the representations of $\rho$ and $E$ is more expensive. The support of many of the functions may overlap, resulting in many non-zero terms. Hence, the representation of $\mathcal{S}$ is no longer sparse. Fortunately, if we are only computing to within some chosen accuracy it may turn out that many of the products in Equation 2 make a negligible contribution to the total. It would be desirable to *only* compute the components that matter.

---

[1]To avoid cluttering the following derivations and help expose the fundamental connections between basis functions, we will ignore all scaling constants and assume an orthogonal basis.

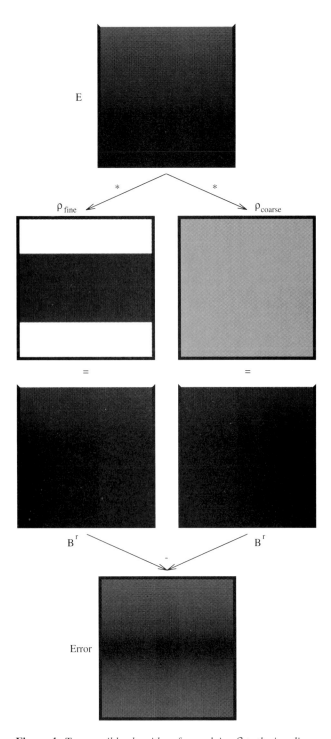

**Figure 4**: *Two possible algorithms for applying $S$ to the irradiance E for an example which exhibits a large difference. The bottom shows error magnitude (white, high error).*

Two observations suggest methods for producing such an algorithm:

1. $S$ may be smooth and if represented in the wavelet basis it may have a sparse representation. If, for example, the texture has regions with fairly little high frequency detail we will be able to adequately represent the texture in those regions with few coefficients. Wavelets afford us one way to optimally take advantage of smoothness if present.

2. The operator $S$ will be followed by the operator $G$ in the

next iteration. Hierarchical radiosity systems [12, 11] use different levels of detail to compute the irradiance from the radiosity. The decision as to how far to subdivide the surfaces is based on the smoothness of $G$. As a result there is no need to compute the radiosity at a finer level of detail than needed in the next iteration. This is distinct from the finest level of radiosity used in a final rendering.

These observations can be formulated into two variants of an algorithm which work directly with the given basis:

**Algorithm nodal:**

1. Push the irradiance to the resolution level of $\rho$
2. Apply $S$
3. Reproject
4. Pull to level of outgoing radiosity

We use the term *outgoing radiosity* to denote the level at which radiosity is needed for the next iteration of the solver. This is distinct from the level at which irradiance was computed, since incoming power may need a finer (or coarser!) subdivision than outgoing power.

**Algorithm wavelet:**

1. Push/pull[2] the irradiance to the radiosity resolution level
2. Apply $S$
3. Reproject

The term *push* denotes transfer (addition) from a parent to children in a subdivision hierarchy, while *pull* refers to averaging a quantity from children to their parent [12].

These two algorithms are illustrated in Figure 4. At the top is the computed irradiance on the far wall due to a light source at the top. On the left $S$ is a applied at the finest level of the $\rho$ texture. The resulting radiosity is reprojected and pulled to the level of outgoing radiosity. On the right the application of $S$ is performed at the level of outgoing radiosity followed by reprojection. The results can be markedly different as shown by the difference between the two at the bottom. Note that it is also possible for radiosity to be computed at a finer level than the reflectance texture. In this case the texture is simply interpolated, or *pushed* in the parlance of wavelet radiosity.

### 2.5 Error analysis

In order to facilitate the following error analysis we define all the terms in the matrix realizations of the operators $G$ and $S$. Replacing $K = S \circ G$ in the traditional form of the linear system we have

$$B_i = B_i^e + \sum_{j=1}^{n} K_{ij} B_j = B_i^e + \sum_{k=1}^{n} S_{ik} \sum_{j=1}^{n} G_{kj} B_j$$

Using $\langle f, g \rangle$ to denote the inner product, we can write $K_{ij} = \langle S \circ G(N_j), N_i \rangle$, $G_{kj} = \langle G(N_j), N_k \rangle$. Finally $S_{ik}$ as given as a function of the coefficients of $\rho$

$$S_{ik} = \langle S(N_k), N_i \rangle = \sum_{l=1}^{n} \rho_l \langle N_l N_k, N_i \rangle \qquad (3)$$

We now analyze the error introduced by the approximate algorithm. In what follows let $P$ denote the projection operator onto the level of the outgoing radiosity, and let $\rho_d(x) = (\rho - P(\rho))(x)$ denote the difference between $\rho$ and its projection at a particular level of detail. This corresponds to the finer levels of detail below the given level. We may then write

$$P \circ S(E) = P(P(\rho)E) + P(\rho_d E)$$

---

[2]We say push/pull since in some regions of the reflectance texture one may need to pull while in other regions one may need to push.

```
Gather( QuadNode p )
  p.E = 0
  ForAllElements( q, p.Interaction )
    p.E += Interaction[i].K * q.B
  Gather( p.sw )
  Gather( p.se )
  Gather( p.nw )
  Gather( p.ne )

PushPull( QuadNode p )
  if( !p.Leaf() )
    p.children.E += WaveletTransformDown( p.E )
    PushPull( p.sw )
    PushPull( p.se )
    PushPull( p.nw )
    PushPull( p.ne )
    p.B = WaveletTransformUp( p.children.B )
  else
    p.B = p.Be + ApplyOpS( p.rho, p.E )
```

**Figure 5**: *Pseudo code for* Gather *and* PushPull. *Note that* B, E, rho, *and* Be *are two dimensional arrays of coefficients and the operations on them are matrix operations. The function* ApplyOpS *is given by Equation 4.*

Examining the right hand side we see two terms. The first, $\mathcal{P}(\mathcal{P}(\rho)E)$, arises from multiplying the approximation of $\rho$ at the chosen subdivision level with the irradiance computed at that level, followed by a reprojection. The second term, $\mathcal{P}(\rho_d E)$, describes the effect of multiplying the finer detail with the irradiance and again reprojecting. Both are potential sources of error. If we only compute $\mathcal{S}$ at the level of the outgoing radiosity we are completely dropping the second term, $\mathcal{P}(\rho_d E)$ (Figure 4 was designed to make this term large). Using the fact that the magnitude of a linearly transformed vector is bounded above by the product of the magnitudes of the vector and the linear operator, $\|Ax\| \leq \|A\| \|x\|$, we may write

$$\|\mathcal{P}(\rho_d E)\| \leq \|\mathcal{P}\| \|\rho_d\| \|E\|$$

For orthogonal projections $\mathcal{P}$ we have $\|\mathcal{P}\| = 1$ and consequently the error in this term can be bounded by the product of the irradiance magnitude and the magnitude of the ignored texture detail. Recall that $\rho_d$ was the detail lost when using $\rho$ as projected at a given level ($\mathcal{P}(\rho)$) compared to the actual $\rho$.

In the standard wavelet radiosity algorithm an *oracle* function is used to decide whether a given interaction needs subdivision to meet the error criterion [11] with regard to $\mathcal{G}$. The presence of reflectance textures requires an additional oracle to decide at what level of detail $\mathcal{S}$ can be executed. This oracle can be based on a test whether $\|\rho_d\| \|E\|$ is less than some error threshold. This is very similar to the BF refinement [12] in ordinary hierarchical radiosity. In BF refinement an interaction between two elements ($\mathcal{G}$) is refined if the product of the magnitudes of radiosity and the form factor error estimate is above the error threshold. This BF refinement also insures the proper handling of emissive textures.

The other source of error arises from the fact that some information is lost in the reprojection step after $\mathcal{P}(\rho)$ and $E$ have been multiplied. This error however, is already implicitly taken into account by the oracle which governs the expansion of $\mathcal{G}$. This oracle decided that the radiosity at the receiving element is only needed to the level of detail at which we computed $E$.

## 3 Implementation

We have added reflectance and emittance textures to a wavelet radiosity system based on [11, 16] and [17]. Pseudo code for the two functions which changed from previous hierarchical radiosity systems, Gather and PushPull is given in Figure 5.

In the paragraphs below we give some more details regarding the following three parts of the overall system

1. functions to build wavelet representations of the texture (image) input files

2. extending the push/pull algorithm to include non-constant emissions and a new function ApplyOpS

3. implementation of RenderMan shaders [19] for final rendering output.

### 3.1 Wavelet encoding of textures

For the encoding of texture maps we used the same basis functions as were used in the rest of the system. These are the multi-wavelets introduced by Alpert [1], which are based on Legendre polynomials up to some order (we used order 0 through 3). The mathematics do not require us to use the same wavelet basis for the textures as for the other parts of the system, but it is a natural choice with the least modifications to the system overall.

After reading in a texture, which is currently limited to have a power-of-2 $u$ and $v$ extent, we pyramid transform it using the low pass and high pass filter sequences associated with the multi-wavelets [16]. This results in averaged representations of the original texture from the finest (input) level all the way to the overall average for use during the solution process. Of the detail information (high pass bands) only a running total of the energy is maintained for use by the oracle.

To start the transform we treat each pixel value as the coefficient of a constant basis function whose domain is the pixel's area. These constant functions are then projected, i.e. taking the inner product with the multi-wavelets, onto the finest level of the hierarchy. This was chosen for simplicity, but other choices are possible. For example, one might use a cubic spline interpolant of the texture values at the finest level and evaluate the integrals of this function with the multi-wavelet bases at the finest level, before beginning the pyramid transform. The rest of the hierarchy is created by running the PyramidUp algorithm described in [11, 16].

At this point we have a full quadtree representation of the texture. For space reasons it may be desirable to prune subtrees in regions which do not have enough spatial detail to warrant finer level descriptions. This is akin to a lossy compression scheme applied to the original texture. During actual production use of our system we have seen a significant savings from this pruning.

### 3.2 Extending push/pull

The modification to the push/pull algorithm only occurs when it reaches the leaves of the hierarchy. After gathering irradiance, which is the $\mathcal{G}$ step, we need to push the irradiance to the leaves of the subdivision as induced by the $\mathcal{G}$ oracle. Ordinarily we would now multiply the coefficients of the basis functions with the scalar $\rho$ before executing the pull to get ready for the next iteration. Instead we apply $\mathcal{S}$ as given by Equation 3 at this level or an even finer level, if required by the original $\rho$ map and the modified oracle. In practice most applications of $\mathcal{S}$ happen at the irradiance level without any need to go to finer levels (Figure 4 shows an extreme case where application of $\mathcal{S}$ must occur at a lower level).

So far we have used a single index on all coefficients to indicate which basis function they belong to. In so doing we have abstracted the fact that all functions are defined with respect to surfaces, i.e. with 2 parameters. We will be explicit about the 2 parameter nature of our basis functions for a moment to give the exact expression for the application of $\mathcal{S}$. Let $\{N_i(u)\}_{i=1,...,M}$

**Figure 6**: *These pictures illustrate the difference in radiosity solutions produced by using true texture maps and approximating them with average values. The left column shows the effect of a reflectance texture with averaging (left half) and without averaging (right half). Similarly the right column shows the difference between averaging and correct solution for emittances. These images were computed with cubic basis functions ($M_4$ multi-wavelets).*

be the multi-wavelets of order $M$. For a moment the index numbering is limited to a *single* element. Surface basis functions are given by $\{N_i(u)N_j(v)\}_{i,j=1,\ldots,M}$ and consequently we use double indices on $B$, $E$, and $\rho$. For example, if we use cubic basis functions with $M = 4$ all the coefficients can be thought of as $4 \times 4$ matrices. We still need the reprojection coefficients $R_{ikm} = \int du\, N_k(u)N_m(u)N_i(u)$. With this notation we have

$$B_{ij}^r = \sum_{kl=1}^{M} \sum_{mn=1}^{M} R_{ikm}R_{jln}\rho_{kl}E_{mn} \quad i,j = 1,\ldots,M \quad (4)$$

Note that $R_{ikm}$ can be precomputed once for a given choice of basis. Taking the example of $M = 4$ again we see that the $4 \times 4$ coefficients $B_{ij}^r$ are a sum over all combinations of the $4 \times 4$ irradiance coefficients with the $4 \times 4$ reflectance coefficients. The weights in this sum are given by the $4 \times 4 \times 4$ reprojection coefficients. Only emittance is left to be added in before executing the pull and starting the next iteration

$$B_{ij} = B_{ij}^e + B_{ij}^r.$$

### 3.3 Final output

As the renderer for final output we use RenderMan [19]. This requires the creation of a RenderMan Interface Bytestream (rib) file containing descriptions of the geometry of each leaf element generated during subdivision, as well as the computed coefficients for the basis functions associated with the element. We have written RenderMan shaders which accept these coefficients as parameters and evaluate the radiosity function at a given point $(u, v)$ in parameter space of the surface element. In the case of multi-wavelets this is achieved by implementing the Legendre basis functions in the shading language. Note that we do no post processing, such as, for example, vertex averaging, as is done in many traditional

radiosity systems. The rendered images show the functions exactly as computed by the radiosity system, because the color of each sample is interpolated using the appropriate basis function during the rendering process.

For surfaces which do not have texture maps associated with them, we write out the coefficients of the *radiosity*. For surfaces with associated texture maps (emittance and/or reflectance) we write out the coefficients of the *irradiance* together with texture coordinates and references to the original texture files. The shaders take this description and for a given $(u, v)$ evaluate the irradiance, multiply with the reflectance texture value, and add the emittance texture value.

Although our final renderings were done with RenderMan, the texture mapping and basis function interpolation scheme used could be easily added to any rendering system.

## 4 Results

Figure 6 shows the difference between using averaged textures and true textures during the radiosity computation:

- The left column demonstrates the case of a reflectance texture mapped onto the floor. The texture map has equal amounts of red, green and blue, and these were chosen so the average texture value is gray and colorless. The left half shows the result of using the average texture color and adding the texture as a post process; the right half shows the result achieved using the true texture map. Below each half images is a cutout of the region just above the floor to show the difference between the two computations more clearly. Note the strong color bleeding near the floor. These colors are absent if the average value is used.

**Figure 7**: *This scene illustrates the visual complexity added to a radiosity simulation by the inclusion of reflectance and emission textures (62). Total simulation time to convergence 10 minutes.*

- The right column shows the results of a similar experiment for emittances. In this case there are 4 ceiling lights with the same texture map, this time used for emittance instead of reflectance. Once again the left half shows the solution when using only the average color, and the right when using the true colors during the simulation itself. In both cases we also have a cutout of the region just below the ceiling lights where the differences are most pronounced. Again, with averaging no colored light is cast onto the ceiling and walls near the lights.

For these examples we used multi-wavelet $M_4$ (piecewise cubic) basis functions.

To test the robustness of the system, and to measure the impact of texturing on the running time of the radiosity algorithm, we computed more complicated scenes shown in Figures 1 and 7. Figure 1 was modeled with 23 quadrilaterals and 10 texture maps. The stained-glass window is a single quadrilateral with the emittance and reflectance maps shown in Figure 9. We solved the system using cubic multi-wavelets. A total of 29 seconds was spent on hierarchy creation for all texture maps (each with a resolution of $128^2$ pixels). The solution was run to convergence in 10 complete gather sweeps. 1795 elements with 12831 interactions were created. The process size reached 51Mb out of which 26Mb were consumed by texture map data. The execution time was 36 minutes on an SGI Indigo (R4000 50MHz) computer. Over 90% of this time was spent computing quadratures. The increased cost in the application of $S$ due to the textures is only felt during the iterations (the remaining 10%), which become approximately 10% more expensive. Figure 7 shows another scene. It contained 99 quadrilaterals and 62 texture maps (most had a resolution of $32^2$ pixels), which resulted in 9515 elements and 90362 interactions using linear basis functions. Total memory size grew to 54Mb of which 9Mb were used for textures. The solution required 10 minutes and 15 complete gather iterations for convergence on an SGI Indigo (R4000 50MHz) computer.

These performance numbers demonstrate that the resulting system can simulate scenes with many textures efficiently incurring

**Figure 8**: *Two details from Figure 7. On top the recessed colored windows on the far wall of the room illustrate the subtle lighting effects possible. Each window is a single polygon. On the bottom the effect of reflectance maps on the staircase. The top of each step has a reflectance map. Notice the patterns in the induced color bleeding.*

**Figure 9**: *The stained glass window was created with the emissive texture on the left and the reflective texture (matte) on the right.*

only a small time penalty. Extending the existing wavelet radiosity system was straightforward since only a few functions needed minor modifications.

Figure 8 shows close-up views of some of the areas that were most influenced by the texture maps. The color changes around the colored glass windows and the reflection off the staircase steps are effects that would have been difficult to model without the use of texture maps. Similarly in Figure 1 the use of texture maps allowed the system to cluster many floor tiles or window panes together when determining interactions by using the standard hierarchical error criteria [12, 11]. The fact that high visual complexity was achieved with only a few quadrilaterals attests to the power of the texture mapping paradigm in the radiosity context.

## 5 Summary and conclusion

We have presented a technique which extends hierarchical radiosity algorithms to include reflectance and emittance textures during the solution process. This extension was facilitated by a careful examination of the radiosity integral equation. We separate the computation of irradiance, a global process, from the computation of reflected radiosity, a local process. In so doing we can take advantage of efficiencies in each step individually. These efficiencies are not available if the two steps are merged, as is normally done. The new method has been implemented in a wavelet radiosity system. The resulting images demonstrate the desired lighting effects with little penalty in performance. As a result increasing the visual complexity of radiosity computations with texture maps is now practical.

Although the computational cost of using texture maps is now quite small, the storage and memory costs may still be large. An interesting research question is how to manage the texture data. Since only limited resolutions are ever needed, and since many radiosity runs may be performed using the same input textures, it is reasonable to precompute and store the wavelet representation of the texture. The radiosity program then need only read in the resolution sets that are required. This also suggests the intriguing possibility of applying a lossy wavelet compression to the texture maps to begin with. The compression would be limited so as to not produce any artifacts to the human observer, but could still reduce the cost of reading the textures, and the amount of disk space needed to store them.

The use of texture mapping techniques in computer graphics has a long tradition and many complex effects can be achieved. One such example has already been demonstrated in Figure 1, where two texture maps, one for emittance and another for reflectance are combined with a matte (see Figure 9). As a result the odd shaped stained glass window is created from texture maps and a single quadrilateral. Other uses for texture maps include environment mapping and bump mapping [4]. The algorithm described in this paper may be easily modified to use environment maps; an interesting application of this would be to the modeling of skylighting, which is currently very expensive. A clever algorithm for approximating bump mapping in the context of radiosity is described in [4]; similar approximations could likely be used in a hierarchical radiosity algorithm, although this would require further research.

Some of these techniques may also be useful for the clustering problem. Imagine a surface described by a displacement map over a regular grid. Now we have actual geometric complexity, yet a multi resolution description still appears promising and could be incorporated in a straightforward manner into the texture mapping system. In fact one might imagine replacing entire complex ensembles of geometry with a "picture" during parts of the radiosity solution process. Another use for this system is in the area of inverse problems. Consider taking a photograph of a diffuse surface, i.e. capturing its radiosity, and using this as a texture in a radiosity simulation. This could be used to match real scenes with computed scenes [9]; and more generally might be useful for problems arising in computer vision, such as the computation of the reflectance map.

The technique we applied in our analysis, separating out the global $G$ part of the computation from the surface local $S$ part, may also be a fruitful analysis technique for other rendering problems. For example, in volume rendering it may yield new insights to separate the representation of the attenuation operator from the representation of the scattering operator. Another example is the computation of radiance, where one might also gain new efficiencies from separating the incident radiance operator from the scattering operator.

## Acknowledgments

We would like to thank Seth Teller and Celeste Fowler for their contributions to the radiosity testbed which greatly facilitated the research reported in this paper. Many thanks also to Don Mitchell, Michael Cohen, and Steven Gortler for stimulating discussions and David Laur for production help. The first author would like to thank Sondra Au for artistic advice and contributions. Thanks to James Shaw for the stained-glass window texture (Figure 1) and SGI for many of the other texture maps used in Figures 1 and 7. Other support came from Apple, Silicon Graphics and the NSF (contract no. CCR 9207966).

## References

[1] ALPERT, B., BEYLKIN, G., COIFMAN, R., AND ROKHLIN, V. Wavelet-like Bases for the Fast Solution of Second-kind Integral Equations. *SIAM Journal on Scientific Computing 14*, 1 (Jan 1993).

[2] BEYLKIN, G., COIFMAN, R., AND ROKHLIN, V. Fast Wavelet Transforms and Numerical Algorithms I. *Communications on Pure and Applied Mathematics 44* (1991), 141–183.

[3] BLINN, J. F., AND NEWELL, M. E. Texture and Reflection in Computer Generated Images. *Communications of the ACM 19*, 10 (October 1976), 542–547.

[4] CHEN, H., AND WU, E.-H. An Efficient Radiosity Solution for Bump Texture Generation. *Computer Graphics 24*, 4 (August 1990), 125–134.

[5] COHEN, M., CHEN, S. E., WALLACE, J. R., AND GREENBERG, D. P. A Progressive Refinement Approach to Fast Radiosity Image Generation. *Computer Graphics 22*, 4 (August 1988), 75–84.

[6] COHEN, M. F., AND GREENBERG, D. P. The Hemi-Cube: A Radiosity Solution for Complex Environments. *Computer Graphics 19*, 3 (July 1985), 31–40.

[7] COHEN, M. F., GREENBERG, D. P., IMMEL, D. S., AND BROCK, P. J. An Efficient Radiosity Approach for Realistic Image Synthesis. *IEEE Computer Graphics and Applications 6*, 3 (March 1986), 26–35.

[8] DORSEY, J. O., SILLION, F. X., AND GREENBERG, D. P. Design and Simulation of Opera Lighting and Projection Effects. *Computer Graphics 25*, 4 (July 1991), 41–50.

[9] FOURNIER, A., GUNAWAN, A. S., AND ROMANZIN, C. Common Illumination between Real and Computer Generated Scenes. In *Proceedings of Graphics Interface 93* (1993), pp. 254–261.

[10] GORAL, C. M., TORRANCE, K. E., GREENBERG, D. P., AND BATTAILE, B. Modelling the Interaction of Light between Diffuse Surfaces. *Computer Graphics 18*, 3 (July 1984), 212–222.

[11] GORTLER, S., SCHRÖDER, P., COHEN, M., AND HANRAHAN, P. Wavelet Radiosity. In *Computer Graphics Annual Conference Series 1993* (August 1993), Siggraph, pp. 221–230.

[12] HANRAHAN, P., SALZMAN, D., AND AUPPERLE, L. A Rapid Hierarchical Radiosity Algorithm. *Computer Graphics 25*, 4 (July 1991), 197–206.

[13] HECKBERT, P. S. Radiosity in Flatland. *Computer Graphics Forum 2*, 3 (1992), 181–192.

[14] KAJIYA, J. T. The Rendering Equation. *Computer Graphics 20*, 4 (1986), 143–150.

[15] NISHITA, T., AND NAKAMAE, E. Continuous Tone Representation of Three-Dimensional Objects Taking Account of Shadows and Interreflection. *Computer Graphics 19*, 3 (July 1985), 23–30.

[16] SCHRÖDER, P., GORTLER, S. J., COHEN, M. F., AND HANRAHAN, P. Wavelet Projections For Radiosity. In *Fourth Eurographics Workshop on Rendering* (June 1993), Eurographics, pp. 105–114.

[17] TELLER, S., AND HANRAHAN, P. Global Visibility Algorithms for Illumination Computations. In *Computer Graphics Annual Conference Series 1993* (August 1993), Siggraph, pp. 239–246.

[18] TROUTMAN, R., AND MAX, N. Radiosity Algorithms Using Higher-order Finite Elements. In *Computer Graphics Annual Conference Series 1993* (August 1993), Siggraph, pp. 209–212.

[19] UPSTILL, S. *The RenderMan Companion*. Addison Wesley, 1992.

[20] ZATZ, H. R. Galerkin Radiosity: A Higher-order Solution Method for Global Illumination. In *Computer Graphics Annual Conference Series 1993* (August 1993), Siggraph, pp. 213–220.

# Error-Bounded Antialiased Rendering of Complex Environments

Ned Greene*    Michael Kass†

Apple Computer

## Abstract

In previous work, we presented an algorithm to accelerate z-buffer rendering of enormously complex scenes [16]. Here, we extend the approach to antialiased rendering with an algorithm that guarantees that each pixel of the output image is within a user-specified error tolerance of the filtered underlying continuous image. As before, we use an object-space octree to cull hidden geometry rapidly. However, instead of using an image-space depth pyramid to test visibility of collections of pixel samples, we use a quadtree data structure to test visibility throughout image-space regions. When regions are too complex, we use quadtree subdivision to simplify the geometry as in Warnock's algorithm. Subdivision stops when the algorithm can either analytically filter the required region or bound the convolution integral appropriately with interval methods. To the best of our knowledge, this is the first algorithm to antialias with guaranteed accuracy scenes consisting of hundreds of millions of polygons.

**CR Categories and Subject Descriptors:** I.3.7 [Computer Graphics]: Three-Dimensional Graphics and Realism - Hidden line/surface removal; I.3.3 [Computer Graphics]: Picture/Image Generation. **Additional Key Words and Phrases:** Antialiasing, Interval Arithmetic, Shaders, Octree, Quadtree.

## 1  Introduction

The fact that computer generated images frequently contain step edges and other high frequency detail has always posed serious aliasing problems for rendering algorithms [11]. Even with special measures to combat aliasing, jaggies and other familiar aliasing artifacts frequently occur. The aliasing difficulties we have with computer graphics today, however, may seem mild compared to the aliasing problems that will become commonplace in a few years. As inexpensive computers become more and more powerful, computer graphics models will become increasingly detailed, and we will regularly be faced with images that contain large numbers of sub-pixel polygons. These sub-pixel polygons will create a great deal of energy at high spatial frequencies and cause severe aliasing for current algorithms.

*Apple Computer and U.C. Santa Cruz, greene@apple.com

†Current Affiliation: FITS Imaging, fits.imaging@applelink.apple.com

The left panel of figure 1 shows the severity of aliasing that can result from standard z-buffer rendering of a 167 million polygon model of the Empire State Building. The exterior skin of the building is represented by large multi-pixel polygons that cause the usual aliasing artifacts we have come to expect from z-buffer rendering. The interior of the building, however, consists of an extremely large number of polygons, and it exhibits a qualitatively different level of aliasing. Each of the floors of the model is populated with hundreds of office cubicles, each consisting of thousands of polygons. A detail of the interior can be seen in figure 3. Through some of the windows in figure 1, large numbers of polygons are visible in a single pixel. With z-buffer rendering, each pixel is colored using just the front-most polygon that crosses the pixel center, but with so many polygons covering portions of a single pixel, the color that happens to occur at the center may differ greatly from the local average, causing a disturbing visual artifact.

Uniform oversampling is often used to combat aliasing, but with a model of this complexity, no reasonable amount of oversampling can be guaranteed to produce good results. Moreover, in many applications, such as animation, it is important to be able to produce an acceptable antialiased result without user intervention. If the geometry becomes very complicated in a particular pixel of a frame, the rendering algorithm should detect the problem and work as hard as necessary on that pixel to avoid aliasing.

Here we present the first rendering algorithm capable of dealing with models as complex as our model of the Empire State Building while guaranteeing proper antialiasing within a desired error tolerance. Our algorithm extends the techniques developed by Greene, Kass and Miller [16] to cull hidden geometry very quickly. Having discarded most hidden geometry, it uses Warnock-style subdivision [25] to bound the convolution integral at each pixel to within the desired error tolerance. For flat-shaded or Gouraud-shaded polygons, it is possible to compute the integral exactly. For more complicated shading functions, we rely on interval arithmetic to provide bounds. In any case, for each pixel, the algorithm terminates when it computes the exact result or when it can prove a sufficiently good error bound that further subdivision is unnecessary.

In section 2, we discuss the aliasing problem in general and the relation of our method to prior work. In section 3, we present the details of our algorithm and describe its two stages. In the first stage, the algorithm culls hidden geometry using an octree, and in the second stage, it uses Warnock-style subdivision to achieve the desired error bound. In section 4, we describe our implementation of the algorithm and show results. Finally, in section 5, we describe extensions of the algorithm which should make it possible to compute motion blur.

# 2  Aliasing

The potential for aliasing arises in computer graphics because the mathematical representations that we ordinarily use to describe images (e.g. polygons) contain energy at arbitrarily high spatial frequencies, while the sampled rasters we use to display and print images are limited to a finite range of spatial frequencies. Let $I(x, y)$ be the vector-valued function that gives the color of each point in $\Re^2$ for the idealized mathematical representation of a computer graphics image. If we compute a raster image by directly sampling $I(x, y)$ at the center of each output pixel, then any spatial frequency content in $I(x, y)$ beyond half the sampling rate will alias to a lower frequency and cause disturbing visual artifacts. There are three approaches for dealing with this problem. The first approach is to adjust the number, locations or weights of the samples to attenuate the visible aliased energy. The second approach is to try to detect aliasing artifacts in the rendered image and remove them by post-processing. The third approach and the only one capable of guaranteed accuracy is to compute or approximate the convolution $I(x, y) * f(x, y)$ of the image $I(x, y)$ with a low-pass filter $f(x, y)$ at each output pixel using analytic or other means.

The first approach, adjusting the number and location of the samples and the filter kernels used to combine them, is probably the most widely used approach and can go a long way toward reducing the severity of aliasing artifacts. Unfortunately, it provides no guarantees about the quality of the result and can produce unacceptable errors in cases where a large number of primitives are visible within a single pixel. For any fixed sampling rate, if we place the samples stochastically rather than using a regular sampling grid, then many of the patterned aliasing artifacts that arise with regular sampling can be converted into less disturbing noise [8, 10, 13]. Nonetheless, the noise may still be unacceptably high in some areas. The problem is that we do not know in advance what sampling rate will be required for any particular region of the image, and any algorithm that uses a fixed sampling rate (e.g. [5]) will be unable to deal with the extreme geometry in figure 1 where large numbers of polygons are frequently visible in a single pixel.

Some authors have suggested using the variance of a collection of rays through a pixel to determine a local sampling rate for ray tracing [19, 13] and this can produce good results in many cases. A serious problem, however, is that the accuracy of the result is proportional to the square root of the number of samples. According to Lee et al. [19], in order to achieve a 95% confidence limit that the pixel value is calculated correctly to within a variance of 1 part in 128 (and hence a standard deviation of about 9%), the maximum number of rays required is 96. Using these figures, if we want the standard deviation of the error to be 1 part in 128, we need a maximum of 12,288 rays per pixel. Rendering figure 1 by casting over twelve thousand rays to antialias each of the complex pixels would be prohibitively expensive. Even if we used that many rays, we would only know that 95% of the output pixels should be within the error bounds implied by the desired standard deviation.

The second approach to combating aliasing, post-processing, has limited potential because it begins after the sampling process. If geometric primitives are large compared to pixels, then a post process can sometimes effectively infer edges from the sampled image and soften them to attenuate aliasing artifacts [4]. However, if large numbers of primitives are visible within individual pixels such as in figure 1, too much information is lost in the sampling process to allow a post process to compute an acceptable reconstruction.

The third approach, convolution before sampling, was first advanced by Crow [11] and Catmull [6] for polygonal images and is the only technique which is, in principle, capable of eliminating aliasing entirely. From a theoretical perspective, if we convolve $I(x, y)$ with the appropriate *sinc* function, it will be low-pass filtered below the Nyquist rate before sampling and no aliasing will occur. From a practical perspective, however, some authors (e.g. [13]) have observed that the ideal *sinc* function generates ringing (Gibbs phenomenon) at step edges, and have suggested other filters such as triangular filters, Gaussians, raised cosine filters, Hamming windows etc. Whatever filter is chosen, rendering with this approach requires (a) identifying the visible geometric primitives affecting each output pixel and (b) filtering them.

Most visible surface algorithms capable of finding all the geometric primitives potentially affecting a single pixel require examining each primitive in the model (e.g. [6, 7, 26, 25, 22]). For ordinary purposes with moderately complex models, this is not a serious limitation. For a model as complex as that of figure 1, however, this poses a major problem. Examining and processing each of the 167 million primitives in the model would take a prohibitively long time on current computers. The only practical way of rendering the model is to use an algorithm which does work roughly proportional to the visible complexity of the scene rather than the size of the entire model. In general, such algorithms are known as *output sensitive*.

Naylor [21] presented a BSP tree visibility algorithm capable of culling hidden subtrees of a model occluded by a single face. The algorithm does not, however, cull subtrees occluded by multiple faces in the final visibility map unless it happens to be possible to merge the multiple faces into a single face at a higher level of the image-space BSP tree. As a result, it seems unlikely that the method, as presented, would cull enough geometry to make it practical to render the model of figure 1.

Airey [2] and subsequently Teller [24] proposed dividing models up into disjoint cells and finding the set of polygons potentially visible from each cell for the purpose of culling hidden geometry. These culling techniques, which vary in effectiveness according to characteristics of the model, are of continuing interest in rendering complex scenes.

Greene, Kass and Miller [16] presented an algorithm to accelerate z-buffer rendering of complex environments which employs an object-space octree and an image-space depth pyramid. The algorithm culls hidden geometry very effectively for scenes with high depth complexity and is well suited to the type of model in figure 1. Here, we modify the basic ideas of this method to support filtering before sampling. With z-buffer rendering, geometry which is hidden on all point samples can be culled whether or not portions of the geometry are visible in between the samples. With antialiased rendering, however, geometry should be culled only if it is completely hidden. To facilitate culling, we insert the model geometry into a quadtree data structure. If the geometry in a quadtree cell is simple, we can quickly determine whether or not the geometry completely hides a given primitive. Otherwise, we use Warnock-style subdivision to create simpler children. Similar data structures were used by Meagher for volume rendering [20].

Once the visible polygons affecting a pixel have been identified, they need to be convolved with the desired filter and summed. Fast algorithms using look-up tables have been developed to compute the convolution quickly for arbitrary filters with flat-shaded polygons [14, 1], and for Gaussian or box filtered texture-mapped polygons [27, 12]. In section 3.5, we show how to use interval arithmetic to extend the range of cases that can be accurately filtered to include Phong highlights, texture mapping and shade trees made up of operations amenable to interval techniques.

# 3 Algorithm

Our algorithm employs two key data structures in order to antialias very complex models with guaranteed accuracy. The first data structure is an object-space octree used to organize the model polygons in world space. The second is an image-space quadtree used to organize information about potentially visible polygons in each region of the screen. With these two data structures, the algorithm culls hidden geometry very quickly and establishes color bounds for each output pixel.

## 3.1 Construction of the Octree

The first step of the algorithm is to organize the model in an octree. Following [16], this can be done with a simple recursive procedure. Beginning with the complete list of model polygons and a root cube large enough to enclose the entire model, we recursively perform the following steps: If the size of the list is sufficiently small, we associate all of the polygons on the list with the cube and exit. Otherwise, we associate with the cube any polygons on the list which intersect at least one of the three axis-aligned planes that bisect the cube. We then subdivide the octree cube and call the procedure recursively with each of the eight child cubes and the polygons on the list that fit entirely in that cube. The details of how we detect cube-polygon intersection (and also cube-frustum and rectangle-polygon intersection) can be found in [17]. The refinement described in [16] that avoids placing some small polygons in large cubes is also useful here.

In building the octree, we expect to do work proportional to $n \log(n)$ where $n$ is the number of polygons in the model. However, if we replicate geometry by instancing sub-octrees, as we have done with our model of the Empire State Building, it is possible to construct an octree in much less time than it would take to traverse all of the polygons in the model. More elaborate instancing involving transformed and unioned octrees is also compatible with our general approach, although this would require changing various details of the algorithm. Even without instancing, for animation purposes static objects need only be inserted into an octree once, so the cost of traversing static geometry can be amortized over all of the frames.

## 3.2 Rendering the Octree

After the model has been organized in an octree, our antialiased rendering algorithm operates in two passes. In the first pass, we traverse the octree in front-to-back order [15], culling sub-octrees which are completely hidden and inserting polygons associated with potentially visible octree cubes into the image-space quadtree. In the second pass, we compute minimum and maximum color bounds for each quadtree cell. Anywhere the color uncertainty at the pixel level is above the user-specified error tolerance, we subdivide in breadth-first order until the uncertainty drops below the error tolerance.

## 3.3 Tiling Pass

As in [16], we cull hidden cubes before processing the polygons they contain by applying the following observation: assuming that the viewpoint is outside a cube, if the front faces of the cube are completely hidden, then all of the geometry contained in the cube is hidden and can be ignored. To use this test effectively, we traverse the octree in front-to-back order, because this guarantees that any geometry that can occlude a cube is represented in the quadtree before the cube is considered. Combining cube culling and front-to-back traversal, we have the following overall control structure for the tiling pass:

```
Tile(OctreeNode N)
```

```
{
    unless CouldCubeBeVisible(N) return
    Q = smallest quadtree cell enclosing N
    for each polygon P on N's list
        InsertPolyIntoQuadtree(P,Q)
    for each child C of N in front-to-back order
        Tile(C)
}

CouldCubeBeVisible(OctreeNode N)
{
    if N is completely outside the viewing frustum
    then return False
    if viewpoint is inside N then return True
    for each front face F of N {
        Q = smallest quadtree cell enclosing F
        if CouldCubeFaceBeVisible(F,Q)
        then return True
    }
    return False
}
```

The test CouldCubeFaceBeVisible returns False if it can prove that a cube face is hidden, and True otherwise. With z-buffer rendering, a cube face (or in fact any polygon) is hidden if its depth at each pixel sample is farther than the value stored in the z-buffer. To cull hidden z-buffered cube faces (and model polygons) efficiently, [16] uses a pyramid of depth values that can often show with a single depth comparison that all the z-buffer values in a region enclosing a cube face are nearer than the face. With antialiased rendering, however, a cube face is hidden only if every point on the face is behind the corresponding point on a model polygon. To establish visibility of faces in this case, we generalize the depth pyramid of [16] to a quadtree data structure containing a value $zfar$ at each cell which is equal to the depth of the farthest visible point within the quadtree cell and a value $znear$ which is equal to the depth of the nearest visible point within the quadtree cell. If the nearest point on a face is farther than $zfar$ of an enclosing quadtree cell, then the face is hidden within the cell. Likewise, if the nearest point on a face is nearer than $znear$ of an enclosing quadtree cell, the face is at least partially visible within the cell. If neither of these two conditions holds, we can obtain a more definitive result by applying the same visibility tests recursively within children of the quadtree cell.

In some cases the amount of computation needed to resolve the visibility of a cube can exceed the cost of rendering the polygons it contains, so we use a computation limit in testing cube faces for visibility. If the number of quadtree cells we visit while testing a cube face for visibility exceeds some constant times the number of polygons within the cell, we stop testing and assume that the cube face is visible. The following pseudocode outlines a visibility test for cube faces that visits quadtree cells in breath-first order.

```
CouldCubeFaceBeVisible(CubeFace F,QuadtreeCell Q)
{
    NumberVisited = 0
    create queue of quadtree cells containing
    only Q
    while queue is not empty {
        NumberVisited = NumberVisited + 1
        if NumberVisited > ComputationLimit
        then return True
        C = Head(queue)
        remove C from queue
        if F intersects C then {
            if nearest point on F within C is nearer
            than C.znear then return True
            unless nearest point on F within C is
            farther than C.zfar {
                if C is a leaf cell
                then SubdivideQCell(C)
                add C's children to end of queue
            }
        }
    }
```

```
    return False
}

SubdivideQCell(QuadtreeCell Q)
{
    create child for each quadrant of Q
    for each child C of Q {
        add each polygon on Q's list that
        intersects C to C's polygon list
        find any covering structures formed by
        polygons on C's list
        if C is covered by polygons on its list {
            find C.zfar
            RemoveHiddenPolys(C)
        }
        else C.zfar = z of far clipping plane
        find C.znear
        PropagateZBounds(C)
    }
    delete Q's poly list
}

PropagateZBounds(QuadtreeCell Q)
{
    if Q is root cell then return
    P = Parent(Q)
    P.znear = nearest znear of Q and its siblings
    P.zfar = farthest zfar of Q and its siblings
    PropagateZBounds(P)
}
```

When the above visibility test fails to prove that a cube is hidden, we insert any polygons associated with the cube into the quadtree. First we test each polygon for visibility using $znear$ and $zfar$ comparisons as we did when testing cube faces for visibility. If the test fails to show that a polygon is hidden, we insert the polygon into the quadtree cell and update $zfar$ if the depth of the farthest visible point within the cell has changed. This only happens if the new polygon, either by itself, or in combination with polygons already stored in the cell, forms a geometric structure which completely covers the cell. Easily detected covering structures include (a) a single polygon, (b) two polygons meeting along an edge and (c) a set of polygons meeting at a single vertex. If the number of polygons in a cell is large, testing for coverage becomes expensive, so we subdivide the quadtree cell whenever the number of polygons on its list exceeds a threshold (ten in our current implementation). Pseudocode for this portion of the algorithm is as follows.

```
InsertPolyIntoQuadtree(Polygon P,QuadtreeCell Q)
{
    if P does not intersect Q then return
    Pznear = z of nearest point on P within Q
    if Pznear is farther than Q.zfar then return
    if P covers Q or forms a covering structure
    with other polygons on Q's list then {
        if zfar of covering structure is nearer
        than Q.zfar then {
            Q.zfar = zfar of covering structure
            PropagateZBounds(Q)
            if Q is a leaf cell
            then RemoveHiddenPolys(Q)
            else for each child C of Q {
                if C.znear is farther than Q.zfar
                then delete C and its subtree
            }
        }
    }
    InsertPoly(P,Q)
}

InsertPoly(Polygon P,QuadtreeCell Q)
{
    if Q is a leaf cell and its polygon list is
    not full then {
        add P to Q's polygon list
        Pznear = z of nearest point on P within Q
        if Pznear is nearer than Q.znear then {
```

```
            Q.znear = Pznear
            PropagateZBounds(Q)
        }
        return
    }
    if Q is a leaf cell then SubdivideQCell(Q)
    for each child cell C of Q
        InsertPolyIntoQuadtree(P,C)
}

RemoveHiddenPolys(QuadtreeCell Q)
{
    for each polygon P on Q's list {
        Pznear = z of nearest point on P within Q
        if Pznear is farther than Q.zfar
        then remove P from Q's list
        if P is behind all planes of a covering
        structure of Q
        then remove P from Q's list
    }
}
```

The tiling pass traverses all cubes of the octree which it is unable to prove are hidden. When it finishes, it has inserted all potentially visible polygons into the quadtree. The tiling pass never visits an octree node more than once and for densely occluded scenes it typically visits only a small subset of all octree nodes.

## 3.4 Refinement Pass

The refinement pass begins after the tiling pass has culled most of the hidden polygons and inserted the remaining polygons into the quadtree. Its task is to evaluate the filtered color $f(x,y) * I(x,y)$ of each output pixel. If the geometry and shading in a quadtree cell are simple enough, the algorithm may be able to compute the required convolution integral exactly or bound it tightly enough to meet the error tolerance. If the geometry or shading is too complex, the quadtree cell is subdivided as in Warnock's algorithm. New color bounds are computed for the children and propagated to coarser levels of the quadtree. Subdivision continues recursively in breadth-first order until the error tolerance is met at the pixel level. The algorithm converges as long as repeated subdivision ultimately improves the error bounds.

At the beginning of the refinement pass, we subdivide the quadtree if necessary so that all leaf cells are no larger than a single pixel. For the purposes of refinement, we associate with each quadtree cell a minimum and maximum bound on each color component of the portion of the convolution integral $f(x,y) * I(x,y)$ within the cell. If the point-spread function $f(x,y)$ is a pixel-sized box filter, then $f(x,y) * I(x,y)$ is just the average value of $I(x,y)$ in each pixel and the filtering is known as area sampling [6]. In this case, the refinement pass is relatively simple and is described by the following pseudocode in which the uncertainty of each quadtree cell is difference between min and max bounds of the portion of the convolution integral within the cell.

```
Refine()
{
    place all quadtree leaf cells in a priority
    queue sorted by uncertainty
    for each cell Q on queue
        PropagateUncertainty(Parent(Q))
    while queue is not empty {
        Q = Head(queue)  /* greatest uncertainty */
        remove Q from queue
        SubdivideQCell(Q)
        for each child C of Q {
            compute C.Uncertainty
            add C to queue
        }
        PropagateUncertainty(Q)
    }
}
```

```
PropagateUncertainty(QuadtreeCell Q)
{
    Q.Uncertainty = sum of uncertainty of Q's
    children
    if Q is sub-pixel
    then PropagateUncertainty(Parent(Q))
    else {
        if Q.Uncertainty < ErrorTolerance
        then remove Q and its subtree from
        the priority queue
    }
}
```

If the point-spread function $f(x, y)$ of the filter extends beyond the boundaries of a pixel, then the algorithm is somewhat more complicated. In general, if $f(x, y)$ is zero beyond some fixed radius, there will be a small maximum number of pixels $k$ that can be affected by the value of $I(x, y)$ in a pixel or sub-pixel region. In this case, with each quadtree cell, we store up to $k$ min and max color bounds corresponding to the portion of the convolution integral $f(x, y) * I(x, y)$ lying inside the quadtree cell for each of the affected pixels. Whenever we subdivide a quadtree cell, for each of the affected pixels, we compute new bounds on $f(x, y) * I(x, y)$ in the children and propagate the changes to the affected pixel-sized quadtree cells. If the point-spread function $f(x, y)$ has negative lobes, we can improve the bounds on $f(x, y) * I(x, y)$ by breaking $f$ into the sum of a positive part $f^+(x, y)$ and a negative part $f^-(x, y)$. Then we can separately bound $f^+(x, y) * I(x, y)$ and $f^-(x, y) * I(x, y)$ and combine them to bound $f(x, y) * I(x, y)$. The control structure for choosing which cell to subdivide next can be the same here as outlined above for area sampling.

## 3.5   Interval Arithmetic

In order to compute each pixel to within the error tolerance with guaranteed accuracy, the refinement pass of the algorithm must be able to integrate $f(x, y) * I(x, y)$ analytically within a quadtree cell or prove sufficiently tight bounds on the integral. For flat shading, Gouraud shading and other polynomial shading functions, the integral can be computed analytically with simple filters. For more general shaders, however, analytic integration may not be possible, so we rely on interval arithmetic [3, 23, 18] to bound the integral. Kass [18] has shown that Cook's shade-tree approach [9] can be extended in a relatively straightforward manner to create interval shaders. An interval shader receives bounds on input parameters such as $u, v$ coordinates, components of the surface normal, the vector to the eye, etc. and uses these bounds to compute a bound on the output color.

Once bounds on color within a quadtree cell have been established they need to be combined with bounds on $f(x, y)$, the point-spread function of the filter. For efficiency, we can precompute a table of intervals for $f(x, y)$ for subdivisions of a canonical pixel down to some fine resolution. We can then use interval multiplication to find bounds on the required convolution $f(x, y) * I(x, y)$.

Interval shaders will drive quadtree subdivision at places like specular highlights because, for this example, the bounds will be loose if a polygon could contain a highlight and much tighter otherwise. Note that some care is required when constructing interval shaders for use with the algorithm. To guarantee convergence, all that is needed is that the intervals get smaller with subdivision. To achieve rapid convergence, however, the intervals must give reasonably tight bounds on the integral.

## 4   Implementation and Results

We have implemented the algorithm described in section 3 using the area sampling technique described in section 3.4. To avoid using excessive amounts of memory, we have found it necessary to render complex images in subwindows. To demonstrate the progressive refinement possibilities of the algorithm, our implementation differs from the pseudocode of section 3.4 in that it does not subdivide down to the pixel level before beginning the refinement pass, and instead of using the priority queue described in section 3.4, it refines the quadtree one level at a time, doing all subdivision at level $k$ before doing any subdivision at level $k + 1$.

We are in the process of adding additional special integration cases to our implementation, but the current list of cases that it integrates exactly is as follows. If a single flat-shaded polygon covers a quadtree cell, the implementation computes the integral as the product of the polygon color and the area of the quadtree cell. If two flat-shaded polygons cover a quadtree cell and either (a) one of the polygons is completely in front of the other or (b) the two polygons meet on an edge, the implementation computes the area of each polygon within the cell, multiplies each area by the corresponding color and sums the results to compute the integral. Additional integration cases would reduce the need for subdivision and improve overall efficiency.

Figure 1 shows the Empire State Building rendered with our error-bounded rendering algorithm (right) and with the hierarchical z-buffer method (left) [16]. At the lower left corner of each image, a small region of the scene has been magnified with pixel replication to show detail. Note that the z-buffered image has white pixels that appear to be randomly scattered along the columns of windows. This severe aliasing artifact is absent from the error-bounded antialiased image on the right. Our unoptimized implementation rendered this 340×512 antialiased image to within an error tolerance of .05 in approximately one hour on a 50 MHz SGI Crimson.

Figure 3 shows an interior view of the Empire State Building model. At top right, we show the result of antialiased rendering within an error tolerance of .05, and at top left we again show an aliased comparison image rendered using the hierarchical z-buffer method. The bottom center panel of figure 3 shows the quadtree subdivision produced in rendering the antialiased image. Note that subdivision is coarse in regions covered by large polygons and becomes very fine along edges and in regions of fine geometric detail. The bottom right panel of figure 3 shows quadtree subdivision in a different way. In this image, intensity encodes the log of the number of quadtree cells created at each pixel. Bright regions indicate where the algorithm is working hardest, for example at the end of the corridor where pixels contain numerous visible polygons. The bottom left panel of figure 3 shows the uncertainty of the antialiased image at each pixel, scaled so the maximum allowable error of .05 is represented as white. Most pixels are black, indicating that the algorithm was able to determine an exact color by integration.   Some of the bright lines in the foreground are caused by slight gaps in the model; others are due to simple cases that our implementation does not yet integrate. Our unoptimized implementation rendered this 512×512 antialiased image in approximately 5 minutes on a 50 MHz SGI Crimson.

Figure 4 illustrates the progressive refinement nature of the algorithm. The images from left to right show the regions of the image known to be within the error tolerance after four consecutive refinement passes. Pixels whose uncertainty exceed the error tolerance are shown in green. As the algorithm progresses, it produces an increasingly accurate image, computing more and more pixels to within the error tolerance. If it were necessary to stop rendering at some point due to a frame-time limit, the remaining pixels could be interpolated quickly from their neighbors.

Our model of the Empire State Building is composed of flat-shaded polygons, so in figures 1 and 3, most of the polygonal fragments in leaf cells of the quadtree were integrated analytically for an exact result. For more complex shaders, we rely on interval arithmetic as described in section 3.5. Figure 2 shows an example in which an interval shader projects a checkerboard texture map and a cycloidal bump map onto a polygon. The bumps refract the texture map and reflect both Phong highlights and a "sky ramp" reflection map indexed by elevation. Each box-filtered pixel in this $512 \times 512$ antialiased image is accurate to within an error tolerance of .025. The left panel of figure 2 is a subdivision image in which, as before, intensity encodes the log of the number of quadtree cells created at each pixel. As expected, this image indicates that the algorithm works hardest in high frequency regions of the output image and does comparatively little work in low frequency regions.

## 5 Further Directions

In principle, it should be possible to extend the algorithm we have presented to do temporal as well as spatial antialiasing (i.e. motion blur). To do this, it would be necessary to add a time dimension to both the object-space octree and the image-space quadtree. Nodes in the new object-space tree would represent cubes of space for intervals of time. Nodes in the new image-space tree would represent regions of screen-space for intervals of time. For visibility purposes, each polygon and cube face would be treated as a space-time polyhedron. Culling would be done in space-time; a polygon would be culled from an image-space cell if no part of its space-time polyhedron was visible in the cell during any of the time interval. Subdivision to meet the error tolerance could take place either in space or time as appropriate. While the details of such an approach remain to be worked out, we are optimistic that it is possible to build a practical and guaranteed spatio-temporal antialiasing algorithm with this approach.

## 6 Conclusion

We have presented an antialiased rendering algorithm capable of rendering models of enormous complexity while producing results that are guaranteed to be correctly filtered to within a user-specified error tolerance. We have implemented the algorithm, shown that it is practical and used it create accurately filtered images of scenes containing over one hundred million polygons. In addition to its value as presented, the algorithm appears to be a good starting point for doing accurate spatio-temporal antialiasing. Beyond this, we have shown that interval arithmetic can be used to guarantee that a wide class of shading functions are accurately filtered.

## Acknowledgements

We thank Frank Crow and the Advanced Technology Group at Apple Computer for supporting this research. We also thank Lance Williams for a critical reading and Steve Rubin and Eric Chen for providing modeling and rendering software used to create the office model.

## References

[1] G. Abram and L. Westover, Efficient alias-free rendering using bit-masks and look-up tables, *Proc. Siggraph '85*, 53–59, July 1985.

[2] J. Airey, Increasing update rates in the building walkthrough system with automatic model-space subdivision and potentially visible set calculations, Tech Report TR90-027, C.S. Dept., U.N.C. Chapel Hill, 1990.

[3] G. Alefeld and J. Herzberger, *Introduction to interval computations*, Academic Press, 1983

[4] J. Bloomenthal, Edge inference with applications to antialiasing, *Proc. Siggraph '83*, 157–162, July 1983.

[5] L. Carpenter, The A-buffer, an antialiased hidden surface method, *Proc. Siggraph '84*, 103–108, July 1984.

[6] E. Catmull, A hidden-surface algorithm with anti-aliasing, *Proc. Siggraph '77*, 6–11, Aug. 1978.

[7] E. Catmull, An analytic visible surface algorithm for independent pixel processing, *Proc. Siggraph '84*, 109–115, July 1984.

[8] R. Cook, T. Porter and L. Carpenter, Distributed ray tracing, *Proc. Siggraph '84*, 137–146, July 1984.

[9] R. Cook, Shade Trees, *Proc. Siggraph '84*, 223–230, July 1984.

[10] R. Cook, Stochastic sampling in computer graphics, *ACM Transactions on Graphics*, 51–72, Jan. 1986.

[11] F. Crow, The aliasing problem in computer-generated shaded images, *CACM*, 799–805, Nov. 1977.

[12] F. Crow, Summed-area tables for texture mapping, *Proc. Siggraph '84*, 207–212, July 1984.

[13] M. Dippé and E. Wold, Antialiasing through stochastic sampling, *Proc. Siggraph '85*, 69–78, July 1985.

[14] E. Feibush, M. Levoy and R. Cook, Synthetic texturing using digital filters, *Proc. Siggraph '80*, 294–301, July 1980.

[15] J. Foley, A. van Dam, S. Feiner and J. Hughes, *Computer graphics principles and practice*, 2nd edition, Addison-Wesley, 695–697, 1990.

[16] N. Greene, M. Kass and G. Miller, Hierarchical z-buffer visibility, *Proc. Siggraph '93*, 231–238, July 1993.

[17] N. Greene, Detecting intersection of a rectangular solid and a convex polyhedron, *Graphics Gems IV*, Ed: P. Heckbert, 71–79, 1994.

[18] M. Kass, CONDOR: Constraint-based dataflow, *Proc. Siggraph '92*, 321–330, July 1992.

[19] M. Lee, R. Redner and S. Uselton, Statistically optimized sampling for distributed ray tracing, *Proc. Siggraph '85*, 61–68, July 1985.

[20] D. Meaghar, Efficient synthetic image generation of arbitrary 3-D objects, *Proc. IEEE Conf. on Pattern Recognition and Image Processing*, 473-478, June 1982.

[21] B. Naylor, Partitioning tree image representation and generation from 3D geometric models, *Proc. Graphics Interface '92*, 201–212, 1992.

[22] M. Sharir and M. Overmars, A simple output-sensitive algorithm for hidden surface removal, *ACM Transactions on Graphics* Vol. 11(1) 1992.

[23] J. Snyder, Interval analysis for computer graphics, *Proc. Siggraph '92*, 121–130, 1992.

[24] S. Teller, Visibility computations in densely occluded polyhedral environments. U.C. Berkeley Report No. UCB/CSD 92/708, Oct. 1992.

[25] J. Warnock, A hidden surface algorithm for computer generated halftone pictures, Computer Science Dept., Univ. of Utah, TR 4-15, June 1969.

[26] K. Weiler and P. Atherton, Hidden surface removal using polygon area sorting, *Proc. Siggraph '84*, 103–108, July 1984.

[27] L. Williams, Pyramidal Parametrics, *Proc. Siggraph '83*, 1–11, July 1983.

**Figure 1.** A model of the Empire State Building consisting of 167 million polygons rendered with z-buffering (left) and with the error-bounded antialiased rendering algorithm (right). Each box-filtered pixel of the antialiased image is accurate to within an error tolerance of .05.

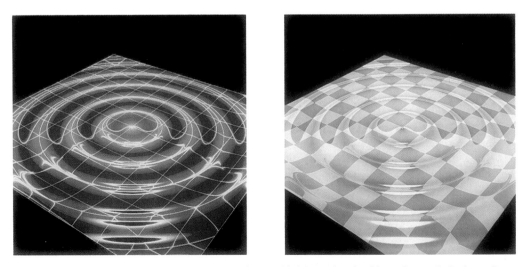

**Figure 2.** Antialiased image of a single polygon (right) rendered with an interval shader using texture mapping, bump mapping, reflection mapping and Phong highlights. Each box-filtered pixel is accurate to within an error tolerance of .025. In the image on the left, intensity encodes the log of the number of quadtree cells created for each pixel. The algorithm works hardest in high frequency regions of the output image and does comparatively little work in low frequency regions.

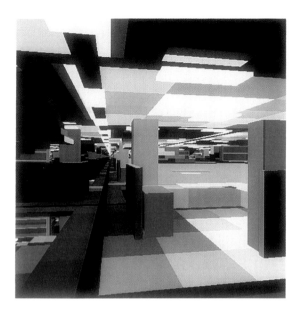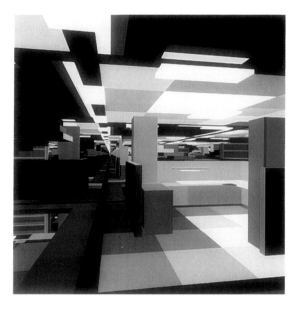

**Figure 3.** An interior view of the Empire State Building model. Above: Z-buffer image (left) and corresponding error-bounded antialiased image (right). Below: Uncertainty image (left), quadtree subdivision (center), and log-scale subdivision image (right). The uncertainty image is scaled so that white corresponds to the error tolerance of .05.

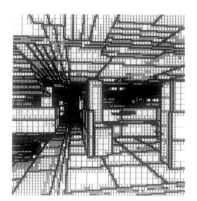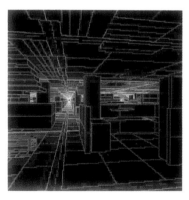

**Figure 4.** Regions known to be within the error tolerance after four consecutive refinement passes for the scene of figure 3. Green indicates pixels with color uncertainty above the error tolerance.

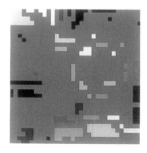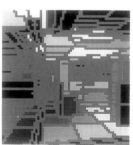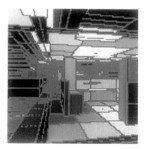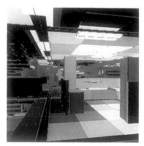

# Bounds and Error Estimates for Radiosity

*Dani Lischinski*      *Brian Smits*      *Donald P. Greenberg*

Program of Computer Graphics*
Cornell University

## ABSTRACT

We present a method for determining *a posteriori* bounds and estimates for local and total errors in radiosity solutions. The ability to obtain bounds and estimates for the total error is crucial for reliably judging the acceptability of a solution. Realistic estimates of the local error improve the efficiency of adaptive radiosity algorithms, such as hierarchical radiosity, by indicating where adaptive refinement is necessary.

First, we describe a hierarchical radiosity algorithm that computes conservative lower and upper bounds on the exact radiosity function, as well as on the approximate solution. These bounds account for the propagation of errors due to interreflections, and provide a conservative upper bound on the error. We also describe a non-conservative version of the same algorithm that is capable of computing tighter bounds, from which more realistic error estimates can be obtained. Finally, we derive an expression for the effect of a particular interaction on the total error. This yields a new error-driven refinement strategy for hierarchical radiosity, which is shown to be superior to brightness-weighted refinement.

**CR Categories and Subject Descriptors:** I.3.3—[**Computer Graphics**]: Picture/Image Generation; I.3.7—[**Computer Graphics**]: Three-Dimensional Graphics and Realism – Radiosity.

**Additional Key Words and Phrases:** *a posteriori* error bounds and estimates, adaptive refinement, global illumination, hierarchical radiosity, importance

## 1   INTRODUCTION

During the past decade, radiosity has become the method of choice for simulating global illumination in environments consisting entirely of Lambertian (ideal diffuse) reflectors and emitters. Global illumination in such environments is governed by a Fredholm integral equation of the second kind:

$$B(x) = E(x) + \rho(x) \int k(x,y)B(y)\, dy, \qquad (1)$$

---

*   580 ETC Building, Cornell University, Ithaca, New York 14853.
E-mail: {danix | bes | dpg}@graphics.cornell.edu

where $B(x)$ is the total radiosity at point $x$, $E(x)$ is the emission, and $\rho(x)$ is the reflectivity[1]. The kernel of the integral operator

$$k(x,y) = \frac{\cos\theta_x \cos\theta_y}{\pi r_{xy}^2} V(x,y)$$

describes the point-to-point transfer from $y$ to $x$: $\theta_x$ and $\theta_y$ are the angles between the surface normals and the line connecting $x$ and $y$, $r_{xy}$ is the distance between the two points, and $V(x,y)$ is 1 if $y$ is visible to $x$ and 0 otherwise.

Radiosity algorithms compute an approximate solution $\widehat{B}(x)$ to equation (1) by projecting the continuous integral equation into a finite dimensional function space. Most radiosity algorithms use spaces of piecewise constant functions, although recently several investigators described radiosity algorithms that use higher order basis functions [12, 21, 22]. The projection of the continuous equation results in a discrete system of $n$ linear equations, where $n$ is the dimension of the finite dimensional space:

$$(I - K)B = E. \qquad (2)$$

Since radiosity algorithms produce only approximate results, reliable error bounds and realistic error estimates are crucial for assessing the acceptability of a particular solution, as well as for automatic adaptive refinement.

The theory of integral equations [1, 10] provides an *a priori* error analysis of computational methods for Fredholm equations of the second kind. This general framework is valuable for analyzing convergence rates [10], and for bounding various components of the error in terms of the corresponding operator norms [3]. However, *a priori* error bounds are typically pessimistic and often difficult to evaluate, requiring information about the operators or the exact solution, which may not be available. In this paper we discuss *a posteriori* methods that bound the combined effect of the various error sources for a particular instance of the problem. Because the analysis takes place after or during the computation of the solution, such methods can provide tighter bounds more easily.

During the 1980's the issues of *a posteriori* error estimation and automatic adaptive refinement received considerable attention in the finite elements literature [4, 19]. Most of the work has related to partial differential equations. More recently, results have become available also for boundary integral equations and boundary element methods [5], which are essentially similar to radiosity methods.

In the radiosity literature, however, very little has been written regarding *a posteriori* error analysis. In particular, current radiosity algorithms can provide the user with neither guaranteed bounds on the total error $\|B(x) - \widehat{B}(x)\|$, for any function norm $\|\cdot\|$, nor reliable

---

[1]All of these quantities depend on the wavelength, but for simplicity we restrict the discussion to a single wavelength throughout this paper.

estimates of the total error. The goal of this paper is to address these deficiencies.

We begin with a brief account of past attempts to estimate the error in radiosity approximations.

In Section 3 we describe an algorithm that computes two piece-wise constant functions that are guaranteed to bound the exact solution $B(x)$ from below and from above. This can be done simultaneously with the computation of the approximate solution $\widehat{B}(x)$. These bounds pertain to both $B(x)$ and $\widehat{B}(x)$, so they can be used to compute a conservative upper bound on the error $\|B(x) - \widehat{B}(x)\|$. Our algorithm resembles the general bracketing technique suggested by Brown [6], but we utilize special properties of equation (1) to produce tighter bounds.

In many instances, a conservative error bound is not required, or is too pessimistic, and a good error estimate is preferable. In Section 4 we describe a non-conservative bounding algorithm that computes tighter "bounds", which are no longer guaranteed to contain the exact solution $B(x)$ everywhere. These non-conservative bounds are much cheaper to compute, and result in more realistic error estimates, i.e., estimates which are closer to the actual errors.

Our final contribution is the derivation of an expression that describes the effect that a particular interaction has on the total error bound. This expression uses bounds on importance and on radiosity that can be computed using our algorithms. This gives rise to a new error-driven refinement strategy for hierarchical radiosity, which is shown to be superior to brightness-weighted refinement.

## 2  ERROR ESTIMATION IN RADIOSITY

Cohen's adaptive subdivision algorithm [8] can be viewed as the first attempt at *a posteriori* error estimation. In this algorithm, elements are subdivided if their radiosity differs from that of their neighbors by more than a certain threshold. Thus, the difference between radiosities of adjacent elements is treated as an indicator of the local error. Note that this heuristic may fail to identify elements that should be subdivided.

A more conservative approach is described by Campbell [7], who uses numerical optimization to find the minimum and the maximum radiosity over each element. The difference between these extrema is used as a criterion for adaptive subdivision.

Among the various radiosity methods, hierarchical radiosity (HR) comes closest to bounding the errors in the solution: a bound is computed on the error in each interaction (link) between patches. Hanrahan et al. [13] compute an approximate upper bound on the form-factor corresponding to the link, and use it to obtain an approximate upper bound on the transferred energy.

Smits et al. [17] obtain an estimate of the error in each interaction by point sampling the kernel function over the areas of the two interacting patches. The difference between the maximum and the minimum values thus obtained is taken to be the error in the form-factor. This error estimate is less conservative than Hanrahan's, but it is generally more accurate.

Given error estimates for all the links in an environment, one can approximate the total error over each patch by summing up the errors associated with all its links. However, this does not take into account propagation of errors, which parallels the propagation of light.

Several other error estimation techniques are surveyed by Cohen and Wallace [9]. These techniques can be classified into two groups: (i) comparing the approximation to a higher order approximation, and (ii) computing the residual

$$r(x) = \widehat{B}(x) - E(x) - \rho(x) \int k(x,y)\widehat{B}(y)\,dy.$$

Both of the above are computationally expensive and do not provide foolproof subdivision criteria.

## 3  A RADIOSITY-BOUNDING ALGORITHM

For simplicity we start with a radiosity-bounding algorithm for full matrix radiosity. Later in this section, we extend this algorithm to work within a more efficient radiosity algorithm, namely hierarchical radiosity.

The goal of the bounding algorithm is to compute two piecewise constant functions $\underline{B}(x)$ and $\overline{B}(x)$ that bound the exact radiosity $B(x)$ from below and from above, respectively. In other words, given a discretization of the environment into a set of $n$ elements $S_1, \ldots, S_n$, we compute $\underline{B}_1, \ldots, \underline{B}_n$ and $\overline{B}_1, \ldots, \overline{B}_n$, such that

$$\underline{B}_i \leq B(x) \leq \overline{B}_i \quad \text{for all } x \in S_i.$$

Roughly, this is achieved by replacing the coefficients of the discrete linear system (2) by infima and suprema bounding the corresponding continuous functions over the areas of the elements $S_1, \ldots, S_n$.

### 3.1  Computing Lower Bounds

Let $\underline{\rho}_i$ and $\underline{E}_i$ denote the infima on the reflectivity and on the emission, respectively, over $S_i$. Also, let $\underline{F}_{ij}$ denote the infimum on the (point-to-area) form-factor from a point on $S_i$ to $S_j$:

$$\underline{F}_{ij} = \inf_{x \in S_i} \int_{S_j} k(x,y)\,dy,$$

and let $\underline{K}_{ij} = \underline{\rho}_i \underline{F}_{ij}$. Then the lower bounds vector $\underline{B} = (\underline{B}_1, \ldots, \underline{B}_n)^{\mathrm{T}}$ can be obtained by solving a linear system of $n$ equations

$$(I - \underline{K})\,\underline{B} = \underline{E},$$

using a standard method such as Jacobi or Gauss-Seidel iteration.

**Proof.** It is easy to see that the matrix $I - \underline{K}$ is strictly diagonally dominant, from which it follows [11] that the spectral radius of $\underline{K}$ is strictly less than 1. Thus, the inverse matrix $(I - \underline{K})^{-1}$ exists, and can be expressed as a Neumann series

$$(I - \underline{K})^{-1} = I + \sum_{i=1}^{\infty} \underline{K}^i.$$

The solution vector $\underline{B}$ can then be written as

$$\underline{B} = (I - \underline{K})^{-1}\underline{E} = \underline{E} + \sum_{i=1}^{\infty} \underline{K}^i \underline{E}.$$

Alternatively, $\underline{B}$ can be expressed as the limit of the series of vectors $\underline{B}^{(k)}$ that are defined by the recurrence relation

$$\begin{aligned}
\underline{B}^{(0)} &= \underline{E} \\
\underline{B}^{(k+1)} &= \underline{E} + \underline{K}\underline{B}^{(k)}.
\end{aligned}$$

Note that the above corresponds to Jacobi iteration in matrix notation. It is easy to see by induction that $\underline{B}^{(k)}$ is a lower bound on the radiosity after $k$ light bounces. Therefore, the limit $\underline{B}$ is a lower bound on the total radiosity function $B(x)$. □

## 3.2 Computing Upper Bounds

Unfortunately, we cannot use the same straightforward approach for computing the upper bounds $\overline{B} = (\overline{B}_1, \ldots, \overline{B}_n)^{\mathsf{T}}$. Let $\overline{K}$ be defined in the same way as $\underline{K}$, except that suprema are taken instead of infima. Then the matrix $I - \overline{K}$ is not necessarily diagonally dominant: the entries of $\overline{K}$ are upper bounds on the form-factors and thus the sum of the absolute values of the entries in a row of $I - \overline{K}$ can exceed 1. In such a case, iterative solution methods such as Jacobi or Gauss-Seidel could diverge. Furthermore, it is possible for $I - \overline{K}$ to be singular.

We now describe an iterative algorithm that transforms $\overline{K}$ into a strictly diagonally dominant matrix $\overline{K}^*$, such that the solution to the linear system of equations

$$\left(I - \overline{K}^*\right) \overline{B} = \overline{E}$$

is a vector of upper bounds. The solution $\overline{B}$ is computed simultaneously with the transformation of $\overline{K}$ into $\overline{K}^*$.

The algorithm starts by forming the matrix $\overline{K}$. We then perform Jacobi iterations using a modified matrix: because the sum of the form-factors from a given element cannot exceed 1, we can zero out elements in each row of $\overline{K}$ until the form-factors corresponding to the remaining non-zero entries sum to at most 1. To ensure that the modified matrix still yields an upper bound on the current light bounce, we zero out those entries corresponding to the dimmest elements. Since the brightness ordering of the elements may change from one iteration to another, different entries on the matrix may be zeroed out in each iteration. However, as the iterates converge to the solution $\overline{B}$, the order of the elements becomes fixed, at which point we obtain $\overline{K}^*$.

More precisely, at each iteration we sort the current solution vector $\overline{B}^{(k)}$ in order of decreasing brightness, and permute the columns of the matrix accordingly. Each entry in the solution vector is updated by:

$$\overline{B}_i^{(k+1)} = \overline{E}_i + \overline{\rho}_i \left[ \sum_{j=1}^{l} \overline{F}_{ij} \overline{B}_j^{(k)} + \left( 1 - \sum_{j=1}^{l} \overline{F}_{ij} \right) \overline{B}_{l+1}^{(k)} \right], \quad (3)$$

where $l$ is the largest index in row $i$ such that

$$\sum_{j=1}^{l} \overline{F}_{ij} \leq 1.$$

It can be shown by induction that, if the iterates are sorted as described above, $\overline{B}^{(k)}$ is an upper bound on the radiosity after $k$ interreflections. Thus, if the iterates converge, they converge to a total upper bound on the radiosity function $B(x)$.

**Proof.** To prove convergence, we must examine the behavior of each entry in the solution vector as the algorithm progresses. Because all the entries in the matrix $\overline{K}$ are non-negative, if $\overline{B}^{(0)}$ is set to $\overline{E}$, each entry in the solution vector increases at each iteration, i.e., for all $i$, $\overline{B}_i^{(k)} \leq \overline{B}_i^{(k+1)}$. Because we do not allow the form-factors in a row to exceed 1, each entry of $\overline{B}^{(k)}$ is bounded from above:

$$\overline{B}_i^{(k)} \leq E_{\max} \left( 1 + \rho_{\max} + \cdots + \rho_{\max}^k \right) < \frac{E_{\max}}{1 - \rho_{\max}},$$

where $E_{\max}$ is the maximum emission and $\rho_{\max}$ the maximum reflectivity in the environment. From elementary analysis, we know that a monotonically increasing series that is bounded from above must converge. Since the vectors $\overline{B}^{(k)}$ are of a finite dimension, it follows that the vector sequence converges. $\square$

```
GatherLowerBounds(node, lower)
foreach  link ∈ node.links do
    lower += node.rho * link.Fmin * link.source.lower
end for
if  IsLeaf(node) then
    node.lower = lower + node.emission
else
    node.lower = ∞
    foreach  child ∈ node.children do
        GatherLowerBounds(child, lower)
        node.lower = min (node.lower, child.lower)
    end for
end if


GatherUpperBounds(node, contribList)
foreach  link ∈ node.links do
    add the pair (link.Fmax, link.source.upper) to contribList
end for
if  IsLeaf(node) then
    ffSum = 0
    node.upper = node.emission
    Sort(contribList)
    foreach  pair (ff, upper) ∈ contribList do
        if  ffSum + ff < 1 then
            ffSum += ff
            node.upper += node.rho * ff * upper
        else
            node.upper += node.rho * (1 − ffSum) * upper
            break
        end if
    end for
else
    node.upper = 0
    foreach  child ∈ node.children do
        GatherUpperBounds(child, contribList)
        node.upper = max (node.upper, child.upper)
    end for
end if
```

Figure 1: *Pseudocode for gathering lower and upper bounds*

### 3.3 A Radiosity-Bounding Algorithm for HR

The algorithms in Sections 3.1 and 3.2 are presented in the context of the full matrix radiosity algorithm. They involve $O(n^2)$ work to compute the bounds on the form-factors, and therefore are not practical. However, they can be modified to work more efficiently within the HR framework. This requires a few changes to the standard HR algorithm. We need to compute and store upper and lower bounds *Fmin* and *Fmax* on the form-factor associated with each link. We can then gather, push, and pull radiosity bounds, in a way similar to that of the patch radiosities themselves. See Figure 1.

Note that gathering, pushing, and pulling are all performed in a single sweep of the hierarchy. Thus, the bounds are updated in place, which makes this a Gauss-Seidel iteration. This iteration converges faster than the Jacobi iteration used in previous HR algorithms. The speedup applies not only to the computation of bounds, but to the computation of the radiosities as well.

Gathering upper bounds is a bit more involved than gathering lower bounds, as can be seen from the pseudocode in Figure 1. *GatherUpperBounds* essentially pushes links down to the leaves, where they are sorted according to the brightnesses of the corresponding source nodes. The upper bound of the leaf node is then updated using equation (3).

One undesirable feature of this algorithm is the sorting of the links, which implies that $O(k \log k)$ work must be done to update the upper bound at each leaf node, where $k$ is the number of the contributing links. However, complete sorting can be avoided in most cases. Sorting is only necessary when the sum of the contributing form-factors exceeds 1. Even then, only a few of the dimmest sources must be removed from the list. This can be done efficiently using a heap data structure with a *DeleteMin* operation. Tarjan [20] provides a detailed description of such data structures.

### 3.4 Bounding Form-Factors

Thus far we have assumed that the bounds $\underline{F}_{ij}$ and $\overline{F}_{ij}$ are available to us. How do we obtain them? We know of no analytical way of computing such bounds. Thus, we must resort to numerical optimization to find the minimum and the maximum values of the point-to-polygon form-factor from points on $S_i$ to $S_j$. Such numerical methods are discussed in detail by Campbell [7]. These methods generally require the computation of form-factor gradients in the presence of occluders, which can be done either using finite differences or analytically, as described by Arvo [2].

In our current implementation we estimate form-factor bounds by evaluating the analytical point-to-polygon form-factor [18] at the center and at the vertices of each receiving patch. In the partially occluded case, the analytical formula is applied only to the visible parts of the source [16]. The upper and lower bounds on the form-factor are then set to the maximum and the minimum of these values. While these bounds are not conservative, as elements decrease in size the point-to-area form-factor function becomes monotonic over most elements, and the heuristic yields accurate bounds. This is particularly so when a discontinuity-driven subdivision strategy [15] is employed.

### 3.5 Results

The plots in Figures 2, 3, and 4 show the piecewise-constant bounding functions computed by the hierarchical bounding algorithm for three simple environments shown in Figure 5. The exact radiosity function is also plotted for each of the three cases. The functions are plotted along the dotted lines across the floor of each environment.

The bounds in Figure 2 were found in a single iteration, since there are no interreflections in this environment, and errors do not propagate. Because of this, the bounds are very tight: in fact, tighter piecewise constant bounds are only possible if more elements are used.

Figures 3 and 4 show two cases with interreflections, which results in looser bounds due to error propagation. As illustrated in the figures, the bounds computed by the algorithm become tighter as the accuracy of the solution increases. Note that the radiosity function and the bounds are not symmetric, because in the corresponding environments the reflectivity of the left wall is higher than that of the right wall.

## 4 COMPUTING REALISTIC ERROR ESTIMATES

Having obtained bounds on the radiosity of each element, we can obtain an upper bound on the local error there. Assuming that the

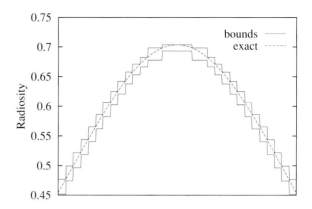

Figure 2: *Upper and lower bounds for the configuration shown in Figure 5a. The smooth curve in the middle is the exact radiosity function.*

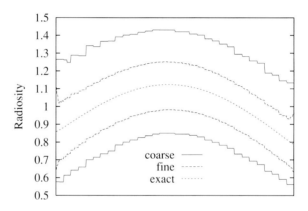

Figure 3: *Nested lower and upper bounds corresponding to two HR solutions for the configuration in Figure 5b. One solution is coarse and the other is fine. The smooth curve in the middle is the exact radiosity function.*

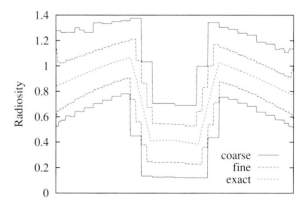

Figure 4: *Nested lower and upper bounds corresponding to two HR solutions for the configuration in Figure 5c. One solution is coarse and the other is fine. The smooth curve in the middle is the exact radiosity function.*

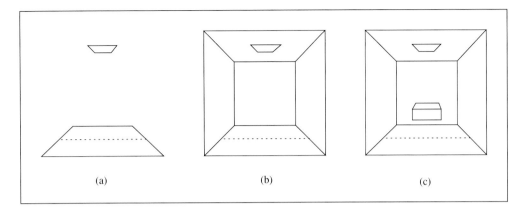

Figure 5: *Three simple test cases: (a) direct illumination only; (b) inter-reflections without occlusion; (c) inter-reflections with occlusion. All the surfaces are grey with reflectivities between 0.3 and 0.7.*

approximate radiosity $B_i$ lies halfway between $\underline{B}_i$ and $\overline{B}_i$, the errors over $S_i$ in the $L_\infty, L_1$, and $L_2$ norms are:

$$\|B(x) - B_i\|_\infty \equiv \max_{S_i} |B(x) - B_i| \leq (\overline{B}_i - \underline{B}_i)/2, \quad (4)$$

$$\|B(x) - B_i\|_1 \equiv \int_{S_i} |B(x) - B_i| \, dx \leq A_i(\overline{B}_i - \underline{B}_i)/2, \quad (5)$$

$$\|B(x) - B_i\|_2^2 \equiv \int_{S_i} |B(x) - B_i|^2 dx \leq A_i(\overline{B}_i - \underline{B}_i)^2/4. \quad (6)$$

However, these error bounds represent a worst case scenario, and do not give an accurate error estimate even when the bounds on radiosity are as tight as in Figure 2. More realistic estimates are obtained if we assume that the values of $B(x)$ over $S_i$ are uniformly distributed between $\underline{B}_i$ and $\overline{B}_i$. Under this assumption the $L_1$ and $L_2$ norm errors are estimated as:

$$\|B(x) - B_i\|_1 \approx A_i(\overline{B}_i - \underline{B}_i)/4, \quad (7)$$

$$\|B(x) - B_i\|_2^2 \approx A_i(\overline{B}_i - \underline{B}_i)^2/12. \quad (8)$$

We compute local error estimates at all the leaves of the hierarchy. These estimates are then pulled up to the roots of the hierarchies, and combined to obtain the estimate for the total error. The error at a parent node is the sum of the children's errors in the $L_1$ norm, and the maximum over the children's errors in $L_\infty$ norm. For the $L_2$ norm, the squares of the children's errors are summed and the square root of the sum is taken.

### 4.1 Obtaining Tighter Non-Conservative Bounds

The conservative algorithm produces bounds which are quite loose even for simple environments, resulting in pessimistic error estimates. For most practical purposes good non-conservative error estimates could prove more useful than conservative error bounds. To quote Delves and Mohamed [10]:

> Given two error estimates of equal realism and equal cost and given that one is also a bound, we would clearly prefer the bound. In practice bounds usually prove expensive and pessimistic. Most users will then usually prefer a cheaper and more realistic error estimate, recognizing and accepting that estimates can sometimes err on the side of optimism.

We now present a way for computing tighter, although not conservative, bounds on radiosity. Error estimates computed from these radiosity bounds are not guaranteed error bounds, but they are much closer to the true errors. To compute these tighter bounds we approximate $\underline{B}$ and $\overline{B}$ as follows:

$$\underline{B} \approx \underline{E} + K\widehat{B}$$
$$\overline{B} \approx \overline{E} + \overline{K}\widehat{B}.$$

This is equivalent to first setting both $\underline{B}$ and $\overline{B}$ to $\widehat{B}$ and then performing a single gathering iteration over the environment using the same *GatherLowerBounds* and *GatherUpperBounds* routines as before. Because only one iteration is performed, error propagation is no longer accounted for, but the computation is significantly simplified. More conservative estimates can be obtained by using two or more iterations, yielding a trade-off between speed and conservativity.

Two additional changes to the algorithm have been used to produce even tighter bounds. First, instead of bounding each form-factor separately and summing the bounds, we directly bound the radiosity contributed to each node through all its links: the contribution is evaluated at the center and at the vertices of the patch, and the extrema values are used as bounds. Second, we set *node.lower* and *node.upper* to the area-weighted averages of the children bounds, rather than to the minimum and the maximum, respectively.

### 4.2 Results

To test the quality of our error estimates we computed an extremely fine radiosity solution for each of the three environments in Figure 5. The floor polygon in each environment was sampled on a 400 by 400 grid to serve as a reference. We then computed a series of radiosity solutions of various degrees of accuracy for each environment. The floor polygon was sampled as before, and the difference between each solution and the reference solution was computed. This difference is referred to as the *measured* error. During each solution, two error estimates were computed: one from the conservative bounds, and the other from the tighter non-conservative bounds. In both cases equations (4), (7), and (8) were used to estimate the errors.

Figure 6 shows plots of the error estimates together with the measured error for each of the three test cases. The left column corresponds to $L_\infty$ norm and the right column to $L_1$ norm. Error plots for $L_2$ norm are not given, since they look almost exactly the same as the $L_1$ plots for these test cases.

In the top pair of plots (corresponding to Figure 5a) the conservative and the non-conservative bounding algorithms yield the same bounds, and therefore the corresponding error estimates are always the same. For the $L_\infty$ norm these estimates follow tightly the measured error, and for the $L_1$ norm they give realistic upper bounds.

In the remaining two cases there is a significant difference between the two types of error estimates. In the $L_\infty$ norm, the non-conservative estimate does not always yield a bound on the error (see lower left plot). In the $L_1$ norm, both estimates bound the measured error from above, but the conservative error estimates are much more pessimistic than their non-conservative counterparts.

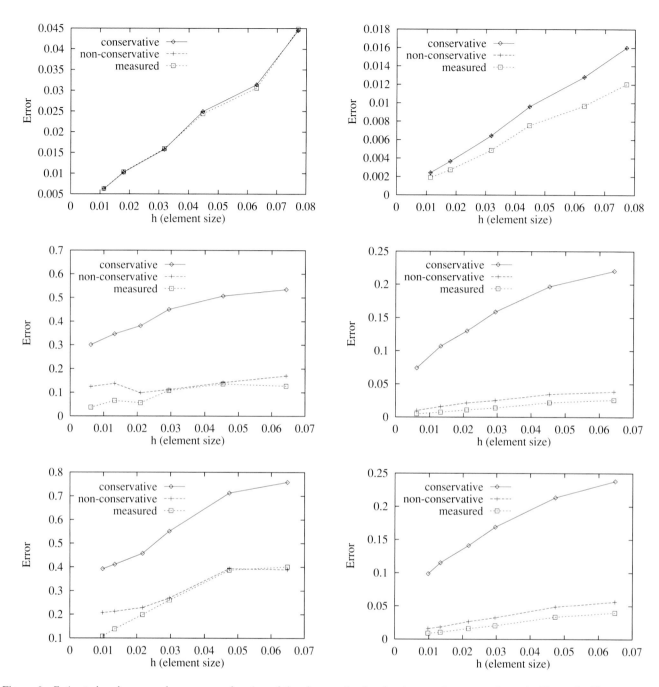

Figure 6: *Estimated and measured errors as a function of the element size for the three environments shown in Figure 5. The top row corresponds to Figure 5a, the middle row to 5b, and the bottom row to 5c. $L_\infty$ errors are shown on the left and $L_1$ errors on the right.*

Both types of estimates become closer to the measured error as the accuracy of the solutions increases. Both the estimated and the measured errors vary linearly in the element size $h$, as expected for piecewise-constant approximations.

## 5   ERROR-DRIVEN REFINEMENT

The original hierarchical radiosity algorithm [13] adaptively improves the accuracy of a solution by estimating the error associated with each link. All links for which this error estimate exceeds a given threshold $\epsilon$ are refined and the solution is recomputed. More specifically, Hanrahan et al. suggest to refine all those links for

which the estimated upper bound on the transferred energy exceeds $\epsilon$. A link is refined by subdividing the node which has the greater form-factor, as seen from the center of the other node. This strategy is referred to as *brightness-weighted* refinement, as it gives priority to links transferring energy from bright sources.

We make two observations with respect to brightness-weighted refinement: (i) The links carrying the largest amount of energy are not necessarily the ones with the greatest errors in the transferred energy. (ii) Due to propagation of errors, refining the link between nodes $i$ and $j$ reduces not only the error over patch $i$, but may also reduce errors on other patches receiving light from it. Thus, to make the most benefit of each link refinement, priority should be given to links with the greatest effect on the total solution error.

The first observation suggests using $\Delta K_{ij} = \overline{K}_{ij} - \underline{K}_{ij}$ as the estimate of the link form-factor error, rather than using an upper bound on the form-factor. The error in the transferred energy is then given by $\Delta K_{ij}\overline{B}_j$.

To address the second observation, we derive an expression that relates $\Delta K_{ij}$ to the overall value of $\|\overline{B} - \underline{B}\|_1$, which is an upper bound on the overall error in $L_1$ norm. This is done by using the concept of importance.

### 5.1 Importance and Linear Functionals

Recall that *importance*, which we shall denote by $Z$, is the solution to the adjoint of the transport equation [14, 17]:

$$M^{\mathrm{T}}Z = R$$

where $M^{\mathrm{T}}$ is the adjoint of the real matrix $M$. In the context of radiosity, $M = I - K$. $R$ is the *receiver* vector, which is dual to the emission vector $E$.

Any linear functional $f(B)$ of the radiosities can be expressed as an inner product $R^{\mathrm{T}}B$, where $R_i$ gives the contribution of $B_i$ to the value of $f(B)$. It can be shown [17] that

$$R^{\mathrm{T}}B = Z^{\mathrm{T}}E.$$

Thus, the $i$-th element of the importance vector gives the contribution made by a unit of emission at patch $i$ to the value of $R^{\mathrm{T}}B$.

Note that because all the entries in the vector $\overline{B} - \underline{B}$ are non-negative, the value of its $L_1$ norm is given by a linear functional:

$$\left\|\overline{B} - \underline{B}\right\|_1 = R^{\mathrm{T}}\left(\overline{B} - \underline{B}\right),$$

where $R = [A_1, \ldots, A_n]^{\mathrm{T}}$ is the vector of patch areas. We can now derive the main result of this section:

$$\left\|\overline{B} - \underline{B}\right\|_1 = \underline{Z}^{\mathrm{T}}\Delta K\overline{B} + \underline{Z}^{\mathrm{T}}\left(\overline{E} - \underline{E}\right). \quad (9)$$

This expression relates $\|\overline{B} - \underline{B}\|_1$ to the link errors $\Delta K$ and to errors in the emission. The term $\underline{Z}^{\mathrm{T}}\Delta K\overline{B}$ is a sum over all links. The values summed are the link form-factor error $\Delta K_{ij}$ weighted by the lower bound on the importance of the receiver $\underline{Z}_i$ and the upper bound on the radiosity of the source $\overline{B}_j$. Intuitively, $\Delta K_{ij}\overline{B}_j$ is an upper bound on the incorrect radiosity that patch $i$ receives from patch $j$, while $\underline{Z}_i$ gives the contribution of this incorrect radiosity on the total error bound. The $\underline{Z}^{\mathrm{T}}(\overline{E} - \underline{E})$ term gives the effect non-constant emission has on the total error bound.

**Proof.** Let $\overline{M} = I - \overline{K}^*$ and $\underline{M} = I - \underline{K}$. The system for lower bounds on the radiosities and its adjoint equation can now be written as

$$\underline{M}B = \underline{E} \quad \text{and} \quad \underline{M}^{\mathrm{T}}Z = R,$$

and the upper bounds system can be written as $\overline{M}\overline{B} = \overline{E}$. Noting that $\Delta K = \overline{K} - \underline{K} = \underline{M} - \overline{M}$, we obtain

$$\overline{M}\overline{B} = (\underline{M} - \Delta K)\overline{B} = \overline{E},$$

from which it follows that

$$\underline{M}\overline{B} = \overline{E} + \Delta K\overline{B}. \quad (10)$$

Since $R^{\mathrm{T}}\underline{B} = \underline{Z}^{\mathrm{T}}\underline{E}$, we can express $R^{\mathrm{T}}(\overline{B} - \underline{B})$ in terms of $\Delta K$ as follows:

$$\begin{aligned} R^{\mathrm{T}}(\overline{B} - \underline{B}) &= R^{\mathrm{T}}\overline{B} - R^{\mathrm{T}}\underline{B} \\ &= R^{\mathrm{T}}\overline{B} - \underline{Z}^{\mathrm{T}}\underline{E} \\ &= (\underline{M}^{\mathrm{T}}\underline{Z})^{\mathrm{T}}\overline{B} - \underline{Z}^{\mathrm{T}}\underline{E} \\ &= \underline{Z}^{\mathrm{T}}\underline{M}\overline{B} - \underline{Z}^{\mathrm{T}}\underline{E}. \end{aligned}$$

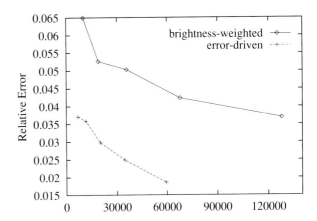

Figure 7: *Relative $L_1$ error as a function of the number of links: brightness-weighted vs. error-driven refinement.*

Substituting equation (10) into the above expression we have

$$\begin{aligned} R^{\mathrm{T}}(\overline{B} - \underline{B}) &= \underline{Z}^{\mathrm{T}}(\overline{E} + \Delta K\overline{B}) - \underline{Z}^{\mathrm{T}}\underline{E} \\ &= \underline{Z}^{\mathrm{T}}\Delta K\overline{B} + \underline{Z}^{\mathrm{T}}(\overline{E} - \underline{E}). \end{aligned}$$

$\square$

Equation (9) is an exact expression relating errors in the transferred energy to the value of any linear functional $R^{\mathrm{T}}(\overline{B} - \underline{B})$. In particular this expression applies to the view-dependent functionals used by Smits et al. [17]. Thus, the expression that Smits et al. used to assess the view-dependent error can be viewed as an approximation to our more conservative bound.

### 5.2 A New Refinement Strategy

Equation (9) suggests a new error-driven refinement strategy for HR. In this strategy we refine all links for which $\underline{Z}_i\Delta K_{ij}\overline{B}_j > \epsilon$, since these links have the greatest effect on the total error bound. In order to evaluate this expression for each link, the routine *GatherLowerBounds* must be modified to solve for the lower bounds on importance in addition to lower bounds on radiosity. These changes are straightforward, and they do not significantly increase the amount of work done in the routine.

When we refine a link between a receiver node $i$ and a source node $j$, we need to decide which node to subdivide to obtain the greatest reduction in the error. We use the following heuristic: node $i$ is subdivided if

$$\left(\overline{K}_{ij} - \underline{K}_{ij}\right)\overline{B}_j \geq \overline{K}_{ij}\left(\overline{B}_j - \underline{B}_j\right),$$

and node $j$ is subdivided otherwise. Intuitively, this means that we subdivide the receiver if the error due to the non-constant form-factor is greater than the error due to non-constant radiosity on the source.

### 5.3 Results

We implemented both brightness-weighted and error-driven refinement strategies and tested them on the simple environment shown in Figure 5c. The plot in Figure 7 shows how the measured relative $L_1$ error on the floor decreases as a function of the number of links. This plot demonstrates clearly that error-driven refinement is much more efficient: it is capable of achieving much smaller errors using only a fraction of the links required by brightness-weighted refinement. Similar results were observed on several other test cases.

## 6 CONCLUSIONS

We have described a hierarchical radiosity algorithm that computes conservative bounds on the exact radiosity function simultaneously with the computation of the approximate solution. In contrast to previous attempts to estimate the errors in radiosity, our algorithm properly accounts for the propagation of errors due to interreflections, and provides conservative upper bounds on the error. We have also presented a non-conservative version of this algorithm that provides tighter bounds and more realistic error estimates. Finally, we have derived a new error-driven adaptive refinement strategy for hierarchical radiosity that significantly outperforms brightness-weighted refinement.

We hope that the results described in this paper will prove useful not only for reliable image synthesis, but also for other fields in which similar integral equations arise. Examples include radiative heat transfer, illumination engineering, and remote sensing. In all these fields numerical accuracy of the results is even more crucial than in image synthesis.

Much further work is needed on *a posteriori* error analysis for radiosity. For instance, we need techniques for efficiently computing reliable tight bounds on form-factors, perhaps using tools such as irradiance Jacobians [2]. Also, we would like to extend the techniques described in this paper to higher order basis functions. While we are able to bound the exact radiosity function, our bounds will not necessarily apply to higher order approximations, as they may exhibit oscillations [22]. Even if the approximation is contained within our bounds, equations (7) and (8) will probably produce pessimistic error estimates, since they assume that the approximation is piecewise-constant.

Prior to rendering an image, the radiosity solution is usually projected onto a new set of basis functions, typically piecewise-linear or piecewise-quadratic [15]. We need to analyze the effect of such projections on the error in order to extend our error estimates from solutions to images.

Finally, we would like to emphasize the need for the development of perceptual error metrics for image synthesis. Fast convergence in a quantitative error metric, such as the $L_1$ norm, does not necessarily imply fast convergence of the resulting images, as perceived by a human observer. Thus, we expect that a perceptual error-driven refinement strategy would be more appropriate for image synthesis.

## ACKNOWLEDGEMENTS

Special thanks go to Jim Arvo: without his encouragement and advice this paper would not have been written. We would also like to thank Richard Lobb and Charlie Van Loan for helpful discussions and for reviewing the manuscript. The comments provided by the anonymous reviewers have helped greatly to improve this paper. This work was supported by the NSF grant, "Interactive Computer Graphics Input and Display Techniques" (CCR-8617880), by the NSF/DARPA Science and Technology Center for Computer Graphics and Scientific Visualization (ASC-8920219), and by generous donations of equipment from Hewlett-Packard.

## REFERENCES

[1] ANSELONE, P. M. Convergence and Error Bounds for Approximate Solutions of Integral and Operator Equations. In *Error in Digital Computation*, L. B. Rall, Ed., vol. 2, John Wiley & Sons, New York, 1965, pp. 231–252.

[2] ARVO, JAMES. The Irradiance Jacobian for Partially Occluded Polyhedral Sources. In *Computer Graphics* Proceedings, Annual Conference Series, 1994.

[3] ARVO, JAMES, KENNETH TORRANCE, AND BRIAN SMITS. A Framework for the Analysis of Error in Global Illumination Algorithms. In *Computer Graphics* Proceedings, Annual Conference Series, 1994.

[4] BABUŠKA, I., O. C. ZIENKIEWICZ, J. GAGO, AND E. R. DE A. OLIVEIRA, EDS. *Accuracy Estimates and Adaptive Refinements in Finite Element Computations*, John Wiley & Sons, Chichester, 1986.

[5] BREBBIA, C. A. AND M. H. ALIABADI, EDS. *Adaptive Finite and Boundary Element Methods*, Computational Mechanics Publications, Southampton, and Elsevier Applied Science, London, 1993.

[6] BROWN, R. W. Upper and Lower Bounds for Solutions of Integral Equations. In *Error in Digital Computation*, L. B. Rall, Ed., vol. 2, John Wiley & Sons, New York, 1965, pp. 219–230.

[7] CAMPBELL, III, A. T. *Modeling Global Diffuse Illumination for Image Synthesis*, PhD dissertation, University of Texas at Austin, Austin, Texas, December 1991.

[8] COHEN, MICHAEL F., DONALD P. GREENBERG, DAVID S. IMMEL, AND PHILIP J. BROCK. An Efficient Radiosity Approach for Realistic Image Synthesis. *IEEE Computer Graphics and Applications*, 6(2), March 1986, pp. 26–35.

[9] COHEN, MICHAEL F. AND JOHN R. WALLACE. *Radiosity and Realistic Image Synthesis*, Academic Press Professional, Cambridge, Massachusets, 1993.

[10] DELVES, L. M. AND J. L. MOHAMED. *Computational Methods for Integral Equations*, Cambridge University Press, Cambridge, Great Britain, 1985.

[11] GOLUB, GENE H. AND CHARLES F. VAN LOAN. *Matrix Computations*, The Johns Hopkins University Press, Baltimore, Maryland, 2nd edition, 1989.

[12] GORTLER, STEVEN J., PETER SCHRÖDER, MICHAEL F. COHEN, AND PAT HANRAHAN. Wavelet Radiosity. In *Computer Graphics* Proceedings, Annual Conference Series, 1993, pp. 221–230.

[13] HANRAHAN, PAT, DAVID SALZMAN, AND LARRY AUPPERLE. A Rapid Hierarchical Radiosity Algorithm. *Computer Graphics*, 25(4), July 1991, pp. 197–206.

[14] LEWINS, JEFFERY. *Importance, The Adjoint Function: The Physical Basis of Variational and Perturbation Theory in Transport and Diffusion Problems*, Pergamon Press, New York, 1965.

[15] LISCHINSKI, DANI, FILIPPO TAMPIERI, AND DONALD P. GREENBERG. Combining Hierarchical Radiosity and Discontinuity Meshing. In *Computer Graphics* Proceedings, Annual Conference Series, 1993, pp. 199–208.

[16] NISHITA, TOMOYUKI AND EIHACHIRO NAKAMAE. Half-Tone Representation of 3-D Objects Illuminated by Area Sources or Polyhedron Sources. Proceedings of COMPSAC '83 (Chicago, Illinois, November 1983), pp. 237–241.

[17] SMITS, BRIAN E., JAMES R. ARVO, AND DAVID H. SALESIN. An Importance-Driven Radiosity Algorithm. *Computer Graphics*, 26(4), July 1992, pp. 273–282.

[18] SPARROW, E. M. A New and Simpler Formulation for Radiative Angle Factors. *ASME Journal of Heat Transfer*, 85(2), May 1963, pp. 81–88.

[19] SZABÓ, BARNA AND IVO BABUŠKA. *Finite Element Analysis*, John Wiley & Sons, New York, 1991.

[20] TARJAN, ROBERT ENDRE. *Data Structures and Network Algorithms*, SIAM, Philadelphia, 1983.

[21] TROUTMAN, ROY AND NELSON L. MAX. Radiosity Algorithms Using Higher Order Finite Elements. In *Computer Graphics* Proceedings, Annual Conference Series, 1993, pp. 209–212.

[22] ZATZ, HAROLD R. Galerkin Radiosity: A Higher Order Solution Method for Global Illumination. In *Computer Graphics* Proceedings, Annual Conference Series, 1993, pp. 213–220.

# A Framework for the Analysis of Error in Global Illumination Algorithms

*James Arvo*
*Kenneth Torrance*
*Brian Smits*

Program of Computer Graphics*
Cornell University

## Abstract

In this paper we identify sources of error in global illumination algorithms and derive bounds for each distinct category. Errors arise from three sources: inaccuracies in the boundary data, discretization, and computation. Boundary data consist of surface geometry, reflectance functions, and emission functions, all of which may be perturbed by errors in measurement or simulation, or by simplifications made for computational efficiency. Discretization error is introduced by replacing the continuous radiative transfer equation with a finite-dimensional linear system, usually by means of boundary elements and a corresponding projection method. Finally, computational errors perturb the finite-dimensional linear system through imprecise form factors, inner products, visibility, etc., as well as by halting iterative solvers after a finite number of steps. Using the error taxonomy introduced in the paper we examine existing global illumination algorithms and suggest new avenues of research.

**CR Categories and Subject Descriptors:** I.3.7 [Computer Graphics]: Three-Dimensional Graphics and Realism.

**Additional Key Words and Phrases:** boundary elements, discretization, error bounds, global illumination, linear operators, projection methods, radiosity, reflectance functions.

## 1 Introduction

The role of global illumination algorithms is to simulate the interaction of light with large-scale geometry for the purpose of image synthesis. The greatest challenges in this endeavor have been those of accuracy and efficiency. While issues of efficiency have been addressed frequently in computer graphics, error analysis has received comparatively little attention. Indeed, the subject is difficult to even approach for several reasons. First, there is no universally accepted definition of accuracy for global illumination. Although accuracy connotes a quantitative comparison with some ideal, the ideal may be either empirical or theoretical, and the comparison may assume a range of forms from purely mathematical to perceptual. A second obstacle has been a lack of mathematical formalisms

*580 Engineering and Theory Center Building, Ithaca, New York 14853

for global error analysis. Thus far, analysis has been confined to specific sub-problems, and no systematic treatment of the subject has been presented.

In this paper we attempt to establish a framework for error analysis within a well-defined class of global illumination problems. Specifically, we address the problem of approximating solutions to a form of the rendering equation [18] given imprecise data for geometry, reflectance functions, and emission functions. We further assume that the approximation is to be assessed quantitatively by its distance from the theoretical solution. By employing radiometric quantities and physically-motivated measures of error we temporarily sidestep the difficult issues of display and perception. Moreover, in the present work we exclude participating media, transparent surfaces, and probabilistic solution methods. The problem domain that we address can be summarized as follows:

- Radiometric quantities (radiance, reflectivities, emission)

- A linear model of radiative transfer

- Direct radiative exchange among opaque surfaces

- Deterministic boundary element formulations

Given these restrictions, we derive error bounds in terms of potentially known quantities, such as bounds on emission, reflectivity, and measurement error. To obtain these error bounds, we draw upon the general theory of integral equations [2] as well as the more abstract theory of operator equations [1, 21].

While the analysis is carried out in an abstract setting, we shall not lose sight of practical considerations. For instance, in simulating a given physical environment, perhaps under varied lighting conditions, how accurately must the reflectance functions be measured? Or, when simulating radiant transfer among diffuse surfaces, how important is it to use higher-order elements? Can we expect higher accuracy by using analytic area-to-area instead of point-to-area form factors? Finally, how accurate must visibility computations be for global illumination? While we do not provide definitive answers to these questions, the analysis presented here introduces a formalism and a starting point for determining quantitative answers.

## 2 Radiative Transfer

Global illumination involves the processes of light emission, reflection, redistribution, shadowing and, ultimately, absorption in an environment. These are physical processes governed by the equations of radiative transfer. In general, radiative transfer equations apply at both microscopic and macroscopic scales and are based primarily on the first and second laws of thermodynamics. These laws respectively affirm that thermal energy is conserved and flows

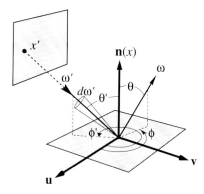

Figure 1: *The local coordinates of a bidirectional reflectance function. The incident vector $\omega'$ and the reflected vector $\omega$ are in world coordinates. The angles define a local coordinate system.*

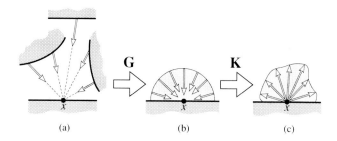

Figure 2: *The actions of $G$ and $K$ at a single point $x$. The operator $G$ converts (a) distant surface radiance directed toward $x$ into (b) local field radiance, where (c) it is again mapped into surface radiance by $K$.*

irreversibly from regions of high potential (temperature) to regions of low potential [30]. The two laws also yield certain reciprocity conditions such as those exhibited by reflection functions and form factors.

In the present paper, we use a geometrical optics formalism to describe radiative transfer processes at the large scale; interference and diffraction are ignored at this scale. We restrict physical or wave optics effects to the level of scattering and emission at surfaces, where the radiative wavelength may be comparable in size to surface features. Further, monochromatic radiation is assumed, and we neglect energy transfer between wavelength bands (for instance, by absorption and re-emission at surfaces). Given the forgoing physical assumptions, we specify in this section the continuous governing equation for global illumination.

Let $\mathcal{M}$ denote the collection of all surfaces in an environment, which we assume to form an enclosure for simplicity. Let $\mathcal{X}$ be a space of real-valued functions defined on $\mathcal{M} \times \mathcal{S}^2$; that is, over all surface points and angular directions in the unit sphere $\mathcal{S}^2$. Given the *surface emission* function $g \in \mathcal{X}$, which specifies the origin and directional distribution of emitted light, we wish to determine the *surface radiance function* $f \in \mathcal{X}$ that satisfies

$$f(x,\omega) = g(x,\omega) + \int_{\Omega_i} k(x; \omega' \to \omega) f(x',\omega') \cos \theta' \, d\omega', \qquad (1)$$

where $\Omega_i$ is the hemisphere of incoming directions, $k$ is a directional reflectivity, $\theta'$ is the angle of the incident beam contained in the solid angle $d\omega'$, and $x'$ is a point on a distant surface determined by $x$ and $\omega'$. See Figure 1. Equation (1) is expressed in radiometric variables but otherwise embodies the same physical principles as the rendering equation introduced by Kajiya [18]. The radiometric formulation is essential for the present error analysis.

The function $k$ appearing in equation (1) is the bidirectional reflectance distribution function at each surface point phrased in terms of direction vectors:

$$k(x; \omega' \to \omega) \equiv \rho_x(\theta', \phi', \theta, \phi) \qquad (2)$$

where $(\theta', \phi')$ and $(\theta, \phi)$ are the polar angles of the incident and reflected directions respectively. The function $k$ has two crucial properties that follow from the thermodynamic principles of energy conservation and reciprocity. By conservation we have that

$$\int_{\Omega_o} k(x; \omega' \to \omega) \cos \theta \, d\omega \leq 1, \qquad (3)$$

where $\omega' \in \Omega_i$ and $\Omega_o$ is the outgoing hemisphere. Equation (3) states that the energy reflected from a surface cannot exceed that of the incident beam. Reciprocity states that

$$k(x; \omega' \to \omega) = k(x; \omega \to \omega') \qquad (4)$$

for all $\omega' \in \Omega_i$ and $\omega \in \Omega_o$. These facts play a major role in the following analysis.

Note that the implicit function $x'$ in equation (1) is the means of constructing the distribution of energy impinging on a surface from the distribution of energy leaving distant surfaces; that is, it constructs local *field radiance* from distant *surface radiance*. The connection afforded by $x'(x, \omega')$ corresponds to the intuitive operation of tracing a ray from $x$ in the direction $-\omega'$. This simple coupling is a consequence of steady-state radiance being invariant along rays in free space; in the presence of participating media the coupling is replaced by the equation of transfer along the ray [6].

The balance equation for direct radiative exchange between surfaces was perhaps first presented in the form of equation (1) by Polyak [31]; in current radiative heat transfer literature this form is used when participating media are ignored [27]. Note that form factors do not appear directly in the integral form of the balance equation, but result from the $\cos \theta' \, d\omega'$ term for certain approximations.

## 2.1 Linear Operators

Integral equations such as equation (1) belong to the more general class of *operator equations*. Operator equations tend to be more concise than their integral counterparts while capturing algebraic properties essential for error analysis. Operator equations were first applied to global illumination by Kajiya [18] although their connection with integral equations of a similar nature has been profitably explored for nearly a century [4].

Equation (1) can be expressed as an operator equation in numerous ways. We shall construct the central operator from two simpler ones, each based on standard radiometric concepts. The representation given here has two novel features: first, it cleanly separates notions of geometry and reflection into distinct linear operators, and secondly, it employs an integral operator with a cosine-weighted measure. Both of these features simplify the subsequent error analysis.

We first define the *local reflection operator* $\mathbf{K}$, an integral operator accounting for the scattering of incident radiant energy at surfaces. This operator is most easily defined by showing its action on an arbitrary field radiance function $h$:

$$(\mathbf{K}h)(x,\omega) \equiv \int_{\Omega_i} k(x; \omega' \to \omega) h(x,\omega') \, d\mu(\omega'). \qquad (5)$$

The $\mathbf{K}$ operator maps the field radiance function $h$ to the surface radiance function after one reflection (Figures 2b-c). The operation is *local* in that the transformation occurs at each surface point in isolation. In equation (5) we have adopted the notation of Lebesgue integration [32] to introduce a measure $\mu$ that incorporates the cosine weighting. The essential relationship with the differential solid angle $d\omega'$ used in equation (1) is

$$d\mu(\omega') \equiv \cos\theta' \, d\omega'. \tag{6}$$

The new notation hides the ubiquitous cosines and, more importantly, emphasizes that the cosine is an artifact of surface integration. This observation allows the kernel $k$ to inherit the reciprocity property of reflectance functions and simplifies some of the following analysis.

Next, we define the *field radiance operator* $\mathbf{G}$, a linear operator that expresses the incident field radiance at each point in terms of the surface radiance of the surrounding environment (Figures 2a-b). Showing the action of $\mathbf{G}$ on a surface radiance function $h$, we have

$$(\mathbf{G}h)(x,\omega) \equiv h(x'(x,\omega),\omega). \tag{7}$$

The $\mathbf{G}$ operator expresses non-local point-to-point visibility operations as a mapping on the space of radiance functions. Defining $\mathbf{G}$ in this way allows us to factor out the implicit function $x'(x,\omega)$ from the integral in equation (1). It is easily verified that $\mathbf{KG}$ is equivalent to the original integral and that both $\mathbf{K}$ and $\mathbf{G}$ are linear. Therefore, we can write equation (1) as

$$f = g + \mathbf{KG}f, \tag{8}$$

which is a linear operator equation of the *second kind*.

To highlight the linear relationship between surface radiance and surface emission, equation (8) can be written more compactly as

$$\mathbf{M}f = g, \tag{9}$$

where the linear operator $\mathbf{M}$ is defined by

$$\mathbf{M} \equiv \mathbf{I} - \mathbf{KG}, \tag{10}$$

and $\mathbf{I}$ is the identity operator. We also note that $\mathbf{K}$ and $\mathbf{G}$ are self-adjoint in a natural sense, so the adjoint of $\mathbf{M}$ can be written

$$\mathbf{M}^* = \mathbf{I} - \mathbf{GK}, \tag{11}$$

which is useful in importance-driven global illumination.

A global illumination problem is essentially a 3-tuple $(\mathcal{M}, \mathbf{M}, g)$ of surfaces, linear operator, and emission function. In the following sections we explore numerical methods for solving equation (9) and investigate sources of error.

## 3 Boundary Elements and Projection Methods

By far the most common methods for solving global illumination problems are those employing surface discretizations, which are essentially *boundary element* methods [26]. In more abstract terms, boundary element methods are themselves *projection methods* whose role is to recast infinite-dimensional problems in finite dimensions. In this section we pose the problem of numerical approximation for global illumination in terms of projections. This level of abstraction will allow us to clearly identify and categorize all sources of error while avoiding implementation details.

The idea behind boundary element methods is to construct an approximate solution from a known finite-dimensional subspace $\mathcal{X}_n \subset \mathcal{X}$, where the parameter $n$ typically denotes the dimension of the subspace. For global illumination the space $\mathcal{X}_n$ may consist of $n$ boundary elements over which the radiance function is constant. Alternatively, it may consist of fewer boundary elements, but with internal degrees of freedom, such as tensor product polynomials [41], spherical harmonics [35], or wavelets [12]. In any case,

each element of the function space $\mathcal{X}_n$ is a linear combination of a finite number of basis functions, $u_1, \ldots, u_n$. That is,

$$\mathcal{X}_n = \text{span}\,\{u_1, \ldots, u_n\}. \tag{12}$$

Given a set of basis functions, we seek an approximation $f_n$ from the space $\mathcal{X}_n$ that is "close" to $f$ in some sense. By virtue of the finite-dimensional space, finding $f_n$ is equivalent to determining $n$ unknown coefficients $\alpha_1, \ldots, \alpha_n$ such that

$$f_n = \sum_{j=1}^{n} \alpha_j u_j. \tag{13}$$

There are many possible methods for selecting such an approximation from $\mathcal{X}_n$, each motivated by a specific notion of closeness and the computational requirements of finding the approximation.

A universal feature of discrete boundary element approaches is that they operate using a finite amount of "information" gathered from the problem instance. For projection methods this is done in the following way. We select $f_n \in \mathcal{X}_n$ by imposing a finite number of conditions on the *residual error*, which is defined by

$$r_n \equiv \mathbf{M}f_n - g. \tag{14}$$

Specifically, we attempt to find $f_n$ such that $r_n$ simultaneously satisfies $n$ linear constraints. Since we wish to make the residual "small", we set

$$\phi_i(r_n) = 0, \tag{15}$$

for $i = 1, 2, \ldots n$, where the $\phi_i : \mathcal{X} \to \mathbb{R}$ are linear functionals. The functionals and basis functions together define a projection operator, as we show in section 6.2.

Any collection of $n$ linearly independent functionals defines an approximation $f_n$ by "pinning down" the residual error with sufficiently many constraints to uniquely determine the coefficients. However, the choice of functionals has implications for the quality of the approximation as well as the computation required to obtain it. Combining equations (13), (14), and (15) we have

$$\phi_i\left(\mathbf{M}\sum_{j=1}^{n}\alpha_j u_j - g\right) = 0, \tag{16}$$

for $i = 1, 2, \ldots, n$, which is a system of $n$ equations for the unknown coefficients $\alpha_1, \ldots, \alpha_n$. Exploiting the linearity of $\phi_i$ and $\mathbf{M}$, we can express the above equations in matrix form:

$$\begin{bmatrix} \phi_1\mathbf{M}u_1 & \cdots & \phi_1\mathbf{M}u_n \\ \vdots & \ddots & \vdots \\ \phi_n\mathbf{M}u_1 & \cdots & \phi_n\mathbf{M}u_n \end{bmatrix} \begin{bmatrix} \alpha_1 \\ \vdots \\ \alpha_n \end{bmatrix} = \begin{bmatrix} \phi_1 g \\ \vdots \\ \phi_n g \end{bmatrix}. \tag{17}$$

As shown below, most global illumination algorithms described in recent literature are special cases of the formulation in equation (17). Specific projection-based algorithms are characterized by the following choices:

1. Choice of basis functions $u_1, \ldots, u_n$

2. Choice of linear functionals $\phi_1, \ldots, \phi_n$

3. Algorithms for evaluating $\phi_i\mathbf{M}u_j$ for $i, j = 1, 2, \ldots, n$

4. Algorithms for solving the discrete linear system

These choices do not necessarily coincide with the sequential steps of an algorithm. Frequently information obtained during evaluation of the linear functionals or during the solution of the discrete linear system is used to alter the choice of basis functions. The essence of adaptive meshing lies in this form of feedback. Regardless of the order in which the steps are carried out, the approximation generated ultimately rests upon specific choices in each of the above categories. Consequently, we can determine conservative bounds on the accuracy of the final solution by studying the impact of these choices independently.

## 4 A Taxonomy of Errors

In the previous section we characterized the fundamental features that distinguish projection-based global illumination algorithms. In this section we introduce a higher-level organization motivated by distinct categories of error; this subsumes the previous ideas and adds the notion of imprecise problem instances. Assuming that accuracy is measured by comparing with the exact solution to equation (1), all sources of error incurred by projection methods fall into one of three categories:

- **Perturbed Boundary Data:**

  *Both the operator **M** and the source term g may be inexact due to measurement errors and/or simplifications made for efficiency.*

- **Discretization Error:**

  *The finite-dimensional space $\mathcal{X}_n$ may not include the exact solution. In addition, satisfying the constraints $\phi_1, \ldots, \phi_n$ may not select the best possible approximation from $\mathcal{X}_n$.*

- **Computational Errors:**

  *The matrix elements $\phi_i \mathbf{M} u_j$ may not be computed exactly, thus perturbing the discrete linear system. Finally, the perturbed linear system may not be solved exactly.*

It is important to note that the above categories are mutually exclusive and account for all types of errors incurred in solving equation (1) with a projection method. The conceptual error taxonomy is shown schematically in Figure 3. In the remainder of this section we illustrate each of these categories of error with examples from existing algorithms.

### 4.1 Perturbed Boundary Data

The idealized problems that we solve in practice are rarely as realistic as we would like. As a rule, we settle for solving "near by" problems for several reasons. First, the data used as input may only be approximate. For instance, reflectance and emission functions obtained through simulation [40] or empirically through measurement of actual materials or light sources [36, 39] are inherently contaminated by error.

A second reason that boundary data may be perturbed is that use of the exact data may be prohibitively expensive or even impossible. Thus, a surface may be treated as a smooth Lambertian reflector for the purpose of simulation, although the actual geometry and material exhibits directional diffuse scattering. Regardless of the source of the discrepancy, the near-by problem can be viewed as a *perturbation* of the original problem.

### 4.2 Discretization Error

To make the problem of global illumination amenable to computer solution, we must recast the problem in terms of finite-dimensional quantities and finite processes. This transition is referred to as

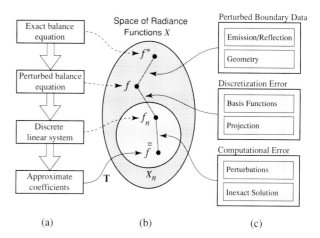

(a)　　　　　　(b)　　　　　　(c)

Figure 3: *(a) The conceptual stages for computing an approximate solution. (b) The function corresponding to each stage is an approximation of the previous stage. (c) Approximations specific to each stage introduce new errors.*

*discretization.* In general, the discrete finite-dimensional problem cannot entirely capture the behavior of the infinite-dimensional problem, and the discrepancy is called *discretization error.* This type of error is particularly difficult to analyze as it inherently involves infinite-dimensional spaces and their relationship to finite-dimensional subspaces. Consequently, most global illumination algorithms rely upon heuristics rather than error bounds to perform discretization tasks such as adaptive meshing.

We now look at how two aspects of discretization have been treated in various algorithms: 1) the choice of basis functions, which determines the finite-dimensional space containing the approximation, and 2) projection, the finite process by which the approximation is selected from this space.

### 4.2.1 Basis Functions

For many global illumination algorithms, the basis functions are completely determined by the geometry of the boundary elements. This is true of any piecewise-constant approximation, such as those employed by Goral et al. [10], Cohen et al.[8], and Hanrahan et al. [13]. Often a smoothing step is applied to piecewise-constant approximations for display purposes, although this does not necessarily improve the accuracy of the approximation. When non-constant elements are employed, such as tensor product polynomials [41, 37] or wavelets [12], the degrees of freedom of the elements add to the dimension of the approximating subspace.

For non-diffuse environments the finite-dimensional space must also account for the directional dependence of surface radiance functions; several avenues have been explored for doing this. Immel et al. [17] used subdivided cubes centered at a finite number of surface points to simultaneously discretize directions and positions. Sillion et al. [35] used a truncated series of spherical harmonics to capture directional dependence and a quadrilateral mesh of surface elements for the spatial dependence. As a third contrasting approach, Aupperle et al. [3] used piecewise-constant functions defined over pairs of patches to account for both directional and spatial variations.

The accuracy of the approximation is limited by the space of basis functions; in general, the exact solution cannot be formed by a finite linear combination of polynomials or other basis functions. The error can be reduced either by expanding the subspace $\mathcal{X}_n$, or by selecting basis functions that fit the solution more closely. Discontinuity meshing [14, 24] is an example of the latter strategy.

### 4.2.2 Projections

Given a set of basis functions, the next conceptual step is to construct a reasonable approximation from it. We now demonstrate how the major projection methods follow from specific choices of the linear functionals $\phi_1, \ldots, \phi_n$ described in section 3. The first technique is *collocation* [22], which follows by defining $\phi_i$ to be an *evaluation functional* at the $i^{th}$ collocation point; that is

$$\phi_i h \equiv h(x_i), \qquad (18)$$

where $x_1, \ldots, x_n$ are distinct points in the domain of the radiance functions chosen so that $\det[u_i(x_j)] \neq 0$. The $ij^{th}$ element of the resulting linear system has the form

$$u_j(x_i) - (\mathbf{K}\mathbf{G}u_j)(x_i). \qquad (19)$$

Collocation has been widely used in global illumination because of the relative simplicity of the above expression. In the case of constant basis functions over planar boundary elements, the resulting matrix has a unit diagonal with point-to-area form factors off the diagonal, which is a widely used radiosity formulation [8]. In general, methods based on a finite number of point-to-area interactions are collocation methods.

A second technique is the *Galerkin method*, which follows by defining $\phi_i$ to be an inner product functional with the $i^{th}$ basis function; that is

$$\phi_i h \equiv \langle u_i \mid h \rangle, \qquad (20)$$

where the inner product $\langle \cdot \mid \cdot \rangle$ denotes the integral of the product of two functions. The $ij^{th}$ element of the resulting linear system has the form

$$\langle u_i \mid u_j \rangle - \langle u_i \mid \mathbf{K}\mathbf{G}u_j \rangle. \qquad (21)$$

The Galerkin method was first employed in global illumination by Goral et al. [10] using a uniform mesh and constant basis functions. The use of higher-order basis functions was investigated by Heckbert [14] and later by Zatz [41] and Troutman and Max [37]. For diffuse environments with constant elements, the second inner product in equation (21) reduces to an area-to-area form factor.

There are other possibilities for the linear functionals $\phi_1, \ldots, \phi_n$. For instance, the inner products in equation (20) may be taken with respect to a different set of basis functions. If we set

$$\phi_i h \equiv \langle \mathbf{M}u_i \mid h \rangle, \qquad (22)$$

we obtain the *least squares* method. With the above functional, the solution to the linear system in equation (17) has a residual error that is orthogonal to the space $\mathcal{X}_n$, which minimizes the residual error in a very natural sense. However, the matrix elements for the least squares method include terms of the form $\langle \mathbf{K}\mathbf{G}u_i \mid \mathbf{K}\mathbf{G}u_j \rangle$, which are formidable to evaluate even with trivial basis functions [15]. Consequently, to our knowledge, there are currently no global illumination algorithms based on the least squares method.

### 4.3 Computational Errors

Given a particular method of discretization, error may be incurred in constructing the discrete (finite-dimensional) linear system, and once formulated, we may fail to solve even the discrete problem exactly. These facts illustrate a third distinct class of errors. Because they arise from the practical limits of computational procedures, this class is called *computational errors* [23]. Computational errors perturb the discrete problem, and then preclude exact solution of the perturbed problem. We now look at examples of each of these.

### 4.3.1 Perturbation of the Linear System

The most computationally expensive operation of global illumination is the evaluation of the matrix elements in equation (17); this is true even of algorithms that do not store an explicit matrix [7]. Furthermore, only in very special cases can the matrix elements be formed exactly, as they entail visibility calculations coupled with multiple integration. Consequently, the computed matrix is nearly always perturbed by computational errors.

A common example of an error in this category is imprecise form factors. The algorithm introduced by Cohen and Greenberg [8] for diffuse environments computed form factors at discrete surface points by means of a hemicube, which introduced a number of errors specific to this approach [5]. Errors are also introduced when form factors are approximated through ray tracing [38] or by using simpler geometries [13]. These errors can be mitigated to some extent by the use of analytic form factors [5, 34], yet there remain many cases for which no analytic expression is known, particularly in the presence of occluders.

For non-constant basis functions the form factor computations are replaced by more general inner products, which require different approximations. For instance, the matrix elements in the Galerkin approach of Zatz [41] required four-fold integrals, which were approximated using Gaussian quadrature. Non-diffuse environments pose a similar difficulty in that the matrix elements entail integration with reflectance functions [35].

Another form of matrix perturbation arises from simplifications made for the sake of efficiency. For example, small entries may be set to zero [25], or the entire matrix may be approximated by one with a more efficient structure, such as a block matrix [13] or a wavelet decomposition [12].

### 4.3.2 Inexact Solution of the Linear System

Once the discrete linear system is formed, we must solve for the coefficients $\alpha_1, \ldots, \alpha_n$. This has been done in a number of ways, including Gaussian elimination [10], Gauss-Seidel [8], Southwell relaxation (shooting) [7, 11], and Jacobi iteration [13]. In any such method, there will be some error introduced in the solution process: direct solvers like Gaussian elimination are prone to roundoff error, whereas interative solvers like Gauss-Seidel must halt after a finite number of iterations.

In approaches where the matrix is constructed in advance, such as "full matrix" radiosity [8] or hierarchical radiosity [13], the iterative solution can be carried out to essentially full convergence. Other approaches, such as progressive radiosity [7], construct matrix elements on the fly and then discard them. The cost of computing these elements generally precludes complete convergence, making this source of error significant.

## 5 Quantifying Error

Thus far the discussion has focused on the sources of error without attempting to quantify them. In this section we introduce the tools that will be used to derive error bounds in subsequent sections.

To quantify error, we require some notion of "size" for the elements of the function space $\mathcal{X}$ as well as a notion of the "distance" between its members. An abstraction that embodies these notions is a real-valued *norm* defined on $\mathcal{X}$, denoted by $\| \; \|$; the ordered pair $(\mathcal{X}, \| \; \|)$ is then called a *normed linear space*. The subject of normed linear spaces is extremely rich, and we shall only touch upon it here. For a more complete discussion see the classic texts by Rudin [32] or Kantorovich [19].

## 5.1 Function Norms

Infinitely many norms can be defined on the space of radiance functions, each conveying a different notion of size, distance, and convergence. Since equation (8) imposes only certain integrability conditions on radiance functions, it is natural to apply the $L^p$-norm defined by

$$\| f \|_p \equiv \left[ \int_{\mathcal{M}} \int_{\mathcal{S}^2} |f(x, \omega)|^p \, d\mu(\omega) \, d\sigma(x) \right]^{1/p}, \qquad (23)$$

where $\sigma$ denotes area measure, and $p$ is a real number in the range $[1, \infty]$. Three of these norms are of particular interest: the $L^1$-norm and $L^\infty$-norm have immediate physical interpretations, while the $L^2$-norm possesses algebraic properties that make it appropriate in some instances; for instance, when the algebraic structure of an inner product space is required.

In the limiting case of $p = \infty$, the $L^p$-norm reduces to

$$\| f \|_\infty \equiv \sup_{x \in \mathcal{M}} \sup_{\omega \in \mathcal{S}^2} |f(x, \omega)|, \qquad (24)$$

where sup denotes the least upper bound. As the *maximum radiance* attained at any surface point and in any direction, $\| f \|_\infty$ has the dimensions of radiance [watts/m$^2$sr]. In contrast, $\| f \|_1$ measures the *total power* of the radiance function $f$, and consequently has the dimensions of power [watts].

To measure the distance between two radiance functions $f$ and $f'$ in $\mathcal{X}$, we use the non-negative quantity $\| f - f' \|$. Similarly, we define the distance between a function and a subspace $Y \subset \mathcal{X}$ by

$$\text{dist}(f, Y) \equiv \inf_{f' \in Y} \| f - f' \|, \qquad (25)$$

where inf denotes the greatest lower bound. When the subscript on the norm is omitted, it is implied that the definition or relation holds for any choice of norm.

## 5.2 Operator Norms

To investigate the effects of perturbing the operators themselves, we must also endow the linear space of operators on $\mathcal{X}$ with a norm. The standard *operator norm* is defined by

$$\| A \| \equiv \sup \left\{ \| Ah \| : \| h \| \leq 1 \right\}, \qquad (26)$$

where the norm appearing twice on the right is the one associated with $\mathcal{X}$; the operator norm is said to be *induced* by the given function norm. Although the theory of linear operators closely parallels that of matrices, there are important differences; for instance, matrix norms are necessarily finite while operator norms need not be. We therefore distinguish the class of *bounded* operators as those with finite norm.

Equation (26) implies that $\| Ah \| \leq \| A \| \| h \|$ for all $h \in \mathcal{X}$. Several useful consequences follow immediately from this inequality. For instance, let $f_n \in \mathcal{X}_n$ be the approximate solution to $Mf = g$ discussed in section 3. Then, whenever $M^{-1}$ exists and is bounded, it follows from equation (14) that

$$
\begin{aligned}
\| f_n - f \| &= \| f_n - M^{-1} g \| \\
&\leq \| M^{-1} \| \| M f_n - g \| \\
&\leq \| M^{-1} \| \| r_n \|, \qquad (27)
\end{aligned}
$$

which justifies the strategy of minimizing the residual error $r_n$ in order to reduce the error $\| f_n - f \|$. Appendix A contains several other inequalities, including Banach's lemma, which will prove useful in deriving error bounds.

## 5.3 Norms of Special Operators K, G, and $M^{-1}$

We now compute bounds for the operators $K$, $G$, and $M^{-1}$, which will be essential for all subsequent bounds. From definitions (5), (23), and (26), we can deduce an explicit formula for $\| K \|_1$. A straightforward manipulation [19, p. 109] shows that

$$\| K \|_1 = \sup_{x \in \mathcal{M}} \sup_{\omega' \in \Omega_i} \int_{\Omega_o} k(x; \omega' \to \omega) \, d\mu(\omega). \qquad (28)$$

This norm is the maximum reflectivity of any surface in the environment which, by equation (3), is necessarily bounded above by 1. If we disallow perfect reflectors and ignore the wave optics effect of specular reflection near grazing, the norm has a bound strictly less than 1; that is, $\| K \|_1 = m < 1$. The $L^\infty$-norm of $K$ is very similar, merely exchanging the roles of the two directions:

$$\| K \|_\infty = \sup_{x \in \mathcal{M}} \sup_{\omega \in \Omega_o} \int_{\Omega_i} k(x; \omega' \to \omega) \, d\mu(\omega'). \qquad (29)$$

By the reciprocity relation in equation (4) we have $\| K \|_1 = \| K \|_\infty$, implying that reflected radiance is everywhere diminished by at least the same factor of $m$. The bound can be extended to all $L^p$-norms by the inequality

$$\| A \|_p \leq \max \left\{ \| A \|_1, \| A \|_\infty \right\}, \qquad (30)$$

which holds for linear integral operators [20, p. 144]. Therefore

$$\| K \|_p \leq m < 1 \qquad (31)$$

for all $1 \leq p \leq \infty$.

Similarly, we can bound the $G$ operator by invoking several physical principles. Because we have assumed no volume emission or absorption, the enclosure $\mathcal{M}$ contains no sources or sinks in its interior. By Gauss's theorem, an analogous statement holds for the boundary of the enclosure; that is, the net flux passing through $\mathcal{M}$ is zero. Because the power entering the enclosure must equal the power leaving it, we have $\| f \|_1 = \| Gf \|_1$. The argument extends immediately to $f^p$ for any $p$, so $\| f \|_p = \| Gf \|_p$. By definition of the operator norm, it follows that

$$\| G \|_p = 1 \qquad (32)$$

for all $1 \leq p \leq \infty$. Note that the norm can be less than 1 if $\mathcal{M}$ does not form an enclosure.

A third operator that we shall need to bound is $M^{-1}$, which maps surface emission functions to surface radiance functions at equilibrium. It follows from bounds (31) and (32) that $M^{-1}$ exists and can be expanded into a Neumann series [20, p. 30]. Taking norms and summing the resulting geometric series, we have

$$\| M^{-1} \|_p \leq 1 + m + m^2 + \ldots = \frac{1}{1 - m} \qquad (33)$$

for all $1 \leq p \leq \infty$. This bound also implies that the space of bounded radiance functions with respect to a given $L^p$-norm is closed under global illumination; that is, if an emission function $g$ has a finite $L^p$-norm, so too will the solution $f$.

## 6 Error Bounds

With the results of the previous section we can obtain bounds for each category of error. Because the methods employed here take account of very little information about an environment, the bounds tend to be quite conservative. The organizational structure of this section follows that of Figure 3 and section 4.

## 6.1 Perturbed Boundary Data

We solve global illumination problems using inexact or noisy data in hopes of obtaining a solution that is close to that of the original problem. But under what circumstances is this a reasonable expectation? To answer this question we analyze the mapping from problem instances $(\mathcal{M}, \mathbf{M}, g)$ to solutions $f$. We shall assume that any input to a global illumination problem may be contaminated by error, and determine the impact of these errors on the solution. We shall show that the problem of global illumination is *well-posed* except in certain extreme and non-realizable cases; that is, "small" perturbations of the input data produce "small" errors in the solution in physically meaningful problems.

To bound the effects of input data perturbations, we examine the quantity $\|f^* - f\|$, where $f^*$ is the solution to the exact or unperturbed system, and $f$ is the solution to a perturbed system

$$\widetilde{\mathbf{M}} f = \widetilde{g}, \qquad (34)$$

where perturbed entities are denoted with tildes.

### 6.1.1 Perturbed Reflectance and Emission Functions

We first investigate the effect of perturbing the reflectance and emission functions. The former is equivalent to perturbing the local reflection operator $\mathbf{K}$. Consider a perturbed operator $\widetilde{\mathbf{K}}$ and a perturbed emission function $\widetilde{g}$ such that

$$\left\| \mathbf{K} - \widetilde{\mathbf{K}} \right\| \leq \delta_k \qquad (35)$$

and

$$\| g - \widetilde{g} \| \leq \delta_g. \qquad (36)$$

Since $\| \mathbf{G} \| = 1$, and $\mathbf{G}$ is not perturbed, it follows that inequality (35) also applies to the corresponding perturbed $\mathbf{M}$ operator:

$$\left\| \widetilde{\mathbf{M}} - \mathbf{M} \right\| = \left\| \mathbf{KG} - \widetilde{\mathbf{K}}\mathbf{G} \right\| \leq \left\| \mathbf{K} - \widetilde{\mathbf{K}} \right\| \, \| \mathbf{G} \| \leq \delta_k.$$

Intuitively, the above inequality holds because the worst-case behavior over all possible field radiance functions is unaffected by $\mathbf{G}$, which merely redistributes radiance.

A bound on $\|f^* - f\|$ in terms of bounds on the perturbations and other quantities is derived in Appendix B. The result is

$$\|f^* - f\| \leq \left( \frac{\delta_k}{1 - m - \delta_k} \right) \left( \frac{\| g \| + \delta_g}{1 - m} \right) + \frac{\delta_g}{1 - m}, \qquad (37)$$

which contains terms accounting for perturbations in the reflectance and emission functions individually as well as a second-order term involving $\delta_k \delta_g$. Note that the reflectance term requires $\delta_k < 1 - m$, indicating that the problem becomes less stable as the maximum reflectivity approaches 1. For highly reflective environments, the results may be arbitrarily bad if the input data are not correspondingly accurate. With perfect reflection the problem is ill-posed. In general, the worst-case absolute error in $f$ depends upon the maximum reflectivity of the environment $m$, the perturbation of the reflection functions $\delta_k$, and the error in the emission function, $\delta_g$.

### 6.1.2 Perturbed Surface Geometry

The effects of imprecise surface geometry are more difficult to analyze than those due to imprecise reflection or emission. While the space of radiance functions has a linear algebraic structure that underlies all of the analysis, no analogous structure exists on the set of possible surface geometries. The analysis must therefore proceed along different lines.

An alternative approach is to study imprecise surface geometry indirectly, by means of the $\mathbf{G}$ operator. That is, we can express the effect of surface perturbations on the field radiance at each point as a perturbation of $\mathbf{G}$. Given a perturbed operator $\widetilde{\mathbf{G}}$, and a bound on its distance from the exact $\mathbf{G}$, the same analysis used in Appendix B for perturbed reflectance functions can be applied. Such an approach may be useful for analyzing schemes in which geometry is simplified to improve the efficiency of global ilumination [33]. However, relating changes in geometry to bounds on the perturbation of $\mathbf{G}$ is an open problem.

## 6.2 Discretization Error

In this section we study discretization errors introduced by projection methods. Clearly, the discretization error $\|f - f_n\|$ is bounded from *below* by $\text{dist}(f, \mathcal{X}_n)$, the distance to the best approximation attainable within the space $\mathcal{X}_n$. To obtain an upper bound, we express equation (15) using an explicit projection operator:

$$\mathbf{P}_n r_n = 0, \qquad (38)$$

where $\mathbf{P}_n$ projects onto the subspace $\mathcal{X}_n$. That is, $\mathbf{P}_n$ is a linear operator with $\mathbf{P}_n^2 = \mathbf{P}_n$ and $\mathbf{P}_n h = h$ for all $h \in \mathcal{X}_n$. Such a projection can be defined in terms of the basis functions $u_1, \ldots, u_n$ and the linear functionals $\phi_1, \ldots, \phi_n$ of section 3. The form of $\mathbf{P}_n$ is particularly simple when

$$\phi_i(u_j) = \begin{cases} 1 & \text{if } i = j \\ 0 & \text{otherwise} \end{cases} \qquad (39)$$

which is commonly the case. For instance, this holds whenever there is exactly one collocation point within the support of each basis function, or when orthogonal polynomials are used in a Galerkin-based approach. When equation (39) holds, $\mathbf{P}_n$ is given by

$$\mathbf{P}_n h = \sum_{i=1}^{n} \phi_i(h) u_i \qquad (40)$$

for any function $h \in \mathcal{X}$ [9]. It is easy to see that the above equation defines a projection onto $\mathcal{X}_n$.

To produce the desired bound, we write equation (38) as

$$\mathbf{P}_n \mathbf{M}(f - f_n) = 0, \qquad (41)$$

then isolate the quantity $\|f - f_n\|$ after taking the norm, as shown in Appendix C. The resulting bounds on discretization error are

$$\text{dist}(f, \mathcal{X}_n) \leq \|f - f_n\| \leq \left( \frac{\text{dist}(f, \mathcal{X}_n)}{1 - m - \delta_P} \right) \left( 1 + \| \mathbf{P}_n \| \right), \qquad (42)$$

where the constant $\delta_P$ is such that

$$\| \mathbf{K} - \mathbf{P}_n \mathbf{K} \| \leq \delta_P. \qquad (43)$$

The bounds in equation (42) depend on both the subspace $\mathcal{X}_n$ and the projection method. Note that if $f$ is in the space $\mathcal{X}_n$, then $\text{dist}(f, \mathcal{X}_n) = 0$, and the upper bound implies that $f_n = f$. Thus, all projection methods find the exact solution when it is achievable with a linear combination of the given basis functions. On the other hand, when $\text{dist}(f, \mathcal{X}_n)$ is large, then the lower bound implies that the approximation will be poor even when all other steps are exact. Unfortunately, this distance is difficult to estimate *a priori*, as it depends on the actual solution.

The dependence on the type of projection appears in the factor of $1 + \| \mathbf{P}_n \|$ and in the constant $\delta_P$. For all projections based on inner products, $\| \mathbf{P}_n \| = 1$ when the basis functions are orthogonal [2, p. 64]. For other methods, such as collocation, the norm of the projection may be greater than one [2, p. 56]. The meaning of the constant $\delta_P$ is more subtle. The norm in equation (43) is a measure of how well the projection $\mathbf{P}_n$ captures features of the reflected radiance.

## 6.3 Computational Errors

The effects of computational errors can be estimated by treating them as perturbations of the *discrete* linear system. The analysis therefore parallels that of perturbed boundary data, although carried out in a finite dimensional space. We shall denote the linear system in equation (17) by $\mathbf{A}\alpha = \mathbf{b}$. In general, the matrix elements as well as the vector $\mathbf{b}$ will be inexact due to errors or simplifications. We denote the perturbed system and its solution by

$$\widetilde{\mathbf{A}}\,\widetilde{\alpha} = \widetilde{\mathbf{b}}. \tag{44}$$

Although the exact matrix is unknown, it is frequently possible to bound the error present in each element. For instance, this can be done for approximate form factors and block matrix approximations [13].

Given element-by-element error bounds, the impact on the final solution can be bounded. From the element perturbations we can find $\delta_A$ and $\delta_b$ such that

$$\left\| \mathbf{A} - \widetilde{\mathbf{A}} \right\| \leq \delta_A, \tag{45}$$

and

$$\left\| \mathbf{b} - \widetilde{\mathbf{b}} \right\| \leq \delta_b, \tag{46}$$

for some vector norm and induced matrix norm. Also, since the perturbed matrix is known, the norm of its inverse can be estimated:

$$\left\| \widetilde{\mathbf{A}}^{-1} \right\| \leq \beta. \tag{47}$$

With the three bounds described above, essentially the same steps used in Appendix B yield the bound

$$\left\| \alpha - \widetilde{\alpha} \right\| \leq \left( \frac{\delta_A \beta^2}{1 - \delta_A \beta} \right) \left( \left\| \widetilde{\mathbf{b}} \right\| + \delta_b \right) + \beta \delta_b. \tag{48}$$

Computing values for $\delta_A$ and $\delta_b$ that are reasonably tight is almost always difficult, requiring error bounds for each step in forming the matrix elements. There is no universal method by which this can be done; each approach to estimating visibility or computing inner products, for example, requires a specialized analysis. In contrast, the bound in equation (47) is more accessible, as it is purely a problem of linear algebra.

Given that equation (44) generally cannot be solved exactly, the solution process is yet another source of error. The result is an approximation of $\widetilde{\alpha}$, which we denote by $\widetilde{\widetilde{\alpha}}$. From equation (27), this last source of error is bounded by

$$\left\| \widetilde{\alpha} - \widetilde{\widetilde{\alpha}} \right\| \leq \beta \left\| \widetilde{\mathbf{A}}\widetilde{\widetilde{\alpha}} - \widetilde{\mathbf{b}} \right\|. \tag{49}$$

When $\widetilde{\mathbf{A}}$ and $\widetilde{\mathbf{b}}$ are stored explicitly, the above expression can be used as the stopping criterion for an iterative solver.

To relate errors in the coefficients $\alpha_1, \ldots, \alpha_n$ to errors in the resulting radiance function, consider the mapping $\mathbf{T} : \mathbb{R}^n \to \mathcal{X}_n$ where

$$\mathbf{T}x \equiv \sum_{j=1}^{n} x_j\, u_j. \tag{50}$$

As a finite-dimensional linear operator, $\mathbf{T}$ is necessarily bounded; its norm supplies the connection between coefficients in $\mathbb{R}^n$ and functions in $\mathcal{X}_n$. Observe that

$$
\begin{aligned}
\left\| f_n - \widetilde{\widetilde{f}} \right\| &= \left\| \mathbf{T}\alpha - \mathbf{T}\widetilde{\widetilde{\alpha}} \right\| \\
&\leq \left\| \mathbf{T} \right\| \left\| \alpha - \widetilde{\widetilde{\alpha}} \right\| \\
&\leq \left\| \mathbf{T} \right\| \left( \left\| \alpha - \widetilde{\alpha} \right\| + \left\| \widetilde{\alpha} - \widetilde{\widetilde{\alpha}} \right\| \right). \quad (51)
\end{aligned}
$$

Equation (51) relates the computational error present in the final solution to inequalities (48) and (49). The value of $\| \mathbf{T} \|$ will depend on the basis functions $u_1, \ldots, u_n$ and the choice of norms for both $\mathbb{R}^n$ and $\mathcal{X}_n$, which need not be related.

## 7 The Combined Effect of Errors

In the previous sections we derived inequalities to bound the errors introduced into the solution of a global illumination problem. Using these inequalities we can now bound the distance between the exact solution and the computed solution. By the triangle inequality we have

$$\left\| f^* - \widetilde{\widetilde{f}} \right\| \leq \left\| f^* - f \right\| + \left\| f - f_n \right\| + \left\| f_n - \widetilde{\widetilde{f}} \right\|, \tag{52}$$

which is the numerical analogue of the chain of approximations shown in Figure 3. The terms on the right correspond to errors arising from perturbed boundary data, discretization, and computation; sections 6.1, 6.2, and 6.3 provide bounds for each of these errors. We note that the first and third terms can be reduced in magnitude by decreasing errors in the emission and reflectance functions and in the computational methods for forming and solving the linear system. The second term, due to discretization error and addressed by equation (42), is more difficult to compute, and is further explored below.

### 7.1 A Numerical Experiment

Using a simple configuration, we compared the discretization errors incurred by two projection methods: collocation and Galerkin. The geometry consisted of a square diffuse light source, with unit side, above and parallel to a rectangular diffuse receiver 10 units on a side. The receiver was discretized using piecewise-constant basis functions over uniform quadrilateral elements. The reflectivity of the light source was set to zero, so interreflection was ignored. For this configuration the projections and the actual solution could be computed analytically using closed-form expressions for point-to-area and area-to-area form factors [16].

Figure 4 shows various errors with respect to three different norms as the number of mesh elements increases. The bottom curve in each plot is the distance between the closest approximation and the analytic solution; by equation (42) this is a lower bound on the the discretization error of any projection method. For each mesh element, the closest approximation follows from the median, the mean, and the extrema of the analytic solution for the $L^1$, $L^2$, and $L^\infty$-norms, respectively. Also shown in the plots are the distances from the analytic solution to the approximations produced by the two projections.

Because the constants $m$ and $\delta_P$ in equation (42) are related to reflectivity, which did not enter into this computation, the theoretical upper bound on discretization error is the lower bound times $1 + \| \mathbf{P} \|$. The top curve in each plot is twice the lower bound, which is the smallest upper bound attainable by the present analysis since $\| \mathbf{P} \| \geq 1$ for any projection. With one exception, the top curve suffices as an upper bound for the discretization error. (The single exception results from a collocation projection with a norm significantly greater than 1.)

The discretization error is one of the more difficult errors to quantify. Note that the discretization errors of the two projections shown in Figure 4 generally fall between the upper and lower curves, and approach the lower bound as the mesh refinement is increased. The two projection methods are very close, and the Galerkin projection exactly achieves the lower bound in the $L^2$-norm.

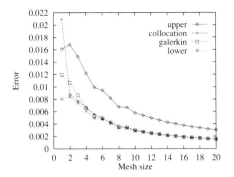 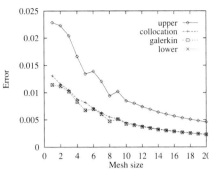 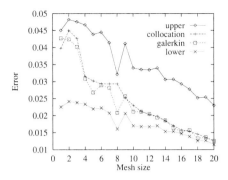

**Figure 4:** *Discretization errors in three different norms for collocation and Galerkin applied to a simple configuration: (a) $L^1$-norm, (b) $L^2$-norm, and (c) $L^\infty$-norm. The lower curve in each plot is the distance to the optimal approximation, and the upper curve is twice this distance.*

## 8  Conclusions and Future Work

We have introduced a new operator equation describing direct radiative transfer among opaque surfaces. The new formulation is appropriate for global illumination, and has several advantages over the rendering equation. First, it is closer to the underlying physical principles, being based on standard radiometric concepts. Second, it is well-suited to the error analysis presented in this paper.

We have identified three sources of error in global illumination algorithms: inaccuracies in the input data, discretization, and computational errors. Input errors result from noise in measurement or simulation, or from simplifications. Discretization errors result from restricting the space of possible approximations and from the method of selecting the approximation. Computational errors form a large class that includes imprecise form factors and visibility, as well as errors introduced by block matrix approximations and iterative matrix methods. To produce a reliable solution, each of these sources of error must be accounted for. Using standard methods of analysis, we have derived worst-case bounds for each category of error based primarily on quantities such as the maximum directional reflectivity of any surface in the environment.

There remains much work to do. Better ways of characterizing environments are needed to obtain more realistic error bounds; constants such as maximum reflectivity are much too coarse. A deficiency of the function norms employed here is that they do not adequately handle the wave optics effect of specular reflection at grazing angles. Other norms should be explored, including those that are in some sense perceptually-based. Also, reliable bounds are needed for a wide assortment of standard computations, such as form factors between partially occluded surfaces and inner products involving higher-order elements. Finally, we need to relate the norms used here and the types of tolerances that can reasonably be obtained through measurement and simulation.

## Acknowledgments

The authors wish to thank Dani Lischinski for many valuable discussions. This work was supported by the NSF grant "Interactive Computer Graphics Input and Display Techniques" (CCR-8617880), and by the NSF/ARPA Science and Technology Center for Computer Graphics and Scientific Visualization (ASC-8920219). The authors gratefully acknowledge the generous equipment grant from Hewlett-Packard Corporation on whose workstations this research was conducted.

## REFERENCES

[1] ANSELONE, P. M. Convergence and error bounds for approximate solutions of integral and operator equations. In *Error in Digital Computation*, L. B. Rall, Ed., vol. 2. John Wiley & Sons, 1965, pp. 231–252.

[2] ATKINSON, K. E. *A Survey of Numerical Methods for the Solution of Fredholm Integral Equations of the Second Kind*. Society for Industrial and Applied Mathematics, Philadelphia, 1976.

[3] AUPPERLE, L., AND HANRAHAN, P. A hierarchical illumination algorithm for surfaces with glossy reflection. In *Computer Graphics Proceedings* (1993), Annual Conference Series, ACM SIGGRAPH, pp. 155–162.

[4] BATEMAN, H. Report on the history and present state of the theory of integral equations. *Report of the 18th Meeting of the British Association for the Advancement of Science* (1910), 345–424.

[5] BAUM, D. R., RUSHMEIER, H. E., AND WINGET, J. M. Improving radiosity solutions through the use of analytically determined form-factors. *Computer Graphics 23*, 3 (July 1989), 325–334.

[6] CHANDRASEKAR, S. *Radiative Transfer*. Dover Publications, New York, 1960.

[7] COHEN, M. F., CHEN, S. E., WALLACE, J. R., AND GREENBERG, D. P. A progressive refinement approach to fast radiosity image generation. *Computer Graphics 22*, 4 (August 1988), 75–84.

[8] COHEN, M. F., AND GREENBERG, D. P. The hemi-cube: A radiosity solution for complex environments. *Computer Graphics 19*, 3 (July 1985), 75–84.

[9] GOLBERG, M. A. A survey of numerical methods for integral equations. In *Solution methods for integral equations: Theory and applications*, M. A. Golberg, Ed. Plenum Press, New York, 1979, pp. 1–58.

[10] GORAL, C. M., TORRANCE, K. E., GREENBERG, D. P., AND BATTAILE, B. Modeling the interaction of light between diffuse surfaces. *Computer Graphics 18*, 3 (July 1984), 213–222.

[11] GORTLER, S. J., AND COHEN, M. F. Radiosity and relaxation methods. Tech. Rep. TR 408-93, Princeton University, 1993.

[12] GORTLER, S. J., SCHRÖDER, P., COHEN, M. F., AND HANRAHAN, P. Wavelet radiosity. In *Computer Graphics Proceedings* (1993), Annual Conference Series, ACM SIGGRAPH, pp. 221–230.

[13] HANRAHAN, P., SALZMAN, D., AND AUPPERLE, L. A rapid hierarchical radiosity algorithm. *Computer Graphics 25*, 4 (July 1991), 197–206.

[14] HECKBERT, P. S. *Simulating Global Illumination Using Adaptive Meshing*. PhD thesis, University of California, Berkeley, June 1991.

[15] HILDEBRAND, F. B. *Methods of Applied Mathematics*. Prentice-Hall, New York, 1952.

[16] HOWELL, J. R. *A Catalog of Radiation Configuration Factors*. McGraw-Hill, New York, 1982.

[17] IMMEL, D. S., COHEN, M. F., AND GREENBERG, D. P. A radiosity method for non-diffuse environments. *Computer Graphics 20*, 4 (August 1986), 133–142.

[18] KAJIYA, J. T. The rendering equation. *Computer Graphics 20*, 4 (August 1986), 143–150.

[19] KANTOROVICH, L., AND AKILOV, G. P. *Functional Analysis in Normed Spaces*. Pergamon Press, New York, 1964.

[20] KATO, T. *Perturbation Theory for Linear Operators*. Springer-Verlag, New York, 1966.

[21] KRASNOSEL'SKII, M. A., VAINIKKO, G. M., ZABREIKO, P. P., RUTITSKII, Y. B., AND STETSENKO, V. Y. *Approximate Solution of Operator Equations*. Wolters-Noordhoff, Groningen, The Netherlands, 1972.

Translated by D. Louvish.

[22] KRESS, R. *Linear Integral Equations.* Springer-Verlag, New York, 1989.

[23] LINZ, P. *Theoretical Numerical Analysis, an Introduction to Advanced Techniques.* John Wiley & Sons, New York, 1979.

[24] LISCHINSKI, D., TAMPIERI, F., AND GREENBERG, D. P. Discontinuity meshing for accurate radiosity. *IEEE Computer Graphics and Applications 12*, 6 (November 1992), 25–39.

[25] LISCHINSKI, D., TAMPIERI, F., AND GREENBERG, D. P. Combining hierarchical radiosity and discontinuity meshing. In *Computer Graphics Proceedings* (1993), Annual Conference Series, ACM SIGGRAPH, pp. 199–208.

[26] MACKERLE, J., AND BREBBIA, C. A., Eds. *The Boundary Element Reference Book.* Springer-Verlag, New York, 1988.

[27] MODEST, M. F. *Radiative Heat Transfer.* McGraw-Hill, New York, 1993.

[28] ORTEGA, J. M. *Numerical Analysis, a Second Course.* Academic Press, New York, 1972.

[29] PHILLIPS, J. L. The use of collocation as a projection method for solving linear operator equations. *SIAM Journal on Numerical Analysis 9*, 1 (1972), 14–28.

[30] PLANCK, M. *The Theory of Heat Radiation.* Dover Publications, New York, 1988.

[31] POLYAK, G. L. Radiative transfer between surfaces of arbitrary spatial distribution of reflection. In *Convective and Radiative Heat Transfer.* Publishing House of the Academy of Sciences of the USSR, Moscow, 1960.

[32] RUDIN, W. *Functional Analysis.* McGraw-Hill, New York, 1973.

[33] RUSHMEIER, H. E., PATTERSON, C., AND VEERASAMY, A. Geometric simplification for indirect illumination calculations. *Graphics Interface '93* (May 1993), 227–236.

[34] SCHRÖDER, P., AND HANRAHAN, P. On the form factor between two polygons. In *Computer Graphics Proceedings* (1993), Annual Conference Series, ACM SIGGRAPH, pp. 163–164.

[35] SILLION, F., ARVO, J., WESTIN, S., AND GREENBERG, D. P. A global illumination solution for general reflectance distributions. *Computer Graphics 25*, 4 (July 1991), 187–196.

[36] TOULOUKIAN, Y. S., Ed. *Retrieval Guide to Thermophysical Properties Research Literature*, second ed. McGraw-Hill, New York, 1968.

[37] TROUTMAN, R., AND MAX, N. L. Radiosity algorithms using higher-order finite element methods. In *Computer Graphics Proceedings* (1993), Annual Conference Series, ACM SIGGRAPH, pp. 209–212.

[38] WALLACE, J., ELMQUIST, K., AND HAINES, E. A ray tracing algorithm for progressive radiosity. *Computer Graphics 23*, 3 (July 1989), 315–324.

[39] WARD, G. J. Measuring and modeling anisotropic reflection. *Computer Graphics 26*, 2 (July 1992), 265–272.

[40] WESTIN, S., ARVO, J., AND TORRANCE, K. Predicting reflectance functions from complex surfaces. *Computer Graphics 26*, 2 (July 1992), 255–264.

[41] ZATZ, H. Galerkin radiosity: A higher order solution method for global illumination. In *Computer Graphics Proceedings* (1993), Annual Conference Series, ACM SIGGRAPH, pp. 213–220.

## Appendix A: Operator-Norm Inequalities

In addition to the properties common to all norms, operator norms also satisfy

$$\| \mathbf{AB} \| \leq \| \mathbf{A} \| \, \| \mathbf{B} \|, \tag{53}$$

which makes them compatible with the multiplicative structure of operators [19]. Additional bounds, such as those pertaining to inverse operators, can be deduced from the basic properties of operator norms. For instance, given a bounded operator $\mathbf{A}$ with an inverse, any operator $\mathbf{B}$ sufficiently close to $\mathbf{A}$ is also invertible, with

$$\| \mathbf{B}^{-1} \| \leq \frac{\| \mathbf{A}^{-1} \|}{1 - \| \mathbf{A} - \mathbf{B} \| \, \| \mathbf{A}^{-1} \|}. \tag{54}$$

This inequality, known as Banach's lemma [28, p. 32], holds whenever $\| \mathbf{A} - \mathbf{B} \| < 1/\| \mathbf{A}^{-1} \|$. A useful corollary of Banach's lemma

is the inequality

$$\| \mathbf{A}^{-1} - \mathbf{B}^{-1} \| \leq \frac{\| \mathbf{A} - \mathbf{B} \| \, \| \mathbf{A}^{-1} \|^2}{1 - \| \mathbf{A} - \mathbf{B} \| \, \| \mathbf{A}^{-1} \|}, \tag{55}$$

which holds under the same conditions [20, p. 31].

## Appendix B: Error Bounds for Perturbed Reflectance and Emission Functions

To bound the error $\| f^* - f \|$ due to perturbations in the reflection and emission functions according to the inequalities (35) and (36) we write

$$\begin{aligned}
\| f^* - f \| &= \| \mathbf{M}^{-1} g - \widetilde{\mathbf{M}}^{-1} \widetilde{g} \| \\
&\leq \| \mathbf{M}^{-1} - \widetilde{\mathbf{M}}^{-1} \| \, \| \widetilde{g} \| + \| \mathbf{M}^{-1} \| \, \| g - \widetilde{g} \|.
\end{aligned}$$

From inequalities inequality (55), (33) and (35), we have

$$\| \mathbf{M}^{-1} - \widetilde{\mathbf{M}}^{-1} \| \leq \left( \frac{\delta_k}{1 - m - \delta_k} \right) \left( \frac{1}{1 - m} \right). \tag{56}$$

Combining the above and noting that $\| \widetilde{g} \| \leq \| g \| + \delta_g$ by inequality (36), we arrive at the bound

$$\| f^* - f \| \leq \left( \frac{\delta_k}{1 - m - \delta_k} \right) \left( \frac{\| g \| + \delta_g}{1 - m} \right) + \frac{\delta_g}{1 - m}. \tag{57}$$

## Appendix C: Bounding Discretization Error

Adding $(\mathbf{I} - \mathbf{P}_n)(f - f_n)$ to both sides of equation (41) and simplifying, using the fact that $(\mathbf{I} - \mathbf{P}_n)f_n = 0$, we have

$$[\mathbf{I} - \mathbf{P}_n \mathbf{KG}] (f - f_n) = (\mathbf{I} - \mathbf{P}_n)f. \tag{58}$$

When the operator on the left of equation (58) is invertible, we obtain the bound

$$\| f - f_n \| \leq \| (\mathbf{I} - \mathbf{P}_n \mathbf{KG})^{-1} \| \, \| f - \mathbf{P}_n f \|. \tag{59}$$

A more meaningful bound is obtained by simplifying both factors on the righthand side [29]. Since $\mathbf{I} - \mathbf{P}_n \mathbf{KG}$ is an approximation of the operator $\mathbf{M}$, let $\delta_P$ be such that

$$\| \mathbf{M} - (\mathbf{I} - \mathbf{P}_n \mathbf{KG}) \| \leq \delta_P, \tag{60}$$

which simplifies to

$$\| \mathbf{K} - \mathbf{P}_n \mathbf{K} \| \leq \delta_P. \tag{61}$$

Because $\mathbf{M}$ is invertible, so is $\mathbf{I} - \mathbf{P}_n \mathbf{KG}$ when $\delta_P$ is sufficiently small. Banach's lemma from Appendix A then provides the bound

$$\| (\mathbf{I} - \mathbf{P}_n \mathbf{KG})^{-1} \| \leq \frac{1}{1 - m - \delta_P}.$$

The second norm on the right of inequality (59) can be simplified as follows. Let $h \in \mathcal{X}_n$. Then $\mathbf{P}_n h = h$, so

$$\begin{aligned}
\| f - \mathbf{P}_n f \| &= \| (f - h) + (h - \mathbf{P}_n f) \| \\
&\leq \| f - h \| + \| \mathbf{P}_n (h - f) \| \\
&\leq (1 + \| \mathbf{P}_n \|) \| f - h \|.
\end{aligned}$$

Since $h \in \mathcal{X}_n$ was chosen arbitrarily, the inequality holds for the least upper bound over $\mathcal{X}_n$, giving

$$\| f - \mathbf{P}_n f \| \leq (1 + \| \mathbf{P}_n \|) \operatorname{dist}(f, \mathcal{X}_n).$$

From the above inequalities we obtain the upper bound

$$\| f - f_n \| \leq \left( \frac{1}{1 - m - \delta_P} \right) \left( 1 + \| \mathbf{P}_n \| \right) \operatorname{dist}(f, \mathcal{X}_n). \tag{62}$$

# Multiresolution Painting and Compositing

*Deborah F. Berman*     *Jason T. Bartell*     *David H. Salesin*

Department of Computer Science and Engineering
University of Washington
Seattle, Washington 98195

## Abstract

We describe a representation for *multiresolution images*—images that have different resolutions in different places—and methods for creating such images using painting and compositing operations. These methods are very easy to implement, and they are efficient in both memory and speed. Only the detail present at a particular resolution is stored, and the most common painting operations, "over" and "erase," require time proportional only to the number of pixels displayed. We also show how *fractional-level zooming* can be implemented in order to allow a user to display and edit portions of a multiresolution image at any arbitrary size.

**CR Categories and Subject Descriptors:** I.3.2 [Computer Graphics]: Picture/Image Generation — Display Algorithms; I.3.6 [Computer Graphics]: Methodology and Techniques — Interaction Techniques.

**Additional Key Words:** compositing, infinite-resolution, multiresolution images, painting, wavelets, zooming.

## 1 Introduction

When editing images, it is important to be able to make sweeping changes at a coarse resolution, as well as to do fine detail work at high resolution. Ideally, the storage cost of the resulting image should be proportional only to the amount of detail present at each resolution; furthermore, the time complexity of the editing operations should be proportional only to the resolution at which the operation is performed. In addition, the user should be able to zoom in to the image to an arbitrary resolution, and to work at any convenient scale.

In this paper, we describe a very simple image painting and compositing system that meets these goals in large part. The system makes use of a Haar wavelet decomposition of the image, which is stored in a sparse quadtree structure. This wavelet representation has many advantages. First, the wavelet representation itself is concise in that it contains the same number of wavelet coefficients as there are pixels in the original image. Second, this representation supports compositing more efficiently than image pyramids. Finally, wavelets can also be used to achieve high compression rates on images [2]. By making use of a wavelet representation on-line, the editing system can be used to operate on compressed images directly, without first having to uncompress and then recompress afterward, making it much more practical for handling large images than a pyramid-based scheme.

The *multiresolution images* produced by our system can be thought of as having different resolutions in different places. There are many applications of these multiresolution images, including:

- Interactive paint systems, allowing an artist to work on a single image at various resolutions.

- Texture mapping, allowing portions of a texture that will be seen up close to be defined in more detail.

- Satellite and other image databases, allowing overlapping images created at different resolutions to be coalesced into a single multiresolution image.

- Storing and viewing the results of "importance-driven" physical simulations [9], which may be computed to different resolutions in different places.

- Virtual reality, hypermedia, and games, allowing for image detail to be explored interactively, using essentially unlimited degrees of panning and zooming.

- Supporting the "infinite desktop" user-interface metaphor [5], in which a single virtual "desktop" with infinite resolution is presented to the user.

The idea of using wavelets for multiresolution painting has also been explored simultaneously but independently by Perlin and Velho [6]. The system we describe differs from theirs in many respects, the most significant being the use of a Haar wavelet basis, support for fractional-level zooming and editing and a variety of compositing operations, and a different use of lazy evaluation in the algorithms employed.

In Section 2, we describe our multiresolution painting and compositing algorithm in detail. The algorithm is very simple, although its derivation requires some fairly sophisticated mathematics, which is deferred to Appendix A. In Section 3, we give examples of how the system can be used. Finally, in Section 4, we suggest directions for future work.

## 2 Algorithm

Here, we briefly describe a set of data structures and algorithms to support multiresolution painting and compositing.

### 2.1 Definitions and data structures

Let $\mathcal{I}$ be a *multiresolution image*—that is, an image with different resolutions in different places. One could think of $\mathcal{I}$ as an image whose resolution varies adaptively according to need.

More formally, we will define $\mathcal{I}$ as a sum of piecewise-constant functions $\mathcal{I}^j$ at different resolutions $2^j \times 2^j$. In this sense, $\mathcal{I}$ can be thought of as having "infinite" resolution everywhere: a user zooming into $\mathcal{I}$ would see more detail as long as higher-resolution detail is present; once this resolution is exceeded, the pixels of the finest-resolution image would appear to grow as larger and larger constant-colored squares.

We store the multiresolution image $\mathcal{I}$ in a sparse quadtree structure $Q$. The nodes of $Q$ have the usual correspondence with portions of the image: the root of $Q$, at level 0, corresponds to the entire image; the root's four children, at level 1, correspond to the image's four quadrants; and so on, down the tree. Thus, each level $j$ of quadtree $Q$ corresponds to a scaled version of multiresolution image $\mathcal{I}$ at resolution $2^j \times 2^j$. Note that, by the usual convention, "higher" levels of the quadtree correspond to lower-resolution versions of the image, and vice versa.

Each node of the quadtree contains the following information:

**type** $QuadTreeNode$ = **record**
    $d_i$: **array** $i \in [1, 3]$ **of** $RGBA$
    $\tau$: *real*
    $child[i]$: **array** $i \in [1, 4]$ **of pointer to** $QuadTreeNode$
**end record**

The $d_i$ values in the $QuadTreeNode$ structure describe how the colors of the children deviate from the color of the parent node. We will call these $d_i$ values the *detail coefficients*. These coefficients allow us to compute the RGBA colors of the four children, given the color of the parent, as described in Section 2.2.1. We will refer to the "alpha" component of a color $c$ or detail coefficient $d_i$ as $c.\alpha$ or $d_i.\alpha$. The $\tau$ value represents the *transparency* of the node, initialized to 1. The $\tau$ values are used to optimize the painting and compositing algorithm, as explained later. The $child[i]$ fields are pointers to the four children nodes. Some of these may be null. To optimize storage, the $child[i]$ fields can alternatively be represented by a single pointer to an array of four children.

Note that each node $N$ of the tree corresponds to a particular region of the display. We will denote this region by $A(N)$. The value $A(N)$ is determined implicitly by the structure of the quadtree and the particular view, and does not need to be represented explicitly in $N$. Except when displaying at fractional levels (Section 2.4), there is a one-to-one correspondence between pixels on the display and nodes at some level $j$ in the quadtree.

The quadtree itself is given by:

**type** $QuadTree$ = **record**
    $c$: $RGBA$
    $root$: **pointer to** $QuadTreeNode$
**end record**

The $c$ value in the quadtree structure supplies the color of the root node; it corresponds to an average of all the colors in the image $\mathcal{I}$.

The quadtree is sparse in that it contains no leaves with detail coefficients that are all 0. Thus, the constant portions of the image at any particular resolution are represented implicitly. This convention allows us to support infinite resolutions in a finite structure. It also allows us to explicitly represent high-resolution details only where they actually appear in the image.

## 2.2 The algorithm

Multiresolution painting is easy to implement. The main loop involves three steps: *Display*, *Painting*, and *Update*.

### 2.2.1 Display

An image at resolution $2^j \times 2^j$ is displayed by calling the following recursive *Display* routine once, passing it the root and color of the overall quadtree:

**procedure** $Display(N : QuadTreeNode; \; c : RGBA)$:
    $c_1 \leftarrow c + d_1 + d_2 + d_3$
    $c_2 \leftarrow c - d_1 + d_2 - d_3$
    $c_3 \leftarrow c + d_1 - d_2 - d_3$
    $c_4 \leftarrow c - d_1 - d_2 + d_3$
    **for** $i \leftarrow 1$ **to** 4 **do**
        **if** $N$ is a leaf **or** $N$ is at level $j - 1$ **then**
            Draw $c_i$ over the region $A(child[i])$
        **else**
            $Display(child[i], \; c_i)$
        **end if**
    **end for**
**end procedure**

For clarity, the pseudocode above recurses to level $j - 1$ for the entire image; in reality, it should only recurse within the bounds of the portion of the image that fits in the display window. Note that if $m$ pixels are displayed, the entire display operation takes just $O(m)$ time. (More precisely, the operation requires $O(m + j)$ time; however, since $j \ll m$ in almost any practical situation, we will ignore this dependency on $j$ in the analyses that follow.)

### 2.2.2 Painting

Painting is implemented by compositing the newly-painted foreground buffer $\mathcal{F}$ with the background buffer $\mathcal{B}$ produced by *Display*, to create a new result image $\mathcal{R}$. We support several binary compositing operations: "over," which places new paint wherever it is applied; "under," which places paint only where the background is transparent; and "in," which places paint only where the background is already painted. We also support a unary "erase" operation, which removes paint from the background. The compositing algebra was originally described by Porter and Duff [7], and first described in the context of digital painting by Salesin and Barzel [8].

No special routines are required to implement painting itself. The only difference with ordinary painting is that in addition to the composited result $\mathcal{R}$, we must keep a separate copy of the foreground buffer $\mathcal{F}$, which contains all of the newly applied paint. This foreground buffer is necessary for updating the quadtree, as described in the next section. Ordinary painting proceeds until the user either changes the painting operation (for example, from "over" to "under"), or changes the view by panning or zooming. Either of these operations triggers an "update."

### 2.2.3 Update

The "update" operation is used to propagate the results of the painting operation to the rest of the multiresolution image, as represented by the quadtree. The update involves two steps: *decomposition*, in which the changes are propagated to all higher levels of the quadtree; and *extrapolation*, in which the changes are propagated to all the lower levels. We will consider each of these in turn.

Let $j$ be the level at which the user has been painting, and let $c_r(x, y)$ be the color of each modified pixel in the result image $\mathcal{R}$. A decomposition of the entire image is performed by calling the following *Decompose* function once, passing the root of the quadtree $Q.root$ as an argument, and storing the result in $Q.c$:

```
function Decompose(N : QuadTreeNode):
    if N is at level j then
        return c_r(x, y)
    end if
    for i ← 1 to 4 do
        c_i ← Decompose(child[i])
    end for
    d_1 ← (c_1 − c_2 + c_3 − c_4)/4
    d_2 ← (c_1 + c_2 − c_3 − c_4)/4
    d_3 ← (c_1 − c_2 − c_3 + c_4)/4
    return (c_1 + c_2 + c_3 + c_4)/4
end function
```

For clarity, the pseudocode above assumes that the sparse quadtree $Q$ already contains all of the nodes corresponding to the pixels in the result image $\mathcal{R}$; however, if $\mathcal{R}$ has been painted at a higher resolution than the existing image, then new nodes may have to be allocated and added to $Q$ as part of the traversal. Furthermore, for efficiency, the Decompose function should be modified to only recurse in regions of the multiresolution image where changes have actually been made. Note that if the portion of the image being edited has $m$ pixels, then the entire decomposition operation takes $O(m)$ time.

Extrapolation is a bit more complicated, and depends on the particular compositing operation used. For binary painting operations, let $c_f(x, y)$ be the color of the foreground image $\mathcal{F}$ at each pixel $(x, y)$, and let $c_f.\alpha(x, y)$ be the pixel's alpha (opacity) value. For the "erase" operation, let $\delta(x, y)$ be the opacity of the eraser at each pixel. Extrapolation can then be performed by calling the following routine for the node $N$ corresponding to each modified pixel $(x, y)$ of the edited image:

```
procedure Extrapolate(N : QuadTreeNode):
    for i ← 1 to 3 do
        switch on the compositing operation
            case "over":
                d_i ← d_i * (1 − c_f.α(x, y))
            case "under":
                d_i ← d_i − d_i.α * c_f(x, y)
            case "in":
                d_i ← d_i * (1 − c_f.α(x, y)) + d_i.α * c_f(x, y)
            case "erase":
                d_i ← d_i * (1 − δ(x, y))
        end switch
    end for
    if N is not a leaf then
        for i ← 1 to 4 do
            Extrapolate(child[i])
        end for
    end if
end procedure
```

Note that the extrapolation procedure takes time proportional to the amount of detail that appears "below" the modified parts of the image. In order to optimize this operation, at least for the most common cases of painting "over" and erasing, we can use a form of lazy evaluation. First, observe that the two formulas for "over" and "erase" in the pseudocode above merely multiply the existing detail coefficients by some constant, which we will call $\tau(x, y)$. (For painting "over," $\tau(x, y) = 1 − c_f.\alpha(x, y)$; for erasing, $\tau(x, y) = 1 − \delta(x, y)$.) Thus, for these two operations, rather than calling the Extrapolate procedure for each node $N$, we can instead just multiply the value $N.\tau$ stored at the node by $\tau(x, y)$. Later, if and when the $d_i$ values for a node $N$ are actually required, they can be lazily updated by multiplying each $N.d_i$ with the $\tau$ values of all of the node's ancestors. This product is easily performed as part of the recursive evaluation.

This very simple form of lazy evaluation is a by-product of the underlying wavelet representation for the image, since the detail coefficients at higher resolutions depend only on the product of the opacities of all the paint applied and removed at lower resolutions. Any sort of lazy evaluation method would be much more complicated with image pyramids, since the high-resolution colors have a much more complex dependence on the colors of the paint applied and removed at lower resolutions. Note also that color correction, an important image operation, is a special case of compositing "over," and so can be performed on an arbitrarily high-resolution image in time proportional only to the resolution actually displayed.

### 2.3 Boundary conditions

Treating boundary conditions correctly introduces a slight complication to the update and display algorithms described in the sections above. The difficulty is that the Decompose function needs to have available to it the colors of the children of every node $N$ that it traverses. However, some of these child nodes correspond to regions that are outside the boundary of the window in which the user has just painted, and therefore are not directly available to the routine. The obvious solution is to store color information in addition to the detail coefficients at every node of the quadtree; however, this approach would more than double the storage requirements of the quadtree, as well as introduce the extra overhead of maintaining redundant representations. Instead, we keep a temporary auxiliary quadtree structure of just the colors necessary for the decomposition; this structure can be filled in during the Display operation at little extra cost. The size of this auxiliary structure is just $O(m)$.

### 2.4 Display and editing at fractional resolutions

So far, we have assumed a one-to-one correspondence between the nodes of the quadtree at level $j$ and the pixels of the image at resolution $2^j \times 2^j$. Since the levels of the quadtree are discrete, this definition only provides for discrete levels of zooming in which the resolution doubles at each level.

From a user-interface point of view, it would be better to be able to zoom in continuously on the multiresolution image being edited. A kind of *fractional-level* zooming can be defined by considering how the square region $A(N)$ corresponding to a given node $N$ at level $j$ in the quadtree would grow as a user zoomed in continuously from level $j$ to $j+1$ to $j+2$. The size of $A(N)$ would increase exponentially from width 1 to 2 to 4 on the display. Thus, when displaying at a fractional level $j + t$, for some $t$ between 0 and 1, we would like $A(N)$ to have size $2^t \times 2^t$.

On workstations that provide antialiased polygon drawing, this fractional zooming is implemented quite simply by drawing each node $N$ as a single square of the proper fractional size. On less expensive workstations that support only integer-sized polygons efficiently, a slightly less pleasing but still adequate display can be achieved by rounding each rendered square to the nearest pixel. In either case, the only change to the Display routine is to bottom out the recursion whenever $N$ is at level $\lceil j + t − 1 \rceil$ instead of at level $j − 1$, and to let the region $A(child[i])$ correspond to the appropriate fractional size.

Of course, from a user's standpoint, if it is possible to display an image at any level $j + t$, then it should also be possible to edit it at that level. This fractional-level editing is also easy to support. To update the quadtree representation, we simply rescale the buffer of newly painted changes $\mathcal{F}$ to the size of the next higher integer level, as if the user had painted the changes at level $j+1$; the scaling factor required is $2^{1−t}$. We can then perform the same update as before, starting from level $j + 1$.

## 3 Results

Figure 1 demonstrates our system with three examples.

In the first example (a)–(d), the user zooms into an image of Mona Lisa (a) and paints on some eye shadow and lipstick at higher resolution (b). To add a glint in the eye, the user zooms in slightly closer (c). Note that any (continuous) level of zooming is supported, so the user need not know anything about the underlying representation, which is actually discrete. The retouched image is then displayed at the original resolution (d).

In the second example (e)–(h), the user paints a tree at multiple resolutions, using different kinds of compositing operations. Most of the tree was painted at a coarse resolution. In the first frame (e), the user zooms way into the upper left corner of the tree and paints some leaves. In the second frame (f), the user zooms out to a coarser scale and changes the color of the leaves, using an "in" brush that only paints where paint has previously been applied. In the third frame (g), the user zooms out to a very coarse resolution and quickly roughs in the sky and grass, using an "under" brush that only deposits color where no paint already appears. Note that even though the sky color is applied coarsely, the new paint respects all of the high-resolution detail originally present in the image (h).

In the third example (i)–(l), we have created a single multiresolution image out of six successive images from the book, *Powers of Ten* [4], by compositing the images together at different scales. In the book, each of the images is a $10\times$ higher-resolution version of the central portion of its predecessor. In our multiresolution system, these six images become a single image with a $10^5$ range of scale. (Note that representing power-of-10 images in our power-of-2 quadtree requires the fractional-level editing capability.) The first frame (i) shows a close-up of the innermost detail. The second frame (j) shows the image after zooming out by a factor of 100,000. In the third frame (k), the user retouches the low-resolution image using an "over" brush to give the impression of smog. This smog affects all of the closer views without eliminating any of the detail present, as demonstrated in the final frame (l).

## 4 Future work

There are many directions for future research, including:

**Compression.** Wavelet image transforms are most commonly used for image compression [2]. Our system already performs a simple kind of lossless compression by pruning any branches of the quadtree whose detail coefficients are all 0. We would also like to incorporate lossy image compression as part of our system. As a further extension, this compression could be applied interactively, with the user selecting increased compression ratios in the less vital parts of the image.

**Progressive refinement.** Another advantage of the wavelet representation is that it provides a natural ordering of the detail coefficients with respect to either $L^2$ (least squares) or $L^\infty$ (max error) metrics. For example, the best $L^2$ approximation to an image using $m$ coefficients is given by the largest $m$ detail coefficients, assuming proper normalization of the basis functions. These largest coefficients, drawn as flat-shaded rectangles using polygon rendering and accumulation hardware, could be used to provide a fast indication of the image during interactive panning and zooming. The image could then be updated progressively from its most important to least important details.

**User-interface paradigms.** Multiresolution images can encode a great deal of complexity. New user-interface paradigms may therefore be required for navigating them. One useful tool would indicate the amount of detail present at different places of the image. Another would provide some measure of context when zoomed far into an image. For moving around, we would like to experiment with a movement akin to "flying," in which the user navigates through a large multiresolution image by smoothly zooming out, panning across, and zooming back in.

**Automatic synthesis of detail.** A fairly straightforward modification to our system would allow it to generate more detail procedurally whenever the user zoomed into an image, allowing for images with essentially infinite detail, such as fractals.

**3-D and video.** We would like to extend this work to three dimensions, allowing direct volumetric painting at arbitrary scales. We would also like to investigate the possibilities of multiresolution video, in which the temporal resolution of an animation might be varied to provide detailed slow-motion sequences, or to provide a low-bandwidth preview mechanism.

**Antialiasing and higher-order wavelets.** One drawback of the simple Haar-basis painting system described in this paper is that when the user zooms into an area where there is no further detail, the pixels of the lower-resolution image are displayed as large constant-colored squares. A number of possibilities exist for alleviating this problem. One approach would be to perform some kind of filtering on the displayed image so as to hide the pixel-replication artifacts; however, the inconsistency between the internal and external representations of the image that such an approach entails will likely be problematic. A more intriguing alternative is to extend the painting and compositing operations to higher-order wavelets, which might be used to achieve higher-order continuity across the image under any level of zooming. However, higher-order wavelets have a number of drawbacks as well. The supports of such wavelets are necessarily overlapping and larger than those of Haar wavelets, leading to a considerably more complex implementation, which is also likely to run at least an order of magnitude slower. More importantly, defining an accurate and basis-independent compositing operation appears to require that the wavelet basis be closed under products, which is not true of any higher-order wavelet basis of which we are aware. This requirement is discussed in more detail in Appendix A.

### Acknowledgements

We would like to thank Tony DeRose for helpful discussions during the development of these ideas. This work was supported by an NSF National Young Investigator award (CCR-9357790), by the University of Washington Graduate Research and Royalty Research Funds (75-1721 and 65-9731), by an Air Force Laboratory Graduate Fellowship, and by industrial gifts from Adobe, Aldus, and Xerox.

### References

[1] Charles K. Chui. *Wavelet Analysis and its Applications,* Volumes 1 and 2. Academic Press, Inc., San Diego, Califorinia, 1992.

[2] Ronald A. DeVore, Björn Jawerth, and Bradley J. Lucier. Image compression through wavelet transform coding. *IEEE Transactions on Information Theory*, 38(2):719–746, March 1992.

[3] Stephane Mallat and Sifen Zhong. Wavelet transform maxima and multiscale edges. In Ruskai et al., editor, *Wavelets and Their Applications*, pages 67–104. Jones and Bartlett Publishers, Inc., Boston, 1992.

[4] Philip Morrison, Phylis Morrison, and The Office of Charles and Ray Eames. *Powers of Ten.* Scientific American Library, New York, 1982.

[5] Ken Perlin and David Fox. Pad: An alternative approach to the user interface. Proceedings of SIGGRAPH 93 (Anaheim, California, August 1-6, 1993). In *Computer Graphics*, Annual Conference Series, 1993, pages 57–64.

[6] Ken Perlin and Luiz Velho. A wavelet representation for unbounded resolution painting. Technical report, New York University, November 1992.

[7] Thomas Porter and Tom Duff. Compositing digital images. Proceedings of SIGGRAPH '84 (Minneapolis, Minnesota, July 23–27, 1984). In *Computer Graphics* 18, 3 (July 1984), pages 253–259.

[8] David Salesin and Ronen Barzel. Two-bit graphics. *IEEE Computer Graphics and Applications*, 6:36–42, 1986.

[9] Brian E. Smits, James R. Arvo, and David H. Salesin. An importance-driven radiosity algorithm. Proceedings of SIGGRAPH '92 (Chicago, Illinois, July 26–31, 1992). In *Computer Graphics* 26, 2 (July 1992), pages 273–282.

## A  Deriving the equations

The multiresolution paint algorithm we have described is an application of *wavelets*, a mathematical tool that has found a wide variety of applications in recent years, including image processing and compression [1, 2, 3]. In this appendix, we briefly describe how our algorithm fits into the larger context of wavelets, and we show how the formulas of Section 2 can be derived.

Let $C^n$ be a matrix of size $2^n \times 2^n$ representing the pixel values of an image. We can associate with $C^n$ a function $\mathcal{I}^n(x, y)$ given by

$$\mathcal{I}^n(x, y) = \Phi^n(y) C^n \Phi^n(x)^{\mathrm{T}}$$

where $\Phi^n(x)$ is a row matrix of basis functions $[\phi_1^n(x), \ldots, \phi_{2^n}^n(x)]$, called *scaling functions*. In our application, we use the *Haar basis*, in which each scaling function $\phi_i^n(x)$ is given by

$$\phi_i^n(x) = \begin{cases} 1 & \text{for } 0 \leq 2^n x - i < 1 \\ 0 & \text{otherwise} \end{cases}$$

The wavelet transform allows us to decompose $C^n$ into a lower-resolution version $C^{n-1}$ and detail parts $D_1^{n-1}$, $D_2^{n-1}$, and $D_3^{n-1}$, using matrix multiplication as follows:

$$C^{n-1} = A^n C^n (A^n)^{\mathrm{T}} \tag{1}$$
$$D_1^{n-1} = A^n C^n (B^n)^{\mathrm{T}} \tag{2}$$
$$D_2^{n-1} = B^n C^n (A^n)^{\mathrm{T}} \tag{3}$$
$$D_3^{n-1} = B^n C^n (B^n)^{\mathrm{T}} \tag{4}$$

In the Haar basis, the matrices $A^n$ and $B^n$ are given by:

$$A^n = \begin{bmatrix} 1/2 & 1/2 & 0 & 0 & \cdots & & 0 \\ 0 & 0 & 1/2 & 1/2 & & & \\ \vdots & \vdots & & & \ddots & & \\ 0 & 0 & & & \cdots & 1/2 & 1/2 \end{bmatrix}$$

$$B^n = \begin{bmatrix} 1/2 & -1/2 & 0 & 0 & \cdots & & 0 \\ 0 & 0 & 1/2 & -1/2 & & & \\ \vdots & \vdots & & & \ddots & & \\ 0 & 0 & & & \cdots & 1/2 & -1/2 \end{bmatrix}$$

The detail coefficients $d_i$ at level $j$ in our algorithm are the entries of the $D_i^j$ matrix. Thus, equations (1)–(4) provide the expressions used in the *Decompose* routine.

The four decomposed pieces can also be put back together again, using two new matrices $P^n$ and $Q^n$:

$$\begin{aligned} C^n = {} & P^n C^{n-1} (P^n)^{\mathrm{T}} + P^n D_1^{n-1} (Q^n)^{\mathrm{T}} \\ & + Q^n D_2^{n-1} (P^n)^{\mathrm{T}} + Q^n D_3^{n-1} (Q^n)^{\mathrm{T}} \end{aligned}$$

This equation provides the expressions used in the *Display* routine. In the Haar basis, these matrices are given by $P^n = 2(A^n)^{\mathrm{T}}$ and $Q^n = 2(B^n)^{\mathrm{T}}$.

The original function $\mathcal{I}^n(x, y)$ can be expressed in terms of the lower-resolution pixel values $C^{n-1}$ and detail coefficients $D_i^{n-1}$ using a new set of basis functions $\Psi^j = [\psi_1^j(x), \ldots, \psi_m^j(x)]$, called *wavelets*, as follows:

$$\begin{aligned} \mathcal{I}^n(x, y) = {} & \Phi^{n-1}(y) C^{n-1} \Phi^{n-1}(x)^{\mathrm{T}} \tag{5} \\ & + \Phi^{n-1}(y) D_1^{n-1} \Psi^{n-1}(x)^{\mathrm{T}} \\ & + \Psi^{n-1}(y) D_2^{n-1} \Phi^{n-1}(x)^{\mathrm{T}} \\ & + \Psi^{n-1}(y) D_3^{n-1} \Psi^{n-1}(x)^{\mathrm{T}} \end{aligned}$$

In the Haar basis, there are $m = 2^j$ wavelets in $\Psi^j$, and each $\psi_i^j(x)$ is given by:

$$\psi_i^j(x) = \begin{cases} 1 & \text{for } 0 \leq 2^j x - i < 1/2 \\ -1 & \text{for } 1/2 \leq 2^j x - i < 1 \\ 0 & \text{otherwise} \end{cases}$$

Decomposing the first term $\Phi^{n-1}(y) C^{n-1} \Phi^{n-1}(x)^{\mathrm{T}}$ of equation (5) recursively allows us to represent a function $\mathcal{I}^n(x, y)$ in its *wavelet basis*, given by the row matrix

$$\begin{bmatrix} \Phi^0 & | & \Psi^0 & | & \cdots & | & \Psi^{n-1} \end{bmatrix}.$$

In order to derive the expressions used for compositing detail coefficients in the *Extrapolate* routine, we must begin by defining compositing operations on functions $\mathcal{F}$, $\mathcal{B}$, and $\mathcal{R}$, built from the pixel values $C_f$, $C_b$, and $C_r$ of the foreground, background, and result images:

$$\begin{aligned} \mathcal{F}^j(x, y) &= \Phi^j(y) C_f^j \Phi^j(x)^{\mathrm{T}} \\ \mathcal{B}^n(x, y) &= \Phi^n(y) C_b^n \Phi^n(x)^{\mathrm{T}} \\ \mathcal{R}^n(x, y) &= \Phi^n(y) C_r^n \Phi^n(x)^{\mathrm{T}} \end{aligned}$$

Note that the foreground image has its highest-resolution components in level $j$, the level at which the user is painting, whereas the background and resulting images have components in a potentially higher-resolution level $n$.

For example, the "over" operation can be defined on functions $\mathcal{F}$, $\mathcal{B}$, and $\mathcal{R}$ as follows:

$$\mathcal{R}^n(x, y) = \mathcal{F}^j(x, y) + (1 - \mathcal{F}^j.\alpha(x, y)) * \mathcal{B}^n(x, y)$$

The expressions for compositing detail coefficients can be derived by writing each function in its wavelet basis, multiplying out, and regrouping terms. The derivation is tedious, but the final expressions are quite simple, as the pseudocode for the *Extrapolate* routine attests.

Note that compositing multiresolution images, as defined here at least, requires taking products of basis functions. While the Haar basis is closed under products, we know of no other finite wavelet basis that has this property. Proving or disproving the existence of non-trivial finite wavelet bases that are closed under products is an interesting (and, as far as we know, open) theoretical question, which this research in compositing multiresolution images suggests.

(a) Mona Lisa.

(e) Close-up of leaves on a tree.

(i) A sunny day in the park.

(b) Adding makeup at higher resolution.

(f) Painting "in" with fall colors.

(j) Zooming out by a factor of 100,000.

(c) Zooming in a little closer for the glint.

(g) Painting "under" with sky and grass.

(k) Adding smog over Chicago.

(d) Mona ready to step out.

(h) Modified close-up view.

(l) Smog affects the park view.

Figure 1: Interactive multiresolution painting. (a)–(d): Adding makeup and a glint in the eye to Mona Lisa. (e)–(h): Painting "in" and "under" at low resolutions. (i)–(l): Adding smog to an image with a 100,000:1 range of scale.

# Computer-Generated Pen-and-Ink Illustration

*Georges Winkenbach*    *David H. Salesin*

Department of Computer Science and Engineering
University of Washington
Seattle, Washington 98195

## Abstract

This paper describes the principles of traditional pen-and-ink illustration, and shows how a great number of them can be implemented as part of an automated rendering system. It introduces "stroke textures," which can be used for achieving both texture and tone with line drawing. Stroke textures also allow resolution-dependent rendering, in which the choice of strokes used in an illustration is appropriately tied to the resolution of the target medium. We demonstrate these techniques using complex architectural models, including Frank Lloyd Wright's "Robie House."

**CR Categories and Subject Descriptors:** I.3.3 [Computer Graphics]: Picture/Image Generation; I.3.5 [Computer Graphics]: Three-Dimensional Graphics and Realism — Color, Shading, Shadowing, and Texture.

**Additional Key Words:** architectural rendering, comprehensible rendering, non-photorealistic rendering, prioritized stroke textures, resolution-dependent rendering, texture indication.

## 1   Introduction

Most of the research in computer graphics rendering over the last twenty years has been devoted to the problem of creating images of physical scenes with ever-increasing complexity and realism. The success of this research has been a well-heralded achievement in graphics.

However, the computer's ability to display images of ever-increasing complexity gives rise to a new problem: communicating this complex information in a comprehensible and effective manner. In order to communicate truly complex information effectively, some form of visual abstraction is required. This type of abstraction has been studied most comprehensively in the fields of graphic design and traditional illustration.

In this paper, we therefore examine algorithms for the "non-photorealistic" rendering of complex forms. While photorealistic images certainly have their place, in many applications, such as architectural and industrial design, a stylized illustration is often more effective.

The advantages of illustration are numerous. Illustrations can convey information better by omitting extraneous detail, by focusing attention on relevant features, by clarifying and simplifying shapes, or by exposing parts that are hidden. In addition, illustrations often consume less storage than realistic images, and are more easily reproduced and transmitted. Illustrations also provide a more natural

vehicle for conveying information at different levels of detail. Finally, in many applications, illustrations can add a sense of vitality difficult to capture with photorealism.

The benefits of illustrations over photographs are well-recognized in many practical contexts. For example, medical texts almost always employ hand-drawn illustrations in place of (or in addition to) photographs, since they allow tiny and hidden structures to be much better described. In addition, most assembly, maintenance, and repair manuals of mechanical hardware employ illustrations rather than photographs because of their clarity. For example, at Boeing, even when CAD databases of airplane parts exist, all high-quality manuals are still illustrated by hand in order to provide more effective diagrams than can be achieved with either photorealistic rendering or simple hidden line drawings [16].

To explore the use of abstraction as a means for conveying information effectively, it makes sense to begin with an area with well established conventions. For this reason, we are beginning our investigation using the domain of pen-and-ink illustrations of architectural forms, for which a great number of well-documented conventions already exist [5, 11, 13, 14, 17, 20]. Restricting the domain to "pen and ink" also has the advantage that no exotic display technology is required to view the algorithms' output: conventional laser printers, even the inexpensive 300 dots-per-inch variety, give quite reasonable results.

In the rest of this paper, we describe a number of principles of traditional pen-and-ink illustration, and we show how a great number of them can be implemented as part of an automated rendering system.

### 1.1   Related work

The area of "non-photorealistic rendering" has received relatively little attention in the computer graphics community. We survey most of the related work here.

Seligmann and Feiner have described methods for automatically constructing illustrations to achieve a particular communicative goal [24]. Their system is primarily concerned with the high-level goal of composing the best model for communicating a particular intent, whereas the system we describe is more concerned with the low-level details of rendering the model once it is built. Thus, our system could serve as a "back-end" for theirs.

With respect to the rendering of architectural forms, Yessios described a prototype "computer drafting" system for common materials in architectural designs, including stones, wood, plant, and ground materials [26], which, like our work, attempts to provide a warmer, hand-drawn appearance as opposed to a mechanical one. Miyata also gave a nice algorithm for automatically generating stone wall patterns [19]; these patterns would make a good starting point for some of the pen-and-ink techniques described in this paper.

With respect to line-drawing techniques, Appel et al. were the first to discuss how a line could be "haloed" automatically to give the appearance of one line passing behind another [2]. Kamada and Kawai generalized this work by showing how different line attributes, such as dashed and dotted line, could be used to give a more informative treatment of hidden lines [12]. Dooley and Cohen later introduced more line qualities, such as thickness, and discussed how the treatment of outline and surface shading could be customized by a user to create more effective illustrations [6, 7]. In the commercial realm, the Premisys Corporation markets a product called "Squiggle" that adds waviness and irregularities to CAD output as a post-process, lending a hand-drawn appearance to the drawings [21]. The Adobe Dimensions program allows PostScript stroke textures to be mapped onto surfaces in three dimensions [1].

The research described in this paper was most directly inspired by the work of Saito and Takahashi, who introduced the concept of a "G-buffer" for creating comprehensible renderings of 3D scenes [22]. Our work takes a somewhat different approach, in that it integrates aspects of 2D and 3D rendering, whereas their method essentially uses image processing techniques once the set of G-buffers are created. In addition, by introducing methods for texturing surfaces with strokes, the work in this paper extends the repertoire of the types of renderings that can be produced in a purely automated way.

In related works, our group is exploring several different aspects of the pen-and-ink illustration problem. This paper describes the overall vision of computer-generated illustration, surveys principles from traditional illustration, and shows how they can be incorporated into an automated system for rendering 3D models. A second paper discusses the issues of creating pen-and-ink illustrations interactively, with an emphasis on using 2D greyscale images as a starting point [23]; in this interactive work, the responsibility of producing an effective illustration is primarily the artist's. A third paper examines the issues involved in representing, editing, and rendering the individual strokes that are the building blocks of any line illustration system [8].

## 1.2 Overview

The rest of this paper is organized as follows. Section 2 surveys the principles of traditional pen-and-ink illustration. Section 3 discusses how these principles can be used to guide the design of an automated system for producing this type of imagery. Section 4 introduces "strokes" and "stroke textures," the building blocks of our system, and describes how they can be used to implement many of the traditional illustration principles. Section 5 discusses some of our results, and Section 6 lays out an agenda for future research in the area. Finally, the appendix gives details about the implementation.

## 2 Principles of pen-and-ink illustration

While pen-and-ink drawing has a long history, dating back to the illuminated manuscripts of the Middle Ages, it is only relatively "recently" — that is, since the end of the 19th century — that pen-and-ink illustration has been developed as an art form in and of itself.

Pen-and-ink illustration is a limiting medium. The pen gives off no color or tone, so both color and shading must be suggested by combinations of individual strokes. Furthermore, when rendered manually, it is very difficult and time-consuming with pen and ink to cover a large area with tone, and it is practically impossible to lighten a tone once it is drawn.

However, pen-and-ink illustrations have some particular qualities that make them especially attractive. First, they are ideal for out-

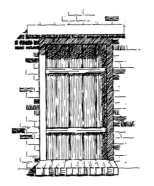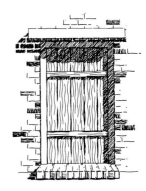

Figure 1: *Two doors. The lines of wood grain are drawn with an even pressure, while the lines between the planks use varying pressure. For wood grain, we typically use the waviness function of the left door, while that of the right door has been exaggerated.*

lines: each individual pen-and-ink stroke can be made expressive by employing small irregularities in its path and pressure. Second, pen and ink provide a real economy of expression in representing tones and texture: the character of a few small strokes can clearly indicate the difference between textures like smooth glass and old knotted wood.

In addition to these concrete advantages, pen-and-ink drawings by their very nature possess some special qualities that are difficult to capture in other media. Their simplicity provides an appealing crispness and directness. Finally, pen-and-ink illustrations blend nicely with text, due to their linear quality and their use of the same ink on the same paper, making them ideal for printed publications.

In the rest of this section, we survey some of the fundamental principles of illustrating in pen and ink. These principles are distilled primarily from Guptill's classic text, *Rendering in Pen and Ink* [11], and also from Lohan's *Pen&Ink Techniques* [17] and several other sources [5, 13, 14, 20]. While the field of pen-and-ink is too vast to allow a comprehensive treatment within the scope of this paper, the principles described here should be sufficient to motivate many of the design choices for a computer-graphics system. We organize our treatment into three parts: Strokes, Tone and texture, and Outline.

## 2.1 Strokes

In classical pen-and-ink illustration, a "stroke" is produced by placing the point, or "nib," of a pen in contact with the paper, and allowing the nib to trace out a path. The thickness of the stroke can be varied by varying the pressure on the nib.

Some principles of stroke-drawing are summarized below:

- *Too thin a stroke can give a washed-out appearance; too coarse can detract from the delicate details.*

- *It is frequently necessary to vary the pen position, with the nib sometimes turning as the stroke is drawn.*

- *Strokes must look natural, not mechanical. Even-weight line drawings appear lifeless; instead, the thickness of a line should vary along its length.*

- *Wavy lines are a good way to indicate that a drawing is schematic and not yet completely resolved.*

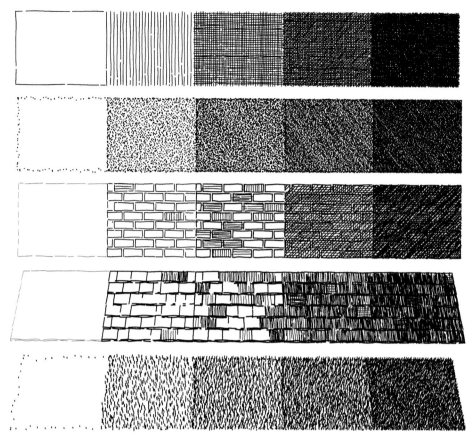

Figure 2: *Using strokes to indicate both texture and tone. The stroke textures used, from top to bottom, are: "cross-hatching," "stippling," "bricks," "shingles," and "grass." Notice how the outline style of the white areas is also particular to each texture.*

## 2.2 Tones and texture

The terms "value" and "tone" are used interchangeably to refer to the amount of visible light reflected toward the observer from a point on a surface. In traditional pen-and-ink illustration, it is impossible to portray the value of each surface precisely; instead, combinations of strokes are used to create an overall impression of the desired tone.

The tone achieved by a combination of strokes is a function of the ratio of black ink to white paper over a given region of the illustration. If the character of the strokes is varied, then the same strokes that are used to achieve a particular tone can also be used simultaneously to indicate the "texture" of the subject being rendered. This dual role of individual strokes to convey both tone and texture is part of the economy of pen-and-ink illustration.

Here are some of the principles of drawing tones and textures with pen-and-ink strokes:

- *Tones should be created from lines of roughly equal weight and spacing.*

- *It is not necessary to depict each individual tone accurately; however, presenting the correct arrangement of tones among adjacent regions is essential.*

- *To disambiguate objects, it is sometimes important to "force tone" by enhancing contrast or inventing shadows.*

- *The character of strokes is important for conveying texture, as well as geometry and lighting. For example:*

   - *Crisp, straight lines are good for "glass."*

   - *Horizontal surfaces should be hatched with predominantly horizontal lines.*

   - *Absence of detail altogether indicates glare.*

   - *A sketchy kind of line is good for "old" materials, while careful stippling is good for "new" materials.*

- *To lend economy to the illustration, it is important to utilize some form of "indication" for conveying the impression of a texture without drawing every single stroke. The method of indication should also be varied across the drawing to avoid monotony.*

## 2.3 Outlines

Realistic scenes contain no real outlines; instead, forms are defined by variations in texture and tone. However, outline is nevertheless a very natural means for portraying objects — for example, most children's drawings utilize outline almost exclusively.

The medium of pen and ink is ideal for creating outlines with an incredible range of expressiveness. The pen allows for outlines that change thickness, sometimes disappearing altogether. In addition, the character of the outline stroke can be a very powerful indicator of texture.

Outline strokes are used not only for the contours of an object, but also for delineating the essentials of its interior. For example, in an illustration of a leaf, the veins are typically rendered in outline, in addition to the contour.

Figure 3: *Creating the same texture and tone at different scales. At the smallest scale, the brick outline strokes are sufficient to build the tone. As the scale increases, the prioritized stroke texture automatically introduces shading inside the bricks to maintain the tone. The same technique applies to generating illustrations at the same scale but for different printer resolutions.*

Different styles of rendering use various combinations of outline and tone; all combinations are possible. Moreover, there exists an entire spectrum between outline and tone illustrations: as outline drawings become increasingly complex, they begin to take on more and more aspects of an illustration with tone.

Here are some of the important classical principles for drawing expressive outlines:

- *The quality of the outline stroke is important for conveying texture. For example, crisp straight lines are good for hard objects, while a greater variety of line quality is better for soft objects.*

- *Thick outlines are used to suggest shadows, or to bring one object or part of an object forward in the scene. Thick line junctions are used to suggest darkness where objects overlap and to add "snappiness" to the illustration.*

- *Outlines should become "haloed" and fade away where one object passes behind another object.*

- *Outlines must be introduced where tones are omitted to convey shape.*

- *Using "indication" for drawing outlines is just as important as for drawing tones.*

## 3 Computer-generated pen-and-ink illustration

Implementing these principles of pen-and-ink illustration as part of an automated system presents an interesting challenge. A reasonable starting point is to take the traditional "graphics rendering pipeline" for photorealistic imagery and see which parts, if any, need to be altered in order to support this style of non-photorealism.

We identified two fundamental differences:

1. *The dual nature of strokes.* In the traditional graphics pipeline, the renderings of texture and tone are completely independent. A texture is typically defined as a set of images assigned to each surface, which affect the shading parameters. Tone is produced by dimming or brightening the rendered shades, while leaving the texture invariant. However, for pen-and-ink illustration, the very same strokes that produce tone must also be used to convey texture. Thus, tone and texture must become more tightly linked in a system for producing this type of imagery.

2. *The need to combine 2D and 3D information.* In the traditional graphics pipeline, the information used for rendering is entirely three-dimensional, with the final projection to two dimensions

largely a matter of sampling the rendered shades. For pen-and-ink illustration, the 2D aspects of the particular projection used are every bit as essential as the 3D information for creating a proper rendering. The necessary 2D information takes a number of forms. First, the size of the projected areas must be used to compute the proper stroke density, in order to accommodate the dual nature of strokes described above. In addition, the 2D adjacencies of the projected geometry must also be used, since outlining depends on such issues as the type of junction between 2D boundaries (whether two adjacent regions in 2D are adjoining in 3D or passing one behind the other), and the level of contrast between tones of adjacent 2D regions.

Thus, our rendering system is a basic graphics pipeline with a few notable changes. The standard aspects of the pipeline include:

- *The model.* Any standard polygonal 3D model will do.

- *The assignment of texture.* Textures are assigned to 3D surfaces in the usual way. However, the textures are no longer described by images, but by "stroke textures," as discussed in the next section.

- *The lighting model.* Any standard illumination model can be employed to compute a "reference solution," which is then used as a target for tone production with strokes. We use the Phong model, which, although not physically-based, appears to be quite adequate for most non-photorealistic rendering.

- *The visible surface algorithm.* Any object-space or list-priority visible surface algorithm will do; we use BSP trees in our implementation.

- *Shadow algorithm.* The shadow algorithm must also use an object-space or list-priority method; we use Chin and Feiner's BSP tree shadow volumes [4].

Here are the notable differences from the standard pipeline:

- *Maintaining a 2D spatial subdivision.* The need to consider 2D adjacency information in rendering suggests the use of some form of spatial subdivision of the visible surfaces. We use a half-edge data structure for maintaining this planar map [18].

- *The rendering of texture and tone.* Polygons are no longer scan converted; instead, both texture and tone must be conveyed with some form of hatching. The stroke textures we define in the next section achieve this effect.

- *Clipping.* The strokes must be clipped to the regions they are texturing. Since so many strokes are drawn, the clipping must be extremely fast. In addition, in order to simulate a hand-drawn effect, the clipping should not be pixel-based — that is, it should not remove just those pixels of the stroke that are outside the clipping region — since this gives an unnatural, mechanical appearance. Instead, the clipping should be stroke-based, allowing a wavy stroke to sometimes stray slightly outside of the clipping region. To achieve this effect, we clip the straight-line paths of our strokes prior to adding in the function for waviness (see Section 4.1). For fast clipping, we use set operations on a 2D BSP tree representation of the planar map [25].

- *Outlining.* Outlines play a significant role in pen-and-ink illustration. Outlines come in two varieties. The "boundary outlines," which surround visible regions, must be drawn in a way that takes into account both the textures of the surrounded regions, and the adjacency information stored in the planar map. In addition, "interior outlines" are used within polygons to suggest shadow directions or give view-dependent accents to the stroke texture.

A brief description of the rendering process follows; more details about the rendering algorithm can be found in the appendix. To render a scene, the system begins by computing the visible surfaces and the shadow polygons. It then uses these polygons, projected to Normalized Device Coordinate (NDC) space, to build the 2D BSP tree and the planar map. Each visible surface is then rendered. The procedural texture attached to each surface is invoked to generate the strokes that convey the correct texture and tone for the surface. All the strokes are clipped to the visible portions of the surface using set operations on the 2D BSP tree. Finally, the outline strokes are drawn by extracting from the planar map all of the outline edges necessary for the illustration, as described in Section 4.3.

## 4 Strokes and stroke textures

In this section we discuss strokes and stroke textures, the essential building blocks of our system.

### 4.1 Strokes

In our system, all strokes are generated by moving a nib along a basic straight path. Character is added to the stroke by perturbing the path with a *waviness function* and by varying the pressure on the nib with a *pressure function*. Figure 1 demonstrates some of the effects that can be achieved with different waviness and pressure functions. A more detailed explanation of our strokes can be found in Appendix A.3.1.

### 4.2 Stroke textures

A *stroke texture* is a collection of strokes used to produce both texture and tone. We define a *prioritized stroke texture* as a set of strokes each with an associated priority. When rendering a prioritized stroke texture, all of the strokes of highest priority are drawn first; if the rendered tone is still too light, the next highest priority strokes are added, and so on, until the proper tone is achieved.

For our stroke textures, we assign different aspects of the texture different priority. For example, for a "brick" texture, the outlines of the individual brick elements have highest priority, the strokes for shading individual bricks have medium priority, and the hatching strokes that go over the entire surface have lowest priority. In the cross-hatching texture, vertical strokes have priority over horizontal strokes, which have priority over the various diagonal stroke directions. Figure 2 demonstrates several greyscales of tone produced using different procedural prioritized stroke textures, including "cross-hatching," "stipple," "brick," "shingle," and "grass." For

Figure 4: *The effect of changing view direction on outline strokes of a shingle texture. Notice how the vertical edges begin to disappear as the texture is viewed from a more edge-on direction.*

each texture, the relative priorities of the strokes can be seen from the collection of strokes used to achieve a particular value of grey. More details about the procedural methods for our stroke textures are given in Appendices A.3.2 and A.3.3.

Although not explored in this paper, the idea of prioritized stroke textures is general enough to support many kinds of non-procedurally generated textures as well, such as textures drawn directly by an artist, or strokes produced through edge extraction from a greyscale image. These kinds of non-procedural stroke textures are explored in more detail by Salisbury et al. [23].

### 4.2.1 Resolution dependence

A common problem with the figures created by existing computer drawing programs is that they do not scale well when printed at different sizes or resolutions. Enlargement is typically performed either by pixel replication, which yields ugly aliasing artifacts, or by drawing the same strokes at higher resolution, which yields thinner strokes and an overall lighter illustration. Reduction is almost always performed by scan-converting the same curves at a lower resolution, often yielding a large black mass of overlapping strokes. Printing speed is also a common problem with illustration reduction, since the same number of strokes needs to be transmitted to and rendered by the printer, even when a smaller number of strokes would have sufficed (and actually have been preferable from an aesthetic standpoint, as well).

The prioritized stroke textures described here do not suffer from these problems. Strokes are chosen to provide the proper texture and tone for a given illustration size and printer resolution, as demonstrated in Figure 3. Note that for smaller images or coarser resolutions, fewer strokes are required, improving printing efficiency. Efficiency can be improved still further by rendering a simplified approximate version of each stroke, accurate to within one printer pixel [8].

### 4.2.2 Indication

As discussed in the principles of texture generation, it is important to suggest texture without drawing every last stroke. This principle of "indication" lends economy to an illustration. It also makes an illustration more powerful by engaging the imagination of the viewer rather than revealing everything.

Indication is one of the most notoriously difficult techniques for the pen-and-ink student to master. It requires putting just enough detail in just the right places, and also fading the detail out into the unornamented parts of the surface in a subtle and unobtrusive way.

Clearly, a purely automated method for artistically placing indication is a challenging research project.

We therefore decided to compromise and implement a semi-automated method, whereby the user specifies at a very high level where detail should appear in the drawing, and indication is used everywhere else. For easy specification of the areas of detail, we borrowed the idea of using "fields" generated by line segments from the morphing paper of Beier and Neely [3]. The user interactively places "detail segments" on the image to indicate where detail should appear. Each segment is projected and attached to the texture of the 3D surface for which indication is being designed.

A field $w(x, y)$ is generated by the detail segment $\ell$ at a point $(x, y)$ in texture space according to

$$w(x, y) = (a + b * distance((x, y), \ell))^{-c}$$

where $a$, $b$, and $c$ are non-negative constants that can be used to change the effect of the field. When several detail segments are present, we define the field at a point $(x, y)$ to be that of the closest segment. So as not to create patterns that are too regular, the field $w(x, y)$ is perturbed by a small random value. Textures such as "bricks" and "shingles" evaluate the strength of the field of indication at the center of each brick or shingle element. The set of strokes for that element is generated only if the indication field is above some preset threshold.

This approach seems to give reasonable results, as demonstrated in Figures 6 and 9. Figure 5 shows the detail segments that were used to generate Figure 6.

### 4.3 Outline

As described in Section 3, outlines come in two varieties: *boundary* and *interior* outlines. The *boundary outlines* surround the visible polygons of the image, and must be drawn in a way that takes into account both the textures of the surrounded regions, and the adjacency information stored in the planar map. The *interior outlines* are used within polygons to suggest shadow directions or to give view-dependent accents to the stroke texture.

In our implementation we have tried to address many of the principles for the effective use of these two types of outline, as described below.

**Expressing texture with outline.** Each stroke texture $T$ has associated with it a *boundary outline texture*, which is used whenever the outline of a polygon textured with $T$ is rendered. The boundary outline textures for some of our procedural textures are demonstrated in the white squares of Figure 2. These boundary outline textures are also displayed with and without their accompanying stroke textures in the illustrations of Figure 7.

**Minimizing outline.** Let $E$ be an edge that is shared by two faces $F$ and $G$ of a planar subdivision. Our rendering algorithm draws $E$ only if the tones of face $F$ and $G$ are not sufficiently different for the two faces to be easily disambiguated by their shading alone. In this sense, we minimize the use of boundary outline strokes. When a boundary outline stroke *is* drawn, it must be rendered according to the boundary outline texture for one of the two faces $F$ or $G$. We choose the texture of the face of the planar subdivision that represents a polygon closer to the viewer. Figure 8 demonstrates how outline is omitted in the presence of sharp changes in tone, and added in the absence of tone changes.

**Accented outlines for shadowing and relief.** "Accenting," or thickening, outline edges is a technique for providing subtle but important cues about the three-dimensional aspects of an illustrated scene. In

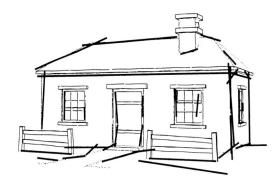

Figure 5: *Detail segments. The user interactively attaches "detail segments" to the surfaces to indicate roughly where details should appear.*

our implementation, the interior outlines of each brick in the "brick" stroke texture are drawn according to their relationship with the direction of the light source: brick edges that cast shadows are rendered with thickened edges, while illuminated brick edges are not drawn at all. Figure 10 demonstrates this effect.

**Dependence of viewing direction.** In addition to the light source direction, the viewing direction is another important parameter that should be taken into account when drawing outline strokes. For example, consider a roof of shingles. Viewed from above, all edges between individual shingles are clearly visible; viewed from more to the side, however, the shingles tend to blend together, and vertical edges begin to disappear, leaving the horizontal edges predominant. This effect is demonstrated in Figure 4. To implement this effect, each stroke texture is outfitted with a very simplified "anisotropic bidirectional reflectance distribution function" (BRDF), to borrow a term from radiometry, which describes its outline features in terms of both the lighting and viewing directions.

## 5 Results

Our computer-generated pen-and-ink illustration system was used to create all the figures in this paper. The system was developed on a Macintosh Quadra 700 using ThinkC.

The only input to the program is the scene geometry, including texture assignments for each surface, and some field lines for specifying the "indication."

We also used the system to generate an image of the top two floors of Frank Lloyd Wright's "Robie House," as shown in Figure 9. The model consist of 1043 polygons. It took 30 minutes to compute and print the image. Of this time, 22 minutes were devoted to computing the planar map from the input geometry, and 8 minutes were required for actually rendering the image at 600 dots per inch.

## 6 Summary and future work

This paper does not propose any radically new algorithms or present any complex mathematics. However, we feel it nevertheless provides a number of contributions to the computer graphics community. These contributions include:

- Surveying established principles from traditional illustration that can be used for communicating visual information effectively.

- Showing that a large number of these principles can be incorporated as part of an automated rendering system, and that the

Figure 6: *Indicating texture. The left house is drawn using "indication"; the right house is not.*

information present for driving the ordinary graphics pipeline is in many respects also sufficient for achieving important non-photorealistic effects.

- Introducing the concept of a "prioritized stroke texture," a general framework for creating textures from strokes, and providing a methodology for building procedural versions of these textures.

- Allowing a form of resolution-dependent rendering, in which the choice of strokes used in an illustration is appropriately tied to the resolution of the target medium.

However, the work described in this paper is just one early step in the exploration of automated non-photorealistic rendering algorithms. There are many ways to extend this work, including:

- Improving the procedural stroke textures, and automating further our methods for creating them.

- Incorporating other illustration effects, such as exploded, cut-away, and peel-back views, for showing parts that are hidden.

- Adding more interactive controls to help in designing 3D illustrations. Also, experimenting with very high-level controls—for

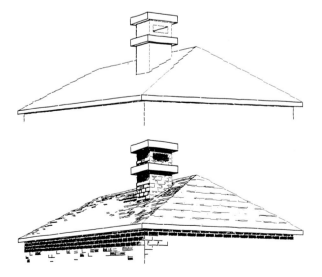

Figure 7: *Indicating texture through outline. Notice how different textures are delineated with different styles of boundary outlines. The upper and lower illustrations are the same, except that all but the boundary outline textures have been removed in the upper illustration to present the different styles more clearly.*

example, a control to add emphasis to parts of an illustration, which would work by automatically accentuating and suppressing detail over different parts of the image.

- Rendering other natural forms that appear in architectural drawings (and for which established conventions also exist), such as trees, grass, water, human figures, etc.

- Rendering other types of databases besides architectural models, such as databases of mechanical parts. Also, applying traditional illustration techniques and principles to databases that are not inherently visual in nature, such as flow simulations or higher-dimensional datasets. (This variety of rendering could be thought of as a form of scientific visualization.)

- Creating animations. Because our system uses randomness profusely, issues in frame-to-frame coherence arise. For instance, large features that are random, such as the selection of bricks that are shaded, should not vary from frame to frame. However, more subtle features, such as the waviness of strokes used to give the hand-drawn appearance, should be allowed to waver [15].

- Exploring other forms of illustration besides pen-and-ink, including traditional forms like watercolor and air brushing, as well as new methods of conveying information visually that may not necessarily mimic traditional forms.

## Acknowledgments

We wish to thank Tony DeRose for many helpful ideas along the way. Thanks also to Dan Ambrosi who advised us on illustration techniques and who also suggested the "Robie House" as a model. We are also grateful to Taweewan Winkenbach who spent many hours building the model for the "Robie House".

This work was supported by NSF Presidential and National Young Investigator awards (CCR-8957323 and CCR-9357790), by the University of Washington Graduate Research and Royalty Research Funds (75-1721 and 65-9731), and by industrial gifts from Adobe, Aldus, and Xerox.

## References

[1] Adobe Systems Incorporated, Mountain View. *Adobe Dimensions*, 1992.

[2] Arthur Appel, F. James Rohlf, and Arthur J. Stein. The haloed line effect for hidden line elimination. Proceedings of SIGGRAPH '79 (Chicago, Illinois, August 8-10, 1979. In *Computer Graphics* 13, 2 (August 1979), 151–157.

Figure 8: *Outline minimization. Notice how the boundary edges on the vertical and horizontal dividers between the panes appear only where contrast with the adjacent surface is low. (These boundary outlines are also omitted when they face the light source.)*

[3] Thaddeus Beier and Shawn Neely. Feature-based image metamorphosis. Proceedings of SIGGRAPH '92 (Chicago, Illinois, July 26-31, 1992). In *Computer Graphics* 26, 2 (July 1992), 35–42.

[4] Norman Chin and Steven Feiner. Near real-time shadow generation using BSP trees. Proceedings of SIGGRAPH '89 (Boston, Massachusetts, July 31 - August 4, 1989). In *Computer Graphics* 23, 3 (July 1989), 99–106.

[5] Frank Ching. *Architectural Graphics*. Van Nostrand Reinhold Company, New York, 1975.

[6] Debra Dooley and Michael F. Cohen. Automatic illustration of 3D geometric models: Lines. *Computer Graphics*, 24(2):77–82, March 1990.

[7] Debra Dooley and Michael F. Cohen. Automatic illustration of 3D geometric models: Surfaces. In *Proceedings of Visualization '90*, pages 307–314, October 1990.

[8] Adam Finkelstein and David H. Salesin. Multiresolution curves. Proceedings of SIGGRAPH 94 (Orlando, Florida, July 24-29, 1994). In *Computer Graphics*, Annual Conference Series, 1994.

[9] H. Fuchs, Z. M. Kedem, and B. F. Naylor. On visible surface generation by a priori tree structures. Proceedings of SIGGRAPH '80 (Seattle, Washington, July 14-18, 1980). In *Computer Graphics* 14, 3 (July 1980), 124–133.

[10] Leonidas Guibas, Lyle Ramshaw, and Jorge Stolfi. A kinetic framework for computational geometry. In *Proceedings of the 24th IEEE Annual Symposium on Foundations of Computer Science*, pages 100–111, 1983.

[11] Arthur Leighton Guptill. *Rendering in Pen and Ink*. Watson-Guptill Publications, New York, 1976.

[12] Tomihisa Kamada and Saturo Kawai. An enhanced treatment of hidden lines. *ACM Transaction on Graphics*, 6(4):308–323, October 1987.

[13] Stephen Klitment. *Architectural Sketching and Rendering: Techniques for Designers and Artists*. Whitney Library of Design, New York, 1984.

[14] Paul Laseau. *Architectural Drawing: Options for Design*. Design Press, New York, 1991.

[15] John Lasseter. Personal communication, January 1994. Pixar, Richmond, California.

[16] John Lewis. Personal communication, November 1993. Boeing Computer Services, Seattle, Washington.

[17] Frank Lohan. *Pen and Ink Techniques*. Contemporary Books, Inc., Chicago, 1978.

[18] Martti Mäntylä. *An Introduction to Solid Modeling*. Computer Science Press, Rockville, Maryland 20850, 1988.

[19] Kazunori Miyata. A method of generating stone wall patterns. Proceedings of SIGGRAPH '90 (Dallas, Texas, August 6-10, 1990). In *Computer Graphics* 24, 4 (August 1990), 387–394.

[20] Tom Porter and Sue Goodman. *Manual of Graphic Techniques 4*. Charles Scribner's Sons, New York, 1985.

[21] The Premisys Corporation, Chicago. *Squiggle*, 1993.

[22] Takafumi Saito and Tokiichiro Takahashi. Comprehensible rendering of 3D shapes. Proceedings of SIGGRAPH '90 (Dallas, Texas, August 6-10, 1990). In *Computer Graphics* 24, 4 (August 1990), 197–206.

[23] Michael P. Salisbury, Sean E. Anderson, Ronen Barzel, and David H. Salesin. Interactive pen-and-ink illustration. Proceedings of SIGGRAPH 94 (Orlando, Florida, July 24-29, 1994). In *Computer Graphics*, Annual Conference Series, 1994.

[24] Dorée Duncan Seligmann and Steven Feiner. Automated generation of intent-based 3D illustration. Proceedings of SIGGRAPH '91 (Las Vegas, Nevada, July 28 - August 2, 1991). In *Computer Graphics* 25, 4 (July 1991), 123–132.

[25] William C. Thibault and Bruce F. Naylor. Set operations on polyhedra using binary space partitioning trees. Proceedings of SIGGRAPH '87 (Anaheim, California, July 27-31, 1987). In *Computer Graphics* 21, 4 (July 1987), 153–162.

[26] Chris I. Yessios. Computer drafting of stones, wood, plant, and ground materials. Proceedings of SIGGRAPH '79 (Chicago, Illinois, August 8-10, 1979). In *Computer Graphics* 13, 2 (August 1979), 190–198.

## A  Implementation Details

### A.1  Overview

Three main global data structures are used by our system:

- *The model $M$.* The model is stored as a collection of polygons in three-space. For convenience, concave polygons and polygons with holes are decomposed into convex polygons.

- BspTree. The 2D BSP tree [25] is a representation of the visible polygons projected to Normalized Device Coordinates (NDC) space. It is used for fast clipping of strokes.

- PlanarMap. The planar map [18] is a partition of the NDC plane into *vertices*, *edges*, and *faces*, according to the NDC projections of the visible polygons. It is used to generate the outline strokes of the surfaces.

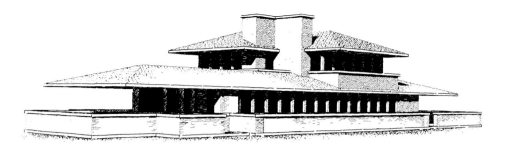

Figure 9: *Frank Lloyd Wright's "Robie House."*

The rendering process is structured as follows:

**procedure** *RenderScene(M)*:
    (*BspTree, PlanarMap*) ← *VisibleSurfaces(M)*
    **for** each visible surface $S \in M$ **do**
        *Strokes* ← *Texture(S, Tone(S))*
        **for** each stroke $s \in$ *Strokes* **do**
            *Render(ClippedStroke(s, BspTree))*
        **end for**
        *Render(ConstructMinimalOutline(S, PlanarMap))*
**end procedure**

The following sections describe the individual stages of the rendering process in more detail.

## A.2  Computing the visible surfaces

We use a 3D BSP tree to compute visibilities [9], and Chin and Feiner's shadow volumes [4] to compute the shadow polygons. The result is a set of convex polygons that can easily be ordered in depth with respect to the view point. To build the 2D BSP tree, the visible polygons are examined in front-to-back order. Each polygon is first projected to NDC space, and then inserted into the 2D BSP tree. The insertion into the 2D BSP tree is equivalent to the set union operation described by Thibault and Naylor [25], except that "in" leaf nodes carry an additional pointer back to the 3D polygon from which they originate. As such, the 2D BSP tree forms a partition of NDC space, with each cell in the partition corresponding either to a unique frontmost polygon in the 3D scene, or to the background.

The planar map data structure is computed with the help of the 2D BSP tree. We begin by inserting a single rectangular region, representing the entire drawing surface in NDC space, into the tree. As each node of the tree is traversed, the original region is partitioned into smaller and smaller faces in each branch of the tree. Faces reaching an "out" leaf node are tagged as background faces. Faces reaching an "in" leaf node receive a pointer to the corresponding 3D polygon in $M$. The BSP tree node also receives a pointer to the planar map face. Because of numerical inaccuracies, it is possible that some leaf nodes in the BSP tree never receive a matching face in the planar map. During clipping, a segment that falls in a leaf node having no planar map pointer is simply discarded. Because such nodes correspond to extremely thin regions, no visible artifacts result.

Geometrically, the planar map and the BSP tree are redundant: they encode the same 2D partition. However, the two data structures are amenable to different tasks. The BSP tree is efficient for clipping strokes through set operations, but does not readily allow searching among neighboring polygons. By contrast, the planar map encodes polygon adjacencies, but does not lend itself as well to clipping.

## A.3  Rendering the textures

### A.3.1  Individual strokes

A *stroke* $S$ consists of three parts:

- a *path* $P(u) : [0, 1] \rightarrow \mathbb{R}^2$, giving the overall "sweep" of the stroke, as a function of the parameter $u$.

- a *nib* $\mathcal{N}(p)$, defining the cross-sectional "footprint" of the stroke, as a function of the pressure $p$ on the nib.

- a *character function* $C(u) = (C_w(u), C_p(u))$, describing the *waviness* of the curve $C_w(u)$ (how the curve departs from its path) and the pressure $C_p(u)$ on the nib.

The stroke $S$ is defined as all pixels in the region

$$\mathcal{S} = (P(u) + C_w(u)) * \mathcal{N}(C_p(u))$$

where $*$ denotes the convolution of two parameterized point sets $A(u)$ and $B(u)$ of the Cartesian plane $\mathbb{R}^2$. This convolution is defined as [10]:

$$A(u) * B(u) = \bigcup_{u \in [0,1]} \{a + b \,|\, a \in A(u) \wedge b \in B(u)\}.$$

A stroke $S$ is rendered by scan-converting the path (after waviness is added) and stamping a copy of the nib, scaled by the pressure value, in place of drawing each pixel. Note that more efficient scan-conversion methods undoubtedly exist. Indeed, the investigation of a good representation for individual strokes, including their overall sweep and character functions, is a sizable research topic in and of itself [8].

All strokes are drawn by a C++ object named *InkPen*. An *InkPen* is in turn composed of three objects: a *Nib*, a *WavinessFunction*, and a *PressureFunction*. Different pens can be created by assembling various combinations of these components. So far, we have only used circular nibs of variable radius, and a sine-wave waviness function with randomly perturbed amplitude and wavelength. Two kinds of pressure functions are used throughout the images in this paper: a simple "broken-line" function that lifts the pen off the paper with some randomness, and a random sine wave function that creates strokes of varying thickness. Although our implementation does not allow for all the generality of real pen and ink as described in Section 2.1, the limited set of functions we have implemented still allows for a fairly wide range of expressiveness.

An *InkPen* supports methods to: scale the nib size; query the amount of ink deposited between two points when using a particular nib size; and draw a stroke between two points to achieve a particular darkness, in which case the darkness of the stroke will be appropriately modulated by the *PressureFunction* of the pen.

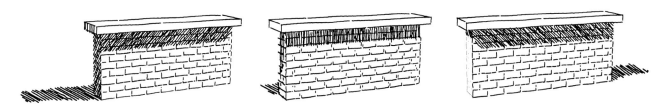

Figure 10: *Illuminated bricks. Notice how the thickened edges change to follow the shadow direction.*

### A.3.2   Building tone from strokes

The first step in building tone is to compute a reference shade $v \in [0 = white, 1 = black]$; we use a simple Phong model in our implementation. A procedural stroke texture is then used to produce a set of strokes that together achieve the target grey value $v$. As a simple example, to achieve a tone $v$ over an area $A$ using a nib of width $w$ with non-overlapping strokes requires drawing strokes of total length $vA/w$.

To compute tone accurately, it is also important to take into account the overlap between strokes that cross each other. Assuming uncorrelated overlap between the strokes of each non-overlapping set seems to work well. For example, for bidirectional hatching, suppose that the strokes in each hatching direction deposit a quantity of ink $x$ on the paper. Then the total ink in the cross-hatched area is given by the sum of the ink from the strokes in each direction $2x$, minus the quantity of ink that is deposited in the same place twice, which, assuming uncorrelated strokes, can be approximated by $x^2$. Thus, in order to achieve a value $v$, we use enough strokes in each direction to achieve a value $x$ that satisfies the quadratic equation $2x - x^2 = v$. The correct level for each set is therefore given by $x = 1 - \sqrt{1-v}$. This expression is used, for example, by the "cross-hatching" texture to achieve the right tone when two different directions of hatching are crossed (Figure 2).

### A.3.3   Stroke textures

To draw more complex textures, we use procedural prioritized stroke textures, as described in Section 4. In this section, we examine the "brick" texture in some detail. The description in this section can readily be extended to other types of stroke textures.

The "brick" texture builds tone out of three sets of strokes: the brick outlines; shading strokes within the bricks; and hatching strokes layered over the whole surface. Each set of strokes is associated with a different *InkPen*.

The rendering process for "brick" textures is summarized below:

**procedure** *RenderBrickTexture(TargetTone, Polygon3D)*
   *Layout* ← *GenerateBricks(Polygon3D, BrickSizes)*
   **for** each brick $B \in Layout$ **do**
      *DrawBrickOutline(B, TargetTone, ViewPoint, Lights)*
      **if** the tone of $B$ is too light **then**
         *ShadeWithinBrick(B, TargetTone)*
      **end if**
   **end for**
   **if** the overall tone is still too light **then**
      *HatchOver(Layout, TargetTone)*
   **end if**
**end procedure**

The brick outlines are generated from a simple layout that is computed on the fly in texture space and then projected into device space

before drawing takes place.

The width of the nib used to draw the outline strokes is scaled according to the tone being rendered: darker tones use the default nib size; for lighter tones, the nib size is scaled down. The same nib size is used for all the bricks in order to achieve a consistent result over the entire surface. The darkness of each stroke is then adjusted so as to take the BRDF and shadow edge effects into account, as described in Section 4.3. The darkness of the strokes may be further reduced, for example, when the area of the bricks becomes smaller due to perspective forshortening.

Let $T_o$ be the tone created by the outline strokes for a given brick $B$. We estimate $T_o$ by taking the sum of the amount of ink deposited by each outline stroke and dividing it by the area covered by the brick on the paper, as discussed in Appendix A.3.2. If $T_o$ is not dark enough to achieve the desired tone, then the interior of the brick is shaded. The darkness of each brick is limited by a constant $T_s$. Rather than shading every brick with the same tone $T = TargetTone - T_o$, we instead shade each brick with probability $\min\{1, T/T_s\}$. If the brick is shaded, enough strokes are used to achieve a tone $T_s$, with some randomness added.

If the shaded bricks still do not achieve the target tone, that is, if $T_o + T_s < TargetTone$, then additional hatching is used over the top of all the bricks. For these hatch lines, we use the method described in Appendix A.3.2 to take into account the overlap between strokes.

### A.3.4   Clipping strokes

The strokes must be clipped to the visible regions they texture. The 2D BSP tree data structure is used for this purpose. The path of each stroke is "pushed" down the BSP tree until it reaches one or more leaf nodes. Only the portions of the path that reach nodes belonging to the region being textured are rendered. Other clipping conditions can also be used. For instance, hatching shadow areas is handled by generating strokes over the entire surface and clipping them to the regions in shadow.

### A.3.5   Constructing the outline strokes

The outlines of visible surfaces are extracted by traversing the set of edges stored in the planar map. As described in Section 4.3, these outline edges are rendered only when the tones on either side of the edge are very similar, and when the edges themselves are not directly illuminated by the light source. Testing the tones of adjacent faces is easily accomplished by searching in the planar map.

# Interactive Pen-and-Ink Illustration

*Michael P. Salisbury    Sean E. Anderson    Ronen Barzel*    David H. Salesin*

Department of Computer Science and Engineering
University of Washington
Seattle, Washington 98195

*Pixar
1001 West Cutting Blvd
Richmond, California 94804

## Abstract

We present an interactive system for creating pen-and-ink illustrations. The system uses *stroke textures*—collections of strokes arranged in different patterns—to generate texture and tone. The user "paints" with a desired stroke texture to achieve a desired tone, and the computer draws all of the individual strokes.

The system includes support for using scanned or rendered images for reference to provide the user with guides for outline and tone. By following these guides closely, the illustration system can be used for interactive digital halftoning, in which stroke textures are applied to convey details that would otherwise be lost in this black-and-white medium.

By removing the burden of placing individual strokes from the user, the illustration system makes it possible to create fine stroke work with a purely mouse-based interface. Thus, this approach holds promise for bringing high-quality black-and-white illustration to the world of personal computing and desktop publishing.

**CR Categories and Subject Descriptors:** I.3.2 [Computer Graphics]: Picture/Image Generation - Display algorithms; I.3.6 [Computer Graphics]: Methodology and Techniques - Interaction techniques; I.4.3 [Image Processing]: Enhancement.

**Additional Key Words:** Comprehensible rendering, non-photorealistic rendering, prioritized stroke textures.

## 1   Introduction

Pen-and-ink is an extremely limited medium, allowing only individual monochromatic strokes of the pen. However, despite the limitations of the medium, beautiful pen-and-ink illustrations incorporating a wealth of textures, tones, and styles can be created by skilled artists. Indeed, partly because of their simplicity and economy, pen-and-ink illustrations are widely used in textbooks, repair manuals, advertising, and many other forms of printed media.

Part of the appeal and utility of pen-and-ink illustrations is that they can be easily printed alongside text, using the same ink on the same paper, without any degradation. For the same reasons, pen-and-ink-style illustrations could also be useful in the domain of desktop publishing and laser printers—especially if the illustrations were generated and manipulated directly on a computer.

While the problem of painting full-color images on a computer has received considerable attention in the computer graphics community, the requirements of an interactive pen-and-ink-style illustration system are different enough to merit special study. Pen-and-ink illustrations have two major properties that distinguish them from other art media:

1. *Every stroke contributes both tone (darkness) and texture.* Since tone and texture are not independent parameters, the pen artist must take care to convey both of these qualities simultaneously.

2. *Strokes work collectively.* In general, no single stroke is of critical importance; instead, strokes work together to express tone and texture.

This paper describes an interactive pen-and-ink-style illustration system. The overall goal of the system is to enable a user to easily generate effective and attractive illustrations directly on a computer. In this work, we are not concerned with creating purely computer-generated images; rather, the computer is utilized as a tool to enhance the speed and ease with which a user can create illustrations.

The interactive illustration system allows a variety of texturing in order to achieve the same range of style and expressive ability that is possible with a physical pen and ink. We do not want to limit the user to any specific algorithmic "look."

The system places a particular emphasis on using continuous-tone images as a reference for the user, and thus provides a form of "interactive digital halftoning" in which the user can introduce texture as an integral part of the resulting illustration. In this sense, the visual artifacts that are necessarily produced in quantizing a greyscale image can be given an artistic or expressive nature. Also, of practical significance, photocopying does not degrade pen-and-ink-style images to the same extent as conventionally-halftoned images.

### 1.1   Background: Pen-and-ink illustration

We give here a brief description of some of the salient features and terminology of hand-drawn pen illustration, relevant to the design of an interactive system. For further discussion and instruction, interested readers should consult Guptill [6], a comprehensive text on pen and ink illustration. In addition, Simmons [16] provides instruction on illustrating using a "technical pen," which draws strokes of constant width. Both books contain dozens of stunning examples. A discussion of pen-and-ink principles as they relate to purely computer-generated imagery can be found in Winkenbach et al. [20].

Because texture in an illustration is the collective result of many pen strokes, each individual stroke is not critical and need not be drawn precisely. Indeed, a certain amount of irregularity in each stroke is desirable to keep the resulting texture from appearing too rigid or mechanical.

The most commonly used textures include: *hatching*, formed by roughly parallel lines; *cross-hatching*, formed by overlapped hatching in several directions; and *stippling*, formed by small dots or very short lines. Textures can also be wavy, scribbly, or geometric and can appear hard or soft, mechanical or organic.

The perceived grey level or *tone* in an illustration depends largely on how dense the strokes are in a region (just like the dots in a dithered halftone image). Although grey-level ramps can be achieved by judiciously increasing stroke density, fine-art illustrations typically emphasize contrast between adjacent regions, and often employ a very limited number of distinct grey levels.

Shapes in an illustration can be defined by *outline* strokes. These strokes are exceptional in that they may be long and individually significant. Often the outline is left implicit by a change in tone or texture. The choice of whether or not to use outlines is largely an aesthetic one, made by the artist, and used to achieve a particular effect. For example, explicit outlines are typically used for hard surfaces, while implied outlines generally convey a softer or more organic object.

Producing fine-art-quality, hand-drawn pen-and-ink illustrations requires a great deal of creativity and artistic ability. In addition, it requires a great deal of technical skill and patience. A real pen and ink have no undo!

## 1.2 Related work

Most of the published work on "digital painting" is concerned with the problem of emulating traditional artists' tools. Only a few of these works take an approach similar to ours of creating higher-level interactive tools that can produce the same results as their predecessors: Lewis [10] describes brushes that lay down textured paint; Haeberli [7] shows how scanned or rendered image information can be used as a starting point for "painting by numbers;" and Haeberli and Segal [8] use hardware texture-mapping for painting and also mention 3D halftoning effects.

Considerable work has also been done for creating black-and-white illustrations, generally for engineering or graphical design work. The earliest such system was Sutherland's "Sketchpad" [18]. Gangnet et al. [5] use planar decomposition to manipulate and clip geometric objects. Pavlidis [11] provides a method for "cleaning up" schematic drawings by removing hand-drawn irregularities. Quite the opposite (and more along the lines of our work), the Premisys Corporation markets a commercial product, "Squiggle," [13] that adds waviness and irregularities to CAD output to augment lines with extra information and to make the results appear more hand-drawn. Saito and Takahashi [14] produce automated black-and-white illustrations of 3D objects.

Our research group is exploring several different aspects of the pen-and-ink illustration problem. This paper discusses the issues of interactively creating pen-and-ink illustrations, with an emphasis on using 2D greyscale images as a starting point. A second paper shows how principles of illustration can be incorporated into an automated system for rendering 3D models [20]. A third paper examines the issues involved in representing, editing, and rendering the individual strokes that are the building blocks of any line illustration system [4].

Figure 1: *A closeup view of several individual pen strokes, with various amounts of curve and waviness.*

## 1.3 Overview

The next section discusses the overall design of our system, as well as its individual capabilities and features. Section 3 presents some example illustrations and describes our experience with using the system. Section 4 suggests directions for future research. The primary data structures and algorithms of our prototype implementation are outlined in appendix A.

## 2 The Illustration System

Full-color paint systems often support direct simulations of traditional artist tools, such as brushes and paint [3, 17]. However, for our application, there is little purpose in providing the user with a simulated "ink pen" to draw the pen strokes, for several reasons:

- A mouse-based interface does not support the fine control needed for detailed stroke work.

- The strokes of an illustration are not of great individual importance.

- Drawing individual strokes is tedious, and we would like our system to reduce much of that tedium.

Thus, rather than focus on the individual strokes, the system tries to directly support the higher-level cumulative effect that the strokes can achieve: texture, tone, and shape. The user "paints" using textures and tones, and the computer draws the individual strokes.

The illustration system cannot completely ignore individual strokes, however. Outlines are the most notable example of strokes that have individual significance; in addition, an artist might occasionally need to touch up fine details of textured work. Therefore, the system also allows users to draw individual strokes and provides controls for modifying stroke character through smoothing and through the substitution of various stroke styles [4].

To further aid users in creating illustrations, the system allows scanned, rendered, or painted images to be used as a reference for tone and shape. The system also supports edge extraction from images, which is useful for outlining. Finally, a range of editing capabilities is supported so that users are free to experiment or make mistakes.

The following sections discuss the capabilities and workings of the system in greater detail.

### 2.1 Strokes

It is important that the strokes automatically generated by the system be irregular. Uneven strokes make an illustration look softer, more natural, and hand-drawn, whereas regular strokes introduce mechanical-looking texture. The use of irregular strokes can be compared to the introduction of randomness in image dithering [19].

Figure 2: *Assorted stored stroke textures.*

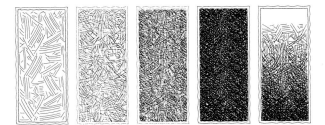

Figure 3: *A single texture drawn with several tone values.*

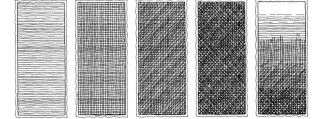

Figure 4: *A prioritized texture. Only the most significant strokes are drawn for light tone values; less important strokes are brought in to darken the texture.*

We cannot simply draw strokes in completely random directions, however—the stroke direction is one of the key elements in defining a texture. Instead, the system perturbs the strokes in a variety of small ways (see Figure 1): strokes can be drawn with a slight wiggle (a wave with slightly randomized frequency and phase); straight strokes can be given a slight overall curvature; and stroke length and direction can be jiggled slightly. Section A.3 describes the stroke-drawing algorithm in greater detail. Currently, strokes in our system are each of constant width, as per a "technical pen" [16].

## 2.2 Textures

The user paints by rubbing a "brush" over the illustration; the strokes that appear in the region under the brush are generated based on a user-selected *stroke texture* (see Figure 2). The system supports a library of user-defined *stored* stroke textures, as well as several built-in *procedural* stroke textures. In this way, a wide variety of illustration styles can be achieved. These two types of stroke textures are described in more detail below.

### Stored stroke textures

A stored texture is simply a collection of strokes. Drawing a texture at a given darkness is a matter of choosing from the collection a subset that has enough strokes to reach the desired tone. (Some textures may be inherently too light—they may not have enough strokes to make dark tones.)

For textures such as stipples and scribbles, the choice of strokes to draw for a given tonality is not critical. In these cases, the system simply selects strokes from the texture in a random sequence, generating candidate strokes and testing the tonal effect of candidate strokes as described in Section A.3. Candidate strokes that pass the tests are drawn, and those that fail are discarded (see Figure 3).

For other textures, however, the system supports a predefined *priority* for each stroke, which specifies an order to use in generating and testing candidate strokes. For example, Figure 4 illustrates a texture in which only horizontal hatches are drawn for light tones,

while cross-hatching strokes are used for darker tones. Another example would be a texture in which larger scribbles are drawn before smaller ones.

Creating a good prioritized stroke texture is not always easy—some design iteration may be required before the strokes and their priorities work well together. Once a texture has been created and perfected, however, it can be archived for repeated use. The system lets the user draw textures interactively and can also support textures that are computed programmatically or that are taken from edges extracted from scanned images.

### Procedural stroke textures

Many interesting texture effects can be computed procedurally. The system currently supports three types of procedural texturing: stippling (randomly distributed points or short strokes), parallel hatching, and curved strokes. The latter two textures can follow along or against the gradient of a reference image. Since these are the only textures truly built into the system, they are the basic building blocks from which user-drawn stored textures are formed.

To draw procedural stroke textures, the system simply generates appropriate candidate strokes under the region of the brush and tests them, as discussed in detail in Section A.3. More intricate prioritized procedural stroke textures, such as "brick," "wood," or "shingle" textures, can also be defined [20], although they are not currently implemented in our interactive system.

## 2.3 Reference images

A scanned, rendered, or digitally painted continuous-tone image can be underlaid "beneath" the illustration being drawn, and displayed faintly. This reference image can be used in several ways (see Figure 5):

Figure 5: *Using a grey scale image for reference. Left to right: Original grey scale image; extracted edges; curved hatching across the gradient.*

Figure 6: *Manipulating curve detail. Left to right: Teapot edges from Figure 5, with detail removed; alternate details applied to the curves.*

- As a visual reference for the artist.

- As a tone reference for painting, in which case the texture darkness will match that of the image.

- As a source image from which edges are extracted to use for outlining and clipping. The user can select edges corresponding to versions of the image at various resolutions.

- As a progenitor of *stencils*. The user can interactively define stencils by specifying ranges of intensities in the reference image; strokes are drawn only where the reference image value is within the specified ranges.

- As a reference for determining stroke and texture orientation. Textures that follow the reference gradient can be particularly useful for conveying curved surfaces.

Note that its extensive support for reference images makes the illustration system a particularly effective tool for interactive digital halftoning. However, it does not provide automatic halftoning—it is up to the user to choose which stroke textures to apply, where to apply them, and how dark to make them, based on the user's intent and aesthetic sense for the final illustration. One could imagine an automated system to extract texture from an image, but there is not always enough information in the image to achieve the desired effect. For example, the original reference photograph for the goose in Figure 9 does not show feathers in any great detail; the artist must choose textures and introduce tone variation to convey the sense of feathering.

### 2.4 Detail manipulation

The illustration system supports multiresolution curves [4], allowing users to add or remove detail from strokes and edges. For example, an illustration can be initially made using smooth strokes, which can later be adjusted in subtle or not so subtle ways, using a variety of wiggly or scribbly detail. Alternatively, detail can be removed from an edge extracted from the tone reference in order to yield smoother outlines (see Figure 6).

### 2.5 Clipping

The user can specify outlines, which may or may not be drawn in the final illustration, but against which strokes (and stroke textures) are clipped. Outlines can be drawn by hand or can be taken from edges in reference images.

Just as individual strokes should not be too regular, the clipped ends of textures should in general be slightly ragged. The system introduces a small amount of random variation by clipping strokes too soon or allowing them to spill beyond the edge of the clipping region (see Figure 7).

Figure 7: *Strokes clipped to an outline. Left: The outline is drawn. Center: The outline has been removed; notice the hard edge caused by exact clipping. Right: A small amount of random sloppiness creates a softer edge.*

### 2.6 Individual strokes

Sometimes individual strokes are important enough to be drawn by hand; for example, the hairs in Figure 11 were individually created. The user can draw individual strokes with a mouse or with a tablet. These strokes can be given waviness and clipped in the same manner as automatically-generated strokes. To overcome the mouse's lack of smoothness, unwanted detail can be removed via the multiresolution curve mechanism, or prestored "artistic" irregularities can be introduced, as described in Section 2.4.

### 2.7 Editing collections of strokes

In addition to modifying individual strokes, the user can edit collections of strokes. Editing operations can be applied to all strokes, to those generated from a given texture, or to strokes selected interactively.

Perhaps the most interesting editing operation is the "lighten" operation. Rather than simply erasing all strokes under the brush, "lighten" incrementally removes strokes. Thus, a textured region that is too dark can be made lighter without destroying the integrity of the texture, instilling pen-and-ink with qualities of a subtractive medium. For example, in the lower left-hand drawing of Figure 8, the mottled effect in the background was created by painting a crosshatch texture to a uniform darkness, then slightly lightening in a few places with touches of the brush.

### 3 Results

The pen-and-ink illustration system is implemented in C++ and runs at interactive speed on an SGI Indigo2 workstation, without any additional hardware assistance. The system has proven quite successful at assisting users in easily producing a variety of illustrations. All figures in this paper were drawn using the illustration system; only a few minutes were required for the simplest figures, and a few hours were required for the goose in Figure 9. All figures were out-

Figure 8: *A single scene, drawn in a variety of styles. Pitz [12] suggests drawing this scene with varying styles, as an exercise for student illustrators. The three drawings on top and left are attempts to closely follow examples given in the book, while the lower right is our own stylistic expression. The illustrations were created using an image of a simple 3D model as a tone reference.*

put in PostScript by our system and printed with the text on a GCC SelectPress 1200dpi printer.

To test the range and quality of the system, we chose to tackle exercises and mimic drawings from illustration texts. Figures 8, 9 and 10 show some of the results. We must admit that the target pen-and-ink drawings in the textbooks are generally finer than ours. However, when we consider that our illustrations were made on a bitmap display, using only a mouse, by programmers who are not trained illustrators, and in a matter of minutes for the simpler drawings, we find our results very encouraging.

## 4 Future work

The illustration system we have built suggests a number of areas for future research:

- *Experimenting with better interaction techniques.* The control panel of our prototype system has a button or slider for nearly every low-level operation and parameter in the program and hence is somewhat cumbersome to use. A better interface would provide support for common illustrator techniques, such as haloed outlines and stippled edges. In addition, we would like to explore adding much higher-level controls for producing illustrations, including commands to "increase contrast" or "focus attention" on certain regions of the illustration.

- *More sophisticated strokes and stroke textures.* Our simple procedural and stored textures do not yet provide all of the subtlety and variety available to the pen. For example, we would like to include the ability to vary the thickness along a stroke, which is supported in other pen-and-ink work [4, 20].

- *Resolution-independence.* The user should be able to work at a convenient screen resolution, while the final output should have strokes drawn with the highest resolution the printer can support. However, changing resolution in a naive fashion may change the appearance of strokes and stroke textures in undesirable ways. We would like to explore methods of storing illustrations not as collections of strokes, but as higher-level descriptions of tone, texture, and clipping information that could be used to generate the image appropriately at any arbitrary resolution.

- *Combining with 3D.* We would like to interface our interactive system with an automatic renderer for creating pen-and-ink illustrations from 3D models [20] to create an integrated interactive 2D and 3D illustration system.

## Acknowledgements

We would like to thank Adam Finkelstein for helping us incorporate his stroke detail research into our editor, and Georges Winkenbach and Tony DeRose for their useful discussion of illustration principles. We would also like to thank SGI for loaning us several machines in order to meet our deadlines.

This work was supported by an NSF National Young Investigator award (CCR-9357790), by the University of Washington Graduate Research and Royalty Research Funds (75-1721 and 65-9731), and by industrial gifts from Adobe, Aldus, and Xerox.

## References

[1] Brian Cabral and Leith (Casey) Leedom. Imaging Vector Fields Using Line Integral Convolution. Proceedings of SIGGRAPH 93 (Anaheim,

Figure 9: *A Canada goose. Simmons [16] uses the goose as a worked example of tight technical pen drawing from a reference photograph; we attempted to mimic the author's final result with our system, using only a mouse. The book includes a reproduction of the author's own reference photograph, which we scanned to use as a tone reference.*

California, August 1–6, 1993). In *Computer Graphics*, Annual Conference Series, 1993, pages 263–272.

[2] John Canny. A Computational Approach To Edge Detection. In Rangachar Kasturi and Ramesh C. Jain, editors, *Computer Vision: Principles*, pages 112–131. IEEE Computer Society Press, Los Alamitos, California, 1991. Reprinted from *IEEE Transactions on Pattern Analysis and Machine Intelligence*, 8(6):679–698, November 1986.

[3] Tunde Cockshott, John Patterson, and David England. Modelling the Texture of Paint. In *Proceedings of EUROGRAPHICS '92*, pages C–217 to C–226, September 1992.

[4] Adam Finkelstein and David H. Salesin. Multiresolution Curves. Proceedings of SIGGRAPH 94 (Orlando, Florida, July 24–29, 1994). In *Computer Graphics*, Annual Conference Series, 1994.

[5] Michel Gangnet, Jean-Claude Herve, Thierry Pudet, and Jean-Manuel Van Thong. Incremental Computation of Planar Maps. Proceedings of SIGGRAPH '89 (Boston, Massachusetts, July 31–August 4, 1989). In *Computer Graphics* 23, 3 (August 1989), pages 345–354.

[6] Arthur L. Guptill. *Rendering in Pen and Ink*. Watson-Guptill Publications, New York, 1976.

[7] Paul Haeberli. Paint by Numbers: Abstract Image Representations. Proceedings of SIGGRAPH '90 (Dallas, Texas, August 6–10, 1990). In *Computer Graphics* 24, 4 (August 1990), pages 207–214.

[8] Paul Haeberli and Mark Segal. Texture Mapping as a Fundamental Drawing Primitive. In *Proceedings of the Fourth Annual EUROGRAPHICS Workshop on Rendering*, pages 259–266, Paris, June 1993. Ecole Normale Superieure.

[9] Douglas Kirkland. *Icons*. Collins Publishers San Francisco, San Francisco, California, 1993.

[10] John-Peter Lewis. Texture Synthesis for Digital Painting. Proceedings of SIGGRAPH '84 (Minneapolis, Minnesota, July 23–27, 1984). In *Computer Graphics* 18, 3 (July 1984), pages 245–252.

[11] Theo Pavlidis. An Automatic Beautifier for Drawings and Illustrations. Proceedings of SIGGRAPH '85 (San Francisco, California, July 22–26, 1985). In *Computer Graphics* 19, 3 (July 1985), pages 225–230.

[12] Henry C. Pitz. *Ink Drawing Techniques*. Watson-Guptill Publications, New York, 1957.

[13] The Premisys Corporation, Chicago. *Squiggle*, 1993.

[14] Takafumi Saito and Tokiichiro Takahashi. Comprehensible Rendering of 3D Shapes. Proceedings of SIGGRAPH '90 (Dallas, Texas, August 6–10, 1990). In *Computer Graphics* 24, 4 (August 1990), pages 197–206.

[15] Robert Sedgewick. *Algorithms*. Addison-Wesley Publishing Company, Reading, Massachusetts, 1983.

[16] Gary Simmons. *The Technical Pen*. Watson-Guptill Publications, New York, 1992.

[17] Steve Strassman. Hairy Brushes. Proceedings of SIGGRAPH '86 (Dallas, Texas, August 18–22, 1986). In *Computer Graphics* 20, 4 (August 1986), pages 225–232.

[18] Ivan E. Sutherland. Sketchpad: A Man-Machine Graphics Communication System. In *Proceedings of the Spring Joint Computer Conference*, pages 329–346, 1963.

[19] Robert Ulichney. *Digital Halftoning*. The MIT Press, Cambridge, 1987.

[20] Georges Winkenbach and David H. Salesin. Computer-Generated Pen-and-Ink Illustration. Proceedings of SIGGRAPH 94 (Orlando, Florida, July 24–29, 1994). In *Computer Graphics*, Annual Conference Series, 1994.

## A    Implementation details

This appendix outlines the implementation of our prototype pen-and-ink illustration system. We will focus on the most significant features: the data structures allowing quick updating and editing of the illustration, and the stroke generation and testing algorithms.

Section A.1 describes the data types used in the system. Section A.2 presents the global data items maintained. The process of generating and using strokes is discussed in Section A.3.

Figure 10: *Close-up of the goose head.*

## A.1 Data Types

The two basic data structures used by the illustration system are the *stroke* and the *stroke database*.

### Stroke

The data type at the heart of the system is the *Stroke*. Each stroke includes the following fields:

- *pixels*: An arbitrary-size array of *(x,y)* pixel coordinate pairs.
- *length*: The size of the *pixels* array.
- *width*: The width of the stroke, in pixels.
- *bbox*: The rectangular bounding box of the stroke's pixels.
- *id*: The texture from which the stroke was derived.
- *priority*: The ranking of a stroke, if in a prioritized texture.

The entries of the *pixels* array contiguously trace the path of the stroke: $x$ and $y$ never change by more than $\pm 1$ from one entry to the next.

The operations supported by the *Stroke* type include: testing to see if a stroke intersects a given rectangular region, circular region, or other stroke; decreasing *length* by trimming entries off the ends of *pixels*; merging two contiguous strokes into a single stroke; and returning the point in the stroke that is closest to a given pixel.

A stroke can be manipulated as a multiresolution curve [4]. Each entry in *pixels* is used as a control point of an interpolating spline, which is subject to multiresolution analysis and can have its detail edited or replaced. The resulting curve is scan-converted to recover the contiguous *pixels* entries required by the *Stroke* type.

### Stroke database

A stroke database maintains a collection of *Stroke* instances, supporting addition and deletion of strokes, and various queries. It is important that the database operations and queries be quick enough to allow painting and editing at interactive speed.

We implement the stroke database using a modified k-D tree (see Sedgewick [15]). Each node of the tree corresponds to a region of the image; the children of the node partition that region. The partition is always horizontal or vertical and is chosen so as to distribute as evenly as possible the strokes of a region between the two children. Each leaf node contains a list of the strokes that intersect its region. For performance purposes, a limit of 10 strokes per leaf and a minimum size of $5 \times 5$ pixels per leaf are maintained (with the area restriction having precedence).

In the modified k-D tree, a given stroke may be referenced by several leaves since a stroke can cross partitions of the tree. The structure allows us to quickly find all strokes that may overlap a specified region by the usual recursion along the limbs of the tree that include the region. Minor extra bookkeeping is required when iterating through the strokes in the leaves to ensure that a stroke is not visited multiple times.

The queries supported by a stroke database include: finding all strokes within a given rectangular or circular region; finding all strokes that overlap a given stroke; and finding the stroke nearest a given pixel. Each query may specify criteria such as a particular *id* value. These queries allow the system to perform operations such as deleting a stroke and updating the screen as follows: first, find the stroke nearest the cursor; next, delete the stroke from the database and erase it from the screen; finally, find all strokes that overlap the deleted stroke and redraw them.

## A.2 Global data objects

The system maintains several global data objects to support the interactive illustration processes:

- *Main stroke database and image bitmap.* The illustration is maintained in a dual representation: a stroke database maintains the collection of *Stroke* instances that make up the illustration; and an image bitmap allows the system to quickly determine if a pixel has been drawn by one or more strokes. When storing to disk, only the stroke database needs to be saved; the image bitmap can be recreated by traversing the database and drawing all the strokes.

- *Clip-edge database and clip-edge bitmap.* To allow fast clipping of drawn strokes to outline edges, the system maintains a global bitmap into which all clipping edges are drawn (clipping is discussed in Section A.3). The clip edges can come from edge detection of the reference image or from freehand drawing. To allow the user to activate and deactivate edges, the edges are stored as *Stroke* instances in a stroke database.

- *Stored stroke textures.* The system loads stored stroke textures on demand from a library on disk. A stored texture is defined as a rectangular region with toroidal wrap-around, so that the texture can seamlessly tile the illustration plane. Each texture is maintained in the system as a stroke database. For a prioritized texture, each stroke has an associated priority value. The stroke database of a stored stroke texture is queried but is not modified when the texture is used.

- *Reference image.* The system stores the reference image in memory, allowing quick pixel-by-pixel tone reference and stenciling. Unlike the image bitmap of the illustration, the reference image is an 8-bit greyscale. When a reference image is loaded from disk, the detected edges in the image are added to a clip-edge database and bitmap. We use a Canny edge extractor [2] to detect edges at several image resolutions. This potentially time-consuming processing is only done the first time a given reference image is used; the resulting edges are saved on disk along with the image, so that they can be loaded quickly in the future.

## A.3 Drawing strokes

The process to "paint" with strokes is similar for the supported procedural textures—stippling, straight hatching, and curved hatching—and for stored stroke textures. The following pseudocode outlines this process:

*Paint:*
```
    for each brush position P
        while S ← GenerateCandidateStroke(P)
            ClipStroke(S)
            if TestStrokeTone(S) then
                DrawStroke(S)
            end if
        end while
    end for
```

The steps of this process are described below.

☞ *GenerateCandidateStroke(P)*: At each brush position $P$, the system may in general try to draw many strokes. Each invocation of *Generate-CandidateStroke* returns the next stroke instance from a set of candidates. The next stroke returned may be generated dynamically based on the success of the previous strokes. The generation of candidate strokes depends on the texture:

- *Stippling.* There is only a single candidate: a stipple dot at a random location under the brush (chosen with uniform distribution in the brush's polar coordinates). The stipple dot is generated as a length 1 stroke.

- *Straight hatching.* The system tries a sequence of line segments with decreasing length, until a segment is drawn or a minimum length is reached. The midpoint of each stroke is a random location under the brush, and the direction and initial length are specified by the user. The direction may be fixed or aligned relative to the gradient of the reference image. The user may request a small randomization of the direction and length. The user may also specify that only full-length strokes be used, in which case if the initial candidate is not drawn, no further strokes are attempted. Each candidate stroke is a perturbed line segment, generated by the following pseudocode:

$PerturbedLineSegment(x_1, y_1, x_2, y_2, a, \omega, c):$
; $(x_1, y_1)$ and $(x_2, y_2)$ are the endpoints of the line segment.
; $a$ is the magnitude and $\omega$ the base frequency of waviness.
; $c$ is the magnitude of curviness.
; $random()$ value has uniform distribution on $[0, 1]$.
; $gaussian()$ value has normal distribution on $[-1, 1]$.
$dx \leftarrow x_2 - x_1$
$dy \leftarrow y_2 - y_1$
$s \leftarrow \sqrt{dx^2 + dy^2}$
$\delta \leftarrow 2\pi\omega \left(1 + \frac{1}{4} gaussian()\right)$
$\gamma \leftarrow \frac{1}{2}\delta gaussian()$
$i \leftarrow 0, \ j \leftarrow 0, \ \phi \leftarrow 2\pi random()$
**for** $\alpha \leftarrow 0$ **to** 1 **step** $1/\max(|dx|, |dy|)$
    ; *perturb line with sine waviness and quarter-wave curve.*
    $b \leftarrow a sin(\phi)/s + c\left(\cos(\frac{\pi}{2}\alpha - \frac{\pi}{4}) - 1\right)$
    $pixels[i] \leftarrow (x_1 + \alpha\,dx + b\,dy, \ y_1 + \alpha\,dy + b\,dx)$
    ; *occasionally shift the sine wave frequency.*
    **if** $j\delta > \frac{\pi}{2}$ **and** $gaussian() > \frac{1}{3}$ **then**
        $\gamma \leftarrow \frac{1}{2}\delta gaussian()$
        $j \leftarrow 0$
    **end if**
    ; *update for next pixel.*
    $\phi \leftarrow \phi + \delta + \gamma$
    $i{+}{+}, \ j{+}{+}$
**end for**

When needed, intermediate pixels are inserted in order to maintain the contiguity requirement of the *Strokes* type.

- *Curved hatching.* Similar to straight hatching, the system tries strokes of decreasing length until one is accepted. The user specifies the initial length and direction relative to the reference image gradient. A curved stroke is generated by following the image gradient as a vector field (much as was done by Cabral and Leedom [1]) forward and backward for the given length.

- *Stored Strokes.* The system queries the texture's database for a list of strokes that lie under the brush, modulo tiling of the image plane with the texture. The strokes of the resulting list are tried in priority order for prioritized textures, or random order for non-prioritized textures. A prioritized texture may be flagged as *strictly prioritized*, in which case if a candidate stroke fails the tone test, the remaining lower-priority strokes are not considered. Each candidate stroke is generated by translating the stored stroke's *pixels* to the proper tile in the image. Our system does not currently add any randomness to the strokes beyond that which was used when the texture was originally defined. Tiling artifacts are typically not objectionable if the illustration feature size is smaller than the tile size, but could be alleviated through random stroke perturbations.

☞ *ClipStroke(S)*: The candidate stroke $S$ is subjected to a series of clipping operations:

1. *To the bounds of the overall image.*

2. *To the brush.* Clip the strokes to the brush for stored stroke textures to give the user a traditional "textured paint." This clipping step is not performed for procedural textures; in this case, the candidate strokes are generated starting under the brush but may extend beyond its bounds.

3. *To clip-edges.* Trace from the center of the stroke out to each end, examining the corresponding pixels of the global clip-edge bitmap, stopping when an edge is met.

4. *To a reference-image stencil.* Trace from the center of the stroke out to each end, examining the corresponding pixels of the reference image. Can stop at black, white, or any of a number of user-defined ranges of image intensities.

The clipping operations return a "first" and a "last" index into the stroke's *pixels* array, but before actually trimming the stroke, these indices are perturbed up or down by a small random amount to achieve ragged clipping as described in Section 2.5. The magnitude of the perturbation is adjustable by the user. If the stroke is clipped to zero length, it can be trivially rejected at this point.

☞ *TestStrokeTone(S)*: Two tests are performed to see how stroke $S$ affects the image. First, the stroke's pixels in the image buffer are tested: if all the pixels are already drawn, the stroke has no effect on the image and is trivially rejected. Next, the effect of the stroke on the image tone is determined: the stroke is temporarily drawn into the image bitmap and the resulting tone is computed pixel-by-pixel along its length, by low-pass filtering each pixel's neighborhood. Depending on the user's specification, the desired tone may be determined from the reference image's value (via similar low-pass filtering along the stroke), or may simply be a constant value. The stroke fails if it makes the image tone darker than the desired tone anywhere along its length.

☞ *DrawStroke(S)*: To draw stroke $S$, its pixels in the image bitmap are set, the display is updated, and an instance of $S$ is added to the main stroke database. For stored stroke textures, the system checks to see if the new stroke $S$ overlays an existing instance of the same stroke—such an occurrence could happen, for example, if the earlier stroke was clipped to the brush and the user has now moved the brush slightly. Rather than adding the new stroke, the previously-drawn stroke is extended to include the new stroke's pixels in order to avoid overwhelming the data structures. Note that for a new instance of a stroke to align with a previous instance, any extra randomness should be exactly repeatable; the values for the stroke perturbations should be derived from a pseudorandom function over the illustration plane.

Figure 11: *An illustrated portrait. The reference image was a photograph by Douglas Kirkland [9].*

# Drawing and Animation Using Skeletal Strokes

Siu Chi HSU
Cambridge University Computer Lab
*sch@cl.cam.ac.uk*

Computer Science Department[†],
Chinese University of Hong Kong, Shatin, Hong Kong
*schsu@cs.cuhk.hk*

†: current correspondence address

Irene H. H. LEE
Creature House Inc.

School of Music,
Hong Kong Academy for Performing Arts

## ABSTRACT

The use of *skeletal strokes* is a new vector graphics realization of the brush and stroke metaphor using arbitrary pictures as 'ink'. It is based on an idealized 2D deformation model defined by an arbitrary path. Its expressiveness as a general brush stroke replacement and efficiency for interactive use make it suitable as a basic drawing primitive in drawing programs as well as windowing and page description systems. This paper presents our drawing and animation system, 'Skeletal Draw', based on skeletal strokes. The effectiveness of the system in stylish picture creation is illustrated with various pictures made with it. Decisions made in the handling of sub-strokes in a higher order stroke and recursive strokes are discussed. The general anchoring mechanism in the skeletal stroke framework allows any arbitrary picture deformation to be abstracted into a single stroke. Its extension to piecewise continuous anchoring and the anchoring of shear angle and stroke width are explained. We demonstrated how this mechanism allows us to build up powerful pseudo-3D models which are particularly useful in the production of 2½D cartoon drawings and animation. Animation sequences have been made to illustrate the ideas, including a vector graphics based motion blurring technique.

## 1 INTRODUCTION

We are proposing *skeletal strokes* as a new vector based drawing primitive for general stroking and picture specification. With the skeletal strokes framework, users are freed from the dependence on the scanner to input expressive brush strokes for further processing; they can create these strokes interactively on the computer. Compared with previously proposed expressive strokes, the skeletal stroke framework has more general applications. It has, for example, an anchoring mechanism which could be applied to 2½D animation. The high level abstraction of skeletal strokes makes it particularly attractive in terms of storage size and transmission efficiency. Its efficient implementation is favourable for incorporation into windowing systems and page description languages.

We shall demonstrate the various techniques with our drawing and animation system, Skeletal Draw, which uses skeletal strokes as the basic primitives. An animation sequence has also been made to show the effectiveness of creating 2½D

animation using pseudo-3D models.

## 2 STROKES, SKELETONS AND ENVELOPES

The constant thickness stroke is still the basic drawing primitive provided by most commercially available vector based drawing packages[34,39]. To create pictures like figures 2, 3, 17 and 19 with these packages usually involves scanning in an original copy (which has already been created on paper) or tracing out its outlines manually or automatically. Indeed, many impressive illustrations that fill the pages of manuals of many market-leading packages are there to demonstrate the package's automatic tracing or photo-retouching capabilities.

### 2.1 What is a Stroke?

Useful as they are for simple designs, constant thickness strokes cannot be compared to more general strokes for convenience and expressiveness. While it is possible to trace out the outlines of a brush trail every time (figure 1), this painstaking drawing method no doubt is a hindrance to the aspiring artist. It is also doubtful whether pictures of reasonable complexity can be managed if all the strokes are traced out this way — consider modifying a few strokes in Figure 3 if the strokes are polygons. In fact, one would not regard such a drawing method as 'drawing with strokes'. If a picture is drawn with strokes, the effects of each stroke should be apparent after a single application of the brush. In this sense, the constant thickness stroke provided by most drawing programs and the bitmap brush (whether antialiased or not) available in paint programs are both considered to be computer strokes. We shall discuss the deficiencies of each shortly.

Figure 1: Tracing out a stylish brush trail with 'primitive' strokes. The letter 'S' in this illustration is drawn with one single skeletal stroke application.

### 2.2 Skeleton verses Envelope

Many drawing/2D warping packages allow the user to specify the deformation of a picture by reshaping an envelope around the undeformed picture. This technique has been advocated for applications in 2D animation in as early as the 70's[15] and is still widely used in the latest systems[32]. A coordinate system transformation based on envelope deformation is quite different from a skeleton based one. The former is much more well defined as the coordinates within an envelope can usually be interpolated bi-parametrically from the bounding curves defining the envelope. To control the whole coordinate system with one single skeleton, however, a proper deformation model must be defined to handle the singularities arising from extreme bending cases. Under this definition, the 'skeleton techniques' described in [15] should not be considered as a skeleton deformation.

Envelope based techniques may be suitable for manipulating a few pictures. When it comes to controlling individual strokes in a complicated drawing, however, it becomes as cumbersome as the use of lines to trace out brush trails. One could see why the place of general brush strokes are not so easily replaceable.

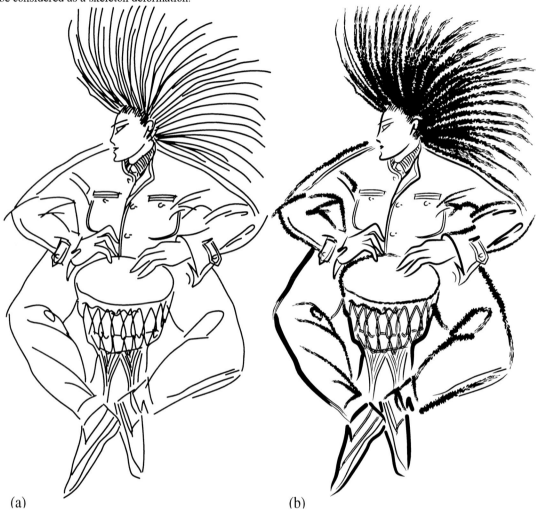

(a)                                    (b)

Figure 2: A stylish figure after Tomio Mohri[35]. (a) With a constant thickness stroke. (b) With 5 types of skeletal strokes.

## 3 EXISTING BRUSH AND STROKE MODELS

### 3.1 Raster Based Strokes

Many powerful and expressive strokes have been proposed before in SIGGRAPH and other literature. Smith[46] and Whitted[50] proposed the use of antialiased Z-buffer images to create strokes with a 3D appearance. Bleser et. al.[10] used a lookup table of bitmaps indexed by the pressure and tilt reading of a 5D digitizer stylus. They effectively recreated a digital charcoal stick. Another system models graphite pencils in a similar way[49]. Greene's drawing prism[24] even allows the capturing of the path of virtually anything which is being dragged over the prism surface. However, strokes created by these systems suffer from the same problem as those provided by paint programs: after being drawn, they are difficult to edit, especially if they are antialiased.

Other physical models exist. Strassmann[47] modelled the ink-laying processes of bristle brush on paper. Guo and Kunii[25] extended them to include ink-diffusion through the paper fabric

mesh. Their results are attractive despite the relatively slow computation speed (1 to 2 minutes per stroke in Strassmann's prototype system). To achieve ultimate authenticity, Pang et.al.[38] even attached real bristle brushes to plotters and defined the strokes by the paths and pen up/down control parameters.

These strokes did reproduce on the digital computer, to a certain extent, the effects made by a brush or pen. Unfortunately, the dexterity demanded of the artist in the handling of the brush or pen is also transferred to the user at the computer, often in an unnatural way. The control parameters (speed of movement, pressure, tilt) of the individual strokes are either dependent on both a powerful input device and a skilful user, or they have to be specified explicitly. If digital strokes are no less difficult to control than real ones, it makes sense to do the drawings on paper and let the computer do the retouching and other post-processing jobs on the scanned-in version. A further problem is that simulation often takes too long for interactive use on small machines.

Figure 3: A picture drawn using nine different types of skeletal strokes after the Lithograph *The Scream* by Edvard Munch (1863-1944).

## 3.2 Vector Based Strokes

As for vector graphics based systems, apart from those which depend on constant thickness strokes, there are others following Knuth's line of using analytical paths defined by the trajectory of some geometrical shapes[21,30,31]. The skeleton based stroke primitives in Berkel's SIAS system[9] allowed the local width of a stroke along the path to vary arbitrarily. They might be suitable for specific applications like digital typography. These strokes are however too restrictive in form as a general brush stroke replacement.

In commercial drawing programs, the option to vary the stroke width is already a feature, yet the controlling of it is still far from satisfactory. For systems without a pressure sensitive digitizer, the stroke width is often determined by the drawing speed alone or with other controls[39]. Again, these rather unnatural means of making expressive strokes are difficult to use and time consuming.

## 3.3 Outcome or the Process?

The monitor screen is not a piece of paper and the digitizer not a pen. Although the brush and stroke metaphor is helpful for understanding the digital drawing process, it may not be wise to strive to model it completely. Since we are usually more interested in the final appearance of the stroke than the physical action of dragging a brush across paper, we might as well try to model the desired look of the stroke in the first place. Of course one could then argue that the mastering of the brush is in itself an art, in which case one should really go back to the use of the physical brush.

In the following sections, we shall first give a brief summary of the key features of skeletal strokes and our drawing program, 'Skeletal Draw'. Then its use as a general drawing tool and its applications in comics and animation making will be explained.

## 4 SKELETAL STROKES

The use of skeletal strokes[27,28] is a new realization of the brush and stroke metaphor. It does not use physical models (e.g.

bristles of brushes or properties of paper) nor use repeated patterns as the basic drawing unit. Instead, an arbitrary picture and its deformation are abstracted into a skeletal stroke to draw with. This structured approach turns out to be far more general than those based on physical models. It is a rich framework for general picture deformation yet the only control parameter required is the brush path itself. The deformation of individual parts of a picture can be independently controlled. Higher order strokes can be used to build up complex pictures, while recursive strokes can be made to generate and manipulate fractals. Some effects that can be achieved include marks made by a bristle brush or a flat nib pen, the effects of wood cut and water-based ink with blotting effects (figure 4). With the use of the higher order anchoring mechanism, it is capable of giving an illusion of objects rotating. This is invaluable in the creation and manipulation of pseudo-3D models.

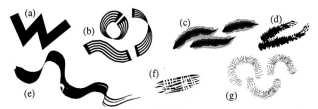

Figure 4: An assortment of effects with skeletal strokes. (a) Constant thickness skeletal stroke, (b) strokes with bending and twisting, (c) water based ink with a blotting effect, (d) 2 applications of a stylish stroke, (e) more than an ordinary flat-nib pen, (f) wood-cut, (g) 3 applications of a stylish stroke.

## 4.1 Review on Skeletal Stroke Deformation

The skeletal stroke deformation has been discussed in detail in [28], here we will only briefly go through the main points but leave out the mathematical details and derivations.

The skeletal stroke deformation is based on localized parametric coordinate system transformation along the stroke application path. A skeletal stroke is defined by specifying a *reference backbone* and a *reference thickness* on any arbitrary picture. The purpose of defining the reference backbone and thickness is for parameterizing the coordinate system of the original picture. On applying the stroke along a path, the original picture is redrawn on the deformed coordinate system defined by the path, the width of the stroke application, and some other optional parameters like shear angle and twist.

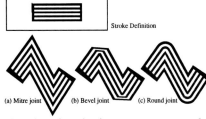

Figure 5: A stroke applied onto the same path with 3 different types of joints.

Naïvely using the instantaneous normals along the application path as the deformed local y axes would cause the flesh (the picture abstracted in a stroke) to wrinkle or fold back onto itself. To eliminate these undesirable effects, we have proposed a deformation model based on an idealized material with non-localized deformation on axial compression. The lateral deformation is handled by spatially constraining the material to the local centre of curvature. In the cases of extreme bending, which is common for thick polyline strokes, we introduced a *macroscopic centre of curvature* (MCC) which is the intersection point of two angle bisectors at two adjacent joints. The coordinate space would converge towards the MCC as in the case for continuous stroke paths. The joint zone coordinate systems for mitre, bevel and round joints are also derived.

If we use an undistorted skeletal stroke as a texture coordinate space[11], sampled images can be deformed with a skeletal stroke application using standard texture mapping techniques. Since the relation between the original (defined by the reference backbone) and the distorted (specified in the stroke application) coordinate systems is well defined, proper filtering of the texture map can be performed.

Normally, the flesh would freely stretch and shrink with the length of the application path. This might not be desirable for special features in a stroke, like serifs or other stroke-end forms. We have therefore defined an anchoring mechanism which allows the aspect ratio of part of the flesh (i.e. a subset of vertices or control points in the original picture) to be retained. This is actually achieved by parameterizing the coordinates to a new coordinate system with a shifted origin known as the *anchor origin*. The final coordinates (both x and y) on application are controlled by the width of the stroke application alone, hence a part of the flesh anchored to a single anchor origin would retain its aspect ratio and would not stretch or shrink with the application path length but would move with the final position of the anchor origin. If we anchor different parts of the flesh to different anchor origins, they would shift to different absolute positions.

Figure 6: Anchoring different parts to different anchor origins.

Stroke definition    Application to paths of different lengths

The effect of anchoring to different anchor origins can be interesting. In figure 6, the figure's pupils (and half of each eye) and the rest of its face are both anchored but to different ends of the stroke. The former is anchored to the point A1; the latter to A2. If we change the stroke length while fixing the stroke width, the eyes will bulge with the end of the stroke while the rest of the face stays with the beginning of the stroke.

If the anchor origins themselves are anchored to other anchor origins, the deformation result would be even more dramatic. In fact, we have proved that for $n$th order anchoring, the final x and y coordinates are actually $n$th degree parametric equations with the coefficients being the respective x and y coordinates of the various anchor origins and the parameter being the changes in aspect ratio from the origin aspect ratio on definition[28]. Therefore we could conveniently encode any subtle deformations to a single stroke definition.

Figure 7: A stroke resembling a head. 2nd order anchoring has been used to control the deformation of the head to give an illusion of rotation. The anchor origins are determined automatically by the system.

The elegance of the general anchoring mechanism lies in its consistency with the intuitive zeroth order anchoring and arbitrary deformation. The extension to piecewise continuous general

anchoring and the use of this mechanism to construct pseudo-3D models shall be described in a subsequent section.

## 5  SKELETAL DRAW: A SKELETAL STROKE BASED DRAWING SYSTEM

Skeletal Draw is an implementation of our vision of a professional drawing system (Figure 21). The current system is implemented on a 486 PC under MS-Windows™, and is derived from a previous Unix™ version on X.

The system consists of less than 15000 lines of C++ code. Basic drawing tools like the free-hand brush, the polygonal pen, rubber rectangles and so on are all available; their uses are basically identical to those in most other drawing systems. The major difference is that the strokes are directional and much more expressive than the usual constant thickness strokes.

### 5.1  Drawing with Skeletal Strokes

Drawing with skeletal strokes is similar to drawing with constant thickness strokes on other systems. To select a stroke to be used for a particular path, there is a repertoire of predefined or user-defined strokes to choose from in the menu. However, choosing from the menu is inconvenient, especially when artists are likely to use a variety of strokes interchangeably. To ensure quick switching between strokes, we therefore allow the binding of 40 different strokes to the numeric keys (together with a combination of the Shift and Control modifier keys). The system can of course take advantage of more powerful input devices like the pressure sensitive stylus. Skilful artists may want to modify the stroke attributes and to switch between strokes based on the pen pressure and speed. It is however worth pointing out that all the illustrations shown in this paper were created with just a modest 2-button stylus.

Besides varying the application path, a stroke application can be modified by specifying the stroke width and shear angle. This is done by interactively pulling out a rubber line from any one end of the stroke (Figure 21) or by specifying explicit numeric values. The length of the line indicates the stroke width and the angle the line makes with the path's normal would give the stroke the same amount of shearing. The direction of application can also be reversed by hitting a key. The colour and fill pattern of a stroke can also be changed without touching the objects in the original definition. Figures 20 and 22 are drawn using the same set of strokes used in Figure 2 and 3. After modifying an applied stroke, the system will immediately redraw on the screen the stroke resulting from the new application.

As is the case with PostScript[2], the stroking process (the application of a skeletal stroke along a path) is separated from the filling process. An area enclosed by a skeletal stroke path can be filled in the same way as polygons enclosed by constant thickness strokes are.

### 5.2  Defining New Strokes

Defining a new stroke is easy. The user simply drags out a stroke definition box in the middle of which is an L-shaped line (Figure 8). The horizontal part and the vertical part of the L-shaped line represents the stroke's reference backbone and the reference thickness respectively. The L-shaped line provides a scale for the new stroke, and everything within the box would be included as part of the stroke. If the orientation of the new design is not aligned with the reference backbone, the user can always transform the box (rotate, translate, scale or even put it in perspective) so that the L-shaped line is aligned with the picture before committing the definition. The inverse of the alignment transformation of the box will be used to transform the coordinates of the vertices or control points of the picture before parametric coordinates of the new stroke are recorded.

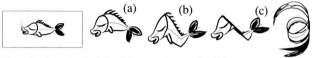

Figure 8: A stroke is defined from a picture of a fish (drawn with skeletal strokes). The stroke is applied (a) on a curved path, (b) on a polyline path, (c) using the ribbon style.

## 5.3 Higher Order Strokes

A stroke can be defined to consist of other skeletal strokes, in which case the stroke defined would be a higher order stroke. Actually, a stroke can even be defined in terms of itself by first laying out the applications of a special stroke named 'self'. Since the appearance of the stroke 'self' is insignificant, it is normally defined as a constant thickness rectangular stroke. It needs to be there for the user to specify the relation between the recursive applications and the entire stroke itself.

### Deferred Application or Not

In the definition of a higher order stroke, we are faced with the question of whether to treat the appearance of the sub-strokes as geometric attributes which deform with the main stroke or just cosmetic attributes akin to pseudo-pen size in the final coordinate space[12]. The answer to this determines whether we apply the sub-strokes before defining the main stroke (sub-strokes being merely geometric objects of the main stroke) or whether we apply them after applying the main stroke (i.e. sub-strokes are applied onto newly deformed application paths). The former option would not involve application of the sub-strokes to potentially curlier paths and are referred to as the *flattened definition*. Flattened definition is easy to handle and is more efficient. It would, however, fail to take advantage of an important feature provided by the skeletal stroke framework: the anchoring mechanism. Furthermore, it cannot be used with self recurring strokes, since it is not possible to determine the 'self' stroke's appearance before it has been applied. In this case, either the *deferred application* (the second option) or the Measured Rendering Algorithm[4,5,6] must be adopted.

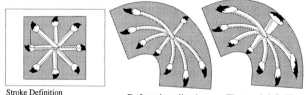

Stroke Definition      Deferred application    Flattened definition

Figure 9: The stroke definition on the left is made up of a square and 8 applications of a stroke resembling a brush. Different results with deferred application (middle) and flattened definition (right) are shown.

In our system, both options are available with deferred application as the default. With the case of deferred application, we still have to decide what to do with the resulting width of the sub-strokes. Under this mode, the resulting widths at different parts of a sub-stroke would differ in relation to the position and orientation of the main stroke. Even for strokes undergoing affine transformations, the determination of the 'correct' width is a

problem. For sub-strokes subjected to highly irregular skeletal transformation, this becomes very difficult. Possible approaches adopted by us are to either reduce the width of sub-strokes to an invariant or to scale it in proportion to the width the resulting main stroke. In general, the results based on the latter (which is the adopted option) are found to be satisfactory. In cases where they are not, we can always go back to a flattened definition.

### Rendering a Recursive Stroke

Rendering a recursive stroke explicitly by determining the resultant geometry is in general impossible. Since a recursive stroke is equivalent to an IFS (Iterated Function System) code (with a condensation set if objects other than itself are present in the definition)[3,4,5,6], the attractor is often a fractal with a fractal dimension less than 2. We therefore have to resort to one of the approximation methods for rendering these fractals. The Escape Time Algorithm[4] would result in a clean and sharp image while the Measured Rendering Algorithm[4,5,6] would give a quick but rough image of the attractor. Here, the decision on which algorithm and level of accuracy to use is left to the discretion of the user. Some sample recursive strokes are shown in Figure 9. One interesting point that is worth a small remark if the Escape Time Algorithm is used: after recurring to a certain stage, something must be drawn out by the system. In our system, this something can be specified by the user to be any arbitrary skeletal stroke. This technique is particularly handy for drawing plants and scattered objects. Furthermore, we could waive the contractive requirement of the transformations (the sub-strokes, in our case) as we are using the IFS to draw pictures but not to encode pictures.

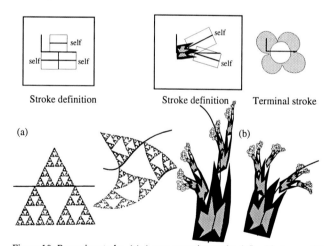

Figure 10: Recursive stroke. (a) A pure recursive stroke defined in terms of 3 instances of itself. On application, it gives a Sierpinski triangle. The stroke can be deformed just like any other stroke. (b) A recursive stroke defined in terms of 2 instances of itself and 2 polygons. The stroke application has recurred to 5 level deep and a terminal stroke of a flower is drawn at the last level. (The flower has been anchored to retain its aspect ratio).

## 5.4 Anchoring the Flesh

Zeroth order anchoring is the more often used anchoring mode. It preserves the aspect ratio of a chosen part of a picture so that after application that part would not stretch or shrink with the length of the application path. To perform a zeroth order anchoring is easy. In the stroke definition box, one just needs to use the Anchor Tool to circle the part of the flesh to be anchored and to specify an anchor origin, the position (within the box) to where that part of the flesh is to be anchored. All the vertices and control points inside the circled region would then be anchored to the anchor origin accordingly.

For higher order anchoring, it is not at all easy to figure out where to put the higher order anchor origins to achieve a particular effect. Instead of leaving the user to do this by trial and error, our solution to this is specification by examples. The user supplies an arbitrary number of instances of the picture, each of which corresponds to a different factor of the aspect ratio of the original picture. The system can then calculate the corresponding anchor origins.

### Anchoring Sub-Stroke Width and Shear Angle

If the given picture instances contain sub-strokes and the width and shear angle of the sub-strokes are not identical in different instances, then we must also find a way to describe these variations. The solution we have adopted is to record the width and shear angle of a stroke in the form of an additional point. The angle of the line joining this special *shear-width point* to the end of the stroke and the tangent of the end would be the shear angle and the length of this line the stroke width. This is identical to our use of a rubber line to interactively specify the width and the shear angle. This special point is then anchored in exactly the same way as other points.

### Piecewise Continuous Anchoring

If $N$ instances are given, it is theoretically possible to use $N$-1 anchor origins to define a deformation that would result in the $N$ given forms at the corresponding aspect ratio factors. Just as in curve fitting, we would not fit a $(n-1)$th degree polynomial to a set of $n$ points because of the over-crookedness of the resultant curve and the lack of localized control over the curve. Instead of determining the multi-level anchor origins which are the coefficients of the two continuous parametric equations, we could also employ piecewise continuous anchoring. In this case, the anchor origins (coefficients of the piecewise continuous parametric equations) can be easily determined from the neighbourhood picture instances. In the Skeletal Draw system, a Catmull-Rom spline interpolation scheme is employed.

Figure 11: Two stylish cartoon figures drawn with skeletal strokes.

### 5.5 Information Recorded in a Stroke

The amount of information that needs to be stored for a skeletal stroke is small. For a stroke definition it is merely the original picture plus the original aspect ratio of the stroke (the ratio of length of reference backbone to reference thickness). If the points

are anchored, the list would include the order of anchoring and the corresponding anchor origins.

For a stroke application, only the application path, its width (and other optional parameters) and its reference to a stroke definition is recorded. If the definition of a stroke is modified, the appearance of all the stroke applications referring to that stroke would reflect the changes immediately on redraw.

## 6 General Drawing Applications

We anticipate that skeletal strokes would have considerable impact on many drawing applications: in fashion design where stylish bold strokes are often used; in interior design where pseudo-3D strokes representing furniture and architectural objects can be laid out with ease; in dynamic clip-arts which can deform dramatically beyond the limits of stretching, shrinking, shearing, twisting and bending. If implemented in windowing system kernels or page description languages like PostScript, the skeletal stroke deformation algorithm would extend the systems to permit expressive strokes to be specified in more or less the same way as the constant thickness strokes currently are, think about windows with borders in stylish strokes. In the case of PostScript, it would be something like:

```
/name setstroke      % select a skeletal stroke
newpath ..moveto
..lineto ..curveto   % path construction
5 setstrokewidth     % optional controls
stroke               % stroke application
```

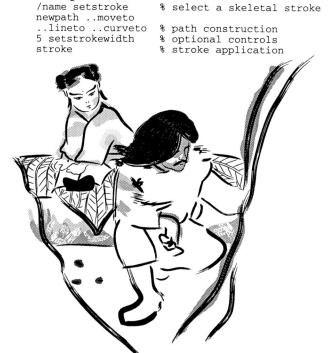

Figure 12: Mimicking Chinese brush painting.

## 7 Comics and Animation

One interesting application of skeletal strokes that we have been exploring is its use in comics and stylish 2½D animation production. Snoopy and the characters in 'The Yellow Submarine' are characters falling under this category[18]. Comics is a now a highly respected sub-culture in many countries especially in Japan. Works by famous comics artists like Tezuka Osamu[37] have even been studied and given literary praise. Pragmatically, comics publishing is also a mega-dollar business. Even though demand for quality comics is high, the production of comics is still mainly a hand craft. Day in and day out, teams of overworked assistants are painstakingly filling in the buildings and pedestrians in the background and drawing in special dramatic effects to meet deadlines. Computers have not yet been able to offer substantial help because of the lack of efficient support for stylish strokes, which are essential for creating variety and atmosphere creating, and hence important to the success of a comics work.

Skeletal strokes with the use of the general anchoring mechanism could provide the comics artist with a library of faces, limbs and features which are pseudo-rotatable (Figure 7). Colour gradation and shading changes of the models can also be encoded into the strokes using gradation lines or points[14]. This library could be created by the artist at the character design process. With it the artist could quickly lay out the characters in various postures and positions. Wildly different looks that are not readily available from the library can be introduced by editing the looks of applied strokes. Without sacrificing the flexibility of hand drawing, this approach not only speeds up the production process dramatically, but also helps to make sure characters have a consistent form. The time consuming task of drawing buildings and other objects in the background can also be sped up with a library of pseudo-3D architectural strokes and recursive plant strokes.

Figure 13: Two figures in bold strokes.

## 7.1 Speed Lines for Motion Blurring

In both comics and animation, fast action is often represented by speed lines, which suggest the distance an object or character has travelled across the camera before its shutter is closed again. Motion blurring is particularly important in animation because it reduces temporal aliasing effects. Its method of generation in vector based cartoon has not been, however, a well addressed problem.

One possible way is to employ temporal antialiasing techniques like stochastic sampling across the time dimension[19,20] or the recently proposed more efficient technique of Spatio-temporal Filtering[45]. These methods involve considerable computational cost which would not be practical for interactive use unless on high-end machines. 2½D image based techniques have also been proposed[33] which are more efficient. However all these techniques require the resultant picture to be a raster image and therefore might not always be appropriate for use in an interactive vector-based drawing system. In traditional comics, the use of crisp lines and strokes to indicate motion is usually the preferred way. We have therefore implemented a simple method to efficiently generate speed lines based on the traditional approach for blurring cartoon objects.

The traditional technique used by famous animators like Shamus Culhane is to do nothing to the leading edge of the moving object but blur the trailing edge with a trail (which is the same colour as the object) along the direction of motion[18]. Based on this approach, our system generates speed lines as follows. The moving object is a polygon enclosed possibly by skeletal strokes (the polygons inside a skeletal stroke are handled in the same way). First we have to determine which points outlining the polygon make up the trailing edge of the object. For each evenly spaced outlining point then, this question is asked: does a point a very small distance away from it along the direction of the velocity lie inside or outside of the polygon? If it lies inside, the outlining point is on the leading edge, and nothing would be done to it. For points on the trailing edge, each would be attached with a thin triangle the colour of the polygon. The base of the triangle would coincide with the outlining point; the apex would lie at a distance proportional to the speed along the velocity direction.

The spacing of the speed lines now varies with the curvature of the trailing edge, or, to be precise, the sine of the angle $\theta$ between the velocity direction and the tangent of the polygon at the base of the speed line. This variation in spacing is annoying especially at curved trailing edges. To achieve uniform spacing between the resultant speed lines, we have to correct the step size of the speed line base point along the polygon by the factor $\sin(\theta)$. We only draw the next speed line when the accumulated corrected spacing is greater than the specified spacing (Figure 14).

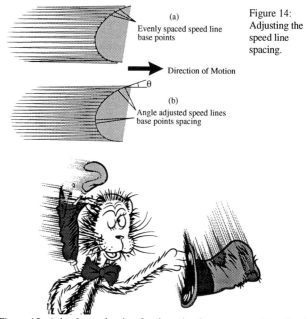

(a)
Evenly spaced speed line base points

Figure 14: Adjusting the speed line spacing.

Direction of Motion

$\theta$

(b)
Angle adjusted speed lines base points spacing

Figure 15: A keyframe drawing for the animation sequence, *The Cat in Skeletal Strokes*. The speed lines in this still picture are generated by manually moving the umbrella and the hat. The ones in the animation are derived automatically from object movements.

To introduce more variety to speed lines, which is particularly important for static pictures, the spacing and length of the speed lines are given a certain randomness (Figure 15). In fact, there is no reason why speed lines cannot be shapes other than triangles. Why not arbitrary skeletal strokes along curved speed lines? So this is what we have done. To give an object drawn with Skeletal Draw a motion blur, the user only needs to transform the object to a new configuration (position and orientation). Using the specified stroke and speed line spacing, the system would create the speed lines from the new configuration to the old one. If a few intermediate configurations are marked before generating the speed lines, their paths would then be Catmull-Rom splines interpolating the various configurations.

## 7.2 Controlling a Pseudo-3D Stroke

We have demonstrated how to create an illusion of rotation by making use of the general anchoring mechanism. To perform that deformation, only one control parameter, the aspect ratio of the stroke, has been used. We could in theory control any kind of deformation of a picture with the aspect ratio alone. If different features in a picture are to change in different ways, however, it would be more convenient to have independent controls.

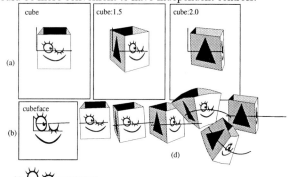

Figure 16: Hierarchical definition allowing independent control of different parts. (a) The definition of the stroke 'cube', 2nd order anchored by providing 3 instances at 1, 1.5 and 2 times its original aspect ratio(i.e. the left most one). (b) The definition of the sub-stroke 'cubeface' used in the definition of the stroke 'cube'. Notice that the eyes in the 'cubeface' stroke are also anchored skeletal strokes. The right eye has been closed by lengthening the application path. (c) Demonstrating how the 'eye' closes on varying its stroke length. (d) Application of the stroke 'cube' at different path lengths. Notice that the closing of the right eye takes effect at any 'angle' of the cube stroke.

We shall explain how to introduce extra independent controls with an example. Figure 16 shows a stroke of a cube which has a face on one of its sides. We can independently control the rotation of the cube and the blinking of the eyes of the face. This is done by defining the cube as a main stroke with the face as its sub-stroke. As was mentioned in Section 5.5, each stroke application is recorded with reference to the stroke definition (or stroke definitions if sub-strokes exist). This means that any changes in the definition of the stroke 'cubeface' would propagate to that of the stroke 'cube' and the changes would be reflected in its resulting stroke applications. Now using general anchoring, we can define the eyes on the stroke 'cubeface' to blink by varying the stroke application length of the 'eye' stroke. Hence by manipulating the lengths of the definitions of the strokes 'cube' and 'eye', we can control the cube rotation and eye blinking actions independently. This feature is particularly attractive for animating stylish cartoon characters which have no actual 3D realization.

This hierarchical way to define skeletal strokes means it is possible to build up powerful 2½D models with an arbitrary number of independent control parameters. Actually, these controls can be raised from the stroke definition level: we can easily set up an external control system by which users can manipulate different features with pop-up sliders, dials or other graphical user interfaces. We shall not go into details here.

Figure 17: A picture after a CACM front cover[1].

## 7.3 Animation with Skeletal Draw

Animation takes full advantage of the picture and deformation abstraction capability provided by skeletal strokes. The Skeletal Draw program has also been built with facilities to generate animation sequences. Traditional key-frame technique is used by Skeletal Draw. To create the key-frames, the user directly manipulates the characters in the scene. The system then calculates the in-betweens by interpolating Catmull-Rom splines. After the keyframes have been laid out, the program can do a quick playback using fewer in-betweens and substituting any skeletal strokes with rectangular (possibly deformed) ones. This quick preview is mainly to let the user to have a feel for the timing and smoothness of the motion. The in-betweens can be recorded in the same formats as the key-frames for inspection or further refinement. Because we are interpolating only the skeletons and they are usually of very simple forms, ensuring a proper interpolation of them is trivial. Furthermore, the shapes of the flesh are totally controlled by the skeletons, no interpolation of the individual points on the flesh is performed. Therefore the ambiguity of the shape blending problem[41,42] on the flesh would not arise at all.

The use of general anchoring is not limited to character creation. Since an arbitrary deformation can be recorded in one single stroke, a skeletal stroke can be viewed as an encapsulated unit of motion. These 'canned' motions can be applied conveniently at any time in a sequence. By redefining the sub-strokes, these motions can be used to animate other objects.

Stylized and complex drawings like those by Maurice Sendak[43] and Dr. Seuss[44] are known to be difficult to animate. It took Oscar winning animator Gene Deitch five years of experimenting before he found a way to transfer Maurice Sendak's drawing techniques to the screen[18]. With skeletal strokes' compact abstraction, complicated hatching or stipples can be condensed into simple units with which to further build up characters.

We have created a 1 minute animation sequence, *The Cat in Skeletal Strokes*, based on Dr. Seuss' *The Cat in the Hat*[44] character using the Skeletal Draw program. Two man days were used to create the sequence, which could have been even shorter had the bugs which appeared then been fixed earlier. Taking into consideration that our system was run on a 486 PC, this efficiency compares even more favourably than the Inkwell system[32]. The most time consuming part in the course of production is actually in the generation of antialiased frames.

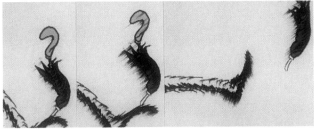

Figure 18: Frames from *The Cat in Skeletal Strokes*. The length and direction of the speed lines changes automatically with object movements.

Figure 19: A picture after Javier Mariscal's *Spain, the New Rising Star* (1990). A few strokes have been specially defined for this picture, e.g. the olive-green wiggly deco on the roof top and the hotel in the backdrop.

Figure 20: After the colour-lithograph *Loge with Golden Mask* (Detail) by Henri de Toulouse-Lautrec (1864-1901).

### 7.4 Incorporating Other Techniques

Metamorphosis or Morphing techniques[8,53] have received great attention lately due to their capability to generate dramatic but convincing deformations to photographic images with relatively simple calculations. By defining skeletal strokes to consist of morphing control lines on sampled images, we could build up

photorealistic pseudo-3D models of images instead of vector based pictures. With the hierarchical control over various parts of the strokes, we could start to make Michael Jackson's eyes blink and his head turn independently instead of our cartoon character's.

Figure 21: The width and shear angle of the yellow 'sausage' stroke (detail of the picture in Figure 19) is being modified.

Figure 22: *Where on Earth is SIGGRAPH94*. After a 'Cobi' poster by Javier Mariscal. Notice the fractal strokes at the lower part of the picture.

There are also published techniques which are useful for high level specification of animation sequences. For example, skeleton based 3D animation techniques based on physical deformations of complex 3D models[16,23]. While these may be useful for realistic deformations, they are not quite applicable to stylish figures, which do not even have a 3D realizable form. Furthermore, physical simulation is often unnecessary in stylish animation, which is the field we have been focusing on.

Techniques like gait control[22], constraint based methods [7,29,36,40,51,52] and dynamics simulation[13,46] are certainly important for creating highly realistic and complex physically based motions. Incorporation of these methods into our system is worth exploring in future.

## 9 CONCLUSION

We have presented in this paper the skeletal strokes framework for general drawing and animation. The framework has been demonstrated with the skeletal stroke based drawing system, Skeletal Draw. The decisions involved in its implementation and the resultant interaction style have been presented. In fact all the pictures and illustrations in this paper are drawn by the authors with the system without the help of a scanner. Figures 2, 3, 12, 19-22 in particular, demonstrate that skeletal strokes can be used to create rich and complex drawings from scratch. In the past, these can only be practically drawn with paint programs.

We have also introduced the combined usage of the hierarchical higher level stroke definition and the general anchoring mechanism to create pseudo-3D models with an arbitrary number of independent controls over different features of the model. The significance of these aspects in sample applications like comics and 2½D animation has also been discussed.

## REFERENCES

[1] Adams, Kathryn. [picture] In *Communications of the ACM*, October 1993, front cover.

[2] Adobe Systems Inc. *PostScript Language: Reference Manual*. Addison-Wesley, 1989.

[3] Barnsley, Michael F. *Fractals Everywhere*. Academic Press, 1988.

[4] Barnsley, Michael F. and L. P. Hurd. *Fractal Image Compression*. AK Peters Ltd., 1993.

[5] Barnsley, Michael F., A. Jacquin, F. Malassenet, L. Reuter and A. D. Sloan. Harnessing Chaos for Image Synthesis. Proceedings of SIGGRAPH88. In *Computer Graphics*, 22, 4 (August 1988).

[6] Barnsley, Michael F. and A. D. Sloan. A Better Way to Compress Images. In *BYTE*, January 1988.

[7] Barzel, Ronen and A. H. Barr. A Modelling System Based on Dynamic Constraints. Proceedings of SIGGRAPH88. In *Computer Graphics*, 22, 4 (August 1988).

[8] Beier, Thaddeus and S. Neely. Feature-Based Image Metamorphosis. Proceedings of SIGGRAPH92. In *Computer Graphics*,26,2 (July 1992).

[9] van Berkel, Pierre. SIAS, Strokes Interpreted Animated Sequences. In *Computer Graphics Forum*, 8, 1989.

[10] Bleser, Teresa W., J. L. Sibert and J. P. McGee. Charcoal Sketching: Returning Control to the Artist. In *ACM Transactions on Graphics*, 7(1):76-81, January 1988.

[11] Blinn, J. F. and M. E. Newell. Texture and Reflection in Computer Generated Images. In *Communications of the ACM*, volume 19, Oct., 1976.

[12] Bresenham, J. E. Ambiguities in Incremental Line Rastering. In *IEEE Computer Graphics and Applications*, volume 7, 1987.

[13] Brunderlin, Armin and T. W. Calvert. Goal-Directed, Dynamic Animation of Human Walking. Proceedings of SIGGRAPH89. In *Computer Graphics*, 23, 3 (July 1989).

[14] Burtnyk, N. and M. Wein. Computer-Generated Key-Frame Animation. In Journal of Society for Motion Picture and Television Engineers, 80:149-153, 1971.

[15] Burtnyk, N. and M. Wein. Interactive Skeleton Techniques for Enhancing Motion Dynamics in Key Frame Animation. In *Communications of the ACM*, volume 19, October 1976.

[16] Chadwick, John E., D. R. Hauman and R. E. Parent. Layered Construction for Deformable Animated Characters. Proceedings of SIGGRAPH89. In *Computer Graphics*, 23, 3 (July 1989).

[17] Chen, Shenchang E. and W. Lance. View Interpolation for Image Synthesis. Proceedings of SIGGRAPH93. In *Computer Graphics*, Annual Conference Series, 1993.

[18] Culhane, Shamus. *Animation from Script to Screen*. Columbus Books, 1989.

[19] Cook, Robert L. Stochastic Sampling in Computer Graphics. In *ACM Transactions on Graphics*, 5(1), January 1986.

[20] Dippé, M. A. Anti-aliasing Through Stochastic Sampling. Proceedings of SIGGRAPH85. In *Computer Graphics*, 19, 3 (July 1985).

[21] Ghosh, Pijush K. and S. P. Mudur. The Brush-Trajectory Approach to Figures Specification: Some Algebraic-Solutions. In *ACM Transactions on Graphics*, 3(2):110-134, April 1984.

[22] Girard, Michael and A. A. Maciejewski. Computational Modelling for the Computer Animation of Legged Figures. Proceedings of SIGGRAPH85. In *Computer Graphics*, 19, 3 (July 1985).

[23] Gourret, Jean-Paul, N. Magnenat Thalmann, D. Thalmann. Simulation of Object and Human Skin Deformation in a Grasping Task. Proceedings of SIGGRAPH89. In *Computer Graphics*, 23,3 (July 1989).

[24] Greene, Richard. The Drawing Prism: A Versatile Graphic Input Device. Proceedings of SIGGRAPH85. In *Computer Graphics*, 19, 3 (July 1985).

[25] Guo, Qinglian and T. L. Kunii. Modelling the Diffuse Paintings of 'Sumie'. In *Modelling in Computer Graphics*. T. L. Kunii, Ed. Springer Verlag. 1991.

[26] Hahn, James K. Realistic Animation of Rigid Bodies. Proceedings of SIGGRAPH88. In *Computer Graphics*, 22, 4 (Aug. 1988).

[27] Hsu, Siu Chi. *Computer Support for Large Character Set Languages*. PhD thesis, University of Cambridge, Computer Laboratory, December 1991.

[28] Hsu, Siu Chi, I. H. H. Lee and N. E. Wiseman. Skeletal Strokes. In *UIST'93 Proceedings of the ACM SIGGRAPH and SIGCHI Symposium on User Interface Software and Technology*, November 1993.

[29] Issacs, Paul M. and M. F. Cohen. Controlling Dynamic Simulation with Kinematic Constraints, Behaviour Functions and Inverse Dynamics. Proceedings of SIGGRAPH87. In *Computer Graphics*,21,4 (July 1987).

[30] Knuth, Donald E. Lessons Learned from METAFONT. In *Visible Language*, 19(1), 1985.

[31] Knuth, Donald E. *The METAFONT Book*. Addison Wesley, 1989.

[32] Litwinowicz, Peter C. Inkwell: A 2½D Animation System. Proceedings of SIGGRAPH91. In *Computer Graphics*, 25, 4 (July 1991).

[33] Max, Nelson L. and D. M. Lerner. A Two-and-a-Half-D Motion-Blur Algorithm. Proceedings of SIGGRAPH85. In *Computer Graphics*, 19, 3 (July 1985).

[34] Miles, Linda and B. Wilson. *Illustration Techniques with Adobe Illustrator for Windows*. Hayden (a Prentice Hall division), 1992.

[35] Mohri, Tomio. Issey Miyaki Advertisement. [picture] In *Joyce Men Spring 1993*. Joyce Publishing Ltd., 1993.

[36] Ngo J. Thomas and J. Marks. Spacetime Constraints Revisited. Proceedings of SIGGRAPH93. In *Computer Graphics*, 1993.

[37] Osamu, Tezuka. Hinotori (Fire Bird). Kadokana Bunko, 1990.

[38] Pang, Y. J. and H. X. Zhong. Drawing Chinese Traditional Painting by Computer. In *Modelling in Computer Graphics*. T. L. Kunii, Ed. Springer Verlag. 1991.

[39] Paulson, Ed. *Using CorelDraw! 4*. Que Corporation, 1993.

[40] Platt, John C. and A. H. Barr. Constraint Methods for Flexible Models. Proceedings of SIGGRAPH88. In *Computer Graphics*,22,4 (Aug 1988).

[41] Sederberg, Thomas W. and E. Greenwood. A Physically Based Approach to 2D Shape Blending. Proceedings of SIGGRAPH92. In *Computer Graphics*, 26, 2 (July 1992).

[42] Sederberg, Thomas W., P. Gao, G. Wang and H. Mu. 2D Shape Blending: An Intrinsic Solution to the Vertex Path Problem. Proceedings of SIGGRAPH93. In *Computer Graphics*, 1993.

[43] Sendak, Maurice. *Where the Wild Things are*. HarperCollins Publishers Ltd., 1992.

[44] Dr. Seuss. *The Cat in the Hat*. Random House, 1958.

[45] Shinya, Mikio. Spatial Anti-aliasing for Animation Sequences with Spatio-temporal Filtering. Proceedings of SIGGRAPH93. In *Computer Graphics*, 1993.

[46] Smith, Alvy Ray. Paint. In *Tutorial: Computer Graphics*, 13(2):501-- 515. IEEE Press, 1982.

[47] Strassmann, Steve. Hairy Brushes. Proceedings of SIGGRAPH86. In *Computer Graphics*, 20, 4 (Aug. 1986).

[48] Terzopoulos, Demetri and K. Fleischer. Modelling Inelastic Deformation: Viscoelasticity, Plasticity, Fracture. Proceedings of SIGGRAPH88. In *Computer Graphics*, 22, 4 (Aug. 1988).

[49] Vermeulen, Allan H. and P. P. Tanner. PencilSketch -- A Pencil-Based Paint System. In *Proceedings of Graphics Interface '89*, May 1989.

[50] Whitted, Turner. Anti-Aliased Line Drawing Using Brush Extrusion. Proceedings of SIGGRAPH83. In *Computer Graphics*,17,3 (July 1983).

[51] Witkin, Andrew, K. Fleischer and A. Barr. Energy Constraints On Parameterized Models. Proceedings of SIGGRAPH87. In *Computer Graphics*, 21, 4 (July 1987).

[52] Witkin, Andrew and M. Kass. Spacetime Constraints. Proceedings of SIGGRAPH88. In *Computer Graphics*, 22, 4 (Aug. 1988).

[53] Wolberg, George. *Digital Image Warping*. IEEE Computer Society Press, 1990.

# Efficient Techniques for Interactive Texture Placement

## Peter Litwinowicz, Gavin Miller
## Apple Computer, Inc.
1 Infinite Loop, MS 301-3J, Cupertino, CA 95014
litwinow@apple.com,  gspm@apple.com

## ABSTRACT
This paper describes efficient algorithms for the placement and distortion of textures. The textures include surface color maps and environment maps. Affine transformations of a texture, as well as localized warps, are used to align features in the texture with features of the model. Image-space caches are used to enable texture placement in real time.

**Keywords:** Texture placement, interaction, image warping, environment mapping.

## 1 Introduction
The use of texture mapping to enhance surface detail is well established [Catmull74]. Environment, or reflectance, mapping is described in [Blinn76]. Few solutions are available which allow interactive alignment of features in a texture with geometric features of a model.

Recently, with the availability of real-time texturing hardware, real-time texture placement is possible on high-end machines [Fuchs89], [Kirk90], [Akeley93]. Such hardware allows the global manipulation of the texture (such as placement and scale) but does not allow the alignment of particular features in the texture and the model.

An alternative approach, taken by [Hanrahan90] was to allow the painting of texture directly onto the surface of objects. Unfortunately, this approach required painterly skill on the part of the user, and did not allow distortion of pre-existing textures to fit a new model.

Warping or "morphing" algorithms have been developed which allow local distortions of pictures [Wolberg90][Beier92]. To date warping algorithms have mostly been used to distort pictures in the image plane. [Williams 90] presented a method for warping texture features into registration with a geometric model but the interaction entailed working with a 2D map of the model.

A way to create a piece-wise bivariate parameterization for a polygonal mesh is given in [Maillot93]. It employed optimization to smooth the regions near the boundaries between different pieces of the mapping chart. Feature alignment involves having a sector boundary for each feature. If there are a large number of features, the number of sectors will grow, thereby increasing the solution time for the smoothness optimization.

Section 2 of this paper describes image buffering schemes and new algorithms to accelerate the placement of textures onto surfaces in 3-space. In Section 3, the use of warping techniques are shown to be useful for aligning textures on surfaces in 3-space directly. In Section 4, an efficient scheme is presented for interactive reflection mapping, allowing the environment map to be rotated relative to the object reflecting it.

## 2 Texture Mapping Using Image Buffers
When placing textures interactively on a surface, it is vital that the display is refreshed at a reasonable frame rate. In order to achieve this on low-end machines, it is necessary to precompute as much of the rendering process as possible. One useful constraint to impose is that the camera and model stay fixed, and only the surface texture is able to move. This means that the model may be scan-converted into a cache or "image buffer" which stores information about the surface at each pixel such as the surface UV values. This was the approach taken in [Hanrahan90] to allow painting directly on surfaces. Assuming that the lights remain fixed during the interaction, the total illumination brightness may also be cached in the buffer. Furthermore, if the surfaces are purely diffuse, then the pixel color may be found by multiplying the illumination brightness by the texture color.

### 2.1 Efficient Parametric Mapping
The first step is to create an image buffer for the visible surfaces. In our approach the image buffer stores only the surface illumination and UV values. Figure 1 shows the UV parameterization of a sphere encoded in the red and green channels and the final texture-mapped sphere.

Once such an image buffer has been created, the process of texture-mapping and shading is given by the following steps:

For each pixel corresponding to the surface of interest:
1. Apply an affine transformation to the buffer UV values.
2. Look up the surface color using the transformed UV value.
3. Combine the surface color with the illumination.
4. Place the result in the corresponding screen pixel.

Step 1 may be optimized in the following way. Rather than applying a general two by two transformation matrix to the UV values, an intermediate texture image may be used. This intermediate image contains a transformed version of the original texture map. To create this intermediate image, the affine mapping is applied to the texture image directly. The image buffer UV values are merely used to index into this intermediate map. When creating the intermediate map, the scaling factor for the texture image is constant for all scanlines. When this scaling is implemented using point sampling, the texture resampling code merely requires adds and shifts in the inner loop.

### 2.2 Efficient Color Scaling
Once the surface color has been determined from the texture map, it must be combined with the total illumination to give the pixel color. This requires the multiplication of the red, green and blue components by the illumination brightness and for the results to be packed into a long word for subsequent placement in the frame-buffer. The traditional implementation requires three multiplies

and several shifts. However, if the brightness values are in a range of 0 to 255, it is possible to compute the same result with just two multiplies. If an approximate result is acceptable, then it is possible to use just one multiply. Pseudo-code for these techniques is given in Appendix 1.

## 3 Interactive Texture Placement Using Image Warping

Scaling, rotating and moving a texture on an object will often be enough control. In many cases, however, the features in the texture will not line up with features in the geometry. We propose a method that permits feature alignment without modifying the object or repainting the texture.

Delineating a set of features in an image is the first step in the warping process. The user then specifies what final shape these features should take. The deformation software then automatically warps the initial texture so that the features take the final shape, interpolating appropriately for the regions between specified features. The implementation described below was chosen among the many techniques available [Beier92][Wolberg90][Litwinowicz94] for its speed.

In Figure 2a, a picture of a checkerboard is shown, with 6 feature points described. The user specifies that the two internal feature points be moved as shown by the red arrows. The four corners are to remain where they are. In our system a Delaunay triangulation [Preparata85] is calculated for the original (non-displaced) feature points, as shown in Figure 2b. The original position of a feature point determines its UV index for texture mapping. Then the feature points are displaced as desired by the user (Figure 2c); note that the topology determined in the prior step is retained. By texture mapping these triangles using the assigned UV texture indices, the original texture is warped into Figure 2d.

In essence, the Delaunay triangulation has been used to interpolate the given displacements. As such, the Delaunay triangulation provides a rather crude interpolant. After the interactive process is completed, the user could be provided with the option of one the earlier referenced smoother, but much slower, warping techniques.

Using a combination of UV image buffering and image deformation, it is possible to warp a texture directly on a 3D object. In our feature alignment tool, users first create a feature point on the texture. Instead of moving a feature point in the image plane, as in the traditional warping application, the user creates a corresponding feature point on the object itself. When the user specifies a point by clicking on the object, the displaced coordinate for the feature point is looked up in the UV buffer (computed before the interactive process). Using corresponding image and UV points as the original and destination features, the image is warped before mapping onto the object. As a user drags around a feature point in object or texture space he sees the resultant texture mapped object at interactive speeds. It should be noted that the warping in our implementation, which entails texture mapping the triangulation derived from the features points, is accomplished with software scan conversion. With texture mapping hardware the warping stage could be done even faster.

Figure 3a shows an object and a texture to be placed on the object. Figure 3b shows the straight one-to-one mapping, and the mapping after the user has found the best fit for the texture using the scaling and offset tool. The user then enters the feature alignment mode and identifies correspondences (right and left pictures of Figure 3c). The four outside points on the texture in Figure 3c, left, define the best scaling and offset fit as specified by

the user in the affine fit step. After the feature correspondence is completed, the original texture is warped (middle, Figure 3c) and then mapped onto the object. Note that the user does not work on an untextured object, but interacts by dragging texture interactively as suggested by the picture on the right in Figure 3c.

As with all image deformation algorithms that use forward mapping it is possible for the warped texture to fold back on itself. Our implementation does not prevent this from occurring, but since the warping is interactive the user can prevent or correct such fold-overs as they occur.

To summarize: We use the global placement technique to provide a good rough placement of the texture for the local refinement process. The local refinement process is initialized with four correspondences between the texture and object which describe the user-applied affine transformation. The four corresponding points are chosen so that they completely surround the part of the texture being mapped. The user can locally match features by adding more correspondences.

Interactive global placement for Figure 1 with a 256x256 texture ran at 6.5 frames/sec with no shading, 4.7 frames/sec with 4-bit shading (see Appendix A1.3) and 4.2 frames/sec with 8-bit shading (see Appendix A1.2) on a Macintosh Quadra™ 950. Global placement for Figure 3 ran at 2.4 frames/sec for translation, 1.42 frames/sec for scaling, and 1.3 frames/sec for warping with 8 feature points.

## 4 Efficient Environment Map Manipulation

Environment mapping samples a texture image using the reflected site vector for each point on an object. For environment map placement we require a way to transform each reflected ray vector so that the environment map may be rotated around the object. In this way, reflections may be moved to desired places on the model.

Doing a full matrix multiply of the reflected vector followed by a texture look-up would be prohibitive. An alternative is to use spherical polar coordinates for the representation of the reflected ray in the image buffer. The reflected ray direction is stored as spherical polar coordinates $(\phi, \theta)$ in the image buffer. The environment map is also stored as a spherical polar map with coordinates $(\phi, \theta)$, as in Figure 4. Figure 5a shows an example surface. In Figure 5b, the $(\phi, \theta)$ values are encoded in the red and green channels. The polar axis for the environment map is pointing directly away from the camera.

By using the image buffer $(\phi, \theta)$ values to index into the environment map directly, it is possible to render an image of the environment map reflected by the object. This is illustrated in Figure 5c. If the $(\phi, \theta)$ values are mapped directly into the environment map, there are no degrees of freedom for interaction. However, adding an offset to the $\phi$ value, before indexing into the environment map, is equivalent to rotating the environment map around the polar axis, by an amount equal to the offset. This provides one rotational degree of freedom.

For a general placement system, more rotational degrees of freedom are required. A way to achieve this is to transform the $(\phi, \theta)$ coordinates for a vertical polar axis into the $(\phi', \theta')$ values which correspond to a horizontal polar axis. Adding to the value of $\phi'$, and then taking the inverse mapping, is equivalent to rotating about the horizontal axis. The mapping between two polar coordinate frames may be stored in a 2-D look-up-table. This table is a map the same size as the spherical environment map and is called the "spherical-to-spherical" map. Details of how to compute the spherical-to-spherical map is given in Appendix 2.

In order to render the scene with three degrees of freedom, the reflected ray vector is stored in the image buffer in terms of $(\phi, \theta)$ where the spherical polar axis is aligned with the camera view direction. Adding an offset to the $\phi$ value is equivalent to rotating about the screen Z-axis, which is also known as "twist". The coordinates $(\phi + twist, \theta)$ are used to index into the spherical-to-spherical map to compute $(\phi', \theta')$. Adding an offset to $\phi'$ is equivalent to rotating about the screen X-axis, which is equivalent to the "pitch" angle. The value coordinates $(\phi' + pitch, \theta')$ are again indexed into the spherical-to-spherical map to compute $(\phi'', \theta'')$. Adding an offset to $\phi''$ is equivalent to rotating about the polar axis of the environment map. The coordinates $(\phi'' + yaw, \theta'')$ are indexed into the spherical-polar environment map to find the color of the screen pixel. This process leads to reflection maps which may be rotated with three degrees of freedom.

If only two degrees of freedom are required in the interface, then the $(\phi, \theta)$ values are stored for a spherical polar axis aligned with the screen X-axis. This then requires only a single use of the spherical-to-spherical map. This more restricted interaction is often adequate and leads to faster performance and less aliasing artifacts. An example teapot rendered using the three degree of freedom algorithm is shown in Figure 5d, which was displayed interactively at 6.0 frames/sec on a Macintosh Quadra™ 950.

When texture-mapping hardware is available, this technique may be modified as follows. Using the above techniques, an image of a sphere is computed which reflects the environment at any orientation. This image of a reflective sphere can then be used as a surface texture . The texture is indexed using the screen X and Y coordinates of the reflected ray vector. These index values are interpolated using the texture-mapping hardware of the workstation.

## 5 Summary
This paper demonstrated a technique that allows intuitive placement of textures on objects. This is achieved using an affine transformation for gross placement, followed by texture warping for local refinement. A technique was also described which permits control over reflection mapping.

## 6 Acknowledgments
Thanks to Subhana Ansari for layout help.

## 7 References

[Akeley93] Akeley, Kurt, "RealityEngine Graphics", Computer Graphics, SIGGRAPH Annual Conference Proceedings, 1993 pp. 109-116.

[Beier92] Beier, Thaddeus and Shawn Neely. "Feature-Based Image Metamorphosis," Computer Graphics, Volume 26, Number 2, July 1992, pp. 35-42.

[Blinn76] Blinn, Jim. and Martin Newell.. "Texture and Reflection in Computer Generated Images." CACM, Vol. 19 Number 10, October 1976, pp. 542-546.

[Catmull74] Catmull, E. , "A Subdivision Algorithm for Computer Display of Curved Surfaces", Ph.D. dissertation, University of Utah, 1974.

[Kirk90] Kirk, David and Douglas Voorhies, "The Rendering Architecture of the DN10000VS", Computer Graphics, Vol. 24, No. 4, August 1990, pp. 299-307.

[Fuchs89] Fuchs, Henry, J. Poulton, J. Eyles, T. Greer, J. Goldfeather, D. Ellsworth, S. Molnar, G. Turk, B. Tebbs, L.

Israel, "Pixel-Planes 5: A Heterogeneous Multiprocessor Graphics System Using Processor-Enhanced Memories" Computer Graphics, Vol. 23, No. 3, July 1989, pp. 79-88.

[Hanrahan90] Hanrahan, Pat and Paul Haeberli,. "Direct WYSIWYG Painting and Texturing on 3D Shapes," Volume 24, Number 4, August 1990, pp. 215-223.

[Litwinowicz94] Litwinowicz, Peter and Lance Williams,. "Animating Images with Drawings," SIGGRAPH 94 proceedings.

[Maillot93] Maillot, Jérome, H. Yahia, A. Verroust, "Interactive Texture Mapping", Computer Graphics, SIGGRAPH Annual Conference Proceedings, 1993 pp. 27-34.

[Preparata85] Preparata, Franco P., Michael Ian Shamos, "Computational Geometry, An Introduction", Springer Verlag, 1985.

[Williams90] Williams, Lance. "Performance-driven Facial Animation," Computer Graphics, Vol. 24, No. 4, pp. 235-242.

[Wolberg90] Wolberg, George. Digital Image Warping. 1990, IEEE Computer Society Press.

### Appendix 1: Pseudo-code for Efficient Color Scaling
In the following pseudo-code fragments, all values are assumed to be contained in longs. The direct approach to color scaling is given in Figure A1.1.

```
// The following is done once per screen pixel
redValue   = ((textureColor & redMask)   >> redBits);
greenValue = ((textureColor & greenMask) >> greenBits);
blueValue  = ((textureColor & blueMask)  >> blueBits);
scaledR = (redValue   * brightness) >> brightnessBits;
scaledG = (greenValue * brightness) >> brightnessBits;
scaledB = (blueValue  * brightness) >> brightnessBits;
compositeColor = (scaledR << 16) | (scaledG << 8) | scaleB;
(The order of R and B may be reversed for
different conventions in the frame-buffer.)
```

Figure A1.1: Color scaling using three multiplies.

In Figure A1.1, the textureColor is three eight bit color values packed into a long. Also, the surface illumination is stored in "brightness" which is defined to have a value between zero and two to the power of "brightnessBits" minus one.

If brightnessBits is defined to be 8, then it is possible to compute the same result with just two multiplies. This is illustrated in Figure A1.2.

```
// The following things can be defined just once
gMask = 255 << 8;
iMask = ((1 << 24) - 1) - gMask;

// The following is done once per screen pixel
compositeColor = (((brightness * (textureColor & iMask)) >> 8) & iMask)
        + (((brightness * (textureColor & gMask)) >> 8) & gMask);
```

Figure A1.2: Color scaling using two multiplies.

It is also possible to compute an approximate scaling of the color using just a single multiply. This may be achieved by masking out the four least significant bits of each color component of the texture and then multiplying by a four bit brightness. Both the color texture values and the brightness can be dithered in a preprocessing step to avoid contouring artifacts. Pseudo-code for this approach is given in Figure A1.3

```
// The following thing can be defined just once
RGBMask = (15 << 16) | (15 << 8) | 15;

// The following is done once per texture pixel in a preprocessing step
fourBitTextureColor = (textureColor >> 4) & RGBMask;

// The following is done once per screen pixel
compositeColor  = (fourBitBrightness * fourBitTextureColor);
```

Figure A1.3: Color scaling using one multiply.

## Appendix 2: The Spherical-to-Spherical Map

To compute the spherical-to-spherical map, the algorithm loops for each pixel in the map computing the $(\phi, \theta)$ angular coordinates linearly from the pixel coordinates.

$D_x = \sin(\theta)\sin(\phi)$; $D_y = \sin(\theta)\cos(\phi)$; $D_z = \cos(\theta)$;
where $0 \leq \theta \leq \pi$ and $0 \leq \phi \leq 2\pi$

The direction vector **D** is then rotated about the Z-axis and the result is used to find a new pair of $(\phi', \theta')$ values which are then encoded in the spherical-to-spherical map:

$d_x = D_y$;   $d_y = -D_x$;   $d_z = D_z$;
$\phi' = \tan^{-1}(d_x / d_z)$;     $\theta' = \sin^{-1}(d_y)$;

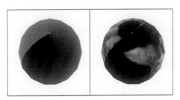

Figure 1. UV-buffer of a sphere and the same sphere texture mapped.

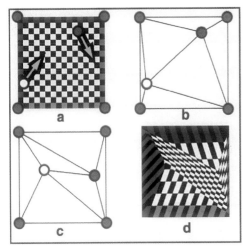

Figure 2. a) Undistorted texture. b) Original feature control points, with Delaunay triangulation. c) Displaced control points d) Locally distorted texture.

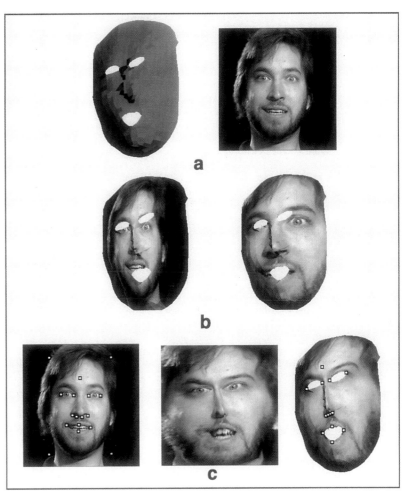

Figure 3. a) Object and image to be textured. b) Textured object using identity UV map and user-applied scale and offset. c) Feature alignment using texture warping.

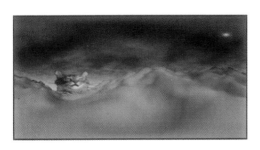

Figure 4. Spherical environment map of terrain with cat.

Figure 5. Teapot: a) Shaded surface. b) Reflected ray as polar coordinates. c) Reflections for default map orientation d) Reflections with map in new orientation.

# Rotated Dispersed Dither: a New Technique for Digital Halftoning

Victor Ostromoukhov, Roger D. Hersch, Isaac Amidror

Swiss Federal Institute of Technology (EPFL)

CH-1015 Lausanne, Switzerland

victor@di.epfl.ch

## ABSTRACT

Rotated dispersed-dot dither is proposed as a new dither technique for digital halftoning. It is based on the discrete one-to-one rotation of a Bayer dispersed-dot dither array. Discrete rotation has the effect of rotating and splitting a significant part of the frequency impulses present in Bayer's halftone arrays into many low-amplitude distributed impulses. The halftone patterns produced by the rotated dither method therefore incorporate fewer disturbing artifacts than the horizontal and vertical components present in most of Bayer's halftone patterns. In grayscale wedges produced by rotated dither, texture changes at consecutive gray levels are much smoother than in error diffusion or in Bayer's dispersed-dot dither methods, thereby avoiding contouring effects.

Due to its semi-clustering behavior at mid-tones, rotated dispersed-dot dither exhibits an improved tone reproduction behavior on printers having a significant dot gain, while maintaining the high detail rendition capabilities of dispersed-dot halftoning algorithms. Besides their use in black and white printing, rotated dither halftoning techniques have also been successfully applied to in-phase color reproduction on ink-jet printers.

## 1   INTRODUCTION

Due to the proliferation of low-cost bi-level desktop printers, converting grayscale images to halftoned black and white images remains an important issue. While significant progress has been made to improve the quality of error-diffusion algorithms, dispersed-dot dither algorithms, which are much faster, have not been substantially improved over the last 20 years. Only recently, a new method for generating well-dispersed dither arrays was reported [14].

This contribution presents a new dispersed-dot dither technique, based on a discrete one-to-one rotation of a conventional dispersed-dot dither threshold array. It will be shown that, compared to Bayer's ordered dither, this new rotated dispersed-dot dither technique produces diagonally oriented small-sized halftone clusters, reduces the power of individual low frequency components, incorporates smooth pattern transitions between neighbouring gray levels and provides an improved tone reproduction curve, halfway between classical clustered-dot and Bayer's dispersed-dot dither techniques.

In section 2, we give a brief survey of the main halftoning techniques and show their respective advantages and drawbacks in terms of computation complexity, tone reproduction behavior and detail resolution. In section 3, the proposed rotated dither method is presented. It is based on a one-to-one discrete rotation of a dither tile made of replicated Bayer dither arrays. In section 4, we compare the proposed rotated dither method with error diffusion and with Bayer's dispersed-dot dither method by showing halftoned images. In section 5, we try to explain why the proposed rotated dither algorithm generates globally less perceptible artifacts than Bayer's by analyzing the frequencies produced by the halftoning patterns at different gray levels. In section 6, we analyze the tone reproduction behavior of the different algorithms and show that the rotated dispersed-dot dither algorithm has a robustness close to that of clustered-dot halftoning, therefore being appropriate for printers with a significant dot gain.

## 2   BACKGROUND

Both classical clustered-dot halftoning [15] and dispersed-dot dither halftoning algorithms [13] are supported by modern PostScript level-2 printers which provide the means to customize their *dither threshold array* by downloading the threshold values used for the halftoning process. With a given dither threshold array, the halftoning process consists of scanning the output bitmap and, for each output pixel, finding its corresponding locations both in the dither array and in the grayscale input pixmap image, comparing corresponding input image pixel intensity values to dither array threshold values, and accordingly writing pixels of one of two possible output intensity levels to the output image bitmap. Dither array based halftoning is very efficient: only one comparison is needed per output device pixel. Furthermore, output device pixels can be computed independently, which enables the halftoning process to be parallelized and pipelined [10]. Patent literature demonstrates that significant efforts have been made for improving the quality of exact angle clustered-dot dithering techniques [11],[5],[12]. However, the only recent effort known to improve the quality of dispersed-dot dither halftoning is the void-and-cluster method proposed by Ulichney [14].

Error diffusion algorithms, first introduced by Floyd and Steinberg [4], are more computationally intensive methods. They require diffusing the error, i.e. the difference between the output device pixel intensity and the original source image intensity, to a certain number of neighbours. In the traditional Floyd-Steinberg algorithm, parallel computation of output device pixels is not possible since each output pixel depends on the error transferred by its neighbours. The dot diffusion method proposed by Knuth [9] and further improved by Zhang and Webber [16] removes these limitations by

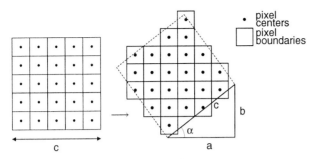

**Figure 1:** Rotating a square array of $c^2$ pixels by a Pythagorean angle $\alpha = \arctan(b/a)$, where $c = 5$, $a = 4$, $b = 3$.

tiling the output bitmap plane into limited size quadratic neighbourhoods, within which the error is allowed to propagate. Nevertheless, these improved error diffusion halftoning methods still require much more computation than dither array based halftoning, since errors must be propagated to several neighbours and since output pixels cannot always be computed in scanline order.

Generally, clustered-dot dither is preferred to Bayer's dispersed-dot dither because of Bayer's dispersed-dot dither artifacts and poor tone reproduction behavior. We will show that the proposed rotated dispersed-dot dither method generates slightly clustered halftone patterns which offer good tone reproduction behavior and at the same time avoid contouring effects by providing patterns which grow into one another smoothly as the intensity level increases.

## 3 THE ROTATED DITHER METHOD

Bayer's dispersed-dot ordered dither method has been shown to be optimal in the sense that in each gray level, the lowest frequency is as high as possible [3]. Nevertheless, as Figure 5b shows, low frequency components given by the dither array period size are quite strong for a large number of gray levels. These low frequency halftoning artifacts are well perceived, since at increasing intensity levels they switch back and forth from horizontal and vertical to diagonal directions. The transition between one intensity level and the next one creates an abrupt pattern change which appears in the halftoned image as a false contour.

Since human eye sensitivity to gratings decreases considerably at oblique orientations [2], we can make the perceived halftoning artifacts less visible by rotating the dispersed dither array. Moreover, we will show in section 5 that the discrete rotation of the dispersed dither array decreases the power of the individual low-frequency components by distributing their low-frequency energy over a larger set of frequencies.

The discrete rotation we intend to apply to dither arrays has some similarities with the rotation of bitmap images. For the sake of simplicity, we will therefore also use in this context the term "pixel" to denote a simple dither array element. The rotating task consists of finding a discrete rotation, which generates a "rotated Bayer threshold array" whose threshold values are exactly the values of the original Bayer dither threshold array. Let us consider rotations of binary pixel grids composed of unit size pixel squares. Exact rotation of a square pixel grid by an angle $\alpha$ around the position $(x_0, y_0)$ can be described by the following transformation applied to the pixel centers $(x, y)$:

$$x' = (x - x_0) \cos \alpha - (y - y_0) \sin \alpha + x_0 \qquad (1)$$

$$y' = (x - x_0) \sin \alpha + (y - y_0) \cos \alpha + y_0$$

In the general case, more than one rotated original pixel center may fall within a single pixel's square boundary in the destination grid, and some destination pixels may remain empty [6]. We therefore

need a one-to-one discrete rotation which unambiguously maps the set of original dither array elements into the new set formed by the rotated dither array.

Let us consider the continuous boundary of a square array of $c^2$ discrete pixels (Figure 1). It can be shown that if this boundary is rotated by a Pythagorean angle $\alpha = \arctan(b/a)$, where $a$ and $b$ are Pythagorean numbers satisfying the Diophantine equation $a^2 + b^2 = c^2$, the resulting rotated square boundary contains the same number of pixel centers as the original pixel array (Figure 1). Therefore, a discrete one-to-one rotation can be obtained by rotating with a Pythagorean angle and by an appropriate one-to-one mapping between the set of dither elements belonging to the original square and the set of dither elements belonging to the rotated square.

Such a discrete one-to-one rotation is obtained by rotating with a Pythagorean angle $\alpha = \arctan(b/a)$, where $c = 5, a = 4$, $b = 3$ and $\alpha = \arctan(3/4) = 36.87°$ and by applying rounding operations. Let us assume that $(i, j)$ is the coordinate system of the original dither array and $(x, y)$ the coordinate system of the rotated dither array, and that $i_0$, $j_0$, and respectively $x_0$, $y_0$ are integer values defining the location of the given original square dither array, respectively the location of the rotated dither array:

$$x = \text{round}\left(\frac{a}{c} * (i - i_0) - \frac{b}{c} * (j - j_0)\right) + x_0 \qquad (2)$$

$$y = \text{round}\left(\frac{b}{c} * (i - i_0) + \frac{a}{c} * (j - j_0)\right) + y_0$$

For this discrete one-to-one rotation, the distance between corresponding rotated and rounded pixel centers is either zero or equal to $1/\sqrt{5} = 0.447214$ (see Figure 3). In order to apply this discrete one-to-one rotation to a square Bayer dither threshold array, we have to consider the Bayer threshold array $D^n$ of size $n \times n$, replicated $c$ times vertically and horizontally, since its side length must be an integer multiple of Pythagorean hypotenuse $c$ (Figure 2a). We will denote the dither tile obtained this way by $D^{c*n}$. In Figures 2 and 4 we use as example the Bayer dither threshold array of size $n = 4$.

The discrete one-to-one rotation described by equations (2) applied to a dither tile $D^{c*n}$ made of a replicated Bayer dither threshold array yields a rotated dither tile $R^{c*n}$ (Figure 2b), which also paves the plane like the original tile $D^{c*n}$. The elements of the rotated dither tile $R^{c*n}$ have the same dither values as the corresponding original dither elements from the dither tile $D^{c*n}$. The subpixel displacements expressing the difference between continuous and discrete rotations are shown in Figure 3. The circle at the top left of Figure 3 shows the repetitive subpixel displacement patterns. Pixel centers of the same color within one oblique row in tile $R^{c*n}$ of Figure 3 correspond to pixel centers in one horizontal row of the original tile $D^{c*n}$.

The rotated dither tile $R^{c*n}$ includes irregularly arranged dither sub-arrays paving the dither plane (one of these sub-arrays is highlighted in blue in Figure 4). Such a diagonally oriented dither sub-array is easily transformed, according to Holladay's algorithm [7], into an equivalent rectangular dither tile paving the plane and containing the same number of dither threshold values (Figure 4).

Let us recall the computational effort required for dither array based halftoning. Once the dither tile containing the dither threshold values has been generated, it can be stored in memory and used for halftoning the grayscale images. Halftoning time is determined by the time required to scan the output image bitmap space, pixel by pixel, maintaining a pointer both at the corresponding places in the grayscale source image and in the Holladay rectangular dither tile and performing comparisons between corresponding dither threshold and input pixel intensity values. Computation time is proportional to the number of output bitmap pixels and is much smaller than the time needed by error-diffusion algorithms requir-

a)

b)

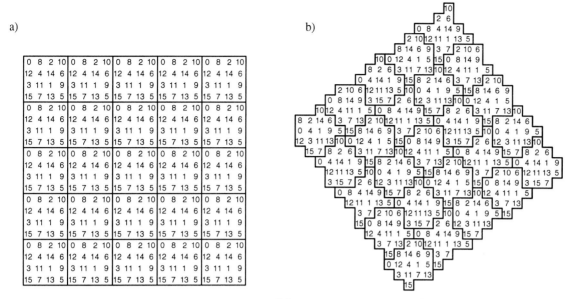

**Figure 2:** (a) Original replicated dither threshold array $D^{c*n}$ and (b) rotated dither tile $R^{c*n}$ obtained by the discrete rotation of tile $D^{c*n}$.

ing at each output bitmap pixel the error to be distributed to several neighbouring pixel elements [16].

## 4  EXPERIMENTAL RESULTS

Let us compare the proposed rotated dither method with standard Bayer dispersed-dot dither, Floyd-Steinberg error diffusion and clustered-dot dither. As can be seen from Figure 5, rotated dispersed-dot halftoning generates less texture artifacts than the standard Bayer method. Moreover, as it can be seen in the gray wedges at the top of the images, the tone reproduction of rotated dither is much better than that of the Bayer dither and slightly better than that of error diffusion.

As can be seen from Figure 5, the detail rendition capabilities of rotated dither are slightly better than those of Bayer dither, and much better than those of clustered-dot dither. It is well known that error diffusion has an inherent sharpening behavior and therefore provides better detail rendition capabilities [8]; nevertheless, it creates visible patterns in constant intensity areas.

In the grayscale wedges produced by rotated dither at consecutive gray levels, especially at intensity levels close to 50%, texture changes produced by rotated dither are smoother than in Floyd-Steinberg's error-diffusion or in Bayer's dispersed-dot dither methods (Figure 6).

Rotated dither halftoning techniques can also be applied both to single orientation multi-color in-phase printing and to increase the number of perceived colors on displays with a limited number of intensity levels.

## 5  FREQUENCY DOMAIN ANALYSIS

In order to compare the proposed rotated dither algorithm with Bayer's dispersed-dot dither algorithm, we analyze their respective halftone patterns at various intensity levels by comparing their frequency amplitude spectra. It is well known that the human eye is most sensitive to the lowest frequency components of screen dot patterns, especially if they have a horizontal or vertical orientation. Bayer demonstrated that his ordered dither algorithm minimizes the occurrence of low-frequency components. However, he didn't take into account the amplitudes of the spectral frequencies, nor

did he consider the anisotropic behavior [2] of the eye's contrast sensitivity function (CSF). In this section, we will show that the rotated dispersed-dot dither algorithm produces halftone patterns with a larger number of frequency components than Bayer's.

To compare the two dither algorithms, we consider halftone cells produced according to the example shown in section 3, representing gray levels $0, \frac{1}{16}, \frac{2}{16}, ..., \frac{15}{16}$. In that example, the Holladay rectangle paving the corresponding rotated dither tile has a size of 20 x 4 pixels. By choosing a sample array of a size which is an integer multiple of the horizontal and vertical replication period of the dither rectangle paving the plane, we ensure that the frequencies present in the Discrete Fourier Transform (DFT) of the sample array are located exactly on the spatial-frequency sampling grid, thereby avoiding leakage effects and ensuring that the spectral impulses fall exactly on the center of DFT impulses [1].

In the examples shown in Figure 9, we consider 80x80 pixel sample halftone arrays created according to Bayer's 4x4 dispersed-dot dither array and according to the rotated dither method, using 4x4 dispersed-dot dither arrays, replicated 5 times and rotated. We compare the amplitude spectrum of the respective halftone arrays for several gray levels. Figure 9 shows the halftone patterns as well as their corresponding DFT impulse amplitudes at grayscale levels $\frac{1}{16}, \frac{3}{16}, \frac{5}{16}$ and $\frac{7}{16}$. The dot surfaces in the spectra are proportional to the amplitude of the corresponding frequency impulses.

The following observations can be made:

– Compared to Bayer's dither, rotated dither incorporates additional lower frequency components having, however, a lower amplitude than the original Bayer frequency component.

– Bayer's original frequency components are present in the rotated dither patterns; they are simply rotated by $\alpha = \arctan(3/4)$, the angle used for the discrete one-to-one rotation. However, their amplitude is considerably lower than that of the corresponding Bayer frequency components. Figure 10 shows the amplitude spectrum for halftone at intensity level $\frac{3}{16}$ generated by the Bayer and the rotated dither methods. The Bayer frequency impulses present in the frequency spectrum of the rotated halftone pattern are marked by rings.

The rotated dither method rotates the frequency impulses present in the Bayer halftone array and splits one part of their amplitude into many lower amplitude distributed impulses. The power of the original Bayer main frequency components is therefore reduced, and additional low energy components are created. Moreover, since the main frequency components are rotated, they are less perceptible to the human eye than the horizontal and vertical components present in most of Bayer's halftone patterns.

## 6 TONE REPRODUCTION BEHAVIOR

The tone reproduction behavior of a given halftoning algorithm is heavily dependent on the dot gain behavior of the considered printer. At levels darker than 50%, dispersed-dot dither as well as error-diffusion halftoning algorithms tend to generate one pixel wide elongated white surface areas which may shrink considerably due to dot gain. We will show that the clustering behavior of rotated dither at mid-tones has a positive impact on its tone reproduction capabilities.

Let us compare the tone reproduction behavior of the rotated dispersed-dot dither algorithm with Bayer's dispersed-dot dither algorithm, error diffusion and clustered-dot halftoning. For this purpose we measure and plot the tone reproduction behavior of a variable intensity grayscale wedge printed on a black and white laser printer. Figure 7 shows the tone reproduction behavior for the considered halftoning techniques and Figure 8 the grayscale wedges printed at 300 dpi on a commercial laser printer.

If we compare the rotated dither method with Bayer's dither and error-diffusion, Figures 7 and 8 clearly show that for printers with a certain dot gain, rotated dispersed-dot dither has a behavior closer to clustered-dot dither, especially at mid-tones. It is therefore a good candidate for dispersed-dot printing on laser or ink-jet printers (300–800 dpi) having a significant dot gain.

While the clustered-dot dither method is the most robust in terms of reproduction behavior at large dot gains, the new rotated dispersed-dot dither method offers both a favorable reproduction behavior and good detail rendition capabilities.

## 7 CONCLUSION

This contribution proposes a new high-speed dispersed-dot dither algorithm whose dither array is obtained by discrete rotation of a conventional Bayer dither array. Discrete rotation attenuates the visible frequency components produced by halftoning, and spreads the power of the visible low frequency artifacts onto additional frequencies, thereby reducing the perception of the produced artifacts.

Furthermore, when rendering images at smoothly increasing intensity levels, rotated dispersed-dot dither generates less contouring effects than Bayer's dither method and less artifacts than Floyd-Steinberg's error-diffusion method.

Due to its additional lower-frequency components, the proposed rotated dispersed-dot algorithm has a more pronounced clustering behavior than both Bayer's dispersed-dot dither and error-diffusion algorithms. It therefore exhibits an improved tone reproduction behavior on printers having a significant dot gain. Rotated dispersed-dot dither is nearly as robust as clustered-dot dither while offering much higher detail rendering capabilities.

Rotated dither halftoning techniques can be applied both to single orientation multi-color in-phase printing and to increase the number of perceived colors on display devices with a limited number of intensity levels.

## ACKNOWLEDGMENTS

We would like to thank the HP Research Labs (Palo Alto, CA) and the Swiss National Fund (grant No. 21-31136.91) for supporting the project.

## REFERENCES

[1] E.O. Brigham, *The Fast Fourier Transform and its Applications.* Prentice-Hall, UK, 1988.

[2] F.W. Campbell, J.J. Kulikowski, J. Levinson, The effect of orientation on the visual resolution of gratings, *J. Physiology*, London, 1966, Vol 187, 427-436.

[3] B.E. Bayer, An Optimum Method for Two-Level Rendition of Continuous-Tone Pictures, *IEEE 1973 International Conference on Communications,* Vol. 1, June 1973, 26-11–26-15.

[4] R.W. Floyd, L. Steinberg, An Adaptive Algorithm for Spatial Grey Scale, *Proc. SID,* 1976, Vol 17(2), 75-77.

[5] Gall, Winrich, "Method and Apparatus for Producing Half-Tone Printing Forms with Rotated Screens on the Basis of Randomly Selected Screen Threshold Values", U.S. Patent No. 4700235 (1987), Assignee: Dr. Ing. Rudolf Hell GmbH. (Fed. Rep. of Germany).

[6] R.D. Hersch, Raster Rotation of Bilevel Bitmap Images, *Eurographics'85 Proceedings,* (Ed. C. Vandoni), North-Holland, 1985, 295-308.

[7] Holladay T. M., "An Optimum Algorithm for Halftone Generation for Displays and Hard Copies," *Proceedings of the Society for Information Display,* 21(2), 1980, 185-192.

[8] K.T. Knox, Edge Enhancement in Error Diffusion, *SPSE's 42nd Annual Conf.,* May 1989, 56-79.

[9] D.E. Knuth, Digital Halftones by Dot Diffusion, *ACM Trans. on Graphics,* 6(4), 1987, 245-273.

[10] M. Morgan, R.D. Hersch, V. Ostromoukhov, Hardware Acceleration of Halftoning, Proceedings SID International Symposium, Anaheim, in *SID 93 Digest,* May 1993, Vol XXIV, 151-154.

[11] Rosenfeld, Gideon, "Screened Image Reproduction", U.S. Patent No. 4456924 (1984). Assignee: Scitex Corporation Ltd. (Israel).

[12] Troxel, D.E., "Method and Apparatus for Generating Digital, Angled Halftone Screens Using Pixel Candidate Lists and Screen Angle Correction to Prevent Moire Patterns", U.S. Patent No. 5124803 (1992). Assignee: ECRM.

[13] R. Ulichney, *Digital Halftoning,* The MIT Press, Cambridge, Mass., 1987.

[14] R. Ulichney, The void-and-cluster method for dither array generation, *IS&T/SPIE Symposium on Electronic Imaging Science & Technology, Proceedings Conf. Human Vision, Visual Processing and Digital Display IV,* (Eds. Allebach, Rogowitz), SPIE Vol. 1913, 1993, 332-343.

[15] J.A.C. Yule, *Principles of Colour Reproduction,* John Wiley & Sons, NY (1967).

[16] Y. Zhang, R.E.Webber, Space Diffusion: An Improved Parallel Halftoning Technique Using Space-Filling Curves, Proceedings of SIGGRAPH'93, In *ACM Computer Graphics,* Annual Conference Series, 1993, 305-312.

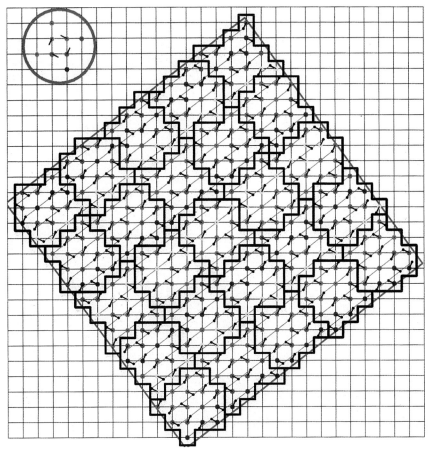

**Figure 3:** Subpixel displacements due to the difference between continuous and discrete rotation.

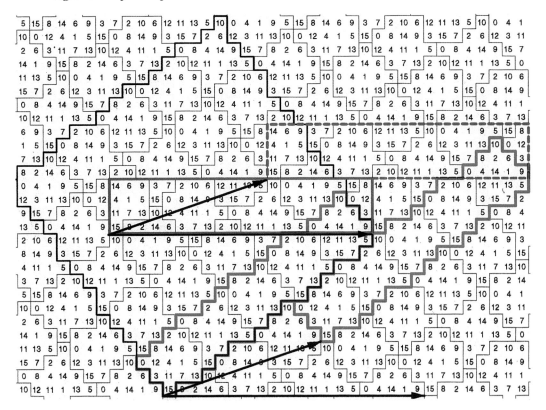

**Figure 4:** Rotated dither sub-tile (blue) and corresponding Holladay rectangle (red).

a)

b)

c)

d)

**Figure 5:** Grayscale image, halftoned at 150 dpi with (a) the 16x16 rotated dither algorithm, (b) 16x16 Bayer's dither algorithm, (c) a conventional diagonally oriented clustered-dot dither array and (d) error diffusion.

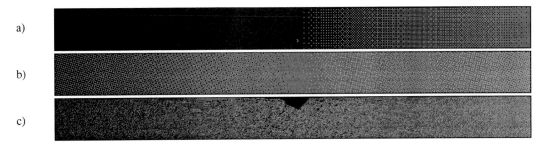

**Figure 6:** Intensity ramp at intensity levels between 37.5% and 62.5% for (a) 16x16 Bayer dither, (b) 16x16 rotated dither and (c) error-diffusion (300 dpi).

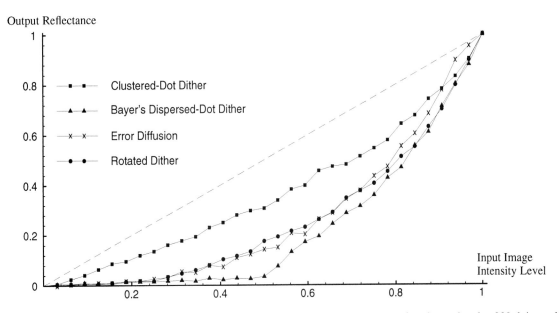

**Figure 7:** Tone reproduction curves obtained from density measurements of wedges printed at 300 dpi on a laser printer.

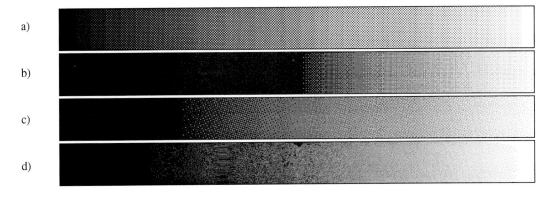

**Figure 8:** Tone reproduction behavior of a a grayscale wedge halftoned with (a) a conventional diagonally oriented clustered-dot dither array (dot area = 32 pixels), (b) Bayer's 16x16 dispersed-dot dither, (c) 16x16 rotated dispersed-dot dither and (d) error diffusion, printed at 300 dpi.

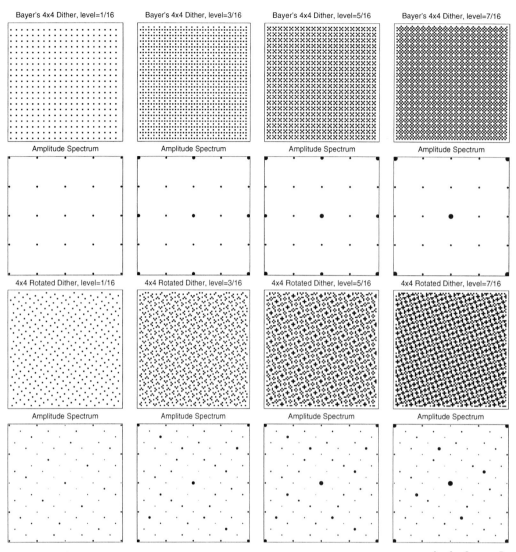

**Figure 9:** Halftone patterns and corresponding DFT impulse amplitudes at gray levels $\frac{1}{16}$, $\frac{3}{16}$, $\frac{5}{16}$ and $\frac{7}{16}$.

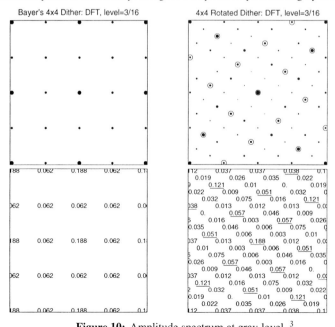

**Figure 10:** Amplitude spectrum at gray level $\frac{3}{16}$.

# Energy Preserving Non-Linear Filters

Holly E. Rushmeier[1]
National Institute of Standards and Technology

Gregory J. Ward [2]
Lawrence Berkeley Laboratory

## ABSTRACT

Monte Carlo techniques for image synthesis are simple and powerful, but they are prone to noise from inadequate sampling. This paper describes a class of non-linear filters that remove sampling noise in synthetic images without removing salient features. This is achieved by spreading real input sample values into the output image via variable-width filter kernels, rather than gathering samples into each output pixel via a constant-width kernel. The technique is non-linear because kernel widths are based on sample magnitudes, and this local redistribution of values cannot generally be mapped to a linear function. Nevertheless, the technique preserves energy because the kernels are normalized, and all input samples have the same average influence on the output. To demonstrate its effectiveness, the new filtering method is applied to two rendering techniques. The first is a Monte Carlo path tracing technique with the conflicting goals of keeping pixel variance below a specified limit and finishing in a finite amount of time; this application shows how the filter may be used to "clean up" areas where it is not practical to sample adequately. The second is a hybrid deterministic and Monte Carlo ray-tracing program; this application shows how the filter can be effective even when the pixel variance is not known.

**CR Categories and Descriptors:** I.3.3 [**Computer Graphics**]: Picture/image generation - *Display algorithms*; I.3.7 [**Computer Graphics**]: Three-Dimensional Graphics and Realism - *shading*
**General Terms:** Algorithms
**Additional Key Words and Phrases:** Monte Carlo, Lighting Simulation, Noise Reduction.

## 1   Introduction

Over the past decade two approaches for computing global illumination for realistic images have emerged – Monte Carlo path tracing and finite element (radiosity) methods. An advantage of the Monte Carlo approach is that the computational work is concentrated in the visible image at image resolution – not distributed throughout the environment. A disadvantage is that Monte Carlo images generated in a fixed length of time appear noisy. In this paper we examine the origins of this noise and develop the idea of energy preserving non-linear filters to reduce noise in post-processing. The filters are energy preserving in that they spread "noisy" samples into small regions rather than throwing them out. The filters are non-linear because the local distribution of samples is based on their magnitudes, hence output pixels will not be tied to a uniformly weighted sum of the input values. (Although such a relation may hold over large portions of the image.) The formulation of the filters is unique in that they are constructed by specifying the influence of each input sample, rather than by specifying the support region for each output pixel.

We begin with a discussion of digital filter applications in computer graphics, and the need for a new filter for synthetic images. We then discuss the source of noise in Monte Carlo images by examining features of this solution to the rendering equation. We develop the overall design of an energy preserving non-linear filter and show implementations of these filters for two different rendering systems. Examples are presented to demonstrate how energy preserving non-linear filters can effectively improve image quality without requiring additional sampling.

## 2   Filters

Generating a synthetic image is a sampling problem. The extensive literature in signal processing provides many useful algorithms and insights for image generation. Principles from signal processing for sampling and reconstructing images have been explored by many researchers (e.g. [6],[9]). Because samples are computationally expensive for global illumination calculations, efficient techniques must be employed in selecting the original samples. However, as noted by Mitchell [10] the problem of sampling global illumination is more complicated than 2-D image sampling because it involves predicting noise in 2-D space resulting from sampling a higher dimensional space. As we will discuss in more detail in the following section, even with sophisticated sampling techniques, excessive supersampling is required to eliminate noise under many common circumstances.

Lee and Redner [8] have studied the problem of noise in

---
[1] Rm. B-146, Bldg. 225, NIST, Gaithersburg, MD 20899
[2] 1 Cyclotron Rd., 90-3111, Berkeley, CA 94720

stochastically sampled synthetic images. They note that the linear filters typically used in computer graphics are unsatisfactory for eliminating the spike noise encountered in images generated using stochastic sampling. Linear filters tend to blur image details that should be kept sharp, while failing to spread the spike noise adequately. To resolve this problem, Lee and Redner proposed using alpha trimmed filters. Alpha trimmed filters have proved successful for eliminating spike noise and preserving edges in image processing applications. Such filters throw out "outlier" sample values when computing filtered pixel values. Lee and Redner demonstrate that alpha trimmed filters produce synthetic images without noticeable noise artifacts. However, they do not address the effect of such filters on the accuracy of the resulting image, and some important features may be lost.

Alpha trimmed and similar non-linear filters (e.g. morphological filters [5]) produce good results for many types of physically recorded images. In physically recorded images, the noise in the image is frequently due to secondary inputs that corrupt the signal of interest. Examples of unwanted secondary inputs are thermal noise in a detector element, and bit errors introduced in image transmission. Throwing out samples from these extraneous sources is desirable. In synthetic images, there are no corrupting secondary inputs. All of the samples carry valid information about the signal, and their effect should be included in the final image.

Another difference between synthetic and recorded images is the confidence we have in the results for some pixels. In recorded images there is frequently a great deal of uncertainty throughout the image. The exact pixel values are often unimportant, since many applications only need to identify objects, rather than examine subtle lighting effects. For synthetic images we have a high level of confidence in the values of some pixels. A great deal of computational effort has been expended to obtain subtle effects. We don't want the values of these pixels altered by a post-process filter.

In effect, we want our rendering process to simulate a sort of "idealized camera" up to and possibly including the storage of our final image. In displaying the image, we may attempt to compensate for human visual response with a tone-mapping operator (as discussed in the following section), but if we do not have a valid physical result, we have nothing to offer as input to such an operator.

The differences between synthetic and recorded images introduce two constraints for a filter for synthetic images that are not usually imposed on filters for physical images – energy preservation and minimal disruption. Energy preservation comes from the consideration that we do not want to throw any samples out. If a sample is contributing to a noisy region, we want to reduce noise by spreading out the energy it carries – not by removing it from the image. Minimal disruption comes from the consideration that we do not want to alter pixels that we have a high level of confidence in. To the greatest extent possible, the radiance of these pixels should be the same in the filtered image as in the unfiltered image.

## 3   The Complete Rendering Equation

The generation of a synthetic image was originally characterized as the solution of a rendering equation by Kajiya [7]. A complete rendering equation gives the values to be set on an image display device as a function of the radiometric properties of the synthetic scene and the display device. For convenience in examining the source of image noise we will examine the rendering equation in three parts:

$$L(x,y,\theta,\phi) = L_e(x,y,\theta,\phi)$$
$$+ \int_i f_r(x,y,\theta_i,\phi_i,\theta,\phi)L_i(x,y,\theta_i,\phi_i)cos\theta_i d\omega_i \qquad (1)$$

$$L_p = \int_{image\_plane} L(x,y,\theta,\phi)g(x,y)dxdy \qquad (2)$$

$$N_p = T(L_p) \qquad (3)$$

Equation 1 is the equation of transport for visible light in the synthetic scene. Equation 1 gives the radiance $L(x,y,\theta,\phi)$ at visible surface point $(x,y)$ in the direction $(\theta,\phi)$ that would reach the observer of a physical realization of the scene. $L_e(x,y,\theta,\phi)$ is the emitted radiance of the point (non-zero only for light sources) and $f_r(x,y,\theta_i,\phi_i,\theta,\phi)$ is the bidirectional reflection distribution function (BRDF) for the point. The integral on the right hand side accounts for all reflection of incident radiance $L_i(x,y,\theta_i,\phi_i)$ from solid angles $d\omega_i$. Radiance has dimensions of energy per unit time, area and solid angle.

Equation 2 expresses the radiance $L_p$ of a discrete pixel from the function $L(x,y,\theta,\phi)$. The function $g(x,y)$ is the 2-D filter used to eliminate spatial aliasing errors. The function $g(x,y)$ has dimensions of 1/area and is normalized so that $L_p$ has the same units and range as $L(x,y,\theta,\phi)$.

Equation 3 expresses the conversion of pixel radiance, which can take on any physically realizable value (i.e. from starlit to sunlit scenes), and converts it to a dimensionless setting for the display device $N_p$ – usually to an integer between 0 and 255. The function $T()$ is the tone operator, which is constructed using properties of human perception and characteristics of the display device. Various forms for $T()$ are discussed in [4], [12], and [13]. Even simple tone operators are inherently non-linear because of quantization effects and clipping of out of range values.

Typical Monte Carlo renderers compute an estimate $\hat{L}_p$ by forming and averaging many sample values $L'_p$. As stated by Purgathofer [11], the number of samples $M_t$ is determined by the number required to reduce the estimated deviation $S_p$ of the average to less than a specified tolerance $d$ with a specified confidence $\alpha$ using the percentage point of the $t$ distribution $t_{1-\frac{\alpha}{2},M_t-1}$. That is:

$$\hat{L}_p = \sum_{q=1}^{M_t} L'_{p,q}/M_t \qquad (4)$$

$$S_p \equiv \sqrt{\frac{1}{M_t(M_t-1)} \sum_{q=1}^{M_t} (L'_{p,q} - \hat{L}_p)^2} \qquad (5)$$

$$S_p < d/t_{1-\frac{\alpha}{2},M_t-1} \qquad (6)$$

The calculation of each value $L'_p$ begins by selecting a random value of $(x,y)$ in the right hand side of Eq. 2. At this location Eq. 1 is estimated by choosing a random direction for evaluating the integral on the right hand side. Since the value of $L_i(x,y,\theta_i,\phi_i)$ is unknown, and also governed by Eq. 1 , this estimation is done recursively, and a path of rays is generated [7]. After values of $\hat{L}_p$ are computed the tone operator in Eq. 3 is applied to display the image.

Using this naive approach, there is often high variance in the estimate of the integral on the right hand side of Eq. 1. This is because the integrand sample values can vary from the light source radiance to the radiance of dark, shaded objects in the room – with a dynamic range of $10^5$ being common [4]. To make Monte Carlo solutions practical, the integral on the right hand side is rewritten as a sum of integrals [3].

$$\int_i f_r(x, y, \theta_i, \phi_i, \theta, \phi) L_i(x, y, \theta_i, \phi_i) cos\theta_i d\omega_i =$$

$$\int_s f_{r,d}(x, y, \theta_i, \phi_i, \theta, \phi) vis(s) L_e(x_s, y_s) cos\theta_i cos\theta_s dA_s / r_s^2$$

$$+ \int_i f_{r,d}(x, y, \theta_i, \phi_i, \theta, \phi) L_{i,not\_s}(x, y, \theta_i, \phi_i) cos\theta_i d\omega_i$$

$$+ \int_{spec\_lobe} f_{r,s}(x, y, \theta_i, \phi_i, \theta, \phi) L_i(x, y, \theta_i, \phi_i) cos\theta_i d\omega_i \quad (7)$$

In Eq. 7, $f_{r,d}$ is the diffuse-like component of the BRDF, and $f_{r,s}$ is the specular-like. The integral for the diffuse-like component is divided into parts. The first is the integral for direct illumination. The direct illumination is an integral over all light sources $s$ in terms of the area of the sources $A_s$, visibility of the source $vis(s)$, emission from the source surface $L_e(x_s, y_s)$, angle from the source $\theta_s$ and distance to the source, $r_s$. The second is an integral for indirect illumination, i.e. over all incident light that does not come directly from the light source. The final integral on the right of Eq. 7 gives the specularly reflected light. Each of the integrals on the right of Eq. 7 generally has a lower variance than the integral on the left of Eq. 1, so the number of trials required is greatly reduced [1].

## 4 Designing a Filter for Synthetic Image Noise

One way to eliminating noise in Monte Carlo images is to increase sampling rates until the estimated error is less than the display device brightness resolution. However, in this section we show that in a typical image there will be regions in which the number of samples required to achieve this goal is impractical.

### 4.1 The Origin of Noisy Regions

A "worst case" estimate of the minimum number of trials $M_t$ required for applying the test in Eq. 6 is given by Purgathofer [11]. Scaling the values so that samples range from 0 to 1, the number of trials required is:

$$M_t > \frac{\log(1 - \alpha)}{\log(1 - d)} \quad (8)$$

For an image anti-aliasing problem with samples that ranged in value from 0 to 255, Purgathofer found that useful results were obtained when an interval of $D = \pm 13$ (i.e. $d = 13/255 = .05$ in Eq. 8) was allowed with a confidence of 80%. These values of $d$ and $\alpha$ give a minimum sampling of 32 trials/pixel.

The sampling rates required when computing radiance in "real world" floating point values and subsequently mapping to the device with a tone operator are much higher. While the form of tone operators varies, a typical radiance value on the order of $10^{-3}$ times the light source radiance is mapped in Eq. 3 to a value $N_p$ on the order of 100. An interval on the order of $\pm 10$ in the final display then requires an interval $d$ equal to $10^{-4}$ times the light source radiance. Scaling the problem so that the light source radiance is 1, a value of $d = 10^{-4}$ with a confidence of 80 % in Eq. 8 gives a **minimum** sampling rate of **16,094** trials per pixel!

The reorganization of the equation of transport given in Eq. 7 reduces the variance so that for most pixels in an image this worst case does not occur. However, there will be small regions in the image in which the "worst case" is encountered. These isolated regions will be noisy because they are undersampled. We summarize these high variance cases in Fig. 1.

Figure 1(a) illustrates the first type of high variance integration. Both light sources and non-light sources can be visible through some pixels. Sampling Eq. 2 for these pixels is essentially sampling a binomial distribution with several orders of magnitude in the two alternatives. Convergence is extremely slow in such cases.

Figure 1(b) illustrates a second high variance case – the integration of direct illumination for a diffuse-like surface (first integral on the right of Eq. 7). For a point which has a full view of the light source, a small number of trials are needed to estimate the cosine and distance terms in the integral. However, when the view of a light source is partially obscured a large number of trials may be required to estimate the visible area. The smaller the fraction of the source that is visible, the larger the number of trials needed. Since a light source has a high radiance, just one "hit" will result in a large sample standard deviation.

Figure 1(c) illustrates the integration of reflected light for a specular-like surface, the third integral on the right of Eq. 7. The BRDF is concentrated on a small lobe near the specular direction. A high variance in samples for this case occurs when a small portion of this lobe is subtended by a light source.

The fourth type of integration with high deviations is the case of "caustic paths", shown in Fig. 1(d). The integral diagrammed in Figure 1(d) is the second term on the right of Eq. 7. A "caustic" appears when a small portion of the incident hemisphere is subtended by the image of a light source in a specular-like reflection. When a sample ray hits this small image, a large deviation in the sample is introduced.

In any of the four cases, high deviations are expected in some region of the scene, not at one point. Light source edges, penumbrae, fuzzy specular reflections and caustics spread through regions. For $Q$ pixels in one of these regions, only a small number of pixels $q$ will have obtained samples hitting the high radiance portion of the domain of integration. The $q$ pixels will *appear* to be adding noise to the region of $Q - q$ pixels that *appear* to be accurate. Actually, all $Q$ pixels are equally valid. Rather than throwing out the $q$ "noise" pixels, the true value that should have been calculated for the whole region should be an average of all $Q$ values.

### 4.2 Filter Design

Our goal then is to design a filter that will spread the influence of $q$ "noise" pixels into a larger region of $Q$ pixels. We want to spread these pixels out without changing the total energy in the image, and without changing any pixel values unnecessarily.

First, to meet the goal of preserving energy, the filter must be applied to floating point sample values before the application of the tone operator. For example, take a simple tone operator that scales values by (128/.001), and clips values over 255. Consider a box filter in 1-D on the three

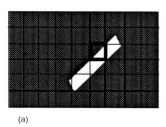 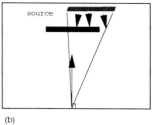 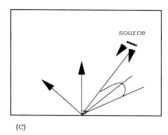 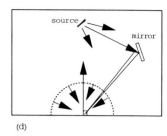

(a)　　　　　　　　(b)　　　　　　　　(c)　　　　　　　　(d)

Figure 1: *High pixel variances result when: (a) a light source is partially visible through a pixel the variance in samples, (b) a diffuse-like surface views only a small fraction of a light source, (c) when a light source subtends a small portion of the specular lobe of a specular surface, or (d) the image of a light source is visible to a diffuse-like surface via specular reflections*

values .0001, .001, and 1. If used before the tone operator, the filter gives 0.3337 and the pixel is clipped to a value of 255. If the tone operator is used first, the values become 13, 128 and 255, and the filter erroneously produces a result of 132.

Because we also want minimal disruption of pixels which are not in noisy areas, we want to design a filter that spreads the influence of "noise" pixels *only*. Because we are working from the point of view of constructing rather than analyzing an image, we construct our filter from a different point of view than usual.

Figure 2 diagrams typical digital filters. A support region is defined for each output pixel. This region may be uniform, as shown in (a). This has the energy preserving property we seek, but has the disadvantages of blurring detail and not adequately distributing some values. A variable width region may be used to change the influence of some input samples [6]. However, as shown in the example in (b), this type of variable width kernel does not preserve all of the energy in the original sample set.

We propose constructing energy preserving filters based on the region of influence of each input sample, rather than defining a support region for each output sample. This is diagrammed in Fig. 3. A region is defined for each input sample. The weights assigned to the sample as it is distributed to the output image sum to one, and energy is preserved. By varying the region of influence for each input sample, large areas of the image can remain unaffected by the filter and the input image is disrupted a minimal amount.

The design of any input based energy preserving filter requires two rules: 1) a rule to identify "noise" inputs, and 2) a rule to determine the region into which the "noise" inputs will be distributed.

## 5　Example Applications

There are many ways that Monte Carlo solutions to the rendering equation can be constructed. Energy preserving filters can be used to reduce noise in any of these methods. We present the application of energy preserving filters to two different rendering methods.

### 5.1　Monte Carlo Path Tracing with a Radiosity Preprocess

The first example we consider is a Monte Carlo path tracing (MCPT) method with a radiosity preprocess to reduce variance. In this method the estimates $\hat{L}_p$ are made as described

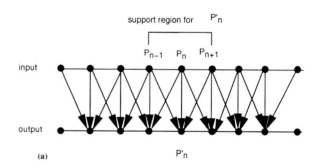

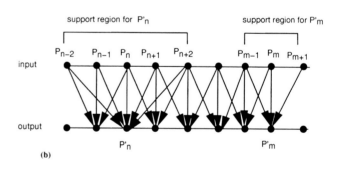

Figure 2: *(a) A constant width filter based on defining the support region for each pixel. The weights assigned to the samples in the support region sum to one, i.e. $P'_n = .25P_{n-1} + .5P_n + .25P_{n+1}$. Energy is preserved since the weight assigned to each input pixel sums to unity for the image as a whole. (b) A variable width filter based on defining the support region for each pixel. The weights assigned to the samples in the support region sum to one. The energy in the input image is not preserved, however. For example, $P_n$ is weighted by .25 for $P'_{n-1}$, by .375 for $P'_n$ and by .25 $P'_{n+1}$, so that 12.5% of the energy from $P_n$ is lost.*

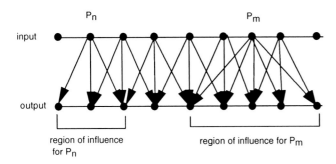

Figure 3: *A variable width filter based on defining the region of influence for each input sample. The sum of weights assigned to a sample as it is distributed to the output image is set to one to guarantee energy preservation. For example, $P_n$ is weighted by .25 in computing $P'_{n-1}$, .5 for $P_n$ and .25 for $P'_{n+1}$. $P_m$ is weighted by .0625 for $P'_{m-2}$, .25 for $P'_{m-1}$, .375 for $P'_m$, .25 for $P'_{m+1}$ and .0625 for $P'_{m+2}$.*

in Section 3, except that in estimating the incident radiance for diffuse-like surfaces in the indirect illumination integral, values from a radiosity preprocess are used. This is essentially the progressive multi-pass method described by Chen et al. [3], except that the "light ray" pass for explicit calculation of caustics is replaced by allowing caustic paths to be followed in the integration of indirect illumination. The "light ray" pass can be extremely costly when many light source/specular surface combinations need to be examined. By using an energy preserving filter, the noise that has been the drawback of including caustic paths in the Monte Carlo integration will be reduced.

For this method, "noise" pixels will be identified as pixels which have not converged to within a user specified interval $\pm D$. To be sure that most pixels have converged, we need a minimum value of $M_t$ that will be valid for the majority of pixels. To predict $M_t$, we need to know typical values of $S_p$ (defined in Eq. 5). We also need to estimate the floating point value visibility threshold $L_{tvis}$ which will translate into a difference of one unit in $N_p$. The threshold depends on the form of T() in Eq. 3.

To predict $S_p$ and $L_{tvis}$ we take a small pilot sample (e.g. similar to the pilot sample suggested in [2]) by rendering a 100x100 pixel image with 16 trials per pixel. Since the deviation in our estimates decreases with the square root of the number of trials, the estimate of $S_{p\_M_t}$ for $M_t$ samples will be the average sample deviation $\bar{S}_{p\_16}$ we calculate for the pilot sample times $\sqrt{16/M_t}$. For the purposes of estimating $L_{tvis}$, we assume a simple linear tone operator in which the average image value $L_{ave}$ will be mapped to the middle of the display range, $N_{MID}$. That is:

$$L_{tvis} = L_{ave}/N_{MID} \qquad (9)$$

Knowing $L_{tvis}$ and an estimate of $S_p$, the number of trials required to obtain a result accurate to $\pm D$ is approximately:

$$M_t = \left(\frac{4\bar{S}_{p\_16}}{DL_{tvis}}\right)^2 \qquad (10)$$

We construct our method to require a minimum of samples $M_t$ as given by Eq. 10. (Note, because $t_{1-\frac{\alpha}{2},M_t-1}$ is near 1.0 for $\alpha = 80\%$ and $M_t > 16$ it does not appear in the estimate in Eq. 10.) Since the value of $M_t$ using this

technique is a typical, rather than maximum value, we multiply this number by heuristically determined value of 4 to establish $M_{t,ceiling}$ to insure that the majority of pixels will converge.

The simple linear tone operator is only assumed for the purpose of estimating the number of samples. The image will still be computed in floating point, and any tone operator can be applied to the result.

For the method just described, a pixel is considered a "noise" pixel to be treated by the filter if its sample variation is larger than the acceptable tolerance after $M_{t,ceiling}$ trials. The excess value at each unconverged pixel is defined as the difference between the pixel radiance and the average of its immediate neighbors. If the excess energy exceeds this average by more than the variation allowed in the original calculations (i.e. $DL_{tvis}$), it is spread into a region around the unconverged pixel.

Energy could be preserved by simply spreading the excess energy over the entire image. However, that would unnecessarily disrupt some pixels, and all definition of features such as caustics would be lost. To determine the size of a smaller region into which the energy should be spread, we use the criterion that we do not want to introduce nonphysical high frequency artifacts into the image. The energy is spread so that the additional radiance at each pixel will be no more than $L_{tvis}$.

Any shape filter could be used. For a simple box shaped filter, the calculation is straightforward. The difference between the radiance of the unconverged pixel $L_u$ and the average of its converged neighbors $\bar{L}_n$ is found. The amount that $L_u - \bar{L}_n$ exceeds the allowable error level $DL_{tvis}$ is the excess value $L_{excess}$ which needs to be distributed. To limit the effect on neighboring pixels, the number of pixels to which the excess is distributed is $ceiling(L_{excess}/L_{tvis})$.

Only converged pixels in the original solution are used to compute the average. The effect of the filter does not depend on the order in which pixels are traversed. In some instances an unconverged pixel will have no converged neighbors. In this case the filter is applied recursively, with pixels that have had excess energy spread out marked as converged in the next iteration.

The method just described doesn't account for the spectral variation of radiance. If the method were applied for each spectral sample individually, wavelengths for which a pixel had a high variance would be smoothed out, while values at other wavelengths would be left untouched. The result would be "noisy" areas tending to turn gray. To avoid this color shift, the luminance of each "noisy" pixel is compared to the average luminance of its neighbors, and excess luminance is distributed with the same spectral distribution as the original "noisy" pixel.

Figure 4 shows the results of applying the simple box filter to an image generated using MCPT with radiosity preprocess. Two small specular boxes, one blue and one red are located in a yellow-brown room. (The specular boxes do not appear shiny because they reflect the featureless walls of the room). An image rendered using Eq. 10 to determine $M_t$ with $D = 5$ for a 0 to 255 display device is shown on the left. There are noisy regions in the image due to caustic paths in the indirect illumination calculation as diagrammed in Fig. 1(d). A noisy caustic due to the blue box can be seen on the ceiling near the light. More subtle noisy caustics due to the red box can be seen on the floor near the red box and on the ceiling above the red box. There is also a large penumbra region (as diagrammed in Fig. 1(a)) on the left wall due to the blue box.

The image after applying the filter is shown in the center.

Figure 4: Application of energy preserving filter to images using Monte Carlo path tracing with radiosity preprocess. Left: Unfiltered image, 60–240 samples. Center: Left image after filtering. Right: Unfiltered image, 1500–6000 samples.

Figure 5: Low resolution images of a light source generated using *Radiance*. Pixels are enlarged to emphasize differences. Left: Uniform Gaussian filter. Right: Non-linear filter.

Figure 6: Images generated using *Radiance* showing noise in specular reflection. Left: Uniform Gaussian filter. Right: Non-linear filter.

A comparison of the unfiltered and filtered images shows that the filter correctly left features outside of the high noise areas undisrupted. Only a small number of pixels in the penumbra region are changed. The large caustic feature due to the blue box is retained and smoothed out, as are the smaller fainter red caustics.

The image in the lower right is the same scene rendered using a minimum sampling rate that is 25 times higher (i.e. $M_t$ set for $D = 1$.) Not surprisingly, the filtered image appears somewhat noisier than the high sampling rate image which took **25** times longer to compute. This is because the filter is designed to affect the unconverged "high noise" pixels only, not to remove the $\pm 5$ units of variation allowed in the original low sampling rate calculation. However, a comparison of the filtered and high sampling rate images does show that the caustic features preserved by the filter are real.

## 5.2 RADIANCE

*Radiance* is a rendering system developed over many years at the Lawrence Berkeley Laboratory. It incorporates most kinds of light transport in a physically-based simulation of architectural (and other) environments, using a hybrid Monte Carlo and deterministic ray tracing approach that has been optimized to provide accurate results quickly in most cases [14]. In general, *Radiance* produces high quality results in much less time than the MCPT method just described.

"Noise" pixels are less common in *Radiance*, but they may still occur because of the Monte Carlo components of the calculation. However, because of the deterministic components of the calculation, an explicit measure of $S_p$ is not available for each input sample. Alternative rules for identifying "noise" pixels and their region of influence are needed.

In *Radiance*, an initial floating-point picture is generated at the super-sample resolution (typically 3x3 times the final image resolution). Anti-aliasing and other filtering operations are carried out by a separate program. Since we do not have an estimate of the variance of each sample, we define "noisy" samples as pixel super-sample values that are very large (or very small) compared to their neighbors. We increase the radius of influence for these samples. The criterion for how much to spread a sample is simply stated:

> Any given super-sample is spread out sufficiently that its influence on any given output pixel is smaller than a specified tolerance.

A "noisy" super-sample is identified as having a greater influence on an output pixel than we can tolerate with the current filter kernel. The amount a given sample affects a weighted average of samples is derived very easily from the formula for weighted averages:

$$\bar{x} = \frac{\sum_i w_i x_i}{\sum_i w_i} \qquad (11)$$

The average without sample $x_k$ is simply:

$$\bar{x}_{k-} = \frac{\bar{x}(\sum_i w_i) - w_k x_k}{\sum_{i \neq k} w_i} \qquad (12)$$

Taking the absolute difference between $\bar{x}$ and $\bar{x}_{k-}$ and dividing by $\bar{x}_{k-}$, we arrive at the absolute relative difference due to a super-sample's influence:

$$D_{ar} = \frac{\left| \frac{x_k}{\bar{x}} - 1 \right|}{\frac{\sum_i w_i}{w_k} - \frac{x_k}{\bar{x}}} \qquad (13)$$

$$\bar{x}, \bar{x}_{k-} > 0$$

Our goal is to find a kernel width that produces a $D_{ar}$ less than or equal to the selected tolerance. In the context of a filter kernel whose weights sum to one, this translates to the following formula:

$$tolerance \geq \frac{\left| \frac{x_0}{\bar{x}} - 1 \right|}{\frac{1}{w_0} - \frac{x_0}{\bar{x}}} \qquad (14)$$

where:

$x_0$ is the super-sample value

$w_0$ is the super-sample weight at the central peak of the filter kernel

$\bar{x}$ is the kernel-weighted average centered on this super-sample

If the effect of a sample is above our tolerance level using the default kernel radius, the radius is expanded until the sample's effect is below tolerance. The tolerance given depends on the expected pixel variance, which is in turn related to the number of super-samples used for each pixel. From experience using a Gaussian kernel, a good tolerance value for 3x3 oversampling is 0.25, and a good tolerance for 4x4 oversampling is 0.15. These tolerance values are typically higher than the $L_{tvis}$ value used for the previously described box filter because the influence of a Gaussian kernel always peaks near the closest output pixel, and drops off rapidly with distance.

The search for a kernel width to satisfy Relation 14 without going too far overboard could be expensive, so we have made a few optimizations. First, we work with pixel luminance values rather than colors, which reduces the number of operations and avoids the color shifting mentioned in the previous section. Second, we compute ring sums about the closest output pixel and use 1-dimensional vector multiplication to compute the different Gaussian-weighted averages, greatly simplifying the calculation of $\bar{x}$. Finally, we use numerical iteration to zero in on the appropriate kernel width more quickly. Treating 14 as an equation, we guess the next kernel width based on the $D_{ar}$ computed for the current width. In most cases, this produces faster convergence than a simple binary search, but care must be taken to avoid infinite iteration on anomalous pixels. In our implementation of this filter, we have found it to take about three times as long as a standard Gaussian kernel, which is still insignificant compared with the overall rendering times.

Examples of applying a filter of this form are shown in Figs. 5 and 6. The examples demonstrate two types of high variance areas that can be encountered in *Radiance* renderings.

As discussed in Section 4.1, light source boundaries (diagrammed in Fig. 1(a)) may cause aliasing in the final image even when many samples are taken at a pixel, because just one sample landing on or off the light source makes a detectable contrast difference in the final result. As mentioned in Section 4.2 the usual solution of clamping before filtering produces incorrect results. It also destroys the physical units of the result. By applying an energy preserving nonlinear filter before mapping to the display device, extreme contrast boundaries are spread out and aliasing is reduced. The effect is a slight fuzziness to light source boundaries in proportion to their brightness, something that in appearance is quite natural because the eye loses acuity in these regions, anyway.

The image on the left of Fig. 5 shows a low-resolution closeup of a pendant fixture, filtered with a linear Gaussian kernel and 9 samples/pixel. Notice the jagged edges caused by inadequate sampling. The image on the right shows the same computation with an energy preserving non-linear filter applied during anti-aliasing. The source boundaries are now softer and smoother, as they would appear in real life. The results have not been changed, only dispersed slightly around the source edges. This is important for later analyses, which might need the absolute radiance values to evaluate glare or other visual quality metrics.

To avoid unpredictably long rendering times, *Radiance* uses a minimal number of shadow rays to light sources plus one specular ray per pixel super-sample per surface interaction, similar to Monte Carlo path tracing. The user chooses an initial sampling density that produces adequate convergence over most of the image, but in areas where the number of samples chosen is not enough, there will be noise. The most frequent source of objectionable sampling noise is rough specular reflection of light sources (diagrammed in Fig. 1(c).) The left image in Fig. 6 shows a rendering of a candle holder with a rough specular surface on a table using 16 samples per pixel and a linear Gaussian filter. In this case, a linear Gaussian filter compounds the sampling artifacts by spreading them out to neighboring pixels without sufficiently reducing their contribution. So, little bright spots become big bright spots. The right image demonstrates how a non-linear filter reduces image noise without compromising the results. The specular highlights that were present in the calculation are still present in the filtered image – only more evenly distributed. This can be compared with alpha trimmed filters that reduce noise simply by removing the offending samples, taking the very real highlight with them. The energy preserving quality of our filter ensures that we do not lose the information we have worked so hard to compute.

## 6    Conclusions

We have introduced a new class of non-linear filters that reduces sampling noise while preserving energy and important image features. In two example applications we have shown that such a filter may be used to clean up unconverged sections of a Monte Carlo image, or reduce artifacts in a hybrid deterministic and stochastic ray tracing system.

The new filtering technique has particular significance for physically-based rendering, where image accuracy is a key goal. Its energy preserving nature means none of the calculations are thrown away, and the filter's non-linear response is critical in a floating-point domain where sample values may differ by several orders of magnitude. Also, the characteristic of minimal disruption guarantees that converged pixels will not be adversely affected.

The key underlying theme in this paper is choosing between what is correct and what is acceptable in a physically-based rendering. The eye's relative sensitivity to high frequency noise tends to undermine the application of Monte Carlo techniques, since reducing variance in some parts of an image can be extremely expensive. Instead, we can recognize these areas as being inadequately sampled, and use a variable-width kernel to reconstruct them in a way that maintains overall accuracy without offending the eye. Our goal is to be as correct as possible and still be acceptable to

the viewer. Since acceptability is such a subjective measure, it is difficult to say when and whether an optimal kernel has been found, but the general approach of scaling kernel width to target a specific variance seems to work quite well.

It is our hope that this new class of filters will help broaden the practical applications of Monte Carlo techniques in rendering by removing one of its principal drawbacks: image noise.

## REFERENCES

[1] J. Arvo and D. Kirk. Particle Transport and Image Synthesis. Proc. of SIGGRAPH '90 (Dallas,TX, Aug. 6-10, 1990. *Computer Graphics*, 24(4):63–66, Aug. 1990.

[2] J. Arvo and D. Kirk. Unbiased Sampling Techniques for Image Synthesis. Proc. of SIGGRAPH '91 (Las Vegas,NV, Jul. 28- Aug. 2). *Computer Graphics*, 25(4):153–156, Jul. 1991.

[3] S. Chen, H. Rushmeier, G. Miller, and D. Turner. A Progressive Multi-Pass Method for Global Illumination. Proc. of SIGGRAPH '91 (Las Vegas,NV, Jug. 28- Aug. 2). *Computer Graphics*, 25(4):165–174, Jul. 1991.

[4] K. Chiu, M. Herf, P. Shirley, S. Swamy, C. Wang, and K. Zimmerman. Spatially Non-Uniform Scaling Functions for High Contrast Images. In *Proc. of Graphics Interface 1993 (Toronto, May 19-21)*, pages 245–253.

[5] C.-H. Chu and E. Delp. Impulsive Noise Suppression and Background Normalization of Electrocardiogram Signals Using Morphological Operators. *IEEE Trans. on Biomedical Engineering*, pages 262–267, Feb. 1989.

[6] M. Dippé and E. Wold. Antialiasing Through Stochastic Sampling. Proc. of SIGGRAPH '85 (San Francisco,CA, Jul. 22- 26, 1991). *Computer Graphics*, 19(3):69–78, Jul. 1985.

[7] J. Kajiya. The Rendering Equation. Proc. of SIGGRAPH '86 (Dallas,TX, Aug. 18-22). *Computer Graphics*, 20(4):143–150, Aug. 1986.

[8] M. E. Lee and R. A. Redner. A Note on the Use of Nonlinear Filtering in Computer Graphics. *IEEE Computer Graphics and Applications*, pages 23–29, May 1990.

[9] D. Mitchell. Generating Antialiased Images at Low Sampling Densities. Proc. of SIGGRAPH '87 (Anaheim,CA, Jul. 27-31). *Computer Graphics*, 21(4):65–72, Jul. 1987.

[10] D. Mitchell. Spectrally Optimal Sampling for Distributed Ray Tracing. Proc. of SIGGRAPH '91 (Las Vegas,NV, Jul. 28- Aug. 2). *Computer Graphics*, 25(4):157–164, Jul. 1991.

[11] W. Purgathofer. A Statistical Method for Adaptive Sampling. *Computers & Graphics*, pages 157–162, 1987.

[12] J. Tumblin and H. Rushmeier. Tone Reproduction for Realistic Images. *IEEE Computer Graphics and Applications*, pages 42–48, Nov. 1993.

[13] G. Ward. A Contrast-Based Scalefactor for Luminance Display. In P. Heckbert, editor, *Graphics Gems IV*. Academic Press, 1994.

[14] G. Ward. The RADIANCE Lighting Simulation and Rendering System. Proc. of SIGGRAPH '94 (Orlando,FL, Jul. 24-29). *Computer Graphics, Annual Conference Series*, 1994.

# Spreadsheets for Images

Marc Levoy
Computer Science Department
Stanford University

## Abstract

We describe a data visualization system based on spreadsheets. Cells in our spreadsheet contain graphical objects such as images, volumes, or movies. Cells may also contain widgets such as buttons, sliders, or curve editors. Objects are displayed in miniature inside each cell. Formulas for cells are written in a general-purpose programming language (Tcl) augmented with operators for array manipulation, image processing, and rendering.

Compared to flow chart visualization systems, spreadsheets are more expressive, more scalable, and easier to program. Compared to conventional numerical spreadsheets, spreadsheets for images pose several unique design problems: larger formulas, longer computation times, and more complicated intercell dependencies. In response to these problems, we have extended the spreadsheet paradigm in three ways: formulas can display their results anywhere in the spreadsheet, cells can be selectively disabled, and multiple cells can be edited at once. We discuss these extensions and their implications, and we also point out some unexpected uses for our spreadsheets: as a visual database browser, as a graphical user interface builder, as a smart clipboard for the desktop, and as a presentation tool.

**CR Categories:** I.4.0 [Image Processing]: General — *Image processing software*; I.3.6 [Computer Graphics]: Methodology and Techniques — *Interaction techniques, Languages*; D.3.2 [Programming Languages]: Language Classifications — *Data-flow languages*

**Additional keywords:** data visualization, user interfaces, flow charts, visual programming languages, spreadsheets

## 1. Introduction

The majority of commercially available image processing and data visualization systems employ a flow chart paradigm. Users select processing modules from a menu and wire them together using a mouse. Although elegant in principle, flow charts are limited in expressiveness and scalability. Useful programming constructs like procedure calls and variable substitution cannot be conveniently expressed in these systems. Flow charts spend their screen real estate on operators and their interconnections, which becomes uninteresting once the flow chart has been

Address: Center for Integrated Systems    Email: levoy@cs.stanford.edu
         Stanford University              Web:   http://www-graphics.stanford.edu
         Stanford, CA 94305-4070

specified, and they run out of screen space if the chart exceeds a few dozen operators. Flow charts also provide no convenient mechanism for managing multiple datasets.

We propose an alternative paradigm based on spreadsheets. Broadly speaking, a spreadsheet is a system for specifying constraints among cells arranged in a grid. Cells may contain a constant data value or a formula that evaluates to a data value. Formulas may reference the value of other cells, but they may not alter the value of other cells. Formulas are typically written in a simple, interpreted language. Examples of spreadsheet systems are Microsoft's Excel, Lotus's 1-2-3, and Borland's Quattro.

We have implemented a spreadsheet for images (henceforth denoted SI) in which we extend the notion of a data value to include graphical objects such as images. These objects are displayed in miniature inside each cell. Double clicking on a cell brings up the full-size object. Cells may also contain interactive widgets. Manipulating a widget modifies the data associated with the cell. If formulas in other cells reference the modified cell, they are recomputed as well.

Formulas in our spreadsheet are written in Tcl, a general-purpose programming language that provides variables, assignment statements, procedures, and a full complement of control structures. The formula for a cell can range from a one-line expression to an entire program. To support editing of such formulas, SI is intimately tied to Emacs, a popular, customizable text editor. Double clicking on a cell brings up an Emacs window devoted to that cell.

Compared to flow chart systems, the presence of an embedded formula language makes SI more expressive. The infinite grid of the spreadsheet, together with the ability to resize cells, gives SI better scalability. SI also spends its screen space on operands rather than operators, which are usually more interesting to the user. Finally, because spreadsheets are two-dimensional, they provide a natural mechanism for applying multiple operators to multiple datasets.

Compared to conventional numerical spreadsheets, SI offers three important extensions. Firstly, a formula in SI can display its result anywhere in the spreadsheet. This allows users to intermix functional and imperative programming styles, simplifying many common tasks. Secondly, SI allows cells to be selectively disabled. This allows users to work on one part of the spreadsheet at a time, a useful feature in the face of long cell computation times. Thirdly, SI allows multiple cells to be edited at once and fired as a group. This simplifies development of complicated spreadsheets. These three extensions complicate the dependency analysis and the cell firing algorithm, as we shall see.

The remainder of the paper is organized as follows. Section 2 presents our reasons for choosing Tcl as our formula language, and it describes how Tcl and SI fit together. Section 3 describes the logical structure and command set of SI. The remaining sections describe SI's implementation, our experiences with SI, comparisons with other systems, and the future of SI.

| Register manipulation | load, store, display, openwindow*, closewindow*, popwindow, pushwindow |
|---|---|
| Spreadsheet services | loadsheet, storesheet, winsize*, titleheight, view-pixel* |
| Cell manipulation | cellsize*, view-cell, cut*, copy*, paste*, delete*, enable*, disable* |
| Data structure queries | regexists, queryreg, codereg, codecell |

**Figure 1:** Commands of the SI kernel. Starred commands are also available using a point and click interface.

| Register creation | scalar, vector, scanline, image, volume |
|---|---|
| Display widgets | button, slider, label, plot, imageviewer, cineviewer |
| Register manipulation | copy, extract, insert, promote, slice, delete |
| Pixel operations | add, subtract, multiply, divide, mod, over, and, or, makeramp, ramp, shift |
| Spatial operations | rotate, convolve, scale, displace, warp, makedisplacement |
| 3D occupancy grids | readabekas, deinterlace, profile, opinion, occupancy |

**Figure 2:** Commands of a prototype image processing package, including the commands for processing 3D occupancy grids that were used to generate figure 5.

## 2. Tcl as a formula language

From a conceptual point of view, the choice of a formula language is unimportant. We envision SI as a kit of parts in which the language is a replaceable module. For our prototype, we sought a language that was powerful, easy to type, and interpreted rather than compiled (for interactivity). Our choice was Tcl (Toolkit Command Language) [3]. Tcl consists of an application-independent embeddable command interpreter, a set of built-in commands for manipulating variables, strings, lists, and files, and a set of C-callable interface routines for adding additional commands. Examples of Tcl code are scattered throughout this paper.

From the user's point of view, Tcl's advantages are that it is easy to type (like UNIX shell commands) and that it provides a variety of control structures and substitution mechanisms (like the UNIX shell but better). From the implementors' point of view, Tcl's advantages are its small code size, its fast execution (fast enough to use for mouse event loops), and its simple interface to C — procedure calls with string arguments.

Tcl has one further advantage: it is the basis for Tk [4], an X11 toolkit similar to Xt. Tk provides a base set of graphics and text-oriented widgets, a mechanism for defining new widgets, and a simplified interface between user applications and the X window system. For SGI users, Tk replaces the window management and event handling services that are present in GL but are missing in OpenGL. As the Tcl/Tk user communities expand, we expect to see Tk widget sets for 3D graphics and image processing.

Tcl appears in two places in SI. Firstly, it is the language in which formulas are written. Secondly, the SI program provides a Tcl command prompt. Users may invoke all of the functionality of SI, including functions normally driven by the mouse, by entering commands at this prompt. This capability allows users to record and play back interactive sessions, to customize SI from an initialization script, and to perform many other useful tasks.

## 3. The structure and commands of SI

SI consists of a kernel and one or more standalone application packages. The kernel manages memory, displays the spreadsheet, and contains the firing algorithm. The application packages create and manipulate data registers and are responsible for defining Tk-compatible widgets to display the registers they create. This modular design reflects one of Ousterhout's goals for Tcl: systems composed of compact, reusable parts.

In this section, we take a tour through the logical structure and command set of the SI kernel. Our examples include commands from a simple image processing application package. The command set of the SI kernel is listed in figure 1. The command set of our image processing package is listed in figure 2.

### 3.1. Registers

The basic unit of storage in SI is called a register. A register is a named allocation of memory. Registers may contain anything: images, volumes, geometry, etc. The SI kernel controls the allocation and deallocation of registers, but the kernel knows nothing about the contents of a register. The contents and interpretation of registers is determined by those application package commands that know how to manipulate them.

Commands in SI generally consist of a command name followed by options and one or more arguments. The argument list for most commands includes the name of one or more registers. For example,

```
rotate -Bspline myreg Y 45 newreg
```

rotates a volume register named `myreg` around its Y-axis by 45 degrees. The command uses a cubic B-spline as its resampling filter, and places its result into a register named `newreg`.

To minimize the number of type coercions a user must perform, most commands accept a variety of register types, performing conversions, applying defaults, or ignoring arguments as appropriate. One very important default is that if the name of the output register (newreg above) is omitted, SI will make up a name. To make this form useful, commands that produce a register as output return a string result giving the name of the output register. The register produced by such a command can be used as the input to another command using Tcl's command substitution mechanism:

```
rotate -Bspline [load head.mri] Y 45 newreg
```

In this formula, the `load` command executes first, generating an arbitrary name for its output register, e.g. `Reg123`. The `rotate` executes next, with arguments `Reg123 Y 45 newreg`. The register produced by the `load` command is never seen by the user and is unimportant. It is deleted automatically by SI when the formula is modified or when the cell is deleted.

## 3.2. Display widgets

The contents of registers are by themselves undisplayable. The second building block in SI is a display widget. It is a view of a register. Some types of registers may have more than one widget that knows how to display them; others may have none. Such a register would need to be converted to a displayable type in order to view it.

Display widgets are associated with registers using a widget command. For example,

```
cineviewer -rocking [load head.mri]
```

loads a volume into a register, then opens a window on the workstation screen that contains an instance of the cine viewer widget. This widget contains image subwindows and interactive controls for viewing slices of a volume as a flipbook animation. The -rocking option specifies that the animation should alternate directions rather than circling from the last frame back to the first frame.

## 3.3. Cells

The third building block in SI is a cell. In addition to their usual appearance, all display widgets in SI know how to draw themselves in miniature inside a spreadsheet cell. Miniature versions of widgets may be live, meaning that they respond to mouse events just like the full-size widget, or dead, in which case double clicking on the miniature version brings up the full-size widget.

Display widgets are associated with cells by adding a cell name argument to the widget command. To display a miniature version of the cine viewer widget in cell a1, we type

```
cineviewer -rocking [load head.mri] a1   (1)
```

So far, we have assumed that all formulas are entered at the SI program prompt. If a formula is instead typed into an Emacs window that is associated with a particular cell, the cell name argument may be omitted:

```
a1: cineviewer -rocking [load head.mri]
```

We use the notation "a1:" (typeset in Times Roman) to signify that the formula that follows (typeset in Courier) is contained in the cell a1. The "a1:" does not appear in the cell. Every type of register has a default display widget. For volumes, it is the cine viewer. Therefore, the formula in cell a1 could be further simplified to read

```
a1: load head.mri
```

Executing this formula would cause the specified file to be loaded into a volume register, and a miniature version of the cine viewer to be displayed in the cell. If the formula contains more than one command separated by newlines, only the register returned by the last command executed will be displayed in the cell.

In the common case, the user doesn't need to think about registers or display widgets when writing formulas. The vast majority of formulas will look like this last example. The key to providing both brevity and flexibility in the formula language lies in the liberal use of defaults.

## 3.4. Chaining formulas together

Cell names may be used in any context in which a register name is valid. This allows us to reference the data in a cell by either its register name or its cell name. Here is a simple three-cell spreadsheet:

```
a1: load alps.rgb
b1: rotate a1 45
c1: ramp b1 [makeramp {{0 255} {255 0}}]
```

The first command loads an image into cell a1. A miniature version of the image is displayed in the cell. The second command rotates the image by 45 degrees and displays the result in cell b1. The third command inverts the pixel values in the rotated image, displaying its result in cell c1. The makeramp command accepts a Tcl list of coordinate pairs and returns a Tcl list of coordinates piecewise linearly interpolated from the specified coordinates. In this example, the command would return the Tcl list {{0 255} {1 254} {2 253}...}}. This list becomes an input argument to the ramp command, which modifies the image from cell b1.

## 3.5. Ways to reference a cell

As in numerical spreadsheets, references to cells can be relative or absolute. b1 is a relative reference. If a formula containing this reference were moved down one row using cut and paste, the reference would be changed to b2. If the formula is being edited in an Emacs window at the time it is relocated, SI sends the updated text to Emacs. In contrast, the notation /b1, b/1, or /b/1 forces the column, row, or both coordinates to be absolute, respectively. Absolute references are not modified if the cells are relocated.

SI also supports arithmetic calculations on cell references. For example, a1+2+3 references the cell two rows down and three columns right from the base address a1. If a formula containing this reference were moved down one row, the base address a1 would be changed to a2, and the reference would stay correct. Note that this construction is similar to Excel's OFFSET(A1,2,3), but is somewhat easier to type.

Finally, all of Tcl's substitution mechanisms can be applied to cell references. Thus, a1+$i+$j references the cell whose row and column offsets from a1 are given by the Tcl variables i and j respectively. Similarly, a1+[foo]+[bar] references the cell whose offsets are the values returned by the Tcl commands foo and bar. Finally, every occupied cell in the spreadsheet has associated with it a Tcl command that returns the contents of the register displayed in that cell. Thus, a1+[b1]+[b2] references the cell whose offsets are the values contained in cells b1 and b2.

## 3.6. Active widgets

In addition to being live or dead, widgets may be passive, meaning that they only display their underlying registers, or active, meaning that they both display and modify their underlying registers. For example:

```
a1: load alps.rgb
b1: slider
b2: rotate a1 [b1]
```

The command slider in cell b1 is a widget command, Since it is invoked without arguments in this example (compare to the cineviewer command in example (1)), a default scalar integer register is created, and the slider displays the contents of that register. The operand [b1] in cell b2 invokes the command b1, which returns the current value of the slider in cell b1, and the rotate command rotates the image in cell a1 by this amount. Since the formula in cell b2 depends on cell b1, moving the slider causes the rotation to be recomputed.

The spreadsheet for this example is shown in figure 3. The slider widget is really Tk's "scale" widget. The options visible on the `slider` command in the figure are options defined by Tk for its `scale` command. In addition to these Tk-defined options, most active widgets accept a `-[no]continuous` option. Specifying `-continuous` means that the widget will fire its descendents repeatedly (as fast as possible) until the mouse button is released. If the slider in the previous example were so defined, dragging the slider bar back and forth would cause the image to rotate back and forth. To reduce computational delays if cell b2 were the beginning of a long sequence of operations, active widgets also accept a `-[no]firedescendents` option. Specifying `-nofiredescendents` means that the widget will fire only its immediate children as long as the mouse button is down. When the button is released, the widget's other descendents will be fired.

## 3.7. Control structures

SI supports all of the control structures in Tcl, including `if`, `while`, `for`, `foreach`, and `case`. Of particular interest are the looping commands. Loops in SI take one of three general forms:

**Single-cell loops.** The easiest way to code a loop is entirely within one cell using the Tcl `for` command:

```
a1: load alps.reg temp
    for {set i 0} {$i <= 90} {incr i 30}
            {rotate temp $i a1}
```

This formula will step the alpine pasture image through four rotational positions, each of which will appear briefly in cell a1.

**Multi-cell for-loop.** If the user has already built a sequence of processing steps and decides retrospectively to iterate one or more parameters of the sequence over a range of values, this can be done without reworking the entire spreadsheet by inserting one additional cell at the beginning of the loop to trigger it:

```
a2: for {set i 0} {$i <= 90} {incr i 30}
            {byte $i a2; fire b2}              (2)

b1: load alps.reg
b2: rotate b1 [a2]
b3: ramp b2 [makeramp {{0 0} {255 100}}]
```

The original spreadsheet consisted of cells b1 through b3. Cell a2 has been added to control the loop. The `byte` command creates a scalar byte register and displays it in a2 using a Tk label widget. The `fire` command executes cell b2 as a subroutine. When cell b2 and its descendents (b3 in this example) have finished executing, control is returned to a2, which increments `i` and loops.

**Multi-cell while-loop.** If the user wishes to predicate loop termination on a value computed by the loop body, two cells are required to control the loop:

```
a1: load alps.reg                              (3)
c1: byte 3
b2: convolve -box [c1] [c1] a1
c3: if {[max [gradient b2]] > 50}
            {byte [expr [c1] + 1] c1}
```

In this example, the `byte` command in cell c1 initializes the loop. The `if` command in cell c3 evaluates a data object computed by the loop body and conditionally modifies cell c1, on which the loop body depends. The loop body will thereby be reexecuted repeatedly until the condition becomes false. In this

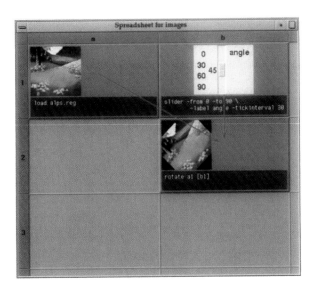

**Figure 3:** Slider widget being used to control a rotation. Cell b2 rotates the image in cell a1 by the angle specified on the slider in cell b1. Each time the slider is moved, cell b2 (and its descendents, if it had any) are recomputed.

example, cell a1 is blurred by a box filter of increasing width (starting at 3x3), stopping when the maximum gradient magnitude in the image drops below 50.

## 4. Selected implementation details

### 4.1. The user interface

SI is implemented in C, C++, Tcl/Tk, and Emacs Lisp. These depend on UNIX and the X window system but are otherwise platform independent. Some of the widgets currently depend on GL — the nonportable version of Silicon Graphics's graphics library — but these will shortly be converted to OpenGL, a platform-independent library.

The unique characteristics of SI pose several challenging user interface design problems. Firstly, our cells are larger than those in numerical spreadsheets, so fewer of them are displayed at once. To make navigation easier, we provide an accelerated scrolling tool and the ability to quickly change the size of all cells. (Individual cells cannot be resized, as this would destroy the regularity of the spreadsheet grid.)

Secondly, our longer formulas and powerful language semantics lead to more complicated intercell dependencies than in numerical spreadsheets. To keep users from getting lost, the formula for each cell is displayed inside the cell. Long formulas can optionally be decimated to fit (see figures 5 and 6). Although the decimated text is not legible, its overall structure is clearly visible. To clarify intercell dependencies, the dependency graph can be displayed as an overlay (see figures 4 and 5).

Thirdly, our cells take longer to compute than cells in numerical spreadsheets — several minutes in extreme cases. To keep the spreadsheet visually consistent during long computations, cells that depend on modified cells are grayed out (in Macintosh style) to indicate that they are out of date. As each cell fires, it is highlighted to provide feedback of its progress. The mouse is alive during cell computations and can be used to navigate through the spreadsheet or abort an errant computation.

As a further response to long cell computation times, SI allows cells to be selectively disabled, allowing the user to work on one part of the spreadsheet at a time. In addition, the user can select a group of cells to edit simultaneously in Emacs, and then fire the entire group at once with a single keystroke. While most of the features described above are cosmetic, these last two profoundly affect the firing algorithm, which is discussed in the next section.

## 4.2. Managing dependencies

The dependency relationships in SI are represented by a directed acyclic graph having two types of nodes, formulas and objects. Objects consist of cell names, register names, Tcl variables, and Tcl procedures. When a formula consumes an object (e.g. specifies a cell as input, invokes a Tcl procedure, etc.), this is represented in the graph by a directed edge from the object to the formula. When a formula produces an object (e.g. specifies a cell as output, defines a Tcl procedure, etc.), this is represented by a directed edge from the formula to the object.

Following user modification of one or more formulas or objects, the dependency graph is traversed as described in Appendix A, and the modified formulas and their descendents are recomputed. The time required to perform a dependency analysis is usually several orders of magnitude smaller than the time required to execute a formula or decimate an image for display, so we do not discuss it further here.

SI's firing algorithm differs from the firing algorithms found in conventional spreadsheets in two ways. Firstly, the ability to specify objects as outputs in formulas forces us to distinguish formulas from objects in the dependency graph and gives rise to producer edges (that is, edges from formulas to objects). Surprisingly, this additional flexibility does not complicate the dependency analysis in any substantive way.

The second difference arises from our ability to selectively disable and reenable cells and to edit several formulas at once. Conventional spreadsheets do not allow either action. As a result, our firing algorithm begins with a queue of edited or reenabled formulas which need to be executed. To further complicate matters, Tcl allows conditionally executed commands and substitutions in command operands (see section 3.5). This prevents us from lexically scanning a formula in advance of execution to determine the set of objects it will consume or produce. Without this information, it is impossible to determine which formula on the queue should be executed first.

This is a standard problem in operating system design, and there are standard solutions to it. The solution used in SI (and described in the appendix) is to execute modified formulas in arbitrary order, requeueing them if they consume undefined or invalid objects. If the dependency relationships are indeed acyclic, this algorithm is guaranteed to find a valid firing order. The presence of a cycle leads to a condition called livelock, and it will be detected by our firing algorithm. This solution can lead to wasted computation if a formula contains a long computation followed by a reference to an invalid object, requiring the formula to be requeued and recomputed from scratch later, but such cases are rare. In practice, formulas usually make their consumer references early, so the time lost to requeueing is negligible, and the user sees only the final firing order. We are currently investigating other solutions, including blocking a formula's execution until the invalid object is available (in this case, cycles lead to a condition called deadlock), lexically scanning the cell to resolve as many references as possible, or allowing formulas to declare a set of objects they might consume or produce when executed.

## 5. Experience and examples

Our experience with SI has been limited but positive. Although its image processing package offers only rudimentary functionality, we have used it in several research projects (see figure 5). We have also found some unexpected uses for SI, such as summarizing research results for colleagues and giving public presentations (see figure 6). Sometimes, we use it simply as a smart clipboard for storing images on our desktop, like the Macintosh clipboard but more powerful. Other plausible applications for SI are as a database browser, as an exposure sheet for computer animation, or as a video postproduction planner.

The ability to specify outputs in formulas makes SI very different from a conventional spreadsheet, so it is worthwhile to consider how this additional power might be used. Consider the spreadsheet shown in figure 4. The user in this example began by building a pipeline for classifying 3D medical datasets. Puzzled by the classified volume displayed in cell d2, the user added the following diagnostic code to the formula in that cell:

```
set means ""
for {set z 0} {$z < [d2 zlen]} {incr z} {
    lappend means [mean [slice d2 $z]]
}
set order [lorder $means]
for {set i 0} {$i < 5} {incr i} {
    slice d2 b4+0+$i [lindex $order $i]
}
```

This code creates a Tcl list containing the mean pixel intensity for each of the [d2 zlen] slices in the classified volume, calls lorder, a Tcl proc (defined elsewhere in the formula) to generate a second list containing slice numbers in order of decreasing mean slice pixel intensity, and displays the brightest 5 slices in cells b4 through f4. Still puzzled, the user created formulas in cells f5 and g5 to analyze one of these slices.

In this example, the ability to display results anywhere in the spreadsheet made it easy to insert the visual equivalent of a printf statement into an existing formula — without having to reorganize the spreadsheet. The ability to define and reference local variables made it easy to write the for-loops needed to sort the slices — conventional spreadsheets don't allow local variables in formulas. The flexibility to use an imperative programming style (that is, with assignment statements) in cell d2 to produce cell f4 and a functional programming style in cell g5 to consume cell f4 extends but does not break the spreadsheet paradigm — on the contrary, it seems very natural. This example would have been difficult to write without this flexibility.

## 6. Comparisons and discussion

Spreadsheets for images are not a new idea. Piersol's ASP package [6], a spreadsheet program based on the Smalltalk-80 object-oriented programming environment, anticipates many of the features of SI. Cells are allowed to contain any sort of object, including images and other spreadsheets, and formulas are written in Smalltalk — a general purpose programming language. In keeping with the conventional spreadsheet paradigm, formulas in cells in ASP are not permitted to alter the value of other cells.

Palaniappan's IISS environment [5] combines a custom Mathematica-like formula language, Mark Overmars's Forms UI toolkit, and the Khoros image processing library. IISS appears to allow assignment statements, but a complete definition of their language and firing algorithm has not yet been published.

A key feature of SI is its ability to intermix functional and imperative programming (see the example in section 5).

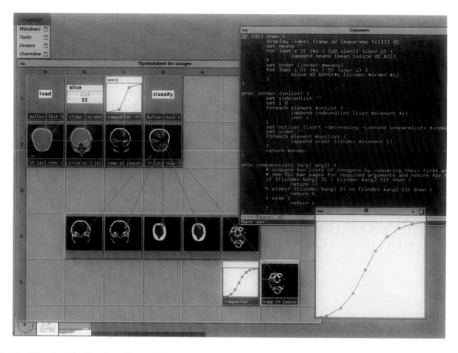

**Figure 4:** A simple classification pipeline for a 3D medical dataset. A slice chosen using the slider in cell b1 is classified according to the transfer function selected in cell c1. The unclassified and classified slices are displayed in cells b2 and c2, respectively. When the user presses the button in cell d1, the entire volume is classified and displayed in cell d2. In addition, the brightest 5 slices are displayed in row 4. The display of these classified slices is controlled by the formula in cell d2 (see section 5). An Emacs editor window is also visible; it is currently editing the contents of the formula in cell d2.

Interestingly, conventional numerical spreadsheets also offer imperative programming, usually in the form of a second, hidden command language that is more flexible than the cell formula language. To write an imperative program using Excel Version 4.0 [2], the user creates an auxiliary spreadsheet called a macro sheet that has special properties. Formulas in a macro sheet can assign values to any cell in the macro sheet using the `SET.VALUE()` function. This notation is not permitted in the main spreadsheet. The advantage of a two-language design is that it presents a simple programming model to the novice computer user. The disadvantage is that the jump in complexity from spreadsheet programming to macro sheet programming is large.

The currently dominant paradigm for visualizing image data is flow charts, so it is worthwhile comparing them to SI. The earliest system to combine a graph-based execution model with a visual programming interface was Paul Haeberli's ConMan [1]. Currently popular flow-chart visualization packages include AVS, Explorer, apE, Khoros, IBM's Data Explorer, PV-Wave, Wavefront's Data Visualizer, FIELDVIEW from Intelligent Light, VoxelView, and many others. SGI's Explorer [7] is perhaps the most highly developed of these packages, so we base our comparisons on it. Three major factors can be identified:

**Expressiveness.** The "repeat" and "while" modules of Explorer approximate the `for` and `while` loops of Tcl. Explorer contains no modules, however, that evaluate conditionals or perform substitutions (unless the user writes a custom module).

**Scalability.** The "micro" form of a module icon in Explorer measures 116 x 40 pixels; 30 modules and their associated wiring makes for a crowded window. Modules may be coalesced into a single icon, but the user must perform this reduction. Cells in SI can be resized down to 12 x 17 pixels simply by dragging the window frame, allowing up to 6000 cells to be displayed at once. Although cells are unreadable at that size, such a view makes it easy to navigate through a large spreadsheet.

**Customization.** Explorer provides extensive support for writing custom modules, but the jump in complexity from visual programming to module programming in C or Fortran is nontrivial. In SI, the formula language is also the customization language. The transition from novice user to expert user is therefore smooth. To facilitate rapid module prototyping, Explorer also offers an interpreted language called Shape. Its power is greater than Tcl because it directly supports array manipulations, but its interface to the flow chart via the encapsulating "LatFunction" module is somewhat cumbersome.

# 7. Status and future work

The kernel of SI is complete and relatively stable. Our efforts are now focused on building application packages. The image processing package used in these examples needs more commands and a richer library of widgets. We plan to soon add a volume visualization package, a polygon mesh package, and a surface fitting package.

The most critical issue for the future of SI is performance. Spreadsheets offer a natural mechanism not present in flow charts — and not yet exploited in SI — for controlling computational expense; images need only be computed at a resolution commensurate with the size of the cells in which they are displayed. In the early stages of a data exploration, miniature images suffice, and computations should be fast. If the user stretches the spreadsheet, images get bigger and computations slow down. If the user double clicks on a cell, that cell is recalculated at full resolution. Many image processing operators lend themselves in an obvious way to such computation shedding; spatial warps can be subsampled; frequency domain operators can be windowed; polygonal meshes can be retiled using fewer polygons. Our goal is to make these optimizations transparent to the user.

Another area for future development is the formula language. Tcl is not an ideal solution in many respects. It offers only one datatype — strings. Because there are no numerical datatypes, arithmetic expressions are cumbersome to write, as the examples in this paper demonstrate. Tcl also does not support multidimensional arrays. All manipulation of arrays (and hence images) in SI must be done through C-language commands. Finally, Tcl does not have the speed of a compiled language like C. We often find ourselves prototyping a computation in Tcl, then rewriting it in a combination of Tcl and C. Alternatives to Tcl include Lisp, a C or C++ interpreter (several now exist), or a new language that combines the simplicity of Tcl with the power of an array manipulation language like Mathematica or MATLAB.

To summarize, SI combines the power of a data analysis language, the interactivity of a flow chart visualizer, and the extemporaneous qualities of a spreadsheet. While the power of SI seems useful and easily manageable in examples such as the one shown in figure 4, SI is nevertheless a general programming environment, and it is possible to create confusing programs using it. In particular, the flow of control in the while-loop in section 3.7 is not obvious. In general, the presence of conditionally executed commands and substitutions in command operands means that the reference patterns of formulas in SI are dynamic; cycles can appear and disappear during spreadsheet recomputation. The ability of SI to display the dependency graph and to detect cycles helps, but it is not foolproof. We are continuing to refine the design of SI as we search for a data analysis paradigm that is simple enough to keep a novice out of trouble yet powerful enough to satisfy the needs of a scientist/programmer.

# 8. Acknowledgements

Discussions with David Heeger, Richard Frank, Bob Brown, and Robert Skinner were useful in the early stages of the project. I wish to particularly acknowledge many fruitful discussions with Philippe Lacroute. This research was supported by the NSF under contract CCR-9157767 and by Software Publishing.

# 9. References

[1]    Haeberli, Paul, "ConMan: A Visual Programming Language for Interactive Graphics," *Computer Graphics (Proc. SIGGRAPH)*, Vol. 22, No. 4, Atlanta, Georgia, August, 1988, pp. 103-111.

[2]    Microsoft Corporation, *Excel User's Guide 2*, Microsoft Corporation, Document Number XL26297-1092, 1992.

[3]    Ousterhout, John K., "Tcl: An Embeddable Command Language," *Proc. 1990 Winter USENIX Conference*.

[4]    Ousterhout, John K., "An X11 Toolkit Based on the Tcl Language," *Proc. 1991 Winter USENIX Conference*.

[5]    Palaniappan, K., Hasler, A.F., Manyin, M., "Exploratory Analysis of Satellite Data Using the Interactive Image Spreadsheet (IISS) Environment," Preprint volume of the *9th Internation Conference on Interactive Information and Processing* Anaheim, California, January, 1993, pp. 145-152.

[6]    Piersol, K.W., "Object Oriented Spreadsheets: The Analytic Spreadsheet Package," *Proc. OOPSLA '86*, September, 1986, pp. 385-390.

[7]    Silicon Graphics Inc., *IRIS Explorer User's Guide* and *IRIS Explorer Module Writer's Guide*, Silicon Graphics Inc., Document numbers 007-1371-020 and -1369-, 1992-1993.

# Appendix A: The firing algorithm

Dependency relationships in SI are represented by by a directed acyclic graph having two types of nodes, formulas and objects, as described in section 4.2. Formula are marked as modified or unmodified, and objects are marked as modified or unmodified, and as valid or invalid. Formulas become modified in one of three ways:

(1)    The user changes a formula using the Emacs text editor.

(2)    The user adds, deletes, cuts, pastes, or loads a cell.

(3)    The user enables for firing a previously disabled cell.

Following user modification of one or more formulas, an execution queue is created and is initialized to the set of modified formulas, arranged in arbitrary order. The firing algorithm then proceeds as follows:

**Step 1: execute a formula.** Remove a formula $i$ from the front of the queue, delete all edges originating or terminating at $i$, and submit it to the Tcl interpreter for execution. For each object $j$ consumed (or produced) by formula $i$ as it executes, add a directed edge from $j$ to $i$ (or from $i$ to $j$) to the graph. If two producer references point to the same object, a collision has occurred; flag it as an error. If $i$ is found to consume an undefined or invalid object (e.g. an empty or invalidated cell, an undefined Tcl procedure, etc.), abort execution and move $i$ to the back of the queue. If no formula on the queue can be executed successfully, the spreadsheet contains a cycle; flag it as an error.

**Step 2: invalidate its descendents.** If formula $i$ executes successfully, mark as invalid all objects $k$ such that there exists a path of length one or more originating from $i$ and terminating at $k$. Allow cycles of length two involving a formula and an object. This allows a formula to read/modify/write a register. Cycles of length greater than two are flagged as errors.

**Step 3: fire its direct consumers.** Add to the execution queue all direct consumers of all objects produced by $i$, i.e. all formulas $m$ for which the graph now contains a directed edge of length two from $i$ to $m$ (passing through an object).

Following user modification of an object (e.g. by manipulating an active widget or by resetting a global variable at SI's Tcl command prompt), all formulas that consume (either directly or indirectly) the object are queued for execution using a similar algorithm.

To avoid introducing cycles into the dependency graph, multi-cell loops require the following special treatment. In the for-loop of example (2) (section 3.7), the `fire` command in cell a2 executes cell b2 and its descendents as a subroutine. The subroutine returns when the execution queue is empty, allowing cell a2 to continue execution. This mechanism bypasses the usual dependency analysis, allowing us to omit from the graph a producer edge from the formula in cell a2 to cell b2 and a consumer edge from cell b3 to the formula in cell a2, which would form a cycle. In the while-loop of example (3), the `byte` command in cell c3 conditionally overwrites cell c1, creating an edge in the graph from c3 to c1 and temporarily creating a cycle. This edge is deleted each time cell c3 begins execution. On the last iteration through the loop, the `byte` command is not executed and no edge is created. Therefore, in the quiescent states that precede and follow execution of the loop, the graph is acyclic.

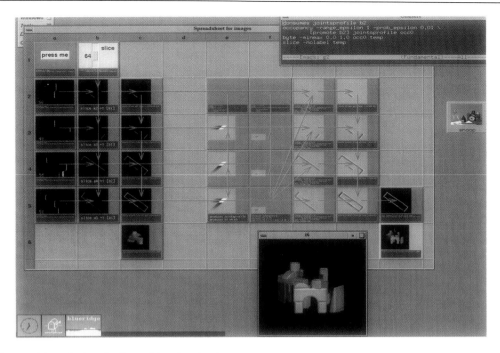

**Figure 5:** This spreadsheet depicts the flow of data in a 3D fax machine - a machine we are building in our lab for digitizing the shape and external appearance of physical objects using a laser scanner and precision motion platform. When the button in cell a1 is pressed, four laser reflection image sequences are loaded into cells a2 through a5, respectively. A cine viewer widget associated with each cell displays a frame from that image sequence in miniature in the cell. The slice specified in the slider in cell b1 is then loaded into cells b2 through b5. Two different occupancy grid algorithms are applied to these slices, leading after some intermediate steps to the results shown in cells c5 and i5. Volume renderings of the complete volumetric occupancy grid have been imported from another spreadsheet and are shown in cells c6 and i6. The user has double clicked on cell i6, so its image is also shown full size at the bottom of the screen. The scene is a pile of wooden children's blocks. An Emacs editor window is also visible; it is currently editing the contents of the formula in cell g2.

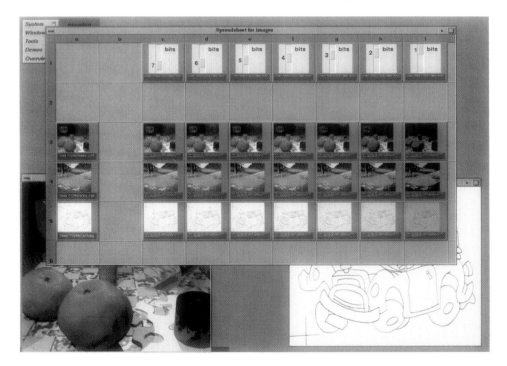

**Figure 6:** This spreadsheet was used to give a live classroom demonstration of the effects of image quantization. The original 8-bit images are in cells a3 through a5. The sliders in cells c1 through i1 are used to set the number of bits to which the images appearing in that column are quantized. This example demonstrates how the two-dimensional grid of a spreadsheet lends itself naturally to visualizing multiple operators applied to multiple datasets. The user has double clicked on cells g3 and c5, so they are also shown at full size. This spreadsheet took about 10 minutes to construct.

# A Model for Efficient and Flexible Image Computing

*Michael A. Shantzis*
*Pixar\**

## - Abstract

*As common as imaging operations are, the literature contains little about how to build systems for image computation. This paper presents a system which addresses the major issues of image computing. The system includes an algorithm for performing imaging operations which guarantees that we only compute those regions of the image that will affect the result. The paper also discusses several other issues critical when creating a flexible image computing environment and describes solutions for these problems in the context of our model. These issues include how one handles images of any resolution and how one works in arbitrary coordinate systems. It also includes a discussion of the standard memory models, a presentation of a new model, and a discussion of each ones' advantages and disadvantages.*

**CR Classification:** I.3.3. [Computer Graphics]: Picture/Image Generation; I.4.9. [Image Processing]: Applications.

**Additional Keywords:** Image computing, special effects, filtering, resampling, compositing.

## 1. Introduction

The topic of image computing refers to the set of manipulations one performs on digital images. This includes all operations commonly associated with image processing (such as filtering, image enhancement, and fourier transforms) [8], and those more typically considered computer graphics techniques (such as multipass geometric transformations [4], color-space manipulations [5], and merge operations [7]). Image computing is the primary task in many graphics environments. In film and video related applications, such as computer-aided animation, one spends a significant amount of time planning and executing imaging operations. One of the earliest video production systems, the Hanna-Barbera cartoon animation system [12], used imaging methods in this manner. Other common applications involve image computing as well, such as publishing and data analysis. Many vendors provide systems for building such

*1001 West Cutting Blvd, Richmond CA, 94804
Phone: (510)215-3503
Electronic mail: mas@pixar.com

applications, such as Silicon Graphics' *ImageVision Library* [10], while others have developed complete systems which use these techniques, such as Alias Research's *Eclipse* [2]. Hence we see that the development of efficient and flexible methods for image computing is a topic worthy of research.

We must address two levels of optimization in order to create an efficient imaging system. First, we must ensure that the individual operations are efficient. We find discussions of this in the literature, although one might consider adding additional, application-specific optimizations to their system. Secondly, we must ensure that we invoke the individual operations only on the regions that affect the final result.

In order to create a flexible image computing environment one should be able to quickly change between different resolutions of both source and result images to provide the typical tradeoffs between precision and speed. Similarly, one should be able to specify imaging operations in whatever coordinate system is most appropriate for the application.

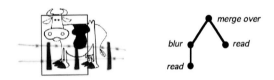

FIGURE 1: Simple Imaging Graph

This paper addresses this set of issues and offers a single solution to them in the form of an imaging paradigm. The paper provides a rigid definition of the image computing problem, and then presents an algorithm for performing such computations. The algorithm addresses three major concerns: correctness of result, efficiency in space, and efficiency in time. The paper then describes how one creates a usable environment given the goals stated above. This involves defining a set of coordinate systems which support multiple resolutions for both the source and result images, and which allow one to specify all operations in an arbitrary space. It also discusses the tradeoffs of the various memory models one might choose in designing an image computing application.

## 2. The Definition of Image Computing

We begin by defining our paradigm for image computing. Let there be an unbounded, two-dimensional lattice of pixels. Attached to the lattice is a coordinate system. For convenience, we map one unit in our coordinate system to one pixel in the lattice.

One may place an *object* in the pixel lattice at any position. Each object is initially either read off of disk (i.e. an image), or generated (e.g. a noise function). We say that the object is *defined* anywhere in the lattice in which its value is explicitly stated. For example, an image is defined everywhere within its bounding box, and a function can possibly be defined in the entire space. Anywhere in which an object is not defined is referred to as the image's *abyss*. One arbitrarily defines an abyss behavior (for simplicity, we define our abyss as clear).

One can perform an *operation* on any object, the result of which is another object, possibly defined in a different region (i.e. the operation can possibly change the geometry of the object). An operation may contain *parameters* used in its execution. If the parameters involve any spatial component, such as a distance, we express them in the lattice's coordinate system.

An *imaging graph* (or simply a *graph*) is a directed acyclic graph where each node represents an operation. Its connectivity expresses the manner in which we execute the operations, with each node pointing to the nodes on which it will operate. Leaf nodes represent operations which generate image data (including the *read* operation, which reads an image off of disk), while non-leaf nodes represent operations which manipulate pre-existing data. An imaging graph contains one root node (i.e. a node with no parents). We define the image computing problem as evaluating a graph at this root node within a stated *region of interest*, or *ROI*, of our pixel lattice. The ROI need not include all the data defined at the root node, as we might be interested in only a subset of what is defined. The result of a computation is an image which is at most the size of the ROI, and which lies at a specific location in our coordinate system. In FIGURE 1, we see an example of an imaging graph, the result of its execution, and one possible ROI.

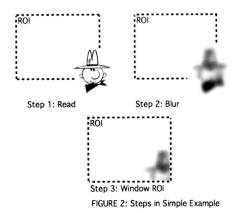

Step 1: Read — Step 2: Blur — Step 3: Window ROI

FIGURE 2: Steps in Simple Example

### 3. Fundamentals of the Image Computing Algorithm

Suppose, for example, we wish to read an image off of disk and blur it by convolving it with a kernel of size $k$ by $k$. Let us say, however, that the ROI does not completely encompass the region in which the blurred image is defined. We see the steps of this evaluation in FIGURE 2. We now explore how to evaluate these operations with two distinct goals in mind: correctness of result, and efficiency in execution.

Without regard to efficiency, we can correctly evaluate this graph by reading the image into a buffer large enough to contain all the pixels defined by the blurred source image (a buffer $(k-1)/2$ pixels larger in all directions than the size of the unblurred image), reading the image into the center of the buffer (i.e. leaving a $(k-1)/2$ pixel boundary around the source image), blurring the entire buffer, and windowing into the region of the buffer which intersects the ROI to obtain our final result, as is shown in FIGURE 3.

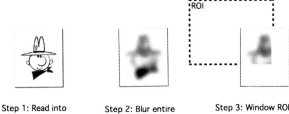

Step 1: Read into middle of buffer — Step 2: Blur entire buffer — Step 3: Window ROI

FIGURE 3: Correct Evaluation of Example

Although this method will give us the correct result, it is not particularly efficient. We have obviously blurred more than was necessary given that we have thrown away part of the blurred result. We have also read more of the image than was necessary.

Consider instead evaluating the graph in the following fashion. Refer to FIGURE 4 in which we have labeled three regions, A, B, and C. Region B is the intersection of the ROI and the image's defined region, A is the region $(k-1)/2$ pixels out from B into the ROI, and C is the region $(k-1)/2$ pixels out from B into the image's defined region. First, declare a buffer large enough to contain all of these three regions. Read into the buffer all of the source image contained in B and C. Inclusion of the data in C assures that the bottom and right edge of the ROI will be correctly blurred. Next, blur the entire buffer (i.e. A, B, and C). Finally, take the data in A and B as our result. We include A in our result to account for the "fadeout" created by the blur. Since we have included all the defined data which affects the final image, this execution is correct. Furthermore, since we excluded all irrelevant data, it is efficient as well.

Let us generalize this method for all possible *read-blur* computations (i.e. for any ROI and a source image anywhere in our space). This problem entails determining the size and position of three separate regions: the region defining the minimum amount of data we must read from disk (B and C from our example), the region on which we perform the blur (A, B, and C), and the region containing the final result (A and B). Stated differently, we must determine the smallest defined region required after we have evaluated each of the two operations and the space required for their execution.

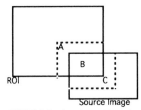

FIGURE 4: Regions in our Example

Let us first consider how we determine the smallest defined region required after evaluating the *blur*. If we had an infinite ROI, we would be interested in all data defined by blurring the source image. But we are only interested in the part of this region which intersects our ROI. Thus, we can compute our desired result by expanding the source image's defined region by $(k-1)/2$ in all directions, giving us the entire defined region of the blurred image, and intersecting it with our ROI. This is shown in the top left of FIGURE 5.

Now let us determine the smallest required region of the read operation. Were our source image defined everywhere, we would be interested only in the region of the source image that would affect the outcome of the *blur*. Since any pixel within $(k-1)/2$ of the ROI affects the blur, we are interested in the all pixels within $(k-1)/$

2 of the ROI. But our image is only defined in a finite region. Hence we can compute this result by expanding the ROI by $(k-1)/2$ in all directions and intersecting it with the defined region of the source image. This is shown in the bottom right of FIGURE 5.

Lastly, we perform the blur operation in a region large enough to contain both of the regions calculated above. We simply compute the bounding box of the two regions as they are positioned relative to one another.

These calculations exhibit the fundamental concepts behind our algorithm. At each node in the imaging graph, calculate the smallest defined region which will maintain correctness of result. This is bounded by two regions: the amount of defined data we *have* at each node as a function of the amount of data defined by our leaf nodes, and the amount of data we *need* at each node as a function of the ROI. Once we know this region for each node, we can proceed in determining how to execute the graph in an optimal fashion, including memory allocation and order of node evaluation.

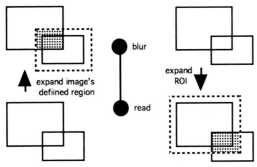

FIGURE 5: Calculating smallest regions

## 4. The Image Computing Algorithm

We now describe the major steps of our image computing algorithm: Defining the regions we need to compute for each node in the graph, calculating how much space we need to execute each operation, allocating the image space, and performing the actual operations.

### 4.1. Region/Rectangle Calculation

Let us generalize the region calculation process to include a graph of any level of complexity. To do this, we examine the calculations for an individual node in the graph. For each node, we compute the have region from its childrens' have regions, taking into account the node's operation type and parameters. In our example, we computed the *blur's* have region by expanding its *read's* have region by $(k-1)/2$ on all sides. Note that a leaf node generates its have region from its own parameters, as with the read node in our example, whose have region is set to the image's bounding box. Likewise, we compute the node's need region from its parents' need regions, given each of its parents' operation type and parameters. In our example, we computed the *read's* need region by expanding the *blur's* need region by $(k-1)/2$. The need region of the root node is set to the ROI, as was the case with our example's *blur* node.

We refer to the intersection of the have and need regions as the *result* region. Finally, as we saw with the *blur* in our example, the execution of the node might require more space than is specified by the result region. Hence we also maintain the *comp* region, which expresses the area we need to compute the node. This comp region is usually set to the union of the node's result region and its childrens' result regions (as we saw in the *blur* example), but it is possible that we need additional space for the node's computation.

All of the regions in our system are possibly non-rectangular. It is both sufficient and convenient, however, to force the regions to be rectangular. Thus, we refer to the above regions as the *haveRec, needRec, compRec,* and *resultRec*.

We set each nodes' four rectangles by traversing the graph four separate times. The dependencies amongst the four rectangles require us to perform these traversals in a certain order. Also note that the rectangle calculation process lends itself very well to an object-oriented implementation, where we associate four rectangle calculation methods with each operation type. Each of the four methods sets its node's appropriate rectangle, except the needRec method, which sets each of its childrens' needRecs.

We first compute the haveRecs, traversing the graph in a depth-first fashion. At each node we call the haveRec calculation method associated with that node's operation type. If the node has more then one child, the routine must take all its childrens' haveRecs into account. Computation is not necessarily as simple as taking the bounding box of all its childrens' haveRecs. For example, consider the binary operation *merge in* [7]. The most data that can result from this operation is the intersection of the childrens' haveRecs.

Secondly, we traverse the graph in a breadth-first manner to set the nodes' needRecs, first setting the root node's needRec to the ROI. We traverse breadth-first as each node is responsible for setting its childrens' needRecs. At each node we call the needRec calculation method associated with that node's operation type.

In the third pass through the graph, we set the nodes' resultRecs. As the resultRec is only a function of the node's haveRec and needRec, it does not matter whether we perform this pass breadth-first or depth-first.

Finally, we traverse the graph to set the compRecs. The order of traversal for the compRec calculation is also inconsequential.

### 4.2. Example Operations

Most imaging operations fit into one of three categories: Unary point operations (such as color space transformations), n-ary point operations (such as merges), and operations that affect the geometry of the image (such as resampling operations, convolutions, and warps). We now present examples of the rectangle calculation methods associated with operations in these three groups.

#### 4.2.1. Unary Point Operations

This category consists of all unary operations (i.e. those which operate on a single child) where the value of a given destination pixel is a function only of the pixel in the source at the same location in the coordinate space. Image tints, range alterations, and color space conversions are all unary point operations.

The haveRec calculation method simply sets the node's haveRec to its child's haveRec. The needRec calculation method sets the child's needRec to the node's needRec. As with all operations, the resultRec calculation method takes the intersection of the node's needRec and haveRec. Finally, we require no extra image space to perform a unary operation, so the compRec calculation method sets the node's compRec to its resultRec.

#### 4.2.2. N-ary Point Operations: *Merge*

This category consists of all n-ary operations (i.e. those which operate on multiple children) where the value of a given destination pixel is a function only of the pixels in the sources at the same location in the coordinate space. The *merge* operations in [7] fall into this category. We shall use them as examples in our discussion.

The added complexity in the rectangle calculation methods for all n-ary point operations is due to the fact that we must take into account all of the childrens' haveRecs. In the merge operations, we see a good case of how this manifests itself. Depending on which merge operation we are interested in, the haveRec calculation method changes. For example, for *merge over*, the node's haveRec is set to the bounding box of the two childrens' haveRecs. For *merge in*, though, it is set to the intersection of the childrens' haveRecs.

The remainder of the rectangle calculation methods for n-ary point operations mimic the methods for unary point operations, with the caveat that they operate on multiple children. The needRec calculation method sets all the childrens' needRecs to the node's needRec. The resultRec and compRec calculation methods both take the intersection of the node's needRec and haveRec.

### 4.2.3. Geometric Transformation Operations : *Affine*

Geometric transformation operations include all convolutions (including *blur*), image warps, and affine transformations (any geometric transformation which preserves parallel lines, such as translates, rotations, stretches, and skews). We shall discuss the rectangle calculation methods for affine transformations.

In [4], Catmull and Smith detail how one decomposes an affine transformation on an image into two scanline-oriented shears, one horizontal and one vertical. We perform each of the two shears by resampling and repositioning [9] every scanline in the image (i.e. $x' = A x + B$, where x is a location in the source, x' is a location in the destination, and A and B are constants), changing the offset from scanline to scanline by a constant amount (if scanline i has an offset of B, then scanline i+1 has an offset of $B + \Delta B$). There are certain situations when the resampling process will produce finer results if we pre-rotate the image by 90 degrees before performing the two shears.

To calculate an *affine* node's haveRec, we express the four corners of its child's haveRec as vectors, and transform them by the affine's matrix. This gives us the position of the child's haveRec after the transformation. Next, we take the bounding box of the four transformed vectors and expand it in all directions by $(k-1)/2$, where $k$ is the width of the filter used in the affine's resampling process. The result is the affine node's haveRec.

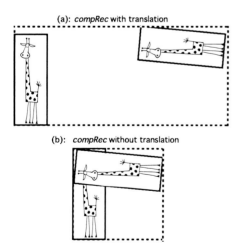

(a): *compRec* with translation

(b): *compRec* without translation

**FIGURE 6:** Optimizing affine's*compRec*

The needRec calculation method is the inverse of the haveRec calculation. We expand the node's needRec by $(k-1)/2$ to account for the filtering, transform the four corners of the node's haveRec by the *inverse* of the node's affine matrix, and take the bounding box of these four transformed vectors. The result is the child's needRec.

The *affine's* compRec calculation method contains some minor subtleties which add to its complexity. First, let us consider an affine whose matrix contains a large translational component. Let us also say that we innocently define the compRec to be the bounding box of the node's resultRec and its child's resultRec, as we typically do for most operations (we see this scenario in FIGURE 6a). Were we to do this, we would end up allocating and operating on a large amount of data that is just part of the image's abyss, wasting both cycles and memory. Therefore it makes sense to force our affine to operate with as little a translational component as possible (see FIGURE 6b). We derive a different matrix for performing the affine than the one that this node represents. The matrix performs all the non-translational operations of the original matrix, but will remove the translation from the child's resultRec to the node's resultRec. The origins of the affine's compRec and resultRec are still set as if we are using the node's original matrix. As a result, we perform a smaller affine, and the node still represents the correct result. The second subtlety in calculating the affine node's compRec has to do with the 90 degree rotation that we might need to perform on the image as part of the affine operation. If we need to pre-rotate the image, the compRec must be large enough to rotate the child's resultRec.

Finally, as with all other operation classes, we compute the resultRec in the usual fashion, by taking the intersection of the node's haveRec and needRec.

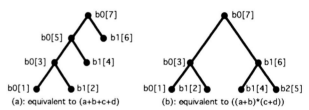

(a): equivalent to (a+b+c+d)   (b): equivalent to ((a+b)*(c+d))

FIGURE 7: Examples of Image buffer assignment

### 4.3. Image Buffers

Next we address how one minimizes the amount of memory required to evaluate an imaging graph. One need not look far to see how simple it would be to waste memory during a graph evaluation. Consider our *read-blur* example. We should be able to perform the blur operation in the same buffer into which we read the image. If we do not, our computation could take almost twice as much memory as necessary. However it is not always possible to perform an operation "in place." Consider the node which has two parents. Only the last parent to reference this node may reuse this node's memory. Therefore, we see that it is necessary to intelligently assign image memory to each node in a graph.

We refer to the object in which we perform our imaging operations as an *image buffer*. An image buffer consists of an image large enough to contain all the compRecs and resultRecs of the nodes to which it is assigned, and also some state information that we will use during the image computation.

### 4.3.1. Image Buffer Assignment

We assign image buffers to nodes in such a way as to minimize the amount of memory required for computing a graph. Let us assume for now that this problem is equivalent to minimizing the number of image buffers we must create, ignoring the size requirements of each of the buffers. The problem of minimizing the number of image buffers is equivalent to the problem in compiler design of minimizing the number of registers required to evaluate a complex arithmetic expression. This algorithm consists approximately of the following steps. Assign a level of complexity to each node (i.e. how many image buffers it will take to evaluate the graph below this node), then traverse the graph depth-first, visiting the children in a descending order of complexity. At each node, assign an image buffer to each node by first attempting to reuse one of the childrens' image buffers and then attempting to use one that already exists but is not currently in use. Finally, if none exist, create a new buffer. The result of this process is both an assignment of buffers to nodes and a specific order of graph traversal to use during image computation. For further details of this process, see [1].

In FIGURE 7 we see two example graph topologies, the buffers we ended up assigning to them (labeled b0, b1, and b2), and the traversal order (shown in brackets). We also see an equivalent arithmetic expression for each of the trees. Note that FIGURE 7a requires two buffers while FIGURE 7b requires three. In general, the "broader" the graph, the more image buffers one needs to declare. Note that it is conceivable that two graphs can represent the same set of operations, as would be the case in FIGURE 7, if all the binary operations were *merge overs*, and all the leafs were *reads*. One might choose to perform a pre-pass on an imaging graph, identifying and removing such inefficiencies.

Let us return to our the assumption we made earlier, that it is sufficient to only minimize the number of image buffers we create. This method will not necessarily lead to the least possible memory usage for our computation. Consider a *merge over* node where the resultRec of the first child completely engulfs the resultRec of the second. Were we to reuse the first child's image buffer, we would only need to declare one large and one small image buffer. Were we to reuse the second child's, though, we would need to declare two larger buffers. Thus, we can further optimize our image buffer assignment by taking the size of the nodes' resultRecs and compRecs into account. If you are willing to assume that all the resultRecs and compRecs in your graph are roughly the same size, the simpler method of image buffer assignment suffices. Since we have been able to make this assumption for all of our image computing applications, we have not explored an algorithm which takes the node's memory requirements into account. Therefore, we present it as a topic of future research.

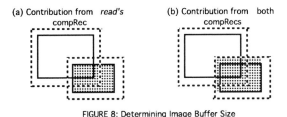

FIGURE 8: Determining Image Buffer Size

### 4.3.2. Image Buffer Usage

Once we have assigned image buffers to each node, we must determine the amount of image memory we must allocate for each buffer. Unfortunately, it will not suffice to simply set the image buffer size to the largest compRec or resultRec of the nodes which reference it. To demonstrate, let us return to our read-*blur* example and add the condition that in order for us to perform the *read*, we must read and decode the entire file before we window into it to obtain the resultRec. Hence we have the compRecs and resultRecs for our two nodes as shown in FIGURE 8. Let us now attempt to calculate the size of the image buffer we will need to perform this computation. In order to execute the re*ad* node, we need a buffer large enough to hold that node's compRec. Once we proceed and execute the *blur* node, however, we must expand the buffer up and to the left in order to

accommodate the blur's compRec. Hence we must effectively mimic the graph evaluation (i.e. how we will reference each buffer as we execute the graph) to correctly calculate the size of each of the image buffers. Finally, as we saw in the "broad" graph of FIGURE 7b, each buffer might be used for more than one sequence of operations (this was the case with buffer b1). We must make sure that we mimic the graph evaluation for each individual sequence of references to a given buffer, and declare enough image buffer space to handle all the buffers' references.

### 4.4. The Imaging Operation

The imaging operation creates subwindows into each of the childrens' image buffers, a subwindow into the node's image buffer and performs the imaging operation. One might choose to put some operation-specific optimizations in at this step. For example, when performing a *merge over*, one might copy over the regions outside of the intersection of the children's resultRecs instead of performing the more expensive merge operation on them.

### 4.5. Pseudocode of the Algorithm

```
computeImage(rootNode,roi) {
    rootNode = buildGraph();
    // Set all the rectangles
    rootNode->needRec = roi;
    setHaveRecs(rootNode);
    setNeedRecs(rootNode);
    // Can do next two recs at once.
    setResultAndCompRecs(rootNode);
    // Assign image buffers & get ordered
    // node list for execution
    orderedList = assignImageBuffers(rootNode);
    evaluateGraph(orderedList);
}

setHaveRecs(node) {
    // Traverse graph depth-first.
    foreach child of node
        setHaveRecs(child);
    node->setHaveRec();  // Set node's haveRec
}

setNeedRecs(node) {
    node->setNeedRec(); // Set childs' needRecs.
    // Traverse graph breadth-first.
    foreach child of node
        setNeedRecs(child);
}

setResultAndCompRecs() {
    // Traverse graph depth-first.
    foreach child of node
        setCompAndResultRecs(child);
    node->setResultRec(); // Set node's resultRec
    node->setCompRec(); // Set node's compRec
}

evaluateGraph(orderedList) {
    foreach node in ordered list
        node->evaluate();
}
```

## 5. Creating a Functional Image Computing System

We now examine two related issues which are critical to the creation of a complete image computing environment. The first issue stems from the desire to operate in arbitrary resolutions and to specify operations in the most convenient coordinate system for the application. Its solution involves the inclusion of certain techniques for managing affine operations within our image computing environment. The second issue involves how we configure image memory within our environment to avoid excessive swapping. We present two models common to imaging environments, discuss some problems with them, and propose a third memory model which is made possible by our image computing algorithm.

## 5.1. Arbitrary Resolutions and Coordinate Systems

In order to support arbitrary resolutions we strategically place *affine* nodes in our graph to compensate for changes in both the sources' and result's resolutions. We account for the use of a lower resolution source by placing an *affine* node above each leaf node. The matrix assigned to this *affine* node compensates for the change in the resolution of the leaf node from its original. For example, if our source image is half the original resolution, the matrix will represent a scale by two. We account for lower resolution in the destination image by placing an affine above the root node. The node's matrix compensates for any change in this computation's resolution from the original resolution. For example, if we wish the result to be half the size as the original, the matrix will represent a scale by one half.

Coincidentally, were we to place an *affine* node above every leaf and above the root, even if we were operating in our original resolution, we could define an arbitrary coordinate system in which we could specify all the graph's spatial parameters. We simply include the transformation into this coordinate system in all the *affine* nodes at the leaf nodes, and include the transformation from this coordinate system in the *affine* added above the root.

We now define three coordinate systems: the *source coordinate system* (the space in which our source images lie), the *master coordinate system* (the space in which we specify all our operations), and the *destination coordinate system* (the space of our final image). The *source-to-master transformation* states where in the master coordinate system we wish to place our source image. Its value changes with the resolution of the source image. The *master-to-destination transformation* states which portion of the master coordinate system we would like placed in the ROI. Its value changes with the resolution of the result image.

Although requiring these additional *affine* nodes in the imaging graph makes the image computing system more flexible, we need to examine its implications. Since the resampling process is not perfect, each time we perform an affine on an image, we degrade it slightly. It is a worthy goal to perform as little resampling of our images as possible, and it is unacceptable to simply require that we perform at least two affine transformations on each image. Furthermore, given that the master coordinate system is truly arbitrary, we should also question the wisdom of transforming our image into it. In order to solve these problems we combine all of the affine transformations from the path from the leaf up to the root and place the resulting matrix in the affine above each respective leaf node. We then remove all other matrices from our graph. Consequently, immediately following the execution of each leaf node, we transform its result into its final position. Note that we end up performing all non-affine imaging operations at an image's final resolution. This gives us an upper bound on the computation time required to evaluate each of them.

The combining of all the affine transformations into a single one creates a new issue that we must address. We have set up the coordinate systems so that we can specify the parameters to all operations in the master coordinate system. As we "commute" the matrices down the imaging graph, we must adjust the parameters of each operation we pass (only those operations whose parameters contain some spatial component will need modification). For example, if we have an *affine* node which describes a resize of $s$ over a *blur* node with a width $w$, and we wish to put the resize below the blur, we must set the blur width to $sw$. Note that this adds a major constraint to all our operations, namely that we can commute the operation over affine transformations simply by modifying the operation's spatial parameters. This is not necessarily trivial. Consider the blur operation. If we only allowed for isotropic resizes (those that scale equally in all directions), any spatially scalable blur kernel would suffice. If we wish to allow for rotations, we would need to provide a radially symmetric blur kernel, such as a gaussian. If we allowed for all possible affine transformations, the blur operation becomes considerably more complex, as the blur kernel must be anisotropic along two arbitrary vectors.

Finally, note that we might push all the affines down our graph and realize that there is more than a single unique affine for one particular leaf node (for example, if one instantiates an image multiple times, giving each a different position). We provide two solutions to this dilemma. We can either replicate the portion of the graph below the *affine* node (or nodes) responsible for creating the discrepancy, or we can simply refrain from pushing the responsible node's matrix downward. The former solution will cause some inefficiencies in computation, as we might need to compute entire subsections of the original graph multiple times. The latter solution will result in a single image being resampled more than once.

## 5.2. Memory Models in Image Computing

Image computation is very memory-intensive. It is highly possible that even a single image is too large to fit completely into physical memory. Hence, we need to examine some of the ramifications of relying on virtual memory in our process. Specifically, we must try to determine how much swapping will result from the execution of typical imaging operations. Throughout this discussion we will use as our benchmark an imaging operation which consists of an x-pass followed by a y-pass (such as an affine transformation). Such operations are the most demanding on the machine's virtual memory, since we can be certain that either x or y accesses will entail referencing memory locations which are spread out amongst many

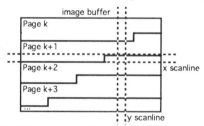

FIGURE 9: Page layout with contiguous memory

pages of virtual memory.

### 5.2.1. Contiguous Memory Model

Say we were to create an image buffer, referencing memory in a simple contiguous fashion. We add the additional constraint that the buffer is large enough to contain many virtual pages. In FIGURE 9 we see how these pages might be laid out within the image buffer. In order to reference a scanline in x, we need to swap in at most two pages. In order to reference a scanline in y, though, we will essentially need to swap in every page within the image. This is unacceptable as all the pages might not fit into physical memory simultaneously. Therefore, laying out memory contiguously is acceptable only if we will be performing x-passes on our images or if all of the image will fit into physical memory.

### 5.2.2. Tiled Memory Model

One common solution to the above problem is to "tile" the memory as seen in FIGURE 10 [6]. In this configuration, memory is not laid out contiguously. In order to reference an entire scanline in either x or y, one must reference several independent pages. We choose a tile width and tile height such that one can have resident all the necessary pages for referencing an entire x or y scanline.

In order to support tiled memory, one must unfortunately choose between requiring all imaging operations to deal with non-contiguous memory, or providing routines for copying from tiled memory into a contiguous block for the scanline routines to operate in. Neither of these alternatives is ideal, as the former leads to a overly complex imaging model and the latter adds inefficiencies to the system.

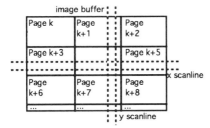

FIGURE 10: Page layout with tiled memory

### 5.2.3. Physical Memory and "Divide and Conquer"

Given the shortfallings of the above two models, we now present a third model which does not rely at all on virtual memory and hence removes issues of swapping. Let us take the tactic that we do not wish to allow any swapping of image memory during the graph evaluation process. In other words, let us reserve some fraction of all physical memory strictly for image computing. The obvious question at this point is what to do when our computation requires more memory than we reserved.

In order to address this, consider the following features of our image computing algorithm. First, we know precisely how much memory it takes to evaluate a graph before we begin evaluating the graph, as we precomputed the size of each image buffer. Secondly, even without a formal proof we can see that if we were to divide our ROI, it would take less memory to compute either of the ROI halves than it would to compute the entire one.

If we find that a given ROI computation requires more memory than we reserved, we simply "divide and conquer" the region. As we finish computing each sub-ROI, we can either cache the result temporarily to disk, or leave it somewhere in our reserved memory space, out of the way. If we cache the sub-ROI to disk, we effectively add an extra read and write of our image to our final computation time. If we leave it in memory, we reduce the amount of memory we have available to perform subsequent sub-ROI computations, which may or may not matter, depending on the particular situation.

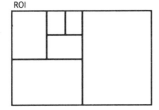

FIGURE 11: Possible subdivisions of the ROI

The most efficient way of subdividing is to keep each sub-ROI as square as possible, as we see in FIGURE 11. A simple example will show why this is true. Consider a computation which entails

reading an image in and rotating it 90 degrees. Let us also say that our ROI is W by H, where W > H. The size of the affine's compRec in this case would roughly be W by W. Were we to subdivide into two long W by (H/2) regions, we will not change the size of the *affine* node's compRec and will not reduce the computation's memory requirements. If we were to keep subdividing with the goal of making each ROI square, we will eventually create one whose *affine's* compRec is roughly H by H.

Some additional computation results from using this divide and conquer scheme. First, for each read node in our graph, we reference the disk an additional time per subdivision. We do not necessarily read the entire image off of the disk an extra time (if the image is stored in a tiled format, we can simply read the tiles which intersect the current resultRec), but we must perform an extra "seek" per subdivision. We might also need to perform additional computations due to the subdivision. Consider an image computation which consists of a k by k convolution of a W by H image (assume an ROI big enough to contain the blur's entire haveRec). As we see from the calculations in FIGURE 12, if we subdivide, we must read in an additional $(k-1)H$ pixels, and convolve an additional $(k-1)H$ pixels.

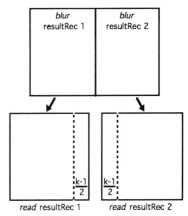

FIGURE 12: Larger resultRecs due to subdivision

There is no single test for comparing the overhead of "divide and conquer" with that of the two virtual memory schemes. Also, the comparison will not yield a single solution as superior to the other. Such analysis might tell us which method is more desirable under which conditions. The comparison must take the following into account: disk read/write/seek speeds as well as operating system overhead for such operations, image storage format (including the granularity of tiling on disk, the compression ratios of source images, and decoding speeds), the ratio of *read* nodes to all other nodes in graph, and the number of nodes in graph which will cause excess calculations as shown in FIGURE 12.

### 6. Similar Systems

Some of the imaging systems we have found use a technique known as *demand-driven execution*. This technique provides optimization methods similar to the ones described above. In demand-driven systems, one builds a network of operations, just as we build a graph. One requests the calculation of a region from the beginning of the network, equivalent in our model to use setting the root's ROI. The operation which receives this request either has the result of the request available, or must recompute some of the desired region. In the latter case it passes the request downstream to the next element in the network. This request is propagated down a string of operations, and the results of the operations are propagated upward. If one alters an operation's parameter, the system is able to reproduce a result from calculating only from that point up. These techniques produce similar results to our rectangle calculation process.

The *ImageVision Library* [10] uses the demand-driven model in the context of image manipulation. The technique also has broader uses in computer graphics, as demonstrated by the *Application Visualization System* [11], where it is used for a larger class of graphics primitives and operations.

Finally, in [3], we see the use of techniques similar to our rectangle calculation methods for the purpose of removing elements from a constructive solid geometry model. The author points out a novel method for paring the pertinent data even further. Expressed in our model's terms, first calculate the nodes' haveRecs. Instead of setting the root's needRec to the ROI, set it to the intersection of the ROI and the root's haveRec. Then compute the nodes' needRecs. Finally, set the leaves' haveRecs to their respective needRecs. Perform these haveRec and needRec calculations ($n$-1) times, where $n$ equals the number of leaf nodes in the graph.

## 7. Conclusions

We have presented an algorithm for the evaluation of image operations which is efficient in both space and time and assures correctness of result. We described a method for dealing with images of different resolutions which also provides the ability to express spatial parameters in an arbitrary coordinate system. This method also enables us to assure that each source image is resampled only once, a desirable feature for many applications. Along with describing two common memory models for image computing, we presented a third which allows one to work completely within physical memory by using a "divide and conquer" scheme.

Our imaging environment supports any operation for which we can bound the result. One does this by providing the four rectangle calculation methods described above, a method for commuting an affine transformation over the operation's parameters, and the imaging operation itself.

We see several areas in which we can improve our computing environment further. As mentioned earlier, our image buffer assignment technique would benefit by taking into account the sizes of the compRecs and resultRecs which reference it. We could also gain further efficiencies by allowing for non-rectangular regions (for example, if we were to describe each region by a set of rectangles instead). It would be useful to analyze more precisely the tradeoffs between the "divide and conquer" memory model and the tiled memory model. Finally, we should analyze the benefits of making multiple passes in the rectangle calculation process, as diagrammed in [3].

## Acknowledgements

The author wishes to thank the following people for their various contributions in both the research and the writing of this work: Ronen Barzel, Ed Catmull, Rob Cook, Tom Hahn, Oren Jacob, Peter Nye, Rick Sayre, Lori Shantzis, Graham Walters, and a special thanks to Jeff Pidgeon for providing the artwork used in this paper.

## References

1. Aho, Alfred, Ravi Sethi, and Jeffrey Ullman. *Compilers: Principles, Techniques, and Tools*, Addison-Wesley, 1986.

2. Alias Research Corp. *Eclipse*. Alias Research Corp., Toronto, Ontario, Canada.

3. Cameron, Stephen. "Efficient Bounds in Constructive Solid Geometry." *IEEE Computer Graphics and Applications*, Vol. 11, No. 3 (May 1991), pp. 68-74.

4. Catmull, Ed and Alvy Ray Smith. "3-D Transformations of Images in Scanline Order." *Computer Graphics* Vol. 14 (1980), pp. 279-284.

5. Foley, James, Andries van Dam, Steven Feiner, and John Hughes. *Computer Graphics: Principles and Practice*. Addison-Wesley, second edition, 1990.

6. Fraser, Donald, Robert Schowengerdt, and Ian Briggs. "Rectification of Multichannel Images in Mass Storage Using Image Transposition." *Computer Vision, Graphics, and Image Processing*, Vol. 29, (1985), pp. 23-36.

7. Porter, Thomas and Tom Duff. "Compositing Digital Images." *Computer Graphics* Vol. 18, No. 3 (1984), pp. 253-259.

8. Pratt, William. *Digital Image Processing* John Wiley & Sons, Inc., 1991.

9. Schumacher, Dale. "General Filtered Image Rescaling" *Graphics Gems III*, (D. Kirk ed.), pp. 8-16, Academic Press, Inc., Boston.

10. Silicon Graphics Inc. *ImageVision Library*. Silicon Graphics Inc., Mountain View, CA.

11. Upson, Craig, Thomas Faulhaber Jr., David Kamins, David Laidlaw, David Schlegel, Jeffrey Vroom, Robert Gurwitz, Andries van Dam. "The Application Visualization System: A Computational Environment for Scientific Visualization." *IEEE Computer Graphics and Applications*, Vol. 9, No. 4 (July 1989), pp. 30-42.

12. Wallace, Bruce. "Merging and Transformation of Raster Images for Cartoon Animation." *Computer Graphics* Vol. 15, No. 3 (1981), pp. 253-262.

# Priority Rendering with a Virtual Reality Address Recalculation Pipeline.

## Matthew Regan,  Ronald Pose

### Monash University *

## Abstract.

Virtual reality systems are placing never before seen demands on computer graphics hardware, yet few graphics systems are designed specifically for virtual reality. An address recalculation pipeline is a graphics display controller specifically designed for use with head mounted virtual reality systems, it performs orientation viewport mapping after rendering which means the users head orientation does not need to be known accurately until less than a microsecond before the first pixel of an update frame is actually sent to the head mounted display device. As a result the user perceived latency to head rotations is minimal.

Using such a controller with image composition it is possible to render different objects within the world at different rate, thus it is possible to concentrate the available rendering power on the sections of the scene that change the most. The concentration of rendering power is known as priority rendering. Reductions of one order of magnitude in the number of objects rendered for an entire scene have been observed when using priority rendering. When non interactive background scenes which are rendered with a high quality rendering algorithm such as ray tracing are added to the world, highly realistic virtual worlds are possible with little or no latency.

CR Descriptors: I.3.1 [Computer Graphics]: Hardware Architecture --- *Raster display devices*; I.3.3 [Computer Graphics]: Picture/image generation --- *Display algorithms*; I.3.6 [Computer Graphics]: Methodology and Techniques;

## 1   Introduction.

The recent popularity of virtual reality has placed extreme pressure on conventional graphics systems to provide realistic real time graphics. In order to maintain the illusion of immersion in a

*Department of Computer Science, Monash University, Wellington Rd, Clayton, Victoria 3168, Australia.
E-mail:  regan@bruce.cs.monash.edu.au

virtual world the user must continually see images from his own vantage point. Any delays between changes in the user's head position and the display of images from that position are very noticeable. To minimise this delay high update rates are required. Conventional film animation rates of 24 frames per second border on adequate. An update rate of 60 or more frames per second is desirable for a good immersion effect. This delay known as latency is one of the most noticeable and undesirable features of many systems.

In order to present the user with 60 updates per second extremely powerful rendering engines are required. These rendering engines draw the scene from the user's viewing position very quickly and present the image to the user. Much academic and commercial research has been done to devise systems which are capable of maintaining high rendering rates [1][4]. One of the reasons such powerful rendering engines are needed is that if a user wearing a head mounted display rotates his head the image changes. Within many applications it is conceivable that the biggest difference between successive frames is due to the viewport orientation. If it were possible to detach the user's head orientation from the rendering process it may be possible to reduce significantly the rendering loads. So instead of drawing the entire scene at 60 frames per second we could draw only the parts of the world that change very fast at 60 frames per second. Initial experiments on a sample world indicate that as little as 1-2% of the objects in a virtual world require updating at 60 frames per second.

A graphics display architecture which will detach user head orientation from the rendering process has been devised and is called an address recalculation pipeline[9][10]. This hardware graphics system performs viewport mapping after rendering and is fundamentally different to conventional display controllers. The location of the user's head does not need to be accurately known until nanoseconds before the first pixel of a frame is displayed on the output devices in the head mounted display unit. This means the lengthy rendering time and the double buffer swap time are removed from latency the user perceives during head rotations, greatly increasing the realism of the virtual world.

There are further advantages to using an address recalculation pipeline when used in conjunction with image composition[7]. This combination allows different objects within the virtual world to be rendered at different rates. Not all objects need to be rerendered at the maximum rate. Initial experiments on a virtual world indicate that many objects within the world only require updating 3.75 to 7.5 times per second, resulting in drastic reductions in rendering loads and overall system cost. Further the combination provides a high quality mechanism for renderer overload. When the renderers are overloaded the user still receives the images using the most up-to-date orientation information from the head tracker, and the latency to head rotations remains minimal. Only fluidity of animation and motion through the scene suffer as a result of renderer overload. Stereoscopic latency is affected by renderer overload, however latency to stereo is often permissible[6].

The subject of this paper will be to examine priority rendering which is a technique for using an address recalculation pipeline with image composition to provide low latency and low rendering loads while maintaining a highly accurate representation of high quality virtual worlds, which are the goals of many virtual reality display systems. The object rendering load for a sample application environment will also be examined.

## 2   The Address Recalculation Pipeline.

An address recalculation pipeline uses hardware which performs orientation viewport mapping post rendering. That is, the orientation mapping occurs after a scene has been rendered rather than as the scene is being rendered. This removes the usually lengthy rendering time from the user perceived latency for head rotations. Some previous work on image warping post rendering has been done [2][12], however these algorithms are usually multiple pass algorithms and are often not directly applicable.

A major feature of the pipeline is that the update rate for user head rotations is bound to the update rate of the display device usually 60+ Hz, instead of the rendering frame rate. Also, with an address recalculation pipeline, the latency does not include the rendering time and doesn't include double buffer swap delays. The orientation of the view the user sees does not need to be known until the first pixel is to be sent to the display device. This means the images the user sees use the most up to date head tracking information. The nature of the latency to head rotations is depicted in Figure 1.

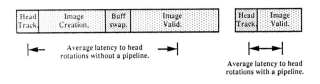

Figure 1:         Latency to head rotations.

In order to perform viewport mapping after rendering, the rendered view must completely encapsulate the user's head, so when the user's head orientation changes the view from the new orientation has already been rendered and the address recalculation pipeline presents the user with the new view computed from the pre rendered image in the system's display memory. The surface of a cube was chosen as the encapsulating rendering surface after considering many possible candidates, as the cube results in a moderately simple hardware implementation and has fewer aliasing artefacts than most other surfaces. The cube's greatest advantage however is in its associated rendering simplicity. The surface of the cube may be rendered to by rendering to six standard viewport mappings. Thus most standard rendering algorithms require little or no modification. Figure 3 depicts an image rendered onto the surface of a cube and Figure 4 depicts a view of an image created by the address recalculation pipeline from the rendered image.

The architecture of the address recalculation pipeline differs from mainstream architectures in the nature of the pixel addressing mechanism. In a conventional display system, pixels to be displayed on the output device are fetched from the display memory sequentially. All adjacent pixels in the display memory appear adjacent on the display device. The address recalculation pipeline is different in that rather than fetching pixels sequentially, pixels are fetched from display memory based on the pixel's screen location, the distortion due to wide-angle viewing lenses and the orientation of the user's head. An overview of the pipeline is given in Figure 2.

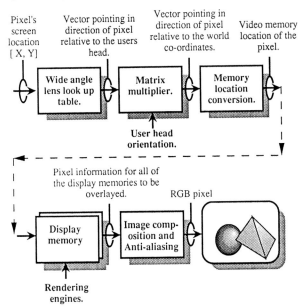

Figure 2:         The address recalculation pipeline.

The pipeline runs at video display rates with the main high speed input being the x-y location of the pixel on the display device. The output from the pipeline is a stream of RGB pixels. The pipeline consists of multiple stages. Each stage performs a unique and necessary function. The first stage of the pipeline converts the screen location of a pixel into a three dimensional vector pointing in the direction at which the pixel is seen relative to the user's head as seen through the wide angle viewing lenses. The next stage of the pipeline multiplies this vector by a matrix containing user head orientation information. The output of the matrix multiplication stage is another three dimensional vector. This new vector points in the direction at which the pixel is seen relative to the world co-ordinate system. The third stage of the pipeline converts the three dimensional vector into a display memory location. Next, four adjacent pixels are fetched from the display memories. Finally the four pixel sets are composed and blended using redundant bits from the matrix multiplication stage. The resulting antialiased pixel is then sent to one of the output devices in the head mounted displays. The hardware is duplicated to obtain a stereo view.

On first examination it may appear that using an address recalculation pipeline would have six times the rendering overheads (scan conversion, clipping etc.) of a conventional system, however this is rarely the case and is only found if the scene has polygons evenly spread out in all three dimensional directions. The address recalculation pipeline must scan convert all polygons it receives which is the worst case scenario for a conventional system. Many conventional rendering systems are

Figure 3:        Image in display memory.

Figure 5:        A wide angle viewing lens distortion.

Figure 4:        An arbitrary view created by pipeline.

Figure 6:        Prototype Address Recalculation Pipeline
                 board.

designed to cope with situations approaching the worst case scenario [8]. The rendering overheads for a conventional system may be reduced if the user is not looking at a complex part of the scene, however as the system has no control over the user's choice of direction for viewing it is fair to assume the user is looking at the most polygonally dense section of the world.

## 2.1    Hardware Implementation.

The current hardware implementation of the address recalculation pipeline uses 16 bit fixed point arithmetic for all computations. The prototype system is designed for medium resolution displays of the order of 640 by 480 pixels with a 60 Hz refresh rate which means each pipeline stage must complete in 40 ns. Many virtual reality systems incorporate wide angle viewing lenses [3][11]. Wide angle viewing lens distortion correction is achieved by means of a hardware look-up table. The wide angle viewing lens look-up table requires one 48 bit entry per display pixel. The resulting look-up table is 3 Mbytes in size. The system may accommodate many different wide angle lens types by down loading different distortions into the look-up table. A possible distortion is depicted in Figure 5. There is no run time rendering penalty for a distorting wide angle viewing lens.

The matrix multiplier stage is implemented with nine 16 bit by 16 bit commercially available multipliers and six 16 bit adders. Some additional 16 bit registers are used for pipeline synchronisation. The vector conversion stage which converts a three dimensional vector into display memory location requires six 16 bit divisions, some programmable logic and buffering circuitry. The divisions are implemented with a reciprocal table look-up followed by a multiplication.

The vector conversion stage produces a display memory location. The display memory itself is organised into six faces, where the faces logically fold to form a cube. Each face of the cube has a display resolution of 512 by 512 pixels. This display resolution results in 1.5 Mpixel display memories. Each display memory is Z buffered and double buffered with a private rendering engine. A stereo system employing multiple display memories for image composition requires vast amounts of memory. To implement high resolution display memories with current technology, static memory is used due to the speed requirements and the non-sequential nature of the memory access. As a result, the cost of display memory tends to dominate the cost of the system. This may change as new memory chip architectures become available. The hardware prototype of the address recalculation pipeline board is given in Figure 6.

## 3    Image Composition.

Image overlaying or image composition [7] is a technique often used to increase the apparent display memory bandwidth as scene from the renderer. Rather than having one display memory (or two for double buffering) the graphics has multiple display memories. Different sections of the visible scene may drawn into separate display memories then overlayed to form a final scene. In many implementations each display memory has a private rendering engine.

As pixels are being fetched from the display memory to be sent to the output device, all the display memories are simultaneously fetched from the same location. Next the Z value associated with each pixel is compared with the Z value of the pixels from the same location in the other display memories. The pixel with the smallest Z value is the winner and is the one that is sent to the output device. Figure 7 illustrates the concept of image composition. Note how one image may cut into another.

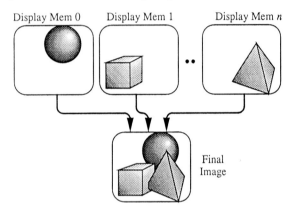

Figure 7:            Image Composition.

In a conventional graphics system image composition uses a factor $n$ redundancy to provide a factor $n$ increase in performance. A side effect of image composition is that each of the display memories may be updated individually and at different rates. In a virtual reality system using image composition alone this side effect is generally of no use as all of the images in the display memories are rendered with the same fixed viewport mapping so when the viewport changes due to a user head rotation all of the images have an incorrect viewport mapping and need re-rendering. A factor $n$ increase in speed is all that may be achieved.

Using an address recalculation pipeline it is possible to make effective use of this side effect of image composition to achieve in certain cases much better than factor n improvement for n display memories in a virtual reality display environment. This is because the images in the display memory of a graphics system with an address recalculation pipeline do not necessarily become invalid when the user's head orientation changes, thus the length of time an image in display memory is valid only loosely depends on the orientation (for a stereo view). For example a non interactive background may never require re-rendering and may thus be pre-rendered with great detail using a high quality rendering technique and a complex model.

## 4    Priority Rendering.

Using an address recalculation pipeline it is possible to render a scene which is largely independent of the user's head orientation. When image composition is combined with the address recalculation pipeline it is possible to render different parts of a scene at different rates. This paper examines a how virtual world may be subdivided into different rendering rates and the effect this has on the overall rendering efficiency.

The orientation independent sections of a static scene that change the most tend to occur during user translations. When the user is stationary within the scene, the renderers must only maintain stereoscopy (which is a form of translation) and animate objects which are changing themselves or change as a result of interaction.

Priority rendering is demand driven rendering. An object is not redrawn until its image within the display memory has changed by a predetermined threshold. In a conventional system this strategy would not be effective as almost any head rotations would cause considerable changes to the image in display memory and the system would have to re-render everything. The images stored in the display memory of a graphics system with an address recalculation pipeline are to a great extent independent of user head orientation which means the renderer doesn't have to redraw the entire scene for head rotations.

The threshold for determining when an object has changed by more than a tolerable amount is determined by the designer of the virtual world and may typically be based on several factors. Usually this threshold is in the form of an angle ($\theta_t$) which defines the minimum feature size of the world. Ideally this angle would be less than the minimum feature size the human eye can detect, approximately one third of an arc minute, however in reality this is impractical. If anti-aliasing of the image in display memory is not used a more sensible threshold may be the inter-pixel spacing in the display memory and if no hardware anti-aliasing is used at all, the pixel spacing in the head set worn by the user may be used. Priority rendering attempts to keep the image in display memory accurate to within $\theta_t$ at the highest possible update rate.

In order to compute the image changes for an object contained within the virtual world we compute how much the object would have changed if it were static and then add an animation component unique to the object as required.

Consider what happens to the display memory image of a static object as the user translates relative to the object. The relative location of the image changes and the image itself may change in size. The rendering strategy must compensate for image changes within display memory. It is possible to predict when these changes occur by observing certain features of a sphere which encapsulates the object.

User translations cause objects to move within the display memory. In order to keep the scene accurate to within $\theta_t$ we need to know how long the image of the object will remain valid at the user's current relative speed. This time is known as the object's translational validity period ($\tau_{translation}$). (See Figure 8) Relative speed is used to compute the object's validity period rather than relative velocity as the resulting world would have several objects caught in slow display memories if the user changes direction significantly. This would result in large temporal errors in the locations of several objects. The relative speed must include a component for the eyes' speed relative to the centre of rotation of the head if the users head is rotating.

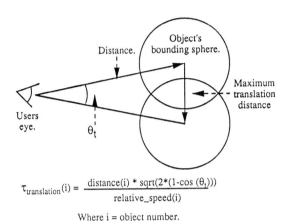

$$\tau_{translation}(i) = \frac{distance(i) * sqrt(2*(1-\cos(\theta_t)))}{relative\_speed(i)}$$

Where i = object number.

Figure 8:      An object's translational validity period ($\tau_{translation}$).

As the user moves towards or away from an object the size of the image of the object changes. We must compute the time that the size of the object is valid and re-render the object when its image size has changed by the predetermined threshold $\theta_t$. Again we use the speed of the object relative to the user rather than the velocity of the object relative to the user for our computations for the same reasons as before. The period for which the size of the image is valid is known as the object's size validity time ($\tau_{size}$). (See Figure 9) Note that as the image size changes by $\theta_t$ there may be several aliases of the object; these have been ignored.

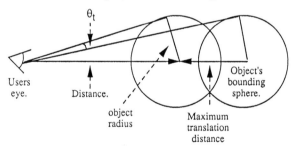

$$\tau_{size}(i) = \frac{distance(i) - radius(i)/\sin(\theta_t + A\sin(radius(i)/distance(i)))}{relative\_speed(i)}$$

Where i = object number.

Figure 9:      An object's size validity period ($\tau_{size}$).

The last factor we consider is any requirement for animation by the object itself. For example a bird flapping its wings requires more updating than a static object like a stationary rock. The period of update for a specific object must be tagged to the object within the database and is defined by the virtual world designer. The period of the current frame of animation for a particular object is known as the object's animation validity time.

$$\tau_{animation} = user\_defined$$

Many other factors may be considered relevant for a highly accurate representation of the scene. For example object rotation

as we translate has not been computed mainly because either size, translational or animation changes tend to dominate the required update rate.

Finally we wish to determine the overall object validity period. This period gives us the amount of time we have until the next update of this object is required. This period also incidentally gives us the latency for a particular object, however, by definition the error in position of the object is less than $\theta_t$. The overall object validity period $\tau_{overall}$ is defined as the smallest of the translational, size and animation periods. Obviously if $\tau_{overall}$ is less than the period of the maximum update rate, $\tau_{overall}$ is assigned the period of the maximum frame rate. This period defines the object's priority and the rendering power devoted to a particular object is based on this priority.

$$\tau_{overall} = min(\tau_{translation}, \tau_{size}, \tau_{animation})$$

Accelerations have not been considered thus far, only relative speed. This may result in latency when accelerating as an object's computed validity period may not accurately reflect the actual validity period. Including acceleration into period computations is possible however the computation is made unnecessarily complex as high accelerations within a virtual world are limited as the sense of heavy acceleration may result in a form of motion sickness known as vection[5].

The previous discussions are based on being able to render all objects completely independently, this would require a pair of display memories per object (for a stereo view). As display memory pricing tends to dominate the overall system cost, providing one display memory per object is obviously impractical. An alternative is to have a limited number of display memories with fixed update periods and attempt to match objects with a particular display memory update rate. The display memory which has the highest update period which is less than the validity period of the object is chosen as the target display memory for a particular object.

Several strategies for dividing the overall system into a set of display memory update rates are possible and the optimal technique will ultimately depend on the nature of the virtual world. For our experiments we have chosen a set of update rates starting at the highest swap rate (for example 60Hz). All other swap rates are some exponential harmonic of the top rate. The display memory update swap strategy is depicted in Figure 10. Using this technique it is possible to swap an object from a low update rate into any of the higher update rates.

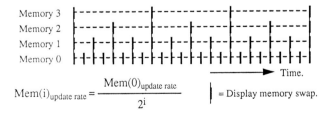

$$Mem(i)_{update\ rate} = \frac{Mem(0)_{update\ rate}}{2^i}$$

      | = Display memory swap.

Figure 10:      Display memory swap strategy.

The fastest display memory is swapping at 60 frames per second and all of the other display memories are swapping at some exponential harmonic of the top rate. The main reason for swapping on harmonics is so objects may be swapped to any faster update rate. The promotion or demotion of an object from one update rate to another occurs on the crossing of the

harmonics, if objects are not swapped on harmonic crossings an object may not be represented or represented twice for a short period of time. This choice of exponential harmonics may not lead to maximum rendering efficiency (the number of times the object needs to be updated compared with the number of times the object is updated) and rendering loads across all display memories may not be distributed evenly. However the optimal configuration is based heavily on the nature of the scene, the rendering power available and the desired overload strategy.

The rendering hardware may have more display memories available than the virtual world requires for high efficiency. In this event, multiple renderers and display memories may be assigned to the one update rate thus devoting more hardware resources to a particular update rate, helping to balance the load.

The previous computations do not take into account stereoscopy. Fortunately the closest objects are most likely be in high speed buffers and it is these objects that are most affected by stereo updates. It may be possible to include a period factor which considers how far the head may rotate within a set period of time, however this is deemed unnecessary as some latency to stereoscopy is acceptable.

## 5   Experimental virtual environment.

Priority rendering may be used to reduce the overall rendering load on the rendering subsystem. The rendering load is based on several features of the scene, where the actual number of polygons is just one of the factors. One of our virtual world applications is a walk through of a forest and is the subject of this investigation. This simulation was performed in order to determine the rendering load on various display memories with various update rates.

The virtual world under investigation contained one thousand trees. Each tree is bounded by a sphere of radius five metres, which implies a maximum tree height of ten metres. The actual number of polygons contained within each tree is arbitrary as we are only considering object rendering load, the number of polygons per tree will eventually be determined by our real rendering power. The trees are randomly placed in a circular forest at a density such that the leaves of the trees may form a continuous canopy. The resulting forest has a radius of one hundred and fifty metres.

The simulation investigates the object rendering loads on various display memories with different update rates. The experiment is conducted as a walk through the world from one side to the other at one metre per second (approximate walking speed), passing through the centre of the world. This gives us statistics on rendering loads for circumstances ranging from being completely surrounded by the objects to being at the edge of the objects.
The chosen allowable error $\theta_t$ is the smallest inter-pixel spacing between the smallest pixels in the display memory. The system is to have a display memory resolution of 512 by 512 pixels per face, this means the smallest distance between any two pixels is approximately six arc minutes. This is an order of magnitude higher than the resolution of the human eye.

All of our comparisons are based on the number of objects that must be redrawn by the rendering system to maintain the approximately the same illusion with an effective update rate of 60 frames per second. We compare how many objects a system with an address recalculation pipeline must redraw against the

number of objects a system without the pipeline must redraw for the entire length of the simulation (both systems are assumed to have multiple display memories and multiple renders). The Relative Object Rendering Load (RORL) is a percentage measurement of this ratio.

$$RORL = \frac{\text{Total number of object updates (with pipeline)}}{\text{Total number of object updates (without pipeline)}} * 100\%$$

With an address recalculation pipeline for the simulation described above the RORL is 15%. That is the system with the pipeline only had to redraw 15 objects for every 100 objects the system without the pipeline had to redraw for a similar illusion. If we make the minimum feature size (maximum error size) $\theta_t$ larger, the RORL reduces further. When $\theta_t$ is increased to be the smallest arc distance between the largest pixels in display memory the RORL is less than 8% of the object rendering load of a conventional system. Figure 11 depicts the relationship between the object rendering load (relative to a conventional system) and minimum feature size.

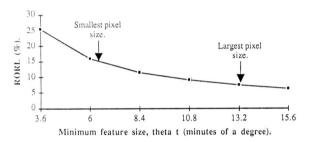

RORL vs Minimum feature size.

Figure 11:      RORL against feature size.

The combination of the address recalculation pipeline with image composition and priority rendering has cut our total object rendering load to 15% of the equivalent object rendering load without the hardware. The main reason for this significant saving is depicted in Figures 12 and 13. Of the total number of object updates required for the walk through, nearly 40% of them were assigned to display memory 3 which is swapping at 7.5 frames per second. So even though display memory 0 is swapping 8 times faster than display memory 3, it is only doing one quarter the work display memory 3 is doing. This means memory 3 is updating $40\%/10\% * 8 = 32$ times the number of objects display memory 0 is updating (at an eighth the rate).

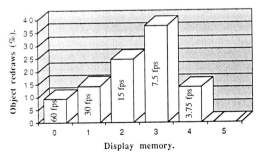

Rendering loads at various display memory update rates.

Figure 12:      Graphical depiction of objects assigned to display memories.

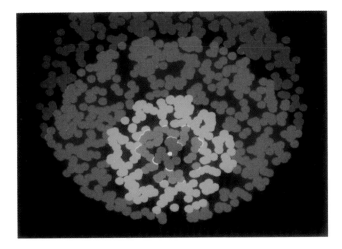

| | |
|---|---|
| White: | User. |
| Red: | Display Memory 0 (60 fps). |
| Cyan: | Display Memory 1 (30 fps). |
| Yellow: | Display Memory 2 (15 fps). |
| Green: | Display Memory 3 (7.5 fps). |
| Blue: | Display Memory 4 (3.75 fps). |

Figure 13    Display memory assignment of trees during a walk through.

Providing a stereo view of the world is highly desirable within a head mounted graphics display system to help with the sense of presence within the world. With an address recalculation pipeline the display memories are not actually centred around the point of rotation of the user's head, rather they are centred around the user's eyes. This means when the user's head rotates while the user is stationary a small amount of translation occurs. This implies the need to re-render some objects which are affected by the translation caused by the head rotation. Although the speed at which the eyes translate during a head rotation must be included into the priority computation for $\tau_{translation}$ and $\tau_{size}$ it is interesting to note the total number of objects that become invalid to head rotations of various angles. Figure 14 shows how many objects become invalid for a particular head rotation. The upper line is when $\theta_t$ = 6 arc minutes (corresponding to the smallest pixel in display memory) while the lower line for when $\theta_t$ = 13 arc minutes (corresponding to the largest pixel in display memory). From this graph we see that head rotations smaller than 45 degrees require few objects to be updated. These figures were generated whilst standing in the middle of the above mentioned scene.

**Objects requiring update vs Angle of head rotation.**

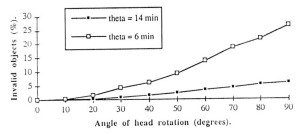

Figure 14:    Invalid objects against Angle of head rotation.

## 6 Conclusion.

We have described a novel display architecture optimised for use in virtual reality systems. This architecture allows us to take advantage of a prioritized rendering technique which was the focus of this paper. Simulation studies have shown that these techniques can provide order of magnitude performance improvements over conventional graphics subsystems applied to virtual reality applications.

Using the address recalculation pipeline it is possible to reduce latency for head rotations to close to theoretical limits. In fact latency to user head rotations is imperceptible since these are handled within the display controller itself without need for re-rendering.

The use of image composition and parallel prioritized rendering techniques in conjunction with the address recalculation pipeline enables one to handle translation through scenes of great complexity without sacrificing frame rate or incurring unacceptable latency. Comparison with conventional approaches illustrated where the performance gains were taking place.

While the address recalculation pipeline itself can provide a significant advantage for virtual reality applications, its use in conjunction with multiple renderers and prioritized rendering techniques forms a significant advance in virtual reality implementation technology.

## 7 Acknowledgements.

Matthew Regan acknowledges the support of an Australian Postgraduate Award (Priority). This research was conducted under an Australian Research Council Small Grant. Datasets courtesy Iain Sinclair.

## References.

[1] Akeley, Kurt. Reality Engine Graphics, Proceedings of SIGGRAPH 93. In *Computer Graphics*, Annual Conference Series 1993. 109-116.

[2] Catmull, Ed. and Smith, Alvy. 3-D Transformations of Images in Scanline Order. Proceedings of SIGGRAPH 80. In *Computer Graphics*, Annual Conference Series 1980. 279-285.

[3] Deering, Michael. High Resolution Virtual Reality, Proceedings of SIGGRAPH 92 In *Computer Graphics*, Annual Conference Series 1992. 195-202.

[4] Fuchs, Henry. et al. Pixel-Planes 5: A Heterogeneous Multiprocessor Graphics System Using Processor Enhanced Memories. Proceedings of SIGGRAPH 89. In *Computer Graphics*, Annual Conference Series 1989. 79-88.

[5] Hettinger, Lawrence and Riccio, Gary. Visually Induced Motion Sickness in Virtual Reality Systems: Implications for training and Mission Rehearsal, Presented at a DoD sponsored Inter agency Tech Simulation, 1-3 Oct, 1991.

[6] Lipton, L. Temporal Artefacts in Field-Sequential Stereoscopic Displays. Proceedings of SID '91 (Anaheim, California, May 6-10, 1991). In Proceedings of the SID 22 (May 1991), 834-835.

[7]   Molnar, Steven, Image Composition Architectures for Real-Time image Generation. Ph.D dissertation, University of North Carolina, 1991.

[8]   Molnar, Steven and Fuchs, Henry. Advanced Raster Graphics Architectures. Chapter 18, Computer Graphics, Foley and VanDam, 872-873.

[9]   Regan, Matthew and Pose, Ronald. A Low Latency Virtual Reality Display System. Tech Report 166, Department of Computer Science, Monash University . September 1992.

[10]  Regan, Matthew and Pose, Ronald. An Interactive Graphics Display Architecture. Proceedings of IEEE Virtual Reality Annual International Synposium. (18-22 September 1993, Seattle USA), 293-299.

11]   Robinett, Warren and Roland, Jannack. A Computational Model for the Stereoscopic Optics for  Head Mounted Display. In Presence 1, (winter 1992), 45-62.

[12]  Smith, Alvy. Planar 2-Pass Texture Mapping and Warping. Proceedings of SIGGRAPH 87.  In Computer Graphics, Annual Conference Series 1987. 263-272.

## Appendix

### Derivation of $\tau_{translation}$ and $\tau_{size}$

For a given $\theta_t$, the smallest maximum translational distance $x$ of an object at distance $d$ will occur when the distance after the translation is also $d$ (ie. no change in size). This means we may use the cosine rule to compute $x$ and then from $x$, given the objects relative speed we may compute $\tau_{translation}$.

$$x^2 = d^2 + d^2 - 2d*d*\cos(\theta_t)$$
$$x^2 = 2d^2(1-\cos(\theta_t)$$
$$x = d*sqrt(2(1-\cos(\theta_t)))$$

$$\tau_{translation} = maximum\_translation / relative\_speed$$
$$\tau_{translation} = d*sqrt(2(1-\cos(\theta_t)))/ relative\_speed$$

When an object changes size the smallest maximum translation distance occurs when the object moves closer.  The maximum translational distance occurs when the angle to the edge of the object $\theta$ changes by $\theta_t$.

$$\theta \text{ at position 1} = Asin (radius/d)$$
$$\theta \text{ at position 2} = Asin (radius/(d-x))$$

$$\theta_t = \theta(pos2) - \theta(pos1)$$
$$\theta_t = Asin (radius/(d-x)) - Asin (radius/d)$$
$$sin (\theta_t + Asin(radius/d)) = radius/(d - x)$$
$$x = d-radius/(sin(\theta_t + Asin(radius/d)))$$

$$\tau_{translation} = maximum\_translation / relative\_speed$$
$$\tau_{translation} = (d-radius/(sin(\theta_t+Asin(radius/d))))/speed$$

# Reflection Vector Shading Hardware

## Douglas Voorhies and Jim Foran

## Silicon Graphics Computer Systems

## Abstract

Surface reflections of an environment can be rendered in real time if hardware calculates an unnormalized reflection vector at each pixel. Conventional perspective-correct texturing hardware can then be leveraged to draw high-quality reflections of an environment or specular highlights in real time. This fully accommodates area light sources, allows a local viewer to move interactively, and is especially well suited to the inspection of surface orientation and curvature. By emphasizing the richness of the incoming illumination rather than physical surface properties, it represents a new direction for real-time shading hardware.

## Introduction

Interactive computer graphics systems have been widely used in industrial design for the modeling, visualization, and manufacture of complex surfaces such as automobile bodies. The models are commonly represented as a mesh of vertex positions, normals, and surface colors[5]. In both real-life and computer graphics, if the surface is shiny and the viewer moves, it is easier to visualize the surface smoothness and curvature[14].

Both reflections and realistic surfaces require extensive calculations. Computer graphics has long sought effective shortcuts to these complexities, but graphics hardware has done little to follow either path.

To correctly model the optical physics would require a bi-directional reflectance function (BDRF)[12] evaluated at each surface point, convolved with the hemispherical illuminating scene visible from that point. This wide convolution and scene re-rendering are, of course, computationally intractable for real-time rendering hardware. Two approximations are commonly employed: point light sources and mirror reflections. Point lights allow the BDRF to be evaluated for only a single entry and single exit direction. (In practice, workstations have employed only the "half-angle" approximation to specular surface behavior.)

Mirror-like reflections are handled by sampling environment maps or by ray tracing. Environment maps are used to model a scene at infinity; they are an arbitrary function of direction alone, and ignore parallax. The map may be precomputed since it is a 360° image of the environment as viewed from only a single reference point. Ray tracing, on the other hand, accounts for the local 3-D position of reflected objects, and is therefore extremely costly. Each reflected

voorhies@sgi.com     (415) 390–1058
foran @sgi.com     (415) 390–3602
2011 N. Shoreline Blvd., Mountain View CA 94039

ray probes surrounding objects, multiplying the already high intersection testing load and making rendering time not linear with complexity. It also requires the full definition of all objects before rendering can begin, preventing an "immediate mode" paradigm and adding a storage-based upper limit on the number of objects.

Environment mapping has proved effective because the eye gets a clear impression of surface curvature from the reflection's distortion of the environment image. Parallax artifacts are a second order effect which requires cognitive analysis across the breadth of the rendered image to be noticed. The reflections are always optically correct and consistent (for a different, distant environment).

Point-light and reflection approximations are expensive for hardware. Even these extreme simplifications are usually implemented only at vertexes, with interpolation of the surface colors or map indexes in between. While effective for diffuse surfaces, Gouraud shading[6] is inadequate for shiny ones. The polygonal nature of the model is accentuated and Mach banding[9] is introduced. Similarly, when indexes into a 360° environment map are linearly interpolated, the reflection can be distorted.

Nonetheless, these two approaches are useful in their primary domains, and can begin to solve the difficult middle ground of partially specular surfaces. A richer illuminating environment can be approximated by summing multiple point lights. The "mirror reflection" of an environment map can approximate a BDRF which is radially symmetric around the reflection vector (e.g., Phong[10]) by blurring the environment in a preprocessing step using a spherical convolution. Point lights and environment maps can be used together, with their results summed, to approximate BDRFs which have both a broad diffuse lobe and a narrow specular lobe.

Much work (such as [3][12]) has been done to more carefully approximate physical surface BDRFs. For example, Torrance and Sparrow developed a physically-based theoretical model for reflected light[11], based on a Gaussian distribution of surface microfacets. The specular reflectance is dependent on the angle between the average surface normal and the "perfect reflection" normal. While these models and much subsequent work are much closer to empirical behavior than Phong highlights, the calculations required are even more extensive.

This paper will focus on communicating surface orientation and curvature in real time by handling reflections using the "mirror reflection" approximation. In this case, having rich illumination information is more useful than rich surface behavior. Mirror-like reflections of large area lights give more effective visual clues than anisotropic patinas or grazing-angle effects. The position-invariant simplification of an environment map makes it practical for real-time hardware, in turn permitting smooth motion which further aids surface orientation and curvature assessment.

## Environment Mapping

First discussed by Blinn and Newell[2], and elaborated by Greene[7], environment maps express source illumination by direction alone. It is built upon texture mapping, which is becoming more common and comparable in performance to linear shading[1].

Software renderers calculate a reflection vector for each pixel, and use this to index into an axis-aligned cube map, a latitude/longitude map, or a *sin*(latitude)/longitude map. Rendering hardware has map -ped an environment texture on to polygons[8] using a circular "reflection-in-a-sphere" texture as in Figure 1. [4] implemented a partial approach: calculation of reflection vectors, but only a color ramp as a degenerate environment.

Figure 1:
Circular Environment Map

None of these are appropriate for local viewer real-time applications. The software calculation of reflection vectors has involved expensive normalization of the eye and surface normal vectors, and a hardware-accessed circular texture map is correct for only orthographic rendering with a fixed, infinite viewer.

This latter limitation is a poor match to emulating the physical inspection of a car body, for example, where the viewer walks around a stationary car. Virtual reality devices such as the stereoscopic boom emphasize this natural "inspection" paradigm, where the object and environment stay fixed, while the viewer roams at will. Altering the eye position requires creation of a new map, which is challenging to do in real time.

Texture index interpolation within a circular map also has two severe artifacts. Grazing reflections map to points near the perimeter, and they are extremely sensitive to object normals. A tiny object rotation can result in a vertex texture index snapping to the opposite side of the map, as illustrated by Figure 2.

 A slight rotation of the object makes one texture index jump →

Figure 2: Perils of the Grazing Reflection Singularity

Secondly, linear texture index interpolation in this "reflection-in-a-sphere" circular map causes severe distortion of the reflection, especially for near-grazing reflections. Although there is sufficient resolution and minimal distortion at the center of the map, the periphery may be very distorted and the mapping extremely anisotropic.

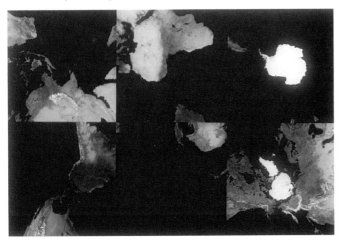

Figure 3: Cube Map Example

## Reflection Vector Shading

If the reflection vector is used as an index into a cube environment map, we can avoid these artifacts. If it is a function of the eye direction, the viewer can be local. The six cube faces capture the environment color for all 3-D reflection directions without singularities.

The cubic environment map is a general table controlling what is reflected by the surface. Because the map is indexed by the reflection vector, specular spread functions can be incorporated into the maps themselves if they are based solely on the relative reflection angle. Thus a Phong highlight can be incorporated, whereas a Torrance-Sparrow function cannot. Since such highlights are precomputed, there is no rendering-time penalty for a high number of light sources. Indeed, maps can contain area lights or photographic environments, or any combination of these. See Figure 3 for an example cube map.

Cubic environment maps pose difficulties for hardware texturing architectures. Since different polygon vertices can map into different cube faces, interpolation between vertex indices often fails. Even within a face, linear interpolation does not accurately correspond to the angular change in the reflection vector across a polygon.

Both of these problems disappear if the reflection direction is recomputed at every pixel. Crossing cube edges is no longer a problem because only the surface normal and eye vectors are interpolated iteratively; the choice of cube face is made afresh for each reflection vector at each pixel. And because the reflection vector is based on a changing eye vector, the viewer can be local. This is especially important for flat surfaces, which would otherwise not reflect an "image".

Surprisingly, the reflection vector can be computed from non-normalized surface normal and eye vectors since the reflection itself does not need to be normalized. Since projecting onto the cube faces involves a division, the absolute reflection vector length cancels out.

Each of the components of the eye and normal vectors ($\mathbf{E}$ and $\mathbf{N}$) iterate linearly in eye space. Commonly, the reflection vector ($\mathbf{R}$) is calculated using a normalized normal vector ($\mathbf{N_N}$) to allow the dot-product projection of $\mathbf{E}$ on to $\mathbf{N}$:

$$\mathbf{R} = 2 * \mathbf{N_N} * (\mathbf{N_N} \cdot \mathbf{E}) - \mathbf{E}$$

We can dramatically reduce the hardware required to synthesize reflection vectors, eliminating this normalization step, by multiplying both sides by the length of the unnormalized normal vector squared ($\mathbf{N_U} \cdot \mathbf{N_U}$):

$$\mathbf{R_U} = 2 * \mathbf{N_U} * (\mathbf{N_U} \cdot \mathbf{E}) - \mathbf{E} * (\mathbf{N_U} \cdot \mathbf{N_U})$$

The result is a unnormalized reflection vector whose length equals the product of the lengths of the normal and eye vectors. Computing

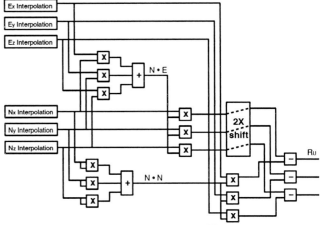

Figure 4: Reflection Vector Hardware

this vector thus requires two dot products, two vector scalings and a vector subtraction.

Figure 4 shows hardware to generate the reflection vector. Since the cube face is chosen by the major axis, it can be determined by an inexpensive three-way comparison. Within a cube face, the indexes (−1...+1) can be obtained by dividing the minor axis values by the major axis value, as in Figure 5, which cancels out the vector length. This requires one division at each pixel, which can conveniently be handled by the per-pixel divider otherwise required for perspective-correct texture mapping.

Figure 6 shows hemispheres tesselated with 60, 240, and 960 triangles per sphere. Even with 960 triangles, Gouraud shading between Phong-lit vertex colors using a specularity exponent of 20 shows Mach bands and a grossly polygonal highlight. Reflection vector shading shows slight highlight distortion at low tesselation and essentially none at medium and high tesselations.

Figure 7 show an automobile body illuminated by a photographic environment image. Here no blurring of the environment is done; this makes the surface appear shiny. In creating this image, we learned how sensitive reflection vector shading can be. Any errors in tesselation or normal vectors are revealed mercilessly as distortion of the reflection. This amplification suggests it will be invaluable in analyzing models to insure their quality. Rendering with lower specularity fails to reveal irregularities in normal vectors which are quire visible with reflection vector shading. This sensitivity is implicit in any method which is very effective at visualizing curvature and orientation.

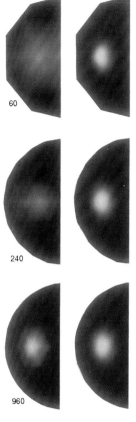

60

240

960

Gouraud-shaded, Phong-lit vertexes    Reflection-mapped

Figure 6: Highlights

## Perspective Viewing

Insuring the reflection vector is correct when viewing the surface in perspective can be accomplished by projecting from screen space back to the world space of the environment. Formally, this is done by substituting N/w and E/w for the normal and eye vectors iterated in screen space, calculating R/w, and dividing it by 1/w at each pixel to return to the world space reflection direction. Here "1/w" is the homogeneous component of each vector, proportional to the eye distance. But there is a second fortuitous advantage of projecting on to the environment cube faces: the w's in the denominators of each component of R/w cancel when the minor axes are divided by the major axis! Therefore the 1/w scaling factor is completely transparent to the hardware and the perspective divider otherwise needed for texturing can be used instead for the index calculation. Its division to project the R/w reflection vector onto the cube implicitly achieves screen space to world space projection.

## Level of Detail

Traditionally level of detail filtering can be handled using mip-maps[13]. The area of the environment subtended by a single square pixel is the quadrilateral enclosed by the reflections of the pixel corners. Since mip-maps are usually isotropic, to avoid undersampling requires selecting the mip-map level based on the largest dimension of the subtended area. This avoids the aliasing inherent in ray tracing, and the slight overfiltering is less of a problem for reflections than it is for surface textures.

To select the map, we use the normal vector alone. Angular change in the eye vector results in an equal angular change in the reflected

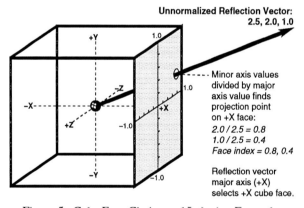

**Unnormalized Reflection Vector: 2.5, 2.0, 1.0**

- - - Minor axis values divided by major axis value finds projection point on +X face:

*2.0 / 2.5 = 0.8*
*1.0 / 2.5 = 0.4*
*Face index = 0.8, 0.4*

Reflection vector major axis (+X) selects +X cube face.

Figure 5: Cube Face Choice and Indexing Example

Data Set courtesy of Viewpoint DataLabs

Figure 7: Shiny surfaces with photographic environment

vector. Angular change in the normal results in twice as large a change in the reflection. These changes can add or cancel. However, the eye vector changes very slowly unless the surface is extremely close to the eye, and so its effect is almost always swamped by the normal vector iteration. The normal vector's rate-of-change is therefore a practical indication of worst-case area to be sampled.

## Future work

We have implemented reflection vector shading in software and are designing it into a high-end workstation. 16-bit vector component precision appears artifact-free, and conventional texture mapping is effective for the cube-face environment mapping.

This new approach invites exploration of additional techniques. Bump mapping seems to be a logical next step since reflection vector shading does not need normalized reflection vectors. Orthogonal tangent vectors could be interpolated or generated, and used to tug the reflection vector based on a 2-component texture or pseudo-random hash. Grazing angle effects might be included by increasing the specular effect if $(N \cdot E)$ is near zero. Local lights or object inter-reflection might be handled by rendering cube faces from the viewpoint of a reflective object.

## Summary

High-quality reflection effects become possible for hardware by using texture maps to hold the faces of a cubic environment map. The map is indexed by a reflection vector calculated per-pixel without requiring any normalization. This makes it practical for VLSI hardware. The result is specular highlights at texturing speed, independent of the number of light sources, as well as local viewer environment mapping. The highlights can be reflections of point lights using Phong-type dropoff functions, or of area lights or photographic environments. Because the reflection vector is recomputed with every pixel, it is relatively free from artifacts. Because it is implemented in hardware, the smooth flow of reflections over a surface as the viewer moves greatly aids assessing the position and curvature. The visual effect is a significant step in the realism and usefulness of interactively-rendered surfaces.

## References

[1] Akeley, Kurt. "RealityEngine Graphics". *Proceedings of SIGGRAPH '93*, (August 1993), pp. 109–116.

[2] Blinn, Jim and Newell, Martin. "Texture and Reflection in Computer Generated Images". *Communications of the ACM*, Vol.19, No. 10 (1976), pp. 542–547.

[3] Cook, Robert and Torrance, Kenneth. "A Reflection Model for Computer Graphics". *ACM Transactions on Graphics,* Vol. 1, No. 1 (1982), pp. 7–24.

[4] Derring, M., Winner, S., Schediwy, B., Duffy, C., and Hunt, N. "The Triangle Processor and Normal Vector Shader: A VLSI System for High Performance Graphics", *Proceedings of SIGGRAPH '88*, (August 88), pp. 21–30.

[5] Foley, J. D., van Dam, A., Feiner S. K, and Hughes J. F. "Computer Graphics, Principals and Practice, 2nd Edition" Addison-Wesley, Reading Mass. 1990.

[6] Gouraud, Henri. "Continuous Shading of Curved Surfaces". *IEEE Transactions on Computers,* Vol. 20, No. 6 (June 1971), pp. 623–628.

[7] Greene, Ned. "Environment Mapping and Other Applications of World Projections". *IEEE Computer Graphics and Applications,* Vol. 6, No. 11, (November 1986), pp. 21–30.

[8] Haeberli, Paul and Akeley, Kurt. "The Accumulation Buffer: Hardware Support for High-Quality Rendering", *Proceedings of SIGGRAPH 90*, (July 1990), pp. 309–318.

[9] Mach, Ernst. "The Analysis of Sensations and the Relation of the Physical to the Psychical". Dover Publications, New York, 1959.

[10] Phong, Bui Thong. "Illumination for Computer Generated Pictures". *Communications of the ACM*, Vol. 18, No. 6 (1975), pp. 311–317.

[11] Torrance, K. and Sparrow, E. "Theory for Off-Specular Reflection from Roughened Surfaces". *Journal Optical Society of America*, Vol. 57, No. 9, (September 1967), pp. 1105–1114.

[12] Westin, Steven, Arvo, James, and Torrance, Kenneth. "Predicting Reflectance Functions from Complex Surfaces". *Proceedings of SIGGRAPH '92,* (July 1992), pp. 255–264.

[13] Williams, Lance. "Pyramidal Parametrics". *Proceedings of SIGGRAPH '83,* (July 1983), pp. 1–11.

[14] Zisserman, A., Giblin, P., and Blake, A. "The Information Available to a Moving Observer from Specularities". *Image and Vision Computing* Vol. 7, No. 1 (1989), pp. 38–42.

# FBRAM: A new Form of Memory
# Optimized for 3D Graphics

*Michael F Deering, Stephen A Schlapp, Michael G Lavelle*
*Sun Microsystems Computer Corporation*[†]

## ABSTRACT

FBRAM, a new form of dynamic random access memory that greatly accelerates the rendering of Z-buffered primitives, is presented. Two key concepts make this acceleration possible. The first is to convert the read-modify-write Z-buffer compare and RGBα blend into a single write only operation. The second is to support two levels of rectangularly shaped pixel caches internal to the memory chip. The result is a 10 megabit part that, for 3D graphics, performs read-modify-write cycles ten times faster than conventional 60 ns VRAMs. A four-way interleaved 100 MHz FBRAM frame buffer can Z-buffer up to 400 million pixels per second. Working FBRAM prototypes have been fabricated.

**CR Categories and Subject Descriptors:** I.3.1 [Computer Graphics]: Hardware Architecture; I.3.3 [Computer Graphics]: Picture/ Image Generation *Display algorithms*; I.3.7 [Computer Graphics]: Three Dimensional Graphics and Realism.

**Additional Keywords and Phrases:** 3D graphics hardware, rendering, parallel graphics algorithms, dynamic memory, caching.

## 1 INTRODUCTION

One of the traditional bottlenecks of 3D graphics hardware has been the rate at which pixels can be rendered into a frame buffer. Modern interactive 3D graphics applications require rendering platforms that can support 30 Hz animation of richly detailed 3D scenes. But existing memory technologies cannot deliver the desired rendering performance at desktop price points.

The performance of hidden surface elimination algorithms has been limited by the pixel fill rate of 2D projections of 3D primitives. While a number of exotic architectures have been proposed to improve rendering speed beyond that achievable with conventional DRAM or VRAM, to date all commercially available workstation 3D accelerators have been based on these types of memory chips.

[†]2550 Garcia Avenue, MTV18-212
Mountain View, CA 94043-1100
michael.deering@Eng.Sun.COM     (415) 336-3017
stephen.schlapp@Eng.Sun.COM     (415) 336-3818
mike.lavelle@Eng.Sun.COM        (415) 336-3103

This paper describes a new form of specialized memory, Frame Buffer RAM (FBRAM). FBRAM increases the speed of Z-buffer operations by an order of magnitude, and at a lower system cost than conventional VRAM. This speedup is achieved through two architectural changes: moving the Z compare and RGBα blend operations inside the memory chip, and using two levels of appropriately shaped and interleaved on-chip pixel caches.

## 2 PREVIOUS WORK

After the Z-buffer algorithm was invented [3], the first Z-buffered hardware systems were built in the 1970's from conventional DRAM memory chips. Over time, the density of DRAMs increased exponentially, but without corresponding increases in I/O bandwidth. Eventually, video output bandwidth requirements alone exceeded the total DRAM I/O bandwidth.

Introduced in the early 1980's, VRAM [18][20] solved the video output bandwidth problem by adding a separate video port to a DRAM. This allowed graphics frame buffers to continue to benefit from improving bit densities, but did nothing directly to speed rendering operations. More recently, rendering architectures have bumped up against a new memory chip bandwidth limitation: faster rendering engines have surpassed VRAM's input bandwidth. As a result, recent generations of VRAM have been forced to increase the width of their I/O busses just to keep up. For the last five years, the pixel fill (i.e. write) rates of minimum chip count VRAM frame buffers have increased by less than 30%.

Performance gains have mainly been achieved in commercially available systems by brute force. Contemporary mid-range systems have employed 10-way and 20-way interleaved VRAM designs [1][14]. Recent high-end architectures have abandoned VRAM altogether in favor of massively interleaved DRAM: as much as 120-way interleaved DRAM frame buffers [2]. But such approaches do not scale to cost effective machines.

More radical approaches to the problem of pixel fill have been explored by a number of researchers. The most notable of these is the pixel-planes architecture [9][16], others include [7][8][11][4]. [12] and [10] contain a good summary of these architectures. What these architectures have in common is the avoidance of making the rendering of every pixel an explicit event on external pins. In the limit, only the geometry to be rendered need enter the chip(s), and the final pixels for video output exit.

These research architectures excel at extremely fast Z-buffered fill of large areas. They achieve this at the expense of high cost, out-of-order rendering semantics, and various overflow exception cases. Many of these architectures ([16][11][4]) require screen space pre-sorting of primitives before rendering commences. As a consequence, intermediate geometry must be sorted and stored in large batches.

Unfortunately, the benefits from the fast filling of large polygons are rapidly diminishing with today's very finely tessellated objects. That is, the triangles are getting smaller [6]. The number of pixels filled per scene is not going up anywhere near as quickly as the total number of polygons. As 3D hardware rendering systems are finally approaching motion fusion rates (real time), additional improvements in polygon rates are employed to add more fine detail, rather than further increases in frame rates or depth complexity.

## 3 Z-BUFFERING AND OTHER PIXEL PROCESSING OPERATIONS

Fundamental to the Z-buffer hidden surface removal algorithm are the steps of reading the Z-buffer's old Z value for the current pixel being rendered, numerically comparing this value with the new one just generated, and then, as an outcome of this compare operation, either leaving the old Z (and RGB) frame buffer pixel values alone, or replacing the old Z (and RGB) value with the new.

With conventional memory chips, the Z data must traverse the data pins twice: once to read out the old Z value, and then a second time to write the new Z value if it wins the comparison. Additional time must be allowed for the data pins to electrically "turn around" between reading and writing. Thus the read-modify-write Z-buffer transaction implemented using a straightforward read-turn-write-turn operation is four times longer than a pure write transaction. Batching of reads and writes ($n$ reads, turn, $n$ writes, turn) would reduce the read-modify-write cost to twice that of a pure write transaction for very large $n$, but finely tessellated objects have very small values of $n$, and still suffer a 3-4× penalty.

This is the first problem solved by FBRAM. Starting with a data width of 32 bits per memory chip, FBRAM now makes it possible for the Z comparison to be performed entirely *inside* the memory chip. Only if the internal 32 bit numeric comparison succeeds does the new Z value actually replace the old value. Thus the fundamental read-modify-write operation is converted to a pure write operation at the data pins.

Because more than 32-bits are needed to represent a double buffered RGBZ pixel, some way of transmitting the results of the Z comparison across multiple chips is required. The Z comparison result is communicated on a single external output signal pin of the FBRAM containing the Z planes, instructing FBRAM chips containing other planes of the frame buffer whether or not to write a new value.

The Z-buffer operation is the most important of the general class of read-modify-write operations used in rendering. Other important conditional writes which must be communicated between FBRAMs include window ID compare [1] and stenciling.

Compositing functions, rendering of transparent objects, and anti-aliased lines require a blending operation, which adds a specified fraction of the pixel RGB value just generated to a fraction of the pixel RGB value already in the frame buffer. FBRAM provides four 8-bit 100 MHz multiplier-adders to convert the read-modify-write blending operation into a pure write at the pins. These internal blend operations can proceed in parallel with the Z and window ID compare operations, supported by two 32-bit comparators. One of the comparators supports magnitude tests ($>, \geq, <, \leq, =, \neq$), the other supports match tests ($=, \neq$). Also, traditional boolean bit-operations (for RasterOp) are supported inside the FBRAM. This collection of processing units is referred to as the pixel ALU.

Converting read-modify-write operations into pure write operations at the data pins permits FBRAM to accept data at a 100 MHz rate. To match this rate, the pixel ALU design is heavily pipelined, and can process pixels at the rate of 100 million pixels per second. Thus in a typical four-way interleaved frame buffer design the max-

imum theoretical Z-buffered pixel fill rate of an FBRAM based system is 400 mega pixels per second. By contrast, comparable frame buffers constructed with VRAM achieve peak rates of 33-66 mega pixels per second [5][14].

Now that pixels are arriving and being processed on-chip at 100 MHz, we next consider the details of storing data.

## 4 DRAM FUNDAMENTALS

Dynamic memory chips achieve their impressive densities (and lower costs) by employing only a single transistor per bit of storage. These storage cells are organized into pages; typically there are several thousand cells per page. Typical DRAM arrays have hundreds or thousands of pages. Per bit sense amplifiers are provided which can access an entire page of the array within 120 ns. These sense amplifiers retain the last data accessed; thus they function as a several thousand bit page buffer. The limited number of external I/O pins can perform either a read or a write on a small subset of the page buffer at a higher rate, typically every 40 ns.

FBRAM starts with these standard DRAM components, and adds a multiported high speed SRAM and pixel ALU. All of this is organized within a caching hierarchy, optimized for graphics access patterns, to address the bandwidth mismatch between the high speed pins and the slow DRAM cells.

## 5 PIXEL CACHING

The cache system design goal for FBRAM is to match the 100 MHz read-modify-write rate of the pixel ALU with the 8 MHz rate of the DRAM cells. Figure 1 illustrates this cache design challenge.

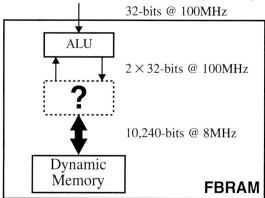

Figure 1. Bandwidth mismatch between pixel ALU and DRAM.

Caches have long been used with general purpose processors; even a small cache can be very effective [17]. But caches have been much less used with graphics rendering systems.

The data reference patterns of general purpose processors exhibit both *temporal* and *spatial* locality of reference. Temporal locality is exhibited when multiple references are made to the same data within a short period of time. Spatial locality is exhibited when multiple references within a small address range are made within a short period of time. Caches also reduce the overall load on the memory bus by grouping several memory accesses into a single, more efficient block access.

Graphics hardware rendering does *not* exhibit much temporal locality, but *does* exhibit spatial locality with a vengeance. Raster rendering algorithms for polygons and vectors are a rich source of spatial locality.

Although the bandwidth available inside a dynamic memory chip is orders of magnitude greater than that available at the pins, this internal bandwidth is out of reach for architectures in which the pixel cache is external to the memory chips. Others have recognized the potential of applying caching to Z-buffered rendering [13], but they were constrained to building their caches off chip. Such architectures can at best approach the rendering rate constrained by the memory pin bandwidth. As a result, these caching systems offer little or no performance gain over SIMD or MIMD interleaved pixel rendering.

With FBRAM, by contrast, the pixel caches are *internal* to the individual memory chips. Indeed, as will be seen, *two* levels of internal caches are employed to manage the data flow. The miss rates are minimized by using rectangular shaped caches. The miss costs are reduced by using wide and fast internal busses, augmented by an aggressive predictive pre-fetch algorithm.

Each successive stage from the pins to the DRAM cells has slower bus rates, but FBRAM compensates for this with wider busses. Because the bus width increases faster than the bus rate decreases, their product (bus bandwidth) increases, making caching a practical solution.

## 6 FBRAM INTERNAL ARCHITECTURE

Modern semiconductor production facilities are optimized for a certain silicon die area and fabrication process for a given generation of technology. FBRAM consists of 10 megabits of DRAM, a video buffer, a small cache, and a graphics processor, all implemented in standard DRAM process technology. The result is a die size similar to a 16 megabit DRAM. A 10 megabit FBRAM is 320×1024×32 in size; four FBRAMs exactly form a standard 1280×1024×32 frame buffer.

Figure 2 is an internal block diagram of a single FBRAM [15]. The DRAM storage is broken up into four banks, referred to as banks A,B,C, and D. Each bank contains 256 pages of 320 words (32 bits per word). Each bank is accessed through a sense amplifier page buffer capable of holding an entire 320 word page (10,240 bits). Banks can be accessed at a read-modify-write cycle time of 120 ns.

Video output pixels can be copied from the page buffer to one of two ping-pong video buffers, and shifted out to the display.

FBRAM has a fast triple-ported SRAM register file. This register file is organized as eight blocks of eight 32-bit words. Capable of cycling at 100 MHz, two of the ports (one read, one write) of the register file allow 10 ns throughput for pipelined 32-bit read-modi-

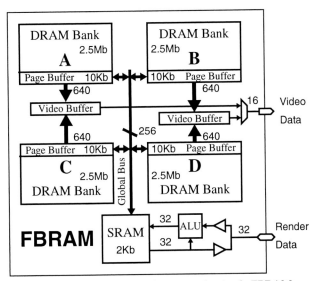

Figure 2. Internal block diagram of a single FBRAM.

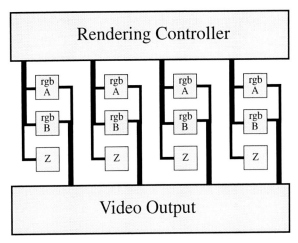

Figure 3. A four-way interleaved frame buffer system composed of 12 FBRAMs (1280×1024, double buffered 32-bit RGBα plus 32-bit Z).

fy-write ALU operations: Z-buffer compare, RGBα blend, or boolean-operations. The third port allows parallel transfer of an entire block (8 words) to or from a page buffer at a 20 ns cycle time via a 256-bit "Global Bus".

FBRAM has two independent sets of control and address lines: one for the two ALU ports of the SRAM register file; the other for operations involving a DRAM bank. This allows DRAM operations to proceed in parallel with SRAM operations. The cache control logic was intentionally left off-chip, to permit maximum flexibility and also to keep multiple chips in lock step.

## 7 FBRAM AS CACHE

Internally, the SRAM register file is a level one pixel cache (L1$), containing eight blocks. Each block is a 2 wide by 4 high rectangle of (32-bit) pixels. The cache set associativity is determined external to the FBRAM, permitting fully associative mapping. The L1$ uses a write back policy; multiple data writes to each L1$ block are accumulated for later transfer to the L2$.

Taken together, the four sense amplifier page buffers constitute a level two pixel cache (L2$). The L2$ is direct mapped; each page buffer is mapped to one of the pages of its corresponding DRAM bank. Each L2$ entry contains one page of 320 32-bit words shaped as a 20 wide by 16 high rectangle of pixels. The L2$ uses a write through policy; data written into a L2$ entry goes immediately into its DRAM bank as well.

The Global Bus connects the L1$ to the L2$. A 2×4 pixel block can be transferred between the L1$ and L2$ in 20 ns.

Four parallel "sense amplifier buses" connect the four L2$ entries to the four DRAM banks. A new 20×16 pixel DRAM page can be read into a given L2$ entry from its DRAM bank as often as every 120 ns. Reads to different L2$ entries can be launched every 40 ns.

## 8 FOUR WAY INTERLEAVED FBRAM FRAME BUFFER

The previous sections described a single FBRAM chip. But to fully appreciate FBRAM's organization, it is best viewed in one of its natural environments: a four way horizontally interleaved three chip deep 1280×1024×96-bit double buffered RGB Z frame buffer. Figure 3 shows the chip organization of such a frame buffer, with two support blocks (render controller and video output). Figure 4 is a *logical* block diagram considering all 12 chips as one system. The discussions of the operations of FBRAM to follow are all based on considering all 12 memory chips as one memory system.

Horizontally interleaving four FBRAMs quadruples the number of data pins; now four RGBZ pixels can be Z-buffered, blended, and written simultaneously. This interleaving also quadruples the size of the caches and busses in the horizontal dimension. Thus the L1$ can now be thought of as eight cache blocks, each 8 pixels wide by 4 pixels high. Taken together, the individual Global Buses in the 12 chips can transfer an 8×4 pixel block between the L1$ and L2$. The four L2$ entries are now 80 pixels wide by 16 pixels high (see Figure 4).

All three levels of this memory hierarchy operate concurrently. When the addressed pixels are present in the L1$, the four way interleaved FBRAMs can process 4 pixels every 10 ns. On occasion, the L1$ will not contain the desired pixels (an "L1$ miss"), incurring a 40 ns penalty ("L1$ miss cost"): 20 ns to fetch the missing block from the L2$ for rendering, 20 ns to write the block back to the L2$ upon completion. Even less often, the L2$ will not contain the block of pixels needed by the L1$ (an "L2$ miss"), incurring a 40-120 ns penalty ("L2$ miss cost") depending upon the scheduling status of the DRAM bank.

This example four way interleaved frame buffer will be assumed for the remainder of this paper.

# 9 RECTANGULAR CACHES REDUCE MISS RATE

The organization so far shows pixels moving between fast, narrow data paths to slow, wide ones. As can be seen in Figure 4, there is sufficient bandwidth between all stages to, in theory, keep up with the incoming rendered pixels, *so long as the right blocks and pages are flowing*. We endeavor to achieve this through aggressive prefetching of rectangular pixel regions.

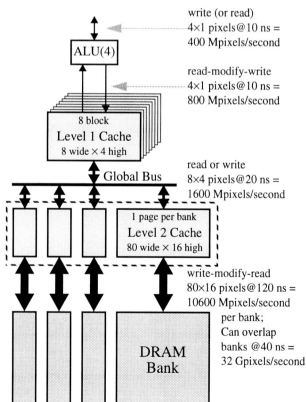

write (or read)
4×1 pixels@10 ns = 400 Mpixels/second

read-modify-write
4×1 pixels@10 ns = 800 Mpixels/second

read or write
8×4 pixels@20 ns = 1600 Mpixels/second

write-modify-read
80×16 pixels@120 ns = 10600 Mpixels/second per bank;
Can overlap banks @40 ns = 32 Gpixels/second

Figure 4. A *logical* representation of a four-way horizontally interleaved frame buffer composed of 12 FBRAMs.

Locality of reference in graphics rendering systems tends to be to neighboring pixels in 2D. Because of this, graphics architects have long desired fast access to square regions [19]. Unfortunately, the standard VRAM page and video shift register dimensions result in efficient access only to long narrow horizontal regions. FBRAM solves this problem by making both caches as square as possible.

Because the L1$ blocks are 8×4 pixels, thin line rendering algorithms tend to pass through four to eight pixels per L1$ block, resulting in a L1$ miss every fourth to eighth pixel (a "miss rate" of 1/4 to 1/8). Parallel area rendering algorithms can aim to utilize all 32 pixels in a block, approaching a miss rate of 1/32.

Similarly, because the L2$ blocks are 80×16 pixels, L2$ miss rates are on the order of 1/16 to 1/80 for thin lines, and asymptotically approach 1/1280 for large areas.

These simplistic miss rate approximations ignore fragmentation effects: lines may end part way through a block or page, polygon edges usually cover only a fraction of a block or page. In addition, fragmentation reduces the effective pin bandwidth, as not all four horizontally interleaved pixels ("quads") can be used every cycle.

FBRAM's block and page dimensions were selected to minimize the effects of fragmentation. Table 1 displays the average number

| | Average Pages/Prim | | | | Average Blocks/Prim | | |
|---|---|---|---|---|---|---|---|
| | 320×4 | 160×8 | 80×16 | 40×32 | 32×1 | 16×2 | 8×4 |
| 10 Pix Vec | 2.61 | 1.84 | 1.48 | 1.36 | 7.57 | 4.58 | 3.38 |
| 20 Pix Vec | 4.21 | 2.68 | 1.97 | 1.71 | 14.1 | 8.15 | 5.76 |
| 50 Pix Vec | 9.02 | 5.20 | 3.42 | 2.78 | 33.8 | 18.9 | 12.9 |
| 100 Pix Vec | 17.1 | 9.42 | 5.85 | 4.57 | 66.6 | 36.8 | 24.9 |
| 25 Pix Tri | 2.96 | 2.02 | 1.60 | 1.46 | 9.75 | 6.12 | 4.68 |
| 50 Pix Tri | 3.80 | 2.45 | 1.89 | 1.67 | 13.8 | 8.72 | 6.67 |
| 100 Pix Tri | 4.97 | 3.05 | 2.24 | 1.94 | 20.0 | 12.8 | 9.89 |
| 1000 Pix Tri | 14.2 | 8.05 | 5.41 | 4.49 | 82.5 | 59.6 | 50.5 |

Table 1 Average number of Pages or Blocks touched per primitive

of L1$ blocks (**B**), and L2$ pages (**P**) *touched* when rendering various sizes of thin lines and right isosceles triangles (averaged over all orientations and positions), for a range of alternative cache aspect ratios. The white columns indicate FBRAM's dimensions. Note that smaller primitives consume more blocks and pages *per rendered pixel*, due to fragmentation effects. Although the table implies that a page size of 40×32 is better than 80×16, practical limitations of video output overhead (ignored in this table, and to be discussed in section 13), dictated choosing 80×16.

# 10 OPERATING THE FRAME BUFFER

For non-cached rendering architectures, theoretical maximum performance rates can be derived from statistics similar to Table 1. This is pessimistic for cached architectures such as FBRAM. Because of spatial locality, later primitives (neighboring triangles of a strip) will often "re-touch" a block or page before it is evicted from the cache, requiring fewer block and page *transfers*. Additional simulations were performed to obtain the quad, page, and block transfer rates. The left half of Table 2 shows the results for FBRAM's chosen dimensions.

Equation 1 can be used to determine the upper bound on the number of primitives rendered per second using FBRAM. The performance is set by the slowest of the three data paths (quads at the pins and ALU, blocks on the global bus, pages to DRAM):

$$\text{primitives/sec} = \min(\frac{R_Q}{Q}, \frac{R_B}{B}, \frac{R_P}{P}) \tag{1}$$

where the denominators **Q**, **B**, and **P** are obtained from the left half of Table 2, and the numerators $R_Q$, $R_B$, $R_P$ are the bus rates for quads, blocks and pages. Referring again to Figure 4, $R_Q$ is 100 million quads/sec through the ALU (4 pixels/quad), $R_B$ is 25 million blocks/sec (40 ns per block, one 20 ns prefetch read plus one 20 ns writeback) and $R_P$ is 8.3 million pages/sec (120 ns per page).

| | Average Misses/Prim | | | Million Prim/sec | | |
|---|---|---|---|---|---|---|
| | **Quad** | **Block** | **Page** | **Quad Perf** | **Block Perf** | **Page Perf** |
| 10 Pix Vec | 8.75 | 2.35 | 0.478 | 11.4 | 10.6 | 17.4 |
| 20 Pix Vec | 16.4 | 4.71 | 0.955 | 6.10 | 5.31 | 8.72 |
| 50 Pix Vec | 38.9 | 11.8 | 2.40 | 2.57 | 2.12 | 3.47 |
| 100 Pix Vec | 76.7 | 23.4 | 4.83 | 1.30 | 1.07 | 1.72 |
| 25 Pix Tri | 11.6 | 1.70 | 0.308 | 8.62 | 14.7 | 27.0 |
| 50 Pix Tri | 20.2 | 3.04 | 0.422 | 4.95 | 8.22 | 19.7 |
| 100 Pix Tri | 36.1 | 6.54 | 0.605 | 2.77 | 3.82 | 13.8 |
| 1000 Pix Tri | 286. | 46.7 | 4.37 | 0.350 | 0.535 | 1.91 |

Table   2 FBRAM Performance Limits

The right half of Table 2 gives the three terms of Equation 1. The white columns indicate the performance limit (the minimum of the three for each case).

Equation 1 assumes that whenever the L1\$ is about to miss, the rendering controller has already brought the proper block in from the L2\$ into the L1\$. Similarly, whenever the L2\$ is about to miss, the rendering controller has already brought the proper page in from the DRAM bank into the L2\$. To achieve such clairvoyance, the controller must know which pages and blocks to prefetch or write back. The FBRAM philosophy assumes that the rendering controller queues up the pixel operations external to the FBRAMs, and snoops this write queue to predict which pages and blocks will be needed soon. These needed pages and blocks are prefetched using the DRAM operation pins, while the SRAM operation pins are used to render pixels into the L1\$ at the same time. Cycle accurate simulation of such architectures have shown this technique to be quite effective.

Although pages can only be fetched to one L2\$ entry every 120 ns, it is possible to fetch pages to *different* L2\$ entries every 40 ns. To reduce the prefetching latency, banks A, B, C and D are interleaved in display space horizontally and vertically, as shown in Figure 5, ensuring that no two pages from the same bank are adjacent horizontally, vertically, or diagonally. This enables pre-fetching any neighboring page while rendering into the current page.

As an example, while pixels of vector **b** in Figure 5 are being rendered into page 0 of bank A, the pre-fetch of page 0 of bank C can be in progress. Usually the pre-fetch from C can be started early enough to avoid idle cycles between the last pixel in page 0 of bank A and the first pixel in page 0 of bank C.

The key idea is that even for vertical vectors, such as vector **d**, we can pre-fetch pages of pixels ahead of the rendering as fast as the rendering can cross a page. Even though vector **c** rapidly crosses three pages, they can still be fetched at a 40ns rate because they are

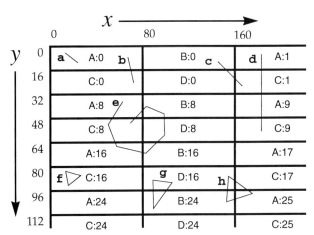

Figure 5. The upper left corner of the frame buffer, showing vertically and horizontally interleaved banks A-D, pages 0-255, and example primitives **a-h**.

from three different banks. Appendix A gives a detailed cycle by cycle example of rendering a 10 pixel vector.

When vectors are chained (vector **e**), the last pixel of one segment and the first pixel of the next segment will almost always be in the same bank and page. Even when segments are isolated, the probability is 75% that the last pixel of one segment and first pixel of next segment will be in different banks, thus enabling overlapping of DRAM bank fetches to L2\$.

## 11 PIXEL RECTANGLE FILL OPERATIONS

As fast as the FBRAM pixel write rate is, it is still valuable to provide optimizations for the special case of large rectangle fill. These specifically include clearing to a constant value or to a repeating pattern. Fast clearing of the RGBZ planes is required to achieve high frame rates during double buffered animation.

FBRAM provides two levels of acceleration for rectangle filling of constant data. Both are obtained by bypassing the bandwidth bottlenecks shown in Figure 4.

In the first method, once an 8×4 L1\$ block has been initialized to a constant color or pattern, the entire block can be copied repeatedly to different blocks within the L2\$ at global bus transfer rates. This feature taps the full bandwidth of the global bus, bypassing the pin/ALU bandwidth bottleneck. Thus regions can be filled at a 4× higher rate (1.6 billion pixels per second, for a four-way interleaved frame buffer).

The second method bypasses both the pin/ALU and the Global Bus bottlenecks, effectively writing 1,280 pixels in one DRAM page cycle. First, the method described in the previous paragraph is used to initialize all four pages of the L2\$, then these page buffers are rapidly copied to their DRAM banks at a rate of 40 ns per page. Thus for large areas, clearing to a constant color or screen aligned pattern can proceed at a peak rate of 32 billion pixels per second (0.25 terabytes/sec), assuming a four-way interleaved design.

## 12 WINDOW SYSTEM SUPPORT

The most important feature of FBRAM for window system support is simply its high bandwidth; however two window system specific optimizations are also included.

Full read-modify-write cycles require two Global Bus transactions: a prefetching read from the L2\$, and copyback write to the L2\$. Most window system operations do not require read-modify-write cycles when rendering text and simple 2D graphics. For such write-only operations, the number of Global Bus transactions can be cut in half, improving performance. This is accomplished by skipping the pre-fetching read of a new block from the L2\$ to L1\$.

Vertical scrolling is another frequent window system operation accelerated by FBRAM. This operation is accelerated by performing the copy internal to the FBRAM. This results in a pixel scroll rate of up to 400 million pixels per second.

## 13 VIDEO OUTPUT

VRAM solved the display refresh bandwidth problem by adding a second port, but at significant cost in die area. FBRAM also provides a second port for video (see Figure 2), but at a smaller area penalty.

Like VRAM, FBRAM has a pair of ping-pong video buffers, but unlike VRAM, they are much smaller in size: 80 pixels each for a four-way interleaved FBRAM frame buffer vs. 1,280 pixels each for a five-way interleaved VRAM frame buffer. These smaller buffers save silicon and enable a rectangular mapping of pages to the display, but at the price of more frequent video buffer loads.

The FBRAM video buffers are loaded directly from the DRAM bank page buffers (L2\$, 80×16 pixels), selecting one of the 16 scan lines in the page buffer. The cost of loading a video buffer in both FBRAM and VRAM is typically 120-200 ns.

To estimate an upper bound for FBRAM video refresh overhead for a 1280×1024 76Hz non-interlaced video display, assume that all rendering operations cease during the 200 ns video buffer load interval. During each frame, a grand total of 3.28 ms (200 ns•1280•1024 pixels / 80 pixels) of video buffer loads are needed for video refresh. Thus 76 Hz video refresh overhead could theoretically take away as much as 25% of rendering performance.

The actual video overhead is only 5-10% for several reasons. First, the pixel ALU can still access its side of the L1\$ during video refresh, because video transfers access the L2\$. Second, although one of the four banks is affected by video refresh, global bus transfers to the other three banks can still take place. Finally, it is usually possible to schedule video transfers so that they do not conflict with rendering, reducing the buffer load cost from 200 to 120 ns.

For high frame rate displays, the raster pattern of FBRAM video output refresh automatically accomplishes DRAM cell refresh, imposing no additional DRAM refresh tax.

## 14 FBRAM PEFORMANCE

The model developed in section 10 gave theoretical upper bounds on the performance of a four-way interleaved FBRAM system. But to quantify the performance obtainable by any real system built with FBRAM, a number of other factors must be considered.

First, a 10% derating of the section 10 model should be applied to account for the additional overhead due to video and content refresh described in section 13.

The sophistication of the cache prediction and scheduling algorithm implemented will also affect performance. Equation 1 assumed that the cache controller achieves complete overlap between the three data paths; this is not always possible. More detailed simulations show that aggressive controllers can achieve 75% (before video tax) of the performance results in table 2.

Taking all of these effects into account, simulations of buildable four-way interleaved FBRAM systems show sustained rates of 3.3 million 50 pixel Z-buffered triangles per second, and 7 million 10 pixel non-antialiased Z-buffered vectors per second. FBRAM systems with higher external interleave factor can sustain performances in the tens of millions of small triangles per second range.

All of our simulations assume that the rest of the graphics system can keep up with the FBRAM, delivering four RGBαZ pixels every 10 ns. While this is a formidable challenge, pixel interpolation and vertex floating point processing ASICs are on a rapidly improving performance curve, and should be able to sustain the desired rates.

FBRAM performance can be appreciated by comparing it with the pixel fill rate of the next generation Pixel Planes rasterizing chips [16], although FBRAM does not directly perform the triangle rasterization function. The pixel fill rate for a single FBRAM chip is only a factor of four less than the peak (256 pixel rectangle) fill rate of a single Pixel Planes chip, but has 400 times more storage capacity.

Next let us contrast the read-modify-write performance of FBRAM to a 60 ns VRAM. Assuming no batching, VRAM page mode requires in excess of 125 ns to do what FBRAM does in 10 ns; a 12.5× speed difference.

Batching VRAM reads and writes to minimize bus-turns, as described in section 3, does not help as much as one might think. Typical VRAM configurations have very few scan lines per page, which causes fragmentation of primitives, limiting batch sizes. Table 1 shows that for a 320×4 page shape, a 50 pixel triangle touches 3.8 pages, averaging 13 pixels per page. For a five way interleaved frame buffer, an average of only 2.6 pixels can be batched per chip.

## 15 OTHER DRAM OFFSHOOTS

A veritable alphabet soup of new forms of DRAM are at various stages of development by several manufactures: CDRAM, DRAM, FBRAM, RAMBUS, SDRAM, SGRAM, SVRAM, VRAM, and WRAM. For 3D graphics, FBRAM is distinguished as the only technology to directly support Z-buffering, alpha blending, and ROPs. Only FBRAM converts read-modify-write operations into pure write operations; this alone accounts for a 3-4× performance advantage at similar clock rates. Other than CDRAM, only FBRAM has two levels of cache, and efficient support of rectangular cache blocks. It is beyond the scope of this paper to derive precise comparative 3D rendering performance for all these RAMs, but FBRAM appears to be several times faster than any of these alternatives.

## 16 FUTURES

The demand for faster polygon rendering rates shows no sign of abating for some time to come. However, as was observed at the end of section 2, the number of pixels filled per scene is not going up anywhere near as rapidly. Future increases in pixel resolution, frame rate, and/or depth complexity are likely to be modest.

Future predictions of where technology is going are at best approximations, and their use should be limited to understanding trends. With these caveats in mind, Figure 6 explores trends in polygon rendering rate demand vs. memory technologies over the next several years. The figure shows the projected pixel fill rate (including fragmentation effects) demanded as the polygon rate increases over time (from the data in [6]). It also displays the expected delivered pixel fill rates of *minimum chip count* frame buffers implemented using FBRAM and VRAM technologies (extrapolating from Equation 1 and from the systems described in [14][5]). The demand curve is above that achievable inexpensively with conventional VRAM or DRAM, but well within the range of a minimum chip count FBRAM system.

The trend curve for FBRAM has a steeper slope because, unlike VRAM, FBRAM effectively decouples pixel rendering rates from the inherently slower DRAM single transistor access rates. This will allow future versions of FBRAM to follow the more rapidly in-

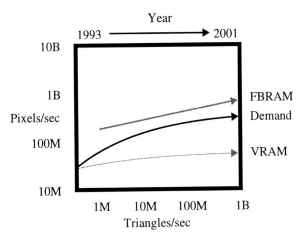

Figure 6. Pixel fill rate needed to match anticipated triangle fill rate demand compared with anticipated delivered pixel fill rate delivered by minimum chip count FBRAM and VRAM systems.

creasing SRAM performance trends. FBRAM still benefits from the inherently lower cost per bit of DRAM technology.

The "excess" pixel fill rate shown for FBRAM in Figure 6 combined with FBRAM's high bit density will permit cost-effective, one pass, full scene antialiasing using super-sampled frame buffers.

## 17 CONCLUSIONS

In the past, the bandwidth demands of video output led to the creation of VRAM to overcome DRAM's limitations. In recent years, the demands of faster and faster rendering have exceeded VRAM's bandwidth. This led to the creation of FBRAM, a new form of random access memory optimized for Z-buffer based 3D graphics rendering and window system support. A ten fold increase in Z-buffered rendering performance for minimum chip count systems is achieved over conventional VRAM and DRAM. Given statistics on the pixel fill requirements of the next two generations of 3D graphics accelerators, FBRAM may remove the pixel fill bottleneck from 3D accelerator architectures for the rest of this century.

## ACKNOWLEDGEMENTS

FBRAM is a joint development between SMCC and Mitsubishi Electric Corporation. The authors would like to acknowledge the efforts of the entire Mitsubishi team, and in particular K. Inoue, H. Nakamura, K. Ishihara, Charles Hart, Julie Lin, and Mark Perry.

On the Sun side, the authors would like to thank Mary Whitton, Scott Nelson, Dave Kehlet, and Ralph Nichols, as well as all the other engineers who reviewed drafts of this paper.

## REFERENCES

1. **Akeley, Kurt and T. Jermoluk.** High-Performance Polygon Rendering, Proceedings of SIGGRAPH '88 (Atlanta, GA, Aug 1-5, 1988). In *Computer Graphics* 22, 4 (July 1988), 239-246.

2. **Akeley, Kurt.** Reality Engine Graphics. Proceedings of SIGGRAPH '93 (Anaheim, California, August 1-6, 1993). In *Computer Graphics*, Annual Conference Series, 1993, 109-116.

3. **Catmull, E.** *A Subdivision Algorithm for Computer Display of Curved Surfaces*, Ph.D. Thesis, Report UTEC-CSc-74-133, Computer Science Dept., University of Utah, Salt Lake City, UT, Dec. 1974.

4. **Deering, Michael, S. Winner, B. Schediwy, C. Duffy and N. Hunt.** The Triangle Processor and Normal Vector Shader: A VLSI system for High Performance Graphics. Proceedings of SIGGRAPH '88 (Atlanta, GA, Aug 1-5, 1988). In *Computer Graphics* 22, 4 (July 1988), 21-30.

5. **Deering, Michael, and S. Nelson.** Leo: A System for Cost Effective Shaded 3D Graphics. Proceedings of SIGGRAPH '93 (Anaheim, California, August 1-6, 1993). In *Computer Graphics*, Annual Conference Series, 1993, 101-108.

6. **Deering, Michael.** Data Complexity for Virtual Reality: Where do all the Triangles Go? Proceedings of IEEE VRAIS '93 (Seattle, WA, Sept. 18-22, 1993). 357-363.

7. **Demetrescu, S.** *A VLSI-Based Real-Time Hidden-Surface Elimination Display System*, Master's Thesis, Dept. of Computer Science, California Institute of Technology, Pasadena CA, May 1980.

8. **Demetrescu, S.** High Speed Image Rasterization Using Scan Line Access Memories. Proceedings of 1985 Chapel Hill Conference on VLSI, pages 221-243. Computer Science Press, 1985.

9. **Fuchs, Henry, and J. Poulton.** Pixel Planes: A VLSI-Oriented Design for a Raster Graphics Engine. In *VLSI Design*, 2,3 (3rd quarter 1981), 20-28.

10. **Foley, James, A. van Dam, S. Feiner and J Hughes.** Computer Graphics: Principles and Practice, 2nd ed., Addison-Wesley, 1990.

11. **Gharachorloo, Nader, S. Gupta, E. Hokenek, P. Balasubramanina, B. Bogholtz, C. Mathieu, and C. Zoulas.** Subnanosecond Rendering with Million Transistor Chips. Proceedings of SIGGRAPH '88 (Boston, MA, July 31, Aug 4, 1989). In *Computer Graphics* 22, 4 (Aug. 1988), 41-49.

12. **Gharachorloo, Nader, S. Gupta, R. Sproull, and I. Sutherland.** A Characterization of Ten Rasterization Techniques. Proceedings of SIGGRAPH '89 (Boston, MA, July 31, Aug 4, 1989). In *Computer Graphics* 23, 3 (July 1989), 355-368.

13. **Goris, A., B. Fredrickson, and H. Baeverstad.** A Configurable Pixel Cache for Fast Image Generation. In *IEEE CG&A* 7,3 (March 1987), pages 24-32, 1987.

14. **Harrell, Chandlee, and F. Fouladi.** Graphics Rendering Architecture for a High Performance Desktop Workstation. Proceedings of SIGGRAPH '93 (Anaheim, California, August 1-6, 1993). In *Computer Graphics*, Annual Conference Series, 1993, 93-100.

15. M5M410092 FBRAM Specification. Mitsubishi Electric, 1994.

16. **Molnar, Steven, J. Eyles, J. Poulton.** PixelFlow: High-Speed Rendering Using Image Composition. Proceedings of SIGGRAPH '92 (Chicago, IL, July 26-31, 1992). In *Computer Graphics* 26, 2 (July 1992), 231-240.

17. **Patterson, David, and J. Hennessy.** Computer Architecture: a Quantitative Approach, Morgan Kaufmann Publishers, Inc., 1990.

18. **Pinkham, R., M. Novak, and K. Guttag.** Video RAM Excels at Fast Graphics. In *Electronic Design* 31,17, Aug. 18, 1983, 161-182.

19. **Sproull, Robert, I. Sutherland, and S. Gupta.** The 8 by 8 Display. In *ACM Transactions on Graphics* 2, 1 (Jan 1983), 35-56.

20. **Whitton, Mary.** Memory Design for Raster Graphics Displays. In *IEEE CG&A* 4,3 (March 1984), 48-65, 1984.

## APPENDIX A: Rendering a 10 pixel Vector

This appendix demonstrates the detailed steps involved in scheduling FBRAM rendering, using the 10 pixel long, one pixel wide vertical Z-buffered vector shown in Figure 7. This figure shows the

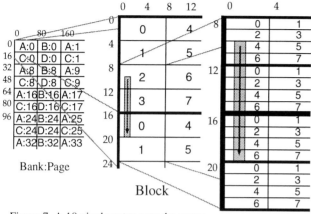

Figure 7. A 10 pixel vector near the upper left corner of the screen, at 3 levels of detail.

memory hierarchy elements touched by the vector at three levels of detail: the coarsest (left most) shows banks (A..D) and pages (0..255), the intermediate detail (middle) shows blocks in the L2$, and the finest (right most) shows pixel quads.

The example vertical vector starts at x=1, y=10, and ends at y=19. Table 3 gives the bank, page, L2$ block, and quad for each pixel in the vector. Note the spatial locality of pixels.

Table 4 below shows the schedule of commands and data issued to the FBRAM, and the resulting internal activities. Note that independent controls are available, and permit parallel L1$ and L2$ activities. The following abbreviations are used in Table 4:

L1$[n]: Block n of the L1$.

L2$[n]: Block n of the L2$.

ACP: Access page (DRAM to L2$ transfer).

| X | Y | Bank | Page | L2$ Block | Quad | L2$ | L1$ |
|---|----|------|------|-----------|------|------|------|
| 1 | 10 | A | 0 | 2 | 4 | miss | miss |
| 1 | 11 |   |   |   | 6 | hit | hit |
| 1 | 12 |   |   | 3 | 0 | hit | miss |
| 1 | 13 |   |   |   | 2 | hit | hit |
| 1 | 14 |   |   |   | 4 | hit | hit |
| 1 | 15 |   |   |   | 6 | hit | hit |
| 1 | 16 | C | 0 | 0 | 0 | miss | miss |
| 1 | 17 |   |   |   | 2 | hit | hit |
| 1 | 18 |   |   |   | 4 | hit | hit |
| 1 | 19 |   |   |   | 6 | hit | hit |

Table 3 Bank, Page, L2$ Block, and Quad for each pixel in the vector

RDB: Read block (L2$ → L1$ transfer).

MWB: Masked write block (L1$ → L2$ transfer).

PRE: Precharge bank (free L2$ entry).

read x: Read pixel x from L1$ to ALU.

write x: Write pixel x from ALU to L1$.

We follow the first pixel at (1, 10) through the cache hierarchy. The pixel's page (page 0 of bank A) is transferred to the L2$ entry A in cycles 1 to 4 (notice that the next 5 pixels are transferred too). The pixel's block is then transferred from L2$ entry A to L1$[0] in cycles 5 and 6 (the next pixel is transferred too). The pixel is read from the L1$[0] to the pipelined ALU in cycle 7. The old and new pixels are merged (Z-buffered, blended) during cycles 8 to 11. The resulting pixel is written back to the L1$[0] in cycle 12. The pixel's block is transferred from the L1$[0] back to the L2$ entry A (and DRAM page 0 of bank A) in cycles 14 and 15.

The second pixel at (1,11) hits in both L1$ and L2$, and can follow one cycle behind the first pixel, arriving back in the L1$ in cycle 13. The pixel at (1,12) misses in the L1$, but hits in the L2$, requiring an RDB from L2$ entry A to L1$[1]. The pixel at (1,16) misses in both caches, requiring a L2$ access of bank C, and followed by a transfer from L2$ entry C to L1$[2]. All the other pixels hit in both caches, and are scheduled like the second pixel.

| | | Commands and Data to FBRAM | | Internal Activities | | | | | | | | | | | |
|---|---|---|---|---|---|---|---|---|---|---|---|---|---|---|---|
| | | L1$ Command and Data | L2$ Command | L2$ Activities | | | | \multicolumn L1$ Activities | | | | | | | |
| | | | | A | B | C | D | 0 | 1 | 2 | 3 | 4 | 5 | 6 | 7 |
| 1 | | | Access Page 0 of Bank A | ACP | | | | | | | | | | | |
| 2 | | | | | | | | | | | | | | | |
| 3 | | | | | | | | | | | | | | | |
| 4 | | | | | | | | | | | | | | | |
| 5 | | | L2$[2] of Bank A → L1$[0] | RDB | | | | RDB | | | | | | | |
| 6 | | | Access Page 0 of Bank C | | | ACP | | | | | | | | | |
| 7 | | Merge data with Quad 4 of L1$[0] | L2$[3] of Bank A → L1$[1] | RDB | | | | read 4 | RDB | | | | | | |
| 8 | | Merge data with Quad 6 of L1$[0] | | | | | | read 6 | | | | | | | |
| 9 | | Merge data with Quad 0 of L1$[1] | | | | | | | read 0 | | | | | | |
| 10 | | Merge data with Quad 2 of L1$[1] | L2$[0] of Bank C → L1$[2] | | | RDB | | | read 2 | RDB | | | | | |
| 11 | | Merge data with Quad 4 of L1$[1] | | | | | | | read 4 | | | | | | |
| 12 | | Merge data with Quad 6 of L1$[1] | | | | | | write 4 | read 6 | | | | | | |
| 13 | | Merge data with Quad 0 of L1$[2] | | | | | | write 6 | | read 0 | | | | | |
| 14 | | Merge data with Quad 2 of L1$[2] | L2$[2] of Bank A ← L1$[0] | MWB | | | | MWB | write 0 | read 2 | | | | | |
| 15 | | Merge data with Quad 4 of L1$[2] | | | | | | | write 2 | read 4 | | | | | |
| 16 | | Merge data with Quad 6 of L1$[2] | | | | | | | write 4 | read 6 | | | | | |
| 17 | | | | | | | | | write 6 | | | | | | |
| 18 | | | L2$[3] of Bank A ← L1$[1] | MWB | | | | | MWB | write 0 | | | | | |
| 19 | | | | | | | | | | write 2 | | | | | |
| 20 | | | Precharge Bank A | PRE | | | | | | write 4 | | | | | |
| 21 | | | | | | | | | | write 6 | | | | | |
| 22 | | | L2$[0] of Bank C ← L1$[2] | | | MWB | | | | MWB | | | | | |
| 23 | | | | | | | | | | | | | | | |

Table 4. Schedule of operations for rendering a 10 pixel vector

# Frameless Rendering: Double Buffering Considered Harmful

Gary Bishop, Henry Fuchs, Leonard McMillan, and Ellen J. Scher Zagier

Department of Computer Science, UNC Chapel Hill

## Abstract

The use of double-buffered displays, in which the previous image is displayed until the next image is complete, can impair the interactivity of systems that require tight coupling between the human user and the computer. We are experimenting with an alternate rendering strategy that computes each pixel based on the most recent input (i.e., view and object positions) and immediately updates the pixel on the display. We avoid the image tearing normally associated with single-buffered displays by randomizing the order in which pixels are updated. The resulting image sequences give the impression of moving continuously, with a rough approximation of motion blur, rather than jerking between discrete positions.

We have demonstrated the effectiveness of this *frameless rendering* method with a simulation that shows conventional double-buffering side-by-side with frameless rendering. Both methods are allowed the same computation budget, but the double-buffered display only updates after all pixels are computed while the frameless rendering display updates pixels as they are computed. The frameless rendering display exhibits fluid motion while the double-buffered display jumps from frame to frame. The randomized sampling inherent in frameless rendering means that we cannot take advantage of image and object coherence properties that are important to current polygon renderers, but for renderers based on tracing independent rays the added cost is small.

**CR Descriptors**: I.3.1 [**Computer Graphics**]: Picture/image generation --- *Display algorithms*; I.3.6 [**Computer Graphics**]: Methodology and Techniques.

## The Motivation: fast interaction

In conventional double-buffered systems each new image is one update interval old when it is first displayed, then it is held for another complete update interval while the next image is computed. For example, at an update rate of 5 Hz an image will be 400 milliseconds old before it is replaced with a new image that is already 200 milliseconds old. In interactive systems, such large delays may cause users to repeatedly overshoot on the inputs resulting in operator induced oscillations. In head-mounted displays, delays cause the virtual world to appear unstable and to swim around as the user moves.

In a 1986 paper on Adaptive Refinement, Bergman, Fuchs, Grant, and Spach[1] suggest that the impact of these delays can be reduced by rapidly displaying a crude image when the scene is changing and progressing through higher quality renderings when

mail: Sitterson Hall CB3175, Chapel Hill, NC 27599-3175; phone: (919) 962-1700; email: lastname@cs.unc.edu.

the inputs are constant. This approach allows timely updates during changes and high-quality images as soon as possible. Their paper also suggests the possibility of a "golden thread", a single step that, if repeated a few times, will generate a crude image, and when repeated further will result in incrementally higher quality images.

## The Idea: randomized immediate pixel update

We are experimenting with an approximation to that "golden thread" that computes a fraction of the pixels in the image and immediately updates them on the display, rather than computing a complete image of lower quality. The order of pixel update is randomized to avoid image tearing and to allow the appearance of simultaneous update everywhere in the image. For each pixel, the latest available input parameters are used so that each pixel accurately represents the time at which it is computed and displayed (this can only be approximated on current raster display systems because of their sequential scan of pixels).

Frames, as in movies and conventional computer displays, lose their meaning in this approach to rendering. When the scene is static, the image quickly converges to the current system state. When the view is changing or objects in the scene are moving, the image continuously blends toward the correct value for current time. At all times, the image on the display represents the most current system state with the available computing power. The image appears blurry, but with smooth and continuous motion. The blur produced is dependent on the rate of change and is a crude approximation to motion blur. Our frameless rendering method can be thought of as a grossly under-sampled version of Cook's Distributed Ray Tracing[2].

If the instantaneous changes in the scene are large (as in a cut from one scene to another) the image momentarily becomes a confusing mixture of past and present images. In order to compensate, the display system might switch to lower resolution or to double-buffering during rapid scene changes. We believe that such dramatic scene changes are rare in most interactive graphics applications and in synthetic environments.

Figure 1 illustrates frameless rendering with a sequence of still images. It should be noted that a user of a frameless rendering system would never see (for long) partially updated static images like those in the figure; instead, the partially updated images only occur when the scene is changing. When motion stops, the system would quickly update all the pixels with the newest values. The bottom row of the figure depicts the intermediate images shown by the frameless display at the times illustrated; the row above depicts the frames from a double-buffered display.

## An Experiment: side-by-side comparison

In order to evaluate the visual effect of this method we implemented an experiment that shows a side-by-side comparison of conventional double-buffering with a simulation of frameless rendering. Each of the displays is given the same computation budget (each is allowed to compute pixels at the same rate). The double-buffered display only switches to the new image after all pixels have been updated; the frameless rendering simulation updates the pixels as soon as possible (though they only become visible at the next video refresh). Thus, the double-buffered display switches from frame to frame at a 5 Hz rate, while the frameless renderer updates about 16% of the pixels at each video frame.

This experiment was done as a proof of concept using mostly tools that were already in place. A set of complete frames were rendered and stored on disk using Rayshade[3], a public domain ray tracer. The disk files were then processed sequentially by replacing a randomly selected fraction of the pixels in the output image with pixels from the current input image file. We used a table to choose random pixels without replacement so update of all pixels was guaranteed. The resulting images were displayed on a conventional workstation using a program that sequentially displays precomputed images. The simulation of the double-buffered display was implemented by switching between the appropriate original images.

The demonstration clearly contrasted the jerky motion of the double-buffered display with the fluid motion of the frameless rendering. The frameless rendering appeared blurred, and careful examination showed that high-contrast edges were ragged. This effect may have been exaggerated by the small size (320 by 240) of the images used in the simulation to allow high update rates on the workstation display.

## Conclusions

We have only begun to explore the potential of this rendering paradigm. An important next step will be to characterize the range of update rates and image rate of change over which the method is applicable. Another area for investigation will be display alternatives for situations in which the instantaneous display change is sufficiently large to produce confusing images.

It may be possible to extend the method to allow inclusion of antialiasing methods based on jittered sampling, thus allowing smooth motion during changes and high-quality images when stationary. This would be one step closer to the "golden thread" mentioned earlier.

It may also be possible to optimize image update based on how the view is changing and on how objects are moving. For example, the samples might be concentrated at moving edges in the image, or old pixels might be moved to new positions before they are combined with newly computed pixels.

Frameless rendering is a simple idea which can be applied to a variety of systems to produce an apparently dramatic improvement in the smoothness of interaction. We are encouraged by these preliminary results and plan to implement frameless rendering in head-mounted display systems for further evaluation.

## Acknowledgments

Support for this research was provided in part by NSF/ARPA Science and Technology Center for Computer Graphics and Scientific Visualization, (NSF Cooperative Agreement #ASC 8920219) and by ARPA Contract DABT63-93-C-C048 "Enabling Technologies and Application Demonstrations for Synthetic Environments."

## References

[1]  Bergman, Larry, Henry Fuchs, Eric Grant, and Susan Spach. Image Rendering by Adaptive Refinement. Proceedings of SIGGRAPH '86. In *Computer Graphics* 20, 4, pp. 29-37, August 1986.

[2]  Cook, Robert L., Thomas Porter, Loren Carpenter. Distributed Ray Tracing. Proceedings of SIGGRAPH '84. In *Computer Graphics* 18, 3, pp. 137-145, July 1984.

[3]  Kolb, Craig E., *Rayshade User's Guide and Reference Manual,* Draft 0.4, January 10, 1992.

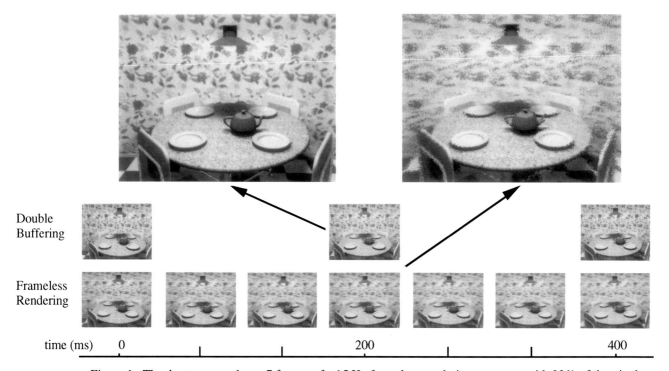

Double Buffering

Frameless Rendering

time (ms)     0                              200                              400

Figure 1. The bottom row shows 7 frames of a 15 Hz frameless rendering sequence with 33% of the pixels updated in each frame. The middle row shows 3 frames of a double-buffering sequence updated at 5 Hz.

# Hardware Accelerated Rendering of CSG and Transparency

Michael Kelley, Kirk Gould, Brent Pease, Stephanie Winner, Alex Yen

Apple Computer, Inc.

## ABSTRACT

This paper describes algorithms for implementing accurate rendering of CSG and transparency in a hardware 3D accelerator. The algorithms are based on a hardware architecture which performs front-to-back Z-sorted shading; a multiple-pass algorithm which allows an unlimited number of Z-sorted object layers is also described. The multiple-pass algorithm has been combined with an image partitioning algorithm to improve efficiency, and to improve performance of the resulting hardware implementation.

**CR Categories and Subject Descriptors: I.3.1** [Computer Graphics]: Hardware Architecture - raster display devices; **I.3.3** [Computer Graphics]: Picture/Image Generation - display algorithms; **I.3.7** [Computer Graphics]: Three-Dimensional Graphics and Realism - visible surface algorithms

**General Terms:** algorithms, architecture

**Additional Key Words and Phrases:** scanline, CSG, transparency, deferred shading, image partitioning

## INTRODUCTION AND BACKGROUND

This paper describes a general purpose hardware accelerator for rendering 3D graphics. In addition to basic operations such as Gouraud and texture-mapped triangles, the system includes support for high-performance rendering of Constructive Solid Geometry (CSG) and transparency. These algorithms, and the system architecture that supports them, are the main topics of the paper.

A variety of hardware algorithms have been proposed and implemented for rendering transparency or CSG, but few have been simple enough to be added to a general purpose accelerator. Ray-casting systems for CSG are slow and too complex to be implemented in hardware as low cost accelerators [13][18]. Enhanced Z-buffer algorithms for CSG often require many rendering passes, reducing performance unless extremely fast (and expensive) rasterizing systems are used [10][17]. Z-buffer transparency algorithms based on sub-pixel screen door algorithms aren't accurate for multiple layers of transparency [2]. Binary space partitioning algorithms allow ordered drawing of transparent objects, but construction overhead makes them slow for dynamic scenes, and intersecting objects aren't rendered correctly [8].

## SYSTEM OVERVIEW

The system described here is a low cost, single-ASIC accelerator designed to be added to a Power Macintosh™ computer. The rasterizer is based on a scanline rendering algorithm. Several scanline based rasterizers have been proposed or built [6][14][16]; the key features of this design are:

- In addition to vertical bucket sorting (which all scanline algorithms perform), each scanline is horizontally partitioned into 16 pixel segments. The small size of this partition allows all sixteen pixels (at 480 bits/pixel) to be stored on-chip, improving performance and substantially reducing cost.

- Rasterization speed is 20M pixels/second, providing throughput of 120K texture-mapped triangles/second[1]. Images of up to 8Kx8K can be rendered in a single pass.

- An unlimited number of visible layers can be sorted by Z prior to compositing. Sorting is performed per pixel, so intersecting objects are rendered correctly.

- Transparency and CSG are performed by the compositing hardware.

- Texture map look-up is deferred until after visible surface determination, improving performance for scenes with layered texture-mapped objects.

These features will be described in more detail throughout the paper.

## Z-ORDERED SHADING

Once it was decided to support rendering of CSG and transparency, it soon became apparent that algorithms based on shading in Z-sorted order (in this system, from front to back) provided the most efficient and accurate solution. The CSG and transparency algorithms themselves are described in the following sections; however, as Z-ordered shading is unusual in hardware accelerators, some background on this is provided first (a detailed discussion is in **IMPLEMENTING Z-ORDERED SHADING**, later in the paper).

Although Z-ordered shading is a common choice for high-quality software renderers [4][20], there are several reasons why it isn't usually implemented in hardware. The first is historical — most hardware acceleration architectures were developed for rendering opaque objects with a single layer Z buffer, a task for which Z-ordered shading offers no advantage. Later implementations of features such as transparency, which would benefit from Z-ordered shading, have been achieved by other algorithms which are a better fit in existing acceleration architectures. An example of this is the Silicon Graphics™ RealityEngine™, which uses sub-pixel screen door coverage masks to implement transparency [2].

In addition to the historical factors, implementing Z-ordered shading in hardware tends to require either large amounts of memory, multiple-pass rendering, or both. The simplest solution is to store multiple Z-ARGB layers per pixel, which allows accurate support of a finite number of layers. However, this requires large amounts of memory, and shows very unpleasant degradation when the number of layers is exceeded. A more elegant solution is a multiple pass algorithm [15]. This provides support of an unlimited number of layers, but it still

---

[1] 100 pixel triangles, with tri-linearly interpolated mip-mapped textures.

requires increased pixel memory, and becomes inefficient for scenes where large numbers of rendering passes are required.

The Z-ordered shading implementation described in the paper uses both multiple Z-ARGB layers and a multiple-pass rendering algorithm. As described later, this hybrid algorithm, combined with the image partitioning algorithm, provides solutions for both of the problems described above.

Because Z-ordered shading was used, the transparency and CSG rendering algorithms described in the next two sections are similar to those used with ray-casting algorithms. In practice, the most challenging part of the design was implementing Z-ordered shading; once that was in place, a wide range of algorithms for CSG and transparency, and potentially for other effects that require multiple visible layers, became applicable.

# FRONT-TO-BACK TRANSPARENCY

The ASIC implements an interpolated transparency model, which includes the simplifying assumption that all component colours are filtered by the same coefficient [7]. This model was chosen because it is accurate, simple, and provides high visual quality. The blending function is expressed as:

$$I_r = I_{rFront} + k_{tFront} I_{rBack}$$

$$I_g = I_{gFront} + k_{tFront} I_{gBack}$$

$$I_b = I_{bFront} + k_{tFront} I_{bBack}$$

$$k_t = k_{tFront} k_{tBack}$$

Where $I_{rBack}$ is the red intensity of the back object, $I_{rFront}$ is the red intensity of the front object with diffuse and ambient contributions pre-multiplied by $(1-k_{tFront})$, and $k_{tFront}$ is the transmission coefficient of the front object. Note that pre-multiplication of $I_{rgbFront}$ is necessary so that the specular component of the front object doesn't diminish as transparency increases [12]. Premultiplication creates the potential for the computed rgb values to exceed 1.0; this implementation avoids overflow of rgb by saturating each component at 255 (the internal equivalent of 1.0).

Clearly, the transparency blending function itself is quite simple — the challenge is that it requires processing the contributing objects from front to back, instead of in object submission order as is more common in hardware accelerators.

# CONSTRUCTIVE SOLID GEOMETRY

Constructive Solid Geometry (CSG) is a modeling method which constructs new geometry from the union, intersection or difference of other geometry. For example, Figure 2a (end of paper) shows a complex shape created by subtracting a torus from a cube. Referring to the cube as **A**, the torus as **B**, and the result as **Result$_a$**, it can be expressed:

$$Result_a = A - B$$

Figure 2b shows the intersection of A and B:

$$Result_b = A \cap B$$

In actual use, many CSG modeling operations are performed on a collection of operand geometries to construct a final object. This resulting object can be represented as an ordered sequence of Boolean set operations on geometry operands, or equivalently as an expression tree with geometry as the leaf nodes [7]. For this paper we've chosen to represent CSG expressions algebraically, like those above, referring to the

Boolean set operations as *operators*, and to the leaf node geometries as *operand geometries*.

In practice, the CSG expressions of objects are usually more complex than the examples above, as the expression often represents the entire construction history of the object.

## Ray Casting CSG

The most natural method for rendering CSG objects is based on ray casting [9][18]. Briefly, a ray is cast through the operand geometries; each intersection corresponds to the entry or exit of a solid operand geometry's space. These intersections allow the projection of the range of each operand's space as a span on the 1D ray. These spans are then combined using the CSG operators. In Goldstein's original paper the operators are applied in the order of the expression tree [9].

Because the ray casting algorithm uses boundary representations of the geometries, the boundary of the resulting CSG object is actually a composite of patches of the boundaries of the operand geometries. When generating images, the natural result of this is illustrated in Figure 2a and 2b — the portions of the constructed geometry that came from the different operand geometries (in this example, a cube and a torus) retain their original appearances.

The extension of this algorithm to a scanline algorithm by Atherton improved performance [3], and was the starting point for the algorithm implemented in the hardware.

## Z-Ordered CSG Evaluation

The algorithm implemented in the hardware evaluates the operand intersections in Z order, rather than in expression order (as is more common in ray-casting implementations). This has two advantages: It reuses the hardware which performs Z-sorting for the transparency implementation, and it dramatically reduces the amount of state that must be stored to evaluate the CSG expression (this is discussed later).

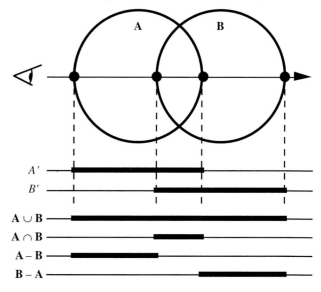

*Figure 3*

Figure 3, above, shows a single ray cast through two circular objects **A** and **B**. The line $A'$ represents a 1 bit state variable that indicates whether the ray is currently inside object **A** (and similarly for $B'$). These state variables are updated whenever an object is intersected — four times in the above example. At any point on the ray, the Boolean CSG function can be applied to these state variables to determine if the point is inside the constructed object. At the bottom of Figure 3 are the results of applying four different Boolean operations.

In practice, because the system renders only the boundary of objects, the Boolean function (which we will call $F_{csg}$) is only evaluated at the intersection points. For example, consider the **B − A** operation, which can be represented as:

$$Fcsg\ (A',B') = B' \bullet \neg A'$$

As the hardware composites the layers from front-to-back, it maintains the $A'$ and $B'$ state variables. At each intersection, it evaluates $F_{csg}$. When $F_{csg}$ changes state, it represents a boundary on the constructed geometry, and the current layer is rendered. If $F_{csg}$ doesn't change, the layer doesn't represent a boundary and is discarded.

In Figure 4, $F_{csg}$ is 0 at the ray origin. The first two intersections $I_1$ and $I_2$ don't change the state of $F_{csg}$ so these boundary layers are discarded — in other words, they don't represent a boundary of the resulting constructed object. $I_3$, however, causes $F_{csg}$ to change from 0 to 1, indicating that the ray has crossed a "real" boundary, so the layer at $I_3$ is rendered. Similarly, $I_4$ causes $F_{csg}$ to change from 1 to 0, so it is also rendered.

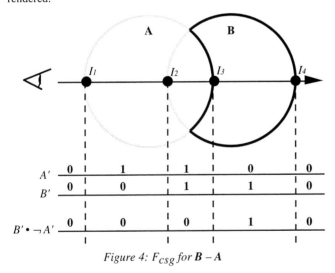

*Figure 4: $F_{csg}$ for **B − A***

### Limitations of Evaluating $F_{csg}$ in Hardware

Because $F_{csg}$ can be arbitrarily complex, we simplified the implementation by limiting the complexity of the function to a maximum of 5 operands. This allows $F_{csg}$ to be implemented as a 32 entry look-up table, using the concatenation of $A'$, $B',C',D',E'$ as the 5 bit index ($2^5$=32). This table is stored in a 32 bit register which the driver software loads before starting the hardware rasterization of the frame.

It is possible, of course, to build hardware that evaluates far more complex expressions than this. We've chosen not to do so for two reasons. This first is cost — this simple evaluator required only ~500 gates, so it was inexpensive and easy to add.

The other reason is that our goal is to accelerate interactive modeling with CSG, not provide a general renderer for arbitrarily complex CSG objects. Even with hardware acceleration, solving the entire CSG expression tree for a complex object can become too slow for interactive use. For real tasks, a hybrid system which uses hardware CSG rendering

for the operands which are being manipulated, while converting the stable portion of the expression tree to a boundary representation, appears to be the most versatile solution [7].

### State Requirements for Implementing CSG

The principal advantage of Z-ordered evaluation of CSG is that very little state (aka memory) is required. In the ASIC, 5 bits are used to store the operand state variables $A'$ to $E'$, and an additional bit stores the last state of $F_{csg}$ so that its changes can be detected — this is even less than is used to store the composited RGB value during transparency blending. (Actually, the multiple pass algorithm requires that these 6 bits be stored for each of the 16 pixels on-chip, so a total of 96 bits are used.)

By comparison, expression ordered evaluation of the CSG expression requires substantially more state storage. Because the Boolean set evaluation at each operand node can produce a virtually unlimited number of separate segments, hardware implementation is much more difficult than for an algorithm with fixed state requirements.

### Z-Ordered CSG vs. Sum of Products

Another popular algorithm for rendering CSG is to decompose the CSG expression into sum-of-products, and then perform multiple-pass rendering of each two-operand expression until the entire CSG expression has been performed. This method is particularly popular with hardware accelerators, because it requires a fixed (and small) amount of per-pixel storage [10][17].

In general, Z-ordered evaluation has an advantage over this method because the entire CSG expression is evaluated in a single rendering pass[2]. Implementations of sum-of-products rendering have varied, but in general they require 2-3 passes for a difference of two objects, with exponential growth as the number of operands increases past two.

An advantage of sum-of-products solutions is that they can render an arbitrarily complex scene (although complex expressions may take a long time).

## IMPLEMENTING Z-ORDERED SHADING

Although Z-ordered shading isn't usually performed in hardware accelerators, many high-quality software rendering algorithms operate in this fashion — in particular, ray-tracing and A-buffer algorithms are very popular [4][20].

Ray-tracing intrinsically operates in front-to-back order, and experimental hardware implementations have been built [13]. However, ray-tracing is still too computationally complex for use in a low cost accelerator.

The A-buffer algorithm generates a front-to-back sorted list of all the pixel fragments that affect each pixel, allowing both transparency and anti-aliasing computations to be performed as the list is composited. Front-to-back ordering is performed by a list sorting operation, which is more suitable for hardware implementation. However, because the layer list can

---

[2] This isn't strictly true when the multiple pass algorithm is added; however, the number of passes is still a fraction of the number of layers, rather than an exponential function of expression complexity.

potentially be quite large, it isn't possible to store it in on-chip RAM, so off-chip memory must be used. Achieving a 40MHz clock speed with the increased latency of off-chip memory proved to be too expensive (and difficult!) to be practical.

Instead, we chose to use a somewhat simpler and less efficient Z-ordered shading algorithm, and then improve the efficiency by combining it with an image space partitioning algorithm. By using a simpler Z sorting algorithm, all the Z and ARGB RAM could be kept on-chip, making a 40MHz clock reasonable. Also, the image space partitioning algorithm reduced system cost substantially by eliminating the system Z-buffer, and by reducing system bandwidth [14][16].

# UNLIMITED VISIBLE LAYERS

The algorithm used is a hybrid of a simple list sorting algorithm, and a multiple pass rendering algorithm similar to that described by Mammen [15]. Very briefly, Mammen's algorithm operated by first rendering the opaque objects in the scene. Then the transparent objects were rendered, retaining only the furthest layer of transparency per pixel. Once all transparent objects were rendered, the transparency layer was composited with the opaque layer, Z values updated, and, if necessary, the transparent objects were re-submitted, rendering another layer of transparency. The process was repeated until all transparent layers were composited, requiring one iteration for each layer of transparency at the deepest point in the image.

This algorithm has the advantage of using a fixed (and small) amount of memory per pixel. However, in the original form it is efficient only for scenes without deeply layered transparency, or where only a small percentage of the objects are transparent. In this system Z sorting is used for both transparency *and* CSG, so it's not unusual for all objects in the scene to require Z sorting — if the original form of the algorithm was used, this would cause many rendering passes and correspondingly low performance.

## Start with the Four Closest Layers

The implementation process began by determining how many layers of sorted Z could be inexpensively supported in hardware, while still providing enough layers to render typical images efficiently. A normal Z-buffer system has a single layer; we simulated designs with 2, 4 and 8 layers on a variety of tests. The goal was to find a depth which could render the common test cases without overflow, or at least with overflow on only a small percentage of the image. *Figure 5*, at the end of the paper, shows a sample test image containing 17 tori, half of which are transparent. Figure 6a (below) is a gray scale rendering of the number of visible layers at each pixel, ranging from zero (black) to six (white).

As the tests were performed, the effect on ASIC cost and performance was evaluated. In the end, a 4 layer deep Z-ARGB buffer provided the best result. For the test image in Figure 5, only the region shown in Figure 6b requires more than four layers to render (Figure 6b will be discussed again later). With double-buffering and miscellaneous control bits added, this implementation worked out to $(24+32+4)*(4*2) = 480$ bits/pixel. For the 16 pixels stored on chip, a total of 7.7 KBits of on-chip RAM were used, well within the cost constraints of the system.

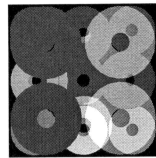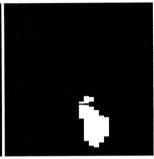

*Figure 6a*　　　　*Figure 6b*
*Number of Visible Layers*　*Region Requiring Two Passes*

## Sort from Front to Back

During rendering, the four layer deep Z-ARGB buffer is used to retain the four closest visible layers per pixel. For simple scenes without transparency or CSG, only the first Z layer is used, and behaviour is identical to a normal Z buffer. However, when transparent or CSG objects are rendered, they are recognized as non-opaque and are inserted into their correct position in each pixel's list. If more than four visible layers are required for any pixel, an overflow flag is set indicating that more than four Z layers will be necessary to complete rendering, and the four closest layers are retained.

## If Necessary, Composite and ReRender

When overflow occurs, the system composites the four closest layers into a single layer, and stores the result, with the backmost Z, into the first layer of the Z buffer. The objects are then resubmitted, and, similarly to [15], the remaining three Z layers are used to capture the *next*-closest three layers of each pixel. This process continues until overflow does not occur, effectively compositing an unlimited number of layers from front to back.

Both the CSG and transparency operations are performed as part of the compositing operation. Note that the CSG operand state bits ($A'$, $B'$...) must be stored per pixel when overflow occurs so processing can be resumed for the next three layers.

## Don't Overflow for Hidden Layers

As is usual in software implementations, the system includes an optimization which stops the compositing process once an opaque layer is reached. This avoids unnecessary overflow to process objects hidden behind an opaque object, and improves compositing performance.

This optimization requires that Z-sorting be performed from front to back.

## Z Sort Performance

When four or fewer visible layers are necessary to render the image, front-to-back sorting speed is governed by the Z list sort-insert time. For random data, the average number of clocks required to insert a pixel into a list of 0, 1, 2 or 3 layers is:

| layers | clocks |
|--------|--------|
| 0 | 1 |
| 1 | 1 |
| 2 | $1 + 1/2(1) = 1.5$ |
| 3 | $1 + 2/3(1 + 1/2(1)) = 2$ |

Assuming that all pixels have 4 visible layers, an average of $1+1+1.5+2 = 5.5$ clocks/pixel are required for Z sorting. Note that this is roughly balanced with compositing speed (1 clock/layer, or 4 clocks/pixel), so Z sort and composite performance stay roughly balanced for up to four visible layers. Also, object processing speed is not too degraded from the opaque object case, with average clocks/pixel layer = 5.5/4 = 1.4.

Increasing the number of layers to 7 both increases the rendering time of the first pass, as the additional 3 layers take an average of 2 clocks/pixel-layer to insert, and requires one additional rendering pass to sort and composite the 3 overflow layers. During the first pass, the average clocks per pixel rises from 5.5 to 11.5 (5.5 + 3*2). During the second pass, the four previously composited layers are discarded in 1 clock/layer, and the three overflow layers are inserted in:

| layers | clocks |
|--------|--------|
| 4 | 1 |
| 5 | 1 + 1/2(1) = 1.5 |
| 6 | 1 + 2/3(1+1/2(1)) = 2 |

Total processing per pixel therefore averages 11.5+4+1+1.5+2 = 20 clocks/pixel. Because seven layers are being processed, this raises the average clocks/pixel layer to 20/7 = 2.8. Although this represents a substantial performance drop, it's much less than the 7X penalty a single layer multiple-pass algorithm would impose.

Of course, real images do not have the homogenous distribution of layers that these calculations have assumed. The next section discusses system performance at the image level.

## IMAGE PARTITIONING

Image partitioning is a well established method used with many software algorithms and hardware architectures [6][14][16]. In general, image partitioning algorithms divide the entire image to be rendered into a number of smaller regions, each of which is rendered separately.

Image partitioning algorithms can have a number of advantages. If the algorithm is designed to render each region independently, it becomes possible to render multiple regions simultaneously, enabling the use of parallel rendering hardware. Alternatively, the algorithm can be designed to share rendering state between the partitions, in which case the main advantage is a reduction of working memory (usually because fewer pixels are stored at once); Watkin's scanline algorithm is a classic example of this [19]. Some systems have exploited both of these advantages [14].

There were two reasons for using an image partitioning algorithm in this system. The first was to reduce working memory to an amount that could be stored in on-chip RAM. Keeping the multiple Z and ARGB layers stored on-chip made it possible to design a Z-sort module that operates at 40M pixel-layer/s, using 400 MB/s of on-chip RAM bandwidth. Although it would have been possible to achieve this performance with off-chip RAM, the system cost would have been substantially higher .

The second reason to use image partitioning was to improve the efficiency of the multiple-pass Z sorting algorithm described earlier. By applying the overflow and re-render tests at a finer level than for the entire image, the efficiency of the algorithm was greatly improved.

In addition to these two performance improvements, image partitioning allowed us to virtually eliminate the limit on image size usually imposed by hardware accelerators. The system can render an image of up to 8Kx8K resolution in a single pass.

### Two Dimensional Bucket Sorting

The image space partitioning algorithm is a variation of the classic scanline algorithm. It begins by bucket sorting all triangles in the image by their first active scanline, a step which has been included in several other hardware accelerators [6][14][16]. Rendering traversal then begins by creating a Y active object list, which is maintained as rendering advances, scanline by scanline, down the image.

At the beginning of each scanline, the Y active list is bucket sorted horizontally (i.e. by X), with each bucket representing a 16 pixel segment of the scanline. (This is variation from the classic scanline algorithm, which performs the X sort by pixel.) Once the X bucket sort is complete, rendering proceeds from left to right across the scanline, maintaining an X active list. Rendering of each 16 pixel segment is completed before advancing to the next segment.

In pseudo-code, and with the multiple-pass algorithm added, the partitioning algorithm can be written as:

```
YBuckets [NScanlines];
XBuckets [ScanlineWidth/16];

ForEachTriangle {
  bucket = FindFirstScanline (tri);
  AddToYBucket (bucket, tri);
}

ForEachScanline {
  AddToYActiveList (YBuckets [scanline]);

  ForEachYActiveTri {
    bucket = FindFirstXSegment (tri);
    AddToXBucket (bucket, tri);
  }

  ForEachSegment{
    AddToXActiveList (XBuckets [segment]);
    do {
      ForEachXActiveTri {
        Render (tri);
      }
    } while (Overflow);
    ScanoutBucket;
  }
}
```

*Figure 7*

Although the code above shows all operations occurring sequentially, whenever possible the hardware overlaps the different phases of the algorithm to avoid idle rasterization time. In particular, for high performance it is necessary to double buffer the Z-ARGB memory so Z sorting can advance to the next segment while the previous segment's compositing is performed.

### Improving Efficiency of the Multiple Pass Algorithm

An advantage of partitioning the image is that the multiple pass algorithm can be applied with much finer granularity than re-rendering the entire image. In many cases only a small percentage of the image will require more than four composited layers; by testing each individual region for overflow and resubmitting only the active objects for that region, overall system efficiency is greatly improved.

Figure 8a and 8b are derived from the test image shown in Figure 5. 8a shows the number of layers per pixel without considering opacity; 8b shows the number of visible layers per pixel. In both cases, the maximum depth is 6 layers, so if the image was rendered using the multiple pass algorithm, two passes would be required (assuming a four layer Z-ARGB buffer). For this test image of 13056 triangles, $N_{TriRend}$, the number of objects * the number of times each object is rendered, can be computed:

$$N_{TriRend} = 2 \text{ passes} * 13056 \text{ tris/pass} = 26112 \text{ tris}$$

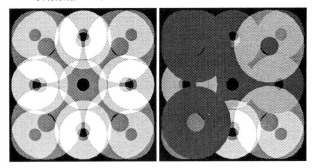

*Figure 8a*          *Figure 8b*

$N_{TriRend}$ can be used to measure the efficiency improvements that result from partitioning the image.

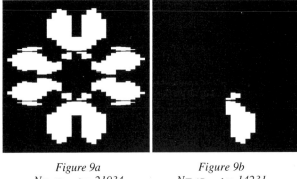

*Figure 9a*          *Figure 9b*
$N_{TriRend} = 21934$          $N_{TriRend} = 14231$

Figure 9a, above, shows the number of rendering passes required for each 16 pixel segment of the scene, assuming the additional optimization of testing for opacity before re-rendering is *not* performed. Even for this simplified algorithm, image partitioning provides an improvement — the simulation measures $N_{TriRend}$ at 21934, a 16% reduction over re-rendering the entire image.

However, the real savings are indicated by Figure 9b, which includes the additional optimization of testing opacity before asserting overflow. In a scene like this test image, where opaque and transparent objects are intermingled, this yields substantial performance improvements — in this case, $N_{TriRend}$ reduces to 14231, a 45% reduction over performing two rendering passes on the entire image.

### Other Image Partitioning Solutions

The efficiency improvements described in the previous section could be further improved by switching to an image partitioning system with better 2D image locality — for example, a 16 pixel partition which was 4x4 pixels instead of 1x16. However, we found that the other advantages of rendering in scanline order (mainly simplicity) outweighed any potential gains.

# SYSTEM ARCHITECTURE

The system splits the rendering task between software and hardware. Transformation, clipping and shading are performed by the PowerMac™ CPU. Rasterization is performed by the ASIC described in this paper. The algorithms used for transformation, clipping and lighting are typical of hardware accelerated workstations; [1][5][11] describe these algorithms in detail. The CPU also performs the initial Y bucket sort of the triangles.

The ASIC rasterizer performs several different tasks, as shown by the pseudo-code in Figure 7 (earlier in the paper). In hardware, these tasks are implemented by multiple modules (shown in Figure 10) which are linked by high speed datapaths. The Z and ARGB RAM are on-chip, as they require very high bandwidth and low latency; system memory is used for triangle storage.

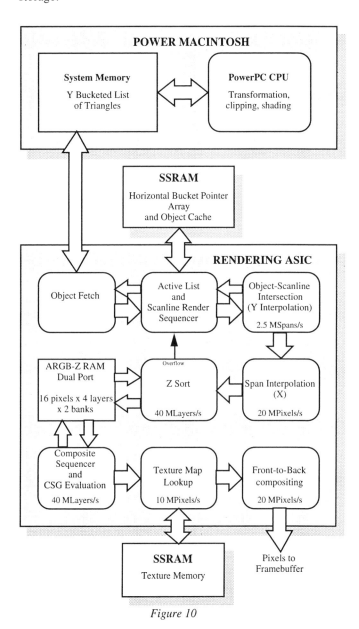

*Figure 10*

## OBJECT FETCH

This module provides the interface to the system bus.

## ACTIVE LIST AND SCANLINE RENDER SEQUENCER

The **Scanline Render Sequencer** controls the rendering of the current scanline, and performs horizontal bucket sorting of the active objects before starting the scanline render. Vertical and horizontal active list maintenance is also performed in this module. The array of object pointers used for the horizontal bucket sort is stored in off-chip SSRAM.

## OBJECT-SCANLINE INTERSECTION

This module intersects triangles with the current scanline, and computes the span endpoint values for the interpolated parameters (such as ARGB and Z). In addition, the X intersect values are fed back to the **Active List** module to allow horizontal bucket sorting of the triangles.

## SPAN INTERPOLATION

This module clips the horizontal span endpoints generated by triangle-scanline intersection to the current X segment, and the parameter values are interpolated for each pixel within the span. As pixels are interpolated, they are output to the **Z Sort** module. Performance is 20 MPixels/s.

## Z SORT

This module inserts the interpolated pixel data into the appropriate layer of the four layer **ARGB-Z RAM**. If overflow occurs, an **Overflow** signal is send to the **Scanline Render Sequencer** indicating that an additional rendering pass will be necessary for the segment. Note that the RAM is double buffered, so that compositing of the previous segment can be performed while the next segment is being sorted.

The **Z Sort** module runs faster than **Span Interpolation** (40 MLayers/s vs. 20 MPixels/s) to compensate for the non-linear increase in sorting operations required for scenes with multiple visible layers per pixel.

## COMPOSITE SEQUENCER AND CSG

The **Composite Sequencer** reads the pixel layers in front-to-back order from the double-buffered **ARGB-Z RAM**, and performs CSG visibility evaluation at 40 MLayers/s. Non-visible layers are discarded.

## TEXTURE MAP LOOKUP

If the incoming pixel layer should be texture mapped, eight texture map values are read from the off-chip RAM and tri-linearly interpolated to generate the diffuse color, after which diffuse and specular lighting are applied. Texture mapping is limited by RAM bandwidth to 10 MPixels/s; however, because texture is applied after hidden surface removal and CSG evaluation, rendering throughput is typically not degraded.

## FRONT-TO-BACK COMPOSITING

The final pixel processing is performed by compositing the incoming pixel layers in front-to-back order, after which the resulting ARGB values are output to the frame buffer.

## CONCLUSIONS

These are the main design goals met by the system:

### CSG and Transparency

An unlimited number of transparent layers can be composited in correct Z order. Z-ordering is performed per-pixel, so intersecting objects are rendered correctly. Arbitrary CSG operations of up to five operands are supported; more complex operations could be implemented if desired.

### Single ASIC Implementation

The entire rasterization engine has been implemented as a single ASIC, with all low latency datapaths on-chip. This resulted in a low-cost implementation, and potential for substantial performance growth as ASIC technology advances. Off-chip Z buffer memory isn't required.

### High Performance

The ASIC can rasterize 120K texture-mapped triangles/s. (This would only qualify as midrange performance by today's workstation standards, but is respectable for a single ASIC rasterizer.) Interestingly, even this basic benchmark (i.e. no CSG or transparency) benefited from Z-ordered shading because the hidden surfaces were discarded before texture mapping was performed.

## FUTURE WORK

Although the implementation described here provides good performance for a single ASIC rasterizer, scaling performance up to higher levels will require additional parallelism. Some form of parallelism at the image partition level would be ideal.

## ACKNOWLEDGEMENTS

The authors wish to thank Kai-Fu Lee and Rick LeFaivre for supporting this research in Apple's Interactive Media Lab.

Thanks to Jill Huchital and Dan Venolia for their reviews.

## REFERENCES

1. Akeley, Kurt and T. Jermoluk, "High-Performance Polygon Rendering", Computer Graphics, Vol. 22, No. 4, August 1988, 239-246

2. Akeley, Kurt, "RealityEngine Graphics", ACM Computer Graphics Conference Proceedings, August 1993, 109-116

3. Atherton, Peter, "A Scan-Line Hidden Surface Removal Procedure for Constructive Solid Geometry", Computer Graphics, July 1983, 73-82

4. Carpenter, Loren, "The A-buffer, an Antialiased Hidden Surface Method", Computer Graphics, Vol. 18, No. 3, July 1984, 103-108

5. Deering, Michael, and S. Nelson, "Leo: A System for Cost Effective 3D Shaded Graphics", ACM Computer Graphics Conference Proceedings, August 1993, 101-108

6. Deering, Michael, S. Winner, B. Schediwy, C. Duffy and N. Hunt, "The Triangle Processor and Normal Vector Shader: A VLSI System for High Performance Graphics", Computer Graphics, Vol. 22, No. 4, August 1988, 21-30

7. Foley, James, A. van Dam, S. Feiner and J. Hughes, "Computer Graphics Principles and Practice, 2nd Edition", Addison-Wesley, 1990, transparency 754-755, CSG tree 557-558, CSG b-rep 546-547

8. Fuchs, Henry, G. Abram, and J. Poulton, "Near Real-Time Shaded Display of Rigid Objects", Computer Graphics, Vol. 17, No. 3, July 1983, 65-72

9. Goldstein, R. and R. Nagel, "3-D Visual Simulation", Simulation 16(1), January 1971, 25-31

10. Goldfeather, Jack and J. Hultquist, "Fast Constructive Solid Geometry Display in the Pixel-Powers Graphics System", Computer Graphics, Vol. 20, No. 4, August 1986, 107-116

11. Harrell, Chandlee, and F. Fouladi, "Graphics Rendering Architecture for a High Performance Desktop Workstation", ACM Computer Graphics Conference Proceedings, August 1993, 93-100

12. Kay, D., "Transparency, Refraction and Ray Tracing for Computer Synthesized Images", Thesis, Cornell University, January 1979

13. Kedem, G. and J. Ellis, "The Raycasting Machine", Proceedings of ICCD, October 1984, 533-538

14. Kelley, Michael, S. Winner, and K. Gould, "A Scalable Hardware Render Accelerator using a Modified Scanline Algorithm", Computer Graphics, Vol. 26, No. 2, July 1992, 241-248

15. Mammen, A., "Transparency and Antialiasing Algorithms Implemented with the Virtual Pixel Maps Technique", Computer Graphics and Applications, 9(4), July 1989, 43-55

16. Niimi, Haruo, Y. Imai, M. Murakami, S. Tomita and H. Hagiwara, "A Parallel Processor System for Three-Dimensional Color Graphics", Computer Graphics, Vol. 18, No. 3, July 1984, 67-76

17. Rossignac, Jaroslaw, and A. Requicha, "Depth-Buffering Display Techniques for Constructive Solid Geometry", IEEE Computer Graphics and Applications, September 1986, 29-39

18. Roth, Scott, "Ray Casting for Modeling Solids", Computer Graphics and Image Processing, 18, 1982, 109-67

19. Watkins, G. "A Real-Time Visible Surface Algorithm", Computer Science Department, University of Utah, UTECH-CSC-70-101, June 1970

20. Whitted, T. "An Improved Illumination Model for Shaded Display", CACM 23(6), June 1980, 343-349

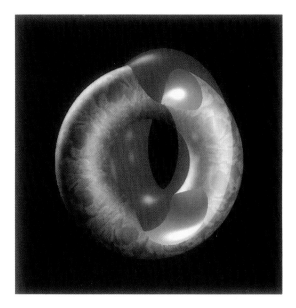

*Figure 1: Difference of Two Tori*

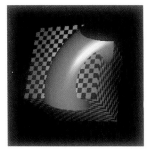 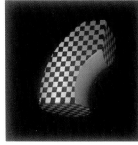

*Figure 2a*
*Cube – Torus*

*Figure 2b*
*Cube ∩ Torus*

*Figure 5: Test Image*

# 3D position, attitude and shape input using video tracking of hands and lips

Andrew Blake[1]and Michael Isard[1]

**Robotics Research Group, University of Oxford.**

## ABSTRACT

Recent developments in video-tracking allow the outlines of moving, natural objects in a video-camera input stream to be tracked
live, at full video-rate. Previous systems have been available to
do this for specially illuminated objects or for naturally illuminated
but polyhedral objects. Other systems have been able to track non-
polyhedral objects in motion, in some cases from live video, but
following only centroids or key-points rather than tracking whole
curves. The system described here can track accurately the curved
silhouettes of moving non-polyhedral objects at frame-rate, for example hands, lips, legs, vehicles, fruit, and without any special
hardware beyond a desktop workstation and a video-camera and
framestore.

The new algorithms are a synthesis of methods in deformable
models, B-spline curve representation and control theory. This
paper shows how such a facility can be used to turn parts of the
body — for instance, hands and lips — into input devices. Rigid
motion of a hand can be used as a 3D mouse with non-rigid gestures
signalling a button press or the "lifting" of the mouse. Both rigid
and non-rigid motions of lips can be tracked independently and used
as inputs, for example to animate a computer-generated face.

## INTRODUCTION

The advent of general-purpose workstations with integral video-
camera and real-time framestore presents an opportunity for a low-
cost approach to position, attitude and shape input. This can be
achieved without special hardware by using software for real-time
tracking of the live video signal, processed at full video-field rate,
50Hz in systems like the one reported here.

Real-time video tracking has been achieved for line-drawings
[15] and polyhedral structures [19] and for simple, natural features
such as road-edges [10]. Commercial systems (e.g. Watsmart, Oxford Metrics) are available which track artificial markers on live
video. Natural point features (e.g. on a face) but not curves,
have been tracked at 10Hz using a workstation assisted by image-
processing hardware [3]. Curve trackers [17] have been demonstrated on modest workstations but slower than frame-rate.

---

[1]Department of Engineering Science, University of Oxford, Parks Rd, Oxford OX1
3PJ, UK.

Two new algorithms are presented in this paper which allow
effective, agile tracking of curves in live video data, at 50Hz, on a
modest workstation (SUN IPX plus Cohu video-camera and Dat-
acell S2200 framestore) without additional hardware. The possibility of tracking curves within a Kalman filtering framework was
raised by Szeliski and Terzopoulos [23]. Kalman filters comprise
two steps: prediction and measurement assimilation. Prediction
employs assumptions about object dynamics to extrapolate past
motion from one video frame to the next. Assimilation blends measurements from a given frame with the latest available prediction.
An excellent introduction to this powerful methodology is given
by Gelb [13]. Our first algorithm applies such a filter to curves
represented by B-splines, to track both rigid and non-rigid motions.

The second algorithm is a "system identification algorithm"
based on ideas from adaptive control theory [2] and "maximum
likelihood estimation" in statistics [22]. Previous approaches to
learning shape variability have used statistical models to represent
a family of possible shapes [14, 9] but statically. In contrast the
learning method reported here is dynamic, using and modelling
*temporal* image sequences. Example motions are tracked by a
general-purpose tracker based on the assumption of default object
dynamics. The tracked motion is used as a training set for the new
algorithm which estimates the underlying dynamics of the training motion. The learned dynamics are then used in the tracker's
predictor which then enjoys enhanced tracking capability for motions similar to those in the training set. The learning process can
be repeated to bootstrap trackers of successively increasing performance.

The effectiveness of the algorithms in generating agile trackers which are resistant to distraction from background clutter is
demonstrated in this paper and on the accompanying video. The
final section of the paper illustrates two of the possible applications
for graphical input: a 3D mouse driven by natural hand movements
and a lip-tracker for use in automating animation.

## PROBLEM FRAMEWORK AND NOTATION

The tracker is an estimator for a moving, piecewise-smooth image-
plane curve:
$$\mathbf{r}(s, t) = (x(s, t), y(s, t)).$$
Following the tracking work of others [21, 8], the curve representation is in terms of B-splines. Quadratic splines with the possibility
of multiple knots for vertices are used here.

A given curve is parameterised as a B-spline
$$x(s) = \mathbf{B}^T(s)\mathbf{X} \text{ and } y(s) = \mathbf{B}^T(s)\mathbf{Y}, \ 0 \leq s \leq N$$
where $\mathbf{X} = (X_1, .., X_{N_c})^T$ and similarly for $\mathbf{Y}$ with $N_c = N$ for
closed curves and $N_c = N + d$ for open ones (with appropriate

variations where multiple knots are used to vary curve continuity). The elements of $\mathbf{X}$ and $\mathbf{Y}$ are simply vectors of $x$ and $y$ coordinates respectively from the set of control points $(X_m, Y_m)$ for the B-spline. The vector $\mathbf{B}(s)$ consists of blending coefficients defined by

$$\mathbf{B}(s) = (B_1(s), ..., B_{N_c}(s))^T \qquad (1)$$

where each $B_m$ is a B-spline basis function [11, 6] appropriate to the order of the curve and its set of knots.

## Tracking

The tracking problem is now to estimate the motion of some curve — in this paper it will be the outline of a hand or of lips. The underlying curve — the physical truth — is assumed to be describable as a B-spline of a certain predefined form with control points $\mathbf{X}(t), \mathbf{Y}(t)$ varying over time. The tracker generates *estimates* of those control points, denoted $\hat{\mathbf{X}}(t), \hat{\mathbf{Y}}(t)$ and the aim is that those estimates should represent a curve that, at each time-step, matches the underlying curve as closely as possible. The tracker consists, in accordance with standard practice in temporal filtering [13, 4], of two parts: a system model and a measurement model. These will be spelt out in detail later. Broadly, the measurement model specifies the positions along the curve at which measurements are made and how reliable they are. The system model specifies the likely dynamics of the curve over time, relative to some average shape or "template" [12] whose control points are given by $(\overline{\mathbf{X}}(t), \overline{\mathbf{Y}}(t))$, and which is generated by an interactive drawing tool, drawing over a single video frame.

## Rigid body transformations

A tracker could conceivably be designed to allow arbitrary variations in control point positions over time. This would allow maximum flexibility in deforming to moving shapes. However, particularly for complex shapes requiring many control points to describe them, this is known to lead to instability in tracking [7]. Furthermore, it is not necessary to allow so much freedom. A moving, outstretched hand, for instance, provided the fingers are not flexing, is an approximately rigid, planar shape. It is known that, under orthographic projection, the image of such a shape has only 6 degrees of freedom [25, 18], so provided perspective effects are not too strong, a good approximation to the curve shape as it changes over time can be obtained by specifying just 6 numbers. They form a vector denoted $\mathbf{Q}$ expressing the affine transformation that is applied to the template to get to the current shape. In this representation, the template itself is simply $\overline{\mathbf{Q}} = (0, 0, 1, 1, 0, 0)^T$. Transformations between $\mathbf{Q}$ and $(\mathbf{X}, \mathbf{Y})$ can be made by applying some matrices $M, W$ (see appendix):

$$\left( \begin{array}{c} \mathbf{X} \\ \mathbf{Y} \end{array} \right) = W\mathbf{Q} \quad \text{and} \quad \mathbf{Q} = M \left( \begin{array}{c} \mathbf{X} \\ \mathbf{Y} \end{array} \right). \qquad (2)$$

Non-planar rigid shapes can also be treated in a similar way to planar ones except that then $\mathbf{Q}$ must be an 8-vector, related to the control points by an appropriately defined $2N_c \times 8$ $W$-matrix. Alternatively, freedom for rigid motion can be restricted, for example to allow only zoom and translation, and then $\mathbf{Q}$ becomes a 3-vector, with an accompanying $2N_c \times 3$ $W$-matrix. Nonrigid motion can also be handled in a similar way, by choosing a $\mathbf{Q}$ representation that represents both the rigid and non-rigid degrees of freedom of the shape. This is needed, for instance, to allow finger movements in hand tracking, or to follow lip movements. It is crucial therefore to allow exactly the right degrees of freedom for nonrigidity, neither too few resulting in excessive stiffness, nor too many leading to instability. Previous snake-based methods for handling non-rigid motion [17] allowed far too many degrees of freedom which leads to instability, quite unusable for real-time

tracking. Further detail on handling of non-rigid motion is given later.

## TRACKER FRAMEWORK

This section describes how the dynamics of the curve are modelled, how the measurement process is modelled, and how the two are brought together to make a curve tracker.

Our model of curve motion is a second order equation driven by noise, as used widely for modelling in control theory [1]. The choice of a second order model includes constant velocity motion, decay and damped oscillation. These motions can be present independently for each of the six degrees of freedom of rigid motion. In the case of oscillation, for instance, there may be 6 independent modes present, each with its own natural frequency and damping rate. In addition to the characteristic oscillation, the "stochastic" element of the model adds in uncertainty, as a smoothed random walk, and so allows a given model to represent a whole *class* of motions. A major attraction of this type of model is compatibility with Kalman filtering. A Kalman filter, consisting of a prediction and a measurement assimilation phase, makes use of just such a model as its predictor.

Second order dynamics are conveniently written in discrete time [1] using a "state vector" $\mathcal{X}_n$, defined in terms of shape $\mathbf{Q}$ *relative* to the template $\overline{\mathbf{Q}}$:

$$\mathcal{X}_n = \left( \begin{array}{c} \mathbf{Q}_{n-1} - \overline{\mathbf{Q}} \\ \mathbf{Q}_n - \overline{\mathbf{Q}}. \end{array} \right) \qquad (3)$$

Successive video frames are indexed $n = 1, 2, 3, ...$

Now the dynamics of the object are defined by the following difference equation:

$$\mathcal{X}_{n+1} = A\mathcal{X}_n + \left( \begin{array}{c} \mathbf{0} \\ \mathbf{w}_n \end{array} \right). \qquad (4)$$

The matrix coefficient $A$ is a $12 \times 12$ matrix, defining the deterministic part of the dynamics; its eigenvectors represent modes, and its eigenvalues give natural frequencies and damping constants [1]. This matrix appears again later, in the tracker, which mirrors equation (4) in its prediction component. At each time $n$, $\mathbf{w}_n$ is an independent, normally distributed, 6-vector of random variables, with *covariance* matrix $C$. It is this covariance matrix $C$ that specifies the random part of the dynamical model — the degree of randomness injected into each of the affine degrees of freedom.

## Measurement of video features

Given an estimated curve $\hat{\mathbf{r}}(s)$, expressed in terms of $\hat{\mathbf{Q}}$, the measurement process at time $t$ consists of casting rays simultaneously along several normals $\mathbf{n}(s)$ to the estimated curve. The normal vectors $\mathbf{n}(s)$ at each measurement point on the curve are calculated in the standard manner for B-spline curves [11], by differentiating to find the tangent vector and then rotating through $90°$. Grey-level values in the video-input framestore are read to measure the (signed) distance $\nu(s)$ of a particular grey-level feature along the curve normal. Typically the feature is a high contrast edge, though other features can also be used [17]. In our system, the highest contrast feature along the normal is chosen within a certain window, typically of width $\pm40$ pixels, on either side of the estimated curve. Each position measurement is assumed to have an associated error distribution, with a root-mean-square value of $\sigma$ pixels. The individual measurements made on each normal are then aggregated to form a combined "virtual" measurement $\mathbf{Z}$ in the $\mathbf{Q}$-space:

$$\mathbf{Z} = \sum_{m=0}^{m=NN_\nu} \nu(m/N_\nu) \mathbf{H}(m/N_\nu)^T$$

where $N_\nu$ is the number of measurements made (at equal intervals) along each B-spline span, $N$ is the number of spans as before, and

$$\mathbf{H}(s) = (\mathbf{n}(s) \otimes \mathbf{B}(s))^T W,$$

where $\mathbf{n}(s)$ is the curve normal vector at a particular point of measurement and $\mathbf{B}(s)$ is the vector of B-spline blending function defined in (1). The projection matrix $W$ that was defined in (2) has the effect here of referring 2D measurements into $\mathbf{Q}$-space, so that they can be applied, in the assimilation phase of the tracker, to update the estimated $\mathbf{Q}$-vector. (Note: the operation $\otimes$ denotes the "Kronecker product"[1].) The $\mathbf{n}(s)$ weighting in the virtual measurement $\mathbf{Z}$ has the effect (and this can be shown rigorously) of "pulling" the tracked curve *along* the normal *only*. Such a weighting along the normal reflects the fact that any displacement *tangential* to a smooth curve is unobservable, the well-known "aperture problem" of visual motion [16].

## Tracking algorithm

The tracking algorithm, a standard "steady state Kalman filter" [13], consists of iterating the following equation:

$$\hat{\mathcal{X}}_{n+1} = A\hat{\mathcal{X}}_n + K \left( \begin{array}{c} \mathbf{Z}_{n+1} \\ \mathbf{0} \end{array} \right),$$

The somewhat non-standard aspect of the algorithm is the $12 \times 12$ "Kalman gain" matrix $K$, defined in the appendix, which has to be designed to match the state-space measurement vector $\mathbf{Z}$. The gain $K$ depends on the system's matrix coefficients $A, C$ and on the reliability and density of measurements along the tracked contour, and is constant over time in the "steady state" case considered here. Allowing time-varying gain is useful to take account of intermittent failures in the measurement process [7], but that is outside the scope of this paper.

## Default tracker

The tracking algorithm described above requires system matrices $A, C$ to be specified. These are not known in advance and the whole purpose of the framework being set up here is to estimate them. However, for the estimation process, a stream of data from a tracked object is needed — for which a tracker is required! Clearly, estimation must be a bootstrap process, beginning with a default tracker based on default values of $A, C$.

A natural default setting for the deterministic part of the dynamics is to assume constant velocity for all degrees of freedom, realised by setting

$$A = \left( \begin{array}{cc} 0 & I \\ -I & 2I \end{array} \right)$$

where $I$ is the $6 \times 6$ identity matrix. A natural default can also be defined for the random part of the dynamics. It is reasonable, as a default, to assume that the magnitude of the random component is uniform over the image plane, with no particular directional bias. For that case, it is known [7] that

$$C = cM\mathcal{H}^{-1}M^T$$

where the "metric" matrix $\mathcal{H}$ is defined in the appendix. This leaves just one constant — $c$ — to be chosen to fix $C$.

Now the default tracker has been specified except for the values of certain constants. Typically the number of measurements per B-spline span is set to $N_\nu = 3$, a value which allows our tracker to

run at video-field rate, on a SUN IPX workstation, with 20 or more control points.

The system and measurement constants $c$ and $\sigma$ also remain to be chosen. The following workable values that were used for the hand-tracking experiments reported later:

$$\sigma = 10.0 \text{ pixels} \quad \text{and} \quad c = 1.0 \text{ pixels}^2$$

— further details on choice of constants are given elsewhere [7].

## LEARNING MOTION AND TRAINING TRACKERS

Training consists of using the default tracker to gather a sequence of $m$ images at the image sampling frequency of 50Hz. The result of tracking is then a sequence of $m$ $\mathbf{Q}$-vectors $\mathbf{Q}_1, ..., \mathbf{Q}_m$, which are the data from which system parameters $A, C$, are estimated. Once $A, C$ are obtained incorporating them in a tracker in the way that was just described.

It follows from definitions in equations (3) and (4) that the $12 \times 12$ matrix $A$ has the form:

$$A = \left( \begin{array}{cc} 0 & I \\ A_0 & A_1 \end{array} \right), \qquad (5)$$

where $A_0, A_1$ are $6 \times 6$ submatrices. Together with $C$, they are estimated as the solution of a least-squares algorithm. Unfortunately, details of the derivation and principles of the algorithm cannot be given here for lack of space. However it is of a type that is somewhat standard in stochastic system identification [2]. It corresponds to maximising the probabilistic "likelihood" [22] of the data with respect to the settings of $A, C$.

Practically, the important point is the algorithm itself, which is straightforward. It should be borne in mind that this algorithm is preparatory to filtering and is therefore done offline. Efficiency is not therefore a major consideration. The algorithm has three steps.

**Step 1: matrix moments** A set of matrix moments

$$S_{ij} = \sum_{n=1}^{m-2} (\mathbf{Q}_{n+i} - \overline{\mathbf{Q}})(\mathbf{Q}_{n+j} - \overline{\mathbf{Q}})^T, \quad i, j = 0, 1, 2$$

is computed from the time-sequence of $\mathbf{Q}$-vectors that serve as the data for learning the parameters $A, C$.

**Step 2: calculate $A$** The $A$-matrix is calculated simply by solving a set of simultaneous equations to obtain the submatrices $A_0, A_1$:

$$S_{20} - A_0 S_{00} - A_1 S_{10} = 0 \qquad (6)$$
$$S_{21} - A_0 S_{01} - A_1 S_{11} = 0. \qquad (7)$$

Now $A_0, A_1$ form the full matrix $A$ as in equation (5).

**Step 3: calculate $C$** Using the value of $A$ just computed, $C$ can be estimated directly:

$$C = \frac{1}{m-2} \sum_{n=1}^{m-2} (\mathbf{Q}_{n+2} - A_0\mathbf{Q}_n - A_1\mathbf{Q}_{n+1}).$$
$$(\mathbf{Q}_{n+2} - A_0\mathbf{Q}_n - A_1\mathbf{Q}_{n+1})^T.$$

---

[1]The Kronecker product [5] $A \otimes B$ of two matrices $A, B$ is obtained by replacing each element $a$ of $A$ with the submatrix $aB$. The dimensions of this matrix are thus products of the corresponding dimensions of $A, B$.

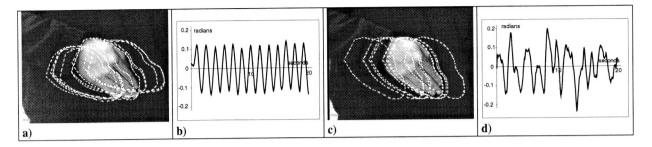

Figure 1: **Learning horizontal oscillation.** *a) Training sequence of a tracked hand captured at 50Hz (full video field-rate) in oscillatory motion. The initial frame of the hand is shown with a subsequence of the positions of the tracked curve overlaid. The centroid's horizontal position is displayed as a time-sequence in b). c) Simulation of the learned system: note that the motion swept out when the learned dynamics are simulated is similar to the motion in the training set. d) Centroid's horizontal position for the sequence in c).*

## LEARNING TRANSLATION

Model parameters are inferred from data by the statistical learning algorithm already described. The resulting tracker is specifically sensitive to a particular motion, in this case translation. This time the learnt motion will also be resynthesised and compared with the original. The horizontal motion training set, shown as a graph in figure 1b, is then used in the estimation procedure of the previous section, to obtain parameters $A, C$. The resulting $A$-matrix has several modes as in the zoom example. The mode which is most significant in the sense that it decays most slowly, represents a damped oscillation whose period is about 1.7 seconds. This is close to the apparent periodicity of the data in which there are between 12 and 13 cycles over 20 seconds, a period of about 1.6 seconds.

As a further check, taking the learned model, we can simulate it by generating pseudo-random gaussian noise and using it to "energise" the model whose coefficients are the learned values of $A, C$. This is illustrated in figure 1c,d. It is clear that the simulated process is similar in amplitude and natural frequency to the data set. However it is more "random" — it does not capture the phase-coherence of the training set. Such behaviour is typical of this algorithm and should be regarded as a feature rather than a bug. It indicates that the algorithm has *generalised* the example motion, capturing its broad characteristics over shorter time-scales without attempting to replicate the entire signal. A stronger model that captured the entire signal would be too strong — the model would compete, in the tracker, with the measurement process and overwhelm it. The remaining influence of the video measurements would then be too weak for effective tracking. (Note: this argument can be put rigorously, but space does not permit.)

### Tracking

The following experiments demonstrate the power of incorporating learned motion into a curve tracker. This time, a training set of *vertical* rigid motion is generated and used to learn motion coefficients $A, C$, much as in the previous example of learned horizontal motion. The trained tracker, incorporating the learned motion is then to be tested against the un-trained, default tracker. It will be clear that the tracker has been trained to track rapid oscillation.

The test sequences are generated consisting of rapid, vertical, oscillatory motions of a hand. The sequences are stored on video so that fair comparisons can be made, using the standard sequences, of the performance of different trackers. Two sequences are made: one of oscillatory motion of gradually increasing frequency — a "chirp" — and the other of regular oscillation against irrelevant background features — "clutter". Results of the tests are shown in figures 2 and 3. The increased agility and robustness of the trained

tracker is also clear in the accompanying video.

## NONRIGID MOTION

The methods illustrated so far for learning and tracking rigid motion can be extended to non-rigid motion. The algorithms described earlier continue to apply, but now the **Q**-space must be redefined to parameterise non-rigid motion of a curve.

### Key-frames

The **Q**-space is extended by redefining the transformation matrices $M, W$ from equation (2). The $W$ matrix (see appendix for details) must be given additional columns each reflecting an additional degree of freedom for non-rigid motion. This then increases the dimension of the **Q** vector from 6 to some larger number. The extra columns of $W$ are derived from "key-frames", typical non-rigid deformations, on which the tracked contour is positioned interactively, as in figure 4. Each of the additional components of the **Q**-vector then represents the proportion of each of the key-frames in the mix. (Note that the template and key-frames do not need to be mutually orthogonal, merely linearly independent). During tracking, the first 6 components of the $\hat{\mathbf{Q}}_n$-vector report on the rigid motion, and the remaining components report on non-rigid motion, so rigid and non-rigid motion can be monitored somewhat independently.

### Lips

The key-frames above generate a **Q**-space that can be used in a default tracker capable of tracking slow speech and sufficient to gather data for training. As a demonstration of the effect of training, trackers were trained for the lip-motions that accompany the sounds "Pah" and "Ooh", and tested on the sound "Pah". The selectivity of the resulting tracker is shown in figure 5. It is clear from these results that the training effect for individual sounds is strong. This suggests that training for typical lip-movements that accompany speech should have a strong effect on tracking speaking lips and this is explored in the next section. The selective training effect could potentially be exploited in its own right for simple lip-reading (e.g. of commands or key-words) an idea that has been explored by others [20] using rather different mechanisms.

## APPLICATIONS

There are potentially many applications for real-time position, attitude and shape input using the new algorithms for learning and tracking. Two are explored here: the use of a hand as a 3D mouse

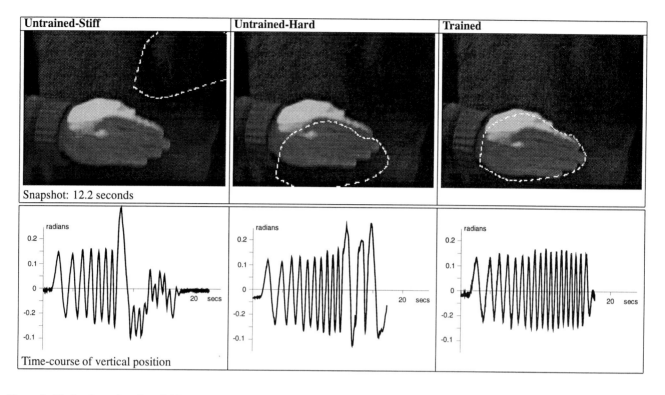

Figure 2: **Trained tracker for rigid motion, tested with rapid oscillations**. *A "chirp" test motion, consisting of vertical oscillations of progressively increasing frequency, is tracked by each of three trackers: untrained-stiff, untrained-hard and trained. For the untrained trackers, lock is lost after 12.2 seconds whereas the trained tracker is still tracking. Graphs of vertical position against time clearly shows the lost lock at about 12 seconds for the untrained trackers. The trained tracker maintains lock throughout the time-sequence.*

and the tracking of lips for control of animation. Of course successful hard-ware realisations of a 3D mouse or "bat" have already been developed [26]. The advantages of the system proposed here is that on the new generation of workstations with built-in cameras it involves *no* additional hardware, and that it is software reconfigurable for example by adding finger-gestures to indicate button presses and perhaps even grasping manoeuvres of the sort used in a "dataglove". Facial animation in real time has been achieved previously using reflective markers [27] but that supplies measurements at distinct points only. The advantage of a system like the one demonstrated here is that it can measure, in real time, the motion of entire curves.

### 3D mouse

Both rigid and nonrigid motion of a hand can be used as a 3D input device. The freedom of movement of the hand is illustrated in figure 6, with rigid motion picked up to control 3D position and attitude, and nonrigid motion signalling button pressing and "lifting". The tracker output — the components of $\hat{Q}$ varying over time — have successfully been used to drive a simulated object around a 3D environment and this is illustrated on the accompanying video.

### Lips

The feasibility of tracking lip movements frontally, when lip high-lighter is worn, was demonstrated by Kass et al [17]. Our system can do this at video-rate. This paradigm can be extended by using high-lighter on a number of facial features, as Terzopoulos and Waters [24] did. It is expected that this could be used with our real-time trainable tracker to build an effective front-end for actor-driven animation, without recourse to expensive virtual-reality input devices.

Tracking lips side-on, whilst arguably less informative, has the advantage of working in normal lighting condition without cosmetic aids. This could be used to turn the mouth into an additional workstation input-device. Learning and selectivity with single sounds were demonstrated earlier. Here, complexity is increased by training on connected speech. Two-stage training was used. In the first stage, the default tracker followed a slow-speech training sequence which is then used, via the learning algorithm, to generate a tracker. This tracker is capable of following speech of medium speed. It is then used to follow a medium-speed training sequence, from which dynamics for a full-speed tracker are obtained.

The trained tracker is then tested against the default tracker, using a test sequence entirely different from the training sequences. Two components of lip motion are extracted from the tracked motion. The larger of these corresponds approximately to the degree to which the lips are parted. This component is plotted both for the default tracker and the trained one in figure 7. It is clear from the figure that the trained filter is considerably more agile. In preliminary demonstrations in which the signal is used to animate a head (frontal view), the default filter is able to follow only very slow speech, whereas the trained filter successfully follows speech delivered at a normal speed. The increased agility and robustness of the trained tracker is made clear in the accompanying video.

## CONCLUSIONS

New algorithms have been described for live tracking of moving objects from video. The first algorithm is a tracker based on the control-theoretic "Kalman filter". It allows particular dynamics, modelled by a stochastic differential equation, to be used predic-

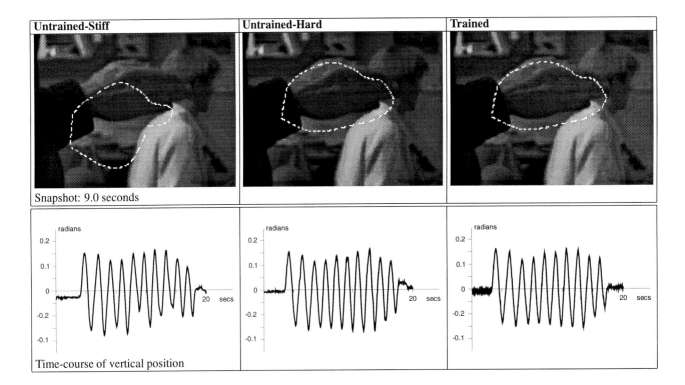

Figure 3: **Trained tracker for oscillatory rigid motion, tested against clutter.** *The two untrained trackers and the trained tracker are compared here using a "clutter" test-sequence. After 9.0 seconds, the stiff-untrained tracker is distracted by background clutter and loses lock, but the hard-untrained and the trained trackers continue to track successfully.*

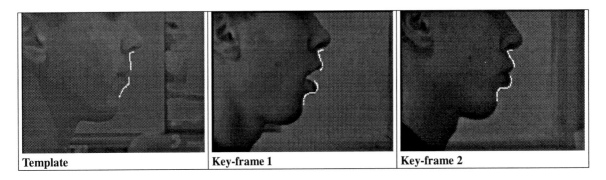

Figure 4: **Keyframes.** *A weighted sum of key-frames is added to the **Q** vector for use in a default tracker for non-rigid motion.*

tively in the tracker. The default tracker, for instance, assumes constant velocity rigid motion driven randomly. It is crucial that the constraints of rigid-body motion are incorporated — represented in our algorithm by the **Q**-space. This is what allows stable tracking, for which free parameters must be limited, to be combined with the apparently conflicting requirement of the large number of control points needed for accurate shape representation.

The second algorithm is the most original contribution. It is a learning algorithm that allows dynamical models to be built from examples. When such a model is incorporated into a tracker, agility and robustness to clutter are considerably increased.

Finally, the advent of workstations with integral cameras and framestores brings an opportunity for these algorithms to be put to work. Unadorned body parts become usable input devices for graphics. This has potential applications in user-interface design, automation of animation, virtual reality and perhaps even low-bandwidth teleconferencing and the design of computer aids for the handicapped.

## Acknowledgements

We are grateful for the use of elegant software constructed by Rupert Curwen, Nicola Ferrier, Simon Rowe, Henrik Klagges and for discussions with Roger Brockett, Yael Moses, David Reynard, Brian Ripley, Richard Szeliski, Andrew Zisserman. We acknowledge the support of the SERC, the EC Esprit programme (SECOND) and the Newton Institute, Cambridge.

## REFERENCES

[1] K. J. Astrom and B. Wittenmark. *Computer Controlled Systems.* Addison Wesley, 1984.

[2] K. J. Astrom and B. Wittenmark. *Adaptive control.* Addison Wesley, 1989.

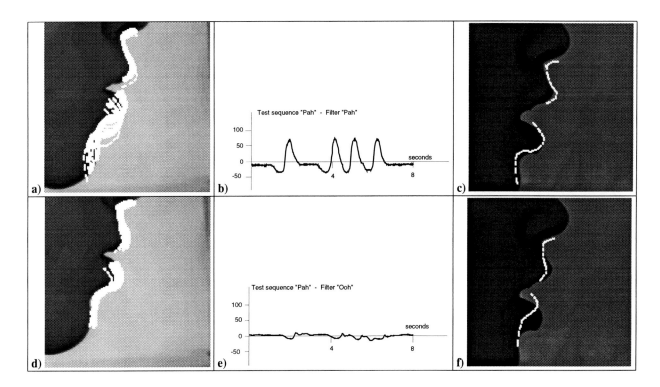

Figure 5: **Filter selectivity for sounds**. *A test sequence in which the sound "pah" is repeated is tracked by a filter trained on the sound "pah". a) shows the area swept out by successive positions of the tracked contour. Note that the filter successfully tracks the opening/shutting deformation of the mouth. The motion signal (b) is plotted in terms of an appropriate scalar component of estimated motion; it shows pairs of troughs (shutting of the mouth) and peaks (opening), one for each "pah". For instance, approximately 4.1s after the start of the signal the tracked contour (c) is clearly still locked. Corresponding pictures for a tracker trained on the sound "Ooh", fed with the same "Pah" test-sequence, are shown in d),e),f). It is clear (d) that only lateral translation is tracked — the nonrigid deformation containing the speech information is lost, as expected. There is minimal opening/shutting response (e). After 4.1s (f) lock has been lost.*

[3] A. Azarbayejani, T. Starner, B. Horowitz, and A. Pentland. Visually controlled graphics. *IEEE Trans. Pattern Analysis and Machine Intell.*, in press, 1993.

[4] Y. Bar-Shalom and T.E. Fortmann. *Tracking and Data Association*. Academic Press, 1988.

[5] Stephen Barnett. *Matrices: Methods and Applications*. Oxford University Press, 1990.

[6] R.H. Bartels, J.C. Beatty, and B.A. Barsky. *An Introduction to Splines for use in Computer Graphics and Geometric Modeling*. Morgan Kaufmann, 1987.

[7] A. Blake, R. Curwen, and A. Zisserman. A framework for spatio-temporal control in the tracking of visual contours. *Int. Journal of Computer Vision*, 11(2):127–145, 1993.

[8] R. Cipolla and A. Blake. The dynamic analysis of apparent contours. In *Proc. 3rd Int. Conf. on Computer Vision*, pages 616–625, 1990.

[9] T.F. Cootes, C.J. Taylor, A. Lanitis, D.H. Cooper, and J. Graham. Buiding and using flexible models incorporating grey-level information. In *Proc. 4th Int. Conf. on Computer Vision*, pages 242–246, 1993.

[10] E.D. Dickmanns and V. Graefe. Applications of dynamic monocular machine vision. *Machine Vision and Applications*, 1:241–261, 1988.

[11] I.D. Faux and M.J. Pratt. *Computational Geometry for Design and Manufacture*. Ellis-Horwood, 1979.

[12] M. A. Fischler and R. A. Elschlager. The representation and matching of pictorial structures. *IEEE. Trans. Computers*, C-22(1), 1973.

[13] Arthur Gelb, editor. *Applied Optimal Estimation*. MIT Press, Cambridge, MA, 1974.

[14] U. Grenander, Y. Chow, and D. M. Keenan. *HANDS. A Pattern Theoretical Study of Biological Shapes*. Springer-Verlag. New York, 1991.

[15] C. Harris. Tracking with rigid models. In A. Blake and A. Yuille, editors, *Active Vision*, pages 59–74. MIT, 1992.

[16] B.K.P. Horn. *Robot Vision*. McGraw-Hill, NY, 1986.

[17] M. Kass, A. Witkin, and D. Terzopoulos. Snakes: active contour models. In *Proc. 1st Int. Conf. on Computer Vision*, pages 259–268, 1987.

[18] J.J. Koenderink and A.J. Van Doorn. Affine structure from motion. *J. Optical Soc. of America A.*, 8(2):337–385, 1991.

[19] D.G. Lowe. Robust model-based motion tracking through the integration of search and estimation. *Int. Journal of Computer Vision*, 8(2):113–122, 1992.

[20] K. Mase and A. Pentland. Automatic lip-reading by optical flow analysis. Media Lab Report 117, MIT, 1991.

[21] S. Menet, P. Saint-Marc, and G. Medioni. B-snakes: implementation and application to stereo. In *Proceedings DARPA*, pages 720–726, 1990.

[22] A. Papoulis. *Probability and Statistics*. Prentice-Hall, 1990.

[23] R. Szeliski and D. Terzopoulos. Physically-based and probabilistic modeling for computer vision. In B. C. Vemuri, editor, *Proc. SPIE 1570, Geometric Methods in Computer Vision*, pages 140–152, San Diego, CA, July 1991. Society of Photo-Optical Instrumentation Engineers.

[24] D. Terzopoulos and K. Waters. Physically-based facial modelling, analysis and animation. *J. Visualization and COmputer Animation*, 11(2), 1990.

[25] S. Ullman and R. Basri. Recognition by linear combinations of models. *IEEE Trans. Pattern Analysis and Machine Intelligence*, 13(10):992–1006, 1991.

[26] C. Ware and D.R. Jessome. Using the bat: a six-dimensional mouse for object placement. In *Proc. Graphics Interface*, pages 119–124, 1988.

[27] L. Williams. Performance-driven facial animation. In *Proc. Siggraph*, pages 235–242. ACM, 1990.

## A. Matrices $M, W$ for rigid planar shape

Matrices $M, W$ convert B-spline control points $(\mathbf{X}, \mathbf{Y})$ to and from

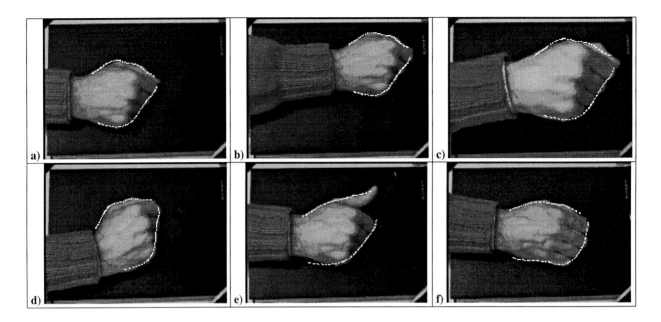

**Figure 6: The unadorned hand as a 3D mouse.** *A hand in its home position (a) can move on the $xy$-plane of the table (b) to act as a regular mouse but can also rise in the $z$ direction (c) and the zooming effect is picked and used to compute $z$. Rotation can also be tracked (d). Note that measured affine distortions in the image plane are straightforwardly translated back into 3D displacements and rotations, as the demonstration of hand-controlled 3D motion on the accompanying video shows. Nonrigid motion tracking can be used to pick up signals. For instance (e) signals a button-press and (f) signals the analogue of lifting a conventional mouse to reposition it.*

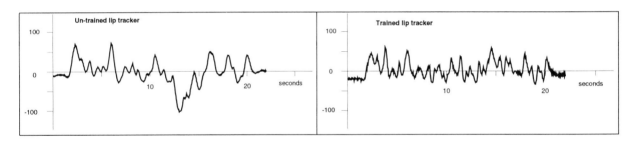

**Figure 7: Trained lip tracker.** *Training a tracker for side-on viewing of speaking lips greatly enhances tracking performance. The graphs show plots from the default and trained filters respectively of one deformation component of the lips during connected speech. The component corresponds to the degree to which the mouth is open — the space of deformations spanned by the first two templates in figure 4. Note the considerable loss of detail in the default filter, and occasional overshoots, compared with the trained filter. (The sentence spoken here was "In these cases one would like to reduce the dependence of a sensory information processing algorithm on these constraints if possible.".)*

the affine 6-vector $\mathbf{Q}$ representation, and are defined to be:

$$W = \begin{pmatrix} 1 & 0 & \overline{\mathbf{X}} & 0 & 0 & \overline{\mathbf{Y}} \\ 0 & 1 & 0 & \overline{\mathbf{Y}} & \overline{\mathbf{X}} & 0 \end{pmatrix}$$

and

$$M = (W^T \mathcal{H} W)^{-1} W^T \mathcal{H}$$

where $N_c$-vectors $\mathbf{0}$ and $\mathbf{1}$ are defined by:

$$\mathbf{0} = (0,0,..,0)^T \quad \mathbf{1} = (1,1,..,1)^T.$$

and

$$\mathcal{H} = \int_0^N \begin{pmatrix} 1 & 0 \\ 0 & 1 \end{pmatrix} \otimes (\mathbf{B}(s)\mathbf{B}(s)^T)\, ds.$$

See also [7].

## B. Calculating the gain

Filter gain $K$ is calculated by iterating to convergence the "discrete Ricatti equation" [13] for this problem, which can be shown to be:

$$P_{n+1} = \left( (AP_n A^T + C')^{-1} + \frac{1}{\sigma^2} J' \right)^{-1}$$

where $C' = \begin{pmatrix} 0 & 0 \\ 0 & C \end{pmatrix}$ and $J' = \begin{pmatrix} J & 0 \\ 0 & 0 \end{pmatrix}$

and $J = \sum_{m=0}^{m=NN_\nu} \mathbf{H}(m/N_\nu)^T \mathbf{H}(m/N_\nu)$

to obtain $P_\infty$. Any reasonable initial condition, such as $P_0 = 0$ will do, and the equation is bound to converge provided the learned dynamics represented by the matrix $A$ are stable. Finally the steady state Kalman Gain for the measurement $\mathbf{Z}$ can be shown to be $K = (1/\sigma^2)P_\infty$.

# Accelerated MPEG Compression of Dynamic Polygonal Scenes

Dan S. Wallach
dwallach@cs.princeton.edu

Sharma Kunapalli
sgk@cs.princeton.edu

Michael F. Cohen
mfc@cs.princeton.edu

Department of Computer Science
Princeton University

## Abstract

This paper describes a methodology for using the matrix-vector multiply and scan conversion hardware present in many graphics workstations to rapidly approximate the optical flow in a scene. The optical flow is a 2-dimensional vector field describing the on-screen motion of each pixel. An application of the optical flow to MPEG compression is described which results in improved compression with minimal overhead.

**CR Categories and Subject Descriptors:** I.2.10 [Artificial Intelligence]: *Vision and Scene Understanding*; I.3.3 [Computer Graphics]: *Picture/Image Generation*; I.3.7 [Computer Graphics]: *Three-Dimensional Graphics and Realism*; I.4.2 [Image Processing]: *Compression (coding)*

**Additional Key Words:** MPEG; optical flow; motion prediction.

## 1 Introduction

The hardware based transformation, scan conversion and Gouraud shading interpolation in modern graphics workstations have been used for purposes beyond their original intent. Another use is described here, that of "rendering" an *optical flow* image[1], that is, an image in which the color of each pixel represents the motion occurring at that location in the image.

Optical flow has been used in computer vision [5, 8] and video compression [6]. It could also be useful for temporal anti-aliasing, providing information for the temporal sampling pattern [12] and for computing the *morph map* as discussed in [2]. After a short discussion of the optical flow computation itself, this paper outlines experiments using the motion information to enhance MPEG compression[2]. An application for this technology would be a networked *game server* in which players with machines containing low-cost MPEG decompression hardware are connected to a high speed graphics server over low bandwidth lines.

Computing the optical flow directly from an image sequence usually requires expensive search algorithms to match corresponding pixels. The approach taken here assumes the input has a polygonal representation and is being rendered on a frame buffer. The flow of vertices can then be calculated by taking the difference between past and present screen coordinates and encoding this information in the color channels. Gouraud shading then rapidly

---

[1] The term *motion field* is sometimes used to distinguish actual motion from apparent motion, e.g., a smooth shiny ball spinning in place in an otherwise static environment is moving but the motion won't be visible.

[2] CAD-based geometrical information has been used in other compression methods [3], however, with the increasing acceptance of the MPEG standard, there is interest in improving MPEG encoding itself.

produces an approximate rendering of the optical flow of each pixel. Workstations equipped with texture mapping hardware can create a more accurate optical flow image.

A significant component of MPEG video compression is motion compensation, enabling one block of an image to point at a similar block in a previous (or future) frame. The optical flow field describes the location of each pixel in a previous frame, and thus provides a good starting point for finding a matching pixel block; using this technique reduces the search range necessary to achieve a desired level of compression.

## 2 Rendering the Optical Flow

When most graphics hardware renders a polygon with local shading, the colors are computed from lighting information at each vertex, and then bi-linearly interpolated across the polygon. Like-

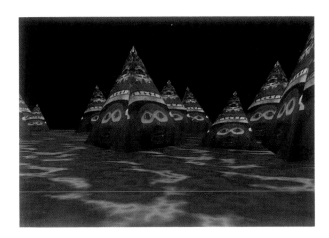

**Figure 1**: Frame from textured test-image sequence.

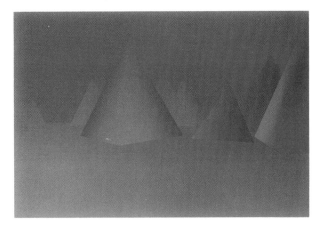

**Figure 2**: Optical flow image between two frames.

wise, for rendering the optical flow field, the optical flow vector is computed for each vertex, encoded as a color, and bi-linearly interpolated across the polygon using the same hardware. This requires knowing the transformation matrices which apply to each point in the previous frame as well as the current frame.

The Gouraud interpolation approach proceeds as follows. For each object, or group of polygons rendered with the same transformation matrix, the previous transformation matrices are saved so differences from them can be computed later. Let $M$ and $M'$ be the current and previous transformation matrices from world coordinates to screen coordinates. Ignoring clipping for the moment, a vertex $v$ is transformed by multiplying by $M$, and dividing by $w$ for the perspective transformation. The optical flow for a vertex going from transformation $M$ to $M'$ is

$$\Delta v_{\mathrm{screen}} = X(v, M) - X(v, M')$$

where $X(v, M)$ represents the transformation operator. Unfortunately, $\Delta v_{\mathrm{screen}} \neq X(v, M - M')$ since $M - M'$ may produce a zero perspective divide term $w$, causing division by zero. Using two 8-bit channels, $\Delta v_{\mathrm{screen}} = (\Delta x, \Delta y)$ is coded into RGB space as:

$$(R, G, B) = (\Delta x + 127, \Delta y + 127, 127)$$

clipping large motions at 0 and 255 (i.e., a maximum of 127 pixels of motion per frame).

A Gouraud-shaded polygon is rendered with these colors at the vertices. Since the geometry and viewing transformations are the same as in normal rendering, polygons occupy the same pixels on the screen. The number of polygons remains the same, thus the optical flow is rendered in a single frame time (Figure 3).

Clipping causes a problem for polygons with some off-screen vertices. If a vertex is near or behind the viewer, the screen coordinates (and optical flow vectors) become extremely large or change sign. To ensure the accuracy of the optical flow vectors, the renderer may subdivide polygons near the viewer. For the experiment in this paper, the floor is subdivided into a regular grid and the pyramids are not subdivided.

However, Gouraud interpolation is only an approximation of the exact answer, for similar reasons that Gouraud shading based on scanline order only approximates object space bilinear interpolation (e.g., it is not rotationally invariant). To be more precise, each pixel would need to be transformed from the current frame to the previous frame, rather than just the vertices. The function to compute this transformation is a *projective mapping*[4].

Projective texture mapping normally utilizes an affine transformation from homogeneous coordinates to texture coordinates. For each polygon, the texture coordinates of the vertices are transformed by the texture matrix resulting in the indices into the texture map. These are then used during rasterization to pull out the texture value at each screen pixel. We can modify this process to encode the pixel's previous location as its texture value. The optical flow vector will then simply be the difference between this value and the new pixel location. This process can be accomplished using current texture mapping hardware [1] in real-time.

The algorithm runs as follows: the polygon's previous and current homogeneous coordinates are used to derive a texture matrix which maps between them. Thus, given the current coordinates, this matrix provides the homogeneous coordinates of the previous frame, and these are then used by the texture mapping hardware to find the "texture coordinates". Each polygon is rendered with an *identity texture*, which maps texture coordinates $(u, v) \rightarrow (u, v, 0)$, a color which directly encodes the texture coordinate[3]. The result is that each pixel's color encodes the screen location of that pixel in a previous frame. The optical flow field, $(\Delta x, \Delta y)$, is then found by subtracting off the pixel location from its encoded value. This too can be done in current hardware with an accumulation buffer:

$$\Delta v_{x,y} = \mathrm{Screen}_{x,y} - (x, y)$$

where $(x, y)$ is simply the identity texture itself. Computing the optical flow correctly with projective mapping is only practical with significant hardware support, but clipping and large polygons will be handled properly.

In general, accurately rendering the optical flow of a polygon is equivalent in complexity to rendering a texture-mapped polygon, and any techniques developed for texture map rendering may be applied to optical flow rendering.

## 3  Some MPEG Basics

This section focuses on the *motion estimation* component of MPEG. For introductory information on MPEG, see [6, 7, 10]. MPEG exploits the general similarity of adjacent picture frames by using *motion vectors* for each $16 \times 16$ pixel *macroblock* to point to another $16 \times 16$ block in a previous or future frame. The MPEG coder records the motion vector itself and the *differences* between previous and current pixels. Since many of the pixels will be largely the same, the difference will contain many zeros or small terms, requiring fewer bits to encode.

MPEG has three frame types:

- *I* (intra-coded or reference) frames are compressed without references to other frames. As a result they consume more bits, but have less error.

- *P* (or predicted) frames contain motion estimations from the preceding *I* frame, along with the difference between the two blocks. Because the difference is usually small, it compresses well.

- *B* (or bi-directional) frames have motion estimations from the nearest *P* or *I* frames in their past *and* future. The difference from the current block to the average of the past and future blocks is encoded. In addition, *B* frames are generally encoded with higher *quantization*, which increases compression at the cost of accuracy.

A typical MPEG sequence will follow a repeating pattern of these frame types such as *I*, *IPPP*, or *IBBPBB*. Figure 4 shows the dependencies in the *IBBPBB* pattern. An arrow from frame A to frame B implies that each macroblock in A should contain a motion vector describing a similar macroblock in B.

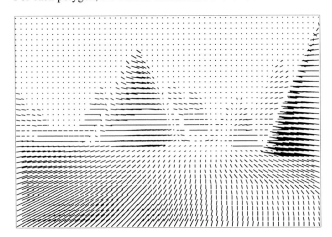

**Figure 3**: Vector-interpretation of an optical flow.

---

[3] Rendering images larger than $256 \times 256$ will require a framebuffer with more than 8 bits per channel to represent the motion vectors with sufficient precision.

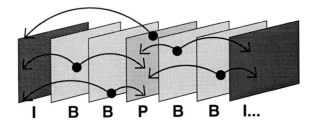

**Figure 4**: MPEG motion vector dependencies.

The literature on motion searching [9] discusses methods to reduce the number and/or cost of comparisons between blocks. Some well-known search techniques are:

- *Exhaustive* – select the best motion vector within a $2N \times 2N$ pixel square of pixels (best compression, but slow)

- *Logarithmic*[6] – first check the corners, sides, and center of a $2N \times 2N$ pixel square range, and recursively (until $N = 0$) repeat the procedure with the best result as the new center and $N$ decremented (fast, but may overlook good solutions)

- *Subsample*[13] – rather than comparing whole macroblocks, only a fraction of the pixels in each macroblock are compared (fast, but may mistake a bad match as a good one)

Under normal circumstances, each algorithm centers its search range on the origin, assuming equal likelihood of motion in any direction.

## 4 Optical Flow and MPEG Compression

Given optical flow information, any of the search algorithms from the previous section can be improved by centering their search at the optical flow's *predicted motion*. This technique should improve *any* block matching scheme with limited search range.

Modifications to the Berkeley MPEG encoder's [11] exhaustive search algorithm were made to measure the effects of shifting the center of the search range. The motion prediction for a macroblock is taken as the *mode* of the associated $16 \times 16$ array of optical flow data. The *mode* rather than the *mean* is used since, if a macroblock contains two or more polygons, the polygon with the largest area is likely to provide a better motion estimate than an average of the two.

Test data from a 30-frame sequence of motion through an environment was used (Figure 1). Experiments included flat-shaded versus textured polygons, and static versus dynamic geometry. The optical flow buffers were rendered with the Gouraud-interpolation method. Camera motion was the same in all cases. Compression was measured as a function of search range[4].

The predicted motion produced modest improvement with flat-shaded input, however, with textures the motion prediction compressed significantly better than the other methods (Figure 6). As the search range increases, the two methods converge as expected (i.e., if searching the whole image, any method could find the best match).

## 5 Conclusion

A fast means to compute approximate optical flow images of polygonal data with minimal changes to the standard graphics pipeline has been demonstrated. One application of the results, MPEG compression, has been shown to benefit from this additional information, particularly for textured scenes.

[4] More results are available through the World Wide Web (e.g.: *xmosaic*). http://www.cs.princeton.edu/grad/dwallach/sg94

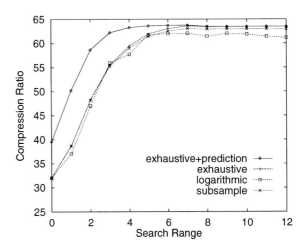

**Figure 5**: Compression vs. search range for texture-mapped polygons with static scenery using an IPPP pattern.

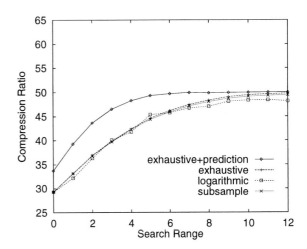

**Figure 6**: Textured polygons, dynamic scenery, IPPP pattern.

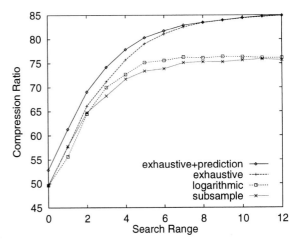

**Figure 7**: Flat-shaded polygons, dynamic scenery, IPPP pattern.

The use of texture mapping hardware to handle the projective mapping of motion coordinates to colors needs to be investigated to fully take advantage of current workstation capabilities.

## Acknowledgements

This work has relied to great extent on the publically available MPEG encoder from U. C. Berkeley. Pat Hanrahan helped work through the equivalence of the mapping to the texture mapping problem. Philip Greenspun provided the Alaskan totem pole picture. The authors would like to thank the reviewers for their excellent suggestions leading to the current paper.

## References

[1] Akeley, K. RealityEngine Graphics. In *Computer Graphics* (Aug. 1993), pp. 109–116.

[2] Chen, S. E., and Williams, L. View Interpolation for Image Synthesis. In *Computer Graphics* (Aug. 1993), pp. 279–288.

[3] Guenter, B. K., Yun, H. C., and Mersereau, R. M. Motion Compensated Compression of Computer Animation Frames. In *Computer Graphics* (Aug. 1993), pp. 297–304.

[4] Heckbert, P. S. Fundamentals of Texture Mapping and Image Warping. Master's thesis, University of California, Berkeley, June 1989.

[5] Horn, B. K. P. *Robot Vision*. MIT Press, 1986.

[6] Coded Representation of Picture, Audio and Multimedia/Hypermedia Information. Committee Draft of Standard ISO/IEC 11172, Dec. 1991.

[7] Legall, D. MPEG – A Video Compression Standard for Multimedia Applications. *CACM 34*, 4 (Apr. 1991), 46–58.

[8] Nagel, H. On the Estimation of Optical Flow: Relations Between Different Approaches And Some New Results. In *Artificial Intelligence* (1987), vol. 33, pp. 299–324.

[9] Orchard, M. A Comparison of Techniques for Estimating Block Motion in Image Sequence Coding. In *Proceedings SPIE, Visual Comm. and Image Proc. I* (1989), vol. 1199, pp. 248–258.

[10] Patel, K., Smith, B. C., and Rowe, L. A. Performance of a Software MPEG Video Decoder. In *Multimedia '93 Proceedings* (Aug. 1993), ACM, Addison-Wesley, pp. 75–82.

[11] Rowe, L. A., Gong, K., Patel, K., and Wallach, D. MPEG-1 Video Software Encoder. Anonymous ftp **mm-ftp.cs.berkeley.edu:/pub/multimedia/mpeg/ mpeg_encode-1.3.tar.Z**, Mar. 1994.

[12] Shinya, M. Spatial Anti-aliasing for Animation Sequences with Spatio-temporal Filtering. In *Computer Graphics* (Aug. 1993), pp. 289–296.

[13] Zaccarin, A., and Liu, B. Fast Algorithms for Block Motion Estimation. In *Proceedings ICASSP'92* (Mar. 1992), pp. III–449 – III–452.

# Improving Static and Dynamic Registration in an Optical See-through HMD

Ronald Azuma[§]          Gary Bishop[†]

Department of Computer Science
University of North Carolina at Chapel Hill

## Abstract

In Augmented Reality, see-through HMDs superimpose virtual 3D objects on the real world. This technology has the potential to enhance a user's perception and interaction with the real world. However, many Augmented Reality applications will not be accepted until we can accurately register virtual objects with their real counterparts. In previous systems, such registration was achieved only from a limited range of viewpoints, when the user kept his head still. This paper offers improved registration in two areas. First, our system demonstrates accurate static registration across a wide variety of viewing angles and positions. An optoelectronic tracker provides the required range and accuracy. Three calibration steps determine the viewing parameters. Second, dynamic errors that occur when the user moves his head are reduced by predicting future head locations. Inertial sensors mounted on the HMD aid head-motion prediction. Accurate determination of prediction distances requires low-overhead operating systems and eliminating unpredictable sources of latency. On average, prediction with inertial sensors produces errors 2-3 times lower than prediction without inertial sensors and 5-10 times lower than using no prediction at all. Future steps that may further improve registration are outlined.

**CR Categories and Subject Descriptors**: I.3.1 [**Computer Graphics**]: Hardware Architecture — *three-dimensional displays*; I.3.7 [**Computer Graphics**]: Three-Dimensional Graphics and Realism — *virtual reality*
**Additional Key Words and Phrases**: Augmented Reality, registration, calibration

## 1   Motivation

Head-Mounted Displays (HMDs) and Virtual Environments have been a subject of great interest in the past few years. Less attention has been paid to the related field of Augmented Reality, despite its similar potential. The difference between Virtual Environments and Augmented Reality is in their treatment of the real world. Virtual Environments immerse a user inside a virtual world that completely replaces the real world outside. In contrast, Augmented Reality uses *see-through HMDs* that let the user see the real world around him. See-through HMDs augment the user's view of the real world by overlaying or compositing three-dimensional virtual objects with their real world counterparts. Ideally, it would seem to the user that the virtual and real objects coexisted. Since Augmented Reality supplements, rather than supplants, the real world, it opens up a different class of applications from those explored in Virtual Environments.

Augmented Reality applications attempt to enhance the user's perception and interaction with the real world. Several researchers have begun building prototype applications to explore this potential. A group at Boeing uses a see-through HMD to guide a technician in building a wiring harness that forms part of an airplane's electrical system [6][33]. Currently, technicians use large physical guide boards to construct such harnesses, and Boeing needs several warehouses to store all of these boards. Such space might be emptied for better use if this application proves successful. Other construction and repair jobs might be made easier if instructions were available, not in the form of manuals with text and 2D pictures, but as 3D drawings superimposed upon real objects, showing step-by-step the tasks to be performed. Feiner and his group demonstrated this in a laser printer maintenance application [11]. Feiner's group is also exploring displaying virtual documents in a sphere around the user, providing a much larger workspace than an ordinary workstation monitor. Medical applications might also benefit from Augmented Reality. A group at UNC scanned a fetus inside a womb with an ultrasonic sensor, then displayed a three-dimensional representation of that data in the same physical location as the fetus [4]. The goal is to provide a doctor with "X-ray vision," enabling him to gaze directly into the body. Conceptually, anything not detectable by human senses but detectable by machines might be transduced into something that we can sense and displayed inside a see-through HMD. Robinett speculates that ultimately Augmented Reality is about augmentation of human perception, about making the invisible visible (or hearable, feelable, etc.) [29].

While promising, Augmented Reality is barely at the demonstration phase today, and its full potential will not be realized until several technical challenges are overcome. One of the most basic is the registration problem. The real and virtual objects must be properly

§† CB 3175 Sitterson Hall; UNC; Chapel Hill, NC 27599
§   (919) 962-1848        azuma@cs.unc.edu
†   (919) 962-1886        gb@cs.unc.edu

Figure 1: Wooden frame for calibration and registration

Figure 2: View seen in HMD, virtual axes on real frame

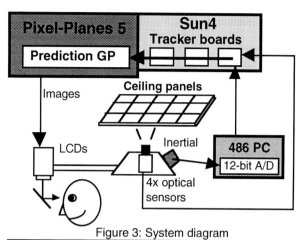

Figure 3: System diagram

aligned with respect to each other, or the illusion that the two coexist will be compromised. This is difficult to do because of the precision required. The human visual system is very good at detecting even small misregistrations, due to the resolution of the fovea and the sensitivity of the visual system to differences. A more tractable bound is provided by the relatively low resolution of the displays in modern HMDs. Errors of just a few pixels are noticeable.

Some applications have strict requirements for accurate registration. For example, imagine a surgeon wearing a see-through HMD displaying virtual objects that identify where and where not to make incisions. Unless the registration errors are kept below a few millimeters, the surgeon is not likely to trust the equipment. Without good registration, Augmented Reality may never be accepted in serious applications.

What causes registration errors? The main sources are:
- Distortion in the HMD optics
- Mechanical misalignments in the HMD
- Errors in the head-tracking system
- Incorrect viewing parameters (field of view, tracker-to-eye position and orientation, interpupillary distance)
- End-to-end system latency

The first four categories may be classified as *static* errors, because they cause registration errors even when the user keeps his head completely still. The 5th category, end-to-end latency, we call a *dynamic* error, because it has no effect until the user moves his head.

No one has achieved perfect registration with a see-through HMD. The current demonstrated state-of-the-art, as reported in the text and pictures of [4][11][18] achieves static errors on the order of 0.5 inches for an object at arm's length away from the HMD, from a small number of viewpoints. Dynamic errors can be much larger. With an end-to-end system latency of 100 ms, and a moderate head rotation rate of 100 degrees/sec, the angular dynamic error will be 10 degrees. At arm's length, this results in registration errors of 5 inches.

## 2  Contribution

This paper describes a system we built that tackles three of the main sources of registration errors: the head tracker, the determination of viewing parameters, and dynamic errors caused by system latency. We demonstrate improved static and dynamic registration as follows:

*Improved static registration:* Pictures and videos of existing Augmented Reality systems show registration from only a small number of viewpoints. The user is not allowed to translate or rotate the HMD very far from the initial viewpoint. There are two reasons for this limitation. First, most commercially available head-tracking systems do not provide sufficient accuracy and range to permit such movement without greatly increasing the static registration errors. Second, determining viewing parameters that work from just one viewpoint is much easier than determining parameters that work from many different viewpoints. We show that parameters yielding good registration from one viewpoint may result in static errors of a few inches at another viewpoint.

Our system is capable of robust static registration: keeping a virtual and real object closely aligned across many widely spaced view-

points and view directions. We use a custom optoelectronic head tracker that provides sufficient range and accuracy. We also developed calibration techniques for determining the viewing parameters. The robust static registration is demonstrated by several still photographs taken from a single video sequence where the user walked 270 degrees around the registration object.

*Improved dynamic registration:* To reduce dynamic errors caused by the end-to-end latency in the system, we use predictive tracking techniques that guess where the user's head will be in the future. We equipped the see-through HMD with inertial sensors to aid head-motion prediction. A method for autocalibrating the orientation of the sensors on the user's head, along with other parameters, was developed. The reduction in dynamic error for three different motion runs is listed in a table.

The rest of the paper is organized as follows: first we give a brief overview of our system. Next, we describe and evaluate the static registration procedure. Then we do the same for dynamic registration. Each section describes problems encountered and points out limitations. The interested reader will find supplementary materials available in the CD-ROM version of this paper and many more details about our work in a technical report (the first author's dissertation) to be released later in 1994 by UNC Chapel Hill.

The main implications of our work are:
- Robust static registration within a few mm is possible, but it requires trackers with higher accuracy than Virtual Environment applications demand.
- Inertial-aided predictors can greatly reduce dynamic registration errors. On average, inertial-based prediction is 5-10 times more accurate than doing no prediction and 2-3 times more accurate than a representative non-inertial predictor.
- Augmented Reality systems that use predictive tracking require low-overhead operating systems and the elimination of unpredictable sources of latency.

## 3  System

Our system uses an optical see-through HMD. Its position and orientation are measured by an optoelectronic tracking system, and the images are generated by the Pixel-Planes 5 graphics engine. Readings taken from inertial sensors mounted on the HMD are digitized by an A/D board in a 486 PC. Figure 10 shows the overall setup, and Figure 3 provides a system diagram.

The optical see-through HMD [16] is shown in Figure 8. Optical combiners placed in front of both eyes overlay images on top of the user's view of the real world. The displays are color LCD monitors containing 340x240 pixels each. The field-of-view in each eye is approximately 30 degrees. We chose an optical see-through approach because it does not delay the user's view of the real world (see Section 7).

Tracking is provided by four optical sensors mounted on the back of the HMD, as seen in Figure 8. These are aimed upwards at an array of infrared LEDs mounted in ceiling panels above the user's head. By sighting several LEDs, and given the known geometry of the sensors on the head and the known locations of the beacons in the ceiling, the system is able to compute the position and orientation of the user's head. The data collection and processing are performed by three single-board 68030 and i860-based computers installed in the VME chassis of a Sun4 host [36].

The inertial sensors consist of three Systron Donner QRS-11 angular rate gyroscopes and three Lucas NovaSensor NAS-CO26 linear accelerometers. The gyros measure angular rates within the range of $\pm300$ degrees/second, and the accelerometers detect acceleration within $\pm2$ $g$. A 12-bit A/D board (National Instruments AT-MIO-16D) in a 486 PC digitizes the signals. To minimize noise, we built special power regulation circuits, used shielded twisted-pair wire, differential-mode A/Ds, and analog prefilters. A Bit3 bus extender sends the digitized readings to the optoelectronic tracker boards in the Sun4.

The virtual images are generated by Pixel-Planes 5 (Pxpl5), a highly parallel graphics engine consisting of i860-based Graphics Processors (GPs) to do geometry transformations and Renderer boards that rasterize primitives [14]. One of the GPs is used to run our prediction routine. The computed head positions and orientations from the optoelectronic tracker and the measured inertial signals are fed to this GP, which uses them to estimate future head locations. The prediction GP also converts the predicted head locations into view matrices that the rest of Pxpl5 uses to generate the graphic images the HMD-wearer sees. Since the normal Pxpl5 software is optimized for maximum throughput and not minimal latency, we use different rendering software written by Mark Olano and Jon Cohen that minimizes Pxpl5 latency [8].

Special care was taken to use fast communication paths and low-overhead operating systems. Interprocessor communication is through shared memory, across Bit3 bus extenders, or through the 640 MByte/sec ring network within Pixel-Planes 5. UNIX is avoided except for initial setup and non-time-critical tasks, like reading buttons. This is discussed more in Section 5.3.

The end-to-end system latency varies from 50-70 ms, with 15-30 ms coming from the tracker, ~12 ms from the predictor, and 16.67 ms from Pxpl5. The rest comes from communication paths and delays caused by the asynchronous nature of our system.

Recording the images that the user sees inside the HMD to create the pictures in this paper was done by mounting a video camera in the right eye of a bust. The HMD was tied to this bust, then carried around.

# 4 Static registration

## 4.1 Previous work

Registration of real and virtual objects is not limited to see-through HMDs. Special effects artists seamlessly blend computer-generated images with live footage for films and advertisements. The difference is in time and control. With film, one can spend hours on each frame, adjusting by hand if necessary, and each shot is carefully preplanned. In Augmented Reality we have no such control: the user looks where he wants to look, and the computer must respond within tens of milliseconds (ms).

Deering [10] demonstrated an impressive registration of a real and virtual ruler in a head-tracked stereo system. Registration is a somewhat easier task in head-tracked stereo vs. an HMD-based system because the images do not change nearly as much for the same amount of head translation or rotation [9].

An extensive literature of camera calibration techniques exists in the robotics and photogrammetry communities (see the references in [21] as a start). These techniques digitize one or more pictures of an object of fixed and sometimes unknown geometry, locate features on the object, then use mathematical optimizers to solve for the viewing parameters. However, it is not clear how to directly apply these techniques to an *optical* see-through HMD, where no camera exists. Asking a user to identify the locations of many different points simultaneously while keeping his head still was judged too difficult to be reliable.

We have already mentioned several papers on Augmented Reality, but most focus on applications rather than on the details of calibration and registration. The sole exceptions are [6][18]. We compare our results with theirs in Section 4.4. Methods used to calibrate helmet-mounted sights on helicopter gunships provided the initial inspiration for our approach.

## 4.2 Problem statement

We reduce the problem to one real object, one set of virtual objects, and a desired registration linking the two. The real object is a wooden frame (Figure 1). The virtual objects are three mutually orthogonal extruded squares that form a coordinate system. The goal is to register the intersection of the three virtual bars with the front left corner of the frame, where the three bars run along the edges that touch the corner (Figures 2 & 14). This task is a good registration test because it's easy to detect small position and orientation errors along the edges of the frame.

Determining parameters that accomplish this task robustly is harder than one might first think. The naive approach, tried by several people in our laboratory, is the following: put a real object at a known or unknown position, wear the see-through HMD, then manually adjust the viewing parameters and the location of the virtual object until the registration "looks right." This rarely yields robust registration, because parameters and locations that work at one viewpoint may generate large registration errors at another. Figure 9 illustrates this. The picture on the left shows good registration at the initial viewpoint. But the same parameters yield a few inches of registration error when used at a different viewpoint, as seen in the picture on the right.

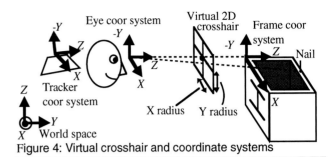

Figure 4: Virtual crosshair and coordinate systems

## 4.3 Procedure

Since camera calibration techniques seemed too difficult to apply in this domain, we thought of ways to directly measure the viewing parameters, using simple tasks that rely on geometric constraints. If the tasks are sensitive enough and our tracker is accurate enough, then this simple approach might work. We now describe these procedures that systematically determine the viewing parameters. The steps in order are:

- Measure the frame's location
- Determine the apparent center of the virtual image
- Measure the transformation between tracker space and eye space
- Measure the field-of-view (FOV)

We use only the right eye of our HMD, due to mechanical misalignments, color mismatches between the two display systems, and because a monocular display is sufficient to demonstrate registration.

*1) Frame measurement:* A digitization probe attached to a "hat" with four optical sensors returns the 3D position of the probe tip (Figure 13). We measure eight points on the frame edges where the red and green bars will lie, fit a pair of orthogonal lines through those points, and those determine the axis going down the third edge.

*2) Apparent center of virtual image:* The center of our 640x512 NTSC frame buffer need not be the center of the virtual image seen by the right eye, requiring off-center projections to properly render the images [12]. Assuming that the frame buffer covers the entire area visible through the optics, we can measure this center by drawing a 2D, non-head-tracked crosshair in the frame buffer (Figure 4). Four numbers specify this crosshair: the $(X,Y)$ center coordinate, and the $X$ and $Y$ radii. The user determines the center by adjusting the $X$ center and radius until the left and rightmost lines are equally spaced from the extreme visible edges of the display. This is tested by increasing the radius; both lines should disappear simultaneously or the center is incorrect. A similar procedure determines the $Y$ center. Our measured center is (330, 255), which differs from the frame buffer center by about 10 pixels.

*3) Eye->Tracker transformation:* This is measured by the boresight operation, where a user wearing the HMD looks straight down the left top edge of the frame with his right eye (Figure 4). A 0.25" diameter pipe sticking out along the edge (Figure 1) helps the user line up accurately. Simultaneously, he centers the virtual crosshair with the corner of the frame and aligns the horizontal and vertical crosshair lines with the edges of the frame (Figure 11). Then the Eye coordinate system has the same orientation as the Frame coordinate system, and the Z axes coincide.

The boresight establishes the following relationship:

$$Q_{wf} = Q_{we}$$

where we define $Q_{wf}$ to be the quaternion that rotates points and vectors from Frame space to World space, and $Q_{we}$ rotates from Eye space to World space [30]. Then the desired Eye->Tracker orientation $Q_{te}$ is computed by:

$$Q_{te} = Q_{tw} * Q_{we}$$
$$Q_{te} = (Q_{wt})^{-1} * Q_{wf}$$

where $Q_{wt}$ is what the head tracker returns, and $Q_{wf}$ is known from step 1.

The Eye->Tracker position offsets are measured by the boresight and one additional task. The position of the corner of the frame in World space is known, due to step 1. The position of the tracker origin in World space is returned by the head tracker. Therefore, we can draw a vector in World space from the corner of the frame to the tracker origin. Rotating this vector by $(Q_{te})^{-1}*Q_{tw}$ transforms it to Eye space. Since Eye space and Frame space share the same orientation and their $Z$ axes coincide, the $X$ and $Y$ values of the vector in Eye space are the $X$ and $Y$ Eye->Tracker offsets, in Eye space. To determine the $Z$ offset, we need one more operation. Two nails are on top of the frame, one in front and one in the rear (Figures 1, 4, & 14). While performing the boresight, the user must also position himself so the front nail covers the rear nail. A red LED mounted on the rear nail helps the user detect when this occurs. The known locations of these two nails identify a specific distance along the frame's $Z$ axis where the user's eye must be. Subtracting that from the corner->tracker vector in Eye space yields the $Z$ component of the Eye->Tracker offset.

The user performs two boresights: one from a few feet away for greater orientation sensitivity, and one less than a foot away (matching the two nails) for greater position sensitivity.

*4) FOV measurement:* It suffices to measure FOV along the vertical $Y$ direction in screen space, since scaling by the frame buffer's aspect ratio yields the horizontal FOV. The crosshair's $Y$ radius is set to 125 pixels so the top and bottom lines are easily visible. The user stands in front of the frame and lines up the top and bottom virtual crosshair lines with corresponding real lines drawn on the frame's front surface (Figures 12, 14). This forces the Eye space $X$ axis to be parallel to the Frame's $X$ axis. From the information in steps 1, 2 and 3, we can compute the locations of the real lines in Eye space. By intersecting the lines with the $X=0$ plane in Eye space, we reduce the geometry to 2D, as shown in Figure 5. We can always get right angles for $y1$ and $y2$ by using the line $Y=0$ as the basis. Then:

$$\beta1 = (-1.0)\ tan^{-1}(y1/z1)$$
$$\beta2 = tan^{-1}(y2/z2)$$

$z1$ and $z2$ are positive, $y2$ is positive and $y1$ is negative as drawn. This still works if the user's eye is above or below both of the real lines: the signs of $y1$, $y2$, $\beta1$ and $\beta2$ change appropriately. Since the crosshair does not cover the entire frame buffer height (512 pixels), we must scale the result to compute the total FOV ß:

$$\beta = (\beta1+\beta2)(512/(2*125))$$

The parameters measured in steps 1-4 are sufficient to implement registration of the virtual axes. Step 1 tells us where to put the virtual axes. The other parameters tell us how to generate view matrices for the right eye, given reports from the head tracker. The only unusual aspect is the need for an off-center projection.

### 4.4 Evaluation

These procedures, used with our optoelectronic tracker, generate parameters that work well from many different viewing angles and positions. To demonstrate this, we recorded a video sequence, using only one set of parameters, of a user walking around and looking at the corner of the frame from many different places. If space allows, excerpts from this will be on the CD-ROM. At several places during the run, the HMD was kept still. These viewpoints are identified by the numbered circles in Figure 14, which correspond with the still images in Figures 2 and 15-22. The red and green bars have a 5x5 mm$^2$ cross-section, while the blue bar is 7x7 mm$^2$ since it's harder to see at long distances. Note that the corner and edges usually stay within the width of the extruded rectangles at the static viewpoints, which puts the registration within $\pm4$ mm for the red and green bars and $\pm5$ mm for the blue bar.

How do these results compare to the two previous works? Janin [18] takes a very different approach. He directly measures parameters with instruments and runs a camera calibration optimizer that requires the user to identify the location of ~20 object points from several different viewpoints. The best accuracy he achieves is $\pm12$mm. In contrast, step 3 of our procedure is similar to Caudell's [6] registration platform, which computes the Eye->Tracker position and orientation offset by having the user line up two circles and two lines. He does not provide any information on how accurate his static registration is, and his registration procedure lacks equivalents to our steps 2 and 4.

Registration accuracy depends on how successfully the user can complete the registration procedures. Users reported difficulty in keeping their heads still during the boresight and FOV operations, because of the weight of the HMD. To compensate, we use the most recent 60 tracker reports to compute each operation, averaging the

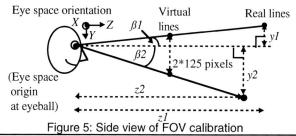

**Figure 5: Side view of FOV calibration**

results. To measure the remaining variation, we had three users repeat the boresight and FOV steps five times, moving their heads away in between each measurement. The average standard deviations in computed orientation, position, and FOV were 0.32 degrees, 4.8 mm (mostly along the $Z$ offset), and 0.1 degrees respectively. While not fatal, this variation does mean users may have to try the procedures more than once to achieve desired results.

## 5 Dynamic registration

The static registration demonstrated in Figures 15-22 holds only when the user stands still. When the user moves and rotates his head, the virtual objects appear to "swim around" the real objects, because of the system latency. The system requires time to measure the head's location, compute the corresponding images for that location, and display those in the HMD. This delay between measuring the head location and displaying the corresponding images means the images will be incorrect if the user moves his head during this delay. The virtual objects appear to lag behind their real counterparts, causing large dynamic registration errors.

To reduce these dynamic errors, we predict head motion. Instead of using the reported head location to generate the graphic images, we predict where the head will be when the displays get updated. If the prediction is correct, the computed virtual images will match reality at the time they are viewed.

### 5.1 Previous work

This paper is not the first to do head motion prediction. Two predict head position with head-tracked stereo displays [10][26]. Several HMD systems predict position and/or orientation by extrapolating readings from the head tracker [1][13][23][25][28][34][35]. Two papers [24][37] add angular accelerometers to a head tracker to aid orientation prediction.

How does our system differ from previous work? One difference is the application. We use prediction to aid registration of real and virtual objects in a see-through HMD and evaluate it in that context, something the other systems did not attempt. We also use gyros and accelerometers to aid *both* orientation and position prediction, which no previous system does. Our work also contributes the following:

- Evaluation of how much inertial sensors help
- Measurement and control of prediction distance
- Autocalibration of inertial sensor parameters

### 5.2 Procedure

We run separate predictors for orientation and position. Each consists of two parts: 1) an estimator that computes our best guess of the current position, velocity, and acceleration, and 2) a predictor that takes those guesses and extrapolates the desired distance into the future. Every time a tracker position and orientation measurement arrives, along with the corresponding inertial measurements, the estimator updates its guesses. Whenever Pxpl5 is ready to compute a new scene, the predictor sends it an output corresponding to the time when that scene will appear.

The estimator used is the Kalman filter [19], which many previous works also use. Space does not permit a detailed description of the filter; please read [22] for that. The Kalman filter is a linear estimator that minimizes the expected mean-square error. For orientation, we use a nonlinear variant called the Extended Kalman Filter (EKF). The filter requires some variables to be estimated, occasional noisy measurements of those variables, and a model of how those variables change with time in the absence of new measurements. It is optimal only if the model is an accurate reflection of reality and if the uncertainty in both the model and the measurements is accurately represented by additive white noise. Even though these assumptions are usually not met, the Kalman filter is still popular because it tends to perform well even with violated assumptions and its recursive formulation makes it efficient to compute.

Building a Kalman filter is easy. The difficult parts are determining an appropriate model and finding good noise parameters. For the latter task, we collected several runs of tracker and inertial data while the HMD-wearer performed "typical" head motions. Then we ran Powell's method [27] to search for parameters that minimized prediction error at a fixed prediction distance. In practice, this heuristic is able to find a fairly wide range of parameters that meet this goal.

We now outline the orientation estimator and predictor, later describing the translation case by how it differs from orientation.

### 5.2.1 Orientation

$\mathbf{Q} = [qw\ qx\ qy\ qz]^T, \quad \mathbf{W} = [w0\ w1\ w2]^T$

$\mathbf{X} = \begin{bmatrix} qw\ qx\ qy\ qz\ w0\ w1\ w2\ \dot{w0}\ \dot{w1}\ \dot{w2} \end{bmatrix}^T$

where $\mathbf{Q}$ is a quaternion rotating points and vectors from Tracker space to World space, $\mathbf{W}$ is omega, the angular rate of rotation in head space, and $\mathbf{X}$ is the $N \times 1$ state vector, where $N=10$. $\mathbf{P}$ is an $N \times N$ covariance matrix representing the uncertainty in $\mathbf{X}$. The initial value of $\mathbf{X}$ holds the starting quaternion and has zeroes for omega and its derivative. $\mathbf{P}$ is initially a diagonal matrix with zeroes in all off-diagonal positions, 1 for the first four diagonal terms (quaternion), and 50 for the remaining six diagonal terms (omega and its derivative). The initial covariances are large so the filter will replace the initial $\mathbf{X}$ with new measurements as they arrive.

$\mathbf{X}$ and $\mathbf{P}$ are maintained at the current time $t$. When each new measurement arrives, say at time $t1$, the filter performs two operations: 1) a time update that advances the state variables to time $t1$ based on the model, and 2) a measurement update that blends in the values measured at time $t1$.

*1) Time update:* A 4th-order Runge-Kutta ODE solver [27] integrates the derivatives of $\mathbf{X}$ and $\mathbf{P}$ from time $t$ to $t1$. The derivatives are:

$\dot{\mathbf{P}} = \mathbf{AP} + \mathbf{PA}^T + \mathbf{E}$
$\dot{\mathbf{X}} = a(\mathbf{X}, t)$  (1)

where $\mathbf{E}$ is an $N \times N$ matrix representing the noise in the model, and $\mathbf{A}$ is the $N \times N$ Jacobian matrix of the nonlinear function $a()$ that returns the derivatives of $\mathbf{X}$ by computing:

$\dot{\mathbf{Q}} = (0.5)(\mathbf{Q})(\mathbf{W}), \quad \dot{\mathbf{W}} = \begin{bmatrix} \dot{w0}\ \dot{w1}\ \dot{w2} \end{bmatrix}^T, \quad \ddot{\mathbf{W}} = 0$

where for the derivative of $\mathbf{Q}$, the multiplications are quaternion multiplications and $\mathbf{W}$ is written as a quaternion with zero $w$ term [7].

*2) Measurement update:* Measurement $\mathbf{Z}$ is an $F \times 1$ matrix, where $F=7$, that holds the measured quaternion $\mathbf{Q_m}$ and omega $\mathbf{W_m}$ reported by our sensors:

$\mathbf{Q_m} = [qw_m\ qx_m\ qy_m\ qz_m]^T, \quad \mathbf{W_m} = [w0_m\ w1_m\ w2_m]^T$

$\mathbf{Z} = [qw_m\ qx_m\ qy_m\ qz_m\ w0_m\ w1_m\ w2_m]^T$

The nonlinear function $h()$ generates $\mathbf{Z} = h(\mathbf{X}(t))$ as follows:

$\mathbf{Q_m} = \text{Normalize}(\mathbf{Q}), \quad \mathbf{W_m} = \mathbf{W}$

and the measurement update itself generates a new $\mathbf{X}$ and $\mathbf{P}$ given $\mathbf{Z}$ as follows:

$\mathbf{K} = \mathbf{PH}^T[\mathbf{HPH}^T + \mathbf{R}]^{-1}$
$\mathbf{P} = [\mathbf{I} - \mathbf{KH}]\mathbf{P}$
$\mathbf{X} = \mathbf{X} + \mathbf{K}[\mathbf{Z} - h(\mathbf{X})]$  (2)

where $\mathbf{K}$ is an $N \times F$ matrix called the Kalman gain, $\mathbf{H}$ is the $F \times N$ Jacobian matrix of the nonlinear function $h()$, and $\mathbf{R}$ is the $F \times F$ covariance matrix representing the noise in the measurements. At the end of the measurement update, we explicitly renormalize the quaternion part of $\mathbf{X}$. This isn't standard, but without it the quaternion terms quickly become unnormalized.

Noise matrices $\mathbf{E}$ and $\mathbf{R}$ are determined during the offline optimization. Both are diagonal matrices with zeroes in all off-diagonal terms. The first six diagonal terms of $\mathbf{E}$ are set to 0.004452: a tiny amount of noise added to the measured quaternion and omega to help the stability of the EKF. The remaining three diagonal terms

are set to 351.0. For $\mathbf{R}$, the first four diagonal terms are 0.0001, representing $\mathbf{Q_m}$ noise, and the remaining three diagonal terms are 0.005921, representing $\mathbf{W_m}$ noise.

*Predictor:* When the scene generator is ready to draw a new image, the predictor bases its extrapolation on the estimated values in $\mathbf{X}$. The predictor is the closed-form solution of integrating the quaternion and omega under the assumption that the derivative of omega is constant over the integration interval $t0$ to $t$. We define a 4x4 matrix $\mathbf{M}(t)$ as satisfying:

$\dot{\mathbf{Q}} = (0.5)(\mathbf{Q})(\mathbf{W}) = (\mathbf{M}(t))(\mathbf{Q})$

where $\mathbf{M}(t)$ essentially rewrites the quaternion multiplication as a matrix multiplication. The solution of this is:

$\mathbf{Q} = \big[(\mathbf{I})\cos(d) + (\mathbf{M})(\sin(d)\,/\,d)\big](\mathbf{Q_{t0}})$

where $\mathbf{Q_{t0}}$ is the original quaternion at time $t0$ and:

$d = \sqrt{a^2 + b^2 + c^2}$
$a = (0.5)\big[(t\text{-}t0)w0 + (0.5)(t - t0)^2(\dot{w0})\big]$
$b = (0.5)\big[(t\text{-}t0)w1 + (0.5)(t - t0)^2(\dot{w1})\big]$
$c = (0.5)\big[(t\text{-}t0)w2 + (0.5)(t - t0)^2(\dot{w2})\big]$

### 5.2.2 Position

The position estimation uses three separate linear Kalman filters, one each for X, Y and Z. Since they are identical in form, we look at the Y case only. This section lists the differences from the orientation case:

$\mathbf{X} = \begin{bmatrix} y\ \dot{y}\ \ddot{y} \end{bmatrix}^T$, where $N = 3$

Initial $\mathbf{X} = [y(0)\ 0\ 0]^T$, $\mathbf{P} = \begin{bmatrix} 2 & 0 & 0 \\ 0 & 500 & 0 \\ 0 & 0 & 500 \end{bmatrix}$

*Time update:* Replace (1) with:

$\dot{\mathbf{X}} = \mathbf{AX}$, where $\mathbf{A} = \begin{bmatrix} 0 & 1 & 0 \\ 0 & 0 & 1 \\ 0 & 0 & 0 \end{bmatrix}$

*Measurement update:* Replace (2) with:

$\mathbf{X} = \mathbf{X} + \mathbf{K}[\mathbf{Z} - \mathbf{HX}]$ where $\mathbf{H} = \begin{bmatrix} 1 & 0 & 0 \\ 0 & 0 & 1 \end{bmatrix}$

and Z is a 2x1 matrix ($F=2$) containing the reported Y position and the linear Y acceleration, in World space. Recovering linear acceleration from the accelerometers is complicated because they detect both linear and angular accelerations, plus gravity. Space does not permit an explanation here; please see Appendix A in the CD-ROM version of this paper for details.

$\mathbf{R} = \begin{bmatrix} .01 & 0 \\ 0 & .05 \end{bmatrix}, \quad \mathbf{E} = \begin{bmatrix} .007 & 0 & 0 \\ 0 & .007 & 0 \\ 0 & 0 & 2000000 \end{bmatrix}$

*Predictor:*

$y(t) = 0.5 * \ddot{y}(t0) * [t - t0]^2 + \dot{y}(t0) * [t - t0] + y(t0)$

### 5.2.3 Autocalibration

The inertial outputs must be rotated into the Tracker coordinate system, because the inertial sensor packs are tilted with respect to Tracker space. To perform these rotations, we must know the orientation of each pack on the HMD. While it is possible to mechanically build a mount that holds each pack at a specified orientation, it's easier to mount the packs at some rigid, but unknown, orientations, then measure them. Also, we would like to measure other sensor parameters, like the biases and scales. Autocalibration refers to mathematical methods that determine such constant parameters by applying geometrical constraints to collected data. One demonstration of this measured the locations of the beacons in the panels of our optoelectronic tracker [15]. Two such methods that we use with our inertial sensors are described in Appendix C on the CD-ROM. They are good at determining the orientation and biases, but not the scales.

### 5.3 Evaluation

From the user's perspective, prediction changes dynamic registration from "swimming around the real object" to "staying close."

| | Walkaround | | | Rotation | | | Swing | | |
|---|---|---|---|---|---|---|---|---|---|
| | Ang | Pos | Screen | Ang | Pos | Screen | Ang | Pos | Screen |
| No prediction (avg) | 1.3 | 14.3 | 9.3 | 2.2 | 6.6 | 33.6 | 2.5 | 17.8 | 37.1 |
| No prediction (peak) | 4.3 | 38.0 | 62.0 | 5.3 | 17.6 | 92.1 | 6.5 | 46.0 | 118.6 |
| Prediction without Inertial (avg) | 0.2 | 2.5 | 4.5 | 0.6 | 3.3 | 13.6 | 0.6 | 5.2 | 16.2 |
| Prediction without Inertial (peak) | 0.8 | 9.0 | 26.7 | 1.6 | 11.7 | 51.0 | 1.8 | 17.1 | 62.8 |
| Prediction with Inertial (avg) | 0.1 | 1.1 | 2.7 | 0.18 | 1.6 | 5.2 | 0.2 | 2.7 | 7.2 |
| Prediction with Inertial (peak) | 0.4 | 6.1 | 15.1 | 0.57 | 9.8 | 36.1 | 0.7 | 17.8 | 30.1 |

☐ Average error    ▨ Peak error

Angular error in degrees, Position error in mm, Screen error in pixels
Prediction distance set at 60 ms for all runs

Figure 6: Performance table of predictors on three motion datasets

Figure 7: Average error vs. prediction distance (Average screen error in pixels vs. Prediction distance in ms; —○— No pred, —●— Pred w/out inertial, —☐— Pred with inertial)

Without prediction, registration errors are large enough to strain the illusion that the real and virtual coexist. With prediction, the real and virtual objects stay close enough that the user perceives them to be together. Although the prediction is not perfect, it demonstrably improves the dynamic registration.

The predictor was run on three recorded motion datasets that are considered representative of this registration task. During each motion sequence, the user keeps the corner of the frame visible in his field-of-view. In the Walkaround dataset, the user walks slowly around the corner of the frame. The Rotation dataset has the user yawing, pitching, and circling his head while standing in place. The Swing dataset combines fast translation and rotation motion.

We compared our inertial-based predictor on these three datasets against doing no prediction and against a predictor that does not use inertial sensors. Directly comparing our predictor against previous work is difficult because our system is unique. Instead, we wrote a Kalman-filter-based predictor that is representative of many previous works that do not use inertial sensors. We ran that on the datasets, keeping all other variables constant. Three error metrics evaluate the accuracy of the predicted outputs vs. the actual tracker measurements. Angular error is computed in degrees as follows:

$$Q_{diff} = (Q_{actual})(Q_{predicted})^{-1}$$
$$angle\_err = (2) acos(Q_{diff}[qw])$$

Position error is the distance between the predicted and actual translations. Screen error combines orientation and translation errors by measuring the difference, in pixels, between the 2D projection of the real frame and the 2D point where the three virtual axes intersect on a hypothetical 512x512 screen. That is, it measures error in terms of what the user sees inside an HMD. The peak and average errors are summarized in Figure 6. On average, our inertial-based predictor is 5-10 times more accurate than doing no prediction and 2-3 times more accurate than prediction without inertial sensors.

Appendix B on the CD-ROM provides additional materials that demonstrate the results of prediction. Depending upon the space allocation on the CD-ROM, these may include error graphs, the motion datasets, and a short QuickTime video.

Figure 7 shows how the average screen-based errors for the Rotation run change as the prediction distance is varied from 25-200 ms. Again, inertial sensors clearly help. But what this graph does not show is that at prediction distances of ~100 ms or more, the jitter in the predicted outputs often reaches objectionable levels. In practice, the only solution is to keep system latency at tolerable levels, below ~80 ms. Thus, prediction cannot compensate for arbitrary amounts of latency; to be effective, it must be combined with efforts that minimize system lag. See Appendix D on the CD-ROM.

Because one cannot accurately predict without knowing how *far* to predict, our system requires accurate clocks and control over latency. Our tracker and graphics engine run asynchronously, requiring an estimation of the prediction distance at each iteration. Miscalculating the prediction distance by as little as 10 ms leads to visible registration errors. The clocks in the tracker boards and Pxpl5 are good to under a millisecond. Synchronization occurs through a message that takes less than 1 ms to make a round trip of all the processors. Since clocks that differ by one second every six hours

change by 8.3 ms every three minutes, skew rate compensation and occasional resynchronizations are performed. Controlling latency means removing all unpredictable delays, so we have direct communication paths not shared with other users, and we run a low-overhead operating system called VxWorks. Processes running on UNIX can suffer unbounded amounts of delay. Pauses of 60-200 ms are common occurrences on our Sun4 host. Therefore, we avoid UNIX for all time-critical tasks, directly injecting data from the tracker into Pxpl5 without going through the Sun4 host. While these steps reduce flexibility and make it harder to debug the system, they are needed to insure accurate prediction. Appendix E on the CD-ROM demonstrates the accuracy of our prediction distance estimation.

## 6 Additional lessons

Augmented Reality demands higher accuracy from head trackers than Virtual Environment applications do [3]. The main difficulty in duplicating our demonstration of static registration is in acquiring a head tracker that one can trust at long ranges. Wooden crates are easy to build, and the calibration techniques are straightforward and applicable to any tracking system or see-through HMD. But many commercially available trackers commonly used for Virtual Environments do not provide sufficient performance. For example, in our laboratory the widely used Polhemus magnetic trackers give distorted outputs at long distances because of the metal in the environment. A coworker experimenting with our optoelectronic tracker discovered a distortion that, when the tracker "hat" yaws 360 degrees about its origin, causes the reported positions to trace an ellipse about an inch wide. Since this distortion seems to be systematic, we were able to compensate for it. The fact that this distortion was undetectable in the Virtual Environment applications we run but was quite noticeable in Augmented Reality only serves to underscore the latter's need for accurate, long-range trackers.

The need to accurately measure time and avoid unpredictable sources of latency has serious ramifications on the design of effective Augmented Reality systems. Tracker measurements must be timestamped, a feature not provided by most commercial trackers. Almost all interactive graphics applications in our laboratory use UNIX because of its convenient programming environment. We build applications to the desired complexity, then we extract as much speed as possible. Flight simulators and some other researchers [20] take the opposite approach: set a minimal standard for performance, then see how much complexity can be supported. Since accurate prediction requires guaranteed performance, future Augmented Reality applications may need to take this latter approach.

## 7 Future work

Much work remains to further improve static registration. We only match one virtual object with one real object, where the real object is the calibration rig itself. Because our optoelectronic tracker loses accuracy when the sensors are not aimed at the ceiling beacons, we cannot move the HMD far away from the wooden frame, nor can we tilt the HMD far from horizontal. Our system is monocular; while our static registration procedure could be applied to both eyes, stereo displays involve additional issues like convergence that we have not addressed. We have not compensated for the optical distortion in the see-through HMD. Because our HMD has narrow field-of-view displays, this distortion is small and detectable only near the edges of the displays. We can eliminate this error by mapping the distortion, then predistorting the graphic images before displaying them [31].

More sophisticated prediction methods might further reduce dynamic registration errors. Adaptive methods that adjust to varying head motion deserve more exploration. Using a nonadaptive predictor is like trying to race a car at constant speed; slowing down on the curves and speeding up on the straight-aways will improve your time. Analyzing head motion for recognizable patterns or high-level characteristics may aid prediction. Other researchers have begun doing this [32], and Fitts' Law has been shown to apply to head motion [2][17].

Our work has not dealt with video see-through HMDs, where a video camera provides a view of the real world and the graphics are composited with the digitized images of the real world. With this class of see-through HMD, standard camera calibration techniques could determine the viewing parameters. And since the computer has digitized images of what the user sees, it may be possible to use image processing or computer vision techniques to detect features in these images and use them to aid registration. The disadvantage of this technology is that the video camera and digitization hardware impose inherent delays on the user's view of the real world. Therefore, even if the graphics are perfectly registered with the digitized images, a problem remains: the latency in the video stream will cause the user to perceive *both* the real and virtual objects to be delayed in time. While this may not be bothersome for small delays, it is a major problem in the related area of telepresence systems and may not be easy to overcome.

## Acknowledgements

This system would not exist without the contributions of many people. We thank Mike Bajura, Suresh Balu, Brad Bennett, Devesh Bhatnagar, Frank Biocca, Fred Brooks, Steve Brumback, Vern Chi, David Ellsworth, Mark Finch, Henry Fuchs, Jack Goldfeather, Stefan Gottschalk, David Harrison, Rich Holloway, John Hughes, Kurtis Keller, Jack Kite, Jonathan Marshall, Carl Mueller, Ulrich Neumann, Mark Olano, Jannick Rolland, Andrei State, Brennan Stephens, Russell Taylor, John Thomas, and Mark Ward for their advice and/or help with this project.

We thank the anonymous reviewers for their helpful comments and constructive criticisms.

Funding was provided by ONR contract N00014-86-K-0680, ARPA contract DABT63-93-C-C048, the NSF/ARPA Science and Technology Center for Computer Graphics and Visualization (NSF prime contract 8920219), and a Pogue Fellowship.

## References

[1] Albrecht, R. E. An adaptive digital filter to predict pilot head look direction for helmet-mounted displays. MS Thesis, University of Dayton, Ohio (July 1989).

[2] Andres, Robert O., and Kenny J. Hartung. Prediction of Head Movement Time Using Fitts' Law. *Human Factors 31,* 6 (1989), 703-713.

[3] Azuma, Ronald. Tracking Requirements for Augmented Reality. *CACM 36,* 7 (July 1993), 50-51.

[4] Bajura, Michael, Henry Fuchs, and Ryutarou Ohbuchi. Merging Virtual Objects with the Real World: Seeing Ultrasound Imagery within the Patient. *Proceedings of SIGGRAPH '92* (Chicago, IL, July 26-31, 1992), 203-210.

[5] Beer, Ferdinand P. and E. Russell Johnston, Jr. *Vector Mechanics for Engineers: Statics and Dynamics (5th ed).* McGraw-Hill, 1988.

[6] Caudell, Thomas P. and David W. Mizell. Augmented Reality: An Application of Heads-Up Display Technology to Manual Manufacturing Processes. *Proceedings of Hawaii International Conference on System Sciences* (Jan. 1992), 659-669.

[7] Chou, Jack C.K. Quaternion Kinematic and Dynamic Differential Equations. *IEEE Trans Robotics and Automation 8,* 1 (Feb. 1992), 53-64.

[8] Cohen, Jonathan, and Mark Olano. Low Latency Rendering on Pixel-Planes 5. UNC Chapel Hill Dept. of Computer Science technical report TR94-028 (1994).

[9] Cruz-Neira, Carolina, Daniel Sandin, and Thomas DeFanti. Surround-Screen Projection-Based Virtual Reality: The Design and Implementation of the CAVE. *Proceedings of SIGGRAPH '93* (Anaheim, CA,

[10] Deering, Michael. High Resolution Virtual Reality. *Proceedings of SIGGRAPH '92* (Chicago, IL, July 26-31, 1992), 195-202.

[11] Feiner, Steven, Blair MacIntyre, and Dorée Seligmann. Knowledge-Based Augmented Reality. *CACM 36,* 7 (July 1993), 53-62.

[12] Foley, James D., Andries van Dam, Steven K. Feiner, and John F. Hughes. *Computer Graphics: Principles and Practice, 2nd edition.* Addison-Wesley (1990), 238-239.

[13] Friedmann, Martin, Thad Starner, and Alex Pentland. Device Synchronization Using an Optimal Filter. *Proceedings of 1992 Symposium on Interactive 3D Graphics* (Cambridge, MA, 29 March - 1 April 1992), 57-62.

[14] Fuchs, Henry, John Poulton, John Eyles, et al. Pixel-Planes 5: A Heterogeneous Multiprocessor Graphics System Using Processor-Enhanced Memories. *Proceedings of SIGGRAPH '89* (Boston, MA, July 31-Aug 4, 1989), 79-88.

[15] Gottschalk, Stefan and John F. Hughes. Autocalibration for Virtual Environments Tracking Hardware. *Proceedings of SIGGRAPH '93* (Anaheim, CA, Aug 1-6, 1993), 65-72.

[16] Holmgren, Douglas E. Design and Construction of a 30-Degree See-Through Head-Mounted Display. UNC Chapel Hill Dept. of Computer Science technical report TR92-030 (July 1992).

[17] Jagacinski, Richard J., and Donald L. Monk. Fitts' Law in Two Dimensions with Hand and Head Movements. *Journal of Motor Behavior 17,* 1 (1985), 77-95.

[18] Janin, Adam L., David W. Mizell, and Thomas P. Caudell. Calibration of Head-Mounted Displays for Augmented Reality Applications. *Proceedings of IEEE VRAIS '93* (Seattle, WA, Sept. 18-22, 1993), 246-255.

[19] Kalman, R. E., and R. S. Bucy. New Results in Linear Filtering and Prediction Theory. *Trans ASME, J. Basic Eng., Series 83D* (Mar. 1961), 95-108.

[20] Krueger, Myron W. Simulation versus artificial reality. *Proceedings of IMAGE VI Conference* (Scottsdale, AZ, 14-17 July 1992), 147-155.

[21] Lenz, Reimar K. and Roger Y. Tsai. Techniques for Calibration of the Scale Factor and Image Center for High Accuracy 3-D Machine Vision Metrology. *IEEE Transactions on Pattern Analysis and Machine Intelligence 10,* 5 (Sept. 1988), 713-720.

[22] Lewis, Frank L. *Optimal Estimation.* John Wiley & Sons, 1986.

[23] Liang, Jiandong, Chris Shaw, and Mark Green. On Temporal-Spatial Realism in the Virtual Reality Environment. *Proceedings of the 4th annual ACM Symposium on User Interface Software & Technology* (Hilton Head, SC, Nov 11-13, 1991), 19-25.

[24] List, Uwe H. Nonlinear Prediction of Head Movements for Helmet-Mounted Displays. Technical report AFHRL-TP-83-45 [AD-A136590], Williams AFB, AZ: Operations Training Division (1984).

[25] Murray, P.M. and B. Barber. Visual Display Research Tool. *AGARD Conference Proceedings No. 408 Flight Simulation* (Cambridge, UK, 30 Sept. - 3 Oct. 1985).

[26] Paley, W. Bradford. Head-Tracking Stereo Display: Experiments and Applications. *SPIE Vol. 1669 Stereoscopic Displays and Applications III* (San Jose, CA, Feb. 12-13, 1992), 84-89.

[27] Press, William H., et al. *Numerical Recipes in C.* Cambridge University Press, 1988.

[28] Rebo, Robert. A Helmet-Mounted Virtual Environment Display System. MS Thesis, Air Force Institute of Technology (Dec 1988).

[29] Robinett, Warren. Synthetic Experience: A Proposed Taxonomy. *Presence 1,* 2 (Spring 1992), 229-247.

[30] Robinett, Warren, and Richard Holloway. Implementation of Flying, Scaling and Grabbing in Virtual Worlds. *Proceedings of 1992 Symposium on Interactive 3D Graphics* (Cambridge, MA, 29 March - 1 April 1992), 189-192.

[31] Robinett, Warren, and Jannick P. Rolland. A Computational Model for the Stereoscopic Optics of a Head-Mounted Display. *Presence 1,* 1 (Winter 1992), 45-62.

[32] Shaw, Chris and Jiandong Liang. An Experiment to Characterize Head Motion in VR and RR Using MR. *Proceedings of 1992 Western Computer Graphics Symposium* (Banff, Alberta, Canada, April 6-8, 1992), 99-101.

[33] Sims, Dave. New Realities in Aircraft Design and Manufacture. *IEEE CG&A 14,* 2 (March 1994), 91.

[34] Smith Jr., B. R. Digital head tracking and position prediction for helmet mounted visual display systems. *Proceedings of AIAA 22nd Aerospace Sciences Meeting* (Reno, NV, Jan. 9-12, 1984).

[35] So, Richard H. Y. and Michael J. Griffin. Compensating Lags in Head-Coupled Displays Using Head Position Prediction and Image Deflection. *Journal of Aircraft 29,* 6 (Nov-Dec 1992), 1064-1068.

[36] Ward, Mark, Ronald Azuma, Robert Bennett, Stefan Gottschalk, and Henry Fuchs. A Demonstrated Optical Tracker With Scalable Work Area for Head-Mounted Display Systems. *Proceedings of 1992 Symposium on Interactive 3D Graphics* (Cambridge, MA, 29 March - 1 April 1992), 43-52.

Aug. 1-6, 1993), 135-142.

[37]  Welch, Brian L., Ron Kruk, et al.  Flight Simulator Wide Field-of-View Helmet-Mounted Infinity Display System.  Technical report AFHRL-TR-85-59, Williams AFB, AZ, Operations Training Division (May 1986).

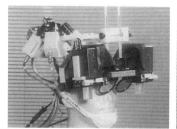

Figure 8: Front and back views of optical see-through HMD

Figure 9: Naive approach yields non-robust registration

Figure 10: Picture of overall system

Figure 11: Boresight view

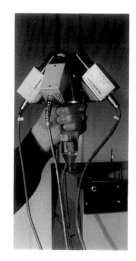

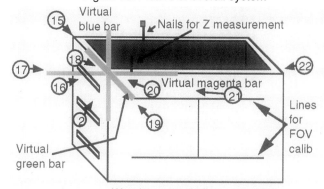

Figure 14: Wooden frame and static registration viewpoints

Figure 12: FOV calib          Figure 13: Measuring frame

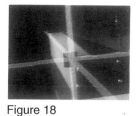

Figure 15          Figure 16          Figure 17          Figure 18

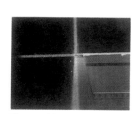

Figure 19          Figure 20          Figure 21          Figure 22

Figures 15-22: Static registration of virtual axes with real frame as seen inside the HMD from viewpoints specified in Figure 14

# A Virtual Environment and Model of the Eye for Surgical Simulation

Mark A. Sagar[1], David Bullivant[2], Gordon D. Mallinson[1], Peter J. Hunter[2]

**The University of Auckland, New Zealand**

Ian W. Hunter[3]

**McGill University, Canada**

## ABSTRACT

An anatomically detailed 3-D computer graphic model of the eye and surrounding face within a virtual environment has been implemented for use in a surgical simulator. The simulator forms part of a teleoperated micro-surgical robotic system being developed for eye surgery. The model has been designed to both visually and mechanically simulate features of the human eye by coupling computer graphic realism with finite element analysis.

The paper gives an overview of the system with emphasis on the graphical modelling techniques and a computationally efficient framework for representing anatomical details of the eye and for finite element analysis of the mechanical properties. Examples of realistic images coupled to a large deformation finite element model of the cornea are presented. These images can be rendered sufficiently fast for the virtual reality application.

**CR Descriptors:** I.3.7 [**Computer Graphics**]: Three-Dimensional Graphics and Realism --- *Virtual Reality;* I.6.3 [**Simulation and Modelling**]: Applications.

## 1. INTRODUCTION

We are developing a teleoperated micro-surgical robot for eye surgery. In order to provide simulation for training and to assist during surgery a virtual environment has been implemented as part of the system. During a simulation, the surgeon operates the robot in exactly the same way as it would be used when performing actual surgery.

[1] Department of Mechanical Engineering,
[2] Department of Engineering Science, The University of Auckland, Private Bag 92019, Auckland, New Zealand.
[3] Biorobotics Laboratory, Department of Biomedical Engineering, McGill University, Montreal, Canada.

Emails: ma.sagar@auckland.ac.nz, d.bullivant@auckland.ac.nz, g.mallinson@auckland.ac.nz, p.hunter@auckland.ac.nz, ian@biorobotics.mcgill.ca

This paper describes our efforts to create anatomical realism in a virtual environment for eye surgery involving visual and mechanical simulation. It provides a framework for the coupling of computer graphics for visual realism with finite element analysis and input from physical instruments.

The creation of a surgical virtual environment to both aid surgeons during operations and provide simulations for training opens up many exciting possibilities. The surgical procedure will be able to be viewed and visualized in new ways providing a new level of surgical experience. During surgery, the predicted mechanical and optical consequences of a particular incision and the optimization of tasks based on underlying mathematical models of tissue can be presented to the surgeon graphically. Operations can be recorded and analysed, and sent to colleagues in electronic form. Before or after surgery the environment can be used as a training simulator.

The use of interactive 3-D graphic modelling for surgical simulation has been gaining popularity. Examples include an endoscopic simulator containing a simplified representation of the colon [1], a system for simulation of tendon transfer operations with simplified geometry [3] and graphic models for simulations generated from CT and MRI scans [4]. Work is also being done on simulating certain laparoscopic surgical procedures in real time [14].

Only a few papers have been published on the realistic display of finite element based biomechanical simulations. Examples are a plastic surgery planning system in which a 3-D surface scan of a patient's face is meshed with finite elements and the displacements resulting from incisions deform the surface scan to show the predicted effects [12] and a simulation of skeletal muscles to provide images for computer animation [2]. In neither case was the time taken to generate each image an issue.

Eye structures such as the sclera and cornea have previously been modelled using analytical techniques [6] or finite element numerical analysis [10,13] but these have used linear elastic deformation theory. Since the cornea is anisotropic and nonlinearly elastic and undergoes large deformations, we have used large deformation elasticity theory with orthotopic and nonlinear material properties in the finite element model.

For the simulation to be most convincing, the surgeon should ideally perform the operation in exactly the same manner and use the same tools as in the actual operation. The display of the subject must look as realistic as possible and the user should be able to manipulate and have a 3-D spatial understanding of the environment. To simulate eye surgery realistically requires the construction of an accurate model of the eye with biomechanically based features. Visually, more realism normally implies more complexity and hence more computer time to generate the image. The graphic modelling challenge is to find fast, simple methods to give the illusion of complexity - which must continue under close scrutiny. Using the finite element approach, the graphic modelling must be coupled with analysis for the key anatomical features being operated on.

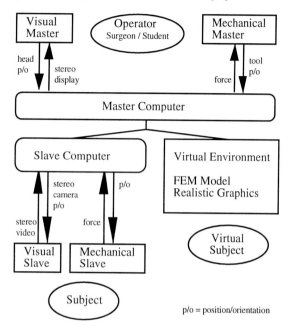

Figure 1: Block diagram of the micro-surgical robotic system.

## 2. OVERVIEW OF THE MICRO-SURGICAL ROBOTIC SYSTEM

Micro-surgery is currently performed by skilled surgeons often using hand crafted tools, where surgical intervention is limited by the dexterity of the surgeon and the available workspace. In the teleoperated micro-surgical robotic system currently being developed, a micro-surgical robot (MSR-1) will perform delicate eye operations under the guidance of a surgeon [8].

The micro-surgical system (see Figure 1) is composed of mechanical and visual master and slave subsystems. The surgeon grasps a handle (such as a micro-scalpel handle) which forms part of the micro-surgical mechanical master. Movements of this handle are monitored by six position transducers and fed to the master computer, where tremor is filtered prior to transmission to the slave computer which reproduces the same movement but scaled down by up to 100 times. The slave micro-surgical robot can hold a variety of micro-tools (diamond knives, probes etc). Forces measured by six transducers in the slave micro-surgical robot are scaled up and reflected back to the six actuators in the mechanical master which then exerts corresponding forces on the handle giving force feedback. The six-axis position/orientation of the surgeon's head (helmet) is used to control the slave stereo camera head. Stereo images from the slave cameras are transmitted back to the surgeon and displayed on either a head mounted display (HMD) or on a large high resolution video rear projection screen.

The modular nature of the Master-Slave arrangement allows the images and forces fed back to the master from the slave to be replaced (or aided) by visual and mechanical computer simulations.

The virtual reality system replaces (or combines) the camera image with computer graphics generated from the eye model. Forces felt by the robot are determined using a finite element model of the tissue and are fed back to the operator via the force reflecting master. In this way both visual and mechanical simulation are achieved, with the surgeon using the same physical equipment as in an actual operation. The graphics can be displayed on either a stereo monitor, video projection screen or HMD.

## 3. GENERAL ANATOMY OF THE EYE

As described in medical texts the eyeball can be considered as being composed of the segments of two slightly deformed spheres of different radii. It consists of three concentric layers which enclose its contents (see Figure 2):

(1) The outermost fibrous layer maintains the shape of the eyeball and is called the sclera save for a transparent section at the front called the cornea which is the major area of refraction for light entering the eye.

(2) The pigmented middle layer is vascular and nutritive in function and comprises the choroid, ciliary body and iris which is visible through the cornea.

(3) The innermost layer is the retina, which consists of nerve elements and is the visually receptive area of the eye.

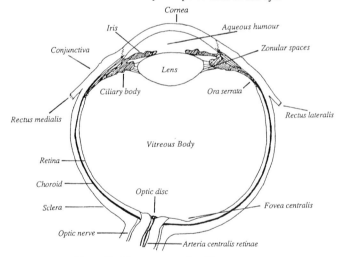

Figure 2: The components of the eye.

## 4. THE 3-D COMPUTER GRAPHIC EYE MODEL

The eye has previously been modelled for computer graphics applications, mainly as part of facial models for animation sequences. Detail has usually been unnecessary because the face has been viewed from a distance, thus specific features of the eye have been simplified or omitted. The iris has normally been treated as a one or two colour annulus and the eyelids and eyelashes (if any) have been simple curves and surfaces, for example [9]. No reference has been found which models the interior of the eye.

The aim here was to produce a fast accurate 3-D model of the eye which holds its detailed appearance even on close up. We chose 10 Hz to be the minimum acceptable display rate for our initial virtual reality applications.

It was necessary to make the model modular, so that aspects of the model, both graphical and analytical could be refined independently as development proceeded, and to allow aspects of the model to be animated such as making the eyelids blink, the eyeball rotate in its orbit and the pupil constrict or dilate.

Another concern was to give the graphics generated from the model parametric complexity so that the same 'model' could be used for rendering at different speeds. Different levels of detail (LOD) can be individually assigned to components of the model.

The above considerations led to a graphical modelling approach based on 3-D graphics primitives rendered by a workstation's graphics pipeline. Quite realistic images and lighting can be generated without the need for more versatile but more compute intensive rendering options such as ray tracing.

A general view of the current model is shown in Figure 6. The eyeball can be seen together with the arrangement of the surface patches used to represent the skin.

## 5. GRAPHICAL FEATURES OF THE MODEL

### 5.1 The sclera and cornea

The cornea is more highly curved than and protrudes from the sclera, which is white and smooth except where the tendons of the ocular muscles are attached. Both are displayed using relatively few polygons which are Gouraud shaded to produce a smoothed effect. For corneal surgery the specific geometry of a particular cornea will be obtained using laser based confocal microscopic imaging systems being developed for use in the micro-surgical robotic system [8].

### 5.2. The iris

The iris is the gemlike adjustable diaphragm around the pupil which controls the amount of light entering the eye. The colour of the iris ranges from light blue to very dark brown and is due to iridial connective tissue and pigment cells, which are often distributed irregularly producing a flecked appearance. The front surface of the iris can be divided into outer, ciliary, and inner, pupillary zones which often differ in colour and are separated by the collarette, a zigzag line, near which there are many pit like depressions called crypts.

Representing the iris parametrically is difficult due to its complex colours and shapes. The approach adopted was to generate two layers (ciliary and pupillary) of wavy radial fibres with each fibre being a single Gouraud shaded polygon with six or more vertices and colours specified by a colour ramp. The co-radial fibre vertices were given slightly different colours to produce a 3-D curved effect. The ciliary fibres were bounded to the collarette which was generated using a periodic function. The ciliary fibre waviness was increased with Gaussian perturbations near the collarette resulting in the formation of crypts between opposed phases. When the pupil dilates in the model, the ciliary fibres become wavy. The pupillary fibres lie slightly below and have the greatest radial retraction.

An alternative method that we have used to generate the iris has been to apply a texture map (from a close up photograph) to

significantly fewer polygons. This speeds up the rendering of the iris on dedicated texture mapping hardware such as Silicon Graphics' Reality Engine. A disadvantage of this approach is that it does not allow the individual components comprising the iris to be manipulated as separate objects. We have chosen a combination of discrete object modelling and texture mapping depending on the level of object manipulation we require and the texture mapping performance of the workstation.

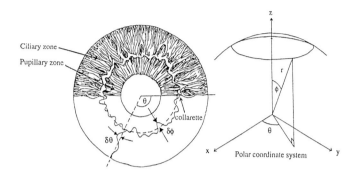

Figure 3: Geometric details of the modelling of the iris.

### 5.3. The retina and retinal blood vessels

The retina is mainly soft and translucent. Near its centre is an oval yellowish area which has a central depression, the fovea centralis, where visual resolution is the highest. This area contains no retinal blood vessels. About 3 mm nasal to this area is the optic disc where the optic nerve joins the retina. The optic disc is slightly puckered and is pierced by the central retinal blood vessels. Usually pink but much paler than the retina, it may be grey or almost white. The general retinal hue is a bright terracotta red which contrasts sharply with the optic disc.

The central retinal artery divides into two equal branches and again in a few mm, each branch supplying its own 'quadrant' of the retina. The central retinal vein is formed correspondingly. The branching of the artery is usually dichotomous with a 45 to 60 degree angle. Smaller lateral branches may leave at right angles. The vessels are visible as they lie close to the retinal surface.

For retinal surgery, in order to accurately model the retina and retinal blood vessel distribution of a specific patient, it would be necessary to stereoscopically scan the retina obtaining 3-D retinal surface estimation and blood vessel form in a similar manner to [15]. At present we are focusing on corneal surgery and retinal and retinal blood vessel positional data are generated using a model which reproduces the fundamental anatomical features and allows the display method to be assessed.

In the model of the fundus the retina has been represented as a deformed spherical segment containing the separately modelled optic disc on the posterior pole. The retinal blood vessels have been generated using a fractal tree [11] originating from the optic disc. The tree is projected onto the retinal sphere (see Figures 4 and 5). A recursive algorithm generated the vessel trees to a specified level of detail, subject to parameters describing mean branching angle, vessel radii and undulation, and creation of fine lateral vessels which branch from the main vessels at right angles. A repulsion factor was added in order to keep the large vessels from growing near the fovea centralis.

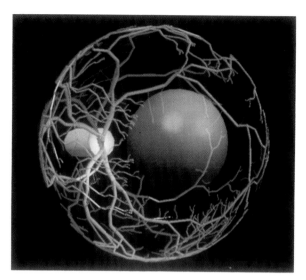

Figure 4: View showing fractal tree of retinal blood vessels (including lens) mapped onto the retinal surface.

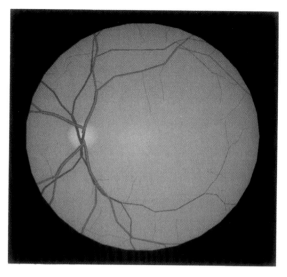

Figure 5: The retina including the optic disc and main blood vessels displayed as would be seen through an ophthalmoscope.

Representing the shape of the surface of the skin around the eye presents several problems. There are large smooth areas of tissue, overlapping folds and areas of sharp curvature between the front and rear surfaces of the eyelids. Parametric complexity is desired and surfaces should be flexible and editable: during surgery the eyelids will be stretched open and fixed. Non-uniform rational B-spline (NURBS) surfaces were chosen to model the facial surface for several reasons:

(1) Surfaces are represented with minimal data. Large data sets from patient facial scans may be reduced dramatically by the least squares fitting of a NURBS surface.

(2) NURBS are implemented in hardware on several graphics workstations and evaluation is reasonably fast and stable.

(3) They have a powerful geometric toolkit. The shape is controlled with control points and the continuity with knots. Refinement can be achieved by subdivision and knot addition.

(4) The net formed by the control points approximates the surface. This allows for fast preliminary collision detection between the robot tools and the face.

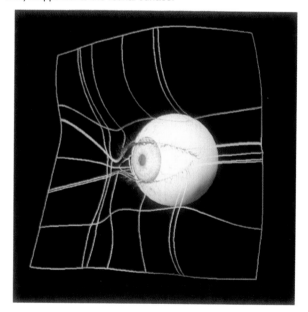

Figure 6: Exterior view of the model with the skin surface rendering omitted.

At the lowest LOD simple line segments are used. At the highest level, the vessels are represented by faceted cylinders replacing the line segments (depending on diameter). At middle levels Gouraud triangular prisms proved to be adequate.

### 5.4. The eyelids and surrounding face

The eyelids are two thin movable folds, adapted to the front of the eyes and forming an elliptical space when parted. The upper eyelid is larger and more mobile. On the nasal side the eyelids are separated by a triangular space, the lacus lacrimalis (tear lake), which contains a small elevation, the caruncle, and a reddish fold, the plica semilinaris. On the lateral side the eyelids meet at a more acute angle.

The initial geometrical data for a patients face is taken from a 3D surface scan. Because the resulting data currently does not give fine enough detail around the eye, and does not give the most efficient representation, a least squares NURBS surface fit of the data is made  This represents the basic characteristic features, but with minimal data. An interactive NURBS facial surface editor was written to refine and manipulate the resulting surface. The refinements are made using anatomical data and pictures. Extra knots and control points were added around the eyelid area for fine control over the eyelids and lacus lacrimalis. The multiplicity of the knots along the rim of the eyelids was increased so that the curve between the front and rear faces could be sharpened.

This approach allows the eyelids to be easily manipulated. By moving only a few control points both eyelids can be drawn together and closed (or stretched open and pinned back for operation). Morphing between different settings produces a blinking effect. The portion of the face from the nose to the eyebrow was defined with a 10 x 14 grid of control points. The caruncle and plica semilinaris were created with a small NURBS patch transformed to lie in the lacus lacrimalis. The amount of tessellation of the NURBS is currently dynamically related to viewpoint using the graphics library routines, but we consider it may be faster in some instances to base tessellation on incoming data. A typical configuration of NURBS surfaces representing the skin is shown in Figures 6 and 8.

*5.5. The eyelashes*

Eyelashes grow as short thick curved hairs from the edges of the eyelids. The upper hairs, more numerous and longer, curve up while those in the lower eyelid curve down so that the upper and lower lashes do not interlace when the eyelids are closed.

The main difficulty in modelling the eyelashes was finding a simple way to describe the length, curl and orientation of each hair. The solution finally arrived at was to represent the 'net' formed by the eyelashes with a piecewise biquadratic mesh having 15 control points (Figure 7), which is attached at one edge via the NURBS eyelid control points in order to move with the eyelids.

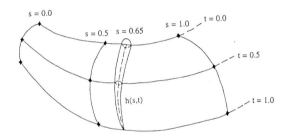

Figure 7: A biquadratic patch used to represent half of the surface used as a basis for constructing the eyelashes.

An editor for the control net was incorporated into the NURBS facial editor. At the highest LOD each hair was then represented by a sequence of truncated cones coaxial with a quadratic curve. A small random factor was added to the quadratic parameters of each hair. The density of hairs is less on the lower eyelid. All these parameters may be adjusted without changing the underlying surface containing the hairs.

## 6. FINITE ELEMENT MODELLING

At present, analytical development has concentrated on the cornea. To obtain stress distributions in the cornea we use large deformation incompressible 3-D elasticity theory with the equations of equilibrium formulated in spherical polar coordinates. The element geometries are defined in spherical polar coordinates $(R,\Theta,\Phi)$ in the undeformed state and $(r,\theta,\phi)$ in the deformed state. The polar coordinates $\Theta,\Phi,\theta$ and $\phi$ have trilinear Lagrange basis functions. The radial coordinates R and r are bicubic Hermite in the normalised material coordinates $(\xi_1, \xi_2)$ lying in the plane of the corneal surface and linear Lagrange in the normalised material coordinate $\xi_3$ directed transmurally through the corneal thickness (see [7] for details of the finite element technique used here).

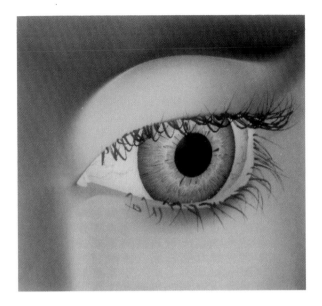

Figure 8: Exterior view of the model showing the NURBS face and the eyelashes.

The material properties are assumed to be homogeneous, orthotropic and nonlinearly elastic with a J-shaped uniaxial stress-strain behaviour along each of the three microstructurally defined axes (assumed to coincide with the $r,\theta,\phi$ directions). Collagen fibres are assumed to lie in the $(\xi_1,\xi_2)$ plane and are given elastic properties typical of the proteoglycan embedded type II collagen fibres found in the bulk of the cornea.

The outside edge of the cornea (limbus) is currently assumed to be fixed in position. In future developments of the model this assumption will be relaxed by including the sclera in the model. Figure 9 shows the finite element model of the cornea with a pressure load applied to the rear surface of the cornea and a point load applied at the centre of the front surface.

## 7. REPRESENTATION OF ROBOT AND SURGICAL ENVIRONMENT

The surgical environment contains graphical object representations of the robot and ophthalmic surgical tools such as scalpels, clamps for pinning back the eyelids and illumination tools. Each tool can be manipulated from the user interface, by the robot, or by hand using an attached position and orientation tracking device. A sample 'tool path' for the surgeon to cut along has been added, and as the scalpel is moved 3-D arrows appear to direct the surgeon when off path. Other information such as depth of cut and hand tremor are shown in a 'head up display' (see Figure 10). The display of graphic information to aid the surgeon is an open area for future investigation.

## 8. VIEWING

The observer has complete freedom of viewing position, orientation and field of view. The contents of the scene are chosen from a list of graphical objects. Visibility determination uses criteria based on the viewer's position relative to the model, and on the content of the scene. The LOD for individual objects can be fixed or made dependent on the estimated proportion of the screen that it occupies. In future developments we wish to investigate more sophisticated adaptive display algorithms.

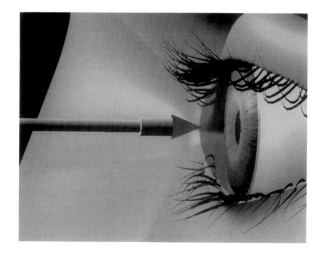

(a)

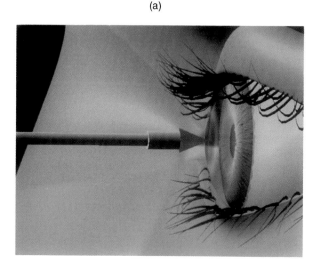

(b)

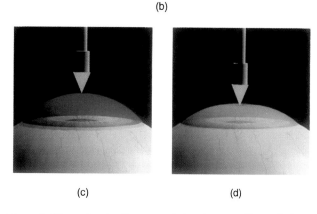

(c)                    (d)

Figure 9: Views showing the cornea being depressed by a robot probe. In the upper pictures the calculated stress field is displayed with banded colour contours. In the lower pictures the stress field is displayed with an alternative colour map and the facial features have been removed for clarity. (a), (c) Undeformed cornea. (b), (d) Deformed cornea.

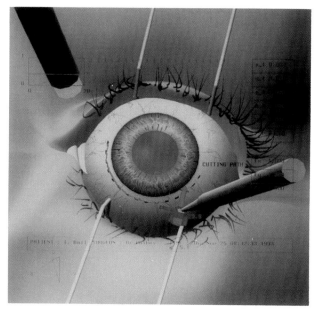

Figure 10: Surgical virtual environment including micro-tools and guidance information. The eyelids have been pulled back as they are during actual surgery. Superimposed on the image is additional information to guide the surgeon. The broken line around the cornea shows a planned cutting path.

At present for stereopsis a time multiplexed stereoscopic display is used with liquid crystal modulator (LCM) shutter glasses. An off-axis projection is made for each eye. Research discussed in [5] has shown that users have differing preferred values for the eye separation parameter usually specified in terms of horizontal viewing angle (HVA), and that this can vary with fatigue. As a result, the user interface includes a control for the HVA. The user interface is included in the stereo display by cloning it for left and right eye views, allowing full control in stereo mode.

## 9. SOFTWARE DESIGN

The design philosophy was to create a fast and flexible modular system to display both pure graphical data, for visual realism, and graphical data generated from the finite element modelling (at various LOD), so that both visual and mechanical simulation can be combined. Processing is distributed between a finite element module and a graphics module, which may be run in parallel on separate processors (see Figure 10).

The finite element module we have developed (CMISS) is a general purpose program designed to handle large deformation nonlinear elasticity problems. The model is stored as 3-D spherical polar nodal coordinates for both deformed and undeformed geometries, including the Hermite arc-length derivatives, element connectivity data and various basis functions and their derivatives evaluated at Gaussian quadrature points.

The graphics module contains its own reduced representation of the finite element structures including basis functions and connectivity information. After each iteration of the finite element module only changed nodal coordinate data need to be transferred to the graphics module. The complete graphic model is stored as a hierarchical list of graphics objects at various LOD comprised of graphical data which may be independently generated by other software (for example the NURBS editor) and graphical data generated from the graphics module's finite element structures.

The user has control over the graphics object list and may assign objects different attributes (for example visibility) for different display windows. Several windows containing the same object list can be created allowing different viewing setups simultaneously The graphic object list is traversed and the selected objects are displayed according to visibility and LOD criteria as described previously. Dynamic data structures are used to store objects and data are referenced through pointer structures for minimum reassignment.

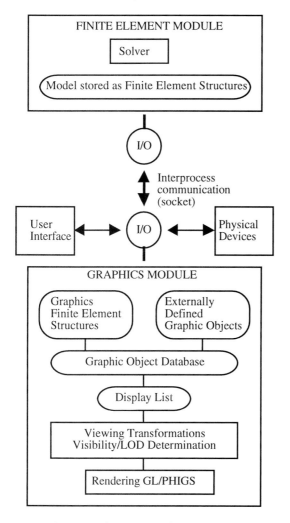

Figure 11: Organisation of the software.

## 10. SOFTWARE IMPLEMENTATION

The graphics module has been written in the C language for environments running the X window system with the Motif widget set for the user interface and Silicon Graphics' GL graphics library. The finite element software (CMISS) has been developed in Fortran.

Hardware resources used during software development included an IBM RISC/6000 Model 730 graphics system and a Silicon Graphics R4000 IRIS Indigo desktop workstation. The latter workstation has a 120 Hz switched display with Crystal EYES

liquid crystal shutter glasses for stereoscopy. A DEC Alpha 3000/300 was also used for the finite element analysis processing. A Silicon Graphics Reality Engine has since been used for a graphics speed trial.

## 11. RESULTS AND DISCUSSION

The virtual environment generates stereoscopic 3-D representations of the robot micro-tools, the main macroscopic features of the eyeball and the surrounding face. The eyeball can move, the eyelids can blink or be stretched open, and the pupil can be made to contract or dilate. The eye model is coupled to a finite element model of the corneal tissue, which can be used to generate realistic deformations and stress fields. Each graphical object has been generated parametrically, allowing arbitrary complexity to be used for differing LOD.

Positional information for the virtual micro-tools from the microsurgical robot and 3-D devices coupled to various hand held surgical tools is used to manipulate the virtual representations.

Initial results indicate a satisfactory level of realism with graphic display speeds on a desktop workstation in the order of what is required. Adequate display speeds are achieved on a high end workstation for the prototype micro-surgical robotic system. At present an incremental update of the computed displacement and stress field takes about one second on an Alpha 3000/300 workstation. This level of performance is acceptable as we anticipate the surgeon making an incision and pausing to evaluate the consequences before proceeding. To assess performance on a high end workstation, the system has been run on a Silicon Graphics Reality Engine. It achieved graphic update rates significantly greater than 10Hz interactively displaying the model together with a 3-D position and orientation tracked surgical tool.

*11.1 Examples*
All examples and display performance times given below were produced on a *desktop* workstation used during the development, a Silicon graphics R4000 IRIS Indigo with a GR2-XS24 graphics board with Z-buffer.

| Example | Polygons (quads) | Line segs. | NURBS tessellation | Update time (s) |
|---|---|---|---|---|
| Figure 12(a) eyeball exterior | 2490 | 900 | - | 0.11 |
| + eyelashes, NURBS | 5690 | 900 | 50 pixels | 0.42 |
| Figure 12(b) eyeball exterior | 1155 | 225 | - | 0.04 |
| + eyelashes, NURBS | 2115 | 225 | 100 pixels | 0.21 |
| Figure 5 eyeball interior | 2280 | 2016 | - | 0.18 |

Table 1: Total display update times on a desktop workstation.

*11.2 Complexity adjustment*
The complexity of all aspects of the model can be easily adjusted. Figure 12 shows two close up views of the front of the eye. The level of detail versus display update time appears to be approximately linear. As shown (see Table 1), for only a slight reduction in apparent quality, the complete image in Figure 12(b) can be rendered in approximately half the time required for Figure 12(a).

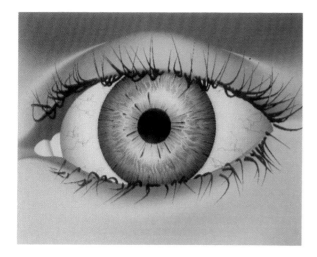

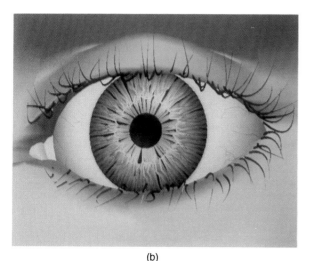

(b)

Figure 12: Close up views of the eye with different complexity parameter values.
(a) Same complexity as used for Figures 8, 9 and 10.
(b) All parameters reduced by a factor of two relative to (a).

## 12. CONCLUSIONS

A surgical virtual environment containing a detailed model of the eye has been implemented for use in a teleoperated micro-surgical robotic system for eye surgery. Visual and mechanical simulations have been combined by the coupling of parametrically defined graphic realism and finite element analysis. The virtual environment produces a fair level of realism (adjustable) for a low display regeneration time on a desktop workstation and gives sufficiently fast performance (>10Hz) on a high end workstation. It now forms part of a prototype micro-surgical robotic system.

Interest has been expressed in using the model for anatomic teaching, as it allows students to select and view each anatomical structure individually.

The model contains a large elastic deformation finite element representation of the cornea which computes the deformation and stress fields for a given displacement or load applied to the cornea. Extensions will include an analysis of the optical properties of the deformed cornea. We will also include tissues surrounding the eye in the graphic model. Eventually we intend to model a number of complete surgical procedures.

## ACKNOWLEDGEMENTS

Financial support from the University of Auckland Research Committee, and the New Zealand Lottery Grants Board is gratefully acknowledged.

## REFERENCES

[1]   Baillie, J., Jowell, P., Evangelou, W. and Bickel, W. Use of computer graphics simulation for teaching of flexible sigmoidoscopy. *Endoscopy 23*, (1991), 126-129.

[2]   Chen, D.T. and Zeltzer, D. Pump it Up: Computer animation of a biomechanically based model of muscle using the finite element method. Proceedings of SIGGRAPH '92 (Chicago, Illinois, July 26-31, 1992), In *Computer Graphics*, 26, 2, (July 1992), 89-98.

[3]   Delp, S. Loan, P., Hoy, M., Zajac, F., Fisher, S. and Rosen, J. An Interactive graphics-based model of the lower extremity to study orthopaedic surgical procedures. *IEEE Transactions on Biomedical Engineering*, 37, 8, (1990).

[4]   Hasimoto, D., Dohi, T., Tzuzuki, M., Horiuchi, Y., Chinzei, K., Suzuki, M. and Idezuki, Y. Development of a computer aided surgery system: Three dimensional graphic reconstruction for treatment of liver cancer. *Surgery*, (1991), 589-596.

[5]   Hodges, L.F. Time multiplexed stereoscopic computer graphics. *IEEE Computer Graphics and Applications*, (March 1992), 20-30.

[6]   Huang, T., Bisarnsin, T., Schachar, R.A., Black, T.D. Corneal curvature change due to structural alternation by radial keratotomy. *Journal of Biomechanical Engineering*, 110, (1988), 249-253.

[7]   Hunter, P.J. and Smaill, B.H. The analysis of cardiac function: a continuum approach. *Prog. Biophys. Molec. Biol. 52*, (1989) 101-164.

[8]   Hunter, I.W., Jones, L.A., Sagar, M.A., Doukoglou, T.D., Lafontaine, S.R., Charette, P.G., Mallinson G.D., Hunter, P.J. A teleoperated microsurgical robot and associated virtual environment for eye surgery, *Presence*, (Accepted 1994)

[9]   Magnenat-Thalmann, N. and Thalmann, D. *Synthetic Actors in Computer Generated 3D films*. Springer-Verlag, (1990).

[10]  Maurice, D.M. Mechanics of the cornea. *The Cornea: Transactions of the World Congress on the Cornea III*. Ed. H. Dwight Cavanagh. Raven Press Ltd., (1988).

[11]  Oppenheimer, P.E. Realtime design and animation of fractal plants and trees. Proceedings of SIGGRAPH '86 (New York). In *Computer Graphics 20, 4*, (1986), 55-64.

[12]  Pieper, S., Rosen, J. and Zeltzer, D. Interactive graphics for plastic surgery, Proceedings of SIGGRAPH '92 (Chicago, Illinois, July 26-31, 1992), In *Computer Graphics*, 26, 2, (July 1992), 127-134.

[13]  Pinksy, P.M.,Datye, D.V. A Microstructurally based finite element model of the incised human cornea. *J. Biomechanics 24*, 10, (1991), 907-922.

[14]  Sims, D. The Point where Lines Converge.. *IEEE Computer Graphics and Applications, 13*, July (1993), 7-9.

[15]  Young, A.A. and Hunter, P.J. Epicardial surface estimation from coronary angiograms. *Computer Vision, Graphics, and Image Processing 47*, (1989) 111-127.

# Wavelength Dependent Reflectance Functions

Jay S. Gondek,  Gary W. Meyer,  Jonathan G. Newman

Department of Computer and Information Science

University of Oregon

## Abstract

A wavelength based bidirectional reflectance function is developed for use in realistic image synthesis. A geodesic sphere is employed to represent the BRDF, and a novel data structure is used to store this description and to recall it for rendering purposes. A virtual goniospectrophotometer is implemented by using a Monte Carlo ray tracer to cast rays into a surface. An optics model that incorporates phase is used in the ray tracer to simulate interference effects. An adaptive subdivision technique is applied to elaborate the data structure from rays scattered into the hemisphere above the surface. The wavelength based BRDF and virtual goniospectrophotometer are utilized to analyze and make pictures of thin films, idealized pigmented materials, and pearlescent paints.

**Categories and Subject Descriptors:** I.3.7 [Computer Graphics]: *Three-Dimensional Graphics and Realism.*
**Additional Key Words and Phrases:** BRDF, full spectral rendering, Monte Carlo.

## 1   Introduction

The appearance of an object is determined by both the spatial distribution and the wavelength composition of the light that is reflected from the object's surface. These geometric and optical properties of the scattered light are what an observer uses to determine what a material looks like. Variation in the spatial distribution of the reflected light causes changes in appearance characteristics such as *gloss, haze, luster,* and *translucency.* Changes in the wavelength composition of the reflected light can alter the *hue, saturation,* and *lightness* that are seen by the observer. Spectrophotometric measurements can be taken to determine the spectral energy distribution of the reflected light and goniophotometric measurements can be made to find the spatial distribution of that light. The *measurement of appearance* is the term that has been coined to identify the family of measurements that are necessary to characterize both the color and the surface finish of an object [13].

While it is possible to separately measure the spatial and spectral distribution of the reflected light, these two dimensions work together to establish the overall appearance of an object. For example, the spectral distribution of the light reflected from a paint or a plastic is not completely determined by the absorptive properties of the pigment particles below the surface of the material. Light that travels into the substance interacts with the pigment particles and this interplay does change the wavelength composition of the light that eventually leaves the material. However, roughening the surface will increase the amount of spectrally nonselective light that is reflected in all directions from the object's surface. This desaturates the color of the object and thus alters its appearance even though the pigment has not been changed. On the other hand, the spatial distribution of the light reflected from multilayer systems (such as an iridescent paint) is only partially determined by the surface roughness of the material. Light that reflects from the topmost surface may be scattered uniformly in all directions. However, light that enters the surface, interacts with the layers below, and emerges from the surface, may have certain wavelengths reinforced while the rest of the spectrum is cancelled. When the reinforcement takes place in the mirror direction, the amount of specularly reflected light is increased and the specular reflection assumes a color that is different than the incident light. As a result, a metallic appearance is produced that might not have been predicted from surface roughness alone.

There are two basic types of local illumination models that are used in computer graphics to control the appearance of an object. In the most widely used approach, separate reflection mechanisms are independently modeled and then linearly combined [1, 5, 11, 16]. The most elaborate of these models, the He model [11], includes directional diffuse and ideal specular terms to account for surface reflection and an ideal diffuse component to accommodate subsurface scattering. The directional diffuse and ideal specular terms in the He model permit spectral reflectance to vary with incident angle, but the wavelength distribution of the ideal diffuse component is modeled as being constant across the scattering hemisphere. Also important amongst the linear combination models are those that include anisotropy in the spatial distribution [14, 17, 22]. The second and most recent type of local illumination model employs a bidirectional reflectance function (BRDF). Data for BRDFs has been generated by performing simulations [4, 23, 10] and by taking measurements [21]. Imaging systems that use BRDFs as their principle local illumination model have been developed [15, 19]. The only BRDF representation scheme proposed thus far for rendering has been the spherical harmonic approach suggested by Cabral et al. [4]. The use of spherical harmonics makes it possible to create reflectance distributions that have arbitrary spatial complexity. However, the use of a separate spherical harmonic representation for each spectral sample is not very efficient.

This paper presents a local illumination model that increases the generality with which an object's appearance can be specified. This is accomplished by adopting a BRDF representation scheme that allows a flexible and efficient representation of spectral as well as spatial information. This spectral BRDF is created by modeling surface and subsurface microstructures and then casting rays at the surface from all positions in the hemisphere above the surface. The rays are traced into the surface where they interact with the subsurface microstructures. An optics model is used that includes phase information. This allows simulation of interference effects due to path length differences and phase changes. A unique data structure is employed to record the rays that are reflected from each incident direction in the hemisphere. The data structure is created by using an adaptive scheme to elaborate the structure for those regions into which the most rays were reflected. This data structure is subsequently used in a shader to create realistic images.

This paper is divided into three additional major sections. In the following section the optics model that incorporates phase information and that was used to create the spectral BRDFs is described. Next, the data structure that was employed to represent the spectral BRDF is discussed. Finally, the simulations that were done to generate the spectral BRDFs are covered. The paper closes with examples that show how the spectral BRDF can be used to capture subtle appearance variations that are the result of both spatial and spectral variation in the light reflected from a surface.

## 2 The Ray Optics Model

In computer graphics, the ray model of light has been successfully used for over a decade to produce realistic images. In ray optics, each ray represents the propagation of a point sample on a wavefront of light. Light waves are generally described in terms of a number of physical properties, including wavelength, amplitude, speed, state of polarization, and phase. Polarization effects can become visible after multiple reflections from dielectrics and metals, as demonstrated in computer graphics by Wolff and Kurlander [24]. The phase of the light wave is needed to compute interference effects. Previous work in rendering the phenomenon of thin film interference has relied on analytical solutions for determining the reflectance from a thin film surface [20, 6]. By introducing the attribute of phase to the current ray model in computer graphics, we are able to predict interference results by simulation rather than relying on analytical solutions. Furthermore, this model allows the computation of reflectance functions from complex interference systems, such as iridescent paint, that defy an analytical solution.

Light is an electromagnetic wave, and thus has an electric and a magnetic field associated with it. Because the electric and magnetic fields are simply related in nonbirefringent dielectric media, the magnetic field can be disregarded and the behavior of light can be described in terms of just the electric field. Natural light can be represented as two arbitrary, incoherent, orthogonal, linearly polarized waves of equal amplitude [12]. Thus, a simulation of natural light is implemented by initially assigning two fields, $E_1$ and $E_2$, to each ray incident from the light source; these fields are plane polarized, orthogonal to each other, and each has an initial amplitude of one. Because the two fields are incoherent with respect to each other, they are treated independently in all subsequent calculations. The propagation of light through the surface model will therefore be described in terms of a single electric field $E$.

### 2.1 The Propagation of Light

The polarization state of $E$ can be modeled by two orthogonal vector components, $E_x$ and $E_y$, that are also both orthogonal to the direction of propagation. Each component may have a unique amplitude and phase. An electric field for a ray that has propagated some distance through the environment is described by the functions

$$E_x = A_x \sin(\omega(t + P/c) + \delta_x) \qquad (1)$$
$$E_y = A_y \sin(\omega(t + P/c) + \delta_y) \qquad (2)$$

where $A$ is the vector component amplitude, $t$ is time, $\omega$ is the angular frequency, $P$ is the optical path length that the ray has traversed from the light source to its current position, $c$ is the speed of light in vacuum, and $\delta$ is a phase offset that results from the

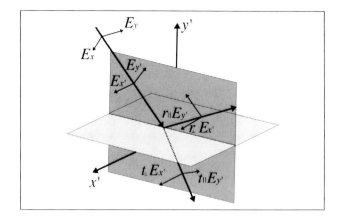

Figure 1: Polarization geometry of incident light.

accumulation of phase jumps that may occur upon reflection, as detailed below.

When a ray strikes a transparent surface, a transmitted ray and a reflected ray are produced, as shown in Figure 1. The components of $E$ for the incident ray ($E_x$ and $E_y$) are re-cast in terms of a new orthogonal basis that coincides with the plane of incidence and the perpendicular to the plane of incidence ($x'$ and $y'$). The amplitudes of the resulting field components are multiplied by the Fresnel amplitude coefficients for reflection and transmission ($r_\perp$, $r_\parallel$, $t_\perp$, and $t_\parallel$ in Figure 1) to give the reflected and transmitted amplitudes [12].

The field components of a ray may undergo independent changes in phase upon reflection. In the case where total internal reflection does not occur, this change in phase is predicted by the signs of the solutions to the Fresnel equations. Otherwise the phase jump is given by the following equations

$$\tan \frac{\delta_\perp}{2} = -\frac{\sqrt{\sin^2 \theta_i - n^2}}{\cos \theta_i} \qquad (3)$$

$$\tan \frac{\delta_\parallel}{2} = -\frac{\sqrt{\sin^2 \theta_i - n^2}}{n^2 \cos \theta_i} \qquad (4)$$

where $\delta_\perp$ and $\delta_\parallel$ are the phase jumps for the reflected fields parallel or perpendicular to the plane of incidence, $\theta_i$ is the incident ray angle, and $n$ is the transmitted index of refraction divided by the incident index of refraction [3]. The new phase offset for each reflected or transmitted component is equal to the sum of the incident phase offset and the phase jump calculated at the time of reflection.

### 2.2 Interference

After a single ray enters the geometric model, the phases associated with the field components of the multiple exiting rays are used to compute interference. This model predicts thin film interference, or, more generally, amplitude splitting interference. Amplitude splitting interference occurs when a wave is divided through reflection and transmission, and later recombines. We do not attempt to model wavefront splitting interference, which is commonly the result of diffraction.

Exiting rays that share the same direction of propagation to within a small tolerance have the potential to interfere. These rays represent partially overlapping wavefronts of light that are focused by the eye or camera lens at an arbitrary distance. According to the Fresnel-Arago laws, interference may be produced in the case where components of electric fields share the same plane of polarization, with the caveat that electric fields originating from different incoherent fields of natural light never produce visible interference and must be treated independently [12] . The coherent field components of parallel rays are summed to produce amplitudes at each

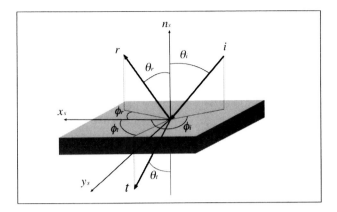

Figure 2: Angles of light scattering.

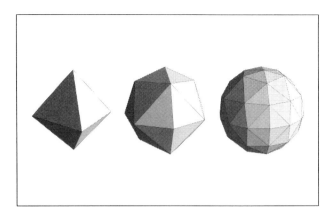

Figure 3: Levels of Geodesic Sphere Construction

wavelength that are the result of interference. This summation is achieved by using a trigonometric identity that is described in optics texts (for example, see [12]).

## 3 Representing the Scattering Function

The ratio of exitance to incident irradiance is computed over the spectrum for all reflected and transmitted rays. Irradiance, $D$, is defined as $D = c\epsilon_0 A^2/2$ for an electric field vector with amplitude $A$ where $\epsilon_0$ is the electric permittivity of free space [12]. Since the two initial fields of white light each had an amplitude of one, the initial spectral irradiance, $D_{\lambda,in}$, is simply $c\epsilon_0$. If $n$ rays are used to represent the incident wavefront of light, then the spectral exitance for each ray is

$$D_{\lambda,out} = \left(\frac{c\epsilon_0}{2n}\right)\left(A_{1,x}^2 + A_{1,y}^2 + A_{2,x}^2 + A_{2,y}^2\right) \quad (5)$$

where $A_{1,x}$, $A_{1,y}$, $A_{2,x}$, and $A_{2,y}$ are the spectral amplitudes of the electric field components of the two incoherent fields associated with the ray. Rays from all sampled incident directions contribute to the final BRDF representation.

The bidirectional spectral reflectivity of a material $\rho''$ is the ratio of reflected radiance $L_{out}$ to incident flux density $D_{in}$, defined for all incident and reflected directions over the hemisphere enclosing a surface element [18]. A BRDF is a function of five variables

$$\rho''(\lambda, \theta_r, \phi_r, \theta_i, \phi_i) = \frac{L_{out}(\lambda, \theta_r, \phi_r, \theta_i, \phi_i)}{D_{in}(\lambda, \theta_i, \phi_i)} \quad (6)$$

for light incident at an elevation angle of $\theta_i$ and an azimuth angle of $\phi_i$, reflected in the direction of $\theta_r$, $\phi_r$ (see Figure 2). In choosing this formulation of $\rho''$, we assume that incident light is unpolarized, and that the sampled surface does not contain florescent material. $L_{out}$ is the radiance of outgoing light, and is expressed in terms of exitance as

$$L_{out} = \frac{D_{out}}{d\omega_{out}\cos\theta_{out}} \quad (7)$$

for flux density propagating through the solid angle $d\omega_{out}$. The bidirectional spectral transmissivity function, or BTDF, is similarly defined for the transmission of light.

Cabral, Max, and Springmeyer [4] used an array as one representation for a BRDF. In their approach, this array essentially represents a set of discrete buckets that cover the hemisphere above a sample element. These buckets are used to capture the scattering of light from each surface element for a particular incident angle. We use an improved data structure that is related to the Cabral et al. method to give a compact and accurate representation of the BRDF and BTDF. Furthermore, this data structure is used directly by a Monte Carlo ray tracer to render images.

### 3.1 The Capture Sphere

An adaptively-built geodesic sphere of unit radius is employed to capture the scattered rays, where facets of this sphere serve as the capture buckets. A single sphere captures the reflectance and transmittance from all incident light angles. Furthermore, this sphere is used to represent the light scattering function upon completion of the simulation. A full sphere is required in the simulation not only to characterize the transmission function, but also because the direction of exiting rays will undergo a transformation, detailed in section 3.3, that may change the orientation of the exiting hemisphere depending on the angle of incidence. Figure 3 shows an example of the recursive subdivision technique that is used to build the sphere geometry. In Figure 3, each facet of the sphere is divided into four smaller facets with each increasing level of recursion. The facets of the sphere serve as buckets to tabulate the ratio of exitant to incident flux density. The ratio $D_{\lambda,k}/D_{\lambda,i}$ for sphere facet $k$ is given by

$$\frac{D_{\lambda,k}}{D_{\lambda,i}} = \frac{1}{D_{\lambda,i}}\sum_R D_{\lambda,R} \quad (8)$$

for all exiting rays $R$ that have direction vectors passing through cell $k$. By substituting Equation 7 into Equation 6, the BRDF for cell $k$ can be expressed as

$$\rho''(\lambda, \theta_k, \phi_k, \theta_i, \phi_i) = \frac{D_{\lambda,k}}{D_{\lambda,i}d\omega_k\cos\theta_k} \quad (9)$$

where $d\omega_k$ is the solid angle of cell $k$.

### 3.2 Adaptive Subdivision

Eight quad-trees are used to represent the triangles that form the geodesic sphere. Each root node denotes a basis triangle (four of these triangles are visible in the left polyhedron of Figure 3). A node at level $i$ represents a triangle that is the result of $i$ subdivisions. An adaptive approach is used to subdivide facets independently, thus providing a variable sampling resolution to capture features in the exitance distribution. Figure 4 shows the steps in adaptive subdivision that occurred when capturing the reflected flux scattered from a Gaussian surface with light incident at 25 degrees.

During subdivision, a facet $k$ is potentially divided into facets $k_1$, $k_2$, $k_3$, and $k_4$. To decide if subdivision is necessary, the root mean squared deviation (RMSD) is computed at each wavelength $\lambda$ for the spectral flux density propagating through cells $k_1, \ldots, k_4$. If the average of the spectral RMSD values is above a small tolerance, then subdivision occurs, and the new cells are recursively tested to see if further subdivision is required. Otherwise, a record containing the incident direction $(\theta_{in}, \phi_{in})$, spectral exitance ratios $(D_{\lambda,k}/D_{\lambda,i})$, and a reflectance or transmittance flag is inserted at the current node (for cell $k$) in the tree structure. The need for identifying the exitance

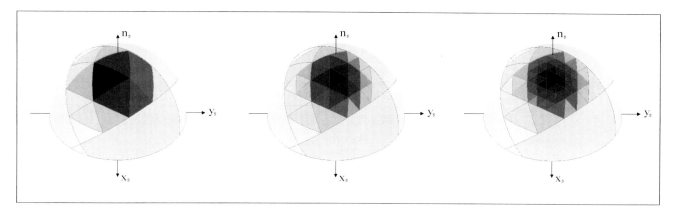

Figure 4: Subdivision for Capturing a Scattering Distribution

as being either reflected or transmitted will be detailed in the next section. Clearly, only the leaf nodes will contain data after the first incident angle is sampled. As more incident angles are sampled, cells represented by interior nodes may obtain data; furthermore, new nodes may be required to capture the additional exitance.

### 3.3 Transforming the Direction Vectors

Consider the problem of accurately characterizing a mirror reflection with this adaptive subdivision method. In this case, all of the rays incident from $\theta_i$, $\phi_i$ will be captured by a small bucket aligned with the $\theta_i$, $\phi_i + \pi$ direction. This implies a high degree of subdivision with every incident angle, impacting storage space and computation time during the simulation. Furthermore, such a representation is difficult to accurately interpolate and creates added time and space expense during rendering.

We define a transformation $T_r$ that is dependent on the angle of incidence, such that $T_r$ is a rotation of $-(\phi_i + \pi)$ about the normal, followed by a rotation of $-\theta_i$ about the $y_s$ axis of the surface (see Figure 2). For the example of capturing a mirror reflection, this transformation rotates every reflected ray into the surface normal, and a single small bucket at the top of the sphere captures the mirror-reflected rays for all incident directions. Transmitted rays are rotated with transformation $T_t$ in a similar way so that the ideal transmission direction is also aligned with the top of the sphere. Thus, for light incident on a smooth pane of glass in air, all reflected and transmitted rays are captured by the same small bucket. Note that multiple records may be associated with each bucket to account for different sample directions.

This method of concisely capturing ideal reflected and transmitted rays extends to any distribution that shows a directional bias for scattering in the mirror or ideal transmission directions. For example, the spatial reflectance distribution from many rough surfaces exhibit a specular lobe that is approximately aligned with the mirror reflectance direction. In such a case, the entire specular lobe is rotated into the direction normal to the surface, substantially localizing the area of high subdivision. For a given bucket and an associated data record the inverse transformations $T_r^{-1}$ and $T_t^{-1}$ can be applied to the vertices of the triangular bucket to recover the cell corresponding to the direction of the unrotated rays.

### 3.4 Interpolating the Function

Because the surface is sampled in a number of discrete incident directions, the tree structure for the capture sphere provides a scattering function that can be evaluated only at these specific directions. From this, we move to a representation of the BRDF and BTDF that is valid over continuous ranges of incident directions. Suppose that we have samples at incident directions $(\theta_1, \phi_1)$, $(\theta_1, \phi_2)$, $(\theta_2, \phi_1)$, and $(\theta_2, \phi_2)$. Given an incident direction $\theta_{in}, \phi_{in}$ such that $\theta_1 \leq \theta_{in} \leq \theta_2$ and $\phi_1 \leq \phi_{in} \leq \phi_2$, an interpolated result

can be found with a two-step process. First, for any cells that are larger for one sample direction than another, a common group of cells is computed by subdividing the cells associated with the four surrounding incident angles. This new group of cells becomes the set of cells associated with $(\theta_{in}, \phi_{in})$. Second, the spectral flux density ratios for these cells are computed with bi-linear interpolation of the values from $(\theta_1, \phi_1)$, $(\theta_1, \phi_2)$, $(\theta_2, \phi_1)$, and $(\theta_2, \phi_2)$. Interpolation of the direction of reflection or transmission simply falls out as a result of assigning $(\theta_{in}, \phi_{in})$ to this group of cells before applying the $T_r^{-1}$ or $T_t^{-1}$ transform. This interpolation method gives a scattering function that can be evaluated for any direction inside the range of sampled incident directions.

### 3.5 Rendering the Data

The above interpolation method is used within the context of a raytracer to render objects constructed from materials that have had their light scattering properties characterized by simulation. Let $(\theta_r, \phi_r)$ be the reflected direction from a surface in the backward raytracing paradigm. Because of reciprocity, the raytracer can "look out" into the scene through the cells that were used to capture the exitance from light incident at $(\theta_r, \phi_r)$. The reflected spectral radiance, $L_\lambda$, for $(\theta_r, \phi_r)$ is given by

$$L_\lambda(\theta_r, \phi_r) = \sum_k \rho''(\lambda, \theta_k, \phi_k, \theta_r, \phi_r) L(\theta_k, \phi_k) \cos \theta_k d\omega_k.$$

(10)

Equation 9 is substituted into Equation 10 to give

$$L_\lambda(\theta_r, \phi_r) = \sum_k \frac{D_{\lambda,k}}{D_{\lambda,i}} L(\theta_k, \phi_k).$$ (11)

In this formulation, both the cosine and solid angle terms cancel. This is one reason why we chose to capture the flux density ratios rather than the actual BRDF in the data structure representation, although the BRDF can easily be computed from the data structure by Equation 9. The flux density ratio for any cell is then used as a measure of the importance of that cell for sampling. To implement this, cells with higher flux ratios are sampled more densely than those with low flux ratios. This gives importance-based sampling of the local scattering function.

## 4 Light Scattering Simulations

The optics model and capture dome described in the previous two sections are used in conjunction with the geometric modeling of surface microstructure to produce a virtual goniospectrophotometer. During the simulation, rays are cast into layered surfaces that may have specific spectral absorption properties. Furthermore, structural colors produced by interference are accounted for, as detailed

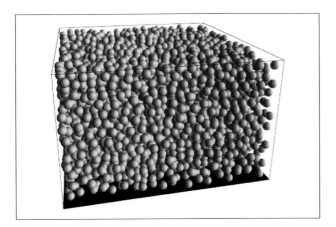

Figure 5: Simple paint microgeometry.

in Section 2. The number of rays per incident angle and the number of sample directions are specified before the simulation begins (although it is conceivable that adaptive sampling techniques could be employed to make these decisions during execution). Twenty wavelength samples spaced over the visible spectrum were used for the simulations and renderings described in the following subsections. All reflection and refraction of rays occur in the ideal mirror and ideal refracted directions, respectively. Any diffuse appearance that is produced from rendering the resulting BRDF and BTDF is fundamentally the accumulation of these reflections and transmissions.

Cabral et al. [4] did some of the early work in characterizing the reflectance functions of modeled surface geometry. Westin et al. [23] introduced the approach of casting rays at complex models of surface microstructure. Hanrahan and Krueger [10] proposed an analytical model of subsurface scattering that more accurately defines the diffuse reflection component, but lacks the generality of simulating actual subsurface microstructure.

In the following simulations, we considered the index of refraction to be constant across the visible spectrum. With this assumption, an entire spectrum can be assigned to each ray. Furthermore, with a wavelength independent index of refraction, Fresnel's equations predict the same amplitude coefficients based on the po-

larization state of the ray, regardless of the wavelength. Thus the electric fields associated with a ray describe the polarization state for the entire spectrum that the ray represents. This simplification was made to decrease the computation time of the simulation. Another option, which would allow for wavelength dependent indices of refraction, could be implemented by storing field representations at each wavelength. More generally, a ray could be cast for each wavelength, facilitating both dispersion and wavelength dependent indices of refraction. To allow for pigments and dyes, spectrally dependent absorption is implemented by maintaining a list of wavelength dependent amplitude coefficients with each ray.

### 4.1 Plastics and Paints

Plastics and paints consist of pigment particles suspended in a transparent matrix. Light scattering qualities of the particles are determined by their geometry and composition. The aggregate result of scattering from numerous particles contributes to the spatial and spectral distribution of reflected light. In many paints, the reflection of light from the surface of each pigment particle is responsible for the change in wavelength composition of incident light. In other paints, the transmission of light through each pigment particle causes spectrally dependent absorption of incoming light; reflection from the surface of the particles simply contributes to the diffusion of light within the substrate [7, 13]. Pigmented surfaces are common in most settings, so it is natural that the problem of rendering such surfaces has received attention in computer graphics [21, 9].

We present a simple model of a paint coating by defining a substrate filled with small pigment-particle microspheres, as shown in Figure 5. These particles are modeled as dielectric spectral filters; attenuation of transmitted light is governed by Bouger's Law [7]. Although this model is not an attempt to rigorously characterize the geometry and material attributes of pigment surfaces, it serves to demonstrate some of the reflective properties that real paints exhibit.

Surface roughness is a significant contributing factor to the appearance of paints and plastics. Smooth surface finishes give a spectrally non-selective mirror reflection for a portion of the incident light. A surface with this property is described as *shiny* or *glossy*. As the texture of the upper surface becomes rough, the spectrally non-selective reflected light assumes a diffuse distribution. In such a case, spectrally dependent scattering from the interior of the surface is combined with the reflectance from the air-surface interface to produce a less saturated, *matte* appearance.

The effect of surface roughness is demonstrated in Figure 6. The

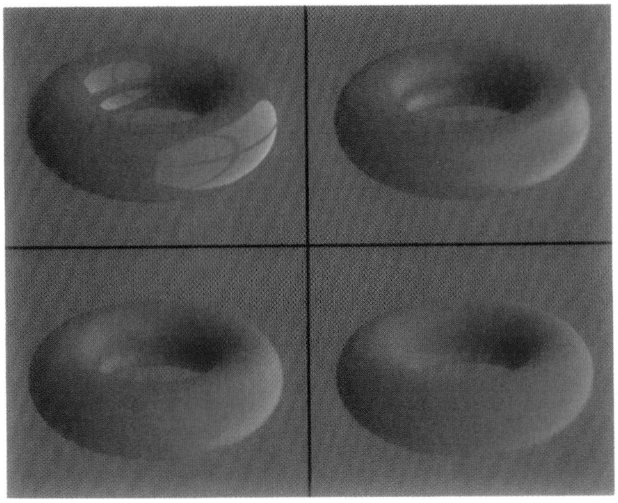

Figure 6: The effect of increasing surface roughness in a simple pigment model.

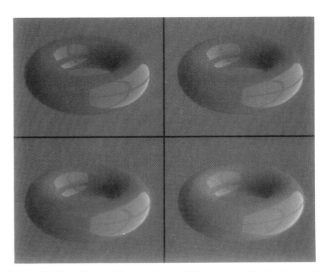

Figure 7: The effect of decreasing particle size in a simple pigment model.

Figure 8: Sunglasses with a thin film coating.

surface microstructures for each of the tori in Figure 6 were modeled as 2 mm wide and 1.2 mm deep sections of paint. Each microsphere had an index of refraction of 2.0 and was 80 $\mu m$ in diameter. The surrounding matrix had an index of refraction of 1.3. The geometry of the air-surface interface for each paint microstructure was defined as a Gaussian surface with an autocorrelation length of $20\mu m$ and RMS surface heights of 0.0, 1.5, 3.0, and 6.0 $\mu m$. The undercoating was an ideal black absorber. Incident rays that happened to exit from the sides of the microstructure instead of the top were not considered valid, and thus did not contribute to the computed reflectance function. The tori in Figure 6 were illuminated with an area light source in the shape of a four-paned window. As the surface roughness increases, the specular highlight makes a transition from glossy to diffuse. Because of the increase in diffuse scattering of white light, there is an observable decrease in the color saturation of the lower-right torus compared to the upper-left torus.

Another interesting property of pigments is the relationship between particle size, absorption, and scattering. Interior scattering events generally occur at the interface between the pigment particle and the surrounding matrix. The nature of the effect depends upon whether the particles are opaque or transparent. In the case where the particles are transparent, the amount of absorption that occurs depends on the path length between the entry and exit points for light passing through each particle. Thus, the ratio of absorption to scattering decreases with a decrease in particle size [7, 13]. The tori in Figure 7 illustrate this phenomenon. In this figure, the surface microstructure for each torus has an identical shape, but the scale of the microstructure decreases from left to right and top to bottom, producing microsphere diameters of 80, 40, 20, and 10 $\mu m$. Because of this shift in scale, the resulting change in the reflectance function is exclusively the effect of the decreasing microsphere diameters. The decline in the ratio of relative absorption to scattering is evidenced by the steps of desaturation that are visible in Figure 7.

## 4.2   Interference Structures

Absorptive pigmentary coloration is but a single class of color producing phenomenon. Colors that are produced entirely by the optical effects of surface geometry are termed *structural colors*. One example of a structural color is the color exhibited by thin film

layers. Section 2 describes the optics model that was used to predict thin film interference during the light scattering simulation.

Figure 9 shows the result of rendering data from the simulation of light incident on eight simple thin films. Each sphere in Figure 9 was illuminated by two window-shaped area light sources. The films have an index of refraction of 2.3 and are surrounded by air. The index of refraction was chosen to approximate that of titanium dioxide, an interference producing agent in iridescent paints. Transmitted rays are absorbed by an ideal black backing so that only the reflected color is observable. This figure depicts the two most brilliant series of interference color. Optical thicknesses for the top row of films, from left to right, are 218.5, 264.5, 310.5, and 345.0 $nm$. The bottom row of films have optical thicknesses of 448.5, 517.5, 586.5, and 667.0 $nm$. Note the change in color as the incident direction goes from normal to oblique. This shift in appearance is due to the change in the optical path of interfering rays as well as the change in Fresnel amplitude coefficients. Figure 8 shows a pair of sunglasses with a thin film coated lens in a texture-mapped environment. In this image, both reflection and transmission are characterized with a full bidirectional scattering function.

Figure 10 compares the analytical solution for thin film reflectance at normal incidence with results from simulation. These

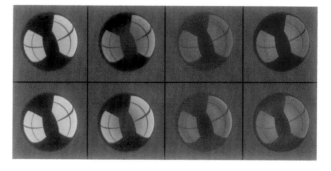

Figure 9: Thin film surfaces showing two orders of interference colors.

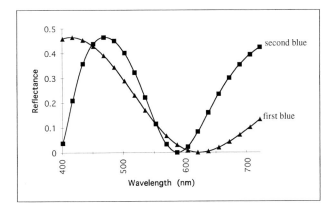

Figure 10: Spectral reflectance for the first and second order blue interference colors. Smooth curves correspond to the analytical solution, discrete points correspond to the results of simulation.

curves correspond to the blue interference films shown in Figure 9 (third column). The discrete points on this graph are data produced by ray sampling; the smooth curves are the result of evaluating the analytical formula for single layer thin film reflectance [18]. The results from the simulation clearly match the analytical solution.

Titanium dioxide ($TiO_2$) coated mica is often used as the color-producing pigment in iridescent and pearlescent paints [2, 8]. The optical thickness of the $TiO_2$ coating is controlled and varies from about 40 to 400 $nm$ for different paints; the thickness of the mica is not controlled and randomly varies from particle to particle in the same paint. For different paints, the $TiO_2$ coated platelets can vary in width from 2 to 50 $\mu m$. As the width increases, the interference paint tends to produce more of a *sparkling* reflection. The platelets in the paint align themselves in a somewhat parallel fashion upon application, and produce a semi-specular metallic appearance when applied to dark surfaces. If this paint is applied to a light surface, then complementary light that is transmitted through the paint and reflected from the undercoating has a tendency to reduce the saturation of the overall spectral scattering distribution.

Figure 12 is an image of an iridescent blue teapot that was rendered with data computed by simulation. Figure 11 shows the geometry of the modeled surface structure. For this simulation, the optical thickness of the $TiO_2$ coating was 310 $nm$, the thickness of the mica enveloped in $TiO_2$ varied from 10 to 300 $nm$, and the width of each platelet was 20 $\mu m$. The index of refraction for the $TiO_2$, mica, and surrounding substrate were 2.3, 1.58, and 1.3, respectively. The platelets were randomly distributed in the medium and randomly rotated slightly out of parallel. The combined effect of the placement and rotation gives the paint a more subtle change in hue with the change in incident angle, and creates a semi-specular reflection.

When the optical thickness of the $TiO_2$ coating is in the range of 80 to 150 nm, constructive interference occurs across most of the incident spectrum, reflecting approximately 30 to 40 percent of the light in the bluish white to yellowish white regime of the incident spectrum [8]. Interference paints with this characteristic are known as pearlescent pigments. Figure 13 shows an image of an artificial pearl that was created by modeling interference pigments. The optical thickness of the $TiO_2$ coating for this example was 122 $nm$. The index of refraction for the matrix surrounding the platelets was set to 1.1, providing a minimal specular contribution and enhancing the luster of the directional diffuse scattering from the platelets. A similar effect could be produced by allowing the platelets to extend out of the matrix, as often occurs in real paints.

Figure 11: Microstructure of interference paint.

## 5  Summary and Conclusions

In this paper we have presented a new computer graphics reflection model that has sufficient generality to represent both light scattering dimensions considered important by those in industry who make careful measurements of appearance. The model accomplishes this by using a wavelength based BRDF to describe the spatial *and* the spectral distribution of the light reflected from a surface. This is a step beyond current BRDF based reflection models in which it is difficult to efficiently incorporate wavelength information. A new method has been introduced to represent this extended BRDF. It employs a data structure to describe a geodesic sphere that has been adaptively subdivided to capture the important features of the BRDF.

We have also described a virtual goniospectrophotometer that was developed to measure these wavelength based BRDFs. The Monte Carlo ray tracer used to simulate this device adopted a ray optics model that kept track of phase information and could perform interference calculations when necessary. Models were constructed of subsurface microstructures and rays were traced beneath an object's surface. The virtual goniospectrophotometer was employed to show how the extended BRDF can be used to model both a spectral change in reflected light caused by a modification to surface roughness and a spatial change in reflected light produced by wavelength based interference below the object's surface. These changes in appearance could not be accurately modeled without including the dimension of wavelength in the BRDF.

This work represents a first step in developing a powerful tool for those interested in exploring how surface and subsurface microstructures affect the appearance of an object. However, to turn it into a true design tool, several important steps must be taken. Comparisons must be performed against goniospectrophotometric data taken from real surfaces for which the surface and subsurface geometries are known. The optical model must be extended to include other effects such as diffraction and dispersion. Improved techniques are necessary to sample the spectrum, control the geodesic sphere subdivision, and interpolate the information stored in the data structure. Even without these improvements, however, the system can generate physically consistent data for realistic imaging applications. This is still quite useful, because in many cases measured appearance data is simply not available.

## 6  Acknowledgements

This work was supported by the ATG Graphics Software Group at Apple Computer and the Oregon Advanced Computing Institute. Additional support was provided by the Hewlett-Packard Company which donated the HP Apollo workstations on which most of the large scale simulations were performed. The authors acknowledge Rob Wicke who wrote a renderer that was used to make some of

Figure 12: Iridescent teapot rendered by simulating interference paint.

the first pictures with the new reflection model. Finally, the authors thank Professor Michael Raymer of the University of Oregon Physics Department for several helpful discussions and for his careful review of Section 2. His comments helped to refine and sharpen several of the concepts presented in this paper.

# 7   References

[1] Blinn, James F. Models of Light Reflection for Computer Synthesized Pictures. Proceedings of SIGGRAPH '77. In *Computer Graphics 11*, 2, (July 1977) 192-198.

[2] Bolomey, R. A. and L. M. Greenstein. Optical Characteristics Of Iridescent And Interference Pigments. *Journal of Paint Technology 44*, 566, (Mar. 1972), 39-50.

[3] Born, Max and Emil Wolf. *Principles of Optics.* 6th Ed. Pergamon Press, Oxford, 1980.

[4] Cabral, Brian, Nelson Max, and Rebecca Springmeyer. Bidirectional Reflection Functions from Surface Bump Maps. Proceedings of SIGGRAPH '87. In *Computer Graphics 21*, 4, (July 1987) 273-281.

[5] Cook, Robert L. and Kenneth E. Torrance. A Reflectance Model for Computer Graphics. *ACM Trans. Graph. 1*, 1, (Jan. 1982), 7-24.

[6] Dias, Maria L. Ray Tracing Interference Color. *IEEE Comput. Graph. Appl. 11*, 2, (Mar. 1991), 54-60.

[7] Evans, R. M. *An Introduction to Color.* John Wiley & Sons, New York, 1948.

[8] Greenstein, L. M. Pearlescence: The Optical Behavior of Nacreous and Interference Pigments. In *Pigment Handbook, Volume III*, T. C. Patton, Ed. John Wiley & Sons, New York, 1973, 357-390.

[9] Haase, Chet S. and Gary W. Meyer. Modeling Pigmented Materials for Realistic Image Synthesis. *ACM Trans. Graph. 11*, 4 (Oct. 1992), 305-335.

[10] Hanrahan, Pat and Wolfgang Krueger. Reflection from Layered Surfaces due to Subsurface Scattering. Proceedings of SIGGRAPH 93 In *Computer Graphics*, Annual Conference Series, 1993 165-174.

[11] He, Xiao D., Kenneth E. Torrance, François X. Sillion, and Donald P. Greenberg. A Comprehensive Physical Model for Light Reflection. Proceedings of SIGGRAPH '91 In *Computer Graphics 25,* 4 (July 1991), 175-186.

[12] Hecht, Eugene. *Optics.* 2nd Ed. Addison-Wesley Publishing Co. Reading, 1987.

[13] Hunter, Richard S. and Richard W. Harold. *The Measurement of Appearance.* 2nd Ed. John Wiley & Sons, New York, 1987.

[14] Kajiya, James T. Anisotropic Reflection Models. Proceedings of SIGGRAPH '85. In *Computer Graphics 19*, 3, (July 1985), 15-21.

[15] Kajiya, James T. The Rendering Equation. Proceedings of SIGGRAPH '86. In *Computer Graphics 20*, 4, (Aug. 1986), 143-150.

[16] Phong, Bui-Tuong. Illumination for Computer Generated Pictures. *Commun. ACM 18*, 6 (June 1975), 311-317.

[17] Poulin, Pierre and Alain Fournier. A Model for Anisotropic Reflection. Proceedings of SIGGRAPH '90. In *Computer Graphics 24*, 4, (Aug. 1990), 273-282.

[18] Siegel, Robert and John R. Howell. *Thermal Radiation Heat Transfer.* McGraw-Hill, New York, 1981.

[19] Sillion, François X., James R. Arvo, Stephen H. Westin, Donald P. Greenberg. Proceedings of SIGGRAPH '91. In *Computer Graphics 25*, 4, (July 1991), 187-196.

[20] Smits, Brian E. and Gary W. Meyer. Newton's Colors: Simulating Interference Phenomena in Realistic Image Synthesis. *Eurographics Workshop on Photosimulation, Realism, and Physics in Computer Graphics Conference Proceedings, 1990*, 185-194.

[21] Takagi, Atsushi, Hitoshi Takaoka, Tetsuya Oshima, and Yoshinori Ogata. Accurate Rendering Technique Based on Colorimetric Conception. Proceedings of SIGGRAPH '90. In *Computer Graphics 24*, 4, (Aug. 1990), 263-272.

[22] Ward, Gregory J. Measuring and Modeling Anisotropic Reflection. Proceedings of SIGGRAPH '92. In *Computer Graphics 26*, 2, (July 1992), 265-272.

[23] Westin, Stephen H., James R. Arvo, and Kenneth E. Torrance. Predicting Reflectance Functions from Complex Surfaces. Proceedings of SIGGRAPH '92. In *Computer Graphics 26*, 2, (July 1992), 255-264.

[24] Wolff, Lawrence B. and David J. Kurlander. Ray Tracing with Polarization Parameters. *IEEE Comput. Graph. Appl. 10*, 6, (Nov. 1990), 44-55.

Figure 13: An artificial pearl produced from a model of pearlescent paint.

# Polarization and Birefringency Considerations in Rendering

David C. Tannenbaum[1]
IBM Corporation

Peter Tannenbaum[2]
Rensselaer Polytechnic
Institute

Michael J. Wozny[3]
National Institute of
Standards and Technology

## ABSTRACT

In this work we render non-opaque anisotropic media. A mathematical formalism is described in which polarization effects resulting from light/material interactions are represented as transformation matrices.

When applying the matrices a skewing is performed to ensure that like reference coordinates are used. The intensity and direction of an extraordinary ray is computed.

**CR Categories and Subject Descriptors:** I.3.7 [**Computer Graphics**]: *Three-Dimensional Graphics and Realism.*
**Additional Key Words and Phrases:** Polarization, Birefringency

## INTRODUCTION

The coherency state of a light wave can be represented in matrix form, a **CM**, [1, 5]. Similarly, a material has associated with it a coherency modification matrix, **CMM**, [2]. Wolf and Kurlander [6] used the **CM** in a ray tracer. Here we extend their work, using a **CMM** to consider birefringent media. Past work has considered surface anisotropy, [4]. Birefringency, in contrast, is a bulk phenomenon.

## COHERENCY AND POLARIZATION

We represent the coherency matrix **CM** [5], as,

$$\mathbf{J} = \left[ \begin{array}{cc} J_{xx} & J_{xy} \\ J_{yx} & J_{yy} \end{array} \right] = \left[ \begin{array}{cc} <E_x E_x^\star> & <E_x E_y^\star> \\ <E_y E_x^\star> & <E_y E_y^\star> \end{array} \right] \quad (1)$$

The $E_x^\star$ symbol denotes the complex conjugate of $E_x$.

[1]Neighborhood Road, Kingston, New York 12401, kt2z@vnet.ibm.com +1 914 385-5267
[2]Troy, New York 12180, tannenp@cs.rpi.edu +1 518 276-4849
[3]Building 220, Room B322, Gaithersburg MD 20899 wozny@cme.nist.gov +1 301 975-3400

Following Parrent et al. [2], we represent the **CMM** for a polarizer making an angle $\theta$ with the ray's X-axis as a matrix applied to the incident **CM** E-field,

$$\mathcal{M}_p = \left[ \begin{array}{cc} \cos^2 \theta & \cos \theta \sin \theta \\ \cos \theta \sin \theta & \sin^2 \theta \end{array} \right] \quad (2)$$

This can be seen by writing out explicitly the product $\mathcal{M}_p \mathcal{E}$,

$$\mathcal{M}_p \mathcal{E} = \left[ \begin{array}{c} \cos \theta (E_x \cos \theta + E_y \sin \theta) \\ \sin \theta (E_x \cos \theta + E_y \sin \theta) \end{array} \right] \quad (3)$$

Notice the E-field is the result of first projecting the initial components $E_x$ and $E_y$ onto the transmission axis of the polarizer, and then finding the X and Y components of this projection. The result of a polarizer on the **CM** is $\mathbf{J}_p = \mathcal{M}_p \mathbf{J} \mathcal{M}_p^\dagger$. This is read: if light of initial coherency **J** passes through a polarizer characterized by a **CMM** $\mathcal{M}_p$, then the transmitted ray has a coherency state $\mathbf{J}_p$ as defined above.

## BIREFRINGENCY

We focus on uniaxial crystals. Strong [3] discusses light propagation in 2d. We solve the 3d configuration and combine the solution with the coherency formalism.

The extraordinary mode of transmission is found by the simultaneous solution of the extraordinary velocity surface and the plane representing the maximal extent of the Huygens' waves. The problem is to compute the point of intersection of an ellipsoid with a plane.

## USING THE CM WITH CALCITE

Before $\mathcal{M}$ can be applied to **J**, the two matrices need to be transformed into a common reference coordinate space. We represent $\mathcal{M}$ with respect to a surface normal vector, considered the Z dimension, and an additional reference vector used to indicate the X direction.

The relationship between the two coordinate systems in terms of the X and Y components is given as,

$$\left[ \begin{array}{cc} \vec{X}_r \bullet \vec{X}_m & \vec{Y}_r \bullet \vec{X}_m \\ \vec{X}_r \bullet \vec{Y}_m & \vec{Y}_r \bullet \vec{Y}_m \end{array} \right] = \left[ \begin{array}{cc} \alpha_1 & \alpha_2 \\ \beta_1 & \beta_2 \end{array} \right] \quad (4)$$

where the subscripts $r$ and $m$ refer respectively to the ray's coordinate system and the **CMM**'s coordinate system.

Before applying a **CMM**, the following skewing transformation is made,

$$\mathbf{J}_{xx}(skew) = \alpha_1^2 \mathbf{J}_{xx} + 2\alpha_1 \alpha_2 \sqrt{\mathbf{J}_{xx}\mathbf{J}_{yy}} + \alpha_2^2 \mathbf{J}_{yy}$$

$$\mathbf{J}_{yy}(skew) = \beta_1^2 \mathbf{J}_{xx} + 2\beta_1\beta_2\sqrt{\mathbf{J}_{xx}\mathbf{J}_{yy}} + \beta_2^2 \mathbf{J}_{yy}$$
$$\Re[\mathbf{J}_{xy}(skew)] = \xi\Re[\mathbf{J}_{xy}] \qquad (5)$$
$$\Im[\mathbf{J}_{xy}(skew)] = \xi\Im[\mathbf{J}_{xy}]$$
$$\mathbf{J}_{yx}(skew) = \mathbf{J}^*_{xy}(skew)$$

$$\text{where,} \qquad \xi = \frac{\mathbf{J}_{xx}(skew)\mathbf{J}_{yy}(skew)}{\mathbf{J}_{xx}\mathbf{J}_{yy}} \qquad (6)$$

When the Z axis of the incident ray and the **CMM** are coincident (or antiparallel) then the transformation reduces to a rotation matrix,

$$\begin{bmatrix} \vec{X}_r\bullet\vec{X}_m & \vec{Y}_r\bullet\vec{X}_m \\ \vec{X}_r\bullet\vec{Y}_m & \vec{Y}_r\bullet\vec{Y}_m \end{bmatrix} = \begin{bmatrix} \cos(\theta) & \sin(\theta) \\ -\sin(\theta) & \cos(\theta) \end{bmatrix} \qquad (7)$$

The **CM** is written in reference to a specific coordinate system associated with a ray and must be aligned with the coordinate system created for the crystal's velocity surfaces.

The dot- and cross-products give the projection of the incident ray's E-field components in the directions both parallel and perpendicular to the optic axis, $\vec{OA}$ and $\vec{OA'}$, respectively. Consider a ray with coherency state **J**, traced backwards, that encounters a calcite obstruction. The intensity of the e-ray is approximated as,

$$I_{e-ray} = \mathbf{J}_{xx}\|\vec{x}^{(\text{ray})} \otimes \vec{OA}\| + \mathbf{J}_{yy}\|\vec{y}^{(\text{ray})} \otimes \vec{OA}\| \qquad (8)$$

Please refer to the Proceedings CD-ROM for an in-depth discussion.

## RESULTS

In Fig. 1 birefringency is evident in the double image of the tiger's mouth and front leg. Note the effect of the polarization filter placed on the disk. Fig. 2 shows a side view of the same scene. The optic axis of the calcite disk is straight up, in the $^+$Z dimension, in both figures.

The tiger images were rendered at $512 \times 512$ resolution with polarization state and birefringency admitted using an otherwise unsophisticated ray-tracer on an IBM Risc System 6000 model 580.

## CONCLUSIONS

Polarization effects are significant because light traveling along one of the modes in a birefringent material becomes polarized orthogonal to the other mode of transmission. The methods we suggest are general and handle polarization changes arriving from any cause.

The method we present is easily added to existing ray tracer systems. Because the changes are localized (*e.g.*, enhancement of the ray definition, modification to the routine used to assign ray intensity, and extension of the ray spawning routine), such extensions can be made without disrupting the fundamental structure of a program.

In the future we hope to address more complex crystalline structures and also to investigate the limited use of forward ray tracing to more accurately model the changes in polarization a light ray encounters in a scene.

## ACKNOWLEDGMENT

We wish to thank IBM for the continued access to numerous workstations and graphics equipment during this work.

## REFERENCES

[1] Max Born and Emil Wolf. *Principles of Optics*. The Macmillan Company, second (revised) edition, 1964.

[2] G. B. Parrent Jr. and P. Roman. On the Matrix Formulation of the Theory of Partial Polarization in Terms of Observables. *Il Nuovo Cimento* (English version), 15(3):370–388, February 1960.

[3] John Strong. *Concepts of Classical Optics*. W. H. Freeman and Company, Inc., 1958.

[4] Gregory J. Ward. Measuring and Modeling Anisotropic Reflection. In *Computer Graphics (SIGGRAPH '92 Proceedings)*, volume 26, No. 2, pages 265–272, July 1992.

[5] Emil Wolf. Coherence Properties of Partially Polarized Electromagnetic Radiation. *Il Nuovo Cimento* (English version), 13(6):1165–1181, September 1959.

[6] Lawrence B. Wolff and David J. Kurlander. Ray Tracing with Polarization Parameters. *IEEE Computer Graphics & Applications*, 10(6):44–55, November 1990.

Figure 1: Ray traced scene including a birefringent disk and rectangular polarization filter.

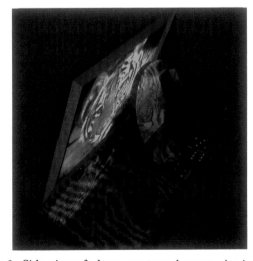

Figure 2: Side view of above ray traced scene. Again note the rectangular polarization filter placed on the disk.

# A Fast Shadow Algorithm for Area Light Sources Using Backprojection

*George Drettakis* [1]
*Eugene Fiume*

Department of Computer Science
University of Toronto,
Toronto, Ontario CANADA M5S 1A4

## Abstract

The fast identification of shadow regions due to area light sources is necessary for realistic rendering and for discontinuity meshing for global illumination. A new shadow-determination algorithm is presented that uses a data structure, called a *backprojection*, to represent the visible portion of a light source from any point in the scene. A complete discontinuity meshing algorithm is described for polyhedral scenes and area light sources, which includes an important class of light/geometry interactions that have not been implemented before. A fast incremental algorithm for computing backprojections is also described. The use of spatial subdivision, and heuristics based on computed statistics of typical scenes, results in efficient mesh and backprojection computation. Results of the implementation show that the use of the backprojection and discontinuity meshing permits accelerated high-quality rendering of shadows using both ray-casting and polygon-rendering with interpolants.

**CR Categories and Subject Descriptors:** I.3.7-[Computer Graphics] Three-Dimensional Graphics and Realism.

**Additional Key Words**: Shadows, umbra, penumbra, discontinuity meshing, global illumination, backprojection.

## 1. Introduction

The accurate depiction of shadows has long been a concern to computer graphics (e.g., [BoKe70][Appe68]). Shadow algorithms are sensitive to underlying geometric models and to light sources. Because a point-light source is either occluded by an object or it is not, transitions from light to umbral shadow are abrupt. An area-light source can be partially occluded, which results in graduated *penumbral* shadow transitions as well. The identification of shadow boundaries is central to computing better-quality discontinuity meshes and to accelerating global-illumination computations.

Shadow algorithms incorporating penumbra for linear and area light sources have been presented in several ray-tracing contexts [Aman84][PoAm90][TaTo91]. Just as visibility algorithms exploit coherence, so too shadows from area sources have coherent structure that can be used by rendering algorithms. Of special interest is the relationship between scene-light geometry and the radiance within shadow regions. Campbell and Fussell [CaFu91] noted that multiple extrema in radiance can arise in a penumbral region. In [LiTG92][Heck92a], it is suggested that reconstruction quality will improve when discontinuity lines are identified.

We shall consider environments of non-interpenetrating, diffusely reflecting polyhedra illuminated by diffusely emitting area

1. First author's current address: iMAGIS/IMAG, BP 53, F-38041 Grenoble Cedex 9, FRANCE. E-mail: George.Drettakis@imag.fr.

light sources. We present an algorithm that partitions the scene into a mesh of faces, so that in each face the view of the source is topologically equivalent. This view is represented by a data structure called the *backprojection*. We develop a set of heuristics based on properties of typical interior scenes that allow this mesh, called the *complete discontinuity mesh*, to be computed efficiently. Once the mesh has been computed and the backprojection calculated in each face of the mesh, scenes involving area light sources can be quickly rendered. An *incremental* backprojection calculation algorithm is used to greatly accelerate illumination computations. In other approaches this expense is at least that of computing the mesh.

The use of the backprojection and the generation of a complete mesh are important contributions for several reasons. Backprojection can be used to compute images with exact radiance values in the penumbra cheaply and view-independently. These images are useful as a reference to evaluate the quality of approximations such as those in [LiTG92][Dret94a]. Incremental backprojection is generally so fast that high-quality rendering is achieved even when using interpolation, at speeds competitive with previous lower-quality interpolatory approaches. A complete discontinuity mesh is essential to computing backprojections, and it provides precise information regarding variation in radiance that is unavailable in other approaches that compute incomplete meshes. This information has been used for the study of radiance properties [Dret94a] in penumbral regions, which was previously prohibitively expensive.

In Section 2, we review discontinuity meshing and its relationship to previous work. In Sections 3-6 the new algorithm to compute the mesh and an efficient incremental backprojection calculation algorithm are presented. We conclude in Section 7. We present statistics from our implementation throughout, substantiating the intuitions used to develop the algorithm.

## 2. The Discontinuity Mesh and Backprojection

Changes in visibility, or *visual events*, are related to the interaction of edges and vertices in the scene [GiMa90][GiCS91]. The visual events of interest are: *EV events*, caused by the interaction of a vertex and an edge; and *EEE events*, caused by the interaction of three edges in environment. An EV event is shown in Figure 1 and a EEE event is shown in Figure 2. In both, the visual event occurs when crossing from the point $P_1$ (red cross) to the point $P_2$ (green cross). For the EV event, visibility changes only when crossing the plane formed by an edge and a vertex, shown as a white triangle. Specifically, vertex $v_1$ is visible at $P_2$, but is not at $P_1$. For EEE events, three edges form a ruled quadric surface shown in white in Figure 2. At $P_2$, the edge $e_1$ of the source is visible, while at $P_1$ it is not. The plane of Figure 1 and the quadric surface of Figure 2 are *discontinuity surfaces*.

The visible regions of a source from a point are polygons whose vertices are either formed by the projection of scene edges onto the source, or vertices of the original light source. A *backprojection instance* at a point $P$, with respect to a source, is the set of polygons forming the visible parts of the source at that point. In Figures 1 and 2, the polygons with color vertices on the source are the backprojection instances at point $P_2$. The *backprojection* in a region is a data-structure containing the set of ordered lists of emitter vertices and edge pairs such that at every point $P$ in that region, the projection through $P$ of these elements onto the plane of the source form the backprojection instance at $P$.

Given a polygonal light source σ and polygonal scene, the partition of the scene into regions having the same backprojection is the *complete discontinuity mesh* of σ. To generate such a mesh, all EV and EEE surfaces that interact with the emitter must be computed. A region of the complete mesh with the *same* backprojection is a *face* of the mesh. Previous algorithms ([LiTG92][Heck92a]) would have missed the EEE curves due to source edges and the corner formed by the two objects in Figure 2 (in red).

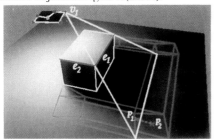

**Figure 1.** EV Discontinuity Surface

***Backprojection Elements***. Backprojection lists are composed of three types of elements, called *bp-elements*, and are illustrated in Figures 1 and 2 with different colors. The three types are:

1. Emitter bp-elements, which are vertices of the emitter (in red).

2. Emitter-edge/scene-edge bp-elements. The projection of a non-emitter scene edge (e.g., edge $e_1$ of the box in Figure 1) through a point $P$ in a face intersects an emitter edge, giving a vertex in the backprojection instance (green vertices).

3. Scene edge/scene edge bp-elements. The projection through a point $P$ of the intersection of two non-emitter edges (e.g., edges $e_1$ and $e_2$ of the box) onto the plane of the emitter is a backprojection vertex that lies within the emitter (in yellow).

**Figure 2.** A EEE Discontinuity Surface

***Computing the backprojection instance***. To compute the instance of a backprojection at a point $P$, each edge of a Type 2 or 3 bp-element is projected through the point $P$ to a point $P'$ on the emitter plane. To perform this projection for Type 2 bp-elements, the plane formed by the scene edge and point $P$ is intersected with the emitter edge. $P'$ is the resulting point of intersection. Similarly, to find the vertex for a Type 3 bp-element the two planes defined by the point $P$ and each of the two scene edges are formed. The intersection of these two planes forms a ray, whose intersection with the emitter plane is $P'$. Thus the list of invariant vertices that form the visible portions of the light source at a given point $P$ can be computed at low cost.

The diffuse illumination at $P$ from each resulting polygonal subsource in the backprojection is

$$L(x,y) = \sum_{i=1}^{n} \gamma_i \cos \delta_i, \qquad (1)$$

where $\gamma_i$ is the angle formed by the point $P(x,y)$ and the vertices of

the source $v_i$, $v_{i+1}$, and $\delta_i$ is the angle between the normal to the receiver, and the plane formed by $v_i$, $v_{i+1}$, and $P$ (e.g., [BaRW89]).

## 2.1. Related Work

The literature contains several partial discontinuity-meshing algorithms. The *extremal penumbral boundary* is the boundary between completely unoccluded regions and penumbral regions. The *extremal umbral boundary* is the boundary between penumbra and umbra. Nishita and Nakamae [NiNa83] directly computed these boundaries for simple environments. Campbell and Fussell [CaFu90] approximated area sources by collections of point light sources, and extended the algorithm in [CaFu91] to area light sources. The extremal penumbral boundary is formed by BSP union operations, but umbral boundaries were not always correctly found, because of the need to compute quadric EEE surfaces. The resulting mesh was represented as a 2-D BSP tree on each receiving surface. Similar mesh computations underlie [ChFe92][ChFe90].

Non-extremal EV surfaces were first calculated in [LiTG92], using BSP trees. Only EV surfaces containing a source edge or vertex were considered, and thus mesh elements often contained subregions with different backprojections. Heckbert considered 2-D discontinuity meshing in [Heck92b], which was extended to 3-D in [Heck92a], in which every EV surface is traced, ignoring EEE surfaces. Teller proposed a similar computation [Tell92], which is equivalent to computing the extremal umbral boundary for such configurations. This is the first treatment of EEE surfaces.

An algorithm to compute the full mesh is proposed by Stewart and Ghali [StGa93][StGa94]. In their algorithm a plane parallel to the source is swept through the scene, and the mesh and the backprojection are built incrementally on this plane. This structure changes during the sweep, requiring more intricate 3-D updates and geometric computations, but guarantees better worst-case behavior than our algorithm. In our case, updates are local and are performed in 2-D, requiring simpler data structures. We also exploit heuristics that, as evidenced below, appear to give excellent results for realistic geometry.

## 3. Efficiently Computing a Complete Mesh

We require some definitions prior to describing our meshing algorithm. A *feature* is either an edge or a vertex. Any EV surface forms a (planar) *wedge*. A *shadow edge* of a polyhedron with respect to a point is an edge that is contained in the silhouette of that polyhedron when viewed from that point. A *shadow vertex* is a vertex that is attached to at least one shadow edge.

Before computing discontinuity surfaces, we compute the lines at which objects touch. These are $D^0$ *events* in [Heck92a]. Each object in the environment is visited, and its neighbors are found using a spatial subdivision structure (see below). Lines are inserted on the faces of objects that touch, denoting radiance discontinuities.

The discontinuity surfaces needed for the complete discontinuity mesh for one emitter are: (a) *emitter-EV surfaces*, of which one feature is on the emitter; (b) *non-emitter EV surfaces*, which do not include an emitter feature, but whose plane intersects the emitter; (c) *emitter EEE surfaces*, that contain an emitter edge, which we call $E_eEE$ surfaces; and (d) *non-emitter EEE surfaces*, that do not contain an emitter edge, but cut the emitter polygon. We have designed efficient algorithms for each type, and we have made an engineering decision to employ algorithms with feasible data structures and solution methods. In doing so we sacrifice worst-case asymptotic complexity for practical performance. As we present our algorithms, heuristic assumptions about scene behavior will be made, and the effect on the resulting complexity presented. Statistics run on typical scenes will be presented to support the assumptions. We now discuss our mesh data structure, and algorithms to handle each type of discontinuity surface.

### 3.1. An Extended Topological Data Structure

We employ a topological, winged-edge data structure to store the mesh (cf. [Glass91]). The structure stores vertices that are connected by edges. These edges enclose faces that can contain edge cycles. This face-edge-vertex structure maintains consistent adjacency information. Each edge has a left and right face pointer, and a twin edge running in the opposite direction.

During the computation of the penumbral boundaries, edges can be added so that the faces of the mesh are not closed. We have augmented the standard data structure to handle such intermediate configurations. Each face of the mesh is bounded by an edge cycle, called a *face boundary*. A *chain* of edges is a sequence of edges that do not necessarily form a closed loop. The following special edges are identified: *lonely edges*, which are not connected to a face boundary, and *dangly edges*, which are connected to a face boundary but are not in any simple cycle. The left and right faces of a lonely or dangly edge are the same, which maintains consistency.

***Computing the arrangement of edges on a receiver.*** In Heckbert's approach [Heck92a], the edges resulting from the intersection of EV-surfaces with receiver objects are associated in an unconnected fashion with the receiver surfaces. A line-sweep step is required to connect these segments. As the sweep-line passes the points, intersections and face structures are built. In our algorithm, the mesh is instead built incrementally as discontinuity surfaces propagate.

EV surfaces are formed by the edges of a blocker polygon and a vertex either of the emitter or other polygon. These edges are traversed in order of the blocker polygon boundary. After each edge insertion, the receiver surface stores the edge as the "last edge inserted". When the next insertion due to the same blocker occurs, it will be connected to the previous vertex (an endpoint of the previous edge), and thus no search time is required to locate the face in which the new edge will be inserted.

When a new blocker is processed, the line connecting the previous insertion point to the current insertion point is followed. In the early stages, no lines will be crossed, and thus the face of insertion will be found without a search. In later stages, the mesh structure may be searched. During this incremental construction, mesh configurations containing lonely and dangly edges often arise. A chain is "closed" to form a closed face, and all dangly and lonely edges are associated with the correct face. The connectivity structure of the faces is thus built incrementally, avoiding some of the numerical robustness problems of the line sweep approach.

In practice, the number of faces traversed to locate the face of insertion is small, as is the number of faces traversed for intersections during edge insertions. Statistics gathered of the number of faces intersected when inserting an edge support this claim. For scenes where $s$ (the total number of faces) was 360, 1256 and 4829 faces, the average number of faces crossed while inserting an edge was 1.19, 1.15 and 1.27 respectively (Table 1).

***Augmenting the mesh to include curved edges.*** Since EEE surfaces are being treated, it is necessary to store curved boundaries of faces. These resulting quadratic curves (see below) are stored symbolically and any operation to determine point-in-face inclusion or line/edge intersections, operates using curved boundaries.

### 3.2. Computing the EV Surfaces

Our algorithm to compute all EV surfaces extends Heckbert's [Heck92a]. Apart from the augmented data structure described above, we also use a voxel-based spatial subdivision structure to greatly decrease the number of intersections of EV surfaces with objects in the environment. The algorithm is completed with the extension to non-emitter EV surfaces. Spatial subdivision is again

used to accelerate the computation of these events.

#### 3.2.1. Casting Emitter-EV Surfaces Through the Environment

To generate the edges of the discontinuity mesh due to emitter EV surfaces, the general structure of Heckbert's algorithm is followed. For each vertex of the emitter and every other shadow edge in the environment (e.g. $v$ and $e$ in Figure 3(a)), and for each edge of the emitter and every shadow vertex in the environment a wedge is formed. Each wedge is potentially intersected with every polygon in the environment. For each such wedge, the line segments corresponding to these intersections are then transformed onto the wedge plane, and inserted into a sorted list (Figure 3(b)). A visibility step is performed that results in the correct segments being inserted into the meshes of the surfaces intersected. These are represented as thick lines in Figure 3(c). The visibility algorithm is a modified 2-D Atherton-Weiler algorithm [AWG78].

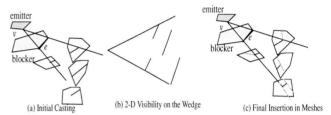

(a) Initial Casting    (b) 2-D Visibility on the Wedge    (c) Final Insertion in Meshes

**Figure 3.** EV surface casting.

Maximal edges are used to determine the boundary between light and penumbra, as described in [CaFu91]. For example, for a specific blocker edge and a source with $p$ vertices, $p$ wedges are formed. At least one of these wedge planes will have all the other wedges in its negative half-space, and is thus maximal. After computing the mesh, the faces are searched to determine those faces whose edges are all due to maximal surfaces. Thus, once the mesh has been computed, the faces that have a completely unoccluded view of the source can be immediately identified.

***Acceleration of emitter-EV computations.*** Since each EV surface needs to be intersected with every object in the environment, the cost of casting one wedge is $O(n)$, where $n$ is the number of objects. Since $m$, the number of resulting wedge/object intersections, is much smaller than $n$ (see Table 1), the cost of 2-D visibility on the wedge plane is unimportant. The total cost of the emitter-EV surface processing is thus heuristically close to $O(n^2)$.

To reduce the number of wedge intersections, we pre-classify objects on a regular grid [AmW87]. The environment is preprocessed once, at which point the objects are inserted into the voxels that they intersect. We can thus restrict object traversal to those in the affected voxels. To intersect an EV wedge with the objects in the scene, we extend and clip it to the bounding box of the environment. The resulting polygon is scan converted on the voxel grid, and a set of candidate objects is created. As seen in Table 1, the casting time for all emitter-EV wedges may approach $O(n)$ in practice, instead of $O(n^2)$, for the class of scenes studied. The performance of voxel spatial subdivision suffers for densely populated scenes requiring high subdivision [PoAm90]. However, since the wedges are distributed in all directions, poor performance for one wedge is likely to be outweighed by economies on many others.

#### 3.2.2. Non-emitter EV Surfaces

Of all possible EV-surfaces, only those that intersect the emitter polygon are relevant. To efficiently identify these surfaces, at each vertex $v$ in the scene, a pyramid is formed with $v$ as its apex and the emitter polygon as its base (see Figure 4(a)). The pyramid is also extended to the other side of the vertex. Objects that intersect the pyramid are added to a list. The list is traversed, and every edge is tested to see if the EV wedge formed with $v$ cuts the source. These additional EV surfaces are collected into a list of candidate non-emitter EV wedges. After the candidate list is formed, the non-emitter EV surfaces in the list are cast, using a modified version of the algorithm used to cast the emitter EV surfaces.

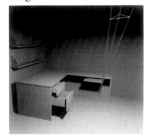 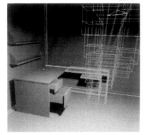

**Figure 4.** (a) the EV pyramid and (b) the voxels visited.

*Acceleration using the voxel structure.* The creation of the candidate lists of non-emitter EV events for all vertices, if performed naively, would be $O(n^2)$ time, where $n$ is the number of edges in the environment. Using the spatial subdivision structure described previously, the voxels that are either internal to the EV-pyramid, or are cut by the bounding planes are found (Figure 4(b)). Subsequently, only the wedges formed by $v$ and the edges of these objects are tested to determine if they cut the source. For each vertex, the number $k$ of edges examined is on average expected to be much smaller than $n$. This is supported by statistics shown in Table 2, run on typical scenes. For a scene of $n = 372$ edges, $k$ was 22.5, while in another scene with $n = 1152$, $k$ was 31.7. In Figure 4(b), only the edges of the highlighted objects are actually tested.

 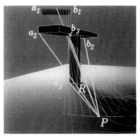

**Figure 5.** (a) $E_e$EE tags; (b) Calculation of $t$

### 3.3. EEE Surface Computation

We now consider separately (a) $E_e$EE surfaces that include an emitter edge, and (b) non-emitter EEE surfaces, which do not include an emitter edge, but cut the emitter polygon.

#### 3.3.1. $E_e$EE Surfaces

The most common EEE curves are caused by discontinuity surfaces that include an emitter edge. Whenever there are more than two skew edges in a scene, these events occur. It is important to identify them efficiently. During the processing of EV surfaces, each mesh vertex receives an integer tag, indicating its generator edges (Figure 5(a)). When two non-adjacent, skew edges meet at a vertex in the mesh, the resulting vertex $v_i$ is inserted in a list. Each such $v_i$ was generated by an emitter vertex $s_i$; thus the EEE conic defined by the triple $\{e_i^s, e_1, e_2\}$ is drawn onto the surface (Figure 5(a)) and similarly for the triple $\{e_{i+1}^s, e_1, e_2\}$. These quadratic curves either join vertices with the same tag, or are appropriately clipped. If a curve is clipped to an occluding edge of a polygon or a mesh edge, the more general solution for non-emitter EEE surfaces is applied.

#### 3.3.2. Non-Emitter EEE Surfaces that Cut the Emitter Polygon

To compute a complete mesh, it is necessary to identify and process EEE surfaces formed by three non-emitter edges that cut the emitter polygon. For scenes of moderate geometric complexity in which

the emitter polygon is small, such events are extremely rare. This is because not only does the ruled quadric surface need to cut the emitter polygon, but the portion that cuts the emitter must be composed of lines that touch the interior of all three defining edges.

*Quadric surfaces arising from EEE events.* The equation of a general quadric surface is

$$Ax^2 + By^2 + Cz^2 + Dyz + Exz + Fxy + Gx + Hy + Iz + J = 0. \quad (2)$$

The coefficients of the ruled quadric formed by three edges can be derived from [GiCS91, Sa1874]. For every point $P$ on the ruled surface defined by edges $e_1, e_2, e_3$, there is a unique line on the surface that passes through $e_1$. If $a_1, b_1$ are the endpoints of $e_1$, then the parametric form for any point $P_t$ on $e_1$ is

$$P_t = a_1 + t(b_1 - a_1), \quad t \in [0,1]. \quad (3)$$

The value of $t$ is used to characterize the point $P$ on the surface given by the other two edges. We call $t$ the *first-edge parameter*. To compute $t$ for a point $P_t$ on the surface, we form the two planes containing $P$ and $e_2$, and $P$ and $e_3$. (If $P$ lies on $e_2$ or $e_3$, then one plane is formed with the other edge, which is then intersected with $e_1$ to find $t$.) Next, we intersect the ray defined by the intersection $R$ of these two planes (yellow line in Figure 5(b)) with the line equation of $e_1$. Then we solve Eq.(3), setting $R = P_t$, for $t \in [0,1]$.

The valid region of the quadric is that for which $t$ varies over $[0,1]$. This region is further limited so that the corresponding ruled lines touch the interior of $e_2$ and $e_3$. To determine the valid region, the first-edge parameter is found for the endpoints $a_2, b_2$ of edge $e_2$ and for the endpoints $a_3, b_3$ of edge $e_3$. The intersection of these intervals is the valid region.

*Processing the quadratic curves on receiver polygons.* The intersection of a plane with the quadric surface is a quadratic curve. To compute this curve, the three generating edges are first transformed into the coordinate system such that the polygon is embedded in the plane $z = 0$. The quadratic curve is now immediately derived from Eq. (2) by keeping only the terms not containing $z$. The quadratic is converted into standard form such that a monotonic parameterization exists [RoAd90]. The quadratic curve is intersected with the edges of the receiver polygon in the $z = 0$ plane, resulting in a collection of segments, possibly clipped to the edges of the receiver polygon. At the endpoint of each segment, two parameter values are computed: the value of the parameter of the curve $s_i$ and the value of the first-edge parameter $t_i$. To determine the valid portions of the curve segments, they are sorted by the curve parameter $s$. The first edge parameters of these segments are computed and only the portions corresponding to valid regions of the quadric are kept.

*Identifying the non-emitter EEE surfaces.* For each edge $e$, a volume is formed between the edge and the convex hull of the emitter polygon, in a manner similar to the EV-pyramid shown in Figure 4(a). This polyhedral volume is used to determine which objects are between the edge and the source, and thus potentially can participate in non-emitter EEE surfaces.

All shadow edges that are not outside the volume, and not parallel to $e$ are inserted into a list. This list contains $k$ edges. For the quadric formed by each non-parallel pair of edges, a trivial culling is performed: if all the vertices of the emitter polygon have the same sign when their coordinates are substituted into Eq. (2), the EEE surface is rejected, since it cannot cut the emitter polygon. A large number of surfaces are culled in this fashion. If some vertices have opposite signs, the curve given by the intersection of the quadric with the emitter plane is formed. If the region of the quadric cutting the emitter polygon is valid (as above), the triple of edges is inserted into the candidate non-emitter EEE surface list.

*Casting EEE surfaces, visibility processing, and EEE curve insertion.* Each EEE surface in the candidate list is intersected with the scene's polygons. The valid segments are stored in a structure including their endpoints, the object they are associated with, and the parameter values $s$ and $t$ for each endpoint. For endpoint $p_i$, the distance $d_i$ along the ruled line from the first-edge is calculated. The coordinate system given by $(t_i, d_i)$ is used to perform visibility processing. Each curve segment now corresponds to a line in $(t, d)$ space (see Figure 6(a,b), where the arrows denote increasing $d$). The lines preserve exact distance only at the endpoints of the curve segments. Relative ordering is maintained because the environment does not include interpenetrating polyhedra.

Once the transformation has been performed, a line sweep visibility processing algorithm is applied. The segments are sorted by increasing first-edge parameter $t$. Each segment has a structure containing "new segments" as they are inserted during the line sweep. A line parallel to the $d$ axis is swept across the plane (Figure 6(b)), and the intersections of the line with the endpoints of the segments are computed. Visibility is calculated and the parameter $t$ recomputed at the resulting new vertices (see Figure 6(c)). Details of the event processing of the sweep can be found in [Dret94a].

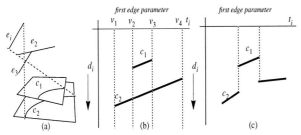

**Figure 6.** Processing the EEE Surfaces

After the visibility step, the curve segments associated with object that are past the third edge in the sense of the distance $d$ are inserted into the corresponding meshes.

***Accelerating EEE surface identification and casting.*** For the EEE surfaces, a volume is formed between the edge $e$ and the emitter polygon. Grid traversal is extended to trace volumes bounded by planes, so that only the objects that are in the voxels that contain the planes, or voxels cut by the planes are processed. The objects in these voxels then comprise a candidate list significantly smaller than the number of objects. As an example (shown in Table 2), for scenes with 372 and 1152 edges, the average number of candidate edges is 46.74 and 67.37 respectively. After rejecting edges outside the volume, and those parallel to edge $e$, the average number of edges $k$ actually examined is usually small. From the statistics, the number $k$ is 6.36 for an environment of 372 edges, and 6.18 for an environment of 1200 edges. The number of EEE surfaces that need to be examined is $k^2$.

When casting the EEE surface, the intersection of the valid region of the quadric surface with the boundaries of the grid is found. The resulting quadratic curves are used to form bounding boxes on the maximal faces of the grid that are then used to form a bounding box of the surface. Within this box, only the objects contained in the voxels cut by the quadric surface are examined.

## 4. Incremental Backprojection Calculation

Since each penumbral face has a unique backprojection, it suffices to create one structure per mesh face, which contains the appropriate lists of emitter vertices and edge pairs. The backprojection instance can then be evaluated at a small cost at any point. In contrast, explicit computation (such as that in [NiNa83]) of the backprojection instance for each point in the face is expensive. The explicit backprojection instance computation at a point $P$, is performed by forming and casting all the EV-wedges defined by $P$ and the edges $e$ lying between $P$ and the emitter. Mesh edges are only

inserted on the plane of the emitter. This creates the correct list of polygons of the backprojection instance on the emitter plane.

With each edge in the mesh, we store the features that induce the corresponding discontinuity surface. The incremental algorithm traverses each edge in the mesh, and uses this information to incrementally update the backprojection from one face to the next. The expensive explicit backprojection calculations in each face are thus avoided.

### 4.1. An Incremental Backprojection Calculation Algorithm

The idea of an incremental algorithm is inspired by [GiCS91]. Our incremental algorithm performs a small number of updates to the backprojection when crossing an edge. The incremental algorithm performs a modified depth-first search of the discontinuity mesh on every receiver surface. Starting from a face in light, for which the "backprojection" is the source itself, every face in each penumbral group is visited. When crossing an edge from one face to another, the appropriate incremental actions are taken. The actions required can be distinguished according to the type of edge being crossed. The discontinuity mesh curves are of two types: (a) *EV induced lines*, caused the intersection of an EV wedge and the scene polygon, (b) *EEE induced curves* that are caused by an EEE surface intersecting the scene polygon. We briefly outline the changes to the backprojections when crossing each edge, depending on its type.

**Figure 7.** Backprojection Updates for EV edges (emitter vertex).

***EV induced edges.*** An EV edge corresponds to the appearance or the disappearance of a vertex behind an edge. For emitter EV-events involving an emitter vertex and scene edge, the updates to the backprojection are shown in Figure 7. For emitter EV-events involving an emitter edge and a scene vertex, the updates required are shown in Figure 8. For non-emitter EV edges, the updates are shown in Figure 9(a).

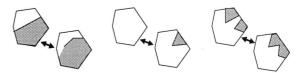

**Figure 8.** Backprojection Updates for EV edges (emitter edge).

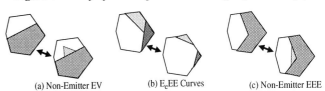

(a) Non-Emitter EV          (b) $E_eEE$ Curves          (c) Non-Emitter EEE

**Figure 9.** Updates for non-emitter EV, $E_eEE$ and EEE edges.

***EEE-induced curves.*** Traversing a EEE curve requires the addition or deletion of up to two scene edge/scene edge elements in the backprojection. For $E_eEE$ edges the update is shown in Figure 9(b), while for non-emitter EEE edges the updates are shown in Figure 9(c). Details of the data structures and their manipulation are presented more fully in [Dret94a].

## 5. Rendering

Once the complete mesh has been computed and the backprojections in each face calculated, an accurate image of direct illumination can be rendered. Rendering is performed either by computing exact radiance values at each pixel, or by interpolation.

## 5.1. Computation of Images with Analytic Radiance Values

To generate an image containing an area light source, previous methods ([CaFu91][LiTG92]) explicitly compute the visible portion of the source at the vertices of the mesh and compute radiance from this. The radiance at other desired points is estimated by interpolation. This is both approximate and expensive. Indeed, the reported cost of computing the illumination at the vertices is at least as large as that of mesh computation.

Given the backprojection in every penumbral face, exact radiance values can be inexpensively computed in penumbral regions. The radiance at any pixel can be computed exactly by finding the instance of the backprojection at the corresponding visible point in the scene, and by applying Eq. (1) for each component of the backprojection, without querying the environment to determine the visible portion of the source. This allows multiple views of scenes with area sources to be computed exactly and cheaply. Examples of such images are shown in Figures 11-14.

## 5.2. Approximate Rendering Using Polynomial Interpolants

Polynomial approximation allows faster rendering and is essential in the context of light transport calculations such as radiosity-based methods. To achieve such an approximation, the penumbral regions of the scene are collected into *groups* of connected penumbral faces. Bounding boxes of these groups are then calculated (see Figure 10(a)). The remaining regular regions of unoccluded illumination are assigned tensor product interpolants of appropriate degree, using the method described in [DrFi93]. The remaining penumbral faces and the light regions not in the tensor product domains, are assigned triangular quadratic interpolants (see Figure 10(b)). Rendering is performed by either querying the interpolants using ray-casting, or by subdividing the polygons of the interpolant domains into smaller polygons, sampling the interpolant at the vertices and rendering in graphics hardware using Gouraud-shaded polygons. The polygons sent to the pipeline and the resulting image are shown in Figures 10(c) and (d).

The hardware rendering allows interactive walkthroughs to be performed with high quality shadows. In addition, by using the incremental algorithm almost-interactive update rates are achieved with a moving source for simple scenes. When moving the source in the table scene of Figure 10 an effective update rate of 5 seconds per frame is achieved using our current implementation. This includes the complete mesh computation, incremental backprojection calculation and the construction, polygonalization and rendering (in hardware) of the interpolants.

# 6. Results and Statistics

All of the above algorithms have been implemented, with the following exceptions: previous-edge caching has been partially implemented, so that explicit searches are sometimes performed to locate the face to insert a new edge; the non-emitter EEE surface processing. The results to follow are strong positive indications that for an interesting classes of scenes drawn from office interiors, the performance of our meshing algorithm is good. All of our computations were performed on an SGI Indigo 2 (R4000).

## 6.1. Performance

In [Dret94a], a simple worst-case complexity analysis of our algorithm shows that it has $O(n^{18})$ time complexity, where $n$ is the number of edges! This is an unrealistic statistic. It is very difficult to construct even an artificial scene for which all worst cases would simultaneously occur. The gap between worst-case analysis and practical performance is worthy of study, but our results suggest that such an analysis may have little to say about real scenes.

In realistic scenes, the use of the voxel grid restricts the number of objects $l$ examined for each surface cast to be much smaller than $n$. The number $m$ of segments for visibility processing is also small, since most often objects are distributed around the scene. The average number $p$ of faces visited when inserting an edge is small due to the mesh connectivity information and because mesh faces are arranged in groups formed as shadows of objects. Thus the surface casting and mesh-edge insertion algorithms perform efficiently. In addition, the number of non-emitter EV and EEE surfaces appears to grow linearly with $n$, and by using the voxel structure they can be identified in $O(n)$ execution time (Table 2).

Our algorithm thus runs in close to $O(n)$ time for an interesting class of interior scenes. It achieves such running times: (a) by taking advantage of expected geometric structure, since the number of non-emitter discontinuity surfaces, the average number of objects tested for intersection by any discontinuity surface, and the actual number of intersections are expected to be small and (b) because it is output sensitive, since the cost of inserting an edge into the mesh depends on the size of the resulting mesh.

## 6.2. Statistics for Emitter EV and $E_eEE$ Implementation

Results are presented in Table 1 for scenes consisting of a table, one complicated desk, the desk and a chair, two desks, and two desks and two chairs respectively. See Figures 10-14 for the rendered scenes. The number of input polygons is $n$, $s$ is the size of the mesh (number of faces), $m$ is the average number of intersections processed in the 2-D visibility step, and max $m$ is the maximum. The average number of objects actually tested for intersection for each wedge is $l$, and $p$ is the average number of faces crossed when inserting an edge. Timings for the use of grid subdivision are given by Grid and NoGrid. The timings include the casting of emitter EV surfaces, the identification and treatment of non-emitter EV surfaces, as well as the treatment of the $E_eEE$ curves.

| Scene | $n$ | $s$ | Time (s) (Grid) | Time (s) (NoGrid) | $m$ | max $m$ | l | $p$ |
|---|---|---|---|---|---|---|---|---|
| Table | 55 | 360 | 6.34 | 9.29 | 1.60 | 5 | 17.89 | 1.19 |
| 1 Desk | 187 | 1256 | 44.42 | 139.07 | 2.09 | 16 | 13.48 | 1.15 |
| 1 Desk 1 Chair | 331 | 2437 | 98.48 | 527.30 | 1.91 | 16 | 16.20 | 1.14 |
| 2 Desks | 349 | 2488 | 89.25 | 626.43 | 2.13 | 29 | 14.07 | 1.15 |
| 2 Desks 2 Chairs | 601 | 4829 | 181.01 | 2302.27 | 1.98 | 29 | 17.80 | 1.27 |

**Table 1.** Statistics from the current implementation the meshing algorithm.

In Table 1, it can be seen that the 2-D visibility step is unimportant, since the average number of segments on the wedge plane is small compared to the scene ($m$ vs. $n$). In addition, the number of faces ($p$) intersected on average during the insertion of each edge into the mesh is small and nearly constant. This suggests that the incremental mesh-building approach will perform well. Also, note that the size of the mesh $s$ grows linearly with $n$.

Observe that the average number of objects in the candidate queue for each wedge cast, $l$, is small compared to $n$, and indeed may not always increase with $n$. If $l$ does not grow with $n$, then the cost of casting a discontinuity surface does not grow either. As more objects were added to the office scenes tested (chairs, shelves, etc.), $l$ did not grow much or even shrunk with $n$, since these objects do not interfere with each other with respect to the light source. This is often the case for scenes of interiors.

## 6.3. Statistics for Non-Emitter Events

The identification steps for non-emitter EEE surfaces were also implemented. In this section we present statistics for the EEE surfaces for the scenes computed above, together with the statistics for the identification of non-emitter EV surfaces. In Table 2, $e$ is the number of edges in the scene. The average number of edges in the EV-pyramid is "EV k", and the number of objects visited in the

EEE-volume, and edges found, are "Queue EEE" and "EEE $k$". These quantities have been discussed in Sections 3.2.2 and 3.3.2.

| Scene | $e$ | EV $k$ | EV Surf. | EV Time | Queue EEE | EEE $k$ | EEE Surf. | EEE Time |
|---|---|---|---|---|---|---|---|---|
| 1 Desk | 372 | 22.45 | 73 | 18.58 | 46.74 | 6.36 | 0 | 25.09 |
| 1 Desk/1 Chair | 636 | 27.33 | 148 | 36.86 | 57.83 | 5.90 | 0 | 52.10 |
| 2 Desks | 696 | 25.56 | 168 | 38.81 | 54.27 | 6.88 | 0 | 47.70 |
| 2 Desks/2 Chairs | 1152 | 31.75 | 394 | 83.93 | 67.37 | 6.18 | 3 | 107.23 |
| 1 Desk (Src 2) | 372 | 18.85 | 457 | 18.95 | 47.94 | 6.22 | 135 | 28.90 |
| 1 Desk/1 Chair (Src 2) | 636 | 28.41 | 2002 | 47.16 | 62.33 | 7.78 | 720 | 61.99 |
| 2 Desks (Src 2) | 696 | 26.10 | 1024 | 45.83 | 67.69 | 7.32 | 324 | 62.52 |
| 2 Desks/2 Chairs (Src 2) | 1152 | 33.24 | 2770 | 91.45 | 73.16 | 6.94 | 1103 | 110.96 |

**Table 2.** Statistics for non-emitter discontinuity surfaces.

The total number of non-emitter EV-surfaces (EV Surf.) was between 73 and 394 for the scenes presented above. The same scenes were run with a bigger source (marked "Src 2" in Table 2), purposely placed so that more of these surfaces cut the emitter. For these new scenes the number of non-emitter EV surfaces was significantly larger (up to 2770), but the average number of edges in the volume was still low. For the first three scenes there were no EEE surfaces cutting the source, while for the scene with two chairs and two desks there were only 3. For "Src 2", the value of $k$ was still small, but the number of potential EEE surfaces was larger.

The cost of identifying all the non-emitter surfaces (EEE time and EV Time) was substantial, but not dominant. The computation time for this step grows slowly in $n$; we do not expect this step to become overwhelming with increased scene complexity, assuming the average number of interactions along each discontinuity surface does not grow significantly.

### 6.4. Results for the Incremental Backprojection Algorithm

The incremental backprojection calculation algorithm has been implemented for relatively simple scenes, in which only EV and $E_eEE$ surface exist in the discontinuity mesh. In Table 3, the time to explicitly compute the backprojections in every face (Time(s) Explicit) is compared to the time taken to compute the backprojections using the incremental algorithm (Time(s) Incremental). The simple scene consists of a parallelepiped floating over a floor and a triangular light source. The table scene is shown in Figure 10, in which the interaction of the table-top and the leg edges create $E_eEE$ surfaces. For both cases the speed-up is immense. For the simple scene the cost of backprojection calculation drops from 2.06 sec. to 0.16 sec., while for the Table scene the cost of computation goes from 9.19 sec. to 0.57 sec., when the incremental algorithm is used. Even better results are expected when the scene is more complex and the explicit computations are thus more expensive.

| Scene | n | s | Mesh Time | Time(s) Explicit | Time(s) Incremental |
|---|---|---|---|---|---|
| Simple Scene (no EeEE) | 19 | 154 | 0.77 | 2.06 | 0.16 |
| Table Scene (w/ EeEE) | 35 | 363 | 2.61 | 9.19 | 0.57 |

**Table 3.** Statistics for the incremental backprojection algorithm.

## 7. Summary and Conclusions

In this paper a complete and efficient discontinuity meshing algorithm based on the fundamental notion of backprojection has been presented. An incremental backprojection calculation algorithm has also been introduced. Our implementation indicates that our algorithm computes the complete discontinuity mesh in time that grows linearly with the number of objects for typical interior office scenes, and that the use of incremental backprojection results in substantial savings in the computation of radiance in the penumbra. Spatial subdivision is used to reduce the number of intersections between objects and discontinuity surfaces. Identification time for non-emitter surfaces is similarly reduced. Our implementation is the first to compute the complete discontinuity mesh for nontrivial scenes involving all classes of EV and EEE events. The only other algorithm that can compute the complete mesh is described in [StGa94]; we shall compare results when that implementation is complete.

The incremental backprojection algorithm allows the backprojection to be computed in an output sensitive manner. This greatly reduces the expense of computing illumination, once the mesh is computed, compared to previous methods where the illumination computation time can surpass that of computing the mesh. Computed radiance is exact at every pixel, not approximate.

The algorithm has been used to study the behavior of radiance in penumbral regions, and to develop efficient representation of illumination for scenes with shadows [Dret94a]. The algorithm has also been used to develop a mesh of varying quality for scenes with multiple light sources [Dret94b]. For the regions in which one source "washes out" the details of the penumbra, only extremal boundaries are computed, while for the regions where the penumbral detail is required, the complete mesh is computed.

### Acknowledgements

The authors wish to acknowledge the financial support of NSERC, ITRC and the University of Toronto. The first author wishes to thank James Stewart for the first implementation of the extended face-edge-vertex structure as well as his helpful insights and suggestions.

### References

[Aman84] Amanatides, John, "Ray Tracing with Cones," *ACM Computer Graphics (Proc. SIGGRAPH '84)*, vol. 18, no. 3, July 1984.

[AmW87] Amanatides, John and Andrew Woo, "A Fast Voxel Traversal Algorithm for Ray Tracing," *Proc. of Eurographics '87*, 1987.

[Appe68] Appel, A., "Some Techniques for Shading Machine Renderings of Solids," *Proc. of AFIPS JSCC*, vol. 32, pp. 37-45, 1968.

[AWG78] Atherton, P., K. Weiler, and Donald P. Greenberg, "Polygon Shadow Generation," *ACM Computer Graphics (Proc. SIGGRAPH '78)*, vol. 12, no. 3, July 1978.

[BaRW89] Baum, Daniel R., Holly E. Rushmeier, and James M. Winget, "Improving Radiosity Solutions Through the Use of Anayticslly Determined Form-Factors," *ACM Computer Graphics (Proc. SIGGRAPH '89)*, vol. 23, no. 3, July 1989.

[BoKe70] Bouknight, W. J. and K. Kelley, "An Algorithm for Producing Half-Tone Computer Graphics Presentations with Shadows and Movable Light Sources," *SJCC, AFIPS*, vol. 36, 1970.

[CaFu90] Campbell, A. T., III and Donald S. Fussell, "Adaptive Mesh Generation for Global Diffuse Illumination," *ACM Computer Graphics (Proc. SIGGRAPH '90)*, vol. 24, no. 4, August 1990.

[CaFu91] Campbell, A. T. III and Donald S. Fussell, "An Analytic Approach to Illumination with Area Light Sources," *Tech. Report TR-91-25*, Comp. Sci. Dept, Univ. of Texas Austin, August 1991.

[ChFe90] Chin, Norman and Steven Feiner, "Near Real-Time Shadow Generation for Global Diffuse Illumination," *ACM Computer Graphics (Proc. SIGGRAPH '90)*, vol. 24, no. 4, August 1990.

[ChFe92] Chin, Norman and Steven Feiner, "Fact Object Precision Shadow Generation for Area Light Source using BSP Trees," *ACM Computer Graphics (SIGGRAPH Symp. on Inter. 3D Graphics)*, 1992.

[Dret94a] Drettakis, George, "Structured Sampling and Reconstruction of Illumination for Image Synthesis," Ph.D. Thesis, Dept. of Computer Sci., University of Toronto, (CSRI T.R. 293 ftp:ftp.csri.toronto.edu:csri-technical-reports/293), January 1994.

[Dret94b] Drettakis, George, "Simplifying the Representation of Radiance from Multiple Emitters," *Submitted for publication*, April 1994.

[DrFi93] Drettakis, George and Eugene Fiume, "Accurate and Consistent Reconstruction of Illumination Functions Using Structured Sampling," *Computer Graphics Forum (Eurographics '93 Conf. Issue)*, vol. 12, no. 3, Barcelona Spain.

[GiCS91] Gigus, Ziv, John Canny, and Raimund Seidel, "Efficiently Computing and Representing Aspect Graphs of Polyhedral Objects," *IEEE Trans. on Pat. Matching & Mach. Intelligence*, vol. 13, no. 6, June 1991.

[GiMa90] Gigus, Ziv and Jitendra Malik, "Computing the Aspect Graph for the Line Drawings of Polyhedral Objects," *IEEE Trans. on Pat. Matching & Mach. Intelligence*, vol. 12, no. 2, February 1990.

[Glass91] Glassner, Andrew S., "Maintaining Winged-Edge Models," *In Graphics Gems II*, edit. by Jim Arvo, Academic Press, 1991.

[Heck92a] Heckbert, Paul, "Discontinuity Meshing for Radiosity," *3rd Eurographics Workshop on Rendering*, Bristol, UK May 1992.

[Heck92b] Heckbert, Paul, "Radiosity in Flatland," *Proc. of Eurographics '92, Cambridge*, Elsevier, September 1992.

[LiTG92] Lischinski, Dani, Fillipo Tampieri, and Donald P. Greenberg, "Discontinuity Meshing for Accurate Radiosity," *IEEE C.G. & Appl.*, vol. 12, no. 6, pp. 25-39, November 1992.

[NiNa83] Nishita, Tomoyuki and Eihchiro Nakamae, "Half Tone Representation of 3-D Objects Illumination By Area Source or Polyhedron Sources," *COMPSAC'83, Proc IEEE 7th Intl. Comp. Soft. and Applications Conf.*, pp. 237-242, November 1983.

[PoAm90] Poulin, Pierre and John Amanatides, "Shading and Shadowing with Linear Light Sources," *Proc. of Eurographics '90*, 1990.

[RoAd90] Rogers, David F. and J. Alan Adams, "Mathematical Elements for Computer Graphics," *(2nd Edition) McGraw-Hill*, 1990.

[Sa1874] Salmon, G., "Analytic Geometry of Three Dimensions," *Metcalfe*, Cambridge, England 1874.

[StGa93] Stewart, A. James and Sherif Ghali, "An Output Sensitive Algorithm for the Computation of Shadow Boundaries," *Fifth Canadian Conference on Computational Geometry*, August 1993.

[StGa94] Stewart, A. James and Sherif Ghali, "Fast Computation of Shadow Boundaries Using Spatial Coherence and Backprojections," *ACM SIGGRAPH Annual Conference Series*, July 1994.

[TaTo91] Tanaka, Toshimitsu and Tokiichiro Takahashi, "Shading with Area Light Sources," *Proc. of Eurographics '91*, 1991.

[Tell92] Teller, Seth, "Computing the Antipenumbra of an Area Light Source," *Computer Graphics (Proc. SIGGRAPH '92)*, vol. 26, no. 2, pp. 139-148, July 1992.

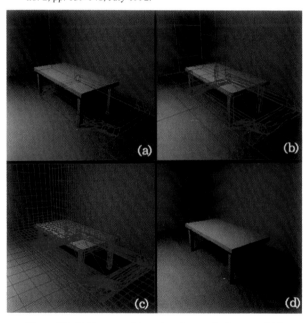

**Figure 10.** Table scene: (a) mesh and penumbral groups (b) interpolant domains (c) polygons sent to pipeline (d) hardware-rendered image.

**Figure 11.** Two desk office scene.

**Figure 12.** One desk office scene.

**Figure 13.** One desk office scene with chair.

**Figure 14.** Two desks with two chairs.

# Fast Computation of Shadow Boundaries
# Using Spatial Coherence and Backprojections

## A. James Stewart and Sherif Ghali

Department of Computer Science
University of Toronto
Toronto, Ontario, Canada M5S 1A4
{jstewart,ghali}@dgp.toronto.edu

## Abstract

This paper describes a fast, practical algorithm to compute the shadow boundaries in a polyhedral scene illuminated by a polygonal light source. The shadow boundaries divide the faces of the scene into regions such that the structure or "aspect" of the visible area of the light source is constant within each region. The paper also describes a fast, practical algorithm to compute the structure of the visible light source in each region. Both algorithms exploit spatial coherence and are the most efficient yet developed.

Given the structure of the visible light source in a region, queries of the form "What specific areas of the light source are visible?" can be answered almost instantly from any point in the region. This speeds up by several orders of magnitude the accurate computation of first level diffuse reflections due to an area light source. Furthermore, the shadow boundaries form a good initial decomposition of the scene for global illumination computations.

**CR category**: I.3.7 [Computer Graphics] Three-Dimensional Graphics and Realism

**Key words**: shadows, backprojections, discontinuity mesh, aspect graphs, radiosity, visual events, efficient surface enumeration, spatial coherence

## 1 Introduction

In a polyhedral scene illuminated by an area light source, discontinuities in illumination must be considered if the scene is to be accurately and quickly rendered. Taking these discontinuities into account goes a long way to producing realistic images.

Discontinuities in illumination occur where the appearance of the visible light source changes abruptly. For example, when a viewpoint crosses from a light area into a shadow, part of the light source disappears and the rate of change of the illumination at the viewpoint diminishes sharply.

Illumination discontinuities form planar or quadric surfaces in space, across which the appearance of the visible light source changes abruptly. When intersected with the faces of the scene, they form linear or quadratic discontinuity curves. The discontinuity curves divide the faces of the scene into cells in which the structure of the visible light source doesn't change. Since the structure of the visible source is constant in each cell, a symbolic description of the structure (called the "backprojection") can be stored in each cell; this allows almost instant reconstruction of the visible areas of the light source at any point in the cell. These concepts will be discussed in more detail later.

In some of the earliest work, Crow computed the shadow volumes made by objects and a point light source [7]. Nishita and Nakamae [18] used shadow volumes from an area light source and classified luminance on each face of the scene as being in umbra, in penumbra, or in light. Radiosity–style algorithms [6; 5] motivated much effort in computing shadows boundaries for use as an initial mesh in radiosity computations. Chin and Feiner [4] and Campbell and Fussell [1] used BSP trees to compute the shadow boundaries in a scene illuminated by a point light source.

Attention has recently turned to computing shadow boundaries for area light sources. Lischinski, Tampieri, and Greenberg [15] classified the types of shadow boundaries that can arise according to the discontinuity in the derivatives of the illumination function on a receiver straddling the boundary. They and Heckbert [14] implemented algorithms that compute the shadow boundaries in a scene illuminated by a polygonal light source. Both algorithms restrict their attention to planar discontinuity surfaces. Algorithms that compute both planar and quadric discontinuity surfaces were given by the authors of the present paper [22] and by Drettakis [8].

Of importance to discontinuity surfaces, Teller recently described how to determine the common stabber to a set of four lines in space using Plücker coordinates [24; 25]. Plücker space provides an elegant parameterization of lines in space that finds the relative orientation of two directed lines using a dot product [21; 23; 3]. We expect Plücker coordinates to become a popular tool in computer graphics.

The discontinuity mesh is related to the aspect graph which is studied in computer vision. Gigus and Malik [12] described an algorithm to compute the aspect graph for planar and quadric discontinuity surfaces. The best algorithm to date for the computation of the aspect graph is due to Gigus, Canny, and Seidel [11].

The results from the present paper can be used in several applications. The discontinuity mesh can be used as the initial mesh for a radiosity–style algorithm. The mesh algorithm can be called before each step of a progressive refinement radiosity using the emitting cell as the light source [15]. Multiple views of the same scene can be computed quickly given the discontinuity mesh, which is independent of the eyepoint and only needs to be computed once.

## 2 Backprojections

This section describes an algorithm that computes the backprojection in every cell of a discontinuity mesh. Construction of the mesh is described in later sections. The algorithm maintains a winged-edge structure to store adjacency information about faces of the scene. and takes advantage of spatial coherence (i.e. the adjacency of faces) to avoid unnecessary computation. The only other algorithm that performs similar processing of the mesh [8] considers each face of the scene separately, but could easily be modified to incorporate our approach. The original work in this area [12] computed the aspect graph (not the discontinuity mesh) and did not need to take advantage of spatial coherence.

### 2.1 Definition of the Backprojection

Recall that the visible source has the same structure or "aspect" from every viewpoint within a cell of the discontinuity mesh, although different areas of the source are visible from different viewpoints

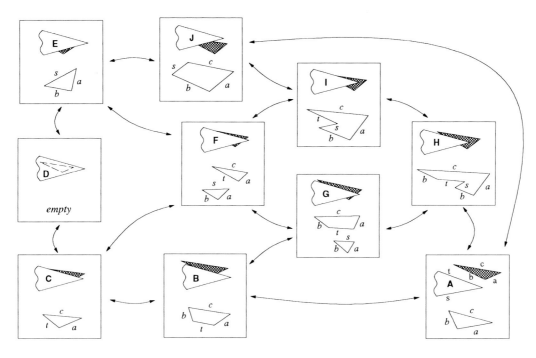

Figure 1: Visible Source and Backprojection in the Mesh Cells

within the cell. Only the position, not the structure, of the area of the visible source varies from viewpoint to viewpoint within a cell.

Figure 2 shows part of a discontinuity mesh formed by a triangular source and a triangular blocker. Each cell of the mesh is labeled with a capital letter. The source edges are $a$, $b$, and $c$; the scene edges of interest are $s$ and $t$. In this example the only discontinuity surfaces that arise are defined by an edge and a vertex and are called EV surfaces. In general, a discontinuity surface is defined by three edges (this is discussed in Section 3).

One such EV surface is formed by vertex $bc$ and edge $t$ and is denoted $\langle b, c, t \rangle$. The discontinuity curve that is the intersection of $\langle b, c, t \rangle$ with the rectangular receiver separates cells $I$ and $H$, $F$ and $G$, and $C$ and $B$ in Figure 2.

Figure 1 shows the visible source for each cell of Figure 2. Each box in Figure 1 corresponds to one cell in Figure 2 and contains (i) the visible source in its upper part as it appears from a viewpoint in the cell, looking upward and (ii) the abstract structure of the visible source in its lower part. The arrows in Figure 1 join adjacent cells. Cell $A$ shows the unoccluded source with labeled edges.

Define a point $u$ to be *visible* from a point $v$ if the line segment $uv$ does not intersect the interior of any polyhedron in the scene. Define the *visible source* at a point $v$ to be the set of points on the source that are visible from $v$. The visible source is a set of polygons and has edges defined by source edges or scene edges. This abstract structure is called the "backprojection" and was described by the authors in [22].

At a viewpoint $v$, define the *backprojection* to be a set of polygons whose edges (i) correspond one-to-one to edges of the visible source at $v$ and (ii) are labeled with the corresponding edges of the scene that bound the visible source. In Figure 1 the top part of each box is the visible source and the bottom part is the backprojection.

Given the backprojection at a particular point, the polygonal boundary of the visible source can be computed as follows: for each backprojection edge, project the corresponding scene edge through the viewpoint onto the plane of the source. Then the exact illumination at the point can be calculated by integrating around the boundary of the visible source.

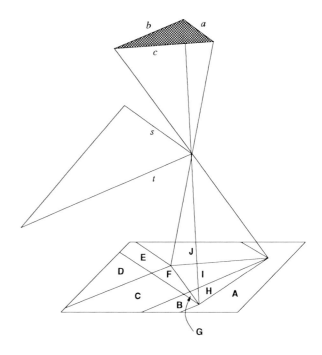

Figure 2: Discontinuity Mesh

## 2.2 Computing the Backprojections

This section describes how to efficiently compute the backprojection for every cell of a mesh. The key insight is the following: *Given the backprojection in one cell, the backprojection in an adjacent cell can be computed by adding or removing a few edges.* For example, in going from cell E to cell J of Figure 1 an edge $c$ is added to the backprojection.

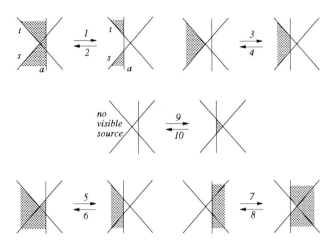

Figure 3: Transitions Across a Discontinuity Surface

To compute the backprojection in every cell of a mesh, the backprojection is computed in an initial cell, then propagated to all adjacent cells, then propagated to all cells adjacent to those cells, and so on. This is a breadth-first traversal of the discontinuity mesh.

To compute the backprojection in the initial cell, a visible surface algorithm (for example, that of McKenna [17]) must be used to determine which parts of the source are visible. However, our algorithm only performs this step at a very few vertices of each polyhedron in the scene.

### 2.3 Updating the Backprojection

This section describes how to update the backprojection from one cell to another. A *visual event* [12] occurs when the viewpoint crosses a discontinuity surface. Since the discontinuity surface intersects the source, some of the three edges that define the surface bound parts of the visible source, as seen from the viewpoint.

For example, consider the transition from cell I to cell F in Figure 2. As the viewpoint crosses the discontinuity surface $\langle a, s, t \rangle$, the vertex $st$ (as seen from the viewpoint) appears to pierce the edge $a$, dividing the visible source into two parts (see Figure 1). The upper left diagram in Figure 3 shows this as an inversion of three lines, following the arrow labeled "1" (the edges $s$ and $t$ are extended past the $st$ vertex and the visible source is shaded).

*All transitions can be thought of in a unified manner as an inversion of three edges.* This unified approach results in a simple implementation. There are only five symmetric pairs of transitions, as shown in Figure 3. All possible combinations of visible source were considered and only these five pairs were physically possible. Each configuration in Figure 3 consists of the three lines that embed the three edges defining the discontinuity surface. Given the three edges of a discontinuity surface and a backprojection on one side of that surface, the transition across the surface can be determined symbolically (with no numeric computation), making the determination robust in the presence of numerical inaccuracy.

Table 1 describes the conditions and actions associated with each transition. The transition is determined by the following two criteria which are listed in the table:

**#E (number of edges)**  The three scene edges that define the discontinuity surface will appear in the backprojection some number of times (0,1,2,3, or 4).

**#V (number of vertices)**  The scene edges that appear in the backprojection will intersect at vertices some number of times (0,1,2, or 3).

Table 1: Transition Conditions and Actions

| #E | #V | type | action |
|---|---|---|---|
| 0 | | 9 | None of $a$, $b$, or $c$ are in the backprojection Create a cycle of $a$, $b$, and $c$. Order is determined numerically. |
| 1 | | 7 | $a$ is in the backprojection. $b$ and $c$ are not. Break $a$ into $a_1 \rightarrow a_2$. Insert $b$ and $c$ between $a_1$ and $a_2$. Determine $b$ and $c$ order numerically. |
| 2 | | 3 or 6 | $a \rightarrow b$. $c$ is not in the backprojection. Insert $c$ between $a$ and $b$. |
| 3 | 1 | 1 | $a \rightarrow b$. $c$ is separate. Split $c$ into $c_1 \rightarrow c_2$. Join $a \rightarrow c_2$ and $c_1 \rightarrow b$. |
| 3 | 2 | 4 or 5 | $a \rightarrow b \rightarrow c$. Delete $b$. |
| 3 | 3 | 10 | $a \rightarrow b \rightarrow c$ in a cycle. Delete $a$, $b$, and $c$. |
| 4 | 2 | 2 | $a \rightarrow c_1$. $c_2 \rightarrow b$. Join $a \rightarrow b$. Merge $c_1$ and $c_2$ into $c$. |
| 4 | 3 | 8 | $a_1 \rightarrow b \rightarrow c \rightarrow a_2$. Delete $b$ and $c$. Merge $a_1$ and $a_2$ into $a$. |

For example, if four edges appear in the backprojection (one appears twice) and they intersect at two vertices then a Type 2 transition applies (shown in Table 1).

Since a scene edge can appear in the backprojection many times, we must be careful to count only those instances that participate in the backprojection update (i.e. those edges shown in Figure 3). From inspection of Figure 3, a backprojection edge $e$ is only counted if either (i) it is attached to another backprojection edge that is labelled with one of the three scene edges, or (ii) it is not attached to any such edge and the two scene edges that do *not* label $e$ meet at a vertex in the scene. Each edge in Figure 3 satisfies condition (i) except for the vertical edges in Type 1 and 7 transitions which satisfy condition (ii).

Table 1 also describes the actions taken for each type of transition. Each entry consists of a description of the configuration of backprojection edges before the transition and an action to perform. The edges that define the discontinuity surface are labeled $a$, $b$, and $c$. Where an edge appears more than once in the backprojection it is labeled with subscripts, like $a_1$ and $a_2$. In Table 1 the notation $x \rightarrow y$ means that edge $x$ precedes edge $y$ in the backprojection. Edges in the backprojection are directed such that the visible part of the source appears to the left of the edge.

For example, consider a Type 2 transition in Table 1. Before the transition the backprojection has four edges, two of which are generated by the same edge on the discontinuity surface (see Figure 3). Keeping in mind that the visible source is to the left of each edge, the edges can be labeled $a$, $b$, $c_1$, and $c_2$ in exactly one way such that $a \rightarrow c_1$ and $c_2 \rightarrow b$. Upon the transition, $a$ and $b$ are joined and $c_1$ and $c_2$ are merged into a single edge.

### 2.4 Computing the Backprojection Across an Edge

The algorithm of the previous section can propagate a backprojection between cells within a single face of the scene. However, when propagating between cells in *two adjacent faces* the backprojection must cross the edge that is shared by the two faces. Since an edge might be embedded in several discontinuity surfaces, the backprojection might have to traverse several surfaces.

For example, Figure 4 shows a source with edges $a$, $b$, and $c$ and a polyhedron with two faces labeled $F$ and $G$ sharing an edge $e$. The edge $e$ is embedded in two discontinuity surfaces:

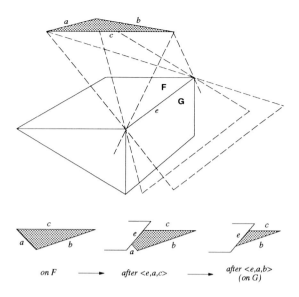

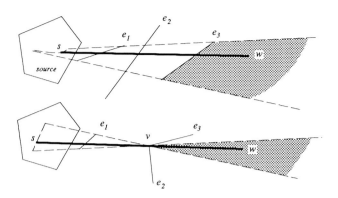

Figure 5: EEE and EV Discontinuity Surfaces

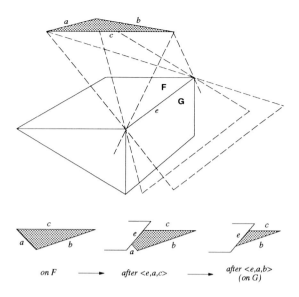

Figure 4: Backprojection Traversing an Edge

$\langle e, a, c \rangle$ and $\langle e, a, b \rangle$ (note that there is no surface $\langle e, b, c \rangle$ since it would intersect the interior of the polyhedron). In face $F$ the backprojection consists of the whole source. In moving to the adjacent face $G$ the backprojection first traverses the surface $\langle e, a, c \rangle$ below $e$ (hiding the vertex $ac$), then traverses the surface $\langle e, a, b \rangle$ below $e$ (hiding the vertex $ab$). The two transitions are shown at the bottom of Figure 4.

The backprojection must cross each discontinuity surface in radial order around the edge. In Figure 4 it would not have made sense to traverse the surface $\langle e, a, b \rangle$ before the surface $\langle e, a, c \rangle$.

In summary, a backprojection can be propagated from one cell of a discontinuity mesh to all connected cells for very little cost, even if cells are on separate faces of the same polyhedron. Drettakis [8] takes a different approach and computes a new backprojection on each polyhedron face.

# 3 Casting Discontinuity Surfaces

This section describes how to *cast* a discontinuity surface through the scene. The casting operation computes the discontinuity curves that are formed by the intersection of a discontinuity surface with the faces of the scene. In this section it is assumed that the three edges defining the surface have already been discovered. Section 4 will describe how to efficiently discover the triples of edges that define discontinuity surfaces.

A discontinuity surface is defined by a triple of edges. In some cases, two of the three edges might meet at a vertex. A surface defined by three edges is denoted EEE; a surface defined by an edge and a vertex is denoted EV. Figure 5 shows two such shaded surfaces.

A *discontinuity surface* is a set of points in space. For any point $w$ on the surface there is a ray that intersects three edges $e_1$, $e_2$ and $e_3$ and the light source at some point $s$ without intersecting the interior of any polyhedron in the scene. If the three edges are skew and distinct, the surface generated is a subset of a quadric [19; 12; 24]. If two of the three edges intersect in a point, the surface is a subset of a plane.

A *discontinuity curve* is the intersection of a discontinuity surface with a face in the scene. If the surface is a quadric, the resulting curve is a conic. If the surface is a plane, the curve is a line segment. For a viewpoint on a face, the appearance of the visible source changes as the viewpoint crosses the discontinuity curve.

A *discontinuity mesh* is the arrangement of discontinuity curves on all faces of the scene.

Heckbert [14] considers only EV surfaces. For every potential EV surface in a scene he computes the intersection of the surface with every face of the scene, resulting in a set of discontinuity segments on various faces. Those segments which are not visible from the light source are removed with a two dimensional visibility algorithm. The remaining segments form the discontinuity mesh. The following sections generalize Heckbert's approach to handle EEE as well as EV surfaces.

## 3.1 Quadrics Defined by Three Edges

Given a point and two lines in space, there exists a single line that touches both lines and pass through the point. The ruled quadric, or *regulus*, formed by the set of lines simultaneously touching three lines in space can be easily synthesized if one thinks of a point moving on one of the three lines. There exists a single line (called the *moveable line* [19]) that passes by each point position and touches the two other lines. The collection of all such lines forms a regulus. This is the basis of a simple parameterization described below. Note that, in general, any line in space pierces such a regulus in *two* points.

The three lines that define the regulus are called *generators* and any line simultaneously touching all three lines is called a *directrix*. The resulting regulus is doubly ruled and if the set of directrices is called the regulus, the set of generators is called the *opposite regulus* [20].

The intersection of a quadric with a plane is, in general, a conic. In affine space, this conic can be an ellipse, a parabola, or a hyperbola depending on whether the line at infinity intersects the conic in zero, one, or two real points in projective space [26]. The section of a conic that arises in our problem is a hyperbola, though it can degenerate into a line segment. We perform all computations using homogeneous coordinates and avoid the need to classify the type of conic in each case.

## 3.2 Computing Surface/Face Intersections

A key operation is to compute the intersection of a discontinuity surface and the scene. First, the equation of the quadric surface is computed. Then this quadric is intersected with each face of the scene to form a conic in each face. The segments of the conic that lie in the face are determined by intersecting the quadric with each edge of the boundary of the face. For each edge of the boundary, this is equivalent to finding the two directrices that simultaneously intersect the three generators of the surface and the line that carries the edge. By substituting the parametric equation of each polygon edge into the equation of a quadric ([19; 12]), we get an equation of the second degree. The real solutions to this equation give the intersection points and the directrices at those points. Each intersection point can be specified by two parameters: the index of the directrix that intersects the point (i.e. the position of the directrix on one of the generators) and the distance along the directrix from the point to the source.

### 3.3 Computing the Visible Conic Segments

Before adding a discontinuity curve to a face, it must be determined that the curve is visible from the light source. Otherwise, the curve is not added to the face. The distances and the indices computed for the endpoints of discontinuity segments are used as input to a sweep line visibility algorithm. This is a simplified version of the hidden surface removal problem (see [14; 8] for details). This approach works whether the quadric is a paraboloid of one sheet or a hyperbolic paraboloid and works whether the conic is a hyperbola or a (subset of a) line.

### 3.4 Computing the Mesh in a Face

After all surfaces have been cast, each face has a list of discontinuity curves associated with it. To this list are added the edges of the face. The arrangement of curves (and the cells defined by the curves) can be computed using a plane sweep algorithm [10]. This is similar to the arrangement Heckbert considers [14]. In our case, we need to make sure, however, that all curves are monotonic in the direction of the sweep. This is clearly true for line segments. For conic segments, check to see if the segment is monotonic and, if it is not, break it into two segments at the point with a derivative parallel to the sweep line.

## 4 Efficient Surface Enumeration

A naive algorithm to build the discontinuity mesh would test *every* triple of edges as a potential discontinuity surface. This section presents a much better algorithm that efficiently determines which triples of edges form discontinuity surfaces. That is, it efficiently enumerates the surfaces.

For an environment of $n$ edges the naive approach considers $\binom{n}{3}$, or about $1/6\, n^3$, triples of edges. For a relatively small environment of 10,000 edges the naive algorithm must consider about 167,000,000,000 such triples. Even if each takes only 0.01 milliseconds to test for validity (about 40 floating point operations at 4 megaflops), it would take 19 days just to enumerate the valid surfaces.

Drettakis [8] uses voxel grid to reduce the number of triples considered, as follows: for each edge $e$, draw the smallest cone that encloses the edge and the source. Only consider those other edges that lie in the voxels that intersect the cone. For each *pair* of such edges, see if it forms a discontinuity surface with the original edge $e$. Drettakis reports that nine tenths of edges are eliminated this way.

Since the number of surfaces is usually much less than $\binom{n}{3}$ an efficient algorithm should not consider a triple of edges unless it actually defines a discontinuity surface. The algorithm presented below uses the backprojection and spatial coherence to accomplish this.

### 4.1 Backprojections and Discontinuity Surfaces

Each discontinuity surface is defined by a triple of edges, two of which might happen to intersect at a vertex. If one of these edges is the most distant from the source it is called the *generating edge*. If two edges intersect at a vertex that is most distant from the source it is called the *generating vertex*. Given three edges, the most distant can be determined by drawing a line that intersects the three edges and the source and ordering the intersection points by increasing distance from the source.

In the following discussion, the light source is assumed to be higher than every polyhedron in the scene. This is not a restriction since nothing above the source (i.e. behind it) is directly illuminated

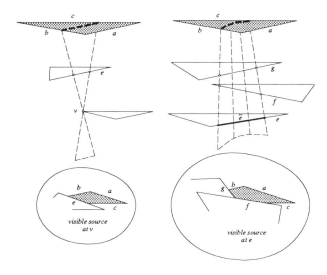

Figure 6: Generating Vertex $v$ and Generating Edge $\tilde{e}$

and can be ignored. *The following observations about generating vertices and generating edges form the core of our approach and allow us to exploit spatial coherence.*

#### 4.1.1 Generating Vertices

If $v$ is the generating vertex of some EV surface $\langle e, v \rangle$ then from the definition of a discontinuity surface there must be a line $\ell$ that simultaneously intersects $v$, $e$, and the source without intersecting the interior of any polyhedron between $v$ and the source. Furthermore, this line must extend below $v$ into empty space; otherwise it would extend into the interior of a polyhedron and the surface would stop at $v$.

For example, consider the left side of Figure 6 in which a vertex $v$, an edge $e$, and a source $abc$ are identified. The backprojection at $v$ is shown to contain four edges: $e$, $c$, $a$ and $b$. There is a line through $v$ and $e$ that intersects the source without intersecting the interior of any polyhedron, so $v$ is the generating vertex of the discontinuity surface $\langle e, v \rangle$. Similarly, $v$ generates the surfaces $\langle a, v \rangle$, $\langle b, v \rangle$, and $\langle c, v \rangle$.

As shown from the example (and proven in our previous work [22]) the vertex $v$ generates a discontinuity surface with exactly those edges that appear in the backprojection at $v$.

**Observation 1** *A vertex $v$ generates a surface $\langle e, v \rangle$ if and only if $e$ is an edge in the backprojection at $v$ and some line intersecting $v$, $e$, and the source extends below $v$ into empty space.*

#### 4.1.2 Generating Edges

On an edge $e$, consider an open subsegment $\tilde{e}$ that does not cross any discontinuity surface (which means that the backprojection is the same at every point on $\tilde{e}$). If $\tilde{e}$ generates a discontinuity surface $\langle \tilde{e}, f, g \rangle$ (where $f$ and $g$ are two edges) then by the definition of a discontinuity surface there must be a line $\ell$ that simultaneously intersects $\tilde{e}$, $f$, $g$, and the source without intersecting the interior of any polyhedron between $\tilde{e}$ and the source. This line must also extend below $\tilde{e}$ into empty space.

For example, consider the right side of Figure 6 in which three edges $e$, $f$, and $g$, and a source $abc$ are shown. The backprojection on $\tilde{e}$ is a polygon with edges $a$, $b$, $g$, $f$, and $c$. Since there is a line simultaneously touching $\tilde{e}$, $f$, $g$, and the source, $\langle \tilde{e}, f, g \rangle$ is a discontinuity surface.

By a similar argument as for generating vertices, whenever a pair of edges $x$ and $y$ meet in the backprojection on $\tilde{e}$ a line can be drawn that simultaneously touches $\tilde{e}$, $x$, $y$, and the source, since the edges of the backprojection define the visible source. Thus $\langle \tilde{e}, g, b \rangle$, $\langle \tilde{e}, b, a \rangle$, $\langle \tilde{e}, a, c \rangle$, and $\langle e, c, f \rangle$ are also discontinuity surfaces generated by $\tilde{e}$ in Figure 6.

**Observation 2** *A subsegment $\tilde{e}$ of an edge $e$ generates a surface $\langle \tilde{e}, x, y \rangle$ if and only if edges $x$ and $y$ meet at a vertex in the backprojection on $\tilde{e}$ and some line intersecting $\tilde{e}$, $x$, $y$, and the source extends below $\tilde{e}$ into empty space. Although $x$ and $y$ meet in the backprojection, the corresponding scene edges do not necessarily meet at a vertex.*

In summary, if the backprojection is known for each vertex and along each edge of the scene, the discontinuity surfaces can be efficiently enumerated simply by looking at the backprojections: At a vertex, all edges in the backprojection are tested; on a subsegment of an edge, all vertices in the backprojection are tested. Since the size of the backprojection is usually very small this testing will be fast. Thus, all discontinuity surfaces can be enumerated efficiently in time approximately proportional to the number of surfaces.

## 4.2 Propagating Backprojections Locally

The algorithm presented below computes the backprojections at a few selected vertices and then propagates them along the edges of the scene to every other edge and vertex. Thus backprojections will be known everywhere and all discontinuity surfaces can be enumerated efficiently. The following sections describe how to propagate the backprojection through the scene.

### 4.2.1 Propagating Along an Edge

An edge $e$ can be subdivided into maximal subsegments in which the backprojection is constant. By definition, these subsegments will be separated by discontinuity surfaces which intersect $e$ but which don't embed $e$. The points of intersection can be ordered from one end of $e$ to the other. Let $s_1, s_2, \ldots s_k$ be the maximal subsegments on $e$, in order.

Given the backprojection at one end of the edge (in $s_1$) it is propagated to the other end (in $s_k$) by crossing the discontinuity surfaces in order. The actions of Table 1 are applied to update the backprojection with each crossing.

To enumerate the discontinuity surfaces generated by $e$, Observation 2 is applied. Let $B_i$ be the backprojection in $s_i$. Every vertex in $B_1$ (the backprojection of the first subsegment) is combined with $e$ according to Observation 2 and the resulting surfaces are cast. Upon updating the backprojection from $B_i$ to $B_{i+1}$ only the *new vertices* in $B_{i+1}$ are combined with $e$ and the resulting surfaces are cast (the old vertices were considered at a previous stage).

Thus the backprojection can be propagated down an edge and all surfaces generated by that edge can be efficiently and easily enumerated.

### 4.2.2 Computing the Backprojection at a Vertex

An edge $(u, v)$ adjacent to a vertex $v$ is said to be *above* the vertex if the other endpoint $u$ is higher than $v$. It will be assumed that $u$ and $v$ are never at the same level (this can be accomplished by imposing a total order on the vertices).

The backprojection at the vertex is the union of the backprojections on the edges immediately above the vertex: If some part of the source (which is above the vertex) is visible at the vertex then it is visible on one of the edges immediately above the vertex. Conversely, if some part of the source is visible on an edge immediately above the vertex then it is visible at the vertex.

To enumerate the surfaces generated by $v$ it is sufficient from Observation 1 to determine which edges are in the backprojection at $v$ (the backprojection does not actually need to be constructed). These are exactly the edges in the union of the backprojections above $v$, minus the set of edges adjacent to $v$. This set can be easily computed and the corresponding surfaces cast.

Thus all surfaces generated by a vertex can be efficiently enumerated, given the backprojections on the edges above the vertex.

### 4.2.3 Propagating Past a Vertex

At a vertex the backprojection is propagated from edge to adjacent edge in *radial order* around the vertex. In this manner the backprojection is propagated from edges above the vertex to edges below.

Let $e_i$ and $e_{i+1}$ be two adjacent edges at a vertex $v$. Let $f_i$ be the face between them and let $f_{i-1}$ be the face on the other side of $e_i$. The propagation from $e_i$ to $e_{i+1}$ consists of three steps: from $e_i$ to $f_i$, across $f_i$, and from $f_i$ to $e_{i+1}$. See Figure 7, which shows a cutaway view of the faces.

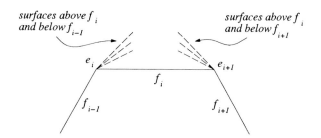

Figure 7: Propagating from Edge to Edge

The first step is similar to the propagation across an edge described in Section 2.4: the backprojection on $e_i$ must be incrementally updated across the surfaces that embed $e_i$ until it reaches $f_i$ (see also Figure 4). To determine these surfaces, consider every vertex in the backprojection at $v$ (which is the union of the backprojections on edges above $v$): Draw a ray from $v$ through the two scene edges that define the backprojection vertex. Order these rays radially around $e_i$ and traverse the corresponding surfaces in radial order.

However, in propagating the backprojection from $e_i$ to $f_i$, it is incorrect to traverse all of the surfaces embedding $e_i$. Only those surfaces that fall below $f_{i-1}$ and above $f_i$ should be traversed (i.e. those surfaces for which the corresponding ray leaving $v$ has a positive dot product with the outward pointing normal of $f_{i-1}$ and a negative dot product with the normal of $f_i$). These are the surfaces encountered as the backprojection moves from $e_i$ to $f_i$. The other surfaces which do not satisfy this condition are those encountered moving from $e_i$ to $f_{i-1}$.

For example, in Figure 4 the surfaces $\langle e, a, b \rangle$ and $\langle e, a, c \rangle$ satisfy this condition (where $F = f_{i-1}$ and $G = f_i$). In propagating the backprojection from $e$ to $G$ both surfaces would be traversed. But in propagating from $e$ to $F$ neither would be crossed. One can think of the propagation from face $F$ to face $G$ in two stages: from $F$ to $e$ and from $e$ to $G$.

The second step involves propagating the backprojection across $f_i$, since the backprojection on $f_i$ adjacent to $e_i$ could be different from that on $f_i$ adjacent to $e_{i+1}$. This only occurs if there are discontinuity curves in $f_i$ which have one endpoint on $v$ (recall that $e_i$ and $e_{i+1}$ meet at $v$). These curves must be traversed in radial order around $v$, from $e_i$ to $e_{i+1}$. Note that these curves will be known when this step takes place.

The third step involves propagating the backprojection from $f_i$ to $e_{i+1}$. This is the same as the first step, but only the surfaces above $f_i$ and below $f_{i+1}$ are traversed.

Thus the backprojection can be propagated from any edge above a vertex to every edge below the vertex. The propagation is fairly easy to implement.

### 4.3 The Global Propagation Algorithm

Define a *peak vertex* to be a vertex with no adjacent edges above it. Since every vertex and edge is reachable from some peak vertex, it is sufficient to compute backprojections for all peak vertices and to propagate them as described above.

However, when propagating along an edge $e$ the discontinuity surfaces that intersect $e$ must be known. The generating edge of any such discontinuity surface must lie above $e$, since it lies between $e$ and the source, which lies above everything. If the edges are processed from top to bottom then the generating edges will be encountered first, ensuring that all surfaces that intersect $e$ are known before $e$ is reached.

The global propagation algorithm operates as follows: Initially, all scene vertices are placed in a priority queue ordered by decreasing height. While the queue is not empty the highest vertex is removed and one of the following operations is applied:

- At a peak vertex, the backprojection is computed with a visible surface algorithm. The backprojection is also computed for one of the edges below the vertex and is propagated to the other edges as described in Section 4.2.3. The surfaces generated by the vertex and its adjacent edge are cast through the scene. Whenever a surface intersects an edge of the scene, the surface/edge intersection point is added to the priority queue.

- At a vertex that is not a peak, the backprojection is propagated from the edges above the vertex to the edges below as described in Section 4.2.3. The surfaces generated by the vertex and the edges below the vertex are cast through the scene, as described in Section 3. Whenever a surface intersects an edge of the scene, the surface/edge intersection point is added to the priority queue.

- At a surface/edge intersection point, the backprojection on the edge is propagated across the discontinuity surface that defines the point. Surfaces are enumerated as described in Section 4.2.1 and are cast through the scene as usual.

When the priority queue becomes empty, all surfaces have been cast and each face of the scene stores an unordered set of discontinuity curves that lie in that face. On each face the mesh is computed from these curves (Section 3.4) and then populated with backprojections using the incremental algorithm of Section 2.3. Note that the backprojection is *already known* for many cells in each face: It was computed when the backprojection was propagated radially around each vertex of the face (Section 4.2.3) and should be stored at that time.

The algorithm is efficient because it does not have to consider all triples of edges as potential discontinuity surfaces, which can be extremely expensive. It enumerates discontinuity surfaces in time approximately proportional to the number of surfaces.

In summary, the algorithm uses spatial coherence to reduce the number of triples of edges considered. Observations 1 and 2 show how to compute the discontinuity surfaces generated by an edge or a vertex, given the backprojection on the edge or vertex. Propagation operations describe how to propagate the backprojection downward through the scene. The algorithm processes points in order of decreasing height so that generating edges of discontinuity surfaces are encountered before the edges intersected by such surfaces.

## 5  Implementation Results

The complete algorithm has been implemented and handles all types of discontinuity surfaces. We believe that any competent programmer can implement the algorithm without difficulty. In fact, the most complicated data structure needed is a winged-edge structure to store the polyhedra, the backprojections, and the mesh.

The algorithm was tested on various scenes, two of which are similar to those of Drettakis and Fiume in these proceedings. One of these two scenes consisted of a rectangular prism suspended between a light source and a receiving surface. The other contained a table, a light source, and a floor.

A third scene, shown in Figure 8, is meant to be a spiral staircase. Notice that discontinuity mesh falls upon the steps as well as the floor. Figure 9 shows a close view of some curved EEE discontinuities from the table scene (which is not shown).

The results are summarized in the following table which lists, for each scene, the number of scene edges, the number of surfaces cast, the time to enumerate the surfaces, the time to cast the surfaces, the time to build the mesh, and the time to populate the mesh with backprojections. These times are from runs on a Silicon Graphics Indigo$^2$ with benchmarks of 59 for SPEC 92 INT and 61 for SPEC 92 FP.

Table 2: Timings (in seconds)

| scene | # edge | # surf | enum time | cast time | mesh time | BP time | total time |
|---|---|---|---|---|---|---|---|
| prism | 19 | 48 | 0.00 | 0.10 | 0.02 | 0.01 | 0.13 |
| table | 67 | 121 | 0.02 | 1.04 | 0.14 | 0.02 | 1.22 |
| spiral | 151 | 433 | 0.20 | 9.48 | 0.69 | 0.20 | 10.57 |
| 4 tables | 247 | 633 | 1.50 | 23.05 | 0.79 | 0.20 | 25.54 |

From Table 2 it is clear that the casting of surfaces takes the most time, and that it is essential to cast the absolute minimum number of surfaces. Even if the surface casting is accelerated with a voxel subdivision as is done by Drettakis and Fiume, it will still be the dominant cost of the algorithm. The primary advantage of our algorithm is that it *does* enumerate the minimum number of surfaces and doesn't take much time doing so.

## 6  Discussion

A fast and practical algorithm has been presented that computes the discontinuity mesh for a polyhedral scene and polygonal light source. Another algorithm has been presented that computes the backprojection in every cell of the discontinuity mesh. These algorithms fully exploit spatial coherence to obtain fast running times.

The implementation of this algorithm has been separate from that of the algorithm by Drettakis and Fiume described in these proceedings. Ideas from both approaches can be combined to yield an algorithm which is more efficient than either. In particular, in our algorithm, the casting of a discontinuity surface can be sped up by using a voxel or BSP approach as is done by Drettakis and Fiume. Their algorithm would be faster if it updated the backprojection from face to face as we describe in Section 2.4.

The most important comparison is in the number of surfaces cast by each algorithm. Surface casting is the most expensive operation, whether or not it is accelerated by a voxel grid. Compared to surface casting, the operations of enumerating the surfaces, building the mesh, and populating it with backprojections take almost no time at all (about one tenth the time for casting).

The heuristic approach of Drettakis and Fiume avoids considering all surfaces with a voxel grid heuristic. Our approach provably considers the minimum number of surfaces [22] by propagating the backprojection through the scene and applying Observations 1 and 2. It is not yet clear which algorithm will perform better in practice.

## Acknowledgements

This research is supported by the Information Technology Research Centre of Ontario, the Natural Sciences and Engineering Research Council of Canada, and the University of Toronto.

# References

[1] A. T. Campbell III and Donald Fussell. Adaptive mesh generation for global diffuse illumination. *Computer Graphics (SIGGRAPH '90 Proceedings)*, 24(4):155–164, August 1990.

[2] A. T. Campbell III and Donald Fussell. An analytic approach to illumination with area light sources. Department of Computer Sciences, University of Texas at Austin, technical report TR-91-25, August 1991.

[3] Bernard Chazelle, Herbert Edelsbrunner, Leonidas Guibas, Micha Sharir, and Jorge Stolfi. Lines in space: Combinatorics and algorithms. New York University, Courant Inst. of Math. Sc. Technical Report No. 491, (also in STOC 1989, pp. 382-393), February 1990.

[4] Norman Chin and Steven Feiner. Near real-time shadow generation using bsp trees. *Computer Graphics (SIGGRAPH '89 Proceedings)*, 23(3):99–106, July 1989.

[5] Michael Cohen, Shenchang Eric Chen, John R. Wallace, and Donald P. Greenberg. A progressive refinement approach to fast radiosity image generation. *Computer Graphics (SIGGRAPH '88 Proceedings)*, 22(4):75–84, August 1988.

[6] Michael Cohen and Donald P. Greenberg. The hemi-cube: A radiosity solution for complex environments. *Computer Graphics (SIGGRAPH '85 Proceedings)*, 19(3):31–40, August 1985.

[7] Franklin C. Crow. Shadow algorithms for computer graphics. *Computer Graphics (SIGGRAPH '77 Proceedings)*, 11(2):242–248, July 1977.

[8] George Drettakis. *Structured Sampling and Reconstruction of Illumination for Image Synthesis*. PhD thesis, University of Toronto, January 1994.

[9] George Drettakis and Eugene Fiume. A fast shadow algorithm for area light sources using backprojections. *COMPUTER GRAPHICS Proceedings, Annual Conference Series 1994*, August 1994.

[10] Herbert Edelsbrunner. *Algorithms in Computational Geometry*. Springer-Verlag, 1987.

[11] Ziv Gigus, John Canny, and Raimund Seidel. Efficiently computing and representing aspect graphs for polyhedral objects. *IEEE Transactions on Pattern Analysis and Machine Intelligence*, 13(6):542–551, June 1991.

[12] Ziv Gigus and Jitendra Malik. Computing the aspect graphs for line drawings of polyhedral objects. *IEEE Transactions on Pattern Analysis and Machine Intelligence*, 12(2):113–122, February 1990.

[13] Pat Hanrahan, David Salzman, and Larry Auperle. A rapid hierarchical radiosity algorithm. *Computer Graphics (SIGGRAPH '91 Proceedings)*, 25(4):197–206, July 1991.

[14] Paul Heckbert. Discontinuity meshing for radiosity. *Third Eurographics Workshop on Rendering*, pages 203–215, May 1992.

[15] Dani Lischinski, Filippo Tampieri, and Donald Greenberg. Discontinuity meshing for accurate radiosity. *IEEE Computer Graphics & Applications*, pages 25–39, November 1992.

[16] Dani Lischinski, Filippo Tampieri, and Donald Greenberg. Combining hierarchical radiosity and discontinuity meshing. *COMPUTER GRAPHICS Proceedings, Annual Conference Series 1993*, pages 199–208, August 1993.

[17] M. McKenna. Worst-case optimal hidden-surface removal. *ACM Trans. Graph.*, 6:19–28, 1987.

[18] Tomoyuki Nishita and Eihachiro Nakamae. Half-tone representation of 3-d objects illuminated by area sources or polyhedron sources. *COMPSAC'83, Proc. IEEE 7th Intl. Conf. Soft. and Appl. Conf.*, pages 237–242, November 1983.

[19] George Salmon. *A treatise on the Analytical Geometry of Three Dimensions*. Longmans, Green and Co., 1912.

[20] Arthur Scherk. personal communications.

[21] Duncan M. Y. Sommerville. *Analytical Geometry in three dimensions*. Cambridge University Press, 1934.

[22] A. James Stewart and Sherif Ghali. An output sensitive algorithm for the computation of shadow boundaries. In *Canadian Conference on Computational Geometry*, pages 291–296, August 1993.

[23] Jorge Stolfi. *Oriented Projective Geometry*. PhD thesis, Stanford University, 1988.

[24] Seth Teller. Computing the antipenumbra of polyhedral holes. *Computer Graphics (SIGGRAPH Procedings)*, August 1992.

[25] Seth Jared Teller. *Visibility Computations in Densely Occluded Polyhedral Environments*. PhD thesis, University of California at Berkeley, 1993.

[26] Oswald Veblen and Wesley Young. *Projective Geometry*. Blaisdell Publishing Co., 1938.

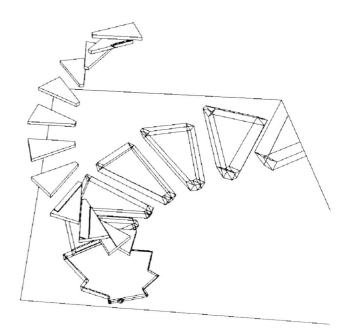

Figure 8: Spiral Staircase and its Discontinuity Mesh

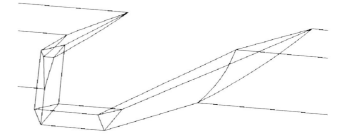

Figure 9: Curved EEE Discontinuities from Table Scene

# Generalization of Lambert's Reflectance Model

Michael Oren    and    Shree K. Nayar

Department of Computer Science, Columbia University

New York, NY 10027

## Abstract

Lambert's model for body reflection is widely used in computer graphics. It is used extensively by rendering techniques such as radiosity and ray tracing. For several real-world objects, however, Lambert's model can prove to be a very inaccurate approximation to the body reflectance. While the brightness of a Lambertian surface is independent of viewing direction, that of a rough surface increases as the viewing direction approaches the light source direction. In this paper, a comprehensive model is developed that predicts body reflectance from rough surfaces. The surface is modeled as a collection of Lambertian facets. It is shown that such a surface is inherently non-Lambertian due to the foreshortening of the surface facets. Further, the model accounts for complex geometric and radiometric phenomena such as masking, shadowing, and interreflections between facets. Several experiments have been conducted on samples of rough diffuse surfaces, such as, plaster, sand, clay, and cloth. All these surfaces demonstrate significant deviation from Lambertian behavior. The reflectance measurements obtained are in strong agreement with the reflectance predicted by the model.

**CR Descriptors:** I.3.7 [**Computer Graphics**]: Three-Dimensional Graphics and Realism; I.3.3 [**Computer Graphics**]: Picture/Image Generation; J.2 [**Physical Sciences and Engineering**]: Physics.

**Additional Key Words:** reflection models, Lambert's model, BRDF, rough surfaces, moon reflectance.

## 1 Introduction

An active area of research in computer graphics involves the creation of realistic images. Images are rendered using one of two well-known techniques, namely, ray tracing [34] or radiosity [6]. The quality of a rendered image depends to a great extent on the accuracy of the reflectance model used. In the past decade, computer graphics has witnessed the application of several physically-based reflectance models for image rendering (see [7], [16], [9], [13]). Reflection from a surface can be broadly classified into two categories: *surface reflectance* which takes place at the interface between two media with different refractive indices and *body* reflectance

which is due to *subsurface scattering*. Most of the previous work on physically-based rendering has focused on accurate modeling of surface reflectance. They predict ideal specular reflection from smooth surfaces as well as wide directional lobes from rougher surfaces [13]. In contrast, the body component has most often been assumed to be Lambertian. A Lambertian surface appears equally bright from all directions. This model was advanced by Lambert [18] more than 200 years ago and remains one of the most widely used models in computer graphics.

For several real-world objects, however, the Lambertian model can prove to be a poor and inadequate approximation to body reflection. Figure 1(a) shows a real image of a clay vase obtained using a CCD camera. The vase is illuminated by a single distant light source in the same direction as the sensor. Figure 1(b) shows a rendered image of a vase with the same shape as the one shown in Figure 1(a). This image is rendered using Lambert's model, and the same illumination direction as in the case of the real vase. As expected, Lambert's model predicts that the brightness

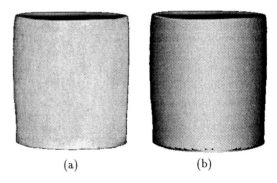

| (a) | (b) |

Figure 1: (a) Real image of a cylindrical clay vase. (b) Image of the vase rendered using the Lambertian reflectance model. In both cases, illumination is from the viewing direction.

of the cylindrical vase will decrease as we approach the occluding boundaries on both sides. However, the real vase is very flat in appearance with image brightness remaining almost constant over the entire surface. The vase is clearly *not* Lambertian [1]. This deviation from Lambertian behavior can be significant for a variety of real-world materials, such as, concrete, sand, and cloth. An accurate model that describes body reflection from such commonplace surfaces is imperative for realistic image rendering.

---

[1]Note that the real vase does not have any significant specular component, in which case, a vertical highlight would have appeared in the middle of the vase.

What makes the vase shown in Figure 1(a) non-Lambertian? We show that the primary cause for this deviation is the roughness of the surface. Figure 2 illustrates the relationship between magnification and reflectance (also see [16]). The reflecting surface may be viewed as a collection of planar facets. At high magnification, each picture element (rendered pixel) includes a single facet. At lower magnifications, each pixel can include a large number of facets. Though the Lambertian assumption is often reasonable when looking at a single planar facet, the reflectance is not Lambertian when a collection of facets is imaged onto a single pixel. This deviation is significant for very rough surfaces, and increases with the angle of incidence. In this paper, we develop a comprehensive model that predicts body reflectance from rough surfaces, and provide experimental results that support the model. Lambert's model is an instance, or limit, of the proposed model.

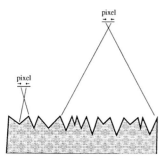

Figure 2: The roughness of a surface causes its reflectance properties to vary with image magnification.

The topic of rough surfaces has been extensively studied in the areas of applied physics, geophysics and engineering. The development of the first few models were primarily motivated to describe the non-Lambertian behavior of the moon. Some of the models are empirical such as Opik's model [22] and its modification by Minnaert [19]. These models do not have any physical foundation and have been found to be incorrect. In contrast, Smith [29] and Buhl et al. [3] attempted to develop theoretical models for reflectance from rough surfaces. Smith modeled the rough surface as a random process and assumed each point on the surface to be Lambertian in reflectance. Smith's analysis, however, was confined to the plane of incidence and is not easily extensible to reflections outside this plane. Moreover, Smith's model does not account for interreflection effects. Buhl et al. [3] modeled the surface as a collection of spherical cavities. They analyzed interreflections using this surface model, but did not present a complete model that accounts for masking and shadowing effects for arbitrary angles of reflection and incidence. Subsequently, Hering and Smith [14] derived a detailed thermal emission model for surfaces modeled as a collection of V-cavities. However, all cavities are assumed to be identical and aligned in the same direction, namely, perpendicular to the source-viewer plane. Further, the model is limited to the plane of incidence.

More recently, body reflection has emerged as a topic of interest in the graphics community. Poulin and Fournier [26] derived a reflectance function for anisotropic surfaces modeled as a collection of parallel cylindrical sections. Addressing a different cause for non-Lambertian reflectance from the one discussed here, Hanrahan and Krueger [10] used linear transport theory to analyze subsurface scattering from a multi-layered surface. Other researchers in graphics have

numerically pre-computed fairly complex reflectance functions and stored the results in the form of look-up tables or coefficients of spherical harmonic expansion (for examples, see [4] [16] [33]). This approach, though practical in many instances, does not replace the need for accurate analytical reflectance models.

The reflectance model developed here can be applied to isotropic as well as anisotropic rough surfaces, and can handle arbitrary source and viewer directions. Further, it takes into account complex geometrical effects such as *masking*, *shadowing*, and *interreflections* between points on the surface. We begin by modeling the surface as a collection of long symmetric V-cavities. Each V-cavity has two opposing facets and each facet is assumed to be much larger than the wavelength of incident light. This surface model was used by Torrance and Sparrow [30] to describe incoherent directional component of surface reflection from rough surfaces. Here, we assume the facets to be Lambertian [2]. First, we develop a reflectance model for anisotropic surfaces with one type (facet-slope) of V-cavities, with all cavities aligned in the same direction on the surface plane. Next, this result is used to develop a model for the more general case of isotropic surfaces that have normal facet distributions with zero mean and arbitrary standard deviation. The standard deviation parameterizes the *macroscopic* roughness of the surface. The fundamental result of our work is that the body reflectance from rough surfaces is not uniform but increases as the viewer moves toward the source direction. This deviation from Lambert's law is not predicted by any previous reflectance model.

We present several experimental results that demonstrate the accuracy of our model. The experiments were conducted on real samples such as sand, plaster, and cloth. In all cases, reflectance predicted by the model was found to be in strong agreement with measurements. The derived model has been implemented as a shading function in RenderMan [32]. We conclude by comparing real and rendered images of a variety of objects. These results demonstrate two points that are fundamental to computer graphics. (a) Several real-world objects have body reflection components that are significantly non-Lambertian. (b) The model presented in this paper can be used to create realistic images of a variety of real-world objects.

## 2  Surface Roughness Model

The effects of shadowing, masking and interreflection need to be analyzed in order to obtain an accurate reflectance model. To accomplish this, we use the roughness model proposed by Torrance and Sparrow [30] that assumes the surface to be composed of long symmetric V-cavities (see Figure 3). Each cavity consists of two planar facets. The width of each facet is assumed to be small compared to its length. We assume each facet area $da$ is small compared to the area $dA$ of the surface patch that is imaged by a single sensor pixel. Hence, each pixel includes a very large number of facets. Further, the facet area is large compared to the wavelength $\lambda$ of incident light, and therefore geometrical optics can be used to derive the reflectance model. The above assumptions can be summarized as: $\lambda^2 \ll da \ll dA$

We denote the slope and orientation of each facet in the V-cavity model as $(\theta_a, \phi_a)$, where $\theta_a$ is the polar angle and

---

[2]This assumption does not limit the implications of the reflectance model presented here. The non-Lambertian behavior reported here is expected for a wide range of local body reflectance models (see [5], for example) since surface roughness is shown to play a dominant role.

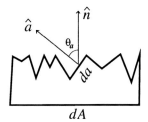

Figure 3: Surface modeled as a collection of V-cavities.

$\phi_a$ is the azimuth angle. Torrance and Sparrow have assumed all facets to have equal area $da$. They use the distribution $N(\theta_a, \phi_a)$ to represent the number of facets per unit surface area that have the normal $\hat{a} = (\theta_a, \phi_a)$. Here, we use a probability distribution to represent the fraction of the surface area that is occupied by facets with a given normal. This is referred to as the *slope-area distribution* $P(\theta_a, \phi_a)$. The facet-number distribution and the slope-area distribution are related as follows:

$$P(\theta_a, \phi_a) = N(\theta_a, \phi_a)\, da\, \cos \theta_a \qquad (1)$$

The slope-area distribution is easier to use than the facet-number distribution in the following model derivation. For isotropic surfaces, $N(\theta_a, \phi_a) = N(\theta_a)$ and $P(\theta_a, \phi_a) = P(\theta_a)$, since the distributions are rotationally symmetric with respect to the global surface normal $\hat{n}$ (Figure 3).

## 3  Reflectance Model

In this section, we derive a reflectance model for rough diffuse surfaces. For lack of space, only important results are discussed. For details we refer the reader to Oren and Nayar [23, 24]. During the derivation, we will draw on several well-known radiometric definitions that are given in [20].

Consider a surface area $dA$ that is imaged by a single sensor element in the direction $\hat{v} = (\theta_r, \phi_r)$ and illuminated by a distant point light source in the direction $\hat{s} = (\theta_i, \phi_i)$. The area $dA$ is composed of a very large number of symmetric V-cavities. Each V-cavity is composed of two facets with the same slope but facing in opposite directions. Consider the flux reflected by a facet with area $da$ and normal $\hat{a} = (\theta_a, \phi_a)$. The projected area on the surface occupied by the facet is $da \cos \theta_a$ (see Figure 3). Thus, while computing the contribution of the facet to the radiance of the surface patch, we need to use the projected area $da \cos \theta_a$ and not the actual facet area $da$. This radiance contribution is what we call the *projected radiance* of the facet:

$$L_{rp}(\theta_a, \phi_a) = \frac{d\Phi_r(\theta_a, \phi_a)}{(da \cos \theta_a) \cos \theta_r\, d\omega_r} \qquad (2)$$

where, $d\omega_r$ is the solid angle subtended by the sensor optics. For ease of description, we have dropped the source and viewing directions from the notations for projected radiance and flux. Now consider the slope-area distribution of facets given by $P(\theta_a, \phi_a)$. The total radiance of the surface can be obtained as the aggregate of $L_{rp}(\theta_a, \phi_a)$ over all facets on the surface:

$$L_r(\theta_r, \phi_r; \theta_i, \phi_i) = \qquad (3)$$
$$\int_{\theta_a=0}^{\frac{\pi}{2}} \int_{\phi_a=0}^{2\pi} P(\theta_a, \phi_a)\, L_{rp}(\theta_a, \phi_a)\, \sin \theta_a\, d\phi_a\, d\theta_a$$

### 3.1  Model for Uni-directional Single-Slope Distribution

The first surface type we consider has all facets with the same slope $\theta_a$. Further, all V-cavities are aligned in the same direction; azimuth angles of all facets are either $\phi_a$ or $\phi_a + \pi$. Consider a Lambertian facet with albedo $\rho$, that is fully illuminated (no shadowing) and is completely visible (no masking) from the sensor direction. The radiance of the facet is proportional to its irradiance and is equal to $\frac{\rho}{\pi} E(\theta_a, \phi_a)$. The irradiance of the facet is $E(\theta_a, \phi_a) = E_0 < \hat{s}, \hat{a} >$, where, $E_0$ is the irradiance when the facet is illuminated head-on (i.e. $\hat{s} = \hat{n}$), and $<, >$ denotes the dot product between two vectors. Using the definition of radiance [20], the flux reflected by the facet in the sensor direction is: $d\Phi_r = \frac{\rho}{\pi} E_0 < \hat{s}, \hat{a} > < \hat{v}, \hat{a} >$. Substituting this expression in (2), we get:

$$L_{rp}(\theta_a, \phi_a) = \frac{\rho}{\pi} E_0 \frac{< \hat{s}, \hat{a} > < \hat{v}, \hat{a} >}{< \hat{a}, \hat{n} > < \hat{v}, \hat{n} >} \qquad (4)$$

The above expression clearly illustrates that the projected radiance of a tilted Lambertian facet is not equal in all viewing directions.

**Geometric Attenuation Factor:** If the surface is illuminated and viewed from the normal direction ($\hat{s} = \hat{v} = \hat{n}$), all facets are fully illuminated and visible. For larger angles of incidence and reflection, however, facets are shadowed and masked by adjacent facets (see Figure 4). Both these geometrical phenomena reduce the projected radiance of the facet. This reduction in brightness can be derived using geometry and incorporated into a single term, called the *geometrical attenuation factor* ($\mathcal{GAF}$), that lies between zero and unity. Several derivations of the $\mathcal{GAF}$ have been presented [30] [2] [23]. The final result can be compactly represented as:

$$\qquad (5)$$
$$\mathcal{GAF} = Min\left[1, Max\left[0, \frac{2< \hat{s}, \hat{n} >< \hat{a}, \hat{n} >}{< \hat{s}, \hat{a} >}, \frac{2< \hat{v}, \hat{n} >< \hat{a}, \hat{n} >}{< \hat{v}, \hat{a} >}\right]\right]$$

The above $\mathcal{GAF}$ is valid for any facet normal, $\hat{a}$, not necessarily the bisector of the angle between the source and the sensor direction.

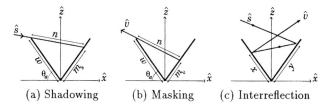

(a) Shadowing     (b) Masking     (c) Interreflection

Figure 4: Shadowing, masking and interreflection in a V-cavity

**Projected Radiance and $\mathcal{GAF}$:** The projected radiance of a Lambertian facet is obtained by multiplying the projected radiance given by (4) with the $\mathcal{GAF}$ given by (5).

$$L_{rp}^1(\theta_a, \phi_a) = \frac{\rho}{\pi} E_0 \frac{< \hat{s}, \hat{a} > < \hat{v}, \hat{a} >}{< \hat{a}, \hat{n} > < \hat{v}, \hat{n} >} \mathcal{GAF}(\hat{s}, \hat{v}, \hat{a}) \qquad (6)$$

Note that the projected radiance is denoted as $L_{rp}^1$; the superscript is used to indicate that the radiance is due to direct illumination by the source. In the following discussion, we will use $L_{rp}^2$ to denote radiance due to interreflections.

**Interreflection Factor:** We have the task of modeling interreflections in the presence of masking and shadowing effects. In the case of Lambertian surfaces, the energy in an incident light ray diminishes rapidly with each interreflection bounce. Therefore, we model only two-bounce interreflections and ignore subsequent bounces. Since the length $l$ of the V-cavity is much larger than its width $w$, i.e. $l \gg w$, it can be viewed as a one-dimensional shape with translational symmetry. For such shapes, the two-bounce interreflection component can be determined as an integral over the one-dimensional cross-section of the shape [28]:

$$L_r^2(x) = \frac{\rho}{\pi} \int K'(x,y) L_r^1(y) dy \qquad (7)$$

where $x$ and $y$ are the shortest distances of facet points from the intersection of the two facets (see Figure 4(c)). $K'$ is the kernel for the translational symmetry case and is derived in [15] and [8] to be:

$$K'(x,y) = \frac{\pi \sin^2(2\theta_a)}{2} \frac{xy}{(x^2 + 2xy\cos(2\theta_a) + y^2)^{3/2}} \qquad (8)$$

We know that the orientation of the considered facet is $\hat{a} = (\theta_a, \phi_a)$ and the orientation of the adjacent facet is $\hat{a}' = (\theta_a, \phi_a + \pi)$. The limits of the integral in the interreflection equation are determined by the masking and shadowing of these two facets. Let $m_v$ be the width of the facet which is visible to the viewer, and $m^s$ be the width of the *adjacent* facet that is illuminated. From the definitions of radiance and projected radiance we get:

$$L_{rp}^2 = \frac{l < \hat{a}, \hat{v} >}{da < \hat{a}, \hat{n} > < \hat{v}, \hat{n} >} \int_{x=m_v}^{w} L_r^2(x)\, dx \qquad (9)$$

Using the following change of variables: $t = \frac{x}{w}$ ; $r = \frac{y}{w}$, the radiance due to two-bounce interreflections given by (7) and (9) can be written as:

$$L_{rp}^2 = \left(\frac{\rho}{\pi}\right)^2 E_0 \frac{< \hat{a}', \hat{s} > < \hat{a}, \hat{v} >}{< \hat{a}, \hat{n} > < \hat{v}, \hat{n} >} \int_{t=\frac{m_v}{w}}^{1} \int_{r=\frac{m^s}{w}}^{1} K'(t,r) dr\, dt \quad (10)$$

Using (8), the above integral is evaluated as:

$$\int_{t=\frac{m_v}{w}}^{1} \int_{r=\frac{m^s}{w}}^{1} K'(r,t) dr\, dt = \qquad (11)$$

$$\frac{\pi}{2}\left[ d\left(1, \frac{m_v}{w}\right) + d\left(1, \frac{m^s}{w}\right) - d\left(\frac{m^s}{w}, \frac{m_v}{w}\right) - d(1,1) \right]$$

where: $d(x,y) = \sqrt{x^2 + 2xy\cos(2\theta_a) + y^2}$. We refer to right hand side of equation (11) as the *interreflection factor* ($\mathcal{IF}$). The total projected radiance of the facet is the sum of two the components, the radiance due to direct source illumination given by equation (6) and the above interreflection component. Therefore, $L_{rp}(\theta_a, \phi_a) = L_{rp}^1(\theta_a, \phi_a) + L_{rp}^2(\theta_a, \phi_a)$. The uni-directional single-slope surface considered here has only two types of facets with normals $(\theta_a, \phi_a)$ and $(\theta_a, \phi_a + \pi)$. Hence, the radiance of the surface for any given source and sensor directions is simply the average of the projected radiances of the two facet types.

## 3.2 Model for Isotropic Single-Slope Distribution

All facets on this isotropic surface have the same slope $\theta_a$ but are uniformly distributed in $\phi_a$. As we did in the previous section, we evaluate the projected radiance as the sum of two components: projected radiance due to direct illumination, $L_{rp}^1(\theta_a)$, and projected radiance due to interreflection, $L_{rp}^2(\theta_a)$. In the previous section, we calculated each of the two components for a single facet with normal $\hat{a} = (\theta_a, \phi_a)$.

Therefore, the radiance of the isotropic surface is determined as an integral of the projected radiance over $\phi_a$:

$$L_{rp}^i(\theta_a) = \frac{1}{2\pi} \int_{\phi_a=0}^{2\pi} L_{rp}^i(\theta_a, \phi_a) d\phi_a \qquad (i = 1,2) \quad (12)$$

Given a source direction $(\theta_i, \phi_i)$ and a sensor direction $(\theta_r, \phi_r)$, we first find the ranges of facet orientation $\phi_a$ for which the facets are masked, shadowed, masked and shadowed, and neither masked nor shadowed[3]. This requires careful geometrical analysis. Then the above integral is decomposed into parts corresponding to masking/shadowing ranges. Each range is evaluated using the corresponding radiance expressions (6) and (11). We refer the interested reader to Oren and Nayar [23, 24] for details.

## 3.3 Model for Gaussian Slope-Area Distribution

The surface considered above consists of V-cavities with a single facet slope. Realistic surfaces can be modeled only if the slope-area distribution $P(\theta_a, \phi_a)$ includes a variety of different facet slopes. If the surface roughness is isotropic, the slope-area distribution can be described using a single parameter namely $\theta_a$ since the facets are uniformly distributed in $\phi_a$. The two components of the radiance of any isotropic surface can therefore be determined as:

$$L_r^i(\theta_r, \theta_i, \phi_r - \phi_i) = \int_0^{\frac{\pi}{2}} P(\theta_a) L_{rp}^i(\theta_a) \sin\theta_a d\theta_a \qquad (13)$$
$$(i = 1,2)$$

where $L_{rp}^i(\theta_a)$ $(i = 1,2)$ are the projected radiance components obtained in the previous section. Here, we assume the isotropic distribution to be Gaussian with mean $\mu$ and standard deviation $\sigma$, i.e. $P(\theta_a; \sigma, \mu)$. Reasonably rough surfaces can be described using a zero mean $(\mu = 0)$ Gaussian distribution: $P(\theta_a) = c \exp\left(-\theta_a^2/2\sigma^2\right)$ where $c$ is the normalization constant.

## 3.4 Functional Approximation

The reflectance model is to be obtained by evaluating integral (13) using the results of section 3.2 and the Gaussian distribution, $P(\theta_a; \sigma, 0)$. The resulting integral cannot be easily evaluated. Therefore, we pursued a functional approximation to the integral that is accurate for arbitrary surface roughness and angles of incidence and reflection. In deriving this approximation, we carefully studied the functional forms of $L_{rp}^i(\theta_a)$ $(i = 1,2)$ which were evaluated in the previous step (the details can be found in Oren and Nayar [23, 24]). This enabled us to identify basis functions that can be used in the approximation. Then, we conducted a large set of numerical evaluations of the integral in (13) by varying surface roughness $\sigma$, the angles of incidence $(\theta_i, \phi_i)$ and reflection $(\theta_r, \phi_r)$. These evaluations and the identified basis functions were used to arrive at an accurate functional approximation for surface radiance. This procedure was applied independently to the source illumination component as well as the interreflection component.

The final approximation results are given below. We define $\alpha = Max[\theta_r, \theta_i]$ and $\beta = Min[\theta_r, \theta_i]$. The source illumination component of radiance of a surface with roughness $\sigma$ is:

---

[3]Imagine a V-cavity rotated about the global surface normal for any given source and sensor direction. Various masking/shadowing scenarios can be visualized.

$$L_r^1(\theta_r, \theta_i, \phi_r - \phi_i; \sigma) = \frac{\rho}{\pi} E_0 \cos\theta_i \left[ C_1(\sigma) + \right.$$

$$\cos(\phi_r - \phi_i) C_2(\alpha; \beta; \phi_r - \phi_i; \sigma) \tan\beta +$$

$$\left. \left(1 - |\cos(\phi_r - \phi_i)|\right) C_3(\alpha; \beta; \sigma) \tan\left(\frac{\alpha + \beta}{2}\right) \right]$$

where the coefficients are:

$$C_1 = 1 - 0.5\frac{\sigma^2}{\sigma^2 + 0.33}$$

$$C_2 = \begin{cases} 0.45\frac{\sigma^2}{\sigma^2 + 0.09}\sin\alpha & \text{if } \cos(\phi_r - \phi_i) \geq 0 \\ 0.45\frac{\sigma^2}{\sigma^2 + 0.09}\left(\sin\alpha - \left(\frac{2\beta}{\pi}\right)^3\right) & \text{otherwise} \end{cases}$$

$$C_3 = 0.125\left(\frac{\sigma^2}{\sigma^2 + 0.09}\right)\left(\frac{4\alpha\beta}{\pi^2}\right)^2$$

The approximation to the interreflection component is:

$$L_r^2(\theta_r, \theta_i, \phi_r - \phi_i; \sigma) = \quad (15)$$

$$0.17\frac{\rho^2}{\pi} E_0 \cos\theta_i \frac{\sigma^2}{\sigma^2 + 0.13}\left[1 - \cos(\phi_r - \phi_i)\left(\frac{2\beta}{\pi}\right)^2\right]$$

The two components are combined to obtain the total surface radiance:

$$L_r(\theta_r, \theta_i, \phi_r - \phi_i; \sigma) = \quad (16)$$

$$L_r^1(\theta_r, \theta_i, \phi_r - \phi_i; \sigma) + L_r^2(\theta_r, \theta_i, \phi_r - \phi_i; \sigma)$$

Finally, the $BRDF$ of the surface is obtained from its radiance and irradiance as $f_r(\theta_r, \theta_i, \phi_r - \phi_i; \sigma) = L_r(\theta_r, \theta_i, \phi_r - \phi_i; \sigma) / E_0 \cos\theta_i$. It is important to note that the approximation presented above obeys Helmholtz's reciprocity principle (see [1]). *Also note that the above model reduces to the Lambertian model when $\sigma = 0$.* Note that by substituting the albedo as function of the wavelength, $\rho(\lambda)$, the dependency of the model on the wavelength comes out explicitly.

In the next section, we present several experimental results that verify the above diffuse reflectance model. Here, we give a brief illustration of the main characteristics of the model. Figure 5 shows the reflectance predicted by the model for a very rough surface with $\sigma = 30°$ and $\rho = 0.9$. The radiance $L_r$ in the plane of incidence ($\phi_r = \phi_i, \phi_i + \pi$) is plotted as a function of the reflection angle $\theta_r$ for incidence angle $\theta_i = 75°$. Two curves are shown in the figure, both obtained by the numerical evaluation of the integral in (13).

The first curve (solid line) includes both direct illumination and interreflection components of radiance, while the second (thin line) is only the direct illumination component. Notice that these radiance plots deviate substantially from Lambertian reflectance. *Surface radiance increases as the viewing direction approaches the source direction.* The curves can be divided into three sections. In the *backward* (source) direction, the radiance is maximum and gets "cut-off" due to strong masking effects when $\theta_r$ exceeds $\theta_i$. This cut-off occurs exactly at $\theta_r = \theta_i$ and is independent of roughness. In the middle section of the plot, radiance varies approximately as a scaled $tan\,\theta_r$ function with constant offset. Finally, interreflections dominate in the *forward* direction where most facets are self-shadowed and the visible facets receive light primarily from adjacent facets. This is illustrated by the difference between the two curves.

In Figure 6(a), the effect of varying the incidence angle $\theta_i$ is shown. Here we have chosen to plot $BRDF$ rather than radiance to better illustrate the effect of varying $\theta_i$. It is

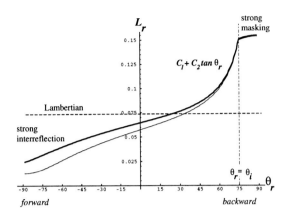

Figure 5: Diffuse reflectance in the plane of incidence for a surface with $\sigma = 30°$, $\rho = 0.90$, and incidence angle $\theta_i = 75°$. The thin line is radiance due to direct illumination (without interreflections).

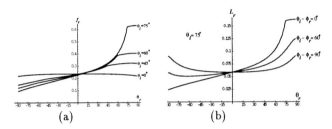

Figure 6: (a) $BRDF$ for different angles of incidence. (b) Radiance outside the plane of incidence. In both plots, $\sigma = 40°$ and $\rho = 0.9$.

interesting to note that the model predicts near-Lambertian behavior for very small incidence angles ($\theta_i \approx 0$). This results from both facets of a V-cavity having nearly equal irradiance for small angles of incidence. As the incidence angle increases, the backscatter phenomenon begins to dominate. Figure 6(b) shows the effect of placing the sensor outside the plane of incidence. When the sensor-normal plane is perpendicular to the source-normal plane, the rough surface again exhibits near-Lambertian characteristics.

## 3.5 Qualitative Model

In this section, we propose a further simplification to the reflectance model presented in the previous section. In order to obtain this simplification, a slight sacrifice in accuracy must be made. In return, some computations can be saved during image rendering. The following simplified model was arrived at by studying, through numerous simulations, the relative significance of various terms in the functional approximation given by (14). The simulations showed that coefficient $C_3$ makes a relatively small contribution to the total radiance. A simpler model is thus obtained by discarding $C_3$ and ignoring interreflections:

$$L_r(\theta_r, \theta_i, \phi_r - \phi_i; \sigma) = \quad (17)$$

$$\frac{\rho}{\pi} E_0 \cos\theta_i (A + B\,Max\left[0, \cos(\phi_r - \phi_i)\right]\sin\alpha\tan\beta)$$

$$A = 1.0 - 0.5\frac{\sigma^2}{\sigma^2 + 0.33}$$

$$B = 0.45\frac{\sigma^2}{\sigma^2 + 0.09}$$

The two coefficients $A$ and $B$ are obtained directly from $C_1$ and $C_2$, respectively. Note that the qualitative model also reduces to the Lambertian model when $\sigma = 0$.

## 4 Experimental Verification

We have conducted several experiments to verify the accuracy of the reflectance model. The experimental set-up ([23, 24]) used to measure the radiance of samples is shown in figure 7.

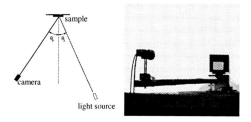

Figure 7: Sketch and photograph of the set-up used to measure reflectance.

Figures 8 and 9 shows results obtained for samples of wall plaster (A) and sand (B). The radiance of each sample is plotted as a function of sensor direction $\theta_r$ for different angles of incidence $\theta_i$. These measurements are made in the plane of incidence ($\phi_r = \phi_i = 0$). The measured brightness values, shown as dots, are compared with those predicted by the model plotted as solid lines. For these two samples (A and B), $\sigma$ and $\rho$ were selected empirically to obtain the best match between measured and predicted reflectance. Here, we have used the numerical evaluation of the model (equation 13). For both samples, radiance increases as the viewing direction $\theta_r$ approaches the source direction $\theta_i$ (backward reflection). This is in contrast to the behavior of rough specular surfaces that reflect more in the forward direction, or Lambertian surfaces where radiance does not vary with viewing direction. For both samples, the model predictions and experimental measurements match remarkably well. In both cases, a small peak is noticed near the source direction. This phenomenon is known as the *opposition effect* or retroreflection. It is a sharp peak close to the source direction and is caused by a different backscattering mechanism from the one described by our model. (see [12, 17, 31, 21, 27, 11]).

Figures 10 and 11 show results for a sample C (foam) and sample D (cloth) that has not only a body reflectance component but also a significant surface reflection component. In this case, the reflectance model used is a linear combination of new model and the Torrance-Sparrow model [30] that describes the incoherent directional component of surface reflection and which is based on the same surface model (long symmetric V-cavities): $L_r = k_b L_r^b + k_s L_r^s$, where $L_r^b$ and $L_r^s$ are the body and surface reflection components, respectively. $k_b$ and $k_s$ are weighting coefficients for the two components. For this experiment, we used the functional approximation and the reflectance parameters $\sigma$, $\rho$, $k_b$, and $k_s$ were estimated by fitting (using non-linear optimization) the model to measured data. Additional experiments are reported in Oren and Nayar [23].

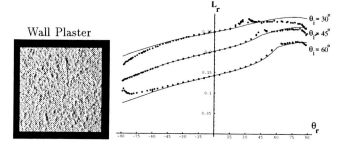

Figure 8: Reflectance measurement and reflectance model (using $\sigma = 30°$, $\rho = 0.90$) plots for wall plaster (sample A). Radiance is plotted as a function of sensor direction ($\theta_r$) for different angles of incidence ($\theta_i = 30°, 45°, 60°$).

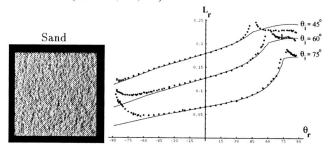

Figure 9: Reflectance measurement and reflectance model (using $\sigma = 35°$, $\rho = 0.80$) plots for white sand (sample B).

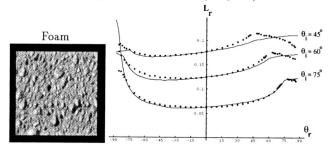

Figure 10: Reflectance measurement and reflectance model ($\sigma = 20°$, $\rho = 0.8$, $k_s/k_b = 0.019$) plots for foam (sample C).

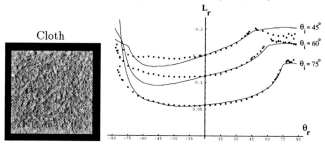

Figure 11: Reflectance measurement and reflectance model ($\sigma = 42°$, $\rho = 0.75$, $k_s/k_b = 0.085$) plots for a cotton towel (sample D).

## 5 Implications for Graphics

In this section, we describe the implications of the proposed model for realistic rendering. Figure 12(a) shows a real image of the rough cylindrical clay vase discussed in the introduction. Figure 12(b) shows a rendered image of the vase using the Lambertian model and its known geometry. Clearly, this rendered image does not match the real image of the vase. On the other hand, the appearance of the rendered vase using the proposed reflectance model, shown in Figure 12(c), closely resembles the real vase. The model parameters $\rho = 0.7$ and $\sigma = 40°$ were chosen empirically to obtain the best fit to the measured brightness values. Figure 13(a) compares brightness values along the cross-section of the three different vase images in Figure 12. It is interesting to note that the brightness of the real vase remains nearly constant over most of the cross-section and drops quickly to zero very close to the limbs. The proposed model does very well in predicting this behavior, while the Lambertian model produces large brightness errors. Figure 13(b) shows similar plots for illumination from 20° to the right of the sensor. In this case, brightness variation on the real vase is asymmetric. Once again, the proposed model closely matches the real image. However, the Lambertian model forces the brightness close to the right limb of the vase to drop much faster than in the real image. As a result, the brightness peak predicted by the Lambertian model is significantly away from the actual peak.

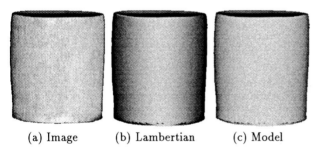

(a) Image     (b) Lambertian     (c) Model

Figure 12: Real image of a cylindrical clay vase compared with images rendered using the Lambertian and proposed models. Illumination is from the camera direction.

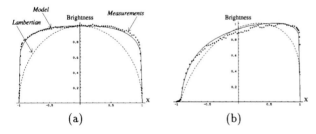

(a)               (b)

Figure 13: Comparison between image brightness along the cross-section of the real vase, and vases rendered using the Lambertian and proposed models. (a) $\theta_i = 0°$. (b) $\theta_i = 20°$.

The functional approximation, given by equation (14), and the qualitative model, given by (17), are easily used for realistic rendering. We have implemented the functional approximation as a "shader" using the RenderMan shading language [32]. Figure 14 shows spheres rendered using the shader. In all four cases, the sphere is illuminated from the viewer direction. In the first case, $\sigma = 0$, and hence the

sphere appears Lambertian. As the roughness increases, the sphere begins to appear flatter. In the extreme roughness case shown in Figure 14(d), the sphere appears like a flat disc with near constant brightness. This phenomenon has been widely observed and reported in the case of the full moon ([25],[28]).

Finally, Figure 15 shows rendered images of a scene with three matte objects, a vase, cylindrical block and a cube. In Figure 15(a), all three objects have zero macroscopic roughness, i.e. they are Lambertian. Illumination in this case is from the viewer direction. Note that the vase and the cylinder have strong brightness variations, and the three visible faces of the cube have distinctly different brightness values. In Figure 15(b), the scene is again illuminated from the viewer direction, but the three objects have roughness $\sigma = 30°$. Consequently, the shading over the vase and the cylinder is diminished considerably. Furthermore, the contrast between the flat and curved sections of the cylindrical block and also the contrast between the three faces of the cube are reduced substantially. It is important to note that the moderate shading is achieved without any ambient component in the illumination, but rather from modeling of roughness effects.

## 6 Summary

In conclusion, we have developed a comprehensive model for body reflectance from surfaces with macroscopic roughness. A model was first derived for anisotropic surfaces that have facets with only one slope. This result was used to develop a model for isotropic surfaces with Gaussian slope-area distribution. We have also presented a qualitative model for diffuse reflection that has a simple functional form. Numerous experiments were conducted to verify the reflectance mechanism described in this paper. Real and rendered images of diffuse objects were compared to demonstrate that the proposed model has important implications for computer graphics.

## REFERENCES

[1] P. Beckmann and A. Spizzichino. *The Scattering of Electromagnetic Waves from Rough Surfaces.* Pergamon, New York, 1963.

[2] J. F. Blinn. Models of light reflection for computer synthesized pictures. *ACM Computer Graphics (SIGGRAPH 77)*, 19(10):542–547, 1977.

[3] D. Buhl, W. J. Welch, and D. G. Rea. Reradiation and thermal emission from illuminated craters on the lunar surface. *Journal of Geophysical Research*, 73(16):5281–5295, August 1968.

[4] B. Cabral, N. Max, and R. Springmeyer. Bidirectional reflection functions from surface bump maps. *ACM Computer Graphics (SIGGRAPH 87)*, 21(4):273–281, 1987.

[5] S. Chandrasekhar. *Radiative Transfer.* Dover Publications, 1960.

[6] M. F. Cohen and D. P. Greenberg. The hemi-cube, a radiosity solution for complex environments. *ACM Computer Graphics (SIGGRAPH 85)*, 19(3):31–40, 1985.

[7] R. L. Cook and K. E. Torrance. A reflection model for computer graphics. *ACM Transactions on Graphics*, 1(1):7–24, 1982.

[8] D. Forsyth and A. Zisserman. Mutual illumination. *Proc. Conf. Computer Vision and Pattern Recognition*, pages 466–473, 1989.

[9] R. Hall. *Illumination and Color in Computer Generated Imagery.* Springer-Verlag, 1989.

[10] P. Hanrahan and W. Krueger. Reflection from layered surfaces due to subsurface scattering. *Computer Graphics Proceedings (SIGGRAPH 93)*, pages 165–174, 1993.

[11] B. W. Hapke, R. M. Nelson, and W. D. Smythe. The opposition effect of the moon: The contribution of coherent backscatter. *Science*, 260(23):509–511, April 1993.

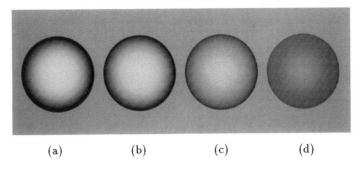

(a)          (b)          (c)          (d)

Figure 14: Images of spheres rendered using the proposed reflectance model: (a) $\sigma = 0$ (Lambertian sphere); (b) $\sigma = 10°$; (c) $\sigma = 20°$; and (d) $\sigma = 40°$.

[12] B. W. Hapke and Huge van Horn. Photometric studies of complex surfaces, with applications to the moon. *Journal of Geophysical Research*, 68(15):4545–4570, August 1963.

[13] X. D. He, K. E. Torrance, F. X. Sillion, and D. P. Greenberg. A comprehensive physical model for light reflection. *ACM Computer Graphics (SIGGRAPH 91)*, 25(4):175–186, 1991.

[14] R. G. Hering and T. F. Smith. Apparent radiation properties of a rough surface. *AIAA Progress in Astronautics and Aeronautics*, 23:337–361, 1970.

[15] M. Jakob. *Heat Transfer*. Wiley, 1957.

[16] J. T. Kajiya. Anisotropic reflection model. *ACM Computer Graphics (SIGGRAPH 91)*, 25(4):175–186, 1991.

[17] Y. Kuga and A. Ishimaru. Retroreflectance from a dense distribution of spherical particles. *Journal of the Optical Society of America A*, 1(8):831–835, August 1984.

[18] J. H. Lambert. Photometria sive de mensure de gratibus luminis, colorum umbrae. *Eberhard Klett*, 1760.

[19] M. Minnaert. The reciprocity principle in lunar photometry. *Astrophysical Journal*, 93:403–410, 1941.

[20] F. E. Nicodemus, J. C. Richmond, and J. J. Hsia. *Geometrical Considerations and Nomenclature for Reflectance*. National Bureau of Standards, October 1977. Monograph No. 160.

[21] P. Oetking. Photometric studies of diffusely reflecting surfaces with application to the brightness of the moon. *Journal of Geophysical Research*, 71(10):2505–2513, May 1966.

[22] E. Opik. Photometric measures of the moon and the moon the earth-shine. *Publications de L'Observatorie Astronomical de L'Universite de Tartu*, 26(1):1–68, 1924.

[23] M. Oren and S. K. Nayar. Generalization of the lambertian model and implications for machine vision. Technical Report CUCS-057-92, Department of Computer Science, Columbia University, New York, NY, USA, 1992.

[24] M. Oren and S. K. Nayar. Generalization of lambert's reflectance model. *Proceedings of SIGGRAPH 94*, 1994. CD-ROM version.

[25] N. S. Orlova. Photometric relief of the lunar surface. *Astron. Z*, 33(1):93–100, 1956.

[26] P. Poulin and A. Fournier. A model for anisotropic reflection. *ACM Computer Graphics (SIGGRAPH 90)*, 24(4):273–282, 1990.

[27] T. Shibata, W. Frei, and M. Sutton. Digital correction of solar illumination and viewing angle artifacts in remotely sensed images. *Machine Processing of Remotely Sensed Data Symposium*, pages 169–177, 1981.

[28] R. Siegel and J. R. Howell. *Thermal Radiation Heat Transfer*. Hemisphere Publishing Corporation, third edition, 1972.

[29] B. G. Smith. Lunar surface roughness: Shadowing and thermal emission. *Journal of Geophysical Research*, 72(16):4059–4067, August 1967.

[30] K. Torrance and E. Sparrow. Theory for off-specular reflection from rough surfaces. *Journal of the Optical Society of America*, 57:1105–1114, September 1967.

[31] L. Tsang and A. Ishimaru. Backscattering enhancement of random discrete scatterers. *Journal of the Optical Society of America A*, 1(8):836–839, August 1984.

[32] S. Upstill. *The RenderMan Companion*. Addison Wesley, 1989.

[33] H.W. Westin, J.R. Arvo, and K.E. Torrance. Predicting reflectance functions from complex surfaces. *ACM Computer Graphics (SIGGRAPH 92)*, 26(2):255–264, 1992.

[34] T. Whitted. An improved illumination model for shaded display. *Communications of the ACM*, 23(6):343–349, 1980.

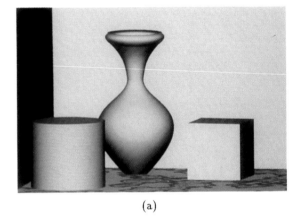

(a)

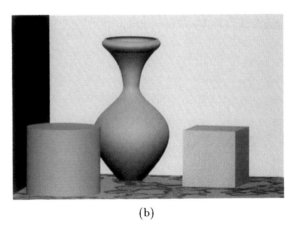

(b)

Figure 15: Scene rendered using the proposed model. All three objects have equal roughness. (a) $\sigma = 0°$; (b) $\sigma = 30°$. The illumination is from the viewing direction.

# Free-Form Shape Design Using Triangulated Surfaces

William Welch and Andrew Witkin
School of Computer Science
Carnegie Mellon University
Pittsburgh, PA 15213

**Keywords:** fair surface design, functional minimization, polygonal models, Delaunay triangulation, adaptive meshing

## Abstract

We present an approach to modeling with truly mutable yet completely controllable free-form surfaces of arbitrary topology. Surfaces may be pinned down at points and along curves, cut up and smoothly welded back together, and faired and reshaped in the large. This style of control is formulated as a constrained shape optimization, with minimization of squared principal curvatures yielding graceful shapes that are free of the parameterization worries accompanying many patch-based approaches. Triangulated point sets are used to approximate these smooth variational surfaces, bridging the gap between patch-based and particle-based representations. Automatic refinement, mesh smoothing, and re-triangulation maintain a good computational mesh as the surface shape evolves, and give sample points and surface features much of the freedom to slide around in the surface that oriented particles enjoy. The resulting surface triangulations are constructed and maintained in real time.

## 1 Introduction

One of the fundamental goals in computer-aided free-form shape design is to offer convenient ways to specify shape and topology. We are concerned here with a truly broad class of surfaces: smooth, doubly curved surfaces, of arbitrary topology (closed or bordered). This generality is what makes representing and controlling such shapes on a computer a difficult problem.

### 1.1 Functional minimization for shape design

Optimization has long been used as a way of describing fair free-form shapes(a good survey is Moreton[23]). More recently, it has come to be used in interactive modelers[4,5,41,18]. Though such approaches are computationally complex, their intent is to create an illusion of simplicity for the designer. Ideally, the designer sees a surface having no particular fixed controls or other representation-specific parameters. Instead, the surface can be directly manipulated, pinned down at points and along curves, and will behave as if made of some infinitely stretchy material. This lets us mimic a style of pen-and-paper design in which important contours of a shape are sketched out as "character lines", with the understanding that a surface passes through them in a fair way[4]. Such shapes are ultimately realized as solutions to constrained functional minimization problems — globally fair surfaces that satisfy geometric interpolation constraints. This approach allows concise descriptions of a

useful class of free-form shapes.

Unfortunately, these approaches have only allowed a designer to interact with pre-fabricated families of shapes, in which the topology remains fixed and surfaces do not stray far from their initial configurations. More drastic, nonuniform deformations are not handled well by the linearized thin plate functional[30] used to fair the piecewise smooth patches making up these surfaces. Further, no real consideration has been given to the problem of creating non-trivial smooth surface topologies interactively. The one approach to fair shape design that has allowed large-scale changes in shape and topology during sculpting is the oriented particle system of Szeliski and Tonnesin[34]. The drawback of this approach is that there is no *explicit* control over surface topology — because there is no actual surface. A surface triangulation can be imposed on the particles strictly as an output, but this has no influence on the particles' subsequent behavior, and no persistence across sculpting operations.

### 1.2 Our approach

In this paper we continue with the agenda set forth in [41] and develop an approach to modeling truly mutable yet completely controllable free-form surfaces.

Our basic approach to shape control will use character lines and curve and surface fairing. To this we add:

- the ability to cut up surfaces and paste them back together smoothly, without topological restriction, thus building up complex topologies incrementally.

- the ability to seamlessly incorporate familiar shape control tools (e.g., generalized cylinders) into more complex faired surface models, using local shape-copying.

- a fairing functional based on geometric surface properties, which yields graceful shapes in the face of large-scale changes to surface shape and topology.

As with previous work, the shape design problem will be cast in terms of functional minimization: the desired shape will be the one that satisfies various geometric constraints while optimizing a measure of surface quality. Since explicit functional solutions to these minimization problems cannot generally be found, we will construct approximate solutions using an explicit surface representation.

In choosing a representation, we bridge the gap between the patch-based and particle-based approaches by adding just enough structure to a particle system to unambiguously fix its topology. To this end, our chosen representation is a set of sample points in three-space, triangulated to yield a 2D manifold topology. Although the resulting surface approximations will be faceted rather than smooth, we never lose sight of the fact that the implicitly defined variational[1] surface is the "real" surface. A designer interacts only with these approximate renderings, but always with the understanding that operations will be interpreted as implicitly defining an ideal variational

---

[1]We use "variational" in its mathematical sense as the solution of a problem in calculus of variations[7]. Unfortunately, this clashes with a different usage common in design literature.

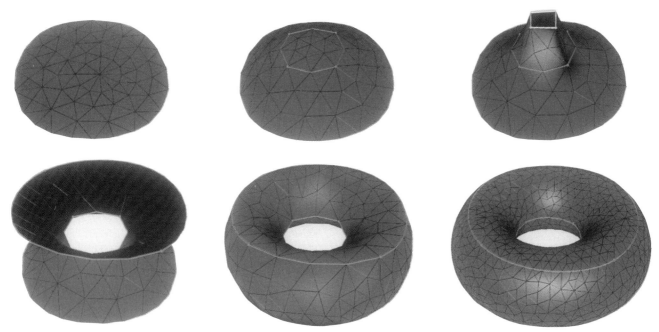

**Figure 1: Making a Torus: 1. A closed curve is skinned to make a disc. 2. another closed curve is drawn on disc and elevated (this will control the inner torus shape). 3. A hole is cut in center of disc and the new boundary curve elevated. 4. The upper curve is expanded to match the lower. 5. Two boundary curves are skinned to make a single toroidal surface passing through the three control curves (200 nodes). 6. Refinement (1300 nodes. All surface meshes are rendered with Gouraud-shaded triangular facets.)**

surface. Such shapes can thus be unambiguously specified and controlled through direct manipulation, regardless of the coarseness of their explicit approximations. If an explicit smooth surface is needed for any reason, it is a straightforward task to fit one to the triangulated surface in a post-processing step[24].

### 1.3 Outline of this paper

After a brief overview of our approach to variational sculpting and its underlying machinery, the bulk of the paper (sections 3–5) develops the mathematics and algorithms needed to construct approximations to these variational surfaces. In section 6 we discuss some specific higher-level shape tools and operations formulated within this variational framework. Section 7 concludes with a discussion of the work's contributions and some suggested directions for future research.

## 2 Overview

### 2.1 Triangulated surface representation

This work develops an approach to interactively sculpting with variational free-form curves and surfaces. Because such shapes generally cannot be explicitly computed, we are concerned with approximating these surface shapes at interactive speeds.

Our representation for the topology and approximate shape of a variational surface is a set of sample points in 3D with an associated surface triangulation (we will often refer to this simply as a mesh). These meshes are represented in our modeler as collections of nodes with radially ordered neighbor relations. Curves are approximated as piecewise-linear (PWL) sequences of nodes joined by edges. We will sometimes need to operate on an embedded curve in a surface, such as a boundary or control curve. In this case the nodes and edges making up the curve must be contained in the mesh as well.

No assumptions are made about the three-dimensional shape of the mesh. In particular, there are no flatness assumptions, and we will not detect or prevent self-intersection. However, the triangulation itself must completely determine the topology of the surface that is being approximated. Regardless of the coarseness of the

sampling, a triangular facet in the mesh should always correspond to a continuous triangular piece of the approximated surface, and a closed PWL boundary curve in the mesh should exist for each boundary curve in the smooth surface.

### 2.2 Approximating surface shapes

A fair amount of computational machinery goes towards maintaining variational shape approximations interactively (in spite of our initial minimalist intentions). We break the approximation problem into a number of reasonably simple pieces, most of them transcending our choice of a point-wise surface (as opposed to, say, smooth triangular patches) as the approximating representation. At the lowest level, local surface reconstruction lets us compute over a mesh as if it were a smooth surface, by estimating surface derivatives at sample points. On top of this is built a surface fairing scheme that minimizes squared principal curvatures. Because an even distribution of samples over a surface improves the results of such fairing computations, we apply techniques from numerical grid generation to keep samples well-dispersed. Finally, automatic refinement and retriangulation processes adapt the mesh density and connectivity as surface shape and area changes, and give sample points and local features much of the freedom to slide around within a surface that oriented particles enjoy. In order to fix some of the ideas, consider the simple construction sequence illustrated in Figure 1, which demonstrates point and curve skinning, automatic shape fairing over wide ranges of deformation, interactive changes to topology, and automatic mesh refinement. Other aspects of our approach — parameterized shaping tools and smooth surface surgery, can be seen in Figures 6 and 7.

In the following sections we detail a collection of robust procedures (some of them new) for controlling the local shape and topology of a mesh. Many schemes for operating on and computing over such unstructured meshes are made with reference to a separate planar domain — either a global parameterization, or a local projection of part of the mesh onto a plane. Such approaches will not be directly useful to us. On the one hand, a well-known result from differential topology implies that we cannot hope to find global pa-

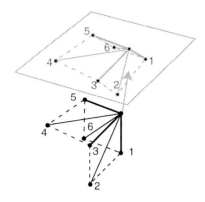

**Figure 2: A failed neighborhood projection.**

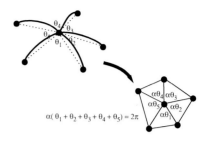

**Figure 3: Surface neighborhood parameterization: angles between neighbors are measured in 3D, then scaled to sum to $2\pi$.**

rameterizations for surfaces of arbitrary genus[2]. On the other hand, local planar projection operations can fail if the mesh is not sufficiently flat (or an unfortunate choice of projection plane is made), for then the projection may scramble the radial order of neighbors about a node (Figure 2). Our modeler must behave robustly in such configurations, always honoring the given neighborhood topology at each node.

## 3 Local shape reconstruction

Fundamental to our approach is the ability to operate on the mesh as a sampling of a smooth surface. To do so, in addition to sample point positions we also need to be able to evaluate surface derivatives at each of these points. This will be done by temporarily fitting a smooth surface to the neighborhood around a sample point.

Because we will ultimately control sample point positions indirectly, by solving for positions that yield desired surface properties, there will be great advantage to having such derivatives be linear functions of the sample point positions. This rules out direct geometric constructions[21] as well as algebraic fitting methods[28]. Algebraic methods have the added drawback that they do not allow us to incorporate topological constraints like radial neighbor ordering into the fit.

Instead, following a standard approach to constructing finite difference stencils over a computational field[12], we will fit a truncated Taylor series expansion at a neighborhood around a point. This approach yields the desired linearity, but it comes at the expense of having to construct a separate bivariate parameterization over which to evaluate the polynomial basis functions. We'll make the most of this by constructing the parameterization in such a way that it gives the fairing functional (Section 4) a particularly simple form.

### 3.1 Neighborhood parameterizations

Much of the theory of curves and surfaces is developed in terms of curves parameterized by arc-length[25]. Geometric quantities, such as curvature, have simple expressions with respect an arc-length parameterization. The geometric fairing functionals of the next section will involve differentiation with respect to arc-length, so we want to use arc-length parameterizations in our local reconstructions to simplify these computations.

For surfaces, there is no corresponding notion of an arc-length parameterization; but there is a construction from differential geometry, the *geodesic polar map*[25], which serves our needs in much the same way. This is simply a generalization to geometric surfaces

of polar coordinates $(r, \theta)$ in the plane. A map is constructed for a neighborhood about a given point on the surface, in such a way that a unit-speed geodesic path is associated with each tangent direction ($\theta$). Directional derivatives computed at the point in any tangent direction are thus taken with respect to an arc-length parameterization.

In fitting a parametric curve to a sequence of scattered points, it is necessary to first assign parametric coordinates to these points. Prior to the fit, we cannot assign these coordinates based on arc-length because we have no curve. So instead, we will make a chord-length approximation to an arc-length parameterization[9,8], in which the parametric interval between two samples is taken to be the 3D Euclidean distance between them.

In constructing a neighborhood parameterization for surface fitting, it is common to project neighboring vertices in 3-space onto, e.g., the node's tangent plane. As was pointed out earlier, this is a hazardous operation. The surface triangulation induces an ordering on neighbors about each node and this order should be reflected in the parameterization, but there is no guarantee that projection will do so. Instead of projecting onto a plane, we measure the angular separation between each neighbor *in 3D*, and then uniformly scale these angles so that they sum to $2\pi$ for nodes in the surface interior and $\pi$ for nodes on the boundary (Figure 3). Using a chord-length approximation to arc-length, the Euclidean distance from the center node to each of its neighbors is taken as the radial parametric separation, mimicking the geodesic polar parameterization.

### 3.2 Local coordinate fitting

Given a suitable parameterization of the neighborhood, it is a straightforward task to fit a truncated Taylor series expansion for each of the surface $x$, $y$, and $z$ coordinate functions about the neighborhood center. In the following, $\mathbf{p}_0$ will designate the position of the node at the neighborhood center, $\mathbf{p}_1...\mathbf{p}_n$ the positions of $\mathbf{p}_0$'s $n$ neighbors, and $(u_0, v_0)...(u_n, v_n)$ their parametric coordinates.

For each of the coordinate functions we seek the coefficients of a biquadratic:

$$s(u,v) = c_0 + c_1 u + c_2 v + \frac{c_3}{2}u^2 + c_4 uv + \frac{c_5}{2}v^2 \quad (1)$$
$$= \mathbf{b}(u,v)\mathbf{c}, \quad (2)$$

where $\mathbf{b}(u,v)$ is the basis row vector $[1, u, v, \frac{1}{2}u^2, uv, \frac{1}{2}v^2]$, and $\mathbf{c}$ a column vector of coefficients. We want $s(u_0, v_0) \equiv s(0,0) = p_0$; this requires $c_0 = p_0$ (here we take $p_i$ to mean one of $p_{ix}, p_{iy}, p_{iz}$, since the same fitting procedure applies to each). The remaining coefficients will be determined such that the $s(u_i, v_i)$ are a least-squares fit to the $p_i$.

Shifting the origin to $p_0$ yields the vector of shifted neighbor positions $\mathbf{q} = [p_1 - p_0, ..., p_n - p_0]^T$. The sample matrix $\mathbf{S}$ for this shifted, center-constrained system is built by evaluating the basis vector $\mathbf{b}(u_i, v_i)$ for each of the neighbors and collecting these rows into a matrix, then deleting its first column. Then $\mathbf{S}[c_1, ..., c_5]^T = \mathbf{q}$, and the least-squares solution for $c_1...c_5$ is

[2]the Poincaré-Hopf Index theorem on the existence of smooth vector-fields over manifolds[15], which says, informally, that you cannot comb the hair on a ball without leaving a crown somewhere.

$$[c_1, ..., c_5]^T \;=\; [\mathbf{S}^T\mathbf{S}]^{-1}\mathbf{S}^T\mathbf{q} \qquad (3)$$
$$\;=\; \mathbf{Z}\mathbf{q}. \qquad (4)$$

To put this in a more convenient form as a linear function of the $p_i$, let $\mathbf{z}$ represent the vector sum of the columns of $\mathbf{Z}$ and $\mathbf{P}$ represent the $n \times 3$ matrix of the $\mathbf{p}_i$'s $x, y, z$ coordinates. The vector form for the reconstructed surface positions $\mathbf{s}(u, v)$ is then

$$\mathbf{s}(u, v) \;=\; \mathbf{b}(u, v)\begin{bmatrix} 1 & 0 \\ -\mathbf{z} & \mathbf{Z} \end{bmatrix}\mathbf{P} \qquad (5)$$
$$\;=\; \mathbf{b}(u, v)\mathbf{BP}. \qquad (6)$$

This fitting procedure is somewhat complicated by the irregular degrees of the triangulated nodes since it requires that every node have at least five neighbors (a radial ordering for nodes beyond the immediate neighbors is not determined by the triangulation, so we do not search beyond the neighborhood to bring in additional samples as is common in least-squares schemes[13]). Worse, even though a node may have five neighbors they may be positioned parametrically so as to make the full biquadratic fit ill-conditioned.

In this case, a reduced polynomial basis function is used. For each node (of sufficient degree), an initial fit of the full basis $[1, u, v, \frac{1}{2}u^2, uv, \frac{1}{2}v^2]$ is attempted. The condition number of this fit, $c = \|\mathbf{S}^T\mathbf{S}\| \cdot \|(\mathbf{S}^T\mathbf{S})^{-1}\|$, is then computed (where the matrix norms are Frobenius norms[14]).

If the fit was ill-conditioned (say, $c > 1000$), or if there were too few neighbors, a fit is attempted with the reduced basis functions $[1, u, v, \frac{1}{2}(u^2 + v^2)]$ for interior nodes[3]. Boundary nodes, which will rarely have enough neighbors for a full fit, are treated specially: the parameterization is constructed so that the two boundary nodes lie on the $\pm u$ axis, and the basis functions $[1, u, v, \frac{1}{2}u^2]$ are used. This lets a surface curve along its boundary while remaining flat in the infield direction. As before, the condition number is evaluated and an ill-conditioned fit rejected. As a last resort, a planar fit (for boundary or infield nodes) is made with the basis functions $[1, u, v]$.

A shortcoming of this approach is that the somewhat arbitrary choice of basis functions could lead to instability over time (though we have not observed this, a neighborhood that is nearly well-conditioned might switch back and forth between different sets of basis functions). Better would be to consistently use the same set of basis functions and optimize some auxiliary norm in the underdetermined case, as in Barth [1]. This requires an orthogonal decomposition of $\mathbf{S}^T\mathbf{S}$, an added computational expense that degrades the overall interactivity of the modeler.

### 3.3 Curve reconstruction

Smooth neighborhoods for PWL curve approximations are computed analogously to the fitting procedure for surfaces. A chord-length parameterization is used, along with the basis functions $[1, u, \frac{1}{2}u^2]$.

## 4 Surface fairing

In this section we formulate constrained fairing for triangulated surfaces. Surfaces will seek shapes that minimize a global measure of curvature, subject to the requirement that they interpolate specified control points and curves.

### 4.1 Smooth surface objective

We take as the surface fairing objective function the integral of the squared principal curvatures over a smooth surface[25]:

---

[3]It is tempting to damp the second-order terms in the system matrix $\mathbf{S}^T\mathbf{S}$ to insure well-conditioning without these repeated fitting attempts, but this noticeably degrades the fairing in Section 4.

$$E = \int_S (\kappa_1^2 + \kappa_2^2)dA, \qquad (7)$$

where $dA$ is the differential area form. Lott and Pullin [20] used this for surface fairing because of its relationship to the strain energy of a thin elastic plate. Unlike the more commonly used linearized thin plate approximation[4,41,35,18], this formulation does not create shape artifacts related to an underlying fixed surface parameterization. $E$ is a geometric quantity whose definition is independent of parameterization.

Recall from the differential geometry of surfaces that information about the curvature of a surface at a point is given by the second fundamental form[32]. The normal section curvature of a surface $\mathbf{s}(u, v)$ in the direction of a parametric unit tangent $\mathbf{t} = [t_u, t_v]$ is given by $\kappa = II(\mathbf{t}, \mathbf{t})$, where

$$II(\mathbf{t}, \mathbf{t}) = \mathbf{t}^T\begin{bmatrix} \mathbf{s}_{uu} \cdot \mathbf{n} & \mathbf{s}_{uv} \cdot \mathbf{n} \\ \mathbf{s}_{vu} \cdot \mathbf{n} & \mathbf{s}_{vv} \cdot \mathbf{n} \end{bmatrix}\mathbf{t}, \qquad (8)$$

$\mathbf{n}$ is the surface unit normal, and subscripts indicate partial differentiation with respect to arc-length. It is straightforward to show that the squared Frobenius norm of the matrix is equivalent to $\kappa_1^2 + \kappa_2^2$. This lets us reformulate the objective function $E$ in terms of the surface derivatives and normals appearing in these matrix elements:

$$E = \int_S ((\mathbf{s}_{uu} \cdot \mathbf{n})^2 + 2(\mathbf{s}_{uv} \cdot \mathbf{n})^2 + (\mathbf{s}_{vv} \cdot \mathbf{n})^2)dA. \qquad (9)$$

### 4.2 Triangulated surface objective

For a triangulated surface this integral is approximated as an area-weighted sum of integrands over sample points:

$$E = \sum_{\text{nodes}} ((\mathbf{s}_{uu}(0, 0) \cdot \mathbf{n})^2 + 2(\mathbf{s}_{uv}(0, 0) \cdot \mathbf{n})^2 + (\mathbf{s}_{vv}(0, 0) \cdot \mathbf{n})^2)a, \qquad (10)$$

where $\mathbf{s}(0, 0)$ is the local surface function (6) evaluated at its node, and $a$ the node's associated area (nominally, $1/3$ the area of each of the triangles in its parametric neighborhood). Because the neighborhood parameterization was constructed so that directional derivatives are computed with respect to an approximate arc-length parameterization, the partial derivatives above are simply taken with respect to the local $u$ and $v$. The assumption here is that these parameterizations are being continually updated as the surface shape changes; whether or not this is a good way to approximate differentiation with respect to arc-length (to be characterized in[40]), the resulting objective function is geometric in nature, so that our surface fairing does not exhibit parameterization artifacts.

Substituting (6) and evaluating the derivatives of the basis functions $\mathbf{b}(0, 0)$ leads to a particularly simple form for $E$:

$$E = \sum_{\text{nodes}} ((\mathbf{B}_3\mathbf{P} \cdot \mathbf{n})^2 + 2(\mathbf{B}_4\mathbf{P} \cdot \mathbf{n})^2 + (\mathbf{B}_3\mathbf{P} \cdot \mathbf{n})^2)a \qquad (11)$$

where $\mathbf{B}_j$ is the $j$th row of the $i$th neighborhood basis matrix.

The dependency of $E$ on the node positions is given by its gradient with respect to $\mathbf{P}$. To make the minimization of $E$ tractable, we take the $\mathbf{n}$ and $a$ to be constant when computing this gradient, and will refer to this modified objective as $\hat{E}$. This makes $\hat{E}$ quadratic and positive definite in $\mathbf{s}$'s parametric derivatives, and similarly in the node positions, thus guaranteeing a unique minimum. Note that the $E$ itself is *not* a quadratic function of the node positions, and so a single minimization of $\hat{E}$ with fixed $\mathbf{n}$ and $a$ will not in general minimize $E$. We will return to this point shortly.

In manipulating gradients of $\hat{E}$ it will be notationally convenient to consider a "flattened" $\mathbf{P}$, formed by concatenating its $x, y, z$ components into a single long vector $\bar{\mathbf{P}}$. Because $\hat{E}$ is purely quadratic in $\mathbf{P}$, it is possible to write it in the form $\hat{E} = \bar{\mathbf{P}}^T\mathbf{H}\bar{\mathbf{P}}$, where $\mathbf{H}$ is a constant, $3n \times 3n$ matrix. In the constrained minimization scheme below, $\mathbf{H}$ will never actually be computed and stored as a monolithic matrix; instead, vector products with $\mathbf{H}$ (and sub-matrices of $\mathbf{H}$) will be computed. This is done by looping over the nodes, accumulating each neighborhood's contribution to the product. Some rearrangement of (11) yields a convenient form for this matrix-vector product:

$$\mathbf{H}\bar{\mathbf{P}} = \sum_{\text{nodes}} \mathbf{n}(\mathbf{P}\,\mathbf{n})^T(\mathbf{B}^T_3\mathbf{B}_3 + 2\mathbf{B}^T_4\mathbf{B}_4 + \mathbf{B}^T_5\mathbf{B}_5)a \qquad (12)$$

(note that the $\mathbf{B}_j$ are row vectors). In addition to saving on the work of constructing $\mathbf{H}$, this multiplication scheme also exploits $\mathbf{H}$'s inherent sparsity without any additional effort on our part.

### 4.3 Curves

Before taking up the constrained minimization of $E$, we briefly mention fairing for point-sampled curves. This is well-trodden ground ([19]), but to keep our presentation self-contained we point out that the geometric curve fairing objective

$$E = \int \kappa^2 ds, \qquad (13)$$

can be formulated analogously to the surface objective above. The shapes of space curves in our modeler are controlled this way, subject to point interpolation constraints, below. They in turn control the shapes of embedded surface curves, with corresponding sequences of surface nodes constrained to track the nodes of freestanding curves.

### 4.4 Geometric constraints

Point and curve interpolation constraints on a surface are enforced by simply freezing the positions of their associated nodes during fairing. A frozen node is no longer considered an independent variable, but it contributes linear terms to $\hat{E}$. Splitting $\bar{\mathbf{P}}$ into unconstrained and constrained parts $\bar{\mathbf{Q}}$ and $\bar{\mathbf{R}}$ and partitioning $\mathbf{H}$ accordingly,

$$\hat{E} = [\bar{\mathbf{Q}}^T\bar{\mathbf{R}}^T] \begin{bmatrix} \mathbf{H}^{QQ} & \mathbf{H}^{QR} \\ \mathbf{H}^{RQ} & \mathbf{H}^{RR} \end{bmatrix} \begin{bmatrix} \bar{\mathbf{Q}} \\ \bar{\mathbf{R}} \end{bmatrix} \qquad (14)$$

The gradient of $\hat{E}$ with respect to the active nodes is then

$$\nabla\hat{E} = \mathbf{H}^{QQ}\bar{\mathbf{Q}} + 2\mathbf{H}^{QR}\bar{\mathbf{R}}. \qquad (15)$$

We mention in passing another useful constraint, the *hinge*[4], which allows cross-boundary tangents along a surface boundary to be controlled. Under our scheme, with boundaries aligned parametrically in the $u$ direction, this amounts to constraining $\mathbf{s}_v(0,0)$ (which is simply $\mathbf{B}_2\mathbf{P}$) at each point on the boundary. This constraint cannot be directly enforced by freezing independent variables, as was done with point constraints, so a penalty[27] or Lagrange multiplier[33] technique should be used.

### 4.5 Minimizing the objective

To minimize $\hat{E}$ subject to the point constraints, we solve for the $\bar{\mathbf{Q}}$ yielding $\nabla\hat{E} = 0$. Rather than form $\mathbf{H}$ explicitly, the system is solved using a conjugate-gradient method[33], which only requires matrix-vector products with $\mathbf{H}$, not an explicit representation $\mathbf{H}$ itself[4].

---

[4]To maintain interactivity as this system increases in size, we allow the conjugate gradient solver only a fixed number of iterations (10–20) per solve/redraw cycle. A (not unpleasant) side-effect of this is an illusion of viscous drag as the solution converges over time.

As was mentioned, a single minimization of $\hat{E}$ does not in general minimize $E$. This minimization will be iterated as the user interacts with the surface, each time reparameterizing neighborhoods then using the current surface normals and areas in evaluating $\hat{E}$. It is tempting to claim that when (if) the surface reaches equilibrium, it will have approached the minimum for $E$; but this disregards the possibility that the ignored gradient terms are nonzero. In any event, the resulting shapes are visually pleasing, and an accurate minimization of $E$ thus seems less important here than the added speed and robustness that have been gained through the linearization.

There is little we can say formally about the conditions under which this iterative scheme converges to an equilibrium; but in our experience the minimization has been well-behaved over a wide range of configurations. As with almost any nonlinear optimization, a caveat is that "reasonable" initial surface shapes must be used. This has not been a problem in our interactive system because changes to shape are generally incremental. There are configurations in which curvature minimization is undesirable as an objective function, as with narrow cylinders (which collapse). A minimum curvature variation functional, as in Moreton and Séquin[22], would remedy this problem; but it is not clear how to compute the curvature derivatives given our local quadratic reconstructions, and we leave this as future work.

## 5 Surface sampling

Taking the view that a mesh is a discrete sampling of some smooth underlying surface, it is important that the surface be sampled sensibly. In our case, "sensibly" means samples are distributed and triangulated so as to give good neighborhood shapes, so that local polynomial fitting is well-conditioned. It also means samples are distributed for speed and accuracy in the global approximation. While there is no numerical harm in having many samples clumped together in an uninteresting place on the surface, their presence needlessly slows down the computation. On the other hand, a large gap in sampling over an area will poorly resolve the shape. Since we generally do not know surface shapes or topologies *a priori*, the surface sampling and triangulation must be controlled dynamically as points move about and neighborhoods change shape.

### 5.1 Sample point distribution

We begin with the problem of maintaining a uniform sampling density over a surface. One approach that has been used successfully for both smooth and polyhedral surfaces is point repulsion[29, 38,39,42]: points move under the influence of mutual repulsive (or attractive) forces between points, constrained to act within the surface. In these schemes, a pair of points' influence on each other falls off as an inverse power of their separation. Ideally, this separation is measured in terms of geodesic distance on the surface, since in a highly curved surface, two points that are nearby geometrically may be far apart geodesically. As a practical matter, these schemes project a 3D neighborhood (there being no triangulation to deliver up a surface neighborhood) onto each sample point's tangent plane and measure these projected distances. Forces are accumulated to produce a velocity for each point, and as points are moved in these directions they must be repeatedly pushed back onto the surface to counter this integration drift.

These schemes work best when sampling is dense enough that repulsion forces are acting over small distances and neighborhoods are not highly curved (these assumptions are implicit in making the above-mentioned projections). Interestingly, these methods do not break down when the assumptions fail. So long as there is a robust procedure for returning points to the surface after integration error has moved them off, it doesn't really matter if some point accidentally lands in a geodesically distant location (assuming this behavior doesn't prevent the method from reaching equilibrium). However,

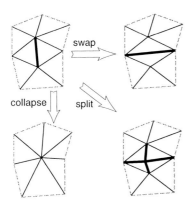

**Figure 4: Mesh transformation operators: edge split, edge collapse, and edge flip. These change the mesh without altering its manifold topology.**

this is behavior is clearly disastrous if we are dragging a triangulation along with the points, as in our application.

We consider instead a parametric repulsion scheme that uses the neighborhood structure given by the triangulation to avoid making wild leaps off the surface. In place of a neighborhood projection onto a node's tangent plane, we use the geodesic polar parameterization of Section 3.1. Since this includes only the neighboring points in the triangulation (whereas a repulsion scheme relies potential interactions between all points) we will optimize the placement of the node within this polygonal neighborhood. Imagining a uniform continuous distribution of samples within the neighborhood, the equilibrium position for the node under an $r^2$ repulsion/attraction scheme would be the centroid of the polygon.

We move the point parametrically towards the neighborhood centroid, then the local surface function is evaluated to determine the new node position in 3D. This avoids the need to project the point back onto the surface after integrating a 3D velocity vector. Thus the scheme will work properly even in situations where a neighborhood's shape is folded over or collapsed. Note that this treats the surface as if it were a (non-smooth) union of quadratic bowls, over which samples are sliding.

As it happens, this method is closely related to a "mesh improvement" scheme called *Laplacian smoothing*[11], so named because its fixed point is an approximate solution to Laplace's equation over the mesh. In fact, Laplace's equation is ubiquitous in computational mesh generation[36,37], arising naturally from a variational formulation of a uniform-density objective. We experimented with forming the Laplacian over a surface mesh, in terms of locally reconstructed neighborhoods[17], and solving the resulting global error minimization for point positions. In practice, we found that this was more robust than the purely local scheme above, but was more expensive to compute, and in the end we reverted to the local scheme.

### 5.2 Sample point density

We use a simple spatial refinement/un-refinement scheme to control the local density of sample points. Node separations are measured in 3D, and an edge-splitting refinement (see Figure 3) is triggered if any two neighbors are too far apart. Similarly, if any node is too close to each of its neighbors, the node is destroyed using an edge-collapse operation. Both of these operations preserve the surface topology, and Hoppe, et. al.[16] showed that they are sufficient to transform any surface triangulation into any other of the same topological type.

### 5.3 Surface triangulation

The sample distribution scheme just presented moves nodes around within their respective triangulated neighborhoods. In ad-

dition to this neighborhood smoothing, we will dynamically maintain a quality triangulation over the nodes as they change position. In addition to the numerical conditioning benefits that result from a good triangulation, this will also have the effect of allowing nodes to migrate across neighborhoods. Surface features like bounded subregions and embedded curves will be free to slide around relative to each other within the surface triangulation (e.g., the final frame in Figure 5).

Field[11] has shown that combining a Laplacian neighborhood smoothing scheme and Delaunay triangulation (DT) tends to produce nice triangulations. For our meshes we will work with a generalization of the planar DT due to Chew[6]. He generalizes the "empty circumcircle" characterization of the planar DT to one of empty circumspheres on a surface, and proves that it retains many of the desirable properties of the planar DT. The surface DT maximizes the minimum angle in the triangulation (measured in 3D), and thus eliminates skinny triangles. Further, this globally optimal triangulation can be constructed from any other surface triangulation by a series of local edge-flip operations(Figure 4), each of which increases the minimum angle within some quadrilateral in the mesh. These edge-flips preserve the topological type of the surface, so there is always a valid mesh as retriangulation progresses.

### 5.4 Constrained triangulation

In constructing the surface DT given an initial surface triangulation, there will be edges that must not be disturbed, such as those that are part of embedded control curves. A scheme that incorporates these *source edges* is referred to as a *constrained Delaunay triangulation*, or CDT [2]. It enjoys the same minimum-angle property as the DT (over all triangulations which include the source edges), and this leads directly to the *flip algorithm* for restoring a CDT given an initial triangulation:

> **Algorithm Restore-CDT:** For an edge $e$ not a source edge, $Q_e$ is the quadrilateral formed by taking the two triangles on either side of $e$. We say that $Q_e$ is *reversed* if $e$ forms a smaller minimum angle with the outside edges than the other diagonal does. Initially, put all non-source edges into a queue. Repeatedly remove the first edge $e$, each time checking to see if $Q_e$ is reversed. If so, $e$ is flipped in the triangulation, replacing it with $Q_e$'s other diagonal. The non-source edges of $Q_e$ are added to the queue (if not already present). When the queue is empty, the CDT has been restored.

This terminates in at most $O(edges^2)$ flips, but in practice we see only a few flips at any one time. We can introduce a bit of hysteresis by only flipping edges if they increase their local minimum-angle by some small minimum. This produces an approximate CDT by making edges somewhat more reluctant to flip.

A technicality of this definition of the surface DT is that the generalization of consistent circumcircles to circumspheres on surfaces depends on a local flatness assumption: that no dihedral angle exceeds $\pi/2$. Rather than enforce this requirement by refining the triangulation in highly curved neighborhoods, we have found that it works well in practice to relax the requirement by maintaining only an approximate DT. Edges with sharp dihedral angles are treated as temporary source edges and are not allowed to be flipped, thus preserving the algorithm's termination guarantee.

In our modeler, Restore-CDT runs continually, interleaved with steps of the shape optimization, so that a quality mesh is always present for computation. An important aspect of this is approach is that we always begin with valid surface triangulation. Improving the quality of a surface triangulation is much simpler than attempting to impose a surface triangulation on a collection of scattered points (hence inferring a surface topology) — and it is guaranteed never to fail. In keeping with this approach, modeling operations which change the mesh structure or surface topology (Section 6.3)

outline. The tool itself then supplies the fitted piece of surface that fills the outline. In this example, the explicit surface is used only for topological information — allowing the user to indicate (e.g., by proximity to the tool) which surface region is to be affected. The result is unambiguous and independent of the resolution of the current surface approximation.

### 6.5 External shape controllers

Because it would be cumbersome to specify all shapes in terms of functional minimization, we also allow externally represented shapes to control the shapes of bounded surface regions. These can be applied to bounded regions of a variational surface to act as local or global shape-control tools. For example, in our sculpting system we define a cylindrical offset tool in terms of a space curve backbone and a radius function (Figure 6). A controlled region may contain sub-regions that are in turn controlled by other shaping tools. This lets us, e.g., attach handles or drill holes in externally controlled regions, so that ultimately their local topology may be very different from that of the shape controller.

Nodes along the boundary between an externally controlled region and a faired region will have a mixture of free and constrained neighbors. This allows the shape of the surface on the controlled side to influence the shape on the faired side up to second-order, so that tangent and curvature information are propagated across the boundary. Since only one shape control tool can drive a given surface point at a time, it is not generally possible to have two tool-controlled regions meet along a shared control curve. In these situations a faired blend region must be installed between them (see, e.g., the body/handle attachment on Figure 7).

In implementing such controllers, there are any number of ways to triangulate and track a tool shape, depending on how the tool surface is represented, and we will not pretend to a complete discussion. As an example from our system, a number of tool shapes are defined as implicit surfaces, and we use the surface-tracking technique from Witkin and Heckbert's point-sampling scheme [42] to keep sample points glued to moving tool surfaces. The sample distribution and triangulation over the tool surface itself is handled just as it was for faired surfaces. Since the the topologies of the implicit surface tools in our system are known *a priori* and remain fixed during sculpting, we avoid the difficult general problem of triangulating an implicit surface by generating a valid initial triangulation when the tool is applied. Nonetheless, it is still possible for points to behave badly by bunching up when a tool surface is moved quickly, and this approach can certainly be improved on. If tool surfaces have an associated parameterization, the sampling and tracking may be done using parametric coordinates and these difficulties do not arise.

### 6.6 Building structured models

The composition of parameterized shapes via blending regions leads naturally to structured free-form models. As in Bonner, *et al*'s work with tubular structures [3], these shape control tools may be organized in a variety of ways through the use of deformation hierarchies (note that the deformations are not applied to the surface itself). In our system the resulting collections of shape control tools and character lines serve as "skeletons" supporting a triangulated surface skin. As the underlying control shapes are changed, the surface tracks them, automatically adjusting blend shapes, refining, unrefining, and re-triangulating to maintain a good approximation to the composite shape.

## 7   Conclusion

We have presented an approach to designing fair, free-form shapes using triangulated surfaces. Our initial implementation of these ideas is a modeler that runs at interactive speeds on a Silicon Graphics Indigo class workstation, for surface models of several hundred nodes (in the illustrations in this paper, any surfaces containing more than 500 nodes were given a final refinement after all interactive shaping was complete).

### 7.1   Contributions

The principal contribution of this work is a scheme for interactively designing fair free-form shapes of arbitrary, mutable topology. Little work has appeared regarding topological design for free-form shapes (though see [10]). Our approach uses a triangulated mesh to represent a surface model's topology, and modeling operations alter the mesh to change this topology in controlled ways.

The positions of the triangulated sample points in 3D approximate the shape of an underlying smooth surface, whose shape is defined as the solution of a functional minimization. To this end, we use a geometric fairness functional based on extrinsic surface curvature, and thus avoid shape artifacts related to surface parameterization. This is a highly non-linear functional, yet we have developed an approach to its optimization that is fast and robust enough to withstand interactive re-shaping.

In order to perform this optimization over a triangulated surface mesh, we perform local smooth surface reconstruction that estimates surface derivatives while honoring the neighborhood topologies induced by the mesh. Our construction of neighborhood parameterizations uses a projection scheme we have not seen elsewhere.

Finally, the fairing computation is interleaved with adaptive refinement, adaptive sample distribution, and re-triangulation. The approach used in this work, while not particularly novel, is used to novel effect: features are free to slide around in a surface so as to minimize the overall fairness functional, rather than being bound by parametric surface coordinates to a fixed place in the surface.

### 7.2   Future Work

Though we formulate surface shape control using interpolated control curves, our scheme does not yet accommodate intersecting control curves. A compatibility condition[26] demands that when control curves meet at a point, they must all fit a common quadratic surface form; otherwise, no there can be no smooth interpolating surface in the neighborhood of the intersection. What is needed is a special intersection node that enforces this compatibility constraint on curves meeting there (like the hub of an umbrella).

It would be interesting to develop a version of this approach using smooth triangular patches. We expect it to be computationally expensive (this was our motivation for using point-sampled approximations), but it may be that a very coarse surface refinement in terms of patches could be made to perform comparably to a more highly refined point-sampled surface, thus offsetting this cost.

Finally, it may be worthwhile to consider a curvature-sensitive scheme for distributing sample points across the surface. The error of our objective function integration in a neighborhood is related to the neighborhood's total curvature, and an adaptive scheme would would tend to distribute this error more evenly across nodes.

## Acknowledgements

The authors would like to thank the Siggraph reviewers for many helpful comments on the early draft of this paper (and to Reviewer #5 — you're welcome). Thanks also to Hans Pedersen and Zoran Popović for their help with the figures. This work was supported in part by the Engineering Design Research Center, an NSF Engineering Research Center at Carnegie Mellon University, by a Science and Technology Center Grant from the National Science Foundation, #BIR-8920118, by a High Performance Computing and Communications Grant from the National Science Foundation, #BIR-9217091, by Apple Computer, Inc., and by an equipment grant from Silicon Graphics, Inc.

must do so in controlled ways that always leave a valid triangulation.

# 6   Operations on surfaces

The three previous sections are sufficient machinery to approximate faired surfaces that interpolate shape control curves. In this section we consider using this machinery as a basic computational substrate for free-form modeling. Recall that in this approach a designer will interact only with approximate renderings of surfaces, but that anything done to a surface model must be interpreted in terms that define an ideal variational shape.

We consider here some basic modeling operations cast in terms of our variational substrate. The intent is to illustrate important considerations in using variational surfaces as a basic shape representation, rather than offer an exhaustive set of sculpting operations. A common theme is that of carving a surface up into disjoint regions and designating a shape controller for the nodes in each region. Mixing explicit shape control for some regions and functional minimization for others will allow us to construct structured models for parameterized free-form shapes.

## 6.1   Embedding control curves

A surface control curve is specified by designating a series of (not necessarily neighboring) points on the surface that the control curve should pass through. *Face splitting* is used to allow such points to be placed at arbitrary locations on the surface. This operation adds a new node in the middle of a triangular face and connects it to each vertex of the triangle (equivalent to an edge-split followed by an edge-flip, with suitable repositioning of the new node). Once the desired anchor nodes have been inserted into the mesh, a sequence of nodes and edges is inserted to join the designated nodes in a PWL curve. One way to insert a curve connecting two nodes is to first find a sequence of abutting faces that connect them; their union then forms a polygonal channel into which a curve connecting the two nodes can be inserted by splitting each edge that crosses the channel. Once the surface curve has been created, a matching space curve is created (with point constraints at the original anchor positions) and the surface curve is constrained to follow it. Note that our procedure needn't create a particularly straight surface curve, or leave a particularly nice triangulation (it does neither), since fairing and Delaunay triangulation will subsequently neaten things up.

## 6.2   Bounded surface regions

Many computations are meant to be performed only on some subset of the surface (e.g., splitting operations, or the application of shaping tools to surface regions). This will require that surface nodes and edges be classified as being inside, outside, or on the boundary of a surface region delineated by an embedded closed curve. The classification is straightforward if performed edge-by-edge:

> **Algorithm Find-Interior-Edges:** Given an edge $e_{seed}$ in the interior of the region to be collected, a closed series of edges representing the region boundary, and a list of surface edges, gather all interior edges into a list. Begin by adding edge $e_{seed}$ to an (initially empty) check queue. Then, while the check queue is not empty, remove the first edge $e_{interior}$ and add it to the list of interior edges. Let $Q_e$ be the quadrilateral formed by taking the two triangles on either side of $e_{interior}$. For each edge $e_{test}$ of $Q_e$, check to see if it is in the list of boundary edges or interior edges. If not, add $e_{test}$ to the check queue. When the check queue is empty, all interior edges have been found.

## 6.3   Changing the topology

We must be able to make controlled changes to surface topology: splitting along an embedded curve to create a new boundary, or stitching two surfaces together along boundary edges. Introducing a crease in a surface along a curve or smoothing such a crease is also implemented in terms of splitting and merging, since such a discontinuity is actually represented using two independent surfaces whose boundary curves are constrained to coincide.

**Curve correspondence:** To merge two surfaces along a pair of boundaries, or skin two boundary curves with a single sheet, the nodes on the two curves must first be put into correspondence. In general, something like Sederberg's scheme [31] might be used to robustly determine this correspondence. A simpler (though by no means fail-safe) procedure is to iteratively refine the curve with fewer edges by splitting its longest edge until both curves have the same number of nodes. Then choose the alignment that minimizes the sum of squared distances between nodes. This works well in our modeler in the common situation where the user brings curves into proximity with each other before triggering a merge. The resampling and Delaunay triangulation processes quickly iron out artifacts that may result from the simpler matching procedure once the merge has been completed.

**Splitting and merging surfaces:** Recall that the triangulated surfaces are represented as a collection of nodes, each with a radially ordered list of neighbors. To merge two boundary curves that have been put into correspondence, for each pair of nodes move the interior edges of one node to the other, preserving their radial order. This will convert the latter nodes from boundary nodes to infield nodes, and leave the former boundary curve completely disconnected from the merged surface, whence its nodes and edges may be destroyed. Splitting a surface along a closed infield curve is the inverse of this: classify the node edges as being part of the region's interior, exterior, or boundary. Clone the boundary nodes and edges. Then delete the interior edge connections from one boundary copy, and the exterior edge connections from the other.

## 6.4   Surface intersections

A limitation of this modeling approach is that we cannot consider operations that depend on approximated shapes to tell us something about ideal shapes. For example, we shouldn't look for points of intersection between two approximate surfaces in order to answer the question, "do the variational surfaces intersect?" Because of discretization error, whether or how two approximate surfaces intersect says nothing about the true intersection topology.

This would seem to rule out an important style of design in which intersecting surfaces are trimmed against each other and joined along their intersection curves. But a version of trim-and-stitch surface composition that is eminently suited for our approach treats such intersection curves as free-standing boundary or character lines in the composite surface. To "intersect" two variational surfaces, a curve is first constructed that approximates the shape of the intersection curve of the explicit surfaces[5]. Then the parent surfaces are *redefined* to interpolate this independent curve as their new boundary. This somewhat backwards notion of trimming has the advantage over passive surface intersection that the trim curve can be directly reshaped by the designer.

This style of surface composition simplifies the implementation of familiar intersection-based operations. For example, consider applying a parameterized embossing tool (a "branding iron" with control knobs) to a curved surface. Implementing such a tool becomes simple if we observe that, since the tool will be given control over the intersection shape, we don't really need to perform the initial surface intersection and trimming. To apply the tool, we can simply specify that a given surface region contains a hole matching the tool

---

[5]In our implementation, the approximate curve is coarsely sampled, and these fixed samples are used as the anchors of a free-standing curve.

Figure 5: Adding a handle: 1. a cylinder and a torus. The red glow indicates they are close enough for an automated join operation. 2. Join complete: a hole has been cut in the torus and a blend region added connecting it to the cylinder. Boundary curves for the blend region control the tightness of the blend. 3. The cylinder is extended to the opposide wall and joined (500 nodes). 4. The handle's far attachment point is dragged towards the initial attachment point (surface refined to 1500 nodes).

Figure 7: A Klein mug. A single, self-intersecting surface whose handle and outside and inside walls are each controlled by cylinder tools (800 nodes).

Figure 6: A branching surface. Three cylinders, controlled by offset cylinder tools, meet in a minimum curvature surface. A hole has been cut in one of the cylinders, and a fourth cylinder attached there using a faired skirt (800 nodes).

# References

[1] Timothy Barth. Higher order solution of the euler equations on unstructured grids using quadratic reconstruction. In *28th Aerospace Sciences Meeting*. AIAA-90-0013, 1990.

[2] Marshall Bern and David Eppstein. Mesh generation and optimal triangulation. Technical Report CSL-92-1, XEROX Palo Alto Research Center, March 1992.

[3] D.L. Bonner, M.J. Jakiela, M. Watanabe, and N. Kishi. Pseudoedge: nonintersected parametric quilt modeling of multiply connected objects. *Computer Aided Design*, 25(7):438–452, July 1993.

[4] George Celniker and Dave Gossard. Deformable curve and surface finite-elements for free-form shape design. *Computer Graphics*, 25(4), July 1991. (Proceedings Siggraph '91).

[5] George Celniker and William Welch. Linear constraints for nonuniform B-spline surfaces. In *Proceedings, Symposium on Interactive 3D Graphics*, 1992.

[6] Paul Chew. Guaranteed quality mesh generation for curved surfaces. In *Proceedings of the ACM Symposium on Computational Geometry*, 1993.

[7] R. Courant and D. Hilbert. *Methods of Mathematical Physics*, volume volume I. Wiley, 1937.

[8] M. Eppstein. On the influence of parameterization in parametric interpolation. *SIAM J. Numer. Anal.*, 13:261–268, 1976.

[9] Gerald Farin. *Curves and Surfaces for Computer Aided Geometric Design*. Academic Press, 1990.

[10] Helaman Ferguson, Alyn Rockwood, and Jordan Cox. Topological design of sculptured surfaces. *Computer Graphics*, 26(2), July 1992. (Proceedings Siggraph '92).

[11] D. A. Field. Laplacian smoothing and delaunay triangulations. *Comm. Appl. Numer. Methods*, 4:709–712, 1984.

[12] G. Forsythe and W. Wasow. *Finite Difference Methods for Partial Differential Equations*, chapter 19, pages 179–182. John Wiley and Sons, 1960.

[13] Richard Franke and Gregory Nielson. Scattered data interpolation and applications: a tutorial and survey. In Hans Hagen and Dieter Roller, editors, *Geometric Modeling*. Springer-Verlag, 1991.

[14] Gene Golub and Charles Van Loan. *Matrix Computations*. Johns Hopkins University Press, 1989.

[15] Victor Guillemin and Alan Pollack. *Differential Topology*. Prentice-Hall, 1974.

[16] Huges Hoppe, Tony DeRose, Tom Duchamp, John McDonald, and Werner Stuetzle. Mesh optimization. In *Proceedings of Siggraph 93*, 1993.

[17] Geertjan Huiskamp. Difference formulas for the surface Laplacian on a triangulated surface. *Journal of Computational Physics*, 95:477–496, 1991.

[18] Michael Kallay. Constrained optimization in surface design. In *Modeling in Computer Graphics*. Springer Verlag, 1993.

[19] Michael Kass, Andrew Witkin, and Dimitri Terzopoulos. Snakes: Active contour models. *International Journal Computer Vision*, 1(4), 1987.

[20] N. J. Lott and D. I. Pullin. Method for fairing b-spline surfaces. *Computer-Aided Design*, 20(10), 1988.

[21] Steve Mann, Charles Loop, Michael Lounsbery, D. Meyers, J. Painter, Tony Derose, and K. Sloan. A survey of parametric scattered data fitting using triangular interpolants. In *Curve and Surface Modeling*. SIAM.

[22] Henry Moreton and Carlo Séquin. Functional minimization for fair surface design. *Computer Graphics*, 26(2), July 1992. (Proceedings Siggraph '92).

[23] Henry P. Moreton. *Minimum Curvature Variation Curves, Networks, and Surfaces for Fair Free-form Shape Design*. PhD thesis, University of California, Berkeley, 1993.

[24] Gregory Nielson. A transfinite, visually continuous, triangular interpolant. In Gerald Farin, editor, *Geometric Modelling*, pages 235–246. SIAM, 1987.

[25] Barrett O'Neill. *Elementary Differential Geometry*. Academic Press, 1966.

[26] Jörg Peters. Smooth interpolation of a mesh of curves. *Constructive Approximation*, 7:221–246, 1991.

[27] John Platt. *Constraint Methods for Neural Networks and Computer Graphics*. PhD thesis, California Institute of Technology, 1989.

[28] Vaughan Pratt. Direct least-squares fitting of algebraic surfaces. *Computer Graphics (SIGGRAPH '87 Proceedings)*, 21(4):145–152, July 1987.

[29] M. M. Rai and D. A. Anderson. Application of adaptive grids to fluid-flow problems with asymptotic solutions. *AIAA J.*, 20:496–502, 1982.

[30] D.G. Schweikert. An interpolation curve using a spline in tension. *Journal of Math and Phys.*, 45:312–317, 1966.

[31] Thomas Sederberg and Eugene Greenwood. A physically based approach to 2D shape blending. *Computer Graphics*, 26(2), July 1992. (Proceedings Siggraph '92).

[32] Michael Spivak. *A Comprehensive Introduction to Differential Geometry*. Publish or Perish, Inc., 1979.

[33] Gilbert Strang. *Introduction to Applied Mathematics*. Wellesley-Cambridge Press, 1986.

[34] Richard Szeliski and David Tonnesen. Surface modeling with oriented particle systems. *Computer Graphics*, 26(2), July 1992. (Proceedings Siggraph '92).

[35] D. Terzopoulos. Multi-level reconstruction of visual surfaces. *MIT Artificial Intelligence Memo Number 671*, April 1981.

[36] J.F. Thompson, Z.U.A. Warsi, and C.W. Mastin. *Numerical Grid Generation: Foundations and Applications*. North-Holland, 1985.

[37] Joe F. Thompson. A survey of dynamically-adaptive grids in the numerical solution of partial differential equations. *Applied Numerical Mathematics*, 1:3–27, 1985.

[38] Greg Turk. Generating textures on arbitrary surfaces using reaction-diffusion. *Computer Graphics (SIGGRAPH '91 Proceedings)*, 25(4):289–298, July 1991.

[39] Greg Turk. Re-tiling polygonal surfaces. *Computer Graphics*, 26(2):55–64, July 1992. (Proceedings Siggraph '92).

[40] William Welch. *Free-Form shape design using triangulated surfaces*. PhD thesis, Carnegie Mellon University, (in preparation) 1994.

[41] William Welch and Andrew Witkin. Variational surface modeling. *Computer Graphics*, 26(2), July 1992. (Proceedings Siggraph '92).

[42] Andrew Witkin and Paul Heckbert. Using particles to sample and control implicit surfaces. *In these proceedings*, July 1994.

# A Generalized de Casteljau Approach to 3D Free-form Deformation

Yu-Kuang Chang and Alyn P. Rockwood

Department of Computer Science and Engineering
Arizona State University
Tempe, AZ 85287-5406

## ABSTRACT

This paper briefly presents an efficient and intuitive 3D free-form deformation approach based on iterative affine transformations, a generalized de Casteljau algorithm, whereby the object warps along a Bézier curve as its skeleton.

**CR Categories and Subject Descriptors:** I.3.5 [Computer Graphics]: Computational Geometry and Object Modeling - Curve, surface, solid, and object representations; Hierarchy and geometric transformations.

**Additional Key Words:** The de Casteljau algorithm, affine transformation, Bézier curve, B-spline, geometric modeling, deformation.

## 1. INTRODUCTION

Free-form deformation (FFD) has become important tool in computer-assisted geometric design and animation. Barr first suggested a set of hierarchical transformations for deforming an object including stretching, bending, twisting, and tapering operators [1]. It is a very efficient and useable method if somewhat constrained. Sederberg and Parry [2] proposed a general technique for deformation which is based on trivariate Bernstein polynomials and enables the deformation of objects by manipulating control points (see also [3]). Another successful approach with an initial lattice and a scheme of B-spline control points that approximate the shape of the intended deformation is given by Coquillart [4].

---

1. TEL: (602)965-4154
   Internet: ychang@enws120.cagd.eas.asu.edu
2. TEL: (602)965-8267
   Internet: rockwood@asu.edu

We propose a technique that deforms by repeatedly applying affine transformations in space. The object warps along a user defined curve. Our approach reduces the definition of the free-form deformation from a crowded set of control points to a single Bézier curve and a few affine maps controlled by readily understood "handles." It also generalizes the well-known de Casteljau algorithm for curve evaluation [5].

## 2. PRELIMINARIES

We assume some familiarity with curves and surfaces (see Farin [5]). The de Casteljau Algorithm for evaluating a Bézier curve of degree n with control points $p_i$ and at a parameter u is

$$p_i^j(u) = (1-u) \cdot p_i^{j-1}(u) + u \cdot p_{i+1}^{j-1}(u), \ 1 \le j \le n, \ 0 \le i \le n-j,$$

where $p_i^0(u) = p_i, \quad 0 \le i \le n.$     (1)

The value $p_0^n(u)$ is the point on the curve at u.

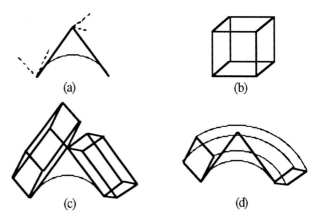

**Figure 1**: (a) Bézier curve, control polygon and user-specified axes, (b) cube primitive, (c) first-level execution of the generalized de Casteljau algorithm, and (d) second-level execution of the generalized de Casteljau algorithm.

Equation (1) consists of repeated univariate linear interpolation. Our approach generalizes the de Casteljau algorithm to a trivariate scheme. Each segment of the Bézier control polygon is given with two user-specified axes, called *handles*, at one endpoint which defines a local coordinate system [2]. Objects in u-v-w space are mapped along an embedded Bézier curve by iterative affine transformations derived from the handles and control polygon segments. For example, Figure 1(a) shows a quadratic Bézier curve, control polygon, and two local axes on each segment. Figure 1(b) is a cube to be deformed. After executing the first level of the generalized de Casteljau algorithm, the cube is mapped affinely to each segment of the control polygon in Figure 1(c). In Figure 1 (d), the second level of the algorithm warps the original cube along the Bézier curve.

## 3. THE DEFORMATION ALGORITHM

Observe that in 3-space each iteration of the de Casteljau algorithm is just the execution of a degenerate affine transformation. It maps space to a line. Therefore the de Casteljau algorithm can be generalized to an iterative transformation scheme simply by raising the rank of the transformation matrix.

If vectors $\underline{r}$, $\underline{s}$, and $\underline{t}$ span an affine space, the function $\Phi[\underline{p},\underline{q}]: R^3 \rightarrow R^3$ is defined as an affine transformation from parameter space into affine space in homogeneous form as

$$\Phi[\underline{p},\underline{q}]\begin{pmatrix} u \\ v \\ w \\ 1 \end{pmatrix} = \begin{pmatrix} q_x - p_x & s_x & t_x & p_x \\ q_y - p_y & s_y & t_y & p_y \\ q_y - p_y & s_z & t_z & p_z \\ 0 & 0 & 0 & 1 \end{pmatrix}\begin{pmatrix} u \\ v \\ w \\ 1 \end{pmatrix} = \begin{pmatrix} x \\ y \\ z \\ 1 \end{pmatrix} \quad (2)$$

where $\underline{r}=(q_x-p_x,q_y-p_y,q_z-p_z)$, $\underline{s}=(s_x,s_y,s_z)$, and $\underline{t}=(t_x,t_y,t_z)$. Note especially that the interval [0,1] on u is mapped to $[\underline{p},\underline{q}]$ on $\underline{r}$. The generalized de Casteljau algorithm is given by

$$\underline{p}_i^0(\underline{u}) = \underline{p}_i, \qquad 0 \le i \le n,$$
$$\tag{3}$$
$$\underline{p}_i^j(\underline{u}) = \Phi\left[\underline{p}_i^{j-1},\underline{p}_{i+1}^{j-1}\right](\underline{u}), \quad 1 \le j \le n, \ 0 \le i \le n-j,$$

where n is the degree and $\underline{p}_0^n(\underline{u})$ is the deformed point on an object at $\underline{u}=(u,v,w)$. The deformation algorithm performs iterative affine transformations and as a result the deformation of space includes the Bézier curve.

In the first level of the generalized de Casteljau algorithm, if $\underline{s}$ in the transformation matrix is a zero vector, then a solid will be mapped into just a surface patch because the depth information is lost. The case where elements of vector $\underline{t}$ are all zero is similar except the degeneration occurs on a different axis. The deformation process is reduced to the classic de Casteljau algorithm if and only if both $\underline{s}$ and $\underline{t}$ are zero vectors. Under these circumstances, the solid is mapped to a curve since the parameter v and w are no longer effective.

For the second level or above, the vectors, $\underline{s}$ and $\underline{t}$, could be zero or nonzero. If they are all zero, the function of second-level execution linearly blends the result of the first-level execution and similarly for higher levels. If $s_x$, $s_y$, or $s_z$ is nonzero, the deformed object is sheared by an amount proportional to the v value along the direction of $(s_x,0,0)$, $(0,s_y,0)$, or $(0,0,s_z)$. The same applies to vector $\underline{t}$ except that the shearing is proportional to w instead of v. The effects of the shearing operations are hierarchical. For instance, there are three levels of affine transformations in the cubic case. A nonzero vector $\underline{s}$ or $\underline{t}$ in second-level transformation matrix shears only a portion of the object related to the appropriate control polygon segments, while one in the third-level affects the whole object.

## 4. IMPLEMENTATION

Figure 2 shows examples of stretch, taper, swell, twist, and bend operations applied to a cube primitive (upper left). They mimic Barr's deformations, but are polynomial.

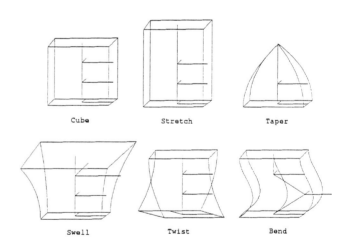

Cube      Stretch      Taper

Swell      Twist      Bend

**Figure 2**: "Barr"-like deformations applied to a cube.

Our deformation algorithm can be applied to any geometric model. Figure 3 and Figure 4 show polygons before and after deformation. A figure similar to Figure 4 could also be generated with the Sederberg and Parry's approach. It would require specification of more, loosely related control points. Moreover, the generalized de Casteljau approach is computationally more efficient than trivariate de Casteljau, because it is an affine transformation plus a univariate interpolation in space vs. one that iterates over three variables. A comparison of computation times is given in Table 1.

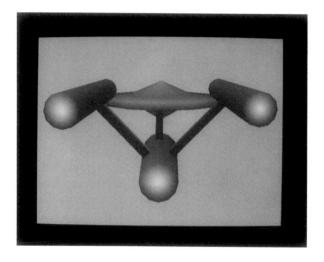

**Figure 3**: Undeformed polygons.

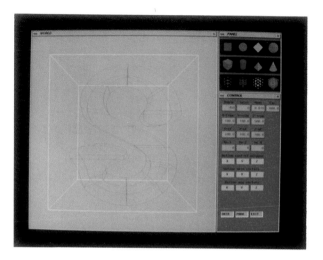

**Figure 5**: The user interface for the free-form deformation.

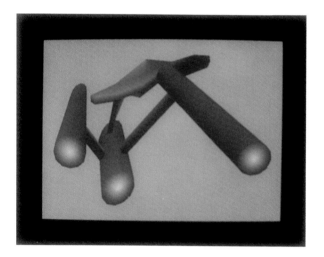

**Figure 4**: Deformed polygons.

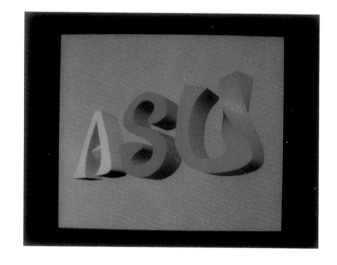

**Figure 6**: The design of a logo.

| Deformation method \ Degree | Linear | Quadratic | Cubic |
|---|---|---|---|
| Bézier lattice method (Sederberg and Parry's approach) | 42 multiplications 21 additions | 90 multiplications 45 additions | 144 multiplications 72 additions |
| Generalized de Casteljau method (Our approach) | 9 multiplications 9 additions | 27 multiplications 27 additions | 54 multiplications 54 additions |

**Table 1**: Comparison of computation complexity.

The design interface supports user two functions: First, specification of a curved spline by Bézier control points and second, definition of two local axes on each control polygon segment. These are intuitive and simple to use (see Figure 5).

Tangent continuity ($C^1$) between two volumes that share local coordinate systems at the endpoints is guaranteed if adjacent local systems are linearly dependent. Figure 7 shows two pieces of cubic Bézier curves which are joined smoothly ($C^2$ with B-splines, for instance). The axis triple ($\underline{r}_i, \underline{s}_i, \underline{t}_i$) is associated with the i[th] segment of control polygon where $\underline{r}_i = \underline{p}_{i+1} - \underline{p}_i$. At the junction point $\underline{p}_3$ of the consecutive Bézier curves, two volumes defined on those two curves are connected with $C^1$ continuity if the derivative vectors at the boundary are the same. By calculating partial derivatives (refer to [5]) at a point on the boundary, it induces the following constraints:

$$\underline{p}_3 = \tfrac{1}{2}(\underline{p}_2 + \underline{p}_4)$$

$$\underline{s}_3 = \tfrac{1}{2}(\underline{s}_2 + \underline{s}_4), \qquad (4)$$

$$\underline{t}_3 = \tfrac{1}{2}(\underline{t}_2 + \underline{t}_4).$$

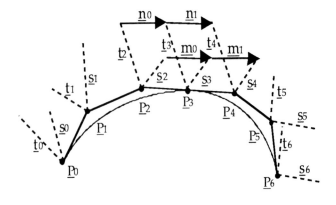

**Figure 7**: Local coordinate systems defined over piecewise Bézier curves.

Tangent direction continuity ($G^1$) requires only the collinearity of the cross-boundary derivatives. It results in

$$\underline{p}_4 - \underline{p}_3 = \mu_0(\underline{p}_3 - \underline{p}_2)$$

$$\underline{m}_1 = \mu_1 \underline{m}_0, \qquad (5)$$

$$\underline{n}_1 = \mu_2 \underline{n}_0,$$

where $\mu_i \neq 0$ for i=0 to 2. It is $C^1$ if $\mu_0 = \mu_1 = \mu_2 = 1$. If $\mu_0$, $\mu_1$, and $\mu_2$ are all equal, then $\underline{s}_2$, $\underline{s}_3$ and $\underline{s}_4$ are linearly dependent as are $\underline{t}_2$, $\underline{t}_3$ and $\underline{t}_4$. However, linear dependence is only the sufficient condition for continuity. For example, if $\mu_0$ and $\mu_1$ differ, then $\underline{s}_3$ and $\underline{t}_3$ are still affine transformations of the adjacent handles.

Figures 6 shows the design of a logo which is generated on a piecewise Bézier (B-spline) basis. The primitives are cubes and the deformed shapes are chosen somewhat arbitrarily.

## 5. CONCLUSIONS

The proposed approach replaces the sometimes overwhelming problem of control point clutter with a simple design scheme for a broadly useful set of deformations, and does so with greater computational efficiency.

We have only used polygons and cube primitives in the paper. Clearly any object defined in $R^3$ could be warped. Extensions in higher dimensions are also straightforward.

Finally and most importantly, the deformation algorithm is just one example of the generalized de Casteljau idea. Other applications such as interpolation to local affine systems are yet to be investigated. The idea is applicable to any iterative scheme like de Casteljau's. One might consider, for instance, a generalized de Boor scheme directly for B-splines or an Aitken scheme for Lagrange interpolation.

## ACKNOWLEDGEMENTS

We thank faculty and students of the Computer Aided Geometric Design (CAGD) group of the Arizona State University for their comments and support.

## REFERENCES

[1] Barr, A. H., Global and Local Deformations of Solid Primitives, Proceedings of SIGGRAPH '84, Computer Graphics 18, 3 (July 1984), 21-30.

[2] Sederberg, T. W. and Parry, S. R., Free-Form Deformation of Solid Geometric Models, Proceedings of SIGGRAPH '86, Computer Graphics 20, 4 (August 1986), 151-159.

[3] Bézier, P., Mathematical and Practical Possibilities of UNISURF, In Barnhill, R. E. and Riesenfeld, R. F. (eds), Computer Aided Geometric Design, Academic Press (1974), New York, 127-152.

[4] Coquillart, S., Extended Free-Form Deformation: A sculpturing Tool for 3D Geometric Modeling, Proceedings of SIGGRAPH '90, Computer Graphics 24, 4 (August 1990), 187-196.

[5] Farin, G. E., Curves and Surfaces for Computer Aided Geometric Design, Academic Press (1993), 3rd Edition, Boston.

# Multiresolution Curves

*Adam Finkelstein*     *David H. Salesin*

Department of Computer Science and Engineering
University of Washington
Seattle, Washington 98195

## Abstract

We describe a multiresolution curve representation, based on wavelets, that conveniently supports a variety of operations: smoothing a curve; editing the overall form of a curve while preserving its details; and approximating a curve within any given error tolerance for scan conversion. We present methods to support continuous levels of smoothing as well as direct manipulation of an arbitrary portion of the curve; the control points, as well as the discrete nature of the underlying hierarchical representation, can be hidden from the user. The multiresolution representation requires no extra storage beyond that of the original control points, and the algorithms using the representation are both simple and fast.

**CR Categories and Subject Descriptors:** I.3.5 [Computer Graphics]: Computational Geometry and Object Modeling — Curve, Surface, Solid, and Object Representations; I.3.6 [Computer Graphics]: Methodology and Techniques — Interaction Techniques.

**Additional Key Words:** curve compression, curve editing, curve fitting, curve smoothing, direct manipulation, scan conversion, wavelets.

## 1  Introduction

A flexible representation for curves should allow editing, smoothing, and scan conversion. In particular, the representation should support:

- the ability to change the overall "sweep" of a curve while maintaining its fine details, or "character" (Figure 3);

- the ability to change a curve's "character" without affecting its overall "sweep" (Figure 6);

- the ability to edit a curve at any continuous level of detail, allowing an arbitrary portion of the curve to be affected through direct manipulation (Figure 4);

- continuous levels of smoothing, in which undesirable features are removed from a curve (Figure 2);

- curve approximation, or "fitting," within a guaranteed maximum error tolerance, for scan conversion and other applications (Figures 8 and 9).

In this paper, we show how a *multiresolution* curve representation can provide a single, unified framework for addressing all of these issues. It requires no extra storage beyond that of the original $m$ control points, and the algorithms that use it are both simple and fast, typically linear in $m$.

There are many applications of multiresolution curves, including computer-aided design, in which cross-sectional curves are frequently used in the specification of surfaces; keyframe animation, in which curves are used to control parameter interpolation; 3D modeling and animation, in which "backbone" curves are manipulated to specify object deformations; graphic design, in which curves are used to describe regions of constant color or texture; font

design, in which curves represent the outlines of characters; and pen-and-ink illustration, in which curves are the basic elements of the finished piece. In all of these situations, the editing, smoothing, and approximation techniques we describe can be powerful tools.

### 1.1  Related work

Some of the algorithms supported by multiresolution curves are new, to our knowledge, such as the ability to edit a curve at any continuous level of detail, and the ability to change a curve's character without affecting its overall sweep. However, the majority of applications described in this paper have already been addressed in one form or another. Although the algorithms we describe compare favorably with most of this previous work, it is the convenience with which the multiresolution representation supports such a wide variety of operations that makes it so useful. We survey here some of these previous techniques.

Forsey and Bartels [13] employ hierarchical B-splines to address the problem of editing the overall form of a surface while maintaining its details. Their original formulation requires the user to design an explicit hierarchy into the model. In later work [14], they describe a method for recursively fitting a hierarchical surface to a set of data by first fitting a coarse approximation and then refining in areas where the residual is large. This construction is similar in spirit to the filter bank process used in multiresolution analysis, as described in Section 2.1. One significant difference is that in their formulation there are an infinite number of possible representations for the same surface, whereas the multiresolution curve representation is unique for a given shape. Fowler [15] and Welch and Witkin [28] also describe methods in which editing can be performed over narrower or broader regions of a surface; however, in neither of these works is there an attempt to preserve the higher-resolution detail beneath the edited region.

Curve and surface smoothing algorithms that minimize various energy norms have also been studied; these are surveyed in Hoschek and Lasser [16]. One example is the work of Celniker and Gossard [7], in which a fairness functional is applied to hand-drawn curves, as well as to surfaces. The method we describe is really a least-squares type of smoothing, which is much simpler but supports continuous levels of smoothing that behave quite reasonably and intuitively in practice.

Many schemes for approximating curves within specified error tolerances have also been explored [2, 20, 23, 27]. Most of this research has centered on various forms of knot removal for representing curves efficiently with non-uniform B-splines. In this paper, we look at the very practical concern of producing a small number of Bézier segments that approximate the curve well, since these segments are the standard representation for curves in PostScript [1], the most common page description language. Our requirements are also somewhat different than those of most previous curve-fitting methods. In particular, for our application of scan conversion we do not require any particular continuity constraints for the approximating curve. Relaxing this condition can allow much higher compression ratios.

### 1.2  Overview

The next section discusses the theory of multiresolution analysis, and develops a multiresolution representation for B-spline curves. Sections 3, 4, and 5 describe how this representation can be used to support efficient smoothing, editing, and scan conversion. Finally, Section 6 suggests some areas for fu-

© 1994     ACM-0-89791-667-0/94/007/0261     $01.50

ture research. The details of the multiresolution curve formulation can be found in the appendices.

## 2 Theory of multiresolution curves

In this section, we discuss the theory of wavelets and multiresolution analysis, and we show how it can be applied to representing endpoint-interpolating B-spline curves.

### 2.1 Wavelets and multiresolution analysis

Wavelets are a simple mathematical tool that have found a wide variety of applications in recent years, including signal analysis [22], image processing [11], and numerical analysis [6]. In this section, we sketch the basic ideas behind wavelets and multiresolution analysis. Rather than presenting the classical multiresolution analysis developed by Mallat [22], we present here a slightly generalized version of the theory, following Lounsbery et al. [19], that is more convenient for our application of representing open curves.[1]

Consider a discrete signal $C^n$, expressed as a column vector of samples $[c_1^n, \ldots, c_m^n]^T$. In our application, the samples $c_i^n$ could be thought of as a curve's control points in $\mathbb{R}^2$.

Suppose we wish to create a low-resolution version $C^{n-1}$ of $C^n$ with a fewer number of samples $m'$. The standard approach for creating the $m'$ samples of $C^{n-1}$ is to use some form of filtering and downsampling on the $m$ samples of $C^n$. This process can be expressed as a matrix equation

$$C^{n-1} = A^n C^n \qquad (1)$$

where $A^n$ is an $m' \times m$ matrix.

Since $C^{n-1}$ contains fewer samples than $C^n$, it is intuitively clear that some amount of detail is lost in this filtering process. If $A^n$ is appropriately chosen, it is possible to capture the lost detail as another signal $D^{n-1}$, computed by

$$D^{n-1} = B^n C^n \qquad (2)$$

where $B^n$ is an $(m - m') \times m$ matrix, which is related to matrix $A^n$. The pair of matrices $A^n$ and $B^n$ are called *analysis filters*. The process of splitting a signal $C^n$ into a low-resolution version $C^{n-1}$ and detail $D^{n-1}$ is called *decomposition*.

If $A^n$ and $B^n$ are chosen correctly, then the original signal $C^n$ can be recovered from $C^{n-1}$ and $D^{n-1}$ by using another pair of matrices $P^n$ and $Q^n$, called *synthesis filters*, as follows:

$$C^n = P^n C^{n-1} + Q^n D^{n-1} \qquad (3)$$

Recovering $C^n$ from $C^{n-1}$ and $D^{n-1}$ is called *reconstruction*.

Note that the procedure for splitting $C^n$ into a low-resolution part $C^{n-1}$ and a detail part $D^{n-1}$ can be applied recursively to the new signal $C^{n-1}$. Thus, the original signal can be expressed as a hierarchy of lower-resolution signals $C^0, \ldots, C^{n-1}$ and details $D^0, \ldots, D^{n-1}$, as shown in Figure 1. This recursive process is known as a *filter bank*.

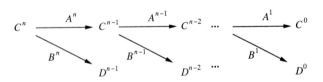

Figure 1: *The filter bank.*

Since the original signal $C^n$ can be recovered from the sequence $C^0, D^0, D^1, \ldots, D^{n-1}$, this sequence can be thought of as a transform of the original signal, known as a *wavelet transform*. Note that the total size of the

transform $C^0, D^0, \ldots, D^{n-1}$ is the same as that of the original signal $C^n$, so no extra storage is required.

Wavelet transforms have a number of properties that make them attractive for signal processing. First, if the filters $A^j$, $B^j$, $P^j$, and $Q^j$ are constructed to be sparse, then the filter bank operation can be performed very quickly — often in $O(m)$ time. Second, for many of the signals encountered in practice, a large percentage of the entries in the wavelet transform are negligible. Wavelet compression methods can therefore approximate the original set of samples in $C^n$ by storing only the significant coefficients of the wavelet transform. Impressive compression ratios have been reported for univariate signals as well as for images [11].

As suggested by the treatment above, all that is needed for performing a wavelet transform is an appropriate set of analysis and synthesis filters $A^j$, $B^j$, $P^j$, and $Q^j$. To see how to construct these filters, we associate with each signal $C^n$ a function $f^n(u)$ with $u \in [0, 1]$ given by

$$f^n(u) = \Phi^n(u) C^n \qquad (4)$$

where $\Phi^n(u)$ is a row matrix of basis functions $[\phi_1^n(u), \ldots, \phi_m^n(u)]$, called *scaling functions*. In our application, for example, the scaling functions are the endpoint-interpolating B-splines basis functions, in which case the function $f^n(u)$ would be an endpoint-interpolating B-spline curve.[2]

The scaling functions are required to be *refinable*; that is, for all $j$ in $[1, n]$ there must exist a matrix $P^j$ such that

$$\Phi^{j-1} = \Phi^j P^j \qquad (5)$$

In other words, each scaling function at level $j - 1$ must be expressible as a linear combination of "finer" scaling functions at level $j$. As suggested by the notation, the refinement matrix in equation (5) turns out to be the same as the synthesis filter $P^j$.

Next, let $V^j$ be the linear space spanned by the set of scaling functions $\Phi^j$. The refinement condition on $\Phi^j$ implies that these linear spaces are nested: $V^0 \subset V^1 \subset \cdots \subset V^n$. Choosing an inner product for the basis functions in $V^j$ allows us to define $W^j$ as the *orthogonal complement* of $V^j$ in $V^{j+1}$, that is, the space $W^j$ whose basis functions $\Psi^j = [\psi_1^j(u), \ldots, \psi_{m-m'}^j(u)]$ are such that $\Phi^j$ and $\Psi^j$ together form a basis for $V^{j+1}$, and every $\psi_i^j(u)$ is orthogonal to every $\phi_i^j(u)$ under the chosen inner product. The basis functions $\psi_i^j(u)$ are called *wavelets*.

We can now construct the synthesis filter $Q^j$ as the matrix that satisfies

$$\Psi^{j-1} = \Phi^j Q^j \qquad (6)$$

Equations (5) and (6) can be expressed as a single equation by concatenating the matrices together:

$$\left[ \Phi^{j-1} \mid \Psi^{j-1} \right] = \Phi^j \left[ P^j \mid Q^j \right] \qquad (7)$$

Finally, the analysis filters $A^j$ and $B^j$ are formed by the matrices satisfying the inverse relation:

$$\left[ \Phi^{j-1} \mid \Psi^{j-1} \right] \left[ \begin{array}{c} A^j \\ \hline B^j \end{array} \right] = \Phi^j \qquad (8)$$

Note that $\left[ P^j \mid Q^j \right]$ and $\left[ A^j \mid B^j \right]^T$ are both square matrices. Thus,

$$\left[ \begin{array}{c} A^j \\ \hline B^j \end{array} \right] = \left[ P^j \mid Q^j \right]^{-1} \qquad (9)$$

from which it is easy to prove a number of useful identities:

$$\begin{aligned} A^j Q^j &= B^j P^j = \mathbf{0} \qquad (10)\\ A^j P^j &= B^j Q^j = P^j A^j + Q^j B^j = \mathbf{1} \end{aligned}$$

where $\mathbf{0}$ and $\mathbf{1}$ are the matrix of zeros and the identity matrix, respectively.

---

[1] The more general theory described here differs from Mallat's original formulation by relaxing his condition that the basis functions must be translates and scales of one another.

[2] For simplicity of notation, we often omit the explicit dependence on $u$ when writing $f^n$ and $\Phi^n$.

## 2.2 Multiresolution endpoint-interpolating B-splines

In our application, we build a multiresolution analysis for B-spline curves. In this paper, we restrict our attention to the common case of cubic B-splines defined on a knot sequence that is uniformly spaced everywhere except at its ends, where its knots have multiplicity 4. Such B-splines are commonly referred to as *endpoint-interpolating* cubic B-splines. These curves are discussed in detail in many texts on computer-aided design [4, 12, 16].

The multiresolution framework described in Section 2.1 is very general. To construct our *multiresolution curves* from endpoint-interpolating cubic B-splines, we need to make several choices, as enumerated below:

1. *Choose the scaling functions $\Phi^j(u)$ for all $j$ in $[0, n]$.*
   This choice determines the synthesis filters $P^j$. For each level $j$, we would like a basis for the endpoint-interpolating cubic B-spline curves with $2^j$ interior segments. The basis functions for these curves are the $2^j + 3$ endpoint-interpolating cubic B-splines, which are refinable, as required by equation (5).

2. *Select an inner product for any two functions $f$ and $g$ in $V^j$.*
   This choice determines the orthogonal complement spaces $W^j$. We use the standard form $\langle f, g \rangle = \int f(u)g(u)du$.

3. *Select a set of wavelets $\Psi^j(u)$ that span $W^j$.*
   This choice determines the synthesis filters $Q^j$. Together, the synthesis filters $P^j$ and $Q^j$ determine the analysis filters $A^j$ and $B^j$ by equation (9). We use the set of $2^j$ *minimally-supported* functions that span $W^j$.

Appendix A contains more details on the specific wavelets we use and their derivation. A similar construction has also been independently proposed by Chui and Quak [9]. Note that multiresolution constructions can be built for other types of splines as well, such as uniform B-splines [8], and non-uniform B-splines with arbitrary knot sequences [21]. A recent construction applicable to subdivision surfaces is discussed by Lounsbery *et al.* [19].

Note that because both the scaling functions and wavelets in our construction have compact support, the synthesis filters $P^j$ and $Q^j$ have a banded structure, allowing reconstruction in $O(m)$ time. However, a potential weakness of our construction is that the analysis filters $A^j$ and $B^j$ are dense, which would seem to imply an $O(m^2)$-time decomposition algorithm. Fortunately, there is a clever trick, due to Quak and Weyrich [25], for performing the decomposition in linear time. The implementation of their algorithm is described in Appendix B.

## 3 Smoothing

In this section, we address the following problem: *Given a curve with $m$ control points $C$, construct a best least-squares-error approximating curve with $m'$ control points $C'$, where $m' < m$.* Here, we will assume that both curves are endpoint-interpolating uniform B-spline curves.

The multiresolution analysis framework allows this problem to be solved trivially, for certain values of $m$ and $m'$. Assume for the moment that $m = 2^j + 3$ and $m' = 2^{j'} + 3$ for some nonnegative integers $j' < j$. Then the control points $C'$ of the approximating curve are given by

$$C' = A^{j'+1}A^{j'+2} \cdots A^j C$$

In other words, we simply run the decomposition algorithm, as described by equation (1), until a curve with just $m'$ control points is reached. Note that this process can be performed at interactive speeds for hundreds of control points using the linear-time algorithm described in Appendix B.

One notable aspect of the multiresolution curve representation is its discrete nature. Thus, in our application it is easy to construct approximating curves with 4, 5, 7, 11, or any $2^j + 3$ control points efficiently, for any *integer level $j$*. However, there is no obvious way to quickly construct curves that have "levels" of smoothness in between.

The best solution we have found is to define a *fractional-level* curve $f^{j+t}(u)$ for some $0 \le t \le 1$ in terms of a linear interpolation between its two nearest

integer-level curves $f^j(u)$ and $f^{j+1}(u)$, as follows:

$$
\begin{aligned}
f^{j+t}(u) &= (1-t)f^j(u) + tf^{j+1}(u) \\
&= (1-t)\Phi^j(u)C^j + t\Phi^{j+1}(u)C^{j+1} \quad (11)
\end{aligned}
$$

These fractional-level curves allow for continuous levels of smoothing. In our application a user can move a control slider and see the curve transform continuously from its smoothest (4 control point) form, up to its finest ($m$ control point) version. Some fractional-level curves are shown in Figure 2.

Figure 2: *Smoothing a curve continuously. From left to right: the original curve at level 8.0, and smoother versions at levels 5.4 and 3.1.*

## 4 Editing

Suppose we have a curve $C^n$ and all of its low-resolution and detail parts $C^0, \ldots, C^{n-1}$ and $D^0, \ldots, D^{n-1}$. Multiresolution analysis allows for two very different kinds of curve editing. If we modify some low-resolution version $C^j$ and then add back in the detail $D^j, D^{j+1}, \ldots, D^{n-1}$, we will have modified the overall sweep of the curve (Figure 3). On the other hand, if we modify the set of detail functions $D^j, D^{j+1}, \ldots, D^{n-1}$ but leave the low-resolution versions $C^0, \ldots, C^j$ intact, we will have modified the character of the curve, without affecting its overall sweep (Figure 6). These two types of editing are explored more fully below.

### 4.1 Editing the sweep

Editing the sweep of a curve at an integer level of the wavelet transform is simple. Let $C^n$ be the control points of the original curve $f^n(u)$, let $C^j$ be a low-resolution version of $C^n$, and let $\widehat{C}^j$ be an edited version of $C^j$, given by $\widehat{C}^j = C^j + \Delta C^j$. The edited version of the highest-resolution curve $\widehat{C}^n = C^n + \Delta C^n$ can be computed through reconstruction:

$$
\begin{aligned}
\widehat{C}^n &= C^n + \Delta C^n \\
&= C^n + P^n P^{n-1} \cdots P^{j+1} \Delta C^j
\end{aligned}
$$

Note that editing the sweep of the curve at lower levels of smoothing $j$ affects larger portions of the high-resolution curve $f^n(u)$. At the lowest level, when $j = 0$, the entire curve is affected; at the highest level, when $j = n$, only the narrow portion influenced by one original control point is affected. The kind of flexibility that this multiresolution editing allows is suggested in Figures 3 and 4.

In addition to editing at integer levels of resolution, it is natural to ascribe meaning to editing at fractional levels as well. We would like the portion of the curve affected when editing at fractional level $j + t$ to interpolate the portions affected at levels $j$ and $j + 1$. Thus, as $t$ increases from 0 to 1, the portion affected should gradually narrow down from that of level $j$ to that of level $j + 1$, as demonstrated in the lower part of Figure 4.

Consider a fractional-level curve $f^{j+t}(u)$ given by equation (11). Let $C^{j+t}$ be the set of control points associated with this curve; that is,

$$f^{j+t}(u) = \Phi^{j+1}(u)C^{j+t} \quad (12)$$

We can obtain an expression for $C^{j+t}$ by equating the right-hand sides of equations (11) and (12), and then applying equations (5) and (3):

$$
\begin{aligned}
C^{j+t} &= (1-t)P^{j+1}C^j + tC^{j+1} \\
&= P^{j+1}C^j + tQ^{j+1}D^j
\end{aligned}
$$

Suppose now that one of the control points $c_i^{j+t}$ is modified by the user. In order to allow the portion of the curve affected to depend on $t$ in the manner described above, the system will have to automatically move some of the nearby control points when $c_i^{j+t}$ is modified. The distance that each of these control points is moved is inversely proportional to $t$: for example,

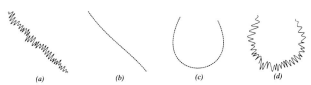

Figure 3: *Changing the overall sweep of a curve without affecting its character. Given the original curve (a), the system extracts the overall sweep (b). If the user modifies the sweep (c), the system can reapply the detail (d).*

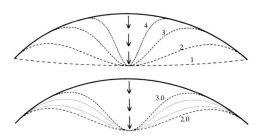

Figure 4: *The middle of the dark curve is pulled. Upper: Editing at integer levels 1, 2, 3, and 4. Lower: Editing at fractional levels between 2.0 and 3.0.*

when $t$ is near 0, the control points in $C^{j+t}$ are moved in conjunction so that the overall effect approaches that of editing a single control point at level $j$; when $t = 1$, the nearby control points are not moved at all, since the modified curve should correspond to moving just a single control point at level $j + 1$.

Let $\Delta C^{j+t}$ be a vector describing how each control point of the fractional-level curve is modified: the $i$-th entry of $\Delta C^{j+t}$ is the user's change to the $i$-th control point; the other entries reflect the computed movements of the other control points. Rather than solving for $\Delta C^{j+t}$ explicitly, our approach will be to break this vector into two components, a vector $\Delta C^j$ of changes to the control points at level $j$, and a vector $\Delta D^j$ of changes to the wavelet coefficients at level $j$:

$$\Delta C^{j+t} = P^{j+1} \Delta C^j + t\, Q^{j+1} \Delta D^j \qquad (13)$$

Next, define $\Delta \acute{C}^{j+t}$ to be the user's change to the control points at level $j + t$, that is, a vector whose $i$-th entry is $\Delta c_i^{j+t}$, and whose other entries are 0. Define also a new vector $\Delta \acute{C}^j$ as a change to control points at level $j$ necessary to make the modified control point $c_i^{j+t}$ move to its new position. We choose the vector that is 0 everywhere, except for one or two entries, depending on the index $i$ of the modified control point. By examining the $i$-th row of the refinement matrix $P^{j+1}$, we can determine whether the modified control point is maximally influenced by either *one* control point $c_k^{j+1}$ or *two* control points $c_k^{j+1}$ and $c_{k+1}^{j+1}$ at level $j + 1$. In the former case, we set $\Delta \acute{c}_k^j$ to be $\Delta c_i^{j+t}/P_{i,k}^{j+1}$. In the latter case, we set $\Delta \acute{c}_k^j$ and $\Delta \acute{c}_{k+1}^j$ to be $\Delta c_i^{j+t}/2P_{i,k}^{j+1}$.

Note that applying either change alone, $\Delta \acute{C}^{j+t}$ or $\Delta \acute{C}^j$, would cause the selected control point to move to its new position; however, the latter change would cause a larger portion of the curve to move. In order to have a "breadth" of change that gradually decreases as $t$ goes from 0 to 1, we can interpolate between these two vectors, using some interpolation function $g(t)$:

$$\Delta C^{j+t} = (1 - g(t))\, P^{j+1} \Delta \acute{C}^j + g(t)\, \Delta \acute{C}^{j+t} \qquad (14)$$

Thus, $\Delta C^{j+t}$ will still move the selected control point to its new position, and it will also now control the "breadth" of change as a function of $t$.

Finally, equating the right-hand sides of equations (13) and (14), multiplying with either $A^{j+1}$ or $B^{j+1}$, and employing the identities (10) yields the two expressions we need:

$$\Delta C^j = (1 - g(t))\, \Delta \acute{C}^j + g(t)\, A^{j+1} \Delta \acute{C}^{j+t} \qquad (15)$$

$$\Delta D^j = \frac{g(t)}{t} B^{j+1} \Delta \acute{C}^{j+t}$$

We now have the choice of any function $g(t)$ that allows $\Delta D^j$ to increase monotonically from 0 to 1. The function $g(t):=t^2$ is an obvious choice that we have found to work well in practice.

The changes to the high-resolution control points are then reconstructed using a straightforward application of equation (3):

$$\Delta C^n = P^n P^{n-1} \cdots P^{j+2} (P^{j+1} \Delta C^j + Q^{j+1} \Delta D^j) \qquad (16)$$

The fractional-level editing defined here works quite well in practice. Varying the editing level continuously gives a smooth and intuitive kind of change in the region of the curve affected, as suggested by Figure 4. Because the algorithmic complexity is just $O(m)$, the update is easily performed at interactive rates, even for curves with hundreds of control points.

### 4.1.1 Editing with direct manipulation

The fractional-level editing described above can be easily extended to accommodate *direct manipulation,* in which the user tugs on the smoothed curve directly rather than on its defining control points [3, 13, 15, 18]. To use direct manipulation when editing at level $j + t$, we make use of the pseudo-inverse of the scaling functions at levels $j$ and $j + 1$.

More precisely, suppose the user drags a point of the curve $f^{j+t}(u_0)$ to a new position $f^{j+t}(u_0) + \delta$. We can compute the least-squares change to the control points $\Delta \acute{C}^j$ and $\Delta \acute{C}^{j+t}$ at levels $j$ and $j + t$ using the pseudo-inverses $(\Phi^j)^+$ and $(\Phi^{j+1})^+$ as follows:

$$\Delta \acute{C}^j = (\Phi^j(u_0))^+ \delta \qquad (17)$$

$$\Delta \acute{C}^{j+t} = (\Phi^{j+1}(u_0))^+ \delta$$

These two equations should be interpreted as applying to each dimension $x$ and $y$ separately. That is, $\delta$ should be a scalar (say, the change in $x$), and the left-hand side and the pseudo-inverses should both be column-matrices of scalars. The modified control points of the highest-resolution curve can then be computed in the same fashion outlined for control-point manipulation, by applying equations (15) and (16).

Note that the first step of the construction, equation (17), can be computed in constant time, since for cubic B-splines at most four of the entries of each pseudo-inverse are non-zero. The issue of finding the parameter value $u_0$ at which the curve passes closest to the selection point is a well-studied problem in root-finding, which can be handled in a number of ways [27]. In our implementation, we scan-convert the curve once to find its parameter value at every illuminated pixel. This approach is easy to implement, and appears to provide a good trade-off between speed and accuracy for an interactive system.

For some applications, it may be more intuitive to drag on the high-resolution curve directly, rather than on the smoothed version of the curve. In this case, even when the curve's display resolution is at its highest level, it may still be useful to be able to tug on the curve at a lower editing resolution. In this way, varying levels of detail on the curve can be manipulated by dragging a single point: as the editing resolution is lowered, more and more of the curve is affected. This type of control can be supported quite easily by setting $\delta$ to be the change in the high-resolution curve at the dragged point $f^n(u_0)$, and using the same equations (17) above.

### 4.1.2 Editing a desired portion of the curve

One difficulty with curve manipulation methods is that their effect often depends on the parameterization of the curve, which does not necessarily correspond to the curve's geometric embedding in an intuitive fashion. The manipulation that we have described so far suffers from this same difficulty: dragging at a particular (possibly fractional) level $\ell = j + t$ on different points along the curve will not necessarily affect constant-length portions of the curve. However, we can use the multiresolution editing control to compensate for this defect in direct manipulation, as follows (Figure 5).

Let $h$ be a parameter, specified by the user, that describes the desired length of the editable portion of the curve. The parameter $h$ can be specified using any type of physical units, such as screen pixels, inches, or percentage of

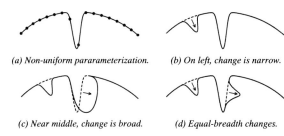

*(a) Non-uniform pararameterization.*          *(b) On left, change is narrow.*

*(c) Near middle, change is broad.*          *(d) Equal-breadth changes.*

Figure 5: *Curve (a) has a parameterization that is non-uniform with respect to its length. Direct manipulation on the left part of the curve (b) affects a much smaller fraction of the curve than does direct manipulation at the same level in the middle (c). The last figure (d) shows that a specified fraction of the curve can be edited, with the system determining the appropriate editing level.*

the overall curve length. The system computes an appropriate editing level $\ell$ that will affect a portion of the curve of about $h$ units in length, centered at the point $f^n(u_0)$ being dragged.

We estimate $\ell$ as follows. For each integer-level editing resolution $j$, let $h^j(u_0)$ denote the length of $f^n(u)$ affected by editing the curve at the point $f^n(u_0)$. The length $h^j(u_0)$ is easily estimated by scan-converting the curve $f^n(u)$ to determine the approximate lengths of its polynomial segments, and then summing over the lengths of the segments affected when editing the curve at level $j$ and parameter position $u_0$. Next, define $j_-$ and $j_+$ to be, respectively, the smallest and largest values of $j$ for which $h^{j-}(u_0) \geq h \geq h^{j+}(u_0)$. To choose the editing level $\ell$, we use linear interpolation between these two bounding levels $j_-$ and $j_+$:

$$\ell = \frac{h - h^{j+}}{h^{j-} - h^{j+}}$$

Finally, by representing $\ell$ in terms of an integer level $j$ and fractional offset $t$, we can again apply equation (17), followed by equations (15) and (16), as before. Though in general this construction does not *precisely* cover the desired portion $h$, in practice it yields an intuitive and meaningful control. Figure 5 demonstrates this type of editing for a curve with an extremely non-uniform geometric embedding.

## 4.2 Editing the character of the curve

Another form of editing that is naturally supported by multiresolution curves is one of editing the character of a curve, without affecting its overall sweep. Let $C^n$ be the control points of a curve, and let $C^0, \ldots, C^{n-1}, D^0, \ldots, D^{n-1}$ denote the components of its multiresolution decomposition. Editing the character of the curve is simply a matter of replacing the existing set of detail functions $D^j, \ldots, D^{n-1}$ with some new set $\widehat{D}^j, \ldots, \widehat{D}^{n-1}$, and reconstructing.

With this approach, we have been able to develop a "curve character library" that contains different detail functions, which can be interchangeably applied to any set of curves. The detail functions in the library have been extracted from hand-drawn strokes; other (for example, procedural) methods of generating detail functions are also possible. Figure 6 demonstrates how the character of curves in an illustration can be modified with the same (or different) detail styles. The interactive illustration system used to create this figure is described in a separate paper [26].

Figure 6: *Changing the character of a curve without affecting its sweep.*

## 4.3 Orientation of detail

A parametric curve in two dimensions is most naturally represented as two separate functions, one in $x$ and one in $y$: $f(u) = (f_x(u), f_y(u))$. Thus, it seems reasonable to represent both the control points $C^j$ and detail functions $D^j$ using matrices with separate columns for $x$ and $y$. However, encoding the detail functions in this manner embeds all of the detail of the curve in a particular $xy$-orientation. As demonstrated in Figure 7, this representation does not always provide the most intuitive control when editing the sweep of the curve.

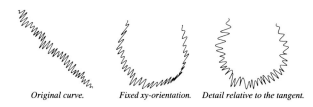

*Original curve.*          *Fixed xy-orientation.*          *Detail relative to the tangent.*

Figure 7: *Editing the sweep of a curve using a fixed $xy$-orientation of detail versus orientation relative to the tangent of the curve.*

As an alternative, we employ a method similar to that of Forsey and Bartels [13] for representing detail with respect to the tangent and normal to the curve at a coarser level. Specifically, for computing the reference frame for orienting a detail coefficient $d_i^j$, we use the tangent and normal of the curve $f^{j-1}(u_0)$ at a parameter position $u_0$ corresponding to the maximum value of the wavelet $\psi_i^j(u)$. Note that the curve $f(u)$ is no longer a simple linear combination of the scaling functions $\Phi^0$ and wavelets $\Psi^j$; instead, a change of coordinates must be performed at each level of reconstruction for the wavelet coefficients $D^j$. However, this process is linear in the number of control points, so it does not increase the computational complexity of the algorithm.

We have experimented with both normalized and unnormalized versions of the reference frame; the two alternative versions yield different but equally reasonable behavior. Figure 6 uses the unnormalized tangents whereas the rest of the figures in this paper use normalized tangents.

## 5 Scan conversion and curve compression

Using "curve character libraries" and other multiresolution editing features, it is easy to create very complex curves with hundreds or potentially thousands of control points. In many cases (such as in this paper), these curves are printed in a very small form. Conventional scan conversion methods that use all the complexity of these curves are wasteful, both in terms of the network traffic to send such large files to the printer, and in terms of the processing time required by the printer to render curves of many control points within a few square pixels. We therefore explore a form of curve compression that is suitable for the purposes of scan conversion. The algorithm requires an approximate curve to have a guaranteed error tolerance, in terms of printer pixels, from the original curve. However, it does not require any particular continuity constraints, as are usually required in data-fitting applications.

As discussed in Section 3, the simple removal of wavelet coefficients can be used to achieve a least-squares, or $L^2$, error metric between an original curve and its approximate versions. However, for scan conversion, an $L^2$ error metric is not very useful for measuring the degree of approximation: an approximate curve $\widetilde{f}(u)$ can be arbitrarily far from an original curve $f^n(u)$ and still achieve a particular $L^2$ error bound, as long as it deviates from the original over a small enough segment. In order to scan convert a curve to some guaranteed precision—measured, say, in terms of maximum deviation in printer pixels—we need to use an $L^\infty$ norm on the error. There are many ways to achieve such a bound. The method described here is a simple and fast one, although methods with higher compression ratios are certainly possible.

Let $s_i^j$ (with $0 \leq i \leq 2^j - 1$) be a segment of the cubic B-spline curve $f^j(u)$, defined by the four control points $c_i^j, \ldots, c_{i+3}^j$. Note that each segment $s_i^j$ corresponds to exactly two segments $s_{2i}^{j+1}$ and $s_{2i+1}^{j+1}$ at level $j+1$.

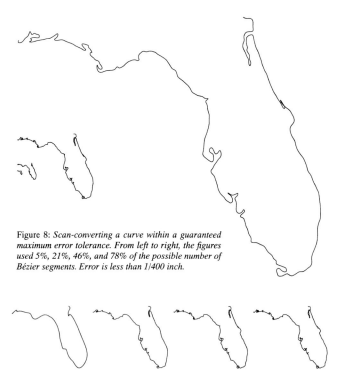

Figure 8: *Scan-converting a curve within a guaranteed maximum error tolerance. From left to right, the figures used 5%, 21%, 46%, and 78% of the possible number of Bézier segments. Error is less than 1/400 inch.*

Figure 9: *Same curves as above, but drawn at constant size.*

Our objective is to build a new approximating curve $\widetilde{f}(u)$ for $f(u)$ by choosing different segments at different levels such that $||\widetilde{f}(u) - f^n(u)||_\infty$ is less than some user-specified $\epsilon$ for all values of $u$.

Assume, for the moment, that we have some function $ErrBound(s_i^j)$ that returns a bound on the $L^\infty$ error incurred from using the segment $s_i^j$ of some approximate curve $f^j(u)$ in place of the original segments of $f^n(u)$ to which it corresponds. We can scan-convert a curve to within any error tolerance $\epsilon$ by passing to the recursive routine *DrawSegment* the single segment $s_0^0$ corresponding to the lowest-level curve $f^0(u)$. This routine recursively divides the segment to varying levels so that the collection of segments it produces approximates the curve to within $\epsilon$.

**procedure** *DrawSegment* $(s_i^j)$:
  **if** $ErrBound(s_i^j) < \epsilon$ **then**
    Output segment $s_i^j$ as a portion of $\widetilde{f}(u)$
  **else**
    *DrawSegment* $(s_{2i}^{j+1})$; *DrawSegment* $(s_{2i+1}^{j+1})$
  **end if**
**end procedure**

To construct the *ErrBound* routine, let $M^j$ be the B-spline-to-Bézier-basis conversion matrix [4] for curves with $2^j + 3$ control points, and let $E^j$ be a column vector with entries $e_i^j$ defined by

$$E^j \quad := \quad M^j Q^j D^{j-1} \qquad (18)$$

The vector $E^j$ provides a measure of the distance that the Bézier control points migrate when reconstructing the more detailed curve at level $j$ from the approximate curve at level $j - 1$. Since Bézier curves are contained within the convex hull of their control points, the magnitudes of the entries of $E^j$ provide conservative bounds on approximations to the curve due to truncating wavelet coefficients.

A bound $\delta_i^j$ on the $L^\infty$ error incurred by replacing segment $s_i^j$ with its approximation at level $j - 1$ is given by

$$\delta_i^j \quad \leq \quad max_{i \leq k \leq i+3} \left\{ \left|\left| e_k^j \right|\right|_2 \right\} \qquad (19)$$

The *ErrBound* routine can then be described recursively as follows:

**procedure** *ErrBound* $(s_i^j)$:
  **if** $j = n$ **then**
    **return** 0
  **else**
    **return** $max \{ ErrBound(s_{2i}^{j+1}) + \delta_{2i}^{j+1}, \ ErrBound(s_{2i+1}^{j+1}) + \delta_{2i+1}^{j+1} \}$
  **end if**
**end procedure**

An efficient implementation of the *ErrBound* routine would use dynamic programming or an iterative (rather than recursive) procedure to avoid re-computing error bounds. In practice, the routine is fast enough in its recursive form that we have not found this optimization to be necessary, at least for scan converting curves with hundreds of control points.

The approximate curve $\widetilde{f}(u)$ is described by a set of Bézier segments, which we use to generate a PostScript file [1]. Note that the scan-conversion algorithm, as described, produces approximate curves $\widetilde{f}(u)$ that are not even $C^0$ continuous where two segments of different levels abut. Since we are only concerned with the absolute error in the final set of pixels produced, relaxing the continuity of the original curve is reasonable for scan conversion. We can achieve $C^0$ continuity, however, without increasing the prescribed error tolerance, by simply averaging together the end control points for adjacent Bézier segments as a post-process. We have found that these $C^0$ curves look slightly better than the discontinuous curves; they also have a more compact representation in PostScript. Figures 8 and 9 demonstrate compression of the same curve rendered at different sizes.

## 6 Extensions and future work

This paper describes a multiresolution representation for endpoint-interpolating B-spline curves, and shows how this single representation supports a variety of display and editing operations in a simple and efficient manner. We believe that the operations described are very general and can be readily extended to other types of objects described by a multiresolution analysis.

There are many directions for future research, including:

**Handling discontinuities.** An important extension is to generalize the multiresolution curve representation and editing operations to respect discontinuities of various orders that have been intentionally placed into a curve by the designer. This extension would allow the techniques to be applied more readily to font design, among other applications. One approach is to try using the multiresolution analysis defined on non-uniform B-splines by Dæhlen and Lyche [10].

**Sparse representations.** Our algorithms have so far used only *complete* wavelet decompositions of the curve's original control points. However, in order to support curve editing at an arbitrarily high resolution, it would be convenient to have a mechanism in place for extending the wavelet representation to a higher level of detail in certain higher-resolution portions of the curve than in others. One such sparse representation might use pruned binary trees to keep track of the various wavelet coefficients at different levels of refinement, in a manner very similar to the one used by Berman *et al.* for representing multiresolution images [5].

**Textured strokes.** For illustrations, it is useful to associate other properties with curves, such as color, thickness, texture, and transparency, as demonstrated by Hsu and Lee [17]. These quantities may be considered extra dimensions in the data associated with each control point. Much of the machinery for multiresolution editing should be applicable to such curves. As a preliminary test of this idea, we have extended our curve editor with a *thickness* dimension. The thickness along the curve is governed by the thick-

Figure 10: *Two curves of varying thickness.*

nesses defined at the control points. It is possible to modify this parameter at any level of resolution, just as one edits the position of the curve. Figure 10 shows curves with varying thickness. Ultimately, we would like to combine stroke editing with multiresolution image editing [5], perhaps providing a unified framework for object-oriented ("MacDraw-like") and image-oriented ("MacPaint-like") interactive design programs.

**Surfaces.** Another obvious extension of these techniques is to surfaces. As a test of multiresolution surface editing, we built a surface editor that allows a user to modify a bicubic tensor-product B-spline surface [4, 12, 16] at different levels of detail. Figure 11 shows several manipulations applied to a surface over 1225 control points modeling a human face. It is worth noting that tensor-product surfaces are limited in the kinds of shapes they can model seamlessly. Lounsbery *et al.* [19] discuss a multiresolution representation for subdivision surfaces of arbitrary topology. Many of the techniques described in this paper should extend directly to their surfaces as well. In particular, fractional-level display and editing are applicable in the same way as for curves and tensor-product surfaces. In addition, the compression technique for scan-converting curves might also be used for rendering simplified versions of polyhedra within guaranteed error tolerances.

Figure 11: *Surface manipulation at different levels of detail. From left to right: original, narrow change, medium change, broad change.*

## Acknowledgements

We would like to thank Tony DeRose, Ronen Barzel, and Leena-Maija Reissell for very helpful discussions during the development of these ideas, and Sean Anderson for implementing the tensor-product B-spline surface editor.

This work was supported by an NSF National Young Investigator award (CCR-9357790), by the University of Washington Graduate Research and Royalty Research Funds (75-1721 and 65-9731), and by industrial gifts from Adobe, Aldus, and Xerox.

## References

[1] *PostScript Language Reference Manual.* Addison-Wesley Publishing Company, Inc., 1985.

[2] M. J. Banks and E. Cohen. Realtime spline curves from interactively sketched data. *Computer Graphics*, 24(2):99–107, 1990.

[3] R. Bartels and J. Beatty. A technique for the direct manipulation of spline curves. In *Proceedings of the 1989 Graphics Interface Conference*, pages 33–39, London, Ontario, Canada, June 1989.

[4] R. Bartels, J. Beatty, and B. Barsky. *An Introduction to Splines for Use in Computer Graphics and Geometric Modeling.* Morgan Kaufmann, 1987.

[5] D. Berman, J. Bartell, and D. Salesin. Multiresolution painting and compositing. Proceedings of SIGGRAPH 94. In *Computer Graphics,* Annual Conference Series, 1994.

[6] G. Beylkin, R. Coifman, and V. Rokhlin. Fast wavelet transforms and numerical algorithms I. *Communications on Pure and Applied Mathematics*, 44:141–183, 1991.

[7] G. Celniker and D. Gossard. Deformable curve and surface finite elements for free-form shape design. *Computer Graphics*, 25(4):257–265, July 1991.

[8] C. K. Chui. *An Introduction to Wavelets.* Academic Press, Inc., Boston, 1992.

[9] C. K. Chui and E. Quak. Wavelets on a bounded interval. In D. Braess and L. L. Schumaker, editors, *Numerical Methods in Approximation Theory*, volume 9, pages 53–75. Birkhauser Verlag, Basel, 1992.

[10] M. Dæhlen and T. Lyche. Decomposition of splines. In T. Lyche and L. L. Schumaker, editors, *Mathematical Methods in Computer Aided Geometric Design II*, pages 135–160. Academic Press, New York, 1992.

[11] R. DeVore, B. Jawerth, and B. Lucier. Image compression through wavelet transform coding. *IEEE Transactions on Information Theory*, 38(2):719–746, March 1992.

[12] G. Farin. *Curves and Surfaces for Computer Aided Geometric Design.* Academic Press, third edition, 1992.

[13] D. Forsey and R. Bartels. Hierarchical B-spline refinement. *Computer Graphics*, 22(4):205–212, 1988.

[14] D. Forsey and R. Bartels. Tensor products and hierarchical fitting. In *Curves and Surfaces in Computer Vision and Graphics II, SPIE Proceedings Vol. 1610*, pages 88–96, 1991.

[15] B. Fowler. Geometric manipulation of tensor product surfaces. In *Proceedings of the 1992 Symposium on Interactive 3D Graphics*, March 1992. Available as Computer Graphics, Vol. 26, No. 2.

[16] J. Hoschek and D. Lasser. *Fundamentals of Computer Aided Geometric Design.* A K Peters, Ltd., Wellesley, Massachusetts, third edition, 1992.

[17] S. Hsu and I. Lee. Skeletal strokes. Proceedings of SIGGRAPH 94. In *Computer Graphics,* Annual Conference Series, 1994.

[18] W. M. Hsu, J. F. Hughes, and H. Kaufman. Direct manipulation of free-form deformations. *Computer Graphics*, 26(2):177–184, 1992.

[19] M. Lounsbery, T. DeRose, and J. Warren. Multiresolution surfaces of arbitrary topological type. Technical Report 93-10-05B, University of Washington, Department of Computer Science and Engineering, January 1994.

[20] T. Lyche and K. Mørken. Knot removal for parametric B-spline curves and surfaces. *Computer Aided Geometric Design*, 4(3):217–230, 1987.

[21] T. Lyche and K. Mørken. Spline-wavelets of minimal support. In D. Braess and L. L. Schumaker, editors, *Numerical Methods in Approximation Theory*, volume 9, pages 177–194. Birkhauser Verlag, Basel, 1992.

[22] S. Mallat. A theory for multiresolution signal decomposition: The wavelet representation. *IEEE Transactions on Pattern Analysis and Machine Intelligence*, 11(7):674–693, July 1989.

[23] M. Plass and M. Stone. Curve-fitting with piecewise parametric cubics. *Computer Graphics*, 17(3):229–239, July 1983.

[24] W. H. Press, B. P. Flannery, S. A. Teukolsky, and W. T. Fetterling. *Numerical Recipes.* Cambridge University Press, Cambridge, second edition, 1992.

[25] E. Quak and N. Weyrich. Decomposition and reconstruction algorithms for spline wavelets on a bounded interval. CAT Report 294, Center for Approximation Theory, Texas A&M University, April 1993.

[26] M. P. Salisbury, S. E. Anderson, R. Barzel, and D. H. Salesin. Interactive pen-and-ink illustration. Proceedings of SIGGRAPH 94. In *Computer Graphics,* Annual Conference Series, 1994.

[27] P. J. Schneider. Phoenix: An interactive curve design system based on the automatic fitting of hand-sketched curves. Master's thesis, Department of Computer Science and Engineering, University of Washington, 1988.

[28] W. Welch and A. Witkin. Variational surface modeling. *Computer Graphics*, 26(2):157–166, 1992.

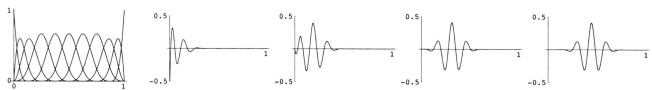

Figure 12: *The B-spline scaling functions and the first four wavelets at level 3.*

## A  Wavelets for endpoint-interpolating B-splines

As discussed in Section 2.1, a multiresolution analysis is completely determined by an initial set of scaling functions $\Phi^0$ and a pair of synthesis filters $P^j$ and $Q^j$ for every level $j$ in $[1, n]$. This appendix supplies these functions and matrices for endpoint-interpolating cubic B-splines, and outlines their derivation. Figure 12 shows some examples of these B-spline scaling functions and wavelets.

Initial scaling functions are given by the four cubic Bernstein polynomials:

$$\Phi^0(u) = \left[(1-u)^3,\ 3u(1-u)^2,\ 3u^2(1-u),\ u^3\right]$$

The matrices $P^j$ and $Q^j$ appear in Figure 13. Note that $P^j$ is a matrix with dimensions $(2^j + 3) \times (2^{j-1} + 3)$ whose middle columns, for $j \geq 3$, are given by vertical translates of the fourth column, shifted down by 2 places for each column. Matrix $Q^j$ has the same structure for $j \geq 4$, except with dimensions $(2^j + 3) \times 2^{j-1}$.

The $P^j$ matrix is straightforward to derive from the Cox-de Boor recursion formula [12]; it encodes how each endpoint-interpolating B-spline can be expressed as a linear combination of B-splines that are half as wide. To derive the $Q^j$ matrix, we use some new notation. Given two row vectors of functions $X$ and $Y$, let $[\langle X \mid Y \rangle]$ be the matrix of inner products $\langle X_k, Y_l \rangle$. Since, by definition, scaling functions and wavelets at the same level $j$ are orthogonal, we have

$$\left[\langle \Phi^j \mid \Psi^j \rangle\right] = \left[\langle \Phi^j \mid \Phi^{j+1} \rangle\right] Q^{j+1} = \mathbf{0},$$

so the columns of $Q^{j+1}$ span the null space of $\left[\langle \Phi^j \mid \Phi^{j+1} \rangle\right]$. We choose a basis for this null space by finding the matrix $Q^{j+1}$ that has columns with the shortest runs of non-zero coefficients; this matrix corresponds to the wavelets with minimal support. The entries of the inner product matrix can be computed exactly with symbolic integration; thus, the fractions reported in Figure 13 are exact (though ugly).

## B  Linear-time filter-bank algorithm

Section 2.2 notes that the obvious filter-bank decomposition algorithm for endpoint-interpolating B-spline curves takes $O(m^2)$-time because $A^j$ and $B^j$ are dense. However, Quak and Weyrich [25] describe an algorithm for performing the algorithm in linear time, using a transformation to the "dual space." The derivation of this idea is beyond the scope of this paper; however, for completeness, we summarize here how the linear-time algorithm can be implemented.

Let $I^j$ and $J^j$ be the inner product matrices $\left[\langle \Phi^j \mid \Phi^j \rangle\right]$ and $\left[\langle \Psi^j \mid \Psi^j \rangle\right]$, respectively. Equations (1) and (2) can then be rewritten:

$$I^{j-1}C^{j-1} = (P^j)^T I^j C^j$$
$$J^{j-1}D^{j-1} = (Q^j)^T I^j C^j$$

Since $P^j, Q^j$, and $I^j$ are banded matrices, the right-hand side of these equations can be computed in linear time. What remains are two band-diagonal systems of equations, which can also be solved in linear time using $LU$ decomposition [24].

The matrices $I^j$ for $j \geq 3$ are given in Figure 13. Note that $I^j$ is a symmetric matrix with dimensions $(2^j + 3) \times (2^j + 3)$ whose middle columns, for $j \geq 3$, are given by vertical translates of the sixth column. The $I^j$ matrices for $j < 3$ and the $J^j$ matrices may be found by:

$$I^j = \left(P^{j+1}\right)^T I^{j+1} P^{j+1}$$
$$J^j = \left(Q^{j+1}\right)^T I^{j+1} Q^{j+1}$$

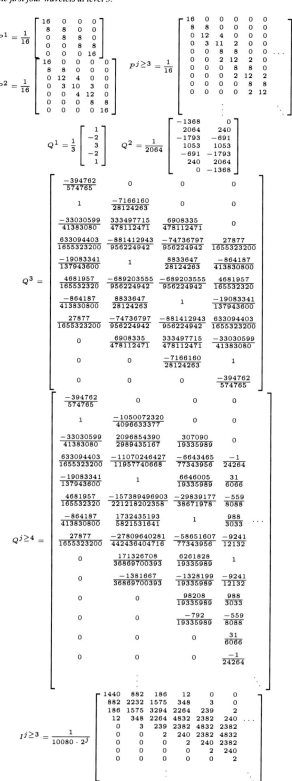

Figure 13: *The synthesis filters $P^j$ and $Q^j$ and the inner product matrices $I^j$.*

# Using Particles to Sample and Control Implicit Surfaces

Andrew P. Witkin
Paul S. Heckbert

Department of Computer Science
Carnegie Mellon University

## Abstract

We present a new particle-based approach to sampling and controlling implicit surfaces. A simple constraint locks a set of particles onto a surface while the particles and the surface move. We use the constraint to make surfaces follow particles, and to make particles follow surfaces. We implement *control points* for direct manipulation by specifying particle motions, then solving for surface motion that maintains the constraint. For sampling and rendering, we run the constraint in the other direction, creating *floater* particles that roam freely over the surface. Local repulsion is used to make floaters spread evenly across the surface. By varying the radius of repulsion adaptively, and fissioning or killing particles based on the local density, we can achieve good sampling distributions very rapidly, and maintain them even in the face of rapid and extreme deformations and changes in surface topology.

**CR Categories:** I.3.5 [**Computer Graphics**]: Computational Geometry and Object Modeling: *Curve, surface, solid, and object representations, Physically based modeling;* I.3.6 [**Computer Graphics**]: Methodologies and Techniques: *Interaction techniques;* G.1.6 [**Numerical Analysis**]: Optimization: *Constrained Optimization.*

**General Terms:** algorithms, design.

**Additional Key Words and Phrases:** physically based modeling, constrained optimization, adaptive sampling, interaction.

## 1   Introduction

Implicit surfaces have proven to be useful for modeling, animation, and visualization. One appeal of implicit models is that new surfaces can be created by adding or otherwise combining the functions that define them, producing a variety of subtle and interesting shape effects. Another is their role in the visualization of volume data. In addition, the implicit representation lends itself to such calculations as ray/surface intersection and inside/outside test. However, implicit surfaces suffer from two serious drawbacks: first, although well suited to ray tracing, they are not easily rendered at interactive speeds, reflecting the underlying problem that it is difficult

Mail to the authors should be addressed to the Department of Computer Science, Carnegie Mellon University, 5000 Forbes Ave, Pittsburgh PA 15213, USA. Email should be addressed to Andrew Witkin as *aw@cs.cmu.edu*, and to Paul Heckbert as *ph@cs.cmu.edu*.

to *sample* them systematically. This is particularly a problem if we wish to render time-varying surfaces in real time, which is vital for interactive sculpting. Second, the shapes of implicit surfaces have proven to be more difficult to specify and control than those of their parametric counterparts.

In this paper, we present a new particle-based approach to sampling and shape control of implicit surfaces that addresses these problems. At the heart of our approach is a simple constraint that locks a collection of particles onto an implicit surface while both the particles and the surface move. We can use the constraint to make the surface follow the particles, or to make the particles follow the surface. Our formulation is differential: we specify and solve for velocities rather than positions, and the behavior of the system is governed by differential equations that integrate these velocities over time.

We control surface shape by moving particles interactively, solving for surface motion that keeps the particles on the surface. This technique lets us pin down the surface at some points while interactively dragging others. These particles act as *control points* for direct manipulation of the surface.

For sampling and rendering, we run the constraint in the other direction, creating particles that may roam freely over the surface, but are compelled to follow it as it moves. We call these particles *floaters*. Our starting point is the idea that uniform sampling density can be achieved by making the particles repel each other. This approach was used by Turk [29] to resample polygon meshes, and by Figueiredo *et al.* [12] to sample implicit surfaces.

Simple repulsion can work quite well for stationary surfaces, but only if a reasonably good initial sampling is available. If large-scale non-uniformities exist, convergence can be extremely slow for even moderate sampling densities. We eliminate the need for a good starting point, and dramatically accelerate convergence, by employing an iterative "fissioning" approach, in which we start with a small number of particles and a large radius of repulsion, allow them to equilibrate, then split each particle in two, reducing the radius of repulsion. We repeat the process until the desired sampling density is reached. Each level thus inherits a distribution that is already uniform at large scale, requiring just a few iterations to iron out the local irregularities.

Global fissioning still fails to handle surfaces that move and deform, since irregularities can arise after the density becomes high. We introduce a local adaptive repulsion algorithm, in which the repulsion radius and particle birth and death are regulated based on local density. This method is fast enough to maintain good sampling even in the face of rapid and extreme surface motion and deformation.

The remainder of the paper is organized as follows: we begin by discussing previous related work. Then we introduce the basic constraint mechanism that attaches particles to surfaces. Next we describe the use of particles for surface shape control. We then explain our adaptive repulsion sampling algorithm. After describing the implementation and results, we conclude with a discussion of future work.

## 2 Previous Work

Related work can be divided into two categories: sampling methods and control methods.

### 2.1 Sampling Methods

Related research on surface sampling includes both particle-based sampling techniques and polygonization techniques for implicit surfaces.

Turk used repelling particles on surfaces to uniformly resample a static surface [28] and to simplify a polygonization by reducing the number of polygons [29]. Hoppe et al. also explored mesh simplification, framing it as an optimization problem with penalties for geometric error, number of samples, and edge length [16]. Their method did not restrict the points to a surface, however, as Turk's and ours do.

Szeliski and Tonnesen used oriented particles to model surfaces [27]. Their technique allowed the user to move the particles interactively, employing short-range repulsion and long-range attraction to keep the particles from clumping or flying apart. The system generated a surface by connecting neighboring particles appropriately, but it did not manipulate a high level representation for a surface, such as a parametric patch or an implicit function, as ours does. The output of their system was a triangulation. Their system bears a superficial resemblance to ours because we both use disks to visualize the surface, but in other respects our techniques are quite different.

An implicit surface, also called an iso-surface, is the set of points $\mathbf{x}$ that satisfy $F(\mathbf{x}) = 0$. Implicit surfaces are typically defined by starting with simple building block functions and by creating new implicit functions using the sum, min, or max of simpler functions. When the building blocks are polynomials in $x$, $y$, and $z$, the resulting surfaces are called *algebraic surfaces*, and when the building blocks are spherical Gaussian functions, the surfaces are called *blobbies* [8], "soft objects", or "metaballs". The use of sums of implicit functions allows blend surfaces to be created [24], and the use of min and max yields the union and intersection of solid objects.

Rendering an implicit surface is often difficult. If a ray tracer is used, intersecting a ray with an implicit surface reduces to one-dimensional root-finding, but this can be very slow for a complex implicit function [8]. To exploit the speed of graphics hardware, we would prefer to render using a z-buffer algorithm. This requires converting the implicit surface into polygons or other parametric surfaces.

Most existing methods for polygonizing implicit surfaces subdivide space into a uniform grid of cubical or tetrahedral voxels, sample the function at the vertices of the voxels, and then, for each voxel whose vertices are not all in or all out, generate polygon(s) approximating the surface [33,18,21,10]. This approach is often called the *marching cubes* algorithm. Improvements on this algorithm use adaptive subdivision based on curvature [9]. Unfortunately, all of these algorithms will miss small surface features if the initial sampling grid is too coarse, except Snyder's, which uses interval arithmetic to guarantee that the topology of the polygonization matches the topology of the real surface [26].

These polygonization algorithms were designed for static surfaces; to polygonize a changing surface with them would require beginning from scratch each time. The algorithm of Jevans et al. is

an exception. It re-polygonizes only those voxels that change [17].

Physically-based approaches to the polygonization of implicit surfaces were pioneered by Figueiredo et al. [12]. One of the two methods they describe starts with particles randomly scattered in 3-D space, subjects them to forces that pull them to the surface (an idea proposed in [11]), and uses repulsion between particles to distribute them uniformly over the surface. Their technique uses penalty methods, however, which lead to stiff differential equations whose solution is generally either slow to repel into a nice pattern, or inaccurate at staying on the surface. Once the particles have reached equilibrium, a polygonization is found using Delaunay triangulation. Their work resembles ours most closely, but our simulation method differs from theirs, and our technique supports interactive control of surfaces and incremental sampling of changing surfaces, while theirs does not.

### 2.2 Control Methods

One of the principal disadvantages of implicit modeling relative to parametric modeling is the difficulty of controlling the shape of an implicit surface [11]. The effect of the parameters of an implicit surface is often non-intuitive.

With algebraic surfaces, for instance, it is hard to predict the surface shape given its coefficients. Modeling is further complicated by the global nature of an algebraic surface's polynomial basis functions, which prevent local shape control. For these reasons and others, piecewise algebraic surfaces have recently become popular [25]. Piecewise algebraic surfaces are typically defined by a weighted sum of Bernstein polynomials over a lattice of tetrahedra. Least squares methods for fitting surfaces to a set of points are available both for standard algebraic surfaces [22] and for piecewise algebraic surfaces [1]. Pratt's algorithm can fit a surface with $m$ parameters to $n$ points $(n > m)$ in time $O((n + m)m^2)$. These methods are limited to algebraic surfaces, however.

Blobby models employ local basis functions, so they are often more intuitive to work with than algebraic surfaces [8]. In an interactive blobby modeling system, a user might use dials or sliders to adjust the position and radius of each blobby center [7], but arriving at a desired surface is a matter of guesswork, and the real time display is typically just a wireframe, with a higher quality rendering requiring off-line ray tracing or polygonization. Some recent work has fit blobby models to a set of surface points, but the method is quite slow, one example requiring days of computer time to fit 2900 control points using 1200 parameters [20]. Direct manipulation of a blobby surface at interactive speeds has remained an open problem.

The differential methods we use to constrain the motion of particles and surfaces are rooted in classical mechanics (see, e.g. [15] for a discussion of mechanical constraints and constraint forces) and are closely related to constraint methods used in physically based modeling for computer graphics [5,2,3,32,31,4]. Allied methods have also been used for interactive geometric modeling [30,14].

## 3 The Particle/Surface Constraint

In this section we derive the basic machinery that allows us to attach moving particles to moving surfaces. First we derive a basic constraint on particle and surface velocities that establishes, then maintains contact as the system evolves over time. We then pose two related problems: solve for particle velocities given time derivatives of the surface parameters, and solve for surface derivatives given particle velocities. Since the problem will generally be underconstrained, we express it as a constrained optimization.

**Notation:** We use boldface to denote vectors, and italics for scalars. Subscripts denote partial differentiation. Superscript $i$ or $j$ denote the $i$th or $j$th member of a collection of objects. E.g. $\mathbf{p}^i$ is the $i$th in a collection of vectors, and $F_{\mathbf{X}}$ is the derivative of scalar $F$ with respect to vector $\mathbf{x}$, hence a vector. Superscripts other than $i$ or $j$ have their usual meaning as exponents, e.g. $|\mathbf{x} - \mathbf{c}|^2$ or $e^{-x^2}$. A dot, as in $\dot{\mathbf{q}}$, denotes a derivative with respect to time.

## 3.1 The Basic Constraint

We represent the moving implicit surface by $F(\mathbf{x}, \mathbf{q}(t)) = 0$, where $\mathbf{x}$ is position in space, and $\mathbf{q}(t)$ is a vector of $m$ time-varying shape parameters. For example, an implicit sphere could be defined by $F = |\mathbf{x} - \mathbf{c}|^2 - r^2$, with center $\mathbf{c}$ and radius $r$. The parameter vector $\mathbf{q}$ would then be the 4-vector $[c_x, c_y, c_z, r]$.

The condition that a collection of $n$ moving particles lie on the surface is

$$F(\mathbf{p}^i(t), \mathbf{q}(t)) = 0, \quad 1 \le i \le n, \qquad (1)$$

where $\mathbf{p}^i(t)$ is the trajectory of the $i$th particle. In order for this condition to be met from some initial time $t_0$ onward, it suffices that equation 1 is satisfied at $t_0$, and that the time derivative $\dot{F} = 0$ thereafter. Since we want to manipulate velocities rather than positions, we obtain an expression for $\dot{F}$ using the chain rule:

$$\dot{F}^i = F_{\mathbf{X}}^i \cdot \dot{\mathbf{p}}^i + F_{\mathbf{q}}^i \cdot \dot{\mathbf{q}}, \qquad (2)$$

where $\dot{F}^i$, $F_{\mathbf{X}}^i$, and $F_{\mathbf{q}}^i$ denote $\dot{F}$, $F_{\mathbf{X}}$, and $F_{\mathbf{q}}$ evaluated at $\mathbf{p}^i$. By setting $\dot{F}^i$ to zero in equation 2, we obtain $n$ linear constraints on the $\dot{\mathbf{p}}^i$s and on $\dot{\mathbf{q}}$. In principle, if we began with a valid state and ensured that these conditions were met at every instant thereafter, we would be guaranteed that the particles remained on the surface. In practice, we might not have valid initial conditions, and numerical integration errors would cause drift over time. We cure these problems using a feedback term [6], setting $\dot{F}^i = -\phi F^i$, where $\phi$ is a feedback constant. This yields the set of $n$ linear constraint equations

$$C^i(\mathbf{p}^i, \dot{\mathbf{p}}^i, \mathbf{q}, \dot{\mathbf{q}}) = F_{\mathbf{X}}^i \cdot \dot{\mathbf{p}}^i + F_{\mathbf{q}}^i \cdot \dot{\mathbf{q}} + \phi F^i = 0 \qquad (3)$$

## 3.2 Constrained Optimization

We employ these constraints in two ways: first, in order to use particles to move the surface, we solve for $\dot{\mathbf{q}}$ given the $\dot{\mathbf{p}}^i$'s. Second, to use mutually repelling particles to sample the surface, we solve for the $\dot{\mathbf{p}}^i$'s given $\dot{\mathbf{q}}$. In either case, we generally wish to solve underconstrained systems. To do so we minimize a quadratic function of $\dot{\mathbf{p}}^i$ and $\dot{\mathbf{q}}$, subject to the constraints. The objective function we use here is

$$G = \frac{1}{2} \sum_{i=1}^{n} |\dot{\mathbf{p}}^i - \mathbf{P}^i|^2 + \frac{1}{2} |\dot{\mathbf{q}} - \mathbf{Q}|^2,$$

where $\mathbf{P}^i$ and $\mathbf{Q}$ are known *desired* values for $\dot{\mathbf{p}}^i$ and $\dot{\mathbf{q}}$ respectively.[1] These desired values can be used in a variety of ways. Setting $\mathbf{P}^i$ to zero minimizes particle velocities. Setting $\mathbf{Q}$ to zero minimizes the surface's parametric time derivative.

In unconstrained optimization we require that the gradient of the objective function vanish. At a *constrained* minimum, we require instead that the gradient of the objective function be a linear

---

[1]Although we do not give the derivation here, a straightforward and useful generalization is to allow error to be measured using an arbitrary symmetric positive-definite metric tensor, e.g. $(\dot{\mathbf{q}} - \mathbf{Q})^T \mathbf{M} (\dot{\mathbf{q}} - \mathbf{Q})$. In particular, it is possible to automatically compute a sensitivity matrix, analogous to the mass matrix in mechanics, that compensates for scale differences among the components of $F_{\mathbf{q}}$ (see [31].)

combination of the gradients of the constraint functions [13]. This condition ensures that no further local improvement can be made without violating the constraints. In the case of a point constrained to a surface, this condition is easily visualized: the gradient of the objective function must lie normal to the surface, so that its orthogonal projection onto the tangent plane vanishes. Though harder to visualize, the idea is the same in higher dimensions.

The classical method of Lagrange multipliers [13] solves constrained optimization problems by adding to the gradient of the objective a linear combination of constraint gradients, with unknown coefficients. One then solves simultaneously for the original unknowns, and for the coefficients. In the case of linear constraints and a quadratic objective, this is a linear problem.

The two problems we wish to solve—obtaining $\dot{\mathbf{p}}^i$ given $\dot{\mathbf{q}}$, and $\dot{\mathbf{q}}$ given $\dot{\mathbf{p}}^i$—seek to minimize the same objective subject to the same constraints, differing only in regard to the knowns and unknowns. Even so, the solutions will turn out to be quite different because of the structure of $C^j$'s dependencies on $\dot{\mathbf{p}}^i$ and $\dot{\mathbf{q}}$. We next consider each problem in turn.

## 3.3 Floaters

In solving for the $\dot{\mathbf{p}}^i$'s, the requirement that the gradient of the objective be a linear combination of the constraint gradients is expressed by

$$G_{\dot{\mathbf{p}}^i} + \sum_j \lambda^j C^j_{\dot{\mathbf{p}}^i} = \dot{\mathbf{p}}^i - \mathbf{P}^i + \lambda^i F_{\mathbf{X}}^i = 0 \qquad (4)$$

for some value of the unknown coefficients $\lambda^i$. The summation over $j$ drops out because $C^j$ cannot depend on $\dot{\mathbf{p}}^i$ unless $i = j$. In addition we require that the constraints be met, i.e. that $C^i = 0$, $1 \le i \le n$. Equation 4 allows us to express the $\dot{\mathbf{p}}^i$'s in terms of the unknown $\lambda^i$'s. Substituting for $\dot{\mathbf{p}}^i$ in equation 3 gives

$$F_{\mathbf{X}}^i \cdot (\mathbf{P}^i - \lambda^i F_{\mathbf{X}}^i) + F_{\mathbf{q}} \cdot \dot{\mathbf{q}} + \phi F^i = 0.$$

We may solve for each $\lambda^i$ independently. Doing so yields

$$\lambda^i = \frac{F_{\mathbf{X}}^i \cdot \mathbf{P}^i + F_{\mathbf{q}} \cdot \dot{\mathbf{q}} + \phi F^i}{F_{\mathbf{X}}^i \cdot F_{\mathbf{X}}^i}.$$

Substituting into equation 4 yields

$$\dot{\mathbf{p}}^i = \mathbf{P}^i - \frac{F_{\mathbf{X}}^i \cdot \mathbf{P}^i + F_{\mathbf{q}} \cdot \dot{\mathbf{q}} + \phi F^i}{F_{\mathbf{X}}^i \cdot F_{\mathbf{X}}^i} F_{\mathbf{X}}^i \qquad (5)$$

which is the particle velocity that solves the constrained optimization problem. Notice that in the case that the surface is not moving and the constraints are met, so that $F^i = 0$ and $\dot{\mathbf{q}} = 0$, this reduces to

$$\dot{\mathbf{p}}^i = \mathbf{P}^i - \frac{F_{\mathbf{X}}^i \cdot \mathbf{P}^i}{F_{\mathbf{X}}^i \cdot F_{\mathbf{X}}^i} F_{\mathbf{X}}^i,$$

which is just the orthogonal projection of $\mathbf{P}^i$ onto the surface's tangent plane at $\mathbf{p}^i$.

## 3.4 Control Points

We follow the same procedure in solving for $\dot{\mathbf{q}}$, except that derivatives of $C^j$ and $G$ are taken with respect to $\dot{\mathbf{q}}$. The condition that the gradient of the objective be a linear combination of the constraint gradients is

$$G_{\dot{\mathbf{q}}} + \sum_j \lambda^j C^j_{\dot{\mathbf{q}}} = \dot{\mathbf{q}} - \mathbf{Q} + \sum_j \lambda^j F_{\mathbf{q}}^j = 0. \qquad (6)$$

This time, the sum does not vanish, because every $C^j$ generally depends on $\dot{\mathbf{q}}$.

We next use equation 6 to substitute for $\dot{\mathbf{q}}$ in equation 3:

$$F^i_{\mathbf{x}} \cdot \dot{\mathbf{p}}^i + F^i_{\mathbf{q}} \cdot \left( \mathbf{Q} - \sum_j \lambda^j F^j_{\mathbf{q}} \right) + \phi F^i = 0.$$

Rearranging gives us the $n \times n$ matrix equation to be solved for $\lambda^j$:

$$\sum_j \left( F^i_{\mathbf{q}} \cdot F^j_{\mathbf{q}} \right) \lambda^j = F^i_{\mathbf{q}} \cdot \mathbf{Q} + F^i_{\mathbf{x}} \cdot \dot{\mathbf{p}}^i + \phi F^i. \qquad (7)$$

Note that element $(i, j)$ of the matrix is just the dot product $F^i_{\mathbf{q}} \cdot F^j_{\mathbf{q}}$. Having solved for the $\lambda^j$'s, we then solve for $\dot{\mathbf{q}}$ using equation 6:

$$\dot{\mathbf{q}} = \mathbf{Q} - \sum_j \lambda^j F^j_{\mathbf{q}}. \qquad (8)$$

### 3.5 Summary

In this section we have given the solutions to two very closely related problems:

- Given the instantaneous surface motion $\dot{\mathbf{q}}$, solve for particle velocities $\dot{\mathbf{p}}^i$ that minimize deviation from desired velocities $\mathbf{P}^i$ subject to the constraint that the particles stay on the surface. Each particle's constrained velocity may be computed independently.

- Given the particle velocities $\dot{\mathbf{p}}^i$, solve for the implicit function time derivative $\dot{\mathbf{q}}$ that minimizes deviation from a desired time derivative $\mathbf{Q}$, again, subject to the constraint that the particles must remain on the surface. Calculating $\dot{\mathbf{q}}$ entails the solution of an $n \times n$ linear system, where $n$ is the number of particles.

We combine these methods by maintaining two populations of particles: *control points* and *floaters*. Control points are moved explicitly by the user, and $\dot{\mathbf{q}}$ is calculated to make the surface follow them. In contrast, floaters' velocities are calculated to make them follow the surface, once $\dot{\mathbf{q}}$ has been computed.

## 4 Adaptive Sampling

In this section we address the problem of sampling implicit surfaces, building on the floater mechanism that we presented in the previous section. Good sampling is a requirement both for quick rendering and for the evaluation of integrals such as surface area or volume.

Our primary goal is to obtain sampling distributions that are either (a) uniform, with user-specified density, (b) or non-uniform, with density based on local criteria such as surface curvature. We wish to reach the specified distribution quickly from a few seed points (ideally, only one per connected component) and to *maintain* a good distribution as the surface moves and deforms. To support interactive sculpting, we must be able to update at least a few hundred sample points at 10Hz or better. Additional goals are that the particles should move as little as possible in response to surface motion, and that only basic and generic information about the function $F$ be required. It should not be necessary to supply a surface parameterization.

The starting point for our approach is the idea, introduced by Turk [28] and by Figueiredo *et al.* [12], that particles can be made to spread out to uniform density by local repulsion, relying on the finiteness of the surface to limit growth. Simple repulsion can do a good job at ironing out local irregularities given a reasonably good initial sampling (as in Turk's application to resampling of a polygon mesh) but is extremely slow to converge if the initial sampling is irregular at large scale, and fails completely to track surface motions and deformations.

After describing our basic repulsion scheme, we introduce the idea of *global fissioning*: we start the sampling process with a very small number of particles but a very large radius of interaction, coming close to equilibrium in just a few iterations. We then fission each particle, imposing random displacements that are smaller than the interaction radius. At the same time, we scale the interaction radius to a smaller value. We now have a new starting point, locally irregular but with nearly uniform large-scale structure. A few iterations suffice to smooth out the small irregularities and reach a new equilibrium. The scaling and fissioning process is repeated until the target sampling density is reached.

Global fissioning still fails to handle surface motion: should new nonuniformities be introduced after the fissioning process terminates, the system suffers all of the shortcomings of simple fixed-scale repulsion. So, for example, the sudden introduction of a bulge in the surface can create a gaping hole in the sampling pattern that will be repaired extremely slowly, if at all. Intuitively, we would like particles at the edge of such voids to "feel" the reduction of density, expand their radii of interaction to quickly fill the hole, then begin fissioning to restore full density. On the other hand, if density becomes too high, we would like particles to die off until the desired density is restored. We will conclude the section by describing a fast and robust adaptive repulsion scheme that provides just this behavior, meeting all of our goals.

### 4.1 Simple Repulsion

As a windowed density measure, we employ a simple Gaussian energy function based on distances between particles in 3-D. We define the *energy* of particle $i$ due to particle $j$ to be:

$$E^{ij} = \alpha \exp\left( -\frac{|\mathbf{r}^{ij}|^2}{2\sigma^2} \right)$$

where $\mathbf{r}^{ij} = \mathbf{p}^i - \mathbf{p}^j$ is the vector between particles, $\alpha$ is a global repulsion amplitude parameter, and $\sigma$, called the global *repulsion radius*, is the standard deviation of the Gaussian. The repulsion radius controls the range of the repulsion "force." Note that $E^{ij} = E^{ji}$.

The energy of particle $i$ in its current position is defined as:

$$E^i = \sum_{j=1}^n E^{ij}$$

Ultimately, we would like to reach the global minimum of each $E^i$ by varying the particle positions on the surface. Finding the global minimum is impractical, but we can find a local minimum by gradient descent: each particle moves in the direction that reduces its energy fastest. We therefore choose each particle's desired velocity to be negatively proportional to the gradient of energy with respect to its position:

$$\mathbf{P}^i = -\sigma^2 E^i_{\mathbf{p}^i} = \sum_{j=1}^n \mathbf{r}^{ij} E^{ij}$$

The formulas for energy and desired velocity have been carefully chosen here so that "energy" is unitless, while desired velocity is proportional to distance. This guarantees that the sampling pattern computed by this simple repulsion method scales with a surface.

If desired particle velocities are set in this way, and constrained particle velocities are computed with equation 5, particles repel, but their behavior is highly dependent on the parameter $\sigma$. The slope of a Gaussian peaks at distances of $\pm\sigma$ and it is near zero at much smaller or much greater distances. When the distance between particles is not between $.03\sigma$ and $3\sigma$, for instance, the repulsion is below 7% of its peak. If $\sigma$ is chosen too small then particles will (nearly) stop spreading when their separation is about $3\sigma$, and if $\sigma$ is chosen too big then distant particles will repel more than nearby ones, and the resulting sampling pattern will be poor. The best value for $\sigma$ is about $.3\sqrt{(\text{surface area})/(\text{number of particles})}$.

## 4.2 Global Fissioning

If a surface is seeded with several floater particles, and an initial value of $\sigma$ can be found that causes these particles to disperse, then the sampling can be repeatedly refined by allowing the particles to reach equilibrium, then simultaneously fissioning each particle into two, giving the new particles a small random displacement, and simultaneously dividing $\sigma$ by $\sqrt{2}$. The particles are considered to be at equilibrium when their net forces, and hence their speeds, get low. With this global fissioning scheme, early generations will spread out sparsely, and succeeding generations will fill in more densely.

Simple repulsion with global fissioning is acceptable for maintaining a good distribution on a very slowly changing surface, but the population is always a power of two, and particles do not redistribute quickly in response to rapid surface changes. Global fissioning fails to adapt to changes in a surface adequately, as mentioned earlier.

## 4.3 Adaptive Repulsion

To develop a more adaptive repulsion scheme, we employ an analogy to a population of organisms distributing itself uniformly across an area. Specifically, imagine a population of pioneers spreading West and colonizing America. In order to settle the entire country as quickly as possible, a good rule is for each male-female pair to spread out as much as possible away from their neighbors, until the encroachment on them is roughly equal in all directions, and only then to homestead and have children. If the encroachment from neighbors is low, then each pair can claim more land (be greedier), but when neighbors are pressing in, each pair must relinquish land. Early pioneers travel great distances and claim huge tracts of land, while later generations move less and divide up successively smaller shares until the desired density is achieved.

These ideas can be applied to particle behavior. To achieve uniform densities quickly, and maintain them as the surface moves or deforms, we will allow each particle to have its own repulsion radius $\sigma^i$, and to decide independently when it should fission or die. A particle's radius should grow when all of the forces on it are small and it should shrink when the forces on it are big. For a particle near equilibrium, birth and death occur when the density is too low or too high, respectively. We now quantify these principles.

Similar to the simple repulsion scheme, we define the energy of particle $i$ due to particle $j$ as:

$$E^{ij} = \alpha \exp\left(-\frac{|\mathbf{r}^{ij}|^2}{2(\sigma^i)^2}\right)$$

Note that the global parameter $\sigma$ has been replaced by the local parameter $\sigma^i$, so that $E^{ij} \neq E^{ji}$ in general.

The energy at particle $i$ is defined as:

$$E^i = \sum_{j=1}^{n}(E^{ij} + E^{ji})$$

The repulsion force and desired velocity is again proportional to the gradient of energy with respect to position:

$$\mathbf{P}^i = -(\sigma^i)^2 E_{\mathbf{p}^i}^i = (\sigma^i)^2 \sum_{j=1}^{n}\left(\frac{\mathbf{r}^{ij}}{(\sigma^i)^2}E^{ij} - \frac{\mathbf{r}^{ij}}{(\sigma^j)^2}E^{ji}\right) \quad (9)$$

The time-varying repulsion radii will be controlled differentially. We want the radius to grow when the energy is too low and to shrink when the energy is too high. This can be done indirectly by controlling the energies.

As stated earlier, our energy measure is scale-invariant. That is, if all surfaces and samples are scaled ($\mathbf{p}^i$ and $\sigma^i$), the $E^i$ will remain constant. Therefore, to ensure that neighboring particles repel each other, we can simply drive all of their energies to a global desired energy level, $\hat{E}$. To arrive at a value for $\hat{E}$, we consider an ideal hexagonal close-packing, which is the best uniform sampling pattern for a planar surface. In this configuration, all $\sigma^i$ should be equal, and the distance between nearest neighbors should be roughly $2\sigma$ to guarantee strong repulsion forces. Since each particle has six nearest neighbors in this configuration, the desired energy should be roughly $\hat{E} = 6\alpha \exp\left(-(2\sigma)^2/(2\sigma^2)\right) = 6e^{-2}\alpha \approx .8\alpha$.

The portion of a particle's repulsion energy that is directly affected by a change in its own repulsion radius is:

$$D^i = \sum_{j=1}^{n} E^{ij}$$

To keep $D^i$ near the desired value, we use the linear feedback equation:

$$\dot{D}^i = -\rho(D^i - \hat{E}) \quad (10)$$

where $\rho$ is the feedback constant.

The change to the repulsion radius of a particle that will yield this change in energy can be derived with the chain rule: $\dot{D}^i = D_{\sigma^i}^i \dot{\sigma}^i + \sum_j D_{\mathbf{p}^j}^i \cdot \dot{\mathbf{p}}^j$, neglecting the latter terms, thus:

$$\dot{\sigma}^i = \frac{\dot{D}^i}{D_{\sigma^i}^i} \quad (11)$$

The rule above works fine for particles that are exerting some force on their neighbors, but it causes infinite radius change when a particle is alone in a sparsely sampled region of a surface (or is the first particle), where $D^i = D_{\sigma^i}^i = 0$. In such cases we want the radius to grow, but not catastrophically, so we modify equation 11:

$$\dot{\sigma}^i = \frac{\dot{D}^i}{D_{\sigma^i}^i + \beta} \quad (12)$$

for some $\beta$. The change in energy with respect to a change in radius is:

$$D_{\sigma^i}^i = \frac{1}{(\sigma^i)^3} \sum_{j=1}^{n} |\mathbf{r}^{ij}|^2 E^{ij} \quad (13)$$

Using equations 9, 12, 10, and 13 to control particle positions and repulsion radii will do a good job of moving particles into sparse regions quickly, but their radii might become very large, and hence the density might remain too low.

## 4.4 Adaptive Fission/Death

To achieve uniform density it is necessary that large-radius particles fission. Likewise, particles that are overcrowded should be considered for death.

We use the following criteria to control birth and death of particles: A particle is fissioned iff:

- the particle is near equilibrium, $|\dot{\mathbf{p}}^i| < \gamma \sigma^i$, and
- either the particle's repulsion radius is huge ($\sigma^i > \sigma^{\max}$), or it is adequately energized and its radius is above the desired radius ($D^i > \nu \hat{E}$ and $\sigma^i > \hat{\sigma}$).

Fission splits a single particle in two. The two particles are given initial radii of $\sigma^i/\sqrt{2}$ and a desired velocity that is a random direction scaled by a fraction of $\sigma^i$. A particle dies iff:

- the particle is near equilibrium, $|\dot{\mathbf{p}}^i| < \gamma \sigma^i$, and
- the particle's repulsion radius is too small, $\sigma^i < \delta \hat{\sigma}$, and
- the following biased randomized test succeeds: $R > \sigma^i/(\delta\hat{\sigma})$, where $R$ is a uniform random number between 0 and 1.

The death criteria are made stochastic to prevent mass suicide in overcrowded regions.

This combination of adaptive repulsion, fissioning, and death is much more responsive to changes in the surface shape than the simple repulsion scheme.

## 5 Implementation and Results

The techniques described above have been implemented in about 3700 lines of C++ code. Particular implicit function classes are derived from a generic implicit function base class. Adding a new implicit function to the system is easy, requiring only the implementation of functions $F$, $F_{\mathbf{X}}$, $F_{\mathbf{q}}$, and bounding box. Each of these except $F_{\mathbf{q}}$ is standard in any system employing implicit functions.

For example, we define the blobby sphere implicit function to be the sum of Gaussians of the distance to each of $k$ center points [8]. The parameter vector $\mathbf{q}$ consists of $4k + 1$ parameters: a bias $b$ plus four parameters for each sphere (a center 3-vector $\mathbf{c}^i$ and standard deviation $s^i$). Thus,

$$\mathbf{q} = [b, \mathbf{c}^1, s^1, \mathbf{c}^2, s^2, \ldots, \mathbf{c}^k, s^k]$$

If we define

$$g^i(\mathbf{x}) = \exp\left(-\frac{|\mathbf{x} - \mathbf{c}^i|^2}{(s^i)^2}\right)$$

then the functions needed by the system are

$$F(\mathbf{x}) = b - \sum_{i=1}^{k} g^i(\mathbf{x})$$

$$F_{\mathbf{X}}(\mathbf{x}) = 2 \sum_i \frac{\mathbf{x} - \mathbf{c}^i}{(s^i)^2} g^i(\mathbf{x})$$

$$F_{\mathbf{q}}(\mathbf{x}) = [F_b, F_{\mathbf{c}^1}, F_{s^1}, F_{\mathbf{c}^2}, F_{s^2}, \ldots, F_{\mathbf{c}^k}, F_{s^k}]$$

where

$$F_b(\mathbf{x}) = 1$$

$$F_{\mathbf{c}^i}(\mathbf{x}) = -2 \frac{\mathbf{x} - \mathbf{c}^i}{(s^i)^2} g^i(\mathbf{x})$$

$$F_{s^i}(\mathbf{x}) = -2 \frac{|\mathbf{x} - \mathbf{c}^i|^2}{(s^i)^3} g^i(\mathbf{x})$$

If we assume that $g^i(\mathbf{x}) = 0$ beyond a radius of $3s^i$, then a conservative bounding box for blobby spheres is the bounding box of non-blobby spheres with centers $\mathbf{c}^i$ and radii $3s^i$.

We have also implemented spheres and blobby cylinders. A blobby cylinder function is defined to be the sum of Gaussians of the distance to each of several line segments. A system of $k$ blobby cylinders has $7k + 1$ parameters: a bias plus seven parameters for each cylinder (two endpoints and a standard deviation).

It is often useful to freeze some of these parameters to a fixed value so that they will not be modified during interaction. This is

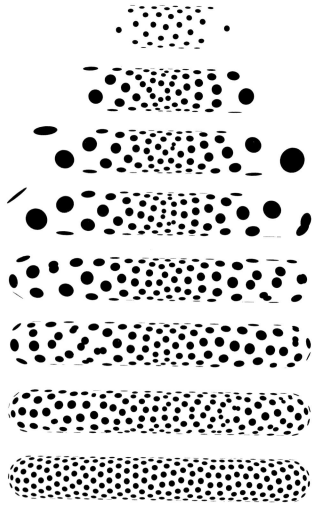

**Figure 1:** This sequence illustrates the adaptive repulsion and fissioning mechanism. The topmost image shows a deliberately poor sampling of a blobby cylinder produced using simple repulsion: the cylinder was rapidly stretched, leaving the sample points behind. The remaining images, from top to bottom, show the recovery of good sampling when adaptive repulsion is enabled. The particles at the frontier increase their radii of repulsion, rapidly filling the voids. As the particles slow down, they fission, restoring the desired sampling density. This process takes about four seconds on an SGI Crimson.

done simply by leaving them out of the $\mathbf{q}$ and $F_{\mathbf{q}}$ vectors. To get blobs of equal radii, for instance, one would omit all $s^i$.

The system starts up with a single floater positioned arbitrarily in the bounding box of the surface and then begins the physical simulation by repeating the following differential step:

- The user interface sets *desired* control point velocities $\mathbf{P}^i$. Stationary control points of course have zero desired velocity, while control points being dragged by the user have desired velocities that are calculated as a function of cursor position.

- Set $\mathbf{Q}$, the *desired* values for the time derivatives of the surface parameters. These are typically set to zero to minimize parametric change in the surface, but they could also be calculated to attract the surface toward a default shape.

- Compute the actual surface parameter changes, $\dot{\mathbf{q}}$, as constrained by the control point velocities, using equations 7 and 8.

- Compute repulsion forces between floaters to set their desired velocities $\mathbf{P}^i$, using equation 9.

- Compute actual floater velocities, as constrained by the already-computed surface time derivatives, using equation 5. (When the gradient $F_{\mathbf{X}}$ is near zero, however, the surface is locally ill-defined, and it is best to leave such floaters motionless, i.e., $\dot{\mathbf{p}}^i = 0$.)

- Compute the change to floater repulsion radii, $\dot{\sigma}^i$, using equations 12, 10, and 13.

- Update the positions of the control points and floaters using Euler's method, that is: $\mathbf{p}^i(t + \Delta t) = \mathbf{p}^i(t) + \Delta t \dot{\mathbf{p}}^i(t)$, and similar formulas to update the surface parameters $\mathbf{q}$ from $\dot{\mathbf{q}}$, and the floater repulsion radii $\sigma^i$ from $\dot{\sigma}^i$.

- Test each floater for possible fission/death.

- Redisplay the floaters and control points as disks tangent to the surface, with normal given by $F_{\mathbf{X}}$ and (for floaters) radius proportional to $\sigma^i$.

Using the mouse, the user can pick a control point and move it in a plane perpendicular to the view direction. Pulling control point $i$ sets the desired control point velocity $\mathbf{P}^i$. Since the velocities feed into the constrained optimization solution, which in turn feeds into a numerical differential equation solver, some care must be taken to ensure that control point motions are reasonably smooth and well behaved, which they might not be if positions were set directly by polling the pointing device. A simple solution which works well is to make the velocity of the dragged particle proportional to the vector from the point to the 3-D cursor position. This in effect provides spring coupling between the cursor and the control point. Although the control point can lag behind the cursor as a result, performance is brisk enough that the lag is barely noticeable. Similar dragging schemes are described in [14,31]. The user can also create and delete control points and adjust the desired repulsion radius $\hat{\sigma}$ through a slider.

The matrix in equation 7 is symmetric and in general positive definite. It thus lends itself to solution by Cholesky decomposition [23], which is easy to implement, robust and efficient. However, the matrix can become singular if inconsistent or redundant constraints are applied, that is if the number of constraints exceeds $m$, or if some of the $F_{\mathbf{q}}^i$'s are linear combinations of others. While the former condition is easy to detect by counting, the latter is not. The problem of singularities can be circumvented by using a least-squares technique, or singular value decomposition [23].

The system is fast enough to run at interactive rates. Let $m$ be the number of degrees of freedom of the implicit surface, let $n$ be the number of control points, and let $r$ be the number of floaters. The most expensive parts of the algorithm are the computation of the $n \times n$ matrix of equation 7, which has cost $O(mn^2)$, the solution of the linear system, which has cost $O(n^3)$, the computation of repulsion forces between all pairs of floaters, which currently has cost $O(r^2)$, and the display of the floaters, which has cost $O(r)$ (with a large constant). Our current system does not handle overconstrained surfaces, so $m \geq n$, thus the total asymptotic cost of the algorithm is $O(mn^2 + r^2)$ per iteration.

We have run simulations as complex as $m = 56, n = 10, r = 500$. Above $r = 250$ floaters, the $O(r^2)$ repulsion cost has dominated, but this could easily be optimized using spatial data structures. For smaller numbers of floaters ($r < 150$), our system runs at interactive rates (10 Hz or faster on a Silicon Graphics workstation with 100 MHz processor).

The following parameter settings are recommended (where $d$ is surface diameter):

| PARAMETER | MEANING |
| --- | --- |
| $\Delta t = .03$ | time step |
| $\phi = \rho = 15$ | feedback coefficients to keep particles from drifting off surface, and keep particles energized, respectively |
| $\alpha = 6$ | repulsion amplitude |
| $\hat{E} = .8\alpha$ | desired energy |
| $\beta = 10$ | to prevent divide-by-zero |
| $\hat{\sigma} = d/4$ or less | desired repulsion radius (user-controllable) |
| $\sigma^{\max} = \max(\frac{d}{2}, 1.5\hat{\sigma})$ | maximum repulsion radius (note that this changes over time) |
| $\gamma = 4$ | equilibrium speed (multiple of $\sigma^i$) |
| $\nu = .2$ | fraction of $\hat{E}$, for fissioning |
| $\delta = .7$ | fraction of $\hat{\sigma}$, for death |

Most of these parameters can be set once and forgotten. The only parameter that a user would typically need to control is the desired repulsion radius, $\hat{\sigma}$.

Overall, the method meets our goals, it is fast, and it has proven to be very robust. It has recovered from even violent user interaction causing very rapid shape change. The adaptive sampling, fission, and death techniques seem to be well tuned and to work well together, as we have not seen the system oscillate, diverge, or die with the current parameter settings. During interaction, $\hat{\sigma}$ is the only parameter that needs to be varied.

Another result of this work is that we have discovered that *implicit surfaces are slippery*: when you attempt to move them using control points they often slip out of your grasp.

# 6 Conclusions

In this paper we have presented a new particle-based method for sampling and control of implicit surfaces. It is capable of supporting real-time rendering and direct manipulation of surfaces. Our control method is not limited to algebraic surfaces as many previous techniques are; it allows fast control of general procedural implicit functions through control points on the surface. We have presented a dynamic sampling and rendering method for implicit surfaces that samples a changing surface more quickly than existing methods. The use of constraint methods allows particles to follow the surface as it changes, and to do this more rapidly and accurately than with penalty methods. Our algorithms for adaptive repulsion, fission, and death of particles are capable of generating good sampling patterns much more quickly than earlier repulsion schemes, and they sample the surface well even during rapid shape changes.

There are a number of directions for future research.

We intend to investigate other uses for the samplings we obtain. One of these is the calculation of surface integrals for area, volume, or surface fairness measures such as those described in [19,30]. Another is the creation of polygon meshes.

To polygonize a surface within the framework presented here it is necessary to infer topology from the sample points. This is more difficult than finding a polygonization from a set of samples on a grid in 3-D, as in marching cubes algorithms, where an approximate topology is suggested by the signs of the samples and by the topology of the grid itself. Delaunay triangulation in 2-D or 3-D is one possible way to extract topology [12,27]. A more robust alternative would employ Lipschitz conditions and interval arithmetic [26]. To preserve the basic advantages of our method, we would require a polygonization algorithm that allows efficient dynamic updates as the surface changes.

Although we developed it to sample implicit surfaces, our adaptive repulsion scheme can be applied to meshing or sampling of parametric surfaces as well: each floater would be defined by its position in the surface's 2-D parameter space, rather than position in 3-D space.

Several performance and numerical issues remain to be addressed. As we tackle more complex models, we could exploit sparsity in $F$'s dependence on $\mathbf{q}$. Notably, with local bases such as blobby models, the dependence of $F$ on faraway elements is negligible. An additional numerical issue is the handling of singular constraint matrices, due to overdetermined or dependent constraints. Excellent results can be obtained using least-squares techniques.

An additional area of investigation is the use of local criteria, notably surface curvature, to control sampling density. Surface curvature can be measured directly, at the cost of taking additional derivatives of $F$. Since this places a considerable extra burden on the implementor of implicit primitives, an alternative is to estimate curvature at each floater based on positions and normals of nearby points. Having established a desired density at each point, based on curvature or any other criterion, relatively simple modifications to the adaptive repulsion scheme will yield the desired nonuniform density. Another possible density criterion is the user's focus of interest, e.g. the neighborhood of a control point being dragged.

Finally, there is room for considerable further work in interactive sculpting of implicit surfaces. Dragging one control point at a time can be somewhat limiting given the slippery behavior of the surface. However, the basic control-point machinery developed here could be used to build more complex sculpting tools that influence multiple surface points in coordinated ways.

## Acknowledgements

The authors wish to thank Scott Draves and Sebastian Grassia for their contributions to this work. This research was supported in part by a Science and Technology Center Grant from the National Science Foundation, #BIR-8920118, by an NSF High Performance Computing and Communications Grant, #BIR-9217091, by the Engineering Design Research Center, an NSF Engineering Research Center at Carnegie Mellon University, by Apple Computer, Inc, and by an equipment grant from Silicon Graphics, Inc. The second author was supported by NSF Young Investigator Award #CCR-9357763.

## References

[1] Chandrajit Bajaj, Insung Ihm, and Joe Warren. Higher-order interpolation and least-squares approximation using implicit

**Figure 2:** This sequence illustrates the construction of a shape composed of blobby cylinders. The shape was created by direct manipulation of control points using the mouse. In the topmost image, all three cylinder primitives are superimposed. Each subsequent image represents the result of a single mouse motion.

algebraic surfaces. *ACM Trans. on Graphics*, 12(4):327–347, Oct. 1993.

[2] David Baraff. Analytical methods for dynamic simulation of non-penetrating rigid bodies. *Computer Graphics*, 23(3):223–232, July 1989.

[3] David Baraff. Curved surfaces and coherence for non-penetrating rigid body simulation. *Computer Graphics*, 24(4):19–28, August 1990.

[4] David Baraff and Andrew Witkin. Dynamic simulation of non-penetrating flexible bodies. *Computer Graphics*, 26(2):303–308, 1992. Proc. Siggraph '92.

[5] Ronen Barzel and Alan H. Barr. A modeling system based on dynamic constaints. *Computer Graphics*, 22:179–188, 1988.

[6] J. Baumgarte. Stabilization of constraints and integrals of motion in dynamical systems. *Computer Methods in Applied Mechanics*, 1972.

[7] Thaddeus Beier. Practical uses for implicit surfaces in animation. In *Modeling, Visualizing, and Animating Implicit Surfaces (SIGGRAPH '93 Course Notes)*, pages 20.1–20.10. 1993.

[8] James F. Blinn. A generalization of algebraic surface drawing. *ACM Trans. on Graphics*, 1(3):235–256, July 1982.

[9] Jules Bloomenthal. Polygonization of implicit surfaces. *Computer Aided Geometric Design*, 5:341–355, 1988.

[10] Jules Bloomenthal. An implicit surface polygonizer. In Paul Heckbert, editor, *Graphics Gems IV*, pages 324–350. Academic Press, Boston, 1994.

[11] Jules Bloomenthal and Brian Wyvill. Interactive techniques for implicit modeling. *Computer Graphics (1990 Symp. on Interactive 3D Graphics)*, 24(2):109–116, 1990.

[12] Luiz Henrique de Figueiredo, Jonas de Miranda Gomes, Demetri Terzopoulos, and Luiz Velho. Physically-based methods for polygonization of implicit surfaces. In *Graphics Interface '92*, pages 250–257, May 1992.

[13] Phillip Gill, Walter Murray, and Margret Wright. *Practical Optimization*. Academic Press, New York, NY, 1981.

[14] Michael Gleicher and Andrew Witkin. Through-the-lens camera control. *Computer Graphics*, 26(2):331–340, 1992. Proc. Siggraph '92.

[15] Herbert Goldstein. *Classical Mechanics*. Addision Wesley, Reading, MA, 1950.

[16] Huges Hoppe, Tony DeRose, Tom Duchamp, John McDonald, and Werner Stuetzle. Mesh optimization. In *SIGGRAPH 93 Proceedings*, pages 19–26, July 1993.

[17] David J. Jevans, Brian Wyvill, and Geoff Wyvill. Speeding up 3-D animation for simulation. In *Proc. MAPCON IV (Multi and Array Processors)*, pages 94–100, Jan. 1988.

[18] William E. Lorensen and Harvey E. Cline. Marching cubes: A high resolution 3D surface reconstruction algorithm. *Computer Graphics (SIGGRAPH '87 Proceedings)*, 21(4):163–170, July 1987.

[19] Henry Moreton and Carlo Séquin. Functional minimization for fair surface design. *Computer Graphics*, 26(2):167–176, 1992. Proc. Siggraph '92.

[20] Shigeru Muraki. Volumetric shape description of range data using "blobby model". *Computer Graphics (SIGGRAPH '91 Proceedings)*, 25(4):227–235, July 1991.

[21] Paul Ning and Jules Bloomenthal. An evaluation of implicit surface tilers. *Computer Graphics and Applications*, pages 33–41, Nov. 1993.

[22] Vaughan Pratt. Direct least-squares fitting of algebraic surfaces. *Computer Graphics (SIGGRAPH '87 Proceedings)*, 21(4):145–152, July 1987.

[23] W.H. Press, B.P. Flannery, S. A. Teukolsky, and W. T. Vetterling. *Numerical Recipes in C*. Cambridge University Press, Cambridge, England, 1988.

[24] A. Ricci. A constructive geometry for computer graphics. *Computer Journal*, 16(2):157–160, May 1973.

[25] T. Sederberg. Piecewise algebraic surface patches. *Computer Aided Geometric Design*, 2(1-3):53–60, 1985.

[26] John M. Snyder. *Generative Modeling for Computer Graphics and CAD*. Academic Press, Boston, 1992.

[27] Richard Szeliski and David Tonnesen. Surface modeling with oriented particle systems. *Computer Graphics (SIGGRAPH '92 Proceedings)*, 26(2):185–194, July 1992.

[28] Greg Turk. Generating textures on arbitrary surfaces using reaction-diffusion. *Computer Graphics (SIGGRAPH '91 Proceedings)*, 25(4):289–298, July 1991.

[29] Greg Turk. Re-tiling polygonal surfaces. *Computer Graphics (SIGGRAPH '92 Proceedings)*, 26(2):55–64, July 1992.

[30] William Welch and Andrew Witkin. Variational surface modeling. *Computer Graphics*, 26(2):157–166, 1992. Proc. Siggraph '92.

[31] Andrew Witkin, Michael Gleicher, and William Welch. Interactive dynamics. *Computer Graphics*, 24(2):11–21, March 1990. Proc. 1990 Symposium on 3-D Interactive Graphics.

[32] Andrew Witkin and William Welch. Fast animation and control of non-rigid structures. *Computer Graphics*, 24(4):243–252, July 1990. Proc. Siggraph '90.

[33] Brian Wyvill, Craig McPheeters, and Geoff Wyvill. Data structure for soft objects. *The Visual Computer*, 2(4):227–234, 1986.

# Displacement Mapping Using Flow Fields

Hans Køhling Pedersen
School of Computer Science
Carnegie Mellon University

hkp@cs.cmu.edu

## Abstract

Existing displacement mapping techniques operate only in directions normal to the surface, a restriction which limits the richness of the set of representable objects. This work removes that restriction by allowing displacements to be defined along curved trajectories of flow fields. The main contribution of this generalized technique, which will be referred to as *flow mapping*, is an alternative model of offset surfaces that extends the class of shapes that can be modelled using displacement maps. The paper also discusses methods for synthesizing homogeneous displacement textures. Finally, it introduces the concept of a *texture atlas* for efficient sampling and reconstruction of distorted textures.

## 1 Introduction

One way to augment the visual richness of an object without increasing the complexity of the underlying mathematical model is to specify a detailed surface description separately in the form of a *displacement texture* [4]. While texture mapping in general has received extensive research interest, the displacement mapping literature has remained comparatively sparse, and existing work [8, 9, 12, 14] has largely been restricted to the following model:

Let the surface $S$ be parameterized by $X : U \subseteq R^2 \mapsto R^3$. The displaced surface $\tilde{S}$ can then be defined by the parameterization

$$\tilde{X}(u,v) = X(u,v) + \mathbf{n}(u,v) \cdot g(u,v) \qquad (1)$$

where $\mathbf{n}$ denotes the local surface normal, and $g : U \mapsto R$ is a continuous displacement map.

Unfortunately, this expression can be problematic, even if $X$ is differentiable and $g$ is constant. First, $\tilde{X}$ will generally be more complex than $X$, e.g. finding ray intersections with an offset surface typically requires sophisticated numerical methods. Second, discontinuities will appear if the magnitude of the displacements is higher than the minimum radius of curvature in some region of the surface (figure 1). Furthermore, if the displacement function $g$ is non-constant, artifacts as shown in figure 2 can occur.

The complexity of the model can be reduced by tessellating the displaced surface into a set of polygons and rendering these. However, if $g$ is a detailed procedural or tiled texture, this may require a very large number of polygons; also, care must be taken to avoid self-intersections. Furthermore, because the nature of the model is fundamentally explicit, it is not naturally compatible with some of the features offered by implicit models, such as diffuse or gaseous phenomena.

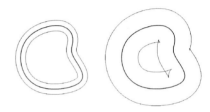

**Figure 1:** *Discontinuities can occur for surface normal displacements where the size of the displacements is higher than than the minimum radius of curvature.*

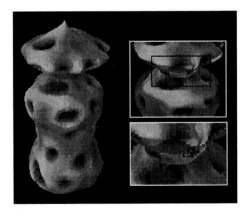

**Figure 2:** *Discontinuities (right) arising from a non-constant displacement function. (A "rough" variation of flow mapping was used to create the leftmost structure).*

In conclusion, despite its obvious potential, the normal offset paradigm suffers from inherent problems, computationally as well as qualitatively, which have limited its use as a practical tool in image synthesis. This paper extends the class of objects that can be displacement mapped by defining and measuring the displacements along flow lines that are not necessarily orthogonal to the surface (see figure 3).

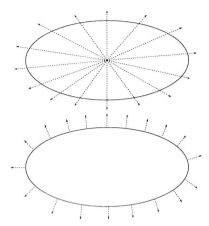

**Figure 3:** *Top: flow field passing through a surface. Bottom: the normal vector field to the same surface.*

The next section describes the flow mapping model and discusses ways to synthesize homogeneous displacement textures. Section 3 addresses the problem of sampling and reconstructing distorted textures. Finally, section 4 discusses the results and suggests topics for future work.

## 2   Flow Mapping

For some surfaces, the problems with normal displacements do not apply. "Displacement mapping" of a plane is trivial, and rendering a displaced sphere requires only simple trigonometric calculations. The desirable property shared by these two cases can be more formally expressed as follows:

Let the surface $S$ be defined explicitly by the surface parameterization $X : U \subseteq R^2 \mapsto R^3$ and implicitly by the point-membership classification function $F : R^3 \mapsto R$ given by:

$$F(p) \begin{cases} < 0, & \text{if p is inside of S} \\ = 0, & \text{if p is on the surface of S} \\ > 0, & \text{if p is outside of S} \end{cases}$$

Let $\Phi : U \times T \mapsto R^3$; $U \subseteq R^2$, $T \subseteq R$ denote a differentiable 3D flow satisfying:

- $\Phi(u, v, t_0) = X(u, v); (u, v) \in U$
- $\left| \frac{\partial \Phi}{\partial t}(u, v, t) \right| > 0; (u, v, t) \in U \times T$
- $\Phi^{-1}(p)$ can be computed "efficiently", $p \in R^3$

Intuitively, $\Phi$ can be thought of as a flow where particles move with velocity vector $\frac{\partial \Phi}{\partial t}$, starting at some source (e.g. the center in the case of a sphere) and passing through $S$ at time $t = t_0$. For example, for the unit sphere, $\Phi$ can conveniently be chosen

$$\Phi_{Sphere}(u, v, t) = t \cdot X(u, v), \text{ with } t_0 = 1$$

where $X$ is the longitude-lattitude parameterization.

$\Phi(u, v, t_0)$ is equivalent to $X(u, v)$, and $\Phi(u^*, v^*, t)$; $t \in T$ and $(u^*, v^*)$ fixed, parameterizes the trajectories of the flow. The projection onto $S$ of a point $p$ at the position $\Phi(u, v, t)$, along the trajectory on which it is located, is $\Phi(u, v, t_0)$. In this notation, the distance between an arbitrary point and its projection onto $S$ is the arc length

$$\int_{\Pi_t \circ \Phi^{-1}(p)}^{t_0} \left| \frac{\partial \Phi}{\partial t}(\Pi_{u,v} \circ \Phi^{-1}(p), s) \right| ds, \qquad (2)$$

where $\Pi_t : R^3 \mapsto R$; $\Pi_t(u, v, t) = t$ and $\Pi_{u,v} : R^3 \mapsto R^2$; $\Pi_{u,v}(u, v, t) = (u, v)$ are selection functions. The above expression (2) is just a convenient reformulation of the definition of arc length for a regular parameterized curve. The relation between $\Phi$, $X$, and the selection functions is illustrated in figure 4.

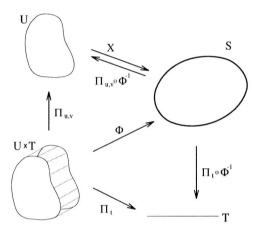

**Figure 4:** *The relationship between the flow, $\Phi$, the surface parameterization, $X$, and the selection functions $\Pi_{u,v}$ and $\Pi_t$.*

The non-Euclidean distance measure (2) defined on the trajectories of $\Phi$ can be used to compute the distance from arbitrary points to the surface. This allows a point-membership classification function $\tilde{F}$ for the displaced surface $\tilde{S}$ to be defined:

$$\tilde{F}(p) = \begin{cases} -1, & d_\Phi(p, X(u^*, v^*)) < g(u^*, v^*) \\ 0, & d_\Phi(p, X(u^*, v^*)) = g(u^*, v^*) \\ 1, & d_\Phi(p, X(u^*, v^*)) > g(u^*, v^*) \end{cases} \qquad (3)$$

where $(u^*, v^*) = \Pi_{u,v} \circ \Phi^{-1}(p)$, $g$ is the displacement map, and $d_\Phi$ is the distance measure defined by

$$d_\Phi(p, S) = sgn(F(p)) \cdot \int_{\Pi_t \circ \Phi^{-1}(p)}^{t_0} \left| \frac{\partial \Phi}{\partial t}(\Pi_{u,v} \circ \Phi^{-1}(p), s) \right| ds, \qquad (4)$$

as demonstrated in figure 5.

The $sgn(F(p))$ term makes (4) positive for points outside of $S$ and negative for interior points. It is necessary to use signed distances as $g$ can take both positive and negative values corresponding to "bumps" and "pits".

The integral in (4) is computationally demanding in the general case, but if the trajectories of $\Phi$ are assumed to be linear, (4) reduces to

$$d_\Phi(p, S) = sgn(F(p)) \cdot d_3(p, X(\Pi_{u,v} \circ \Phi^{-1}(p))), \qquad (5)$$

where $d_3$ denotes the Euclidean distance. Under the same assumption, the explicit expression for $\tilde{S}$ becomes

$$\tilde{X}(u, v) = X(u, v) + \frac{\frac{\partial \Phi}{\partial t}(u, v, t_0)}{\left| \frac{\partial \Phi}{\partial t}(u, v, t_0) \right|} \cdot g(u, v), \qquad (6)$$

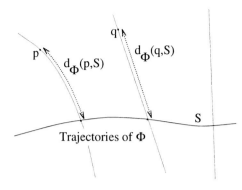

**Figure 5:** *The distance from a point to the surface S is measured along the trajectories of* $\Phi$.

Given $\tilde{F}$ and $\tilde{X}$, the displaced surface can be rendered directly using techniques from volume rendering [6, 7] or it can be tessellated and rendered as a set of triangles [2, 3, 19].

## 2.1 Deformed objects

The preceding discussion described how displacements can be measured along the trajectories of simple flows with linear trajectories. In the following, the model will be generalized to allow arc-length displacements along curved trajectories.

The idea is to deform a simple surface into a more complex one. If the displaced surface $\tilde{S}$ with parameterization $\tilde{X}$ is mapped into the surface $\hat{S}$ by an invertible mapping $M : R^3 \mapsto R^3$, the model becomes

$$\hat{\Phi} = M \circ \Phi \qquad (7)$$
$$\hat{X} = M \circ \tilde{X} \qquad (8)$$
$$\hat{F} = \tilde{F} \circ M^{-1} \qquad (9)$$

If $M$ is continuous, two points located on the same trajectory of the undeformed flow $\Phi$ will also be located on the same trajectory of the deformed flow $\hat{\Phi}$. This property makes the model applicable to a variety of complex geometrical objects. For the model to be practical, however, $M$ and $M^{-1}$ must both be easily computable: $M$ is used to estimate surface normals and tangents, and $M^{-1}$ occurs in the point-membership classification function for the displaced surface (3). The subspace of 3D mappings with these properties contains a variety of global and local, linear and non-linear deformations, some of which are described in [1]. A detailed description of 3D deformations is beyond the scope of this paper, but the use of successive simplified *free-form deformations* [13] has produced interesting results (general FFDs have non-trivial inverse mappings, but similar results can be achieved using suitable invertible deformations, e.g. generalized Gaussian bumps).

## 2.2 Non-linear arc-length displacements

If the displacements are defined relative to the undeformed surface, the model offers little control over displacement texture after the deformation. To reduce the distortion, the values of the displacement mapping, which will be denoted $\hat{g}$ in the deformed model, are measured in arc length along the trajectories of $\hat{\Phi}$. For non-linear flows, the evaluation of $\hat{F}$ would require the calculation of the integral in (4), but as $\hat{F}$ may need to be determined many times for each pixel in the image (e.g. if implicit rendering techniques are utilized), it is critical that it can be estimated efficiently.

This problem is avoided by pre-computing an *anti-distorted* displacement map $g$ so

$$d_{\hat{\Phi}}(\hat{X}(u, v), \bar{S}) = \hat{g}(u, v), \qquad (10)$$

where $g$ occurs in the definition of $\hat{X}$ (see equations (8) and (6)) and $\bar{S}$ denotes the deformed undisplaced surface (parameterized by $M \circ X$).

This condition just means that $g(u, v)$ must be estimated so that the arc length between $\hat{X}(u, v)$ and its projection onto $\bar{S}$ is $\hat{g}(u, v)$ for all $(u, v) \in U$.

As $p$ and $M(p)$ have the same projection onto $S$ and thus the same $(u, v)$-coordinates for every point $p$, the anti-distortion mechanism operates by perturbing the amplitudes of the displacement map $\hat{g}$. The algorithm looks like this:

**for** $(u, v) \in U$ **do**
    $p = X(u, v)$
    $\hat{p} = M(p)$
    $\hat{q} = \hat{p}$ displaced by $\hat{g}(u, v)$ along trajectory of $\hat{\Phi}$
    $q = M^{-1}(\hat{q})$
    $g(u, v) = d_{\Phi}(q, S) = sgn(F(q)) \cdot d_3(q, p)$

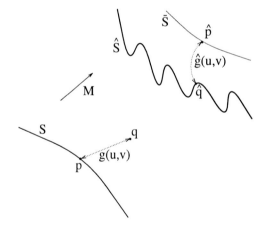

**Figure 6:** *Computing the anti-distorted displacement map g. See text for reference.*

Every point in texture space is mapped onto $\bar{S}$ and displaced along the trajectory of $\hat{\Phi}$ on which it is located using a suitable numerical approximation (e.g. measuring the displacement along a piecewise linear approximation to the trajectory produces an acceptable result). The resulting point is mapped back to the original coordinates by $M^{-1}$, and as the the trajectories of $\Phi$ were assumed to be straight lines, the anti-distorted displacement can now be computed as the Euclidean distance between the initial point $p$ and the final point $q$. Figure 7 shows an example of this process.

When $g$ is so computed, the point-membership classification function $\hat{F}$, (9), for the deformed and arc-length displaced surface $\hat{S}$ no longer involves the estimation of a non-Euclidean arc length. Instead,

$$\hat{F}(p) = \tilde{F} \circ M^{-1}(p)$$

requires only the calculation of the Euclidean distance

$$d_{\Phi}(M^{-1}(p), X(\Pi_{u,v} \circ \Phi^{-1} \circ M^{-1}(p))),$$

where the last expression is obtained directly from the definition of $\hat{F}$ and the conditionals in (3).

This result makes displacement mapping along the curved trajectories of a deformed flow simple and practical.

### 2.3 Dealing with texture distortion

To make the displacement texture itself appear homogeneous on the deformed object, it is necessary to compensate for the distortion introduced by $\hat{X}$. Doing this manually can be a tedious and difficult process, but recent progress in texture synthesis [15, 18] allows attractive *reaction-diffusion* textures to be synthesized automatically. Though space does not permit a detailed description of this topic, one simple observation should be mentioned, as it significantly extends the scope of reaction-diffusion textures.

While Turk's method [15] works for arbitrary surfaces, but has difficulties dealing with anisotropic patterns, Witkin & Kass' approach [18] facilitates anisotropic diffusion, but can only be applied to a restricted class of parametric surfaces. If the two methods are combined, however, it is possible to obtain anisotropic reaction-diffusion textures for arbitrary parametric surfaces. This can be accomplished by applying Turk's *point repulsion* algorithm to parametric surfaces (this idea will be explained in section 3.2), and then using one of the partial derivatives as a reference direction for anisotropic diffusion. An example of an anisotropic displacement texture for a complex parametric surface can be seen in figure 7.

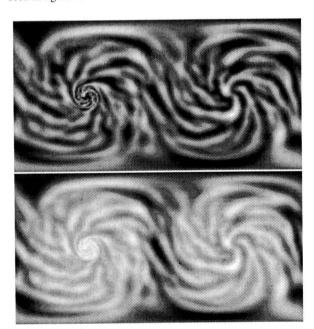

**Figure 7:** *Displacement texture before and after anti-distortion of the amplitude. The amplitude of the lower texture will appear homogeneous after the deformation $M$ has been applied. Figure 10a shows this texture mapped onto the correspondingly deformed 3D object.*

The model is, however, compatible with all standard texture mapping techniques. In particular, the use of *solid textures* [10, 11] restricted to the surface has produced interesting results. As it is important that $g$ can be evaluated efficiently, it is typically best to project the solid texture to $(u, v)$-space in a pre-processing

step and then interpolate from the resulting sample values.

### 2.4 Summary

This section has described the flow mapping model and explained how it can be used to generate complex homogeneous shapes. To make this technique practical, however, the texture $g$ must be represented efficiently. As the proposed solution to this problem is new, the next section will give a detailed presentation of the algorithm.

## 3 Distorted texture mappings

When a 2-dimensional texture is mapped onto a complex 3D surface, the texture will be stretched and compressed according to the variations in the metric tensor of the mapping function. While recent research [17, 18] has illuminated the visual problems associated with parametric distortion, little interest has been devoted to the question of how to represent distorted textures. The latter problem can be broken into:

1. Sampling the texture signal across a 3D surface.

2. Reconstructing the continous texture from the discrete sample values.

The most frequently used solution to this problem is to define one global mapping between the 2D texture space and the 3D object. The texture is sampled over a regular grid and reconstructed using linear interpolation. For surfaces locally isometric to a plane, i.e. those with angular and distance preserving parameterizations, this approach will produce a uniform sampling rate, but if the mapping introduces distortion, a high sampling frequency may be necessary in order to achieve the desired resolution globally. As a result, the texture will not only take up an unnecessarily large amount of memory, but if it is to be enhanced, e.g. anti-distorted as described in section 2.2 or filtered, the processing time will increase. As the deformations described in section 2.1 may introduce a significant amount of distortion, we designed an alternative representation inspired by the idea of an *atlas* from differential geometry [5].

### 3.1 A texture atlas

The idea of an atlas is to cover a surface with a number of local mappings instead of one global. This section will explain how a *texture atlas* allows adaptive sampling to be combined with easy reconstruction.

For an invertible mapping $X : U \mapsto S$ with continuous partial derivatives in a neighborhood of $(u_0, v_0)$, the first order Taylor expansion about $(u_0, v_0)$ is

$$X(u_0, v_0) + (u - u_0) \cdot X_u + (v - v_0) \cdot X_v,$$

where $X_u$ and $X_v$ denote the partial derivatives of $X$.

For our purpose, the key observation is that a sufficiently small "neighborhood" surrounding a point $(u_0, v_0) \in U$ will map onto some neighborhood of $X(u_0, v_0)$ with only first order distortion. If a set of samples is selected uniformly in some appropriate neighborhood around $(u_0, v_0)$ with compensation for this distortion, the samples will be uniformly distributed after they are mapped onto the surface. If the surface is divided into a sufficient number of patches, and a local mapping is constructed for every patch, we would expect to obtain a better distribution of the samples than if just one global mapping were used. The next section will describe how this idea can be implemented efficiently.

## 3.2 Computing the mappings for an atlas

Originally, our idea was to subdivide the parameter space recursively using standard pyramidal techniques. This strategy, however, performed poorly for a wide range of distorted mappings as it produced a large number of small sectors corresponding to patches of negligible surface area. This led us to investigate a more direct approach that would subdivide the actual surface rather than its parameter space. This alternative method relies on the observation that the Voronoi diagram of a uniformly distributed point set on a surface will have Voronoi patches with approximately the same shape and area.

Turk [15, 16] developed a technique for positioning samples uniformly over a polygonal surface. A randomly distributed point set is subjected to a relaxation process where each point is repelled by its neighbors. If the repelling forces are computed appropriately, the points will eventually settle down in a homogeneous distribution. This idea can easily be adapted for parametric surfaces: If Turk's point repulsion algorithm is applied in parameter space instead of object space, i.e. by representing the repulsion forces as 2D parametric offsets instead of 3D vectors, the resulting process will produce a uniform distribution that is independent of the parameterization[1]. The next step is to construct a texture mapping for the Voronoi patch corresponding to each point. This requires computing the inverse image of each patch, but as these inverse images can be complex curvilinear regions (see figure 8), we choose to bound each inverse image by a rectangle. More specifically, for each point $p$ on the surface, the problem is to bound the set of points in the parameter space which, when mapped onto the surface, will have $p$ as their closest neighbor. The set of bounding rectangles can be estimated numerically in a pre-processing step: First, the lengths of $X_u$ and $X_v$ are used to compute an initial guess for the dimensions of the rectangle. If the border contains points $(u^*, v^*)$ so the closest neighbor to $X(u^*, v^*)$ is $p$, the rectangle is expanded, otherwise it is contracted. This process continues until the bounding box covers the patch with the desired accuracy.

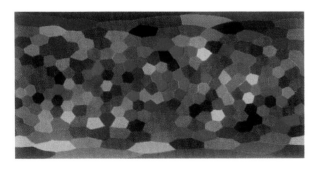

**Figure 8:** *Inverse Voronoi diagram to 256 uniformly distributed points on a sphere (using the longitude-latitude parameterization).*

When all the bounding rectangles are computed, each local mapping is sampled in a miniature $N \times N$ grid. The motivation

---

[1] This algorithm is robust, but works best when the tangent vectors are not degenerate. In the case of a sphere, improved performance can be achieved by using two different parameterizations, one tilted 90 degrees relative to the other. If a point is close to a singularity/pole in one parameterization, the repulsion forces are computed relative to the other.

---

for using identical square grids is that 1) the point repulsion step guarantees that the Voronoi patches will have approximately the same area and shape, and 2) the bounding rectangle algorithm described above automatically compensates for first order distortion.

For efficient look-ups, the maps are stored in a hash table. As the bounding rectangles are not disjoint, each entry in the table is sorted to avoid large bounding boxes obscuring smaller ones.

Since the displacement function must be continuous to avoid discontinuities in the displaced surface, linear interpolation is used inside each patch. To avoid discontinuities at the borders between different mappings, a modified bilinear interpolation scheme can be used, but as these discontinuities are negligible and have not produced visible artifacts, we have not found it necessary to implement this feature.

## 3.3 A Texture Atlas - Discussion

A texture atlas is a relatively efficient way of storing a distorted texture. The main advantage from existing sampling methods is that the signal can be reconstructed efficiently. The combination of these properties makes the texture atlas well suited for representation of moderately to severely distorted textures.

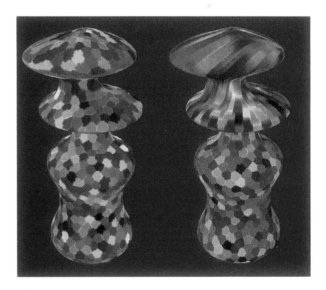

**Figure 9:** *The difference between one global mapping (right) and an atlas of 1024 local mappings (left) of the same resolution. Note the more uniform sampling rate on the leftmost image.*

Figure 9 shows a comparison between a texture atlas, $(a)$, and regular grid sampling, $(b)$. The two textures have the same resolution: the atlas has $1024 \times 9 \times 9 = 82.944$ samples and the grid $408 \times 204 = 83.232$ samples. The object is a parameterized sphere subjected to a series of non-linear deformations. As the Jacobian of the deformed parameterization varies significantly, grid sampling gives a poorly distributed population compared to the atlas: to achieve the same resolution as the atlas, the number of samples in the grid would have to be increased almost 100 times.

The algorithm works robustly for arbitrary parameterizations, provided the surface does not deviate too much from its first order approximation within each local mapping. It has been tested successfully on a wide variety of parameterizations, including cubic splines and pathologically deformed mappings with different kinds of singularities; for deformed mappings, a reduction of 2 or 3 orders of magnitude in the number of samples is not unusual. The algorithm is general and requires virtually no user intervention: it takes an arbitrary parameterization and the desired number of local mappings as input, and produces an atlas as output. The algorithm is linear in the number of local mappings, though the complexity of the parameterization also affects the performance. For the atlas shown in figure 9a, 1000 local mappings and 5 non-linear deformations were applied, and the pre-computation time was approximately 10 minutes on a SUN4 SPARC-station. Once an atlas is computed for a shape, it can be used with arbitrary textures. Look-ups are made efficient by a hash-table, and the average reconstruction time compares to that of linear interpolation from a 2D grid.

In conclusion, the texture atlas provides a general, efficient, and reliable representation for distorted texture mappings. In particular, it makes the enhanced displacement mapping strategy practical for a wider range of objects.

# 4 Conclusion

The generalized displacement mapping model presented in this paper improves on a classic tool in image synthesis. It allows a new range of geometrically complex shapes to be displacement mapped, reduces the difficulties with self-intersections, allows very large or even infinite displacements, offers easily computable implicit and explicit object representations, and facilitates gaseous effects such as diffuse or glowing objects.

The combination of these properties and the compatibility with all standard texture mapping techniques makes flow mapping a general and useful contribution to state-of-the-art image synthesis.

Currently, the main limitation of the technique is that it is restricted to objects that can be modeled by deforming flow fields. This paper has not attempted an in depth exploration of the set of modeling primitives that can be applied, and further work is needed to illuminate this question. The current implementation supports flows emanating from points, lines , conic intersections, and piecewise quadratic curves, and includes a library of linear and non-linear deformations. However, the quality of the results obtained with these simple tools suggests a rich new subspace of detailed and visually interesting objects.

# 5 Acknowledgments

Thanks to Andy Witkin, Carnegie Mellon University, and the Fulbright Commission.

# References

[1] Alan H. Barr. Global and local deformations of solid primitives. In Hank Christiansen, editor, *Computer Graphics (SIGGRAPH '84 Proceedings)*, volume 18, pages 21–30, July 1984.

[2] Jules Bloomenthal. Polygonization of implicit surfaces. *Computer Aided Geometric Design*, 5(4):341–356, 1988.

[3] Jules Bloomenthal. Simplicit: A simple implicit surface polygonizer. *In Paul Heckbert, editor, Graphics Gems IV*, pages 324–350, Academic Press Inc., Boston, 1994.

[4] Robert L. Cook. Shade trees. In Hank Christiansen, editor, *Computer Graphics (SIGGRAPH '84 Proceedings)*, volume 18, pages 223–231, July 1984.

[5] Manfredo P. do Carmo. *Differential Geometry of Curves and Surfaces*. Prentice-Hall Inc., 1976.

[6] Robert A. Drebin, Loren Carpenter, and Pat Hanrahan. Volume rendering. In John Dill, editor, *Computer Graphics (SIGGRAPH '88 Proceedings)*, volume 22, pages 65–74, August 1988.

[7] James T. Kajiya and Brian P. Von Herzen. Ray tracing volume densities. In Hank Christiansen, editor, *Computer Graphics (SIGGRAPH '84 Proceedings)*, volume 18, pages 165–174, July 1984.

[8] J. W. Patterson, S. G. Hoggar, and J. R. Logie. Inverse displacement mapping. *Computer Graphics Forum*, 10(2):129–139, June 1991.

[9] Bradley A. Payne and Arthur W. Toga. Distance field manipulation of surface models. *IEEE Computer Graphics and Applications*, 12(1):65–71, January 1992.

[10] Darwyn R. Peachey. Solid texturing of complex surfaces. In B. A. Barsky, editor, *Computer Graphics (SIGGRAPH '85 Proceedings)*, volume 19, pages 279–286, July 1985.

[11] Ken Perlin. An image synthesizer. In B. A. Barsky, editor, *Computer Graphics (SIGGRAPH '85 Proceedings)*, volume 19, pages 287–296, July 1985.

[12] Stan Sclaroff and Alex Pentland. Generalized implicit functions for computer graphics. In Thomas W. Sederberg, editor, *Computer Graphics (SIGGRAPH '91 Proceedings)*, volume 25, pages 247–250, July 1991.

[13] Thomas W. Sederberg and Scott R. Parry. Free-form deformation of solid geometric models. In David C. Evans and Russell J. Athay, editors, *Computer Graphics (SIGGRAPH '86 Proceedings)*, volume 20, pages 151–160, August 1986.

[14] John M. Snyder. *Generative Modeling for Computer Graphics and CAD*. Academic Press Inc., 1992.

[15] Greg Turk. Generating textures for arbitrary surfaces using reaction-diffusion. In Thomas W. Sederberg, editor, *Computer Graphics (SIGGRAPH '91 Proceedings)*, volume 25, pages 289–298, July 1991.

[16] Greg Turk. Re-tiling polygonal surfaces. In Edwin E. Catmull, editor, *Computer Graphics (SIGGRAPH '92 Proceedings)*, volume 26, pages 55–64, July 1992.

[17] Jarke J. van Wijk. Spot noise-texture synthesis for data visualization. In Thomas W. Sederberg, editor, *Computer Graphics (SIGGRAPH '91 Proceedings)*, volume 25, pages 309–318, July 1991.

[18] Andrew Witkin and Michael Kass. Reaction-diffusion textures. In Thomas W. Sederberg, editor, *Computer Graphics (SIGGRAPH '91 Proceedings)*, volume 25, pages 299–308, July 1991.

[19] Brian Wyvill, Craig McPheeters, and Geoff Wyvill. Data structure for soft objects. *The Visual Computer*, 2(4):227–234, 1986.

**Figure 10:** Deformed objects. Notice the smooth and discontinuity-free appearance. These objects are represented by a sphere, a few non-linear deformations, and a texture atlas. The texture used for a) is shown in figure 7.

**Figure 11:** Reaction-diffusion texture on a yellow thing.

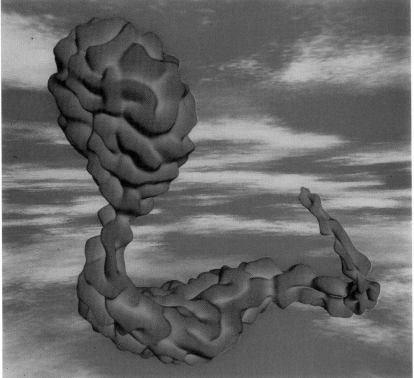

**Figure 12:** Solid textures displaced along a flow emanating from a piecewise quadratic curve.

**Figure 13:** Image texture mapped to a simple curve.

# NC Milling Error Assessment and Tool Path Correction

## Yunching Huang [†] and James H. Oliver [††]

Iowa Center for Emerging Manufacturing Technology
Department of Mechanical Engineering
Iowa State University
Ames, IA

## ABSTRACT

A system of algorithms is presented for material removal simulation, dimensional error assessment and automated correction of five-axis numerically controlled (NC) milling tool paths. The methods are based on a spatial partitioning technique which incorporates incremental proximity calculations between milled and design surfaces. Hence, in addition to real-time animated five-axis milling simulation, milling errors are measured and displayed simultaneously. Using intermediate error assessment results, a reduction of intersection volume algorithm is developed to eliminate gouges on the workpiece via tool path correction. Finally, the view dependency typical of previous spatial partitioning-based NC simulation methods is overcome by a contour display technique which generates parallel planar contours to represent the workpiece, thus enabling dynamic viewing transformations without reconstruction of the entire data structure.

CR Categories and Subject Descriptors: I.3.3 [Computer Graphics]: Picture/Image Generation; I.3.5 [Computer Graphics]: Computational Geometry and Object Modeling; J.6 [Computer-Aided Engineering]: Computer-aided Manufacturing

# 1 INTRODUCTION

Numerically controlled (NC) milling technology is a production process that directs a cutter through a set of prescribed sequential trajectories to fabricate a desired part from raw stock. The technology is capable of producing free-form sculptured surfaces while maintaining tight milling error tolerance. NC milling technology is, therefore, widely used in the production of complicated, high precision, low quantity products such as molds, dies, aerospace parts, etc. These products, especially molds and dies, typi-

cally affect many other subsequent production processes. Thus the influence of NC milling on product development and quality control is significant.

In order to improve the accuracy and reliability of the NC milling process, verification methods are used prior to actual production, to check milling tool paths for potential problems such as milling error, collision, improper machining parameters, tool wear, etc. These problems typically produce undesirable consequences such as unqualified products, machine damage, and personnel injuries. Hence, NC milling verification is a critical procedure for actual production. Traditionally, milling verification is conducted by observing line drawings of tool paths and performing test milling on soft, inexpensive materials. Since these methods are time-consuming, expensive, and prone to error. They are gradually being replaced by analytical methods.

## 1.1 Analytical NC Milling Simulation and Verification Methods

Analytical methods of NC milling simulation and verification are generally distinct from techniques used to model milling phenomenon and formulate milling problems. These methods can be categorized into three approaches — direct solid modeling, discrete vector intersection, and spatial partitioning representation. Each of these approaches has been applied to five-axis NC verification with varying ranges of applicability and degrees of success. The following discussion summarizes the research underlying each approach.

### 1.1.1 Direct solid modeling approach

The direct solid modeling approach is typically implemented by using constructive solid geometry or boundary representation solid modeling systems [21]. Since regularized Boolean set operations are supported in these modeling systems, a milling simulation is implemented via a series of regularized Boolean difference operations to subtract successive tool swept volumes from the workpiece. The result is an explicit solid model of the milled workpiece.

The direct solid modeling approach is theoretically capable of providing accurate NC milling simulation and verification. However, its application remains limited by the complexity of five-axis

[†]  6 Chung-Hsing Street, Hsin-Chuang, Taipei, Taiwan 24209, R.O.C.
e-mail: yhuang@iastate.edu, phone: 011-886-2-991-5796

[††]  2078 H.M. Black Engineering Building, Ames, Iowa 50011-2160
e-mail: oliver@iastate.edu, phone: (515) 294-1745

tool swept volume formulation and the Boolean set operations. Although solid primitives combined by means of regularized Boolean set operators can be displayed via ray casting techniques without explicit evaluation [1,22], ray-intersecting five-axis swept volumes is still a time-consuming process [16].

### 1.1.2 Discrete vector intersection approach

The discrete vector intersection approach assesses milling error by computing distances between a set of pre-selected points on design surfaces and tool swept surfaces [4,10,17]. Each design surface point has an associated vector, typically the outward normal, as shown in Figure 1. Verification is performed by calculating the intersection between the point-vector pairs (rays) and the tool swept surfaces.

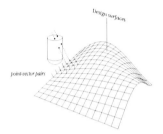

*Figure 1   Illustration of discrete vector intersection approach*

The discrete vector intersection approach is best described in terms of three sub-tasks: discretization, localization, and intersection [17]. The discretization task transforms the design surfaces into a sufficiently dense distribution of surface rays to approximate the original design surfaces. The localization process extracts a plausible subset of rays for each tool motion. Finally, the intersection calculation determines the directed distance (cut value) between each surface point in the subset and the tool swept surfaces, i.e., an indication of the milling error at the surface point. Graphical display of computed milling errors is typically presented by a color map depicting a range of cut values superimposed on the design surfaces. The severity of milling errors on the design surfaces can be visually depicted.

Since this technique addresses only the design surface, the discrete vector intersection approach is not capable of performing milling simulation or computing material removal rate. Also, computation of intersection between rays and the five-axis tool swept volumes is expensive.

### 1.1.3 Spatial partitioning representation approach

The primary disadvantage of the direct solid modeling method for NC milling verification, i.e., the computational complexity of regularized Boolean set operations, motivates the use of the spatial partitioning approach. This method decomposes a solid object into a collection of basic elemental components thus simplify the processes of regularized Boolean set operations to one-dimensional computations. Several proposed implementations differ in the type of basic element used to approximate the solid, including the dexel data structure [20], the G-buffer data structure [19], the octree data structure [3,11], and the ray-representation [13].

These spatial partitioning representation implementations share the advantage of efficient regularized Boolean set operations which facilities realistic milling simulation. Some even provide specialized hardware implementations to increase performance [13,20]. These advantages are very useful in visual detection of gross milling errors and in milling process animation. Furthermore, the volume removed at each tool motion can be easily calculated with user-specified accuracy depending on the size of the basic element. Despite these advantages, however, the spatial partitioning approach has failed to address dimensional milling verification capabilities of comparable complexity and accuracy as those provided by the discrete vector intersection approach.

### 1.2   Motivation

To maintain the advantages and overcome limitations of previous milling simulation and error assessment approaches, this research adopts the spatial partitioning approach as the basis for a comprehensive system which also incorporates the advantages of the discrete vector intersection approach. The goal is to develop a platform independent NC milling verification system that is capable of providing realistic simulation, dimensional error assessment and tool path correction. Finally, a contour display method is introduced to ameliorate the view dependency problem typically associated with application of the spatial partitioning representation. Thus dynamic viewing transformations of the milled and verified part is achieved.

## 2 DEXEL REPRESENTATION OF SOLID GEOMETRY

A dexel representation derived from the dexel data structure of Van Hook [20] is introduced to approximate free-form solid geometry as sets of rectangular solid elements. The dexel representation of a solid is constructed in a dexel coordinate system via ray intersection and is manipulated using dexel-based Boolean set operations. A major distinction between this approach and the original dexel data structure described by Van Hook is that the construction of dexels is not limited by the viewing vector. An independent dexel coordinate system is used to support dynamic viewing transformations. Furthermore, five-axis tool motions, dimensional error assessment, and tool path correction are implemented based on the dexel representation.

### 2.1   Dexel Coordinate System

The left-handed dexel coordinate system is defined by an origin point $O$, a depth vector $v_d$, and an orientation vector $v_o$ in the world coordinate system. Basis vectors of the dexel coordinate system are given by,

$$\begin{bmatrix} v_x \\ v_y \\ v_z \end{bmatrix} = \begin{bmatrix} v_d \times v_o \\ -v_x \times v_d \\ v_d \end{bmatrix} \quad (1)$$

The vectors $v_d$ and $v_o$ are analogous to the vectors typically required to define a viewing transformation in computer graphics applications, i.e., the viewing direction and the view-up vector [7], respectively. In Van Hook's dexel data structure, the depth vector $v_d$ is limited to the viewing direction, thus the view is fixed once dexel data structure has been constructed. In the current implementation, the properties of each dexel are stored relative to an independent dexel coordinate system and can be transformed into either the world coordinate system or the screen coordinate system via coordinate transformations.

Dexel locations are referenced by a two-dimensional grid in the $xy$-plane of the dexel coordinate system, called the *dexel plane*. Each grid point is addressed by an integer pair, e.g., $(I_x\ I_y)$ as illustrated in Figure 2. Assuming the grid points are uniformly spaced along the $x$- and $y$-axis by distances $w_x$ and $w_y$, respectively, the dexel coordinate values of each grid point are computed by $(I_x w_x,\ I_y w_y)$. To simplify dexel operations and display tasks, in this implementation, $w_x$ and $w_y$ are assumed equal, and set to a value $w$.

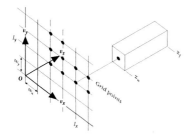

*Figure 2  Dexel coordinate system*

Each dexel is physically a rectangular solid located on a dexel plane grid point extending along the $z$-axis of the dexel coordinate system. The $x$- and $y$-dimension of each dexel is fixed and the length of a dexel is determined by a $z$-depth pair $(z_n, z_f)$, where the subscripts $n$ and $f$ denote near and far values, respectively.

The accuracy of a dexel representation of any object is determined by the dexel plane orientation and the dexel size $w_0$. Two methods are provided for specification of the dexel coordinate system. The first is via interactive selection, i.e., the user chooses a coordinate orientation in which essential areas of the design surfaces are exposed. The second approach automates this procedure by calculating the dexel coordinate system orientation that produces the maximum projected area of the design surfaces on the dexel plane [9].

The size of each dexel face is calculated from a user-specified approximation tolerance, $E$. In this application, the size of the milling tool determines the minimum feature size of the resulting part. Therefore, as shown in Figure 3, the dexel size is computed relative to tool radius, $R$,

$$w = 2R - 2\sqrt{R^2 - E^2} \qquad (2)$$

Finally, the ratio of $E$ to $R$ characterizes the relative accuracy of a tool-based dexel representation. In this implementation, an $E/R$

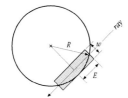

*Figure 3 Maximum dexel approximation error of a circle*

value of 0.2 provides real-time performance at reasonable accuracy. This corresponds to a $w/R$ value of 0.04.

## 2.2  Ray Intersection of Dexel Models

A ray intersection process is used to convert solid objects into the dexel representation. Parallel rays are fired from a sub-set of grid points on the dexel plane to intersect solid objects, and dexels are formed from the segments of rays that are in the interior of the objects. Thus, a set of dexels is generated to represent the object.

The ray intersection procedure also generates the object's outward surface normal corresponding to each dexel face (grid point). The surface normals are used to determine the intensity of each dexel face by computing the scalar product of the normal vector and a light source vector. The light intensity is recorded in the data structure, hence each dexel face may be realistically shaded. In addition to the $z$-depth pair and light intensity, several auxiliary parameters are recorded, including dexel type, (e.g., cutter, workpiece, fixture, etc.) and a pointer to the next dexel, if any, at the grid address.

## 2.3  Regularized Boolean Set Operations on Dexel Models

Regularized Boolean set operations are simple to implement for dexel-based solid objects. Since dexel faces are uniform, the operations are reduced to one-dimensional depth comparisons. The union operation either merges two intersecting dexels if the depths overlap, or, otherwise, constructs a link between the two component dexels. The intersection operation generates a dexel from the overlapping range, or null if there is no intersection. The difference operation removes the intersecting portion. An example of the dexel-based Boolean set operations is shown in Figure 4. Such operations are used intensively for milling simulation.

*Figure 4  Shaded image illustration of Boolean operations*

## 2.4  Display of Dexel Models

The image-space display method proposed by Van Hook [20] is very efficient for visualizing dexel-based objects. This method aligns the depth vector of the dexel coordinate system with the viewing vector of the screen coordinate system, so only the near face of each dexel is visible and each grid point on the dexel plane corresponds to a constant number of pixels on the display device. Figure 5 demonstrates a one-to-one mapping between the dexel plane and the viewing screen, the color index of the nearest dexel at each address is written directly to the frame buffer of the display device. However, since dexels are aligned with the viewing vector,

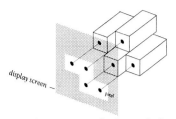

*Figure 5  Image-space display method*

only the front and the back views can be efficiently displayed. To display dexel-based objects in other viewing directions the entire dexel representation must be reconstructed which severely limits applications in manufacturing and engineering.

To overcome this limitation, a *contour display* method is developed to provide an efficient dynamic viewing capability. This method generates contours that connect dexel faces (center points) along constant *x* and *y* grid addresses. Thus two sets of equally spaced planar contours are displayed to represent dexel-based objects. Alternatively, the contour points could be used to construct a triangular mesh for a smoother rendering of dexel-based objects [6,14].

Assuming a constant *x*-contour is to be generated, contour generation proceeds by first selecting a starting dexel that has the smallest *y* coordinate value, then it sequentially traverses through all dexels with the same *x* address. The basic rule of the traversal is, from the current dexel point, step to the next higher grid point in the *y*-direction if the current dexel point is on the near side, otherwise, step to the next lower one. Several cases of dexel point connection, as illustrated in Figure 6, are classified in the contour generation process. In case 1, dexels *A* and *B* overlap and thus the next dexel point to be connected from $A_n$ is $B_n$ (the near dexel point at the next higher *y*). Case 4 is similar to case 1 except it handles the dexel points at the far side. In case 2, there is no dexel at the next higher grid point, thus the far dexel point is connected. Similarly, case 5 handles far dexel points. In case 3, dexel *C* and *D* are connected by dexel *B*, and there is no dexel above *C*, so the next dexel point to be connected from the far side of *C* is the near side of *D*. Case 6 addresses dexel near-to-far connection in a similar fashion.

As illustrated in Figure 6, only six cases can occur during contour generation, however, internal voids that do not connect to any outer contour are possible. Thus after each contour is generated, dexels are scanned to identify dexel points that are not included in the contours. Such dexel points are used as starting points for the contour generation process to create additional internal contours.

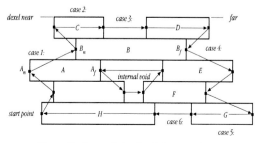

*Figure 6  Cases of dexel point connection*

A typical dexel representation of solid geometry can easily generate thousands of dexel points on the contours. However, not all dexel points are necessary for the contours, e.g., sequential dexel points that have the same color and are nearly colinear can be reduced to two end points. Thus intermediate dexel points are eliminated by a culling process that checks sequential dexel points, of the same color, against a linearity tolerance. Since the dexel model is displayed as a set of planar contours, dynamic graphical viewing of the model is achievable with commonly available graphics hardware. Figure 7 demonstrates an example of the contour display method in which 71% of the original 195,767 dexel points are eliminated, to facilitate efficient dynamic viewing.

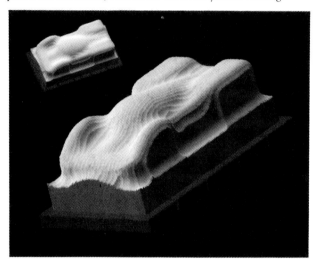

*Figure 7  Contour display of dexel representation*

## 3  NC MILLING SIMULATION AND DIMENSIONAL ERROR ASSESSMENT

The NC milling simulation algorithm utilizes the dexel representation of solid geometry to model cutters, workpiece stock and fixtures in a milling setup. It applies regularized Boolean difference operations to simulate the material removal process between a moving tool and workpiece during the milling process. A moving tool is represented by an *instances of motion* approach which successively updates the workpiece model. Thus the computational expense of ray intersecting a swept volume is eliminated without sacrificing accuracy, and realistic, real-time milling simulation is achieved.

### 3.1  NC Milling Simulation

The instances of motion approach approximates tool swept volumes to dexel resolution by a finite set of tool instances. Let the start and end cutter location (CL) points of a tool motion be denoted by $P$ and $Q$, respectively, and the corresponding unit tool axes by $u$ and $v$. Transforming the CL points and axes into the dexel coordinate system yields $P'$, $Q'$, $u'$, and $v'$, respectively, as shown in Figure 8. To model a tool swept volume using instances of motion, the maximum distance between adjacent instances must be less than the dexel size $w$, so the number of instances $n$ between the CL points is given by,

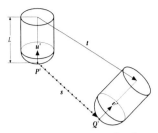

Figure 8 *Computing instances of tool motion*

$$n = \frac{max\,(|s_x|,\ |s_y|,\ |s_z|,\ |t_x|,\ |t_y|,\ |t_z|)}{w} \qquad (3)$$

where $s$ and $t$ are linear sweeping vectors of the tool top and bottom center points in the dexel coordinate system, i.e.,

$$\begin{aligned} s &= Q' - P' \\ t &= s + L\,(v' - u') \end{aligned} \qquad (4)$$

where $L$ is the length of the tool.

The dexel-space tool location and non-normalized tool axis at each instance of motion, denoted by $I^d$, is given by linear interpolation,

$$I_i^d = [\ P' + \frac{i}{n}\,s\ ,u' + \frac{i}{n}\,(v' - u')\ ] \qquad (5)$$

where $i = 1, \ldots, n$. Note that for three-axis motion, the tool axis is fixed so the tool axis interpolation portion of Equation (5) is omitted and the computation of $n$ is simplified. During the simulation, a dexel representation of the tool model is generated at every instance to sequentially update the workpiece by Boolean difference operations thus simulating the material removal process.

An example of three-axis milling simulation representing a typical rough milling process is demonstrated in Figure 9. The computation time for this example is 47 seconds for 3324 instances, or 68.6 instances per second, on a Silicon Graphics (SGI) Indy with a 150MHz MIPS R44000 CPU. Note that the initial shape of the workpiece is not limited to blocks, more complicated parts can be constructed via ray intersection with quadric or sculptured surfaces.

The accuracy of the dexel-based instances of motion approach can be evaluated by comparing it with the results of an equivalent approach based on ray intersection with the actual tool swept volume. Assume that point $P$ is generated from the intersection of a tool swept volume and a ray originating at a dexel grid point [16]. In this intersection process, the member (instance) of the family of tool positions on which $P$ lies is com-

puted. Note that the density of intersection points on the tool swept volume is limited by the density of grid points on the dexel plane. Since the instance of motion approach creates at least as many tool instances as the maximum number of grid points along the tool trajectory, as indicated in Equation (3), the resulting intersections are equivalent to those computed via the swept volume approach.

## 3.2 Milling Error Assessment

An important property of the dexel representation is that dexel points lie on the surface of the represented object. This property results from the ray intersection process to convert objects into a dexel representation. Furthermore, since the dexel coordinate system is fixed for all dexel-based objects, this property also holds for dexel-based objects generated from regularized Boolean set operations. The milling error assessment algorithm exploits this property and is capable of computing the discrepancy between the dexel-based milled surfaces and actual design surfaces with high accuracy.

The algorithm is essentially an inverse formulation of the discrete vector intersection approach, i.e., instead of calculating milling errors from the design surfaces to the tool swept volume, this method computes the errors from the milled part to the design surfaces. Thus the localization and intersection sub-tasks of the former approach are replaced by a surface near point calculation between dexel points and design surfaces. The surface near point calculation is performed only on dexels that are updated during simulation, thus no additional localization effort is needed. Figure 10 illustrates an instance of the verification algorithm, in which a dexel is updated by a regularized Boolean difference operation and the new dexel point $C$ is assessed for milling error by the surface near point calculation algorithm.

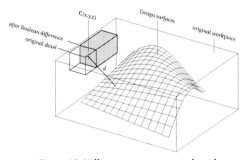

Figure 10 *Milling error assessment algorithm*

### 3.2.1 Surface near point calculation

The surface near point calculation algorithm computes the distance $d$, as shown in Figure 10, between each updated dexel point and the design surfaces. The sign of $d$ is determined by the direction of corresponding surface normal vector. Since the design surfaces are not discretized for error assessment, any of a number of near point algorithms for sculptured surfaces can be employed [2,15,18]. These algorithms are based on the fact that the minimum distance between a space point $P$ and a surface $S$ occurs at a surface point $Q$ at which the vector $(P\text{-}Q)$ is perpendicular to the sur-

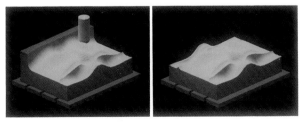

Figure 9 *Three-axis milling simulation*

face tangent plane. This property forms a system of non-linear equations and is solved by using a Newton/Raphson search procedure [12].

Since the robustness and efficiency of the Newton/Raphson method depend on the choice of an initial point, a voxel data structure is implemented as a preprocessing step to supply candidate initial surface points for any given dexel point. The voxel data structure also provides for localization of candidate surfaces for each near point computation, i.e., only those surfaces nearest the given dexel point are stored in the voxel data structure. Hence the minimum distance is computed only among these surfaces.

The initial surface near point lookup algorithm first discretizes each design surface into a set of $N$ points based on a given chordal deviation tolerance [5,8]. These surface points form a triangular mesh that approximates the original surfaces. Each triangle of the mesh is then inserted in a voxel data structure [4,7] constructed in a bounding box of all design surfaces in the world coordinate system. Voxels that intersect with the surface triangular mesh are populated with the surface index and the $(u, v)$ parameters of corresponding vertices. Since more than one vertex may be contained in a voxel, each voxel records the root index of a point list. Thus all surface points in a given voxel may be accessed via a linked list.

Two additional parameters complete the definition of the initial surface near point data structure: the dimension of a voxel and a range of projection. The voxel size affects the efficiency of surface near point computation, i.e., the larger the voxel, the more candidate initial surface points it contains. However, the accuracy of surface near point computation is typically not affected by the voxel size. The following heuristic relationship is generally effective for specification of voxel size $d_v$,

$$d_v = \frac{B_{max}}{\sqrt{N}} \qquad (6)$$

where $B_{max}$ is the maximum dimension of the design surface bounding box.

The range of projection parameter sets upper and lower offset bounds from the triangular mesh, so that only space points within this range are considered for surface near point calculation. To build the range of projection into the voxel data structure, additional voxels on both sides of each triangle are filled with the corresponding surface information if they lie within the range of projection (measured with respect to the triangle normal). Note that the range of projection must be larger than the chordal deviation tolerance to cover hills and valleys missed in surface discretization. An example of the voxel data structure is illustrated in Figure 11 which shows the original design surface and all filled voxels. Only voxels that are close to the surface are filled with surface near point data.

To lookup initial surface near points a space point is converted into integer voxel indices $(I_x, I_y, I_z)$ to obtain the surface near point list of the corresponding voxel address. Surface near point calculations are then performed from each of the initial points in the voxel list, and the minimum of all candidate solutions is taken as the milling error.

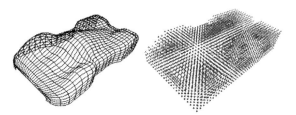

Figure 11 A design surface and associated voxel data

### 3.2.2 Graphical representation of milling errors

The results of milling error assessment are displayed by several hues depicting the depth of cut. A lookup table is prepared to interpret a cut value into a proper hue value for dexel display. The intensity of each hue is obtained from the dexel data structure, (based on normal and light source vectors described above). Figure 12 demonstrates an example of the graphical representation of milling error during a milling simulation process. In this figure, milling error information is encoded and displayed on the milled surface and the color bar shown at the left-hand side depicts the range of milling error. The computation time for this example running on the same SGI Indy is 606 seconds for 4624 instances of motion, or 7.6 instances per second.

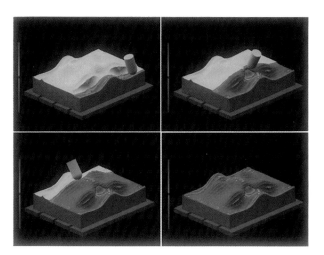

Figure 12 NC milling simulation with error assessment

Assuming a tolerance is given by $[t_l, t_h]$, a gouge is a cut deeper than the lower tolerance bound, and, an undercut is a cut above the higher tolerance bound. In Figure 12, the green color represents errors that are within the tolerance range (-0.01 to 0.01, in this example) relative to the nominal design surfaces; the upper blue colors represent the amount of undercut; and the warmer red colors represent gouge. The tool color (yellow) on the part indicates that the dexel points are outside of a range of interest [17]. The range of interest specifies the maximum and minimum magnitudes of distinguishable undercut and gouge (-0.04 to 0.04 in this case). Hence given a depth of cut, the corresponding color depicting its error is obtained from the color map. For cut values deeper than the lower bound of the range of interest, the color depicting the deepest gouge is used. For undercut larger than the highest bound, the milling tool color is displayed.

Note that the computation time for surface near point calculation is proportional to the number of updated dexels. Hence, a post-process error assessment that computes dimensional milling errors after milling simulation is completed is generally more efficient. The post-process milling error assessment scans through all dexels of the workpiece model and verifies dexel points that have been updated in the milling process. Hence it eliminates unnecessary surface near point computation during the simulation process. The reduction of computational cost can be significant. For example, a result identical to Figure 12 can be obtained in 160 seconds: 119 seconds for five-axis simulation (38.8 instances per second) and 41 seconds for the post-process verification task.

## 4 TOOL PATH CORRECTION

The NC milling error assessment system identifies potential problems in tool paths so that NC programmers can modify the paths to avoid errors. However, these problems require either manually changing the CL data of the tool paths or changing the design surface model and generating new tool paths. Such processes are generally time-consuming, inaccurate, and may introduce more problems. Therefore, to reduce the difficulty of tool path modification, a *reduction of intersecting volume* algorithm is developed to eliminate gouges.

### 4.1 Gouge Elimination

The objective of the reduction of intersection volume algorithm is to reduce the depth of cut to meet the lower limit of a specified tolerance range via tool path modification. The algorithm computes the intersection volume of the tool and workpiece using the regularized Boolean intersection operation, then checks the intersection volume for gouge using the milling error assessment algorithm. Detected gouges are removed by translating the tool position along a *guide vector*. The gouge elimination algorithm is employed recursively to ensure the new CL data is gouge-free.

Assuming $m$ gouged dexel points are detected at an instance of tool motion, the guide vector $G$, as illustrated in Figure 13, is computed by,

$$G = \sum_{i=1}^{m} (d_i - t_l)\, n_i \tag{7}$$

where $d_i$ is the depth of cut at a gouged dexel point, $n_i$ is the outward normal vector generated from the surface near point algorithm at each dexel point, and $t_l$ is the lower bound of the tolerance. If the length of $G$ in Equation (7) is zero or within a range $[-\varepsilon, \varepsilon]$, where $\varepsilon$ is a small value, then the tool axis is used as

the guide vector. Finally, the magnitude of the guide vector is set to the value of the maximum gouge. The tool is translated by G and the process is repeated iteratively until the gouge is eliminated.

An illustration of the gouge elimination algorithm is shown in Figure 14. In this figure, a tool motion is defined by a pair of CL points $P$ and $Q$, and it is assumed that the start point $P$ is gouge-free. The algorithm first iteratively eliminates the gouge at $Q$, and hence generates a new CL point $Q'$. The entire tool motion between $P$ and $Q'$ is then evaluated and the first gouge point is discovered at $S$. Let $S'$ be the CL point corresponding to $S$ that avoids the gouge and denote the previous instance of motion as $R$ ($R$ is gouge-free). The remaining tool motion is broken into two motions and the gouge elimination algorithm is applied recursively to each segment. Thus segments $R$ through $S'$ and $S'$ through $Q'$ are recursively checked for gouges and subdivided, until the entire motion is gouge free.

An application of this algorithm is demonstrated in Figure 15. A Comparison with Figure 12, shows that the gouges are completely eliminated and a modified tool path has been generated to replace the original. The computation time for this example is 799 seconds for 4716 instances, or 5.9 instances per second. During the gouge elimination process, 138 gouge CL points are detected and 426 iterations are taken to correct them, or 3.1 iterations per gouge elimination. Note that the total instances of motion is increased (originally 4624 instances the original tool path) in the corrected tool path.

*Figure 14 A 2D example of the gouge elimination algorithm*

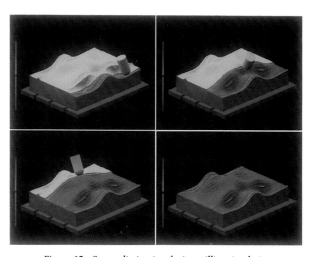

*Figure 15   Gouge elimination during milling simulation*

## 5 CONCLUSION AND FUTURE WORK

An integrated system is presented for material removal simulation, dimensional error assessment and automated correction of gen-

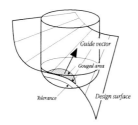

*Figure 13   Gouge elimination using the guide vector*

eral five-axis NC milling tool paths. The error assessment algorithm combines the advantages of the discrete vector intersection approach and the spatial partitioning representation method, and thus is capable of efficiently simulating and precisely verifying milling tool paths. The dexel-based geometry is constructed in a coordinate system that is independent of screen space, and a contour generation algorithm supports dynamic viewing transformations. Based on the milling error assessment results, a gouge elimination algorithm is developed.

One opportunity for future research is to incorporate an incremental triangulation algorithm [6,14] to generate a polygonal mesh over the emerging workpiece. This may facilitate a smoother rendering for dynamic viewing than the current contour display implementation. In addition, research is underway toward incorporation of tool feed rate with the volume and geometry of material removed from the workpiece to assess machine dynamic performance.

## ACKNOWLEDGEMENT

Research support provided by the Office of Naval Research (Grant No. N00014-92-J-4092) is gratefully acknowledged. The authors are also grateful to the Iowa Center for Emerging Manufacturing Technology and the Iowa State University Research Foundation[1]. Special thanks are due to Professors James Bernard, Martin Vanderploeg, and Lin-Lin Chen for their constructive comments and advice. The authors also thank Patrick Bergan, James Schlosser, and Kevin Renze for their support during paper preparation.

## REFERENCES

1.  Atherton, P. R., "A Scan-Line Hidden Surface Removal Procedure for Constructive Solid Geometry," Proceedings of SIGGRAPH '83. In *Computer Graphics,* 17, 3 (July 1983), pp. 73-82

2.  Barnhill, R. E. and Kersey, S. N., "A Marching Method for Parametric Surface/Surface Intersection," *Computer Aided Geometric Design*, 7, 1990, pp. 257-280

3.  Brunet P. and Navazo, I, "Solid Representation and Operation Using Extended Octrees," *ACM Transactions on Graphics*, 9, 2, April 1990, pp. 170-197

4.  Chang, K. Y. and Goodman, E. D., "A Method for NC Tool Path Interference Detection for A Multi-Axis Milling System," *ASME Control of Manufacturing Process*, DSC-Vol. 28/PED-Vol. 52, 1991, pp. 23-30

5.  Drysdale, R. L. and Jerard R. B., "Discrete Simulation of NC Machining," *Algorithmica, Special Issue on Computational Geometry* 4, 1, 1989, pp. 33-60

6.  Ekoule, A. B., Peyrin, F. C., and Odet, C. L., "A Triangulation Algorithm From Arbitrary Shaped Multiple Planar Contours," *ACM Transactions on Graphics*, 10, 2, April 1991, pp. 182-199

7.  Foley, J. D., Van Dam, A., Feiner, S. K. and Hughes, J. F., *Computer Graphics Principles and Practice*, 1990, Addison-Wesley Publishing Company, New York, NY

8.  Huang, Y. and Oliver, J. H., "Non-Constant Parameter NC Tool Path Generation on Sculptured Surfaces," *Proceedings of ASME International Computers in Engineering*, 1992, pp. 411-419

9.  Huang, Y. *Dimensional verification and correction of five-axis numerically controlled tool paths*, Ph.D. Dissertation, 1993, Iowa State University, 1993

10.  Jerard, R. B., Hussaini, S. Z., Drysdale, R. L., and Schaudt, B., "Approximate Methods for Simulation and Verification of Numerically Controlled Machining Programs," *The Visual Computer*, 4, 1989, pp. 329-348

11.  Kawashima, Y., Itoh, K., Ishida, T, Nonaka, S., and Ejiri, K, "A Flexible Quantitative Method for NC Machining Verification Using a Space-Division Based Solid Model," *The Visual Computer*, 7, 1991, pp. 149-157

12.  Kincaid, D. and Cheney, W., *Numerical Analysis, Mathematics of Scientific Computing*, 1991, Brooks/Cole Publishing Company, Pacific Grove, CA

13.  Menon, J. P. and Robinson, D. M., "Advanced NC Verification Via Massively Parallel Raycasting: Extensions to New Phenomena and Geometric Domains," *ASME Manufacturing Review*, 6, 2, June 1993, pp. 141-154

14.  Meyers, D., Skinner, S., and Sloan, K., "Surfaces from Contours," *ACM Transactions on Graphics*, 11, 3, July 1992, pp. 228-258

15.  Mortenson, M. E., *Geometric Modeling*, 1985, John Wiley & Sons Inc., New York, NY

16.  Narvekar, A., Huang, Y. and Oliver, J. H., "Intersection of Rays with Parametric Envelope Surfaces Representing Five-Axis NC Milling Tool Swept Volumes," *Proceedings of ASME Advances in Design Automation* Vol 2, 1992, pp. 223-230

17.  Oliver, J. H. and Goodman, E. D., "Direct Dimensional NC Verification," *Computer Aided Design*, 22, 1, 1990, pp. 3-10

18.  Pegna, J. and Wolter, F.-E., "Designing and Mapping Trimming Curves on Surfaces Using Orthogonal Projection," *Proceedings of ASME Advances in Design Automation*, Computer Aided and Computational Design, DE-Vol. 23-1, 1990, pp. 235-245

19.  Saito, T. and Takahashi, T., "NC Machining with G-buffer Method," Proceedings of SIGGRAPH '91. In *Computer Graphic,* 25, 4 (July 1991), pp. 207-216

20.  Van Hook, T., "Real-Time Shaded NC Milling Display," Proceedings of SIGGRAPH '86. In *Computer Graphics* 20, 4 (August 1986), pp. 15-20

21.  Voelcker, H. B. and Hunt, W. A., "The Role of Solid Modeling in Machine-Process Modeling and NC Verification," SAE Technical Paper No810195, Feb. 1981

22.  Wang, W.P. and Wang K.K., "Geometric Modeling for Swept Volume of Moving Solids," *IEEE Computer graphics and Applications*, 6, 12, 1986, pp. 8-17

1.  The ISU Research Foundation has applied for a US patent on this technology and has licensed it to Arete Software Company.

# Piecewise Smooth Surface Reconstruction

Hugues Hoppe[*]    Tony DeRose[*]    Tom Duchamp[†]    Mark Halstead[‡]
Hubert Jin[§]    John McDonald[§]    Jean Schweitzer[*]    Werner Stuetzle[§]

University of Washington
Seattle, WA 98195

## Abstract

We present a general method for automatic reconstruction of accurate, concise, piecewise smooth surface models from scattered range data. The method can be used in a variety of applications such as reverse engineering — the automatic generation of CAD models from physical objects. Novel aspects of the method are its ability to model surfaces of arbitrary topological type and to recover sharp features such as creases and corners. The method has proven to be effective, as demonstrated by a number of examples using both simulated and real data.

A key ingredient in the method, and a principal contribution of this paper, is the introduction of a new class of piecewise smooth surface representations based on subdivision. These surfaces have a number of properties that make them ideal for use in surface reconstruction: they are simple to implement, they can model sharp features concisely, and they can be fit to scattered range data using an unconstrained optimization procedure.

**CR Categories and Subject Descriptors:** I.3.5 [Computer Graphics]: Computational Geometry and Object Modeling. - surfaces and object representations; J.6 [Computer-Aided Engineering]: Computer-Aided Design (CAD); G.1.2 [Approximation]: Spline Approximation.

**Additional Keywords:** Geometric modeling, surface fitting, shape recovery, range data analysis, subdivision surfaces.

## 1 Introduction

In this paper, we present a new representation for piecewise smooth surfaces of arbitrary topological type,[1] and a method for fitting such surface models to scattered range data, where neither the topological type of the surface, its geometry, nor the location of its sharp features are known in advance. We also present examples showing that the surface representation and fitting method are useful for im-

portant applications such as *reverse engineering* — the automatic generation of CAD models from laser range data.

In previous work [4, 10, 11], we developed a method for fitting compact, accurate piecewise linear surfaces to scattered range data. The generalization to piecewise smooth surfaces is a natural and necessary extension. Many objects of interest are piecewise smooth; their surfaces consist of smoothly curved regions that meet along sharp curves and at sharp corners. Modeling such objects as piecewise linear surfaces requires a large number of triangles, whereas curved surface models can provide both a more accurate and a more compact representation of the true surface. It is critical, however, to use a surface representation that is capable of explicitly modeling sharp features. Using an everywhere smooth surface representation to model sharp features either results in a large number of surface elements, or in a poor geometric fit, as illustrated in Color Plate 1m. Additionally, the surface representation should be capable of modeling surfaces of arbitrary topological type.

The most popular smooth surface representations are tensor product NURBS. However, NURBS can only represent surfaces of arbitrary topological type by partitioning the model into a collection of individual NURBS patches. Adjacent patches must then be explicitly stitched together using geometric continuity conditions [6]. A large number of parameters (the B-spline coefficients) are therefore introduced, most of which are constrained by the continuity conditions. As a consequence, fitting NURBS in general requires high-dimensional constrained optimization.

Subdivision surfaces, first introduced by Doo/Sabin [5] and Catmull/Clark [3], offer a promising alternative. They are capable of modeling everywhere smooth surfaces of arbitrary topological type using a small number of unconstrained parameters.

Our surface representation is a generalization of the subdivision surface scheme introduced by Loop [13]. Loop's scheme, like all subdivision schemes to date, produces tangent plane continuous surfaces of arbitrary topological type. A principal contribution of our work is to show that it is possible to locally modify Loop's subdivision rules to model sharp features such as creases and corners. The modified subdivision rules also model boundary curves, as shown for instance in the spout of the Utah teapot (Color Plate 2).

Our reconstruction method consists of three major phases, the first two of which have been described elsewhere:

**1. Estimation of topological type** [10]: Given an unorganized set of points (Color Plate 1j) on or near some unknown surface (Color Plate 1i), phase 1 constructs a triangular mesh consisting of a relatively large number of triangles (Color Plate 1k). This phase determines the topological type of the surface and produces an initial estimate of the geometry.

**2. Mesh optimization** [4, 11]: Starting with the output of phase 1, phase 2 reduces the number of triangles and improves the fit to

---

[*]Department of Computer Science and Engineering, FR-35

[†]Department of Mathematics, GN-50

[‡]Apple Computer

[§]Department of Statistics, GN-22

   This work was supported in part by IBM, Silicon Graphics Inc., the Xerox Corporation, and the National Science Foundation under grants CCR-8957323 and DMS-9103002.

[1]The topological type of a surface refers to its genus, the presence of boundaries, etc.

the data (Color Plate 1l). Our approach to this phase is to cast the problem as optimization of an energy function that explicitly models the trade-off between the competing goals of concise representation and good fit. The free variables in the optimization procedure are the number of vertices in the mesh, their connectivity, and their positions.

**3. Piecewise smooth surface optimization**: Phase 3 is the subject of this paper. Starting with the optimized mesh (a piecewise linear surface) produced in phase 2, this phase fits an accurate, concise piecewise smooth subdivision surface (Color Plate 1o), again by optimizing an energy function that trades off conciseness and fit to the data. The phase 3 optimization varies the number of vertices in the control mesh, their connectivity, their positions, and the number and locations of sharp features. The automatic detection and recovery of sharp features in the surface is an essential part of phase 3. Our piecewise smooth subdivision surface scheme is introduced in Section 3. The optimization problem and algorithm are described in Section 4.

Phase 2 can in principle be eliminated, but has proven to be convenient for two reasons: first, is it computationally more efficient to optimize over a piecewise linear surface in the early stages of optimization, and second, initial estimates of sharp features are much more robust when obtained from the phase 2 mesh.

The principal evidence for our method's success is its application to a wide variety of data, including simulated and real laser scanner data. A number of examples, shown in the Color Plates, are discussed in Section 5.

## 2  Background on subdivision surfaces

A subdivision surface is defined by repeatedly refining an initial control mesh as indicated in Color Plates 1a–1d. (Formally, a *mesh* $M$ is a pair $(K, V)$, where: $K$ is a *simplicial complex* specifying the connectivity of the vertices, edges, and faces, and thus determining the topological type of the mesh; $V = \{\mathbf{v}_1, \ldots, \mathbf{v}_m\}$, $\mathbf{v}_i \in \mathbf{R}^3$ is a set of vertex positions defining the shape of the mesh in $\mathbf{R}^3$.) The first and most popular subdivision surface schemes, introduced by Doo/Sabin [5] and Catmull/Clark [3], are based on quadrilateral meshes, and generalize biquadratic and bicubic tensor product B-splines, respectively. A subdivision scheme based on triangles is more convenient for our purposes. We use a generalization of the triangular scheme introduced by Loop [13], as it is the simplest known scheme leading to tangent plane smooth surfaces.

**2.1  Loop's subdivision:** Loop's subdivision scheme is a generalization of $C^2$ quartic triangular B-splines. The refinement step proceeds by splitting each triangular face into four subfaces. The vertices of the refined mesh are then positioned using weighted averages of the vertices in the unrefined mesh. Formally, starting with the initial control mesh $M = M^0$, each subdivision step carries a mesh $M^r = (K^r, V^r)$ into a refined mesh $M^{r+1} = (K^{r+1}, V^{r+1})$ where the vertices $V^{r+1}$ are computed as affine combinations of the vertices of $V^r$. Some of the vertices of $V^{r+1}$ naturally correspond to vertices of $V^r$ — these are called *vertex points*; the remaining vertices in $V^{r+1}$ correspond to edges of the mesh $M^r$ — these are called *edge points*. Let $\mathbf{v}^r$ denote a vertex of $V^r$ having neighbors $\mathbf{v}_1^r, \ldots, \mathbf{v}_n^r$ as shown in Figure 1a. Such a vertex is said to have valence $n$. Let $\mathbf{v}_i^{r+1}$ denote the edge point of $V^{r+1}$ corresponding to the edge $\mathbf{v}^r \mathbf{v}_i^r$, and let $\mathbf{v}^{r+1}$ be the vertex point of $V^{r+1}$ associated with $\mathbf{v}^r$. The positions of $\mathbf{v}^{r+1}$ and $\mathbf{v}_i^{r+1}$ are computed according to the subdivision rules

$$
\begin{aligned}
\mathbf{v}^{r+1} &= \frac{\alpha(n)\mathbf{v}^r + \mathbf{v}_1^r + \cdots + \mathbf{v}_n^r}{\alpha(n) + n} \\
\mathbf{v}_i^{r+1} &= \frac{3\mathbf{v}^r + 3\mathbf{v}_i^r + \mathbf{v}_{i-1}^r + \mathbf{v}_{i+1}^r}{8}, \quad i = 1, \ldots, n
\end{aligned} \tag{1}
$$

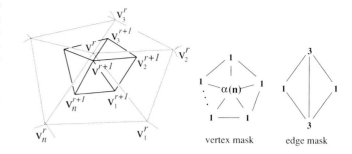

Figure 1: The neighborhood around a vertex $\mathbf{v}^r$ of valence $n$ (left); Loop's vertex mask (center); Loop's edge mask (right).

where subscripts are taken modulo $n$, and where $\alpha(n) = \frac{n(1-a(n))}{a(n)}$ with $a(n) = \frac{5}{8} - \frac{(3+2\cos(2\pi/n))^2}{64}$. Affine combinations such as those in Equation 1 can be nicely visualized by diagrams called *masks*, as shown in Figure 1.

**2.2  Computing surface points and tangent vectors:** Loop's surfaces in particular, and subdivision surfaces in general, are defined only as the limit of an infinite refinement process. In most cases closed form expressions for the limit surfaces are not known, but somewhat surprisingly, various properties of subdivision surfaces, such as exact points on the surface and exact tangent planes, can nonetheless be computed.

To study the properties of subdivision surfaces, it is convenient to write Equation 1 in matrix form as

$$
\begin{aligned}
(\mathbf{v}^{r+1}, \mathbf{v}_1^{r+1}, \ldots, \mathbf{v}_n^{r+1})^T &= S_n(\mathbf{v}^r, \mathbf{v}_1^r, \ldots, \mathbf{v}_n^r)^T \\
&= S_n^{r+1}(\mathbf{v}^0, \mathbf{v}_1^0, \ldots, \mathbf{v}_n^0)^T
\end{aligned} \tag{2}
$$

where superscript $T$ denotes matrix transpose. The matrix $S_n$ is called the *local subdivision matrix* [5].

As $r \to \infty$, each point $\mathbf{v}^r$ approaches a point on the limit surface. Equation 2 suggests that the limit point can be obtained by analyzing the eigenstructure of the local subdivision matrix. Indeed, the limit point can be expressed as an affine combination of the initial vertex positions [8]:

$$
\mathbf{v}^\infty = \frac{\ell_1 \mathbf{v}^0 + \ell_2 \mathbf{v}_1^0 + \cdots \ell_{n+1}\mathbf{v}_n^0}{\ell_1 + \ell_2 + \cdots \ell_{n+1}}
$$

where $(\ell_1, \ldots, \ell_{n+1})$ is the dominant left eigenvector of $S_n$. For Loop's surfaces this affine combination can be expressed as the *position mask* shown in Figure 2 [13].

Eigenanalysis of the local subdivision matrix can also be used to establish smoothness. It can be shown, for instance, that Loop's surfaces are indeed tangent plane continuous [13, 19]. Moreover, Halstead *et al.* [8] show that the tangent vectors to the limit surface at $\mathbf{v}^\infty$ can be computed using the two left eigenvectors of $S_n$ corresponding to the second largest eigenvalue (this eigenvalue has multiplicity 2). For Loop's surfaces the vectors

$$
\begin{aligned}
\mathbf{u}_1 &= c_1 \mathbf{v}_1^0 + c_2 \mathbf{v}_2^0 + \cdots + c_n \mathbf{v}_n^0 \\
\mathbf{u}_2 &= c_2 \mathbf{v}_1^0 + c_3 \mathbf{v}_2^0 + \cdots + c_1 \mathbf{v}_n^0,
\end{aligned} \tag{3}
$$

with $c_i = \cos(2\pi i/n)$ span the tangent plane of the surface. Their cross product therefore gives an exact normal vector to the surface which is useful, for example, to create Phong-shaded renderings such as those shown in the Color Plates. The formulas given in Equation 3 can be visualized as the *tangent masks* shown in Figure 2.

Eigenanalysis will again be used in Section 3.2 to study the properties of piecewise smooth subdivision surfaces.

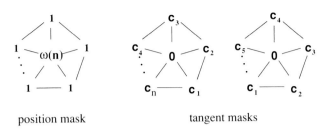

position mask                    tangent masks

Figure 2: Masks for computing positions and tangents to Loop's surfaces, where $\omega(n) = \frac{3n}{8a(n)}$, and where $c_i = \cos(2\pi i/n)$.

# 3 Piecewise smooth subdivision surfaces

Fitting smooth surfaces to non-smooth objects often produces unacceptable results. As an example, fitting an everywhere smooth subdivision surface to the points in Color Plate 1j produces the surface shown in Color Plate 1m.

In this section we develop new subdivision rules to accurately model objects with tangent discontinuities. These subdivision rules produce commonly occurring sharp features that we call *creases*, *corners*, and *darts*, as illustrated in Color Plate 1e–h. A crease is a tangent line smooth curve along which the surface is $C^0$ but not $C^1$; a corner is a point where three or more creases meet; finally, a dart is an interior point of a surface where a crease terminates. Although this list of sharp features is not exhaustive (for instance, we cannot model a cone or two coincident darts), it has proven sufficient for the examples we have encountered.

Subdivision surfaces produced by the new rules are tangent plane smooth everywhere except along creases and at corners. A detailed theoretical analysis of the behavior along creases and at corners is beyond the scope of this paper and will be presented in subsequent work. In Section 3.2 we summarize the relevant results of the analysis.

**3.1 Subdivision rules:** To model creases, corners, and darts using subdivision surfaces, a subset $L$ of edges in the simplicial complex $K$ is tagged as *sharp*. We refer to the pair $(K, L)$ as a *tagged simplicial complex*. The subdivision masks are modified so that tangent plane continuity across sharp edges is relaxed. Boundary curves are produced by tagging all boundary edges of the mesh as sharp.[2] In the subdivision process, edges created through refinement of a sharp edge are tagged as sharp.

Subdivision rules at crease vertices must be chosen carefully in order for the surface on each side of the crease to have a well-defined tangent plane at each point along the crease. Similar considerations apply to corners and darts. It should be noted that the specific subdivision masks we use are by no means unique. Indeed, there is considerable flexibility in selecting them. The masks we present here are simple and have worked well in practice, but further research should be done to explore other alternatives.

We classify vertices into five different types based on the number and arrangement of incident edges. A *smooth vertex* is one where the number of incident sharp edges $s$ is zero; a *dart vertex* has $s = 1$; a *crease vertex* has $s = 2$; and a *corner vertex* has $s > 2$. Crease vertices are further classified as *regular* and *non-regular* depending on the arrangement of smooth edges. An interior crease vertex is regular if it has valence 6 with exactly two smooth edges on each side of the crease; a boundary crease vertex is regular if it has valence 4. All other crease vertices, whether interior or boundary, are non-regular.

Figure 3 shows our vertex and edge subdivision masks. As in-

---

[2]In related work, Nasri [15, 16] developed a method to model boundary curves in a Doo-Sabin subdivision procedure by augmenting the control mesh rather than by modifying the subdivision masks.

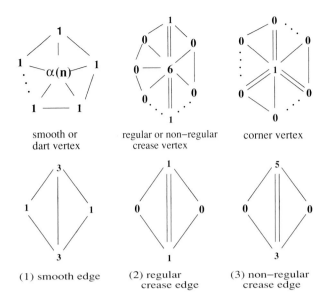

smooth or              regular or non-regular          corner vertex
dart vertex                crease vertex

(1) smooth edge        (2) regular             (3) non–regular
                           crease edge             crease edge

Figure 3: Vertex and edge subdivision masks. Double lines denote sharp edges.

|  | dart | reg crease | non-reg crease | corner |
|---|---|---|---|---|
| dart | 1 | 1 | 1 | 1 |
| reg crease | 1 | 2 | 3 | 3 |
| non-reg crease | 1 | 3 | 2 | 2 |
| corner | 1 | 3 | 2 | 2 |

Table 1: Assignment of sharp edge subdivision masks as a function of the types of the two incident vertices. Masks are numbered as shown in Figure 3.

dicated in the figure, vertex subdivision masks are chosen based on the type of the vertex.

We use three different types of edge subdivision masks. A smooth edge (one not tagged as sharp) is subdivided using the smooth edge mask. The mask used to subdivide a sharp edge depends on the types of the incident vertices as shown in Table 1. When applying edge subdivision mask 3, the regular crease vertex incident to the edge receives the weight 5.

Those familiar with B-spline curve subdivision may recognize that the crease subdivision masks have been designed so that the sharp edges converge to uniform cubic B-splines except near non-regular crease and corner vertices. The zeros in the crease subdivision masks completely decouple the behavior of the surface on one side of the crease from the behavior on the other side.

**3.2 Computing surface points and tangent vectors:** As explained in Section 2.2, limiting points and tangent planes can be computed using masks. These masks are determined by the eigenstructure of local subdivision matrices, which depend on the type of the vertex (smooth, dart, regular and non-regular crease, and corner).

**Smooth and dart vertices:** At smooth and dart vertices, our local subdivision matrix is identical to Loop's matrix. The position and tangent masks are therefore as in Figure 2.

**Crease vertices:** Since the zeros in the crease subdivision masks (Figure 3) decouple the behavior of the surface on one side of the crease from the behavior on the other side, we can decouple the analysis, focusing on a local subdivision matrix that describes the behavior on one side of the crease. As indicated earlier, boundary curves are modeled as one-sided creases.

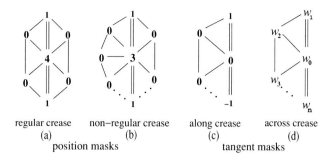

regular crease  non-regular crease  along crease  across crease
(a)           (b)                  (c)          (d)
position masks                     tangent masks

Figure 4: Position and tangent masks for crease vertices.

In the following, we assume that the vertices $\mathbf{v}_1^0, ..., \mathbf{v}_n^0$ surrounding one side of a crease vertex $\mathbf{v}^0$ of valence $n$ are indexed as shown in Figure 4d.

At a regular crease vertex, the dominant left eigenvector of the local subdivision matrix yields the position mask shown in Figure 4a, meaning that

$$\mathbf{v}^\infty = \frac{1}{6}(4\mathbf{v}^0 + \mathbf{v}_1^0 + \mathbf{v}_n^0)$$

is a point on the limit crease. Similarly, when the crease vertex is non-regular, we obtain the position mask shown in Figure 4b.

For crease vertices of valence 4 or higher, the subdivision rules described in the previous section give rise to well-defined tangent planes on both sides of the crease.[3] As for smooth vertices, tangent masks are again determined by the two left eigenvectors corresponding to the 2nd and 3rd largest eigenvalues. For both regular and non-regular crease vertices, a tangent along the crease is obtained by the tangent mask shown in Figure 4c. To compute a tangent vector transverse to the crease, we use the tangent mask shown in Figure 4d, where the weights are defined as follows. At a regular crease vertex, the valence is 4 and the mask is given by $(w_0, ..., w_4) = (-2, -1, 2, 2, -1)$. At a non-regular crease vertex, for $n \geq 4$, $w_0 = 0$, $w_1 = w_n = \sin\theta$, and $w_i = (2\cos\theta - 2)(\sin(i-1)\theta)$ for $i = 2, ..., (n-1)$ where $\theta = \pi/(n-1)$; for $n = 3$, $(w_0, ..., w_3) = (-1, 0, 1, 0)$; finally, for $n = 2$, $(w_0, w_1, w_2) = (-2, 1, 1)$.

**Corner vertices:** The subdivision masks at a corner vertex are much like those at a crease vertex. If the corner vertex has $s$ sharp edges, the local subdivision matrix decouples into $s$ separate matrices (or $s - 1$ matrices if the corner vertex lies on a boundary), each describing a smooth region of the surface. Since the corner vertex does not move during subdivision, it is itself a point on the surface (equivalently, $(1, 0, ..., 0)$ is the dominant left eigenvector). The tangent masks in this case reduce to simple differences: $(1, -1, 0, ..., 0)$ and $(1, 0, 0, ..., -1)$.

# 4 Fitting piecewise smooth subdivision surfaces

In this section, we describe an algorithm for phase 3 of the reconstruction problem as outlined in Section 1.

The input to phase 3 is an unstructured collection $X = \{\mathbf{x}_1, ..., \mathbf{x}_n\}$ of data points scattered in three dimensions, together with the mesh obtained from phase 2. Edges are initially tagged as sharp if the dihedral angle of the faces incident to the edge is above a threshold (e.g. 40 degrees). The output of phase 3 is a concise piecewise smooth surface that accurately fits the data.

As in phase 2 (mesh optimization), we cast the problem as one of minimizing an energy function that captures the competing goals of conciseness and accuracy.

---

[3]The techniques we use to prove smoothness do not apply to vertices of valence 2 and 3, although numerical experiments suggest that tangent planes are well-defined in these cases, too.

## 4.1 Definition of the energy function:

The energy function is given by

$$E(K, L, V) = E_{dist}(K, L, V) + c_{rep}m + c_{sharp}e$$

where $E_{dist}$ is the total squared distance from the data points to the subdivision surface; $c_{rep}m$ is a penalty on the number $m$ of vertices; and $c_{sharp}e$ is a penalty on the number $e$ of sharp edges.

The parameter $c_{rep}$ controls the trade-off between conciseness and fidelity to the data and should be set by the user. The parameter $c_{sharp}$ controls the tradeoff between smoothness of the surface and fidelity to the data. Setting $c_{sharp} = c_{rep}/5$ has worked well in all our examples.

We minimize the energy function over the space $\mathcal{M}$ of *tagged meshes* $M = (K, L, V)$ where $K$ is of the same topological type as the phase 2 mesh, and $L$ is the subset of sharp edges of $K$. The goal is to find the tagged mesh in $\mathcal{M}$ that minimizes $E$.

The reader familiar with Hoppe *et al.* [11] will notice the absence of a "spring energy" term, which was introduced to guide the mesh optimization algorithm into a good local energy well. For the type of examples shown in the Color Plates, that energy term has been unnecessary in phase 3.

## 4.2 Minimization:

Our algorithm for energy minimization closely parallels the one presented in Hoppe *et al.* [11]. We decompose the problem into two nested subproblems: an inner, continuous optimization over the control vertex positions $V$ for fixed $(K, L)$, and an outer, discrete optimization over $(K, L)$.

### 4.2.1 Optimization over $V$ for fixed $(K, L)$:

We want to determine

$$E(K, L) = \min_V E_{dist}(K, L, V) + c_{rep}m + c_{sharp}e,$$

the minimum energy for fixed $(K, L)$. Since $m$ and $e$ are fixed, this is equivalent to minimizing the distance energy over the vertex positions $V$. In the following, $V$ is treated as an $m \times 3$ matrix whose rows contain the $(x, y, z)$ coordinates of the vertices.

Computing the distance energy $E_{dist}$ involves projecting the data points $\mathbf{x}_i$ onto the subdivision surface $S$. This is not feasible in practice as the surface is defined only as the limit of an infinite process. Instead, we project onto a piecewise linear approximation $\tilde{S}$ to $S$ obtained by subdividing the original mesh $r$ times to produce a refined mesh $M^r$, then pushing all the vertices of $M^r$ to their limit positions using the position masks. (Typically we use $r = 2$.) Since each of the vertices of $M^r$ can be written as an affine combination of the vertices $V$ of $M$ (using the subdivision rules), and since the limit position of any vertex can be obtained using the position masks, each of the vertices of $\tilde{S}$ can be written as an affine combination of the vertices $V$. That is, each vertex $\tilde{\mathbf{v}}$ of $\tilde{S}$ can be written as $\tilde{\mathbf{v}} = \mathbf{y}V$, where the entries of the row vector $\mathbf{y}$ can be computed by combining the effects of $r$-fold subdivision followed by application of a position mask. Moreover, since $\tilde{S}$ is piecewise linear, every point on $\tilde{S}$ — not just the vertices — can be written as an affine combination of the vertices $V$.

For each data point $\mathbf{x}_i$, let $\mathbf{w}_i$ be the closest point on $\tilde{S}$. As argued above, $\mathbf{w}_i$ can be written as $\mathbf{y}_i V$, meaning that $E_{dist}$ can be expressed as

$$E_{dist} = \sum_{i=1}^n \|\mathbf{x}_i - \mathbf{y}_i V\|^2 .$$

This expression for $E_{dist}$ is quadratic in $V$. Hence, for fixed $\mathbf{y}_i$, optimizing over $V$ is a linear least-squares problem. Moreover, the vectors $\mathbf{y}_i$ are sparse since the subdivision rules are local.

This suggests an iterative minimization scheme alternating between the following steps:

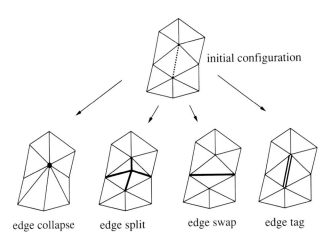

initial configuration

edge collapse    edge split    edge swap    edge tag

Figure 5: Elementary mesh transformations.

1. For fixed $V$, compute the projections $\mathbf{y}_i V$ of the data points $\mathbf{x}_i$ onto $\tilde{S}$.

2. For fixed $\mathbf{y}_1, \cdots, \mathbf{y}_n$, optimize $E_{dist}$ over $V$.

Step 2, which is a sparse linear least squares problem, can be solved as described in [11].

**4.2.2 Optimization over $(K, L)$:** Our algorithm for solving the outer minimization problem, minimizing $E(K, L)$, again closely parallels the algorithm of [11].

We define a set of four elementary mesh transformations, *edge collapse*, *edge swap*, *edge split*, and *edge tag*, taking a tagged simplicial complex $(K, L)$ to another tagged simplicial complex $(K', L')$, as shown in Figure 5. The first three transformations are discussed in [11]. The fourth transformation, edge tag, is a toggle that either adds an edge to the set $L$ of sharp edges, or removes one from it. These four transformations are complete in the sense that they form a transitive set of transformations on the set of tagged simplicial complexes (of a given topological type).

A *legal move* is the application of one of these elementary transformations to an edge of $K$ that leaves the topological type of $K$ unchanged. The criterion for determining whether a move is legal is given in [11]. Our goal is to find a sequence of legal moves taking us from an initial tagged simplicial complex $(K_0, L_0)$ to one for which a minimum of $E$ is achieved.

This is accomplished via a variant of random descent: We form a candidate set, initially consisting of all edges of $K$. We randomly select an edge from the candidate set and try the four elementary transformations in turn until we find a legal move $(K, L) \Rightarrow (K', L')$ with $E(K', L') < E(K, L)$. If none is found, we remove the edge from the candidate set; otherwise, we accept the move and expand the candidate set to include edges whose vertices were affected by the transformation. The process is repeated until the candidate set is empty.

Due to the expense of computing $E(K', L')$ for each speculative move, the idealized algorithm just described is too inefficient to be of practical use. We therefore replace the exact computation of $E(K', L')$ by an approximate one.

Our approximate computation of $E$ is based on the observation that the effect of an elementary transformation on the geometry of the subdivision surface is localized to a neighborhood of the affected edge. Thus, when speculating upon an elementary transformation, we only optimize over the positions of control vertices in a neighborhood of the affected edge, and recompute projections of data points originally projecting onto the neighborhood of $\tilde{S}$ supported by these control vertices. For details, see [9, 12].

## 5 Results

The main motivation for moving from piecewise linear to piecewise smooth surfaces is to obtain more accurate and concise models of point sets. The last row of Color Plate 1 and the first 2 rows of Color Plate 2 show results of our experiments with range data. The leftmost column shows the original point sets; the second column shows the optimized piecewise linear surfaces obtained from phase 2 (mesh optimization); the third column shows the optimized tagged meshes resulting from phase 3 (subdivision surface optimization), with sharp edges $L$ highlighted in yellow; finally, the rightmost column shows the subdivision surfaces associated with these control meshes. Modeling surfaces such as the one shown in Color Plate 1t using NURBS would be very cumbersome and would likely require significant user intervention. In contrast, our subdivision surface approach is both simple and automatic.

Our method can also be used for the approximation of known surfaces. To this end, we first generate a set of points on the surface to be approximated, and then run the three phases of the reconstruction procedure. The lower three rows of Color Plate 2 show the resulting approximations of a dense triangular mesh, a swept surface, and a NURBS surface. Since the NURBS teapot was defined as a set of mutually intersecting patches, we had to manually remove some of the sample points. Note how this teapot is modeled as a single subdivision surface of genus 1 (the handle of the teapot makes it homeomorphic to a torus), without resort to explicit continuity constraints or trimming curves.

Another advantage of optimizing using a piecewise smooth model is that the resulting surface not only fits the data more accurately than a piecewise linear model, but also is a better predictor of the true underlying surface. As a validation, we sampled a different set of 10,000 points from the swept surface (knot). As shown in Table 2, even though the subdivision control mesh has a fifth as many vertices as the mesh from phase 2, the subdivision surface fits the new set of points with one fourth the distance energy.

| | $c_{rep}$ | $m$ # vertices | $E_{dist}$ original points | new points |
|---|---|---|---|---|
| phase 2 | $10^{-5}$ | 975 | .00308 | .00934 |
| phase 3 | $10^{-5}$ | 363 | .00042 | .00054 |
| | $10^{-4}$ | 207 | .00216 | .00251 |

Table 2: Validation results

| Color Plate | $n$ | $c_{rep}$ ph2 | $c_{rep}$ ph3 | $m$ (#vertices) ph2 | ph3 | $\frac{ph2}{ph3}$ | $E_{dist}$ ph2 | ph3 | $\frac{ph2}{ph3}$ | Time hrs |
|---|---|---|---|---|---|---|---|---|---|---|
| 1j | 4,102 | $10^{-5}$ | $10^{-5}$ | 163 | 112 | 1.5 | $4.86\ 10^{-4}$ | $1.53\ 10^{-4}$ | 3.2 | 0.9 |
| 1q | 30,937 | $10^{-5}$ | $10^{-5}$ | 891 | 656 | 1.4 | $4.93\ 10^{-3}$ | $4.14\ 10^{-3}$ | 1.2 | 7.7 |
| 2.1 | 16,864 | $10^{-5}$ | $10^{-5}$ | 262 | 156 | 1.7 | $2.19\ 10^{-3}$ | $1.33\ 10^{-3}$ | 1.6 | 2.8 |
| 2.2 | 12,745 | $10^{-5}$ | $10^{-5}$ | 685 | 507 | 1.4 | $4.05\ 10^{-3}$ | $3.85\ 10^{-3}$ | 1.1 | 4.1 |
| 2.3 | 16,475 | $10^{-5}$ | $10^{-4}$ | 184 | 87 | 2.1 | $9.68\ 10^{-4}$ | $1.65\ 10^{-3}$ | 0.6 | 2.2 |
| 2.4 | 10,000 | $10^{-5}$ | $10^{-4}$ | 975 | 205 | 4.8 | $3.08\ 10^{-3}$ | $2.32\ 10^{-3}$ | 1.3 | 2.2 |
| 2.5 | 26,103 | $10^{-5}$ | $10^{-4}$ | 623 | 152 | 4.1 | $3.17\ 10^{-3}$ | $2.62\ 10^{-3}$ | 1.2 | 5.3 |

Table 3: Parameter settings and optimization results

In most examples, the representation constant $c_{rep}$ was set to $10^{-5}$, the same value that was used in phase 2. As indicated in Table 3, the control meshes obtained from phase 3 are more concise than those of phase 2, and at the same time, the subdivision surfaces fit the points more accurately than the triangular meshes of phase 2. Because the point sets for the swept surface and the NURBS teapot are sampled without error from piecewise smooth surfaces, we could afford to raise $c_{rep}$ in order to produce very concise control meshes, while still reducing $E_{dist}$.

The phase 3 execution times listed in Table 3 were obtained

on a DEC Alpha workstation. In all test cases we set $c_{sharp} = c_{rep}/5$ and the number of subdivision iterations (referred to in Section 4.2.1) to $r = 2$.

## 6 Related work

There is a large body of literature on reconstructing surfaces of fixed topological type. Bolle and Vemuri [1] review methods for fitting embeddings of a rectangular domain. Schudy and Ballard [22, 23], Brinkley [2], and Sclaroff and Pentland [24] fit embeddings of a sphere. Schmitt et al. [20, 21] fit embeddings of a cylinder to data from cylindrical range scans. Goshtasby [7] works with embeddings of cylinders and tori.

There is also extensive literature on smooth interpolation of triangulated data of arbitrary topological type using parametric surface patches; see Lounsbery et al. [14] for a survey. These schemes are designed to interpolate sparse data, rather than to fit dense, noisy point sets of the type obtained from range scanners.

Two recent articles describing methods for fitting either piecewise linear or everywhere smooth surfaces of arbitrary topological type are Veltkamp [27] and Szeliski et al. [26].

We are not aware of any previous method for fitting piecewise smooth surface models of arbitrary topological type to dense, noisy data, although one could imagine developing such a procedure based on a piecewise smooth triangular patch method such as Nielson's side-vertex patch [17], or Shirman and Séquin's split domain scheme [25].

In many respects, our work can be considered a generalization to surfaces of the parametric curve fitting method of Plass and Stone [18]: they cast the fitting process as non-linear optimization, and they also produce piecewise smooth, rather than everywhere smooth models.

## 7 Summary and future work

We have described a piecewise smooth surface reconstruction procedure that produces concise and accurate surface models from unorganized points. Our method automatically determines the topological type of the surface, and the presence and location of sharp features. A key ingredient of the method is a new subdivision surface scheme that allows the modeling of surface features such as corners, boundaries, creases, and darts. Finally, we have demonstrated the effectiveness of the subdivision surface optimization procedure in recovering piecewise smooth models from range data, and in approximating other surface forms such as swept surfaces and NURBS.

There are a number of areas for future research, including:

1. Development of subdivision rules that can model a wider variety of sharp features such as cones, multiple darts meeting at a smooth vertex, and darts meeting at a corner.

2. Development of alternative optimization algorithms that allow direct control over maximum error.

3. Speedup of the algorithm and implementations on parallel architectures.

4. Development of an on-line algorithm for use in real-time data capture.

5. Experimentation with sparse, non-uniform data.

**Acknowledgments**   We wish to thank the Ford Motor Co. for providing the cross section data, Technical Arts Co. for the laser range data, Rob Sharein for the swept surface, and Pratt & Whitney for the dense tessellation of the gas turbine engine component.

## References

[1] Ruud M. Bolle and Baba C. Vemuri. On three-dimensional surface reconstruction methods. *IEEE Trans. Pat. Anal. Mach. Intell.*, 13(1):1–13, January 1991.

[2] James F. Brinkley. Knowledge-driven ultrasonic three-dimensional organ modeling. *IEEE Trans. Pat. Anal. Mach. Intell.*, 7(4):431–441, July 1985.

[3] E. Catmull and J. Clark. Recursively generated B-spline surfaces on arbitrary topological meshes. *Computer-Aided Design*, 10:350–355, September 1978.

[4] T. DeRose, H. Hoppe, T. Duchamp, J. McDonald, and W. Stuetzle. Fitting of surfaces to scattered data. *SPIE*, 1830:212–220, 1992.

[5] D. Doo and M. Sabin. Behaviour of recursive division surfaces near extraordinary points. *Computer-Aided Design*, 10(6):356–360, September 1978.

[6] G. Farin. *Curves and Surfaces for Computer Aided Geometric Design.* Academic Press, 3rd edition, 1992.

[7] Ardeshir Goshtasby. Surface reconstruction from scattered measurements. *SPIE*, 1830:247–256, 1992.

[8] Mark Halstead, Michael Kass, and Tony DeRose. Efficient, fair interpolation using Catmull-Clark surfaces. *Computer Graphics (SIGGRAPH '93 Proceedings)*, pages 35–44, August 1993.

[9] H. Hoppe, T. DeRose, T. Duchamp, H. Jin, J. McDonald, and W. Stuetzle. Piecewise smooth surface reconstruction. TR 94-01-01, Dept. of Computer Science and Engineering, University of Washington, January 1994.

[10] H. Hoppe, T. DeRose, T. Duchamp, J. McDonald, and W. Stuetzle. Surface reconstruction from unorganized points. *Computer Graphics (SIGGRAPH '92 Proceedings)*, 26(2):71–78, July 1992.

[11] H. Hoppe, T. DeRose, T. Duchamp, J. McDonald, and W. Stuetzle. Mesh optimization. *Computer Graphics (SIGGRAPH '93 Proceedings)*, pages 19–26, August 1993.

[12] Hugues Hoppe. *Surface reconstruction from unorganized points.* PhD thesis, Department of Computer Science and Engineering, University of Washington, In preparation.

[13] Charles Loop. Smooth subdivision surfaces based on triangles. Master's thesis, Department of Mathematics, University of Utah, August 1987.

[14] Michael Lounsbery, Stephen Mann, and Tony DeRose. Parametric surface interpolation. *IEEE Computer Graphics and Applications*, 12(5):45–52, September 1992.

[15] Ahmad H. Nasri. Polyhedral subdivision methods for free-form surfaces. *ACM Transactions on Graphics*, 6(1):29–73, January 1987.

[16] Ahmad H. Nasri. Boundary-corner control in recursive-subdivision surfaces. *Computer Aided Design*, 23(6):405–410, July-August 1991.

[17] G. Nielson. A transfinite, visually continuous, triangular interpolant. In G. Farin, editor, *Geometric Modeling: Algorithms and New Trends*, pages 235–246. SIAM, 1987.

[18] Michael Plass and Maureen Stone. Curve-fitting with piecewise parametric cubics. *Computer Graphics (SIGGRAPH '83 Proceedings)*, 17(3):229–239, July 1983.

[19] Ulrich Reif. A unified approach to subdivision algorithms. Mathematisches Institut A 92-16, Universität Stuttgart, 1992.

[20] F. Schmitt, B.A. Barsky, and W. Du. An adaptive subdivision method for surface fitting from sampled data. *Computer Graphics (SIGGRAPH '86 Proceedings)*, 20(4):179–188, 1986.

[21] F. Schmitt, X. Chen, W. Du, and F. Sair. Adaptive $G^1$ approximation of range data using triangular patches. In P.J. Laurent, A. Le Mehaute, and L.L. Schumaker, editors, *Curves and Surfaces*. Academic Press, 1991.

[22] R. B. Schudy and D. H. Ballard. Model detection of cardiac chambers in ultrasound images. Technical Report 12, Computer Science Department, University of Rochester, 1978.

[23] R. B. Schudy and D. H. Ballard. Towards an anatomical model of heart motion as seen in 4-d cardiac ultrasound data. In *Proceedings of the 6th Conference on Computer Applications in Radiology and Computer-Aided Analysis of Radiological Images*, 1979.

[24] S. Sclaroff and A. Pentland. Generalized implicit functions for computer graphics. *Computer Graphics (SIGGRAPH '91 Proceedings)*, 25(4):247–250, July 1991.

[25] L. Shirman and C. Séquin. Local surface interpolation with Bézier patches. *Computer Aided Geometric Design*, 4(4):279–296, 1988.

[26] R. Szeliski, D. Tonnesen, and D. Terzopoulos. Modeling surfaces of arbitrary topology with dynamic particles. In *1993 IEEE Computer Society Conference on Computer Vision and Pattern Recognition*, pages 82–87. IEEE Computer Society Press, 1993.

[27] R.C. Veltkamp. 3D computational morphology. *Computer Graphics Forum*, 12(3):116–127, 1993.

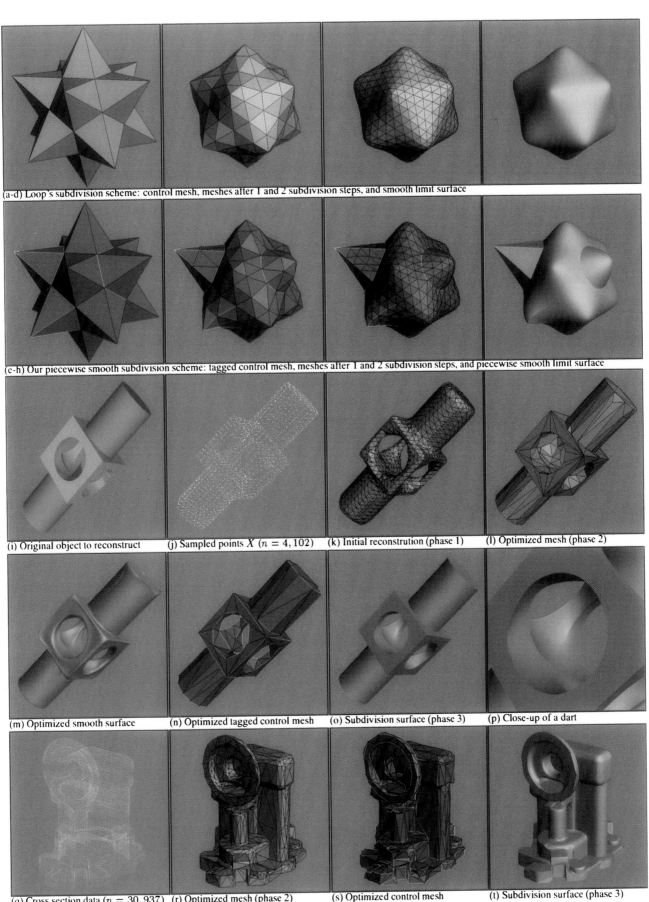

(a-d) Loop's subdivision scheme: control mesh, meshes after 1 and 2 subdivision steps, and smooth limit surface

(e-h) Our piecewise smooth subdivision scheme: tagged control mesh, meshes after 1 and 2 subdivision steps, and piecewise smooth limit surface

(i) Original object to reconstruct  (j) Sampled points $X$ $(n = 4,102)$  (k) Initial reconstruction (phase 1)  (l) Optimized mesh (phase 2)

(m) Optimized smooth surface  (n) Optimized tagged control mesh  (o) Subdivision surface (phase 3)  (p) Close-up of a dart

(q) Cross section data $(n = 30,937)$  (r) Optimized mesh (phase 2)  (s) Optimized control mesh  (t) Subdivision surface (phase 3)

Color Plate 1: Examples of Loop's subdivision scheme, our piecewise smooth subdivision scheme, phases 1–3 of surface reconstruction on a simulated data set, and surface reconstruction with real scanned data.

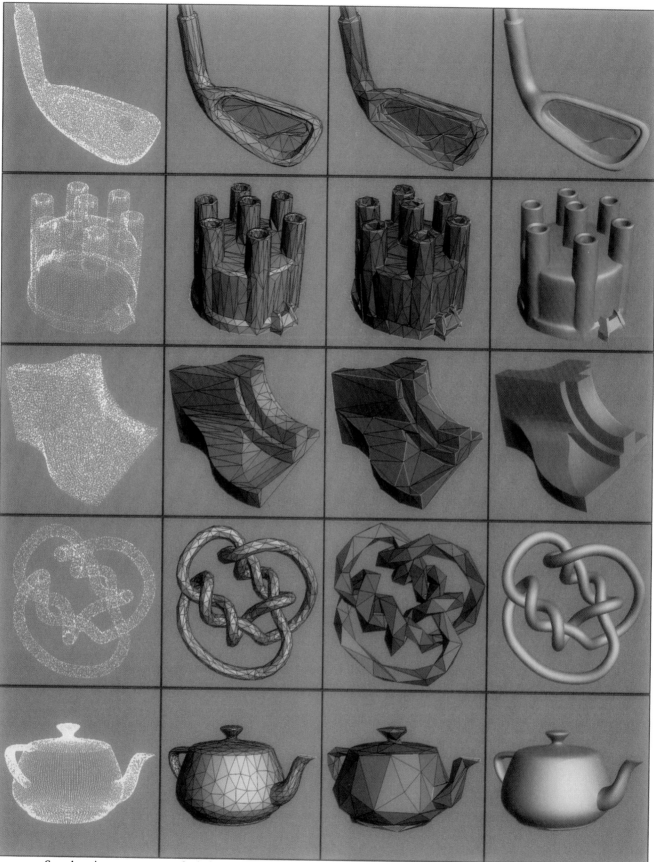

Sample points      Optimized mesh (phase 2)      Optimized control mesh      Subdivision surface (phase 3)

Color Plate 2: Top two rows show examples of surface reconstruction from range data; bottom three rows show subdivision surface approximations to existing surfaces (a dense mesh, a swept surface, and a NURBS surface).

# Smooth Spline Surfaces over Irregular Meshes

## Charles Loop
## Apple Computer, Inc.

## Abstract

An algorithm for creating smooth spline surfaces over irregular meshes is presented. The algorithm is a generalization of quadratic B-splines; that is, if a mesh is (locally) regular, the resulting surface is equivalent to a B-spline. Otherwise, the resulting surface has a degree 3 or 4 parametric polynomial representation. A construction is given for representing the surface as a collection of tangent plane continuous triangular Bézier patches. The algorithm is simple, efficient, and generates aesthetically pleasing shapes.

**CR Categories and Subject Descriptors:** I.3.5 [**Computer Graphics**]: Computational Geometry and Object Modeling - *Curve, Surface, Solid, and Object representations;* J.6 [**Computer-Aided Engineering**]: Computer-Aided Design (CAD); G.1.2 [**Approximation**]: Spline Approximation.

**Additional Key Words and Phrases:** Computer-aided geometric design, B-spline surfaces, Triangular patches, Geometric continuity, Irregular meshes, Aribitrary topology.

## 1 Introduction

The B-spline paradigm for modeling smooth surfaces is limited by the requirement that the control point mesh must be organized as a regular rectangular structure. Ignoring this requirement by collapsing control mesh edges leads to surfaces with ambiguous surface normals and degenerated parameterizations. A more general method is to construct a surface from a mesh of points without degeneracy. By constructing this surface using piecewise polynomials, familiar algebraic tools can be brought to bear for analysis. This is the approach taken in this paper.

A new type of spline surface is presented for modeling surfaces of arbitrary topological type by smoothly approximating an irregular control mesh. The advantage of this technique over existing schemes is simplicity, efficiency, and piecewise polynomial form. The spline surface is simply constructed by computing a triangular Bézier representation of a network of surface patches. Being of

Author's address: Apple Computer, Inc., 1 Infinite Loop, MS:301-3J, Cupertino, CA 95014; loop@apple.com

fairly low polynomial degree (at most 4), these patches are efficient to compute and evaluate. The spline surface is smooth, since the patches fit together with tangent plane continuity. Another advanage of this scheme is a close relationship to quadratic B-spline surfaces. In regular regions of the mesh, the surface is equivalent to a B-spline represented by bi-quadratic Bézier patches. This property can represent a considerable savings in time and space, since in practice control meshes often have few irregularities.

The spline algorithm takes an irregular control mesh as input. A new refined mesh is created with more faces, vertices, and edges than the original. The new mesh has a simpler structure since every vertex has exactly four edges incident upon it. Next, an intermediate form called a "quad-net" is constructed corresponding to each vertex of the refined mesh. The quad-nets characterize local 4-sided regions of the surface in a uniform way. Finally, a group of four quartic triangular patches are constructed for each quad-net as output. The union of these patches constitutes a smooth spline surface.

This paper is organized as follows: previous work is surveyed in § 2. Relevant background material, including Bézier forms and B-splines are covered in § 3. The spline algorithm is presented as a sequence of pipeline stages in § 4. A detailed development of the smoothness constraints used to construct the surface is presented in § 5. Concluding remarks are found in § 6. Special techniques for dealing with meshes with boundaries (i.e., meshes that are not closed) are given in Appendix A.

## 2 Previous Work

The earliest attempts to overcome the topological limitations of B-spline surfaces were based on the refinement principle[1, 4]. The idea is to refine, or subdivide, an irregular mesh by creating a new mesh, with more faces and vertices, that approximates the old. By repeating this process, a smooth surface is formed in the limit. Subdivision algorithms are conceptually quite simple and generally generate nice shapes. However, subdivision surfaces do not admit an analytic form, complicating their use in many practical applications. Despite this, algorithms based on subdivision surfaces continue to appear[7].

Gregory patches have been used to interpolate the vertices of an irregular mesh[2]. These patches have singularities at corners and are not polynomial. Other non-polynomial surface patches used to define B-spline-like surfaces over irregular meshes include the 3 and 5-sided patches defined in[17], and $n$-sided S-patches[9, 12]. S-patch based schemes can be inefficient (in both time and space) for $n > 5$ or 6. A generalization of quartic triangular B-splines to strictly triangular meshes using degree six polynomial patches appears in [11]. Other schemes use tensor product polynomials, but require the connectivity of the control mesh to be restricted[6, 18].

More recent approaches to the problem assume that irregular vertices (a vertex with other than 4 edges incident upon it) are isolated. That is, every irregular vertex is surrounded by one or more layers of quadrilaterals and regular vertices. G-splines[8, 16] take this approach. Severals schemes by Peters[13, 14, 15] isolate irregularities by applying one or more refinement steps to an irregular mesh. The approach taken in this paper is similar. The distinguishing features are that only one refinement step is required, and the mesh does not have to be preprocessed to have excusively 3 or 4-sided faces. The trade-off for this simplification is fewer patches of higher degree. The patches computed here are at most polynomial degree 4, as opposed to degree 3 in [10, 13, 14].

# 3  Background

This section gives a brief review of Bézier curves and surfaces, and B-spline surfaces. Consult [5] for additional details.

## 3.1  Bézier forms

A degree $d$ *Bézier curve* is defined

$$B(t) = \sum_{i=0}^{d} \mathbf{b}_i B_i^d(t),$$

where $t \in [0, 1]$, the points $\mathbf{b}_i$ form the Bézier *control polygon*, and

$$B_i^d(t) = \binom{d}{i}(1 - t)^{d-i} t^i,$$

are degree $d$ Berstein polynomials. As a convenient notation, a Bézier curve will be identified by its control polygon represented by the vector $[\mathbf{b}_0, \mathbf{b}_1, \ldots, \mathbf{b}_d]$.

A degree $r$ by $s$ *tensor product Bézier patch* is defined

$$B(u, v) = \sum_{i=0}^{r} \sum_{j=0}^{s} \mathbf{b}_{ij} B_i^r(u) B_j^s(v),$$

where $u, v \in [0, 1]$, and the $\mathbf{b}_{ij}$ are a rectangular array of points forming the Bézier *control net*.

A degree $d$ *Bézier triangle* is defined

$$B(u, v) = \sum_{i+j+k=d} \mathbf{b}_{ijk} B_{ijk}^d(u, v),$$

where $u, v, (1-u-v) \in [0, 1]$, $ij$, and $k$ are non-negative integers that sum to $d$, the $\mathbf{b}_{ijk}$ form a triangular Bézier control net, and

$$B_{ijk}^d(u, v) = \binom{d}{ijk}(1 - u - v)^i u^j v^k,$$

are the degree $d$ bi-variate Bernstein polynomials where $\binom{d}{ijk}$ is the trinomial coefficient $\frac{d!}{i!j!k!}$.

Bézier surfaces are a convenient representation for individual polynomial patches. Algorithms for rendering, raytracing, and surface intersection often utilize the Bézier form. When constructing smooth composite surfaces consisting of several patches, satisfying the necessary smoothness constraints among Bézier surfaces can be quite complex. In this setting, it is preferable to use B-spline surfaces.

## 3.2  B-splines

A *tensor product B-spline surface* is defined

$$S(u, v) = \sum_{i} \sum_{j} \mathbf{d}_{ij} N_i^r(u) N_j^s(v),$$

where the $\mathbf{d}_{ij}$ form a rectangular control mesh and the $N_k^d$ are order $d$ (degree $d - 1$) B-spline *basis functions*. Each basis function is defined over a partition of the real axis called a *knot vector* (see [5] for details).

Two particular properties of B-splines are of interest here. First, by introducing a new knot between each pair of existing knots, the control mesh is refined, or subdivided, without changing the shape of the surface. Second, B-splines are piecewise polynomial, therefore it is possible to represent a B-spline surface as a collection of individual polynomial patches. The spline surface presented in this paper is closely related to quadratic B-spline surfaces with uniform knots.

A quadratic B-spline can be represented as a composite of bi-quadratic tensor product Bézier patches. A single such patch is constructed corresponding to each vertex $\mathbf{d}_{ij}$ of the control mesh as illustrated in Figure 1. The corner points $\mathbf{b}_{00}$, $\mathbf{b}_{20}$, $\mathbf{b}_{02}$, and $\mathbf{b}_{22}$ are found as the centroids of the four faces surrounding $\mathbf{d}_{ij}$. The points $\mathbf{b}_{10}$, $\mathbf{b}_{01}$, $\mathbf{b}_{21}$, and $\mathbf{b}_{12}$ are found as midpoints of the four edges incident on $\mathbf{d}_{ij}$, and the point $\mathbf{b}_{11}$ is equivalent to $\mathbf{d}_{ij}$.

The refinement algorithm for quadratic B-splines involves computing a new vertex corresponding to each {vertex, face} pair of the original mesh. The new vertices are found as weighted averages of the points belonging to each face of the original mesh. For the quadratic B-spline case, these weights (going around a face) are $\{\frac{9}{16}, \frac{3}{16}, \frac{1}{16}, \frac{3}{16}\}$. The newly created vertices are then connected to form the faces of the refined control mesh.

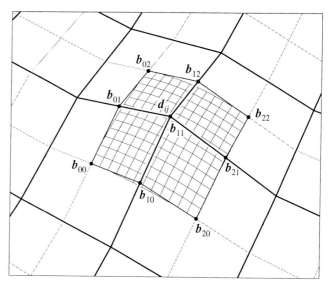

Figure 1: The bi-quadratic Bézier patch corresponding to the B-spline control mesh point $\mathbf{d}_{ij}$.

A B-spline surface is smooth because adjacent patches share positions and first derivatives at all points along common boundaries. This notion of matching derivatives along patch boundaries is sufficient because the domain of each patch lies in a single $uv$ plane. Therefore, a B-spline surface is a deformation of this domain plane. For this reason, B-spline surfaces can only model shapes that are topologically planar[†].

---

[†]B-spline surfaces may also be defined over cylinders and tori, as these domains can tile the plane.

Under a less restrictive definition, a surface is considered *smooth* if at all points it has a continuous, well-defined tangent plane. This notion is known as first order *geometric continuity*[3] and denoted $G^1$. In the next section, a spline surface is created by constructing a collection of patches over independent domains such that the union of this collection is $G^1$.

## 4 Constructing the Spline

Constructing the spline surface begins with a user-defined *control mesh* denoted $\mathcal{M}^0$. A control mesh is a collection of vertices, edges, and (not necessarily planar) faces that can intuitively be thought of as a polygonal surface that may, or may not, be closed.[‡] The term *valance* is used to denote the number of edges incident on a vertex.

The spline surface is constructed in the following stages:

Input: *irregular control mesh*

1. refine mesh

2. construct quad-nets

3. construct patches

Output: *collection of triangular patches*

The mesh $\mathcal{M}^0$ is passed to a refinement procedure that creates a new mesh $\mathcal{M}^1$. The purpose of the refinement procedure is to isolate irregularities. After the refinement step, the mesh $\mathcal{M}^1$ is used to construct a set of *quad-nets*. The quad-nets characterize the surface locally, and provide a uniform structure for the third and final step. From each quad-net, a collection of four quartic triangular Bézier patches is constructed and output. The details of each step are described in the next three sections, followed by some examples.

### 4.1 Mesh Refinement

The first step takes a user-defined control mesh $\mathcal{M}^0$ and creates a new refined mesh $\mathcal{M}^1$. The vertices of $\mathcal{M}^1$ are constructed to corresponded to each {vertex, face} pair of $\mathcal{M}^0$. Let $F$ be a face of $\mathcal{M}^0$ consisting of vertices $\{P_0, P_1, \ldots, P_{n-1}\}$ with centroid $O$ (the average of the $P_i$'s). The point $P_i'$ of $\mathcal{M}^1$ corresponding to $\{P_i, F\}$ is found by

$$P_i' = \tfrac{1}{4}O + \tfrac{1}{8}P_{i-1} + \tfrac{1}{2}P_i + \tfrac{1}{8}P_{i+1},$$

where all subscripts are taken modulo $n$.

The faces of $\mathcal{M}^1$ are constructed corresponding to a vertex, face, or edge of $\mathcal{M}^0$. Each $k$-valant vertex of $\mathcal{M}^0$ will generate a $k$-sided face belonging to $\mathcal{M}^1$. Similarly, each $n$-sided face of $\mathcal{M}^0$ will generate an $n$-sided face belonging to $\mathcal{M}^1$. Finally, each edge of $\mathcal{M}^0$ will generate a 4-sided face belonging to $\mathcal{M}^1$. This construction is illustrated in Figure 2. Note that all the vertices of $\mathcal{M}^1$ are 4-valant, and every non-4-sided face is surrounded by 4-sided faces. Special consideration for vertices and edges that belong to the boundary of $\mathcal{M}^0$ can be found in Appendix A.

**Remark :** The refinement rule given here is equivalent to quadratic B-spline refinement for regular meshes. A more general construction of the refined mesh points due to Peters[13] associates a pair of scalar values $u$ and $v$ with each point $P_i'$ such that

$$P_i' = (1-u)(1-v)O + \tfrac{(1-u)v}{2}P_{i-1} + \tfrac{u+v}{2}P_i + \tfrac{u(1-v)}{2}P_{i+1}.$$

The parameters $u$ and $v$ are similar to knots of a B-spline in that they may be used to locally adjust the shape of the surface.

[‡]More technically, a control mesh is a tessellated, oriented 2-manifold (possibly with boundary).

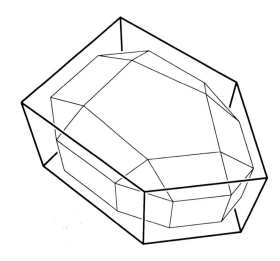

Figure 2: Mesh refinement: The vertices of the refined mesh $\mathcal{M}^1$ (thin lines) correspond to {vertex,face} pairs of the original mesh $\mathcal{M}^0$ (bold lines).

### 4.2 Quad-Nets

In the second step, 16 points and a pair of integers collectively referred to as a *quad-net* are constructed corresponding to each vertex of $\mathcal{M}^1$. Though quad-nets are in many ways like the control nets of Bézier patches, their purpose here is only as an intermediate stage between the refined mesh and the final triangular Bézier surface patches. A quad-net and its labeling scheme are illustrated in Figure 3.

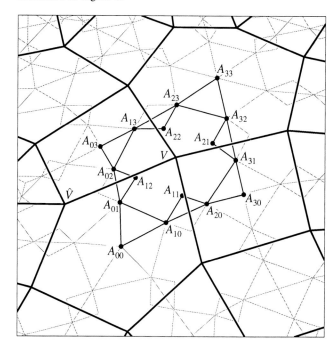

Figure 3: The quad-net corresponding to the vertex $V$ of $\mathcal{M}^1$.

A quad-net locally characterizes a piece of the spline surface bounded by the four cubic Bézier curves $[A_{00}, A_{10}, A_{20}, A_{30}]$, $[A_{30}, A_{31}, A_{32}, A_{33}]$, $[A_{33}, A_{23}, A_{13}, A_{03}]$, and $[A_{30}, A_{02}, A_{01}, A_{00}]$. The corners $A_{00}$, $A_{30}$, $A_{03}$ and $A_{33}$ lie at the centroids of the four faces surrounding a vertex $V$. The interior points $A_{11}$, $A_{12}$, $A_{21}$, and $A_{22}$ help specify the tangent plane along each of the four boundary curves.

In order to ensure that the spline surface is $G^1$, some constraints must be satisfied between the points of a pair of adjacent quad-nets. These constraints are as follows:

$$(1 - c)A_{00} + cA_{01} = \tfrac{1}{2}A_{10} + \tfrac{1}{2}\hat{A}_{10}, \qquad (1)$$

$$\tfrac{1}{2}A_{01} + \tfrac{1}{2}A_{02} = \tfrac{1}{2}A_{12} + \tfrac{1}{2}\hat{A}_{12}, \qquad (2)$$

$$A_{03} = \tfrac{1}{2}A_{13} + \tfrac{1}{2}\hat{A}_{13}, \qquad (3)$$

where $\hat{A}_{10}$, $\hat{A}_{12}$ and $\hat{A}_{13}$ are points of an adjacent quad-net, and $c$ is a scalar to be determined. Similar constraints apply for the other three boundary curves in a symmetric manner. Justification for Constraints (1), (2), and (3) is provided in § 5.

Constraint (1) must hold between all pairs of adjacent quad-nets that share the point $A_{00}$. This implies that all quad-net points surrounding $A_{00}$ must be co-planar. The following theorem is the key to constructing quad-net points that satisfy this requirement:

**Theorem 4.1** *Let $P_0, \ldots, P_{n-1} \in \Re^3$ be a set of points in general position. The set of points $Q_0, \ldots, Q_{n-1}$ found by*

$$Q_i = \tfrac{1}{n}\sum_{j=0}^{n-1} P_j(1 + \beta(\cos\tfrac{2\pi(j-i)}{n} + \tan\tfrac{\pi}{n}\sin\tfrac{2\pi(j-i)}{n})), \quad (4)$$

*satisfy*

$$(1 - \cos\tfrac{2\pi}{n})O + \cos\tfrac{2\pi}{n}Q_i = \tfrac{1}{2}Q_{i-1} + \tfrac{1}{2}Q_{i+1}, \qquad (5)$$

*where*

$$O = \tfrac{1}{n}\sum_{j=0}^{n-1} P_j,$$

*and are therefore co-planar.*

**Proof :** See Appendix B. □

The factor $\beta$ in Equation (4) is a free parameter that may be set arbitrarily. Theorem 4.1 applies to the construction at hand by setting

$$\beta = \tfrac{3}{2}(1 + \cos\tfrac{2\pi}{n}),$$

and interpreting the points $P_0, \ldots, P_{n-1}$ as the vertices of a face belonging to mesh $\mathcal{M}^1$, the point $O$ as $A_{00}$, and the points $Q_0, \ldots, Q_{n-1}$ as the quad-net points surrounding $A_{00}$. Under this interpretation it is immediately clear from (5) that Constraint (1) is satisfied with $c = \cos\tfrac{2\pi}{n}$. Constructing the points $A_{30}$, $A_{03}$, and $A_{33}$ and the surrounding quad-net points is similar. The observation that every n-sided face of $\mathcal{M}^1$ ($n \neq 4$) is surrounded by 4-sided faces, indicates that faces containing $A_{30}$ and $A_{03}$ are always 4-sided. Constraint (3) is satisfied since $\cos\tfrac{2\pi}{n} = 0$ when $n = 4$.

Applying Theorem 4.1 to each of the four faces surrounding a vertex of $\mathcal{M}^1$ will produce all of the quad-net points except for the four interior points $A_{11}$, $A_{12}$, $A_{21}$, and $A_{22}$. The construction for the point $A_{12}$ is as follows: let $V$ be the vertex about which the quad-net is constructed, and let $\hat{V}$ be an edge sharing neighbor of $V$ (see Figure 3). Compute

$$A_{12} = \tfrac{1}{2}A_{01} + \tfrac{1}{2}A_{02} + \tfrac{1}{6}(V - \hat{V}), \qquad (6)$$

and by symmetry

$$\hat{A}_{12} = \tfrac{1}{2}A_{01} + \tfrac{1}{2}A_{02} + \tfrac{1}{6}(\hat{V} - V). \qquad (7)$$

Averaging Equations (6) and (7) shows that Constraint (2) is satisfied. The construction of the other three interior quad-net points is symmetric.

The sixteen quad-nets points do not by themselves give enough information to construct surface patches that meet neighboring patches smoothly. The pair of integers $n_0$ and $n_1$ that correspond to the number of sides belonging to the faces that contain points $A_{00}$ and $A_{33}$ respectively are also needed. These two integers characterize the relationship between a quad-net and its neighbors when $\cos\tfrac{2\pi}{n_0}$ or $\cos\tfrac{2\pi}{n_1}$ are substituted for $c$ in Constraint (1). The quad-nets are now passed to the next step where patches are constructed.

## 4.3 Constructing Patches

In the third and final step, parametric surface patches are constructed that interpolate the information encoded by the quad-nets constructed in step 2. A single bi-cubic patch is not sufficient to interpolate this data in general, since the mixed partial or *twist* terms at the corners of a quad-net may not be consistent (i.e., $\tfrac{\partial^2}{\partial u\,\partial v} \neq \tfrac{\partial^2}{\partial v\,\partial u}$, where $u$ and $v$ correspond to boundary curve parameters).

This difficulty can be eliminated by using four triangular patches that form an 'X' with respect to the four quad-net boundary curves. Cubic triangular patches suffice to interpolate the quad-net boundary curves, but do not have enough degrees of freedom to satisfy smoothness constraints across quad-nets boundaries. By using quartic patches, additional degrees of freedom are introduced that can be used to ensure smooth joins between adjacent triangular patches. The labeling scheme used for the Bézier control nets of the four quartic patches is as follows:

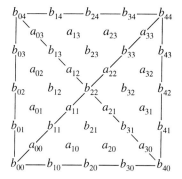

Formulas for the Bézier control points of one of the triangular patches are now given. Similar formulas for the other three patches can be found by symmetry. Interpolating the cubic boundary curves of a quad-net is achieved by degree raising, resulting in

$$b_{00} = A_{00},$$
$$b_{01} = \tfrac{1}{4}A_{00} + \tfrac{3}{4}A_{01},$$
$$b_{02} = \tfrac{1}{2}A_{01} + \tfrac{1}{2}A_{02},$$
$$b_{03} = \tfrac{3}{4}A_{02} + \tfrac{1}{4}A_{03},$$
$$b_{04} = A_{03}.$$

Tangent plane continuity is maintained across quad-net boundaries by setting

$$a_{00} = \tfrac{1}{2}b_{10} + \tfrac{1}{2}b_{01},$$
$$a_{01} = \tfrac{c}{8}A_{00} + \tfrac{3-3c}{8}A_{01} + \tfrac{c}{4}A_{02} + \tfrac{1}{8}A_{10} + \tfrac{1}{2}A_{12},$$
$$a_{02} = \tfrac{3-c}{8}A_{02} + \tfrac{c}{8}A_{03} + \tfrac{1}{2}A_{12} + \tfrac{1}{8}A_{13},$$
$$a_{03} = \tfrac{1}{2}b_{03} + \tfrac{1}{2}b_{14},$$

where $c = \cos\tfrac{2\pi}{n_0}$ (note that $c = \cos\tfrac{2\pi}{n_1}$ when constructing $a_{31}$, $a_{32}$, $a_{13}$, and $a_{23}$). These formulas are derived in § 5.

The points $b_{12}$, $b_{21}$, $b_{23}$, and $b_{32}$ do not affect tangent plane behavior across quad-net boundaries, and may be chosen arbitrarily. Some care should be taken in determining the position of these points so that the resulting surface is free of unwanted undulations or other artifacts. A reasonable construction is:

$$b_{12} = \tfrac{7}{8}A_{12} + \tfrac{1}{8}(A_{21} - A_{11} - A_{22}) + \tfrac{3}{16}(A_{10} + A_{13}) - \tfrac{1}{16}(A_{00} + A_{03}).$$

The remaining Bézier control points are computed by

$$
\begin{aligned}
b_{11} &= \tfrac{1}{2}a_{10} + \tfrac{1}{2}a_{01}, \\
a_{11} &= \tfrac{1}{2}b_{21} + \tfrac{1}{2}b_{12}, \\
b_{22} &= \tfrac{1}{2}a_{12} + \tfrac{1}{2}a_{21}.
\end{aligned}
$$

These constructions ensure that the triples $\{b_{01}, a_{00}, b_{10}\}$, $\{a_{01}, b_{11}, a_{10}\}$, $\{b_{12}, a_{11}, b_{21}\}$, and $\{a_{12}, b_{22}, a_{21}\}$ are colinear and share affine ratios. Therefore, the four triangular patches are $C^1$ along the boundaries internal to a quad-net.

The collection of quartic Bézier triangles constructed in this step are output as the final step in the spline algorithm. Figures 5 and 6 show several control meshes and the corresponding spline surfaces generated by the algorithm.

## 4.4 Special Cases

The construction just presented generates a smooth spline surface over any control mesh that is topologically a 2-manifold. However, there are certain optimizations that can be implemented to generate patches of lower degree. These special cases arise when $n_0$ and $n_1$ equal 3 or 4. In each case, the boundary curves of a quad-net are quadratic rather than cubic. If $n_0 = n_1 = 4$, a single bi-quadratic Bézier patch can be used in place of the four quartic triangles. Otherwise, the four quartic Bézier triangles can be replaced by cubics.

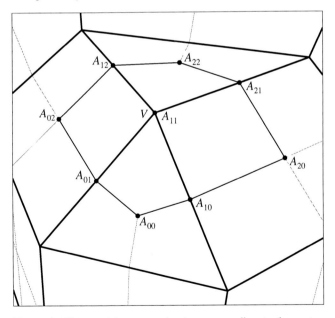

Figure 4: The special case quad-net corresponding to the vertex $V$.

To take advantage of these optimizations, the special case quad-net shown in Figure 4 corresponding to the $V$ of $\mathcal{M}^1$ is used. The points $A_{00}$, $A_{20}$, $A_{02}$, and $A_{22}$, are the centroids of the four faces surrounding $V$. The points $A_{10}$, $A_{01}$, $A_{12}$, and $A_{21}$, are the midpoints of the four edges incident on $V$, and the point $A_{11}$ is

equivalent to $V$. This special case quad-net must also know about the integers $n_0$ and $n_1$ (equal to the number of sides belonging to the faces surrounding $A_{00}$ and $A_{22}$ respectively).

The four cubic Bézier triangular patches constructed from the special case quad-net are labeled as:

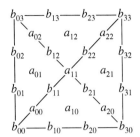

Formulas for the Bézier control net of one of these patches are given. The other three control nets are found by symmetry. The boundary curve is found by

$$
\begin{aligned}
b_{00} &= A_{00}, \\
b_{01} &= \tfrac{1}{3}A_{00} + \tfrac{2}{3}A_{01}, \\
b_{02} &= \tfrac{2}{3}A_{01} + \tfrac{1}{3}A_{02}, \\
b_{03} &= A_{02}.
\end{aligned}
$$

Tangent plane continuity is maintained across quad-net boundaries by setting

$$
\begin{aligned}
a_{00} &= \tfrac{1}{2}b_{10} + \tfrac{1}{2}b_{01}, \\
a_{01} &= \tfrac{1}{6}A_{00} + \tfrac{2-c}{6}A_{01} + \tfrac{1+c}{6}A_{02} + \tfrac{1}{3}A_{11}, \\
a_{02} &= \tfrac{1}{2}b_{02} + \tfrac{1}{2}b_{13},
\end{aligned}
$$

where $c = \cos\frac{2\pi}{n_0}$. A smooth join across the internal boundaries is ensured by setting:

$$
\begin{aligned}
b_{11} &= \tfrac{1}{2}a_{10} + \tfrac{1}{2}a_{01}, \\
a_{11} &= \tfrac{1}{2}b_{21} + \tfrac{1}{2}b_{12}.
\end{aligned}
$$

If $n_0 = n_1 = 4$, then the special case quad-net is output as the control net of a bi-quadratic tensor product Bézier patch.

## 5 Smoothness Conditions

The purpose of this section is to derive the constraints imposed on the quad-net construction (§ 4.2), and the formulas for Bézier control points that affect tangent plane behavior along quad-net boundaries (§ 4.3 and 4.4). This section is included for completeness; it is not crucial to understanding the results of this paper.

The purpose of the quad-nets is to characterize the curves and tangent planes along the boundaries of a quadrilateral piece of the spline surface. One such boundary curve is represented by the cubic Bézier curve $[A_{00}, A_{01}, A_{02}, A_{03}]$ constructed in § 4.2. Adjacent quad-nets sharing these points will clearly lead to a continuous (but not necessarily smooth) surface. To see how adjacent quad-nets give rise to surfaces that are tangent plane continuous, it must be demonstrated how a quad-net encodes a tangent plane along a boundary.

The tangent plane at a point on a surface can be represented as the span of a pair of vectors. Along a quad-net boundary, one of these vectors is the derivative of the boundary curve written in Bézier form as

$$R = 3[A_{01} - A_{00}, A_{02} - A_{01}, A_{03} - A_{02}].$$

The other vector points inward along the boundary and is defined

$$S = 3[A_{10} - (1 - c)A_{00} - cA_{01}, 2A_{12} - A_{01} - A_{02}, A_{13} - A_{03}],$$

where $c = \cos\frac{2\pi}{n_0}$. The tangent plane encoded by the quad-net along the boundary is the span of $R$ and $S$. Similar expressions hold for the other three edges of a quad-net.

To see that a pair of adjacent quad-nets encode the same tangent plane along a common boundary, consider the pair of quad-nets that share the boundary $[A_{00}, A_{01}, A_{02}, A_{03}]$. Let $A_{10}$, $A_{12}$, and $A_{13}$ be the 'first row' of points belonging to the first quad-net adjacent to the common boundary, and let $\hat{A}_{10}$, $\hat{A}_{12}$, and $\hat{A}_{13}$ be the first row of the second quad-net. Clearly, both quad-nets will share the tangent vector $R$ since they share a common boundary curve. By definition

$$\hat{S} = 3[\hat{A}_{10} - (1 - c)A_{00} - cA_{01}, 2\hat{A}_{12} - A_{01} - A_{02}, \hat{A}_{13} - A_{03}],$$

is the inward pointing tangent vector of the second quad-net. Adjacent quad-nets will encode the same tangent plane along the common boundary if $R$, $S$, and $\hat{S}$ are linearly dependent. This follows by construction, since it is easily verified that Constraints (1-3) are equivalent to the condition

$$S = -\hat{S}.$$

Therefore, the quad-nets constructed in § 4.2 encode identical tangent planes along common boundaries.

Next, it is shown that the triangular patches constructed in § 4.3 interpolate the tangent planes encoded along quad-net boundaries. Let $P$ be the quartic triangular patch constructed to interpolate a quad-net boundary curve. The tangent plane of $P$ along this boundary is the span of the partial derivatives

$$P^u = 4[b_{01} - b_{00}, b_{02} - b_{01}, b_{03} - b_{02}, b_{04} - b_{03}],$$

and

$$P^v = 4[a_{00} - b_{00}, a_{01} - b_{01}, a_{02} - b_{02}, a_{03} - b_{03}]. \quad (8)$$

The tangent plane of $P$ will interpolate the quad-net tangent plane if $R$, $S$, $P^u$, and $P^v$ are linearly dependent. By construction

$$
\begin{aligned}
P^u &= R, \quad \text{and} \\
P^v &= \phi R + \psi S, \quad (9)
\end{aligned}
$$

where

$$\phi = [\tfrac{1+c}{2}, \tfrac{1}{2}] \quad \text{and} \quad \psi = [\tfrac{1}{2}],$$

are scalar valued functions in Bézier form. Therefore $P$ will interpolate the tangent plane along the boundary of the quad-net. Expanding the right hand side of (9) and equating this result to the right hand side of (8) gives the formulas used to construct points $a_{00}$, $a_{01}$, $a_{02}$, and $a_{03}$.

## 5.1  Smoothness in Special Cases

The special case outlined in § 4.4 is similar except the tangent plane encoded by the special case quad-net is the span of the vectors

$$R = 2[A_{01} - A_{00}, A_{02} - A_{01}],$$

and

$$S = 2[A_{10} - (1 - c)A_{00} - cA_{01}, A_{11} - A_{01}, A_{12} - A_{02}].$$

Expanding the right hand side of (9) with these definitions of $R$ and $S$, and equating this result to

$$P^v = 3[a_{00} - b_{00}, a_{01} - b_{01}, a_{02} - b_{02}],$$

gives the formulas used to construct points $a_{00}$, $a_{01}$, and $a_{02}$.

It must also be demonstrated that a special case quad-net of § 4.4 encodes the same boundary curve and tangent plane as a normal quad-net. Let $A$ be a normal quad-net and $\tilde{A}$ be a special case quad-net defined over the same vertex. By construction

$$A_{00} = \tilde{A}_{00}, \quad \text{and} \quad A_{03} = \tilde{A}_{02}.$$

The weights from Theorem 4.1 for the cases $n = 3$ and $n = 4$ are $\{\frac{4}{9}, \frac{4}{9}, \frac{1}{9}\}$ and $\{\frac{5}{12}, \frac{5}{12}, \frac{1}{12}, \frac{1}{12}\}$ respectively. Since these weights are used to construct $A_{10}$, $A_{01}$, $A_{02}$, and $A_{13}$, it is straightforward to show that in either case

$$
\begin{aligned}
A_{10} &= \tfrac{1}{3}\tilde{A}_{00} + \tfrac{2}{3}\tilde{A}_{10}, & A_{01} &= \tfrac{1}{3}\tilde{A}_{00} + \tfrac{2}{3}\tilde{A}_{01}, \\
A_{02} &= \tfrac{1}{3}\tilde{A}_{02} + \tfrac{2}{3}\tilde{A}_{01}, & A_{13} &= \tfrac{1}{3}\tilde{A}_{02} + \tfrac{2}{3}\tilde{A}_{12},
\end{aligned}
$$

and

$$A_{12} = \tfrac{1}{6}\tilde{A}_{00} + \tfrac{1}{3}\tilde{A}_{01} + \tfrac{1}{6}\tilde{A}_{02} + \tfrac{1}{3}\tilde{A}_{11}.$$

Substituting these equations (for $A_{00}, \ldots, A_{12}$) into the definition of the tangent vector $S$ for the normal case yields the definition of $S$ for the special case. Therefore, both types of quad-nets encode the same tangent planes and may be used interchangably when $n_0$ and $n_1$ are equal to 3 or 4.

## 6  Conclusions

An algorithm has been presented for constructing a tangent plane smooth spline surface that approximates an irregular control mesh. The spline surface is in general a composite of quartic triangular Bézier patches. In certain special cases, cubic triangular patches may be used in place of the quartics. Over regular regions of the mesh, a bi-quadratic Bézier patch may be used in place of four quartic triangular patches. In fact, the four quartic triangular patches constructed over a regular region represents exactly the same polynomial map as the single bi-quadratic Bézier patch. Although this has not been proved, its plausability is evident since the total degree of a bi-quadratic surface is 4.

The spline algorithm as presented was factored into 3 steps. Each of these steps was a geometric construction that involved taking weighted averages (affine combinations) of points. Therefore, the spline surface is *affine invariant* (i.e., independent of any affine transformation applied to the control mesh). It is not clear that the concatenation of the geometric constructions leads to *convex combinations* in all cases (although the special case constructions of § 4.4 are convex).

Over regular regions of a mesh, the refinement step (§ 4.1) is not needed and will result in more patches being constructed than are actually required. It should be possible to avoid this unnecessary 'splitting' of patches as an optimization.

## Appendix

## A  Treatment of Boundaries

A method of dealing with mesh boundaries in a reasonable way is now presented. The problem is that quad-nets are not defined over boundary vertices of $\mathcal{M}^1$. As a result, the boundary of the spline surface does not approximate the boundary of the $\mathcal{M}^0$ very well. A solution is to modify step 1 (§ 4.1) so that new faces are added to $\mathcal{M}^1$ that correspond to vertices and edges belonging to the boundary of $\mathcal{M}^0$. The following construction has the property that the boundary of the resulting spline surface will be the quadratic B-spline curve corresponding to the boundary vertices of $\mathcal{M}^0$. There are two cases to consider, faces of $\mathcal{M}^1$ corresponding to boundary edges of $\mathcal{M}^0$, and faces of $\mathcal{M}^1$ corresponding to boundary vertices of $\mathcal{M}^0$.

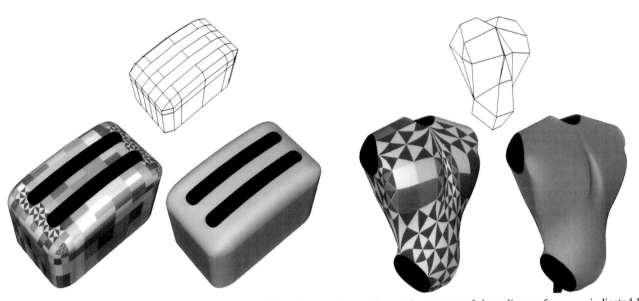

Figure 5: A pair of irregular control meshes and resulting spline surfaces. The patch structure of the spline surfaces are indicated by color: blue and yellow patches are quartic, red and green patches are cubic, and gray patches are bi-quadratic.

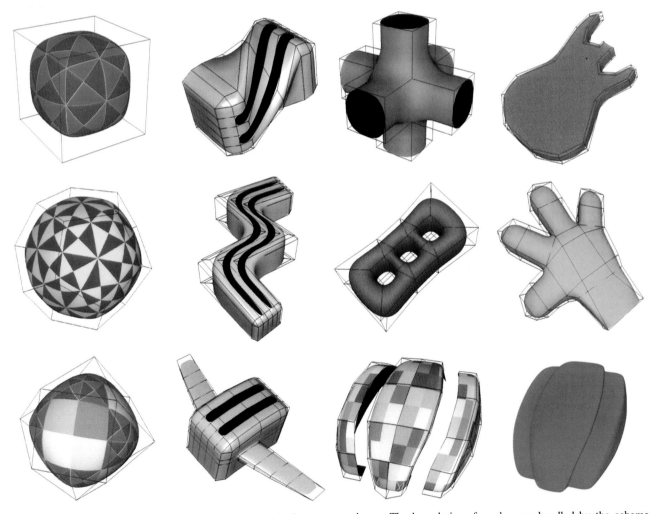

Figure 6: More examples: the color coding of patches is the same as above. The boundaries of meshes are handled by the scheme outlined in Appendix A. This approach may be used to create creases on a surface as illustrated by the two shapes in the lower right hand corner. Disjoint meshes that share boundary geometry will result in a crease.

## A.1  Boundary Edges

Let the vertex pair $\{V_0, V_1\}$ be a boundary edge of $\mathcal{M}^0$ belonging to face $F$. Let $P_0$ and $P_1$ be the vertices of $\mathcal{M}^1$ constructed in step 1 corresponding to the vertex-face pairs $\{V_0, F\}$ and $\{V_1, F\}$ respectively. Two new vertices

$$
\begin{aligned}
Q_0 &= \tfrac{3}{2}V_0 + \tfrac{1}{2}V_1 - P_0, \\
Q_1 &= \tfrac{1}{2}V_0 + \tfrac{3}{2}V_1 - P_1,
\end{aligned}
$$

and one new face $\{P_0, P_1, Q_1, Q_0\}$ are added to $\mathcal{M}^1$.

## A.2  Boundary Vertices

Let $V$ be a vertex on the boundary of $\mathcal{M}^0$. Let $k$ be the number of faces incident on $V$. Let $P_1, \ldots, P_k$ be the vertices of $\mathcal{M}^1$ corresponding to $V$ constructed in step 1, and let $P_0$ and $P_{k+1}$ be the vertices found by the boundary edge construction given in Appendix A.1.

When $k = 1$, $V$ is a corner of $\mathcal{M}^0$. By treating this vertex as a discontinuity in the boundary B-spline curve, the spline surface boundary will have a corner. A new face $\{P_0, P_1, P_2, P_3\}$ is added to $\mathcal{M}^1$ where

$$
P_3 = 4V - P_0 - P_1 - P_2.
$$

When $k > 1$ a new $n = 2k$-sided face $\{P_0, \ldots, P_{n-1}\}$ is added to $\mathcal{M}^1$ where

$$
P_i = 2(uQ_0 + (1-u)Q_1) - P_{n-i+1}, \quad i = k+2, \ldots, n-1,
$$

with

$$
Q_0 = \tfrac{1}{2}P_0 + \tfrac{1}{2}P_1, \quad Q_1 = \tfrac{1}{2}P_k + \tfrac{1}{2}P_{k+1},
$$

and

$$
u = \tfrac{1}{2}\left(1 + \cos\tfrac{2\pi i}{n} + \tan\tfrac{\pi}{n}\sin\tfrac{2\pi i}{n}\right).
$$

These constructions, offered without proof, are included because they are of practical value. The boundaries of the spline surfaces illustrated in Figures 5 and 6 were dealt with using this technique.

## B  Proof of Theorem 4.1

Let $M_k = \beta(\cos\tfrac{2\pi k}{n} + \tan\tfrac{\pi}{n}\sin\tfrac{2\pi k}{n})$. Expand the right hand side of Equation (5) as follows:

$$
\begin{aligned}
&\tfrac{1}{2}Q_{i-1} + \tfrac{1}{2}Q_{i+1} \\
={} &\tfrac{1}{2n}\sum_{j=0}^{n-1} P_j\left(1 + M_{j-(i-1)}\right) + \tfrac{1}{2n}\sum_{j=0}^{n-1} P_j\left(1 + M_{j-(i+1)}\right), \\
={} &\tfrac{1}{2n}\sum_{j=0}^{n-1} P_j\left(2 + M_{j-i+1} + M_{j-i-1}\right), \\
={} &\tfrac{1}{2n}\sum_{j=0}^{n-1} P_j\left(2 + 2\cos\tfrac{2\pi}{n}M_{j-i}\right), \\
={} &\tfrac{1}{n}\sum_{j=0}^{n-1} P_j\left(1 - \cos\tfrac{2\pi}{n}\right) + \tfrac{1}{n}\sum_{j=0}^{n-1} P_j\cos\tfrac{2\pi}{n}\left(1 + M_{j-i}\right), \\
={} &\left(1 - \cos\tfrac{2\pi}{n}\right)O + \cos\tfrac{2\pi}{n}Q_i.
\end{aligned}
$$

The key step of combining $M_{j-(i-1)} + M_{j-(i+1)}$ to get $2\cos\tfrac{2\pi}{n}M_{j-i}$ comes about using the well known trigonometric identities:

$$
\begin{aligned}
\cos\theta + \cos\phi &= 2\cos\tfrac{1}{2}(\theta+\phi)\cos\tfrac{1}{2}(\theta-\phi), \quad \text{and} \\
\sin\theta + \sin\phi &= 2\sin\tfrac{1}{2}(\theta+\phi)\cos\tfrac{1}{2}(\theta-\phi).
\end{aligned}
$$

Clearly the points $Q_i$ are co-planar since from (5) any $Q_i$ can be found as a linear combination of $O, Q_0$, and $Q_1$, and must therefore lie in the plane spanned by these three points.

## References

[1] E. Catmull and J. Clark. Recursively generated B-spline surfaces on arbitrary topological meshes. *Computer Aided Design*, 10(6):350–355, 1978.

[2] H. Chiyokura and F. Kimura. Design of solids with free-form surfaces. In *Proceedings of SIGGRAPH '83*, pages 289–298. 1983.

[3] T. DeRose. *Geometric Continuity: A Parametrization Independent Measure of Continuity for Computer Aided Geometric Design*. PhD thesis, Berkeley, 1985.

[4] D. Doo. A subdivision algorithm for smoothing down irregularly shaped polyhedrons. In *Proceedings on Interactive Techniques in Computer Aided Design*, pages 157–165. Bologna, 1978.

[5] G. Farin. *Curves and Surfaces for Computer Aided Geometric Design*. Academic Press, third edition, 1993.

[6] T. N. T. Goodman. Closed biquadratic surfaces. *Constructive Approximation*, 7(2):149–160, 1991.

[7] M. Halstead, M. Kass, and T. DeRose. Efficient, fair interpolation using Catmull-Clark surfaces. In *Proceedings of SIGGRAPH '93*, pages 35–44. 1993.

[8] K. Höllig and Harald Mögerle. G-splines. *Computer Aided Geometric Design*, 7:197–207, 1990.

[9] C. Loop. *Generalized B-spline Surfaces of Arbitrary Topological Type*. PhD thesis, University of Washington, 1992.

[10] C. Loop. Smooth low degree polynomial spline surfaces over irregular meshes. Technical Report 48, Apple Computer Inc., Cupertino, CA, January 1993.

[11] C. Loop. A $G^1$ triangular spline surface of arbitrary topological type. *Computer Aided Geometric Design*, 1994. to appear.

[12] C. Loop and T. DeRose. Generalized B-spline surfaces of arbitrary topology. In *Proceedings of SIGGRAPH '90*, pages 347–356. 1990.

[13] J. Peters. $C^1$ free-form surface splines. Technical Report CSD-TR-93-019, Dept. of Comp. Sci., Purdue University, W-Lafayette, IN, March 1993.

[14] J. Peters. Smooth free-form surfaces over irregular meshes generalizing quadratic splines. *Computer Aided Geometric Design*, 10:347–361, 1993.

[15] J. Peters. Constructing $C^1$ surfaces of arbitrary topology using biquadratic and bicubic splines. In N. Sapidis, editor, *Designing Fair Curves and Surfaces*. 1994. to appear.

[16] U. Reif. Biquadratic G-spline surfaces. Technical report, Mathematisches Institut A, Universität Stuttgart, Pfaffenwaldring 57, D-7000 Stuttgart 80, Germany, 1993.

[17] M. Sabin. Non-rectangular surface patches suitable for inclusion in a B-spline surface. In P. ten Hagen, editor, *Proceedings of Eurographics '83*, pages 57–69. North-Holland, 1983.

[18] J. van Wijk. Bicubic patches for approximating non-rectangular control-point meshes. *Computer Aided Geometric Design*, 3(1):1–13, 1986.

# Zippered Polygon Meshes from Range Images

Greg Turk and Marc Levoy

Computer Science Department

Stanford University

## Abstract

Range imaging offers an inexpensive and accurate means for digitizing the shape of three-dimensional objects. Because most objects self occlude, no single range image suffices to describe the entire object. We present a method for combining a collection of range images into a single polygonal mesh that completely describes an object to the extent that it is visible from the outside.

The steps in our method are: 1) align the meshes with each other using a modified iterated closest-point algorithm, 2) zipper together adjacent meshes to form a continuous surface that correctly captures the topology of the object, and 3) compute local weighted averages of surface positions on all meshes to form a consensus surface geometry.

Our system differs from previous approaches in that it is incremental; scans are acquired and combined one at a time. This approach allows us to acquire and combine large numbers of scans with minimal storage overhead. Our largest models contain up to 360,000 triangles. All the steps needed to digitize an object that requires up to 10 range scans can be performed using our system with five minutes of user interaction and a few hours of compute time. We show two models created using our method with range data from a commercial rangefinder that employs laser stripe technology.

**CR Categories:** I.3.5 [Computer Graphics]: Computational Geometry and Object Modelling.
**Additional Key Words:** Surface reconstruction, surface fitting, polygon mesh, range images, structured light range scanner.

## 1 Introduction

This paper presents a method of combining multiple views of an object, captured by a range scanner, and assembling these views into one unbroken polygonal surface. Applications for such a method include:

- Digitizing complex objects for animation and visual simulation.
- Digitizing the shape of a found object such as an archaeological artifact for measurement and for dissemination to the scientific community.

E-mail: turk@redclay.stanford.edu, levoy@cs.stanford.edu
Web site: www-graphics.stanford.edu

- Digitizing human external anatomy for surgical planning, remote consultation or the compilation of anatomical atlases.
- Digitizing the shape of a damaged machine part to help create a replacement.

There is currently no procedure that will allow a user to easily capture a digital description of a physical object. The dream tool would allow one to set an industrial part or a clay figure onto a platform, press a button, and have a complete digital description of that object returned in a few minutes. The reality is that much digitization is done by a user painstakingly touching a 3D sensing probe to hundreds or thousands of positions on the object, then manually specifying the connectivity of these points. Fortunately range scanners offer promise in replacing this tedious operation.

A *range scanner* is any device that senses 3D positions on an object's surface and returns an array of distance values. A *range image* is an $m \times n$ grid of distances (*range points*) that describe a surface either in Cartesian coordinates (a height field) or cylindrical coordinates, with two of the coordinates being implicitly defined by the indices of the grid. Quite a number of measurement techniques can be used to create a range image, including structured light, time-of-flight lasers, radar, sonar, and several methods from the computer vision literature such as depth from stereo, shading, texture, motion and focus. The range images used to create the models in this paper were captured using structured light (described later), but our techniques can be used with any range images where the uncertainties of the distance values are smaller than the spacing between the samples.

Range scanners seem like a natural solution to the problem of capturing a digital description of physical objects. Unfortunately, few objects are simple enough that they can be fully described by a single range image. For instance, a coffee cup handle will obscure a portion of the cup's surface even using a cylindrical scan. To capture the full geometry of a moderately complicated object (e.g. a clay model of a cat) may require as many as a dozen range images.

There are two main issues in creating a single model from multiple range images: *registration* and *integration*. Registration refers to computing a rigid transformation that brings the points of one range image into alignment with the portions of a surface that is shares with another range image. Integration is the process of creating a single surface representation from the sample points from two or more range images.

Our approach to registration uses an iterative process to minimize the distance between two triangle meshes that were created from the range images. We accelerate registration by performing the matching on a hierarchy of increasingly more detailed meshes. This method allows an object to be scanned from any orientation without the need for a six-degree-of-freedom motion device.

We separate the task of integration into two steps: 1) creating a mesh that reflects the topology of the object, and 2) refining the vertex positions of the mesh by averaging the geometric detail that is present in all scans. We capture the topology of an object by merging pairs of triangle meshes that are each created from a single range image. Merging begins by converting two meshes that may have considerable overlap into a pair of meshes that just barely overlap along portions of their boundaries. This is done by simultaneously eating back the boundaries of each mesh that lie directly on top of the other mesh. Next, the meshes are *zippered* together: the triangles of one mesh are clipped to the boundary of the other mesh and the vertices on the boundary are shared. Once all the meshes have been combined, we allow all of the scans to contribute to the surface detail by finding the *consensus geometry*. The final position of a vertex is found by taking an average of nearby positions from each of the original range images. The order in which we perform zippering and consensus geometry is important. We deliberately postpone the refinement of surface geometry until after the overall shape of the object has been determined. This eliminates discontinuities that may be introduced during zippering.

The remainder of this paper is organized as follows. Section 2 describes previous work on combining range images. Section 3 covers the basic principles of a structured light range scanner. Section 4 presents the automatic registration process. Section 5 describes zippering meshes into one continuous surface. Section 6 describes how surface detail is captured through consensus geometry. Section 7 shows examples of digitized models and compares our approach to other methods of combining range data. Section 8 concludes this paper by discussing future work.

## 2 Previous Work

There is a great deal of published work on registration and integration of depth information, particularly in the vision literature. Our literature review only covers work on registration or integration of dense range data captured by an active range scanner, and where the product of the integration is a polygon mesh.

### 2.1 Registration

Two themes dominate work in range image registration: matching of "created" features in the images to be matched, and minimization of distances between all points on the surface represented by the two images. In the first category, Wada and co-authors performed six degree of freedom registration by matching distinctive facets from the convex hulls of range images [Wada 93]. They computed a rotation matrix from corresponding facets using a least squares fit of the normal vectors of the facets.

In the second category, Champleboux and co-workers used a data structure called an octree-spline that is a sampled representation of distances to an object's surface [Champleboux 92]. This gave them a rapid way to determine distances from a surface (and the distance gradient) with a low overhead in storage. Chen and Medioni establish a correspondence between points on one surface and nearby tangent planes on the other surface [Chen 92]. They find a rigid motion that minimizes the point-to-tangent collection directly and then iterate. Besl and McKay use an approach they call the *iterated closest-point* algorithm [Besl 92]. This method finds the nearest positions on one surface to a collection of points on the other surface and then transforms one surface so as to minimize the collective distance. They iterate this procedure until convergence.

Our registration method falls into the general category of direct distance minimization algorithms, and is an adaptation of [Besl 92]. It differs in that we do not require that one surface be a strict subset of the other. It is described in Section 4.

### 2.2 Integration

Integration of multiple range scans can be classified into *structured* and *unstructured* methods. Unstructured integration presumes that one has a procedure that creates a polygonal surface from an arbitrary collection of points in 3-space. Integration in this case is performed by collecting together all the range points from multiple scans and presenting them to the polygonal reconstruction procedure. The Delaunay triangulation of a set of points in 3-space has been proposed as the basis of one such reconstruction method [Boissonnat 84]. Another candidate for surface reconstruction is a generalization of the convex hull of a point set known as the alpha shape [Edelsbrunner 92]. Hoppe and co-authors use graph traversal techniques to help construct a signed distance function from a collection of unorganized points [Hoppe 92]. An isosurface extraction technique produces a polygon mesh from this distance function.

Structured integration methods make use of information about how each point was obtained, such as using error bounds on a point's position or adjacency information between points within one range image. Soucy and Laurendeau use a structured integration technique to combine multiple range images [Soucy 92] that is similar in several respects to our algorithm. Given *n* range images of an object, they first partition the points into a number of sets that are called *common surface sets*. The range points in one set are then used to create a grid of triangles whose positions are guided by a weighted average of the points in the set. Subsets of these grids are stitched together by a constrained Delaunay triangulation in one of *n* projections onto a plane. We compare our method to Soucy's in Section 7.

## 3 Structured Light Range Scanners

In this section we describe the operating principles of range scanners based on structured light. We do this because it highlights issues common to many range scanners and also because the range images used in this article were created by such a scanner.

### 3.1 Triangulation

Structured light scanners operate on the principle of triangulation (see Figure 1, left). One portion of the scanner projects a specific pattern of light onto the object being scanned. This pattern of light is observed by the sensor of the scanner along a viewing direction that is off-axis from the source of light. The position of the illuminated part of the object is determined by finding the intersection of the light's projected direction and the viewing direction of the sensor. Positions can be accumulated across the length of the object while the object is moved across the path of the projected light. Some of the patterns that have been used in such scanners include a spot, a circle, a line, and several lines at once. Typically the sensor is a CCD array or a lateral effect photodiode.

The scanner used for the examples in this paper is a Cyberware Model 3030 MS. It projects a vertical sheet of He-Ne laser light onto the surface of an object. The laser sheet is created by spreading a laser beam using a cylindrical lens into a sheet roughly 2 mm wide and 30 cm high. The sensor of the Cyberware scanner is a $768 \times 486$ pixel CCD array. A typical CCD image shows a ribbon of laser light running from the top to the bottom (see Figure 2). A range point is created by looking across a scanline for the peak intensity of this ribbon. A range point's distance from the scanner (the "depth") is given by the horizontal position of this peak and the vertical position of the range point is given by the number of the scanline. Finding the peaks for each scanline in one frame gives an entire column of range points, and combining the columns from multiple frames as the object is moved through the laser sheet gives the full range image.

### 3.2 Sources of Error

Any approach to combining range scans should attempt to take into account the possible sources of error inherent in a given scanner. Two sources of error are particularly relevant to integration. One is a result of light falling on the object at a grazing angle. When the projected light falls on a portion of the object that is nearly parallel to the light's path, the sensor sees a dim and stretched-out version of the pattern. Finding the center of the laser sheet when it grazes the

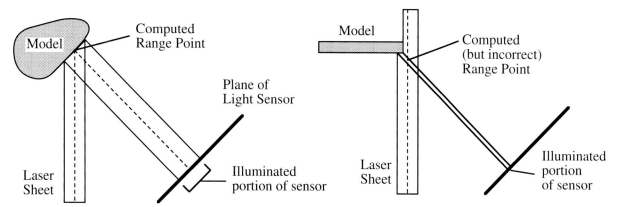

**Figure 1:** Structured light triangulation (left) and false edge extension in the presence of a partially illuminated edge (right).

object becomes difficult, and this adds uncertainty to the position of the range points. The degree of uncertainty at a given range point can be quantified, and we make use of such information at several stages in our approach to combining range images.

A second source of inaccuracy occurs when only a portion of the laser sheet hits an object, such as when the laser sheet falls off the edge of a book that is perpendicular to the laser sheet (see Figure 1, right). This results in a false position because the peak-detection and triangulation method assumes that the entire width of the sheet is visible. Such an assumption results in edges of objects that are both curled and extended beyond their correct position. This false extension of a surface at edges is an issue that needs to be specifically addressed when combining range images.

### 3.3 Creating Triangle Meshes from Range Images

We use a mesh of triangles to represent the range image data at all stages of our integration method. Each sample point in the $m \times n$ range image is a potential vertex in the triangle mesh. We take special care to avoid inadvertently joining portions of the surface together that are separated by depth discontinuities (see Figure 3).

To build a mesh, we create zero, one or two triangles from four points of a range image that are in adjacent rows and columns. We find the shortest of the two diagonals between the points and use this to identify the two triplets of points that may become triangles. Each of these point triples is made into a triangle if the edge lengths fall below a distance threshold. Let $s$ be the maximum distance between adjacent range points when we flatten the range image, that is, when we don't include the depth information (see Figure 3). We take the distance threshold be a small multiple of this sampling distance, typically $4s$. Although having such a distance threshold may prevent joining some range points that should in fact be connected, we can rely on other range images (those with better views of the location in question) to give the correct adjacency information.

This willingness to discard questionable data is representative of a deliberate overall strategy: to acquire and process large amounts of data rather than draw hypotheses (possibly erroneous) from sparse data. This strategy appears in several places in our algorithm.

## 4 Registration of Range Images

Once a triangle mesh is created for each range image, we turn to the task of bringing corresponding portions of different range images into alignment with one another. If all range images are captured using a six-degree of freedom precision motion device then the information needed to register them is available from the motion control software. This is the case when the object or scanner is mounted on a robot arm or the motion platform of a precision milling machine. Inexpensive motion platforms are often limited to one or two degrees of freedom, typically translation in a single direction or rotation about an axis. One of our goals is to create an inexpensive system. Consequently, we employ a registration method that does not depend on measured position and orientation. With our scanner, which offers translation and rotation around one axis, we typically take one cylindrical and four translational scans by moving the object with the motion device. To capture the top or the underside of the object, we pick it up by hand and place it on its side. Now the orientation of subsequent scans cannot be matched with those taken earlier, and using a registration method becomes mandatory.

### 4.1 Iterated Closest-Point Algorithm

This section describes a modified iterated closest-point (ICP) algorithm for quickly registering a pair of meshes created from range images. This method allows a user to crudely align one range image with another on-screen and then invoke an algorithm that snaps the position of one range image into accurate alignment with the other.

The iterated closest-point of [Besl 92] cannot be used to register range images because it requires that *every* point on one surface have

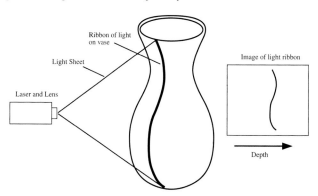

**Figure 2:** Light-stripe projected on vase (left) and corresponding CCD image (right).

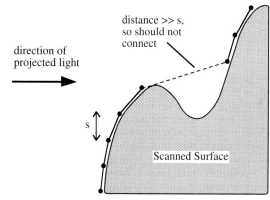

**Figure 3:** Building triangle mesh from range points.

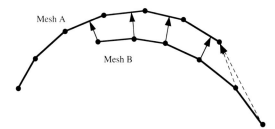

**Figure 4:** Finding corresponding points for mesh registration. Dotted arrows show matches that should be avoided because they will cause mesh *B* to be erroneously dragged up and left.

a corresponding point on the other surface. Since our scans are overlapping, we seldom produce data that satisfies this requirement. Thus we have developed our own variant of this algorithm. Its steps are:

1) Find the nearest position on mesh *A* to each vertex of mesh *B*.
2) Discard pairs of points that are too far apart.
3) Eliminate pairs in which either points is on a mesh boundary.
4) Find the rigid transformation that minimizes a weighted least-squared distance between the pairs of points.
5) Iterate until convergence.
6) Perform ICP on a more detailed mesh in the hierarchy.

In step 1, it is important to note that we are looking for the 3-space position $A_i$ on the surface of mesh *A* that is closest to a given vertex $B_i$ of mesh *B* (see Figure 4). The nearest point $A_i$ may be a vertex of *A*, may be a point within a triangle, or may lie on a triangle's edge. Allowing these points $A_i$ to be anywhere on a $C^0$ continuous surface means that the registration between surfaces can have greater accuracy than the spacing *s* between range points.

## 4.2 Constraints on ICP

Our ICP algorithm differs from Besl's in several ways. First, we have added a distance threshold to the basic iterated closest-point method to avoid matching any vertex $B_i$ of one mesh to a remote part of another mesh that is likely to not correspond to $B_i$. Such a vertex $B_i$ from mesh *B* might be from a portion of the scanned object that was not captured in the mesh *A*, and thus no pairing should be made to any point on *A*. We have found that excellent registration will result when this distance threshold is set to twice the spacing *s* between range points. Limiting the distance between pairs of corresponding points allows us to perform step 2 (eliminating remote pairs) during the nearest points search in step 1.

The nearest points search can be accelerated considerably by placing the mesh vertices in a uniform subdivision of space based on the distance threshold. Because the triangle size is limited in the mesh creation step, we can search over all triangles within a fixed distance and guarantee that we miss no nearby portion of any triangle. Because we will use this constrained nearest-point search again later, it is worth giving a name to this query. Let nearest_on_mesh(*P*,*d*,*M*) be a routine that returns the nearest position on a mesh *M* to a given point *P*, or that returns nothing if there is no such point within the distance *d*.

Second, we have added the restriction that we never allow boundary points to be part of a match between surfaces. Boundary points are those points that lie on the edge of a triangle and where that edge is not shared by another triangle. Figure 4 illustrates how such matches can drag a mesh in a contrary direction to the majority of the point correspondences.

## 4.3 Best Rigid Motion

The heart of the iterated closest-point approach is in finding a rigid transformation that minimizes the least-squared distance between

the point pairs. Berthold Horn describes a closed-form solution to this problem [Horn 87] that is linear in time with respect to the number of point pairs. Horn's method finds the translation vector *T* and the rotation **R** such that:

$$E = \sum_{i=1}^{n} \left\| A_i - \mathbf{R}(B_i - B_c) - T \right\|^2$$

is minimized, where $A_i$ and $B_i$ are given pairs of positions in 3-space and $B_c$ is the centroid of the $B_i$. Horn showed that *T* is just the difference between the centroid of the points $A_i$ and the centroid of the points $B_i$. **R** is found by constructing a cross-covariance matrix between centroid-adjusted pairs of points. The final rotation is given by a unit quaternion that is the eigenvector corresponding to the largest eigenvalue of a matrix constructed from the elements of this cross-covariance matrix. Details can be found in both [Horn 87] and [Besl 92].

As we discussed earlier, not all range points have the same error bounds on their position. We can take advantage of an optional weighting term in Horn's minimization to incorporate the positional uncertainties into the registration process. Let a value in the range from 0 to 1 called *confidence* be a measure of how certain we are of a given range point's position. For the case of structured light scanners, we take the *confidence* of a point *P* on a mesh to be the dot product of the mesh normal *N* at *P* and the vector *L* that points from *P* to the light source of the scanner. (We take the normal at *P* to be the average of the normals of the triangles that meet at *P*.) Additionally, we lower the confidence of vertices near the mesh boundaries to take into account possible error due to false edge extension and curl. We take the confidence of a pair of corresponding points $A_i$ and $B_i$ from two meshes to be the product of their confidences, and we will use $w_i$ to represent this value. The problem is now to find a *weighted* least-squares minimum:

$$E = \sum_{i=1}^{n} w_i \left\| A_i - \mathbf{R}(B_i - B_c) - T \right\|^2$$

The weighted minimization problem is solved in much the same way as before. The translation factor *T* is just the difference between the weighted centroids of the corresponding points. The solution for **R** is described by Horn.

## 4.4 Alignment in Practice

The above registration method can be made faster by matching increasingly more detailed meshes from a hierarchy. We typically use a mesh hierarchy in which each mesh uses one-forth the number of range points that are used in the next higher level. The less-detailed meshes in this hierarchy are constructed by sub-sampling the range images. Registration begins by running constrained ICP on the lowest-level mesh and then using the resulting transformation as the initial position for the next level up in the hierarchy. The matching distance threshold *d* is halved with each move up the hierarchy.

Besl and McKay describe how to use linear and quadratic extrapolation of the registration parameters to accelerate the alignment process. We use this technique for our alignment at each level in the hierarchy, and find it works well in practice. Details of this method can be found in their paper.

The constrained ICP algorithm registers only two meshes at a time, and there is no obvious extension that will register three or more meshes simultaneously. This is the case with all the registration algorithms we know. If we have meshes *A*, *B*, *C* and *D*, should we register *A* with *B*, then *B* with *C* and finally *C* with *D*, perhaps compounding registration errors? We can minimize this problem by registering all meshes to a single mesh that is created from a cylindrical range image. In this way the cylindrical range image acts as a common anchor for all of the other meshes. Note that if a cylindrical scan covers an object from top to bottom, it captures all the surfaces that lie on the convex hull of the object. This means that, for almost all objects, there will be some common portions between the cylindrical scan and all linear scans, although the degree of this overlap depends on the extent of the concavities of the object. We used such a cylindrical scan for alignment when constructing the models shown in this paper.

# 5 Integration: Mesh Zippering

The central step in combining range images is the integration of multiple views into a single model. The goal of integration is to arrive at a description of the overall topology of the object being scanned. In this section we examine how two triangle meshes can be combined into a single surface. The full topology of a surface is realized by zippering new range scans one by one into the final triangle mesh.

Zippering two triangle meshes consists of three steps, each of which we will consider in detail below:

1) Remove overlapping portions of the meshes.
2) Clip one mesh against another.
3) Remove the small triangles introduced during clipping.

## 5.1 Removing Redundant Surfaces

Before attempting to join a pair of meshes, we eat away at the boundaries of both meshes until they just meet. We remove those triangles in each mesh that are in some sense "redundant," in that the other mesh includes an unbroken surface at that same position in space. Although this step removes triangles from the meshes, we are not discarding data since all range points eventually will be used to find the consensus geometry (Section 6). Given two triangle meshes $A$ and $B$, here is the process that removes their redundant portions:

Repeat until both meshes remain unchanged:
    Remove redundant triangles on the boundary of mesh $A$
    Remove redundant triangles on the boundary of mesh $B$

Before we can remove a given triangle $T$ from mesh $A$, we need to determine whether the triangle is redundant. We accomplish this by querying mesh $B$ using the nearest_on_mesh() routine that was introduced earlier. In particular, we ask for the nearest positions on mesh $B$ to the vertices $V_1$, $V_2$ and $V_3$ of $T$. We will declare $T$ to be redundant if the three queries return positions on $B$ that are within a tolerance distance $d$ and if none of these positions are on the boundary of $B$. Figure 7 shows two overlapping surfaces before and after removing their redundant triangles. In some cases this particular decision procedure for removing triangles will leave tiny gaps where the meshes meet. The resulting holes are no larger than the maximum triangle size and we currently fill them in an automatic post-processing step to zippering. Using the fast triangle redundancy check was an implementation decision for the sake of efficiency, not a necessary characteristic of our zippering approach, and it could easily be replaced by a more cautious redundancy check that leaves no gaps. We have not found this necessary in practice.

If we have a measure of confidence of the vertex positions (as we do for structured light scanners), then the above method can be altered to preserve the more confident vertices. When checking to see if the vertices $V_1$, $V_2$ and $V_3$ of $T$ lie within the distance tolerance of mesh $B$, we also determine whether at least two of these vertices have a lower confidence measure than the nearby points on $B$. If this is the case, we allow the triangle to be removed. When no more triangles can be removed from the boundaries of either mesh, we drop this confidence value restriction and continue the process until no more changes can be made. This procedure results in a pair of meshes that meet along boundaries of nearly equal confidences.

## 5.2 Mesh Clipping

We now describe how triangle clipping can be used to smoothly join two meshes that slightly overlap. The left portion of Figure 5 shows two overlapping meshes and the right portion shows the result of clipping. Let us examine the clipping process in greater detail, and

for the time being make the assumption that we are operating on two meshes that lie in a common plane.

To clip mesh $A$ against the boundary of mesh $B$ we first need to add new vertices to the boundary of mesh $B$. Specifically, we place a new vertex wherever an edge of a triangle from mesh $A$ intersects the boundary of mesh $B$. Let $Q$ be the set of all such new vertices. Together, the new vertices in $Q$ and the old boundary vertices of mesh $B$ will form a common boundary that the triangles from both meshes will share. Once this new boundary is formed we need to incorporate the vertices $Q$ into the triangles that share this boundary. Triangles from mesh $B$ need only to be split once for each new vertex to be incorporated (shown in Figure 5, right). Then we need to divide each border triangle from $A$ into two parts, one part that lies inside the boundary of $B$ that should be discarded and the other part that lies outside of this boundary and should be retained (See Figure 5, middle). The vertices of the retained portions of the triangle are passed to a constrained triangulation routine that returns a set of triangles that incorporates all the necessary vertices (Figure 5, right).

The only modification needed to extend this clipping step to 3-space is to determine precisely how to find the points of intersection $Q$. In 3-space the edges of mesh $A$ might very well pass above or below the boundary of $B$ instead of exactly intersecting the boundary. To correct for this we "thicken" the boundary of mesh $B$. In essence we create a wall that runs around the boundary of $B$ and that is roughly perpendicular to $B$ at any given location along the boundary. The portion of the wall at any given edge $E$ is a collection of four triangles, as shown in Figure 6. To find the intersection points with the edges of $A$, we only need to note where these edges pass through the wall of triangles. We then move this intersection point down to the nearest position on the edge $E$ to which the intersected portion of the wall belongs. The rest of the clipping can proceed as described above.

## 5.3 Removing Small Triangles

The clipping process can introduce arbitrarily small or thin triangles into a mesh. For many applications this does matter, but in situations where such triangles are undesirable they can easily be removed. We use vertex deletion to remove small triangles: if any of a triangle's altitudes fall below a user-specified threshold we delete one of the triangle's vertices and all the triangles that shared this vertex. We then use constrained triangulation to fill the hole that is left by deleting these triangles (see [Bern 92]). We preferentially delete vertices that were introduced as new vertices during the clipping process. If all of a triangle's vertices are original range points then the vertex opposite the longest side is deleted.

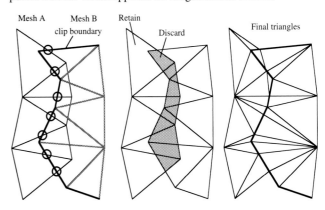

**Figure 5:** Mesh $A$ is clipped against the boundary of mesh $B$. Circles (left) show intersection between edges of $A$ and $B$'s boundary. Portions of triangles from $A$ are discarded (middle) and then both meshes incorporate the points of intersection (right).

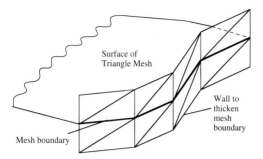

**Figure 6:** Thickened boundary for clipping in 3-space.

### 5.4 False Edge Extension

As described in Section 3.2, range points from a structured light scanner that are near an object's silhouette are extended and curled away from the true geometry. These extended edges typically occur at corners. If there is at least one scan that spans both sides of the corner, then our method will correctly reconstruct the surface at the corner. Since we lower the confidence of a surface near the mesh boundaries, triangles at the false edge extensions will be eliminated during redundant surface removal because there are nearby triangles with higher confidence in the scan that spans the corner. For correct integration at a corner, it is the user's responsibility to provide a scan that spans both sides of the corner. Figure 7 illustrates correct integration at a corner in the presence of false edge extension. Unfortunately, no disambiguating scan can be found when an object is highly curved such as a thin cylinder.

Although the problem of false edge extension is discussed in the structured light literature [Businski 92], we know of no paper on surface integration from such range images that addresses or even mentions this issue. We are also unaware of any other integration methods that will correctly determine the geometry of a surface at locations where there are false extensions. Our group has developed

a method of reducing false edge extensions when creating the range images (to appear in a forthcoming paper) and we are exploring algorithms that will lessen the effect of such errors during integration. It is our hope that by emphasizing this issue we will encourage others to address this topic in future research on range image integration.

## 6 Consensus Geometry

When we have zippered the meshes of all the range images together, the resulting triangle mesh captures the *topology* of the scanned object. This mesh may be sufficient for some applications. If surface detail is important, however, we need to fine-tune the *geometry* of the mesh.

The final model of an object should incorporate all the information available about surface detail from each range image of the object. Some of this information may have been discarded when we removed redundant triangles during mesh zippering. We re-introduce the information about surface detail by moving each vertex of our zippered mesh to a consensus position given by a weighted average of positions from the original range images. Vertices are moved only in the direction of the surface normal so that features are not blurred by lateral motion. This is in contrast to unstructured techniques which tend to blur small features isotropically. Our preference for averaging only in the direction of the surface normal is based on the observation that most points in range scans are generally accurately placed with respect to other points in the same scan, but may differ between scans due to alignment errors such as uncorrected optical distortion in the camera. Let $M_1$, $M_2$,..., $M_n$ refer to the original triangle meshes created from the range images. Then the three steps for finding the consensus surface are:

1) Find a local approximation to the surface normal.
2) Intersect a line oriented along this normal with each original range image.
3) Form a weighted average of the points of intersection.

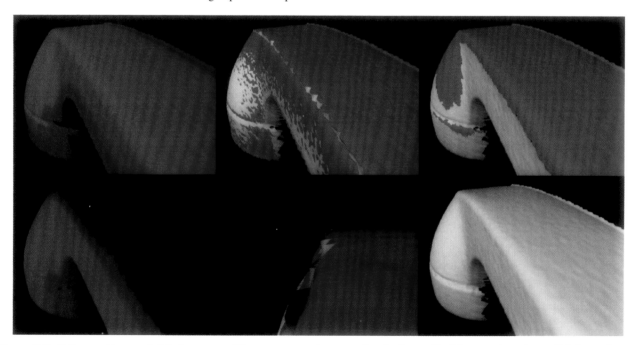

**Figure 7:** Left (top and bottom): Meshes created from two range images of a telephone. Red denotes locations of high confidence and blue shows low confidence. Note the low confidence at the edges to account for false edge extensions. Top middle: The two meshes (colored red and white) after alignment. Bottom middle: Close-up of aligned meshes that shows a jagged ridge of triangles that is the false edge extension of the white mesh at a corner. Top right: The meshes after redundant surface removal. Bottom right: The meshes after zippering.

**Figure 8:** Photograph of a plastic dinosaur model (left) and a polygon mesh created by registering and zippering together 14 range images that were taken of the model (right). The mesh consists of more than 360,000 polygons.

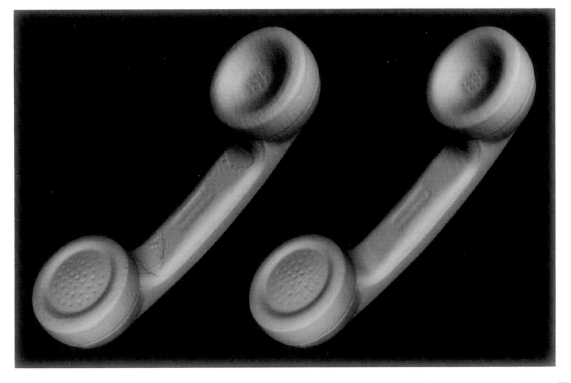

**Figure 9:** Left: This model of a telephone handset was created by zippering together meshes from ten range images. The mesh consists of more than 160,000 triangles. Right: The final positions of the vertices in the mesh have been moved to an average of nearby positions in the original range images. We call this the consensus geometry.

We approximate the surface normal $N$ at a given vertex $V$ by taking an average over all vertex normals from the vertices in all the meshes $M_i$ that fall within a small sphere centered at $V$. We then intersect each of the meshes $M_i$ with the line passing through $V$ along the direction $N$. Let $P$ be the set of all intersections that are near $V$. We take the consensus position of $V$ to be the average of all the points in $P$. If we have a measure of confidence for positions on a mesh we use this to weight the average.

## 7  Results and Discussion

The dinosaur model shown in Figure 8 was created from 14 range images and contains more than 360,000 triangles. Our integration method correctly joined together the meshes at all locations except on the head where some holes due to false edge extensions were filled manually. Such holes should not occur once we eliminate the false extensions in the range images. The dinosaur model was assembled from a larger quantity of range data (measured either in number of scans or number of range points) than any published model known to us. Naturally, we plan to explore the use of automatic simplification methods with our models [Schroeder 92] [Turk 92] [Hoppe 93]. Figure 9 shows a model of a phone that was created from ten range images and contains over 160,000 triangles. The mesh on the right demonstrates that the consensus geometry both reduces noise from the range images without blurring the model's features and also that it eliminates discontinuities at zippered regions.

A key factor that distinguishes our approach from those using unstructured integration ([Hoppe 92] and others) is that our method attempts to retain as much of the triangle connectivity as is possible from the meshes created from the original range images. Our integration process concentrates on a one-dimensional portion of the mesh (the boundary) instead of across an entire two-dimensional surface, and this makes for rapid integration.

Our algorithm shares several characteristics with the approach of Soucy and Laurendeau, which is also a structured integration method [Soucy 92]. The most important difference is the order in which the two methods perform integration and geometry averaging. Soucy's method first creates the final vertex positions by averaging between range images and then stitches together the common surface sets. By determining geometry before connectivity, their approach may be sensitive to artifacts of the stitching process. This is particularly undesirable because their method can create seams between as many as $2^n$ common surface sets from $n$ range images. Such artifacts are minimized in our approach by performing geometry averaging after zippering.

In summary, we use zippering of triangle meshes followed by refinement of surface geometry to build detailed models from range scans. We expect that in the near future range image technology will replace manual digitization of models in several application areas.

## 8  Future Work

There are several open problems related to integration of multiple range images. One issue is how an algorithm might automatically determine the next best view to capture more of an object's surface. Another important issue is merging reflectance information (including color) with the geometry of an object. Maybe the biggest outstanding issue is how to create higher-order surface descriptions such as Bezier patches or NURBS from range data, perhaps guided by a polygon model.

## Acknowledgments

We thank David Addleman, George Dabrowski and all the other people at Cyberware for the use of a scanner and for educating us about the issues involved in the technology. We thank all the members of our scanner group for numerous helpful discussions. In particular, Brian Curless provided some key insights for interpreting the range data and also wrote code to help this work. Thanks to Phil Lacroute for help with the color figures. This work was supported by an IBM Faculty Development Award, The Powell Foundation, and the National Science Foundation under contract CCR-9157767.

## References

[Bern 92]  Bern, Marshall and David Eppstein, "Mesh Generation and Optimal Triangulation," Technical Report P92-00047, Xerox Palo Alto Research Center, March 1992.

[Besl 92]  Besl, Paul J. and Neil D. McKay, "A Method of Registration of 3-D Shapes," *IEEE Transactions on Pattern Analysis and Machine Intelligence*, Vol. 14, No. 2 (February 1992), pp. 239–256.

[Boissonnat 84]  Boissonnat, Jean-Daniel, "Geometric Structures for Three-Dimensional Shape Representation," *ACM Transactions on Graphics*, Vol. 3, No. 4 (October 1984), pp. 266–286.

[Businski 92]  Businski, M., A. Levine and W. H. Stevenson, "Performance Characteristics of Range Sensors Utilizing Optical Triangulation," *IEEE National Aerospace and Electronics Conference*, Vol. 3 (1992), pp. 1230–1236.

[Champleboux 92]  Champleboux, Guillaume, Stephane Lavallee, Richard Szeliski and Lionel Brunie, "From Accurate Range Imaging Sensor Calibration to Accurate Model-Based 3-D Object Localization," *Proceedings of the IEEE Computer Society Conference on Computer Vision and Pattern Recognition*, Champaign, Illinois, June 15-20, 1992, pp. 83–89.

[Chen 92]  Chen, Yang and Gerard Medioni, "Object Modelling by Registration of Multiple Range Images," *Image and Vision Computing*, Vol. 10, No. 3 (April 1992), pp. 145–155.

[Edelsbrunner 92]  Edelsbrunner, Herbert and Ernst P. Mücke, "Three-dimensional Alpha Shapes," *Proceedings of the 1992 Workshop on Volume Visualization*, Boston, October 19-20, 1992, pp. 75–82.

[Hoppe 92]  Hoppe, Hugues, Tony DeRose, Tom Duchamp, John McDonald and Werner Stuetzle, "Surface Reconstruction from Unorganized Points," *Computer Graphics*, Vol. 26, No. 2 (SIGGRAPH '92), pp. 71–78.

[Hoppe 93]  Hoppe, Hugues, Tony DeRose, Tom Duchamp, John McDonald and Werner Stuetzle, "Mesh Optimization," *Computer Graphics Proceedings*, Annual Conference Series (SIGGRAPH '93), pp. 19–26.

[Horn 87]  Horn, Berthold K. P., "Closed-Form Solution of Absolute Orientation Using Unit Quaternions," *Journal of the Optical Society of America. A*, Vol. 4, No. 4 (April 1987), pp. 629–642.

[Schroeder 92]  Schroeder, William J., Jonathan A. Zarge and William E. Lorensen, "Decimation of Triangle Meshes," *Computer Graphics*, Vol. 26, No. 2 (SIGGRAPH '92), pp. 65–70.

[Soucy 92]  Soucy, Marc and Denis Laurendeau, "Multi-Resolution Surface Modeling from Multiple Range Views," *Proceedings of the IEEE Computer Society Conference on Computer Vision and Pattern Recognition*, Champaign, Illinois, June 15-20, 1992, pp. 348–353.

[Turk 92]  Turk, Greg, "Re-Tiling Polygonal Surfaces," *Computer Graphics*, Vol. 26, No. 2 (SIGGRAPH '92), pp. 55–64.

[Wada 93]  Wada, Nobuhiko, Hiroshi Toriyama, Hiromi T. Tanaka and Fumio Kishino, "Reconstruction of an Object Shape from Multiple Incomplete Range Data Sets Using Convex Hulls," *Computer Graphics International '93*, Lausanne, Switzerland, June 21-25, 1993, pp. 193–203.

# Efficient Algorithms for Local and Global Accessibility Shading

## Gavin Miller
## Apple Computer, Inc.

1 Infinite Loop, MS 301-3J, Cupertino, CA 95014
gspm@apple.com

### ABSTRACT
This paper discusses the use of two different approaches for computing the "accessibility" of a surface. These metrics characterize how easily a surface may be touched by a spherical probe. The paper also presents various acceleration techniques for accessibility. The idea of surface accessibility is extended to include "global accessibility" which measures the ability of a spherical probe to enter a structure from outside as well as to fit locally on the surface. The visual effect of shading using accessibility is shown to resemble the patina on certain tarnished surfaces which have then been cleaned.

Keywords: Surface accessibility shading, visualisation, aging.

## 1.0 Introduction
Most synthetic images look as though they are pictures of "new" objects. Visual cues to the aging of man-made products include the accumulation of dust on surfaces, the oxidation of metals (also known as tarnish), and the accumulation of dents and scratches. To counteract the effects of the aging process, many objects in the real world are cleaned and polished. This involves moving a soft rag over dust covered objects, or an abrasive rag over tarnished metals. Typically the cleaning surface, such as the rag, is unable to reach into sharply concave or otherwise inaccessible areas. Concave corners and creases tend to retain dirt or tarnish. To render these effects convincingly, it is necessary to formulate a mathematical definition of how accessible such regions are.

Fortunately, researchers in molecular modeling have long been concerned with defining surface "accessibility", since many chemical reactions depend on the access of one molecule to the surface of another. In Lee and Richards '71, the problem was first addressed in terms of a "solvent-accessible surface." (The original definition was replaced with the following one in Richards '77.) The solvent molecule is considered to be a spherical probe of fixed size, and is not allowed to intersect any of the original surface. The solvent accessible surface is the boundary of the volume which may be occupied by the solvent molecules. In geometrical terms the solvent accessible surface is found by offsetting the molecule outward by the probe radius and then offsetting inward by the same amount. In regions of concavity, the first offset surface will be self-intersecting. By trimming away the self-intersecting regions, the true offset envelope may be found. Because of this trimming, offsetting inwards does not restore the original surface. Instead, a constant radius fillet is introduced. In the case of a molecule with just two atoms, the fillet will be a portion of a torus. See Figure 1.

Connolly '83 described a graphics system for displaying solvent-accessible surfaces in real-time using a vector representation and for rendering shaded surfaces on a raster display. Edelsbrunner and Mucke '92, defined three-dimensional "alpha shapes" which, like solvent-accessible surfaces, are defined as the boundary of a volume inaccessible to a spherical probe of a given size. They simplify the resultant surface by "substituting straight edges for the circular ones and triangles for the spherical caps." They present an algorithm for creating approximate solvent-accessible surfaces as polygonal meshes.

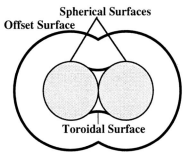

Figure 1. The solvent-accessible surface for a pair of spheres.

Unfortunately, we wish to shade the original surface with a measure of accessibility, rather than create a new surface. Kuhn et al '92 described a way to do this. They defined surface accessibility to be the radius of a sphere which may touch the surface tangentially and not intersect any other surface. Kuhn's definition will be referred to in this paper as "tangent-sphere accessibility". Kuhn et al '92 only described the computation of tangent-sphere accessibility when the original surface is a collection of spheres.

In Connolly '86, a different measure of surface shape is described. A sphere is centered on the surface point and the fraction of the sphere enclosed by the surface is a measure of the surface's curvature. The size of the sphere can be changed, effectively changing the filter size for the surface. While this is a useful shape analysis tool, it is not the best analogy for the tarnish cleaning process. Related work in Bloomenthal '91 creates smooth surfaces by convolving a binary volume representation with a Gaussian kernel and then finding the iso-surface. If the convolution value was used to shade the original surface, the results would be very similar to Connolly '86.

Work has also been described in the molecular modeling literature to determine whether solvents can reach inside a structure from outside. Connolly '91 describes the construction of a "molecular interstitial skeleton". The resultant skeletal structure gives an exhaustive measure of the radius of a sphere which could reach into interstitial regions. Unfortunately, the algorithm is restricted to surfaces made up of spheres, but it does test global accessibility for every size of probe simultaneously. For certain applications, however, measuring global accessibility for a probe with a fixed radius is quite satisfactory. Richards '79 described how to use a cube-connectedness algorithm to determine accessible regions within a structure when using a voxel representation.

## 2.0 Tangent Sphere Accessibility
We start by defining "tangent-sphere accessibility" as the radius of a sphere which may touch a surface point and not intersect any surface. The size of such a sphere will depend on the surface curvature (Figure 2) and the proximity of other surfaces (Figure 3). Note that the radius goes to zero where two surfaces intersect.

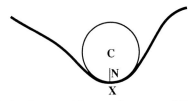

Figure 2. A sphere touching a surface tangentially with the maximum allowed radius.

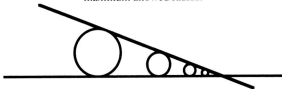

Figure 3. Accessibility for two intersecting planes.

## 2.1 Accessibility in the Presence of Other Geometry

When computing accessibility at a particular surface point, the surface normal and position is known. The accessibility could be computed by iterating on the sphere radius using a sphere-object intersection test (Figure 4). Unfortunately, this approach would be very time consuming since the intersection tests need to be done once per iteration. A second approach is to compute the accessibility directly from the geometry.

Figure 4. Nested tangential spheres

## 2.2 Accessibility in the Presence of Spheres

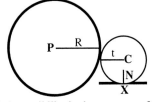

Figure 5. Accessibility in the presence of a sphere.

The accessibility, when the other surface in question is a sphere, is illustrated in Figure 5. The center of the tangential sphere C lies along the line formed by the surface position X, and the surface normal vector N. The radius of the tangential sphere is called t. This relationship is given by Equation (1).

$$C = X + t\,N \tag{1}$$

For the tangential sphere to also touch the other sphere, whose center is P and whose radius is R, Equation (2) must also hold.

$$(C - P) \cdot (C - P) = (R + t)^2 \tag{2}$$

By substituting for C and then solving for t, it turns out that t can be computed directly using Equation (3).

$$t = \frac{R^2 - (X - P) \cdot (X - P)}{2\,(N \cdot (X - P) - R)} \tag{3}$$

If t is found to be less than zero, then the normal must point away from the other sphere enough that the accessibility is actually infinite. The two cases of finite and infinite accessibility are illustrated in Figures 6 and 7.

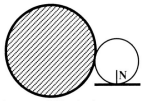

Figure 6. Finite accessibility in the presence of a sphere.

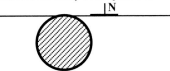

Figure 7. Infinite accessibility in the presence of a sphere.

The accessibility at a surface point is a value which can range between zero and infinity. To use this value as part of a shader, the accessibility needs to be used to generate a blend value between zero and one. This may be done using a linear or polynomial function, or using a negative exponential function. If there are more than two objects in the scene, the resultant accessibility is defined as the minimum of the accessibility values computed for each of the other objects in turn.

## 2.3 Accessibility in the Presence of Lines and Cylinders

Once again, the center of the tangential sphere is given by Equation 1. Given the center of the sphere C, we want to find the distance between this center and the nearest point on the axis of a cylinder. We define the cylinder to have a center P, a length l, and an axis unit vector L.

The nearest point to the sphere on the cylinder axis Q is defined by Equations (8 ) and (9).

$$u = (C - P) \cdot L \tag{8}$$

Where u is the distance along the axis vector from the center of the cylinder and

$$Q = u\,L + P \tag{9}$$

The condition that the tangential sphere also just touches the cylinder is given by Equation (10).

$$(C - Q) \cdot (C - Q) = (t + R)^2 \tag{10}$$

Where R is the radius of the cylinder.

Substituting in Equation (10) for C using Equation 1 and for Q using Equation 9 leads to a quadratic in t.

For the sake of clarity we define intermediate variables V and W in Equations (11) and (12).

$$V = N - (N \cdot L)\,L \tag{11}$$
$$W = ((X - P) \cdot L)L - (X - P) \tag{12}$$

Then the quadratic in t is of the form given by Equation (13).

$$a\,t^2 + b\,t + c = 0 \tag{13}$$

Where

$$a = 1 - V \cdot V \tag{14}$$
$$b = 2\,(R + V \cdot W) \tag{15}$$
$$c = R^2 - W \cdot W \tag{16}$$

The value of t is given by Equation (17).

$$t = \frac{-b \pm (b^2 - 4\,a\,c)^{\frac{1}{2}}}{2\,a} \tag{17}$$

The smallest positive value of t is used. If a is very close to zero, then Equation (18) is used.

$$t = \frac{-c}{b} \qquad (18)$$

So far we have treated the cylinder as if it was of infinite length. For a cylinder of finite length we need to take the end points into consideration. To see if the tangential sphere touches the cylinder within the end caps, we use the computed value of t to find the center of the tangential sphere C using Equation 1. The value of C is then used in Equation (8) to compute a value of u, the distance parameter along the cylinder axis. If the absolute value of u is less than half the cylinder length, then the value of t is valid. If this condition fails, then we ignore t and compute the accessibility for a sphere placed at the nearest end of the cylinder. This assumes that cylinders have spherical end caps.

### 2.4 Accessibility in the Presence of Polygons

To compute the accessibility for a surface element in the presence of polygons, we first consider the accessibility computation for an unbounded infinite plane. This geometry is illustrated in Figure 8.

Once again, the center of the tangential sphere is given by Equation 1. The infinite plane has a point P and a plane normal M. The distance between the infinite plane and the center of the tangential sphere must be equal to the radius of the tangential sphere, as defined by Equation (19).

$$t = (C - P).M \qquad (19)$$

Substituting for C using Equation 1 gives the value of t in Equation (20).

$$t = \frac{(X - P).M}{(1 - N.M)} \qquad (20)$$

Figure 8. Accessibility in the presence of an infinite plane.

In the case of a finite convex polygon, the value of t is then used to compute Q, which is the point on the infinite plane which is closest to the center of the tangential sphere. This is done in Equation (21).

$$Q = X + t(N - M) \qquad (21)$$

The point Q is then tested to see if it lies within the edges of the polygon. If it does, then the value of t is used. If it lies outside the boundary of the polygon, the edges and vertices of the polygon are used to compute the tangential radius. The latter computation is done by treating the polygon edges as cylinders of zero radius, and the polygon vertices as spheres of zero radius. For the case of a convex polyhedron, some of the edge and vertex computation only needs to be done once for the whole object, rather than for each polygonal face. Color Plate 1 shows a rectangular box intersecting with a sphere.

A "clock" made from a large number of spheres, cylinders and polygons is shown in Color Plate 2. Color Plate 2a shows the accessibility shading value and Color Plate 2b shows a diffusely shaded version of the clock. The accessibility shading is used to blend between the shaded surface and black (Color Plate 2c.) Color Plate 3 shows the combination of accessibility shading and environment mapping.

### 3.0 Efficient Tangent-Sphere Accessibility

As the number of objects increases, the cost of computing the tangent-sphere accessibility increases. For the naive algorithm, the cost is linear with the number of objects and proportional to the number of visible pixels. One way to reduce this cost is to reduce the number of objects used to compute the accessibility. This may be achieved by reducing the computation of accessibility to objects which lie within a certain spatial bound. This bound is then used to compute a list of potentially overlapping surfaces. This is an area which has been the study of computational geometers and a number of schemes have been suggested in the literature [Preparata '85].

### 3.1 Pixel-to-Pixel Coherence

A second class of optimization is possible using pixel-to-pixel coherence. Pixel-to-pixel coherence is like scan-line coherence in that results of the previous pixel are used to accelerate the computation for the current pixel. However, pixel-to-pixel coherence, as presented here, may carry over from one scan-line to the next and even between different primitives if they are close enough together, and have a similar enough normal vector.

For two adjacent pixels, the tangential spheres will largely overlap. Put another way, if we slightly enlarge the bound for one of the spheres, it will contain the sphere for the adjacent pixel. This coherence may be used by always employing an enlarged or "sloppy" bound to find the list of overlapping objects. For the next pixel, the new sphere is tested against the old sloppy bound. If the new sphere fits entirely within the old bound, then the old list of overlapping surfaces may be used for this pixel. This process continues until a sphere occurs which does not fit within the sloppy bound. In that case, a new sloppy bound is computed for the current tangential sphere, along with a new list of overlapping primitives. The sloppy bound is given by expanding the exact bound by a "slop margin".

If the chosen slop margin is too large, the returned list will have many surfaces which do not overlap the original bound. If the margin is too small, then the list will have to be recomputed from scratch for a high proportion of adjacent pixels. The optimal margin will depend on the resolution of the image. Coherence will increase as the image resolution increases, so a smaller margin will be optimal for larger images.

For the purposes of an initial evaluation, the clock image was rendered using tangent-sphere accessibility shading at a resolution of 128 by 256 pixels. The strategy used to find overlapping bounds was simply a linear search of the entire model. The slop margin was expressed in terms of a multiple of the maximum accessibility value which could affect the shading. Figure 9 shows the results of using differing values for the slop margin. (The timings are in seconds on an Apple Macintosh Quadra™ 900, which has a 25 MHz Motorola 68040.) The timings are for the portion of the computation concerned with finding the accessibility.

As expected, the rendering time decreased when the slop margin was increased from zero. The rendering time increased again when the margin of slop was very large. Most savings occurred for a margin of about four. This is unexpectedly large, and may be seen as a result of the rather low resolution of the image. The maximum savings due to using a sloppy bound for this image size was about a factor of six to one.

The results for an image resolution of 256 by 512 show that the minimum time occurs for a margin of error of about two. The greater degree of coherence means that a smaller margin will still query the database less frequently. The increase in speed due to the use of a sloppy bound for this higher resolution image is about ten to one. In general, the use of a sloppy bound becomes more effective as the image resolution increases.

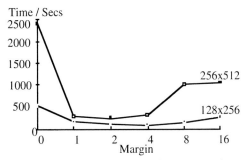

Figure 9. A graph of the rendering time vs. slop margin.

## 3.2 Limitations of Tangent-Sphere Accessibility

Unfortunately, tangent-sphere accessibility has a few computational disadvantages. Concave creases between adjacent polygons in a mesh will always have an inaccessible region. As the polygons become more parallel, the inaccessible region shrinks in size but never disappears. This leads to the very fine black lines and aliased "dots" visible in Color Plate 4. Unfortunately, this means that a smooth surface may not be approximated by a polygonal mesh in order to compute the accessibility. To overcome this problem, accessibility must either be computed for a mesh of normal-continuous patches, or redefined so that it is more forgiving of polygonal mesh approximations.

## 4.0 Surface Shading Using Offset-Distance Accessibility

An alternative definition for accessibility is to say it is equal to the distance to the nearest point on an offset of the surface, minus the offset radius. This definition is analogous to using a spherical cleaning device with an outer layer of abrasive bristles, as is shown in Figure 10.

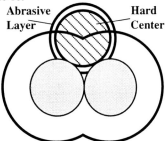

Figure 10. Spherical cleaning probe with abrasive layer.

In convex regions with no intersections, the distance is equal to the offset radius. In concave regions this value will increase depending on how inaccessible the surface is.

Figure 11. Positive offset of a height-field.

If a height field is represented by samples in a rectangular buffer A, then an offset of the surface may be computed in a second buffer B as follows:

• Buffer B is initialized to have the minimum value of buffer A at every sample.
• For each sample point in Buffer A, a sphere centered at that pixel's depth and location is scan-converted into Buffer B taking the maximum of the existing value and the value for the sphere.

This process is illustrated in Figure 11. To compute the offset-offset surface, the offsetting is now done in reverse:

• Buffer C is initialized to have the maximum value of buffer B at every sample.
• For each sample point in Buffer B, a sphere centered at that pixel's depth and location is scan-converted into Buffer C taking the minimum of the existing value and the value for the sphere. pixel.
• The distance to the nearest point on the offset-offset surface may then be approximated by taking the difference between Buffer C and the original height field in Buffer A.

This series of steps is called the offset-offset difference algorithm. It may be optimized by storing the depth of the offset sphere samples in a table.

An alternative algorithm is to compute the distance to the nearest pixel in the offset buffer (Buffer B) for every pixel in the original height field (Buffer A). At first glance this nearest distance calculation might require searching every pixel in Buffer B. This can be avoided by noting that the 3-D distance to the offset pixel is always greater than the 2-D distance in the plane of the buffer. Thus the pixels are tested in a spiral outward from the location of the sample in Buffer A, until the 3-D distance to the nearest sample in the offset buffer is closer than the radius of the spiral. In practice the spiral is a rectangular spiral aligned with the sample grid. This second approach is called the spiral search algorithm. If an upper limit is placed on distance values of interest, then the search may be terminated when the radius of the spiral reaches this distance value.

The offset-offset difference algorithm maintains the depth values at higher precision than the horizontal resolution of the buffer. Since, for certain applications, much of the important detail is in small variations in depth, this algorithm is preferable to the spiral search algorithm. It does slightly over-estimate the distance to the nearest point in the offset surface, but the errors are acceptable.

Color Plate 5 shows the offset-offset difference algorithm applied to a depth map. The depth map has been Lambert shaded, the accessibility computed, and then the results of the two calculations multiplied together. Color Plate 6 shows the accessibility map of a flower molding. By doing a color fill on the background, and then inverting the intensities, the impression of a wood-block print is created.

It is possible to use the same algorithm to approximate the accessibility for a surface when it is a mesh other than a height field. Color Plates 7 and 8 show Cyberware scans of human heads shaded using offset-offset difference accessibility. (The Cyberware scans were in the form of radial displacements to a cylindrical surface.) The banding artifacts on the neck in Color Plate 7 are in the original data.

The effect of changing the offset radius is compared in Color Plate 9. The display shading range was kept in a constant ratio to the offset radius. As the offset radius was increased, the border around the nose increased and the interior of the mouth vanished completely in the last two images. The times taken for the algorithm are shown in Table 2. They increased as the square of the offset radius, as was to be expected.

| Offset Radius/pixels | Time/seconds |
|---|---|
| 1 | 16.3 |
| 2 | 35.8 |
| 4 | 112.4 |
| 8 | 407.1 |
| 16 | 1547.6 |
| 32 | 5925.7 |

Table 2: Offset-offset times for increasing offset radius.

A disadvantage of the offset-offset difference algorithm is that it is parametric on the surface and does not compute the effect of intersections between different pieces of geometry. To compute offset-distance accessibility for intersecting objects, a new approach is required. If objects are represented as the boundaries of volumes stored in a voxel array, then offsetting operations may be applied to the volumetric representation as easily as for height fields. The model is considered to be contained within a three dimensional rectangular array of samples. These samples only need to be one-bit since they represent only the presence or absence of material.

To offset the volume in Voxel Buffer A, the following steps are taken:

• A second voxel buffer, Voxel Buffer B, is first initialized to be a copy of Voxel Buffer A.
• Then, for every voxel in Voxel Buffer A which has a value of one and has a zero neighbor, a sphere is scan-converted into Voxel Buffer B. The scan-conversion sets voxels which lie along the span to have a value of one.
• Voxel Buffer B then represents the offset volume.

To render the original surface with accessibility shading, the surface is scan-converted into a Z-buffer. For each surface point visible in the screen image, a corresponding point is found in the offset voxel buffer (Voxel Buffer B). This buffer is then searched in an expanding sphere until a zero-valued pixel is encountered. The distance between this zero-valued pixel and the original surface point is then used as the accessibility. The results of this algorithm are shown in Color Plate 10a. The shading range for the accessibility has been set to be equal to one voxel spacing. This was done to highlight the nature of the error in approximating the offset volume with a voxel map. An interesting pattern of Vornoi-diagram-like regions appears. These mark the areas for which the nearest zero-valued voxel in the offset surface is the same. In practice, the accessibility shading range is set to several voxel spacings and then the errors become acceptable.

Color Plate 11 compares parametric offset-offset difference shading, and volumetric offset-distance accessibility shading based on the voxel representation. The differences between the two techniques correspond intuitively with changing the offset radius slightly in different regions. From this experiment, it is clear that the results of the parametric and volumetric algorithms are not significantly different for the example chosen. The parametric technique, which is much faster, may be employed usefully on data-sets of this type.

As defined above, the volumetric offsetting algorithm takes time which increases as the cube of the offset radius. In practice this may be reduced to a quadratic dependence on the radius by using different representations for the voxel buffer. One approach is to represent the buffer as one bit numbers packed into long words. This means that 32 voxels may be scan-converted in one instruction. Logical operations on sets of voxels may be computed by applying the same operations to the long words which represent them. (Carpenter '84 used this approach successfully in implementing bit-mask operations as part of the A-buffer algorithm.) This representation does not eliminate the radius-cubed dependence theoretically, but in practice the offset radius is rarely set to more than one hundred or so voxel spacings, so computing the ends of the spans swamps the cost of scan-conversion.

A second possible representation, is to have a two-dimensional array of lists. For each X-axis aligned row in the voxel space, a list of transitions between one and zero could be stored. Scan-converting into such a list then only depends on the depth complexity of the list rather than the length of the span. It should also have memory savings for all but the most pathological volume sets, but might take longer to interrogate for the nearest zero-valued pixel compared to the optimized one-bit representation for practical ranges of offset radius.

A different technique for optimization is to compute the offset distance at voxel locations around the original surface, and then to interpolate the results for intermediate positions. The results of this algorithm are shown in Color Plate 10b. The errors are largely unchanged. A sparse voxel data-structure is needed to store the distance values for voxels which are adjacent to the original surface. Such a representation may also be used to render the surface multiple times when only the viewing transformation is changed. It is the voxel equivalent of storing the surface color in a parametric texture map.

The naive way to compute the distance to the nearest zero-valued pixel in the offset volume also increases as the cube of the offset radius. In practice this may be reduced to the square of the radius either by changing to the 2-D array of lists or by treating the 1-bit representation in slice order as follows:

• Loop from top to bottom for each horizontal slice of the voxel buffer.
• For each pixel in the horizontal slice, compute for each voxel the location of the nearest zero-valued pixel above it. This will either be the location of the nearest zero-valued voxel for the same location in the previous slice, or it will be the location of the current voxel (if it has a value of one).
For this slice we now have a 2-D array of samples which represent the height of the nearest zero-valued voxel above each slice voxel.
• For each slice voxel which is adjacent to the original surface, compute the distance to the nearest zero-valued voxel in the offset volume by using the spiral search algorithm applied to the 2-D array of samples. This corresponds to examining the entire offset voxel buffer above the surface point and finding the nearest non-zero voxel.
• The resultant accessibility value is placed in the sparse voxel representation.

To complete the calculation, the algorithm is repeated, but sweeping from bottom to top. This time the algorithm keeps track of the position of the nearest zero-valued pixel below the current slice. The distance from the top-down sweep is compared to the distance from the bottom-up sweep. The smaller of the two is the valid 3-D distance to the nearest zero-valued voxel in the offset volume. The original surface is then scan-converted using accessibility values interpolated from the sparse voxel representation. The times taken to compute volumetric accessibility for the head in Color Plate 10, for different offset radii are given in Table 3. The voxel set is 512 voxels on a side.

| Offset Radius/pixels | Offset / secs | Shading / secs |
|---|---|---|
| 3 | 298 | 217 |
| 6 | 599 | 404 |
| 12 | 1967 | 1045 |
| 24 | 8173 | 3396 |

Table 3. Volumetric accessibility times for different offset radii.

## 4.1 Global Accessibility using a Voxel Representation

Volumetric rather than parametric accessibility is clearly required if objects intersect in a scene. An example is shown in Color Plate 12.a It shows the effect of shading the volumetric accessibility as a red pigmentation. Locally inaccessible regions are emphasized. However, the interior of the structure is shown to be accessible, as is the small sphere in the center. This is because there is room inside the structure for a probe sphere to touch the surface without intersecting any other surface. To prevent these regions from being accessible, it is required to compute whether the probe sphere could enter the structure from outside. How to compute this is simplified by the observation that testing the intersection of a sphere with a volume is equivalent to testing a point at the center of the sphere against an offset of the volume, where the offset radius is the sphere radius.

Computing global accessibility merely requires that we replaced the test for the nearest zero-valued voxel in the offset buffer with a test for the nearest zero-valued voxel which is connected to a point outside of the structure. This may be computed using a seed-fill algorithm applied to the offset volume. The resultant volume is then used for the offset distance calculation. For a 512-cubed voxel space, a simple seed-fill algorithm takes about 2 minutes on an Iris Crimson with a 66 MHz R4000 processor.

Color Plate 12b shows a global accessibility-based pigmentation for the same model. The small sphere and interior regions of the large spheres are now inaccessible, as expected. A more complex example is shown in Color Plate 13a, where a set of random cylinders has been shaded with diffuse shading. The local accessibility shading in Color Plate 13b shows white regions in the body of the set of cylinders. The global accessibility shown in Color Plate 13c eliminates these regions, providing a strong visual indication that such a structure would be impermeable to spherical probes of that size. Color Plate 13d shows the difference between the local and global accessibility values, and so highlights regions accessible to only those spheres which would be trapped inside the lattice.

## 5.0 Conclusions

A variety of definitions of surface accessibility were explored. New analytical results were derived for "tangent-sphere accessibility" in the presence of cylinders and polygons. An algorithm was also devised which accelerated the computation of tangent-sphere accessibility for large numbers of objects. However, tangent-sphere accessibility was found to be inappropriate for shading polygonal meshes.

A second definition of accessibility was introduced based on the distance to the nearest point on the offset of a surface. This algorithm yielded interesting visual effects which suggested an aged or tarnished appearance. The algorithm was extended to deal with general 3-D surfaces using an efficient voxel representation. The voxel-based approach was expanded to compute "global accessibility" which took into account the ability of a probe of fixed size to travel into a structure from outside.

## 6.0 References

Bloomenthal, Jules, "Convolution Surfaces", Computer Graphics, Vol. 25, No. 4, July 1991 pp 251-256.

Carpenter, Loren, "The A-buffer, An Anitialiased Hidden Surface Method", Computer Graphics, Vol. 18, No. 3, July 1984 pp 103-108.

Connolly, M., "Solvent-accessible surfaces of proteins and nucleic acids", Science, Vol. 221, No. 4612 (19 August 1983) p 303.

Connolly, M. L., "Measurement of protein surface shape by solid angles", Journal of Molecular Graphics, Vol. 4, No. 1, March 1986.

Edelsbrunner, Herbert and Ernst P. Mucke, "Three-dimensional Alpha Shapes", Proceedings of 1992 Workshop on Volume Visualisation, Boston, October 19-20, 1992.

Kuhn, Leslie A., Michael A. Siani, Michael E. Pique, Cindy L. Fisher, Elizabeth D. Getzoff, and Joan A. Tainer, "The Interdependence of Protein Surface Topography and Bound Water Molecules Revealed by Surface Accessibility and Fractal Density Measures", J. Mol. Biol., (1992) 228, pp 13-22.

Lee, B. and F. M. Richards, "The Interpretation of protein structures: estimation of static accessibility", J. Mol. Biol., Vol. 55 (1971) p 151.

Preparata, Franco P., Michael Ian Shamos, "Computational Geometry, An Introduction", Springer Verlag, 1985.

Richards, F. M., Annu. Rev. Biophysics. Bioeng. 6. 151 (1977)

Richards, F. M., "Packing Defects, Cavities, Volume Fluctuations, and Access to the Interior of Proteins, Including Some General Comments on Surface Area and Protein Structure", Carlsberg Res. Commun. 44, (1979) pp 47-63.

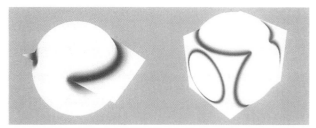

Plate 1. Tangent-sphere accessibility for a sphere intersecting a) a polygon, b) a rectangular box.

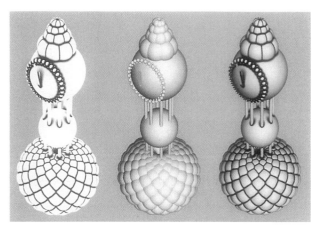

Plate 2 Clock model with a) Tangent-sphere acessibility b) Lambert Shading, c) Composite Shading.

Plate 3: Tangent-sphere accessibility with environment mapping.

Plate 4: Polygonal Mesh with a) Tangent-sphere accessibility shading, b) Lambert shading, c) composite shading.

Plate 6: Flower mould as a) Offset-offset accessibility map, b) Inverted map with background fill.

Plate 5: Height field with a) Lambert Shading, b) Offset -offset accessibility shading , c) Composite shading.

Plate 8: Greek Gods.

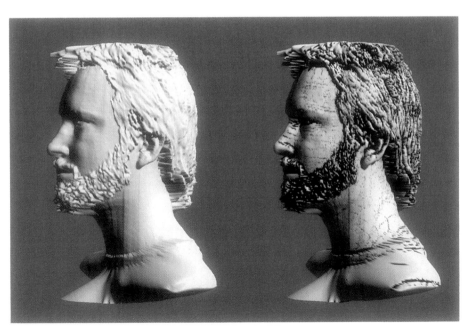

Plate 7: Cyberware scan with a) Lambert shading, b) Offset-offset accessibility shading.

Plate 9: Changing the offset radius for accessibility shading.

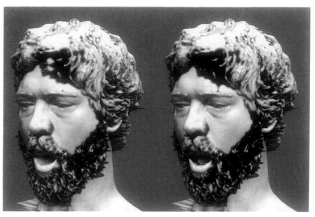

Plate 11: a) Parametric Accessibility b) Volumetric Accessibility.

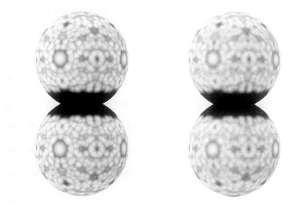

Plate 10: Error for voxel-based accessibility  a) Computed at each
pixel, b) Interpolated from lattice.

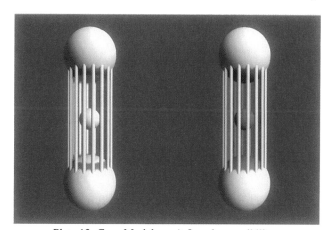

Plate 12: Cage Model  as a)  Local accessibility ,
b) Global  accessibility.

Plate 13: Random Cylinders as a)  Lambert shading,
b) Local accessibility, c) Global accessibility,
d) Local  and not global accessibility.

# Illumination In Diverse Codimensions

David C. Banks

Institute for Computer Applications in Science and Engineering

## ABSTRACT

This paper considers an idealized subclass of surface reflectivities; namely, a simple superposition of ideal diffuse and ideal specular, restricted to point light sources. The paper derives a model of diffuse and specular illumination in arbitrarily large dimensions, based on a few characteristics of material and light in 3-space. It describes how to adjust for the anomaly of excess brightness in large codimensions. If a surface is grooved or furry, it can be illuminated with a hybrid model that incorporates both the 1D geometry (the grooves or fur) and the 2D geometry (the surface).

**CR Categories and Subject Descriptors**: I.3.7 [Computer Graphics]: Three-Dimensional Graphics and Realism – color, shading, shadowing and texture.

**Additional Keywords and Phrases**: manifold, anisotropic reflection, hair, fur.

## 1 Introduction

When a geometric object possesses a distinct (outward) unit normal at each point, the familiar models of illumination can be applied to the object. When the object is in a large dimensional space, the space of unit normals has two or more dimensions and the illumination model must be extended; examples include curves in 3-space and 4-space, or surfaces in 4-space and higher.

This paper addresses the problem of applying light in large codimensions. Consider an object of dimension $k>0$ in Euclidean space of dimension $n>k$. The difference $n-k$ is the *codimension* of the object. Mathematicians use the term $k$-*manifold* to denote the $k$-dimensional generalization of curves (1-manifolds) and surfaces (2-manifolds). Every neighborhood of a $k$-manifold is homeomorphic with Euclidean $k$-space.

Regarding codimension 1, popular texts on computer graphics [Foley90, Rogers85] handle the special case of $k=2$ and $n=3$: these are ordinary surfaces in 3-space. Other authors [Carey87] [Steiner87] have noted that whenever the codimension is 1, each point of a manifold can be naturally assigned a normal vector. The usual lighting equations then prevail. (Special care is required for non-orientable manifolds or manifolds with boundary, since their "frontfacing" elements are not well defined.)

Regarding codimension 2, several authors have considered the case of $k=1$, $n=3$ for illuminating fur [Kajiya85], hair [Anjyo92, Miller88, LeBlanc91, Watanabe92], or anisotropic grooves on a surface [Kajiya89, Poulin90, Westin92, Ward92]. The case $k=2$, $n=4$ has been studied in the "Fourphront" system [Banks92, Banks93] and elsewhere [Hanson93] for examining a variety of

surfaces in 4-space. Kajiya and Hanson each testify that their model is not based on physical principles; Kajiya calls it "ad hoc" and Hanson calls it a "heuristic" result. But in fact the Kajiya-Hanson model can be derived from a few physical principles. This is the subject of section 2.

In daily life one encounters illuminated surfaces everywhere. It is reasonable to believe that the human visual system is especially well designed to infer shape from the shading of 2-dimensional surfaces in 3-space [Horn89]. If surfaces in 3-space represent the ideal for visual comprehension, the Kajiya-Hanson model suffers from a peculiar drawback: manifolds are "too bright" when the codimension grows larger. The increase in brightness in higher-dimensional spaces is not caused by any defect in the ideal diffuse model, but is caused instead by the increasing proportion of unit vectors that lie near the normal space. Section 3 discusses the problem and section 3.4 presents a simple remedy.

Kajiya [Kajiya85] noted the importance of global illumination effects (in the form of attenuation and shadows) for rendering textured volume elements. Section 4 shows how the combination of a manifold together with a vector field (like a surface together with fur) can be illuminated to simulate global effects. The technique can be incorporated into a simple object-order (e.g., polygon) renderer.

That reader should note that more complete reflection models are available; in particular, models that accurately describe the form of the specularly-reflected energy and the shape of the diffusely-reflected energy. The quantity of specular and diffuse reflection depends on the solid angle of the incident irradiation. In particular, the reflected intensity is not finite at grazing angles of reflection, but goes to zero. Examples of more comprehensive reflection models for surfaces in 3-space can be found elsewhere [Kajiya86, He92, Hanrahan93].

## 2 The Model for Large Codimensions

The final results of this section will be equations for diffuse and specular illumination that are equivalent to the results that Kajiya and Hanson have presented [Kajiya89] [Hanson93]. The new contribution that this section offers is a physical motivation to the derivation. The conventional motivation begins by promoting the dimension of a manifold, illuminating the promoted manifold, and integrating. The new motivation dispenses with the promotion and integration steps altogether. It proceeds directly from the geometry to the illumination solution, without regard to the participating dimensions.

The following discussion makes heavy use of the tangent space $\mathbf{T}$ and the normal space $\mathbf{N}$ at a point $\mathbf{p}$ on a $k$-manifold $M$ in $n$-space (see Figure 1). The space $\mathbf{T}$ is the vector space tangent to a point in $M$. It has dimension $k$, matching that of the manifold $M$. The space $\mathbf{N}$ is orthogonal to $\mathbf{T}$ and has dimension $c$ (the codimension of $M$). The dimensions of $\mathbf{T}$ and $\mathbf{N}$ add up to the dimension of the entire space (that is, $k+c = n$).

Mail Stop 132C, NASA Langley Research Center
Hampton, Virginia 23681-0001   (banks@icase.edu)

## 2.1 Conventional Motivation

The benefit of codimension 1 is that there exist only two unit normals in a point's 1-dimensional normal space. The usual illumination equations require the modest choice of one of the two. If the codimension is large, there is no clear way to select one unit normal from the infinitude that are available. There is a clever solution that other authors have adopted: the dimension of the manifold can be promoted to reduce the codimension.

Let $S^n(r)$ denote an $n$-sphere of radius $r$. A circle of radius 10 is then $S^1(10)$; a unit sphere is $S^2(1)$, or simply $S^2$. Kajiya, Hanson, and others have proposed that illuminating a $k$-manifold $M$ of codimension $c > 1$ can be accomplished after forming the Cartesian product of $M$ with $S^{c-1}(r)$. It is required that $S^{c-1}(r)$ lie within the normal space $\mathbf{N}$. A point is thus promoted to a circle in 2-space or to a sphere in 3-space; a curve is promoted to a tube in 3-space; a surface is promoted to a volume in 4-space.

The advantage of promoting $M$ to $M' = M \times S^{c-1}(r)$ is that the promoted manifold has codimension 1. This represents the simple case where the usual lighting equations prevail. The promoted manifold $M'$ can provide an effective representation of $M$ with no further processing. But to render $M$ itself, one must employ a scheme whereby a point $\mathbf{p}$ in $M$ inherits the illumination of its fiber $\mathbf{p} \times S^{c-1}(r)$ in $M'$. A reasonable way to accomplish that goal is to integrate the intensity of the reflected light over $\mathbf{p} \times S^{c-1}(r)$ and then to average it. The average intensity is obtained by dividing the integrated intensity by the measure of the fiber as seen by the eye. This measure can be a length, an area, a volume, or so forth, in accordance with the dimension $c-1$ of the sphere $S^{c-1}(r)$ (used in the cross product) over which the average is taken. The limit of the average, as $r \to 0$, yields a reasonable intensity for the point $\mathbf{p}$.

There are two drawbacks to this approach of promoting $M$ to $M'$, integrating, and then averaging. First, the integration is unwieldy for $c > 1$, due to the specular term in the integrand. Second, the projected measure of $S^{c-1}(r)$ is view-dependent. This opposes the notion that diffuse reflection is view-independent. For example, in derivation (13) of [Kajiya89], the integrated intensity over a fiber $\mathbf{p} \times S^1(r)$ of $M'$ is calculated to be

$$I'_{diffuse} = k_d r \, \mathbf{L} \cdot \mathbf{L_N} \int_0^\pi \sin\theta \, d\theta$$

$$= k_d \, 2r \, \mathbf{L} \cdot \mathbf{L_N}$$

where $k_d$ is the diffuse coefficient, $\mathbf{L}$ is the light vector, and $\mathbf{L_N}$ is the projection of $\mathbf{L}$ onto $\mathbf{N}$ (Figure 1). Under a parallel projection,

the arclength of the circle can vary from $2r$ (viewing the tube from the side) to $\pi r$ (viewing the tube end-on). So the average intensity ranges between a minimum of $2/\pi \, k_d \, \mathbf{L} \cdot \mathbf{L_N}$ and a maximum of $k_d \, \mathbf{L} \cdot \mathbf{L_N}$ according to the viewing angle. Kajiya avoided this problem by treating the quantity $k_d \, 2r / \text{projectedArclength}(r)$ as a constant, so that a point on the original manifold M has intensity

$$I_{diffuse} = K_d \, \mathbf{L} \cdot \mathbf{L_N}$$

## 2.2 Principles for Diffuse Reflection

One can, in fact, justify Kajiya's result by characterizing diffuse reflection in the following way. A neighborhood of a point $\mathbf{p}$ absorbs energy from the incoming light (which delivers $I_{source}$ per unit cross section), and then it re-radiates a fraction $k_d$ of the absorbed energy. How much energy does the beam deliver to a unit-neighborhood of $\mathbf{p}$? That depends on the cross section of the beam and the angle it makes with the tangent plane (Figure 2).

Suppose an incident light beam strikes $M$ at $\mathbf{p}$. The light vector $\mathbf{L}$ (pointing in the direction that the beam propagates) projects orthogonally onto the tangent space $\mathbf{T}$ at $\mathbf{p}$ to produce the vector $\mathbf{L_T}$. The two vectors form an angle $a(\mathbf{L}, \mathbf{L_T})$. Simple trigonometry shows that a unit neighborhood of the tangent space intercepts a beam whose cross-section has measure $\sin(a)$. Note that this quantity is never negative, since a vector can be no more than 90° from the tangent space. The manifold re-radiates $k_d$ of the energy delivered by the beam's cross-section. Thus the diffuse component of reflection at $\mathbf{p}$ is given by

$$(1) \qquad I_{diffuse} = k_d \, I_{source} \sin a(\mathbf{L}, \mathbf{L_T}).$$

This solution is essentially the same as Kajiya's: the sine (measured against $\mathbf{T}$) and cosine (measured against $\mathbf{N}$) are equal.

The principles for this result are (1) the re-radiated light's intensity varies with the energy delivered by the incident beam; and (2) the manifold re-radiates isotropically.

Equation (1) is purely local, neglecting any effects of shadowing (even self-shadowing). For a closed surface in 3-space, it is common practice to clamp the diffuse term to zero when the surface normal points away from the light source. This is best regarded as a "global" calculation. A very thin surface *does* re-radiate light both forward and backward, as the local model predicts. Moreover, when the codimension is larger than 1, the unit normals form a connected set. In that case there is no "front" or "back" side of the manifold. Local two-sidedness is an exclusive property of codimension 1.

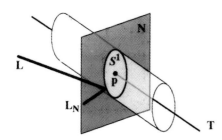

*Figure 1. Light shines in direction $\mathbf{L}$ at a point $\mathbf{p}$ on a tube. $\mathbf{L_N}$ is the projection of the light onto the normal space $\mathbf{N}$. The diffuse reflection is integrated over the visible portion of the circle $S^1$.*

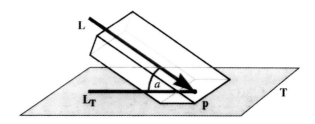

*Figure 2. Light shines in direction $\mathbf{L}$ at a point $\mathbf{p}$. $\mathbf{L_T}$ is the projection of the light onto the tangent space $\mathbf{T}$. The beam strikes a unit neighborhood of $\mathbf{p}$ at an angle $a$.*

## 2.3 Principles for Specular Reflection

A specular highlight is most intense where a reflection vector $\mathbf{R}$ and the view vector $\mathbf{V}$ are aligned. One can use a power function to condense the reflected intensity within a neighborhood where the angle between $\mathbf{R}$ and $\mathbf{V}$ is small (Phong lighting). The only problem is how to determine an appropriate unit-length reflection vector $\mathbf{R}$ when the codimension exceeds 1: there are infinitely many to choose from.

Deriving a solution has two parts. First, one determines the set of candidate reflection vectors $R$. By Fermat's principle, light follows a path of minimal length. Even in large codimensions this principle implies that the angle of incidence (measured against the tangent space) equals the angle of reflection. Section 2.3.1 derives this relation as $\mathbf{R_T} = \mathbf{L_T}$. The second step is to compute the distance between $\mathbf{V}$ and the space $R$ of reflection vectors. Section 2.3.2 computes that distance by means of a "dot product" $\mathbf{V} \cdot R$.

### 2.3.1 Angle of Reflection and the Family of Reflection Vectors

To see how Fermat's principle applies to a ray of light reflecting from a tangent space $\mathbf{T}$, consider a point source $\mathbf{q}$ that shines on the point $\mathbf{p}$ and bounces to reach a point $\mathbf{u}$ (Figure 3). The segments from $\mathbf{q}$ to $\mathbf{p}$ and from $\mathbf{p}$ to $\mathbf{u}$ are straight-line paths, satisfying Fermat's principle. But for fixed $\mathbf{q}$ and $\mathbf{u}$, where does $\mathbf{p}$ lie?

In 2-dimensional space the problem is easy and the solution obvious: the angles $a = \angle(\mathbf{q}\ \mathbf{p}\ \mathbf{q_T})$ and $b = \angle(\mathbf{u}\ \mathbf{p}\ \mathbf{u_T})$ are equal, with $\mathbf{q_T}$ and $\mathbf{u_T}$ lying on opposite sides of $\mathbf{p}$. The situation in $n$-dimensional space is nearly this simple.

If $\mathbf{u} - \mathbf{p}$ really is a reflection vector then a path from $\mathbf{q}$ to $\mathbf{u}$ via a nearby point $\mathbf{s}$ in $\mathbf{T}$ must be longer than the path via $\mathbf{p}$. Thus $\mathbf{q_T}$, $\mathbf{p}$, and $\mathbf{u_T}$ must be collinear. To see why, consider choosing $\mathbf{s}$ off of the line $\overline{\mathbf{u_T}\ \mathbf{q_T}}$. For each of the two triangles (figure 3), the base would be shortened by moving $\mathbf{s}$ to its projection onto $\overline{\mathbf{u_T}\ \mathbf{q_T}}$ (because of the triangle inequality), as would each hypotenuse. So the total path-length through $\mathbf{s}$ is not minimal, defying Fermat's principle. Thus the base of each triangle lies on the line $\overline{\mathbf{u_T}\ \mathbf{q_T}}$.

Suppose that $a = b$ and consider what happens when $\mathbf{p}$ is then perturbed (in the line $\overline{\mathbf{u_T}\ \mathbf{q_T}}$) over to some $\mathbf{p} + s(\mathbf{q_T} - \mathbf{u_T})$. The total distance $D(s)$ is parametrized by $s$:

$$D(s) = d(\mathbf{q},\ \mathbf{p} + s(\mathbf{q_T} - \mathbf{u_T})) + d(\mathbf{p} + s(\mathbf{q_T} - \mathbf{u_T}),\ \mathbf{u})$$

A straightforward application of trigonometry and calculus demonstrates that the total distance is a local minimum exactly when $b = a$. One must simply verify that $\frac{d}{ds}D(s) = 0$ when $s = 0$.

The unit vectors $\mathbf{L}$ and $\mathbf{R}$ consequently have identical tangent components, so the first requirement on a unit reflection vector $\mathbf{R}$ is that $\mathbf{R_T} = \mathbf{L_T}$. If the codimension is 1, there are two such "reflection" vectors, $\mathbf{R^+}$ and $\mathbf{R^-}$; $\mathbf{R^+}$ is the continuation of $\mathbf{L}$ transmitted through $\mathbf{T}$ (for opaque manifolds of codimension 1, this solution is ignored). When the codimension is 2, the set of all reflection vectors forms a cone-shaped family $R$ (Figure 4). The unit reflection vectors from $R$ project to a circle in the normal space $\mathbf{N}$. In general, the unit reflection vectors project to $S^{c-1}(r)$ in $\mathbf{N}$ when the codimension is $c$.

### 2.3.2 Angle Between the View Vector and the Reflection Vector

What is the angle between the view vector $\mathbf{V}$ and the space $R$ of reflections? It is the angle between $\mathbf{V}$ and the closest vector $\mathbf{R}$ in $R$. This vector is easy to find. A unit reflection $\mathbf{R}$ can be expressed by its tangent and normal components $\mathbf{R_T} = \mathbf{L_T}$ and $\mathbf{R_N}$. The unit view vector can be likewise decomposed into $\mathbf{V_T}$ and $\mathbf{V_N}$.

The components $\mathbf{V_T}$, $\mathbf{V_N}$, and $\mathbf{R_T}$ are all fixed, so the distance between $\mathbf{R}$ and $\mathbf{V}$ is minimized when $\|\mathbf{R_N} - \mathbf{V_N}\|$ is minimized. That occurs when $\mathbf{R_N}$ and $\mathbf{V_N}$ are collinear: $\mathbf{R_N} = \lambda \mathbf{V_N}$ for some scalar $\lambda$. To see why this is minimal, recall that the vector $\mathbf{R_N}$ is also perpendicular to the point $\mathbf{R_N}$ on the sphere $S^{c-1}$ in the normal space. It is a familiar result from calculus that if the distance from a point $\mathbf{p}$ (off of $S^{c-1}$) to a point $\mathbf{q}$ (on $S^{c-1}$) is minimal, the vector $\mathbf{p} - \mathbf{q}$ is perpendicular to $S^{c-1}$.

In particular, the reflection $\mathbf{R}$ is found by requiring its normal component to be

$$\mathbf{R_N} = -\|\mathbf{R_N}\| \frac{\mathbf{V_N}}{\|\mathbf{V_N}\|} = -\|\mathbf{L_N}\| \frac{\mathbf{V_N}}{\|\mathbf{V_N}\|}$$

This aligns $\mathbf{R}$ with the projection of the view vector onto the normal space (Figure 3). The cosine of the angle between $\mathbf{R}$ and $\mathbf{V}$ is just the dot product

$$\begin{aligned} \mathbf{V} \cdot \mathbf{R} &= (\mathbf{V_T} + \mathbf{V_N}) \cdot (\mathbf{R_T} + \mathbf{R_N}) \\ &= \mathbf{V_T} \cdot \mathbf{R_T} + \mathbf{V_N} \cdot \mathbf{R_N} \end{aligned}$$

The two inner terms of the expansion are zero because the tangent and normal spaces are orthogonal. By substituting for the components $\mathbf{R_T}$ and $\mathbf{R_N}$ of the reflection vector, one finds the projection formula

$$\mathbf{V} \cdot \mathbf{R} = \mathbf{V_T} \cdot \mathbf{L_T} - \mathbf{V_N} \cdot \|\mathbf{L_N}\| \frac{\mathbf{V_N}}{\|\mathbf{V_N}\|}$$

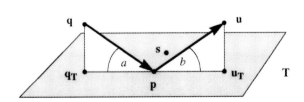

*Figure 3. A ray of light emanates from $\mathbf{q}$, strikes the tangent space $\mathbf{T}$ at $\mathbf{p}$, and reflects to $\mathbf{u}$. If the total path has minimum length, angles $a$ and $b$ are equal.*

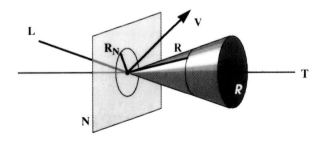

*Figure 4. The light vector $\mathbf{L}$ reflects off a tangent line $\mathbf{T}$ in 3-space, forming a cone $R$ of reflections. The view vector $\mathbf{V}$ projects to $\mathbf{R}$ in $R$. The components of $\mathbf{V}$ and $\mathbf{R}$ in the normal space $\mathbf{N}$ are aligned.*

which simplifies to produce the specular term for large codimensions:

$$(2) \qquad \mathbf{V} \cdot R \;=\; \mathbf{V_T} \cdot \mathbf{L_T} \;-\; \|\mathbf{V_N}\| \, \|\mathbf{L_N}\|$$

It is convenient to use $\mathbf{V} \cdot R$ to denote this dot product between $\mathbf{V}$ and the nearest unit vector in $R$.

### 2.3.3 Summary of Specular Model

Even when the codimension of the manifold is 1, equation (2) ignores which side of the manifold is being illuminated, reminiscent of the diffuse reflection in equation (1). When $\mathbf{V}$ is more than $90°$ away from the reflection space $R$, the quantity $\mathbf{V} \cdot R$ becomes negative. The fact that it can be negative is unrelated to the codimension, and it is reasonable to clamp it to zero. The rationale is that when $\mathbf{V} \cdot R$ is less than zero, $\mathbf{V}$ is so far from the reflection space that it receives no reflected light at all.

The Phong model for calculating the specular intensity is therefore

$$(3) \qquad I_{specular} = k_s \, I_{source} \, (\text{clamp}(\mathbf{V} \cdot R))^{power}$$

where $\text{clamp}(x) = 0$ when $x < 0$. The principles for specular illumination are thus (1) light travels in paths of locally minimal length; and (2) the specular reflection is maximized exactly when the view vector nears the reflection space.

This seems like a lot of effort to expend just to end up with the same equation used by Hanson [Hanson93]. But the purpose of this derivation was not to replace the equations. The purpose was to replace the descriptions "ad hoc" and "heuristic" by means of a physically-motivated derivation of the geometric behavior of light, arguing from principles independent of any particular dimension.

## 3 Excess Brightness in Big Dimensions

When the diffuse model is applied to a $k$-manifold in $n$-space, under different values of $k$ and $n$, a curious phenomenon occurs: the overall brightness of a manifold increases with the codimension. The torus $T^2$ is a convenient test object for demonstrating the effect. The surface can be imbedded in 4-space as the cross-product of two circles by the parametrization

$$(x, y, z, w) \;=\; (r_1 \cos\theta, \; r_1 \sin\theta, \; r_2 \cos\phi, \; r_2 \sin\phi)$$

where $r_1$ and $r_2$ are the "outer" and "inner" radii. One can wrap a curve around the torus $T^2$ by letting $\phi = A\theta$ for some constant $A$. The curve or surface can be illuminated in 4-space, or else projected to 3-space and then illuminated there. Illustration 1 (top row) shows the result. Notice, especially, how uniformly bright the case $k = 1$, $n = 4$ is.

In order to understand the brightness phenomenon, first suppose there are light sources uniformly distributed in all directions. How bright is a point $\mathbf{p}$ on a surface or a curve? The answer requires integrating the illumination term over all directions of incoming light. In $n$-space, these directions cover the unit $(n\text{-}1)$-sphere.

### 3.1 Uniform Illumination of a Surface in 3-space

To integrate the uniform illumination of a point on a surface, let the tangent space $\mathbf{T}$ be the $xz$-plane and let the light vectors fill a unit sphere. The sphere $S^2$ has the following parametrization and area element $dS^2$.

$$(x, y, z) \;=\; (\sin\phi \cos\theta, \; \sin\phi \sin\theta, \; \cos\phi)$$

$$dS^2 = |\sin\phi| \, d\phi \, d\theta$$

The total area $A(S^2)$ of the sphere is $4\pi$. The area-averaged diffuse illumination $I^{2,3}$ at $\mathbf{p}$ (with $k = 2$, $n = 3$) is given by

$$I^{2,3} = \frac{1}{A(S^2)} \, k_d \, I_{source} \int\limits_{\mathbf{L} \,\in\, S^2} \sin a(\mathbf{L}, \mathbf{L_T}) \, dS^2$$

The constants $k_d$ and $I_{source}$ will clutter the ensuing calculations; it is convenient to just ignore them (by assuming they are both equal to 1, say). The rest of the computations follow this convention.

Evaluating the integral requires finding an expression for $\sin a$. It is easier to first find $\cos^2 a(\mathbf{L}, \mathbf{L_T}) = \mathbf{L} \cdot \mathbf{L_T} \,/\, \|\mathbf{L_T}\|$. If $\mathbf{L} = (x, y, z)$ then $\mathbf{L_T} = (x, 0, z)$. The sine can be computed from the cosine as

$$\cos^2 a(\mathbf{L}, \mathbf{L_T}) = 1 - \sin^2\theta \, \sin^2\phi$$

$$\sin a(\mathbf{L}, \mathbf{L_T}) \;=\; |\sin\theta \, \sin\phi|$$

The total illumination for a point on a surface is therefore

$$I^{2,3} = \frac{1}{4\pi} \int\limits_{\phi=0}^{\pi} \int\limits_{\theta=0}^{2\pi} |\sin\theta \, \sin\phi| \; |\sin\phi| \, d\theta \, d\phi = 0.5$$

### 3.2 Uniform Illumination of a Curve in 3-space

Compare the value $I^{2,3}$ to the average illumination of a point on a 1-dimensional curve whose tangent lies in the $(0, 0, 1)$-direction. The area-averaged illumination $I^{1,3}$ is given by the integral

$$I^{1,3} = \frac{1}{A(S^2)} \int\limits_{\mathbf{L} \,\in\, S^2} \sin a(\mathbf{L}, \mathbf{L_T}) \, dS^2$$

The light's tangent component is $\mathbf{L_T} = (0, 0, z)$, so the sine can be easily calculated from the cosine.

$$\cos a(\mathbf{L}, \mathbf{L_T}) = |\cos\phi|$$

$$\sin a(\mathbf{L}, \mathbf{L_T}) = |\sin\phi|$$

The total illumination for a point on a curve is therefore

$$\begin{aligned}
I^{1,3} &= \frac{1}{4\pi} \int\limits_{\phi=0}^{\pi} \int\limits_{\theta=0}^{2\pi} |\sin\phi| \; |\sin\phi| \, d\theta \, d\phi \\
&= \frac{1}{4\pi} \, 2 \int\limits_{\phi=0}^{\pi/2} \int\limits_{\theta=0}^{2\pi} \sin^2\phi \, d\theta \, d\phi = \frac{\pi}{4} \approx 0.785
\end{aligned}$$

The point is nearly 60% brighter just because the curve has a lower dimension than the surface does.

### 3.3 Uniform Illumination of a Curve in 4-space

If the curve is in 4-space, the point becomes brighter still. The 3-sphere $S^3$ has the following parametrization and volume element.

$$(x, y, z, w) \;=\; (\sin\chi \sin\phi \cos\theta, \; \sin\chi \sin\phi \sin\theta, \; \sin\chi \cos\phi, \; \cos\chi)$$

$$dS^3 = |\sin\phi \, \sin^2\chi| \, d\theta \, d\phi \, d\chi$$

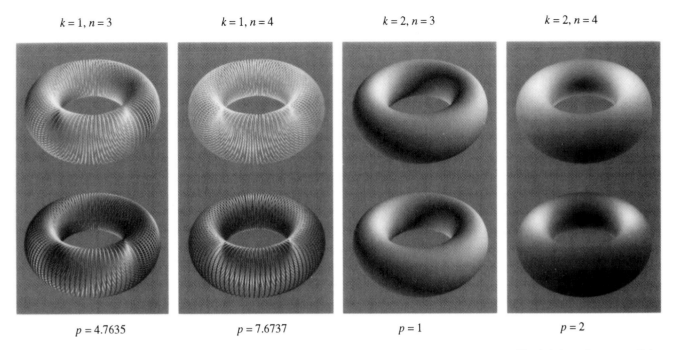

$k = 1, n = 3$  $k = 1, n = 4$  $k = 2, n = 3$  $k = 2, n = 4$

$p = 4.7635$  $p = 7.6737$  $p = 1$  $p = 2$

*Illustration 1. Local diffuse illumination (without self-shadowing) of a k-manifold in Euclidean n-space. The infinite point-source light vector in these images has direction (0.7 0.6 0.38) in 3-space and (0.7 0.6 0.38 0.0) in 4-space. The upper set of images use the diffuse model of equation (1). The bottom set compensates for excess brightness by using equation (5) with an exponent p as in Table 1.*

The total "surface area" $A(S^3)$ of the 3-sphere is $2\pi^2$. If the tangent is aligned with the $(0, 0, 0, 1)$ direction, the uniformly-lit point $\mathbf{p}$ has an area-averaged intensity which is calculated as follows.

$$I^{1,4} = \frac{1}{A(S^3)} \int_{\mathbf{L} \in S^3} \sin a(\mathbf{L}, \mathbf{L_T}) \, dS^3$$

$$= \frac{1}{2\pi^2} \int_{\chi=0}^{\pi} \int_{\phi=0}^{\pi} \int_{\theta=0}^{2\pi} |\sin\chi| \, |\sin\phi \, \sin^2\chi| \, d\theta \, d\phi \, d\chi = \frac{8}{3\pi} \approx 0.849$$

Similar calculations show that $I^{1,2} = 2/\pi \approx 0.673$ (a curve illuminated in 2-space), and $I^{2,4} = 2/3 \approx 0.667$ (a surface illuminated in 4-space).

## 3.4 Compensating for Excess Brightness

Why does the average reflected intensity of a manifold increase with the dimension of the space that the manifold occupies? Consider a $k$-manifold with codimension greater than $k$. For most light vectors $\mathbf{L}$, the large-dimensional normal space $\mathbf{N}$ is closer to $\mathbf{L}$ than the $k$-dimensional tangent space $\mathbf{T}$ is. Light vectors that are in, or near, the normal space make a point look bright, so most light vectors reflect brightly when the codimension is large. Conversely, if the codimension is smaller than $k$ most light vectors are closer to $\mathbf{T}$ than they are to $\mathbf{N}$: a point is likely to look dim.

It is not enough simply to adjust the diffuse coefficient $k_d$ to compensate for the codimension. Consider what it means for the average illumination to approach the limit of 1: the integrand is bounded above by 1, so it must in fact attain that bound almost everywhere. In almost every direction that light shines, it brightly illuminates almost all of the manifold.

Probably no one is very interested in illuminating a flat object using infinitely many point-light sources distributed uniformly in all directions. The typical situation is complementary to it: there may be a single light source, but the manifold's tangents vary continuously over many (if not all) directions. The visual result is generally the same as the theory predicts: a manifold becomes more uniformly bright when its codimension increases.

A simple way to increase the contrast is to exponentiate using a power $p(k, n)$. This changes the diffuse term in equation (1) to be

$$(5) \qquad I_{comp} = k_d I_{source} \sin^{p(k, n)} a(\mathbf{L}, \mathbf{L_T})$$

The brightness is thereby balanced so that a $k$-manifold in $n$-space approximates the contrast displayed by a surface in 3-space. Whereas the diffuse model could be derived from physical principles, there is no physical motivation for this tactic of exponentiation. Its merits are that it opposes the tendency for large codimensions to increase the average brightness of a manifold, and that it yields an integrable expression for the average illumination of a point on a manifold. The only difficulty is in choosing a suitable value of the exponent $p(k, n)$.

It is natural to set $p(2, 3) = 1$ since surface-shading in 3-space is the standard for visual comprehension. For other values of $k$ and $n$, one proceeds by comparing the averaged integrated intensities $I^{k, n}$ to the averaged integrated intensities $I^{2, 3}$ under the new compensating model of equation (5), finding a value of $p(k, n)$ that makes them equal. The integration is somewhat laborious even for low dimensions, so it is relegated to the appendix. The results are summarized in Table 1, and are applied in Illustration 1 (bottom row). As evidence that this normalization technique works, note that the images on the bottom row of Illustration 1 all look very similar in the amount of brightness and contrast they exhibit.

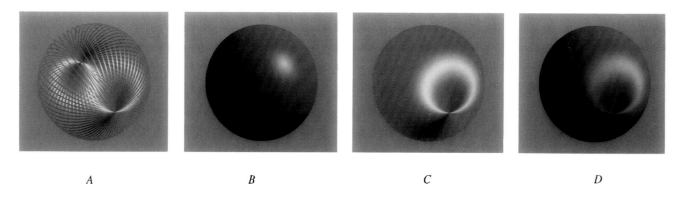

$A$          $B$          $C$          $D$

*Illustration 2. Different vector spaces can combine illumination effects. (A) Integral curves (of codimension 2) through a vector field $\mathbf{V}$ on a sphere. (B) The sphere $S^2$ (of codimension 1) with self-shadowing. (C) Illuminating all of $\mathbf{V}$, neglecting any self-shadowing from $S^2$. (D) Illuminating $\mathbf{V}$, conditioned by the surface normals of $S^2$ according to equation (6).*

|       | $n = 2$ | $n = 3$ | $n = 4$ |
|-------|---------|---------|---------|
| $k = 1$ | $p = 2$ | $p = 4.7635$ | $p = 7.6737$ |
| $k = 2$ | ——— | $p = 1$ | $p = 2$ |

*Table 1. Values of the power $p$ used by equation (5) for compensated diffuse illumination of a $k$-manifold in $n$-space.*

## 4 Mixing Dimensions for Global Effects

This section describes how the large-codimension model for illumination (equations *1* and *2*) can be used to render anisotropic reflectors and furry surfaces. These two examples exhibit a mix of diverse codimensions: 1-dimensional grooves on a 2D surface, or 1-dimensional fibers protruding from a 2D surface. The solution presented here applies to other combinations of codimensions as well.

A manifold may be supplied with one or more vector fields. For example, an isosurface of constant pressure in a fluid flow might possess 1D velocity vectors at every point together with a 2D tangent plane. If vector spaces of different dimensions are associated with a point, one is free to select which space will participate in the lighting calculation. In the case of the pressure-surface, the tangent space reflects like a 2-manifold, whereas the velocity field reflects like a 1-manifold at each sample point.

### 4.1 Anisotropy: Inheritance of Self-shadowing

Section 2.2 noted that a manifold of codimension 1 enjoys the special property of possessing, at most, two sides. The local illumination model can thus simulate the "global" effect of self-shadowing. Consider a surface $M$ with a 2D tangent space $\mathbf{T}$ and a 1D vector field $\mathbf{V}$ in 3-space. A point $\mathbf{p}$ in $M$ is in shadow if its outward normal aims away from the light source. With the light vector directed away from the source, $-\mathbf{N} \cdot \mathbf{L}$ is negative for a self-shadowed point. Assigning a unique normal vector is only possible when $\mathbf{T}$ (of codimension 1) governs the illumination, not $\mathbf{V}$ (of codimension 2). That is unfortunate when one desires to use $\mathbf{V}$, since self-shadowing enhances the fidelity of a rendered image.

The remedy is to let $\mathbf{V}$ inherit the quantity (namely $\mathbf{N} \cdot \mathbf{L}$) that informs the model of self-shadowing. To illuminate $\mathbf{p}$ using $\mathbf{V}$, the reflection terms arising from $\mathbf{V}$ are conditioned by the clamped cosine term arising from the 2-dimensional space $\mathbf{T}$:

$$(6) \qquad I_{conditioned} = (\text{clamp}(-\mathbf{N} \cdot \mathbf{L})\,(I_{diffuse} + I_{specular})$$

The diffuse and specular terms are calculated using equations (*1*) and (*3*) for the vector space of high codimension. The vector space of codimension 1 is consulted in order to provide the normal vector that offers a global effect (self-shadowing).

Illustration 2 shows various renderings of a sphere in 3-space endowed with a vector field $\mathbf{V}$ which is tangent to the sphere and aligned in "north-south" directions. Intuitively, this is like a satin ball used as a Christmas ornament. The satin fibers are integral curves (of codimension 2) through $\mathbf{V}$. The material properties are defined by the coefficients $k_{ambient} = 0.1$, $k_d = 0.5$, $k_s = 1.0$ and an intrinsic color $(r, g, b) = (1.0, 0.25, 0.30)$. In the first image, $A$, the Kajiya-Hanson model is applied to integral curves through $\mathbf{V}$. In the second image, $B$, the surface is illuminated in the usual way, using the tangent space $\mathbf{T}$ (of codimension 1) and applying the clamp function to $-\mathbf{N} \cdot \mathbf{L}$ to produce self-shadowing. The third image, $C$, shows the result of illuminating according to $\mathbf{V}$ and interpolating the result over the polygon mesh (but without the benefit of any such dot product $-\mathbf{N} \cdot \mathbf{L}$ to be clamped). The fourth image, $D$, shows the result of conditioning the solution of image $C$ according to equation (*6*) in order to produce the global effect of self-shadowing.

### 4.2 Fur: Attenuation by a Vector Field

Equation (*6*) shows how the tangent space $\mathbf{T}$ can be used to simulate global effects in illuminating the vector $\mathbf{V}$ space over $\mathbf{p}$. The roles of $\mathbf{T}$ and $\mathbf{V}$ can be reversed as well. In the "satin ball" example, each fiber $\mathbf{V_p}$ lay in the tangent space $\mathbf{T_p}$ at each point $\mathbf{p}$. That is, each fiber was constrained to fit the underlying surface. But that need not be the case. Real, physical fibers may protrude outward from a surface, partially shadowing the surface from light. It is possible to simulate this global effect by attenuating the light that reaches $\mathbf{T_p}$. A simple model for attenuation requires the incoming energy to decay exponentially with the distance that it passes through an absorbing medium of density $\rho$ ($\rho$ being

# Low Cost Illumination Computation

## using an

## Approximation of Light Wavefronts [1]

## Gershon Elber[2]
## Technion, Israel Institute of Technology

### Abstract

We present an efficient method to simulate the propagation of wavefronts and approximate the behavior of light in an environment of freeform surfaces. The proposed method can emulate the behavior of a wavefront emanating from a point or spherical light source, and possibly refracted and/or reflected from a freeform surface. Moreover, it allows one to consider and to render images with extreme illumination conditions such as caustics.

The proposed method can be embedded into rendering schemes that are based on scan conversion. Using a direct freeform surface Z buffer renderer, we also demonstrate the use of the wavefront approximation in illumination computation.

**Key Words:** Wavefronts, Caustics, Spot light source, Illumination, Freeform surfaces.

## 1 Introduction

Synthetic images created by modern computer graphics techniques are sometimes indistinguishable from real imagery. A vast set of algorithms has been developed in the last two decades to simulate the physical behavior of light such as refraction, reflection, caustics, and shadows on one hand and to emulate surface characteristics such as texture and bump mapping on the other.

In recent years, research has also focused on direct rendering of freeform surfaces. Freeform surfaces are traditionally preprocessed and approximated using a large set of polygons before they can be rendered. Alternatives are actively being pursued. In [4, 11], isoparametric curves are employed

as basic rendering primitives instead of polygons. In addition, while direct ray tracing of freeform surfaces is numerically difficult, some encouraging results can be found [20].

In recent years, more accurate models were developed to more precisely simulate the physical behavior of light, in synthetically generated images. In [14], closed form representations for the caustic of wavefronts propagating in homogeneous medium and reflected from quadratic curves (surfaces) are derived. The caustics are the locus of centers of the principal curvatures of the wavefront [23], as is the evolute [10] for curves [14].

In [19], two physical laws, Fermat's principle and the intensity law of light, are exploited. The former states that light travels along extremal paths. The latter shows the connection between the irradiance, or power per unit area, of a light wavefront to the Gaussian [10] curvature of the wavefront. These two principles are combined with ray tracing and used in [19] to simulate the physical phenomena of caustics. Unfortunately, the approach taken in [19] is slow and a significant effort is invested in finding the extremal paths of rays, time that is measured in days of computation, for a single image.

All these methods compute the radiance, or power per surface area taking into account the angle of radiation, on the *surfaces of the objects*. Ultimately, one would like to compute a vector valued function, $\mathcal{I}(x, y, z)$, that can be used to represent the irradiance that reaches a surface at $(x, y, z)$. $\mathcal{I}$ should accumulate both the direct effect of the light sources and the indirect influence of the light reflected from the surfaces. Not only that most illumination models and lighting techniques in computer graphics fit into the model of $\mathcal{I}$, but $\mathcal{I}$ also provides additional strength. The computation of the illumination and lighting of transient objects passing through the environment becomes less expensive, for if the transient object has a negligible affect on $\mathcal{I}$, no computation is necessary. Otherwise, only the incremental change, which is the result of the motion of the transient object, needs to be computed for $\mathcal{I}$. By computing $\mathcal{I}$, we represent the irradiance of *every* location throughout space. Given $\mathcal{I}$, one can immediately derive the radiance at every surface location that is arbitrary oriented, including the surfaces of the objects in the scene. This added strength is of great importance for dynamic environments and animation.

For example, for a simple environment, a point light source that is located at the origin and no occluding objects, the trivariate irradiance function, $\mathcal{I}$, is equal to, $\mathcal{I}(x, y, z) = \frac{\mathcal{I}_0}{4\pi(x^2+y^2+z^2)}$, where $\mathcal{I}_0$ is the flux, or the total power, emitted. Unfortunately, $\mathcal{I}$ can be extremely difficult to compute, in general. In this paper, we discuss an explicit representation to the irradiance function in the environment, $\mathcal{I}$, and will attempt to model $\mathcal{I}$ as a light wavefront. A wavefront emanating from a point light source or a spherical light

---

[1] This work was supported in part by grant No. 92-00223 from the United States-Israel Binational Science Foundation (BSF), Jerusalem, Israel. However, opinions, conclusions or recommendations arising out of supported research activities are those of the author or the grantee and should not be presented as implying that they are the views of the BSF.

[2] Department of Computer Science, Technion, Israel Institute of Technology, Haifa 32000, Israel. Email: gershon@cs.technion.ac.il

source and possibly reflected from a freeform surface, is considered. The presented approach is able to closely represent wavefronts that are emitted from area light sources of two shapes: a sphere or a spot light source of unidirectional emission. We call such a wavefront, a *primary wavefront*, because it represents the radiant intensity that has been originated from the light sources of the environment. Much like progressive radiosity [8], these wavefronts are most likely to have the dominant effect on the illumination of the environment. Given a surface $S(u,v)$, we consider a wavefront emanating from a point light source, $L_p$, and possibly reflected from $S$ as a trivariate function $W(u,v,t)$. $W(u,v,t_k)$ is the state of the wavefront at time $t_k$.

In the following sections, we develop a method to approximate $W(u,v,t)$. In section 2, we present the view independent stage of the computation of the approximation of $W$ while in section 3, the second, view dependent stage that exploits the approximation of $W$ in scenes rendered via a Z buffer, is discussed. Using the proposed approximation method of $W$, one can render and simulate the effects of caustics and illumination using point and spot light sources in a freeform surface environment, as is demonstrated in section 4. Finally, some concluding remarks and suggestions for further research are made in section 5.

The proposed approach was tested using the Alpha_1 solid modeling system which was also used to create all the figures in this paper. The Alpha_1 is being developed at the University of Utah.

## 2 Construction of Wavefronts

In this section, we present a method to approximate a wavefront, $W(u,v,t)$, that is possibly reflected from a freeform shape. The irradiance function, $\mathcal{I}(x,y,z)$, or the propagating wavefront, $W(u,v,t)$, are trivariate functions that are difficult to represent and process in current rendering schemes.

However, one can approximate the trivariate function, $W(u,v,t)$, using a set of bivariate constant set functions, $W(u,v_i,t)$. Fix value of parameter $v$, $v = v_i$. $W(u,v_i,t)$ becomes a bivariate function of the other parameter of surface $S(u,v)$, $u$, and of the time, $t$. Differently considered, $W(u,v_i,t)$ is a wavefront that is emitted or reflected from a single isoparametric curve, $C_{v_i}(u)$, of $S$. By computing $W(u,v_i,t)$ and $W(u,v_{i+1},t)$, one might be able to approximate $W(u,v,t)$ for $v \in [v_i, v_{i+1}]$, provided that $|v_{i+1} - v_i|$ is sufficiently small.

The difficulty in this approximation arises from the need to continuously interpolate between adjacent bivariate constant set functions while its simplicity is in the need to process entities that are of one dimension less. $W(u,v_i,t)$ can be treated as a bivariate surface, a prospect that will be exploited shortly.

Given a freeform surface, $S$, and a point light source, $L_p$, one would like to approximate the way $S$ reflects the coming wavefront. By reducing the dimensionality of the problem, the computation of the reflected wavefront of the entire surface is reduced to the computation of the reflected wavefront of a single isoparametric curve. In section 2.1, we consider the representation of a bivariate wavefront of a single isoparametric curve of surface $S$. Then, in section 2.2, we extend the representation to approximate a wavefront, $W(u,v,t)$, of the entire surface $S$. Finally in 2.3, we discuss how the irradiance of the wavefront can be estimated.

### 2.1 Bivariate Wavefront

Let $L_p$ be a point light source (see Figure 1). Let $C_{v_i}(u)$, $u \in [u_0, u_1]$, be a constant $v$ isoparametric curve of surface $S(u,v)$ and let $n_{v_i}(u) = \frac{\partial S(u,v)}{\partial u} \times \frac{\partial S(u,v)}{\partial v}\big|_{v=v_i}$ be the non normalized normal vector field of $S$ along $C_{v_i}(u)$. Denote

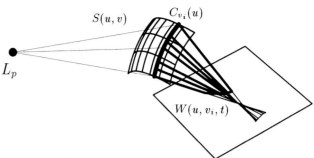

Figure 1: A bivariate wavefront, $W(u,v_i,t)$, emanates from a point light source, $L_p$, and then reflected from a single isoparametric curve, $C_{v_i}(u)$, of surface $S(u,v)$.

by $\vec{v}$ the unit length vector in the direction of $v$, a notation that will be used hereafter. The unit normal of $S$ at $C_{v_i}(u)$ is equal to $\vec{n}_{v_i}(u) = \frac{n_{v_i}(u)}{\|n_{v_i}(u)\|}$, where $\|\cdot\|$ denotes the $L_2$ norm.

Denote by $\mathcal{W}_{v_i}(u,t) = W(u,v_i,t)$ the bivariate function representing the wavefront reflected from $C_{v_i}(u)$. Let

$$\mathcal{D}(u) = (L_p - C_{v_i}(u)), \tag{1}$$

be the vector from a point on the curve, $C_{v_i}(u)$, to the point light source, $L_p$. Let $st$ be the distance that the wavefront travelled, up to time $t$, at speed $s$, assuming a homogeneous medium. Then,

$$\|\mathcal{E}(u,t)\| = st - \|\mathcal{D}(u)\|, \tag{2}$$

is the distance the wavefront travelled after it was reflected from the surface (see Figure 2). $\|\mathcal{E}(u,t)\|$ can be negative suggesting the wavefront has yet to reach the surface.

Given the unit normal of $S$ at $C_{v_i}(u)$, $\vec{n}_{v_i}(u)$, and a point light source, $L_p$, the wavefront is reflected from the isoparametric curve, $C_{v_i}(u)$, in the direction,

$$\vec{r}(u) = 2\left\langle \vec{\mathcal{D}}(u), \vec{n}_{v_i}(u) \right\rangle \vec{n}_{v_i}(u) - \vec{\mathcal{D}}(u), \tag{3}$$

where $\langle \cdot, \cdot \rangle$ denotes the inner product.

At time $t_0$, the wavefront reflected from the isoparametric curve $C_{v_i}(u)$ is,

$$\begin{aligned} \mathcal{W}_{v_i}(u,t_0) &= C_{v_i}(u) + \vec{r}(u) \|\mathcal{E}(u,t)\|\big|_{t=t_0} \\ &= C_{v_i}(u) + \vec{r}(u) (st_0 - \|\mathcal{D}(u)\|). \end{aligned} \tag{4}$$

Constrain $\mathcal{W}_{v_i}(u,t_0)$ to be equal to $C_{v_i}(u)$ at $u = u_0$,

$$\begin{aligned} C_{v_i}(u_0) &= \mathcal{W}_{v_i}(u_0,t_0) \\ &= C_{v_i}(u_0) + \vec{r}(u_0) (st_0 - \|\mathcal{D}(u_0)\|), \end{aligned} \tag{5}$$

where $s$ is the constant propagation speed of the wavefront, assuming a homogeneous medium. For the equality in equation (5) to hold at $t = t_0$, $st_0 - \|\mathcal{D}(u_0)\|$ must vanish,

$$t_0 = \frac{\|\mathcal{D}(u_0)\|}{s}. \tag{6}$$

Hence, we define time $t_0$ to be the time that $\mathcal{W}_{v_i}(u_0,t)$ reaches $C_{v_i}(u_0)$. $\mathcal{W}_{v_i}(u_0,t_0)$ is not equal to $C_{v_i}(u)$, in general (see Figure 2). For $\mathcal{W}_{v_i}(u,t_0)$ to be equal to $C_{v_i}(u)$, $\|\mathcal{D}(u)\|$ must be constant,

$$\begin{aligned} \mathcal{W}_{v_i}(u,t_0) &= C_{v_i}(u) + \vec{r}(u) (st_0 - \|\mathcal{D}(u)\|) \\ &= C_{v_i}(u) + \vec{r}(u) (st_0 - \|\mathcal{D}(u_0)\|) \\ &= C_{v_i}(u). \end{aligned} \tag{7}$$

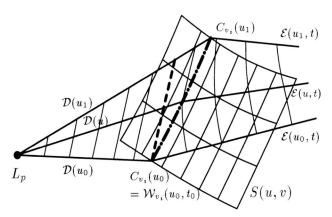

Figure 2: The distance that the wavefront travels in a homogeneous medium, $\|\mathcal{D}(u)\| + \|\mathcal{E}(u, t_k)\|$, is the same for any location $u$ on isoparametric curve $C_{v_i}(u)$, and a fix time $t_k$. $\mathcal{W}_{v_i}(u, t_0)$ and $C_{v_i}(u)$ are shown in dashed and dotted-dashed lines, respectively.

Intuitively, (7) constrains the wavefront, $\mathcal{W}_{v_i}(u, t)$, to reach all the points of $C_{v_i}(u)$ simultaneously, at time $t_0$. Provided the medium is homogeneous, once the wavefront is fully reflected from the surface, it propagates in *straight lines*, in directions that are specified by $\vec{r}(u)$ (equation (3)) and at a constant speed. Therefore, one can reconstruct the bivariate wavefront surface, $\mathcal{W}_{v_i}(u, t)$ as a *ruled surface* between the curve representing the state of the wavefront at time $t_1$, $\mathcal{W}_{v_i}(u, t_1)$ and the curve representing the state of the wavefront at a later time $t_2$, $\mathcal{W}_{v_i}(u, t_2)$,

$$\mathcal{W}_{v_i}(u, t) = (1 - t)\mathcal{W}_{v_i}(u, t_1) + t\mathcal{W}_{v_i}(u, t_2). \qquad (8)$$

Let $C_{v_i}(u)$ be a (piecewise) polynomial or rational function. Neither $\mathcal{W}_{v_i}(u, t_k)$, $k = 1, 2$ nor $\mathcal{W}_{v_i}(u, t)$ will be rational functions, in general, because of the square root terms in the normalization factors (equations (3) and (7)). Offsets of freeform curves and surfaces is a similar mapping that introduces a square root term for normalization. The computation of approximation of offsets of curves and surfaces has been extensively investigated [6, 9, 12, 17, 22]. Fortunately, one can exploit the knowledge that was developed for the offset approximation of freeform curves and surfaces and use it to derive techniques to approximate the propagation of wavefronts.

In [6], a simple method to approximate offsets of freeform curves and surfaces is proposed. Each control point of a Bézier or a NURBs curve is translated in the direction of the normal of the curve at the node parameter value that is associated with the control point. One can directly exploit the techniques that have been developed for approximation of freeform curves to approximate $\mathcal{W}_{v_i}(u, t)$. If $\mathcal{W}_{v_i}(u, t)$ is reflected from surface $S$, one can generalize the offset algorithm and translate each control point in the direction that is specified by $\vec{r}(u)$ (equation (3)) instead of the normal direction. Algorithm 1 summarizes this first order wavefront approximation of an isoparametric curve that is reflected from surface $S$.

Algorithm 1 neither estimates nor bounds the error of the approximation of $\mathcal{W}_{v_i}(u, t)$, $\widehat{\mathcal{W}}_{v_i}(u, t)$. In [6], it is pointed out that using refinement [3, 7] one can improve the approximation and converge to the exact offset. Numerous methods [6, 9, 12, 17, 22] have been proposed to exploit refinement [3, 7] and subdivision [13] and adaptively improve the

**Algorithm 1**

**Input:**
    $C_{v_i}(u)$, isoparametric curve of surface
$$S(u, v);$$
    $L_p$, point light source location;
    $t_1$ and $t_2$, time domain of wavefront;
**Output:**
    $\widehat{\mathcal{W}}_{v_i}(u, t)$, an approximation to
$$\mathcal{W}_{v_i}(u, t), \ t_1 \le t \le t_2;$$
**Algorithm:**
    `ConstructIsoWaveFront(` $C_{v_i}(u)$, $L_p$, $t_1$, $t_2$ `)`
    `begin`
        $\mathcal{D}(u) \Leftarrow (L_p - C_{v_i}(u))$;
        $\{u_{n_j}\} \Leftarrow$ set of node parameter values
                 of $C_{v_i}(u)$'s control points;
        $\{\vec{n}(u_{n_j})\} \Leftarrow$ set of unit normals of $S$
                 at $(u_{n_j}, v_i)$, $\forall u_{n_j}$;
        $\{\vec{r}(u_{n_j})\} \Leftarrow$ set of
            $2\langle \vec{\mathcal{D}}(u_{n_j}), \vec{n}(u_{n_j})\rangle \vec{n}(u_{n_j}) - \vec{\mathcal{D}}(u_{n_j})$, $\forall u_{n_j}$;
        $\widehat{\mathcal{W}}_{v_i}(u, t_1) \Leftarrow C_{v_i}(u)$ with its $j$th
            control point translated in direction
            $\vec{r}(u_{n_j})$ amount equal to $(st_1 - \|\mathcal{D}(u_{n_j})\|)$;
        $\widehat{\mathcal{W}}_{v_i}(u, t_2) \Leftarrow C_{v_i}(u)$ with its $j$th
            control point translated in direction
            $\vec{r}(u_{n_j})$ amount equal to $(st_2 - \|\mathcal{D}(u_{n_j})\|)$;
        $\widehat{\mathcal{W}}_{v_i}(u, t) \Leftarrow (1 - t)\mathcal{W}_{v_i}(u, t_1) + t\mathcal{W}_{v_i}(u, t_2)$;
    `end`

approximation of the offset. The improvement methods can be equally applied to the approximation of a wavefront of a single isoparametric curve that is described in Algorithm 1, yielding a wavefront approximation with a measurable and boundable error.

## 2.2 Trivariate Wavefront

In section 2.1, a method to approximate a single bivariate wavefront, $\mathcal{W}_{v_i}(u, t)$, of a single isoparametric curve, $C_{v_i}(u)$, was described. One may extend the bivariate wavefront approximation of a single isoparametric curve and use a set of adjacent bivariate wavefronts to approximate the trivariate wavefront, $W(u, v, t)$. In [11], a method to adaptively extract isoparametric curves and compute a *coverage* to a surface is described. Quoting from [11],

**Definition 1** *A set of curves* $\mathcal{C}$ *in a given surface* $S$ *is called a* valid coverage *for* $S$ *with respect to some constant* $\delta$ *if, for any point* $p$ *on* $S$, *there is a point* $q$ *on one of the curves in* $\mathcal{C}$, *such that* $\|p - q\| < \delta$.

The surface coverage provides a tool to approximate the trivariate wavefront using a set of adjacent bivariate wavefronts. A trivariate wavefront, $W(u, v, t)$, can be approximated using a set of adjacent bivariate wavefront functions, $W(u, v_i, t)$, constructed using curves that form a valid coverage of $S$. Figure 3 (a) shows a surface with a valid coverage of *isoparametric* curves, extracted adaptively, using the algorithm described in [11]. In Figure 3 (b) a wavefront is approximated using this coverage as a set of bivariate functions.

In the following section, section 2.3, we will demonstrate how one can estimate the irradiance of the wavefront at a certain $(u, v)$ location and at a given time $t$.

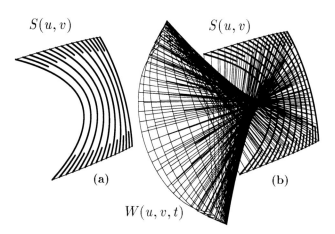

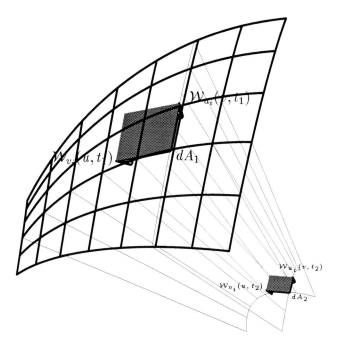

Figure 3: A valid coverage of surface $S(u,v)$ with respect to some $\delta$ of isoparametric curves that were extracted adaptively (a) is used to approximate a wavefront, $W(u,v,t)$, that is emanating from the surface (b).

Figure 4: The area of an area-element of a wavefront can be derived from the two partials of the wavefront $W(u,v,t)$ with respect to $u$ and $v$.

## 2.3 Irradiance Estimation of Wavefront

As the wavefront propagates, its irradiance varies. The irradiance is inverse proportion to the size of an area-element, $dA$, in the wavefront. As the wavefront diverges (converges) the power per unit area decreases (increases) from consideration of conservation of energy. This is known as the intensity law of light,

$$\frac{\mathcal{I}_2}{\mathcal{I}_1} = \frac{dA_1}{dA_2}. \tag{9}$$

This ratio is also proportional to the Gaussian curvature [10], $K$, of the propagating light wavefront. Unfortunately, a trivariate wavefront that is approximated using a set of bivariate wavefronts of isoparametric curves, as in section 2.2, cannot provide the necessary information to compute the area ratio, $\frac{dA_2}{dA_1}$, or the Gaussian curvature, $K$. A two dimensional area entity cannot be derived from the isoparametric information available from the coverage. Further, partial derivatives can be computed in one isoparametric direction only, making it impossible to compute either $K$ or size of area-elements.

Let $W(u,v,t)$ be the trivariate wavefront reflected from a regular surface [10] $S(u,v)$ and let $W(u,v,t_k)$ be the bivariate function representing the state of the wavefront, at time $t_k$. Then, the size of an area-element can be computed as,

$$dA_k = \left\| \frac{\partial W(u,v,t_k)}{\partial u} \times \frac{\partial W(u,v,t_k)}{\partial v} \right\| \tag{10}$$

and the ratio of two area-elements (equation (9)) of a propagating wavefront can be computed as,

$$
\begin{aligned}
\mathcal{R} &= \frac{\mathcal{I}_2}{\mathcal{I}_1} \\
&= \frac{dA_1}{dA_2} \\
&= \frac{\left\| \frac{\partial W(u,v,t_1)}{\partial u} \times \frac{\partial W(u,v,t_1)}{\partial v} \right\|}{\left\| \frac{\partial W(u,v,t_2)}{\partial u} \times \frac{\partial W(u,v,t_2)}{\partial v} \right\|} \\
&= \frac{\left\| \frac{\partial W(u,v,t_1)}{\partial u} \right\| \left\| \frac{\partial W(u,v,t_1)}{\partial v} \right\| \sin(\theta_1)}{\left\| \frac{\partial W(u,v,t_2)}{\partial u} \right\| \left\| \frac{\partial W(u,v,t_2)}{\partial v} \right\| \sin(\theta_2)},
\end{aligned} \tag{11}
$$

where $\theta_k$, $k = 0, 1$ is the angle between the two partials,

$$\sin(\theta_k) = \frac{\left\| \frac{\partial W(u,v,t_k)}{\partial u} \times \frac{\partial W(u,v,t_k)}{\partial v} \right\|}{\left\| \frac{\partial W(u,v,t_k)}{\partial u} \right\| \left\| \frac{\partial W(u,v,t_k)}{\partial v} \right\|}, \tag{12}$$

while it is guaranteed that $\sin(\theta_k)$ will never vanish, because of the regularity condition on $S$.

We already realized that a single coverage of $S$ is not sufficient to compute the size of an area-element or $K$. In order to compute the two partials of $W$ with respect to $u$ and $v$, we employ *two approximations* of the propagating trivariate wavefront. One is defined with a coverage of constant $u$ isoparametric curves and one is defined with a coverage of constant $v$ isoparametric curves (See Figure 4).

Once the wavefront is fully reflected from a surface, at time $t_1$, the wavefront $W(u,v,t)$, $t > t_1$ is an offset of $W(u,v,t_1)$,

$$W(u,v,t) = W(u,v,t_1) + t\vec{n}(u,v), \quad t \in [0, t_2 - t_1]. \tag{13}$$

where $\vec{n}(u,v)$ is a vector field representing the unit normal of $W(u,v,t_1)$. With the clear geometrical interpretation of the offset surface definition, it is interesting that the offset is not conformal [10], in general. On the other hand, two directions in the tangent plane of the surface are fully preserved by the offset and these are the directions of the principal curvatures [23]. Differentiate equation (13) with respect to $u$ and $v$ and represent the partials of $n(u,v)$ using the coefficients of the first and second fundamental forms of $W(u,v,t_1)$ (with what is known as Weingarten equations [10]). Then, if the surface parametrization is along the principal curvatures, $\theta_1$ is equal to $\theta_2$. Otherwise, $\theta_2$ needs to be computed from the first and second fundamental forms of $W(u,v,t_1)$ and $t$. Using two sets of approximations of the wavefront, one reflected along the $u$ and one reflected along the $v$ isoparametric curves of surface $S$, one can rewrite equation (11) for location $(u_j, v_i)$ to be,

$$\mathcal{R} = \frac{\mathcal{I}_2}{\mathcal{I}_1} = \frac{\left\|\frac{\partial \mathcal{W}_{v_i}(u,t)}{\partial u}\right\| \left\|\frac{\partial \mathcal{W}_{u_j}(v,t)}{\partial v}\right\|_{t=t_1}}{\left\|\frac{\partial \mathcal{W}_{v_i}(u,t)}{\partial u}\right\| \left\|\frac{\partial \mathcal{W}_{u_j}(v,t)}{\partial v}\right\|_{t=t_2}} \mathcal{A}(u,v,t), \quad (14)$$

where $\mathcal{A}(u,v,t)$ is the angular ratio that is a constant one for a parametrization along the principal curvatures.

The change of irradiance as the wavefront propagates can then be computed using equation (14). One can separate the multiplicative function $\mathcal{R}$ into two functions in the two parameters,

$$
\begin{aligned}
\mathcal{R} &= \frac{\left\|\frac{\partial \mathcal{W}_{v_i}(u,t)}{\partial u}\right\|_{t=t_1}}{\left\|\frac{\partial \mathcal{W}_{v_i}(u,t)}{\partial u}\right\|_{t=t_2}} \frac{\left\|\frac{\partial \mathcal{W}_{u_j}(v,t)}{\partial v}\right\|_{t=t_1}}{\left\|\frac{\partial \mathcal{W}_{u_j}(v,t)}{\partial v}\right\|_{t=t_2}} \mathcal{A}(u,v,t) \\
&= \mathcal{R}(u)\mathcal{R}(v)\mathcal{A}(u,v,t). \quad (15)
\end{aligned}
$$

Propagating from location $p = \mathcal{W}(u_j, v_i, t_1)$, the wavefront reaches point $q = \mathcal{W}(u_j, v_i, t_2)$ at time $t_2$. In order to estimate the irradiance of the wavefront at a point $q$, the magnitudes of the two partial derivatives of the wavefront with respect to $u$ and $v$ at $p$ for time $t_1$ and at $q$ for time $t_2$ are evaluated. $\mathcal{R}$ can then be computed as the product of the ratios, $\mathcal{R}(u)\mathcal{R}(v)$, and $\mathcal{A}(u,v,t)$. Assume a homogeneous radiant intensity of the wavefront at time $t_1$, as is the situation for a spherical light source. Then, at time $t_2$, the irradiance that reaches $p$ is in inverse proportion to the ratio of the *size* of the area-elements, $\mathcal{R}$, by the intensity law. In section 3, we will discuss an implementation of a rendering algorithm that exploits the two approximations of the wavefront and computes both $\mathcal{R}(u)$ and $\mathcal{R}(v)$ to estimate $\mathcal{R}$.

The number of bivariate surfaces constructed in the approximation of the wavefront depends on the accuracy required and can be quite large. However, once the wavefront approximation is constructed using a surface coverage of isoparametric curves, the approximation can be further optimized. Regions in the reflecting surface that do not face the light source could be immediately purged. This test is performed by computing the zero set of $\xi(u) = \langle n_{v_i}(u), \mathcal{D}_{v_i}(u)\rangle$ (see equation (1)) and purging the regions in $C_{v_i}(u)$ for which $\xi(u)$ is negative.

Figure 5 (a) shows a reflected wavefront only from the regions that faces the light source. Further, if only the regions of high power of the wavefront, $W$, are of interest, regions of $W$ with low irradiance can be immediately eliminated. Let $\mathcal{W}_{u_j}(v,t)$ be the wavefront reflected from isoparametric curve $C_{u_j}(v)$ of surface $S$. By setting a threshold, $\tau$, on $\mathcal{R}(u)$ and $\mathcal{R}(v)$, one can eliminate all regions in $\mathcal{W}_{u_j}(v,t)$ for which the following inequality holds,

$$\tau > \mathcal{R}(v) = \frac{\left\|\frac{\partial \mathcal{W}_{u_j}(v,t)}{\partial v}\right\|}{\left\|\frac{\partial \mathcal{W}_{u_j}(v,t_1)}{\partial v}\right\|}, \quad (16)$$

provided that $\overline{\mathcal{R}(u)\mathcal{A}(u,v,t)}\tau$, where $\overline{f(t)}$ denotes an upper bound of $f(t)$, has a negligible flux density, or irradiance. One can bound from above the range of values that either $\mathcal{R}(u)$ or $\mathcal{R}(v)$ can assume using their coefficients, exploiting the convex hull property of the surface representation. Moreover, because $\mathcal{A}(u,v,t)$ is monotone in $t$, establishing its upper bound is greatly simplified. A recursive subdivision test can be applied to $\mathcal{W}_{u_j}(v,t)$ to eliminate the low energy regions, applying equation (16) as a test at each level. Only the two isoparametric curves at the boundary of the time domain, $t_{min}$ and $t_{max}$, of $\mathcal{W}_{u_j}(v,t)$ should be tested

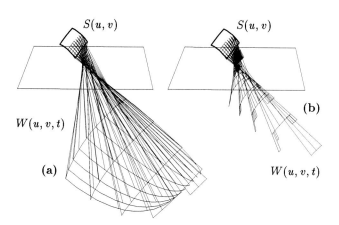

Figure 5: The reflected wavefront, in (a), includes only the regions in the reflecting surface $S$, that face the light source. In (b), the reflected wavefront from (a) is further optimized to remove the regions in the wavefront with low irradiance.

against $\mathcal{W}_{u_j}(v, t_1)$, because $\mathcal{W}_{u_j}(v,t)$ is a ruled surface. Figure 5 shows one example. A wavefront reflected from an isoparametric curve of surface $S$ is shown with and without the $\tau > \mathcal{R}(v)$ optimization.

In this section, a preprocessing stage that creates an approximation of a wavefront that is propagating through space was discussed. This stage is view independent and needs to be computed only once for a given scene. In section 3, we will discuss an implementation that exploits the representation of the approximation of the wavefront for rendering.

## 3  Rendering with Wavefronts

The trivariate wavefront is approximated using a set of bivariate wavefronts reflected from a coverage of isoparametric curves. Armed with this approximation, one can render the bivariate surfaces of the wavefront in virtually the same way the original surfaces of the scene, $\mathcal{S}$, are rendered. Algorithm 2 summarizes the rendering algorithm. The renderer of our implementation processes freeform surfaces directly. Instead of polygons, isoparametric curves that form an almost optimal valid coverage with $\delta < pixel$ (Definition 1) to surface $S$ are scan converted [4, 11].

The rendering is performed in three distinct stages. The set of original surfaces, $\mathcal{S}$, is rendered in the first stage of the algorithm. Each pixel that has been painted in the first stage from a surface in $\mathcal{S}$ is initialized to accumulate the energy information of the wavefronts that are processed in the second stage. Each such pixel accumulates, in the second stage, the information on wavefronts that are found to be close enough in $Z$ to the pixel. This goal is achieved by scan converting the bivariate wavefront surfaces and updating the $Z$ buffer accordingly. We use two sets of isoparametric curves that form a coverage for surface $S \in \mathcal{S}$, one using constant $u$ isoparametric curves and one using constant $v$ isoparametric curves. With the aid of the direct freeform surface renderer, one can estimate $\mathcal{R}$ via the evaluation of the magnitudes of the partial derivatives as in equation (15). The intensity of the bivariate wavefront, light source of origin, reflecting surface if any, and isoparametric direction of coverage are all accumulated in the pixel and kept in a similar way to the z-list used for shadow generation in [1]. Finally, in the last stage, the accumulated irradiance information is processed and $\mathcal{R} = \mathcal{R}(u)\mathcal{R}(v)\mathcal{A}(u,v,t)$ is derived. This process is performed for each wavefront that is uniquely identified by the light source the wavefront originated from and, optionally,

**Algorithm 2**

**Input:**
   $\mathcal{S}$, set of freeform surfaces describing the
                          scene;
   $L_p$, point light source;
**Output:**
   Rendered image;
**Algorithm:**
   RenderSrfsAndWaveFront( $\mathcal{S}$, $L_p$ )
   begin
(1) for each $S$ in $\mathcal{S}$ do
    begin
       Render surface $S$;
    end
(2) for each $S$ in $\mathcal{S}$ do
    begin
      $\left\{ \widehat{\mathcal{W}}_{u_j}(v,t) \right\}$, $\forall j \Leftarrow W(u,v,t)$
          approximated from $C_{u_j}(v)$, $\forall j$,
          a coverage of $S$ using constant
          $u$ isoparametric curves;
      Render and accumulate $\mathcal{R}(v)$ from
                      $\widehat{\mathcal{W}}_{u_j}(v,t)$, $\forall j$;
      $\left\{ \widehat{\mathcal{W}}_{v_i}(u,t) \right\}$, $\forall i \Leftarrow W(u,v,t)$
          approximated from $C_{v_i}(u)$, $\forall i$,
          a coverage of $S$ using constant
          $v$ isoparametric curves;
      Render and accumulate $\mathcal{R}(u)$ from
                      $\widehat{\mathcal{W}}_{v_i}(u,t)$, $\forall i$;
    end
(3) Process accumulated information, compute
    $\mathcal{R}$, and update image;
  end

the reflecting surface.

The radiance at an arbitrary surface location, $p$, and a unit normal, $\vec{n}_p$, in the environment is an accumulative result of all wavefronts passing through this point. The radiance at $p$ can be evaluated by taking into account all wavefronts affecting $p$, and their orientation with respect to $\vec{n}_p$. Alternatively, one can accumulate only the closest wavefronts (in $Z$) to a pixel $(i,j)$ that are below and above the $Z$ depth of the pixel. Then, a linear interpolation that weighs the $Z$ values with the $Z$ depth of the pixel will provide an approximation to $\mathcal{R}(u)$ and $\mathcal{R}(v)$. For each wavefront affecting pixel $(i,j)$, one needs to save a fixed amount of information. $\mathcal{R}(u)$ of the wavefronts below and above the pixel, $\mathcal{R}(v)$ of the wavefronts below and above the pixel, $\mathcal{A}(u,v,t)$, and the $Z$ depth of all these wavefronts. By taking into account only the two closest wavefronts, we significantly reduce the memory requirements, an important consideration in our implementation which is based on a full screen $Z$ buffer. However, we also compromise the quality of the rendering of the wavefront, if the reflecting surface $S$ is not convex with respect to the point light source $L_p$. This consideration will be further discussed in section 5.

## 4   Examples and Results

The direct freeform surface renderer converts a freeform surface into a set of isoparametric curves that form a coverage to the surface (Definition 1) with $\delta$ that is less than

a pixel. Instead of rendering a polygonal approximation, the isoparametric curves of the coverage are scan converted. With the aid of this renderer, one can scan convert the bivariate surfaces approximating the trivariate wavefront and compute the relative area and irradiance of the wavefront, as discussed in previous sections. Based on the same surface coverage, the isoparametric curves can be used to not only render the surface, but also to compute the set of bivariate functions, $\mathcal{W}_{v_i}(u,t)$, approximating the trivariate wavefront, $W(u,v,t)$. The wavefront propagating from an area light source can be closely emulated in two special yet common cases. The first is for a (region of a) spherical light source, a case equivalent to a point light source at the center of the sphere. The second is for an area light source with each point on the surface emanating light in only the direction of the normal of the surface, creating a spot light source if the surface is planar. Alternatively, if $S$ reflects a wavefront, $\vec{r}(u)$ (equation (3)) is used as the propagation direction of the wavefront. In Figure 3, we showed a coverage with of a freeform surface and its reflected wavefront. In practice, a coverage tolerance $\delta$ which is less than a size of a pixel was used for the rendering of the surfaces and a subset with $\delta > pixel$ was used to construct $\mathcal{W}_{v_i}(u,t)$.

In Figure 6, several snapshots are shown from a short movie of a freeform convex surface reflecting a wavefront that is converging in the neighborhood of an underneath plane. The location of the point light source is continuously modified, affecting the illumination of the underneath plane.

Figure 7 shows a spherical light source radially illuminating a partially planar domain. In this example, the bivariate surfaces approximating the propagating wavefronts are diverging away from each other, as time advances and the light energy decays.

## 5   Conclusion

We have presented an efficient method to emulate light wavefront propagation in a freeform surface environment, that is based on a coverage of isoparametric curves. All the images presented in this paper were computed in less than an hour on a 100MHz R4000 SGI Indigo system, at a resolution of 750 by 750 pixels, one sample per pixel. This method accommodates scenes with freeform surfaces that either reflect or, to a limited extent, emanate light energy. One can emulate the emission of light sources of arbitrary freeform shape, but accurately represent only the wavefront of the spot and spherical sources. Moreover, wavefronts emanating from point light sources and reflected from a freeform surface are also representable.

One can present the technique developed herein as a generalization of the shadow volume technique developed for shadow emulation [2, 5, 16]. A shadow volume becomes a predicate wavefront with an intensity function denoting whether or not the point in space is illuminated.

This method can be improved and enhanced in several ways. The coverage of isoparametric curves is computed for the original surface $S$. If the wavefront is diverging, as is for the spherical light source in Figure 7, the accuracy of the coverage is reduced with no bound, affecting the correctness of the rendered image. One might need to adaptively introduce intermediate bivariate wavefronts between adjacent wavefronts that the distance between them is more than allowed by the prescribed tolerance. The adaptive insertion of intermediate bivariate wavefronts elevates a dimension the idea of using the coverage of adaptive isoparametric curve in [11].

The implementation we selected, accumulated wavefront information in each pixel only on the two closest wavefronts. If the reflecting surface is not convex with respect to the point light source, the wavefronts might intersect themselves. By selecting the closest wavefronts, we give up all information regarding nearby wavefronts that might contribute significantly more energy. This difficulty can be al-

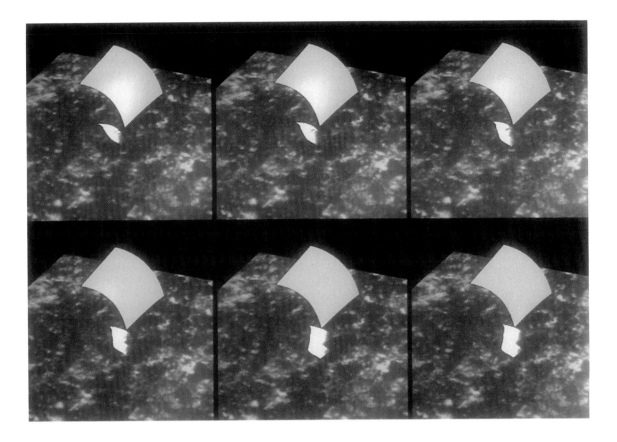

Figure 6: Several snapshots of a short animation sequence of a wavefront of a point light source that is reflected from a freeform surface onto a plane. See also Figure 3.

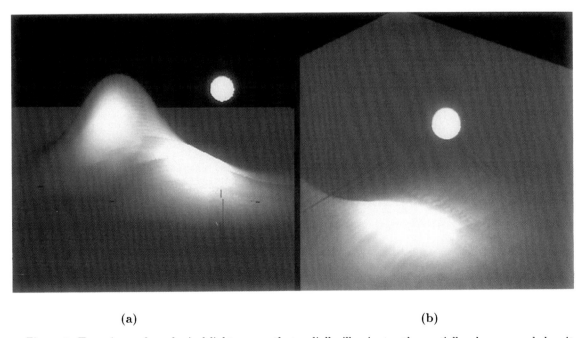

(a)                     (b)

Figure 7: Two views of a spherical light source that radially illuminates the partially planar area below it.

leviated by accumulating in each pixel all the information on all the wavefronts affecting it, for the price of an enlarged memory requirement.

In the implementation discussed, light sources that emit monochrome energy were assumed. One can extend the developed method to support frequency dependent wavefronts by propagating three (or more) sets of wavefronts for three (or more) independent colors that form a color basis. Further, one can consider handling inhomogeneous medium, or allowing discontinuous medium such as glass and water refraction. A propagating bivariate wavefront will become a piecewise ruled surface for the case of piecewise-homogeneous medium, and will become a general bivariate function in the case of a continuous but inhomogeneous medium.

The angle that the wavefront approaches the surface affects the power per unit area that the surface absorbs. This angle can be computed as the inner product of the normal of the surface and the wavefront's normal, both computable in our model. This consideration should also be modeled into the approximation.

The rendering of wavefronts is view dependent, as are the Gouraud and Phong interpolation schemes [15]. In some degenerate orientation, it is possible that we will fail to compute either $\mathcal{R}(u)$ or $\mathcal{R}(v)$ because the viewing direction is coplanar with the wavefronts of the isoparametric curves. This failure manifests itself in the missing vertical line in the illumination of the sphere light source in the bottom of Figure 7 (a). This deficiency should be further investigated and solved.

The natural representation of the wavefront as a trivariate function should also be investigated. Somewhat explored [18, 21], the trivariates are not only difficult to process and render, but trimmed trivariates are required for light/shadow discontinuity emulation and hence, the representation can be highly complex. However, the ability to naturally represent the wavefront propagation as a trivariate strongly motivates this research direction.

We allowed only one level of reflected wavefronts. Either a light energy wavefront emanating from an area light source with a freeform shape, or a freeform surface reflecting a wavefront from a point light source were allowed. Extending these limited cases will bring us closer to the ability to compute the full trivariate irradiance function $\mathcal{I}$.

## 6 Acknowledgments

I would like to thank Elaine Cohen, and the entire Alpha_1 group at the University of Utah, for empowering this research by creating this excellent solid modeling system and making it available.

The author is also grateful to the anonymous reviewers of this paper for their valuable remarks.

## REFERENCES

[1] P. Atherton, K. Weiler, D. Greenberg. Polygon Shadow Generation. Computer Graphics, Vol. 12, No. 3, pp 275-281, 1978.

[2] P. Bergeron. A General Version of Crow's Shadow Volumes. IEEE CG&A Vol 6, No. 9, pp. 17-28, 1986.

[3] W. Boehm. Inserting New Knots into B-spline Curves. Computer Aided Design, vol. 12, No. 4, pp. 199-201, July 1980.

[4] S. Chang, M. Shantz, and R. Rocchetti. Rendering Cubic Curves and Surfaces with Integer Adaptive Forward Differencing. Computer Graphics, Vol. 23, No. 3, pp. 157-166, July 1989.

[5] N. Chin, S. Feiner. Fast Object-Precision Shadow Generation for Area Light Source. Computer Graphics Special Issue, Symposium on Interactive 3D Graphics, March 1992.

[6] B. Cobb. Design of Sculptured Surfaces Using The B-spline Representation. Ph.D. Thesis, University of Utah, Computer Science Department, June 1984.

[7] E. Cohen, T. Lyche, and R. Riesenfeld. Discrete B-splines and Subdivision Techniques in Computer Aided Geometric Design and Computer Graphics. Computer Graphics and Image Processing, 14, pp. 87-111, 1980.

[8] M. F. Cohen, S. E. Chen, J. R. Wallace, D. P. Greenberg. A Progressive Refinment Approach to Fast Radiosity Image Generation. Computer Graphics, Vol. 22, No. 4, pp. 75-84, August 1988.

[9] S. Coquillart. Computing Offset of Bspline Curves. Computer Aided Design, vol. 19, No. 6, pp. 305-309, July/August 1987.

[10] M. P. DoCarmo. Differential Geometry of Curves and Surfaces. Prentice-Hall 1976.

[11] G. Elber and E. Cohen. Adaptive Iso-Curves Based Rendering for Free Form Surfaces. Technical Report UUCS-92-040, Department of Computer Science, Univeristy of Utah.

[12] G. Elber and E. Cohen. Error Bounded Variable Distance Offset Operator for Free Form Curves and Surfaces. International Journal of Computational Geometry & Applications, Vol. 1, Num. 1, March 1991, pp. 67-78

[13] G. Farin. Curves and Surfaces for Computer Aided Geometric Design. Academic Press, Inc. Second Edition 1990.

[14] R. T. Farouki and J. C. A. Chastang. Curves and Surfaces in Geometrical Optics. Mathematical Methods in Computer Aided geometric Design II. T. Lyche and L. L. Schumaler (Eds.), pp. 239-260, Academic Press, 1992.

[15] J. D. Foley et al. Computer Graphics, Principles and Practice, Second Edition. Addison-Wesley Systems Programming Series, Jul. 1990.

[16] G. Heflin and G. Elber. Shadow Volume Generation from Free Form Surfaces. Communicating with Virtual Worlds, Nadia Magnenat Thalmann and Daniel Thalmann (Eds.), Computer Graphics Internation 1993 (CGI 93), Lausanne Switzerland, June 1993.

[17] J. Hoschek. Spline Approximation of Offset Curves. Computer Aided Geometric Design 5, pp. 33-40, 1988.

[18] J. Hoschek and D. Lasser. Fundamentals of Computer Aided Geometric Design. A. K. Peters, English edition, 1993.

[19] D. Mitchell and P. Hanrahan. Illumination from Curved Reflectors. Computer Graphics, Vol. 26, No. 2, pp. 283-291, July 1992.

[20] T. Nishita, T. W. Sederberg and M. Kakimoto. Ray Tracing Trimmed Rational Surface Patches. Computer Graphics, Vol. 24, No. 4, pp. 337-345, August 1990.

[21] K. L. Paik. Trivariate B-Splines. Ms.Sc. Thesis, University of Utah, Computer Science Department, December 1991.

[22] B. Pham. Offset Approximation of Uniform B-splines. Computer Aided Design, vol. 20, No. 8, pp. 471-474, October 1988.

[23] O. N. Stavroudis. The optics of Ray, Wavefronts, and Caustics. Academic, 1972.

# The Irradiance Jacobian for Partially Occluded Polyhedral Sources

*James Arvo*

Program of Computer Graphics*
Cornell University

## Abstract

The irradiance at a point on a surface due to a polyhedral source of uniform brightness is given by a well-known analytic formula. In this paper we derive the corresponding analytic expression for the *irradiance Jacobian*, the derivative of the vector representation of irradiance. Although the result is elementary for unoccluded sources, within penumbrae the irradiance Jacobian must incorporate more information about blockers than either the irradiance or vector irradiance. The expression presented here holds for any number of polyhedral blockers and requires only a minor extension of standard polygon clipping to evaluate. To illustrate its use, three related applications are briefly described: direct computation of isolux contours, finding local irradiance extrema, and iso-meshing. Isolux contours are curves of constant irradiance across a surface that can be followed using a predictor-corrector method based on the irradiance Jacobian. Similarly, local extrema can be found using a descent method. Finally, iso-meshing is a new approach to surface mesh generation that incorporates families of isolux contours.

**CR Categories and Subject Descriptors:** I.3.3 [Computer Graphics]: Picture/Image Generation, I.3.5 [Computational Geometry and Object Modeling]: Geometric Algorithms.

**Additional Key Words and Phrases:** irradiance gradient, irradiance Jacobian, isolux contours, light field, mesh generation, vector irradiance.

## 1 Introduction

A perennial problem of computer graphics is the accurate representation of light leaving a surface. In its full generality, the problem entails both local reflection phenomena and the distribution of light reaching the surface. Frequently the problem is simplified by assuming polyhedral environments or Lambertian (diffuse) emitters and reflectors. With these simplifications the remaining challenges are in simulating interreflections and acurately modeling shadows and penumbrae from area light sources.

---

*580 Engineering and Theory Center Building, Ithaca, New York 14853, email: arvo@graphics.cornell.edu

Many aspects of surface illumination have been studied in order to accurately model features of the reflected light. In previous work, Heckbert [8] and Lischinski et al. [12] identified derivative discontinuities to produce efficient surface meshes. Nishita and Nakamae [14, 15] located penumbrae in polyhedral environments, while Teller [19] computed antipenumbrae for sequences of portals. Ward and Heckbert [22] computed irradiance gradients from random samples of the environment to accurately interpolate irradiance functions. Drettakis and Fiume [5] also estimated gradients from samples and used them to guide subsequent sampling.

The present work introduces a new tool based on the concept of *vector irradiance*, a natural representation of irradiance defined at all points in space. The central contribution of the paper is a closed-form expression for the derivative of the vector irradiance, which we call the *irradiance Jacobian*. The new expression properly accounts for occlusion and subsumes the irradiance gradient as a special case.

In Section 2 we derive the irradiance Jacobian for polygonal sources of uniform brightness starting with an analytic expression for the vector irradiance. The same expression has been used in scalar form by Nishita and Nakamae [14] to accurately simulate polyhedral sources, and by Baum et al. [2] for the computation of form factors. Section 3 introduces a method for characterizing changes in the apparent shape of a source due to differential changes in the receiving point, which is the key to handling occlusions. In Section 4 basic properties of the irradiance Jacobian are discussed, including existence and the connection with gradients.

To illustrate the potential uses of the irradiance Jacobian, Section 5 describes several computations that employ irradiance gradients. We describe a method for direct computation of isolux contours, which are curves of constant irradiance on a surface. Each contour is expressed as the solution of an ordinary differential equation which is solved numerically using a predictor-corrector method. The resulting contours can then be used as the basis of a meshing algorithm. Finding local extrema is a related computation that can be performed using a descent method. Finally, Section 6 describes other potential applications of the irradiance Jacobian.

### 1.1 Radiometric Preliminaries

All radiometric quantities may be defined in terms of *radiance*: radiant power per unit projected area per unit solid angle [watts/m$^2$sr]. Any collection of light sources in an optical medium uniquely defines a non-negative radiance function over all spatial positions and directions. At the macroscopic level, this function completely specifies the distribution of radiant energy in the medium. We shall denote the radiance at the point $r$ and in the direction $\omega$ by $L(r, \omega)$.

Central to the present work is a vector field $\Phi : \mathbb{R}^3 \to \mathbb{R}^3$ known

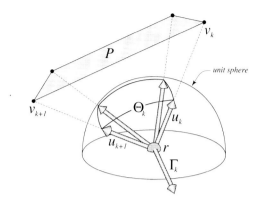

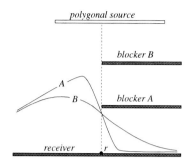

Figure 1: *(a) The vector irradiance at point r due to polygon P can be written in closed-form. (b) The contribution due to edge k is the product of the angle $\Theta_k$ and the unit vector $\Gamma_k$.*

Figure 2: *The irradiance at point r due to source P is the same with either blocker, but the slopes of the irradiance curves are different.*

as the *light field* [7]. In terms of radiance, the light field is given by

$$\Phi(r) \equiv \int_{\mathcal{S}^2} L(r,\omega)\,\omega\,d\sigma(\omega), \tag{1}$$

where $\mathcal{S}^2$ is the unit sphere in $\mathbb{R}^3$, and $\sigma$ is the canonical measure on the sphere [3]. That is, $\Phi(r)$ is the integral over all unit vectors through $r$ weighted by the radiance in each direction. At each point in space $\Phi(r)$ is a vector quantity known as the *light vector* [7] or the *vector irradiance* [17]; we adopt the latter terminology in this paper.

From vector irradiance we can derive other radiometric quantities, such as the *net flux* [watts/m²]. At any point $r$ on a hypothetical surface $\mathcal{M}$, the net flux $\phi(r)$ is the net flow of radiant energy across $\mathcal{M}$ per unit area [9]. By definition,

$$\phi(r) \equiv \int_{\mathcal{S}^2} L(r,\omega)\,\cos\theta\,d\sigma(\omega), \tag{2}$$

where $\theta$ is the angle of incidence relative to the surface. It follows that $\phi$ and $\Phi$ are related by

$$\phi(r) = -\Phi(r) \cdot \mathbf{n}(r), \tag{3}$$

where $\mathbf{n}(r)$ is the surface normal at the point $r$. The vector irradiance at $r$ therefore defines a linear mapping that relates surface normals to net flux.

At real surfaces, the net flux accounts for energy arriving from the hemisphere above the surface, in which case $\phi(r)$ is called *irradiance*. Equivalently, the irradiance at a point $r$ on a surface follows from equation (3) if the vector irradiance is computed using sources that are visible and lie above the tangent plane through $r$.

Although vector irradiance is a very general radiometric quantity defined in any optical medium, it is particularly useful in certain restricted settings. For instance, at diffuse receivers the reflectivity, surface orientation, and vector irradiance completely determine the reflected radiance at every point. Moreover, when the sources are polyhedral, the vector irradiance can be expressed in closed form.

## 1.2 Polyhedral Sources

For sources of uniform brightness, $\Phi$ can be expressed analytically for a number of simple geometries including spheres and infinite strips [7]. Polygonal sources are another important class with known closed-form expressions, and are the focus of this paper. Suppose $P$ is a simple planar polygon in $\mathbb{R}^3$ with vertices $v_1, v_2, \ldots, v_n$. If

$P$ is a diffuse source with constant emission $M$ [watts/m²], then the light field due to $P$ is given by

$$\Phi(r) = \frac{M}{2\pi} \sum_{i=1}^{n} \Theta_i(r)\,\Gamma_i(r), \tag{4}$$

where $\Theta_1, \ldots, \Theta_n$ are the angles subtended by the $n$ edges as seen from the point $r$, or equivalently, the arclengths of the edges projected onto the unit sphere about $r$. The vectors $\Gamma_1, \ldots, \Gamma_n$ are unit normals of the polygonal cone with cross section $P$ and apex $r$. See Figure 1. For any $1 \le k \le n$ the functions $\Theta_k$ and $\Gamma_k$ can be written

$$\Theta_k(r) = \cos^{-1}\left( \frac{v_k - r}{\|v_k - r\|} \cdot \frac{v_{k+1} - r}{\|v_{k+1} - r\|} \right), \tag{5}$$

and

$$\Gamma_k(r) = \frac{(v_k - r) \times (v_{k+1} - r)}{\|(v_k - r) \times (v_{k+1} - r)\|}, \tag{6}$$

where $\|\cdot\|$ is the Euclidean norm and $v_{n+1} \equiv v_1$. Equation (4) most commonly appears in scalar form [2, 6, 14]. With $M = 1$, the corresponding expression $-\Phi(r) \cdot \mathbf{n}(r)$ is the form factor between a differential patch at $r$ and the polygonal patch $P$. This scalar expression was first derived by Lambert in the 18th century [18].

Because the light field is a true vector field, the vector irradiance due to multiple sources may be obtained by summing the contributions from each source individually. Thus, polyhedral sources can be handled by applying equation (4) to each face and summing the resulting vectors. Alternatively, when the faces have equal brightness, equation (4) can be applied to the outer contour of the polyhedron as seen from the point $r$ [14]. Partially occluded sources are handled similarly by summing the contributions of all the visible portions. Determining the visible portions of the sources in polyhedral environments is analogous to clipping polygons for hidden surface removal [23].

The closed-form expression for vector irradiance in equation (4) provides an effective means of computing related expressions, such as derivatives. In the remainder of the paper we derive closed-form expressions for derivatives of the irradiance and vector irradiance due to polyhedral sources in the presence of occluders, and describe several applications.

## 2 The Irradiance Jacobian

The derivative $DF$ of a differentiable function $F : \mathbb{R}^3 \to \mathbb{R}^3$ is represented by a $3 \times 3$ Jacobian matrix. We shall denote the Jacobian

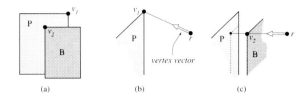

(a)            (b)            (c)

Figure 3: *(a) The view from r of the two types of "intrinsic" vertices. (b) The vertex vector for the unoccluded source vertex $v_1$. (c) The vertex vector for the blocker vertex $v_2$ in the interior of source P.*

matrix of $F$ at $r$ by $\mathbf{J}_r(F)$. That is,

$$\mathbf{J}_r(F) \equiv DF(r) = \left[ \frac{\partial F_i(r)}{\partial x_j} \right]. \tag{7}$$

In this section we derive the Jacobian matrix of the vector irradiance $\Phi$, or more briefly, the *irradiance Jacobian*. The obvious approach is to differentiate equation (4) with respect to the point $r$; a straightforward exercise easily performed by a symbolic manipulator. The result holds for unoccluded polygonal sources.

To see why the irradiance Jacobian is more difficult to compute when blockers are present, consider the arrangement in Figure 2. First, observe that the irradiance at the point $r$ can be computed by applying equation (4) to the visible portion of the source, which is the same in the presence of either blocker $A$ or blocker $B$. Although the resulting expression can be differentiated, this does not result in the irradiance Jacobian. Because the two blockers produce irradiance functions with different slopes at $r$, the irradiance Jacobians must also differ to account for blocker position.

To derive an expression that applies within penumbrae, we express $\Phi(r)$ in terms of *vertex vectors*, which correspond to vertices of the spherical projection of the polygon, as depicted in Figure 1. Vertex vectors may point toward vertices of two distinct types: *intrinsic* and *apparent*. An intrinsic vertex exists on either the source or the blocker, as shown in Figure 3. An apparent vertex results when the edge of a blocker, as seen from $r$, crosses the edge of the source or another blocker, as shown in Figure 4. We shall express $\mathbf{J}_r(\Phi)$ in terms of derivatives of the vertex vectors, viewing them as mappings from points in $\mathbb{R}^3$ to unit vectors. The derivative of a vertex vector is a $3 \times 3$ matrix, which we call the *vertex Jacobian*. Vertex Jacobians hide the geometric details of each vertex, yielding a relatively simple closed-form expression for $\mathbf{J}_r(\Phi)$.

Let $v'_1, v'_2, \ldots, v'_m$ be the vertices of $P'$, the source $P$ after clipping away portions that are occluded with respect to the point $r$. Without loss of generality, we may assume that $P'$ is a single polygon; if it is not, we simply iterate over the pieces. The vertex vectors $u_1(r), u_2(r), \ldots, u_m(r)$ are defined by

$$u_k(r) \equiv \frac{v'_k - r}{\|v'_k - r\|}. \tag{8}$$

We also define $w_1(r), \ldots, w_m(r)$ to be the cross products

$$w_k(r) \equiv u_k(r) \times u_{k+1}(r). \tag{9}$$

Henceforth, we assume that $u_k$ and $w_k$ are functions of position and omit the explicit dependence on $r$. Expressing $\Theta_k$ and $\Gamma_k$ in terms of $w_k$, we have

$$\Theta_k = \sin^{-1} \|w_k\|, \tag{10}$$

and

$$\Gamma_k = \frac{w_k}{\|w_k\|}. \tag{11}$$

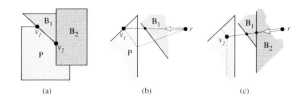

(a)            (b)            (c)

Figure 4: *(a) The view from r of the two types of "apparent" vertices. (b) The vertex vector for $v_1$ resulting from a blocker edge and a source edge. (c) The vertex vector for $v_2$ resulting from two blocker edges.*

The form of equation (10) simplifies the following development, although it is equivalent to equation (5) only for acute angles; that is, only when $u_k \cdot u_{k+1} \geq 0$. This restriction will be removed below.

To compute $\mathbf{J}(\Phi)$ in terms of the vertex Jacobians $\mathbf{J}(u_1), \ldots, \mathbf{J}(u_m)$ we first consider the $k^{\text{th}}$ term of the summation in equation (4). Differentiating, we have

$$\mathbf{J}(\Theta_k \Gamma_k) = \Gamma_k \nabla \Theta_k + \Theta_k \mathbf{J}(\Gamma_k), \tag{12}$$

where $\Gamma_k \nabla \Theta_k$ is the outer product of the vector $\Gamma_k$ and the gradient $\nabla \Theta_k$. We now compute $\nabla \Theta_k$ and $\mathbf{J}(\Gamma_k)$. For brevity, we denote the vertex vectors $u_k$ and $u_{k+1}$ by $a$ and $b$ respectively, and the cross product $a \times b$ by $w$. Then the gradient of $\Theta_k$ with respect to $r$ is

$$\begin{aligned} \nabla \Theta_k &= \nabla \sin^{-1} \|w\| \\ &= \frac{1}{\sqrt{1 - w^{\mathsf{T}} w}} \left( \frac{w^{\mathsf{T}}}{\|w\|} \right) \mathbf{J}(w) \\ &= \left( \frac{w^{\mathsf{T}}}{a^{\mathsf{T}} b} \right) \frac{\mathbf{J}(w)}{\|w\|}. \end{aligned} \tag{13}$$

Similarly, differentiating $\Gamma_k$ with respect to $r$ we have

$$\begin{aligned} \mathbf{J}(\Gamma_k) &= D \left( \frac{w}{\|w\|} \right) \\ &= \frac{\mathbf{J}(w)}{\|w\|} - \frac{w w^{\mathsf{T}}}{\|w\|^3} \mathbf{J}(w) \\ &= \left( \mathbf{I} - \frac{w w^{\mathsf{T}}}{w^{\mathsf{T}} w} \right) \frac{\mathbf{J}(w)}{\|w\|}. \end{aligned} \tag{14}$$

From Equations (10)-(14), we obtain an expression for $\mathbf{J}(\Theta_k \Gamma_k)$ in terms of $\mathbf{J}(w)$ and the vertex vectors $a$ and $b$:

$$\mathbf{J}(\Theta_k \Gamma_k) = \left[ \frac{w}{\|w\|} \left( \frac{w^{\mathsf{T}}}{a^{\mathsf{T}} b} \right) + \sin^{-1} \|w\| \left( \mathbf{I} - \frac{w w^{\mathsf{T}}}{w^{\mathsf{T}} w} \right) \right] \frac{\mathbf{J}(w)}{\|w\|}.$$

If the factor of $\sin^{-1} \|w\|$ is now replaced by the angle between $a$ and $b$, the expression will hold for all angles, removing the caveat noted earlier. The above expression may be written compactly as

$$\mathbf{J}(\Theta_k \Gamma_k) = \mathbf{E}(a, b) \, \mathbf{J}(a \times b), \tag{15}$$

where the function $\mathbf{E}$ is the *edge matrix* defined by

$$\mathbf{E}(a, b) \equiv \left( \frac{1}{a^{\mathsf{T}} b} \right) \frac{w w^{\mathsf{T}}}{w^{\mathsf{T}} w} + \frac{\cos^{-1} a^{\mathsf{T}} b}{\|w\|} \left( \mathbf{I} - \frac{w w^{\mathsf{T}}}{w^{\mathsf{T}} w} \right). \tag{16}$$

In equation (16) we have retained $w$ as an abbreviation for $a \times b$. Because the edge matrix contains no derivatives, it can be computed directly from the vertex vectors $a$ and $b$. To simplify the Jacobian of $a \times b$, we define another matrix-valued function $\mathbf{Q}$ by

$$\mathbf{Q}(p) \equiv \begin{bmatrix} 0 & p_z & -p_y \\ -p_z & 0 & p_x \\ p_y & -p_x & 0 \end{bmatrix}. \qquad (17)$$

Then for any pair of vectors $p$ and $q$, we have $p \times q = \mathbf{Q}(p)q$. Writing the cross product as a matrix multiplication leads to a convenient expression for the Jacobian matrix of $F \times G$, where $F$ and $G$ are vector fields in $\mathbb{R}^3$. Thus,

$$\mathbf{J}(F \times G) = \mathbf{Q}(F)\mathbf{J}(G) - \mathbf{Q}(G)\mathbf{J}(F). \qquad (18)$$

Applying the above identity to equation (15), summing over all edges of the clipped source polygon $P'$, and scaling by $M/2\pi$, we arrive at an expression for the irradiance Jacobian due to the visible portion of polygonal source $P$:

$$\mathbf{J}(\Phi) = \frac{M}{2\pi} \sum_{i=1}^{m} \mathbf{E}(u_i, u_{i+1}) \left[ \mathbf{Q}(u_i)\mathbf{J}(u_{i+1}) - \mathbf{Q}(u_{i+1})\mathbf{J}(u_i) \right]. \qquad (19)$$

This expression can be simplified somewhat further by collecting the factors of each $\mathbf{J}(u_i)$ into a single matrix. We therefore define the *corner matrix* $\mathbf{C}$ to be the matrix-valued function

$$\mathbf{C}(a,b,c) \equiv \mathbf{E}(a,b)\mathbf{Q}(a) - \mathbf{E}(b,c)\mathbf{Q}(c). \qquad (20)$$

Then the final expression for the irradiance Jacobian can be written as a sum over all the vertex Jacobians transformed by corner matrices:

$$\mathbf{J}(\Phi) = \frac{M}{2\pi} \sum_{i=1}^{m} \mathbf{C}(u_{i-1}, u_i, u_{i+1}) \, \mathbf{J}(u_i), \qquad (21)$$

where we have made the natural identifications $u_0 \equiv u_m$ and $u_{m+1} \equiv u_1$. Note that each corner matrix $\mathbf{C}$ depends only on the vertex vectors, and not their derivatives; all information concerning apparent motion due to changing the position $r$ is embodied in the vertex Jacobians $\mathbf{J}(u_1), \ldots, \mathbf{J}(u_m)$, which we now examine in detail.

# 3 Vertex Jacobians

To apply equation (21) we require the vertex Jacobians, which we now construct for both unoccluded and partially occluded polygonal sources. First, observe that each vertex vector $u(r)$ is a smooth function of $r$ almost everywhere; that is, $u(r)$ is differentiable at all $r \in \mathbb{R}^3$ except where two or more edges of distinct polygons appear to coincide, as described in section 4. Differentiability follows from the smoothness of the Euclidean norm and the fact that the apparent point of intersection of two skew lines varies quadratically in $r$ along each of the lines [16]. From this it is evident that the vertex Jacobian exists whenever the real or apparent intersection of two edges exists and is unique.

When the vertex Jacobian exists, it can be constructed by determining its action on each of three linearly independent vectors; that is, by determining the instantaneous change in the vertex vector $u$ as a result of moving $r$. Differential changes in $u$ are orthogonal to $u$ and collectively define a disk, or in the case of partial occlusion, an ellipse. See Figure 5. The directions that are easiest to analyze are the axes of the ellipse, which are the eigenvectors of the vertex Jacobian. We first treat intrinsic vertices and then generalize to the more difficult case of apparent vertices.

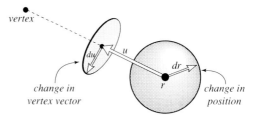

Figure 5: *A differential change in the position $r$ results in a change in the unit vertex vector $u$. The locus of vectors $du$ forms a disk, or more gnerally, an ellipse in the plane orthogonal to $u$.*

## 3.1 Intrinsic Vertices

Suppose that $u$ is the vertex vector associated with an unoccluded source vertex, as shown in Figure 3b. In this case the vertex Jacobian $\mathbf{J}(u)$ is easy to compute since it depends solely on the distance between $r$ and the vertex, which we denote by $\alpha$. Moving $r$ in the direction of the vertex leaves $u$ unchanged, while motion perpendicular to $u$ causes an opposing change in $u$. The changes in $u$ are inversely proportional to the distance $\alpha$. This behavior completely determines the vertex Jacobian. Thus, we have

$$\mathbf{J}(u) = -\frac{1}{\alpha} \left( \mathbf{I} - uu^{\mathsf{T}} \right), \qquad (22)$$

where the matrix $\mathbf{I} - uu^{\mathsf{T}}$ is a projection onto the tangent plane of $\mathcal{S}^2$ at the point $u$, which houses all differential motions of the unit vector $u$. The same reasoning applies to vertex vectors defined by a blocker vertex, as in Figure 3c. In this case $\alpha$ is the distance along $u$ to the blocker vertex.

## 3.2 Apparent Vertices

Within penumbrae, apparent vertices may be formed by the apparent crossing of non-coplanar edges. The two distinct cases are depicted in Figure 4. Let $u$ be the vertex vector associated with such a vertex, where the determining edges are segments of skew lines $\mathcal{L}_1$ and $\mathcal{L}_2$. Let $s$ and $t$ be vectors parallel to $\mathcal{L}_1$ and $\mathcal{L}_2$, respectively, as depicted in Figure 6. As in the case of intrinsic vertices, moving $r$ toward the apparent vertex leaves $u$ unchanged, so $\mathbf{J}(u)u = 0$. To account for other motions, we define the vectors $\widehat{s}$ and $\widehat{t}$ by

$$\begin{aligned} \widehat{s} &\equiv (\mathbf{I} - uu^{\mathsf{T}})s \\ \widehat{t} &\equiv (\mathbf{I} - uu^{\mathsf{T}})t, \end{aligned}$$

which are projections of $s$ and $t$ onto the plane orthogonal to $u$. Now consider the change in $u$ as $r$ moves parallel to $\widehat{s}$, as shown in Figure 6a. In this case the apparent vertex moves along $\mathcal{L}_1$ while remaining fixed on $\mathcal{L}_2$. Therefore, the change in $u$ is parallel to $\widehat{s}$ but opposite in direction to the change in $r$. If $\alpha_t$ is the distance to $\mathcal{L}_2$ along $u$, we have

$$\mathbf{J}(u)\widehat{s} = -\frac{\widehat{s}}{\alpha_t}. \qquad (23)$$

Evidently, $\widehat{s}$ is an eigenvector of $\mathbf{J}(u)$ with associated eigenvalue $-1/\alpha_t$. A similar argument holds when $r$ moves along $\widehat{t}$, as shown in Figure 6b. Here the apparent vertex moves along $\mathcal{L}_2$ while remaining fixed at $\mathcal{L}_1$. If $\alpha_s$ is the distance to $\mathcal{L}_1$ along $u$, we have

$$\mathbf{J}(u)\widehat{t} = -\frac{\widehat{t}}{\alpha_s}, \qquad (24)$$

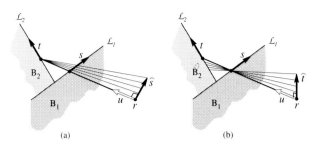

Figure 6: *The vertex Jacobian $\mathbf{J}(u)$ with respect to two skew lines $\mathcal{L}_1$ and $\mathcal{L}_2$ is found by determining how the vertex vector $u$ changes as $r$ moves parallel to (a) the vector $\widehat{s}$, and (b) the vector $\widehat{t}$.*

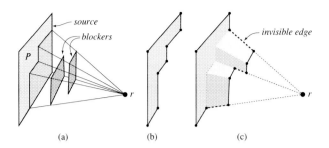

Figure 7: *(a) Source $P$ is partially occluded by two blockers as seen from $r$. (b) The vector irradiance at $r$ due to $P$ can be computed using the simply-clipped polygon. (c) The irradiance Jacobian at $r$ requires the depth-clipped polygon.*

which provides the third eigenvector and corresponding eigenvalue. Collecting these relationships into a matrix equation, we have

$$\mathbf{J}(u) \begin{bmatrix} \widehat{s} & \widehat{t} & u \end{bmatrix} = \begin{bmatrix} -\dfrac{\widehat{s}}{\alpha_t} & -\dfrac{\widehat{t}}{\alpha_s} & 0 \end{bmatrix}. \qquad (25)$$

It follows immediately that whenever the lines $\mathcal{L}_1$ and $\mathcal{L}_2$ are distinct and non-colinear as viewed from the point $r$, then

$$\mathbf{J}(u) = \mathbf{A} \begin{bmatrix} -1/\alpha_t & & \\ & -1/\alpha_s & \\ & & 0 \end{bmatrix} \mathbf{A}^{-1} \qquad (26)$$

where $\mathbf{A} \equiv \begin{bmatrix} \widehat{s} & \widehat{t} & u \end{bmatrix}$. Note that equation (26) reduces to equation (22) when $\alpha_s = \alpha_t$. Equation (26) therefore suffices for all vertex vectors, but the special case for intrinsic vertices can be used for efficiency.

### 3.3 Polygon Depth-Clipping

To compute the irradiance or vector irradiance at a point $r$, it suffices to clip all sources against all blockers, as seen from $r$, and apply equation (4) to the resulting vertex lists. This operation is also sufficient to compute the corner matrices and the vertex Jacobians at unoccluded source vertices. However, the vertex Jacobians for the cases illustrated in Figures 3c, 4b, and 4c all require information about the blockers that is missing from traditionally-clipped polygons. Specifically, the distances to blocker edges defining each vertex are needed to form the matrices in Equations (22) and (26).

Thus, additional depth information must be retained along with the clipped polygons for use in computing vertex Jacobians. We propose a simple mechanism, called *depth clipping*, by which the required information appears as additional vertices. The idea is to construct the clipped polygon using segments of source and blocker edges and joining them by segments called *invisible edges*, which cannot be seen from the point $r$. See Figure 7. The resulting non-planar contour is identical to that of the traditionally-clipped polygon when viewed from $r$. Each invisible edge produces a vertex Jacobian of the form in equation (26); its end points encode the distances from $r$ while the adjacent edges provide the two directions. Each vertex not adjacent to an invisible edge produces a vertex Jacobian of the form in equation (22).

The depth-clipped polygon and the emission $M$ completely specify the irradiance Jacobian. Most polygon clipping algorithms can be extended to generate this representation using the plane equation of each blocker. The depth-clipped polygon also clearly illustrates the information required for irradiance Jacobians.

## 4 Properties of the Irradiance Jacobian

In this section we list some of the basic properties of the irradiance Jacobian, beginning with existence. By definition, the Jacobian $\mathbf{J}_r(\Phi)$ exists wherever $\Phi$ is differentiable, which requires the existence of each directional derivative at $r$. Because we consider only area sources, the variation of $\Phi$ is *continuous* along any line except when a blocker is in contact with the receiving surface. Instantaneous occlusion causes discontinuous changes in the vector irradiance. In the absence of contact occlusions, the variation of $\Phi$ is not only continuous but *differentiable* everywhere except along lines where edges appear to coincide; that is, points at which a source or blocker edge appears to align with another blocker edge [12]. For instance, when both blockers are present simultaneously in Figure 2, the irradiance curve coincides with curve $B$ to the left of $r$, and with curve $A$ to the right. Therefore, the irradiance at $r$ has a discontinuity in the first derivative. Only contact occlusion and edge-edge alignments cause the Jacobian to be undefined; other types of events cause higher-order discontinuities in the vector irradiance, but are first-order smooth.

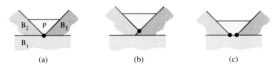

Figure 8: *(a) The vertex Jacobian does not exist at the intersection of three edges. A small change can produce (b) a single apparent vertex, or (c) two apparent vertices.*

From equation (21) it would appear that the irradiance Jacobian does not exist if any one of the vertex Jacobians fails to exist; this is not always so. A vertex Jacobian may be undefined because the vertex lies at the intersection of three edges, as shown in Figure 8a. In cases such as this, a minute change in $r$ can lead to several possible configurations with different vertex Jacobians. See Figures 8b and 8c. However, the unoccluded area of the source still changes smoothly despite such a difficulty at a single vertex. To ensure that equation (21) is valid wherever $\Phi$ is differentiable, we simply restrict the edges that are used in computing the vertex Jacobians to those that actually bound the clipped source. Thus, in Figure 8, blocker $B_1$ is ignored until it makes its presence known by the addition of a new edge, as in Figure 8c.

One of the most useful properties of the Jacobian matrix is its connection with directional derivatives. For any $\xi \in \mathcal{S}^2$, the directional derivative of $\Phi$ at $r$ in the direction $\xi$ is

$$D_\xi \Phi(r) = \mathbf{J}_r(\Phi)\, \xi. \qquad (27)$$

Although directional derivatives of $\Phi$ may be approximated to second order with central differences, using the irradiance Jacobian has several advantages. First, all directional derivatives of $\Phi(r)$ are easily obtained from the irradiance Jacobian at $r$, which requires a single global clipping operation; that is, sources need only be clipped against blockers once. In contrast, difference approximations require at least two clipping operations per directional derivative. More importantly, directions of maximal change follow immediately from the Jacobian but require multiple finite differences to approximate.

A final property, which we build upon in the next section, is the connection with the rate of change of surface irradiance. Differentiating equation (3) with respect to position, we have

$$\nabla\phi = \Phi^{T}\mathbf{J}(\mathbf{n}) + \mathbf{n}^{T}\mathbf{J}(\Phi), \tag{28}$$

which associates the irradiance gradient with the irradiance Jacobian. Note that $\mathbf{J}(\mathbf{n})$ is related to the curvature of the surface at each point $r \in \mathcal{M}$. For planar surfaces $\mathbf{J}(\mathbf{n}) \equiv 0$, so equation (28) reduces to

$$\nabla\phi = \mathbf{n}^{T}\mathbf{J}(\Phi), \tag{29}$$

which is the form we shall use to compute isolux contours on polygonal receivers. When evaluating equation (29) several optimizations are possible by distributing the vector multiplication across the terms of equation (21), which changes the summation of matrices into a summation of row vectors.

## 5    Applications of the Irradiance Jacobian

In the first portion of the paper, we have seen how to compute the irradiance Jacobian and the irradiance gradient. The steps can be summarized as follows:

**Matrix** IrradianceJacobian( **Point** $r$ )

> **Matrix** $\mathbf{J} \leftarrow 0$
> **for each** source $P$ with emission $M$
> > **begin**
> > $\widehat{P} \leftarrow P$ depth-clipped against all blockers, as seen from $r$
> > **for each** $i$: $\mathbf{J}_i \leftarrow$ vertex Jacobian for the $i^{\text{th}}$ vertex of $\widehat{P}$
> > **for each** $i$: $\mathbf{E}_i \leftarrow$ edge matrix for the $i^{\text{th}}$ edge of $\widehat{P}$
> > **for each** $i$: $\mathbf{C}_i \leftarrow$ corner matrix using $\mathbf{E}_{i-1}$ and $\mathbf{E}_i$
> > $\mathbf{J} \leftarrow \mathbf{J} + \frac{M}{2\pi}$ (sum of all $\mathbf{C}_i\mathbf{J}_i$)
> > **end**
> **return** $\mathbf{J}$

Here the inner loops all refer to the vertices as seen from $r$; pairs of vertices associated with invisible edges are counted as one. Gradients can then be computed using equation (28) or equation (29). The procedure above is a general-purpose tool with many applications, several of which are described in the remainder of this section.

### 5.1    Finding Local Extrema

The first application we examine is that of locating irradiance extrema on surfaces, which can be used in computing bounds on the transfer of energy between surfaces [11]. Given the availability of gradients, the most straightforward approach to locating a point of maximal irradiance is with an ascent method of the form

$$r^{i+1} \equiv r^{i} + \gamma_{i}\left(\mathbf{I} - \mathbf{nn}^{T}\right)\nabla\phi^{T}(r^{i}), \tag{30}$$

where $r^{0}$ is a given starting point, and the factor $\gamma_{i}$ is determined by a line search that insures progress is made toward the extremum. For example, the line search may simply halve $\gamma_{i}$ until an increase

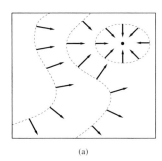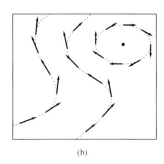

(a)                                        (b)

Figure 9: *(a) Projecting the gradient onto a surface defines a 2D vector field everywhere orthogonal to the level curves. (b) Rotating the projected gradients by $-\pi/2$ creates a vector field whose flow lines are isolux contours. Local maxima are then encircled by clockwise loops.*

in irradiance is achieved. The extremum has been found when no further progress can be made. Minima are found similarly. The principle drawbacks of this method are that it finds only local extrema, and convergence can be very slow when the irradiance function is flat. In the absence of a global method for locating all extrema, seed points near each of the relevant extrema must be supplied.

### 5.2    Direct Computation of Isolux Contours

Curves of constant irradiance over surfaces are known as *isolux contours* [20]. Applications of isolux contours in computer graphics include visualizing irradiance distributions [21, 15] and simplifying shading [4] and sampling [5]. In computer vision isolux contours have been used to perform automatic image segmentation [10]. In this section we show how isolux contours can be computed directly.

Every isolux contour on a surface $\mathcal{M}$ can be represented by a function $r : [0, \infty) \to \mathcal{M}$ that satisfies

$$\phi(r(s)) = \phi(r(0)) \tag{31}$$

for all $s \geq 0$. To compute such a curve we construct a first-order ordinary differential equation (ODE) to which it is a solution, and solve the ODE numerically.

The direction of most rapid increase in $\phi(r)$ at a point $r \in \mathcal{M}$ is given by the gradient $\nabla\phi(r)$, which generally does not lie in the tangent plane of the surface. The projection of the gradient onto the surface is a tangent vector that is orthogonal to the isolux curve passing through its origin. See Figure 9a. If the projected gradient is rotated by 90 degrees, we obtain a direction in which the irradiance remains constant to first order. See Figure 9b. Thus, we define the *isolux differential equation* by

$$\dot{r} = \mathbf{P}(r)\,\nabla\phi^{T}(r), \tag{32}$$

with the initial condition $r(0) = r_0$, where

$$\mathbf{P}(r) \equiv \mathbf{R}(\mathbf{n}(r))\left[\mathbf{I} - \mathbf{n}(r)\mathbf{n}^{T}(r)\right], \tag{33}$$

and $\mathbf{R}(z)$ is a rotation by $-\pi/2$ about the vector $z$. The matrix $\mathbf{P}(r)$ is constant for planar surfaces. The solution of this ODE is an isolux contour with irradiance $c = \phi(r_0)$.

### 5.2.1    Solving the Isolux Differential Equation

Any technique for solving first-order ordinary differential equations can be applied to solving the isolux differential equation. The overriding consideration in selecting an appropriate method is the number of irradiance values and gradients used in taking a step along the curve. Obtaining this information involves a global clipping operation, which is generally the most expensive part of the algorithm.

Multistep methods are particularly appropriate for solving the isolux ODE since they make efficient use of the recent history of the curve. For example, Milne's predictor-corrector method is a multistep method that predicts the point $r_{k+1} \equiv r(s_{k+1})$ by extrapolating from the three most recent gradients and function values using a parabola. When the matrix $\mathbf{P}$ is fixed, Milne's predictor is given by

$$r_{k+1}^0 \equiv r_{k-3} + \frac{4h}{3}\mathbf{P}\left(2g_{k-2} - g_{k-1} + 2g_k\right), \qquad (34)$$

where $g_k$ denotes the gradient at the point $r_k$, and $h$ is the step size [1]. Given the predicted value, a corrector is then invoked to find the nearest point on the curve. Because the contour is the zero set of the function $\phi(r) - c$, the correction can be performed very efficiently using Newton's method. Beginning with the predicted point $r_k^0$, a Newton corrector generates the sequence $r_k^1, r_k^2, \ldots$ by

$$r_k^{i+1} \equiv r_k^i + \left[c - \phi(r_k^i)\right] \frac{\nabla\phi^{\mathrm{T}}(r_k^i)}{||\nabla\phi^{\mathrm{T}}(r_k^i)||^2}, \qquad (35)$$

which converges quadratically to a point on the curve. The iteration is repeated until

$$|c - \phi(r_k^i)| \leq \epsilon, \qquad (36)$$

where $\epsilon$ is a preset tolerance. With this corrector, accurate polygonal approximations can be generated for arbitrarily long isolux contours. This would not be possible with the traditional Milne corrector, for example, which would eventually drift away from the curve. With a good predictor, very few correction steps are required, which saves costly gradient evaluations.

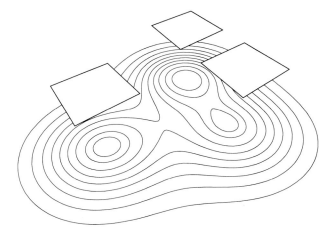

Figure 10: *A family of isolux contours for three unoccluded sources.*

### 5.2.2 Examples of Isolux Contours

The predictor-corrector method described above was used to compute isolux contours for simple test cases with both unoccluded and partially occluded sources. The step size $h$ and the tolerance for the corrector were user-supplied parameters. Use of the Newton corrector made the curve follower fairly robust; even abrupt turns at or near derivative discontinuities in the irradiance function were automatically compensated for.

To generate a family of curves depicting equal steps in irradiance, similar to a topographic map, we must find starting points for each

curve with the desired irradiance values $c_1 > c_2 > \cdots > c_k$. The Newton corrector can be used to find a point on the $(k+1)^{\mathrm{st}}$ curve by finding a root of the equation $\phi(r) - c_{k+1}$ beginning at any point on the $k^{\mathrm{th}}$ curve. The curve families in Figures 10 and 11 were automatically generated in this way. Figure 10 shows a family of isolux contours resulting from three unoccluded rectangular sources. Three distinct families were generated, starting at each of the three local maximuma, which were found by the ascent method described in section 5.1. Figure 11 shows a family of isolux contours resulting from a rectangular source and a simple blocker. These contours surround both a peak and a valley.

Because distinct isolux contours cannot cross, any collection of closed contours has an obvious partial ordering defined by containment. To display filled contours, as shown in Figures 12a and 12b, the regions can be painted in back-to-front order after sorting according to the partial order.

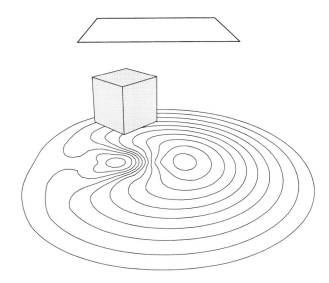

Figure 11: *Isolux contours on a planar receiver due to a rectangular source and simple blocker above the plane of the receiver.*

### 5.3 Iso-Meshing

Because the isolux contours described in the previous section are generated by direct computation rather than by post-processing an image, they may be used in the image generation process. For example, isolux contours can be used to drive a meshing algorithm for global illumination.

The idea is similar to that of discontinuity meshing [8, 13], which can identify important discontinuities in the radiance function over diffuse surfaces. Isolux contours provide additional information about radiance functions, and can be employed for mesh generation either in a preprocessing step for modeling direct illumination, or as part of a radiosity post-process to create a high-quality mesh for rendering a final image [13].

To best exploit the information in the contours, the mesh elements of an *iso-mesh* should follow the contours. To generate a mesh with this property from isolux contours, we have applied the constrained Delaunay triangulation algorithm used earlier by Lischinski et al. [13] for discontinuity meshing. This approach forces the edges of the mesh elements to align with the isolux contours rather than crossing them. It also creates triangles with good aspect ratios. Figure 13 shows the result of applying this algorithm to the families of isolux contours shown in Figure 12. Meshes of varying coarseness can be generated by selecting subsets of the points along the contours.

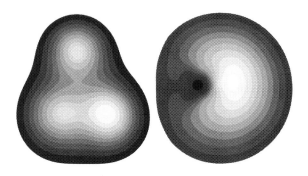

Figure 12: *Filled isolux contours corresponding to the previous figures. Each region is shaded according to the constant irradiance of its contour.*

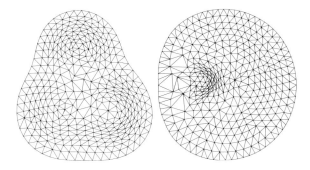

Figure 13: *Iso-meshes generated from families of isolux contours using constrained Delaunay triangulation.*

## 6   Conclusions and Future Work

We have presented a closed-form expression for the irradiance Jacobian due to polygonal sources of uniform brightness in the presence of arbitrary polygonal blockers. The expression is closely related to the well-known analytic formula for point-to-patch form factors, and is evaluated in much the same way when blockers are present; only a minor extension of standard polygon clipping is required.

Several applications that make use of gradients obtained from the irradiance Jacobian have been demonstrated, including the computation of isolux contours and local irradiance extrema, both in the presence of occluders.

Isolux contours provide a useful characterization of irradiance in regions away from the derivative discontinuities that can be handled with discontinuity meshing. We have demonstrated how a family of isolux contours can form the basis of a mesh generated with constrained Delaunay triangulation. This is one means of interpolating isolux contours, and also demonstrates a new approach to meshing for global illumination.

The irradiance Jacobian may also find other applications in global illumination. In approaches that do not employ an explicit mesh, gradients can be used to guide sampling in a spirit similar to previous approaches [22, 5], but using analytically computed gradients. Alternatively, irradiance gradients can be used to define higher-order interpolants within the elements of an existing mesh.

## Acknowledgments

The author owes many thanks to Ken Torrance for his advice and encouragement, and to Steve Westin for his invaluable suggestions. Thanks also to Dani Lischinski for useful discussions and for providing the Delaunay triangulation code, and to Don Greenberg, Brian Smits, Jim Ferwerda, Jed Lengyel, and Erin Shaw for their helpful comments. This work was supported by the NSF grant "Interactive Computer Graphics Input and Display Techniques" (CCR-8617880), and by the NSF/ARPA Science and Technology Center for Computer Graphics and Scientific Visualization (ASC-8920219). Hewlett-Packard Corporation generously provided the workstations used in this research.

## REFERENCES

[1] ACTON, F. S. *Numerical Methods that Work.* Harper & Row, New York, 1970.

[2] BAUM, D. R., RUSHMEIER, H. E., AND WINGET, J. M. Improving radiosity solutions through the use of analytically determined form-factors. *Computer Graphics 23*, 3 (July 1989), 325–334.

[3] BERGER, M. *Geometry, Volume II.* Springer-Verlag, New York, 1987. Translated by M. Cole and S. Levy.

[4] CONWAY, D. M., AND COTTINGHAM, M. S. The isoluminance contour model. In *Proceedings of Ausgraph '88* (Melbourne, Australia, September 1988), pp. 43–50.

[5] DRETTAKIS, G., AND FIUME, E. L. Concrete computation of global illumination using structured sampling. In *Proceedings of the Third Eurographics Workshop on Rendering, Bristol, United Kingdom* (1992).

[6] FOK, V. A. The illumination from surfaces of arbitrary shape. *Transactions of the Optical Institute, Leningrad 28* (1924), 1–11. (Russian).

[7] GERSHUN, A. The light field. *Journal of Mathematics and Physics 18*, 2 (May 1939), 51–151. Translated by P. Moon and G. Timoshenko.

[8] HECKBERT, P. S. *Simulating Global Illumination Using Adaptive Meshing.* PhD thesis, University of California, Berkeley, June 1991.

[9] HOPF, E. *Mathematical Problems of Radiative Equilibrium.* Cambridge University Press, New York, 1934.

[10] LIFSHITZ, L. M., AND PIZER, S. M. A multiresolution hierarchical approach to image segmentation based on intensity extrema. *IEEE Transactions on Pattern Analysis and Machine Intelligence 12*, 6 (June 1990), 529–540.

[11] LISCHINSKI, D., SMITS, B., AND GREENBERG, D. P. Bounds and error estimates for radiosity. In *Computer Graphics Proceedings* (1994), Annual Conference Series, ACM SIGGRAPH.

[12] LISCHINSKI, D., TAMPIERI, F., AND GREENBERG, D. P. Discontinuity meshing for accurate radiosity. *IEEE Computer Graphics and Applications 12*, 6 (November 1992), 25–39.

[13] LISCHINSKI, D., TAMPIERI, F., AND GREENBERG, D. P. Combining hierarchical radiosity and discontinuity meshing. In *Computer Graphics Proceedings* (1993), Annual Conference Series, ACM SIGGRAPH, pp. 199–208.

[14] NISHITA, T., AND NAKAMAE, E. Half-tone representation of 3-D objects illuminated by area sources or polyhedron sources. In *Proceedings of the IEEE Computer Software and Applications Conference* (Chicago, November 1983), pp. 237–242.

[15] NISHITA, T., AND NAKAMAE, E. Continuous tone representation of 3-D objects taking account of shadows and interreflection. *Computer Graphics 19*, 3 (July 1985), 23–30.

[16] PLANTINGA, H., AND DYER, C. R. Visibility, occlusion, and the aspect graph. *International Journal of Computer Vision 5*, 2 (1990), 137–160.

[17] PREISENDORFER, R. W. *Hydrologic Optics, Volume II. Foundations.* National Oceanic & Atmospheric Administration, Honolulu, Hawaii, 1976. (Available as NTIS PB-259 794).

[18] SCHRÖDER, P., AND HANRAHAN, P. On the form factor between two polygons. In *Computer Graphics Proceedings* (1993), Annual Conference Series, ACM SIGGRAPH, pp. 163–164.

[19] TELLER, S. Computing the antipenumbra of an area light source. *Computer Graphics 26*, 2 (July 1992), 139–148.

[20] TROTTER, A. P. *Illumination: Its Distribution and Measurement.* The Macmillan Company, London, 1911.

[21] VERBECK, C. P., AND GREENBERG, D. P. A comprehensive light-source description for computer graphics. *IEEE Computer Graphics and Applications 4*, 7 (July 1984), 66–75.

[22] WARD, G. J., AND HECKBERT, P. S. Irradiance gradients. In *Proceedings of the Third Eurographics Workshop on Rendering, Bristol, United Kingdom* (May 1992).

[23] WEILER, K., AND ATHERTON, P. Hidden surface removal using polygon area sorting. *Computer Graphics 11*, 3 (1977), 214–222.

# Synthetic Topiary

**Przemyslaw Prusinkiewicz, Mark James, and Radomír Měch**

Department of Computer Science
University of Calgary
Calgary, Alberta, Canada T2N 1N4

## ABSTRACT

The paper extends Lindenmayer systems in a manner suitable for simulating the interaction between a developing plant and its environment. The formalism is illustrated by modeling the response of trees to pruning, which yields synthetic images of sculptured plants found in topiary gardens.

**CR categories:** F.4.2 [**Mathematical Logic and Formal Languages**]: Grammars and Other Rewriting Systems: *Parallel rewriting systems*, I.3.7 [**Computer Graphics**]: Three-Dimensional Graphics and Realism, I.6.3 [**Simulation and Modeling**]: Applications, J.3 [**Life and Medical Sciences**]: Biology.

**Keywords:** image synthesis, modeling of plants, L-system, topiary.

## 1 INTRODUCTION

One classification of visual plant models introduces a distinction between *structure-oriented* and *space-oriented* models [26]. The first class is characterized by the assumption that the developmental process and the resulting structure are under the control of *endogenous* mechanisms, inherent in the growing structure and internal to it. *Lineage*, or the transfer of information from mother to daughter *modules* (components of the model) at the time of daughter creation, is the most frequently simulated form of endogenous control, although many models have been formulated without referring to this term explicitly. For example, tree models proposed by Aono and Kunii [1], Bloomenthal [5], Reeves and Blau [32], Oppenheimer [25], and de Reffye and his collaborators [10, 19] are all controlled by lineage. In contrast, *interactive* mechanisms involve information flow between coexisting adjacent components of the developing structure. In a growing plant, this information may be represented by phytohormones, nutrients, or water. *Context-sensitive L-systems* [22] provide a formally defined framework for simulating interactive control mechanisms, and have been used for image synthesis purposes by Smith [33] and Prusinkiewicz *et al.* [28, 29]. Outside the domain of L-systems, models of interactive endogenous control have been investigated by Borchert and Honda [6].

In contrast to structure-oriented models, space-oriented models capture the entire environment of a growing plant, and emphasize *exogenous* control, in which information is transferred through the environment enclosing the modeled structure. This class includes the models of climbing plants introduced by Arvo and Kirk [2] and Greene [12], as well as the models of roots growing around obstacles, also created by Greene [13].

The dichotomy between the structure-oriented and space-oriented models makes it difficult to faithfully capture plants in which the internally controlled development is modified by environmental factors. Such a combination of endogenous and exogenous mechanisms is manifested, for instance, in plant responses to collisions with obstacles, presence or absence of light, pruning, and attacks by insects. Several techniques were proposed to simulate these phenomena. For example, Honda *et al.* [18] used proximity of branches as a factor inhibiting their further growth and bifurcation. Kanamaru *et al.* [21] devised a convincing model of tree architecture in which the development of individual branches is controlled by the amount and direction of incoming light. A variety of factors, including the availability of light and the presence of mechanical obstacles, was assumed by Dabadie [9]. Mechanical obstacles to the development of branching patterns were also considered by Kaandorp [20].

In spite of these results, the problem of specifying and constructing plant models that integrate endogenous and exogenous mechanisms has not yet been completely resolved, because the reported techniques do not combine exogenous and *interactive* endogenous control. We address this limitation by introducing an *environmentally-sensitive* extension of L-systems, based on earlier results by Prusinkiewicz and McFadzean [30], and MacKenzie [24]. According to this extension, selected modules of a growing structure may access information about their position and orientation in space. We illustrate the operation of environmentally-sensitive L-systems by modeling plant response to the extensive pruning found in topiary and knot gardens. This application is motivated by the visual appeal of the resulting forms and their potential relevance to computer-assisted landscape design.

The paper is organized as follows. Background information regarding L-systems is presented in Section 2. On this basis, environmentally sensitive L-systems are defined and illustrated using simple examples in Section 3. Section 4 introduces a more realistic tree model, needed to create synthetic topiary forms. A mechanism that governs the response to pruning is incorporated into this model in Section 5. The resulting topiary forms are presented in Section 6. Section 7 contains conclusions, and lists directions for future work.

## 2  L-SYSTEMS

As the point of departure, we use parametric L-systems with turtle interpretation, described in detail in [16, 27, 28]. The essential aspects of this formalism relevant to the environmentally-sensitive extension are summarized below.

An L-system is a parallel rewriting system operating on branching structures represented as *bracketed strings* of modules. Matching pairs of square brackets enclose branches. Simulation begins with an initial string called the *axiom*, and proceeds in a sequence of discrete *derivation steps*. In each step, *rewriting rules* or *productions* replace all modules in the predecessor string by successor modules. The applicability of a production depends on a predecessor's context (in context-sensitive L-systems), values of parameters (in productions guarded by conditions), and on random factors (in stochastic L-systems). In the most extensive case, a production has the format:

$$id : lc < pred > rc : cond \rightarrow succ : prob$$

where $id$ is the production identifier (label), $lc$, $pred$, and $rc$ are the left context, the strict predecessor, and the right context, $cond$ is the condition, $succ$ is the successor, and $prob$ is the probability of production application. The strict predecessor and the successor are the only mandatory fields. For example, the L-system given below consists of axiom $\omega$ and three non-identity productions $p_1$, $p_2$, and $p_3$.

**L-system 1**

$$
\begin{aligned}
\omega \ : \quad & A(1)B(3)A(5) \\
p_1 \ : \quad & A(x) \rightarrow A(x+1) : 0.4 \\
p_2 \ : \quad & A(x) \rightarrow B(x-1) : 0.6 \\
p_3 \ : \quad & A(x) < B(y) > A(z) : y < 4 \rightarrow B(x+z)[A(y)]
\end{aligned}
$$

The stochastic productions $p_1$ and $p_2$ replace module $A(x)$ either by $A(x+1)$ or by $B(x-1)$, with probabilities equal to 0.4 and 0.6, respectively. The context-sensitive production $p_3$ replaces a module $B(y)$ with left context $A(x)$ and right context $A(z)$ by module $B(x+z)$ supporting branch $A(y)$. The application of this production is guarded by condition $y < 4$. Consequently, the first derivation step may have the form:

$$A(1)B(3)A(5) \implies A(2)B(6)[A(3)]B(4)$$

It was assumed that, as a result of random choice, production $p_1$ was applied to the module $A(1)$, and production $p_2$ to the module $A(5)$. Production $p_3$ was applied to the module $B(3)$, because it occurred with the required left and right context, and the condition $3 < 4$ was true.

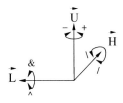

Figure 1: Controlling the turtle in three dimensions

In contrast to the parallel application of productions in each derivation step, the interpretation of the resulting strings proceeds sequentially, with the reserved modules acting as commands to a LOGO-style turtle [27, 28, 29]. At any time, the turtle is characterized by a position vector $\vec{P}$ and three mutually perpendicular orientation vectors $\vec{H}$, $\vec{U}$, and $\vec{L}$, indicating the turtle's heading, the up direction, and the direction to the left. Module $F$ causes the turtle to draw a line in the current direction. Modules $+$, $-$, $\&$, $\wedge$, $/$ and $\backslash$ rotate the turtle around one of the vectors $\vec{H}, \vec{U}$, or $\vec{L}$, as shown in Figure 1. The length of the line and the magnitude of the rotation angle can be given globally or specified as parameters of individual modules. During the interpretation of branches, the opening square bracket pushes the current position and orientation of the turtle on a stack, and the closing bracket restores the turtle to the position and orientation popped from the stack. A two-symbol module @o draws a sphere at the current position. A special interpretation is reserved for the module %, which cuts a branch by erasing all symbols in the string from the point of its occurrence to the end of the branch. The meaning of many symbols depends on the context in which they occur; for example, $+$ and $-$ denote arithmetic operators as well as modules that rotate the turtle.

## 3  ENVIRONMENTALLY-SENSITIVE L-SYSTEMS

The turtle interpretation of L-systems described above was designed to visualize models in a postprocessing step, with no effect on the L-system operation. Position and orientation of the turtle are important, however, while considering environmental phenomena, such as collisions with obstacles and exposure to light. Consequently, the *environmentally-sensitive extension* of L-systems makes these attributes accessible during the rewriting process. To this end, the generated string is interpreted after each derivation step, and turtle attributes found during the interpretation are returned as parameters to reserved *query modules* in the string. Each derivation step is performed as in parametric L-systems, except that the parameters associated with the query modules remain undefined. During the interpretation, these modules are assigned values that depend on the turtle's position and orientation in space. Syntactically, the query modules have the from $?X(x, y, z)$, where $X = P, H, U$, or $L$. Depending on the actual symbol $X$, the values of parameters $x$, $y$, and $z$ represent a position or an orientation vector. In the two-dimensional case, the coordinate $z$ may be omitted.

The operation of the query module is illustrated by a simple environmentally-sensitive L-system, given below.

**L-system 2**

$$
\begin{aligned}
\omega \ : \quad & A \\
p_1 \ : \quad & A \quad \rightarrow \quad F(1)?P(x, y) - A \\
p_2 \ : \quad & F(k) \quad \rightarrow \quad F(k+1)
\end{aligned}
$$

The following strings are produced during the first three derivation steps.

$$
\begin{aligned}
\mu_0' \ : \quad & A \\
\mu_0 \ : \quad & A \\
\mu_1' \ : \quad & F(1)?P(\star, \star) - A \\
\mu_1 \ : \quad & F(1)?P(0, 1) - A \\
\mu_2' \ : \quad & F(2)?P(\star, \star) - F(1)?P(\star, \star) - A \\
\mu_2 \ : \quad & F(2)?P(0, 2) - F(1)?P(1, 2) - A \\
\mu_3' \ : \quad & F(3)?P(\star, \star) - F(2)?P(\star, \star) - F(1)?P(\star, \star) - A \\
\mu_3 \ : \quad & F(3)?P(0, 3) - F(2)?P(2, 3) - F(1)?P(2, 2) - A
\end{aligned}
$$

Strings $\mu_0'$, $\mu_1'$, $\mu_2'$, and $\mu_3'$ represent the axiom and the results of production application before the interpretation steps. Symbol $\star$ indicates an undefined parameter value in a query module. Strings $\mu_1$, $\mu_2$, and $\mu_3$ represent the corresponding strings after interpretation. It has been assumed that the turtle is initially placed at the origin of the coordinate system, vector $\vec{H}$ is aligned with the $y$ axis, vector $\vec{L}$ points in the negative direction of the $x$ axis, and the angle

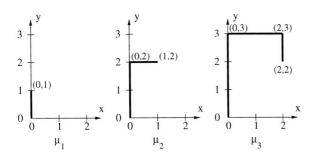

Figure 2: Assignment of values to query modules

of rotation associated with module "$-$" is equal to $90°$. Parameters of the query modules have values representing the positions of the turtle shown in Figure 2.

The next example illustrates an abstract developmental process influenced by the environment.

**L-system 3**

$$\omega : \quad A$$
$$p_1 : \quad A \rightarrow [+B][-B]F?P(x,y)A$$
$$p_2 : \quad B \rightarrow F?P(x,y)@oB$$
$$p_3 : \quad ?P(x,y) : 4x^2 + (y-10)^2 > 10^2$$
$$\rightarrow [+(2y)F][-(2y)F]\%$$

Module $F$ represents a line of unit length, and modules $+$ and $-$ without parameters represent left and right turns of $60°$.

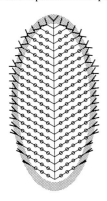

Figure 3: A branching structure pruned to an ellipse

The development begins with module $A$, which creates a sequence of opposite branches $[+B][-B]$ separated by internodes (branch segments) $F$ (production $p_1$). The branches elongate by addition of segments $F$, delimited by markers $@o$ (production $p_2$). Both the main apex $A$ and the lateral apices $B$ create query modules $?P(x,y)$, which return the corresponding turtle positions. If a query module is placed beyond the ellipse $4x^2 + (y-10)^2 = 10^2$, production $p_3$ creates a pair of "tentacles," represented by the substring $[+(2y)F][-(2y)F]$. The angle $4y$ between these tentacles depends on the vertical position $y$ of the query module. Production $p_3$ also inserts cutting symbol $\%$, which terminates branch growth by removing its apex. In summary, L-system 3 produces a branching structure confined to an ellipse, with tentacles placed at the boundary of the structure, and the angle between the tentacles depending on the turtle's position in space, as shown in Figure 3.

The final example of this section presents a simple two-dimensional model of tree response to pruning. As described, for example, by Hallé *et al.* [15, Chapter 4] and Bell [3, page 298], during the normal development of a tree many buds do not produce new branches and remain dormant. These buds may be subsequently activated by the removal of leading buds from the branch system (*traumatic reiteration*), which results in an environmentally-adjusted tree ar-

chitecture. The model given below represents the extreme case of this process, where buds are activated only as a result of pruning.

**L-system 4**

$$\omega : \quad FA?P(x,y)$$
$$p_1 : \quad A > ?P(x,y) : !\text{prune}(x,y) \rightarrow @oF/(180)A$$
$$p_2 : \quad A > ?P(x,y) : \text{prune}(x,y) \rightarrow T\%$$
$$p_3 : \quad F > T \rightarrow S$$
$$p_4 : \quad F > S \rightarrow SF$$
$$p_5 : \quad S \rightarrow \epsilon$$
$$p_6 : \quad @o > S \rightarrow [+FA?P(x,y)]$$

The user defined function

$$\text{prune}(x,y) = (x < -L/2) \| (x > L/2) \| (y < 0) \| (y > L),$$

where $\|$ stands for the logical OR operator, defines a square *clipping box* of dimensions $L \times L$ that bounds the growing structure. According to axiom $\omega$, the development begins with an internode $F$ supporting apex $A$ and query module $?P(x,y)$. The initial development of the structure is described by production $p_1$. In each step, the apex $A$ creates a dormant bud $@o$ and an internode $F$. The module $/(180)$ rotates the turtle around its own axis (the heading vector $\vec{H}$), thus laying a foundation for an alternating branching pattern. The query module $?P(x,y)$, placed by the axiom, is the right context for production $p_1$ and returns the current position of apex $A$. When a branch extends beyond the clipping box, production $p_2$ removes apex $A$, cuts off the query module $?P(x,y)$, and generates the pruning signal $T$. In presence of this signal, production $p_3$ removes the last internode of the branch that extends beyond the clipping box and creates bud-activating signal $S$. Productions $p_4$ and $p_5$ propagate this signal basipetally (downwards), until it reaches a dormant bud $@o$. Production $p_6$ induces this bud to initiate a lateral branch consisting of internode $F$ and apex $A$ followed by query module $?P(x,y)$. According to production $p_1$, this branch develops in the same manner as the main axis. When its apex extends beyond the clipping box, it is removed by production $p_2$, and signal $S$ is generated again. This process may continue until all dormant buds have been activated.

Selected phases of the described developmental sequence are illustrated in Figure 4. In derivation step 6 the apex of the main axis grows out of the clipping box. In step 7 this apex and the last internode are removed from the structure, and the bud-activating signal $S$ is generated. As a result of bud activation, a lateral branch is created in step 8. As it also extends beyond the bounding box, it is removed in step 9 (not shown). Signal $S$ is generated again, and in step 10 it reaches a dormant bud. The subsequent development of the lateral branches, shown in the middle and bottom rows of Figure 4, follows a similar pattern.

L-system 4 simulates the response of a tree to pruning using a schematic branching structure. A more realistic model is needed to synthesize visually convincing images of pruned trees. A suitable model of free-standing trees is presented in the next section, and applied to simulate the response to pruning in Sections 5 and 6.

## 4 A STOCHASTIC TREE MODEL

As a first approximation, the development of a free-standing woody plant — a tree or a shrub — can be described as a process in which new branches are successively added to the structure. Early tree

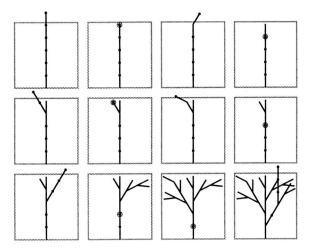

Figure 4: A simple model of a tree's response to pruning. Top row: derivation steps 6,7,8, and 10; middle row: steps 12, 13, 14, and 17; bottom row: steps 20, 40, 75, and 94. Small black circles indicate dormant buds, the larger circles indicate the position of signal $S$.

models emphasized the repetitive character of this process. For example, Honda [17] described a tree as a recursive branching structure, in which the *bifurcation ratio* (the number of branches originating at the mother branch), the branching angles, and the proportions between the lengths of the mother branch and the daughter branches do not depend on the position of the branches in the crown nor on the age of the simulated tree. Tree models of Aono and Kunii [1] and Oppenheimer [25] satisfy similar assumptions. The resulting structures are self-similar, which implies that the number of branches increases exponentially with the age of the structure.

Using morphometric data of young cottonwood (*Populus deltoides*) and observations of the tropical tree *Tabebuia rosea*, Borchert and Slade [7] showed that the exponential growth of the number of terminal branches yields unnaturally dense crowns in models of older trees. In reality, as soon as trees surpass a certain, relatively small size, the rate of branching decreases. Based on the analysis of this phenomenon presented by Borchert and Slade, we present here a model of trees suitable for computer graphics purposes. It is constructed to meet the following botanically justifiable postulates:

- The development begins in season $k = 1$ with the formation of a single nonbranching shoot (branch segment bearing leaves).

- In each subsequent growth season, new shoots grow from the buds situated near the distal ends of last year's segments. There is a constant, $b_{max} > 1$, that determines the maximum bifurcation ratio.

- All branch segments have approximately the same length $l$, independent of their position and the age of the tree, and reach out forming a hemispherical crown.

- Leaves are produced on the terminal (current year) branch segments, thus forming a hemispherical layer of leaves near the perimeter of the crown. There is a constant, $\sigma_{min}$, that determines the minimum area of leaves that must be exposed to light coming from the outside in order to create a viable shoot.

According to these postulates, the radius of a tree crown after $k \geq 1$ growth seasons is limited by $R_k = lk$. A hemispherical crown of this radius has surface area $S_k = 2\pi R_k^2 = 2\pi l^2 k^2$, and this value determines the upper bound on the crown area exposed to direct light. The number $N_{k+1}$ of branch segments added to the tree in year $k + 1$ is limited, on the one hand, by the number of last year's segments $N_k$ multiplied by the maximum bifurcation ratio $b_{max}$, and on the other hand, by the maximum number $v_{k+1} = S_{k+1}/\sigma_{min}$ of shoots that may be produced without excessively obscuring each other. Thus,

$$N_{k+1} = \min\{b_{max}N_k, v_{k+1}\} = \min\{b_{max}N_k, \frac{2\pi l^2}{\sigma_{\min}}(k + 1)^2\}.$$

Let us assume that the minimum leaf area exposed to light per shoot is small compared to the crown area, $\sigma_{min} \ll 2\pi l^2$. In a young tree (during the first few growth seasons), the maximum number of new shoots does not suffice to cover the available crown surface ($b_{max}N_k < v_{k+1}$), and the number of new shoots will increase exponentially with the age of the tree: $N_{k+1} = b_{max}N_k = b_{max}^k$. Since the crown area is proportional only to the square of the age of the tree, at some age $t$ the potential number of new shoots will exceed the number that can be sufficiently exposed to direct light: $b_{max}N_t \geq v_t$. From then on, branching will be limited by the crown area, with the average bifurcation ratio $b_k$ at age $k \geq t$ equal to:

$$b_k = \frac{N_{k+1}}{N_k} = \frac{2\pi l^2(k + 1)^2/\sigma_{min}}{2\pi l^2 k^2/\sigma_{min}} = 1 + \frac{2k + 1}{k^2}.$$

Different branching patterns may satisfy this general formula. For example, if each segment from the previous year gives rise either to one or to two new shoots, the fraction of segments supporting two shoots will be equal to:

$$\frac{N_{k+1} - N_k}{N_k} = \frac{2k + 1}{k^2}. \qquad (1)$$

The stochastic L-system below has been constructed to satisfy this equation.

**L-system 5**

$\omega : \quad FA(1)$

$p_1 : \quad A(k) \rightarrow /(\phi)[+(\alpha)FA(k + 1)] - (\beta)FA(k + 1) :$
$$\min\{1, (2k + 1)/k^2\}$$

$p_2 : \quad A(k) \rightarrow /(\phi)B - (\beta)FA(k + 1) :$
$$\max\{0, 1 - (2k + 1)/k^2\}$$

The generation of the tree begins with a single internode $F$ terminated by apex $A(1)$. The parameter of the apex acts as a counter of derivation steps. Production $p_1$ describes the creation of two new branches, while production $p_2$ describes the production of a branch segment and a dormant bud $B$. Probabilities of these events are equal to $p = \min\{1, (2k + 1)/k^2\}$, and $q = 1 - p$, respectively. This corresponds to the assumption that the departure from exponential bifurcation occurs in step $k = 3$, and in subsequent steps the probability of bifurcation is determined by Equation 1. Figure 5 shows side views of three sample trees after 18 derivation steps. The branching angles, equal to $\phi = 90°, \alpha = 32°$, and $\beta = 20°$, yield a sympodial branching structure (new shoots do not continue the growth direction of the preceding segments). This structure is

Figure 5: Sample tree structures generated using L-system 5

representative to the Leeuwenberg's model of tree architecture identified by Hallé *et al.* [15], although no attempt to capture a particular tree species was made. The same values of branching angles can be found in all the tree models shown in this paper.

## 5  SIMULATION OF PRUNING

L-system 5 generates structures with many dormant buds, and therefore can be used to simulate tree response to pruning in a manner similar to that implemented in L-system 4. The resulting integrated model is given below.

**L-system 6**

$$
\begin{aligned}
\omega : \quad & FA(1)?P(x,y,z) \\
p_1 : \quad & A(k) > ?P(x,y,z) : \ !\mathrm{prune}(x,y,z) \rightarrow \\
& /(\phi)[+(\alpha)FA(k+1)?P(x,y,z)] - (\beta)FA(k+1) : \\
& \qquad\qquad \min\{1, (2k+1)/k^2\} \\
p_2 : \quad & A(k) > ?P(x,y,z) : \ !\mathrm{prune}(x,y,z) \rightarrow \\
& /(\phi)B(k+1,k+1) - (\beta)FA(k+1) : \\
& \qquad\qquad \max\{0, 1 - (2k+1)/k^2\} \\
p_3 : \quad & A(k) > ?P(x,y,z) : \ \mathrm{prune}(x,y,z) \rightarrow T\% \\
p_4 : \quad & F > T \rightarrow S \\
p_5 : \quad & F > S \rightarrow SF \\
p_6 : \quad & S \rightarrow \epsilon \\
p_7 : \quad & B(m,n) > S \rightarrow [+(\alpha)FA(am+bn+c)?P(x,y,z)] \\
p_8 : \quad & B(m,n) > F \rightarrow B(m+1,n)
\end{aligned}
$$

According to axiom $\omega$, the development begins with a single internode $F$ supporting apex $A(1)$ and query module $?P(x,y,z)$. Productions $p_1$ and $p_2$ are similar to those in L-system 5 and describe the spontaneous growth of the tree within the volume characterized by a user-defined clipping function $\mathrm{prune}(x,y,z)$. Productions $p_3$ to $p_7$ are similar to productions $p_2$ to $p_6$ in L-system 4. Specifically, production $p_3$ removes the apex $A()$ after it has crossed the clipping surface, cuts off the query module $?P(x,y,z)$, and creates pruning signal $T$. Next, $p_4$ removes the last internode of the pruned branch and initiates bud-activating signal $S$, which is propagated basipetally by productions $p_5$ and $p_6$. When $S$ reaches a dormant bud $B()$, production $p_7$ transforms it into a branch consisting of an internode $F$, apex $A()$, and query module $?P(x,y,z)$.

The parameter value assigned by production $p_7$ to apex $A()$ is derived as follows. According to production $p_2$, both parameters associated with a newly created bud $B()$ are set to the age of the tree at the time of bud creation (expressed as the the number of derivation steps). Production $p_8$ updates the value of the first parameter $(m)$, so that it always indicates the actual age of the tree. The second parameter $(n)$ remains unchanged. The initial *biological age* [3, page 315] of the activated apex $A()$ in production $p_7$ is a linear combination of parameters $m$ and $n$, calculated using the expression

$am + bn + c$. Since rule $p_1$ is more likely to be applied for young apices (for small values of parameter $k$), by manipulating constants $a$, $b$, and $c$ it is possible to control the bifurcation frequency of branches created as a result of traumatic reiteration. This is an important feature of the model, because in nature the reiterated branches tend to be more juvenile and vigorous than the remainder of the tree [3, page 298].

The operation of this model is illustrated in Figure 6. The clipping form is a cube with an edge length 12 times longer than the internode lengh. The constant values used in production $p_7$ are $a = 0$, $b = 1$, and $c = -5$. The structures shown have been generated in 3, 6, 9, 13, 21, and 27 steps. Leaves were defined using Bézier surfaces, as described in [28, Section 5.1].

The impact of constants $a$, $b$, and $c$ on tree structures is further illustrated in Figure 7. All trees have been generated in 31 steps. In the pair of trees shown on the left-hand side, the initial age of the activated apices is equal to the actual age of the tree minus 5 ($a = 1$, $b = 0$, and $c = -5$). In the middle pair, the initial age is equal to the time of bud creation minus 5 ($a = 0$, $b = 1$, and $c = -5$). Finally, in the rightmost pair the reiterated branches are assigned an initial age of 1 ($a = 0, b = 0, c = 1$). In all cases, the density of the branches is increased near the boundary of the clipping box, compared to a non-pruned tree. As a result, a pruned tree acquires a shape that closely resembles that of its bounding volume, defined by the clipping function. This effect is most pronounced when the reiterated branches are assigned an initial age of 1, which results in the most vigorous branching.

By changing the clipping function, one can shape plant models generated by L-system 6 to a variety of artificial forms. Selected examples are presented in the next section. In all cases the initial age of activated apices is calculated using the set of parameters $a = 0$, $b = 1$, and $c = -5$.

## 6  EXAMPLES OF SYNTHETIC TOPIARY

The term *topiary* denotes the art (or craft) of clipping suitable trees and shrubs into elaborate ornamental shapes, most frequently free-standing [23, pages 132, 183]. These shapes range from purely geometric ones, such as spheres, cones, or spirals, to depictions of "hunting scenes, fleets of ships, and imitations of real objects." [14, page 11]. Related to topiary is the ornamental use of hedges, which includes tall structures intended to obscure the view in *labyrinths*, and intricate patterns of low shrubs designed to be viewed from above in *knot gardens* or *parterres*.

Given a flexible model of tree response to pruning, the main remaining issue is the specification of the clipping surface. *Implicit surfaces* [4, 36] are particularly suitable for this purpose, since they provide a simple method for checking whether a query point lies inside or outside the defined surface. The clipping forms can be blended together and combined using constructive solid geometry operations [35].

The Levens Hall garden in England, laid out at the beginning of the 18th century, is considered the most famous topiary garden in the world [8, pages 52–57]. It contains many geometric forms, two of which have been reproduced in Figures 8 and 9. Specifically, Figure 8 illustrates the use of constructive solid geometry operations to define the clipping form, in this case, the union of a parallelepiped and a cylinder. The spirals shown in Figure 9 have been obtained by pruning a tree to the shape of a seashell. An implicit repre-

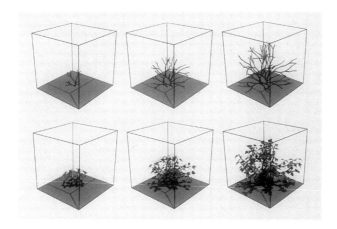

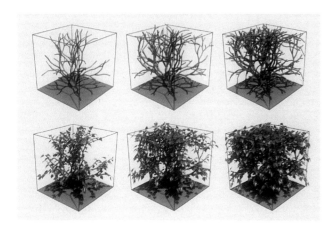

Figure 6: Simulation of tree response to pruning

Figure 8: A tree pruned to a union of a parallelepiped and a cylinder

Figure 7: Impact of vigor of reiterated branches (shown in red) on the appearance of a pruned tree

Figure 9: Trees pruned to a spiral shape

sentation of the seashell was obtained by converting the parametric representation described by Fowler *et al.* [11].

Another application of implicit surface definition is shown in Figures 10 and 11. In this case, the clipping form of a "topiary dinosaur" was obtained as an implicit surface defined by a skeleton of lines and ellipsoids. Two trees were used to facilitate the growth of branches into the elongated shapes of neck and tail.

The large number of primitives representing individual plants makes

it difficult to combine them into complex scenes. The reuse (instantiation) of models provides a simple solution in the case of repetitive designs. For example, the hedges shown in Figure 12 have been composed of rectangular and circular segments, replicated to create the complete scene. The images are relatively faithful synthetic representations of the knot garden at Moseley Old Hall, reconstructed in England in 1960 from a seventeenth-century design [34, page 50] (see also [23, page 122]).

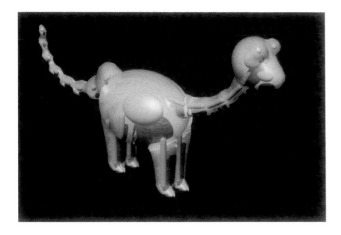

Figure 10: An implicit surface defined by a skeleton of lines and ellipsoids

Figure 11: Topiary dinosaur

Figure 12: A model of the knot garden at Moseley Old Hall

field values may represent concentrations of nutrients and water in soil. This field may be assumed to be stationary, or change dynamically to reflect the absorption of substances by the growing plant. Above the ground, a dynamically changing field may be used to distinguish areas exposed to light from those in shade, and specify areas occupied by other objects for collision detection purposes. We hope that such simulations will lead to a better understanding of the underlying phenomena, increase the predictive value of plant models, and result in more realistic synthetic images of plants.

## 7  DISCUSSION

In this paper, we extended L-systems with a mechanism for simulating the impact of the environment on plant development. The resulting formalism was explained using simple geometric examples, then applied to simulate plant response to pruning. A biologically-motivated tree model incorporating this mechanism served as a basis for creating models of sculptured plants found in topiary gardens. One prospective application of such models is in computer-assisted landscape design.

We have not found much published information characterizing the impact of pruning on tree architecture. More data would be necessary to construct faithful models of particular tree species. As described in [31], construction of visual models of plants provides a valuable guideline for collecting field data. Consequently, the mathematical framework introduced in the present paper may assist in biological studies of the effects of pruning on plant development.

Pruning is only one of a range of phenomena that can be modeled using environmentally-sensitive L-systems. The values returned by the query modules may not only indicate whether a query point is inside or outside a clipping volume, but also to return, through properly defined *field functions*, other values characterizing the space in which the plant develops. For example, in a model of roots, the

### Acknowledgements

We would like to thank Jim Hanan for his essential work on the plant modeling software *cpfg*, which provided the basis for our implementation of the environmentally-sensitive extension of L-systems. Brian Wyvill created the implicitly defined pruning surface for the dinosaur. All images were rendered using the ray-tracer `rayshade` by Craig Kolb. Brian Gaines kindly made his compute server available to us. Keith Ferguson, Lynn Mercer, and the anonymous referees provided many useful comments, which we tried to incorporate into the final version of the paper. This research was sponsored by operating and equipment grants from the Natural Sciences and Engineering Research Council of Canada, and a grant from the Josefa, Marie a Zdeňky Hlávkových Foundation.

### REFERENCES

[1] M. Aono and T. L. Kunii. Botanical tree image generation. *IEEE Computer Graphics and Applications*, 4(5):10–34, 1984.

[2] J. Arvo and D. Kirk. Modeling plants with environment-sensitive automata. In *Proceedings of Ausgraph '88*, pages 27–33, 1988.

[3] A. Bell. *Plant form: an illustrated guide to flowering plants*. Oxford University Press, Oxford, 1991.

[4] J. Blinn. A generalization of algebraic surface drawing. *ACM Transactions on Graphics*, 1(3), 1982.

[5] J. Bloomenthal. Modeling the Mighty Maple. Proceedings of SIGGRAPH '85, in *Computer Graphics*, 19(3):305–311, 1985.

[6] R. Borchert and H. Honda. Control of development in the bifurcating branch system of *Tabebuia rosea*: A computer simulation. *Botanical Gazette*, 145(2):184–195, 1984.

[7] R. Borchert and N. Slade. Bifurcation ratios and the adaptive geometry of trees. *Botanical Gazette*, 142(3):394–401, 1981.

[8] P. Coats. *Great gardens of the Western world*. G. P. Putnam's Sons, New York, 1963.

[9] P. Dabadie. *Contribution à la modélisation et simulation de la croissance des végétaux*. PhD thesis, Université Montpellier II, October 1991.

[10] P. de Reffye, C. Edelin, J. Françon, M. Jaeger, and C. Puech. Plant models faithful to botanical structure and development. Proceedings of SIGGRAPH '88, in *Computer Graphics*, 22(4):151–158, 1988.

[11] D. R. Fowler, H. Meinhardt, and P. Prusinkiewicz. Modeling seashells. Proceedings of SIGGRAPH '92, in *Computer Graphics*, 26(2):379–387, 1992.

[12] N. Greene. Voxel space automata: Modeling with stochastic growth processes in voxel space. Proceedings of SIGGRAPH '89, in *Computer Graphics*, 23(4):175–184, 1989.

[13] N. Greene. Detailing tree skeletons with voxel automata. SIGGRAPH '91 Course Notes on Photorealistic Volume Modeling and Rendering Techniques, 1991.

[14] M. Hadfield. *Topiary and ornamental hedges*. A. & C. Black, London, 1971.

[15] F. Hallé, R. A. A. Oldeman, and P. B. Tomlinson. *Tropical trees and forests: An architectural analysis*. Springer-Verlag, Berlin, 1978.

[16] J. S. Hanan. *Parametric L-systems and their application to the modelling and visualization of plants*. PhD thesis, University of Regina, June 1992.

[17] H. Honda. Description of the form of trees by the parameters of the tree-like body: Effects of the branching angle and the branch length on the shape of the tree-like body. *Journal of Theoretical Biology*, 31:331–338, 1971.

[18] H. Honda, P. B. Tomlinson, and J. B. Fisher. Computer simulation of branch interaction and regulation by unequal flow rates in botanical trees. *American Journal of Botany*, 68:569–585, 1981.

[19] M. Jaeger and P. de Reffye. Basic concepts of computer simulation of plant growth. *Journal of Biosciences*, 17(3):275–291, 1992.

[20] J. Kaandorp. Modelling growth forms of sponges with fractal techniques. In A. Crilly, R. Earnshaw, and H. Jones, editors, *Fractals and chaos*. Springer-Verlag, 1991.

[21] N. Kanamaru and K. Takahashi. CG simulation of natural shapes of botanical trees based on heliotropism. *The Transactions of the Institute of Electronics, Information, and Communication Engineers*, J75-D-II(1):76–85, 1992. In Japanese.

[22] A. Lindenmayer. Mathematical models for cellular interaction in development, Parts I and II. *Journal of Theoretical Biology*, 18:280–315, 1968.

[23] R. Llewellyn. *Ellegance and eccentricity: Ornamental and architectural features of historic British gardens*. Ward Lock Limited, London, 1989.

[24] C. MacKenzie. Artificial evolution of generative models in computer graphics. Master's thesis, University of Calgary, 1993.

[25] P. Oppenheimer. Real time design and animation of fractal plants and trees. Proceedings of SIGGRAPH '86, in *Computer Graphics*, 20(4):55–64, 1986.

[26] P. Prusinkiewicz. Modeling and visualization of biological structures. In *Proceedings of Graphics Interface '93*, pages 128–137, 1993.

[27] P. Prusinkiewicz and J. Hanan. Visualization of botanical structures and processes using parametric L-systems. In D. Thalmann, editor, *Scientific Visualization and Graphics Simulation*, pages 183–201. J. Wiley & Sons, Chichester, 1990.

[28] P. Prusinkiewicz and A. Lindenmayer. *The algorithmic beauty of plants*. Springer-Verlag, New York, 1990. With J. S. Hanan, F. D. Fracchia, D. R. Fowler, M. J. M. de Boer, and L. Mercer.

[29] P. Prusinkiewicz, A. Lindenmayer, and J. Hanan. Developmental models of herbaceous plants for computer imagery purposes. Proceedings of SIGGRAPH '88, in *Computer Graphics*, 22(4):141–150, 1988.

[30] P. Prusinkiewicz and D. McFadzean. Modeling plants in environmental context. In *Proceedings of the Fourth Annual Western Computer Graphics Symposium*, pages 47–51, Banff, 1992.

[31] P. Prusinkiewicz, W. Remphrey, C. Davidson, and M. Hammel. Modeling the architecture of expanding *Fraxinus pennsylvanica* shoots using L-systems. To appear in the *Canadian Journal of Botany*, 1994.

[32] W. T. Reeves and R. Blau. Approximate and probabilistic algorithms for shading and rendering structured particle systems. Proceedings of SIGGRAPH '85, in *Computer Graphics*, 19(3):313–322, 1985.

[33] A. R. Smith. Plants, fractals, and formal languages. Proceedings of SIGGRAPH '84, in *Computer Graphics*, 18(3):1–10, 1984.

[34] R. Verey. *Classic garden design*. J. Murray Limited, London, 1989.

[35] G. Wyvill. Implicit surfaces in CSG systems. In *SIGGRAPH 1990 course notes: Modeling and animating with implicit surfaces*, pages 3.1–3.7, 1990.

[36] G. Wyvill, C. McPheeters, and B. Wyvill. Data structure for soft objects. *The Visual Computer*, 2(4):227–234, 1986.

# Visual Simulation of Lightning

Todd Reed and Brian Wyvill

The University of Calgary[1]

## ABSTRACT

A method for rendering lightning using conventional raytracing techniques is discussed. The approach taken is directed at producing aesthetic images for animation, rather than providing a realistic physically based model for rendering. A particle system is used to generate the path of the lightning channel, and subsequently to animate the lightning. A technique, using implicit surfaces, is introduced for illuminating objects struck by lightning.

**CR Categories:** I.3.3 [**Computer Graphics**]: Picture/Image Generation; I.3.7 [**Computer Graphics**]: Three-Dimensional Graphics and Realism, *Animation*.

**Keywords:** Computer Graphics, Lightning, Raytracing, Implicit Surfaces.

## 1 INTRODUCTION

The synthetic reproduction of natural scenes has been a primary goal of the computer graphics community. Much attention has been given to the problem of rendering plant life, mountainous terrain, clouds, fire, etc. Surprisingly, lightning, one of nature's most spectacular phenomena, has been largely ignored. This paper presents a simple method for modeling and rendering lightning and objects struck by lightning, using raytracing techniques. Lightning is represented as a collection of connected, finite length rays in 3D space. A particle system is used to generate the segments for a complete lightning stroke, and subsequently for animating a lightning strike. For some time we have been working on skeletal-implicit surface modeling techniques and have built a number of models [7]. Such models are represented as an iso-surface in a scalar field. A method is presented for using the scalar field to provide a value for the brightness of the glow around an object that has been struck by lightning.

The best understood source of lightning is cumulonimbus, ordinary thunderstorm clouds. The majority of cloud related lightning discharges are intracloud, and are not visible from earth. Visible types of discharges include cloud-to-cloud, cloud-to-air, ground-to-cloud, and cloud-to-ground[2]. Research on lightning has focused on the familiar cloud-to-ground lightning for the practical reason of minimizing its damaging effect on our environment. This interaction with our environment is also what makes cloud-to-ground lightning so visually stimulating. Photographs of lightning strikes that encounter "ground zero" are among the best[3] (see Figure 9), and provided the inspiration for rendering lightning.

Research in physically based lightning models has been reported (see [2], for example). However, the mathematical complexity and the numerous parameters required to describe the complete lightning environment make these models impractical for the computer artist.

The primary goal of this research is to produce visually realistic images of lightning with minimal complexity and computational cost. Hence, the technique developed in this paper does not attempt to model cloud physics, atmospheric conditions, or the physics of lightning discharges. Photographs of lightning from [4, 5] provided a yardstick for measuring the accuracy of the images produced.

## 2 A TYPICAL LIGHTNING STRIKE

Even though our model is not physically based, a short discussion of lightning physics is essential to introduce terminology and concepts.

A typical (negative) cloud-to-ground lightning strike is initiated within a cloud that is positively charged in its upper region, and negatively charged in its lower region; sparse positive charges also occupy the lowest region of the cloud (see Figure 1). The *stepped leader*, a negative stream of electrons, propogates toward ground zero in discrete steps. The stepped leader itself is initiated by an unknown process termed the *preliminary breakdown* (a). The descending stepped leader forms a jagged and branching channel, still invisible, that attracts an *upward positive leader* from the ground, thus starting the *attachment process* (b). The meeting of the downward and upward leaders triggers the first *return stroke*, which is responsible for illuminating the channel, and creating thunder (c). The return stroke begins at the point of contact between the downward and upward leader, usually close to the ground. If sufficient charge remains in the cloud, *dart leaders* may travel through the residual channel and create subsequent return strokes (d). A lightning strike will typically have less than five return strokes, but can have many more. Returns strokes subsequent to the first usually do not illuminate branches off the main channel. The entire discharge, termed a *flash*, lasts about half a second.

---

[1] Department of Computer Science, The University of Calgary, 2500 University Drive NW, Calgary, Alberta, Canada T2N 1N4, E-mail: reedt@cpsc.ucalgary.ca, blob@cpsc.ucalgary.ca

[2] If you happen to be a shuttle astronaut, include cloud-to-space lightning in this list of visible discharges. On April 28, 1990, a cloud-to-space discharge was recorded for the first time by a payload-bay camera aboard the space shuttle. See [6] for details.

[3] See [4] for an excellent collection of lightning photographs.

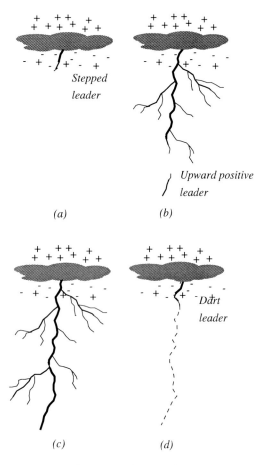

Figure 1: A lightning flash.

The above description is admittedly scant. Readers interested in the physical details of the lightning phenomena are referred to [5].

## 3   LIGHTNING MODEL

The skeletal structure of lightning is generated by a particle system which simulates the stepped leader progression toward ground zero. Starting with a seed segment (in the clouds), new segments are spawned and randomly rotated about the seed segment. Always rotating children segments with respect to the initial seed segment guarantees the channel assumes a linear shape[4]. The segments are concatenated to form a complete channel. Enough segments are generated so that the main channel hits ground zero. During the leader progression, branches are recursively generated. Branches are allocated a number of segments, chosen from a uniform distribution, and grow until its segments are depleted, or ground zero is encountered.

Uman reports that the directional changes between successive channel segments are randomly distributed, independent of segment length, with a mean absolute value of about 16 degrees [5]. This is simulated by rotating non-seed segments $\pm\alpha$ degrees with respect to the seed segment, where $\alpha$ is chosen from a normal distribution with mean 16 degrees and variance of about $0.1$[5]. In three dimensions, two rotations in orthogonal planes are required. Segment lengths

are chosen from a uniform distribution; segment lengths reportedly vary from less than 1 metre to over 1 kilometre. For the purpose of rendering, small segments provide more visually realistic results.

Branching is controlled by a probability function. From the main channel, branching is usually more frequent near the ground. In practice, the erratic behavior of the pseudo-random number generator used[6] made it difficult to consistently control branching. The lightning strokes generated were very sensitive to the seed selected for the number generator. Some seeds completely eliminated branching, while others produced excessive branching (see Figure 2).

Figure 2: Various lightning skeletons obtained with different seeds for the pseudo-random number generator.

## 4   RENDERING

Although conventional raytracing techniques are used for rendering, the line-segment representation of lightning prevents us from treating lightning strokes as geometric objects. The usual shading methods employed by raytracers are inappropriate because lightning does not have a definable surface.

The proposed shading method modifies the conventional shading algorithm by adding a color contribution from the lightning. For each ray, $r$, the following shading calculation is made:

$$I_{total_\lambda} = \sum I_{i_\lambda} \quad I_{i_\lambda} = m_{i_\lambda} \exp\left(-\left(\frac{d_i}{w_{i_\lambda}}\right)^{n_{i_\lambda}}\right) \quad (1)$$

where

- $\lambda$ is the wavelength (*red*, *green* or *blue*).

- $I_{i_\lambda}$ is the light contribution from segment $S_i$ for wavelength $\lambda$.

- $m_{i_\lambda} \epsilon [0, 1]$ is the maximum value of $I_{i_\lambda}$

- $d_i$ is the shortest distance between the ray $r$ and the segment $S_i$.

- $w_{i_\lambda} > 0$ is half the width of the lightning channel segment $S_i$. If $d_i > w_{i_\lambda}$, then $I_{i_\lambda}$ is essentially zero.

- $n_{i_\lambda} > 1$ controls the contrast of the lightning channel with respect to the background. Small values of $n$ create fuzzy lightning channels, and large values ($n > 8$) create sharp lightning channels.

---

[4] Lightning usually obeys the philosophy that the shortest path is the best path, so most channels are linear. Nonetheless, it is not difficult to find photographs showing channels of irregular shape.

[5] The variance was experimentally determined.

[6] The random number generator and distributions used are from GNU's libg++.

Most photographs of lightning show a strong glow surrounding the main channel of the lightning stroke. Reproducing this effect is achieved by a secondary illumination function which is added to equation 1:

$$G_{total_\lambda} = \sum_i G_{i_\lambda} \tag{2}$$

$$G_{i_\lambda} = g_\lambda l_i \exp\left(-\left(\frac{d_i}{W}\right)^2\right) \tag{3}$$

where

- $G_{i_\lambda}$ is the glow light contribution for wavelength $\lambda$.

- $g_\lambda$ is the maximum value of $G_{i_\lambda}$.

- $l_i \epsilon [0,1]$ is a "life" factor that describes the brightness of segment $S_i$.

- $W$ is half the width of the glow (when $l = 1$).

- $d_i$ is the shortest distance between the ray $r$ and the segment $S_i$.

The left-most image of Figure 5 was generated with equation 1; the second and third images show the effect of adding a blue and red glow with equation 2 to the lightning channel.

The calculation of $d_i$ [3] for each segment $S_i$ is a computational bottleneck. By generating the lightning in a plane parallel to the view plane, the rendering process can be optimized by simplifying the calculation of $d_i$. If $L$ is the plane containing the lightning stroke to render, and $p$ is the point where the ray $r$ intersects $L$, then let $d_i$ be the shortest distance between the segment $S_i$ and the point $p$. Using this technique, rendering time can be reduced by a factor of 2-5. While a boon to the time conscious artist, this method has the disadvantage of requiring the plane $L$ to be oriented perpendicular to the line of sight. For the purposes of animation, the more general approach is adopted, thus allowing free motion of the camera.

As the particle system proceeds, appropriate values for $m$, $w$, $n$, and $l$ are assigned to each segment. Seed values for $m$, $w$, and $n$ are input parameters, and $l$ is automatically initialized to 1.

For the main channel, the width attribute, $w$, is fixed for all segments, thus maintaining a uniform thickness for the entire channel. To simulate the gradual narrowing of branches, $w = 0.95 w_{predecessor}$ for branch segments. For a primary branch seed segment[7], $w = cw_{parent}$, where $c \epsilon [a,b]$ is chosen from a uniform distribution, and $0 < a < b < 1$. Branches off the main channel are consistently less than half as thick as the main channel, so $b < 0.5$ is appropriate. For branch seeds not attached to the main channel, $w = w_{parent}$.

The "life" factor, $l$, which controls the glow around a segment, is modified in a similar fashion, except for all branch seeds, $l = c^2 l_{parent}$, where $c$ is defined as above.

All segments share the same values for $m$ and $n$.

## 5    MAKING LIGHTNING A LIGHT SOURCE

Employing the method described above produces realistic lightning images which provide a good background for raytracing scenes. However, if other objects surround the lightning channel, then the lightning must behave as a light source. An expensive, but adequate solution is to add line-segment light sources to each segment. The light source for segment $S_i$ is scaled by $l_i$, so that the main channel contributes more light than the branches. When calculating the

light contribution from segment $S_i$ to point $p$ on some object the light intensity is attenuated by the scalar $1/d_i^2$, where $d_i$ is the shortest distance between $S_i$ and $p$; this attenuation factor prevents the lightning from illuminating distant objects.

## 6    ANIMATION

A single lightning flash, lasting about 0.5 seconds, is composed of at least one return stroke, and possibly subsequent return strokes. Each return stroke is identified by a surge of light illuminating the channel. The first return stroke illuminates the main channel and the branches, while subsequent return strokes typically illuminate only the main channel. Numerous return strokes account for the flickering of lightning. This can be simulated by appropriately modulating the attributes $l_i$ and $m_i$ over time.

For animation, additional attributes are assigned to each segment:

- the age of the segment (one unit of time = one frame)

- the branch level (0 for the main channel, 1 for branches off the main channel, etc.)

- the position of the segment within a branch (0 for the first segment, 1 for the next segment, etc.)

The particle system used for generating the segments is extended to account for time. The animation of a lightning strike is done in two distinct phases:

*Progression* In this phase, the lightning is initiated from a seed segment, and propogates toward ground zero, as described above. Traveling up to 160,000 kilometres per hour, the appearance of a lightning stroke is instantaneous to the human eye. However, for an animation, this gives unsatisfactory results. Recall that a lightning channel is not illuminated until the first return stroke is initiated by the contact of the downward and upward leaders. Rather than replicate this process, we have adopted to illuminate the channel as it progresses toward the ground. This technique, although not physically accurate, is effective for animation because it agrees with people's intuition of how lightning should appear.

*Regression* The flickering of lightning is a result of multiple return strokes down the main channel (but not the branches). To simulate this effect, a positive, decaying, sinusoidal function is used to calculate the intensity of main-channel segments for each frame. The intensity of branch segments decreases monotonically.

To enhance the visual impression of a lightning stroke, we have doubled the time duration of a typical flash to one second, or 30 frames. Figure 6 shows selected frames from a lightning animation. The first five images correspond to the *progression* stage, and the last image starts the *regression* phase.

## 7    GLOWING OBJECTS

The visual effects of lightning striking an object depend on a number of factors, such as the shape of the object, the material from which it is made, etc. Since our goal is to provide a reasonable visual impression of lightning, particularly for animation, making an object glow when it is struck is sufficient for our purposes. Since we already have a skeletal implicit surface system, a value for the glow can be obtained directly from the field in which such models are defined. Readers unfamiliar with implicit surface modeling are directed to [1, 7].

---

[7] A branch off the main channel.

Given a scalar field defined by the implicit function $F$, an implicit surface is defined by the set of points $\{p : F(p) = k\}$, where $k\epsilon(0,1)$ is a chosen constant. For a non-trivial model, $F$ is the aggregate of several fields, each associated with a primitive skeletal element. The train and coach in Figure 6, for example, are composed of several ellipsoids, each with its own field, $F_i$. Hence, the surface of the train is defined by the implicit function

$$F(p) = \sum_{i=1}^{N} c_i F_i(p) \qquad (4)$$

where $N$ is the number of ellipsoids, and $c_i$ is a scalar value used to adjust the contribution of $F_i$.

In our system, $k$ is conventionally 0.5. Thus, if $F(p) < 0.5$, $p$ is outside the surface, and if $F(p) > 0.5$, $p$ is inside the surface. The objective is to make the field between the surfaces defined by $\{p : F(p) = 0.5\}$ and $\{p : F(p) = 0.0\}$ glow; the latter surface, the zero-contour, defines the outer extent of the glow.

For each ray $r$ spawned by the raytracer, the closest point on $r$ to each primitive is found, giving $N$ points, $p_1, p_2, \ldots, p_N$. For each point $p_i$, the implicit value $v_i = F_i(p_i)$ is calculated. The largest $v_i$, $v_{max}$, is used to calculate the brightness of the glow as follows:

$$G_\lambda = m_\lambda v' \qquad (5)$$

where

$$v' = \begin{cases} 0 & \text{if } v_{max} < 0 \\ k & \text{if } v_{max} > k \\ v_{max} & \text{otherwise} \end{cases} \qquad (6)$$

and $m_\lambda \epsilon [0,1]$ are scalars controlling the intensity of independent wavelengths. If $m_\lambda = g_\lambda$ (from equation 3), then the glow around the implicit surface will coincide with the lightning channel glow, if this is desired.

Figure 7 illustrates the glowing effect on two spherical implicit surfaces blending. The animation frames in Figure 6 show lightning striking the train's coach, causing it to glow.

The advantage of using implicit surface models is that the glow can be calculated directly from the field as shown above. However, the technique can produce undesirable results in certain instances. Problems arise when the zero-contour surface, which defines the edge of the glow, does not faithfully follow the $k$-contour surface, which defines the model. This problem is especially evident when negative primitives, obtained by setting $c_i$ in equation 4 to a negative value, are used.

## 8  CONCLUSION

We have presented a workable model of lightning, which produces aesthetic images sufficient for most animation requirements. Our lightning model takes account of the following features of real lightning:

- Accurate shape according to statistical data available.

- The glow around lightning which is often observed.

- Glow around objects that are struck (provided that they are modeled as implicit surface objects).

- Lightning as a light source.

The following points still require further attention:

- Implementing a physically based model and formalizing the branching algorithm used to generate lightning channels.

- Improving the appearance of objects struck by lightning; investigating further how glowing objects can be modeled with implicit surfaces.

- Improving rendering time.

## 9  ACKNOWLEDGEMENTS

We would like to thank the members of the *Graphics Jungle* research lab at the University of Calgary and the support of the computer science department. We would also like to thank Andrew Glassner of Xerox PARC for his encouragement and advice. Thanks go to all those who have contributed to Rayshade development, particularly Craig Kolb and Rod Bogart, at Yale and Princeton Universities respectively.

This work is partially supported by the Natural Sciences and Engineering Research Council of Canada.

## A  LIGHTNING SPECIFICATION

Figure 3 shows an example of the new commands added to the Rayshade input language to specify the lightning and glow around implicit surfaces.

The contents of the file `light.zap` are shown in Figure 4. The file `train.soft` is a binary file generated by the implicit surface editing system. This file contains the specifications of the skeletal elements which define the train model.

```
/* Lightning specification */
lightning light.zap

/* Implicit surface description
   for glow */
glow train.soft
```

Figure 3: An example of the new commands added to Rayshade for rendering lightning and glowing objects.

## REFERENCES

[1] Jules Bloomenthal and Brian Wyvill. Interactive Techniques for Implicit Modeling. *Computer Graphics*, 24(2):109–116, 1990.

[2] L Dellera and E. Garbagnati. Lightning stroke simulation by means of the leader progression model. *IEEE Transactions on Power Delivery*, 5(4):2009–22, October 1990.

[3] Ronald Goldman. Intersection of Two Lines in Three-Space. *Graphics Gems*, page 304, 1992. Edited by David Krik.

[4] William Newcott. Lightning, nature's high-voltage spectacle. *National Geographic*, 184(1):83–103, July 1993. Photographs by Peter Menzel.

[5] Martin A. Uman. *The Lightning Discharge*. Academic Press, Inc., 1987.

[6] O.H. Vaughan, R. Blackesleee, et al. A cloud-to-space lightning as recorded by the Space Shnuttle payload-bay TV cameras. *Monthy Weather Review*, 120(7):1459–61, July 1992.

[7] Brian Wyvill, Craig McPheeters, and Geoff Wyvill. Animating Soft Objects. *The Visual Computer*, 2(4):235–242, February 1986.

```
LIGHTNING(
  -- seed point
  POINT{830.0,1150.0,3800.0},
  -- random number generator seed
  2,
  -- ground elevation,
  1055.0,
  -- initial value for w parameter
  VECTOR{0.4, 0.4, 0.64},
  -- value for m parameter
  VECTOR{0.7, 1.0, 0.7},
  -- value for n parameter
  VECTOR{10.0, 10.0, 4.0},
  -- colour of glow
  COLOUR{0.1, 0.05, 0.07},
  -- width of glow
  3.84,
  -- angle (in radians) and std. deviation
  -- for tortuosity (twist) of channel
  NORMAL{0.179, 0.1},
  -- length of each segment; uniform
  -- distribution
  UNIFORM{0.1, 0.25},
  -- number of branch segments; discrete
  -- uniform distribution
  DISC_UNIFORM{10,20},
  -- angle of branches wrt
  -- parent segment;
  UNIFORM{0.18, 0.75},
  -- width of branch relative
  -- to parent
  UNIFORM{0.45, 0.6},
  -- branch probability
  0.025,
)
```

Figure 4: Sample input for lightning specification.

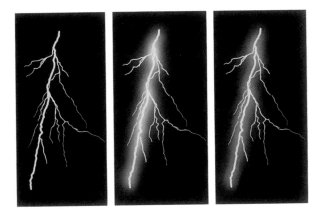

Figure 5: Various lightning images; the left-most lightning image was generated without the additional glow.

Figure 6: Selected frames from a lightning animation.

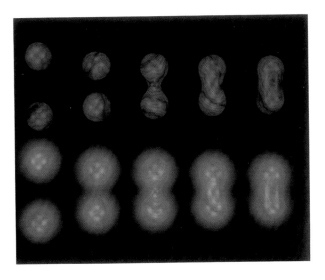

Figure 7: Glowing "soft" objects.

Figure 8: Lightning over a plane of water.

Figure 9: A real photograph of lightning striking a tree; courtesy of Johnny Autery.

# Predicting the Drape of Woven Cloth Using Interacting Particles

David E. Breen†       Donald H. House‡       Michael J. Wozny§

†European Computer-Industry Research Centre, Munich
‡Visualization Laboratory, Texas A&M University
§Manufacturing Engineering Laboratory, National Institute of Standards and Technology, Washington

†§formerly of Design Research Center, Rensselaer Polytechnic Institute
‡formerly of Department of Computer Science, Williams College

## Abstract

We demonstrate a physically-based technique for predicting the drape of a wide variety of woven fabrics. The approach exploits a theoretical model that explicitly represents the microstructure of woven cloth with interacting particles, rather than utilizing a continuum approximation. By testing a cloth sample in a Kawabata fabric testing device, we obtain data that is used to tune the model's energy functions, so that it reproduces the draping behavior of the original material. Photographs, comparing the drape of actual cloth with visualizations of simulation results, show that we are able to reliably model the unique large-scale draping characteristics of distinctly different fabric types.

**Keywords:** cloth, drape, physically-based modeling, particle systems, Kawabata Evaluation System.

## 1 Introduction

The vast number of uses for cloth are mirrored in the extraordinary variety of types of woven fabrics. These range from the most exquisite fine silks, to the coarsest of burlaps, and are woven from such diverse fibers as natural wool and synthetic polyester. Each of these unique fabrics has its own distinguishing characteristics, and is recognizable to the trained eye, perhaps most easily, by the way it drapes. It is not surprising, then, that image makers, designers, and engineers have had a keen interest in characterizing the draping properties of cloth.

In this paper we report on a new technique for reliably reproducing the characteristic drape of particular fabrics. Here, drape means the final configuration of a cloth placed over a solid object. We attempt to answer questions like "What would this shirt look like made from cotton rather than from polyester?" or "Would this dress have a more pleasing drape if made from silk rather than a light wool?". Our work on this problem began several years ago with the development of a theoretical model of woven cloth based on interacting-particle methods [8], that we used to model such complex draping configurations as those in Figure 1. More recently we have been working on a technique for using empirical data from the *Kawabata Evaluation System* [29] fabric measuring equipment to tune the model. With this technique we can now test a particular cloth sample, derive energy functions based on the sample's non-linear mechan-

Figure 1: Draping cloth objects

ical properties, and then use the model to reproduce the fabric's characteristic large-scale draping behavior.

To date, most of the efforts to create a model of cloth have employed continuum mechanics, with simulations utilizing finite element or finite difference techniques. These models have provided less then satisfactory results when attempting to accurately reproduce the characteristic folds and buckles found in specific types of cloth. In the introduction to a 1978 study on textile mechanics Shanahan, Lloyd and Hearle [39] express the opinion that

> "Because of the relative coarse structure of textile materials, ... it might be more profitable ... to use noncontinuum systems directly in the problems of complex (fabric) deformation."

Despite their reservations, they explored continuum methods for many years, but Hearle finally abandoned this approach, stating that [1]

> "In dealing with 3-dimensional buckling of textile fabrics, neither the terminology nor the methodology of established (continuum) theory of bending plates and shells is of much help."

The problem is that cloth is a complex mechanical mechanism whose components are at a scale that is close to the scale of a typical simulation mesh element. Fine fibers are spun into yarns or threads, and these threads are woven into an interlocking network. Significantly, this assemblage is held together not by molecular bonds or welds, but simply by friction. The complexity and variety of the resulting mechanical systems are evident in the magnified views of small pieces of cotton, wool, and polyester/cotton cloth shown in Figure 2. The cotton material is woven with the coarsest thread and has doubled weft threads. The wool material is

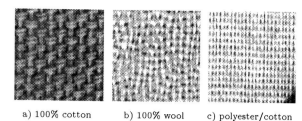

a) 100% cotton    b) 100% wool    c) polyester/cotton

Figure 2: Magnified views of 3 samples of woven cloth

the most irregular in structure and appears to have the loosest weave. The polyester/cotton is the most regular, is of the finest thread, and has the most open space between parallel threads. The behavior of each of these "mechanisms" depends upon all of these factors, as well as fiber type, and ambient conditions such as humidity and temperature.

Our experience is that it is now both possible and practical to construct a model that captures key elements of the small-scale structure of woven cloth. In contrast to continuum techniques, our model utilizes interacting particles. This approach is founded on the premise that by modeling the low-level structures of a material and computationally aggregating their small-scale interactions, correct macroscopic behavior will emerge.

## 2    Background

Our approach to cloth modeling builds upon and merges concepts developed for particle systems and previous cloth models. The following summary of particle system and cloth modeling work is necessarily brief. For further information, we refer the reader to the extensive particle system bibliography found in [9], and to the detailed review of cloth modeling work found in [11].

### 2.1    Particle systems

Particle Systems were first used in computer graphics by Reeves in 1983 [36]. He defined a particle system model as "a cloud of primitive particles," where each particle is generated into the system, moves, ages, and then dies. This work was later extended by Reeves and Blau [37], Fournier and Reeves [20], Sims [42], and many others to model such diverse phenomena as trees and grass, ocean spray, fireworks, waterfalls, fire, snowstorms and explosions. Reynolds [38], in his work on flocking behavior, greatly enhanced the power of the particle system as a modeling tool. He proposed the idea of coupling the particles so that they interact with each other as well as with their environment, and demonstrated that it is possible to exploit simple local rules of interaction between large numbers of simple primitives to produce complex aggregate behaviors. Miller and Pearce [32], Terzopoulos, Platt and Fleischer [46], and Tonnesen [48] all explored coupled particle systems as a way to model liquid-like and melting materials. Miller et al. [33], Szeliski and Tonnesen [44], and van Wijk [49] proposed particle interactions that are a function of direction, producing deformable sheets and surfaces of particles. Our own interest in coupled particle systems has lead to a variety of explorations into specialized modeling and visualization tools [6, 24, 25, 47], into computational issues [26, 27, 34], and CAD technologies [3, 4].

### 2.2    Cloth modeling
#### 2.2.1    computer animation models

The first computer animation model of cloth was by Weil [50], who used a two-step geometric process to model a rectangular cloth hanging from several constraint points. Dhande et al. [17] present a hybrid drape model, which relates the parameters of a swept surface to fabric mechanical properties. Feynman [19] developed the first true physically-

based cloth model. His model utilizes a set of energy equations based on the theory of elastic shells, distributed over a grid of points. Haumann and Parent [23] produced several cloth animations, including a flag waving and curtains blowing in a breeze. Terzopoulos and Fleischer [45] developed a wide range of models for computer graphics based on elasticity theory. Their finite difference and finite element simulations demonstrated 3-D cloth-like structures that bend, fold, wrinkle, interact with solid geometry, and tear. Others have extended their model to simulate complete sets of clothing [13], and how cloth responds to air flow [30]. Aono [2] also used elasticity theory to simulate ripples in cloth-like structures.

#### 2.2.2    engineering and design models

The first cloth draping work published in the engineering community was by Shanahan et al. [39], who used the theory of sheets, shells and plates to characterize a matrix of elastic parameters for a sheet of material. Lloyd [31] later provided non-linear extensions to the matrix and used finite element methods to simulate a 3-D circular cloth being deformed by a projectile. Eischen et al. [18] modeled cloth structures using a large deformation beam and shell theory recently proposed by Simo et al. [41]. Collier et al. [15] present a finite element approach to modeling draping behavior. They also tested fabric using a drape measuring device called the Drapemeter [14], and showed that coefficients produced by their simulations compared favorably with measured values. As part of an apparel CAD system [35], Imaoka et al. [28] developed a continuum mechanics model of cloth based on the large deformation shell theory of Green and Zerna [22]. They also attempted to incorporate data from the Kawabata mechanical tester, but were unable to find a clear mapping of test data into their model.

## 3    A Particle-Based Model of Cloth

The fundamental principles of our particle-based model of cloth have been fully described elsewhere [8, 27], but they are briefly reviewed here, since a basic understanding is essential to the theme of this paper.

We model cloth as a collection of particles that conceptually represents the crossing points of warp and weft threads in a plain weave. Important mechanical interactions that determine the behavior of woven fabric occur at these points. Most significantly, the tension is typically so great at crossings that the threads are clamped together, providing an axis around which bending can occur in the plane of the cloth. Other more distributed interactions, such as stretching of threads and out of plane bending, can be conveniently discretized and lumped at the crossing points.

In the model, we represent the various thread-level structural constraints with energy functions that capture simple geometric relationships between particles within a local neighborhood. These energy functions are meant to encapsulate four basic mechanical interactions: thread collision, thread stretching, out-of-plane bending, and trellising. These are shown graphically in Figure 3, and are captured in the energy equation for particle $i$,

$$U_i = U_{repel_i} + U_{stretch_i} + U_{bend_i} + U_{trellis_i} + U_{grav_i}. \quad (1)$$

In this equation, $U_{repel_i}$ is an artificial energy of repulsion, that effectively keeps every other particle at a minimum distance, providing some measure of thread collision detection, helping prevent self intersection of the cloth. $U_{stretch_i}$ captures energy of tensile strain between each particle and its four-connected neighbors. $U_{bend_i}$ is the energy due to threads bending out of the local plane of the cloth, and $U_{trellis_i}$ is the energy due to bending around a thread crossing in the plane. $U_{grav_i}$ is the potential energy due to gravity.

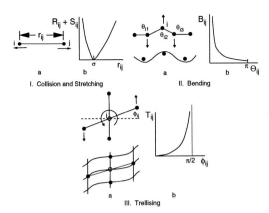

Figure 3: Cloth model energy functions

Repelling and stretching are functions only of interparticle distance $r_{ij}$ (Figure 3-Ia), whereas bending and trellising are functions of various angular relationships between segments joining particles (Figure 3-IIa and 3-IIIa). $U_{grav_i}$ is a function of the height of the particle. Trellising occurs when threads are held fast at a crossing and bend to create an "S-curve" in the local plane of the cloth, and is related to shearing in a continuous sheet of material, but since our model treats cloth as an interwoven grid of threads, trellising is a more descriptive term.

We assume that the threads in the fabric do not stretch significantly when a cloth is simply draping under its own weight. Therefore, the combined stretching and repelling energy function $R + S$ shown in Figure 3-Ib is not empirical, and is meant only to provide collision prevention and a steep energy well that acts to tightly constrain each particle to a nominal distance $\sigma$ from each of its 4-connected neighbors. We have had good success with the functions

$$R(r_{ij}) = \begin{cases} C_0[(\sigma - r_{ij})^5 / r_{ij}] & r_{ij} \leq \sigma \\ 0 & r_{ij} > \sigma, \end{cases} \qquad (2)$$

and

$$S(r_{ij}) = \begin{cases} 0 & r_{ij} \leq \sigma \\ C_0[((r_{ij} - \sigma)/\sigma)^5] & r_{ij} > \sigma, \end{cases} \qquad (3)$$

where $C_0$ is a scale parameter.

The function $U_{repel_i}$ prevents collision and self intersection, so it is calculated by summing over all particles, as given by

$$U_{repel_i} = \sum_{j \neq i} R(r_{ij}). \qquad (4)$$

In practice, our simulation algorithm maintains a spatial enumeration, so that the summation need only be done over near neighbors. An energy well is produced by directly coupling each particle with the stretching function $S$ only to its 4-connected neighbors, as given by

$$U_{stretch_i} = \sum_{j \in N_i} S(r_{ij}), \qquad (5)$$

where $N_i$ is the set of particle $i$'s four-connected neighbors.

The particle energy due to gravity is simply defined as

$$U_{grav_i} = m_i g h_i, \qquad (6)$$

where $m_i$ and $h_i$ are the mass and height of particle $i$, and $g$ is gravitational acceleration. The mass is of the small patch of cloth represented by the particle.

In contrast to stretching, we assume that bending and trellising are the significant contributors to the overall drape of cloth, when it is simply draping under its own weight.

We define a unit of the bending energy $B$ shown in Figure 3-IIb as a function of the angle formed by three particles along a weft or warp "thread line", as shown in Figure 3-IIa. The complete bending energy is

$$U_{bend_i} = \sum_{j \in M_i} B(\theta_{ij}), \qquad (7)$$

where $M_i$ is the set of six angles $\theta_{ij}$ formed by the segments connecting particle $i$ and its eight nearest horizontal and vertical neighbors. This definition is used so that the derivative of bending energy reflects the total change in bending energy due to change in position of particle $i$. The redundancy in this formulation is taken care of later by proper scaling.

The phenomenon of trellising is diagramed in Figure 3-IIIa and a corresponding unit of the trellising energy $T$ is shown in Figure 3-IIIb. Two segments are formed by connecting the two pairs of neighboring particles surrounding a central particle. An equilibrium crossing angle of 90° is assumed, but this angle could easily change over the course of a simulation to model slippage. The trellis angle $\phi$ is then defined as the angle formed as one of the line segments moves away from this equilibrium. The complete function for our energy of trellising is

$$U_{trellis_i} = \sum_{j \in K_i} T(\phi_{ij}), \qquad (8)$$

where $K_i$ is the set of four trellising angles $\phi_{ij}$ formed around the four-connected neighbors of particle $i$. As with bending, this redundant formulation was chosen so that change in total energy with change in the particle's position is completely accounted for locally.

The simulation of the model is implemented as a three-phase process operating over a series of small discrete time steps [27]. The first phase for a single time step calculates the dynamics of each particle as if it were falling freely under gravity in a viscous medium, and accounts for collisions between particles and surrounding geometry. The second phase performs an energy-minimization to enforce interparticle constraints. A stochastic element of the energy minimization algorithm serves to both avoid local minima and to perturb the particle grid, producing a more natural asymmetric final configuration. The third phase corrects the velocity of each particle to account for particle motion during the second phase.

The energy functions indicated in the curves in Figure 3 are similar in shape to those that we first used to verify the theoretical model. These initial functions were simply convenient ones that we knew would smoothly interpolate reasonable boundary conditions. Even with these "sketched-in" energy functions, the simple interactions governing the particles aggregate to produce a macroscopic draping behavior that is convincingly close to that of cloth. We were able to produce visually satisfying results, such as the cloths draped over both the easy-chair and end-table in Figure 1, after just a few runs to tune constants.

## 4  The Kawabata Evaluation System

Even though early experiments confirmed that we could generate reasonable looking draping behavior, there were many things about our simulated cloth that we did not know. The model was not based on physical units, so we did not know the actual size of our simulated cloth sample, and we could not query the model for any kind of mechanical information. Most importantly, we did not have a methodical means of tuning the model to simulate particular kinds of cloth.

In order to tie the model directly to the draping behavior of actual cloth, we have developed a method for deriving the model's energy equations from empirical mechanical data produced by the Kawabata Evaluation System [29]. This

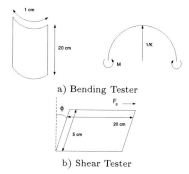

a) Bending Tester

b) Shear Tester

Figure 4: Kawabata Evaluation System measurements

system is a standard set of fabric measuring equipment that can measure the bending, shearing and tensile properties of cloth, as well as its surface roughness and compressibility. For bending, shearing and tensile properties, the equipment measures what force or moment is required to deform a fabric sample of standard size and shape, and produces plots of force or moment as a function of measured geometric deformation. Since we assume that threads do not stretch significantly when a cloth is simply draping under its own weight, we make use only of the Kawabata bending and shear plots. There is, however, no reason why Kawabata tensile data could not be used if one wished to model fabric under tensile load.

The Kawabata bending measurement is done by clamping a 20 cm × 1 cm sample of cloth along both its long edges. The sample is then bent between the clamps, as diagramed in Figure 4a, and the moment necessary to accomplish the bending is recorded. A plot of bending moment $M$ versus curvature $K$ is produced by assuming that the 1 cm cross-section bends with constant curvature. The shearing measurement is done by applying a shearing force along one of the long edges of a 20 cm × 5 cm cloth sample, as diagramed in Figure 4b. A plot of the force $F_s$ versus shear angle $\phi$ is produced. By cutting samples out of the original cloth in two orthogonal directions, it is possible to measure bending and shear in both the warp and weft directions.

Kawabata bending and shear plots for the 100% cotton, 100% wool, and cotton/polyester samples of Figure 2 are shown in Figure 5. Each curve plots a full deformation cycle for fabric oriented in both the warp (solid curve) and weft (dashed curve) directions. The curves are produced by applying a force (or moment) in one direction, releasing the force, reversing the direction of the force, and releasing the force once again. The plots clearly show the hysteretic behavior of cloth – the path of deformation when the cloth is stressed is different from the path when the stress is released, producing a loop in the plot.

The plots for each type of cloth are obviously quite different. Although the shear plots differ little between warp and weft, there are dramatic differences between warp and weft bending for both the 100% cotton and the polyester/cotton materials. In the 100% cotton this is due to the doubling of weft threads, and in the polyester/cotton this is due to the differing warp and weft materials. The shallower shear curve for the 100% wool indicates that it will be the most limp and easily shaped.

We have found it useful to think of the bending and shearing as being divided into three loosely defined regions, a region of initial resistance to deformation, a region of low deformation, and a region of high deformation. The mechanical behavior of cloth throughout its range of deformation is non-linear, especially during initial deformation. The mechanical properties of cloth in the low-deformation region

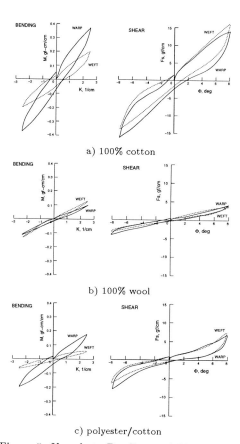

a) 100% cotton

b) 100% wool

c) polyester/cotton

Figure 5: Kawabata Bending and Shear Plots

are usually well-behaved. This is why the assumption of linear elasticity made in continuum cloth models yields a reasonable "cloth-like" behavior. The mechanical properties in the initial-resistance and high-deformation regions are not as well-behaved, and defy a simple, general mathematical description. The Kawabata plots provide information only in the initial-resistance, and low-deformation regions.

## 5 Derivation of the Energy Equations

The process of generating particle energy functions for woven cloth from Kawabata data has three steps. First, we determine functions that approximate the Kawabata plots. Next, we relate these approximating functions to the model's energy functions. This is crucial, since in the case of bending, the approximating functions relate bending moment to curvature, and in the case of trellising, they relate force to shear angle, but what is needed is energy as a function of the bending and trellising angles shown in Figures 3-II and 3-III. Finally, we scale the resulting equations so that they will produce energy values in standard physical units.

### 5.1 Approximating the Kawabata curves

For purposes of calculating drape, we assume that the hysteresis of cloth does not play an important role. Thus, in approximating the Kawabata curves, we look only at the first of the four stages of the deformation cycles shown in Figure 5.

The most convenient way to approximate these curves is with piecewise polynomial functions. This can be done in any number of ways, but the important thing is that we obtain reasonable approximating functions $M(K)$ for bending moment, and $F(\phi)$ for shear force. We decided to interpolate the inflection points of the curves using the lowest order polynomials that were practical, and the Kawabata plots are sufficiently simple that we were able to do this with quadratic and linear segments. In each case, we first fit a function to the outer, more stable segment of the Kawabata curve, then fit additional segments to the initial segment maintaining position and slope continuity at the segment boundaries, using standard interpolation techniques [12]. In general, the slope of the Kawabata plots is difficult to determine at the origin. Therefore, although the first segment must pass through the origin, we did not enforce any slope constraint there.

## 5.2 The bending energy equations

Within the low deformation region within a single thread, we assume that the theory of elastic bending beams [40] is applicable, and can be used to calculate the energy of bending. The strain energy $dU$ due to bending stored in a segment $dS$ of an elastic beam is given by

$$dU = \frac{M\,dS}{2\rho},\qquad(9)$$

where $M$ is the bending moment acting on the segment and $\rho$ is its radius of curvature, which is related to curvature $K$ by $K = 1/\rho$. Within our model, each particle is separated from its 4-connected neighboring particles by the equilibrium distance $\sigma$, which is a function of the grid dimensions and particle density. Therefore each particle represents a $\sigma \times \sigma$ square of cloth. This square of cloth can be thought of as a series of elastic beams (threads) lined parallel to each other. The energy of bending in one of these threads is defined by the integral

$$U = \int_0^\sigma \frac{MK}{2}\,dS.\qquad(10)$$

We assume that within one $\sigma \times \sigma$ patch that the moment and the curvature are constant, simplifying the energy equation for a single thread to

$$U = \frac{MK}{2}\sigma.\qquad(11)$$

Since $M$ is given in units of moment per unit width of sample, we can simply multiply Equation 11 by the width $\sigma$ of each patch, in order to sum up the contributions of each beam (thread) within the $\sigma \times \sigma$ patch. The energy of bending in just one direction then becomes

$$B = \frac{MK}{2}\sigma^2\qquad(12)$$

for each particle. This calculation is performed twice for each particle, once for bending in the warp direction, and once for bending in the weft direction. Recall that our approximation of the Kawabata bending plot provides bending moment $M$ as a function of curvature $K$, so that equation 12 yields bending energy $B$ as a function only of curvature. Thus, we need only relate curvature to the bending angles of the model.

Curvature, along a thread, at the position of a single particle can be approximated by assuming that the curvature is constant from the particle to its two neighbors. Given this assumption, a circle can be fit to the three points and the circle's curvature can be calculated [5]. Unfortunately, this assumption becomes poor as the bending angle $\theta$ becomes small (i.e. as the threads bend in on one another). We would like the curvature $K$ to become arbitrarily large for small bending angle, in order to give reasonable high-deformation behavior. As an approximation, we fit the curve $a/\theta + b$ to the small-angle portion of the curvature equation to yield the complete curvature equation

$$K(\theta) = \begin{cases} \frac{2}{\sigma}\cos(\theta/2), & \pi/4 < \theta \le \pi \\ -\left(\frac{\pi}{4}\right)^2 \beta/\theta + \alpha + \frac{\pi}{4}\beta, & 0 \le \theta \le \pi/4, \end{cases}\qquad(13)$$

where the constants $\alpha = \frac{2}{\sigma}\cos(\pi/8)$ and $\beta = \frac{1}{\sigma}\sin(\pi/8)$ were chosen to maintain $C_0$ and $C_1$ continuity at $\theta = \pi/4$.

## 5.3 The trellising energy equations

We can calculate the energy stored in the 20 cm × 5 cm cloth sample that is sheared in a Kawabata Shear Tester from the work $W$ produced by a force $F$ acting over a displacement $dS$,

$$W = \int F\,dS.\qquad(14)$$

If we assume that the width $l$ of the sample remains constant during shearing, then the path traveled by the point at which the shearing force is applied is a circular arc whose length is defined by $S = l\phi$, where $\phi$ is the shearing angle. If the force point is moving along a circular arc, the component of the applied shearing force in the direction of motion is $F\cos(\phi)$. Applying these results to Equation 14 yields the equation for shearing energy as a function of shear angle first derived by Cusick [16],

$$T = \int F\cos(\phi)l\,d\phi.\qquad(15)$$

Recall that the Kawabata shearing plots provide the shearing force $F$ as a function of shearing angle $\phi$. Therefore, substituting the approximating equation for $F$ into Equation 15 and integrating yields the required energy of shearing strictly as a function of angle.

Once again we are faced with the problem of defining energy curves in the high deformation region not covered by the Kawabata data. Skelton [43] states that most woven materials cannot shear more than 45°. We approximate this constraint by introducing a singularity in the trellising energy curve at about 60°. The extra 15° permits the material to shear all the way to 45° if necessary. This singularity is introduced by fitting the function $a/(1.05 - \phi) + b$ to the slope and position at the endpoint of the Kawabata-derived energy curve (the magic number 1.05, is simply a rough approximation to $\pi/3 = 60°$).

## 5.4 Scaling the energy equations

Up to this point no attention has been paid to the physical units of the energy equations, although we would like them to be in CGS units.

The Kawabata bending plots (see Figure 5) give moment $M$ in units of gf-cm[1]/cm and curvature $K$ in cm$^{-1}$. If we take interparticle distance $\sigma$ to be in cm, then from equation 12 we see that the units for bending energy are gf-cm. Thus, scaling equation 12 by 978.80 will yield energy in ergs.

The Kawabata shearing plots (see Figure 5) give shearing force in units of gf/cm. Scaling this force by 978.80 yields dyne/cm, and multiplying the measured force by the 20 cm length of the sample gives force in dynes. Since the trellising energy is produced by a moment, the energy unit is dyne-cm or ergs. Since one particle represents a $\sigma \times \sigma$ patch of cloth, we want the trellising energy per unit area. This can be computed by dividing the total energy stored in the 20 cm × 5 cm sample by the area of the sample. Therefore the scale factor that converts energy $T$ of equation 15 into trellising energy in ergs is $195.76\sigma^2$.

# 6 Experimental Results

We derived energy equations for the 100% cotton, 100% wool, and polyester/cotton cloth samples shown in Figure 2 using the Kawabata data shown in Figure 5. A full derivation may be found in [10].

---

[1]The unit gf, or gram-force, is the Earth weight of one gram. It is equivalent to 978.80 dynes, and one gf-cm is equivalent to 978.80 ergs.

Given the energy equations for all three samples, we performed two sets of experiments to verify that the model was able to capture the characteristic draping behavior of each type of cloth. The first experiment was to drape real cloth over a cube and then perform the same drape in simulation, using computer visualizations of the simulation results to make visual comparisons with the actual cloth. The second experiment was to recreate the Kawabata Bending and Shear Testers in simulation, to show that the model can accurately reproduce physical measurements. Results of the first set of experiments are of most interest to the computer graphics community and are detailed below. The second set of experiments produced excellent results that are of most interest to the engineering and design community, and are detailed in [10].

In the actual draping experiments, 1 m × 1 m sections of our three cloth samples were draped over a 0.5 m × 0.5 m × 0.5 m cube. The results of these drapings were photographed and are presented in the left column of Figure 6. The same scenario was recreated in simulation. Models of 1 m × 1 m samples of 100% cotton, 100% wool and polyester/cotton, represented by a 51 × 51 particle grid, were draped over a 0.5 m × 0.5 m × 0.5 m geometric model of a cube. Each simulation started with a flat cloth positioned just above and centered over the cube. The simulation was allowed to run until the cloth had draped over the cube and had settled into an equilibrium position. Equilibrium was judged manually, by examining the maximum particle movement between successive time steps. The final drapings produced by the simulations are shown in the computer graphic visualizations in the right column of Figure 6. Camera positions were chosen to accentuate the unique draping characteristics of each type of cloth.

The similarities between the actual and simulated drapings are quite evident in Figure 6. Each kind of material has a characteristic drape that is captured by the simulation. Both the actual and simulated 100% cotton develop a single large billow that comes out from the corner of the cube at a 45° angle. By contrast, the bending stiffness of the wool sample is significantly weaker than the cotton's. Therefore, it does not have the bending strength needed to support a single large billow and the corner structure collapses into two smaller folds, as seen in both the actual and simulated views. In the polyester/cotton material, the bending stiffness is significantly stronger in the warp than in the weft direction. The effect on the draping of the cloth can be clearly seen. Since bending is so much stronger in one direction than the other, the billow is literally pushed around the corner by the warp threads. This produces an asymmetric structure that wraps around the corner of the cube, as can be seen by comparing the front and side views.

## 7  Discussion

The draping experiments show that the model can be used to reproduce the large-scale draping behavior of specific types of cloth, but the cloth simulations do not exactly produce the drape of the actual cloth in Figure 6. This, in a sense, would be impossible, since cloth will never drape twice in exactly the same way. Instead, what we found when working with real materials is that each material does have its own "preferred" draping tendency. For example, at the corner of the cube, the cotton sample usually produced a single draping structure, the wool would form either a single fold or would collapse into more than one fold, and the polyester/cotton always produced an asymmetric fold. Of course, each material could be forced into many kinds of draping configurations, but when allowed to drape naturally, they generally

produced their own characteristic structures.

Another difference evident in Figure 6 between the simulated and real drapings is in the sharpness of edges and corners. The simulated samples appear to have "soft" folds, as if being draped over a rounded cube. These differences are related to the fineness of the particle grid. A 51 × 51 grid is capable of reproducing large-scale draping structures, but it is not sufficient for capturing the sharp bends over the edges or at the corners of a cube. We believe that utilizing a finer particle grid will remove these differences, and are currently working on an adaptive scheme that will sample a region of the cloth more or less finely based on the region's total energy.

The computational speed of our implementation is currently its major drawback. Each simulation, starting with a flat cloth placed above the cube and falling to its final draped configuration, required about 1 CPU-week on an IBM RS/6000 workstation. The issue of speed is one that we chose to ignore for a period while developing and proving the model. There are several ways to improve speed, the most obvious being to write custom simulation code. Currently we work in an object-oriented, message-passing environment that has been excellent for rapid prototyping, but entails a heavy overhead [7, 21]. A more fundamental speed improvement could be had by improving the simulation technique. We currently use a stochastic method that follows a numerically-determined approximation to the energy gradient at each particle [27]. We have begun work custom coding an efficient implementation of our model, that uses precalculated tables to more exactly and efficiently determine energy gradients, and are experimenting with a pure gradient-descent approach to energy minimization. Preliminary results indicate speed-ups well beyond an order of magnitude. Another approach would be to use an approximate, purely-geometric predrape, followed by the physical simulation to perfect the drape. This has already been tried with success by others [35, 51]. Finally, parallelism has been shown to be an especially efficient way of computing uncoupled particle systems [42]. The highly distributed form of our particle model, with its simple local computations and well defined neighbor interactions, should also be especially amenable to this approach [26].

To designers, one of cloth's most important characteristics is its ability to be shaped and creased. Since we ignore hysteresis, our model, as it stands, is conservative – no energy is lost during a deformation. One consequence of this is that we cannot yet mimic shaping and creasing. This has not been an important issue in the kinds of free-draping studies that we have conducted, but would be of very great importance when looking at fabric under the high stresses that occur in manufacturing. It should, however, be relatively easy to extend our model in a natural way to simulate non-conservative deformation. The stretching, bending, and trellising energy functions all either explicitly or implicitly represent a "rest" value for their independent variables. It would be straightforward to represent all of these rest values explicitly, and then vary them as a function of local strain, thus mimicing the effects of slippage within the weave. This could be put on a firm physical basis, at least for the low deformation region, by adjusting "slippage" so that the full hysteresis curves from the Kawabata tester are matched.

## 8  Conclusion

We have presented a particle-based model capable of being tuned to reproduce the static draping behavior of specific kinds of woven cloth. There are several significant aspects to the work. It has demonstrated that a microstructural model may be used to reproduce the macroscopic mechanical behavior of real flexible materials. It has shown that the use of such an approach can allow for the straightforward incorporation of non-linear empirical test data. The model has been verified by experiments. One generates the low-level mechanical properties of real fabrics, and the other recreates the distinctive macroscopic geometric structures of draping cloth and compares them to actual cloth drapings. This kind of evidence has not been presented in previous cloth modeling studies. With this approach, real materials may now be measured, and the measured data used to derive energy equations, allowing the draping behavior of specific materials to be confidently simulated on a computer.

## Acknowledgements

Figure 1 was produced by Gene Greger and David Breen. The Kawabata measurements were provided by Ms. Janet Bulan-Brady and Mr. Herbert Barndt of the Grundy Center for Textile Evaluation at the Philadelphia College of Textiles and Science. We would like to thank Masaki Aono for translating reference [28], Charles Gilman for assisting with the derivation of the bending equations, and David Gordon for assisting in the construction of the Drape-O-Matic Cube. This work was partially supported by the Industrial Associates Program of the Rensselaer Design Research Center, DLA contract No. DLA900-87-D-0016, and NSF grant No. CDR-8818826.

## References

[1] Amirbayat, J. and J.W.S. Hearle, "The Anatomy of Buckling of Textile Fabrics: Drape and Conformability," Journal of the Textile Institute, Vol. 80, pp. 51-69, 1989.

[2] Aono, M., "A Wrinkle Propagation Model for Cloth," Computer Graphics Around the World (Proc. CG International), eds. T.S. Chua and T.L. Kunii (Springer-Verlag, Tokyo, 1990) pp. 95-115.

[3] Aono, M., D.E. Breen and M.J. Wozny, "A Computer-Aided Broadcloth Composite Layout Design System," Geometric Modeling for Product Realization (Proc. IFIP Conference on Geometric Modeling), eds. P.R. Wilson, M.J. Wozny and M.J. Pratt (North-Holland, Amsterdam, September 1992) pp. 223-250.

[4] Aono, M., D.E. Breen and M.J. Wozny, "Fitting a Woven Cloth Model to a Curved Surface: Mapping Algorithms," Computer-Aided Design, Vol. 26, No. 4, pp. 278-292, April 1994.

[5] Beyer, W.H. (ed.), CRC Standard Mathematical Tables, 26th Edition (CRC Press, Inc., Boca Raton, FL, 1981) p. 120.

[6] Breen, D.E. and V. Kühn, "Message-Based Object-Oriented Interaction Modeling," Eurographics '89 Proceedings (Elsevier Science Publishers B.V., Amsterdam, September 1989) pp. 489-503.

[7] Breen, D.E., P.H. Getto and A.A. Apodaca, "Object-Oriented Programming in a Conventional Programming Environment," 13th Annual International Computer Software and Applications Conference Proceedings (IEEE Computer Society Press, Orlando, FL, September, 1989) pp. 334-343.

[8] Breen, D.E., D.H. House and P.H. Getto, "A Physically-Based Particle Model of Woven Cloth," The Visual Computer, Vol. 8, No. 5-6 (Springer-Verlag, Heidelberg, June 1992) pp. 264-277.

[9] Breen, D.E., D. Tonnesen and B. Gates (eds.), "Particle Systems Bibliography," Rensselaer Design Research Center Technical Report TR-92029 (Rensselaer Polytechnic Institute, December 1992).

[10] Breen, D.E., "A Particle-Based Model for Simulating the Draping Behavior of Woven Cloth," Ph.D. Thesis, Rensselaer Design Research Center Technical Report TR-93011 (Rensselaer Polytechnic Institute, June 1993).

[11] Breen, D.E., "A Survey of Cloth Modeling Research," Rensselaer Design Research Center Technical Report TR-92030 (Rensselaer Polytechnic Institute, July 1993).

[12] Burden, R.L. and J.D. Faires, Numerical Analysis, Third Edition (Prindle, Weber & Schmidt, Boston, 1985).

[13] Carignan, M., Y. Yang, N. Magnenat-Thalmann and D. Thalmann, "Dressing Animated Synthetic Actors with Complex Deformable Clothes," Computer Graphics (Proc. SIGGRAPH), Vol. 26, No. 2, pp. 99-104, 1992.

[14] Chu, C.C, C.L. Cummings and N.A. Teixeira, "Mechanics of Elastic Performance of Textile Materials, Part V: A Study of the Factors Affecting the Drape of Fabrics - The Development of a Drape Meter," Textile Research Journal, Vol. 20, pp. 539-548, 1950.

[15] Collier, J.R., B.J. Collier, G. O'Toole and S.M. Sargand, "Drape Prediction by Means of Finite-Element Analysis," Journal of the Textile Institute, Vol. 82, No. 1, pp. 96-107, 1991.

[16] Cusick, G.E., "The Resistance of Fabrics to Shearing Forces," Journal of the Textile Institute, Vol. 52, No. 9, pp. T395-T406, September 1961.

[17] Dhande, S.G., P.V.M. Rao and C.L. Moore, "Geometric Modeling of Draped Fabric Surfaces," Graphics, Design and Visualization (Proc. International Conference on Computer Graphics), eds. S.P. Mudur and S.N. Pattanaik (Jaico Publishing House, Bombay, February 1993) pp. 173-180.

[18] Eischen, J.W., Y.G. Kim, T.G. Clapp and T.K. Ghosh, "Computer Simulation of the Large Motions of Fabric Structures," Proceedings of the 15th SECTAM Conference, College of Engineering at Georgia Institute of Technology, Atlanta, GA, pp. 119-126, 1990.

[19] Feynman, C.R., Modeling the Appearance of Cloth, Master's Thesis, Massachusetts Institute of Technology, 1986.

[20] Fournier, A. and W. Reeves, "A Simple Model of Ocean Waves," Computer Graphics (Proc. SIGGRAPH), Vol. 20, No. 4, pp. 75-84, August 1986.

[21] Getto, P.H. and D.E. Breen, "An Object-Oriented Architecture for a Computer Animation System," The Visual Computer, Vol. 6, No. 2, pp. 79-92, 1990.

[22] Green, A.E. and W. Zerna, Theoretical Elasticity (Oxford University Press, Ely House, London, 1968).

[23] Haumann, D.R. and R.E. Parent, "The Behavioral Test-bed: Obtaining Complex Behavior From Simple Rules," The Visual Computer, Vol. 4, pp. 332-347, 1988.

[24] Hersh, J.S., "Tools for Particle Based Geometric Modeling," Master's Thesis, Rensselaer Design Research Center Technical Report TR-88050 (Rensselaer Polytechnic Institute, December 1988).

[25] House, D.H. and D.E. Breen, "Particles As Modeling Primitives For Surgical Simulation," 11th Annual International IEEE Engineering in Medicine and Biology Conference Proceedings, pp. 831-832, 1989.

[26] House, D.H. and D.E. Breen, "Particles: A Naturally Parallel Approach to Modeling," 3rd Symposium on the Frontiers of Massively Parallel Computation Proceedings, pp. 150-153, 1990.

[27] House, D.H., D.E. Breen and P.H. Getto, "On the Dynamic Simulation of Physically-Based Particle-System Models," Third Eurographics Workshop on Animation and Simulation Proceedings (Cambridge, UK, September 1992).

[28] Imaoka, H., H. Okabe, H. Akami, A. Shibuya and N. Aisaka, "Analysis of Deformations in Textile Fabric," Sen-i Gakkaishi, Vol. 44, No. 5, pp. 217-228, 1988.

[29] Kawabata, S., The Standardization and Analysis of Hand Evaluation (The Textile Machinery Society of Japan, Osaka, 1980).

[30] Ling, L., M. Damodaran and R.K.L. Gay, "A Quasi-Steady Force Model for Animating Cloth," Graphics, Design and Visualization (Proc. International Conference on Computer Graphics), eds. S.P. Mudur and S.N. Pattanaik (Jaico Publishing House, Bombay, February 1993) pp. 181-188.

[31] Lloyd, D.W., "The Analysis of Complex Fabric Deformations," Mechanics of Flexible Fibre Assemblies, eds. J.W.S. Hearle, J.J. Thwaites and J. Amirbayat, (Sijthoff & Noordhoff, Alphen aan den Rijn, The Netherlands, 1980) pp. 311-342.

[32] Miller, G. and A. Pearce, "Globular Dynamics: A Connected Particle System for Animating Viscous Fluids," Computers and Graphics, Vol. 13, No. 3, pp. 305-309, 1989.

[33] Miller, J.V., D.E. Breen, W.E. Lorensen, R.M. O'Bara and M.J. Wozny, "Geometrically Deformed Models: A Method of Extracting Closed Geometric Models from Volume Data," Computer Graphics (Proc. SIGGRAPH), Vol. 25, No. 4, pp. 217-226, July 1991.

[34] Müller, L. and W. Müller, "An Object-Oriented Implementation of The Fast Multipole Method," Rensselaer Design Research Center Technical Report TR-90030 (Rensselaer Polytechnic Institute, July 1990).

[35] Okabe, H., H. Imaoka, T. Tomiha and H. Niwaya, "Three Dimensional Apparel CAD System," Computer Graphics (Proc. SIGGRAPH), Vol. 26, No. 2, pp. 105-110, 1992.

[36] Reeves, W.T., "Particle Systems - A Technique for Modeling a Class of Fuzzy Objects," ACM Transactions on Graphics, Vol. 2, No. 2, pp. 91-108, April 1983.

[37] Reeves, W.T. and R. Blau, "Approximate and Probabilistic Algorithms for Shading and Rendering Structured Particle Systems," Computer Graphics (Proc. SIGGRAPH), Vol. 19, No. 3, pp. 313-322, July 1985.

[38] Reynolds, C.W., "Flocks, Herds and Schools: A Distributed Behavioral Model," Computer Graphics (Proc. SIGGRAPH), Vol. 21, No. 4, pp. 25-34, July 1987.

[39] Shanahan, W.J., D.W. Lloyd and J.W.S. Hearle, "Characterizing the Elastic Behavior of Textile Fabrics in Complex Deformation," Textile Research Journal, Vol. 48, pp. 495-505, 1978.

[40] Shigley, J.E. and L.D. Mitchell, Mechanical Engineering Design, Fourth Edition (McGraw-Hill Book Company, New York, 1983).

[41] Simo, J.C., D.D. Fox and M.S. Rifai, "On a Stress Resultant Geometrically Exact Shell Model. Part III; Computational Aspects of the Nonlinear Theory," Computer Methods in Applied Mechanics and Engineering, Vol. 79, No. 1, pp. 21-70, March 1990.

[42] Sims, K., "Particle Animation and Rendering Using Data Parallel Computation," Computer Graphics (Proc. SIGGRAPH), Vol. 24, No. 4, pp. 405-413, 1990.

[43] Skelton, J., "The Fundamentals of Fabric Shear," Textile Research Journal, Vol. 46, pp. 862-869, December 1976.

[44] Szeliski, R. and D. Tonnesen, "Surface Modeling With Oriented Particles," Computer Graphics (Proc. SIGGRAPH), Vol. 26, No. 2, pp. 185-194, July 1992.

[45] Terzopoulos, D. and K. Fleischer, "Deformable Models," The Visual Computer, Vol. 4, pp. 306-331, 1988.

[46] Terzopoulos, D., J. Platt and K. Fleischer, "From Gloop to Glop: Heating and Melting Deformable Models," Graphics Interface '89 Proceedings, pp. 219-226, June 1989.

[47] Tonnesen, D., "Ray Tracing Implicit Surfaces Resulting From the Summation of Polynomial Functions," Rensselaer Design Research Center Technical Report TR-89003 (Rensselaer Polytechnic Institute, January 1989).

[48] Tonnesen, D., "Modeling Liquids and Solids Using Thermal Particles," Graphics Interface '91 Proceedings, pp. 255-262, 1991.

[49] van Wijk, J.J., "Flow Visualization with Surface Particles," IEEE Computer Graphics and Applications, Vol. 13, No. 4, pp. 18-24, July 1993.

[50] Weil, J., "The Synthesis of Cloth Objects," Computer Graphics (Proc. SIGGRAPH), Vol. 20, No. 4, pp. 359-376, 1986.

[51] Werner, H.M., N. Magnenat Thalmann and Daniel Thalmann, "User Interface for Fashion Design," Graphics, Design and Visualization (Proc. International Conference on Computer Graphics), eds. S.P. Mudur and S.N. Pattanaik (Jaico Publishing House, Bombay, February 1993) pp. 165-171.

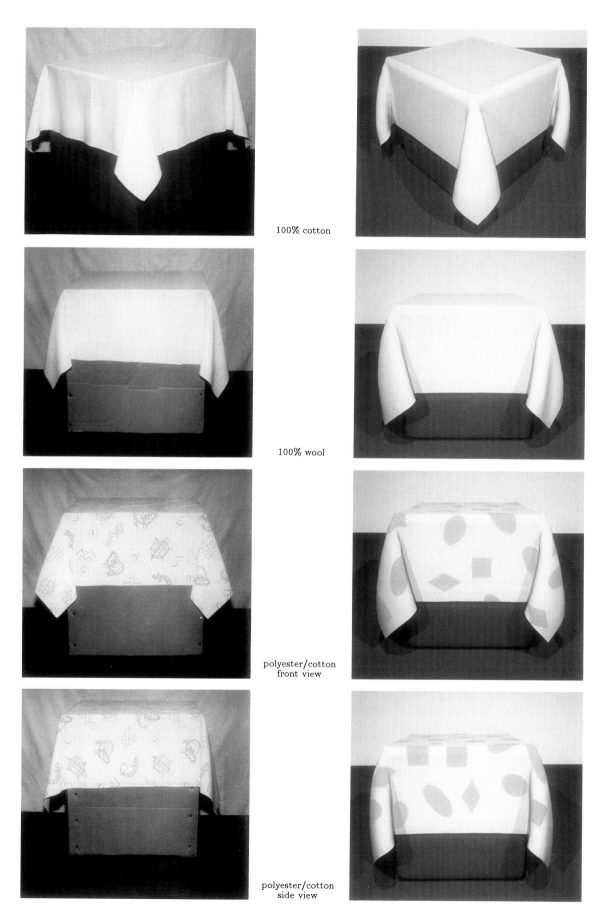

100% cotton

100% wool

polyester/cotton
front view

polyester/cotton
side view

Figure 1: Actual (left) vs. simulated (right) cloth drape

# Method of Displaying Optical Effects within Water using Accumulation Buffer

**Tomoyuki Nishita**
Fukuyama University
Higashimura-cho, Fukuyama, 729-02 Japan
nis@eml.hiroshima-u.ac.jp

**Eihachiro Nakamae**
Hiroshima Prefectural University
Nanatsuka-cho, Shoubara City, 727 Japan
600234@sinet.ad.jp

## Abstract

A precise shading model is required to display realistic images. Recently research on global illumination has been widespread. In global illumination, problems of diffuse reflection have been solved fairly well, but some optical problems after specular reflection and refraction still remain. Some natural phenomena stand out in reflected/refracted light from the wave surface of water. Refracted light from water surface converges and diverges, and creates shafts of light due to scattered light from particles. The color of the water is influenced by scattering/absorption effects of water molecules and suspensions. For these effects, the intensity and direction of incident light to particles plays an important role, and it is difficult to calculate them in conventional ray-tracing because light refracts when passing through waves. Therefore, the pre-processing tracing from light sources is necessary.

The method proposed here can effectively calculate optical effects, shafts of light, caustics, and color of the water without such pre-processing by using a scanline Z-buffer and accumulation buffer.

**CR Categories and Subject Descriptors:**
I.3.3 [**Computer Graphics**]: Picture/Image Generation
I.3.7 [**Computer Graphics**]: Three-Dimensional Graphics and Realism
**Key Words:** Shaft of light, Caustic, Color of Water, accumulation buffer, Optical Length, Photo-realism

## 1 INTRODUCTION

Image synthesis of natural phenomena is one of the most popular field these days; displays of mountains, trees, the earth, waves, the atmosphere have been attempted. This paper is concerned with optical effects within water: the proposed method calculates and displays shafts of light, caustics due to refracted light passing through waves, and the color of water.

Creatures in water and illumination effects onto them are spectacular; Such images are often used in commercials these days, though they are not physically-based images.

In the discussion of optical effects under water, the following three factors must be carefully taken into account; shafts of light and caustics due to refracted light from waves and the color of water due to scattering/absorption of particles.

Concerning caustics due to waves, Shinya[21] precalculated illumination distribution on surfaces by using *grid-pencil tracing*. Watt[22] developed *backward beam tracing*. These methods are 2 pass solutions and require storage memory for an illumination map or caustic polygons. The backward beam tracing method is the improved version of the beam tracing method[6] which can handle reflection/refraction light for polygonal objects. Therefore the method can only handle polygons. Heckbert[7] has developed a method which can calculate caustics due to refracted light from transparent objects such as lenses; the illumination distribution on surfaces is stored as textures. Chen[3] calculates an illumination map by using the *multi-pass method*. But these methods using maps have difficulties in resolution and aliasing (artifact). Mitchel[13] calculated caustics from curved reflectors (limited to implicit surfaces) by using the numerical methods. However, none of these methods have discussed shafts of light.

Concerning shafts of light, Blinn[1], Max[12], Nishita[16], and Klassen[11] have all developed methods for atmospheric scattering. Watt[22], as mentioned above, realized the display of shafts of light underwater by using Nishita's method[16] based on ray-tracing.

Concerning the display of a water surface, Max[12], Fournier[4] and Ts'o[20] have all made an attempt, but they didn't take into account scattering effects due to particles in the water, instead discussing shapes of waves. The authors have developed calculation methods for the color of water surface such as ponds[9] and the color of the sea as viewed from outer space[18]. None of them have discussed the color when viewed from a point within the water.

For displaying creatures in the water, free-form surfaces are indispensable, and the display of caustics on such curved surfaces is desired. The method proposed here can handle free-form surfaces, and is a combined method of scanline based Z-buffer, shadow volume and A-buffer[5]; the method can calculate shafts of light and caustics without the ray-tracing methods used in previous methods. In our method, as a side effect of calculation of shaft of light, caustics on objects can be obtained; in previous work, the shafts of light were calculated by the integration of scattered light on a viewing ray at each pixel, whereas in this method the intensity at every pixel on each scanline is obtained by scanning the intensities passing through the scan plane by the following reasoning. The particle density (mainly water molecules) in the water is assumed as uniform, so the intensity due to scattered light can be obtained as an analytical function of distance between the particles and the viewpoint.

In this paper, to represent curved surfaces the improved method[19] of *metaball*[14] (or referred as blobs[2]) is used.

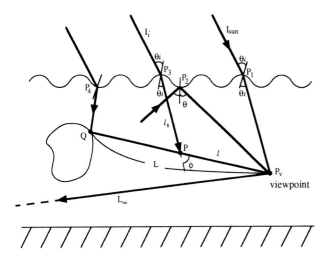

Figure 1: The optical paths arriving at the viewpoint.

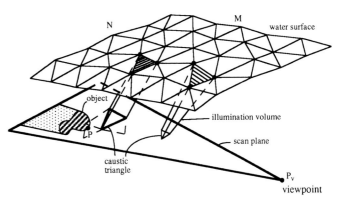

Figure 2: Geometry of illumination volumes and caustic triangles on a scan plane.

## 2 PROPOSED MODEL

The main purpose in the proposed model is to display the following optical effects; (a) shafts of light due to the convergence/diversion depending on wave shape, and (b) caustics on curved surfaces. This model takes into account scattering/absorption due to particles (water molecules and suspensions) in the water, and assumes uniform intensity distribution within visible regions and ignore multiple scattering. For light sources, direct sunlight and skylight outdoor, and point light sources and ambient light indoor are taken into account, even though only the former is discussed in this paper. As our topic is optical effects within water, shadows caused by objects above water surfaces are ignored.

### 2.1 Optical-path model

As shown in Fig.1, when one's viewpoint is located within the water, we can categorize the optical paths arriving at the viewpoint into the following three.

(a) Viewing ray intersecting with objects: The refracted light after passing through the water surface is reflected by an object (point $Q$ in Fig.1), and arrive at the viewpoint. The light is scattered and attenuated by particles (e.g., $P$ in Fig.1) on its way.

(b) Viewing ray intersecting with water surface: The refracted light after passing through the water surface, incoming light (direct sunlight and skylight) arrives at the viewpoint directly. The optical paths are classified into the following depending on the angle between the normal of the wave surface and the viewing ray.

(b.1) the angle is less than critical angle ($P_1$ in Fig.1): the component of refracted light in the incident light at a point on the water surface arrive at the viewpoint.

(b.2) the angle is larger than critical angle ($P_2$ in Fig.1): the light which perfectly reflects at a point on the water surface arrives at the viewpoint.

(c) Viewing ray having no intersection ($L_\infty$ in Fig.1): As the viewpoint is located within the water, the ray usually intersects with something such as the bottom of water. Strictly, the light path belongs to either case (a) or (b). As the extinction coefficients of particles in

water is high in general[8], the light from distant intersection points can be ignored.

### 2.2 Basic ideas

Concerning light refracted after passing through waves, the following conditions should be considered. (i) The intensity distribution of the light in space is not uniform because refracted light converges and/or diverges. (ii) The intensity of reflected light from objects consisting of two component, diffuse and specular reflection, depends on the incident direction of light. (iii) The intensity of scattered light from particles strongly depends on the phase angle between the incident direction and the scattering direction; this effect is called phase function.

It is very difficult to know the path of light arriving at an object ($Q$ in Fig.1) and a particle ($P$ in Fig.1) and the intensity distribution due to caustic effect because of refraction. To solve this problem, previous methods (e.g., [22]) employ an illumination map, whereas our method does not need such a map, as is described below.

Let's consider subdivided triangle elements from a lattice after meshing a water surface (see Fig.2). The refraction vectors are calculated at every lattice point and swept, and a swept volume of a triangle along the refracted vectors is called the *illumination volume*.

For visualization of transparent objects with non-uniform density such as clouds, smoke or haze, numerical integration of the densities on the ray is required. However, this is unnecessary as the density of particles in water is uniform. In the proposed model, for the calculation of the intensity distribution of light in a uniform density medium, that is in water, an analytical function can be used. Our method can be applied not only to water but also to an atmosphere with uniform density.

The calculation of shafts of light and caustics is equivalent to calculating the intensity distribution of flux of light in space. It is difficult that the space to be calculated is limited to the visible regions within the field of view, which is filled with water. To obtain this space, the Z-buffer method can be used. The visible space within the water at each pixel can be obtained as the front part of the depth of the objects stored in the Z-buffer. That is, the invisible regions on a scan plane (e.g., the dotted region in Fig.2) can be discarded.

The intensity of light is inversely propotional to the intersection area between scan plane and illumination volume.

Then, the intensities of scattered light due to particles can be obtained by applying scan conversion on the illumination volumes. That is, after calculation of intensity distribution on a scan line, these intensities are stored in an accumulation buffer.

In this paper, metaballs are employed for displaying curved surfaces. In the method used here, the intersection test between the viewing ray and iso-potential surface can be done through ray-tracing, in which it is effectively executed because the density function on the ray is represented by degree six Bézier curves. The intersection test is performed by *Bézier clipping*[17].

## 2.3  Optical model

In water the light arriving at the viewpoint has two components; the light arriving at the viewpoint directly from light refracted after passing through waves, and the indirect light arriving from light reflected from objects and from scattered light from particles. For the latter, the calculation is done by taking into account light distribution within water. The following conditions also need to be taken into account.

(a)  Even though the distribution of light within water is determined by the incident light, direct sunlight and skylight over the water onto wave surfaces, the shaft of light can be regarded as being generated only by strong direct sunlight; i.e., skylight can be neglected. In our model the illumination volumes caused by refracted light consist of only direct sunlight.

(b)  The scattered light from outside of the viewing field can't arrive at the viewpoint because multiple scattering due to particles is ignored. Light from distant points can't arrive at the viewpoint because the extinction coefficient of particles within the water is large. Defining the maximum distance of light arriving as visible length, the space to be calculated is finite; the viewing pyramid with the height of the visible length.

(c)  The space to be calculated is completely filled by illumination volumes. Defining the triangle as a *caustic triangle* which is the intersected area between an illumination volume and a scan plane (see Fig.2), every point on the scan plane is included in at least one caustic triangle because every edge of the illumination volume is shared by adjacent illumination volumes (there is no gap between the triangles).

(d)  The intensity of light in the caustic triangle is inversely propotional to its area. Usually illumination volumes are very thin, so their caustic triangles are very small; the intensity of scattered light from particles in the caustic triangle is assumed as uniform.

(e)  The light arriving at the viewpoint is determined only by the distance between the caustic triangle and the viewpoint, since the density of particles in water is uniform. That is, the intensity can be calculated by an analytical function (exponential function) of the distance.

(f)  It is difficult to calculate intensity distribution within the water due to skylight as it incidents onto wave surface from various directions. This light after passing through wave surfaces is treated as an ambient light, the intensity of which is defined by the exponential function of its depth.

# 3   OUTLINE OF THE PROCEDURE

First, we prepare the following:  The water surface is subdivided into an $N \times M$ mesh, and illumination volumes, the number of which is $2NM$, are generated by subdivision of the mesh. The refracting direction of incident light at each lattice point is calculated where the direction is influenced by the wave shapes. A 2-dimensional array is prepared to store these refracting directions. A Z-buffer to store depths on the scanline and an accumulation buffer to store intensities are prepared. The visible length is calculated by using the extinction coefficient.

The outline of the procedure is as follows:

(1)  Calculate the normal vector of the wave at each lattice point and store the refracting direction at each point.

(2)  Execute the following processes for each scanline which moves from top to bottom :

(2.1)  After hidden surface removal, store the depths of objects(or water surface) in Z-buffer.

(2.2)  Calculate the intersection points between the edges of illumination volumes and the scan plane.

(2.3)  Execute the following processes for each caustic triangle. Hence, caustic triangles lying outside of the view pyramid and behind objects tested by the Z-buffer are discarded.

(2.3.1) Calculate the maximum intensity of scattered light for the caustic triangle

(2.3.2) Calculate the projected range of the triangle on the screen by means of perspective transformation, calculate the intensity at each pixel in the range by using linear interpolation, and store them in the accumulation buffer.

(3)  Display every pixel color stored in the accumulation buffer.

The method described above is superior to previous methods by virtue of the following: In the previous methods (e.g., Watt[22] employed Nishita's method[16]), ray-tracing is used for the calculation of shafts of light in space. There are huge number of illumination volumes (e.g., more than 100,000 triangular prisms in our examples). This results in the number of intersection tests between rays and illumination volumes becoming huge because intersection tests are required for each pixel on the screen, and the intersection test for illumination volumes is included in the loop of the ray. The proposed method, however, is very effective because the calculation of intensity at every pixel is done in the loop of each illumination volume.

# 4   INTENSITY CALCULATION

Let's consider the light arriving from point $Q$ on an object or a wave surface; the light is influenced by scattering/absorption of particles along its ray. As the intensity within a caustic triangle is assumed as uniform, intensity at each pixel in the projected range of the triangle can be calculated as follows: The intensity at each pixel is calculated by multiplying the intensity of the triangle and the intersection length between the ray and the triangle, and is accumulated in the accumulation buffer. Let's discuss the detail of the method.

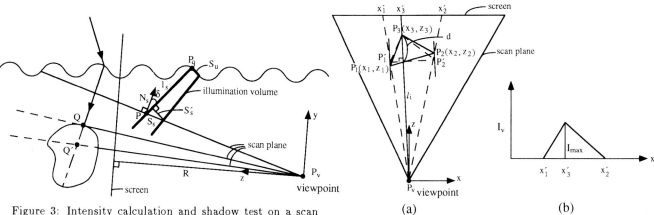

Figure 3: Intensity calculation and shadow test on a scan plane.

Figure 4: Calculation of intensities due to a caustic triangle.

The scattered intensity from particles at point $P$ on the ray is given by (see Fig.1)

$$I_P(\lambda) = (I_i T(\theta_i, \theta_t) F_p \beta(\phi, \lambda) exp(-c(\lambda)l_s) + I_a)\rho, \quad (1)$$

where $\lambda$ is the wavelength, $I_i$ the intensity of incident light onto the water surface ($I_i$ the irradiance of sunlight just above the water surface), $T$ the transmittance of the incident light which obeys Fresnel's law of reflection, $\theta_i$ and $\theta_t$ the incident angle and the refracted angle, respectively; these angles obey Snell's law. $\beta$ a volume scattering function (this is the function of angle $\phi$ between the incident direction and scattering direction: see Fig.1 ), $c(\lambda)$ the attenuation coefficient of light which expresses the ratio of lost energy of light when the light travels a unit length, $\rho$ the density, and $I_a$ ambient light (see 2.3(f)). The color of the water is determined by $c(\lambda)$ and $\beta$. (Data of $\beta$ and $c$ used in this paper is employed from [8].) $F_p$ is the flux ratio between the intensity at just beneath the water surface and at point $P$, $F_p = S_u/S_s'$, which is equivalent to form factor in the radiosity method. $S_u$ and $S_s'$ are areas of cross sections at water surface and at point $P$, respectively. $S_s'$ is determined by the area of the caustic triangle on the scan plane and cosine of angle $\delta$ (see Fig.3). That is,

$$S_s' = S_s cos\delta. \quad (2)$$

As the intensities of scattered light from every particle on the ray are attenuated, the intensity at the viewpoint, $I_v$, is given by

$$I_v(\lambda) = I_q(\lambda)exp(-c(\lambda)L) + \int_0^L I_p exp(-c(\lambda)l)dl, \quad (3)$$

where $I_q$ is the reflected intensity from the object (or refracted light from wave surface), $I_p$ the scattered light from particles, and $l$ the distance between $P$ and the viewpoint, $L$ the distance between the object and the viewpoint.

In the case of point $Q$ being on the wave surface and $\theta_t$ is less than the critical angle(48.6°), $I_p$ is given by

$$I_q(\lambda) = T(\theta_i, \theta_t)(I_{sun}\delta(\theta_i - \theta_t) + I_{sky}(\theta_i)), \quad (4)$$

where $I_{sun}$ is the incident intensity, $\delta(\theta_i - \theta_t)$ the delta function (1 for $\theta_i = \theta_t$). $I_{sky}(\theta_i)$ is the intensity of skylight in angle $\theta_i$ (see [15]).

In the case where the incident ray from the viewpoint is larger than the critical angle (see $P_2$ in Fig.1), the light

from the underside of the water surface reflects perfectly, that is, the scattered light from particles on the reflecting line is reflected. As this reflected light is attenuated when it arrives at the viewpoint, it is not necessary to calculate precisely. These intensities depend on each reflecting angle, then these values are precalculated for several angles and are stored in a table-lookup.

When the light does not intersect with any objects (or the water surface) any great distance away, the visible length is set as $L = \infty$. The attenuation effect in water is large, the light from distant position doesn't arrive at the viewpoint; this means the integration range(interval) is limited. For a given tolerance $\epsilon$, the integration range, i.e., visible length $L_\infty$, can be defined by the relation of $exp(-c(\lambda)L) < \epsilon$ ( $c(\lambda)$ for blue is used because it is small). $I_q$ at this point is assumed as zero.

The calculation method for reflected light from a point $Q$ on an object is described in section 4.2.

## 4.1 Intensity calculation using caustic triangles

The calculation for the intensity distribution of light in space is similar to that of shadow calculation using *shadow volumes*. In the method proposed here, illumination volumes are prepared to calculate the intensity distribution of light. These are scan converted (i.e., extracting intersected triangles on the scan plane), and the intensity distribution are calculated scanline by scanline.

As every point on the ray is included in at least one caustic triangle, the 2nd term of equation (3), $I_v'$, is rewritten as follows:

$$I_v'(\lambda) = \sum_{i=0}^K (I_{pi}d_i + I_q H_i)exp(-c(\lambda)l_i), \quad (5)$$

where $K$ is the number of caustic triangles on the visible range(interval) of the ray, $I_{pi}$ the average intensity of each caustic triangle (per unit length), $d_i$ the intersected length with each triangle and the ray, $l_i$ the distance between each triangle and the viewpoint (see Fig.4). $H_i$ is binary function (0 or 1); 1 in the case when the triangle $i$ intersect with objects (visible surface or water surface)(see 4.2). Triangles whose depths are larger than the visible length are discarded. Equation (5) gives $I_v$ for one ray. By taking into account every triangle on the scan plane, $I_v$ at every pixel on the scanline can be calculated. The shaft of light in space is obtained by applying this to every scanline.

**(1)** Extraction of caustic triangles on the scan plane

The coordinates of each caustic triangle on a scan plane can be calculated as follows (see Fig.3): Let's consider a lattice point $P_u(x_u, y_u, z_u)$ on a wave surface and unit vector of its refraction $\mathbf{L_u}(L_x, L_y, L_z)$ in an eye-point coordinates system. If the distance between the viewpoint and the screen is $R$, y coordinate of the scan line is $y_s$, and x, y, z components of the normal vector $\mathbf{N_S}$ are $(0, 1, -r_s)$, here $r_s = \frac{y_s}{R}$. The length $l_s$ between lattice point $P_u$ and the intersection point between the scan plane and the refracted ray is given by

$$l_s = \frac{y_u - r_s z_u}{L_y - r_s L_z}, \qquad (6)$$

where the refracted ray intersects with the scan plane when the numerator is positive ($P_u$ exists below the scan plane when it is negative). By using the obtained $l_s$, intersection point $P$ can be calculated by using the equation $\mathbf{P} = l_s \mathbf{L_u} + \mathbf{P_u}$. The denominator is propotional to the cosine of angle $\delta$ between the normal of the scan plane and the refracted vector (see Fig.3), and $cos\delta$ is given by

$$cos\delta = (L_y - r_s L_z)a_s, \qquad a_s = (1 + r_s^2)^{-1/2}, \qquad (7)$$

where $a_s$ is constant for the same scan plane. Eqs. (6) and (7) are used effectively because $cos\delta$ and $l_s$ can be used in equations (2) and (1), respectively.

**(2)** Calculation of scattered light within a caustic triangle

The intensity of light in a caustic triangle can be calculated by using its area. If we calculate the areas of every caustic triangle on each scan plane, it is time consuming. So we use the approximation method for calculation of the intensity of light at each pixel, in which area calculation can be avoided.

Let's consider the first term in eq. (5). Fig.4 (a) shows the top view of a scan plane in eye-coordinate systems. Let's consider caustic triangle $P_1(x_1, z_1), P_2(x_2, z_2), P_3(x_3, z_3)$ on the scan plane, where the area of the triangle is $S_s$, and the vertices are sorted in order $x_1 \leq x_3 \leq x_2$. As shown in Fig.4(a), points $P_1$ and $P_2$ are moved parallel with the line $P_v P_3$, and $P_1 P_2$ is perpendicular to $P_v P_3$; these moved points are denoted by $P_1'$ and $P_2'$. In this case, the area of $P_1 P_2 P_3$ equals that of $P_1' P_2' P_3$ (i.e., $S_s$). The area of the triangle, which is half of the parallelogram, is expressed by $\overline{P_1' P_2'} \times d/2$. We need the intersected length between the ray and the triangle to calculate intensity. When the ray passes through $P_3$, the length is maximum. The length of the intersection between the triangle and $P_v P_3$, $d$, is expressed by $\frac{2S_s}{P_1' P_2'}$. The length $\overline{P_1' P_2'}$ can be obtained by adding distance $P_1'$ from the line $P_v P_3$ and the distance $P_2'$ from the same line, and is expressed by $((x_2 - x_1) - (z_2 - z_1)(\frac{x_3}{z_3}))/b$, where $b = \sqrt{1 + (\frac{x_3}{z_3})^2}$. Let's denote projected x-coordinates of triangle $P_1 P_2 P_3$ on the screen as $x_1', x_2', x_3'$. After projection, the triangle affects to the intensity at pixels between $x_1'$ and $x_2'$, and the intensity at $x_3'$ has a maximum value because the intensity depends on the intersected length of the ray and the triangle. That is, as shown in Fig.4(b), the intensity distribution between $x_1'$ and $x_2'$ is approximated by two liner functions. For simple calculation, $x_3'$ is slightly moved to the center of pixel which includes $x_3'$. The distribution function can be determined uniquely by the maximum intensity. As described previously in 2.3(a), for calculating the intensity of a shaft of light only direct sunlight is taken in account; the second term in eq.(1) can be neglected. By assuming

$I_s'$ except for $F_p$ in the first term of eq.(1) ($I_p = I_s' F_p$), $I_p$ is expressed by $I_s' \frac{S_u}{S_s}$. Then the maximum intensity of $I_{pi} d_i$ of the first term of equation (5) is given by (see 4.2 for 2nd term)

$$I_{max} = I_s' \frac{S_u}{S_s} \frac{2S_s}{P_1' P_2'} = \frac{2I_s' S_u b}{(x_2 - x_1) - (z_2 - z_1)(\frac{x_3}{z_3})}. \qquad (8)$$

That is, $S_s$ is canceled; area calculation of the caustic triangle is unnecessary. As $(\frac{x_3}{z_3})$ is small, $b$ is approximated by $1 + (\frac{x_3}{z_3})/2$. For very small $(\frac{x_3}{z_3})$ (i.e., around center on the screen), the intensity of the triangle is inversely propotional to the width $(x_2 - x_1)$ of triangle viewed from the viewpoint. Intensity at every pixel in the interval $[x_1', x_2']$ except $x_3'$ is calculated by linear interpolation.

Let's consider a accumulation buffer, $I(x)$ ($x = 1, 2, ...n$ : $n$ =screen width), to be stored intensities. After initializing the accumulation buffer, the accumulation process to the accumulation buffer is done by the following quasi-code.

```
d1 = I_max/(x'_3 - x'_1);
d = d1([x'_3] + 1 - [x'_1]);
for x = [x'_1] + 1, [x'_3];
{ if (z(x) > z_max) I(x) = I(x) + d ;
  d = d + d1;
}
d2 = I_max/(x'_2 - x'_3) ;
for x = [x'_3] + 1, [x'_2]
{ if (z(x) > z_max) I(x) = I(x) + d;
  d = d - d2;
}
```

where [ ] is the symbol of truncated fractions, $d$ the intensity at pixel $x$. $z(x)$ is the depth at pixel $x$ which is stored in the Z-buffer, and $z_{max}$ the maximum depth of the triangle. In the above process, if the triangle is nearer than the depth of the object at the pixel, the intensity at the pixel is stored in the accumulation buffer like the Z-buffer algorithm.

### 4.2 Intensity calculation on objects

To calculate intensity of reflected light from point $Q$ on an object, illumination volumes hitting $Q$ have to be extracted; at least one illumination volume exists. In previous methods, the intensity distribution is calculated beforehand and stored in an illumination map. Then they require substantial storage memory, and their shape is limited to polygons: even intensities of invisible parts are calculated. If an illumination map is not used, it is time consuming because intensity tests between objects and illumination volumes are executed at every point on the objects.

However our method makes both illumination map and intersection tests between objects and illumination volumes unnecessary. As shown in Fig.2, if a caustic triangle on a scan plane contains point $Q$ on the object ($x$ and $z$ components are enough to test), the illumination volume including the caustic triangle illuminates point $Q$. As the depth of the object at each pixel is stored in the Z-buffer, this test is performed simply by comparing the depth of the triangle with the depth of the object.

The intensity of reflected light is determined by the intersection area between the object and the illumination volume (the ratio of focus is determined by the area), the angle between the normal of the object and the ray, and the attribute of its material (such as reflectance). In previous method [22] handling polygonal objects, the intersected area(i.e., a casuistic polygon) between the object and the illumination volume should be calculated. For curved surfaces, such a calculation is difficult. In the proposed method, the density ratio of flux, $F$ in eq.(1), can be calculated by using the area of the caustic triangle on the scan plane instead of the intersected area on the object. The area of the triangle is calculated just for the intensity calculation of objects, in general the area of caustic triangle is not calculated (see 4.1). The intensity of reflected light, $I_q$, is given by

$$I_q = I_i T(\theta_i, \theta_t) F_p exp(-c(\lambda)l_q)(k_d cos\alpha + k_s(cos\gamma)^n), \quad (9)$$

where $k_d$ and $k_s$ are diffuse reflectance and specular reflectance, respectively. $l_q$ is the distance between the calculation point and the water surface, $\alpha$ the angle between the normal of the object and the incident ray, $\gamma$ the angle between the viewing direction and the reflection direction, $n$ the specular-reflection exponent: we employed Phong's model.

## 4.3 Shadow processing

For the case where light sources are located above the water surface, the calculation method for shafts of light within the water are described here. As the shafts of light stream from top to bottom on the screen, the scanlines are processed from the top to the bottom. As the shadow effects of objects located above the water surface are ignored, if the starting point of illumination volume (on the water surface) is visible from the viewpoint, this point is not in shadow; the test is easily done by using values of Z-buffer. When the starting point is outside of the screen, the shadow test (i.e., inclusion test whether objects include the point or not) is done. During the proceeding of scanlines, once the caustic triangle on the scan plane intersects with an object (see $Q$ in Fig.3), the illumination volume is cut away in the next scanline because of it being in shadow. In the case of the triangle existing behind the value of Z-buffer, the illumination volume intersects with some object (see shaded region in Fig.2) or passes through behind the object (see dotted region in Fig.2). In this case, shadow testing is executed. That is, if the illumination volume intersects with some object, the illumination volume is cut away.

In water the extinction coefficient is large in general. Scattered light from particle far from the water surface do not arrive at the viewpoint, so the illumination volume is assumed to have a limited length. The distant part of it, therefore, is cut away as in shadow processing.

## 5 EXAMPLES

Fig. 5 shows some scenes from an animation of optical effects within water. Fig.(a) shows the shafts of light and caustics on a creature in water; the killer whale consists of 890 metaballs. Fig.(b) shows the killer whale viewed from the bottom of water. Fig.(c) is a close up of Fig.(a) in order to observe caustics on curved surfaces. In these examples, 125,000 illumination volumes are used. The waves are composited by the four different wavelength of waves[9]. The size of the illumination volume is equivalent to 1/36 of the shortest wavelength. The calculation was done on an IRIS CRIMSON. The computation times for Fig.5 (a) and (b) were 6.2 minutes and 7.4 minutes, respectively (image size=512 × 400).

(a)

(b)

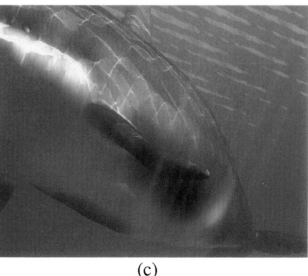

(c)

Figure 5: Examples of optical effects within water.

# 6  CONCLUSION

We have proposed an algorithm for rendering the optical effects such as shafts of light, caustics, and the color of the water. As shown in the examples, the proposed method gives us photo-realistic images taking into account scattering characteristic of particles and intensity distribution of light within the water. The advantages of the proposed method are as follows:

(1) For calculation of caustics on objects, the method proposed here doesn't need any illumination map used in previous methods. The method can display caustics on curved surfaces such as metaballs.

(2) The method proposed here can calculate optical effects, shaft of light, caustics, and color of water, effectively by using a scanline Z-buffer and accumulation buffer.

(3) The shadow effects of shafts of light can be calculated simply by using Z-buffer.

Even though we did not show images viewed from above the water surface, the method proposed here can be applied to atmospheres including caustics on objects due to reflected light from water surfaces.

**Acknowledgment**

The authors would like to acknowledge Mr. T. Maeda for his help in making the data for the killer whale.

# References

[1] J.F. Blinn, "Light Reflection Functions for Simulation of Clouds and Dusty Surfaces," *Computer Graphics*, Vol. 16, No. 3, (1982),pp. 21-29.

[2] J.F. Blinn, "A Generalization of Algebraic Surface Drawing," *ACM Transaction on Graphics*, Vol. 2, (1980),pp. 235-256.

[3] S.E. Chen, H.E. Rushmeier, G. Miller, D. Turner, "A Progressive Multi-Pass Method for Global Illumination," *Computer Graphics*, Vol. 25, No. 4, (1991),pp. 165-174.

[4] A. Fournier, " A Simple Model of Ocean Waves," *Computer Graphics*, Vol. 20, No. 4, (1986),pp. 75-84.

[5] P. Haeberli, K. Akeley, "The Accumulation Buffer: Hardware Support for High Quality Rendering," *Computer Graphics*, Vol. 24, No. 4,(1990),pp. 309-313.

[6] P. Heckbert, P. Hanrahan, "Beam Tracing Polygonal Objects," *Computer Graphics*, Vol. 18, No. 3, (1984),pp. 11-127.

[7] P. Heckbert, "Adaptive Radiosity Textures for Bidirectional Ray Tracing," *Computer Graphics*, Vol. 24, No. 4,(1990),pp. 145-154.

[8] N. G. Jerlov, "Optical Oceanography," Elsevier, Amsterdam (1968).

[9] K. Kaneda, G. Yuan, E. Nakamae, T. Nishita, "Realistic Visual simulation of Water Surfaces Taking into account Radiative Transfer," *Proc. of CAD/Graphics'91*, (1991) pp.25-30.

[10] J.T. Kajiya, "Ray tracing Volume Densities, *Computer Graphics*, Vol. 18, No. 3,(1984),pp.165-174.

[11] R.V. Klassen, "Modeling the Effect of the Atmosphere on Light," *ACM Transaction on Graphics*, Vol. 6, No. 3,(1987),pp. 215-237.

[12] N. Max, "Light Diffusion through Clouds and Haze," *Graphics and Image Processing*, Vol. 33, No. 3, (1986) pp.280-292.

[13] D. Mitchel, P. Hanrahan, "Illumination from Curved Reflectors," *Computer Graphics*, Vol. 16, No. 2, (1992) pp.283-291.

[14] H. Nishimura, M. Hirai, T. Kawai, T. Kawata, I. Shirakawa, K. Omura, "Object Modeling by Distribution Function and a Method of Image generation,", Journal of papers given by at the Electronics Communication Conference '85 J68-D(4) pp.718-725 (in Japanese)

[15] T. Nishita, and E. Nakamae, "Continuous tone Representation of Three-Dimensional Objects Illuminated by Sky Light," *Computer Graphics*, Vol. 20, No. 4,(1986),pp. 125-132.

[16] T. Nishita, Y. Miyawaki, E. Nakamae, "A Shading Model for Atmospheric Scattering Considering Distribution of Light Sources," *Computer Graphics*, Vol. 21, No. 4,(1987),pp. 303-310.

[17] T. Nishita, T.W. Sederberg, M. Kakimoto, "Ray Tracing Rational Trimmed Surface Patches," *Computer Graphics*, Vol. 24, No. 4,(1990), pp.337-345.

[18] T. Nishita, T. Shirai, K. Tadamura, E. Nakamae, "Display of The Earth Taking into Account Atmospheric Scattering," *Proc. of SIGGRAPH'93*, (1993),pp. 175-182.

[19] T. Nishita, E. Nakamae, "A Method for Displaying Metaballs using Bézier Clipping," *Computer Graphics Forum (Proc. of EUROGRAPHICS'94)*, (1994) (to be appear).

[20] P. Y. Ts'o, and B. A. Barsky,. " Modeling and Rendering Waves: Wave-Tracing Using Beta-Splines and Reflective and Refractive Texture Mapping," *ACM Transactions on Graphics*, Vol. 6, No. 3,(1987),pp. 191-214.

[21] M. Shinya, T. Saito, T. Takahashi, "Rendering Techniques for Transparent Objects," *Proc. of Graphics Interface'89*, (1989), pp.173-181.

[22] M. Watt, "Light-Water Interaction using Backward Beam Tracing," *Computer Graphics*, Vol. 24, No. 4, (1990),pp. 377-376.

# IRIS Performer: A High Performance Multiprocessing Toolkit for Real-Time 3D Graphics

## John Rohlf and James Helman
### Silicon Graphics Computer Systems*

## Abstract

This paper describes the design and implementation of IRIS Performer, a toolkit for visual simulation, virtual reality, and other real-time 3D graphics applications. The principal design goal is to allow application developers to more easily obtain maximal performance from 3D graphics workstations which feature multiple CPUs and support an immediate-mode rendering library. To this end, the toolkit combines a low-level library for high-performance rendering with a high-level library that implements pipelined, parallel traversals of a hierarchical scene graph. While discussing the toolkit architecture, the paper illuminates and addresses performance issues fundamental to immediate-mode graphics and coarse-grained, pipelined multiprocessing. Graphics optimizations focus on efficient data transfer to the graphics subsystem, reduction of mode settings, and restricting state inheritance. The toolkit's multiprocessing features solve the problems of how to partition work among multiple processes, how to synchronize these processes, and how to manage data in a pipelined, multiprocessing environment. The paper also discusses support for intersection detection, fixed-frame rates, run-time profiling and special effects such as geometric morphing.

Keywords: Real-time graphics, multiprocessing, visual simulation, virtual reality, interactive 3D graphics

CR Categories and Subject Descriptors: I.3.2 Graphics Systems; I.3.3 Picture/Image Generation; I.3.4 Graphics Utilities, Application Packages, Graphics Packages; I.3.7 Three-Dimensional Graphics and Realism

## 1    Introduction

Recently, multipurpose workstations have attained graphics performance levels that have customarily been the province of expensive, special-purpose image generators (IGs). Consequently, many visual simulation applications are migrating from IGs to graphics workstations. Additionally, the decrease in the cost/performance ratio of current-generation workstations has opened the door to non-traditional visual simulation applications such as virtual reality and location-based entertainment. These applications are often very cost-sensitive and so demand every drop of speed from the machine.

*2011 N. Shoreline Blvd., Mountain View, CA 94043 USA
jrohlf@sgi.com, jimh@sgi.com.

### 1.1    Motivation

In our experience, application developers often have problems extracting graphics performance due to inexperience with the system and ignorance of the "new set of rules", some of them quite arcane, which must be followed for peak performance on each new graphics platform. Also, applications often forgo multiprocessing simply because the development of a multiprocessed application proves too difficult or time-consuming. The resulting single-threaded applications sequentially process all tasks, leaving an expensive graphics subsystem idle while the application carries out non-graphics processing.

Existing general purpose 3D libraries and toolkits tend to address different problems. Immediate-mode rendering libraries such as OpenGL[9], Starbase[6], and XGL provide an efficient interface to hardware, but leave the definition of geometry, scene content and multiple eye points to the application. Object-oriented toolkits such as PHIGS+[13], HOOPS, Doré[7] and IRIS Inventor[12] provide scene structures based on display lists and objects, but for most efficient rendering they retain an internal copy of the geometric data. Since applications often need access to the original data for other purposes, a second inaccessible copy inside the toolkit can substantially increase memory usage. In addition, when the application dynamically changes geometry, the retained data must be edited or rewritten. Depending on the toolkit, this can increase program complexity, degrade performance, or both.

Most importantly, none of the aforementioned toolkits addresses multiprocessing. And from our experience, retrofitting a retained-database toolkit with efficient multiprocessing support and parallel traversals proves difficult at best.

In addition to demanding maximum performance, visual simulation and virtual reality applications have real-time requirements and must run at fixed frame rates to avoid the distractions and artifacts caused by frame rate variations. To achieve reasonable performance, these applications require efficient database culling to the viewing frustum, scene complexity management through level-of-detail switching, intersection testing, and run-time profiling for application and database tuning. Toolkits written specifically for visual simulation such as VisionWorks[10] and GVS[8] partially address many of these issues, but neither offers a fully multiprocessed solution.

### 1.2    Purpose

The fundamental design goal of the toolkit is to provide a software development layer that delivers the greatest possible performance from the graphics workstation, freeing the application developer to concentrate on other matters. We achieve this primarily through:

- Graphics optimizations
- Multiprocessing

Another goal is to simplify the development of virtual reality and visual simulation applications by providing intrinsic support for common graphics and database operations such as multiple views, level-of-detail switching, morphing, intersection testing, picking, and run-time profiling. However, the toolkit does not provide direct support for I/O devices, audio, or motion systems since these are not directly related to the core functions of a rendering platform or a multiprocessing framework. Some applications, such as the fly-through system shown in Figure 17, have added their own device support to IRIS Performer, as have developers of toolkits for particular application domains, e.g. dVS[5] and WorldToolkit[8].

The graphics optimizations and multiprocessing features of the toolkit are targeted for workstations which support immediate-mode graphics and small-scale, symmetric, shared memory multiprocessing.

## 1.3 Overview

The toolkit's core consists of two libraries: **libpf** and **libpr**. **libpr** consists primarily of optimized graphics primitives as well as intersection, shared memory, and other basic functions. **libpf** is built on top of **libpr** and adds database hierarchy, multiprocessing, and real-time features. This arrangement is illustrated in Figure 1 below:

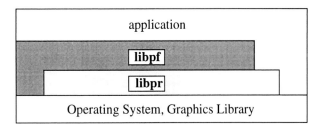

Figure 1.    Library Layering

The two-library approach allows developers to choose which layer they wish to program to and also avoids "black box" limitations to flexibility by allowing an application which uses **libpf** to access the underlying **libpr** primitives. An application is also free to access the immediate-mode graphics library and operating system directly for customized rendering or control.

In keeping with our bottom-up design methodology, we discuss **libpr** first, then follow with **libpf** and finish with a description of run-time profiling utilities which facilitate performance tuning.

## 2    libpr - Efficient Rendering

The **libpr** library provides the high-performance foundation for IRIS Performer. Its specialized graphics primitives are designed to squeeze the highest level of performance from the graphics pipeline by efficiently managing geometry and graphics state for immediate-mode rendering. In addition, **libpr** supports intersection and shared memory utilities that facilitate a multiprocessed visual application.

### 2.1    pfGeoSet - Efficient Geometry Primitive

In our experience, the data structures used to represent geometry and the code which transfers that data to the graphics hardware very often make or break an immediate-mode graphics application. Scattered memory organizations can result in poor cache behavior and inefficient rendering loops can starve a fast graphics pipeline.

**Immediate Mode vs. Display List Mode**

The pfGeoSet's purpose is to achieve maximum immediate-mode performance for 3D geometry. In *immediate mode*, the host CPU must feed the graphics subsystem with primitive, vertex, and attribute commands. An alternative to immediate mode is *display list mode* which compiles a list of commands into a data structure that can be very efficiently transferred to the graphics subsystem.

However, display list mode has some significant disadvantages that immediate mode does not have:

- A display list is a closed data structure. Geometry data must be duplicated at substantial memory penalty for database queries like intersections which require read access.

- Display lists are costly to compile. This generally requires that geometry be static. Techniques requiring vertex manipulation such as animation do not lend themselves to display list mode.

pfGeoSets utilize application-supplied arrays for attributes such as coordinates and colors, consequently avoiding these disadvantages. Applications are free to modify these arrays for dynamic effects without experiencing degraded rendering performance.

A pfGeoSet is a collection of geometric primitives of a single type defined by its:

- primitive type: points, lines, line strips, triangles, quads, or triangle strips

- attribute lists: coordinates, colors, normals, texture coordinates

- attribute bindings: per-vertex, per-primitive, overall, off.

Figure 2 illustrates a pfGeoSet consisting of two triangles with a per-primitive color binding: the first is red and the second is blue.

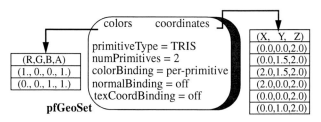

Figure 2.    pfGeoSet Structure

On high-end machines in particular, care must be taken to ensure that immediate-mode data transfer is efficient or else the graphics hardware will be starved. pfGeoSets guarantee efficient data transfer by enforcing an *a priori* grouping of geometry by type that facilitates the use of customized, extremely tight rendering loops. Since all primitives within a pfGeoSet are homogeneous, a single, well-tuned rendering routine that is tailored to the specific pfGeoSet type can quickly transfer the primitives with a minimum of overhead. For example, if a pfGeoSet is a collection of triangles which have colors defined per-primitive (i.e., one color per triangle), its corresponding rendering routine doesn't waste precious if-tests determining whether or not a color should be sent down with each vertex. Over 700 of these specialized rendering routines exist (macro-generated) to handle all combinations of primitive types and attribute bindings, and all are indirectly accessed through the single pfDrawGSet() routine.

**pfGeoSet Construction**

Developers may find pfGeoSet construction messy and may sometimes generate pfGeoSets with sub-optimal performance, e.g., pfGeoSets with a small number of primitives may suffer from excessive setup overhead when transferring them to the graphics subsystem. Or an application may fail to use triangle meshes where possible. Connecting triangles together into a mesh can significantly reduce the amount of data transfer from the CPU to the graphics subsystem as well as the amount of processing required in the graphics hardware. Unfortunately, most databases do not utilize triangle meshing and automatic meshing algorithms are complex. To avoid these pitfalls, the pfuBuilder utility functions provide convenient meshing and performance-oriented construction of pfGeoSets. The application simply feeds independent, potentially concave polygons to a pfuBuilder which returns sorted, meshed, and optimized pfGeoSets on request.

## 2.2 Efficient Graphics State Management

Unlike geometry, graphics state commands do not modify the frame buffer; they do not "draw" anything, but instead configure the graphics hardware with a particular mode (e.g. shading model) or attribute (e.g. texture) that modifies the appearance of geometry. Like geometry, efficient management of graphics state is required for optimal graphics performance.

In **libpr** there are 3 ways to set graphics state, each of which offers significant performance advantages:

- Immediate mode
- Display list mode
- Encapsulated mode

In general, applications use immediate mode to set global state such as enabling fog and use encapsulated mode to specify the appearance of geometry at database creation time. Display list mode is primarily intended for use by the **libpf** library to accommodate multiprocessing.

### 2.2.1 pfState - Immediate Mode

The state management provided by the pfState object is useful for avoiding redundant mode changes. A pfState object maintains all current and previous graphics state in a state stack. The set of managed graphics state is that which can be modified through **libpr** routines and is a subset of that provided by the graphics library. Graphics state is partitioned into:

- Modes such as backface culling, gouraud shading, wireframe on/off
- Attributes such as texture, material parameters

*Modes* are generally simple integer values that are set by single commands such as pfShadeModel() while *attributes* are objects like pfTexture that encapsulate many graphics characteristics. Modes are "set" and attributes are "applied" by their immediate-mode routines: pfShadeModel() and pfApplyTex() for example.

By shadowing the state of the graphics hardware, a pfState can eliminate costly mode changes. For example, if the current shading model is FLAT then a subsequent attempt at setting a FLAT shading model should be intercepted before being sent to the graphics hardware. Avoiding mode changes is especially useful for parallelized geometry engines which become essentially single-threaded during a mode change because mode changes must be broadcast to all engines. Redundant mode changes become particularly prevalent if the database is sorted by mode (See Section 3.1.3).

### 2.2.2 pfDispList - Display List Mode

The primary purpose of the pfDispList is to capture an entire frame's worth of data for use in multiprocessing. It captures and buffers **libpr** rendering commands such as pfShadeModel() and pfApplyTex(). As will be discussed in Section 3.2.2, two processes can communicate via a pfDispList to increase throughput. One *producer* process fills the pfDispList and a *consumer* process draws it by traversing it and sending appropriate commands to the graphics subsystem. Throughput is enhanced because the producer process off-loads expensive database processing from the time-critical consumer process which performs immediate-mode rendering. A pfDispList may be configured as a FIFO or ring buffer for concurrent producer/consumer configurations.

A pfDispList is different from a typical display list in that it captures only references to **libpr** objects and does not contain individual vertex or primitive commands; instead the **libpr** objects themselves contain and transfer these commands. Consequently a pfDispList can be quickly built and traversed. Additionally, a pfDispList is somewhat editable (it may be reused and appended

to) and can also contain references to function callbacks for user-defined rendering.

### 2.2.3 pfGeoState - Encapsulated Mode

The pfGeoState object provides the primary mechanism for specifying graphics state in an IRIS Performer application. It encapsulates all state modes and attributes managed by **libpr**. For example, a pfGeoState may be configured to enable lighting and reference a wood pfTexture and a shiny pfMaterial. Then after it is applied to the graphics subsystem, subsequent geometry will have the appearance of a finished wood surface. A pfGeoState can be attached to a pfGeoSet so that together they define geometry with a specific appearance.

The pfGeoState has some special features that either directly or indirectly enhance rendering performance:

**Locally Set vs. Globally Inherited State**

It is possible to specify every **libpr** mode and attribute of a pfGeoState, in which case the pfGeoState becomes a true graphics context that fully defines the appearance of geometry. However, a full graphics context is fairly expensive to evaluate and is almost never required. The key observation is that many state settings apply to most geometry in the database. For example: fog, lighting model, light sources and lighting enable flag are often applied to the entire scene since they are global effects by nature. Conversely, attributes such as materials and textures are likely to change often within a database. pfGeoStates support these two kinds of state by distinguishing between *globally inherited* and *locally set* state respectively. By globally inheriting state, a pfGeoState can reduce the amount of state it sets, i.e.- it becomes sparse. A sparse pfGeoState is more efficiently managed because fewer pieces of state need be examined. State is inherited simply by not specifying it. However, an important point discussed below is that state is *never* inherited between pfGeoStates. As an important result, pfGeoState rendering becomes order-independent.

**Order Independence**

In many immediate-mode graphics libraries, geometry inherits previously set graphics modes. As a result, rendering is order-dependent; graphics state and geometry must be organized in a specific order to produce the desired appearance. Order dependence is undesirable for high-level database manipulations such as view culling and sorting which frequently modify rendering order.

To ensure order independence, the application must either completely specify the graphics state of all geometry or it must be aware of the current graphics state and change state when necessary. The former solution seriously compromises performance if the graphics context is non-trivial and the latter is a bookkeeping nightmare.

pfGeoStates guarantee order independence for rendering as a direct consequence of not inheriting state from each other. When applied, a pfGeoState implicitly saves and restores state so that its state modifications are insulated from other pfGeoStates. Furthermore, if a global state element is modified by a pfGeoState, it will be restored for those pfGeoStates which inherit that element.

**Lazy Push/Pop**

If a pfGeoState explicitly pushed and popped all graphics state, significant performance would be lost due to unnecessary mode setting. Instead, a pfGeoState pushes only those global state elements that it needs to change and pops only those global state elements that it needs to inherit and that were changed by a previously-applied pfGeoState. Lazy popping eliminates useless mode changes since a mode is not restored if a pfGeoState is going to change it anyway.

## 2.3 Multiprocessing Support

The **libpr** library is designed to fully support, but not require, a multiprocessing environment. To this end, **libpr** provides mechanisms for creating and maintaining shared data.

### 2.3.1 Shared Memory

**libpr** provides mechanisms for sharing memory between related (forked from the same image) and unrelated processes. Allocations are reference counted to support operations such as deletion in a multiprocessed environment (See Section 3.2.3).

### 2.3.2 pfMultibuffer - Multibuffered Arrays

When a process needs to modify a piece of data for consumption by other processes, data must be passed or multiple copies (buffers) must be maintained. To facilitate this, **libpr** provides multiprocessing constructs such as queues and multibuffered memory. The pfMultibuffer object provides data synchronization and data exclusion for multi-stage software pipelines by managing multiple copies of a single data array. pfMultibuffer is particularly useful for dynamic and morphing geometry. A global index for each process indicates the currently active pfMultibuffer buffer, e.g., process A may be working on buffer0 while process B is simultaneously working on buffer2. By changing the global index, processes can "pass" work to each other, simulating a processing pipeline. Since buffers are recycled rather than copied, the mechanism is efficient regardless of the amount of data which changes and independent of the number of consuming processes. When the contents of a pfMultibuffer stop changing, the most recent version is copied into each buffered instance so the application does not need to write every pfMultibuffer every frame.

## 2.4 Database Intersection

Most applications require intersection testing for purposes such as picking and collision detection. Since the target of these tests is often the visual data already represented in pfGeoSets, **libpr** provides the ability to intersect line segments against the polygons inside a pfGeoSet, thereby avoiding expensive duplication of the database. We chose line segments as the first primitive to implement because the tests are fast and they provide the most natural expression of common queries such as picking, line-of-sight visibility, and terrain following. Many simple collision detection mechanisms can be implemented by intersecting a set of line segments that describe the swept volume of a moving object with the database. The racing car simulator shown in Figure 15 uses two segments for following the track height and four segments for detecting collisions with walls and other cars. Several line segments can be grouped into a single intersection request to reduce processing overhead. Performance may be further improved by specifying an optional bounding cylinder which encompasses all line segments and by caching plane equations for static pfGeoSets.

pfSegsIsectGSet() returns the nearest or farthest intersection along each line segment. Applications can use a *discriminator callback* to examine each intersection individually during traversal of the geometry. Discriminator callbacks can direct the intersection traversal and/or modify the intersecting line segments for fine-grained intersection control. Intersection information available to the application includes the actual triangle within the hit pfGeoSet, the intersection position and geometric normal.

## 3 libpf - Adds Database Hierarchy and Automated Multiprocessing to libpr

Representing a visual database involves more than just geometry and its associated graphics state. A higher-level library, **libpf**, built on top of **libpr** provides a hierarchical scene graph of nodes which organizes **libpr** geometry for improved modeling and processing

efficiency.

IRIS Performer accomplishes most database processing through *traversals* of the scene graph hierarchy. Much of **libpf**'s programming interface handles traversal configuration and control. Typically, an application updates scene graph and viewing parameters for a frame and then activates one or more processing traversals. For improved performance on multiprocessor systems, **libpf** can automatically execute these traversals in parallel with little extra programming burden on the application.

## 3.1 Database

A *scene graph* consists of *nodes* connected in a directed, acyclic fashion. Geometry lies at the leaves of the scene graph while internal nodes support notions such as grouping, transformation, selection, and sequencing as well as special operations such as level-of-detail switching, and morphing.

### 3.1.1 Class Hierarchy

While both **libpf** and **libpr** libraries are object-oriented, the flat class hierarchy of **libpr** allowed us to write it in C. However, the natural expression of scene graph nodes requires a deeper class hierarchy as shown in Figure 3. Consequently **libpf** is written in C++.

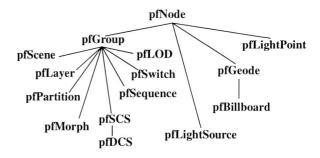

Figure 3.    Node Class Hierarchy

Nodes fall into three groups: abstract, internal and leaf. pfNode is the abstract base class for all nodes and is itself derived from an internal class called pfUpdatable which creates and maintains multiple copies of the node for multiprocessing as described in Section 3.2.

The internal node types are:

- pfGroup: references pfNodes as children
- pfScene: group that roots a scene graph.
- pfSwitch: group with none, one, or all children active
- pfSequence: sequences through its children for animation effects
- pfSCS: applies an unchangeable transformation (static coordinate system) to its children
- pfDCS: applies a changeable transformation to its children (dynamic coordinate system)
- pfLayer: renders coplanar geometry, e.g. pictures on a wall.
- pfLOD: selects one or more children based on distance to eye, viewport pixel size, and field-of-view (level-of-detail).
- pfMorph: interpolates geometry, color, etc. between models
- pfPartition: spatially partitions geometry beneath it into an efficient data structure

The leaf node types are:

- pfGeode: references zero or more pfGeoSets
- pfBillboard: rotates pfGeoSets to face the eyepoint

- pfLightPoint: draws visible, but non-illuminating points of light, e.g. stars, runway lights
- pfLightSource: non-visible but illuminating light source

In a scene graph, pfGeodes typically contain most of the visual geometry. Each pfGeode references a set of **libpr** pfGeoSets. Specialized geometry is contained within pfLightPoints and pfBillboards.

### 3.1.2  Node Hierarchy

**State Inheritance**

In addition to providing organizational and instancing capability, a hierarchy of nodes (scene graph) also allows state inheritance. Within a scene graph, inheritance is strictly top-down. The absence of any left-right or bottom-up inheritance allows arbitrary pruning of the scene graph during traversal. This also facilitates parallelization of a single traversal because subgraphs of the scene graph can be traversed independently. The primary type of inherited state is 3D transformations, although user callbacks may also affect inherited state during traversals. Graphics state such as that defined by the pfGeoState primitive is *not* inherited through the scene graph. Grouping the primary specification of graphics state with leaf geometry rather than with internal nodes of the scene graph greatly facilitates tasks such as sorting by graphics mode.

**Bounding Volume Hierarchy**

The node hierarchy also defines a hierarchy of bounding volumes which are used to accelerate intersection and culling. Each node has a bounding sphere which encloses the node as well as any children it may have. The toolkit automatically recalculates these bounding volumes when geometry or scene graph topology changes.

All node types except pfScene retain parent lists. This allows a change to a child in a scene graph, such as a bounding volume change, to be propagated to all its ancestors in the scene graph. To eliminate redundant updates, internal state is marked using dirty bits which are propagated to the root of the scene graph so the cleaning of dirty state can be deferred until required.

### 3.1.3  Traversals

After the application configures the scene graph and viewing parameters, three basic traversals may process the scene graph:

- Intersection traversal (ISECT) — processes intersection requests for collision detection and terrain following.
- Culling traversal (CULL) — rejects objects outside the viewing frustum, computes level-of-detail switches, sorts geometry by modes
- Drawing traversal (DRAW) — sends geometry and graphics commands to the graphics subsystem.

**TABLE 1.**   Traversal Characteristics

|  | ISECT | CULL | DRAW |
|---|---|---|---|
| Controller | pfSegSet | pfChannel | pfChannel |
| Global Activation | pfSegsIsectNode | pfCull | pfDraw |
| Modes | pfSegSet mode | pfChanTravMode | pfChanTravMode |
| Masks | pfNodeTravMask pfSegSet mask | pfNodeTravMask pfChanTravMask | pfNodeTravMask pfChanTravMask |
| Process Callback | pfIsectFunc | pfChanCullFunc | pfChanDrawFunc |
| Node Callbacks | pfNodeTravFuncs | pfNodeTravFuncs | pfNodeTravFuncs |

Table 1 lists the **libpf** routines which define major characteristics of these 3 traversals

The default CULL and DRAW traversals are completely automatic and are triggered by pfFrame() (See Section 3.2.2). However, pfFrame() first triggers a partial traversal of the scene graph which cleans the internal state of the scene graph. Portions of the scene graph may have already been cleaned if the application called a routine which attempted to read a piece of state which was dirty.

**Cull Traversal**

The CULL traversal precedes the DRAW and uses many techniques to improve rendering performance by reducing load on both the DRAW traversal and on the graphics subsystem:

- Culling to the viewing frustum (pfChannel)
- Computing state specific to a pfChannel, e.g. level-of-detail
- Sorting for performance and visual quality
- Generating a simple display list (pfDispList) for the DRAW traversal

For applications with an eye point in the midst of the database, culling to the viewing frustum can reject the majority of geometry, substantially reducing the amount of data sent to the graphics subsystem. Viewing state and frustum are encapsulated by the pfChannel object. IRIS Performer supports multiple views, e.g. stereo, through multiple pfChannels which may view the same or different pfScenes.

The CULL traversal uses the hierarchical bounding volumes provided by the scene graph (See Section 3.1.2). Bounding spheres are used within the scene graph because they are fast to update, transform and test against. Axially aligned bounding boxes are used for each pfGeoSet to provide tighter bounds around the actual geometry.

During the CULL traversal the bounding sphere of each node is transformed as necessary and compared against the viewing frustum. The action taken depends on the result of the bounding volume test as follows:

- Completely outside the frustum: traversal continues without traversing any of the node's children — the node is *pruned*
- Completely inside the frustum: continue down the scene graph with no further culling tests
- Partially or potentially intersecting: continue testing and traversing down the scene graph

The ultimate output of the CULL traversal is the geometry and graphics state information to be sent to the graphics hardware. When enabled to do so, the CULL traversal first generates sorted lists of the pfGeoSets to be rendered. Each frame, these lists are sorted by graphics mode to increase rendering performance by minimizing expensive graphics mode changes such as transformation and texture changes. It is here that the order-independence offered by pfGeoStates (see Section 2.2.3) is especially useful. Next, the CULL traversal converts these sorted lists into a single pfDispList which eventually contains the entire frame. Transparent geometry is placed into the display list last, after a limited depth sort which improves both pixel-fill performance and the visual quality of the transparency. In our experience, mode sorting can significantly improve rendering throughput, sometimes more than 50%.

**Draw Traversal**

For each visual channel, the DRAW traverses the display list generated by its associated CULL traversal and sends commands to the graphics subsystem. The DRAW traversal differs from the CULL and ISECT traversals in that it does not involve traversing the actual scene graph. We designed the pfDispList format to be very simple, so the DRAW traversal has very little work other than issuing graphics calls. The scene graph traversal overhead is absorbed by the CULL which increases rendering throughput when multiprocessing. When not multiprocessing, we can combine the CULL and DRAW traversals into a single traversal which both culls and issues graphics commands to avoid the small overhead of pfDispList generation.

## Traversal Control

Nodes have separate traversal masks for each traversal type to allow the application to "mask off" subgraphs of the scene for traversal. A node is only traversed if the logical AND of the traversal mask and the node mask is non-zero. This allows multiple databases to coexist in the same scene graph. For example, a scene graph may contain simpler geometry for collisions than for rendering in order to reduce intersection times. In this case, the DRAW traversal mask for the collision geometry and the ISECT traversal mask for the visual geometry would both be zero.

## Traversal Callbacks

Traversal callbacks provide even finer control on traversals. Each node can have its own pre- and post-traversal callbacks corresponding to each traversal type. These allow the application to prune or terminate the traversal at any time. The pre-CULL callback also allows the application to specify the result of the cull test for customized culling. The application may use the pre- and post-DRAW callbacks for custom rendering using **libpr** or the underlying graphics library, or to change and restore the graphics state for a portion of the scene graph. Figure 16 shows a real-time video effects program which uses DRAW callbacks to apply video texturing.

## Intersection Traversal

ISECT traversals differ from the CULL and DRAW in that they are not automatic but are directly invoked by the application. Currently, intersections are based entirely on sets of line segments. The pfSegSet structure embodies an intersection request as a group of line segments, an intersection mask, discriminator callback, and traversal mode. The traversal consists of testing the pfSegSet against the hierarchical bounding volumes in the scene graph. Intersection "hits" can be returned for pfNode bounding volumes, pfGeoSet bounding boxes and the actual geometry inside pfGeoSets. In addition to the traversal callbacks described above, intersections also provide a discriminator callback so that the application can examine each "hit" during traversal and accept or reject the intersection as well as terminate traversal. Because ISECT traversals usually require a pfSegSet to be tested against many triangles, the traversal transforms the pfSegSet into local object coordinates rather than transforming the bounding volumes and pfGeoSets into world coordinates. Since intersections do not modify the database, applications may invoke many intersection requests in parallel.

## Efficiency of Bounding Volume Hierarchy

The efficiency of both CULL and ISECT traversals is largely dependent on the depth and balance of the scene graph hierarchy. For example, a scene graph arranged as a balanced octree will cull more quickly than a flat scene graph. A scene graph with poor spatial hierarchy can be rearranged as a result of database profiling as described in Section 4.2 or be imposed with an improved secondary partitioning with pfPartition as described in Section 3.1.4.

### 3.1.4 Performance Optimizations

#### pfFlatten - Eliminating Transformations

Taking a single model and placing it under multiple static transformations (e.g. trees, houses) in the scene graph is convenient for modeling, but not always necessary at run time. During rendering, a transformation typically requires the hardware matrix stack to be pushed, the new transformation applied, the geometry drawn and then the matrix stack to be popped. For small models, these matrix operations can consume as much time or more than the actual rendering. pfFlatten() can improve graphics performance at a cost in memory usage by duplicating static, instanced geometry, applying the current static transform to the geometry, and setting all static coordinate systems (pfSCSes) to the identity matrix.

#### pfLOD - Level of Detail

Next to view frustum culling, the most important mechanism for reducing and managing the graphics load is level-of-detail (LOD) switching. When an object is only a few pixels large on the screen, it's wasteful to render a model with a high polygon count; rather, a coarser model with a lower level-of-detail should be rendered instead. The pfLOD node uses distance to the eye point, field-of-view, viewport pixel size, and graphics stress (see Section 3.3.2) to select among models of varying geometric complexity.

To make LOD changes as inconspicuous as possible, the pfLOD node can gradually fade between two models when switching. A drawback to fade LOD is that it requires rendering both models during the transition which temporarily increases the graphics load. An alternative LOD mechanism provided by the pfMorph node is described in Section 3.1.5 and can avoid this penalty by smoothly migrating vertices from one LOD to another.

#### pfSequence - Animation Sequences

Most high-quality animation requires moving vertices every frame. But for the highest performance with minimal CPU loading, most real-time applications make extensive use of precomputed animation sequences such as a sequence of textures to simulate a flickering torch. The pfSequence node supports this by automatically sequencing through its children. Each child is assigned a period of time, rather than a number of frames, during which it should be displayed so that the sequence is immune to frame rate variations. An example of pfSequence use is the dragon seen in the background of Figure 13.

#### pfBillboard - Billboarded Geometry

Rotating geometry, usually a single textured polygon, so that it always faces the eye is a trick from visual simulation used for axially and radially symmetric objects such as trees, clouds and special effects such as smoke or fire. Using a billboarded polygon instead of a full three-dimensional model reduces both geometry and pixel fill demands on the graphics pipe. A pfBillboard can be constrained to rotate about an axis or a point. The trees and lamp posts in Figure 14 are examples of pfBillboards.

#### pfPartition - Spatial Data Structure

IRIS Performer relies on the hierarchical bounding volumes of a scene graph to accelerate intersection and culling traversals. However, a user-constructed scene graph may exhibit poor spatial arrangement, obviating the benefits of hierarchical bounding volumes. In this case a specialized spatial data structure imposed on the default scene graph can provide much higher performance, particularly for intersections. The pfPartition group node analyzes geometry underneath it at database load time and partitions pfGeoSets into a 2D grid with multiple membership. During the intersection traversal, line segments in a pfSegSet are scan converted onto the grid to quickly determine which pfGeoSets need to be tested against. Other types of spatial data structures may be added in the future.

### 3.1.5 Special Features

#### pfMorph - Morphing

The pfMorph node provides a mechanism for interpolating geometry between many sources. A pfMorph takes a set of input arrays and weights and places the linear combination of the input arrays into an output array. Typically, the morphed arrays are the vertex, color, normal or texture coordinate arrays of a pfGeoSet in the scene graph beneath the pfMorph node. The two main applications are for continuously varying animated geometry such as the head of the creature in the foreground of Figure 13 and for continuous LOD switching [3]. The latter allows nearly invisible LOD transitions and can be more efficient than fade LOD if the cost of morphing is small compared to the cost of drawing two models during a fade transition.

### 3.1.6  Database Importation

IRIS Performer is strictly a runtime programming interface with an in-memory scene representation and currently has no database file format. An application calls toolkit routines to create and assemble a scene graph from various elements such as pfNodes, pfGeoSets and pfGeoStates. Because the task of creating pfGeoSets can be tedious, a utility library built on top of the toolkit provides routines (pfuBuilder) to simplify the construction and triangle meshing of pfGeoSets. Using these, database loaders have been written for various database formats including Autodesk DXF, Wavefront OBJ, Software Systems FLT, Coryphaeus DWB, and LightScape LSB. Database formats with a hierarchical scene graph and visual simulation extensions (e.g. level-of-detail, billboards) map directly to the toolkit scene graph. For those database formats without any hierarchy, the utility library provides spatial octree-based breakup of geometry (pfuBreakup) so that even large, monolithic models can be organized into a scene graph for efficient culling and intersecting.

## 3.2  Multiprocessing

A fundamental design criterion of the toolkit was to improve performance through multiprocessing while hiding the programming complexities that multiprocessing creates. This section describes our solutions to the following multiprocessing problems:

- How to partition work among multiple processes
- How to synchronize process execution
- How to manage data in a pipelined, multiprocessing environment

### 3.2.1  Pipelined Multiprocessing

IRIS Performer employs a *coarse-grained, pipelined,* multiprocessing scheme, i.e., a relatively small number of processes work concurrently on different stages of one or more processing pipelines. This configuration favors workstations with a relatively small number of processors (tens) over massively parallel systems (thousands). The partitioning of work into multiple processes is based on *processing stages.* A processing stage is a discrete section of a processing pipeline and encompasses specific types of work. Processing stages are tightly coupled to the scene graph traversals described in Section 3.1.3. The ISECT, CULL, and DRAW processing stages consist of zero or more intersection, culling, and drawing traversals respectively in addition to application-specific processing that is accessed through function callbacks. An additional processing stage, the APP, consists primarily of application code as well as database, viewpoint, and system modifications made through toolkit routines. Together, these four stages define two kinds of processing pipelines:

- rendering pipeline: APP → CULL → DRAW
- intersection pipeline: APP → ISECT

### pfPipe - Rendering Pipeline

The APP stage is the head of all pipelines and controls their execution. A rendering pipeline consists of the CULL and DRAW stages and is encapsulated by the pfPipe primitive. An application may use one or more parallel pfPipes that each renders zero or more viewpoints into a single graphics window. The multipipe feature is provided for machines with multiple graphics subsystems and includes support for time-multiplexing the output of multiple hardware renderers to a single display. The intersection pipeline consists of the ISECT stage. Only one intersection pipeline is supported.

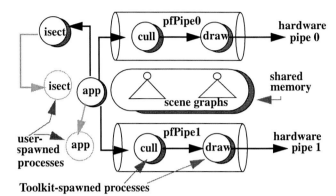

Figure 4.    Multiprocessing Multipipe Configuration

### Multiprocess Partitioning - pfMultiprocess

Multiprocessing in IRIS Performer is achieved by splitting the rendering and intersection pipelines at stage boundaries into multiple processes. For example, the APP and CULL stages may be combined into a single process while the DRAW stage is split into a separate process, resulting in a 2-process configuration which is suitable for a 2-processor machine. The application specifies this partitioning through pfMultiprocess(), allowing applications to choose a process partitioning based on the number of available CPUs. Figure 4 illustrates a processing configuration consisting of two rendering pipelines and an intersection pipeline where each stage has been split into a separate process. Figure 5 illustrates different multiprocess partitionings of the rendering pipeline that range from 1 to 3 processes.

### Multiprocessing With Shared vs. Non-shared Address Space

All pipelined processes are created by pfConfig() using the fork() mechanism. We chose fork() over mechanisms which allow a fully shared virtual address space so we could selectively share memory and support multiple graphics pipes, since not all immediate-mode graphics libraries allow multiple rendering contexts within a single virtual address space. Synchronization for all processes created by pfConfig() is handled internally.

### Additional Multiprocessing

Additional multiprocessing is easily acquired if the application itself creates extra processes. The ISECT and APP stages particularly lend themselves to this kind of multiprocessing. For example, multiple ISECT processes may concurrently execute calls to pfSegsIsectNode() which intersects a set of line segments with a scene graph (see Section 3.1.3). However, synchronization for these processes is the responsibility of the application. The stippled circles in Figure 4 depict these user-spawned processes.

### 3.2.2  Process Synchronization

*Process synchronization* defines the execution order of multiple processes. It is responsible for enforcing periods of mutual exclusion between processes and for ensuring concurrent execution of processes. Most process synchronization in the toolkit is achieved through well-known mechanisms such as semaphores and locks.

### Throughput vs. Latency

IRIS Performer enforces pipelined synchronization of processes created by pfConfig(). Pipelined multiprocessing trades increased throughput for increased latency. *Rendering latency* is defined as the time elapsed from viewpoint specification until the display is completed for that viewpoint. *Rendering throughput* is defined as the amount of geometry processed in unit time. The size of the throughput vs. latency trade-off is dictated by the number of processes in the pipeline (its *depth*) and increases with process count. Pipeline depth is configurable and can range from 1 to 3. For example, a configuration combining the APP and CULL into a single process and separating the DRAW will generate a rendering pipeline whose depth is 2. If all pipeline stages are well-utilized, performance can be increased over the single-processed case by a factor equal to the pipeline depth.

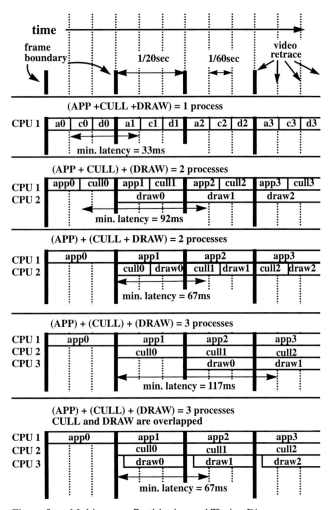

Figure 5.    Multiprocess Partitioning and Timing Diagram

Figure 5 illustrates timing diagrams for different multiprocess configurations ranging from 1 to 3 processes that are running at 20Hz. Boxes represent the execution time of individual stages and each row of boxes corresponds to a single process. Thus, multiple rows of timing boxes illustrate parallel execution of pipeline stages. The text inside the boxes specify the stage or stages that the process handles while the numbers indicate the frame that the process is currently working on. Notice how the amount of time available to each stage (throughput) increases as the number of processes (pipeline depth) increases.

### Frame Control

The toolkit typically synchronizes the application to a user-specified frame rate, e.g. 30Hz. This frame rate defines a series of frame boundaries that demarcate the beginning and ending of a frame. The APP stage is responsible for synchronizing to the specified frame rate and for triggering all processing pipelines once per

frame by calling pfSync() and pfFrame() respectively.

pfSync() suspends the calling process until the next frame boundary and is discussed in more detail in Section 3.3.1. pfFrame() indicates that all rendering and intersection pipelines should begin processing a new frame. If a pipeline stage is not ready to begin processing a new frame because the processing time for the previous frame exceeded the allotted frame time, the stage has *frame-extended*. In this event, pfFrame() does not block but returns control to the application. If the APP process frame-extends, then pfFrame() is not called often enough and the update rate drops even if the rendering pipeline can keep up. For this reason, application processing *must* be kept to within a frame time.

### Improving Latency

Certain applications like "man-in-the-loop" flight simulation and virtual reality applications utilizing a head-tracked display require very low latencies [14]. The latencies listed in Figure 5 are timed from the end of the APP processing until video scanout of the last pixel. To ensure this minimal latency even in cases when the APP takes less than its full allotment of time, the toolkit allows latency-critical updates such as the viewpoint to be made just before kicking off the CULL traversal with pfFrame(). Figure 6 depicts a close-up view of how pfSync() and pfFrame() work together to synchronize process execution. Latency-critical updates are made in the shaded portions of the APP processing time and may reduce throughput by delaying the triggering of the processing pipelines.

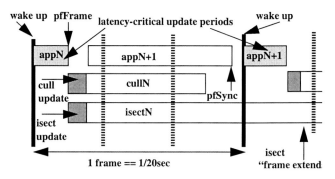

Figure 6.    pfSync and pfFrame

The following pseudo-code fragment illustrates the use of pfSync() and pfFrame() in a typical simulation loop:

```
while(!Done)
{
    updateSim();     /* Make non-latency-critical updates */
    pfSync();        /* Sleep until next frame boundary */
    updateView();    /* Read input devices and update eyepoint */
    pfFrame();       /* Trigger new frame */
}
```

A special multiprocessing mode illustrated by the last timing diagram of Figure 5 eliminates an entire frame of latency by overlapping the CULL and DRAW processes that are working on the same frame. The two processes communicate via a FIFO which stalls a process on empty and full conditions. Although the DRAW has to wait for the CULL to begin filling the FIFO and will stall if it is faster than the CULL, in practice neither of these drawbacks are significant. In this overlapped case, latency is reduced to a single frame, generally the lowest possible. When CULL and DRAW are not overlapped, latency can still be reduced to a single frame by culling to a slightly larger viewing volume and sampling a new viewing position just before drawing.

A lower latency alternative to pipelined multiprocessing would be a single, multithreaded scene graph traversal. We chose against this method due to the *much* higher complexity and overhead arising from the necessary fine-grained synchronization. Also, the threads would have to be single-threaded when the application makes random access modifications to the database and when rendering, if the graphics pipeline does not allow multiple writers.

**Pipeline Bottlenecks**

Ideally, each process in the pipeline takes exactly one frame time to complete its work. This situation indicates a balanced pipeline that is getting maximum utilization of its processors and is the one depicted in Figure 5. An out-of-balance situation arises when a particular process takes longer than all other processes in the pipeline and becomes a bottleneck. In most graphics intensive applications, the process handling the DRAW stage is the bottleneck. In this case, draw times can be reduced through the stress management techniques described in Section 3.3.2. If the bottleneck is due to the CULL stage, times can be reduced by disabling one or more culling modes. Bottlenecks due to the APP stage are largely the responsibility of the application.

**Process Callbacks**

By default, IRIS Performer performs all rendering processing when triggered by pfFrame(); culling and drawing functions are carried out in "black box" fashion. *Process callbacks* provide the user with the ability to execute custom code both before and after default processing, and to execute the code in the appropriate process when multiprocessing.

Process callbacks are provided for the ISECT, CULL, and DRAW stages. Default processing for these stages is triggered by pfSegsIsectNode, pfCull, and pfDraw respectively. If a callback is specified, default processing is disabled and must be explicitly triggered by the callback. This arrangement allows the user to "wrap" default processing with custom code, allowing save/restore, before/after, and multipass rendering methods which use techniques such as projective textures [11]. Figure 12 is from an application which uses multipass renderings with projective textures to simulate a spotlight with real-time shadows. In practice, the DRAW callback is often used for 2D graphics, textual annotations and specialized rendering that requires the full flexibility of the underlying graphics library. A typical DRAW callback is illustrated below:

```
void
drawCallback(pfChannel *chan, void *data)
{
    clearFrameBuffer();
    pfDraw();
    drawSpecialStuff();
}
```

**3.2.3 Data Management**

Three problems plague data management in a pipelined multiprocessing environment:

1) Data visibility. Processes need to share data.
2) Data exclusion. A process must not modify data while other processes are simultaneously reading and/or writing it.
3) Data synchronization. Data modifications must be propagated down processing pipelines in a "frame-accurate" fashion.

**1)** is handled by the shared memory mechanisms described in Section 2.3.1. **2)** can be handled with hardware spin locks but fine-grain locking becomes expensive and as we shall see, the data exclusion problem is solved by the solution to **3)**. First, let us examine the data synchronization problem more closely.

**Data Synchronization**

In the toolkit's multiprocessing pipelines, multiple processes work on different frames at the same time. For example, the APP process works on frame 33 while the DRAW is on frame 31. Suppose a single matrix in shared memory represents the position of a database model. If the APP process updates this matrix while the DRAW process is sending it to the graphics hardware, the matrix might be partially updated when sent to the graphics, resulting in an unin-

tended combination of two matrices. Alternatively, the model might be drawn at the position it should have at frame 33, rather than frame 31. In this case we say that the matrix update is not *frame-accurate* since it does not affect the displayed model at the appropriate time.

Note that hardware pipelines exemplified by graphics subsystems such as RealityEngine[1] solve the data synchronization problem by copying the entire database down through the pipeline. While wide, fast data paths make this practical for hardware pipelines, software pipelines do not have this luxury and require another approach.

**Multibuffering**

We solve the problem of data exclusion and data synchronization with a technique called *multibuffering*. Multibuffering employs multiple copies of data structures known as pfUpdatables (or updatables) that are logically partitioned into buffers known as pfBuffers. All **libpf** objects including pfNodes are pfUpdatables so that each pfBuffer contains a full copy of the scene graph. A pfBuffer is associated with a single process and that process may access only those pfUpdatables in its pfBuffer, thereby solving the data exclusion problem.

Modifications made to pfUpdatables by the APP process are recorded in an update list. Each frame these updates are applied to all downstream pfUpdatables so the updates propagate down all pipelines in frame-accurate fashion, thereby solving the data synchronization problem. Propagating only database modifications significantly reduces the amount of data that flows through the processing pipelines.

This update-based multibuffering mechanism is most useful when making sparse modifications to largely static data structures. This is in contrast to the pointer-switching type of multibuffering provided by pfMultibuffer (see Section 2.3.2) which is most suitable for data structures with large changes, such as vertex arrays used in morphing. In this case, swapping pointers is much more efficient than copying large amounts of data.

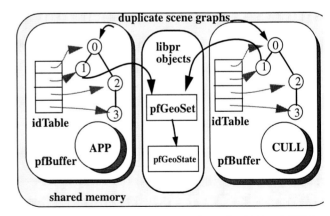

Figure 7.    Multibuffering of a Scene Graph for APP and CULL

**pfBuffer and pfUpdatable**

In addition to forking multiple processes, pfConfig() creates and associates a pfBuffer with each process (except the DRAW as is discussed below). Each pfBuffer has an id table which associates the address of a pfUpdatable with its id. When created, a pfUpdatable is assigned a unique integer id and is added to the id table of the creating process' pfBuffer. Then during the period when updates are exchanged, corresponding pfUpdatables are created in all downstream pfBuffers. Figure 7 depicts the referencing of two copies of the scene graph (one each for the APP and CULL processes) through the pfBuffer's idTable.

## Selective Multibuffering

The net result is that N "images" of each pfUpdatable are created: one for each pfBuffer in use. At first glance this may seem to be an extravagant use of memory. However, only pfUpdatables are multibuffered and only **libpf** objects are pfUpdatables, e.g. pfNodes, pfChannels. Thus all **libpr** primitives such as pfGeoSets and pfGeoStates are *not* multibuffered and do not suffer the memory penalty that multibuffering introduces. This design decision relies on the following assumptions:

- Geometric primitives like pfGeoSets and pfGeoStates represent the vast majority of database memory. Thus, duplicating only the scene graph skeleton does not drastically increase memory usage.

- Most geometry is static and does not require the frame-accurate behavior provided by multibuffering. (In Figure 7 the pfUpdatable numbered "1" is a pfGeode that references a non-multibuffered pfGeoSet.)

Although the first assumption has proven reasonable in most circumstances, we are currently exploring a "copy-on-write" extension to the multibuffering mechanism which would create extra copies only when an updatable is modified. The second assumption however, is restrictive in applications which use sophisticated morphing techniques like continuous terrain level-of-detail that require vertex-level manipulations of geometry [3]. Without multibuffering, the APP process may modify geometry at the same time the DRAW is sending the geometry to the graphics subsystem, resulting in cracks between adjacent polygons. To solve this problem we have offered a solution with the pfMultibuffer primitive described in Section 2.3.2.

## Data Exclusion Revisited

In addition to frame-accurate behavior, multibuffering provides data exclusion which is essential to robust multiprocessing. Since each process is guaranteed exclusive access to updatables in its pfBuffer, it need not worry for example, that the APP process has removed a node from the scene graph. Otherwise, the process might collide with the modification and dereference a bad pointer with disastrous results.

## Update List

An *update* consists of an updatable id and another integer id which defines what has changed. For example an update of [31, 12] might mean "update the transform of the pfDCS whose id is 31." Recording updates by reference has significant advantages over recording updates by value, which in the above example would mean copying the transformation matrix into the update list:

- Updates are homogeneous, thereby simplifying code and data structures

- Updates are small, resulting in quick recording and memory conservation

- Updates have a unique key which allow them to be efficiently managed by a hash table. Specifically, duplicate updates are discarded, keeping the update list from growing without bound.

The primary disadvantage of this update form is that it requires blocking the upstream process during the update period described below.

In order to provide frame-accurate behavior, updates must propagate in an orderly fashion down all processing pipelines. This propagation period occurs during pfFrame(). At this point all processes downstream of the APP (all CULL and ISECT processes) traverse the update list generated by the APP process and update their pfUpdatables. Each update consists of copying a portion of a pfUpdatable in the upstream pfBuffer into the corresponding pfUpdatable in the downstream pfBuffer. For the pfDCS example mentioned above, we would copy only the transformation matrix

between pfDCS copies. At the end of the update period, all pfUpdatables in the downstream pfBuffer are identical to those in the upstream pfBuffer.

During the update period, the upstream process (the APP) must be blocked so that it cannot modify updatables in its buffer and possibly corrupt the update data exchange; we must ensure data exclusion. This update period is illustrated in Figure 6 as the shaded portions of the CULL and ISECT processes.

Figure 8 illustrates an APP feeding two pipelines: one intersection and one rendering pipeline. In this case there are three pfBuffers - one each for the APP, ISECT, and CULL processes.

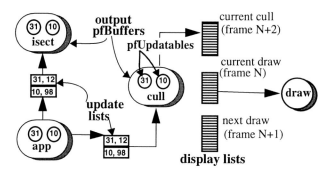

Figure 8. Interprocess Communication for Processing Pipelines Using Update Lists and Display Lists

## Pipeline Frame Extension

The APP pfBuffer maintains an update list for each processing pipeline and appends all updates to all update lists. If a downstream pipeline is not ready to accept the update list when pfFrame() is called because it has frame-extended, the APP does not block but continues with the next frame. In this case, the update list corresponding to the frame-extended pipeline is not reset so that further updates are appended to the list and previous updates are not lost; they will be consumed later when the pipeline is ready. If the APP is feeding multiple pipelines, all ready pipelines update themselves in parallel.

## Cull/Draw Communication

Note however that the DRAW process in Figure 8 does not have a pfBuffer and uses a different communication mechanism with the upstream CULL process. This is not precluded by the pfBuffer/ pfUpdatable mechanism but was chosen to reduce memory requirements and performance degradation. When the CULL and DRAW stages are in separate processes, the CULL process traverses the scene graph and renders visible geometry into a **libpr** display list (See pfDispList in Section 2.2.2). This is very important because it off-loads scene graph traversal overhead from the time-critical DRAW process. However, this means that there is no need for a scene graph in the DRAW process. Also, maintaining a pfBuffer in the DRAW process would require an update period that would steal precious drawing time.

As illustrated in Figure 8, the CULL and DRAW communicate via three display lists. In a perfectly balanced pipeline, only two display lists would be required — the classic double-buffered configuration. However, both CULL and DRAW processes may frame-extend. As a result, a third display list is required to keep the non-extending process from waiting until the extending process is finished with its display list.

## pfDelete - Object Deletion

Deletion of a hierarchical scene or subgraph that supports instancing can be tricky. Care must be taken to ensure that an object's memory is not freed until all references to it are removed. To do otherwise would open the possibility of corrupted memory and ungraceful program cessation. IRIS Performer employs a reference counting scheme to avoid such results.

Whenever an "attachment" is made between two objects, the reference count of the "attachee" is incremented by one. Reference count modifications are locked to ensure data exclusion between multiple processes. pfDelete() deletes objects whose reference counts are non-positive and follows all reference chains, deleting objects until it reaches one whose reference count is greater than zero. The reference count of a pfNode is simply the number of its parents. User-allocated memory such as the attribute arrays of pfGeoSets (See Section 2.1) are reference-counted if the memory is allocated by **libpr** routines since they maintain internal reference counts.

### Multiprocessed Delete

Unfortunately, multiprocessing adds another dimension to reference counting. Non-multibuffered objects such as pfGeoSets are "referenced" by the processes which are accessing them. For example, the ISECT and DRAW processes may be concurrently intersecting with, and rendering a given pfGeoSet. Consequently, a simple reference counting scheme is inadequate.

One possibility would be for processes to reference/dereference objects as they need them. This is unacceptable from a performance standpoint since locks are not free and the number of objects needing locking is large. IRIS Performer's solution takes advantage of its pipelined configuration. An object is not immediately deleted; rather, a frame-stamped deletion request is added to a special list. Meanwhile, the back ends of all pipelines (ISECT and DRAW processes) record the frame count of their most-recently-completed frame. Then when pfFrame() is called, each deletion request on the list is examined. If its frame stamp is less than the frame counts of all pipelines, the deletion request is safely carried out since all pipelines have flushed themselves of the object.

## 3.3 Achieving Real-Time

### 3.3.1 Achieving Real-time Synchronization

Real-time behavior is often required of graphics applications, both for human and hardware (sensor) perception. Real-time in this context implies more than a reasonable frame rate. Equally important is a *fixed frame rate* which ensures a solid, consistent update rate without glitches or hiccups. In fact, many visual simulation applications sacrifice peak frame rates for a fixed frame rate.

The first step in achieving real-time behavior is accessing a timer that runs at wall-clock time, i.e., it runs at the same rate as the clock on your office wall. Since the graphics update rate is restricted to integral fractions of the video refresh rate, the video clock provides a natural real-time clock for synchronizing a graphics application.

### pfVClockSync - Synchronizing to Video Retrace

The kernel maintains a video retrace counter and also provides a synchronizing feature that is accessed through the pfVClockSync() call. This routine takes two arguments, [*interval, offset*] that together specify the frame synchronization boundary. Put arithmetically, pfVClockSync() puts the calling process to sleep until the video retrace count modulo the *interval* equals the *offset*. For example, if pfVClockSync() is called with arguments of [3, 0] when the current video clock is 658, the process will sleep until the video clock is 660.

An application specifies its desired fixed frame rate and synchronizes the APP process to that rate by invoking pfSync() which calls pfVClockSync() to sleep until the next frame boundary. Note that pfSync() alone does not guarantee a fixed frame rate. First, the APP cannot take longer than a frame time because it would then synchronize to an integral multiple of the desired field rate such as 30Hz dropping to 15 Hz or even 10Hz. Second, the processing pipelines must be able to complete their work within a frame time as is discussed in more detail below.

### 3.3.2 Achieving A Fixed-Frame Rate

Once synchronization to wall-clock time is achieved, the next step in attaining real-time behavior is to ensure a fixed frame rate. Many things can compromise a fixed frame rate on a multiuser workstation:

1) Graphics context switching
2) Process context switching
3) Process frame extension (e.g. APP, CULL extensions)
4) Graphics pipeline frame extension (DRAW extension)

**1)** can be remedied by ensuring that only the application of interest is running: no clocks or performance meters allowed. **2)** may be solved by running the application with super-user privileges and using OS commands to isolate and restrict processors. **3)** is more difficult to solve and requires rearranging database hierarchies, disabling of modes, and further multiprocessing to unload the burdened process(es). **4)** is often the most prevalent enemy to a fixed frame rate and it is that which we address in this section.

Graphics pipelines have hard limits on the amount of geometry they can process in a given time. Ideally, the throughput of a graphics pipeline is always enough to render the desired amount of scene geometry in the desired amount of time. In this case a fixed frame rate is easily achieved. However, most scenes have varying geometric complexities due to varying scene density and/or moving models which may come into view. If a frame rate is chosen such that the view of highest complexity may be rendered within a frame time, then the expensive graphics hardware will be underutilized for less complex scenes. On the other hand, if a higher frame rate is chosen, complex scenes will take longer to render than the allowed frame time and distracting visual anomalies, technically referred to as "hiccups", will occur. Consequently, many applications choose a frame rate that can handle the average scene and rely on other mechanisms to artificially reduce more complex scenes so that they can be rendered within a frame time.

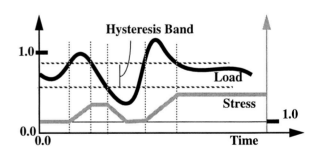

Figure 9.     Stress Feedback Filtering

*Stress management* is the technique used to reduce scene complexity that relies on the level-of-detail mechanism described in Section 3.1.4. When the system is in stress, LODs are artificially reduced; coarser than normal models are chosen, so that overall graphics load is reduced. Stress is based on *load*, the fraction of a frame time taken to render a frame, and increases as load exceeds a user-specified threshold. The load for frame N is used in conjunction with user-specified parameters to define the stress value for frame N+1, thus defining a feedback network. As discussed in [4], this method works reasonably well for relatively constant scene densities but suffers because the stress is always a frame late and can exhibit oscillatory behavior. As illustrated in Figure 9, a hysteresis band can reduce stress oscillations but a more sophisticated stress management technique such as that described in [4] has better characteristics.

### 3.3.3 Overload Management

While stress management seeks to fit DRAW processing into a frame time, *overload management* dictates what happens when stress management has failed and the DRAW exceeds a frame time — it has frame extended. The application may choose differing overload behavior by selecting the *phase* of the DRAW process. Phase dictates the type of synchronization used by the DRAW process: if the phase is *locked*, the DRAW process is guaranteed to begin only on a frame boundary. Thus if the DRAW takes just slightly longer than a frame time, the aggregate frame rate will drop in half. If the phase is *floating*, a frame-extended DRAW will start to draw again as soon as it can (at the next vertical retrace) and try to "catch up", relying on stress management to reduce scene complexity. In practice, floating phase is used more often than locked phase since it does not sacrifice an entire frame time if the DRAW takes just slightly longer than a frame. However, locked phase offers deterministic latencies and can produce a steadier frame rate.

## 4  Run-Time Profiling

Without proper profiling and diagnostic utilities, it is difficult to ascertain the performance of a given application. "Is it running as fast as it can go?" is the most pertinent question. To answer, the developer must be able to answer other questions concerning potential bottleneck areas:

- CPU processing, e.g., is the APP taking longer than the DRAW?
- CPU to graphics transfer, e.g., is the bus saturated or is the DRAW suffering from overhead due to small pfGeoSets?
- Geometry transform, e.g., are excessive mode changes thrashing the Geometry Engines? Are my triangle strips too short?
- Geometry fill, e.g., is the pixel depth complexity too high?

To further complicate matters, bottlenecks change and shift as the visual scene changes, making them moving targets for the tuner.

To aid application and database tuning, IRIS Performer provides extensive profiling information that is collected at run-time and may be graphically displayed for easy comprehension. Run-time collection provides a display of up-to-date information as you fly through the database, facilitating an interactive and time-saving approach to tuning. Figure 10 is the statistics display for the scene in Figure 14 and shows both process and database statistics measurements that are examined in the following sections.

### 4.1  Process Statistics

Due to the concurrent, time-dependent nature of multiprocessing, it is often difficult to understand the behavior of a multiprocessed application. IRIS Performer records the times spent by each processing stage and displays the results in a timing diagram which quickly exposes any bottlenecks. In Figure 10, the upper portion of the display defines a timing diagram analogous to those in Figure 5. Vertical lines indicate vertical retrace and frame boundaries. Horizontal lines indicate the processing times for different stages and their color indicates the stage's frame count.

#### Example Analysis

From Figure 10 we see that the application is configured as 4 processes, one each for ISECT, APP, CULL and DRAW, which all run in parallel. Additionally, the processing times for CULL and DRAW are roughly equivalent and occupy most of a frame time indicating that 30Hz is a reasonable frame rate and load balancing is good. (Note that the time required to draw the statistics display itself pushes the draw time over 1/30 sec.) However, the APP and

ISECT stages take little time so we could free a CPU by combining these two stages into a single process.

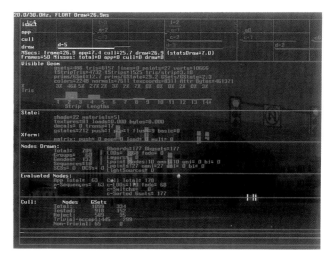

Figure 10.   Display of Process and Database Statistics

### 4.2  Database Statistics

Although the toolkit strives to achieve maximum performance with a given database, a significant amount of performance gain may lurk within the database itself. For example, a scene graph without hierarchy will suffer from poor intersection and culling performance, both of which rely on hierarchical bounding volumes to accelerate processing. Also, a pfGeoSet which contains few triangles will suffer from overhead in pfDrawGSet(). These problems and more can be easily inferred from the statistics display of Figure 10.

#### Example Analysis

The ratios of primitives to pfGeoState (12.7) and pfGeoSets to pfGeoState (2.3) are reasonably high, indicating that pfGeoSet and pfGeoState overhead is not likely a problem. However, the average number of triangles per strip is low at 3.1 which indicates that the hardware geometry processing stage may be a bottleneck. This fragmentation of the database is likely due to the large number of textures (81) since a strip cannot span multiple textures.

Figure 11.   Profiling Display Depicting Pixel Depth Complexity

Although Figure 10 reveals much about the database, it says nothing about the pixel fill bottleneck which is the most important one for the majority of full-screen applications. The toolkit provides a special mode for visualizing pixel *depth complexity*, the number of times each pixel is touched. Figure 11 is a false-color visualization of the depth complexity for the scene of Figure 14. Depth complexities of up to 7 are represented by colors of increasing brightness (some areas have complexities > 7 and wrap). Additionally, the total number of pixels rendered and the average depth complexity is displayed. All of these statistics are computed and displayed at a run-time, albeit at a reduced frame rate.

### 4.3  Future Work

Our design approach has been to focus on the performance and structure of the toolkit's rendering and multiprocessing core. Because of this, we believe the toolkit provides a good foundation for additional functionality.

**Database Paging**

Many applications use databases which are too large to fit in main RAM memory or even a 32-bit virtual address space so portions of the database must reside on disk. The avoidance of distracting pauses when loading from disk requires a quick-loading database format as well as run-time logic which anticipates the viewpoint so the toolkit can begin paging database regions before they come into view.

**Traversals**

While the current 3-process rendering pipeline (APP, CULL, DRAW) is adequate for most applications, some require extensive application and cull processing. The addition of an APP traversal would allow user callbacks to be invoked each frame to control object behavior or trigger activity outside the toolkit. And currently, each pipeline's CULL traversal is restricted to a single process. Implementing parallelized traversals for both APP and CULL, where multiple processes concurrently carry out the same traversal, would improve throughput for both. The strict top-down inheritance of state in the scene graph eases this task since multiple processes can traverse individual subgraphs without requiring state information from other subgraphs. However, load balancing issues and allowing APP processing to be conditional on the results of visibility and level-of-detail computations are problematic since these computations are currently made *after* APP processing.

**Collision Detection**

While intersecting with line segments is useful for terrain following and simple collisions, collisions between objects of substantially different sizes and more detailed interference checking can require very large numbers of segments for adequate spatial coverage. Graph-to-graph intersections of volumes, geometry, and line segments represented by nodes within the scene graph would greatly benefit applications such as MCAD.

## 5  Conclusions

In this paper, we have presented a toolkit with a novel architecture for building high performance, multiprocessed graphics applications. We have described how the toolkit extracts maximal performance from multiprocessor, immediate-mode graphics workstations primarily through:

- geometric data structures designed for efficient immediate-mode data transfer
- reduction of graphics mode changes
- pipelined multiprocessing for parallel scene graph traversal
- efficient host-based view frustum culling
- stress modified level-of-detail switching
- run-time database and process statistics for tuning

By emphasizing immediate-mode performance without caching, the toolkit lends itself to techniques such as character animation and morphing which require intensive vertex-level modifications.

In the course of writing the toolkit, we developed a number of useful techniques for efficient task and data synchronization in a pipelined, multiprocessing system including a configurable software pipeline with update-driven multibuffering.

Without these performance optimizations, expensive hardware can be substantially underutilized. Since the optimizations described in this paper are non-trivial to implement, providing this functionality in a layered toolkit makes it substantially easier for application and other toolkit developers to reap significant performance benefits.

## 6  Acknowledgments

We would like to thank both present and past IRIS Performers: Michael Jones, Sharon Fischler, Chris Tanner, Allan Schaffer, Rob Mace, Ben Garlick and especially Craig "Crusty" Phillips and George Kong for their contributions. We would also like to thank Wade Olsen for the video application in Figure 16, Computer Arts and Entertainment of Madrid for the race simulator in Figure 15, Angel Studios and GreyStone Technology for Figure 13, and Paul Mlyniec of Software Systems for Figure 17.

## 7  References

1. Akeley, Kurt. Reality Engine Graphics. Proceedings of SIGGRAPH 93 (Anaheim, California, August 1-6, 1993). In *Computer Graphics*, Annual Conference Series, 1993, 109-116.

2. Craig, Edgar Phillip. Micropoly 2 vs. Stargazer: the Search for an Exoteric Image Generator. *Proceedings of the 1996 Image VIII Conference,* Dallas, Texas, 26-29 June, 1996. 370-371.

3. Ferguson, Robert, et al. Continuous Terrain Level of Detail for Visual Simulation. In *Proceedings of the 1990 Image V Conference, Phoenix, Arizona, 19-22 June, 1990*, 144-151.

4. Funkhouser, Thomas and Carlo Sequin. Adaptive Display Algorithms for Interactive Frame Rates During Visualization of Complex Virtual Environments. Proceedings of SIGGRAPH 93 (Anaheim, California, August 1-6, 1993). In *Computer Graphics*, Annual Conference Series, 1993, 247-254.

5. Grimsdale, Charles, dVS - Distributed Virtual Environment System. In *Proceedings of Computer Graphics '91 Conference*, London, 1991.

6. Hewlett-Packard Company, *Starbase Graphics Techniques and Display List Programmer's Guide,* Hewlett-Packard, Fort Collins, Colorado, 1991.

7. Kaplan, Michael. The design of the Doré graphics system, *Advances in Object-Oriented Graphics I, Konigswinter, Germany, 6-8 June 1990.* Springer-Verlag, 1991. 177-198.

8. Kawalsky, Roy, *The Science of Virtual Reality and Virtual Environments,* Addison-Wesley, Wokingham, England, 1993.

9. Neider, Jackie, Tom Davis and Mason Woo, *OpenGL Programming Guide*, Addison-Wesley, Reading, Mass, 1993.

10. Paradigm Simulation Inc., *VisionWorks Programming Guide*, Paradigm Simulation, Dallas, Texas, 1992.

11. Segal, Mark, et al. Fast Shadows and Lighting Effects Using Texture Mapping, Proceedings of SIGGRAPH '92 (Chicago, Illinois, July 26-31, 1992). In *Computer Graphics* 26,2 (July 1992, 249-252.

12. Strauss, Paul and Rikk Carey, *An Object-Oriented 3D Graphics Toolkit*, Proceedings of SIGGRAPH 93 (Anaheim, California, August 1-6, 1993). In *Computer Graphics*, Annual Conference Series, 1993, 341-349.

13. van Dam, Andries, et al., PHIGS+ Functional Description Revision 3.0, *Computer Graphics* 22, 3 (July 1988), 124-218.

14. Ward, Mark, et al. A Demonstrated Optical Tracker with Scalable Work Area for Head-Mounted Display Systems, Proceedings of 1992 Symposium on Interactive 3D Graphics (Cambridge, Massachusetts, March 29 - April 1, 1992), 43-52.

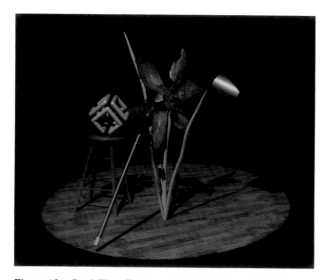

Figure 12.   Real-Time Shadows Using Multipass Rendering

Figure 15.   Racing Simulator with Collision Detection

Figure 13.   Precomputed and Dynamic Geometry Animations

Figure 16.   Video Special Effects Using Draw Callbacks

Figure 14.   Visual Simulation Scene

Figure 17.   Fly Through with Virtual Reality Interface

# Planning Motions with Intentions

Yoshihito Koga[†], Koichi Kondo[‡], James Kuffner[†] and Jean-Claude Latombe[†]

[†] Robotics Laboratory, Department of Computer Science, Stanford University
Stanford, CA 94305, USA

[‡] R & D Center, Toshiba Corporation, 4-1 Ukishima-cho, Kawasaki, 210, Japan

## Abstract

We apply manipulation planning to computer animation. A new path planner is presented that automatically computes the collision-free trajectories for several cooperating arms to manipulate a movable object between two configurations. This implemented planner is capable of dealing with complicated tasks where regrasping is involved. In addition, we present a new inverse kinematics algorithm for the human arms. This algorithm is utilized by the planner for the generation of *realistic* human arm motions as they manipulate objects. We view our system as a tool for facilitating the production of animation.

**Keywords:** Task-level graphic animation, automatic manipulation planning, Human arm kinematics.

## 1   Introduction

Mundane details keep us from vigorously attacking bigger ideas. This is the motivation for achieving task-level animation. From task-level descriptions, the animation of figures in a scene can be automatically computed by an appropriate motion planner. The animator can thereby concentrate on creating imaginative graphics, rather than labouring over the chore of moving these figures in a realistic and collision-free manner. In this paper we present

yotto@flamingo.stanford.edu
kondo2@mel.uki.rdc.toshiba.co.jp
kuffner@flamingo.stanford.edu
latombe@flamingo.stanford.edu

our efforts towards realizing a subset of this ultimate goal - the automatic generation of human and robot arm motions to complete manipulation tasks.

Why study manipulation with arms? Human figures often play an integral role in computer animation. Consequently, there are arm motions and more specifically manipulation motions to animate. Another major application is in ergonomics. Since most products are utilized, assembled, maintained, and repaired by humans, and require for most cases some action by the human arms, by simulating and viewing these arm motions through computer graphics, one can evaluate the design of the product in terms of its usability. This will reduce the number of mock-up models needed to come up with the final design. Again, this would allow the designer more time towards creating high-quality products.

Unlike the motion of *passive* systems like falling objects or bouncing balls, the motion of human and robot arms for the purpose of manipulation are "motions with intentions". The arms move not through some predictable trajectory due to the laws of physics (as is the case with a falling object [2, 9]) but with the *intention* of completing some task. A planner is needed to determine how the arms must move to complete the task at hand. Although there has been previous work on simulating walking and lifting motions, this is the first attempt to automatically generate complex manipulation motions.

Our problem is thus to find a collision-free path for the arms to grasp and then carry some specified movable object from its initial location to a desired goal location. This problem is known as the multi-arm manipulation planning problem [12, 7]. A crucial difference, relative to more classical path planning, is that we must *account for the ability of the arms to change their grasp of the object*. Indeed, for some tasks the arms may need to ungrasp the object and regrasp it in a new manner to successfully complete the motion.

We present a new planner that solves this multi-

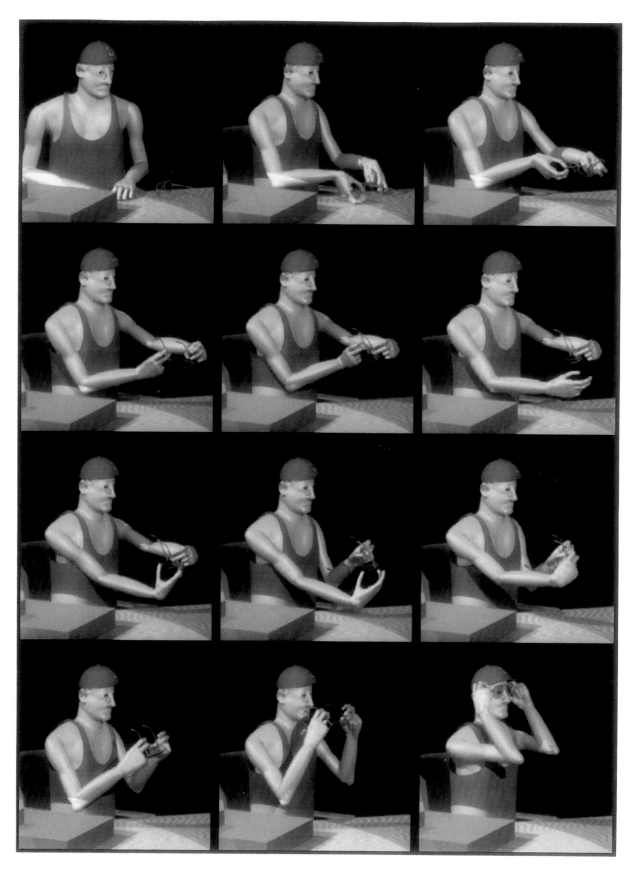

Figure 1. Planned path for manipulating eye glasses.

arm manipulation problem [12]. The planner needs as input the geometry of the environment, the initial and goal configurations of the movable object and arms, a set of potential grasps of the movable object, and the *inverse kinematics of the arms*. With appropriate book-keeping, the animator would simply specify the goal configuration of the movable object (a task-level description) to generate the desired animation.

The planning approach is flexible in regards to the arm types that can be considered. The only restriction is that the arms must have an inverse kinematics algorithm. Thus, in addition to the planner, we present a new inverse kinematics algorithm for the human arms based on results from neurophysiology. This algorithm resolves the redundancy of the human arms by utilizing a sensorimotor transformation model [29, 30]. The result is the automatic animation of human arm manipulation tasks.

In addition to the motion planning aspect, we address the issue of producing natural motions when human figures are animated. By applying results from neurophysiology to various parts of the planner, for instance the inverse kinematics, we hope to achieve a good approximation of naturalness. We believe that the geometry of the motions produced by the planner are in fact quite natural.[1]

Fig. 1 is a series of snapshots along a manipulation path computed by our planner. Once the necessary models of the environment are read by the planner, the input from the animator is simply the goal location for the eye glasses, in this case getting placed on the head. Note, the planner found automatically that the arms must ungrasp and regrasp the glasses in order to complete the task.

Section 2 relates our efforts to previous work. Section 3 describes the details of our motion planner. Section 4 is the derivation of the human arm inverse kinematics. Section 5 is a discussion of how our system takes natural human arm motion into consideration. Finally, Section 6 presents results obtained with the planner.

# 2   Related Work

Planning *motions with intentions* for robot and human arm manipulation is related to several different areas of research. We roughly classify this related work into three categories, manipulation planning, animation of human figures, and neurophysiology.

---

[1] This paper does not consider the velocity distribution along the planned motions.

**Manipulation Planning:** The use of path planning to automatically generate graphic animation was already suggested in [18]. Research strictly addressing manipulation planning is fairly recent. The first paper to tackle this problem is by Wilfong [34]. It considers a single-body robot translating in a 2D workspace with multiple movable objects. The robot, the movable objects and obstacles are modelled as convex polygons. In order for the movable objects to reach their specified goal the robot must "grasp" and carry them there. Wilfong shows that planning a manipulation path to bring the movable objects to their specified goal locations is PSPACE-hard. When there is a single movable object, he proposes a complete algorithm that runs in $O(n^3 \log^2 n)$ time, where $n$ is the total number of vertices of all the objects in the environment. Laumond and Alami [15] propose an $O(n^4)$ algorithm to solve a similar problem where the robot and the movable object are both discs and the obstacles are polygonal.

Our work differs from this previous research in several ways. Rather than dealing with a single robot, we consider the case of multiple human and robot arms manipulating objects in a 3D workspace. In addition, whereas the previous work is more theoretical in nature, our focus is more on developing an effective approach to solving manipulation tasks of a complexity comparable to those encountered in everyday situations (e.g. picking and placing objects on a table).

Regrasping is a vital component in manipulation tasks. Tournassoud, Lozano-Pérez, and Mazer [32] specifically address this problem. They describe a method for planning a sequence of regrasp operations by a single arm to change an initial grasp into a goal grasp. At every regrasp, the object is temporarily placed on a horizontal table in a stable position selected by the planner. We too need to plan regrasp operations. However, the only regrasping motions we consider avoid contact between the object and the environment; they necessarily involve multiple arms (e.g. both human arms).

Grasp planning is potentially an important component of manipulation planning. In our planner, grasps are only selected from a finite predefined set. An improvement for the future will be to include the automatic computation of grasps. A quite substantial amount of research has been done on this topic. See [22] for a commented list of bibliographical references.

**Animation of Human Figures:** Human gaits have been successfully simulated. For example, Bruderlin and Calvert [5] have proposed a hybrid approach to the animation of human locomotion which combines goal-directed and dynamic motion control. McKenna and Zeltzer [21] have successfully simulated the gait of a virtual insect by combining forward dynamic simulation and a biologically-based motion coordination mechanism. Control algorithms have been successfully applied to the animation of dynamic legged locomotion [25]. While dynamic models and the use of motor coordination models have been successfully applied to a wide range of walking motions, such a strategy has yet to be discovered to encompass human arm motions.

For simulating the motion of human arms, there exist methods for specific tasks. For example, Lee et al. [17] have focused on the simulation of arm motions for lifting based on human muscle models. Their method considers such factors as comfort level, perceived exertion, and strength. Our approach is to simulate natural arm motions from the point of view of kinematics, that is we make no consideration of dynamics and muscle models. We justify this approach in Section 5.

There has been previous work in applying motion planning algorithms to animating human figures. Ching and Badler [6] present a motion planning algorithm for anthropometric figures with many degrees of freedom. Essentially, they use a sequential search strategy to find a collision-free motion of the figure to a specified goal configuration. They do not consider manipulation or imposing naturalness on the motions.

The AnimNL project at the University of Pennsylvania [33] is working to automate the generation of human figure movements from natural language instructions. Their focus is mainly on determining the sequence of primitive actions from a high-level description of the task. They utilize models to create realistic motions, however they do not consider complex manipulation motions.

**Neurophysiology:** There are many scientists in psychology and neurophysiology working to determine how the human brain manages to coordinate the motion of its limbs. Soechting [31] gives a good survey of various empirical studies and their results for human arm motions.

One relevant finding is the sensorimotor transformation model devised by Soechting and Flanders [29, 30]. They found that the desired position of the hand roughly determines the arm posture. Our inverse kinematics algorithm for the human arm is based on this result.

# 3   Manipulation Planner

In this section we present our manipulation planning algorithm. The method applies to any system of arms as long as they have an inverse kinematics solution.

## 3.1   Problem Statement

We now give a rather formal formulation of the multi-arm manipulation planning problem. We consider only a single movable object, but for the rest, our presentation is general.

The environment is a 3D workspace $\mathcal{W}$ with $p$ arms $\mathcal{A}_i$ $(i = 1, \cdots, p)$, a single movable object $\mathcal{M}$, and $q$ static obstacles $\mathcal{B}_j$ $(j = 1, \cdots, q)$. The object $\mathcal{M}$ can only move by having one or several of the arms grasp and carry it to some destination.

Let $\mathcal{C}_i$ and $\mathcal{C}_{obj}$ be the C-spaces (configuration spaces) of the arms $\mathcal{A}_i$ and the object $\mathcal{M}$, respectively [19, 16]. Each $\mathcal{C}_i$ has dimension $n_i$, where $n_i$ is the number of degrees of freedom of the arm $\mathcal{A}_i$, and $\mathcal{C}_{obj}$ has dimension 6. The *composite C-space* of the whole system is $\mathcal{C} = \mathcal{C}_1 \times \cdots \times \mathcal{C}_p \times \mathcal{C}_{obj}$. A configuration in $\mathcal{C}$, called a *system configuration*, is of the form $(\boldsymbol{q}_1, \cdots, \boldsymbol{q}_p, \boldsymbol{q}_{obj})$, with $\boldsymbol{q}_i \in \mathcal{C}_i$ and $\boldsymbol{q}_{obj} \in \mathcal{C}_{obj}$.

We define the *C-obstacle region* $\mathcal{CB} \subset \mathcal{C}$ as the set of all system configurations where two or more bodies in $\{\mathcal{A}_1, \cdots, \mathcal{A}_p, \mathcal{M}, \mathcal{B}_1, \cdots, \mathcal{B}_q\}$ intersect.[2] We describe all bodies as closed subsets of $\mathcal{W}$; hence, $\mathcal{CB}$ is a closed subset of $\mathcal{C}$. The open subset $\mathcal{C} \setminus \mathcal{CB}$ is denoted by $\mathcal{C}_{free}$ and its closure by $cl(\mathcal{C}_{free})$.

For the most part we require that the arms, object, and obstacles do not contact one another. However, $\mathcal{M}$ may touch stationary arms and obstacles for the purpose of achieving static stability. $\mathcal{M}$ may also touch arms when it is being moved. This is to achieve grasp stability and $\mathcal{M}$ can only make contact with the end-effector of each grasping arm (grasping may involve one or several arms). No other contacts are allowed.

This leads us to define two subsets of $cl(\mathcal{C}_{free})$:
- The *stable space* $\mathcal{C}_{stable}$ is the set of all legal configurations in $cl(\mathcal{C}_{free})$ where $\mathcal{M}$ is statically stable. $\mathcal{M}$'s stability may be achieved by contacts between $\mathcal{M}$ and the arms and/or the obstacles.
- The *grasp space* $\mathcal{C}_{grasp}$ is the set of all legal configurations in $cl(\mathcal{C}_{free})$ where one or several arms rigidly grasp $\mathcal{M}$ in such a way that they have sufficient torque to move $\mathcal{M}$. $\mathcal{C}_{grasp} \subset \mathcal{C}_{stable}$.

There are two types of paths, transit and transfer paths, which are of interest in multi-arm manipulation:
- A *transit path* defines arm motions that do not move $\mathcal{M}$. Along such a path $\mathcal{M}$'s static stability must be achieved by contacts with obstacles and/or stationary arms. Examples of such a path involve moving an arm to a configuration where it can grasp $\mathcal{M}$ or moving an arm to change its grasp of $\mathcal{M}$. A transit path lies in

---

[2]We regard joint limits in $\mathcal{A}_i$ as obstacles that only interfere with the arms' motions.

the cross-section of $\mathcal{C}_{stable}$ defined by the current fixed configuration of $\mathcal{M}$.

- A *transfer path* defines arm motions that move $\mathcal{M}$. It lies in the cross-section of $\mathcal{C}_{grasp}$ defined by the attachment of $\mathcal{M}$ to the last links of the grasping arms. During a transfer path, not all moving arms need grasp $\mathcal{M}$; some non-grasping arms may be moving to allow the grasping arms to move without collision.

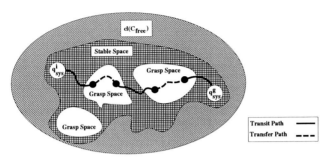

Figure 2. Components of a manipulation path and their relation to the subspaces of $cl(\mathcal{C}_{free})$.

A *manipulation path* is an alternate sequence of transit and transfer paths that connects an initial system configuration, $q_{sys}^{i}$, to a goal system configuration, $q_{sys}^{g}$ (see Fig. 2). Some paths in this sequence may be executed concurrently as long as this does not yield collisions.

In a multi-arm manipulation planning problem, the geometry of the arms, movable object, and obstacles is given, along with the location of the obstacles. The goal is to compute a manipulation path between two input system configurations.

## 3.2 Planning Approach

We now describe our approach for solving the multi-arm manipulation planning problem. This approach embeds several simplifications. As a result the corresponding planner is not fully general. Throughout our presentation, we carefully state the simplifications that we make. Some of them illustrate the deep intricacies of multi-arm manipulation planning.

**Overview:** A manipulation path alternates transit and transfer paths. Each path may be seen as the plan for a subtask of the total manipulation task. This yields the following two-stage planning approach: first, generate a series of subtasks to achieve the system goal configuration; second, plan a transit or transfer path for each subtask. An informal example of a series of subtasks is: grab $\mathcal{M}$, carry it to an intermediate location, change grasp, carry $\mathcal{M}$ to its goal location, ungrasp.

Unfortunately, planning a series of subtasks that can later be completed into legal paths is a difficult problem. How can one determine whether a subtask can be completed without actually completing it? We settle for a compromise. Our approach focuses on planning a sequence of transfer tasks that are guaranteed to be completed into transfer paths. In fact, in the process of identifying these tasks, the planner also generates the corresponding transfer paths. With the transfer tasks specified, the transit tasks are immediately defined: they link the transfer paths together along with the initial and goal system configuration. It only remains to compute the corresponding transit paths.

The assumption underlying this approach is that there exists a legal transit path for every transit task. Actually, in a 3D workspace, this is often the case. If the assumption is not verified, the planner may try to generate another series of transfer tasks, but in our current implementation it simply returns failure.

**Restrictions on grasps:** To simplify the selection of transfer tasks, we impose a restriction on grasps. The various possible grasps of $\mathcal{M}$ are given as a finite *grasp set*. Each grasp in this set describes a rigid attachment of the end-effector(s) of one or several arms with $\mathcal{M}$. For example, if $\mathcal{M}$ is considered too heavy or too bulky to be moved by a single arm, each grasp in the grasp set may indicate the need for a two-arm grasp. If the end-effector consists of multi-joint fingers, their joint values to achieve the particular grasp are specified.

**Generating transfer tasks:** The generation of the transfer tasks is done by planning a path $\tau_{obj}$ of $\mathcal{M}$ from its initial to its goal configuration. During the computation of $\tau_{obj}$, all the possible ways of grasping $\mathcal{M}$ are enumerated and the configurations of $\mathcal{M}$ requiring a regrasp are identified.

The planner computes the path $\tau_{obj}$ so that $\mathcal{M}$ avoids collision with the static obstacles $\mathcal{B}_{j}$. This is done using RPP (Randomized Path Planner), which is thus a component of our planner. RPP is described in detail in [3, 16].

RPP generates $\tau_{obj}$ as a list of adjacent configurations in a fine grid placed over $\mathcal{C}_{obj}$ (the 6D C-space of $\mathcal{M}$), by inserting one configuration after the other starting with the initial configuration of $\mathcal{M}$. The original RPP only checks that each inserted configuration is collision-free. To ensure that there exists a sequence of transfer paths moving $\mathcal{M}$ along $\tau_{obj}$, we have modified RPP. The modified RPP also verifies that at each inserted configuration, $\mathcal{M}$ can be grasped using a grasp from the input grasp set. This is done in the following way. A *grasp assignment* at some configuration of $\mathcal{M}$

is a pair associating an element of the grasp set defined for $\mathcal{M}$ and the identity of the grasping arm(s). Note that the same element of the grasp set may yield different grasp assignments involving different arms. The planner enumerates all the grasp assignments at the initial configuration of $\mathcal{M}$ and keeps a list of those which can be achieved without collision between the grasping arm(s) and the obstacles, and between the grasping arms should there be more than one. We momentarily ignore the possibility that the grasping arm(s) may collide with the other non-grasping arms. The list of possible grasp assignments is associated with the initial configuration. Prior to inserting any new configuration in the path being generated, RPP prunes the list of grasp assignments attached to the previous configuration by removing all those which are no longer possible at the new configuration. The remaining sublist, if not empty, is associated with this configuration which is appended to the current path.

If during a down motion of RPP (a motion along the negated gradient of the potential field used by RPP) the list of grasp assignments pruned as above vanishes at all the successors of the current configuration (call it $q_{obj}$), the modified RPP resets the list attached to $q_{obj}$ to contain all the possible grasp assignments at $q_{obj}$ (as we proceed from the initial configuration). During a random motion (a motion intended to escape a local minimum of the potential), the list of grasp assignments is pruned but is constrained to never vanish. In the process of constructing $\tau_{obj}$, the modified RPP may reset the grasp assignment list several times.

If successful, the outcome of RPP is a path $\tau_{obj}$ described as a series of configurations of $\mathcal{M}$, each annotated with a grasp assignment list. The path $\tau_{obj}$ is thus partitioned into a series of subpaths, each connecting two successive configurations. It defines as many transfer tasks as there are distinct grasp assignments associated with it. By construction, *for each such transfer task, there exists a transfer path satisfying the corresponding grasp assignment.* The number of regrasps along the generated path $\tau_{obj}$ is minimal, but RPP does not guarantee that this is the best path in that respect.

**Details and comments:** The condition that the same grasp assignment be possible at two neighboring configurations of $\mathcal{M}$ does not guarantee that the displacement of $\mathcal{M}$ can be done by a short (hence, collision-free) motion of the grasping arm(s). An additional test is needed when the set of grasps between two consecutive configurations is pruned. In our implementation, we assume that each arm has an inverse kinematics solution. Thus, an arm can attain a grasp with a finite set of different postures, determined by

using the arm's inverse kinematics. We include the posture of each involved arm in the description of a grasp assignment. Hence the same combination of arms achieving the same grasp, but with two different postures of at least one arm, defines two distinct grasp assignments. Then a configuration of $\mathcal{M}$, along with a grasp assignment, uniquely defines the configurations of the grasping arms. The resolution of the grid placed across $\mathcal{C}_{obj}$ is set fine enough to guarantee that the motion between any two neighboring configurations of $\mathcal{M}$ results in a maximal arm displacement smaller than some prespecified threshold.

In addition, we make considerations for sliding grasps. Indeed, for some manipulation tasks, the object must be allowed to slide in the grasp of the arms to achieve the goal. For the grasp assignments in the grasp list, we identify their feasible neighbors and add them to the list. A neighboring grasp assignment is one where the grasp location and orientation is within some threshold distance from the original grasp assignment, and the same arm(s) and posture(s) is utilized. We choose a threshold distance that is small enough to ensure that it is feasible to slide between neighboring grasp assignments. By updating the grasp list in this manner, directions where a sliding grasp is necessary can then be explored during the search for an object path.

A transfer path could be obstructed by the arms not currently grasping $\mathcal{M}$. Dealing with these arms can be particularly complicated. In our current implementation, we assume that each arm has a relatively non-obstructive configuration given in the problem definition (in the system shown in Fig. 1, the given non-obstructive configuration of each arm is when they are held out to the side). Prior to a transfer path, all arms not involved in grasping $\mathcal{M}$ are moved to their nonobstructive configurations. The planner nevertheless checks that no collision occurs with them during the construction of $\tau_{obj}$.

Perhaps the most blatant limitation of our approach is that it does not plan for regrasps at configurations of $\mathcal{M}$ where it makes contact with obstacles (as we said, $\tau_{obj}$ is computed free of collisions with obstacles). Since the object cannot levitate, we require that $\mathcal{M}$ be held at all times during regrasp. We assume that if $\mathcal{M}$ requires more than one arm to move, any subset of a grasp is sufficient to achieve static stability during the regrasp. For example, if a grasp requires two arms, any one of these arms, alone, achieves static stability, allowing the other arm to move along a transit path. An obvious example where this limitation may prevent our planner from finding a path is when the system contains a single arm; no regrasp is then possible.

RPP is only probabilistically complete [3]. If a path exists for $\mathcal{M}$, it will find it, but the computation time cannot be bounded in advance. Furthermore, if no path exists, RPP may run forever. Nevertheless, for a rigid object (as is the case for $\mathcal{M}$), RPP is usually very quick to return a path, when one exists. Hence, we can easily set a time limit beyond which it is safe to assume that no path exists.

RPP requires a postprocessing step to smooth the jerky portions of the path, due to the random walks. Other path planners could possibly be used in place of RPP.

**Generation of transit paths:** The transfer tasks identified as above can be organized into successive layers, as illustrated in Fig. 3. Each layer contains all the transfer tasks generated for the same subpath of $\tau_{obj}$; the transfer tasks differ by the grasp assignment. Selecting one such task in every layer yields a series of transit tasks: the first consists of achieving the first grasp from the initial system configuration; it is followed by a possibly empty series of transit tasks to change grasps between two consecutive transfer tasks; the last transit task is to achieve the goal system configuration. Hence, it remains to identify a grasp assignment in each layer of the graph shown in Fig. 3, such that there exist transit paths accomplishing the corresponding transit tasks.

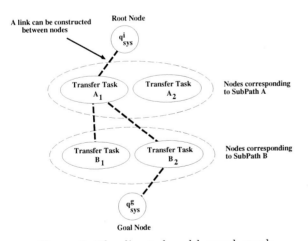

Figure 3. The directed and layered graph.

Assume without loss of generality that all arms are initially at their non-obstructive configurations. Our planner first chooses an arbitrary transfer task in the first layer. Consider the transit task of going from the initial system configuration to the configuration where the arms achieve the grasp assignment specified in the chosen transfer task, with $\mathcal{M}$ being at its initial configuration. The coordinated path of the arms is generated using RPP. If this fails, a new attempt is made with another transfer task in the first layer; otherwise, a transfer task is selected in the second layer. The connection of the system configuration at the end of the first transfer task to the system configuration at the start of this second transfer task forms a new transit task.

The transit task between two transfer tasks is more difficult to solve. Actually, the difficulty arises when an ungrasp/regrasp is required. If the initial and goal grasp assignments are neighbors, then we simply slide the grasp. To understand the difficulty of the case where an ungrasp/regrasp is required, imagine the situation where $\mathcal{M}$ is a long bar requiring two arms to move. Assume that the system contains only two arms and that the bar can be grasped at its two ends and at its center. Consider the situation where the bar is grasped at its two ends and the regrasp requires swapping the two arms. This regrasp is not possible without introducing an intermediate grasp. For example: arm 1 will ungrasp one end of the bar and regrasp it at its center (during this regrasp, arm 2 will be holding the bar without moving); then arm 2 will ungrasp the bar and regrasp it at the other end; finally, arm 1 will ungrasp the center of the bar and will regrasp it at its free end.

We address this difficulty by breaking the transit task between two transfer tasks into smaller transit subtasks. Each transit subtask consists of going from one grasp assignment to another in such a way that no two arms use the same grasp at the same time. In this process, we allow arms not involved in the first and last assignment to be used. We start with the first grasp assignment and generate all of the potential grasp assignments that may be achieved from it (assuming the corresponding transit paths exist). We generate the successors of these new assignments, and so on until we reach the desired assignment (the one used in the next transfer task). For each sequence that achieves this desired assignment, we test that it is actually feasible by using RPP to generate a transit path between every two successive grasp assignments. We stop as soon as we obtain a feasible sequence. The concatenation of the corresponding sequence of transit paths forms the transit path connecting the two considered transfer tasks. We then proceed to link to the next layer of transfer tasks.

When we reach a transfer path in the last layer, its connection to the goal system configuration is carried out in the same way as the connection of the initial system configuration to the first layer.

The result is an alternating sequence of transit and transfer paths that connects the initial configuration $q^i_{sys}$ to the goal configuration $q^g_{sys}$.

# 4    Human-Arm Kinematics

We now outline the method by which we determine the arm posture for a human arm given the position and orientation of its hand. We present the algorithm using the right arm for illustration purposes. We assume that the torso and the shoulder positions are given.

The algorithm is based on two results from neurophysiology. The first result has to do with decoupling the problem into two more manageable subproblems. Lacquaniti and Soechting have shown that the arm and wrist posture are for the most part independent of each other [14]. This allows us to decouple the problem into finding first, the forearm and upper arm posture to match the hand position, and then determining the joint angles for the wrist to match the hand orientation. This is exactly the approach taken in solving the inverse kinematics of a robot manipulator with six degrees of freedom and whose wrist joints intersect at a point [23].

It is also known in neurophysiology that the arm posture for pointing is mainly determined by a simple sensorimotor transformation model. Soechting and Flanders [29, 30] conducted experiments where the test subject was instructed to move the end of a pen-sized stylus to various targets in their vicinity. From this study, they have devised a model that determines the posture of the forearm and upper arm given the position of the end of the stylus. We use this model to determine the shoulder and elbow joint angles given the position of the hand. Then, determining the wrist joint angles is a simple additional step.

## 4.1    Arm posture

Using the sensorimotor transformation model of Soechting and Flanders [29, 30] we determine the arm posture given the location of the hand. To explain their model we first define some generalized coordinates.

Denote the coordinate frame centered on the shoulder as the *shoulder frame*. The $x$-axis is along the line that connects the two shoulders, the $y$-axis is parallel to the outward normal from the chest, and the $z$-axis points upwards towards the head. The parameters for the elevation and yaw of the upper arm are $\theta$ and $\eta$, respectively, and the parameters for the elevation and yaw of the forearm are $\beta$ and $\alpha$, respectively. The position of the wrist (or hand frame) is expressed in terms of the spherical coordinates, azimuth $\chi$, elevation $\psi$, and radial distance $R$. The spherical coordinates are related to the cartesian coordinates of the shoulder

frame by the equations

$$\begin{cases} R^2 = & x^2 + y^2 + z^2 \\ \tan \chi = & x/y \\ \tan \psi = & z/\sqrt{x^2 + y^2} \end{cases} \qquad (1)$$

These arm parameters are illustrated in Fig. 4.

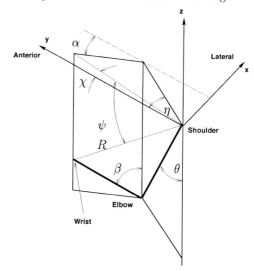

Figure 4. The parameters for the arm posture

The sensorimotor transformation model suggests that the parameters for arm posture are approximated by a linear mapping from the spherical coordinates of the hand frame (actually, Soechting and Flanders report this mapping from the position of the end of the stylus held by the test subject, but we simplify this to the hand). The relation is

$$\begin{cases} \theta = & -4.0 + 1.10R + 0.90\psi \\ \beta = & 39.4 + 0.54R - 1.06\psi \\ \eta = & 13.2 + 0.86\chi + 0.11\psi \\ \alpha = & -10.0 + 1.08\chi - 0.35\psi \end{cases} \qquad (2)$$

where the units of measure are centimeters and degrees. Since this is only an approximation, plugging the arm posture parameters back into the forward kinematics of the arm results in a positional error of the hand frame. This is compensated for in the final stage of the inverse kinematics algorithm.

Once the generalized coordinates $\theta$, $\beta$, $\eta$, and $\alpha$ are obtained, they are transformed into the four joint angles of the forearm and the upper arm. We check to see if they violate any of their limits. If they are within their limits we proceed to find the wrist joint angles. In the event that a limit is violated (an illegal posture), an adjustment phase is initiated.

For an illegal posture obtained from Eq. 2, it turns out that the joint angle $\xi$ (the rotation around the upper arm as shown in Fig. 5) is the only one to violate its limits. We correct for this in the following manner. Consider a new set of generalized coordinates of the arm, consisting of the wrist position and the angle $\phi$ (the rotation of the elbow around the axis between the shoulder and wrist as shown in Fig. 5). By decreasing the value of $\phi$ from the initial illegal posture (moving the elbow upward), $\xi$ will move back into the feasible joint range without ever changing the wrist position. Note that $\xi$ is obtained by transforming the wrist position and $\phi$ into the joint angles of the arm.

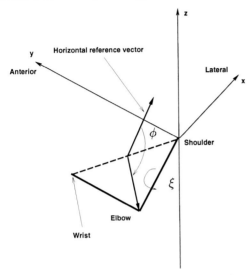

Figure 5. The elbow and shoulder rotation.

To summarize, the arm posture is estimated in the following way:

1. The arm posture is obtained using the transformation of Eq. 2.

2. The values for $\xi$ and $\phi$ are calculated.

3. If $\xi$ violates its joint limit, then $\phi$ is decreased until the corresponding $\xi$ satisfies its joint limit.

## 4.2 Wrist joints

The next step is to obtain the joint angles for the wrist.

We assume that the three wrist joint angles intersect at a point, consequently their values can be determined using basic inverse kinematics techniques. If the resulting wrist angles violate their limits, we adjust the posture of the arm until a feasible joint value is obtained. As before, this is achieved by incrementally changing the angle $\phi$ (rotation of the elbow) until either a feasible solution is obtained or we have exhausted the possible values for $\phi$. In the case where this step fails, we take the closest feasible answer to the desired hand orientation and proceed to the final adjustment step.

## 4.3 Final adjustment

The final step is to adjust the joint angles such that the exact position and orientation of the hand is obtained (recall that the sensorimotor transformation model leaves the hand position slightly off from the desired location). Let $e$ be the $6 \times 1$ vector containing the position and orientation error of the hand frame, and $q$ be the $7 \times 1$ vector of arm joint angles. The relation between these two vectors is

$$e = J(q)\dot{q} \qquad (3)$$

where $J(q)$ is the $6 \times 7$ Jacobian matrix. By solving for $\dot{q}$ we can iteratively change the joint angles to zero the error.

This simultaneous equation has only six linear constraints, thus resulting in an infinite number of solutions. We remedy this situation by utilizing a solution of Eq. 3 expressed as

$$\dot{q} = \dot{q}_0 + r\,n \qquad (4)$$

where $\dot{q}_0$, $r$, and $n$ are respectively, an instance of $\dot{q}$, a scalar parameter, and the null space of Eq. 3. In this case, the null space is one dimensional and is expressed by the multiplication of the scalar $r$ and its basis vector $n$. We employ a constrained optimization to select the $\dot{q}$ which minimizes its norm while satisfying the arm joint limits. The joint angles are then incrementally adjusted accordingly. This ensures that the modification to the hand position and orientation occurs with minimal joint movement. This procedure is iteratively applied until the desired position and orientation of the hand is obtained. The resulting joint angles comprise the posture of the arm for the given hand position and orientation.

The algorithm does not return an answer if the hand frame is out of the workspace of the arms, or if the method fails to correct for a set of joint angles which violates its limits.

## 5 Natural Motion

The multi-arm manipulation planner works regardless of whether the arms are human or robotic. In its most basic state, there is no consideration of producing realistic motions for the arms. Only kinematic constraints are recognized, for example: requiring the motion to be collision free and allowing the arms to grasp the movable object at all times.

However, for the purpose of computer animation the motions must appear natural. For robot arms, since they are undeniably artificial, there is no notion of what comprises natural movement. Though we may need to time parameterize their path to yield realistic animation (i.e. reasonable acceleration and decceleration of the arms) there is no need to impose a naturalness constraint on the planner. In contrast, for human arms there is clearly a natural manner in which they move. Fortunately, neurophysiology gives us a reference to which we can compare our methods and results with experimental data on human motions. In this section, we discuss how our planner with the human-arm inverse kinematics satisfies applicable naturalness constraints one derives from neurophysiology.

**Dynamics versus Kinematics:**  We make no consideration of dynamics in our planning. From the neurophysiological viewpoint this is not a problem. It is widely agreed upon that arm movement is represented kinematically [26]. It is then a postprocessing step, where the dynamics or muscle activation patterns are determined. With our method, by applying the appropriate time parameterization to the planned path [8, 1] one can emulate results found in neurophysiology. However, this is not done in our current planner yet.

**Inverse Kinematics:**  The sensorimotor transformation model is derived from static arm postures. To verify that our inverse kinematics algorithm is applicable to manipulation motions, we consider the experimental results of Soechting and Terzuolo [27]. Their experiment is for curvilinear wrist motions in an arbitrary plane. They find that humans exhibit the following behavior:

1. The modulation in the elevation and yaw angles of the upper arm and forearm ($\theta$, $\eta$, $\beta$, and $\alpha$) are close to sinusoidal.

2. The phase difference between $\theta$ and $\beta$ is 180°, at least for elevation angles of the plane between 0° and 45°.

3. The phase difference between $\alpha$ and $\theta$ is close to $180° - \sigma$, where $\sigma$ is the slant parameter describing the curvilinear wrist motion.

We reproduced their experiment by tracing curvilinear wrist motions and generating the arm parameters using the human arm inverse kinematics algorithm. Our finding is that the computed and experimental values match quite nicely. We refer the reader to [13] for a detailed explanation. Furthermore, Soechting and Terzuolo find that for learned trajectories, their results for curvilinear wrist motions in a plane hold true in three-dimensional space [28]. We justify the use of our inverse kinematics algorithm for manipulation planning based on these experimental results. Note, we do not claim that the posture found by our algorithm is the *only one* that is natural. Clearly, there are other postures that humans assume depending upon the situation. For example, the redundant degree of freedom could be used to posture the arm such that it avoids obstacles. By having a library of different inverse kinematics algorithms for human arms, the planner could consider a variety of natural postures for a given hand position and orientation.

**Point to Point Arm Motion:**  When the arms move to grasp or regrasp an object, the planning is done in the joint space of the arms. Since RPP is utilized to find the path, postprocessing is required to transform the collision free but jerky motion into a smooth one (the jerky motion is due to the random walks utilized by RPP). This smoothing is achieved by attempting to shorten the path by interpolating between its points. The result is essentially a piecewise joint interpolated path. Hollerbach and Atkeson speculate that the underlying planning strategy for such arm motions is a staggered joint interpolation [10]. Staggered joint interpolation is a generalization of joint interpolation introduced by Hollerbach and Atkeson to fit a greater range of experimental data. We have yet to implement a staggered joint interpolation scheme for the "smoother", but at present we are content with the arm motions produced thus far (i.e. joint interpolation appears to be a close enough approximation).

We were unable to find any studies on human regrasping. Thus, no comment can be made on how reasonable the planning strategy is from this viewpoint.

# 6  Experimental Results

We implemented the above approach in a planner written in C and running on a DEC Alpha workstation under UNIX. Experiments were conducted with a seated human figure and a robot arm. Each human arm has seven degrees of freedom, plus an additional nineteen degrees of freedom for each hand. The non-obstructive configurations for the human arms are ones in which they are held out to the side. The robot has six revolute joints and three degrees of freedom for the end-effector. The non-obstructive configuration for the robot is one in which it stands vertically. In addition, we seat the human on a swivel chair. By adding this extra degree of freedom, we allow the arms to access a greater region, and hence tackle more interesting manipulation tasks. The rotation of the chair tracks the object to keep it, essentially, in an optimal position with respect to the workspace of the arms [20].

Fig. 1 shows a path generated by the planner for

Figure 6. Planned path for human/robot arm cooperative manipulation.

the human arms to bring the glasses on the table to the head of the human figure. We specify that both arms should be used to manipulate the glasses (this is defined in the grasp set). Notice that during the regrasping phase, at least one arm is holding the glasses at all times. For this path it took one minute to identify the transfer tasks and an additional two minutes to complete the manipulation path. For the generation of $\tau_{obj}$, the object's C-space was discretized into a $100 \times 100 \times 100$ grid. For the generation of the transit paths, the joint angles of the arms were discretized into intervals of 0.05 radians. The grasp set contained 212 grasps, yielding grasp assignment lists with up to 424 elements.

Fig. 6 shows a path generated by the planner for the human arms and the robot arm cooperating to manipulate a chess box. Having the different arms working together presents no difficulty to our planning approach. The planner simply needs to know the correct inverse kinematics algorithm to apply to each arm. For this example, in defining the grasp set, we specify two classes of grasps, one in which all three arms are used, and another in which only the two human arms are utilized. For this path it took about one and a half minutes to identify the transfer tasks and an additional two minutes to complete the manipulation path. The same discretizations as above were used. The grasp set of the box contained 289 grasps yielding grasp assignment lists with up to 2600 elements.

For manipulation planning with human arms, our current implementation is unable to plan motions where the arms are required to use their redundant degree of freedom to avoid obstacles. For example, a task where the arms must place an object deep into a tight box is almost impossible for our planner. The reason is simply that the sensorimotor transformation model does not consider obstacle avoidance. To tackle this class of problem, we will need to devise another inverse kinematics algorithm that *does* utilize the redundant degree of freedom for the purpose of avoiding obstacles. Again, some sort of naturalness constraint would need to be satisfied.

For these examples, in computing the transit paths RPP uses the sum of the angular joint distances to the goal configuration as the guiding potential. Note that the motion of the fingers for the human and the robot are considered in the transit paths (in moving from one grasp to another the fingers may change their posture). In computing $\tau_{obj}$ RPP uses an NF2-based potential with three control points [16]. In finding both the transit paths and $\tau_{obj}$, we limit the amount of computation spent in RPP to three backtrack operations [16], after which the planner returns failure. Failure to find $\tau_{obj}$

results in the immediate failure to find a manipulation path. Similarly, a failure to find transit paths to link together the layers of transfer paths results in a failure to find a manipulation path. The time for the planner to report failure depends on the problem, with some examples ranging from 30 seconds to a few minutes. The collision checking algorithm utilized is that of Quinlan [24].

# 7 Conclusion

We have presented a novel approach for solving the complicated multi-arm manipulation planning problem. Our approach embeds several simplifications yielding an implemented planner that is not fully general. However, experiments with this planner show that it is quite reliable and efficient in finding manipulation paths, when such paths exist, making it suitable as part of an interactive tool to facilitate the animation of scenes. We believe the robust nature of the planner is the result of careful consideration of the general manipulation problem, the introduction of reasonable simplifications, and the appropriate utilization of the efficient randomized path planner.

We have also presented a new inverse kinematics algorithm for human arms based on neurophysiological studies. This algorithm, in conjunction with the planner, automatically generates natural arm motions for a human figure manipulating an object.

In the future we hope to include the ability to regrasp the movable object by having the arms place it in a stable configuration against some obstacles. We also plan to use existing results to automatically compute the grasp set of an object from its geometric model. The technique described in [11] to deal with multiple movable objects in a 2D space should also be applicable to our planner. Furthermore, we hope to time parameterize the motion paths to yield realistic velocities, by implementing one of the many such algorithms for robot and human arms [8, 1, 4]. Finally, we hope to explore and devise other inverse kinematics algorithms for the arms, as well as incorporating twisting and bending of the torso. Ultimately, we aim to create a task-level animation package for human motions.

**Acknowledgments**

Y. Koga is supported in part by a Canadian NSERC fellowship. The use of Sean Quinlan's collision checking software is gratefully acknowledged.

# References

[1] Atkeson, Christopher and Hollerbach, John. *Kinematic Features of Unrestrained Arm Movements*. MIT AI Memo 790, 1984.

[2] Baraff, David. Analytical Method for Dynamic Simulation of Non-Penetrating Rigid Bodies. Proceedings of SIGGRAPH'89 (Boston, Massachusetts, July 31 - August 4, 1989). In *Computer Graphics* 23, 3 (July 1989), 223-232.

[3] Barraquand, Jerome and Latombe, Jean-Claude. Robot Motion Planning: A Distributed Representation Approach. *Int. J. Robotics Research*, 10(6), December 1991, 628-649.

[4] Bobrow, J.E., Dubowsky, S., Gibson, J.S. Time-Optimal Control of Robotic Manipulators Along Specified Paths. *Int. J. Robotics Research*, Vol. 4, No. 3, 1985, 3-17.

[5] Bruderlin, Armin and Calvert, Thomas. Goal-directed, dynamic animation of human walking. Proceedings of SIGGRAPH'89 (Boston, Massachusetts, July 31 - August 4, 1989). In *Computer Graphics* 23, 3 (July 1989), 233-242.

[6] Ching, Wallace and Badler, Norman. Fast motion planning for anthropometric figures with many degrees of freedom. *Proc. 1992 IEEE Int. Conf. on Robotics and Automation,* Nice, France, 1992, 2340-2345.

[7] Ferbach, Pierre and Barraquand, Jerome. *A Penalty Function Method for Constrained Motion Planning*. Rep. No. 34, Paris Research Lab., DEC, Sept. 1993.

[8] Flash, T. and Hogan, N. *The Coordination of Arm Movements: An Experimentally Confirmed Mathematical Model*. MIT AI Memo 786, 1984.

[9] Hahn, James K. Realistic Animation of Rigid Bodies. Proceedings of SIGGRAPH'88 (Atlanta, Georgia, August 1-5, 1988). In *Computer Graphics* 22, 4 (August 1988), 299-308.

[10] Hollerbach, John and Atkeson, Christopher. Deducing Planning Variables from Experimental Arm Trajectories: Pitfalls and Possibilities. *Biological Cybernetics*, 56(5), 1987, 279-292.

[11] Koga, Y., Lastennet, T., Latombe, J.C., and Li, T.Y. Multi-Arm Manipulation Planning. *Proc. 9th Int. Symp. Automation and Robotics in Construction*, Tokyo, June 1992, 281-288.

[12] Koga, Yoshihito. *On Computing Multi-Arm Manipulation Trajectories*. Ph.D. thesis, Stanford University (in preparation).

[13] Kondo, Koichi. *Inverse Kinematics of a Human Arm*. Rep. STAN-CS-TR-94-1508, Department of Computer Science, Stanford University, CA, 1994.

[14] Lacquaniti, F. and Soechting, J.F. Coordination of Arm and Wrist Motion During A Reaching Task. *The Journal of Neuroscience,* Vol. 2, No. 2, 1982, 399-408.

[15] Laumond, Jean-Paul and Alami, Rachid. *A Geometrical Approach to Planning Manipulation Tasks: The Case of a Circular Robot and a Movable Circular Object Amidst Polygonal Obstacles.* Rep. No. 88314, LAAS, Toulouse, 1989.

[16] Latombe, Jean-Claude. *Robot Motion Planning*. Kluwer Academic Publishers, Boston, MA, 1991.

[17] Lee, P., Wei, S., Zhao, J., and Badler, N.I. Strength guided motion. Proceedings of SIGGRAPH'90 (Dallas, Texas, August 6-10, 1990). In *Computer Graphics* 24, 4 (August 1990), 253-262.

[18] Lengyel, J., Reichert, M., Donald, B.R., and Greenberg, D.P. Real-Time Robot Motion Planning Using Rasterizing Computer Graphics Hardware. Proceedings of SIGGRAPH'90 (Dallas, Texas, August 6-10, 1990). In *Computer Graphics* 24, 4 (August 1990), 327-335.

[19] Lozano-Pérez, Tomas. Spatial Planning: A Configuration Space Approach. *IEEE Tr. Computers,* 32(2), 1983, pp. 108-120.

[20] McCormick, E.J. and Sanders, M.S. *Human Factors in Engineering and Design*. McGraw-Hill Book Company, New York, 1982.

[21] McKenna, Michael and Zeltzer, David. Dynamic simulation of autonomous legged locomotion. Proceedings of SIGGRAPH'90 (Dallas, Texas, August 6-10, 1990). In *Computer Graphics* 24, 4 (August 1990), 29-38.

[22] Pertin-Troccaz, Jocelyn. Grasping: A State of the Art. In *The Robotics Review 1*, O. Khatib, J.J. Craig, and T. Lozano-Pérez, eds., MIT Press, Cambridge, MA, 1989, 71-98.

[23] Pieper, D. and Roth, B. The Kinematics of Manipulators Under Computer Control. *Proceedings*

*of the Second International Congress on Theory of Machines and Mechanisms*, Vol. 2, Zakopane, Poland, 1969, 159-169.

[24] Quinlan, Sean. Efficient Distance Computation Between Non-Convex Objects. To appear in *Proc. 1994 IEEE Int. Conf. on Robotics and Automation*, San Diego, CA, 1994.

[25] Raibert, Marc and Hodgins, Jessica. Animation of Dynamic Legged Locomotion. Proceedings of SIGGRAPH'91 (Las Vegas, Nevada, July 28 - August 2, 1991). In *Computer Graphics* 25, 4 (July 1991), 349-358.

[26] Smith, A.M. et al. Group Report: What Do Studies of Specific Motor Acts Such as Reaching and Grasping Tell Us about the General Principles of Goal-Directed Motor Behaviour? *Motor Contro: Concepts and Issues*, D.R Humphrey and H,J, Freund, eds., John Wiley and Sons, New York, 1991, 357-381.

[27] Soechting, J.F. and Terzuolo, C.A. An Algorithm for the Generation of Curvilinear Wrist Motion in an Arbitrary Plane in Three Dimensional Space. *Neuroscience,* Vol. 19, No. 4, 1986, 1393-1405.

[28] Soechting, J.F. and Terzuolo, C.A. Organization of Arm Movements in Three Dimensional Space. Wrist Motion is Piecewise Planar. *Neuroscience,* Vol. 23, No. 1, 1987, 53-61.

[29] Soechting, J.F. and Flanders, M. Sensorimotor Representations for Pointing to Targets in Three Dimensional Space. *Journal of Neurophysiology,* Vol. 62, No. 2, 1989, 582-594.

[30] Soechting, J.F. and Flanders, M. Errors in Pointing are Due to Approximations in Sensorimotor Transformations. *Journal of Neurophysiology,* Vol. 62, No. 2, 1989, 595-608.

[31] Soechting, J.F. Elements of Coordinated Arm Movements in Three-Dimensional Space. *Perspectives on the Coordination of Movement,* edited by S.A. Wallace, Elsevier Science Publishers, Amsterdam, 1989, 47-83.

[32] Tournassoud, P., Lozano-Pérez, T., and Mazer, E. Regrasping. *Proc. IEEE Int. Conf. Robotics and Automation*, Raleigh, NC, 1987, 1924-1928.

[33] Webber, B., Badler, N., Baldwin, F.B., Beckett, W., DiEugenio, B., Geib, C., Jung, M., Levinson, L., Moore, M., and White, M. Doing what you're told: following task instructions in changing, but hospitable environments. *SIGGRAPH '93 Course note 80 "Recent Techniques in Human Modeling, Animation and Rendering",* 1993, 4.3-4.31.

[34] Wilfong, G. Motion Planning in the Presence of Movable Obstacles. *Proc. 4th ACM Symp. Computational Geometry*, 1988, 279-288.

# Animating Images with Drawings

Peter Litwinowicz[†]

Lance Williams[†]

**Apple Computer, Inc.**

## ABSTRACT

The work described here extends the power of 2D animation with a form of texture mapping conveniently controlled by line drawings. By tracing points, line segments, spline curves, or filled regions on an image, the animator defines features which can be used to animate the image. Animations of the control features deform the image smoothly. This development is in the tradition of "skeleton"-based animation, and "feature"-based image metamorphosis. By employing numerics developed in the computer vision community for rapid visual surface estimation, several important advantages are realized. Skeletons are generalized to include curved "bones," the interpolating surface is better behaved, the expense of computing the animation is decoupled from the number of features in the drawing, and arbitrary holes or cuts in the interpolated surface can be accommodated. The same general scattered data interpolation technique is applied to the problem of mapping animation from one image and set of features to another, generalizing the prescriptive power of animated sequences and encouraging reuse of animated motion.

**Keywords:** Image warping, animation, scattered data interpolation.

## Background

Rich detail and texture are usually reserved for the background paintings in an animation. Production economics do not permit the foreground figures to be dressed in plaid, for example, and such effects are difficult to achieve by traditional means. Three-dimensional computer animation offers shading and texture, but the stylization of form possible in traditional cel animation has proved more elusive. Much of the motivation for the work described here comes from the technique of traditional animation, where all action is portrayed by drawings -- points, lines, and curves -- defined at arbitrary instants of time. Interpolation defines the full sequence from the sparse keys. We envision a similar interpolation in space, embedding the objects and characters the artist has drawn in a surface controlled by the lines of the drawings. The interpolated motion of corresponding

[†] c/o Apple Computer, Inc.
1 Infinite Loop, MS 301-3J
Cupertino, CA 95014 USA
email:     Pete Litwinowicz: litwinow@apple.com
          Lance Williams: lance.w@apple.com

keyframe drawings is used to define spatial deformations which may be applied to other images. "Feature-based" deformations, controlled by the motion of arbitrarily-placed points, curves, and regions, offer a direct and natural method of animating complex images and forms. An earlier attempt at animating drawings by their features [Litw91] required the user to define a mesh of bilinear Coons patches [Forr72]. The curved boundaries of the patches could be aligned with features of interest to the animator, and subsequently animated to control the image. Although the Coons patches are inexpensive to evaluate, the manual division of the image into a mesh, and the necessity of animating all of the patch boundaries to control the motion, require substantial time and effort. Specifying and animating only the features of interest is both vastly more general and a great deal easier for the animator.

Deformations based on tensor-product splines [Sed86][Farin90] are actually a more recent development than "feature based" deformations defined by line segments, which were introduced by Burtnyk and Wein in [Burtn76]. The goal of that work was to permit an animated "skeleton" of linked line segments to drive the animation of a drawing, in this case by polygonal tessellation of regions around the "bones" of the skeleton. An alternate parametrization, based on a skeleton derived from the shape of the matte or support of the image region to be animated, has been described by Wolberg [Wolb89]. In this case, the skeleton is the result of successive thinning operations applied to the original shape. The image warping algorithm is specialized for morphing, that is, for transforming between two image/shapes. Driving an image warp by modifying the skeleton alone would require a slightly different algorithm. Automatic "medial axis" skeletons of this type might be useful for some purposes, but there is no guarantee that the "bones" will align with features the animator is interested in controlling directly.

More recent skeleton animation work appeals to smoother interpolation functions. Van Overveld [vanO90] describes a physical simulation which is calculated for a simple skeleton, then applied to a more complex model by a distance-weighted "force field." The field is defined by a dense set of points on the limbs of the skeleton. The formula used is equivalent to Shepard's interpolation, a simple scattered data interpolant originally developed for terrain surfaces [Shep68]. In [Beier92], Beier and Neely developed an algorithm for image morphing based on Shepard's interpolation, with a significant novelty: the control primitives were extended to include line segments as well as points. Since the line segments can be aligned with important edges in the image, the metamorphosis was termed, "feature based." At edge-like features of the image, a single line segment does the work of dozens of points, and offers a natural and intuitive means of interpolating local orientations.

Thin-plate spline surfaces were introduced to computer-aided geometric design by Harder and Desmarais [Hard72]. Application of finite-element methods to computing smooth surfaces over scattered data for CAGD purposes was first essayed by Pilcher [Pilch74]. Smooth scattered data interpolants, introduced as analogues of physical surfaces, have more recently been applied in vision and image reconstruction [Grim81]. The demands of rapid processing for practical vision systems has motivated attempts to compute some of these surfaces using fast numerical methods [Terz88], and our animation system utilizes these techniques. We have implemented a system which performs the scattered data interpolation for animated deformations or morphing by using multigrid finite-difference evaluation of a thin-plate spline surface. This approach extends the "feature" primitives to curves and solid regions, realized as densely sampled points. In addition to generalizing the control primitives, the underlying surface which defines the deformation is better behaved than a Shepard's interpolant. This is particularly important when deformations are used for animation, without the texture interpolation invoked in a "morph."

## Description of the problem and our solution

Given starting and ending shapes for a set of primitives in the plane, such as curves, lines and points, we would like to calculate a warp that transforms regions between the primitives in a well-behaved and intuitive way. By aligning curves, lines and points with features in an image, intuitive controls for image warping are easily constructed. Deformation of an image can then be accomplished by applying the warp defined by the original drawing and any other drawing of the same features. It is then possible to animate an image simply by animating the drawing, and applying the corresponding image warp at each frame.

From a control primitive's original and final shape we can derive a set of displacements. For a point the displacement is simply a $(\Delta x, \Delta y)$ pair. For a line or polyline, continuous displacements all along the length are defined by the initial and final shape. Not only the "skeleton animation" of Burtnyk and Wein [Burtn76], but a number of subsequent facial animation systems and morphing programs are based on triangulation of displaced points [Gosh86]. For interpolating a set of scattered points, Delaunay triangulation is frequently used. A triangulation is defined for the original feature set, then the vertices are interpolated toward the final shape, and the triangles texture-mapped from the original image. While rapid to compute, the warp is generally not as smooth as desired. The triangulation can be seen in the resulting animation, as the texture map shears along the edges of the triangles.

Beier and Neely [Beier92] advanced a modified Shepard's interpolant which added line segments as control primitives. This method interpolates displacements using a distance-weighted technique and produces smoother interpolations than triangulation. The usual difficulty with these distance-weighted interpolants is trading off "cusps" against "flats" at the data points. In addition, the interpolation may become very expensive as the number of primitives increases, since each contributes at every point on the surface. To give the animator local control, Beier and Neely associate a finite region of influence -- a threshold distance from a point or line segment -- with each primitive. The process of specifying the region size for each primitive can potentially be tedious, and for many warps, no combination of region extents and inverse-distance weighting exponents yields the desired result [Rupr92].

Instead of explicit control over the size of the basis functions used in the interpolation process, our goal was to provide a technique which automatically extended regions of influence to the next user-defined primitive. Another goal was to have a nice "smooth" interpolant, but at the same time provide a mechanism for intuitively introducing discontinuities in the interpolant where appropriate. Finally, we wished to provide curves as deformation primitives.

The thin-plate spline provided a nice compromise for our goals. The region of influence for a particular primitive is global, but the region most affected is the area between a primitive and its nearest neighbors. The thin-plate spline is $C^1$ continuous, certainly smoother than a piecewise planar triangulated surface, and not so potentially cuspy as a Shepard's interpolant.

The thin-plate spline is one solution to a class of scattered data interpolation problems that have the following problem statement (from [Franke79]): "Construct a smooth bivariate function, $F(x,y)$, which takes on certain prescribed values, $F(x_k,y_k) = f_k$, k = 1, . . . , N. The points $(x_k,y_k)$ are not assumed to satisfy any particular conditions as to spacing or density, hence the term 'scattered.'"

How does our problem map onto the scattered data problem? For a number of known $(x_k,y_k)$ positions in the image plane, we have known displacements $(\Delta x_k, \Delta y_k)$ as defined by our original and destination drawings. Substituting $\Delta x_k$ for $f_k$ above, we calculate a smooth interpolating function for the x-displacements for an entire image, and similarly for the y-displacements. The thin plate also has the added constraint that the surface everywhere should minimize the following smoothness functional:

$$\iint_\Omega \frac{\partial^2 F}{\partial^2 u} + 2 \frac{\partial^2 F}{\partial u \partial u} + \frac{\partial^2 F}{\partial^2 v} \, du \, dv$$

where $\Omega$ is the domain of the surface, and F is the surface itself. Encoded in $\Omega$ are the cuts and holes in the surface.

The thin plate spline can be solved by using a $d^2 \log d$ basis function at each point (where d is the distance from the point), and solving the linear system. This becomes extremely expensive as the number of known points increases. By solving the problem on a discrete grid, the solution time is dependent on the strain energy in the plate and not on the number of data points (beyond a small initialization cost). Another advantage to discretizing the problem is that discontinuities in the interpolant are easy to handle. In the continuous problem, it is not obvious how to change the basis function $d^2 \log d$ to handle irregular discontinuities. Our grid sizes are on the order of the image size, in pixels; we make sure that we have at least one grid element per pixel in the image. Finally, we use a coarse-to-fine multiresolution method to calculate our interpolants [Terz88].

We present the animator with curves, polylines, and points as deformation primitives. When solving the problem on a discrete grid we must scan convert the primitives' displacements onto the grid. In practice, we discretize the primitives into equidistant samples.

The animator specifies discontinuities in the surface by supplying an extra black-and-white matte; an image pixel is "connected" to neighboring pixels labeled "nonzero" in this matte. For most purposes, the animator uses the ordinary alpha matte in the role of discontinuity matte as well, but they may be specified separately. For instance, the eyes and mouth of the characters in Figure (1) are on a separate cel level, with holes specified in the top layer. These holes also specify discontinuities in the interpolant, so when the top eyelid closes, it does not affect the lower eyelid.

In applying the displacements we use a forward mapping technique, as opposed to the inverse mapping technique implemented by Beier and Neely (the former is a "many to one" mapping, the latter, "one to many"). All the warped images in the color plates illustrating this paper were generated using a forward mapping, including the pictures demonstrating Beier-Neely interpolation. The Beier interpolation picture actually uses 2 points for the interior points and four lines along the edges; the displacements for the points are weighted with Shepard's formula and the edges with the Beier-Neely modifications for lines. The checkerboards warped with thin-plate interpolation have displaced interior feature points and four stationary lines along the edges.

The interpolated displacements for the entire surface are applied to the image at each pixel. The image is rendered as a polygon mesh; each original pixel becomes a polygon vertex in the mesh, except where the discontinuity matte breaks the connections. Subpixel positioning of the displaced quadrilateral endpoints is important for good results.

## Observations

Our experience suggests that the imposition of a structure to animate the image, such as a grid or mesh of polygons, can impose a heavy burden on the animator. It is far more intuitive to specify, and animate, a simple drawing which parametrizes and controls the image.

Polygonal texturing may not be smooth enough for the extreme deformations used in animation. Distance-weighted interpolants may not be smooth enough, either, and may limit the number of control primitives for practical purposes.

A very valuable feature of the thin-plate spline surface is its *idempotency*. New features can be added at any time without modifying the current mapping, and subsequently serve as handles for further animation. With a polygonal mapping, this can be ensured by subdividing only triangles in which new control points are introduced. With a distance weighted mapping, this property is impossible to achieve, and one must settle for gradually, over time, blending in the contribution of newly introduced control features.

The iterative relaxation used to compute the multigrid spline surface can profit from frame-to-frame coherence in animation. By using the last surface computed as an estimate for the next frame, the expense for the sequence is greatly reduced. The first frame of the example animated cat sequence took 5 min., 34 sec.; subsequent frames, on average, 3 min., 30 sec. (surface computed as a 513x513 grid on a MIPS 36Mhz R3000).

There are several ways to trade off computation and quality in the surface. One is to evaluate the surface on a coarse grid, and use tensor-product interpolation to upsample it. Another is to increase the error permitted when iteration is ceased, or to perform a fixed number of iterations. In this case, a modified form of Southwell iteration [Gera94] offers improved results for the same number of cycles. We implemented this option at the suggestion of Eric Chen, who was inspired by the "shooting" method of computing radiosity [Gortler93].

## Acknowledgments

The authors would like to extend heartfelt thanks to Laurence Arcadias for the cartoon face animated in our illustrations, and to Subhana Ansari for layout.

## References

[Beier92] Beier, T. and S. Neely. "Feature-Based Image Metamorphosis," Computer Graphics, Volume 26, Number 2, July 1992, pp. 35-42.

[Burtn76] Burtnyk, N. and M Wein. "Interactive Skeleton Techniques for Enhancing Motion Dynamics in Key Frame Animation," CACM, Vol. 19, Number 10, October 1976.

[Farin90] Farin, G. Curves and Surfaces for Computer Aided Geometric Design, A Practical Guide, Second Edition. Academic Press, NY, 1990.

[Forr72] Forrest, A. "On Coons and Other Methods for the Representation of Curved Surfaces," Computer Graphics and Image Processing, 1, 1972, pp. 341-369.

[Franke79] Franke, R. "A Critical Comparison of Some Methods for Interpolation of Scattered Data," Report NPS-53-79-03 of the Naval Postgraduate School, Monterey, CA. Obtained from U.S. Department of Commerce, National Technical Information Service.

[Gera94] Gerald, Curtis and P. Wheatley, Applied Numerical Analysis, Fifth Edition, Addison-Wesley Publishing Company, pp. 159-164.

[Gortler93] Gortler, Steven, Michael Cohen and Philipp Slusallek, "Radiosity and Relaxation Methods: Progressive Refinement is Southwell Relaxation," Princeton University Research Report CS-TR-408-93, February 1993.

[Gosh86] Goshtasby, A., "Piecewise Linear Mapping Functions for Image Registration," Pattern Recognition 19:6, 1986, pp. 459-466.

[Grim81] Grimson, W., From Images to Surfaces, MIT Press, 1981.

[Hard72] Harder, R., and R. Desmarais, "Interpolation Using Surface Splines," J. Aircraft, Vol. 9, February 1972, pp. 189-191.

[Litw91] Litwinowicz, P. "Inkwell: A $2^1/2$-D Animation System," Computer Graphics, Volume 25, Number 4 , 1991, pp. 113-121.

[Patterson91] Patterson, E., P. Litwinowicz and N. Greene, "Facial Animation by Spatial Mapping," Computer Animation 1991, Springer-Verlag, NY 1991, pp. 31-44.

[Pilch74] Pilcher, David, "Smooth Parametric Surfaces," in Computer Aided Geometric Design, by Barnhill and Riesenfeld, Academic Press, NY, 1974, pp. 237-253.

[Rupr92] Ruprecht, D., and H. Müller, "Image Warping with Scattered Data Interpolation Methods," Research Report 443, Dortmund University, November 6, 1992.

[Shep68] Shepard, D., "A Two-Dimensional Interpolation Function for Irregularly Spaced Data," Proceedings of the 23rd Nat. Conf. ACM, 1968, pp. 517-523.

[Sed86] Sederberg, T. and S. Parry. "Free-Form Deformation of Solid Geometric Models," *Computer Graphics*, Volume 20, Number 4, August 1986, pp. 151-160.

[Terz88] Terzopoulos, D. "The Computation of Visible-Surface Representations," IEEE Transactions on Pattern Analysis and Machine Intelligence, Vol. 10, No.4, July 1988.

[Wolb89] Wolberg, George. "Skeleton Based Image Warping," The Visual Computer, Vol. 5, Number 1/2, March 1989, pp. 95-108.

[vanO90] van Overveld, C. W. A. M., "A technique for motion specification in computer animation," The Visual Computer, Number 6, 1990, pp. 106-116.

# Animation

The top row of pictures shows sample frames from a video sequence. Key features of the subject have been rotoscoped to extract animated line drawings. Using cross-synthesis procedures described in [Patterson91], and the line drawings of the actor and cat in the leftmost column, the animation for the other line drawings has been automatically generated for the cat. Using these animated line drawings and the original cat photograph (shown in the leftmost column), thin-plate spline surfaces are used to compute each frame of the animation. The final two rows of frames, at left, show two more characters animated in this way, with the original faces shown in the leftmost column. The eyes and teeth are animated on a separate layer.

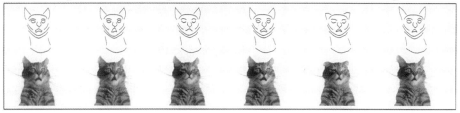

Key features of the subject have been traced by hand as line drawings.

The leftmost drawings define an automatic mapping to the cat's face.

Thin-plate spline surfaces animate images from drawings.

## Holes and Cuts

The two columns of pictures on the far left show the relative smoothness of image warps based on various scattered data interpolation methods. At near left, we show the process of introducing deliberate "holes" or "cuts" in interpolating surfaces:

<u>Top left test image</u> (closing gap in checkerboard). The six red control points are moved to the tips of the yellow arrows. The blue points, as well as each edge of the square, are held in place. <u>Top right</u>, the map which controls the continuity of the surface.

<u>Polygonal interpolation.</u> Triangulation results in sharp bends within the checkerboard as it stretches. Interpolation is local, however, with no influence across the gap.

<u>Beier interpolation.</u> Folds and creases appear in the checkerboard, and the left edge of the hole folds under as the right edge approaches. The "hole" in this and the next example is simply a matte (transparency map) which makes part of the surface transparent.

<u>Thin-plate spline, with no holes in the surface.</u> As the right edge is stretched, the left edge folds under.

<u>Thin-plate spline, with an actual "hole" in the interpolated displacement surface.</u> As the right edge is stretched, the left edge is relatively unaffected. This type of control is necessary for the animation examples at the top of the page. When closing an eyelid, the animator doesn't want to affect the region below the eye. Continuity and translucency are specified with independent maps.

2 displaced points;        triangulation.

Polygonal mapping;        ΔX surface.

Beier interpolation;        ΔX surface.

Thin-plate spline;        ΔX surface.

6 displaced points;        discontinuity map.

Polygonal interpolation.

Beier interpolation.

without "hole"        with "hole"

Thin-plate spline.

# ANIMATED CONVERSATION:
## Rule-based Generation of Facial Expression, Gesture & Spoken Intonation for Multiple Conversational Agents

Justine Cassell   Catherine Pelachaud   Norman Badler   Mark Steedman

Brett Achorn   Tripp Becket   Brett Douville   Scott Prevost   Matthew Stone [1]

**Department of Computer & Information Science, University of Pennsylvania**

### Abstract

We describe an implemented system which *automatically* generates and animates conversations between multiple human-like agents with appropriate and synchronized speech, intonation, facial expressions, and hand gestures. Conversation is created by a dialogue planner that produces the text as well as the intonation of the utterances. The speaker/listener relationship, the text, and the intonation in turn drive facial expressions, lip motions, eye gaze, head motion, and arm gesture generators. Coordinated arm, wrist, and hand motions are invoked to create semantically meaningful gestures. Throughout we will use examples from an actual synthesized, fully animated conversation.

## 1   Introduction

When faced with the task of bringing to life a human-like character, few options are currently available. Either one can manually and laboriously manipulate the numerous degrees of freedom in a synthetic figure, one can write or acquire increasingly sophisticated motion generation software such as inverse kinematics and dynamics, or one can resort to "performance-based" motions obtained from a live actor or puppet. The emergence of low-cost, real-time motion sensing devices has led to renewed interest in active motion capture since 3D position and orientation trajectories may be acquired directly rather than from tedious image rotoscoping [34]. Both facial and gestural motions are efficiently tracked from a suitably harnessed actor. But this does not imply that the end of manual or synthesized animation is near. Instead it raises the challenge of providing a sophisticated toolkit for human character animation that does not require the presence nor skill of a live actor [2], thus freeing up the craft of the skilled animator for more challenging tasks.

In this paper we present our system for *automatically animating conversations between multiple human-like agents with appropriate and synchronized speech, intonation, facial expressions, and hand gestures.* Especially noteworthy is the linkage between speech and

gesture which has not been explored before in synthesizing realistic animation. In people, speech, facial expressions, and gestures are physiologically linked. While an expert animator may realize this unconsciously in the "look" of a properly animated character, a program to automatically generate motions must know the rules in advance. This paper presents a working system to realize interacting animated agents.

Conversation is an interactive dialogue between two agents. Conversation includes spoken language (words and contextually appropriate intonation marking topic and focus), facial movements (lip shapes, emotions, gaze direction, head motion), and hand gestures (handshapes, points, beats, and motions representing the topic of accompanying speech). Without all of these verbal and nonverbal behaviors, one cannot have realistic or at least believable autonomous agents. To limit the problems (such as voice and face recognition) that arise from the involvement of real human conversants, and to constrain the dialogue, we present the work in the form of a dialogue generation program in which two copies of an identical program having different knowledge of the world must cooperate to accomplish a goal. Both agents of the conversation collaborate via the dialogue to develop a simple plan of action. They interact with each other to exchange information and ask questions.

In this paper, we first present the background information necessary to establish the synchrony of speech, facial expression, and gesture. We then discuss the system architecture and its several subcomponents.

## 2   Background

Faces change expressions continuously, and many of these changes are synchronized to what is going on in concurrent conversation. Facial expressions are linked to the content of speech (scrunching one's nose when talking about something unpleasant), emotion (wrinkling one's eyebrows with worry), personality (frowning all the time), and other behavioral variables. Facial expressions can replace sequences of words ("she was dressed [wrinkle nose, stick out tongue]") as well as accompany them [16], and they can serve to help disambiguate what is being said when the acoustic signal is degraded. They do not occur randomly but rather are synchronized to one's own speech, or to the speech of others [13], [20].

Eye gaze is also an important feature of non-verbal communicative behaviors. Its main functions are to help regulate the flow of conversation, signal the search for feedback during an interaction (gazing at the other person to see how she follows), look for information, express emotion (looking downward in case of sadness), or influence another person's behavior (staring at a person to show power)[14].

People also produce hand gestures spontaneously while they

---

[1]The authors would like to thank Francisco Azuola, Chin Seah, John Granieri, Ioi Kim Lam, and Xinmin Zhao.

speak, and such gestures support and expand on information conveyed by words. The fact that gestures occur at the same time as speech, and that they carry the same meaning as speech, suggests that the production of the two are intimately linked. In fact, not only are the meaning of words and of gestures intimately linked in a discourse, but so are their functions in accomplishing conversational work: it has been shown that certain kinds of gestures produced during conversation act to structure the contributions of the two participants (to signal when an utterance continues the same topic or strikes out in a new direction), and to signal the contribution of particular utterances to the current discourse. It is clear that, like facial expression, gesture is not a kinesic performance independent of speech, or simply a 'translation' of speech. Rather, gesture and speech are so intimately connected that one cannot say which one is dependent on the other. Both can be claimed to arise from a single internal encoding process ([8], [21], [27]).

## 2.1   Example

In this section of the paper we present a fragment of dialogue (the complete dialogue has been synthesized and animated), in which intonation, gesture, head and lip movements, and their inter-synchronization were automatically generated. This example will serve to demonstrate the phenomena described here, and in subsequent sections we will return to each phenomenon, to explain how rule-generation and synchronization are carried out.

In the following dialogue, imagine that Gilbert is a bank teller, and George has asked Gilbert for help in obtaining $50. The dialogue is unnaturally repetitive and explicit in its goals because the dialogue generation program that produced it has none of the conversational inferences that allow humans to follow leaps of reasoning. Therefore, the two agents have to specify in advance each of the goals they are working towards and steps they are following (see section 4.1).

| | |
|---|---|
| Gilbert: | Do you have a blank check? |
| George: | Yes, I have a blank check. |
| Gilbert: | Do you have an account for the check? |
| George: | Yes, I have an account for the check. |
| Gilbert: | Does the account contain at least fifty dollars? |
| George: | Yes, the account contains eighty dollars. |
| Gilbert: | Get the check made out to you for fifty dollars and then I can withdraw fifty dollars for you. |
| George: | All right, let's get the check made out to me for fifty dollars. |

When Gilbert asks a question, his voice rises. When George replies to a question, his voice falls. When Gilbert asks George whether he has a blank check, he stresses the word "check". When he asks George whether he has an account for the check, he stresses the word "account".

Every time Gilbert replies affirmatively ("yes"), or turns the floor over to Gilbert ("all right"), he nods his head, and raises his eyebrows. George and Gilbert look at each other when Gilbert asks a question, but at the end of each question, Gilbert looks up slightly. During the brief pause at the end of affirmative statements the speaker (always George, in this fragment) blinks. To mark the end of the questions, Gilbert raises his eyebrows.

In saying the word "check", Gilbert sketches the outlines of a check in the air between him and his listener. In saying "account", Gilbert forms a kind of box in front of him with his hands: a metaphorical representation of a bank account in which one keeps money. When he says the phrase "withdraw fifty dollars," Gilbert withdraws his hand towards his chest.

## 2.2   Communicative Significance of the Face

Movements of the head and facial expressions can be characterized by their placement with respect to the linguistic utterance and their significance in transmitting information [35]. The set of facial movement clusters contains:

- *syntactic functions* accompany the flow of speech and are synchronized at the verbal level. Facial movements (such as raising the eyebrows, nodding the head or blinking while saying "do you have a blank CHECK") can appear on an accented syllable or a pause.

- *semantic functions* can emphasize what is being said, substitute for a word or refer to an emotion (like wrinkling the nose while talking about something disgusting or smiling while remembering a happy event: "it was such a NICE DAY.").

- *dialogic functions* regulate the flow of speech and depend on the relationship between two people (smooth turns[1] are often co-occurrent with mutual gaze; e.g at the end of "do you have a blank check?", both interactants look at each other).

These three functions are modulated by various parameters:

- *speaker and listener characteristic functions* convey information about the speaker's social identity, emotion, attitude, age (friends spend more time looking at each other while talking than a lying speaker who will avoid the other's gaze).

- *listener functions* correspond to the listener's reactions to the speaker's speech; they can be signals of agreement, of attention, of comprehension (like saying "I see", "mhmm").

## 2.3   Communicative Significance of Hand Gestures

Gesture too can be described in terms of its intrinsic relationship to speech. Three aspects of this relationship are described before we go on to speak about the synchronization of the two communicative channels.

First of all, four basic types of gestures occur only during speech ([27] estimates that 90% of all gestures occur when the speaker is actually uttering something).

- *Iconics* represent some feature of the accompanying speech, such as sketching a small rectangular space with one's two hands while saying "do you have a blank CHECK?"

- *Metaphorics* represent an abstract feature concurrently spoken about, such as forming a jaw-like shape with one hand, and pulling it towards one's body while saying "then I can WITHDRAW fifty dollars for you".

- *Deictics* indicate a point in space. They accompany reference to persons, places and other spatializeable discourse entities. An example might be pointing to the ground while saying "do you have an account at THIS bank?".

- *Beats* are small formless waves of the hand that occur with heavily emphasized words, occasions of turning over the floor to another speaker, and other kinds of special linguistic work. An example is waving one's left hand briefly up and down along with the phrase "all right".

In some discourse contexts about three-quarters of all clauses are accompanied by gestures of one kind or another; of these, about 40% are iconic, 40% are beats, and the remaining 20% are divided between deictic and metaphoric gestures [27]. And surprisingly, although the proportion of different gestures may change, all of these types of gestures, and spontaneous gesturing in general, are found in discourses by speakers of most languages.

There is also a semantic and pragmatic relationship between the two media. Gesture and speech do not always manifest the same information about an idea, but what they convey is always complementary. That is, gesture may depict the way in which an action was carried out when this aspect of meaning is not depicted in speech. For example, one speaker, describing how one deposits checks into a bank account, said "you list the checks" while she

---

[1]Meaning that the listener does not interrupt or overlap the speaker.

depicted with her hands that the deposit slip is to be turned over and turned vertically in order for the checks to be listed in the spaces provided on the back of the slip.

Finally, the importance of the interdependence of speech and gesture is shown by the fact that speakers rely on information conveyed in gesture – sometimes even to the exclusion of information conveyed by accompanying speech – as they try to comprehend a story [9].

Nevertheless, hand gestures and gaze behavior have been virtually absent from attempts to animate semi-autonomous agents in communicative contexts.

## 2.4 Synchrony of Gesture, Facial Movements, and Speech

Facial expression, eye gaze and hand gestures do not do their communicative work only within single utterances, but also have inter-speaker effects. The presence or absence of confirmatory feedback by one conversational participant, via gaze or head movement, for example, affects the behavior of the other. A conversation consists of the exchange of meaningful utterances and of behavior. One person punctuates and reinforces her speech by head nods, smiles, and hand gestures; the other person can smile back, vocalize, or shift gaze to show participation in the conversation.

Synchrony implies that changes occurring in speech and in body movements should appear at the same time. For example, when a word begins to be articulated, eye blinks, hand movement, head turning, and brow raising can occur and can finish at the end of the word.

Synchrony occurs at all levels of speech: the phonemic segment, word, phrase or long utterance. Different facial motions are characteristic of these different groups [13], [20]. Some of them are more adapted to the phoneme level, like an eye blink, while others act at the word level, like a frown. In the example "Do you have a blank check?", a raising eyebrow starts and ends on the accented syllables "check", while a blink starts and ends on the pause marking the end of the utterance. Facial expression of emphasis can match the emphasized segment, showing synchronization at this level (a sequence of head nods can punctuate the emphasis). Moreover, some movements reflect encoding-decoding difficulties and therefore coincide with hesitations and pauses inside clauses. Many hesitation pauses are produced at the beginning of speech and correlate with avoidance of gaze (the head of the speaker turns away from the listener) as if to help the speaker to concentrate on what she is going to say.

Gestures occur in synchrony with their semantically parallel linguistic units, although in cases of hesitations, pauses or syntactically complex speech, it is the gesture which appears first ([27]). At the most local level, individual gestures and words are synchronized in time so that the 'stroke' (most energetic part of the gesture) occurs either with or just before the phonologically most prominent syllable of the accompanying speech segment ([21], [27]). At the most global level, we find that the hands of the speaker come to rest at the end of a speaking turn, before the next speaker begins her turn. At the intermediate level, the phenomenon of co-articulation of gestural units is found, whereby gestures are performed rapidly, or their production is stretched out over time, so as to synchronize with preceding and following gestures, and the speech these gestures accompany. An example of gestural co-articulation is the relationship between the two gestures in the phrase "get the check MADE OUT TO YOU for fifty dollars and then I can WITHDRAW fifty dollars for you". During the phrase 'made out to you', the right hand sketches a writing gesture in front of the speaker. However, rather than carrying this gesture all the way to completion (either both hands coming to rest at the end of this gesture, or maintaining the location of the hands in space), the hand drops slightly and then pulls back towards the speaker to perform the 'withdraw' gesture. Thus, the occurrence of the phrase 'made out to you', with its

accompanying gesture, affected the occurrence of the gesture that accompanied "withdraw".

## 3 Computer Animation of Conversation

### 3.1 Literature on Facial Control Systems

Various systems have been proposed to integrate the different facial expression functions. Most of the systems use **FACS** (Facial Action Coding System) as a notational system [17]. This system is based on anatomical studies, and describes any visible facial movements. An action unit **AU**, the basic element of this system, describes the action produced by one or a group of related muscles.

The multi-layer approach [19] allows independent control at each level of the system. At the lowest level (geometric level), geometry of the face can be modified using free form deformation techniques. At the highest level, facial animation can be computed from an input utterance.

In M. Patel's model [28] facial animation can also be done at different levels of representation. It can be done either at the muscle level, the **AU** level or the script level. For each **AU** the user can select starting and ending points of action, the intensity of action, the start and end tensions and the interpolation method to compute the in-between frames. An alternative approach is proposed by [11] with good results.

Building a user-interface, [37] propose a categorization of facial expressions depending on their communicative meaning. For each of the facial functions a list of facial displays is performed (for example, remembering corresponds to eyebrow action, eye closure and one side of mouth pull back). A user talks to the 3D synthetic actor. A speech system recognizes the words and generates an answer with the appropriate facial displays. Grammar rules, a small vocabulary set and a specific knowledge domain are part of the speech analysis system. The responses by the 3D actor are selected from a pre-established set of utterances. The appropriate facial displays accompanying the answer follow the analysis of the conventional situation (e.g. if the user's speech is not recognized the 3D actor will answer with a "not-confident" facial display).

### 3.2 Literature on Gesture Animation

The computer graphics literature is rather sparse on the topic of gesture animation. Animators frequently use key parameter techniques to create arm and hand motions. Rijpkema and Girard [33] created handshapes automatically based on the object being gripped. The Thalmanns [18, 26] improved on the hand model to include much better skin models and deformations of the finger tips and the gripped object. Lee and Kunii [22] built a system that includes handshapes and simple pre-stored facial expressions for American Sign Language (ASL) synthesis. Dynamics of arm gestures in ASL have been studied by Loomis et al [25]. Chen et al [10] constructed a virtual human that can shake hands with an interactive participant. Lee et al [23] automatically generate lifting gestures by considering strength and comfort measures. Moravec and Calvert [5] constructed a system that portrays the gestural interaction between two agents as they pass and greet one another. Behavioral parameters were set by personality attribute "sliders" though the interaction sequence was itself pre-determined and limited to just one type of non-verbal encounter.

## 4 Overview of System

In the current system, a model of face-to-face interaction is used to generate all of the behaviors implemented, from the informational status of intonation to the communicative function of head nods, gaze, and hand gestures. Additionally, however, this system implements two agents whose verbal and nonverbal behaviors are integrated not only within turns, but across speakers.

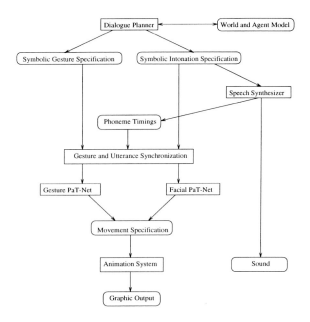

Figure 1: Interaction of components

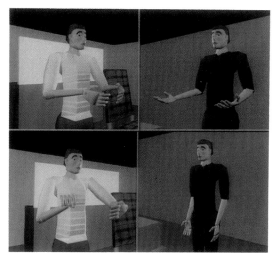

Figure 2: Examples of symbolic gesture specification

In the remaining parts of the paper we explain the different boxes of Figure 1. We start from the top of the figure and work towards its bottom. Currently, gesture is generated by the dialogue planner, while facial expression and gaze are generated by the facial PaT-Net.

## 4.1 Dialogue Planner

The text of this dialogue is automatically generated on the basis of a database of facts describing the way the world works, a list of the goals of the two agents, and the set of beliefs of those two agents about the world, including the beliefs of the agents about one another [30], [7]. In this instance the two agents have goals that change over the course of the dialogue (Gilbert comes to have the goal of helping George get $50; George comes to have the goal of writing a check).

Text is generated and pitch accents and phrasal melodies are placed on generated text as outlined in [36] and [31]. This text is converted automatically to a form suitable for input to the AT&T Bell Laboratories TTS synthesizer ([24]). When the dialogue is generated, the following information is saved automatically: (1) the timing of the phonemes and pauses, (2) the type and place of the accents, (3) the type and place of the gestures.

This speech and timing information will be critical for synchronizing the facial and gestural animation.

## 4.2 Symbolic Gesture Specification

The dialogue generation program annotates utterances according to how their semantic content could relate to a spatial expression (literally, metaphorically, spatializeably, or not at all). Further, references to entities are classified according to discourse status as either new to discourse and hearer (indefinites), new to discourse but not to hearer (definites on first mention), or old (all others) [32]. According to the following rules, these annotations, together with the earlier ones, determine which concepts will have an associated gesture. Gestures that represent something (iconics and metaphorics) are generated for rhematic verbal elements (roughly, information not yet spoken about) and for hearer new references, provided that the semantic content is of an appropriate class to receive such a gesture: words with literally spatial (or concrete) content get iconics (e.g. "check"); those with metaphorically spatial (or abstract) content get metaphorics (e.g. "account"); words with physically spatializeable content get deictics (e.g. "this bank"). Meanwhile, beat gestures are generated for such items when the

semantic content cannot be represented spatially, and are also produced accompanying discourse new definite references (e.g. "fifty dollars"). If a representational gesture is called for, the system accesses a dictionary of gestures (motion prototypes) that associates semantic representations with possible gestures that might represent them[2] (for further details, see [7]).

In Figure 2, we see examples of how symbolic gestures are generated from discourse content.

1. "Do you have a BLANK CHECK?"

   - In the first frame, an iconic gesture (representing a rectangular check) is generated from the first mention (new to hearer) of the entity 'blank check'.

2. "Will you HELP me get fifty dollars?"

   - In the second frame, a metaphoric gesture (the common *propose* gesture, representing the request for help as a proposal that can be offered to the listener) is generated because of the first mention (new to hearer) of the request for help.

3. "You can WRITE the check."

   - In the third frame, an iconic gesture (representing writing on a piece of paper) is generated from the first mention of the concrete action of 'writing a check'.

4. "I will WAIT for you to withdraw fifty dollars for me."

   - In the fourth frame, a beat gesture (a movement of the hand up and down) is generated from the first mention of the notion 'wait for', which cannot be represented spatially.

After this gestural annotation of all gesture types, and lexicon look-up of appropriate forms for representational gestures, information about the duration of intonational phrases (acquired in speech generation) is used to time gestures. First, all the gestures in each intonational phrase are collected. Because of the relationship between accenting and gesturing, in this dialogue at most one representational gesture occurs in each intonational phrase. If there is a representational gesture, its preparation is set to begin at or before the beginning of the intonational phrase, and to finish at or before the next gesture in the intonational phrase or the nuclear stress of the phrase, whichever comes first. The stroke phase is then set to coincide with the nuclear stress of the phrase. Finally, the relaxation is set to begin no sooner than the end of the stroke or the end of

---

[2]This solution is provisional: a richer semantics would include the features relevant for gesture generation, so that the form of the gestures could be generated algorithmically from the semantics. Note also, however, that following [21] we are led to believe that gestures may be more standardized in form than previously thought.

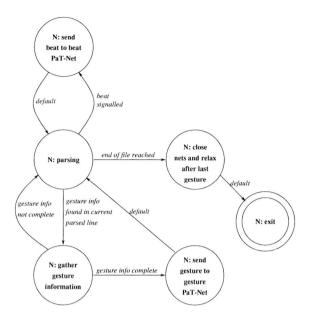

Figure 3: Pat-Net that synchronizes gestures with the dialogue at the phoneme level.

the last beat in the intonational phrase, with the end of relaxation to occur around the end of the intonational phrase. Beats, in contrast, are simply timed to coincide with the stressed syllable of the word that realizes the associated concept. When these timing rules have been applied to each of the intonational phrases in the utterance, the output is a series of symbolic gesture types and the times at which they should be performed. These instructions are used to generate motion files that run the animation system ([3]).

### 4.3 The Underlying Coordination Model

Interaction between agents and synchronization of gaze and hand movements to the dialogue for each agent are accomplished using Parallel Transition Networks (PaT-Nets), which allow coordination rules to be encoded as simultaneously executing finite state automata ([4]). PaT-Nets can call for action in the simulation and make state transitions either conditionally or probabilistically. Pat-Nets are scheduled into the simulation with an operating system that allows them to invoke or kill other PaT-Nets, sleep until a desired time or until a desired condition is met, and synchronize with other running nets by waiting for them to finish or by waiting on a shared semaphore.

In addition, the PaT-Net notation is object oriented with each net defined by a *class* with actions and transition conditions as *methods*. The running networks are instances of the PaT-Net class and can take parameters on instantiation. This notation allows Pat-Nets to be hierarchically organized and allows constructing new nets by combining existing nets or making simple modifications to existing nets.

Behaviors are implemented as specified in the following sections, with all head, eye and hand movement behavior for an individual encoded in PaT-Nets. A PaT-Net instance is created to control each agent with appropriate parameters. Then as agents' PaT-Nets synchronize the agents with the dialogue and interact with the unfolding simulation they schedule activity that achieves a complex observed interaction behavior.

### 4.4 Gesture Generator

The gesture PaT-Net sends information about the timing, shape, and position of the hands and arms to the animation system. The animation process produces a file of motions to be carried out by the two figures. Starting with a given gesture and its timing, speech rate and surrounding gestures constrain the motion sequence for a

proper co-articulation effect. As depicted in Figure 3, upon the signalling of a particular gesture, parse-net will instantiate one of two additional PaT-Nets; if the gesture is a beat, the finite state machine representing beats ("beat-net") will be called, and if a deictic, iconic, or metaphoric, the network representing these types of gestures ("gest-net") will be called. This separation is motivated by the "rhythm hypothesis" ([38]) which posits that beats arise from the underlying rhythmical pulse of speaking, while other gestures arise from meaning representations. In addition, beats are often found superimposed over the other types of gestures, and such a separation facilitates implementation of superposition. Finally, since one of the goals of the model is to reflect differences in behavior among gesture types, this system provides for control of freedom versus boundedness in gestures (e.g. an iconic gesture or emblem is tightly constrained to a particular standard of well-formedness, while beats display free movement); free gestures may most easily be generated by a separate PaT-Net whose parameters include this feature.

Gesture and beat finite state machines are built as necessary by the parser, so that the gestures can be represented as they arise. The newly created instances of the gesture and beat PaT-Nets do not exit immediately upon creating their respective gestures; rather, they pause and await further commands from the calling network, in this case, parse-net. This is to allow for the phenomenon of gesture coarticulation, in which two gestures may occur in an utterance without intermediary relaxation, i.e. without dropping the hands or, in some cases, without relaxing handshape. Once the end of the current utterance is reached, the parser adds another level of control: it forces exit without relaxation of all gestures except the gesture at the top of the stack; this final gesture is followed by a relaxation of the arms, hands, and wrists.

Consider the following data from the intonation and gesture streams. Let us examine a gesture PaT-Net that acts on this input.
*Intonation:* Do you have a blank CHECK
*Gesture:*          pr    beat   sk    rx
In this example, the primary intonational stress of the phrase falls on 'check', but there is a secondary stress on 'blank'. The gesture line of the example shows that the preparation ('pr') of the gesture begins on 'have', that the stroke of the gesture ('st') falls on check, and that the gesturing relaxes ('rx') after 'check'. Because of the secondary stress on the new informational item 'blank', a beat gesture falls there, and it is found superimposed over the production of the iconic gesture.

Due to the structure of the conversation, where the speakers alternate turns, we assume similar alternation in gesturing. (Gesturing by listeners is almost non-existent [27].) For the purposes of gesture generation, phoneme information is ignored; however, utterance barriers must be interpreted both to provide an envelope for the timing of a particular gesture or sequence of gestures and to determine which speaker is gesturing. Timing information, given in the speech file, also allows the PaT-Net to determine whether there is enough time for a complete gesture to be produced. For example, the iconic gesture which accompanies the utterance *"Do you have a blank [check]?"* has sufficient time to execute: it is the only (non-beat) gesture occurring in the phrase, as shown above. However, if this timing is insufficient to allow for full gesture production, then the gesture must be foreshortened to allow for the reduced available timing (because beat gestures are produced by a separate PaT-Net system, they do not enter into questions of co-articulation).

The most common reason for foreshortening is anticipation of the next gesture to be produced in a discourse. In anticipatory co-articulation effects, most often the relaxation phase of the foreshortened iconic, metaphoric or deictic gesture and preparation phase of the next gesture become one. This process can be seen in the gestures accompanying the phrase *"Get the check [made out to you] for fifty dollars and then I can [withdraw] fifty dollars for you"*. "[Made out to you]" is produced .90 seconds into the phrase, and "[withdraw]" is generated at 1.9 seconds. This causes some fore-shortening in the relaxation process during the first gesture, from which the second gesture is then produced.

Co-articulation constraints – synchronizing the gestures with intonational phrases and surrounding gestures – may actually cause the given gestures to be aborted if too little time is available for production given the physical constraints of the human model.

## 4.5 Gesture Motion Specification

The graphics-level gesture animation system accepts gesture instructions containing information about the location, type, timing, and handshape of individual gestures. Based on the current location of the hands and arms in space, the system will attempt to get as close as possible to the gesture goals in the time allowed, but may mute motions or positionings because it cannot achieve them in time (co-articulation effects). This animation system calls upon a library of predefined handshapes which form the primitives of hand gesture. These handshapes were chosen to reflect the shapes most often found in gesture during conversational interaction ([21]). The animation system also calls upon separate hand, arm and wrist control mechanisms.

The gesture system is divided into three parts: hand shape, wrist control, and arm positioning. The first, hand shape, relies on an extensible library of hand shape primitives for the basic joint positions, but allows varying degrees of relaxation towards a neutral hand position. The speed at which the hand may change shape is also limited to allow the modelling of hand shape co-articulation. Large changes in hand position are restricted as less time is allotted for the hand movement, forcing faster hand gestures to smooth together.

The wrist control system allows the wrist to maintain and change its position independently of what complex arm motions may be occurring. The wrist is limited within the model to a physically realistic range of motion. Wrist direction is specified in terms of simple directions relative to the gesturer, such as "point the fingers of the left hand forward and up, and the palm right".

The arm motion system accepts general specifications of spatial goals and drives the arms towards those goals within the limits imposed by the arm's range of motion. The arm may be positioned by using general directions like "chest-high, slightly forward, and to the far left".

The expressiveness of an individual's gesturing can be represented by adjusting the size of the gesture space of the graphical figure. In this way, parameters such as age (children's gestures are larger than adults') and culture (in some cultures gestures tend to be larger) can be implemented in the gesture animation.

## 4.6 Symbolic Facial Expression Specification

In the current system, facial expression (movement of the lips, eyebrows, etc.) is specified separately from movement of the head and eyes (gaze). In this section we discuss facial expression, and turn to gaze in the next section.

P. Ekman and his colleagues characterize the set of semantic and syntactic facial expressions depending on their meaning [15]. Many facial functions exist (such as manipulators that correspond to biological needs of the face (wetting the lips); emblems and emotional emblems that are facial expressions replacing a word, an emotion) but only some are directly linked to the intonation of the voice. In this system, facial expressions connected to intonation are automatically generated, while other kinds of expressions (emblems, for example) are specified by hand [29].

## 4.7 Symbolic Gaze Specification

Gaze can be classified into four primary categories depending on its role in the conversation [1], [12]. In the following, we give rules of action and the functions for each of these four categories (see Figure 4). The nodes of the Pat-Net they refer to is also indicated.

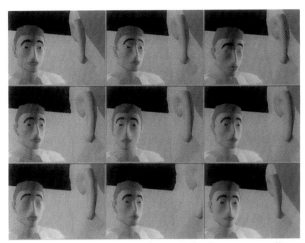

Figure 4: Facial expressions and gaze behavior corresponding to: "All right. <pause> You can write the check".

planning : corresponds to the first phase of a turn when the speaker organizes her thoughts. She has a tendency to look away in order to prevent an overload of information (beginning of turn). On the other hand, during the execution phase, the speaker knows what she is going to say and looks more at the listener. For a short turn (duration less than 1.5 sec.), the speaker and the listener establish eye contact (mutual gaze) [1] (short-turn).

comment : accompanies and comments speech, by occurring in parallel with accent and emphasis. Accented or emphasized items are punctuated by head nods; the speaker looks toward the listener (accent). The speaker also gazes at the listener more when she asks a question. She looks up at the end of the question (utterance: question). When answering, the speaker looks away (utterance: answer).

control : controls the communication channel and functions as a synchronization signal: responses may be demanded or suppressed by looking at the listener. When the speaker wants to give her turn of speaking to the listener, she gazes at the listener at the end of the utterance (end of turn). When the listener asks for the turn, she looks up at the speaker (turn request).

feedback : is used to collect and seek feedback. The listener can emit different reaction signals to the speaker's speech. Speaker looks toward the listener during grammatical pauses to obtain feedback on how utterances are being received (within-turn). This is frequently followed by the listener looking at the speaker and nodding (back-channel). In turn, if the speaker wants to keep her turn, she looks away from the listener (continuation signal). If the speaker doesn't emit a within-turn signal by gazing at the listener, the listener can still emit a back-channel which in turn may be followed by a continuation signal by the speaker. But the probability of action of the listener varies with the action of the speaker [14]; in particular, it decreases if no signal has occurred from the speaker. In this way the listener reacts to the behavior of the speaker.

## 4.8 Gaze Generator

Each of the dialogic functions appears as a sub-network in the PaT-Net. Figure 5 outlines the high-level PaT-Net for gaze control for a single agent. It contains the four dialogic functions, their nodes that define each function, and their associated actions. From the definitions given above, we extract the conditions and the actions characterizing the dialogic functions. For this current version of the

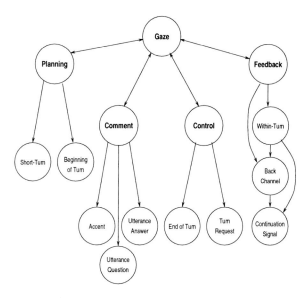

Figure 5: The gaze movement PaT-Net: actions are defined in the nodes; conditional and probabilistic transitions occur on arcs. All leaf nodes also branch back to the root node unconditionally.

program we do not differentiate head movement and eye movement. That is the eyes follow the head. Moreover, in the literature this difference is rarely made. In what follows, we use "gaze" to refer to head and eye movement.

Each node is characterized by a probability. A person can have the floor talking or pausing, but loses it as soon as the other person starts talking. There are 3 possible states per person while having the floor. If Speaker has the floor: Speaker talks and Listener pauses, both of them are talking, or both of them are pausing. For each of these states, Speaker and Listener can gaze at each other or not. This gives us 12 possibilities, or 24 per dyad. We can then compute the probability of being in each of these states [6]. Most of the nodes of the Pat-Net can be characterized by a certain set of states. For example the occurrence of a "within-turn signal" as we defined it corresponds to the action: person1 looks at the person2 while having the floor and pausing. These state sets correspond to a sub-matrix. We compute the probability of each sub-matrix in relation to the particular state (having the floor and pausing) to arrive at a probability of occurrence. We do such a computation for all the other nodes of the Pat-Net. Probabilities appropriate for each agent given the current role as listener or speaker are set for the PaT-Net before it executes. At each turn change, the probabilities change values accordingly. This information is used to determine the rules and transitional probabilities for actions in Pat-Nets.

For each phoneme, the GAZE Pat-Net is entered. A transition is made on the node whose condition is true. If the probability of the nodes allows it, the action is performed. The action of the different nodes of the Pat-Net is illustrated in the following with the example:

```
Gilbert:  Get the chEck made OUt to you
for fifty dollars <pause> And thEn <pause>
I can withdrAw fifty dollars for you.
```

planning: For the first few phonemes of the beginning of the example utterance [3] (in our example it corresponds to "Get the ch"), the sub-network **planning** is applied. This utterance is not short so the node short-turn is not entered.

But the node beginning-turn is entered; the condition of being in a beginning of turn is true but its probability

did not allow the action speaker gazes away to be applied. Therefore the speaker (Gilbert) keeps his current gaze direction (looking at George).

comment: In our example, on accented items ("chEck", "thEn" and "withdrAw"), the node accent of the sub-network **comment** is reached; the actions speaker gazes at the listener and head nod are performed by Gilbert. As before, the instantiation of an action depends on its probability. The system easily represents the parallel agent actions.

control: In our example at the end of the utterance[4] (corresponding to "fifty dollars for you" here) the sub-network **control** is entered. Two actions are considered. The node end of turn corresponds to action performed by the speaker: speaker gazes at listener. The other node turn request affects the listener; the action listener gazes at the speaker and up is performed.

feedback: The two intonational phrases of our example (*get the check made out to you for fifty dollars* and *and then*) are separated by a pause; this corresponds to a within-turn situation. The sub-network **feedback** is entered. If the probability allows it, the action speaker gazes at the listener is performed[5]. After a delay (0.2 sec., as specified by the program), the node back-channel is reached. Once more the program checks the probabilities associated with the actions. Two actions can happen: listener gazes at the speaker and/or the listener nods. In either case, the final step within the **feedback** sub-network is reached after some delay. The action speaker gazes away from the listener is then performed.

### 4.9 Facial Expression Generator

Facial expressions belonging to the set of semantic and syntactic functions (see section 4.6) are clustered into functional groups: lip shape, conversational signal, punctuator, manipulator and emblem. We use **FACS** to denote facial expressions. Each is represented by two parameters: *its time of occurrence* and *its type*. Our algorithm [29] embodies rules as described in Section 4.6 to automatically generate facial expressions, following the principle of synchrony.

The program scans the input utterance and computes the different facial expressions corresponding to these functional groups. The computation of the lip shape is made in three passes and incorporates coarticulation effects. Phonemes are associated to some characteristic shapes with different degree of deformability. For deformable elements, temporal and spatial constraints modify these shapes to consider their surrounding context. A conversational signal (movements occurring on accents, like the raising of an eyebrow) starts and ends with the accented word; while punctuator signal (movement occurring on pause, like frowning) happens on the pause. When a blink is one of these signals it is synchronized at the phoneme level. Other signals such as emblems and emotional emblems are performed consciously and must be specified by the user.

By varying the two parameters defining a facial expression, different speaker personalities can be obtained. For example a persuasive person can punctuate each accented word with raising eyebrows, while another person might not.

### 4.10 Gaze and Facial Motion Specification

The gaze directions generated in a previous stage can now be instantiated. As discussed earlier, the GAZE PaT-Net in Figure 5 is run for each agent at the beginning of every phoneme. Depending on the course taken through the GAZE network due to probabilistic

---

[3]A beginning of a turn is defined as all the phonemes between the first one and the first accented segment.

[4]End of turn is defined as all the phonemes between the last accented segment and the last phonemes.

[5]In the case the action is not performed, the arc going to the node back-channel is immediately traversed without waiting for the next phonemic segment.

branching and environmental state, the net may commit its agent to a variety of actions such as a head nod or a change in the gaze point. A change in the gaze is accomplished by supplying the human model with a 3D coordinate at which to look and a time in which to move – the scheduled motion then begins at the current point in the simulation and has the specified duration. A head nod is accomplished by scheduling a sequence of joint motions for the neck, supplying both the angle and the angular velocity for each nod cycle. Note that the gaze controller schedules motions as they are necessary by reacting to the unfolding simulation (in fact, it does this in semi-real time) and does not have to generate all motions in advance. This makes the gaze controller easy to extend and easy to integrate with the rest of the system.

Different functions may be served by the same action, which differ only in their timing and amplitude. For example, when punctuating an accent, the speaker's head nod will be of larger amplitude than the feedback head nods emitted by the listener. Different head nod functions may also be characterized by varying numbers of up/down cycles. The gaze direction is sustained by calling for the agent to look at a pre-defined point in the environment until a change is made by another action.

For facial expressions, the program outputs the list of **AUs** that characterize each phonemic element and pause [29].

After scanning all the input utterances, all the actions to be performed are specified. Animation files are output. The final animation is done by combining the different output files for the gesture, face and gaze in *Jack*.

## 5   Conclusions

Automatically generating information about intonation, facial expression, head movements and hand gestures allows an interactive dialogue animation to be created; for a non-real-time animation much guess-work in the construction of appropriate motions can be avoided. The resulting motions can be used as is – as demonstrated in the video – or the actions and timings can be used as a cognitively and physiologically justified guide to further refinement of the conversation and the participants' interactions by a human animator.

## REFERENCES

[1] M. Argyle and M. Cook. *Gaze and Mutual gaze*. Cambridge University Press, 1976.

[2] N. I. Badler, B. A. Barsky, and D. Zeltzer, editors. *Making Them Move: Mechanics, Control, and Animation of Articulated Figures*. Morgan-Kaufmann, San Mateo, CA, 1991.

[3] N. I. Badler, C. Phillips and B. L. Webber. *Simulating Humans: Computer Graphics, Animation, and Control*. Oxford University Press, June 1993.

[4] Welton M. Becket. The *jack lisp api*. Technical Report MS-CIS-94-01/Graphics Lab 59, University of Pennsylvania, 1994.

[5] Tom Calvert. Composition of realistic animation sequences for multiple human figures. In Norman I. Badler, Brian A. Barsky, and David Zeltzer, editors, *Making Them Move: Mechanics, Control, and Animation of Articulated Figures*, pages 35–50. Morgan-Kaufmann, San Mateo, CA, 1991.

[6] J. Cappella. personal communication, 1993.

[7] Justine Cassell, Mark Steedman, Norm Badler, Catherine Pelachaud, Matthew Stone, Brett Douville, Scott Prevost and Brett Achorn. *Modeling the interaction between speech and gesture*. Proceedings of the Cognitive Science Society Annual Conference, 1994.

[8] Justine Cassell and David McNeill. Gesture and the poetics of prose. *Poetics Today*, 12:375–404, 1992.

[9] Justine Cassell, David McNeill, and Karl-Erik McCullough. Kids, don't try this at home: Experimental mismatches of speech and gesture. presented at the International Communication Association annual meeting, 1993.

[10] D. T. Chen, S. D. Pieper, S. K. Singh, J. M. Rosen, and D. Zeltzer. The virtual sailor: An implementation of interactive human body modeling. In *Proc. 1993 Virtual Reality Annual International Symposium*, Seattle, WA, September 1993. IEEE.

[11] M.M. Cohen and D.W. Massaro. Modeling coarticulation in synthetic visual speech. In N.M. Thalmann and D.Thalmann, editors, *Models and Techniques in Computer Animation*, pages 139-156. Springer-Verlag, 1993.

[12] G. Collier. *Emotional expression*. Lawrence Erlbaum Associates, 1985.

[13] W.S. Condon and W.D. Osgton. Speech and body motion synchrony of the speaker-hearer. In D.H. Horton and J.J. Jenkins, editors, *The perception of Language*, pages 150–184. Academic Press, 1971.

[14] S. Duncan. Some signals and rules for taking speaking turns in conversations. In Weitz, editor, *Nonverbal Communication*. Oxford University Press, 1974.

[15] P. Ekman. Movements with precise meanings. *The Journal of Communication*, 26, 1976.

[16] P. Ekman. About brows: emotional and conversational signals. In M. von Cranach, K. Foppa, W. Lepenies, and D. Ploog, editors, *Human ethology: claims and limits of a new disipline: contributions to the Colloquium*, pages 169–248. Cambridge University Press, Cambridge, England; New-York, 1979.

[17] P. Ekman and W. Friesen. *Facial Action Coding System*. Consulting Psychologists Press, Inc., 1978.

[18] Jean-Paul Gourret, Nadia Magnenat-Thalmann, and Daniel Thalmann. Simulation of object and human skin deformations in a grasping task. *Computer Graphics*, 23(3):21–30, 1989.

[19] P. Kalra, A. Mangili, N. Magnenat-Thalmann, and D. Thalmann. Smile: A multilayered facial animation system. In T.L. Kunii, editor, *Modeling in Computer Graphics*. Springer-Verlag, 1991.

[20] A. Kendon. Movement coordination in social interaction: some examples described. In Weitz, editor, *Nonverbal Communication*. Oxford University Press, 1974.

[21] Adam Kendon. Gesticulation and speech: Two aspects of the process of utterance. In M.R.Key, editor, *The Relation between Verbal and Nonverbal Communication*, pages 207–227. Mouton, 1980.

[22] Jintae Lee and Tosiyasu L. Kunii. Visual translation: From native language to sign language. In *Workshop on Visual Languages*, Seattle, WA, 1993. IEEE.

[23] Philip Lee, Susanna Wei, Jianmin Zhao, and Norman I. Badler. Strength guided motion. *Computer Graphics*, 24(4):253–262, 1990.

[24] Mark Liberman and A. L. Buchsbaum. Structure and usage of current Bell Labs text to speech programs. Technical Memorandum TM 11225-850731-11, AT&T Bell Laboratories, 1985.

[25] Jeffrey Loomis, Howard Poizner, Ursula Bellugi, Alynn Blakemore, and John Hollerbach. Computer graphic modeling of American Sign Language. *Computer Graphics*, 17(3):105–114, July 1983.

[26] Nadia Magnenat-Thalmann and Daniel Thalmann. Human body deformations using joint-dependent local operators and finite-element theory. In Norman I. Badler, Brian A. Barsky, and David Zeltzer, editors, *Making Them Move: Mechanics, Control, and Animation of Articulated Figures*, pages 243–262. Morgan-Kaufmann, San Mateo, CA, 1991.

[27] David McNeill. *Hand and Mind: What Gestures Reveal about Thought*. University of Chicago, 1992.

[28] M. Patel. *Making FACES*. PhD thesis, School of Mathematical Sciences, University of Bath, Bath, AVON, UK, 1991.

[29] C. Pelachaud, N.I. Badler, and M. Steedman. Linguistic issues in facial animation. In N. Magnenat-Thalmann and D. Thalmann, editors, *Computer Animation '91*, pages 15–30. Springer-Verlag, 1991.

[30] Richard Power. The organisation of purposeful dialogues. *Linguistics*, 1977.

[31] Scott Prevost and Mark Steedman. Generating contextually appropriate intonation. In *Proceedings of the 6th Conference of the European Chapter of the Association for Computational Linguistics*, pages 332–340, Utrecht, 1993.

[32] Ellen F. Prince. The ZPG letter: Subjects, definiteness and information status. In S. Thompson and W. Mann, editors, *Discourse description: diverse analyses of a fund raising text*, pages 295–325. John Benjamins B.V., 1992.

[33] Hans Rijpkema and Michael Girard. Computer animation of hands and grasping. *Computer Graphics*, 25(4):339–348, July 1991.

[34] Barbara Robertson. Easy motion. *Computer Graphics World*, 16(12):33–38, December 1993.

[35] Klaus R. Scherer. The functions of nonverbal signs in conversation. In H. Giles R. St. Clair, editor, *The Social and Physhological Contexts of Language*, pages 225–243. Lawrence Erlbaum Associates, 1980.

[36] Mark Steedman. Structure and intonation. *Language*, 67:260–296, 1991.

[37] Akikazu Takeuchi and Katashi Nagao. Communicative facial displays as a new conversational modality. In *ACM/IFIP INTERCHI'93*, Amsterdam, 1993.

[38] K. Tuite. The production of gesture. *Semiotica*, 93(1/2), 1993.

## 6   Research Acknowledgments

This research is partially supported by NSF Grants IRI90-18513, IRI91-17110, CISE Grant CDA88-22719, NSF graduate fellowships, NSF VPW GER-9350179; ARO Grant DAAL03-89-C-0031 including participation by the U.S. Army Research Laboratory (Aberdeen); U.S. Air Force DEPTH contract through Hughes Missile Systems F33615-91-C-000; DMSO through the University of Iowa; National Defense Science and Engineering Graduate Fellowship in Computer Science DAAL03-92-G-0342; and NSF Instrumentation and Laboratory Improvement Program Grant USE-9152503.

# TBAG: A High Level Framework for Interactive, Animated 3D Graphics Applications

**Conal Elliott, Greg Schechter, Ricky Yeung, and Salim Abi-Ezzi**
SunSoft, Inc. [*]

## Abstract

We present a paradigm and toolkit for rapid prototyping of interactive, animated 3D graphics programs. The paradigm has its roots in declarative programming, emphasizing immutable values, first class functions, and relations, applying these concepts to a broad range of types, including points, vectors, planes, colors, transforms, geometry, and sound. The narrow role of modifiable state in this paradigm allows applications to be run in a collaborative setting (multi-user and multi-computer) without modification.

**CR Categories and Subject Descriptors**: I.3.7 [**Computer Graphics**]: Three-Dimensional Graphics and Realism; I.3.6 [**Computer Graphics**]: Methodology and Techniques; D.1.1 [**Programming Techniques**] Applicative (Functional) Programming; D.2.m [**Software Engineering**] Miscellaneous *Rapid Prototyping*; G.1.7 [**Mathematics of Computing**] Ordinary Differential Equations.

**Additional Keywords and Phrases**: Local Propagation Constraints

## 1 Introduction

TBAG is a paradigm and toolkit for rapid prototyping of interactive, animated 3D graphics programs, based on two broadly applied design principles: graphical ADTs (abstract data types), and explicit functions of time. TBAG attempts to make parameterized geometric models as easy to express as mathematical formulas, by providing a set of *high level graphical ADTs* and functions and operators for constructing graphical values. These types include points, vectors, planes, colors, transforms, geometry, and sound. Values of these types are immutable, ensuring that different uses of a value, even ones occurring in parallel, cannot interfere with each other.

A single type of entity, the *constrainable*, represents modeling animation parameters of all types, user interaction, and even entire animations. Constrainables explicitly represent functions of time,

to be sampled automatically by TBAG, thus relieving application programmers from involvement with frame generation and input device "motion events". Functions and operators that have been defined to work on basic types, including TBAG's high level graphical types, are automatically overloaded to work on constrainables over those types, producing new constrainables. The result is an almost invisible syntax for constructing interactive animations.

Other features of TBAG include lights, shadows, and even sound integrated with geometry in conceptually consistent manner. Also, velocity, gravitational and spring forces, etc., can be specified with ADTs (ordinary differential equations), which are formulated as equality expressions involving the constrainable derivatives. Finally, TBAG supports networked distribution transparently.

While other computer graphics researchers have done much good work to extend the might of numerical constraint solvers, our own work is complementary. It shows how to take a simple and efficient constraint solver, apply it uniformly to a multitude of types (including very high level types), make it support a continuous time model, and provide an almost invisible syntactic interface to it. Future work could merge these two research paths.

In this paper, we present details of TBAG's design, and how we resolved the implementation challenges that resulted. We then discuss TBAG's support for transparent and efficient distribution. Next support for derivatives and ODEs are described. A collection of sample applications is then presented. Finally, we make comparisons with related work.

## 2 The TBAG Programmer's Model

In this section, we describe TBAG's conceptual model and the C++ interface that embodies it. We also discuss how TBAG applications are developed. Implementation issues are discussed in later sections.

### 2.1 Graphical Data Types

TBAG programs perform geometry-specific operations by constructing and manipulating instances of high-level graphical data types. In the design of these types, TBAG leaves generally useful facilities to the host programming language wherever possible. Thus, type-specific support is distilled into as simple a form as possible, while allowing great flexibility and ease of expression. For instance, in TBAG,

- *Definition of reusable geometry* is handled by programming language support for definition of constants of arbitrary types.

[*]2550 Garcia Avenue, M/S MTV10-228, Mountain View, CA 94025 USA.
phone:415-336-{3086,6950,1791,2141}.
email:{conal,gds,ryeung,salim}@eng.sun.com.

- *Parameterized reusable geometry* is handled by definition and invocation of functions that produce geometry. The resulting customization power is not found in currently available graphics packages. Moreover, parameters may be of any type, including the geometry type itself.

- *Attributes and their scoping* are supported by functions that take the involved geometry and attributes as parameters (using a convenient infix notation), and yield a new geometry value.

To see how this approach works in practice, suppose one wants to construct several "block with ball" geometry values, consisting of a rectangular block of a specified color and a yellow sphere on top of it, together transformed according to some specified modeling transformation. In order to create several of these assemblies instead of just one, the programmer would define a C++ function[1]:

```
Geometry
block_with_ball(Transform& xform, Color& color)
{ return
  ( unit_cube * scale(1,4,1) * color +
    unit_sphere * xlt(0,2,0) * yellow ) *
  xform;
}
```

Comments:

- The types Geometry, Transform, and Color are predefined abstract data types. TBAG supplies these types and others, such as Point, Vector, and Axis, together with constants and functions for constructing values of those types.[2]

- The constants unit_cube and unit_sphere, each of type Geometry, are unit-dimensioned shapes, centered at the origin. The constant yellow is of type Color.

- The functions scale and xlt take three real numbers and construct a modeling transform, i.e., a value of the abstract type Transform, to scale or translate, respectively, the specified amounts along the $x$-, $y$-, and $z$-axes. There are also functions to create rotation and uniform scaling transforms, compositions of transforms, and transforms defined by matrices.

- The overloaded operator "*", when applied to a geometry value and a transform value, yields a transformed geometry value. In this example, the first application yields a non-uniformly scaled cube. The same operator is also overloaded to take a geometry value and a color and produce a colored geometry. In fact, both of these operations are special cases of a general attribution operation, which is based on an abstract type Attributer. (Other, less commonly used, attributers do not have additional overloadings, and instead are constructed via functions that indicate the specific attributes involved. For instance, edge_color is a function from colors to attributers, so cube * edge_color(red) evaluates to a cube with red edges.)

- The overloaded operator "+", when applied to two geometry values, yields a geometry value that is the union of the two given geometry values. (Hence any operation that can be applied to geometry values can be applied to unions formed by "+".) The final use of "*" transforms this geometric union.

It is important to keep in mind that, conceptually, every step involved in this definition creates a new value rather than side-effecting an existing one. Different uses of the same value, therefore, cannot interfere with each other, and so TBAG programmers need not be concerned with the order or frequency of evaluation of their definitions.

Geometry values support several operations, including rendering, picking, and bounding-box determination. Most TBAG programmers, however, need not even be aware of these operations, which are invoked automatically by *viewer* objects, and automatically supported by geometry values built up with the primitive geometry values, functions and operators provided in TBAG.

## 2.2 Constrainables

The style of expressions used for creating the static, non-interactive values described above may also be used to create dynamic, interactive *"constrainables"*. A constrainable represents a conceptually continuous flow of values, out of which the application (or the system) can retrieve a value corresponding to a specific time using the type-parameterized function value_at:[3]

```
template<class T>
T value_at(Constrainable<T> cbl, Real time)
```

A TBAG application creates constrainables that embody portions of the desired animation and interaction. Animated, interactive geometry is represented by a Geometry-valued constrainable, i.e., a value of type Constrainable<Geometry&>. A TBAG *viewer* object simply invokes value_at repeatedly on a Geometry-valued constrainable with the current time, and renders the result to a window on the screen, thus producing animation.

The remainder of this section describes how applications introduce constrainables, how constrainables get their values, and how constrainables are put into relationships with other constrainables.

## 2.2.1 Primitive Constrainables

Constrainables are built up compositionally, out of a few types of primitive constrainables, representing time and both physical and virtual input devices. The Real-valued constrainable Time, when asked for its value at a given time (supplied by a viewer), returns that time.

As an example of an input device, consider a window-system slider:

```
Valuator<Real>& hue_slider =
  real_slider("Hue", 0, 2 * pi, 0);
```

The function real_slider creates a labeled slider on the screen with a minimum, maximum, and initial value. The resulting object contains a public instance variable, value, which is a Real-valued constrainable representing the setting of the on-screen slider at all points in time. (Without infinite buffering, only part of the past of an input device may be accurately queried.) The TBAG system ensures that the position of the on-screen slider and the value constrainable always remain consistent.

---

1. C++ note: "T&" is the type of references to values of type T.

2. Each of these types is defined by a C++ abstract class, and some built-in subclasses, which makes TBAG conveniently extensible at this level of "predefined" types, constants, and functions. For ease of extensibility, the Geometry class's main method is actually a multi-method, choosing the actual code that is executed based upon the run-time types of more than one argument. See [20] for more details.

---

3. C++ note: this kind of declaration can be interpreted as an infinite family of function declarations, with T ranging over all types.

Similarly, a constrainable representing the time-varying position of a 2D mouse relative to an on-screen window can be accessed as:

```
Valuator<Point2D&>& mouse_val =
  mouse_constrainable_from_x_window(x_window_id);
```

Now, `mouse_val.value` is a Point2D-valued constrainable representing the position of the mouse relative to the specified window at all points in time. Primitive constrainables representing input devices are used to drive interactive applications.

## 2.2.2 Compound Constrainables

The TBAG system includes a tool that processes C and C++ header files and produces C++ overloaded functions that will accept constrainables as arguments and return properly typed constrainables. Thus, any function that was defined to operate on a type of value may be used to operate on constrainables over that type. For instance, evaluating the expression `sin(Time)` produces a Real-valued constrainable $c$ such that, `value_at(c, t)`, returns `sin(t)`. The standard file `math.h` was processed through the overloading tool to provide the overloading for the `sin` function.

These expressions may be nested to an arbitrary depth. For instance:

```
xlt(sin(Time), cos(Time * 2.0), 1.0)
```

produces a Transform-valued constrainable that, at time $t$, evaluates to `xlt(sin(t), cos(2t), 1.0)`.

Time-varying, interactive geometry is created in a similar fashion. Consider the `block_with_ball` function defined in Section 2.1. Once its header file has been processed through the overloading tool, it may be used with constrainables as arguments:

```
block_with_ball(uniform_scale(fabs(sin(Time))),
                hsv_color(hue_slider.value, 1, 1))
```

The result is a Geometry-valued constrainable representing a block-with-ball that is scaling according to the sine of time, and whose hue is determined by the setting of the slider built in Section 2.2.1.

The importance of the overloading tool cannot be overemphasized. With it, we have automatically turned hundreds of functions that were written without regard to constrainables into functions that can take constrainables as arguments and produce new constrainables (including all of TBAG's geometry-related functions).

Since TBAG allows time-varying and interactive values to be expressed directly, the programmer need not be concerned with many issues relating to flow of control. In most other systems, the application programmer needs to take one of two approaches:

- Explicitly poll for changes on input devices and explicitly update animation parameters.

- More commonly, use an event-driven system, and would register interest in input and timer events, with the registered callback procedures taking responsibility for correctly updating the relevant parameters.

In TBAG, neither approach is necessary, since the desired behavior is explicitly encoded into the constrainables. (In Section 2.3 we shall see that inherently discrete input events, such as a mouse button click, are treated differently.)

## 2.2.3 Establishing Relationships Among Constrainables

A constrainable may be related to other constrainables by setting up *constraints* among them (hence the name "constrainable"). The following code sets up a geometry consisting of a red and a blue block-with-ball, each positioned according to a Transform-valued constrainable:

```
Constrainable<Transform&> xform1, xform2;
Constrainable<Geometry&> scene =
  block_with_ball(xform1, red) +
  block_with_ball(xform2, blue);
```

At this point, the two blocks in `scene` have no connection with each other, so they may be manipulated independently (via `xform1` and `xform2`). Next, we can make these two transforms interdependent, with their composition being the identity transform:

```
assert(xform1 * xform2 == identity_trans);
```

The == operator returns a *constraint*, and `assert` tells TBAG to enforce the specified constraint. The `assert` function returns an *assertion*, which may later be retracted.

Once this constraint is asserted, changes to one of the transform constrainables result in changes to the other. For instance, moving one causes the other to be moved in the opposite direction; shrinking one causes the other to grow; and rotating one causes the other to perform the opposite rotation.

In TBAG, constraints may be asserted on constrainables of any type, and the system determines the appropriate values the constrainables should take on in order to satisfy the required constraints. From the programmer's point of view, constraints are continuously maintained among continuously time-varying values.

## 2.2.4 Multidirectionality

In the above example, we do not say that `xform1` is dependent upon `xform2`, or vice versa. Rather, we say that `xform1` and `xform2` are interdependent. This symmetry allows us to exploit *multidirectionality* — a powerful feature of the constraint engine that underlies TBAG. Thus, `xform1` can be altered and we would expect `xform2` to vary accordingly in order to maintain the relationship, or `xform2` can be altered and `xform1` remains consistent. One way to visualize this situation is to consider the code in Section 2.2.3 as creating the undirected constraint graph in Figure 1. [1]

When the application assigns a value to `xform1`:

```
// assign time-varying rotation:
Assertion *ast = assert(xform1 == rot(y_axis, Time));
```

the constraint engine produces the directed constraint solution graph shown in Figure 2, causing `xform2` to be dependent upon `xform1`. Since the transform composition operation can run in any of three directions (given any two inputs, calculate the third as output), the application can retract the above assertion and assign a value to `xform2`:

---

1. "Constant constrainables" are shown as dashed circles.

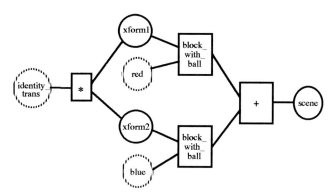

**Figure 1. An Undirected Constraint Graph**

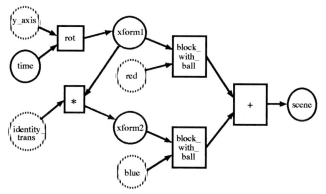

**Figure 2. Figure 1 with** `xform1` **determining** `xform2`

```
retract(ast);
// assign time-varying uniform scale
ast = assert(xform2 == uniform_scale(Time));
```

thus producing the new graph shown in Figure 2.

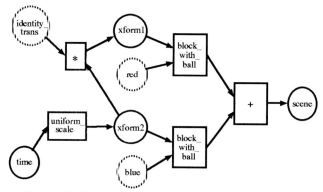

**Figure 3. Figure 1 with** `xform2` **determining** `xform1`

Note that if `ast` had not been retracted prior to the second assertion, the application would have been notified of a conflict (because the composition operation would have three inputs and no outputs).

## 2.2.5 Constraint Generality vs. Efficiency

When considering the use of constraints in an interactive context, it is vital to find a good compromise between generality and efficiency. Ideally, one would like extreme generality, but that choice leads to computationally intractable (and even undecidable) prob-

lems. On the other hand, a constraint system that sacrifices too much power for the sake of efficiency will not satisfy programmers' needs for expressiveness.

One approach for dealing with this problem would be to extend the constraint system to deal with new situations as they arise. In general, this is not a satisfactory approach since: it may require indepth knowledge of the constraint system to solve new problems; *ad hoc* extensions to the constraint system may result in decreased efficiency for the system in general; and the designer of a system cannot possibly predict all the situations an application programmer might encounter.

TBAG has adopted a pragmatic approach to dealing with this problem. Rather than forcing the constraint system to be extended for each new situation encountered, TBAG makes it straightforward and convenient for an application programmer to create and register application-specific functions and constraint-solution methods for those functions. These methods are invoked by the underlying constraint system at the appropriate time.

## 2.3 General Approach for Interaction

As noted above, interaction that is conceptually continuous is encoded directly into constrainables, and thus the application doesn't need to deal with tracking events from conceptually continuous devices. Examples of conceptually continuous interaction include window system slider motion, mouse motion, the turning of a dial, and six degree-of-freedom head tracking.

There are, however, other interactions that are fundamentally discrete (event based). Examples include button presses and menu choices. TBAG applications generally deal with such discrete input events by retracting some existing assertions and asserting new constraints. For instance, in a slight variation of the "opposite block-with-ball" example above, clicking on a block causes that block's position to be related to the mouse position (and, because of the relationship between transforms, the other block moves in the opposite direction). Releasing the mouse button removes the relationship between the mouse and the block. As in this example, discrete events tend to alter the topology of the constraint graph.

### 2.3.1 Manipulators

In the above scenario, the application does not need to watch for "motion events", but it does need to watch for discrete events, like a mouse button press or release. To help applications respond to discrete events, TBAG packages up common interaction paradigms into "manipulators" that may be used to attribute Geometry values, thus making the attributed Geometry obey a particular interaction paradigm. For instance, while the geometry given by

```
block_with_ball(xform1, red)
```

does not know how to respond to the mouse, the result of

```
block_with_ball(xform1, red) *
xform_manipulator(xform1)
```

does. The function `xform_manipulator` takes a Transform-valued constrainable and returns an Attributer that, when attached to a geometry, causes the transform (value of the constrainable) to become constrained to the mouse when the geometry is picked, and releases the transform from the mouse when the geometry is released.

## 2.4 Constraint Classes

Some TBAG programs introduce hundreds or thousands of constrainables and similar numbers of constraints. To make TBAG scalable, there needs to be a way to manage this complexity. Fortunately, as pointed out in [3], there is an elegant idiom for dealing with this complexity problem, combining the use of classes with constraints. TBAG applications make frequent use of these *constraint classes*, which define, as instance data, constrainables representing the object's constrainable properties. Thus, instantiating such a class automatically creates a new set of constrainables. Class initialization code (the C++ constructor method), assert constraints that relate properties of these constrainables. Other constraints relating the newly created object to the outside world are added outside of the class initialization code. Furthermore, class inheritance results in "constraint inheritance" for free. The reason is that if a class B derives from a class A, then initialization of objects of class B will include their initialization as A objects, including the assertion of A's constraints. As an example, Figure 4 shows a hierarchy of geometric constraint classes. Note how the subclasses inherit the constraints of the parent classes.

```
class GeometricObject {
  public:
    Constrainable<Geometry&> geometry;
    // No constraints
};

class XformedGeometricObject: public
                     GeometricObject {
  public:
    Constrainable<Geometry&> base_geom;
    Constrainable<Transform&> model_trans;
    // Constraints:
    XformedGeometricObject() {
      assert(geometry == base_geom *
                       model_trans); }
};

class AffineGeometricObject : public
                     XformedGeometricObject
{
  public:
    Constrainable<Point&>      position;
    Constrainable<Quaternion&> orientation;
    Constrainable<Vector&>     scale_vector;
    Constrainable<Vector&>     shear_vector;
    // Constraints:
    AffineGeometricObject();{
      assert(model_trans ==
        scale_by_vector(scale_vector) *
        shear_by_vector(shear_vector) *
        orient_by_quat(orientation) *
        translate_to_position(position)); }
};
```

**Figure 4. Some geometric object classes**

## 2.5 Lights

In TBAG, lights are simply geometry values. Unlike PHIGS [17] and immediate-mode graphics libraries [27,6], lights may be embedded in scene geometry, subject to that geometry's modeling transforms. This ability facilitates creation of richly articulated geometric assemblies that contain light sources that move appropriately. Lights influence the appearance of all geometric objects in the same scene. (In contrast, programmers of IRIS Inventor must worry about order of traversal, since lights only affect objects "later" than them in traversal order. On the other hand, in TBAG, there is no way to limit the scope of influence of a light.) The implementation price paid for this convenience is that two traversals of the geometry are made. In the first, lights are accumulated and transformed to world coordinates (WC), and non-light geometry is ignored. In the second traversal, the previously ignored geometry is rendered as lit by the accumulated WC lights.

There are four geometry-creating functions corresponding to light types (ambient, directional, positional, and spot lights). Each has useful defaults for all arguments.

As an example, consider the following C++ function:

```
Geometry&
directional_light_shaped_as_cone(
     Color& col, Vector& light_direction)
{ return
  (cone * col + directional_light(col)) *
  align_vectors(light_direction, z_vector);
}
```

This function takes a color and a direction and produces a cone of the specified color emitting a light of that color, all aligned with the specified direction. (The utility function `align_vectors` takes two Vector values and produces a transform that maps the first vector to the second.)

TBAG is not the only system that treats lights as first-class objects (e.g., Mirage [24] and DIVER [10] also do), but it is the only system that we know of that allows such succinct integration of lights with scene geometry.

## 2.6 Shadows

The interface for shadows is based on the notion of a *shadow plane*, which is an invisible, oriented plane that catches shadows. If a scene contains shadow planes, then by default, every pair of non-ambient light and visible geometry casts a shadow onto every shadow plane. With the current renderer, shadows are simply black, semi-transparent, singular transformations of the visible geometry.

The programming interface for shadows consists of a new Geometry constant, `shadow_plane`, and a few new constant attributers.

- The constant `shadow_plane` is a shadow plane situated in the $XZ$ plane, oriented so that shadows are cast on the positive $Y$ side. To create shadow planes with other locations and orientations, one applies transforms to this canonical shadow plane.

- The geometric attributes `light_creates_shadow` and `light_creates_no_shadow` control whether lights in their scope create shadows, with the former being the default.

- The geometric attributes `cast_shadow` and `cast_-no_shadow` control whether visible geometry in their scope cast shadows onto shadow planes.

Figures 7, 8, and 13 show examples of shadow planes in use.

## 2.7 Sound

TBAG makes it easy to add synchronized sound to geometric animations. Sound support is based on the following principles:

- Sound is an abstract data type, like Geometry, with primitives, attributes, and combination.

- Interactive, animated sounds (sounds that are changing based on time and other parameters) are supported as Sound-valued constrainables.

- Synchronization between geometry and sound works simply by relating geometry constrainables and sound constrainables to some of the same parameter constrainables.

To illustrate this last point, the following code fragment constructs a rotatable cube whose rotation angle is determined by a slider. The rotating cube emits the sound of a flute with the pitch modified by the angle's rate of change.

```
Constrainable<Real> angle =
  real_slider("Rotate cube:", 0, 2*pi, 0).value;
Constrainable<Geometry&> scene =
  cube * rot(y_axis,angle) +
  sound_at_origin(f lute*frequency(derivative(angle)));
```

Some comments:

- `flute` is a constant Sound of a flute playing with a canonical pitch and volume.

- The function `frequency` takes a real number and produces a sound attributer that when applied to a sound value multiplicatively modifies the frequency of that sound. Other sound attributers include phase and amplitude.

- The function `sound_at_origin` takes a sound value and produces a geometry value, which is the sound argument embedded into geometric space at the origin. As such it has no visual appearance but may be heard. Such geometries may then be transformed elsewhere in 3D, and renderers may choose to perform audio spatialization on the sound to impart a sense of position to the sound. The current TBAG renderer performs very basic audio spatialization.

# 3 Implementation

The programmer's model presented above has an efficient implementation that makes a number of non-obvious design choices. This section presents that implementation and discusses some of the design choices.

## 3.1 Behaviors

TBAG was designed to provide a fundamentally *continuous*, rather than discrete, treatment of naturally continuous phenomena such as time and motion. The basis for implementing TBAG's continuous approach efficiently is the *behavior*, a type-parameterized family of immutable data types that represent first-class functions of time. The notion of behaviors applies pervasively, for all types and at all levels, from individual parameters to entire animations. For instance, a time-varying angle is represented as a Real-valued behavior, the position and orientation of a geometric component as a transform behavior, and an entire animated scene, as well as each of its geometric components, as geometry behaviors. Behaviors are

purely an implementation device, being constructed invisibly during constraint solution, as will be described below in Section 3.2.

Behaviors support a *sampling* operation, which produces a value for a given time $t$. For instance, consider an animation, which is represented via a geometry behavior. An application or user creates any number of viewer objects, connected to the same geometry behavior. Each of these viewers iteratively samples the geometry behavior according to some criterion, such as maintaining a desired frame rate. In addition, each viewer also has a (viewing) transform behavior, which it samples for the same sequence of times. Each geometry and viewing transform sample pair is rendered to produce a frame of animation. Various viewers of a single geometry behavior may sample it completely independently, e.g., with different frame rates. No interference among these viewers is possible, due to the immutability of TBAG values.

In addition to sampling, behaviors also support differentiation, integration, and fairly general systems of first-order and higher-order ODEs, all over an extensible collection of types. For instance, the derivative of a point behavior is a vector behavior. (See Section 5.) Differentiation is done analytically when possible, and numerically otherwise (when differentiating input devices or functions whose analytic derivatives are not known). Integration and ODE solution is done analytically when of a very simple form, and otherwise using a standard efficient and accurate numerical technique (fourth order Runge-Kutta with adaptive step-size determination).

## 3.2 Continuous Constraints

Our goal with respect to constraints has been to explore easy expression and application to high level (non-numeric) types, rather than powerful numerical constraint solution techniques. TBAG currently uses the SkyBlue constraint satisfaction algorithm [19], which is a descendent of DeltaBlue [14]. Constraints may be specified on arbitrary types of (immutable) values, and may be given different strengths. This efficient, incremental algorithm ensures that a globally optimal subset of specified constraints are satisfied. As explained below, efficiency of TBAG's constraint maintenance is also significantly enhanced by an unconventional use of the underlying constraint satisfaction algorithm, which allows it to be invoked relatively infrequently.

TBAG's design imposes unusual requirements for the constraint system.

- In order to support a fundamentally continuous model of time and interaction, TBAG's constraint system must ensure that the constraints involving continuously changing values are continuously maintained.

- Efficient prediction of constrained values must be possible (and is in fact the typical case).[1]

- The instantaneous rate of change of a constrained value must be available, in order to support derivative constraints. As will be described in Section 5, derivative constraints allow natural expression of behaviors governed by derivatives, integrals, and differential equations.

None of these requirements hold in typical constraint-based systems, because such systems are usually data-driven, i.e., input values are allowed to change discretely, after which the system makes other discrete value changes to resatisfy the constraints. One could satisfy the first requirement by changing the constraint system from data-driven to demand-driven, propagating value demands backwards, rather than propagating value changes forwards. This change would be based on the observation that while, conceptually, values (such as the geometry of a scene) are continuously changing, these values will be sampled discretely (e.g., by viewers during automatic frame generation). The second and third requirement, however, would still not hold in this hypothetical constraint system.

TBAG's answer to the three requirements above is to make the values contained in constrainables and manipulated by the discrete constraint system be *behaviors* instead of base-level values. The constraint engine responds to assertions and retractions by constructing new behaviors for constrainables (typically corresponding to user interactions and other significant events), and propagates such (discrete) changes forward to cause related constrainables to take on new behaviors. (Interestingly, the underlying data-driven constraint system's type-genericity allowed it to be used in this unusual way without modification.) The first requirement is satisfied because the desired constraints hold among the related behaviors, and hence among all corresponding samples. The second requirement follows from the fact that behaviors support arbitrary time-sampling. (Actually, the prediction is only correct as long as the constrainable has its current behavior, which is a useful approximation of prediction of constrained values.) The third requirement follows because derivative is a well-defined concept on behaviors.

A significant performance benefit of this approach is that it allows the constraint engine to run infrequently. The constraint system is only invoked when an application changes underlying relationships in the system. Because the constraint system relates behaviors, its results tend to be valid for a significant amount of time. Section 2.3 illustrated how this characteristic is exploited during user interaction.

Keep in mind that the TBAG programmer is unaware of the fact that constrainables actually contain behaviors and are modified discretely, and instead think of constrainables informally as containing basic values and being modified continuously.

## 3.3 Efficiency Techniques

Any high level paradigm naturally raises concerns about performance. Although TBAG is quite high level, it is nonetheless satisfactorily efficient. The following subsections describe our efficiency techniques. Note that all of these optimizations are possible precisely because of the immutable nature of graphical data and behaviors.

---

1. To appreciate the motivation for prediction, consider that a frame of animation is computed starting at some earlier time $t_C$, but will be rendered at some later time $t_R$, so the system should compute what the geometry and viewing transform will be at time $t_R$, rather than what they are at time $t_C$. This discrepancy is especially noticeable with user interaction, because both the geometry and the viewing transform may be dependent on continuous input devices (such as a 2D or 6D mouse). In particular, when the viewing transform is derived from a head tracker, users are extremely sensitive to any lag in response to head motion. This "interaction lag" is avoided by the fact that all behaviors, including input device behaviors, are capable of doing prediction. Of course neither input values nor the time $t_R$ can be predicted with certainty. However, the alternative of not doing prediction is equivalent to predicting that the input values will remain constant between $t_C$ and $t_R$.

### 3.3.1 Efficient Memory Allocation

Conceptually, for any given viewer object, a scene's geometry and viewing transform are computed from scratch at each frame. (Much per-frame construction can often be avoided, as described in Section 3.3.2 below.) Because the nature and size of the geometry representations are not known *a priori* and because they outlive the function calls that construct them, they must be allocated dynamically (not on the stack) each frame. In order to reduce program complexity and error, TBAG frees the programmer from the need to explicitly free up the allocated storage for abstract values.

At first glance, this approach would seem to require prohibitively expensive use of garbage collection. Fortunately, this is not the case. Due to the side-effect-free nature of behavior execution, any memory allocated during the computation and rendering of a single frame becomes unreferenced after the frame's rendering is complete. Thus, TBAG viewers use a very efficient form of allocation, which we refer to as *transient allocation*. While in "transient mode" (e.g., during frame generation), abstract TBAG values are allocated sequentially from a small number of large chunks of memory. Leaving transient mode (e.g., at the end of a frame) causes these chunks to be made available for future reuse, at the cost of resetting a few pointers.

### 3.3.2 Dynamic Constant Folding

Geometric objects tend to contain many more potential degrees of freedom (represented as constrainables) than are being varied at any one time. Thus, most behaviors are potentially varying but currently constant. A naive implementation of a continuous, demand-driven constraint system, however, would result in repeated evaluation of all behaviors, even the constant ones. Such an implementation would preclude scalability. The TBAG approach of immutable behaviors contained in mutable constrainables allows for a simple solution to this problem. When a compound behavior is constructed, the argument behaviors are checked. If they are all constant behaviors, a new constant behavior is created (for which the result value is computed lazily). Since compound behaviors may be arbitrarily nested, this constant behavior creation may trickle up to larger and larger portions of the constructed behavior. We call this process "dynamic constant folding." Note that explicit invalidation is never necessary, since it happens automatically when the constraint engine recomputes behaviors.

### 3.3.3 Explicit Geometry Optimization

The TBAG function `optimize_geometry` takes a geometry value $g$ and returns a geometry value $g'$ that responds to geometry operations indistinguishably from $g$ but more efficiently. As usual, there is a trade-off to consider: more time is needed to construct the optimized geometry value $g'$ than to simply use $g$ instead, so the optimization is only worthwhile if the result will be used repeatedly.

Different optimizations are done for different operations. For instance, to support rendering, flattening of geometric hierarchy is done to (a) reduce run-time stacking and composition of transforms, and (b) present large graphics primitives (e.g., triangle strips and quadrilateral meshes) to the rendering engine. The actual optimization for each operation is postponed until the operation is first used.

Although not done currently, geometry optimization could apply automatically, e.g., in conjunction with dynamic constant folding.

# 4 Distribution and Collaboration

TBAG provides a simple way to create distributed, collaborative applications. Examples of such applications include:

- *Collaborative design*: three designers are all viewing the same geometry on computers around the country. Modifications that any of the three make are witnessed by all, as they are happening.

- *Remote tutoring*: a professor is teaching a undergraduate physics course and presents an electronic illustration of spring forces in action. Students are watching this experiment live from their homes, in the classroom, or distributed throughout the state, and may interact with the experiment on their computers, to get a better understanding of the physics of springs.

Not only are the distribution and collaboration aspects of these types of applications simple to construct in TBAG, but they also execute quite efficiently, using very little network bandwidth.

## 4.1 Writing Collaborative Applications in TBAG

Distribution and collaboration are facilitated by the addition of a few functions to the TBAG programming interface. One group of functions allow constrainables and assertions to be mapped into machine-independent identifiers that can be passed to different processes on different machines. These are known as "externalization" functions. The other group of functions "internalizes" the externalized identifiers back into C++ constrainables and assertions. The programmer thinks of the externalize/internalize sequence of calls as providing access to an existing constrainable or assertion in a separate process, thus allowing constraints to be asserted on and values to be retrieved from those remote constrainables.

These functions tend to be used as follows. A TBAG application has created a constrainable that produces an interesting animated, interactive geometry. To publish its existence, the application externalizes the constrainable, and communicates the machine-independent identifier to other TBAG applications (perhaps via electronic mail, RPC, ToolTalk™, CORBA™, etc). After receiving the externalized version of the constrainable, these other TBAG applications internalize the identifier and are left with what appears to be a standard C++ constrainable. The application may then do what it pleases with that constrainable. Any changes made to the constrainable are reflected in all processes that are accessing that constrainable.

## 4.2 An Efficient Implementation of Distribution

The above description can be implemented in a number of ways. An obvious approach would be to have process B's internalized constrainable identifier simply contain a reference to the original constrainable on process A. While this approach could work, it would suffer considerable performance penalties. Specifically, each time process B does a `value_at` on the constrainable, a net-

work round trip will need to be made to A to retrieve the value, incurring an unacceptable amount of latency and network usage.

Our approach to implementing distribution avoids these inefficiencies by using replication and local execution where possible. Whenever a process creates a constrainable, all other involved TBAG processes create "clones" of that constrainable. Then, whenever a constraint is asserted in any process, all related TBAG processes are informed of that assertion and perform it themselves locally. Similarly, when a constraint is retracted, related processes perform the retraction locally. Thus, each process has a semantically identical copy of the entire constraint network. As explained in Section 3.2, because interaction and animation are encoded directly in constrainables, applications tend to make assertions and retractions relatively infrequently. Therefore, the expense of keeping the constraint graphs consistent is small.

Not all constraint graphs can be entirely replicated via cloning on all machines involved in a collaboration. Consider the collaborative scenario in Figure 5. This figure represents the programmer's

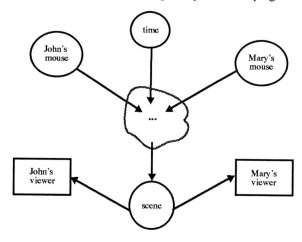

Figure 5. Programmer's view of collaborative application

view of a collaborative application, with the nebulous blob in the center representing a single constraint graph that, from the two mice and time, is determining a geometry to display on both John and Mary's computers. The naive implementation discussed earlier would produce each "frame" of geometry and send it to each display, thus using considerable bandwidth.

However, what our implementation actually does is reflected in Figure 6, where the constraint graph inside the nebulous blob has been replicated onto both machines, and the only information that needs to flow from one machine to the other are mouse positions.

This approach to efficient distribution via replication depends on the ability to distribute constraint assertions and retractions between processes. Such a requirement forces the "values" that constrainables hold to be able to produce a machine-independent representation of themselves. Thus, if an application executes `assert(geom == unit_cube * red)`, the implementation needs to be able to communicate a machine-independent representation of `unit_cube * red` to other processes. Our system achieves this by requiring every implementation subclass of an abstract data type to know how to "print" its instances. This "printed" representation can later be evaluated on another machine to produce a new value that behaves identically to the original one.

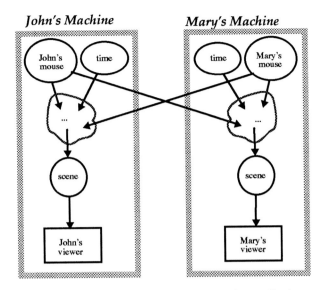

Figure 6. Implementation's view of collaborative application

There is one troublesome aspect to the implementation approach for distribution described above. Every constrainable gets replicated on every participating process, and every assertion and retraction is performed on every participating process, whether or not the process is interested in the constrainables involved. For larger-scale distributed applications with many participants entering and leaving at will, there needs to be a better way, such a "lazy cloning" of constraint graphs.

# 5 Derivatives, Integrals, and ODEs

The combination of derivatives and constraints is a very powerful specification tool for animation and interaction. In fact, our desire to support derivative constraints originally motivated TBAG's behavior-centered internal design. As a simple example, the following lines create two Real-valued slider widgets and constrain the value property of one to be equal to the derivative of the value property of the other.

```
Valuator<Real>& val_slider =
    real_slider("Value", -10, 10, 0);
Valuator<Real>& rate_slider =
    real_slider("Rate", -10, 10, 0);

assert( derivative(val_slider.value) ==
    rate_slider.value )
```

The derivative of a constrainable $v$ is another constrainable $v'$ with the constraint that the derivative of $v$ (considered as a function of time) is equal to $v'$. Consequently, after this constraint is asserted, when a user grabs and moves the value slider, the rate slider continuously moves to reflect the instantaneous rate of change of the value. When the value slider is not moving, the rate slider stays at zero. Also, however, the user may grab and move the rate slider and see the value slider gradually increase and decrease its value at a rate controlled by the rate slider. The constraint system automatically chooses between differentiation (in the first case) and integration (in the second).

To illustrate how derivatives can be used in interaction, one can relate the value slider to a modeling transform of a geometric object being viewed, as follows.

```
assert(my_xform == rot(y_axis, val_slider.value));
```

The result is that a user may control the model's rotation angle via the value slider, or its rotational velocity via the rate slider.

Higher-order derivatives are easy to express, simply as repeated applications of `derivative`, or as a chain of derivative constraints, as follows.

```
Valuator<Real> accel_slider =
    real_slider("Acceleration", -10, 10, 0);
assert(derivative(rate_slider.value) ==
    accel_slider.value));
```

After performing this assertion, all three sliders affect each other and the model's rotation appropriately.

As illustrated above, two techniques to solve derivative constraints are *differentiation* and *integration*. Another technique that turns out to be very powerful is the extraction and solution of systems of ordinary differential equations (ODEs). The need to solve ODE systems arises when there are *cyclic* sets of derivative constraints — a situation that occurs quite frequently in practice.

As an example of derivative constraints requiring ODE solution, consider Newton's law of linear motion, $f = m\,a$. This physical law could be encapsulated as a class that introduces the notions of force and mass:

```
class ParticleObject : public Aff ineGeometricObject {
    public:
        Constrainable<Real> mass;
        Constrainable<Vector&> velocity;
        Constrainable<Vector&> force;
};

ParticleObject::ParticleObject ()
{
    assert( velocity == derivative(position)
            && force == mass * derivative(velocity) );
}
```

Two comments here: (a) recall that the `position` property is inherited from `AffineGeometricObject`, and (b) the `&&` operator takes two constraints and forms a single conjunction constraint with the obvious semantics.

For convenience, TBAG uses a slightly different formulation of `ParticleObject` that contains a set of component force constrainables and automatically maintains the constraint that the net force equals the sum of the component forces. These component forces may come from a variety of physical sources. For instance, there is a utility function `spring_force` that computes the force generated at one end of a spring given that end's position, the spring's stiffness, rest length, and the position of the spring's opposite end.

```
Vector&
spring_force(Point& pos, Real stiffness,
            Real rest_length, Point& opp_end)
{
    Vector& sep = opp_end - pos;
    Real length = vector_magnitude(sep);
    return stiffness * sep * (rest_length - length) /
        length;
}
```

Another simple component force generator is drag, which is based on a particle's velocity and a drag coefficient.

```
Vector&
drag_force(Real drag_coeff, Vector& vel)
{ return -drag_coeff * vel; }
```

Once the header files for these force-producing functions are processed by the overloading tool described in Section 2.2.2, the generated overloadings may be applied to constrainable arguments. In particular, for the `spring_force` function, the particle's position and the position of the spring's opposite end are usually constrainables.

Figure 7 shows a spring toy that was constructed out of a few simple geometrically realized particles and springs. Any of the balls may be grabbed, moved, and even thrown. They then bounce around in a physically realistic looking manner. The posts may also be moved, and are constrained so that their bases remain in the ground plane. The forces acting on each ball are gravity, drag, and two spring forces. Figure 8 shows a construction set that allows the user to add balls and anchors and place springs to connect balls to each other or to anchors.

In these examples, the user may grab and pull on a ball. Rather than overriding the Newtonian constraint, we chose to implement such manipulation of physical objects by means of a transient anchor-and-spring pair. When a physical object is grabbed, an anchor and spring are created and added to the physical object's geometry and the resulting spring force is added to the set of component forces.

In order to handle systems of ODEs, the basic constraint engine [19] was extended with a facility for detecting cyclic constraint subgraphs and then attempting to apply constraint-specific resolution techniques. Extraction of ODE systems is the only such resolution technique we have added. Systems of linear or non-linear equations could be handled in the same way. Briefly, ODE resolution works as follows: each cycle in the identified constraint subgraph is checked to make sure it has at least one derivative constraint for which the integration function has been chosen to satisfy it (i.e., the derivative constraint is being "executed backwards"). If not, cycle resolution fails. Otherwise, a system of simultaneous ODEs is constructed and the identified constraint subgraph is replaced by one that executes the ODE solver and extracts the results for each involved constrainable.

## 5.1 Multi-type Differentiation

TBAG's notion of derivative, and hence integration and ODE solution, are not limited to Real-valued constrainables. Rather, derivatives are defined on many types, including `Real`, `Point`, `Vector`, `Quaternion`, and `Transform`. These types are supported, and more may be added, via an extension mechanism in which the basic operations underlying differentiation and integration are defined. For each such type $T$ (e.g., `Point`), a "delta type" $T'$ (e.g., `Vector`) is identified, together with functions including subtraction (mapping two $T$ values to a $T'$ value), addition (mapping a $T$ value and a $T'$ value to a $T$ value), and scalar multiplication (mapping a real number and a $T'$ value to a $T'$ value). The definition of these operations for the `Quaternion` is particularly interesting. Rather than using subtraction, addition and scaling on quadruples, we use quaternion division, multiplication, and exponentiation, respectively. We find these definitions to yield much more useful results. For instance, the virtual trackball algorithm used by TBAG's geometry viewer is expressed in terms of a quaternion derivative constraint and solved by the ODE engine via quaternion integration. Finally, the operations on affine transforms are based on corresponding operations on scale, shear, rotation and translation components.

The sets of functions needed to support differentiation also suffice to support multi-type interpolation. Thus, TBAG supports a very

general form of linear interpolation: given two values of type $T$, say $v_0$ and $v_1$, and a real number $t$, compute a new value corresponding to $v_0 + (v_1 - v_0) * t$. The +, -, and * operations refer to the corresponding operations on types $T$ and $T'$. Interpolation on the above mentioned types is thus supported. System extenders interested in adding operations such as 3D "morphing" would simply need to provide the appropriate +, -, and * functions on the Geometry type.

## 5.2 Incremental Evaluation

Sampling of constrainables that are driven by integration or ODE solution is side-effect-free, like all sampling in TBAG. A simplistic implementation would be to perform numerical iteration from the initial time and value for each sample, but of course such an approach would be too expensive. Instead, in our implementation, integral and ODE behaviors transparently cache the time and value of the latest sample. Because behaviors are almost always successively sampled at times that differ by a small amount, the iterative numerical algorithm typically requires only a few iterations per behavior sample. Of course, the use of state is far from unusual in uses of differential equation solvers. The difference in TBAG is that the use of state is automatic and transparent.

# 6 A Collection of TBAG Applications

A variety of applications have been written using the TBAG system. This section briefly describes some of them.

The **SoundScape** application in Figure 9 presents a three dimensional landscape of 3D icons, each of which represents a sound being emitted from that point in space. The user may manipulate two microphones (representing the user's left and right ears) and any of the 3D icons, resulting in the user perceiving the sounds in the vicinity of the left and right microphones. In a distributed setting, two separate users can each grab one microphone, thus effecting what they and the other user are hearing in one of their two ears.

The **EagleWatcher** application in Figure 10 (inspired by an interactive animation done at Brown University) presents four "watchers" whose eyes continually track the position of the eagle. The gaze is maintained as the eagle and watchers move. This application was constructed by establishing a constraint relationship between the watcher's head and eye angle, the position of the watcher and the position of the eagle. Additionally, each watcher is emitting a voice, and the user of the application hears the voices that the eagle might hear through its ears, based upon the distance of each watcher to the eagle.

The **ColorView** application shown in Figure 11 (also inspired by an example done at Brown University) presents three interactive views of a color based on its RGB representation: a color cube, three 3D sliders, and three 2D GUI sliders (not shown). Any view may be controlled with the mouse, causing the other two change accordingly. In the color cube case, the RGB components are constrained to the *relative* position of the ball within the cube. As a pleasantly surprising consequence of multi-directionality, the color will change continuously if the cube frame is spun and the ball grabbed and held still..

The **MortgageTool** application in Figure 12 uses multidirectional constraints to allow flexible analysis of the variables that go into a mortgage. The user may vary any subset of the Principal, Interest Rate, Number of Periods, and Payment per Period variables, result-

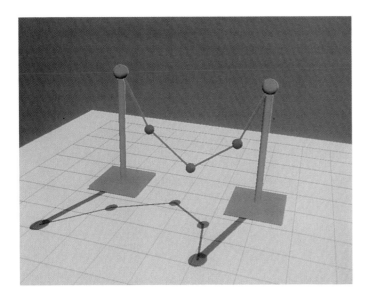

**Figure 7. A Spring Toy**

**Figure 9. SoundScape**

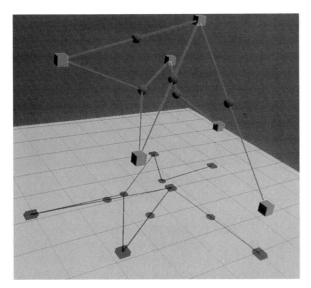

**Figure 8. Spring and Ball Construction Kit**

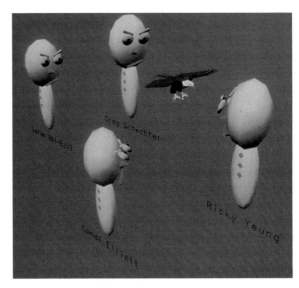

**Figure 10. EagleWatcher**

ing in changes to the remaining variables. (Contrast this with a traditional spreadsheet based approach, where the designer of the spreadsheet is forced, in designing the spreadsheet, to specify which variables are to be input variables, and which are to be output variables.) MortgageTool provides a direct manipulation interface in which the bars of the chart may be directly grabbed and moved. The third dimension is exploited to provide a side-by-side visual comparison of independent scenarios.

The application shown in Figure 13 provides an animated view of various sorting algorithms. Shown here is a MergeSort. Comparisons and swaps are animated and have sound effects.

Finally, Figure 14 shows an implementation of a Xerox PARC-style ConeTree [4]. This fully animated version (with slow-in/slow-out animation) was implemented in less than one day by a summer intern.

# 7 Related Work

**3D Programming Systems.** Also aimed at simplifying construction of interactive 3D programs, Inventor [22] provides a gallery of standardized interaction techniques. Following PHIGS PLUS, Doré, and others, Inventor adopts a procedural, state-based, and discrete approach. Unlike TBAG, these systems are heavily order-dependent and reliant on side-effects (similar to PHIGS structure editing), to achieve application goals.

Mirage [24] is a high level 3D object-oriented graphics system that supports a hierarchical temporal coordinate system, but, unlike TBAG, does not treat time-varying values as a first-class notion.

The UGA [29] work appears to be the first 3D programming framework that supports direct expression of time-varying values as functions of time and input. While both UGA and TBAG are

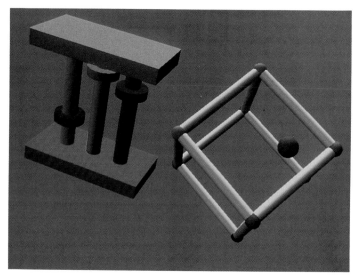

**Figure 11. ColorView**

**Figure 13. Sorting Algorithm Animation**

**Figure 12. MortgageTool**

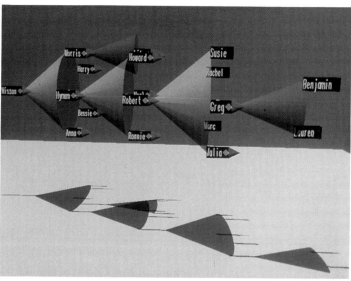

**Figure 14. Xerox ConeTree**

fundamentally continuous, TBAG has focused more on the integration of high-level data types while UGA has focused more on language mechanisms such as delegation hierarchies.

**Animation Systems.** Traditional animation systems support mostly key-frame animation. This discrete frame-based approach is also reflected in many existing animation languages. Descriptions of systems that embed animation capability within a general-purpose programming language can be found in Reynolds' [18] and Thalmann's [25] work. Some interesting variations include S-Dynamics [21], which allows time dependent parametric descriptions of actions, and Arya's lazy functional approach to animation, based on infinite sequences [1]. TBAG, on the other hand, supports a fundamentally continuous model of animation, and does so in the context of a production programming language (C++).

**Applications of Constraints to Graphics.** Constraint technology has long been applied in 2D drawing systems, such as Sketchpad [23] and Juno [16], and in 2D user interfaces, such as ThingLab II [14] and Garnet [15]. In 3D graphics systems, the use of data-flow or unidirectional dependency networks is common; examples can be found in UGA [29], CONDOR [13], AVS [26], and ConMan [11]. In contrast to these systems, TBAG combines the use of multi-directional constraints with the ability to involve high level types in continuous constraint relationships, and does so via a simple syntax.

Developed independently, VB2 [9] also applies the SkyBlue incremental constraint resolution algorithm to 3D graphics. In contrast to TBAG, however, VB2 does not support a continuous time model, high level data types, or a succinct syntax for building up constraint networks.

QOCA [12] independently used overloading to simplify expression of constraints. Unlike TBAG, QOCA supported only Real-valued constraints and supports overloading of the four basic arithmetic operators.

Much good work has gone into extending the might of numerical constraint solvers and applying them to interactive graphics (e.g. [28,2,7,8]). Our own work is complementary, exploring the application of constraints to a multitude of types (including very high level types), and providing an almost invisible programming interface to it.

The Animus system [5] embodies some of the earliest research done on considering time in constraint programming. Its notion of temporal constraints is based on a discrete history mechanism, as opposed to TBAG's fundamentally continuous approach. Consequently, ODE-based applications must express the numerical integration algorithm used (Euler's in the examples given) rather than simply the differential equations themselves.

# 8 Conclusions

This paper has presented TBAG, a paradigm and toolkit for rapid prototyping of interactive, animated 3D graphics programs. The fundamental aspects of TBAG, high level graphical abstract data types, and explicit functions of time, are applied broadly, treating, e.g., points, planes, colors, transforms, geometry, lights, shadows, and sound, in a consistent manner. The immutability of these types and functions allows for efficient automatic memory management and distributed execution. Automatically generated overloading of existing functions and operators give rise to succinctly expressed interactive animations.

Our current direction is in applying these same concepts uniformly to other media types, in pursuit of a coherent framework for distributed integrated media.

# 9 Acknowledgments

The authors would like to thank Leon Shirman, Srikanth Subramaniam, and Michael Deering for their contributions to the ideas and implementation of TBAG, Tom Meyer and Ajay Sreekanth for stress-testing TBAG and developing sample applications during their summer internships, and Matt Peréz for his support of this work.

Finally, we would like to thank the Brown University Graphics Group under Andries van Dam and John Hughes for their pioneering work on UGA, for a very fruitful collaborative relationship, and for comments on an earlier draft of this paper. In particular, work with Matthias Wloka contributed toward our current notion of behaviors; several discussions with John Hughes helped to correct and refine our current and future work with derivatives, and the whole group worked with the TBAG system and made extensive comments on its design.

# 10 References

[1] Kavi Arya. A Functional Approach to Animation. In *Computer Graphics Forum*, 5(4):297-311, December 1986.

[2] Ronen Barzel and Alan H. Barr. A Modeling System based on Dynamic Constraints. Proceedings of SIGGRAPH '88. In *Computer Graphics* 22, 4 (August, 1988).

[3] Alan Borning. The Programming Language Aspects of ThingLab, A Constraint-Oriented Simulation Laboratory. *ACM Transactions on Programming Languages and Systems*, 3(4), October, 1981.

[4] S.K. Card, G.G. Robertson, and J.D. Mackinlay. The Information Visualizer, an Information Workspace. In *Proceedings of the ACM SIGCHI Conference on Human Factors in Computing Systems*, pages 181-188. 1991.

[5] Robert A. Duisberg. Animated Graphical Interfaces using Temporal Constraints. In *CHI'86 Conference Proceedings*, pages 131-136, Boston, April 1986.

[6] *Graphics Library Programming Guide*, Silicon Graphics Computer Systems, Mountain View, Calif., 1991.

[7] Michael Gleicher and Andrew Witkin. Differential manipulation, *Graphics Interface*, June 1991.

[8] Michael Gleicher and Andrew Witkin. Through-the-lens Camera Control. Proceedings of SIGGRAPH '92. In *Computer Graphics*, 26, 2 (July, 1992).

[9] Enrico Gobbetti, Jean-Francis Balaguer, and Daniel Thalmann. VB2: An Architecture for Interaction in Synthetic Worlds. In *Proceedings of the ACM Symposium on User Interface Software and Technology*, 167-178, November, 1993.

[10] Rich Gossweiler, Chris Long, Shuichi Koga, and Randy Pausch. DIVER: A Distributed Virtual Environment Research Platform. In *IEEE Symposium on Research Frontiers in Virtual Reality*, October, 1993.

[11] Paul E. Haeberli. ConMan: A Visual Programming Language for Interactive Graphics. Proceedings of SIGGRAPH '88. In *Computer Graphics* 22, 4 (August, 1988).

[12] Richard Helm, Tien Huynh, Kim Marriott, and John Vlissides. An Object-Oriented Architecture for Constraint-Based Graphical Editing. *Eurographics Object-Oriented Graphics Workshop*, pages 1-22, 1992.

[13] Michael Kass. CONDOR: Constraint-Based Dataflow. Proceedings of SIGGRAPH '92. In *Computer Graphics*, 26, 2 (July, 1992), 321-330.

[14] John H. Maloney, Alan Borning, and Bjorn N. Freeman-Benson. Constraint Technology for User-Interface Construction in ThingLab II. In *OOPSLA '89 Proceedings*, October 1989.

[15] Brad A. Myers, Dario A Guise, Roger B. Dannenberg, Brad Vander Zanden, David S. Kosbie, Edward Pervin, Andrew Mickish, and Philippe Marchal. Garnet: Comprehensive Support for Graphical, Highly Interactive User Interfaces. *IEEE Computer*, November, 1990.

[16] Greg Nelson. Juno, A Constraint-Based Graphics System. Proceedings of SIGGRAPH '88. In *Computer Graphics* 22, 4, (August, 1988), 235-243.

[17] Programmer's Hierarchical Interactive Graphics System (PHIGS). International Standard ISO/IEC 9592.

[18] Craig W. Reynolds. Computer Animation with Scripts and Actors. Proceedings of SIGGRAPH '82. In *Computer Graphics*, 289-296.

[19] Michael Sannela. The SkyBlue Constraint Solver. TR-92-07-02, Department of Computer Science, University of Washington.

[20] Greg Schechter, Conal Elliott, Ricky Yeung, and Salim Abi-Ezzi. Functional 3D Graphics in C++ – with an Object-Oriented, Multiple Dispatching Implementation. To appear in the proceedings of the *1994 Eurographics Object-Oriented Graphics Workshop*.

[21] *S-Dynamics*, Symbolics, Inc., Cambridge, MA. 1985.

[22] Paul S. Strauss and Rikk Carey. An Object-Oriented 3D Graphics Toolkit. In *Computer Graphics (SIGGRAPH '92 Proceedings)*, volume 26(2), July 1992.

[23] Ivan E. Sutherland. Sketchpad: A Man-Machine Graphical Communication System. In *Spring Joint Computer Conference*, pages 329-345, 1963.

[24] Mark A. Tarlton and P. Nong Tarlton. A framework for dynamic visual applications. In *1992 Symposium on Interactive 3D Graphics*, pages 161-164, 1992.

[25] Nadia Magnenat-Thalmann and Daniel Thalmann. *Computer Animation: Theory and Practice*. Springer-Verlag, Tokyo, 1985.

[26] Craig Upson, Thomas Faulhauber, Jr., David Kamins, David Laidlaw, David Schlegel, Jeffrey Vroom, Robert Gurwitz, and Andries van Dam. The Application Visualization System: A Computational Environment for Scientific Visualization. *IEEE Computer Graphics and Applications*, pages 30-42, July, 1989.

[27] *XGL 3.0 Reference Manual*. Sun Microsystems, Inc. 1992.

[28] Andrew Witkin, Kurt Fleischer, and Alan Barr. Energy Constraints on Parameterized Models. Proceedings of SIGGRAPH '87. In *Computer Graphics* 21, 4, (July, 1987).

[29] Robert C. Zeleznik, D. Brookshire Connor, Andries van Dam, Matthias M. Wloka, Daniel G. Aliaga, Nathan T. Huang, Philip M. Hubbard, Brian Knep, Henry E. Kaufman, and John F. Hughes. An Object-Oriented Framework for the Integration of Interactive Animation Techniques. Proceedings of SIGGRAPH '91. In *Computer Graphics* 25, 4, (August, 1991), 105-112.

# A Clustering Algorithm for Radiosity in Complex Environments

*Brian Smits*          *James Arvo*          *Donald Greenberg*

Program of Computer Graphics*
Cornell University

## Abstract

We present an approach for accelerating hierarchical radiosity by clustering objects. Previous approaches constructed effective hierarchies by subdividing surfaces, but could not exploit a hierarchical grouping on existing surfaces. This limitation resulted in an excessive number of initial links in complex environments. Initial linking is potentially the most expensive portion of hierarchical radiosity algorithms, and constrains the complexity of the environments that can be simulated. The clustering algorithm presented here operates by estimating energy transfers between collections of objects while maintaining reliable error bounds on each transfer. Two methods of bounding the transfers are employed with different tradeoffs between accuracy and time. In contrast with the $O(s^2)$ time and space complexity of the initial linking in previous hierarchical radiosity algorithms, the new methods have complexities of $O(s \log s)$ and $O(s)$ for both time and space. Using these methods we have obtained speedups of two orders of magnitude for environments of moderate complexity while maintaining comparable accuracy.

**CR Categories and Subject Descriptors:** I.3.7 [Computer Graphics]: Three-Dimensional Graphics and Realism.

**Additional Key Words:** clustering, error bounds, hierarchical radiosity, global illumination.

## 1  Introduction

Recent trends in realistic image synthesis have been towards a separation of the rendering process into two or more stages[10, 2, 9]. One of these stages solves for the global energy equilibrium throughout the environment. This process can be very expensive and its complexity grows rapidly with the number of objects in the environment. These computational demands generally limit the level of detail of environments that can be simulated. Furthermore, a solution to this problem must be computed before anything useful can be displayed.

Radiosity algorithms attempt to solve the global illumination problem by discretizing the environment and solving a linear system to approximate the transfer of energy between the elements [5]. For complex environments, the large number of interactions is expensive

*580 ETC Building, Cornell University, Ithaca, NY 14853
E-mail: {bes | arvo | dpg}@graphics.cornell.edu

to compute, as each requires form factor and visibility calculations. The challenge is to reduce the computational complexity of this process. In one of the early approaches, Cohen et al. [3] reduced the number of interactions by imposing a two-level hierarchy of patches and elements on the environment. Although the number of interactions was reduced, the approach was still $O(p^2)$ in the number of elements in the environment.

Currently, the best radiosity algorithms are analogous to linear-time algorithms for charged particle simulation [6]. These algorithms work by clustering particles together so that the mutual effect of well-separated collections can be approximated with a single interaction. Hanrahan et al. [7] used a similar strategy to reduce the number of interactions needed for a radiosity solution. A hierarchical structure was imposed on each surface in an environment and interactions were allowed to occur between the appropriate levels on each. This approach works well when the number of initial surfaces is small, as hierarchical radiosity (HR) algorithms can "subdivide" large surfaces into smaller ones, but cannot "group" smaller elements into larger ones. The initial linking phase of HR must check all pairs of initial surfaces for potential interactions; without grouping surfaces together the algorithm is quadratic in the number of initial surfaces. Because complexity in environments is often a result of replacing large surfaces with many small surfaces, this inability to group objects together is a major obstacle in conventional HR algorithms.

Several methods have been developed to increase the efficiency of HR algorithms for complex environments. Global visibility [13] is effective for computing the initial links for environments in which only a small number of "cells" see each other. Many environments, however, also contain large collections of objects that are mutually visible. In such cases, global visibility algorithms do not suffice.

Importance [12] is another method that reduces computation in areas that have little or no noticeable effect on the surfaces of interest. This approach is effective once the initial interactions have been computed, but does nothing to reduce the time of the initial linking phase. Importance driven hierarchical radiosity stands to gain even more from clustering than standard hierarchical radiosity. Because it attempts to compute the radiance very coarsely in some regions of the environment, some means of clustering is needed if it is to do less work than that required for the initial linking.

An approach to clustering was developed by Rushmeier et al. [11] in which the effect of complex groups of surfaces is approximated by simpler representations resembling BRDF's obtained through Monte Carlo sampling. One disadvantage of this approach is that it is not automatic; appropriate clusters must be specified and approximated in advance. Also, no hierarchy is maintained, so the coarsest representation used by the algorithm is that of the selected clusters. Another clustering approach was proposed by Kok[8], which extended progressive radiosity so that patches could transfer energy to

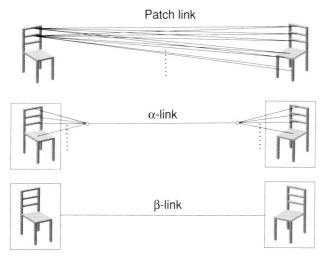

Patch link

α-link

β-link

Figure 1: *Two collections of objects can interact at different levels: a) conventional HR links, b) an α-link requiring linear time and space, and c) a β-link requiring constant time and space.*

groups of surfaces at once. Neither of these approaches analyze the error of the approximations used for the transfers.

To illustrate why clustering is important, consider a simple configuration consisting of two chairs, each containing 100 surfaces. HR would check the 10,000 potential interactions between the two chairs and would create in the neighborhood of 2,500 patch links (Figure 1). However, if the chairs are well separated, then it is unlikely that the energy transfer between them will have a significant effect on the illumination of either. If we can guarantee this throughout the entire solution, we can gain efficiency by coarsely approximating the transfer of energy between them. We shall present a new strategy for linking that would handle this configuration by creating a single link with a cost comparable to either 1 or 200 conventional links, depending on the separation of the objects. By reducing the total cost of the links created between two collections of objects, we reduce the algorithmic complexity of the $O(s^2)$ initial linking step in HR.

## 1.1 Overview

Hierarchical algorithms for radiosity have three components: 1) a hierarchical description of the environment, 2) a criterion for determining the level in the hierarchy at which two objects can interact, and 3) a means of estimating the energy transfer between the objects.

As our criterion for interaction, we use bounds on the potential error in the transfer of energy between two objects. We first describe hierarchical radiosity using this approach, and then present two efficient techniques for bounding the transfers between clusters. The first technique is a fairly accurate approach which we call α-linking. The second is a faster but less accurate approach which we call β-linking. Corresponding to these methods for determining bounds are two ways of estimating the transfer of energy between clusters. We also describe the method used to create the hierarchy of clusters, which is the starting point for the cluster-based linking strategies. Finally we give theoretical bounds on the complexity and results of our implementation demonstrating dramatic speedups over conventional HR in complex environments.

## 2 Hierarchical Radiosity

The value of the radiance function $L$ on a surface at a point $x$ due to another surface $S_i$ can be expressed as

$$L(x) = \int_{S_i} k(x, y) L(y) dy$$

where the kernel $k(x, y)$ expresses the radiance at $x$ due to a differential area at the point $y$. The kernel can be written

$$k(x, y) \equiv \rho(x) \frac{\cos \theta_1 \cos \theta_2}{||x - y||^2} \text{vis}(x, y)$$

where $\theta_1$ is the angle formed by the normal of the differential area at $x$ and the direction given by $y - x$ and $\theta_2$ is the angle formed by the normal of the differential area at $y$ and the the direction given by $x - y$. Also $\rho$ is the bidirectional reflectance distribution function (BRDF). In this paper we shall only address ideal diffuse scattering, although much of the analysis extends to general reflectance functions.

To compute the exact radiance function across the receiver, $L(x)$ must be evaluated at every point on the receiver. In general, some set of basis functions are used to represent the radiance functions and quadrature rules are used to compute the coefficients for the basis functions. This reduces the problem to evaluating $L(x)$ at some fixed number of points.

For an environment meshed to a fixed number of patches $p$, there are potentially $p^2$ interactions. HR maintains a hierarchical representation of each initial surface; for example, by means of a quadtree. HR then allows surfaces interact at a level in the hierarchy where all the interactions have an error less than some bound. This requires bounding the error in the transfer between two patches, which can be done by bounding the difference between the maximum and minimum transfers[12]. The maximum transfer can be computed by finding the maximum value of $k(x, y)$ over all points on the two patches and then integrating the product of this with the radiance of the source. We will denote the maximum value of a function $f$ over some range $A \times B$ as

$$\lceil f \rceil_{A,B} \equiv \max_{\substack{x \in A \\ y \in B}} f(x, y).$$

Using this notation the bound on the energy transfer may be written

$$\max L(x) \leq \lceil k \rceil_{R_j, S_j} \int_{S_i} L(y) dy.$$

This expression allows for arbitrary distributions of radiance across the source. The minimum can be computed similarly, with the minimum set to zero if any two points are occluded. The maximum and minimum values of $k$ are computed by taking a set of jittered samples on both the source and receiver and computing the maximum and minimum values of the kernel between all pairs of samples [12]. Occasionally, this approach greatly underestimates the maximum, such as when a small patch is very close to a large patch. Such an underestimate usually will not prevent further subdivision, however, and the problem diminishes as the two patches approach the same size. Bounding the error in the transfer of energy and only computing interactions to a given accuracy results in a linear number of interactions [7]. The transfer of energy between the two surfaces can then be determined using any of the various form-factor methods.

The main deficiency of HR is that the coarsest representation is the initial surfaces. By collecting a group of these surfaces together, we obtain an even coarser representation. To make use of this coarser representation, we require a bound on the transfer of energy between two such clusters. This bound must be computed in less

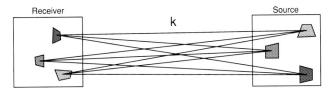

Figure 2: *Straightforward approach to bounding error. Each link represents a maximum value for k.*

Figure 3: *More efficient $\alpha$-link between two clusters.*

than $O(s^2)$ time if we are to gain an improvement over the brute force method of checking all pairs of interactions. We now describe two ways of bounding error, each with a time complexity better than $O(s^2)$.

## 3 Bounding error on clusters

In this section we describe two strategies for computing bounds on the energy transfer between clusters; one requiring linear time and space, and one requiring constant time and space. The strategies are derived by systematically introducing approximations into the exact expression for energy transfer. The first level of approximation results in a type of link we call an $\alpha$-link. By introducing further approximations we produce $\beta$-links. Although these bounds are coarse, they often suffice for a very large fraction of the interactions.

### 3.1 $\alpha$-links

The transfer of energy from a cluster of patches $\mathcal{S}$ to a point can be computed by summing over the $n$ patches in the source cluster

$$L(x) = \sum_{i=1}^{n} \int_{S_i} k(x, y) L(y) dy.$$

Since $k(x, y)$ is a function of the position and orientation of the receiver as well as the source and of the visibility between them, computing the transfer of radiance between two clusters requires evaluating $L(x)$ at least once on each of the $m$ receivers, resulting in $O(mn)$ work.

Applying the same approach used for HR to two clusters is relatively expensive. To bound the transfer between the clusters with this approach, we can use the maximum value of $k(x, y)$ over pairs of patches to bound the transfer. The maximum radiance over all receivers due to the source cluster can be bounded by

$$\max L(x) \leq \max_j \sum_{i=1}^{n} \lceil k \rceil_{R_j, S_i} \int_{S_i} L(y) dy.$$

The maximum value of the kernel function must be computed for each pair of patches, so the time complexity is $O(mn)$. (See Figure 2.)

To improve the time complexity, we split the kernel function into two simpler functions $k^r(x, y)$ and $k^s(x, y)$ given by

$$k^r(x, y) \equiv \rho(x) \cos \theta_1$$
$$k^s(x, y) \equiv \frac{\cos \theta_2}{||x - y||^2}.$$

Then

$$k(x, y) = k^r(x, y) k^s(x, y) \text{vis}(x, y).$$

Each of the new functions depends on two points, but each requires information about the orientation of only one surface. $k^r$

accounts for the projected area and reflectivity of a differential area around $x$ and $k^s$ corresponds to the differential solid angle subtended by a differential area around $y$. We now show that the above separation of the kernel can be used to conservatively bound the interaction between the source cluster and the receiver cluster. This is done by bounding the energy that reaches the receiving cluster from the source, and then determining how much of this energy potentially reaches each receiving patch. (See Figure 3.)

We now use these pieces of the kernel to bound the radiance function at a point $x$. First, $k^r(x, y)$ is replaced by the maximum value it attains over all $y$ in the volume $B(\mathcal{S})$ containing all the source patches. Then, for each of the sources, we replace $k^s(x, y)$ by the maximum value it attains over all $y$ on the source patch. We can also assume that the visibility term is always 1. These steps produce the following conservative upper bound:

$$\begin{aligned}
L(x) &= \sum_{i=1}^{n} \int_{S_i} k^r(x, y) k^s(x, y) \text{vis}(x, y) L(y) dy \\
&\leq \lceil k^r \rceil_{x, B(\mathcal{S})} \sum_{i=1}^{n} \int_{S_i} k^s(x, y) L(y) dy \\
&\leq \lceil k^r \rceil_{x, B(\mathcal{S})} \sum_{i=1}^{n} \lceil k^s \rceil_{x, S_i} \int_{S_i} L(y) dy.
\end{aligned}$$

We can apply this idea to obtain upper bounds on the transfer between the two clusters. The quantity $k^s(x, y)$ can be maximized over all points in the receiving volume $B(\mathcal{R})$ making $k^s(x, y)$ independent of any particular receiver. The factor $k^r(x, y)$ can now be maximized over each receiving patch separately. Thus, the radiance function can be bounded as follows

$$\max L(x) \leq \max_j \lceil k^r \rceil_{R_j, B(\mathcal{S})} \sum_{i=1}^{n} \lceil k^s \rceil_{B(\mathcal{R}), S_i} \int_{S_i} L(y) dy.$$

This expression can be separated into two pieces by defining

$$L_{S_{\max}} \equiv \sum_{i=1}^{n} \lceil k^s \rceil_{B(\mathcal{R}), S_i} \int_{S_i} L(y) dy,$$

which is a bound on the flux density incident upon the receiving bounding volume. Then

$$\max L(x) \leq \max_j \lceil k^r \rceil_{R_j, B(\mathcal{S})} L_{S_{\max}}.$$

Maximizing over all of the receiving patches in $\mathcal{R}$ requires $O(m)$ work. Therefore the time complexity of computing this bound has been reduced from $O(mn)$ to $O(m + n)$.

The bounds needed for HR can be computed from upper and lower bounds on the transfer. We have given upper bounds; a trivial lower bound of zero can always be used. This lower bound is attained when the visibility between all points in the two clusters is zero. Now we have a bound on the error in the interaction between two clusters, which allows us to determine when an interaction is accurate enough. This bound on clusters determines if an $\alpha$-link is an acceptable approximation for the interaction.

In addition to the error bound, we require an estimate for the energy transferred to each receiving patch across the $\alpha$-link. We do this by computing an estimate as well as the bound for the $k^r(x, y)$ associated with each receiving patch and the $k^s(x, y)$ associated with each source patch. Let

$$\langle f \rangle_{A,B} \equiv \mathrm{avg}_{\substack{x \in A \\ y \in B}} f(x, y)$$

Now the radiance on receiving patch $j$ can be estimated by

$$L_j = \langle k^r \rangle_{R_j, B(\mathcal{S})} L_{S_{\mathrm{avg}}}$$

where

$$L_{S_{\mathrm{avg}}} = \sum_{i=1}^{n} \langle k^s \rangle_{B(\mathcal{R}), S_i} \int_{S_i} L(y) dy.$$

Each average is bounded above by the maximum transfer and therefore falls within the error bounds; hence it is sufficiently accurate. In fact, it is quite likely far *more* accurate than the conservative bounds indicate.

We now show that the $\alpha$-link clustering approach has time and space complexity of $O(s \log s)$. First, assume we have $s$ initial patches stored in a hierarchy of clusters with each cluster containing two smaller clusters or, at the leaves, a single patch. This structuring results in a binary tree with a depth of $\log s$. The total number of clusters at level $d$ is $2^d$ and each cluster at level $d$ has $s/2^d$ patches. Now, following Hanrahan et al. [7] and Greengard [6], we assume each cluster is linked to a constant $c_1$ number of other clusters resulting in $c_1 2^d$ $\alpha$-links on level $d$. We can also assume that each cluster is linked to other clusters at approximately the same level in the tree. An $\alpha$-link between two clusters requires space and time proportional to the size of the clusters. Summing the costs for each of the $\log s$ levels of the hierarchy gives

$$\sum_{d=0}^{\log s} \mathrm{num\_links}_d \; * \; \mathrm{link\_cost}_d = \sum_{d=0}^{\log s} c_1 2^d c_2 \frac{s}{2^d} = Cs \log s.$$

Therefore, rather than the $O(s^2)$ work required for a direct approach, clustering using $\alpha$-links gives a time and space complexity of $O(s \log s)$.

### 3.2 $\beta$-Links

For many transfers, the previous technique is still too expensive. Often large numbers of interactions are insignificant and can be treated very coarsely or ignored altogether [9]. In this section we introduce a more efficient but cruder method for bounding the interaction between two clusters. We do this using a very simple bound on the kernel $k(x, y)$ which we denote $k^d(x, y)$,

$$k(x, y) \leq k^d(x, y) \equiv \frac{1}{||x - y||^2}.$$

This bound requires no knowledge about the orientation of the surfaces. We can bound the transfer of energy between two clusters by replacing $k$ by the maximum value of $k^d$ over all points $x$ in the receiving cluster and all points $y$ in the source cluster. (See Figure 4.) Thus,

$$\max L(x) \leq \lceil k^d \rceil_{B(\mathcal{R}), B(\mathcal{S})} \sum_{i=1}^{n} \int_{S_i} L(y) dy.$$

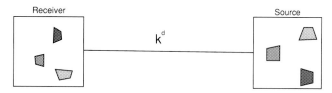

Figure 4: *$\beta$-link between clusters.*

This is a worst-case bound on the transfer between two clusters; it is only achieved when all surfaces are as close as possible to the other cluster, and each source directly faces all the receivers. The virtue of this bound is that it requires no knowledge of the surfaces. If the integral of the radiance over all the source patches has been computed in advance, during the sweep operation described in section 5.1, then the bound can be computed in constant time. As with the $\alpha$-links, we can use the average value of $k^d$ over the two clusters as an estimate of the energy transferred between them. Again, since the average value lies within the range given by the maximum transfer and a minimum transfer of zero, it meets the error tolerance.

The time and space complexity of a system with $\beta$-links is equivalent to the complexity of the standard hierarchical radiosity method. As with linking patches, the error term decreases rapidly with distance, so each cluster will be linked to a constant number of other clusters. Since the number of clusters is linear in the number of initial surfaces, and the cost of a $\beta$-link is independent of the size of the clusters, the complexity is $O(s)$ where $s$ is the number of initial surfaces.

### 3.3 Strategies for linking

We have described two different approaches for linking clusters. The more accurate clustering technique tends to be too expensive for many clusters in a large environment. The faster clustering technique is too coarse to eliminate many of the negligible interactions. Our approach is to exploit the strengths of both strategies. If the coarse approach does not produce an acceptable bound then the more accurate technique is invoked. If neither are accurate enough, then the clusters are recursively subdivided. Only when the level of individual patches is reached does the algorithm resort to conventional HR.

### 4 Linking Criteria

Norms provide a measure of the "size" of a function. We shall use two different norms to quantify error in the energy transfer between two patches or clusters. In the previous section we computed a bound on the maximum possible difference between the approximated radiance and the actual radiance over all points on the receiving object. This corresponds to computing a bound on the $\infty$-norm of the radiance function on the receiver due to the source. More formally, if $L$ is the exact radiance function over the receiver, and $\widetilde{L}$ is the computed radiance function then

$$||L - \widetilde{L}||_\infty = \max_{x \in \mathcal{R}} (L(x) - \widetilde{L}(x)) \leq M$$

where $M$ is one of the previous bounds on the transfer.

The $\infty$-norm gives a bound on the variation between the computed radiance and the actual radiance. Another useful bound is the energy of the difference between the computed and actual radiance functions due to a link. This bound corresponds to the 1-norm.

More formally,

$$||L - \widetilde{L}||_1 = \pi \int_{\mathcal{R}} |L(x) - \widetilde{L}(x)| dx$$

The 1-norm can be bounded by weighting each term of the receiver by the area of the receiver and summing instead of finding the maximum value. We can write this bound for $\alpha$-links as

$$||L - \widetilde{L}||_1 \leq \pi \sum_{j=1}^{m} \left( A_j \lceil k^r \rceil_{R_j, B(\mathcal{S})} \sum_{i=1}^{n} \left( \lceil k^s \rceil_{B(\mathcal{R}), S_i} \int_{S_i} L(y) dy \right) \right)$$

where $A_j$ is the area of receiver $j$. Coarse bounds and patch-to-patch bounds are computed similarly. In a hierarchical solution both norms are easily accommodated, but the norm used affects the subdivision strategy. After performing a local pass to display a solution, the error at each pixel is important, which implies that the $\infty$-norm is most appropriate. However, during the global propagation of energy throughout an environment, it may be more useful to minimize the 1-norm of the error. Intuitively, this is because large surfaces will often have a much more significant effect on the local pass than the smaller ones.

Another useful norm is obtained from the importance weighting [12]. This corresponds to a norm very similar to the 1-norm; rather than weighting each receiver by the area, the receiver is weighted by its importance.

## 5  Implementation

### 5.1  Clustering

Most ray tracing acceleration techniques collect nearby objects together into groups. Some of these, such as octrees and hierarchical bounding volumes, form a natural hierarchy. The same hierarchy can be used to identify clusters. For simplicity, each object should appear in only one cluster. Otherwise, some method of eliminating copies of objects is needed to prevent an object from contributing to a cluster twice. For these reasons we chose to use bounding volume hierarchies [4] instead of octrees to generate our hierarchy of clusters. We use axis-aligned rectangular bounding boxes for both the clusters and for ray casting.

The HR algorithm can be combined with a bounding volume hierarchy to perform clustering fairly easily. The bounds on the error given earlier fit naturally into the brightness-weighted refinement scheme of Hanrahan et al. [7]. This approach first links the surfaces together, then performs several iterations of energy propagation and refinement of the system. The error tolerance is gradually reduced until the final error tolerance is reached. This approach is a variation on the "multigridding" method for iteratively solving systems of linear equations.

Very few modifications are needed to make to the bounding volume data structures useful for clustering. For the more accurate clustering approach, we must loop over all of the patches in the bounding volume. Each link will contain four arrays that hold both the maximum and average values of $k^s$ for all the source patches as well as the maximum and average values of $k^r$ for all of the receiving patches. In our implementation the maximum values are approximated by taking a fixed number of jittered samples on the patch and bounding volume, then finding the maximum value of the kernel at these points. Although this method does not produce a guaranteed bound, it tends to produce a good approximation. If two bounding volumes overlap, the maximum values can be unbounded. In this case we can choose a maximum based on the maximum potential transfer of energy in the environment. We store an estimate of the inter-cluster visibility in the link as well. Visibility is estimated using ray casting. The following pseudocode shows the steps needed to compute an $\alpha$-link between two clusters.

```
Create-α-link(Src, Rec)
α-link T
T.Vis = EstimateVisibility(Src,Rec)
foreach patch i in Src
    T.SrcMax[i] ← ⌈k^s⌉_{B(Rec),S_i}
    T.SrcAvg[i] ← ⟨k^s⟩_{B(Rec),S_i}
foreach patch j in Rec
    T.RecMax[j] ← ⌈k^r⌉_{R_j,B(Src)}
    T.RecAvg[j] ← ⟨k^r⟩_{R_j,B(Src)}
if α-Bound(T) < ε then return TRUE
else return FALSE
```

Procedure $\alpha$-Bound(T) computes the bound on the maximum amount of energy transferred across $\alpha$-link T. We have estimates of the maximum values of $k^s$ and $k^r$ stored in the link. The integral of the radiance function $L_i$ over patch $i$ for constant patches is the product of the radiance $L_i$ and the area $A_i$ of the patch. The procedure for computing the error incurred by an $\alpha$-link between clusters is shown in the following pseudocode:

```
α-Bound(T)
SrcErr ← 0
MaxErr ← 0
foreach patch i in T.Src
    SrcErr ← SrcErr + T.SrcMax[i] * A_i * L_i
foreach patch j in T.Rec
    MaxErr ← Max(MaxErr, T.RecMax[j] * SrcErr)
return MaxErr
```

In addition to computing the error on the links, energy must be transferred between the two clusters. During the gather step of HR, energy is transferred across each link, including all cluster links. The gather across an $\alpha$-link T is performed as follows.

```
α-Gather(T)
SrcRad ← 0
foreach patch i in T.Src
    SrcRad ← SrcRad + T.SrcAvg[i] * A_i * L_i
SrcRad ← SrcRad * T.Vis
foreach patch j in T.Rec
    L_j ← L_j + T.RecAvg[i] * SrcRad
```

For the coarse approach to clustering using $\beta$-links, we store the sum of the areas of all the patches in the bounding volume. We also store the radiance of the bounding volume for use as a source, and the irradiance striking the bounding volume for use as a receiver. If the radiance on each patch of the receiving cluster were updated each time a link was used in a gather, then gathering through a single link would require linear time, resulting in worse complexity bounds for coarse links. As in HR, after transferring energy across the links the radiances must be swept to each object's parents and children. For clusters, this sweep is a slightly different from the sweep described in HR since each cluster holds the irradiance $I$ incident upon it, and the radiance leaving it. Irradiance is pushed down the bounding volume hierarchy to the patches. The incident irradiance is then weighted by the reflectance of the patch and the resulting radiance is pushed down the patches as in HR. Pulling radiance up from the children to the parents is the same as in HR. Each parent receives the area-weighted average of the radiances of its children. The following pseudocode is used when solving the linear system to redistribute the energy gathered across the links. HSweep is the conventional HR sweep procedure.

Sweep($C, I_{down}$)
$\overline{I_{down} \leftarrow I_{down} + I_C}$
**if** $C$ is a leaf **then**
    **foreach** patch $R_j$ in $C$
        $L_j \leftarrow L_j + I_{down} * \rho_j$
        $L_{up} \leftarrow L_{up} + \text{HSweep}(R_j) * A_j / A_C$
**else foreach** $C'$ in $C$
        $L_{up} \leftarrow L_{up} + \text{Sweep}(C', I_{down}) * A_{C'} / A_C$
$L_C \leftarrow L_{up}$
**return** $L_{up}$

The $\beta$-links between clusters are computed in a similar fashion to the $\alpha$-links. They are easier to compute, however, as no looping over the contents of the bounding volume is required. Also, the maximum value for $k^d$ is the inverse of the square of the minimum distance between the clusters, which can be computed with little work for axis aligned bounding volumes. Each $\beta$-link stores only the maximum value and the best computed value of $k^d$ for the two clusters.

Create-$\beta$-link(Src,Rec)
$\overline{\beta\text{-link } T}$
vis $\leftarrow$ EstimateVisibility(Src,Rec)
$\text{T.Max} \leftarrow \left\lceil k^d \right\rceil_{B(Rec),B(Src)}$
$\text{T.Avg} \leftarrow \text{vis} * \left\langle k^d \right\rangle_{B(Rec),B(Src)}$
**if** $\beta$-Bound(T) $< \epsilon$ **then return** TRUE
**else return** FALSE

The error in a $\beta$-link between clusters is also straightforward, following directly from the bounds on the transfer and the previous discussion for higher accuracy links. Computing the error on a $\beta$-link T can be implemented as:

$\beta$-Error(T)
$\overline{\textbf{return } \text{T.Max} * L_{\text{T.Src}} * A_{\text{T.Src}}}$

During the gather phase of the algorithm, each $\beta$-link transfers energy to the receiving cluster. It is stored there as irradiance until the sweep phase when it is scaled by the BRDF.

$\beta$-Gather(T)
$\overline{I_{\text{T.Rec}} = I_{\text{T.Rec}} + \text{T.Avg} * L_{\text{T.Src}} * A_{\text{T.Src}}}$

The above procedures allow the clusters and patches of the environment to be linked together. When two bounding volumes are to be linked it is possible to first check for complete occlusion. This can be done conservatively by checking to see if a convex object completely obstructs the shaft between the source and the receiver. If the two bounding volumes are not completely occluded, then the $\beta$-bound between the clusters is checked. When that is not sufficiently accurate the $\alpha$-bound is checked. If this is still not accurate enough, then the children of the larger cluster are recursively refined against the smaller cluster. If neither of the clusters has children, then the patches in both are refined against each other using the patch refinement from HR. The clustering algorithm begins by using the top-level bounding box both as source and as receiver, which triggers the recursive refinement.

### 5.2 Local Pass

Once a global solution has been computed, displaying the result usually involves smoothing the values computed for each patch so that patch boundaries are not visible. This can be done by Gouraud-shading the surfaces, however this is very prone to artifacts in hierarchical systems [12]. A better approach is to use the techniques of Lischinki et al. [9] and create a separate mesh for display purposes, using the information obtained by the global solution, and recomputing some parts of the illumination on each surface. Our approach is based on this method as well as on the method proposed by Reichert [10]. Given a view, we approximate the intensity

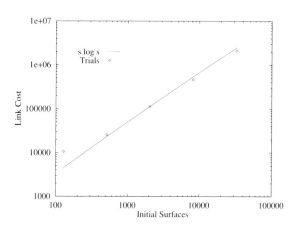

Figure 5: *Link cost for environments of different sizes compared with the function* $s \log(s)$.

by reconstructing the radiance function at each visible point in the environment. This is done by taking the collection of links at all levels of the hierarchy that directly affect this point, and for each link recomputing the form factor from the source to the point. The accuracy is determined by the magnitude of the error on the links, and can result in either recomputing just the unoccluded form factor, or both the form factor and the visibility from each source to the point. Although this method produces high quality results, it is computationally expensive. The techniques of this paper only address methods for efficiently computing the global pass. Further research is required to accelerate the local pass.

## 6 Results

HR has a complexity bound (ignoring the visibility term) of $O(s^2 + p)$ where $s$ is the number of initial surfaces and $p$ is the number of resulting patches. The $O(s^2)$ term comes from computing the initial links between all initial surfaces. Using clustering we do not need to check all pairs of surfaces even if they are mutually visible. Clustering replaces the expensive initial linking step with an algorithm that is $O(s \log s)$ in the number of initial surfaces. This results in an algorithm with an overall complexity of $O(s \log s + p)$. The sections that follow report results for several different environments and refinement strategies.

### 6.1 Link Complexity

We first show how the cost of the links grows with the size of the environment. As a first example, the inside of a sphere was tessellated into triangles. Each triangle was given the same emissive power and reflectance. This allowed us to vary $s$ over a large range of values without really changing the geometry. Also, because every surface can see every other surface, it is easy to determine exactly how many initial links would be needed without clustering. It is also a challenging environment for clustering because every cluster overlaps with several other clusters. We assign a cost of 1 for patch links and $\beta$-links. The cost for $\alpha$-links is $m + n$ where $m$ is the number of patches in the receiving cluster and $n$ is the number of patches in the source cluster. The total link cost is the sum of the link costs for each link computed for the environment. The model was refined using the $\infty$-norm criterion on the links. The graph in figure 5 shows the link cost for five tessellations ranging from 128 patches to 32768 initial patches, as well as the function $y = s \log s$. The costs closely match the function.

For the largest tessellation a conventional HR algorithm would need to create and store over one billion initial links before it could

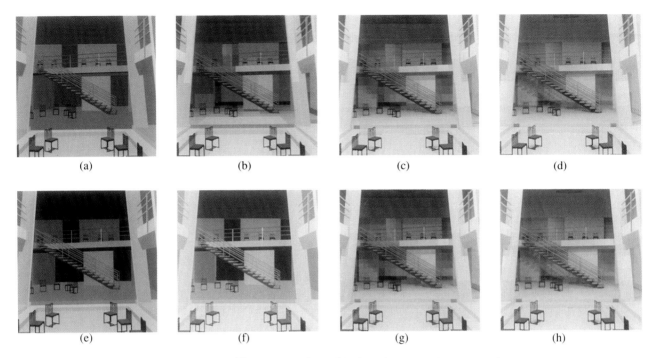

Figure 7: Solutions at different accuracies. With clustering (a-d), without clustering (e-h).

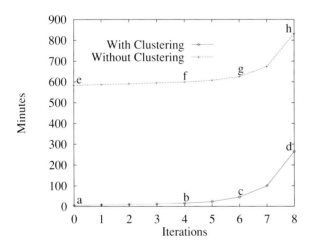

Figure 6: *Time for solutions of increasing accuracy, both with and without clustering.*

compute a solution. With clustering the links cost only about 0.2% of this, a reduction in both time and space of approximately 500.

## 6.2 Refinement Complexity

We now show how a solution refines over time both with and without clustering. We start with an environment of 4170 initial surfaces, illuminated by three directional lights and 8 emitting cubes, and refine the solution from the initial linking stage through eight iterations of successively smaller error tolerances. In this example we used a 1-norm bound on the error for each interaction. A graph of the times for the global solution as the accuracy increases appears in figure 6. These solutions were computed on an HP 755 with 384 megabytes of memory to prevent swapping while computing the solution without clustering. Images of the flat shaded patches

are shown for several different levels of accuracy in figure 7. The long thin polygons in the model do not create ideal clusters because of the large variation in position. Neither algorithm grows linearly with the number of iterations, the algorithms are simply linear with the number of resulting patches.

With clustering, HR becomes more of a progressive algorithm since initial results can be seen relatively quickly. Without clustering it took 583 minutes for the first solution to appear. Clustering reduced that time to 5.35 minutes, a speed up of over one hundred times. Both solutions refine at about the same rate once they are linked. After eight iterations, the clustering solution resulted in 114554 patches. Without clustering there were 114410 patches. These numbers are very close because subdivision can only occur by refining a patch link, and this is done the same way in both algorithms. Bounds on the various kernels were estimated using 81 samples. Visibility was checked with 81 rays.

Clustering amortizes the cost of initial linking over many refinements and except for simple environments, the amortization continues well beyond the required levels of accuracy. This amortization has some cost associated with it, but it is compensated for by reduced link maintenance; that is, there is no need to maintain the $O(s^2)$ initial links through all the early iterations where high accuracy is unnecessary

## 6.3 Importance

We also tested our algorithm using importance weighted refinement. We used the same environment shown in figure 7, with a view of the group of chairs near the stairs. The upper image shown in figure 8 was created with the view-dependent local pass described earlier in the paper. The global solution used for the local pass is shown below the image. The global pass with clustering took about 3 minutes for the initial solution and 53 minutes for the entire global solution, creating 27318 patches. Without clustering, the initial linking took 728 minutes and the entire global pass took 790 minutes. (Estimates of form factor and visibility error were computed with more samples

Figure 8: *Image resulting from local pass (above) and solution used for the local pass (below)*

to make the local pass more effective, causing the initial linking to take longer than it did in the previous example.)

## 7    Conclusions and Future Work

Clustering is an effective technique for accelerating HR. By using two different error bounds on the energy transfer between collections of surfaces, two types of links between cluster were described. Using both of these approaches in an HR algorithm reduces the asymptotic complexity from $O(s^2+p)$ to $O(s \log s+p)$ in addition to making HR a more progressive algorithm. In environments of moderate complexity we obtained speedups of two orders of magnitude. The approach presented here enables HR to work effectively even when there are many mutually visible initial surfaces.

The hierarchy of clusters presented in this paper were fairly straightforward modifications to traditional bounding volume hierarchies. Our current research shows that it is beneficial to build 5D hierarchies in the spirit of [1], to bound direction of the patch

normals as well as position. This can be used to obtain tighter bounds on the transfers since patch orientations are constrained. In the implementation described here, two clusters with even one pair of patches facing each other may be linked with a relatively expensive $\alpha$-link. A 5D hierarchy seems to reduce this problem.

Although a lower bound of zero on energy transfers is always valid, tighter lower bounds between two clusters would improve overall performance of the algorithm. Unlike upper bounds, this requires computing guaranteed bounds on visibility, a potentially expensive operation. Currently, our implementation uses a sampling approach to determine the upper bound on the transfer between two patchs as well as the transfer between patches and clusters. Although we have not noticed any serious problems as a result of this approximation, analytic bounds on these transfers would produce guaranteed bounds. Guaranteed bounds on transfers make it possible to examine the global error in the solution. As mentioned in [12] bounds on transfers between surfaces do not immediately provide a bound on the total error in the solution.

## Acknowledgments

We would like to thank Dani Lischinski for discussions on complexity and for helpful comments on the paper. Also thanks go to Greg Spencer for his software for handling high dynamic range images. This work was supported by the NSF grant "Interactive Computer Graphics Input and Display Techniques" (CCR-8617880), and by the NSF/DARPA Science and Technology Center for Computer Graphics and Scientific Visualization (ASC-8920219). The authors gratefully acknowledge the generous equipment grant from Hewlett-Packard Corporation.

## REFERENCES

[1]  ARVO, J., AND KIRK, D. Fast ray tracing by ray classification. *Computer Graphics 21*, 4 (July 1987), 55–64.

[2]  CHEN, S. E., RUSHMEIER, H. E., MILLER, G., AND TURNER, D. A progressive multi-pass method for global illumination. In *Proceedings of SIGGRAPH'91 (Las Vegas, Nevada, July 28–August 2, 1991)* (July 1991), vol. 25, ACM, pp. 165–174.

[3]  COHEN, M. F., GREENBERG, D. P., IMMEL, D. S., AND BROCK, P. J. An efficient radiosity approach for realistic image synthesis. *IEEE Computer Graphics and Applications 6*, 2 (March 1986), 26–35.

[4]  GOLDSMITH, J., AND SALMON, J. Automatic creation of object hierarchies for ray tracing. *IEEE Computer Graphics and Applications 7*, 5 (May 1987), 14–20.

[5]  GORAL, C. M., TORRANCE, K. E., GREENBERG, D. P., AND BATTAILE, B. Modeling the interaction of light between diffuse surfaces. *Computer Graphics 18*, 3 (July 1984), 213–222.

[6]  GREENGARD, L. *The Rapid Evaluation of Potential Fields in Particle Systems*. MIT Press, Cambridge, Massachusetts, 1988.

[7]  HANRAHAN, P., SALZMAN, D., AND AUPPERLE, L. A rapid hierarchical radiosity algorithm. *Computer Graphics 25*, 4 (July 1991), 197–206.

[8]  KOK, A. J. Grouping of patches in progressive radiosity. In *Proceedings of the Fourth Eurographics Workshop on Rendering (Paris, France, June 14–16, 1993)* (June 1993), pp. 221–231.

[9]  LISCHINSKI, D., TAMPIERI, F., AND GREENBERG, D. P. Combining hierarchical radiosity and discontinuity meshing. In *Computer Graphics Proceedings* (1993), Annual Conference Series, ACM SIGGRAPH, pp. 199–208.

[10]  REICHERT, M. C. A two-pass radiosity method driven by lights and viewer position. Master's thesis, Program of Computer Graphics, Cornell University, Ithaca, New York, January 1992.

[11]  RUSHMEIER, H. E., PATTERSON, C., AND VEERASAMY, A. Geometric simplification for indirect illumination calculations. *Graphics Interface '93* (May 1993), 227–236.

[12]  SMITS, B., ARVO, J., AND SALESIN, D. An importance-driven radiosity algorithm. *Computer Graphics 26*, 4 (July 1992), 273–282.

[13]  TELLER, S., AND HANRAHAN, P. Global visibility for illumination computations. In *Computer Graphics Proceedings* (1993), Annual Conference Series, ACM SIGGRAPH, pp. 239–246.

# Partitioning and Ordering
# Large Radiosity Computations

**Seth Teller**[†]     **Celeste Fowler**[†]     **Thomas Funkhouser**[⋆]     **Pat Hanrahan**[†]

## Abstract

We describe a system that computes radiosity solutions for polygonal environments much larger than can be stored in main memory. The solution is stored in and retrieved from a database as the computation proceeds. Our system is based on two ideas: the use of visibility oracles to find source and blocker surfaces potentially visible to a receiving surface; and the use of hierarchical techniques to represent interactions between large surfaces efficiently, and to represent the computed radiosity solution compactly. Visibility information allows the environment to be *partitioned* into subsets, each containing all the information necessary to transfer light to a cluster of receiving polygons. Since the largest subset needed for any particular cluster is much smaller than the total size of the environment, these subset computations can be performed in much less memory than can classical or hierarchical radiosity. The computation is then *ordered* for further efficiency. Careful ordering of energy transfers minimizes the number of database reads and writes. We report results from large solutions of unfurnished and furnished buildings, and show that our implementation's observed running time scales nearly linearly with both local and global model complexity.

**CR Categories and Subject Descriptors:** I.3.7 [Computer Graphics]: *Three-Dimensional Graphics and Realism –Radiosity*; J.2 [Physical Sciences and Engineering]: *Engineering*.

**Additional Key Words and Phrases:** Multigridding; equilibrium methods; spatial subdivision.

---

† Computer Science Dept., Princeton University, Princeton NJ 08544

⋆ AT&T Bell Laboratories, Murray Hill, NJ 07974

## 1   Introduction

An important application of computer graphics is the modeling of lighting in buildings. In fact, such interior lighting simulations are the major application of the radiosity method. Unfortunately, radiosity algorithms still are not fast and robust enough to handle standard building databases. Evidence of this is that previous radiosity images typically show a solution for only a single room of modest geometric complexity. Furthermore, "tricks" are often used to hide artifacts and to cope with even this low level of model complexity. In this paper we describe radiosity computations on very large databases.

There are three basic measures of the complexity of a radiosity solution: the input complexity, the output complexity, and the intermediate complexity.

- The *input complexity* is related to the number of geometric primitives, textures, and light sources present.

- The *output complexity* is related to the number and type of elements required to represent the computed radiosity solution. Note that the output complexity is much, much greater than the input complexity, as it includes the input model plus a representation of the radiosity on all surfaces. The radiosity function may be very complex due to shadowing and lighting variations, and much recent research has concerned its compact, accurate representation. The optimal output complexity is that which represents the radiosity solution to within a specified error with a minimal amount of information.

- The *intermediate complexity* is related to the size of the data structure needed to perform the radiosity computation. The major components of the intermediate complexity are the form factor matrix and any data structures used to accelerate visibility computations. Since the form factor matrix may grow quadratically in the output complexity, and since accelerated visibility queries may involve sophisticated data structures, the intermediate complexity may be even greater than the output complexity, and is, in fact, usually the limiting factor in performing large radiosity simulations. When storage is unlimited, the optimal intermediate complexity is that associated with the most rapidly converging iterative scheme.

| Model | Surfaces | Patches | Elements | Time |
|-------|----------|---------|----------|------|
| Theater [1] | ∼5K | ∼80K | ∼1M | 192 H |
| Mill [5] | | ∼30K | ∼50K | 195 H |
| Cathedral [28] | ∼10K | | ∼75K | 1 H |

**Table 1**: Previous complex radiosity solutions.

Several complex radiosity computations have been reported in the literature (Table 1). Perhaps the most complex is the Candlestick Theater reported in Baum *et al* [1]. This simulation generated over a million elements, performed 1600 iterations of a progressive refinement algorithm (shooting from a single source), and took approximately 8 days to compute. Other reported complex radiosity simulations each generated less than 100,000 elements. Our goal is to render complete buildings at one square inch effective resolution, obviously a very resource-intensive computation. For example, consider the model of the University of California, Berkeley Computer Science Building. The furnished building model contains more than 8,000 light sources and 1.4 million surfaces and requires approximately 350 megabytes of storage [9]. We estimate that 10 to 100 million elements may be required to represent a high-fidelity radiosity solution throughout the model.

Intermediate memory demands often determine the limits on the size of the model used in a radiosity system. The intermediate memory usage depends on the representation of the form factor matrix. Two general approaches have emerged for coping with the size of the form factor matrix: hierarchical radiosity

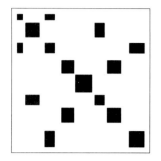

**Figure 1:** A locally dense, globally sparse interaction block matrix.

and visibility subspaces. Hierarchical radiosity (and its relative, wavelet radiosity) efficiently approximate form factor matrices in situations where a set of large surfaces are mutually visible. Techniques are only recently emerging for handling large numbers of small, mutually visible surfaces, for example by clustering. The problem of efficiently computing cluster-cluster interactions is not addressed in this paper. However, our visibility subspace methods do exploit the fact that in many environments, particularly building interiors, only a small percentage of the environment is visible from any particular surface. A global visibility precomputation constructs this potentially visible set for each surface, and the subspace methods maintain the set throughout hierarchical refinement.

Figure 1 depicts a sparse block-structured form factor matrix. Each diagonal block represents a dense interaction within a cluster of surfaces, e.g., the polygons comprising a room. Each off-diagonal block represents the coupling between these clusters, e.g. the rooms visible from a given room. Thus each block is locally dense, but the matrix is globally sparse.

In this paper we describe our system to compute radiosity solutions in such environments. The environment is assumed to be very large and hence is stored in a database as the computation proceeds. The ensuing radiosity computation is *partitioned* into subsets. Each subset contains the information needed to perform a transfer of light to a cluster of polygons. These subset computations are *ordered* to perform the light transfers efficiently by reducing the number of database reads and writes. We report the results of simulations run for models of varying density (local complexity) and overall size (global complexity).

This system is built upon previously described hierarchical radiosity methods, global and local visibility algorithms, and database and walkthrough implementations.

## 2 Prior Work

The problem of increasing the speed and accuracy of radiosity solutions has been addressed on many fronts.

- **Visibility.** One of the most expensive operations in global illumination is visibility computation. For a given surface, the set of surfaces that illuminate (or are illuminated by) it must be efficiently identified. Clearly this requires global knowledge of the model.

  Classical radiosity algorithms used a "hemicube" algorithm to approximate each surface's occluded view of the model as an environment map onto faces of a cube centered on a surface point [6]. The projection operation involved the whole model and respected depth, producing discretized surface fragments visible to the sample point. This and other point-sampling techniques (e.g., [4]) may not detect relevant light sources and/or blockers, however.

  Shaft culling recast global visibility into a collection of visibility subspaces by generating a common shaft volume for each interacting pair, and treating as blockers only those ob-

jects (potentially) intersecting the shaft [14, 18]. Finally, preprocessing and incremental maintenance techniques used a coherent global pass through the model to generate initial blocker lists, then maintained the lists incrementally under link subdivision [25]. These techniques, in contrast to those based on point-sampling, are *conservative* in the sense that they never wrongly exclude a blocker or light source from an interaction.

- **Solution Methods.** Classical radiosity algorithms generate a row-diagonally dominant interaction matrix [6]. The radiosity matrix equation is then solved by repeatedly updating the matrix entries using a numerical solution technique, typically Gauss-Seidel iteration. Several proposed improvements address the order in which the matrix entries are updated. Progressive radiosity techniques choose sources in brightness order and *shoot* their energy into the environment [5]. This may involve considerable bookkeeping, since each shoot updates many brightnesses, and the relative priorities of queued shooters may change considerably. Parallel implementations of progressive refinement have been reported [2, 19]. "Super-shoot gather" techniques repeatedly (over)shoot from and gather to a small number of surfaces, ignoring any interactions not involving the shooters [7, 12].

- **Hierarchical Approaches and Clustering.** Matrix-based solutions consider the matrix at a single *granularity*, namely the correspondence between each matrix entry and pair of surfaces in the environment. The hierarchical radiosity algorithm applied techniques developed for the $n$-body problem, incorporating a global error bound and allowing surfaces to exchange energy whenever they could do so within the specified error [15]. Thus, wherever sufficiently far-apart or dim surfaces interact, hierarchical methods essentially compact a block of the form-factor matrix into a scalar. Recursive application of this idea yielded a radiosity algorithm with running time that grows linearly with the number of output elements. The hierarchical radiosity algorithm did not address the "clustering" problem of efficiently handling interactions among surfaces composed of many small surfaces; some techniques have been recently proposed to do so [20, 22, 29].

- **Meshing and Finite Element Methods.** Finally, meshing and finite-element techniques have been employed to improve the accuracy of radiosity solutions. Classical and hierarchical solution algorithms represented radiosity as constant over each surface. Galerkin-based methods use finite element techniques to represent radiosities more generally, as weighted sums of smoothly varying basis functions defined over each surface [16, 17, 27, 30]. The resulting solutions have better smoothness and convergence behavior than those of classical radiosity. Recently, the wavelet radiosity method [13, 21] combined hierarchical radiosity with Galerkin techniques.

## 3 Basic Ideas

Our system is based on two ideas: partitioning and ordering.

**Partitioning** decomposes the database into subsets. Each subset contains the information needed to gather all the energy destined for a cluster of receivers. We assume that the largest subset, including the sources, receivers, and visibility and interaction information, requires fewer resources than would be required for the whole model. Performing energy transfers for a partition amounts to a single *block iteration* of an iterative solution of the radiosity system of equations. Partitioning is implemented by finding those clusters of source polygons visible to a cluster of receiving polygons. Only light originating from the sources may directly illuminate the receivers. Furthermore, *only polygons visible to the receivers may block light transfers from the sources.* Therefore, the visibility and light transfer computations may use the same database.

The goal of partitioning is to reduce the solver's *working set* to a manageable size. Receiver clusters may have dense interactions in a local region, but should have sparse interactions with the remainder of the environment. Our implementation inherits clustering information (and thus local density) from the modeling hierarchy, and achieves global sparseness by partitioning according to visibility.

**Ordering** is scheduling radiosity subcomputations –the energy transfers– to achieve rapid convergence. An example of an ordering algorithm is the progressive radiosity algorithm, in which the source with the largest unshot radiosity is selected to "shoot" its energy into the environment. In our system, the order must also be chosen so that the memory "footprint" changes slowly; that is, the working set needed for the next transfer should differ little from that of the current transfer. Successful ordering strategies reduce the read and write traffic of the working set from and to external storage, while maintaining rapid convergence properties.

In this paper we analyze several methods for ordering the energy transfers: random order; model definition order; source order; and spatial cell order. We also briefly discuss optimal orderings.

## 4 System Architecture

Our system is designed to solve the following problem: in practice, hierarchical radiosity is limited either by its intermediate complexity (i.e., the number of links) or by its output complexity (the description of the radiosity solution), or both. We address both limitations by constructing small but complete *working sets* (Figure 2) for the hierarchical algorithm, then invoking a radiosity solver and storing away the result – an improved, typically larger, answer – in a spatial database that can grow incrementally and arbitrarily large. This *partitioning* of hierarchical radiosity is shown in §5 to preserve its correctness and convergence properties.

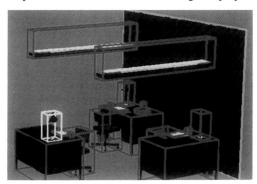

**Figure 2**: A working set of source cluster (white outline), receiver cluster (yellow outline), and blocker polygons (green outline) for a solver invocation. The braid and links are not shown.

The types *surface*, *patch*, *element*, and *link* are familiar to radiosity practitioners. The types *blocker*, *shaft*, and *tube* arise in recent related work on shaft-culling and visibility subspaces [14, 18, 25]. The novel types described here are *clusters* and *braids*, defined analogously to *surfaces* and *links* in existing hierarchical radiosity systems.

- A **tube** is a list of blockers for a pair of geometric entities $p$ and $q$, and a **shaft** volume, the convex hull of $(p \cup q)$. For any tube $T$, VARIETY$(T)$ lazily computes one of IN-VISIBLE, VISIBLE, or PARTIAL, when $p$ and $q$ are totally

mutually invisible, visible, or only partially visible, respectively. Tubes can also subdivide themselves and reclassify their child tubes' VARIETIES when one of $p$ or $q$ subdivides. Only entities that impinge upon the shaft may be **blockers**.

- A **braid** is a list of links between two clusters. A **link** is a directed edge to a patch $p$ from a patch $q$, associating with $p$ and $q$ a form factor estimate and other coupling information. Every link contains a tube. Given the tube $T$ describing the shaft and blockers of clusters $R$ and $S$, the braid over this cluster-cluster interaction is simply the set of all links between *patches* in clusters $R$ and $S$, and a reference to $T$.

- A **cluster** is a list of surfaces and a bounding volume. Note that a cluster may braid with itself if contains any patches $p$ and $q$ such that VARIETY$(p, q) \neq$ INVISIBLE.

The system has six principal computational modules. Five exist in previous work, and have been adopted here with only slight changes. The remaining component, the *radiosity scheduler*, is the main novelty of our system. We describe each module in top-down fashion (Figure 3).

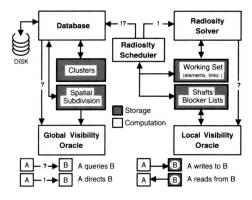

**Figure 3**: System block diagram.

- The **radiosity scheduler** is the conceptual center of the system. It mediates between the database and the radiosity solver, selecting a cluster for refinement and transfer operations (*ordering*), extracting a small portion of the model from the database (*partitioning*), manipulating the solver's working set, invoking the solver, extracting the modified, refined clusters, and returning them to the database.

- The **database** contains a persistent (disk) representation of all clusters and a hierarchical spatial subdivision comprised of convex *cells* and *portals* that connect cells [26]. The database supports the operations of *reading*, *dirtying*, and *releasing* clusters [9, 11]. Releases of dirty data result in deferred writes to persistent storage.

- The **global visibility oracle**, given a receiver cluster, identifies those clusters potentially visible to the receiver, i.e., those clusters that may illuminate the receiver, or block energy transfers to it [23, 25]. A cluster may be visible to itself.

- The **hierarchical wavelet radiosity solver** generates high-quality radiosity solutions using wavelet bases of general order and Gaussian quadrature [13, 15, 21].

- The **local visibility oracle** supports operations for allocating and subdividing tubes, and accelerating point-to-point visibility queries for quadrature [25]. The global oracle supplies the initial blocker list for each tube.

- The **visualization** module employs the Silicon Graphics IRIS GL$^{\text{TM}}$ to facilitate interaction, inspection, and animation of geometric data structures and algorithms [24]. It has proven indispensable to developing a working system.

# 5  Partitioning

We wish to partition a huge radiosity computation into a sequence of small *gathers* to individual receivers, each of which can fit into a small amount of memory. What information must be maintained in order to schedule and perform each gather correctly? Clearly the receiver and source cluster involved must be memory resident, as must their braid (links) and blocker polygons (cf. Figure 2). We compile this *working set* for each transfer, and supply it to the radiosity solver.

Our system constructs partitioning information from three sources. First, the modeling instantiation hierarchy yields clusters of polygons that separately comprise the structural elements, furnishings, light fixtures, etc., of the model. Second, a spatial subdivision groups clusters into cells by proximity, separating them along major sources of occlusion. Third, a visibility computation identifies all cluster pairs that may exchange energy [11, 23, 26].

The final tool is a flexible database from which individual portions of the model may be extracted, modified and replaced [11]. We adapted the database to support the new datatypes required for radiosity.

## 5.1  The Algorithm

Our algorithm: extracts each receiver and its visible set from the spatial database; links them; refines and gathers across the links; and returns the modified clusters to the database. A hierarchical wavelet radiosity *solver* performs the refinement and gather operations. Our algorithm loops over receiver clusters $R$ in the database until convergence, executing the following actions:

---

1. *Read R*
2. *Install R into working set*
3. *For each source cluster S visible to R*
   - (a) *Read S*, blockers $B(R,S)$
   - (b) *Install S*, blockers $B(R,S)$ into working set
   - (c) $T = Tube(R, S, B(R,S))$
   - (d) *Install*( links in $Braid(R, S, T)$ ) into working set
   - (e) Invoke **solver** *Gather*( each patch of $R$ )
   - (f) *Discard* newly refined links from working set
   - (g) *Delete* Tube $T$
   - (h) *Remove S*, blockers $B(R,S)$ from working set
   - (i) *SetDirty(S)*
   - (j) *Release(S)* and blockers $B(R,S)$
4. Invoke **solver** *PushPull*( each patch of $R$ )
5. *Extract(R)* from working set
6. *SetDirty(R)*
7. *Release(R)*

---

The function $Braid(R, S, T)$ in line $3-d$ simply generates top-level links between visible patch pairs from $R$ and $S$, using blocker information from the tube $T$. Refined links are discarded (line $3-f$), since A) they cannot be reused until the next full database iteration, and B) they are so numerous that, at $\sim$250 bytes/link, they do not fit in a 32-bit (4Gb) address space.

## 5.2  Iteration Methods, Correctness, and Convergence

Hierarchical radiosity performs *Jacobi iteration*. That is, only after a complete update of *all* patch's gather slots are *any* patch's shoot slots updated (by *Push* and *Pull* [15]). Jacobi iteration is clearly an untenable strategy for extremely large models, since it would necessitate reading and writing every patch twice per update. Moreover, hierarchical radiosity is often memory-bound in

practice, i.e., limited by the number and computational complexity of its active set of links, or by the size of the solution in progress. Our partitioning scheme eliminates Jacobi iteration altogether, and entirely removes the memory limitations on hierarchical radiosity for environments of sufficiently limited visibility.

The correctness of the partitioned solver is easily shown. During any gather to a cluster $R$, the only patches excluded as sources are INVISIBLE from $R$, and therefore cannot affect the computed solution on $R$.

The convergence of the partitioned solver follows from a numerical argument. The scheduler solves the radiosity matrix equation as does traditional hierarchical radiosity, but for one difference: each receiver sees a combination of old and updated shoot slots on other clusters, rather than seeing uniformly old slots. The scheduler is therefore performing Gauss-Seidel iteration of the linear system, rather than Jacobi iteration as in hierarchical radiosity. Since both methods converge for row-diagonally dominant systems of radiosity equations [6], convergence of the partitioning algorithm is assured.

## 5.3  Partitioning Results

We studied the performance of our system for models of varying complexity. In one test, we increased *local* complexity using models *Office*, *Office Low*, and *Office High* which represent the same office without furniture, with coarsely modeled furniture, and with very detailed furniture. These three models contain roughly one hundred, fifteen hundred, and thirty-five hundred input patches, respectively. In a second test, we increased *global* complexity using the unfurnished models *Office*, *Floor*, and *Building* which represent an office, one entire floor of a building, and finally an entire five floor building (including an atrium and many offices, open areas, stairwells, and classrooms). These models contain roughly one hundred, seven thousand, and forty thousand input patches, respectively.

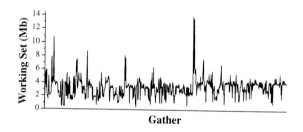

**Figure 4**: Working set size while solving the *Building* model.

We measured the input, intermediate, and output complexity, as well as working set memory requirements, for solutions of these test models. Statistics for three complete iterations (gathers to all clusters) of the radiosity solver are shown in Tables 2 and 3. The minimum allowable element area was one square inch for all runs. All times are wall-clock measurements using a 16 $\mu$-sec timer, on a lightly loaded SGI Crimson Reality Engine with a 50 MHz R4000 CPU, 256Mb memory, and 8Gb local disk. Figure 4 charts the size of the solver working set during one full iteration of the most complex model, *Building*.

Several trends can be gleaned from the measurements. First, the visibility and hierarchical radiosity techniques compacted large numbers of potential elements and interactions to manageable sizes. Second, partitioning techniques successfully bounded the working set size at a few tens of megabytes, even for models demanding several gigabytes of intermediate solution data. Third, intermediate and output complexity and running time appear to vary nearly linearly with input complexity. Thus, partitioning

| Input | | | Intermediate | | | | | Output | | | Observed | |
|---|---|---|---|---|---|---|---|---|---|---|---|---|
| | | | Working Set (Mb) | | # Links | | | # Elements | | | Elapsed Time (s) | |
| Model | Clusters / Patches / Lights | | WS | Total | WS | Total | / Patch | WS | Total | / Patch | Total | / Patch |
| Office | 36 | 127 | 18 | 1.3 | 9.5 | 3,914 | 36,186 | 285 | 1,445 | 3,142 | 24.7 | 180 | 1.4 |
| Office Low | 70 | 1,418 | 21 | 11.1 | 239.9 | 38,593 | 960,432 | 677 | 7,081 | 36,377 | 25.7 | 7,111 | 5.0 |
| Office High | 70 | 3,466 | 21 | 14.1 | 414.4 | 48,784 | 1,678,105 | 484 | 8,975 | 42,400 | 12.2 | 13,051 | 3.8 |

**Table 2**: Input, intermediate, and output complexities, and observed solution times, for models of increasing local complexity. The tabulated quantities are divided into: **WS** (the largest working set processed by the solver); **Total** (the total data processed throughout the run); and **Per Patch** (the total amount divided by the number of input patches). The intermediate working set **WS** was defined as the size of the links (including tubes, shafts, and kernel coefficients), elements (including wavelet coefficients), and blocker polygons.

| Input | | | Intermediate | | | | | Output | | | Observed | |
|---|---|---|---|---|---|---|---|---|---|---|---|---|
| | | | Working Set (Mb) | | # Links | | | # Elements | | | Elapsed Time (s) | |
| Model | Clusters / Patches / Lights | | WS | Total | WS | Total | / Patch | WS | Total | / Patch | Total | / Patch |
| Office | 36 | 127 | 18 | 1.3 | 9.5 | 3,914 | 36,186 | 285 | 1,445 | 3,142 | 24.7 | 180 | 1.4 |
| Floor | 1,761 | 7,054 | 788 | 3.7 | 1,116.1 | 12,532 | 4,307,705 | 611 | 2,686 | 250,933 | 35.6 | 56,712 | 8.0 |
| Building | 9,625 | 39,979 | 7,826 | 14.5 | 6,063.0 | 52,454 | 23,528,943 | 589 | 7,104 | 1,265,843 | 31.7 | 491,040 | 12.2 |

**Table 3**: Input, intermediate, and output complexities, and observed solution times, for models of increasing global complexity.

successfully exploited the global sparsity of the interaction matrix to achieve radiosity solutions for very large models, while maintaining quite small working sets.

# 6 Ordering

Partitioning alone is not sufficient to produce a practical system for large radiosity solutions. The partitioned transfers must be *ordered* so as to minimize expensive reads and writes of partial solution data from and to the database.

To be effective, an ordering algorithm must schedule successive gathers so as to minimize disk accesses, while maintaining rapid convergence properties. Much work has focused on the effects of ordering on convergence rates for the radiosity computation [5, 7, 12]; here we concentrate on the effect of ordering on disk accesses.

A good ordering algorithm maintains a high degree of coherence among the working sets of successive cluster interactions. Unfortunately, finding an optimal ordering is intractable. The problem is computationally equivalent to finding a solution to the traveling salesman problem. As a practical simplification, we have considered only orderings in which all gathers to a single cluster are performed successively (i.e., complete gathers). These orderings are particularly efficient and easy to implement because all sources and blockers for a complete gather to a single cluster are contained in the gatherer's visible set. Our implementation reads the entire set of clusters visible from the gatherer into the memory resident cache before performing any transfers to the gatherer.

We experimented with several ordering algorithms:

- **Random order** gathers to clusters in random order.

- **Model order** gathers to clusters in the order in which they were instantiated by the modeler. In most cases, this is not a random order since models are often constructed by successive addition of related parts. For instance, in the Berkeley Computer Science building model, walls, ceilings and floors were instantiated first (grouped roughly by room), followed by patches representing light fixtures and furniture.

- **Source order** gathers to that cluster which has most often acted as a source (ties are broken by proximity to the most recent gatherer). This strategy is based on the intuition that the working set of a cluster that has been visible to many

previous receivers is likely to have a large overlap with the current working set.

- **Cell order** schedules clusters by traversing cells of the wall-aligned BSP-tree [8] spatial subdivision [23, 26]. Consecutive cells are chosen by selecting the neighbor cell whose intervening boundary has the largest transparent area. This approach exploits the visibility coherence of clusters due to proximity and local intervisibility.

Figure 5 illustrates the effect that ordering can have on the coherence of the working set during an actual radiosity computation involving almost 2,000 clusters. The figure depicts matrices with a dot at position $(i, j)$ if clusters $C_i$ and $C_j$ were potentially visible to each other. Otherwise, no interaction between $C_i$ and $C_j$ was possible, and the space $(i, j)$ is left blank. Four permutations of the underlying interaction matrix were generated, by numbering clustering according to the order in which they were gathered to. Thus, the position of a cluster along the axes of the matrix depends on the gather order. Figure 5 depicts the permuted matrix resulting from gathers in A) random order, B) model order, C) source order and D) cell order, respectively.

In the case of random and model orders, the interactions are spread uniformly over the matrix. No block structure is evident, indicating that objects with similar visibility characteristics are gathered to at very different times. When gathering in source order the matrix appears much more block structured, especially in the early iterations. However, as gathering proceeds the coherence appears to degrade as evidenced by the fact that the block structure disappears in the upper right. The best ordering strategy appears to be cell order, yielding a matrix in natural block diagonal form, as would be expected in a building model. Note the horizontal and vertical stripes; these correspond to clusters in long corridors with many interactions.

## 6.1 Ordering Results

We studied the effects of ordering algorithms on cache performance by restricting the memory resident cache size to 32Mb while solving a one-floor building model. In each test, every cluster gathered exactly once. We logged statistics regarding cluster reads, writes, cache hit ratio, and I/O time during the third complete iteration of the radiosity computation (Table 4). All runs were executed on a 100 MHz R4000 SGI Indigo[2] with 160Mb of fast memory and 1Gb of local disk.

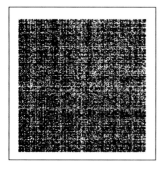

A) Random

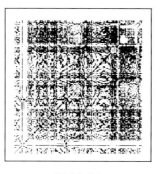

B) Model

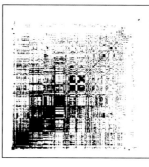

C) Source

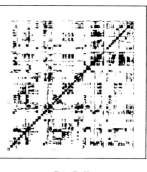

D) Cell

**Figure 5**: Matrices depicting permutations of the cluster-cluster interaction matrix. A dot at position $(i, j)$ denotes potential intervisibility of $C_i$ and $C_j$. Cluster position along axes corresponds to gather order during a complete radiosity iteration in A) random order, B) model order, C) source order, and D) cell order.

| Order | Clusters Read | Mb Read | Cache Hit Ratio | I/O Time(s) | Total Time(s) |
|---|---|---|---|---|---|
| Random | 77,916 | 4,374 | 35.4% | 23,330 | 49,111 |
| Model | 44,163 | 2,376 | 63.4% | 12,806 | 43,685 |
| Source | 30,798 | 1,708 | 74.4% | 8,912 | 33,815 |
| Cell | 11,312 | 617 | 90.6% | 3,180 | 26,454 |

**Table 4**: I/O statistics for various ordering algorithms.

There are significant differences in the I/O overhead incurred by each ordering algorithm. Figure 6 shows the percentage of total execution time spent on I/O (transfers between the disk and memory resident cache) for different gather orders. Random order had a 35.4% cache hit ratio, spending 23,330 seconds (47.5% of the total execution time) on more than 4.3GB of I/O between the disk and memory resident cache. In contrast, cell ordering achieved a 90.6% hit ratio, spending only 3,180 seconds on I/O (12.0% of the execution time). We conclude that the order in which clusters are processed can greatly affect performance during radiosity computations on very large models. We are currently investigating other possible ordering algorithms, including ones derived from progressive radiosity [5], nearest neighbors, and minimum spanning trees [3]. We expect that the best ordering algorithms will take into account both cache coherence and convergence behavior.

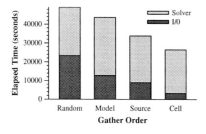

**Figure 6**: Time distributions for various gather orders.

## 7  Results

Using a Silicon Graphics Crimson workstation with a single 50 MHz processor and 256 megabytes of main memory, we computed three complete iterations of a radiosity solution on the entire unfurnished Berkeley Computer Science Building model to one inch resolution. The input model had 9,625 clusters comprising a total of 39,979 polygons. Of these polygons, 7,826 were emissive and served as light sources.

To give an idea of scale, the total area of all polygons in the unfurnished building model is 64,517,972 square inches. Therefore,

without the use of visibility-based partitioning and hierarchical techniques, the numbers of elements and links potentially created during the radiosity computation at one inch resolution are approximately $6.4 \times 10^7$ and $4.2 \times 10^{15}$, respectively – unmanageably high.

Statistics regarding the time and space complexity of the radiosity solution for the entire unfurnished building model are shown in Table 5. To our knowledge, this is the most complex model for which a radiosity solution has been computed. The entire radiosity computation took 136.4 hours and created 1,265,843 elements and 23,528,943 links – 2.0% and 0.00000056% of the potential numbers at one inch resolution, respectively. The partitioning techniques yielding a maximum working set size of 14.5MB, or 0.24% of the 6.1GB of total intermediate and output data. Cell ordering yielded a total I/O time of 14.2 hours, or 10.4% of the total execution time.

| # Iter | # Elements | # Links | Max WS | Solver Time | I/O Time | Total Time |
|---|---|---|---|---|---|---|
| 0 | 39,979 | - | - | - | - | - |
| 1 | 295,039 | 2,649,521 | 2.0 | 3.3 | 0.2 | 5.1 |
| 2 | 884,905 | 15,860,111 | 11.2 | 40.6 | 3.2 | 47.0 |
| 3 | 1,265,843 | 23,528,943 | 14.5 | 69.9 | 10.8 | 84.3 |
| Total | 1,265,843 | 23,528,943 | 14.5 | 113.8 | 14.2 | 136.4 |

**Table 5**: Complexity of radiosity solution for the unfurnished building model (times are in hours).

The five color plates on the next page show images of a radiosity solution for one furnished floor of the Berkeley Computer Science Building model, after two complete iterations. The solution contains 734,665 elements and took 48.5 hours to compute. Plate I shows an overhead view of the furnished floor. Plates II and III show interior views of a typical furnished office, shaded and with an overlaid quadtree mesh, respectively. The global and local complexities of the radiosity solution are readily apparent from these views. Plates IV and V show a typical work area and hallway view, respectively.

The radiosity solutions generated by this system are used as input for the real-time walkthrough program (the color plates were generated using screen-captures from this program). The same visibility information and computations used to determine source and receiver interactions are used to maintain an interactive frame rate in the walkthrough. The hierarchical (quadtree) representation of radiosity on each polygon is particularly useful, as it allows easily selectable levels of detail [10] for each polygon.

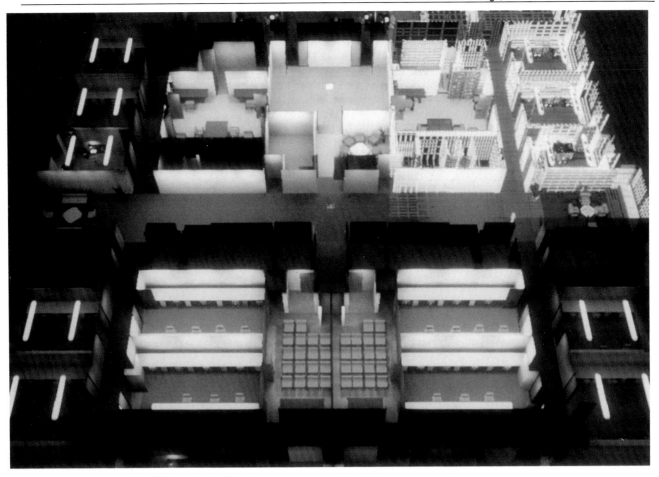

Plate I. The entire furnished floor, solved to one inch effective resolution (734,665 elements).

Plate II: Office, gouraud shaded.

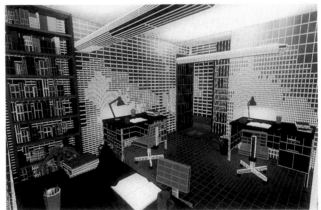

Plate III: Office, meshed.

Plate IV: Workroom, gouraud shaded.

Plate V: Hallway, gouraud shaded.

## 8 Summary and Discussion

This paper presented a system that exploits visibility and coherence information to compute radiosity solutions for very large geometric databases, using existing high-quality global illumination algorithms. Physically-based lighting simulation is more challenging than standard rendering algorithms in that the output complexity is very high, and the intermediate complexity and calculation costs are even higher. However, in the future there are likely to be many applications requiring display of complex, realistic virtual environments, such as the building used in this study. To achieve such complexity requires advances at both the theoretical and the practical level. The theoretical advances discussed in this paper are the visibility and hierarchical radiosity algorithms. The practical advances include the use of system techniques such as databases, scheduling, and caching.

Specifically, we have implemented a system capable of computing radiosity solutions from large models residing in a database stored on a disk. We show how partitioning the model leads to small working sets, allowing us to process databases much larger then those we could handle without partitioning. Poor partitioning of the database can cause it to be read and written many times. We show how clever ordering can significantly reduce disk traffic. The combination of these two techniques allow us to handle very large geometric models.

Given our experience with the system to date, the following research directions seem promising. First, the tradeoffs between gathering and shooting algorithms in hierarchical radiosity should be investigated, as preliminary results indicate that shooting converges more rapidly in some situations. Second, interactions among objects comprised of many small polygons must be handled more efficiently, perhaps by incorporating the notion of levels of detail into the radiosity solution method. Third, the visibility calculations used to determine soft shadows are still very expensive, and should be improved. Finally, the refinement oracle employed by the hierarchical radiosity algorithm is far too conservative. Rather than relying solely on estimates of form factor and transport error, it should incorporate a term based upon representation error over each receiver surface.

## Acknowledgments

Carlo Séquin founded the Building Walkthrough Group at Berkeley, and generously shared the latest model of Berkeley's (now-built) Computer Science Building, Soda Hall. David Laur's help with system administration and color figures was indispensable. Peter Schröder contributed to a C++ reimplementation of the wavelet radiosity solver. Michael Cohen shared his insights about iterative radiosity solution methods. Finally, Dan Wallach helped with video production for the paper submission, and Tamara Munzner helped process statistics for the final version.

We are grateful to the National Science Foundation (contract No. CCR 9207966) and to DIMACS for their support, and to Silicon Graphics, Forest Baskett, and Jim Clark for their gift of a Reality Engine.$^{\text{TM}}$

## References

[1] BAUM, D., MANN, S., SMITH, K., AND WINGET, J. Making Radiosity Usable: Automatic Preprocessing and Meshing Techniques for the Generation of Accurate Radiosity Solutions. *Computer Graphics (Proc. Siggraph '91) 25*, 4 (1991), 51–60.

[2] BAUM, D., AND WINGET, J. Real Time Radiosity Through Parallel Processing and Hardware Acceleration. *Computer Graphics (1990 Symposium on Interactive 3D Graphics) 24*, 2 (March 1990), 67–75.

[3] BENTLEY, J. Experiments on Geometric Traveling Salesman Heuristics. Tech. Rep. Computing Science (No. 151), AT&T Bell Laboratories, 1990.

[4] CAMPBELL III, A., AND FUSSELL, D. Adaptive Mesh Generation for Global Diffuse Illumination. *Computer Graphics (Proc. Siggraph '90) 24*, 4 (1990), 155–164.

[5] COHEN, M., CHEN, S., WALLACE, J., AND GREENBERG, D. A Progressive Refinement Approach to Fast Radiosity Image Generation. *Computer Graphics (Proc. Siggraph '88) 22*, 4 (1988), 75–84.

[6] COHEN, M., AND GREENBERG, D. The Hemi-Cube: A Radiosity Solution for Complex Environments. *Computer Graphics (Proc. Siggraph '85) 19*, 3 (1985), 31–40.

[7] FEDA, M., AND PURGATHOFER, W. Accelerating radiosity by overshooting. In *Proc. $3^{rd}$ Eurographics Workshop on Rendering* (May 1992), pp. 21–31.

[8] FUCHS, H., KEDEM, Z., AND NAYLOR, B. Predetermining visibility priority in 3-D scenes. *Computer Graphics (Proc. Siggraph '79) 13*, 2 (1979), 175–182.

[9] FUNKHOUSER, T. *Database and Display Algorithms for Interactive Visualization of Architectural Models.* PhD thesis, (Also TR UCB/CSD 93/771) CS Dept., UC Berkeley, 1993.

[10] FUNKHOUSER, T., AND SÉQUIN, C. Adaptive display algorithm for interactive frame rates during visualization of complex virtual environments. *Computer Graphics (Proc. Siggraph '93) 27* (1993), 247–254.

[11] FUNKHOUSER, T., SÉQUIN, C., AND TELLER, S. Management of Large Amounts of Data in Interactive Building Walkthroughs. In *Proc. 1992 Workshop on Interactive 3D Graphics* (1992), pp. 11–20.

[12] GORTLER, S., COHEN, M., AND SLUSALLEK, P. Radiosity and relaxation methods – Progressive refinement in Southwell relaxation. Technical Report TR-408-93, Department of Computer Science, Princeton University, 1993.

[13] GORTLER, S., SCHRÖDER, P., COHEN, M., AND HANRAHAN, P. Wavelet radiosity. *Computer Graphics (Proc. Siggraph '93)* (August 1993), 221–230.

[14] HAINES, E., AND WALLACE, J. Shaft Culling for Efficient Ray-Traced Radiosity. In *Proc. $2^{nd}$ Eurographics Workshop on Rendering* (May 1991).

[15] HANRAHAN, P., SALZMAN, D., AND AUPPERLE, L. A Rapid Hierarchical Radiosity Algorithm. *Computer Graphics (Proc. Siggraph '91) 25*, 4 (1991), 197–206.

[16] HECKBERT, P., AND WINGET, J. Finite element methods for global illumination. Tech. Rep. UCB/CSD 91/643, CS Department, UC Berkeley, 1991.

[17] LISCHINSKI, D., TAMPIERI, F., AND GREENBERG, D. P. Combining Hierarchical Radiosity and Discontinuity Meshing. *Computer Graphics (Proc. Siggraph '93) 27* (1993).

[18] MARKS, J., WALSH, R., CHRISTENSEN, J., AND FRIEDELL, M. Image and Intervisibility Coherence in Rendering. In *Proc. of Graphics Interface '90* (May 1990), pp. 17–30.

[19] RECKER, R., GEORGE, D., AND GREENBERG, D. Acceleration Techniques for Progressive Refinement Radiosity. *Computer Graphics (1990 Symp. on Interactive 3D Graphics) 24*, 2 (1990), 59–66.

[20] RUSHMEIER, H., PATTERSON, C., AND VEERASAMY, A. Geometric simplification for indirect illumination calculations. In *Proc. Graphics Interface '93* (1993), pp. 227–236.

[21] SCHRÖDER, P., GORTLER, S., COHEN, M., AND HANRAHAN, P. Wavelet projections for radiosity. In *Eurographics Workshop on Rendering* (1993), pp. 105–114.

[22] SMITS, B., ARVO, J., AND GREENBERG, D. A Clustering Algorithm for Radiosity in Complex Environments. *Computer Graphics (Proc. Siggraph '94) 28* (1994).

[23] TELLER, S. *Visibility Computations in Densely Occluded Polyhedral Environments.* PhD thesis, (Also TR UCB/CSD 92/708) CS Dept., UC Berkeley, 1992.

[24] TELLER, S. A Methodology for Geometric Algorithm Development. In *Proc. Computer Graphics International '93* (1993), N. and D. Thalmann, Eds., pp. 306–317.

[25] TELLER, S., AND HANRAHAN, P. Global Visibility Algorithms for Illumination Computations. *Computer Graphics (Proc. Siggraph '93) 27* (1993), 239–246.

[26] TELLER, S., AND SÉQUIN, C. H. Visibility Preprocessing for Interactive Walkthroughs. *Computer Graphics (Proc. Siggraph '91) 25*, 4 (1991), 61–69.

[27] TROUTMAN, R., AND MAX, N. Radiosity algorithms using higher order finite element methods. *Computer Graphics (Proc. Siggraph '93)* (1993), 209–212.

[28] WALLACE, J., ELMQUIST, K., AND HAINES, E. A Ray Tracing Algorithm for Progressive Radiosity. *Computer Graphics (Proc. Siggraph '89) 23*, 3 (1989), 315–324.

[29] XU, H., PENG, Q.-S., AND LIANG, Y.-D. Accelerated radiosity method for complex environments. *Computers and Graphics 14*, 1 (1990), 65–71.

[30] ZATZ, H. Galerkin radiosity: A higher order solution method for global illumination. *Computer Graphics (Proc. Siggraph '93) 27* (1993), 213–220.

# Fast Volume Rendering Using a Shear-Warp Factorization of the Viewing Transformation

Philippe Lacroute

Computer Systems Laboratory
Stanford University

Marc Levoy

Computer Science Department
Stanford University

## Abstract

Several existing volume rendering algorithms operate by factoring the viewing transformation into a 3D shear parallel to the data slices, a projection to form an intermediate but distorted image, and a 2D warp to form an undistorted final image. We extend this class of algorithms in three ways. First, we describe a new object-order rendering algorithm based on the factorization that is significantly faster than published algorithms with minimal loss of image quality. Shear-warp factorizations have the property that rows of voxels in the volume are aligned with rows of pixels in the intermediate image. We use this fact to construct a scanline-based algorithm that traverses the volume and the intermediate image in synchrony, taking advantage of the spatial coherence present in both. We use spatial data structures based on run-length encoding for both the volume and the intermediate image. Our implementation running on an SGI Indigo workstation renders a $256^3$ voxel medical data set in one second. Our second extension is a shear-warp factorization for perspective viewing transformations, and we show how our rendering algorithm can support this extension. Third, we introduce a data structure for encoding spatial coherence in unclassified volumes (i.e. scalar fields with no precomputed opacity). When combined with our shear-warp rendering algorithm this data structure allows us to classify and render a $256^3$ voxel volume in three seconds. The method extends to support mixed volumes and geometry and is parallelizable.

**CR Categories:** I.3.7 [Computer Graphics]: Three-Dimensional Graphics and Realism; I.3.3 [Computer Graphics]: Picture/Image Generation—Display Algorithms.

**Additional Keywords:** Volume rendering, Coherence, Scientific visualization, Medical imaging.

## 1 Introduction

Volume rendering is a flexible technique for visualizing scalar fields with widespread applicability in medical imaging and scientific visualization, but its use has been limited because it is

Authors' Address: Center for Integrated Systems, Stanford University,
Stanford, CA 94305-4070
E-mail: lacroute@weevil.stanford.edu, levoy@cs.stanford.edu
World Wide Web: http://www–graphics.stanford.edu/

computationally expensive. Interactive rendering rates have been reported using large parallel processors [17] [19] and using algorithms that trade off image quality for speed [10] [8], but high-quality images take tens of seconds or minutes to generate on current workstations. In this paper we present a new algorithm which achieves near-interactive rendering rates on a workstation without significantly sacrificing quality.

Many researchers have proposed methods that reduce rendering cost without affecting image quality by exploiting coherence in the data set. These methods rely on spatial data structures that encode the presence or absence of high-opacity voxels so that computation can be omitted in transparent regions of the volume. These data structures are built during a preprocessing step from a *classified* volume: a volume to which an opacity transfer function has been applied. Such spatial data structures include octrees and pyramids [13] [12] [8] [3], k-d trees [18] and distance transforms [23]. Although this type of optimization is data-dependent, researchers have reported that in typical classified volumes 70-95% of the voxels are transparent [12] [18].

Algorithms that use spatial data structures can be divided into two categories according to the order in which the data structures are traversed: image-order or object-order. Image-order algorithms operate by casting rays from each image pixel and processing the voxels along each ray [9]. This processing order has the disadvantage that the spatial data structure must be traversed once for every ray, resulting in redundant computation (e.g. multiple descents of an octree). In contrast, object-order algorithms operate by splatting voxels into the image while streaming through the volume data in storage order [20] [8]. However, this processing order makes it difficult to implement early ray termination, an effective optimization in ray-casting algorithms [12].

In this paper we describe a new algorithm which combines the advantages of image-order and object-order algorithms. The method is based on a factorization of the viewing matrix into a 3D shear parallel to the slices of the volume data, a projection to form a distorted intermediate image, and a 2D warp to produce the final image. Shear-warp factorizations are not new. They have been used to simplify data communication patterns in volume rendering algorithms for SIMD parallel processors [1] [17] and to simplify the generation of paths through a volume in a serial image-order algorithm [22]. The advantage of shear-warp factorizations is that scanlines of the volume data and scanlines of the intermediate image are always aligned. In previous efforts this property has been used to develop SIMD volume rendering algorithms. We exploit the property for a different reason: it allows efficient, synchronized access to data structures that separately encode coherence in the volume and the image.

The factorization also makes efficient, high-quality resampling possible in an object-order algorithm. In our algorithm the re-

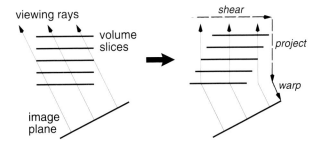

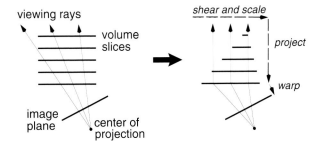

Figure 1: A volume is transformed to sheared object space for a parallel projection by translating each slice. The projection in sheared object space is simple and efficient.

Figure 2: A volume is transformed to sheared object space for a perspective projection by translating and scaling each slice. The projection in sheared object space is again simple and efficient.

sampling filter footprint is not view dependent, so the resampling complications of splatting algorithms [20] are avoided. Several other algorithms also use multipass resampling [4] [7] [19], but these methods require three or more resampling steps. Our algorithm requires only two resampling steps for an arbitrary perspective viewing transformation, and the second resampling is an inexpensive 2D warp. The 3D volume is traversed only once.

Our implementation running on an SGI Indigo workstation can render a $256^3$ voxel medical data set in one second, a factor of at least five faster than previous algorithms running on comparable hardware. Other than a slight loss due to the two-pass resampling, our algorithm does not trade off quality for speed. This is in contrast to algorithms that subsample the data set and can therefore miss small features [10] [3].

Section 2 of this paper describes the shear-warp factorization and its important mathematical properties. We also describe a new extension of the factorization for perspective projections. Section 3 describes three variants of our volume rendering algorithm. The first algorithm renders classified volumes with a parallel projection using our new coherence optimizations. The second algorithm supports perspective projections. The third algorithm is a fast classification algorithm for rendering unclassified volumes. Previous algorithms that employ spatial data structures require an expensive preprocessing step when the opacity transfer function changes. Our third algorithm uses a classification-independent min-max octree data structure to avoid this step. Section 4 contains our performance results and a discussion of image quality. Finally we conclude and discuss some extensions to the algorithm in Section 5.

## 2 The Shear-Warp Factorization

The arbitrary nature of the transformation from object space to image space complicates efficient, high-quality filtering and projection in object-order volume rendering algorithms. This problem can be solved by transforming the volume to an intermediate coordinate system for which there is a very simple mapping from the object coordinate system and which allows efficient projection.

We call the intermediate coordinate system "sheared object space" and define it as follows:

> Definition 1: By construction, in sheared object space all viewing rays are parallel to the third coordinate axis.

Figure 1 illustrates the transformation from object space to sheared object space for a parallel projection. We assume the volume is sampled on a rectilinear grid. The horizontal lines in the figure represent slices of the volume data viewed in cross-section. After transformation the volume data has been sheared parallel to the set of slices that is most perpendicular to the viewing direction and

the viewing rays are perpendicular to the slices. For a perspective transformation the definition implies that each slice must be scaled as well as sheared as shown schematically in Figure 2.

Definition 1 can be formalized as a set of equations that transform object coordinates into sheared object coordinates. These equations can be written as a factorization of the view transformation matrix $M_{\text{view}}$ as follows:

$$M_{\text{view}} = P \cdot S \cdot M_{\text{warp}}$$

$P$ is a permutation matrix which transposes the coordinate system in order to make the $z$-axis the principal viewing axis. $S$ transforms the volume into sheared object space, and $M_{\text{warp}}$ transforms sheared object coordinates into image coordinates. Cameron and Undrill [1] and Schröder and Stoll [17] describe this factorization for the case of rotation matrices. For a general parallel projection $S$ has the form of a shear perpendicular to the $z$-axis:

$$S_{\text{par}} = \begin{pmatrix} 1 & 0 & 0 & 0 \\ 0 & 1 & 0 & 0 \\ s_x & s_y & 1 & 0 \\ 0 & 0 & 0 & 1 \end{pmatrix}$$

where $s_x$ and $s_y$ can be computed from the elements of $M_{\text{view}}$. For perspective projections the transformation to sheared object space is of the form:

$$S_{\text{persp}} = \begin{pmatrix} 1 & 0 & 0 & 0 \\ 0 & 1 & 0 & 0 \\ s'_x & s'_y & 1 & s'_w \\ 0 & 0 & 0 & 1 \end{pmatrix}$$

This matrix specifies that to transform a particular slice $z_0$ of voxel data from object space to sheared object space the slice must be translated by $(z_0 s'_x, z_0 s'_y)$ and then scaled uniformly by $1/(1 + z_0 s'_w)$. The final term of the factorization is a matrix which warps sheared object space into image space:

$$M_{\text{warp}} = S^{-1} \cdot P^{-1} \cdot M_{\text{view}}$$

A simple volume rendering algorithm based on the shear-warp factorization operates as follows (see Figure 3):

1. Transform the volume data to sheared object space by translating and resampling each slice according to $S$. For perspective transformations, also scale each slice. $P$ specifies which of the three possible slicing directions to use.

2. Composite the resampled slices together in front-to-back order using the "over" operator [15]. This step projects the volume into a 2D intermediate image in sheared object space.

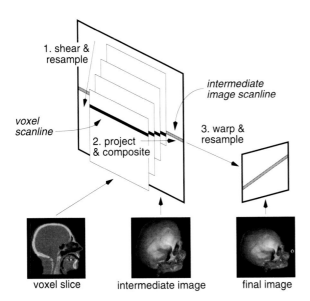

voxel slice      intermediate image      final image

Figure 3: The shear-warp algorithm includes three conceptual steps: shear and resample the volume slices, project resampled voxel scanlines onto intermediate image scanlines, and warp the intermediate image into the final image.

3. Transform the intermediate image to image space by warping it according to $M_{warp}$. This second resampling step produces the correct final image.

The parallel-projection version of this algorithm was first described by Cameron and Undrill [1]. Our new optimizations are described in the next section.

The projection in sheared object space has several geometric properties that simplify the compositing step of the algorithm:

Property 1: Scanlines of pixels in the intermediate image are parallel to scanlines of voxels in the volume data.

Property 2: All voxels in a given voxel slice are scaled by the same factor.

Property 3 (parallel projections only): Every voxel slice has the same scale factor, and this factor can be chosen arbitrarily. In particular, we can choose a unity scale factor so that for a given voxel scanline there is a one-to-one mapping between voxels and intermediate-image pixels.

In the next section we make use of these properties.

## 3 Shear-Warp Algorithms

We have developed three volume rendering algorithms based on the shear-warp factorization. The first algorithm is optimized for parallel projections and assumes that the opacity transfer function does not change between renderings, but the viewing and shading parameters can be modified. The second algorithm supports perspective projections. The third algorithm allows the opacity transfer function to be modified as well as the viewing and shading parameters, with a moderate performance penalty.

### 3.1 Parallel Projection Rendering Algorithm

Property 1 of the previous section states that voxel scanlines in the sheared volume are aligned with pixel scanlines in the intermediate image, which means that the volume and image data structures can

Figure 4: Offsets stored with opaque pixels in the intermediate image allow occluded voxels to be skipped efficiently.

both be traversed in scanline order. Scanline-based coherence data structures are therefore a natural choice. The first data structure we use is a run-length encoding of the voxel scanlines which allows us to take advantage of coherence in the volume by skipping runs of transparent voxels. The encoded scanlines consist of two types of runs, transparent and non-transparent, defined by a user-specified opacity threshold. Next, to take advantage of coherence in the image, we store with each opaque intermediate image pixel an offset to the next non-opaque pixel in the same scanline (Figure 4). An image pixel is defined to be opaque when its opacity exceeds a user-specified threshold, in which case the corresponding voxels in yet-to-be-processed slices are occluded. The offsets associated with the image pixels are used to skip runs of opaque pixels without examining every pixel. The pixel array and the offsets form a run-length encoding of the intermediate image which is computed on-the-fly during rendering.

These two data structures and Property 1 lead to a fast scanline-based rendering algorithm (Figure 5). By marching through the volume and the image simultaneously in scanline order we reduce addressing arithmetic. By using the run-length encoding of the voxel data to skip voxels which are transparent and the run-length encoding of the image to skip voxels which are occluded, we perform work only for voxels which are both non-transparent and visible.

For voxel runs that are not skipped we use a tightly-coded loop that performs shading, resampling and compositing. Properties 2 and 3 allow us to simplify the resampling step in this loop. Since the transformation applied to each slice of volume data before projection consists only of a translation (no scaling or rotation), the resampling weights are the same for every voxel in a slice (Figure 6). Algorithms which do not use the shear-warp factorization must recompute new weights for every voxel. We use a bilinear interpolation filter and a gather-type convolution (backward projection): two voxel scanlines are traversed simultaneously to compute a single intermediate image scanline at a time. Scatter-type convolution (forward projection) is also possible. We use a lookup-table based system for shading [6]. We also use a lookup table to correct voxel opacity for the current viewing angle

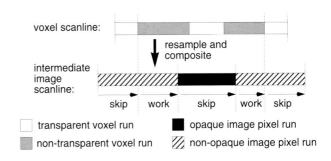

Figure 5: Resampling and compositing are performed by streaming through both the voxels and the intermediate image in scanline order, skipping over voxels which are transparent and pixels which are opaque.

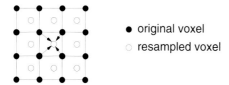

Figure 6: Since each slice of the volume is only translated, every voxel in the slice has the same resampling weights.

since the apparent thickness of a slice of voxels depends on the viewing angle with respect to the orientation of the slice.

The opaque pixel links achieve the same effect as early ray termination in ray-casting algorithms [12]. However, the effectiveness of this optimization depends on coherence of the opaque regions of the image. The runs of opaque pixels are typically large so that many pixels can be skipped at once, minimizing the number of pixels that are examined. The cost of computing the pixel offsets is low because a pixel's offset is updated only when the pixel first becomes opaque.

After the volume has been composited the intermediate image must be warped into the final image. Since the 2D image is small compared to the size of the volume this part of the computation is relatively inexpensive. We use a general-purpose affine image warper with a bilinear filter.

The rendering algorithm described in this section requires a run-length encoded volume which must be constructed in a preprocessing step, but the data structure is view-independent so the cost to compute it can be amortized over many renderings. Three encodings are computed, one for each possible principal viewing direction, so that transposing the volume is never necessary. During rendering one of the three encodings is chosen depending on the value of the permutation matrix $P$ in the shear-warp factorization. Transparent voxels are not stored, so even with three-fold redundancy the encoded volume is typically much smaller than the original volume (see Section 4.1). Fast computation of the run-length encoded data structure is discussed further at the end of Section 3.3.

In this section we have shown how the shear-warp factorization allows us to combine optimizations based on object coherence and image coherence with very low overhead and simple, high-quality resampling. In the next section we extend these advantages to a perspective volume rendering algorithm.

## 3.2  Perspective Projection Rendering Algorithm

Most of the work in volume rendering has focused on parallel projections. However, perspective projections provide additional cues for resolving depth ambiguities [14] and are essential to correctly compute occlusions in such applications as a beam's eye view for radiation treatment planning. Perspective projections present a problem because the viewing rays diverge so it is difficult to sample the volume uniformly. Two types of solutions have been proposed for perspective volume rendering using ray-casters: as the distance along a ray increases the ray can be split into multiple rays [14], or each sample point can sample a larger portion of the volume using a mip-map [11] [16]. The object-order splatting algorithm can also handle perspective, but the resampling filter footprint must be recomputed for every voxel [20].

The shear-warp factorization provides a simple and efficient solution to the sampling problem for perspective projections. Each slice of the volume is transformed to sheared object space by a translation and a uniform scale, and the slices are then resampled and composited together. These steps are equivalent to a ray-casting algorithm in which rays are cast to uniformly sample the first slice of volume data, and as each ray hits subsequent (more

distant) slices a larger portion of the slice is sampled (Figure 2). The key point is that within each slice the sampling rate is uniform (Property 2 of the factorization), so there is no need to implement a complicated multirate filter.

The perspective algorithm is nearly identical to the parallel projection algorithm. The only difference is that each voxel must be scaled as well as translated during resampling, so more than two voxel scanlines may be traversed simultaneously to produce a given intermediate image scanline and the voxel scanlines may not be traversed at the same rate as the image scanlines. We always choose a factorization of the viewing transformation in which the slice closest to the viewer is scaled by a factor of one so that no slice is ever enlarged. To resample we use a box reconstruction filter and a box low-pass filter, an appropriate combination for both decimation and unity scaling. In the case of unity scaling the two filter widths are identical and their convolution reduces to the bilinear interpolation filter used in the parallel projection algorithm.

The perspective algorithm is more expensive than the parallel projection algorithm because extra time is required to compute resampling weights and because the many-to-one mapping from voxels to pixels complicates the flow of control. Nevertheless, the algorithm is efficient because of the properties of the shear-warp factorization: the volume and the intermediate image are both traversed scanline by scanline, and resampling is accomplished via two simple resampling steps despite the diverging ray problem.

## 3.3  Fast Classification Algorithm

The previous two algorithms require a preprocessing step to run-length encode the volume based on the opacity transfer function. The preprocessing time is insignificant if the user wishes to generate many images from a single classified volume, but if the user wishes to experiment interactively with the transfer function then the preprocessing step is unacceptably slow. In this section we present a third variation of the shear-warp algorithm that evaluates the opacity transfer function during rendering and is only moderately slower than the previous algorithms.

A run-length encoding of the volume based upon opacity is not an appropriate data structure when the opacity transfer function is not fixed. Instead we apply the algorithms described in Sections 3.1–3.2 to unencoded voxel scanlines, but with a new method to determine which portions of each scanline are non-transparent. We allow the opacity transfer function to be any scalar function of a multi-dimensional scalar domain:

$$\alpha = f(p, q, ...)$$

For example, the opacity might be a function of the scalar field and its gradient magnitude [9]:

$$\alpha = f(d, |\nabla d|)$$

The function $f$ essentially partitions a multi-dimensional feature space into transparent and non-transparent regions, and our goal is to decide quickly which portions of a given scanline contain voxels in the non-transparent regions of the feature space.

We solve this problem with the following recursive algorithm which takes advantage of coherence in both the opacity transfer function and the volume data:

Step 1: For some block of the volume that contains the current scanline, find the extrema of the parameters of the opacity transfer function $(\min(p), \max(p), \min(q), \max(q), ...)$. These extrema bound a rectangular region of the feature space.

Step 2: Determine if the region is transparent, i.e. $f$ evaluated for all parameter points in the region yields only transparent

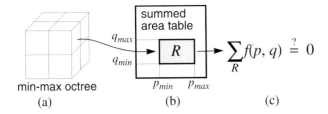

min-max octree  summed area table
(a)  (b)  (c)

Figure 7: A min-max octree (a) is used to determine the range of the parameters $p, q$ of the opacity transfer function $f(p, q)$ in a subcube of the volume. A summed area table (b) is used to integrate $f$ over that range of $p, q$. If the integral is zero (c) then the subcube contains only transparent voxels.

opacities. If so, then discard the scanline since it must be transparent.

Step 3: Subdivide the scanline and repeat this algorithm recursively. If the size of the current scanline portion is below a threshold then render it instead of subdividing.

This algorithm relies on two data structures for efficiency (Figure 7). First, Step 1 uses a precomputed min-max octree [21]. Each octree node contains the extrema of the parameter values for a subcube of the volume. Second, to implement Step 2 of the algorithm we need to integrate the function $f$ over the region of the feature space found in Step 1. If the integral is zero then all voxels must be transparent.* This integration can be performed in constant time using a multi-dimensional summed-area table [2] [5]. The voxels themselves are stored in a third data structure, a simple 3D array.

The overall algorithm for rendering unclassified data sets proceeds as follows. The min-max octree is computed at the time the volume is first loaded since the octree is independent of the opacity transfer function and the viewing parameters. Next, just before rendering begins the opacity transfer function is used to compute the summed area table. This computation is inexpensive provided that the domain of the opacity transfer function is not too large. We then use either the parallel projection or the perspective projection rendering algorithm to render voxels from an unencoded 3D voxel array. The array is traversed scanline by scanline. For each scanline we use the octree and the summed area table to determine which portions of the scanline are non-transparent. Voxels in the non-transparent portions are individually classified using a lookup table and rendered as in the previous algorithms. Opaque regions of the image are skipped just as before. Note that voxels that are either transparent or occluded are never classified, which reduces the amount of computation.

The octree traversal and summed area table lookups add overhead to the algorithm which were not present in the previous algorithms. In order to reduce this overhead we save as much computed data as possible for later reuse: an octree node is tested for transparency using the summed area table only the first time it is visited and the result is saved for subsequent traversals, and if two adjacent scanlines intersect the same set of octree nodes then we record this fact and reuse information instead of making multiple traversals.

This rendering algorithm places two restrictions on the opacity transfer function: the parameters of the function must be precomputable for each voxel so that the octree may be precomputed, and the total number of possible argument tuples to the function (the cardinality of the domain) must not be too large since the

summed area table must contain one entry for each possible tuple. Context-sensitive segmentation (classification based upon the position and surroundings of a voxel) does not meet these criteria unless the segmentation is entirely precomputed.

The fast-classification algorithm presented here also suffers from a problem common to many object-order algorithms: if the major viewing axis changes then the volume data must be accessed against the stride and performance degrades. Alternatively the 3D array of voxels can be transposed, resulting in a delay during interactive viewing. Unlike the algorithms based on a run-length encoded volume, it is typically not practical to maintain three copies of the unencoded volume since it is much larger than a run-length encoding. It is better to use a small range of viewpoints while modifying the classification function, and then to switch to one of the previous two rendering methods for rendering animation sequences. In fact, the octree and the summed-area table can be used to convert the 3D voxel array into a run-length encoded volume without accessing transparent voxels, leading to a significant time savings (see the "Switch Modes" arrow in Figure 12). Thus the three algorithms fit together well to yield an interactive tool for classifying and viewing volumes.

## 4 Results

### 4.1 Speed and Memory

Our performance results for the three algorithms are summarized in Table 1. The "Fast Classification" timings are for the algorithm in Section 3.3 with a parallel projection. The timings were measured on an SGI Indigo R4000 without hardware graphics accelerators. Rendering times include all steps required to render from a new viewpoint, including computation of the shading lookup table, compositing and warping, but the preprocessing step is not included. The "Avg." field in the table is the average time in seconds for rendering 360 frames at one degree angle increments, and the "Min/Max" times are for the best and worst case angles. The "Mem." field gives the size in megabytes of all data structures. For the first two algorithms the size includes the three run-length encodings of the volume, the image data structures and all lookup tables. For the third algorithm the size includes the unencoded volume, the octree, the summed-area table, the image data structures, and the lookup tables. The "brain" data set is an MRI scan of a human head (Figure 8) and the "head" data set is a CT scan of a human head (Figure 9). The "brainsmall" and "headsmall" data sets are decimated versions of the larger volumes.

The timings are nearly independent of image size because this factor affects only the final warp which is relatively insignificant. Rendering time is dependent on viewing angle (Figure 11) because the effectiveness of the coherence optimizations varies with viewpoint and because the size of the intermediate image increases as the rotation angle approaches 45 degrees, so more compositing operations must be performed. For the algorithms described in Sections 3.1–3.2 there is no jump in rendering time when the major viewing axis changes, provided the three run-length encoded copies of the volume fit into real memory simultaneously. Each copy contains four bytes per non-transparent voxel and one byte per run. For the 256x256x226 voxel head data set the three run-length encodings total only 9.8 Mbytes. All of the images were rendered on a workstation with 64 Mbytes of memory. To test the fast classification algorithm (Section 3.3) on the $256^3$ data sets we used a workstation with 96 Mbytes of memory.

Figure 12 gives a breakdown of the time required to render the brain data set with a parallel projection using the fast classification algorithm (left branch) and the parallel projection algorithm (right branch). The time required to warp the intermediate image into the final image is typically 10-20% of the total rendering time for the parallel projection algorithm. The "Switch Modes" arrow

---

*The user may choose a non-zero opacity threshold for transparent voxels, in which case a thresholded version of $f$ must be integrated: let $f' = f$ whenever $f$ exceeds the threshold, and $f' = 0$ otherwise.

| Data set | Size (voxels) | Parallel projection (§3.1) | | | Perspective projection (§3.2) | | | Fast classification (§3.3) | | |
|---|---|---|---|---|---|---|---|---|---|---|
| | | Avg. | Min/Max | Mem. | Avg. | Min/Max | Mem. | Avg. | Min/Max | Mem. |
| brainsmall | 128x128x109 | 0.4 s. | 0.37–0.48 s. | 4 Mb. | 1.0 s. | 0.84–1.13 s. | 4 Mb. | 0.7 s. | 0.61–0.84 s. | 8 Mb. |
| headsmall | 128x128x113 | 0.4 | 0.35–0.43 | 2 | 0.9 | 0.82–1.00 | 2 | 0.8 | 0.72–0.87 | 8 |
| brain | 256x256x167 | 1.1 | 0.91–1.39 | 19 | 3.0 | 2.44–2.98 | 19 | 2.4 | 1.91–2.91 | 46 |
| head | 256x256x225 | 1.2 | 1.04–1.33 | 13 | 3.3 | 2.99–3.68 | 13 | 2.8 | 2.43–3.23 | 61 |

Table 1: Rendering time and memory usage on an SGI Indigo workstation. Times are in seconds and include shading, resampling, projection and warping. The fast classification times include rendering with a parallel projection. The "Mem." field is the total size of the data structures used by each algorithm.

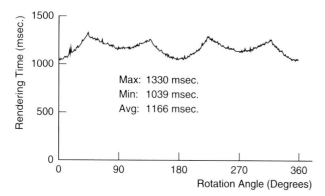

Figure 11: Rendering time for a parallel projection of the head data set as the viewing angle changes.

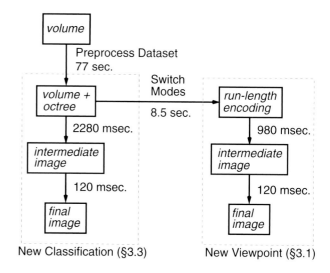

Figure 12: Performance results for each stage of rendering the brain data set with a parallel projection. The left side uses the fast classification algorithm and the right side uses the parallel projection algorithm.

shows the time required for all three copies of the run-length encoded volume to be computed from the unencoded volume and the min-max octree once the user has settled on an opacity transfer function.

The timings above are for grayscale renderings. Color renderings take roughly twice as long for parallel projections and 1.3x longer for perspective because of the additional resampling required for the two extra color channels. Figure 13 is a color rendering of the head data set classified with semitransparent skin which took 3.0 sec. to render. Figure 14 is a rendering of a 256x256x110 voxel engine block, classified with semi-transparent and opaque surfaces; it took 2.3 sec. to render. Figure 15 is a rendering of a 256x256x159 CT scan of a human abdomen, rendered in 2.2 sec. The blood vessels of the subject contain a radio-opaque dye, and the data set was classified to reveal both the dye and bone surfaces. Figure 16 is a perspective color rendering of the engine data set which took 3.8 sec. to compute.

For comparison purposes we rendered the head data set with a ray-caster that uses early ray termination and a pyramid to exploit object coherence [12]. Because of its lower computational overhead the shear-warp algorithm is more than five times faster for the $128^3$ data sets and more than ten times faster for the $256^3$ data sets. Our algorithm running on a workstation is competitive with algorithms for massively parallel processors ([17], [19] and others), although the parallel implementations do not rely on coherence optimizations and therefore their performance results are not data dependent as ours are.

Our experiments show that the running time of the algorithms in Sections 3.1–3.2 is proportional to the number of voxels which are resampled and composited. This number is small either if a significant fraction of the voxels are transparent or if the average voxel opacity is high. In the latter case the image quickly becomes opaque and the remaining voxels are skipped. For the data sets and classification functions we have tried roughly $n^2$ voxels are both non-transparent and visible, so we observe $O(n^2)$ performance as shown in Table 1: an eight-fold increase in the

number of voxels leads to only a four-fold increase in time for the compositing stage and just under a four-fold increase in overall rendering time. For our rendering of the head data set 5% of the voxels are non-transparent, and for the brain data set 11% of the voxels are non-transparent. Degraded performance can be expected if a substantial fraction of the classified volume has low but non-transparent opacity, but in our experience such classification functions are less useful.

## 4.2 Image Quality

Figure 10 is a volume rendering of the same data set as in Figure 9, but produced by a ray-caster using trilinear interpolation [12]. The two images are virtually identical.

Nevertheless, there are two potential quality problems associated with the shear-warp algorithm. First, the algorithm involves two resampling steps: each slice is resampled during compositing, and the intermediate image is resampled during the final warp. Multiple resampling steps can potentially cause blurring and loss of detail. However even in the high-detail regions of Figure 9 this effect is not noticeable.

The second potential problem is that the shear-warp algorithm uses a 2D rather than a 3D reconstruction filter to resample the volume data. The bilinear filter used for resampling is a first-order filter in the plane of a voxel slice, but it is a zero-order (nearest-neighbor) filter in the direction orthogonal to the slice. Artifacts are likely to appear if the opacity or color attributes of the volume contain very high frequencies (although if the frequencies exceed the Nyquist rate then perfect reconstruction is impossible).

Figure 17 shows a case where a trilinear interpolation filter outperforms a bilinear filter. The left-most image is a rendering by the shear-warp algorithm of a portion of the engine data set which has been classified with extremely sharp ramps to produce high frequencies in the volume's opacity. The viewing angle is set to 45 degrees relative to the slices of the data set—the worst case—and aliasing is apparent. For comparison, the middle image is a rendering produced with a ray-caster using trilinear interpolation and otherwise identical rendering parameters; here there is virtually no aliasing. However, by using a smoother opacity transfer function these reconstruction artifacts can be reduced. The right-most image is a rendering using the shear-warp algorithm and a less-extreme opacity transfer function. Here the aliasing is barely noticeable because the high frequencies in the scalar field have effectively been low-pass filtered by the transfer function. In practice, as long as the opacity transfer function is not a binary classification the bilinear filter produces good results.

## 5   Conclusion

The shear-warp factorization allows us to implement coherence optimizations for both the volume data and the image with low computational overhead because both data structures can be traversed simultaneously in scanline order. The algorithm is flexible enough to accommodate a wide range of user-defined shading models and can handle perspective projections. We have also presented a variant of the algorithm that does not assume a fixed opacity transfer function. The result is an algorithm which produces high-quality renderings of a $256^3$ volume in roughly one second on a workstation with no specialized hardware.

We are currently extending our rendering algorithm to support data sets containing both geometry and volume data. We have also found that the shear-warp algorithms parallelize naturally for MIMD shared-memory multiprocessors. We parallelized the resampling and compositing steps by distributing scanlines of the intermediate image to the processors. On a 16 processor SGI Challenge multiprocessor the 256x256x223 voxel head data set can be rendered at a sustained rate of 10 frames/sec.

## Acknowledgements

We thank Pat Hanrahan, Sandy Napel and North Carolina Memorial Hospital for the data sets, and Maneesh Agrawala, Mark Horowitz, Jason Nieh, Dave Ofelt, and Jaswinder Pal Singh for their help. This research was supported by Software Publishing Corporation, ARPA/ONR under contract N00039-91-C-0138, NSF under contract CCR-9157767 and the sponsoring companies of the Stanford Center for Integrated Systems.

## References

[1] Cameron, G. G. and P. E. Undrill. Rendering volumetric medical image data on a SIMD-architecture computer. In *Proceedings of the Third Eurographics Workshop on Rendering*, 135–145, Bristol, UK, May 1992.

[2] Crow, Franklin C. Summed-area tables for texture mapping. Proceedings of SIGGRAPH '84. *Computer Graphics*, 18(3):207–212, July 1984.

[3] Danskin, John and Pat Hanrahan. Fast algorithms for volume ray tracing. In *1992 Workshop on Volume Visualization*, 91–98, Boston, MA, October 1992.

[4] Drebin, Robert A., Loren Carpenter and Pat Hanrahan. Volume rendering. Proceedings of SIGGRAPH '88. *Computer Graphics*, 22(4):65–74, August 1988.

[5] Glassner, Andrew S. Multidimensional sum tables. In *Graphics Gems*, 376–381. Academic Press, New York, 1990.

[6] Glassner, Andrew S. Normal coding. In *Graphics Gems*, 257–264. Academic Press, New York, 1990.

[7] Hanrahan, Pat. Three-pass affine transforms for volume rendering. *Computer Graphics*, 24(5):71–77, November 1990.

[8] Laur, David and Pat Hanrahan. Hierarchical splatting: A progressive refinement algorithm for volume rendering. Proceedings of SIGGRAPH '91. *Computer Graphics*, 25(4):285–288, July 1991.

[9] Levoy, Marc. Display of surfaces from volume data. *IEEE Computer Graphics & Applications*, 8(3):29–37, May 1988.

[10] Levoy, Marc. Volume rendering by adaptive refinement. *The Visual Computer*, 6(1):2–7, February 1990.

[11] Levoy, Marc and Ross Whitaker. Gaze-directed volume rendering. *Computer Graphics*, 24(2):217–223, March 1990.

[12] Levoy, Marc. Efficient ray tracing of volume data. *ACM Transactions on Graphics*, 9(3):245–261, July 1990.

[13] Meagher, Donald J. Efficient synthetic image generation of arbitrary 3-D objects. In *Proceeding of the IEEE Conference on Pattern Recognition and Image Processing*, 473–478, 1982.

[14] Novins, Kevin L., François X. Sillion, and Donald P. Greenberg. An efficient method for volume rendering using perspective projection. *Computer Graphics*, 24(5):95–102, November 1990.

[15] Porter, Thomas and Tom Duff. Compositing digital images. Proceedings of SIGGRAPH '84. *Computer Graphics*, 18(3):253–259, July 1984.

[16] Sakas, Georgios and Matthias Gerth. Sampling and antialiasing of discrete 3-D volume density textures. In *Proceedings of Eurographics '91*, 87–102, Vienna, Austria, September 1991.

[17] Schröder, Peter and Gordon Stoll. Data parallel volume rendering as line drawing. In *Proceedings of the 1992 Workshop on Volume Visualization*, 25–32, Boston, October 1992.

[18] Subramanian, K. R. and Donald S. Fussell. Applying space subdivision techniques to volume rendering. In *Proceedings of Visualization '90*, 150–159, San Francisco, California, October 1990.

[19] Vézina, Guy, Peter A. Fletcher, and Philip K. Robertson. Volume rendering on the MasPar MP-1. In *1992 Workshop on Volume Visualization*, 3–8, Boston, October 1992.

[20] Westover, Lee. Footprint evaluation for volume rendering. Proceedings of SIGGRAPH '90. *Computer Graphics*, 24(4):367–376, August 1990.

[21] Wilhelms, Jane and Allen Van Gelder. Octrees for faster isosurface generation. *Computer Graphics*, 24(5):57–62, November 1990.

[22] Yagel, Roni and Arie Kaufman. Template-based volume viewing. In *Eurographics 92*, C-153–167, Cambridge, UK, September 1992.

[23] Zuiderveld, Karel J., Anton H.J. Koning, and Max A. Viergever. Acceleration of ray-casting using 3D distance transforms. In *Proceedings of Visualization in Biomedical Computing 1992*, 324–335, Chapel Hill, North Carolina, October 1992.

Figure 8: Volume rendering with a parallel projection of an MRI scan of a human brain using the shear-warp algorithm (1.1 sec.).

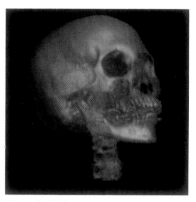

Figure 9: Volume rendering with a parallel projection of a CT scan of a human head oriented at 45 degrees relative to the axes of the volume (1.2 sec.).

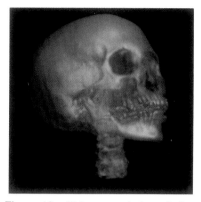

Figure 10: Volume rendering of the same data set as in Figure 9 using a ray-caster [12] for quality comparison (13.8 sec.).

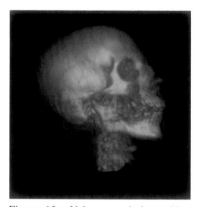

Figure 13: Volume rendering with a parallel projection of the human head data set classified with semitransparent skin (3.0 sec.).

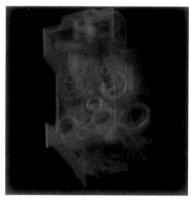

Figure 14: Volume rendering with a parallel projection of an engine block with semitransparent and opaque surfaces (2.3 sec.).

Figure 15: Volume rendering with a parallel projection of a CT scan of a human abdomen (2.2 sec.). The blood vessels contain a radio-opaque dye.

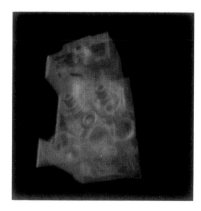

Figure 16: Volume rendering with a perspective projection of the engine data set (3.8 sec.).

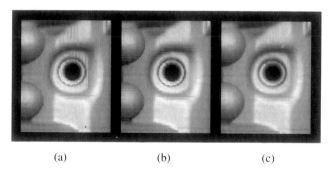

(a)                    (b)                    (c)

Figure 17: Comparison of image quality with bilinear and trilinear filters for a portion of the engine data set. The images have been enlarged. (a) Bilinear filter with binary classification. (b) Trilinear filter with binary classification. (c) Bilinear filter with smooth classification.

# The RADIANCE Lighting Simulation and Rendering System

*Gregory J. Ward*

Lighting Group
Building Technologies Program
Lawrence Berkeley Laboratory
(e-mail: GJWard@Lbl.Gov)

## ABSTRACT

This paper describes a physically-based rendering system tailored to the demands of lighting design and architecture. The simulation uses a light-backwards ray-tracing method with extensions to efficiently solve the rendering equation under most conditions. This includes specular, diffuse and directional-diffuse reflection and transmission in any combination to any level in any environment, including complicated, curved geometries. The simulation blends deterministic and stochastic ray-tracing techniques to achieve the best balance between speed and accuracy in its local and global illumination methods. Some of the more interesting techniques are outlined, with references to more detailed descriptions elsewhere. Finally, examples are given of successful applications of this free software by others.

**CR Categories**: I.3.3 [Computer Graphics]: Picture/image generation - *Display algorithms*; I.3.7 [Computer Graphics]: Three-Dimensional Graphics and Realism - *Shading*.
**Additional Keywords and Phrases**: lighting simulation, Monte Carlo, physically-based rendering, radiosity, ray-tracing.

## 1. Introduction

Despite voluminous research in global illumination and radiosity over the past decade, few practical applications have surfaced in the fields that stand the most to benefit: architecture and lighting design. Most designers who use rendering software employ it in a purely illustrative fashion to show geometry and style, not to predict lighting or true appearance. The designers cannot be blamed for this; rendering systems that promote flash over content have been the mainstay of the graphics industry for years, and the shortcuts employed are well-understood by the software community and well-supported by the hardware manufacturers.

Why has radiosity not yet taken off in the rendering market? Perhaps not enough time has passed since its introduction to the graphics community a decade ago [8]. After all, it took ray-tracing nearly that long to become a mainstream, commercial rendering technique. Another possibility is that the method is too compute-intensive for most applications, or that it simply does not fulfill enough people's needs. For example, most radiosity systems are not well automated, and do not permit general reflectance models or curved surfaces. If we are unable to garner support even from the principal beneficiaries, designers, what does that say of our chances with the rest of the user community?

Acceptance of physically-based rendering is bound to improve†, but researchers must first demonstrate the real-life applicability of their techniques. There have been few notable successes in applying radiosity to the needs of practicing designers [6]. While much research has focused on improving efficiency of the basic radiosity method, problems associated with more realistic, complicated geometries have only recently gotten the attention they deserve [2,19,22]. For whatever reason, it appears that radiosity has yet to fulfill its promise, and it is time to reexamine this technique in light of real-world applications and other alternatives for solving the rendering equation [10].

There are three closely related challenges to physically-based rendering for architecture and lighting design: accuracy, generality and practicality. The first challenge is that the calculation must be accurate; it must compute absolute values in physical units with reasonable certainty. Although recent research in global illumination has studied sources of calculation error [1,20], few researchers bother to compute in physical lighting units, and even fewer have compared their results to physical experiments [15]. No matter how good the theory is, accuracy claims for simulation must ultimately be backed up with comparisons to what is being simulated. The second challenge is that a rendering program must be general. It is not necessary to simulate every physical lighting phenomenon, but it is important to do enough that the unsolvable rendering problems are either unimportant or truly exceptional. The third challenge for any rendering system is that it be practical. This includes a broad spectrum of requirements, from being reliable (i.e. debugged and tested) to being application-friendly, to producing good results in a reasonable time. All three of the above challenges must be met if a physically-based rendering package is to succeed, and all three must be treated with equal importance.

*Radiance* is the name of a rendering system developed by the author over the past nine years at the Lawrence Berkeley Laboratory (LBL) in California and the Ecole Polytechnique Federale de Lausanne (EPFL) in Switzerland. It began as a study in ray-tracing algorithms, and after demonstrating its potential for saving energy through better lighting design, acquired funding from the U.S. Department of Energy and later from the Swiss government. The first free software release was in 1989, and since then it has found an increasing number of users in the research and design community. Although it has never been a commercial product, *Radiance* has benefited enor-

---

†The term "physically-based rendering" is used throughout the paper to refer to rendering techniques based on physical principles of light behavior for local and global illumination. The term "simulation" is more general, referring to any algorithm that mimics a physical process.

mously from the existence of an enthusiastic, active and growing user base, which has provided invaluable debugging help and stress-testing of the software. In fact, most of the enhancements made to the system were the outcome of real or perceived user requirements. This is in contrast to the much of the research community, which tends to respond to intriguing problems before it responds to critical ones. Nine years of user-stimulated software evolution gives us the confidence to claim we have a rendering system that goes a long way towards satisfying the needs of the design community. Further evidence has been provided by the two or three design companies who have abandoned their own in-house software (some of which cost over a million dollars to develop) in favor of *Radiance*.

In this paper, we describe the *Radiance* system design goals, followed with the principal techniques used to meet these goals. We follow with examples of how users have applied *Radiance* to specific problems, followed by conclusions and ideas for future directions.

## 2. System Design Goals

The original goals for the *Radiance* system were modest, or so we thought. The idea was to produce an accurate tool for lighting simulation and visualization based on ray-tracing. Although the initial results were promising, we soon learned that there was much more to getting the simulation right than plugging proper values and units into a standard ray-tracing algorithm. We needed to overcome some basic shortcomings. The main shortcoming of conventional ray-tracing is that diffuse interreflection between surfaces is approximated by a uniform "ambient" term. For many scenes, this is a poor approximation, even if the ambient term is assigned correctly. Other difficulties arise in treating light distribution from large sources such as windows, skylights, and large fixtures. Finally, reflections of lights from mirrors and other secondary sources are problematic. These problems, which we will cover in some detail later, arose from the consideration of our system design goals, given below.

The principal design goals of *Radiance* were to:

1. Ensure accurate calculation of luminance
2. Model both electric light and daylight
3. Support a variety of reflectance models
4. Support complicated geometry
5. Take unmodified input from CAD systems

These goals reflect many years of experience in architectural lighting simulation; some of them are physically-motivated, others are user-motivated. All of them must be met before a lighting simulation tool can be of significant value to a designer.

### 2.1. Ensure Accurate Calculation of Luminance

Accuracy is one of the key challenges in physically-based rendering, and luminance (or the more general "spectral radiance") is probably the most versatile unit in lighting. Photometric units such as luminance are measured in terms of visible radiation, and radiometric units such as radiance are measured in terms of power (energy/time). Luminance represents the quantity of visible radiation passing through a point in a given direction, measured in lumens/steradian/meter$^2$ in SI units. Radiance is the radiometric equivalent of luminance, measured in watts/steradian/meter$^2$. Spectral radiance simply adds a dependence on wavelength to this. Luminance and spectral radiance are most closely related to a pixel, which is what the eye actually "sees." From this single unit, all other lighting metrics can be derived. Illuminance, for example, is the integral of luminance over a projected hemisphere (lumens/meter$^2$ or "lux" in SI units). Luminous intensity and luminous flux follow similar derivations. By computing the most basic lighting unit, our simulation will adapt more readily to new applications.

To assure that a simulation delivers on its promise, it is essential that the program undergo periodic validation. In our case, this means comparing luminance values predicted by *Radiance* to measurements of physical models. An initial validation was completed in 1989 by Grynberg [9], and subsequent validations by ourselves and others confirm that the values are getting better and not worse [14].

### 2.2. Model Both Electric Light and Daylight

In order to be general, a lighting calculation must include all significant sources of illumination. Daylight simulation is of particular interest to architects, since the design of the building facade and to a lesser degree the interior depends on daylight considerations.

Initially, *Radiance* was designed to model electric light in interior spaces. With the addition of algorithms for modeling diffuse interreflection [25], the software became more accurate and capable of simulating daylight (both sun and sky contributions) for building interiors and exteriors. The role of daylight simulation in *Radiance* was given new importance when the software was chosen by the International Energy Agency (IEA) for its daylight modeling task* [4].

### 2.3. Support a Variety of Reflectance Models

Luminance is a directional quantity, and its value is strongly determined by a material's reflectance/transmittance distribution function. If luminance is calculated using a Lambertian (i.e. diffuse) assumption, specular highlights and reflections are ignored and the result can easily be wrong by a hundred times or more. We cannot afford to lose directional information if we hope to use our simulation to evaluate visual performance, visual comfort and aesthetics.

A global illumination program is only as general as its local illumination model. The standard model of ambient plus diffuse plus Phong specular is not good enough for realistic image synthesis. *Radiance* includes the ability to model arbitrary reflectance and transmittance functions, and we have also taken empirical measurements of materials and modeled them successfully in our system [29].

### 2.4. Support Complicated Geometry

A lighting simulation of an empty room is not very interesting, nor is it very informative. The contents of a room must be included if light transfer is to be calculated correctly. Also, it is difficult for humans to evaluate aesthetics based on visualizations of empty spaces. Furniture, shadows and other details provide the visual cues a person needs to understand the lighting of a space. Modeling exteriors is even more challenging, often requiring hundreds of thousands of surfaces.

Although we leave the definition of "complicated geometry" somewhat loose, including it as a goal means that we shall not limit the geometric modeling capability of our simulation in any fundamental way. To be practical, data structure size should grow linearly (at worst) with geometric complexity, and there should be no built-in limit as to the number of surfaces. To be accurate, we shall support a variety of surface primitives, also ensuring our models are as memory-efficient as possible. To be general, we shall provide N-sided polygons and a mechanism for interpolating surface normals, so any reasonable shape may be represented. Finally, computation time should have a sublinear relationship to the number of surfaces so that the user does not pay an unreasonable price for accurate modeling.

---

*The IEA is a consortium of researchers from developed nations cooperatively seeking alternative energy sources and ways of improving energy efficiency in their countries.

## 2.5. Take Unmodified Input from CAD Systems

If we are to model complicated geometry, we must have a practical means to enter these models into our simulation. The creation of a complicated geometric model is probably the most difficult task facing the user. It is imperative that the user be allowed every means to simplify this task, including advanced CAD systems and input devices. If our simulation limits this process in any way, its value is diminished.

Therefore, to the greatest degree possible, we must accept input geometry from any CAD environment. This is perhaps the most difficult of the goals we have outlined, as the detail and quality of CAD models varies widely. Many CAD systems and users produce only 2D or wireframe models, which are next to useless for simulation. Other CAD systems, capable of producing true 3D geometric models, cannot label the component surfaces and associate the material information necessary for an accurate lighting simulation. These systems require a certain degree of user intervention and post-processing to complete the model. Even the most advanced CAD systems, which produce accurate 3D models with associated surface data, do not break surfaces into meshes suitable for a radiosity calculation. The missing information must either be added by the user, inferred from the model, or the need for it must be eliminated. In our case, we eliminate this need by using something other than a radiosity (i.e. finite element) algorithm.

CAD translators have been written for *AutoCAD, GDS, ArchiCAD, DesignWorkshop, StrataStudio, Wavefront,* and *Architrion,* among others. None of these translators requires special intervention by the user to reorient surface normals, eliminate T-vertices, or mesh surfaces. The only requirement is that surfaces must somehow be associated with a layer or identifier that indicates their material type.

## 3. Approach

We have outlined the goals for our rendering system and linked them back to the three key challenges of accuracy, generality and practicality. Let us now explore some of the techniques we have found helpful in meeting these goals and challenges.

We start with a basic description of the problem we are solving and how we go about solving it in section 3.1, followed by specific solution techniques in sections 3.2 to 3.5. Sections 3.6 to 3.9 present some important optimizations, and section 3.10 describes the overall implementation and use of the system.

### 3.1. Hybrid Deterministic/Stochastic Ray Tracing

Essentially, *Radiance* uses ray-tracing in a recursive evaluation of the following integral equation at each surface point:

$$L_r(\theta_r,\phi_r) = L_e(\theta_r,\phi_r) + \tag{1}$$

$$\int_0^{2\pi}\int_0^{\pi} L_i(\theta_i,\phi_i)\,\rho_{bd}(\theta_i,\phi_i;\theta_r,\phi_r)\,|\cos\theta_i|\,\sin\theta_i\,d\theta_i\,d\phi_i$$

where:

$\theta$      is the polar angle measured from the surface normal

$\phi$      is the azimuthal angle measured about the surface normal

$L_e(\theta_r,\phi_r)$
       is the emitted radiance (watts/steradian/meter$^2$ in SI units)

$L_r(\theta_r,\phi_r)$
       is the reflected radiance

$L_i(\theta_i,\phi_i)$
       is the incident radiance

$\rho_{bd}(\theta_i,\phi_i;\theta_r,\phi_r)$
       is the bidirectional reflectance-transmittance distribution function (steradian$^{-1}$)

This equation is essentially Kajiya's rendering equation [10] with the notion of energy transfer between two points replaced by energy passing through a point in a specific direction (i.e. the definition of radiance). This formula has been documented many times, going back before the standard definition of $\rho_{bd}$ [16]. Its generality and simplicity provide the best foundation for building a lighting simulation.

This formulation of the rendering problem is a natural for ray tracing because it gives outgoing radiance in terms of incoming radiance over the projected sphere, without any explicit mention of the model geometry. The only thing to consider at any one time is the light interaction with a specific surface point, and how best to compute this integral from spawned ray values. Thus, no restrictions are placed on the number or shape of surfaces or surface elements, and discretization (meshing) of the scene is unnecessary and even irrelevant.

Although it is possible to approximate a solution to this equation using uniform stochastic sampling (i.e. Monte Carlo), the convergence under most conditions is so slow that such a solution is impractical. For example, a simple outdoor scene with a ground plane, a brick and the sun would take days to compute using naive Monte Carlo simply because the sun is so small (0.5° of arc) in comparison to the rest of the sky. It would take many thousands of samples per pixel to properly integrate light coming from such a concentrated source.

The key to fast convergence is in deciding *what* to sample by removing those parts of the integral we can compute deterministically and gauging the importance of the rest so as to maximize the payback from our ray calculations. In the case of the outdoor scene just described, we would want to consider the sun as an important contribution to be sampled separately, thus removing the biggest source of variance from our integral. Instead of relying on random samples over the hemisphere, we send a single sample ray towards the sun, and if it arrives unobstructed, we use a deterministic calculation of the total solar contribution based on the known size and luminosity of the sun as a whole. We are making the assumption that the sun is not partially occluded, but such an assumption would only be in error within the penumbra of a solar shadow region, and we know these regions to represent a very small portion of our scene.

Light sources cause peaks in the incident radiance distribution, $L_i(\theta_i,\phi_i)$. Directional reflection and transmission cause peaks in the scattering function, $\rho_{bd}$. This will occur for reflective materials near the mirror angle, and in the refracted direction of dielectric surfaces (e.g. glass). Removing such peak reflection and transmission angles by sending separate samples reduces the variance of our integral at a comparatively modest cost. This approach was introduced at the same time as ray-tracing by Whitted [31]. Further improvements were made by adding stochastic sampling to the deterministic source and specular calculations by Cook in the first real linking of stochastic and deterministic techniques [5]. *Radiance* employs a tightly coupled source and specular calculation, described in [29].

### 3.2. Cached Indirect Irradiances for Diffuse Interreflection

No matter how successful we are at removing the specular reflections and direct illumination from the integral (1), the cost of determining the remaining diffuse indirect contributions is too great to recalculate at every pixel because this requires tracing hundreds of rays to reduce the variance to tolerable levels. Therefore, most ray-tracing calculations ignore diffuse interreflection between surfaces, using a constant "ambient" term to replace the missing energy.

Part of the reason a constant ambient value has been accepted for so long (other than the cost of replacing it) is that diffuse interreflection changes only gradually over surfaces. Thus, the contrast-sensitive eye usually does not object to the loss of subtle shading that accompanies an ambient approximation. However, the inaccuracies that result *are* a problem if one wants to know light levels or see the effects of daylight or indirect lighting systems.

Since indirect lighting changes gradually over surfaces, it should be possible to spread out this influence over many pixels to obtain a result that is smooth and accurate at a modest sampling cost. This is exactly what we have done in *Radiance*. The original method for computing and using cached irradiance values [25] has been enhanced using gradient information [28].

The basic idea is to perform a full evaluation of Equation (1) for indirect diffuse contributions only as needed, caching and interpolating these values over each surface. Direct and specular components are still computed on a per-pixel basis, but hemispherical sampling occurs less frequently. This gives us a good estimate of the indirect diffuse contribution when we need it by sending more samples than we would be able to afford for a pixel-independent calculation. The approach is effectively similar to finite element methods that subdivide surfaces into patches, calculate accurate illumination at one point on each patch and interpolate the results. However, an explicit mesh is not used in our method, and we are free to adjust the density of our calculation points in response to the illumination environment. Furthermore, since we compute these view-independent values only as needed, separate form factor and solution stages do not have to complete over the entire scene prior to rendering. This can amount to tremendous savings in large architectural models where only a portion is viewed at any one time.

Figure 1 looks down on a diffuse sphere in a room with indirect lighting only. A blue dot has been placed at the position of each indirect irradiance calculation. Notice that the values are irregularly spaced and denser underneath the sphere, on the sphere and near the walls at the edges of the image. Thus, the spacing of points adapts to changing illumination to maintain constant accuracy with the fewest samples.

To compute the indirect irradiance at a point in our scene, we send a few hundred rays that are uniformly distributed over the projected hemisphere. If any of our rays hits a light source, we disregard it since the direct contribution is computed separately. This sampling process is applied recursively for multiple reflections, and it does not grow exponentially because each level has its own cache of indirect values.

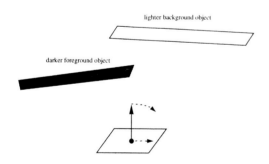

Figure 2: Irradiance gradients due to bright and dark objects in the environment.

Our hemisphere samples not only tell us the total indirect illumination, they also give us more detailed information about the locations and brightnesses of surfaces visible from the evaluation point. This information may be used to predict how irradiance will change as a function of point location and surface orientation, effectively telling us the first derivative (gradient) of the irradiance function. For example, we may have a bright reflecting surface behind and to the right of a darker surface as shown in Figure 2. Moving our evaluation point to the right would yield an increase in the computed irradiance (i.e. the translational gradient is positive in this direction), and our samples can tell us this. A clockwise rotation of the surface element

would also cause an increase in the irradiance value (i.e. the rotational gradient is positive in this direction), and our hemisphere samples contain this information as well. Formalizing these observations, we have developed a numerical approximation to the irradiance gradient based on hemisphere samples. Unfortunately, its derivation does not fit easily into a general paper, so we refer the reader to the original research [28].

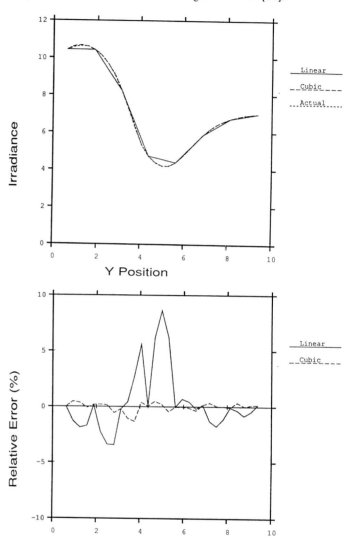

**Figure 3a,b**. *Plots showing the superiority of gradient interpolation for indirect irradiance values. The reference curve is an exact calculation of the irradiance along the red line in Figure 1. The linear interpolation is equivalent to Gouraud shading between evenly spaced points, as in radiosity rendering. The Hermite cubic interpolation uses the gradient values computed by Radiance, and is not only smoother but demonstrably more accurate than a linear interpolation.*

Knowing the gradient in addition to the value of a function, we can use a higher order interpolation method to get a better irradiance estimate between the calculated points. In effect, we will obtain a smoother and more accurate result without having to do any additional sampling, and with very little overhead. (Evaluating the gradient formulas costs almost nothing compared to computing the hemisphere samples.)

Figure 3a shows the irradiance function across the floor of Figure 1, along the red line. The exact curve is shown overlaid with a linearly interpolated value between regularly spaced cal-

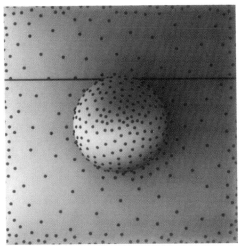

Figure 1. Blue dots show calculation points for diffuse interreflection. (See Figure 3 regarding red line.)

Figure 5. A theater house lighting simulation. The striated shadows on the floor are cast by the catwalks above.

Figure 9a. A drafting office with a mirror light shelf slicing the window and redirecting light upwards.

Figure 9b. A Monte Carlo simulation rendered in the same time as 9a, showing the resulting noise.

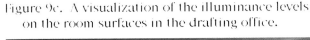

Figure 9c. A visualization of the illuminance levels on the room surfaces in the drafting office.

Figure 11. A cabin in a forest using hierarchical octrees to model over a million pine needles.

culation points, and a Hermite cubic interpolation using computed gradients. The cubic interpolation is difficult to separate from the exact curve. Figure 3b shows the relative error for these two interpolation methods, clearly demonstrating the advantage of using gradient information.

Caching indirect irradiances has four important advantages over radiosity methods. First, no meshing is required, since a separate octree data structure is used to hold the calculated values. This lifts restrictions on geometric shapes and complexity, and greatly simplifies user input and scene analysis. Second, we only have to compute those irradiances affecting the portion of the scene being viewed. This speeds rendering time under any circumstance, since our *view-independent* values may be reused in subsequent images (unlike values computed with importance-driven radiosity [20]). Third, the density of irradiance calculations is reduced at each level of interreflection, maintaining constant accuracy while reducing the time required to compute additional bounces. Fourth, the technique adapts to illumination by spacing values more closely in regions where there may be large gradients, without actually using the gradient as a criterion. This eliminates errors that result from using initial samples to decide sampling density [12], and improves accuracy overall. The gradient *is* used to improve value interpolation, yielding a smoother and more accurate result without the Machbands that can degrade conventional radiosity images.

### 3.3. Adaptive Sampling of Light Sources

Although sending one sample ray to each light source is quite reasonable for outdoor scenes, such an approach is impractical for indoor scenes that may have over a hundred light sources. Most rays in a typical calculation are in fact shadow rays. It is therefore worth our while to rule out light sources that are unimportant and avoid testing them for visibility.

The method we use in *Radiance* for reducing the number of shadow rays is described in [26]. A prioritized list of potential source contributions is created at each evaluation of Equation (1). The largest potential contributors (contribution being a function of source output, proximity and $\rho_{bd}$) are tested for shadows first, and we stop testing when the remainder of the source list is below some fraction of the unoccluded contributions. The remaining source contributions are then added based on statistical estimates of how likely each of them is to be visible.

Figure 4 shows a simple example of how this works. The left column represents our sorted list of potential light source contributions for a specific sample point. We proceed down our list, checking the visibility of each source by tracing shadow rays, and summing together the unobstructed contributions. After each test, we check to see if the remainder of our potential contributions has fallen below some specified fraction of our accumulated total. If we set our accuracy goal to 10%, we can stop testing after four light sources because the remainder of the list is less than 10% of our known direct value. We could either add all of the remainder in or throw it away and our value would still be within 10% of the correct answer. But we can do better than that; we can make an educated guess at the visibility of the remaining sources using statistics. Taking the history of obstructed versus unobstructed shadow rays from previous tests of each light source, we multiply this probability of hitting an untested source by the ratio of successful shadow tests at this point over all successful shadow tests (2/(.9+.55+.65+.95) == 0.65 in this example), and arrive at a reasonable estimate of the remainder. (If any computed multiplier is greater than 1, 1 is used instead.) Our total estimate of the direct contribution at this point is then the sum of the tested light sources and our statistical estimate of the remainder, or 1616 in this example.

We have found this method to be very successful in reducing the number of shadow test rays required, and it is possi-

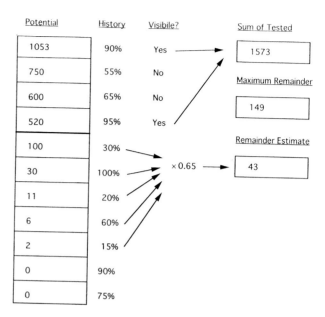

Figure 4: Adaptive shadow testing algorithm, explained in Section 3.4.

ble to place absolute bounds on the error of the approximation. Most importantly, this type of adaptive shadow testing emphasizes contrast as the primary decision criterion. Contrast is defined as the difference between the luminance at a point and the background luminance divided by the background luminance. If a shadow boundary is below the visible contrast threshold, then an error in its calculation is undetectable by the viewer. Thus, this method produces no *visible* artifacts in its tradeoff of speed for accuracy. Accuracy is still lost in a controlled way, but the resulting image is subjectively flawless, due to the eye's relative insensitivity to absolute light levels.

Figure 5 shows a theater lighting simulation generated by *Radiance* in 1989. This image contains slightly over a hundred light sources, and originally took about 4 days to render on a Sun-4/260. (The equivalent of about 5 Vax-11/780's.) Using our adaptive shadow testing algorithm reduced the rendering time to 2 days for the same image†. The time savings for scenes with more light sources can be better than 70%, especially if the light sources have narrow output distributions, such as the spotlights popular in overlighted retail applications.

A different problem associated with ray-per-source shadow testing is *inadequate sampling* of large or nearby sources, which threatens simulation accuracy. For example, a single ray cannot adequately sample a fluorescent desk lamp for a point directly beneath it. The simplest approach for sources that are large relative to their distance is to send multiple sample rays. Unfortunately, breaking a source into pieces and sending many rays to it is inefficient for distant points in the room. Again, an adaptive sampling technique is the most practical solution.

In our adaptive technique, we send multiple rays to a light source if its extent is large relative to its distance. We recursively divide such sources into smaller pieces until each piece satisfies some size/distance criterion. Figure 6a shows a long, skinny light source that has been broken into halves repeatedly until each source is small enough to keep penumbra and solid

---

†The theater model was later rendered in [2] using automatic meshing and progressive radiosity. Meshing the scene caused it to take up about 100 Mbytes of memory, and rendering took over 18 hours on an SGI R3000 workstation for the direct component alone, compared to 5 hours in 11 Mbytes using *Radiance* on the same computer.

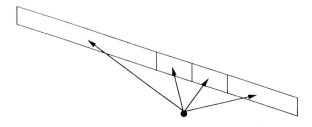

Figure 6a: Linear light source is adaptively split to minimize falloff and visibility errors.

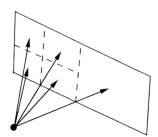

Figure 6b: Area light source is subdivided in two dimensions rather than one.

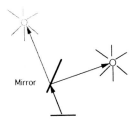

Figure 7a: Virtual source caused by mirror reflection.

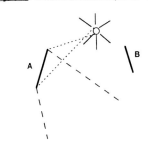

Figure 7b: Source reflection in mirror **A** cannot intersect mirror **B**, so no virtual-virtual source is created.

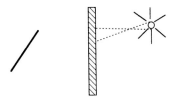

Figure 7c: Source rays cannot reach mirror surface, so no virtual source is created.

angle errors in check. Figure 6b shows a similar subdivision of a large rectangular source. A point far away from either source will not result in subdivision, sending only a single ray to some (randomly) chosen location on the source to determine visibility.

### 3.4. Automatic Preprocessing of "Virtual" Light Sources

Thus far we have accounted for direct contributions from known light sources, specular reflections and transmission, and diffuse interreflections. However, there are still transfers from specular surfaces that will not be handled efficiently by our calculation. A mirror surface may reflect sunlight onto a diffuse or semispecular surface, for example. Although the diffuse interreflection calculation could in principle include such an effect, we are returning to the original problem of insufficient sampling of an intense light source. A small source reflected specularly is still too small to find in a practical number of naive Monte Carlo samples. We have to know where to look.

We therefore introduce "virtual" light sources that do not exist in reality, but are used during the calculation to direct shadow rays in the appropriate directions to find reflected or otherwise transferred light sources. This works for any planar surface, and has been implemented for mirrors as well as prismatic glazings (used in daylighting systems [4]). For example, a planar mirror might result in a virtual sun in the mirror direction from the real sun. When a shadow ray is sent towards the virtual sun, it will be reflected off the mirror to intersect the real sun. An example is shown in Figure 7a. This approach is essentially the same as the "virtual worlds" idea put forth by Rushmeier [18] and exploited by Wallace [24], but it is only carried out for light sources and not for all contributing surfaces. Thus, multiple transfers between specular surfaces can be made practical with this method using intelligent optimization techniques.

The first optimization we apply is to limit the scope of a virtual light source to its affected volume. Given a specific source and a specific specular surface, the influence is usually limited to a certain projected volume. Points that fall outside this volume are not affected and thus it is not necessary to consider the source everywhere. Furthermore, multiple reflections of the source are possible only within this volume. We can thus avoid creating virtual-virtual sources in cases where the volume of one virtual source fails to intersect the second reflecting sur-

face, as shown in Figure 7b. The same holds for thrice redirected sources and so on, and the likelihood that virtual source volumes intersect becomes less likely each time, provided that the reflecting surfaces do not occupy a majority of the space.

To minimize the creation of useless virtual light sources, we check very carefully to confirm that the light in fact has some free path between the source and the reflecting surface before creating the virtual source. For example, we might have an intervening surface that prevents all rays from reaching a reflecting surface from a specific light source, such as the situation shown in Figure 7c. We can test for this condition by sending a number of presampling rays between the light source and the reflecting surface, assuming if none of the rays arrives that the reflecting path must be completely obstructed. Conversely, if none of the rays is obstructed, we can save time during shadow testing later by assuming that any ray arriving at the reflecting surface in fact has a free path to the source, and further ray intersection tests are unnecessary. We have found presampling to be very effective in avoiding wasteful testing of completely blocked or unhindered virtual light source paths.

Figure 8 shows a cross-section of an office space with a light shelf having a mirrored top surface. Exterior to this office is a building with a mirrored glass facade. Figure 9a shows the interior of the office with sunlight reflected by the shelf onto the ceiling. Light has also been reflected by the exterior, glazed building. Light shelf systems utilize daylight very effectively and are finding increasing popularity among designers.

To make our calculation more efficient overall, we have made additional use of "secondary" light sources, described in the next section.

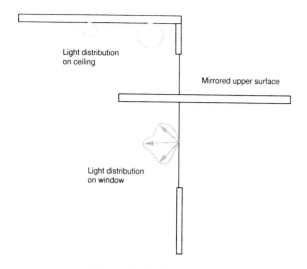

Figure 8: Crossection of office space with mirrored light shelf.

### 3.5. User-directed Preprocessing of "Secondary" Sources

What happens when daylight enters a space through a skylight or window? If we do not treat such "secondary" emitters specially in our calculation, we will have to rely on the ability of the naive Monte Carlo sampling to find and properly integrate these contributions, which is slow. Especially when a window or skylight is partially obscured by venetian blinds or has a geometrically complex configuration, computing its contribution requires significant effort. Since we know a priori that such openings have an important influence on indoor illumination, we can greatly improve the efficiency of our simulation by removing them from the indirect calculation and treating them instead as part of the direct (i.e. source) component.

*Radiance* provides a practical means for the user to move such secondary sources into the direct calculation. For example, the user may specify that a certain window is to be treated as a light source, and a separate calculation will collect samples of the transmitted radiation over all points on the window over all directions, a 4-dimensional function. This distribution is then automatically applied to the window, which is treated as a secondary light source in the final calculation. This method was used in Figure 9a not only for the windows, but also for light reflected by the ceiling. Bright solar patches on interior surfaces can make important contributions to interior illumination. Since this was the desired result of our mirrored light shelf design, we knew in advance that treating the ceiling as a secondary light source might improve the efficiency of our calculation. Using secondary light sources in this scene reduced simulation time to approximately one fifth of what it would have been to reach the same accuracy using the default sampling techniques.

Figure 9b shows a Monte Carlo path tracing calculation of the same scene as 9a, and took roughly the same amount of time to compute. The usual optimizations of sending rays to light sources (the sun in this case) and in specular directions were used. Nevertheless, the image is very noisy due to the difficulty of computing interreflection independently at each pixel. Also, locating the sun reflected in the mirrored light shelf is hopeless with naive sampling; thus the ceiling is extremely noisy and the room is not as well lit as it should be.

An important aspect of secondary light sources in *Radiance* is that they have a dual nature. When treated in the direct component calculation, they are merely surfaces with precalculated output distributions. Thus, they can be treated efficiently as light sources and the actual variation that may take place over their extent (e.g. the bright and dark slats of venetian blinds) will

not translate into excessive variance in the calculated illumination. However, when viewed directly, they revert to their original form, showing all the appropriate detail. In our office scene example, we can still see through the window despite its treatment as a secondary light source. This is because we treat a ray coming from the eye differently, allowing it to interact with the actual window rather than seeing only a surface with a smoothed output distribution. In fact, only shadow rays see the simplified representation. Specular rays and other sampling will be carried out as if the window was not a light source at all. As is true with the computation of indirect irradiance described in section 3.2, extreme care must be exercised to avoid double-counting of light sources and other inconsistencies in the calculation.

### 3.6. Hierarchical Octrees for Spatial Subdivision

One of the goals of our simulation is to model very complicated geometries. Ray-tracing is well-suited to calculations in complicated environments, since spatial subdivision structures reduce the number of ray-surface intersection tests to a tiny fraction of the entire scene. In *Radiance*, we use an octree spatial subdivision scheme similar to that proposed by Glassner [7]. Our octree starts with a cube encompassing the entire scene, and recursively subdivides the cube into eight equal subcubes until each voxel (leaf node) intersects or contains less than a certain number of surfaces, or is smaller than a certain size.

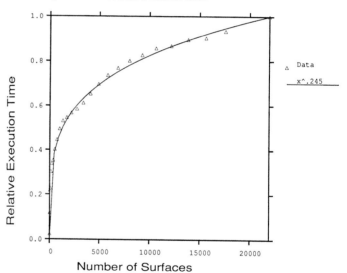

**Figure 10.** *Plot showing sublinear relationship of intersection time to number of surfaces in a scene. The best fit for $\gamma$ in this test was 0.245, meaning the ray intersection time grew more slowly than the fourth root of $N$. The spheres were kept small enough so that a random ray sent from the field's interior had about a 50% chance of hitting something. (I.e. the sphere radii were proportional to $N^{1/3}$.) This guarantees that we are really seeing the cost of complicated geometry, since each ray goes by many surfaces.*

Although it is difficult to prove in general, our empirical tests show that the average cost of ray intersection using this technique grows as a fractional power of the total number of surfaces, i.e. $O(N^{\gamma})$ where $\gamma < \frac{1}{2}$. The time to create the octree grows linearly with the number of surfaces, but it is usually only a tiny fraction of the time spent rendering. Figure 10 shows the relationship between ray intersection time and number of surfaces for a uniformly distributed random field of spheres.

The basic surface primitives supported in *Radiance* are polygons, spheres and cones. Generator programs provide conversion from arbitrary shape definitions (e.g. surfaces of revolution, prisms, height fields, parametric patches) to these basic types. Additional scene complexity is modeled using hierarchical *instancing*, similar to the method proposed by Snyder [21]. In our application of instancing, objects to be instanced are stored in a separate octree, then this octree is instanced along with other surfaces to create a second, enclosing octree. This process is repeated as many times and in as many layers as desired to produce the combined scene. It is possible to model scenes with a virtually unlimited number of surfaces using this method.

Figure 11 shows a cabin in a forest. We began with a simple spray of 150 needles, which were put into an octree and instanced many times and combined with twigs to form a branch, which was in turn instanced and combined with larger branches and a trunk to form a pine tree. This pine tree was then put in another octree and instanced in different sizes and orientations to make a small stand of trees, which was combined with a terrain and cabin model to make this scene. Thus, four hierarchical octrees were used together to create this scene, which contains over a million surfaces in all. Despite its complexity, the scene still renders in a couple of hours, and the total data structure takes less than 10 Mbytes of RAM.

### 3.7. Patterns and Textures

Another practical way to add detail to a scene is through the appropriate infusion of surface detail. In *Radiance,* we call a variation in surface color and/or brightness a *pattern,* and a perturbation of the surface normal a *texture.* This is more in keeping with the English definitions of these words, but sometimes at odds with the computer graphics community, which seems to prefer the term "texture" for a color variation and "bump-map" for a perturbation of the surface normal. In any case, we have extended the notion somewhat by allowing patterns and textures to be functions not only of surface position but also of surface normal and ray direction so that a pattern, for example, may also be used to represent a light source output distribution.

Our treatment of patterns and textures was inspired by Perlin's flexible shading language [17], to which we have added the mapping of lookup functions for multi-dimensional data. Using this technique, it is possible to interpret tabulated or image data in any manner desired through the same functional language used for procedural patterns and textures.

Figure 12 shows a scene with many patterns and textures. The textures on the vases and oranges and lemons are procedural, as is the pattern on the bowl. The pattern on the table is scanned, and the picture on the wall is obviously an earlier rendering. Other patterns which are less obvious in this scene are the ones applied to the three light sources, which define their output distributions. The geometry was created with the generator programs included with *Radiance,* which take functional specifications in the same language as the procedural patterns and textures. The star patterns are generated using a *Radiance* filter option that uses the pixel magnitude in deciding how much to spread the image, showing one advantage of using a floating-point picture format [27]. (The main advantage of this format is the ability to adjust exposure after rendering, taking full advantage of tone mapping operators and display calibration [23,30].)

### 3.8. Parallel Processing

One of the most practical ways to reduce calculation time is with parallel processing. Ray-tracing is a natural for parallel processing, since the calculation of each pixel is relatively independent. However, the caching of indirect irradiance values in *Radiance* means that we benefit from sharing information between pixels that may or may not be neighbors in one or more images. Sharing this information is critical to the efficiency of a parallel computation, and we want to do this in a system-independent way.

We have implemented a coarse-grained, multiple instruction, shared data (MISD) algorithm for *Radiance* rendering†. This technique may be applied to a single image, where multiple processes on one or more machines work on small sections of the image simultaneously, or to a sequence of images, where each process works on a single frame in a long animation. In the latter case, we need only worry about the sharing of indirect irradiance values on multiple active invocations, since dividing the image is not an issue. The method we use is described below.

Indirect irradiance values are written to a shared file whose contents are checked by each process prior to update. If the file has grown, the new values (produced by other processes) are read in before the irradiances computed by this process are written out. File consistency is maintained through the NFS lock manager, thus values may be shared transparently across the network. Irradiance values are written out in blocks big enough to avoid contention problems, but not so big that there is a lot of unnecessary computation caused by insufficient value sharing. We found this method to be much simpler, and about as efficient, as a remote procedure call (RPC) approach.

Since much of the scene information is static throughout the rendering process, it is wasteful to have multiple copies on a multi-processing platform that is capable of sharing memory. As with value sharing, we wished to implement memory sharing in a system-independent fashion. We decided to use the memory sharing properties of the UNIX *fork(2)* call. All systems capable of sharing memory do so during fork on a copy-on-write basis. Thus, a child process need not be concerned that it is sharing its parent's memory, since it will automatically get its own memory the moment it stores something. We can use this feature to our advantage by reading in our entire scene and initializing all the associated data structures before forking a process to run in parallel. So long as we do not alter any of this information during rendering, we will share the associated memory. Duplicate memory may still be required for data that is generated during rendering, but in most cases this represents a minor fraction of our memory requirements.

### 3.9. Animation

*Radiance* is often used to create walk-through animations of static environments. Though this is not typically the domain of ray-tracing renderers, we employ some techniques to make the process more efficient. The most important technique is the use of recorded depth information at each pixel to interpolate fully ray-traced frames with a z-buffer algorithm. Our method is similar to the one explained by Chen et al [3], where pixel depths are used to recover an approximate 3-dimensional model of the visible portions of the scene, and a z-buffer is used to make visibility decisions for each intermediate view. This makes it possible to generate 30 very good-looking frames for each second of animation while only having to render about 5 of them. Another technique we use is unique to *Radiance,* which is the sharing of indirect irradiance values. Since these values are view-independent, there is no sense in recomputing them each time, and sharing them during the animation process distributes the cost over so many frames that the incremental cost of simulating diffuse interreflection is negligible.

Finally, it is possible to get interactive frame rates from advanced rendering hardware using illumination maps instead of ray-tracing the frames directly. (An illumination map is a 2-dimensional array of color values that defines the surface shading.) Such maps may be kept separate from the surfaces' own patterns and textures, then combined during rendering. Specular

---

†Data sharing is of course limited in the case of distributed processors, where each node must have its own local copy of scene data structures.

Figure 12. A still life image showing examples of procedural and scanned textures and patterns.

Figure 13. A comparison of three lighting schemes for a hotel lobby space.

Figure 14. An indirect lighting system was designed to reduce glare on monitors in the London Underground control center.

Figure 15. Stage lighting simulation.

| RADIANCE File Types | | | |
|---|---|---|---|
| Data Type | Format | Created by | Used for |
| Scene Description | ASCII text | text editor, CAD translator | geometry, materials, patterns, textures |
| Function File | ASCII text | text editor | surface tessellation, patterns, textures, scattering functions, coordinate mappings, data manipulation |
| Data File | ASCII integers and floats | luminaire data translator, text editor | N-dimensional patterns, textures, scattering functions |
| Polygonal Font | ASCII integers | Hershey set, font design system, font translator, text editor | text patterns, label generator |
| Octree | Binary | scene compiler (**oconv**) | fast ray intersection, incremental scene compilation, object instancing |
| Picture | run-length encoded 4-byte/pixel floating-point | renderer, filter, image translator | interactive display, hard copy, lighting analysis, material pattern, rendering recovery |
| Ambient File | Binary | renderer, point value program | sharing view-independent indirect irradiance values |

**Table 1.** *All binary types in Radiance are portable between systems, and have a standard information header specifying the format and the originating command(s).*

surfaces will not appear correct since they depend on the viewer's perspective, but this may be a necessary sacrifice when user control of the walk-through is desired. Interactive rendering has long been touted as a principal advantage of radiosity, when in fact complete view-independence is primarily a side-effect of assuming diffuse reflection. *Radiance* calculates the same values using a ray-tracing technique, and storage and rendering may even be more efficient since large polygons need not be subdivided into hundreds of little ones -- an illumination map works just as well or better.

### 3.10. Implementation Issues

*Radiance* is a collection of C programs designed to work in concert, communicating via the standard data types listed in Table 1. The system may be compiled directly on most UNIX platforms, including SGI, Sun, HP, DEC, Apple (A/UX), and IBM (RS/6000). Portability is maintained over 60,000+ lines of code using the Kernighan and Ritchie standard [11] and conservative programming practices that do not rely on system-specific behaviors or libraries. (In addition to UNIX support, there is a fairly complete Amiga port by Per Bojsen, and a limited MS-DOS port by Karl Grau.)

A typical rendering session might begin with the user creating or modifying a geometric model of the space using a CAD program. (The user spends about 90% of the time on geometric modeling.) The CAD model is then translated into a *Radiance* scene description file, using either a stand-alone program or a function within the CAD system itself. The user might then create or modify the materials, patterns and textures associated with this model, and add some objects from a library of predefined light sources and furnishings. The completed model would then be compiled by **oconv** into an octree file, which would be passed to the interactive renderer, **rview,** to verify the desired view and calculation parameters. Finally, a batch rendering would be started with **rpict,** and after a few minutes or a few hours, the raw picture would be filtered (i.e. anti-aliased via image reduction) by **pfilt** using a suitable exposure level and target resolution. This finished picture may be displayed with **ximage,** translated to another format, printed, or further analyzed using one of the many *Radiance* image utilities. This illustrates the basic sequence of:

model $\rightarrow$ convert $\rightarrow$ render $\rightarrow$ filter $\rightarrow$ display

all of which may be put in a single pipelined command if desired.

As *Radiance* has evolved over the years, it has become increasingly sophisticated, with nearly 100 programs that do everything from CAD translation to surface tessellation to lighting calculations and rendering to image filtering, composition and conversion. With this sophistication comes great versatility, but learning the ins and outs of the programs, even the few needed for simple rendering, is impractical for most designers.

To overcome system complexity and improve the reliability of rendering results, we have written an executive control program, called **rad.** This program takes as its input a single file that identifies the material and scene description files needed as well as qualitative settings related to this environment and the simulation desired. The control program then calls the other programs with the proper parameters in the proper sequence.

The intricacies of the *Radiance* rendering pipeline are thus replaced by a few intuitive variable settings. For example, there is a variable called "DETAIL", which might be set to "low" for an empty room, "medium" for a room with a few pieces of furniture and "high" for a complicated room with many furnishings and textures. This variable will be used with a few others like it to determine how many rays to send out in the Monte Carlo sampling of indirect lighting, how closely to space these values, how densely to sample the image plane, and so on. One very important variable that affects nearly all rendering parameters is called "QUALITY". Low quality renderings come out quickly but may not look as good as medium quality renderings, and high quality renderings take a while but when they finish, the images can go straight into a magazine article.

This notion of replacing many algorithm-linked rendering parameters with a few qualitative variables has greatly improved the usability of *Radiance* and the reliability of its output. The control program also keeps track of octree creation, secondary source generation, aborted job recovery, image filtering and anti-aliasing, and running the interactive renderer. The encoding of expertise in this program has been so successful, in fact, that we rely on it ourselves almost 100% for setting parameters and controlling the rendering process.

Although the addition of a control program is a big improvement, there are still many aspects of *Radiance* that are not easily accessible to the average user. We have therefore added a number of utility scripts for performing specific tasks from the more general functions that constitute the system. One example of this is the **falsecolor** program, which calls other image filter programs and utilities to generate an image showing luminance contours or other data associated with a scene or rendering. Figure 9c shows our previous rendering (Figure 9a) superimposed with illuminance contours. These contours tell the lighting designer if there is enough light in the right places or too much light in the wrong places -- information that is difficult to determine from a normal image†.

Even with a competent rendering control program and utility scripts for accomplishing specific tasks, there are still many designers who would not want to touch this system with an extended keyboard. Modern computer users expect a list of pull-down menus with point-and-click options that reduce the problem to a reasonably small and understandable set of alternatives. We are currently working on a graphical user interface (GUI) to the **rad** control program, which would at least put a friendlier face on the standard system. A more effective long-term solution is to customize the rendering interface for each problem domain, e.g. interior lighting design, daylighting, art, etc. Due to our limited resources and expertise, we have left this customization task to third parties who know more about specific applications, and who stand to benefit from putting their GUI on our simulation engine. So far, there are a half dozen or so developers working on interfaces to *Radiance.*

## 4. Applications and Results
The real proof of a physically-based rendering system is the problems it solves. Here we see how well we have met the challenges and goals we set out. *Radiance* has been used by hundreds of people to solve thousands of problems over the years. In the color pages we have included some of the more recent work of some of the more skilled users. The results have been grouped into two application areas, electric lighting problems and daylighting problems.

### 4.1. Electric Lighting
Electric lighting was the first domain of *Radiance,* and it continues to be a major strength. A model may contain any number of light sources of all shapes and sizes, and the output distributions may be entered as either near-field or far-field data. The dual nature of light sources (mentioned in section 3.5) also permits detailed modeling of fixture geometry, which is often important in making aesthetic decisions.

There are several application areas where electric lighting is emphasized. The most obvious application is lighting design. Figure 13 shows a comparative study between three possible lighting alternatives in a hotel lobby space. Several other designs were examined in this exploration of design visualization. With such a presentation, the final decision could be safely left to the client.

One design application that requires very careful analysis is indirect lighting. Figure 14 shows a simulation of a new control center for the London Underground. The unusual arrangement of upwardly directed linear fluorescents was designed to provide general lighting without affecting the visibility of the central display panel (image left).

Stage lighting is another good application of physically-based rendering. The designs tend to be complex and changing, and the results must be evaluated aesthetically (i.e. visually). Figure 15 shows a simulation of a scene from the play *Julius Caesar*. Note the complex shadows cast by the many struts in the stage set. Computing these shadows with a radiosity algorithm would be extremely difficult.

---

†Actually, *Radiance* pictures do contain physical values through a combination of the 4-byte floating-point pixel representation and careful tracking of exposure changes [27], but the fidelity of any physical image presentation is limited by display technology and viewing conditions. We therefore provide the convenience of extracting numerical values with our interactive display program.

### 4.2. Daylighting
Daylight poses a serious challenge to physically-based rendering. It is brilliant, ever-changing and ever-present. At first, the daylight simulation capabilities in *Radiance* were modest, limited mostly to exteriors and interiors with clear windows or openings. Designers, especially architects, wanted more. They wanted to be able to simulate light through venetian blinds, intricate building facades and skylights. In 1991, the author was hired on sabbatical by EPFL to improve the daylight simulation capabilities of *Radiance,* and developed some of the techniques described earlier in this paper. In particular, the large source adaptive subdivision, virtual source and secondary source calculations proved very important for daylighting problems.

The simplest application of daylight is exterior modeling. Many CAD systems have built-in renderers that will compute the solar position from time of day, year, and location, and generate accurate shadows. In addition to this functionality, we wanted *Radiance* to show the contributions of diffuse skylight and interreflection. Figure 16 shows the exterior of the Mellencamp Pavillion, an Indiana University project that recently acquired funding (along with its name).

A more difficult daylighting problem is atrium design*. Designing an atrium requires thorough understanding of the daylight availability in a particular region to succeed. Figure 17 shows an atrium space modeled entirely within *Radiance,* without the aid of a CAD program [13]. The hierarchical construction of *Radiance* scene files and the many programmable object generators makes text-editor modeling possible, but most users prefer a "mousier" approach.

Daylighted interiors pose one of the nastiest challenges in rendering. Because sunlight is so intense, it is usually diffused or baffled by louvers or other redirecting systems. Some of these systems can be quite elaborate, emphasizing the need for simulation in their design. Figure 18 shows the interior of the pavillion from Figure 16. Figure 19 shows a library room illuminated by a central skylight. Figure 20a shows a simulation of a daylighted museum interior. Daylight is often preferred in museums as it provides the most natural color balance for viewing paintings, but control is also very important. Figure 20b shows a false color image of the illuminance values on room surfaces; it is critical to keep these values below a certain threshold to minimize damage to the artwork.

## 5. Conclusion
We have presented a physically-based rendering system that is accurate enough, general enough, and practical enough for the vast majority of lighting design and architectural applications. The simulation uses a light-backwards ray-tracing method with extensions to handle specular, diffuse and directional-diffuse reflection and transmission in any combination to any level in any environment. Not currently included in the calculation are participating media, diffraction and interference, phosphorescence, and polarization effects. There is nothing fundamental preventing us from modeling these processes, but so far there has been little demand for them from our users.

The principle users of *Radiance* are researchers and educators in public and private institutions, and lighting specialists at large architectural, engineering and manufacturing firms. There are between 100 and 200 active users in the U.S. and Canada, and about half as many overseas. This community is continually growing, and as the Radiance interface and documentation improves, the growth rate is likely to increase.

---

*An atrium is an enclosed courtyard with a glazed roof structure for maximizing daylight while controlling the indoor climate.

Figure 16. Design of the Mellencamp Pavillion, currently under construction at Indiana University.

Figure 17. U.K. Atrium design modeled without the benefit of a CAD system, using only Radiance scene generation utilities.

Figure 18. Interior view of Mellencamp Pavillion, above.

Figure 19. Indiana University library space, illuminated by a central skylight.

Figure 20a. Art gallery illuminated by skylights.

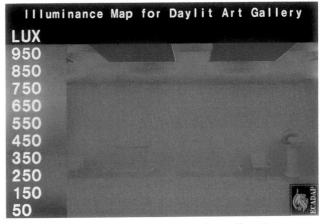

Figure 20b. Corresponding surface illuminances.

For the graphics research community, we hope that *Radiance* will provide a basis for evaluating new physically-based rendering techniques. To this end, we provide both the software source code and a set of precomputed test cases on our ftp server. The test suite includes diffuse and specular surfaces configured in a simple rectangular space with and without obstructions. More complicated models are also provided in object libraries and complete scene descriptions.

## 6. Acknowledgements

Most of the color figures in this paper represent the independent work of *Radiance* users, and are reprinted with permission. Figure 5 was created by Charles Ehrlich from a design by Mark Mack Architects of San Francisco. Figure 11 was created by Cindy Larson. Figures 12 and 13 were created by Martin Moeck of Siemens Lighting, Germany. Figure 14 was created by Steve Walker of Ove Arup and Partners, London. Figure 15 was created by Robert Shakespeare of the Theatre Computer Visualization Center at Indiana University. Figures 16, 18 and 19 were created by Scott Routen and Reuben McFarland of the University Architect's Office at Indiana University. Figures 17 and 20 were created by John Mardaljevic of the ECADAP Group at De Montfort University, Leicester.

The individuals who have contributed to *Radiance* through their support, suggestions, testing and enhancements are too numerous to mention. Nevertheless, I must offer my special thanks to: Peter Apian-Bennewitz, Paul Bourke, Raphael Compagnon, Simon Crone, Charles Ehrlich, Jon Hand, Paul Heckbert, Cindy Larson, Daniel Lucias, John Mardaljevic, Kevin Matthews, Don McLean, Georg Mischler, Holly Rushmeier, Jean-Louis Scartezzini, Jennifer Schuman, Veronika Summeraur, Philip Thompson, Ken Turkowski, and Florian Wenz.

Work on Radiance was sponsored by the Assistant Secretary for Conservation and Renewable Energy, Office of Building Technologies, Buildings Equipment Division of the U.S. Department of Energy under Contract No. DE-AC03-76SF00098. Additional funding was provided by the Swiss federal government as part of the LUMEN Project.

## 7. Software Availability

Radiance is available by anonymous ftp from two official sites:

| | | |
|---|---|---|
| hobbes.lbl.gov | 128.3.12.38 | Berkeley, California |
| nestor.epfl.ch | 128.178.139.3 | Lausanne, Switzerland |

For convenience, *Radiance 2.4* has been included on the CD-ROM version of these proceedings.

From **Mosaic,** try the following URL:

file://hobbes.lbl.gov/www/radiance/radiance.html

## 8. References

[1]   Baum, Daniel, Holly Rushmeier, James Winget, "Improving Radiosity Solutions Through the Use of Analytically Determined Form-Factors," *Computer Graphics*, Vol. 23, No. 3, July 1989, pp. 325-334.

[2]   Baum, Daniel, Stephen Mann, Kevin Smith, James Winget, "Making Radiosity Usable: Automatic Preprocessing and Meshing Techniques for the Generation of Accurate Radiosity Solutions," *Computer Graphics*, Vol. 25, No. 4, July 1991.

[3]   Chen, Shenchang Eric, Lance Williams, "View Interpolation for Image Synthesis," *Computer Graphics*, August 1993, pp. 279-288.

[4]   Compagnon, Raphael, B. Paule, J.-L. Scartezzini, "Design of New Daylighting Systems Using ADELINE Software," *Solar Energy in Architecture and Urban Planning*, proceedings of the 3rd European Conference on Architecture, Florence, Italy, May 1993.

[5]   Cook, Robert, Thomas Porter, Loren Carpenter, "Distributed Ray Tracing," *Computer Graphics*, Vol. 18, No. 3, July 1984, pp. 137-147.

[6]   Dorsey, Julie O'B., Francois Sillion, Donald Greenberg, "Design and Simulation of Opera Lighting and Projection Effects," *Computer Graphics*, Vol. 25, No. 4, July 1991, pp. 41-50.

[7]   Glassner, Andrew S., "Space subdivision for fast ray tracing" *IEEE Computer Graphics and Applications* Vol. 4, No. 10, October 1984, pp. 15-22.

[8]   Goral, Cindy, Kenneth Torrance, Donald Greenberg, Bennet Battaile, "Modeling the Interaction of Light Between Diffuse Surfaces," *Computer Graphics*, Vol. 18, No. 3, July 1984, pp. 213-222.

[9]   Grynberg, Anat, *Validation of Radiance*, LBID 1575, LBL Technical Information Department, Lawrence Berkeley Laboratory, Berkeley, California, July 1989.

[10]  Kajiya, James T., "The Rendering Equation," *Computer Graphics*, Vol. 20, No. 4, August 1986.

[11]  Kernighan, Brian, Dennis Ritchie, *The C Programming Language*, Prentice-Hall, 1978.

[12]  Kirk, David, James Arvo, "Unbiased Sampling Techniques for Image Synthesis," *Computer Graphics*, Vol 25, No. 4, July 1991, pp. 153-156.

[13]  Mardaljevic, John and Kevin Lomas, "Creating the Right Image," *Building Services / The CIBSE Journal*, Vol 15, No. 7, July 1993, pp. 28-30.

[14]  Mardaljevic, John, K.J. Lomas, D.G. Henderson, "Advanced Daylighting Design for Complex Spaces" *Proceedings of CLIMA 2000*, 1-3 November 1993, London UK.

[15]  Meyer, Gary, Holly Rushmeier, Michael Cohen, Donald Greenberg, Kenneth Torrance, "An Experimental Evaluation of Computer Graphics Imagery," *ACM Transactions on Graphics*, Vol. 5, No. 1, pp. 30-50.

[16]  Nicodemus, F.E., J.C. Richmond, J.J. Hsia, *Geometrical Considerations and Nomenclature for Reflectance*, U.S. Department of Commerce, National Bureau of Standards, October 1977.

[17]  Perlin, Ken, "An Image Synthesizer", *Computer Graphics*, Vol. 19, No. 3, July 1985, pp. 287-296.

[18]  Rushmeier, Holly, *Extending the Radiosity Method to Transmitting and Specularly Reflecting Surfaces*, Master's Thesis, Cornell Univ., Ithaca, NY, 1986.

[19]  Rushmeier, Holly, Charles Patterson, Aravindan Veerasamy, "Geometric Simplification for Indirect Illumination Calculations," *Proceedings of Graphics Interface '93*, May 1993, pp. 227-236.

[20]  Smits, Brian, James Arvo, David Salesin, "An Importance-Driven Radiosity Algorithm," *Computer Graphics*, Vol 26, No. 2, July 1992, pp. 273-282.

[21]  Snyder, John M., Alan H. Barr, "Ray Tracing Complex Models Containing Surface Tessellations," *Computer Graphics* Vol. 21, No. 4, pp. 119-128, July 1987.

[22]  Teller, Seth and Pat Hanrahan, "Global Visibility Algorithms for Illumination Computations," *Computer Graphics*, pp. 239-246, August 1993.

[23]  Tumblin, Jack, Holly Rushmeier, "Tone Reproduction for Realistic Images," *IEEE Computer Graphics and Applications*, Vol. 13, No. 6, November 1993, pp. 42-48.

[24]  Wallace, John, Michael Cohen, Donald Greenberg, "A Two-Pass Solution to the Rendering Equation: A Synthesis of Ray Tracing and Radiosity Methods," *Computer Graphics*, Vol. 21, No. 4, July 1987.

[25]  Ward, Gregory, Francis Rubinstein, Robert Clear, "A Ray Tracing Solution for Diffuse Interreflection," *Computer Graphics*, Vol. 22, No. 4, August 1988.

[26]  Ward, Gregory, "Adaptive Shadow Testing for Ray Tracing," *Second EUROGRAPHICS Workshop on Rendering*, Barcelona, Spain, April 1991.

[27]  Ward, Gregory, "Real Pixels," *Graphics Gems II*, Edited by James Arvo, Academic Press 1991, pp. 80-83.

[28]  Ward, Gregory, Paul Heckbert, "Irradiance Gradients," *Third EUROGRAPHICS Workshop on Rendering*, Bristol, United Kingdom, May 1992.

[29]  Ward, Gregory, "Measuring and Modeling Anisotropic Reflection," *Computer Graphics*, Vol. 26, No. 2, July 1992, pp. 265-272.

[30]  Ward, Gregory, "A Contrast-Based Scalefactor for Luminance Display," *Graphics Gems IV*, Edited by Paul Heckbert, Academic Press, 1994.

[31]  Whitted, Turner, "An Improved Illumination Model for Shaded Display," *Communications of the ACM*, Vol. 23, No. 6, June 1980, pp. 343-349.

# Research Frontiers in Virtual Reality

Chairs

Steve Bryson, CSC/NASA Ames Research Center
Steven K. Feiner, Columbia University

Panelists
Frederick P. Brooks, Jr., University of North Carolina at Chapel Hill
Philip Hubbard, Brown University
Randy Pausch, University of Virginia
Andries van Dam, Brown University

In the late 70's and early 80's, SIGGRAPH and computer graphics were still sufficiently young that an often-heard theme was that computer graphics was "just around the corner." Of course, computer graphics is now one of the successes of computer science, touching our lives daily in ways ranging from video games and movies to graphical UIs. Is virtual reality (VR) in the same situation that computer graphics was a decade or two ago? While VR has thus far delivered far less than it has promised, several research conferences have been initiated. The first IEEE VRAIS (Virtual Reality Annual International Symposium) symposium met in September 1993 and the IEEE Symposium on Research Frontiers in Virtual Reality was held the following month during Visualization '93. IEEE VRAIS '95, the follow-on to both these conferences, has already been announced, and the first ACM VRST (Virtual Reality Software and Technology) will take place a month after SIGGRAPH '94. If virtual reality is truly "just around the corner," then what is keeping us from developing and building useful, working virtual environments? This panel is intended to help answer that question.

The panel's participants consist of the organizers, invited speakers, and several selected speakers from the 1993 IEEE Symposium on Research Frontiers in Virtual Reality. Among the issues to be discussed are software, hardware, and human factors challenges raised by the special demands of virtual reality. Software challenges include language models, operating system design, time-critical computation and rendering support, and development system design. Hardware challenges include haptic-feedback devices, high-quality comfortable displays, and fast and accurate 3D trackers. Human-factors challenges include determining how to use 3D input and output effectively, incorporating sound and speech in the user interface, and performing the cognitive research necessary to understand human interaction within virtual environments. The need to develop useful metrics for evaluating virtual environments cuts across all of these issues.

In addition to the specific topics covered by the panelists, the organizers believe that there are a variety of general issues that must be addressed to make VR "real." These include:

- designing distributed architectures: How can we best exploit the potential of large numbers of networked computers to meet the real-time requirements of multiple interacting users and applications?
- structuring real applications: What can we do now to cope with the need for extremely large data sets, massive amounts of computation, and high-throughput networking?
- modeling interactive environments: How can we build tools that assist us in designing and maintaining large, complex, interactive environments?
- creating augmented realities: Augmented realities supplement our interaction with the real world, rather than replacing it. How can we meet their demands for the precise registration required to blend real and virtual worlds seamlessly?

- crafting effective user interfaces: When should an environment attempt to mimic the real world and when should it not? What tasks are most effective in environments that try to act "real," but fail in different ways? How can we represent abstract worlds physically or physical worlds abstractly?
- building multimodal worlds: VR is far more than just graphics! How can we incorporate other input and output modalities besides the visual, such as speech, audio, haptics, and eye tracking?

## Frederick P. Brooks, Jr.

Virtual reality is today a technology that almost works. With off-the-shelf head-mounted displays, the resolution is so poor that the wearer has 20/200 vision; he is legally blind. Field of view is typically less than half that of a normal human being. Trackers keep viewers tethered within a few cubic meters. End-to-end lags in tracking, in image generation, in display, and in communication among components mean that scenes swim about. Registration of real-world images and virtual-world images is still coarse and unreliable. Nevertheless, we are so close that we can at least see into the promised land and imagine ourselves there, and these imagination-stirred hopes excite both professionals and the public.

What's real about virtual reality? We really can today, with commercial equipment:

- change the viewpoint and lighting in real time of fairly complex model worlds,
- manipulate objects in the model world and have them respond in real time,
- build, explore, and comprehend 3D worlds, both real and abstract,
- hear localized sounds from virtual objects,
- feel synthetic forces that accurately represent real-world forces.

Moreover, we can generalize some conclusions about participation in such experiences:

- people really do feel as if present, although no one is fooled very long, except in vehicle simulators.
- experiencing synthetic environments helps people's perception and helps them form accurate 3-D world models.
- interacting with the synthetic environment improves perception. If one of two viewers of the same scene is interacting, and the other is not, the manipulator perceives better.
- synthetic environments can accomplish important training tasks as surrogates for real experience.
- force display has been shown to improve performance on meaningful tasks.

What will it take to make the technology really work? When can we get past the "almost" stage?

One can enumerate the technical tasks, and they are substantial. I think it will take a lot of work by many people (and a fair amount of money), but I believe we will see high-resolution, low-lag systems doing serious applications within three years. Then comes the task of learning how people effectively navigate, wayfind, manipulate, design, and build in synthetic environments. All along the way, it is important that we measure how well we are (or are not) doing and that we report the lessons learned from failures as quickly and accurately as the lessons learned from success. Meanwhile, we are finally seeing the realization of the most powerful mind-machine interface. Isn't it wonderful!

### Philip Hubbard

Real-time performance is essential for virtual reality systems. If a VR system runs too slowly, a user will lose the sense of interaction and immersion that is so important for VR. Despite recent advances in computer technology, current VR systems can give real-time performance for only simple virtual worlds. To handle richer worlds, improved performance must come from somewhere.

A promising solution is to selectively trade detail or accuracy for speed. A VR application gives a user several forms of sensory information, and in some cases the user will tolerate (or not notice) degraded information. If degraded information is faster to compute, this approach improves performance. Variations on this theme are known as "progressive refinement," "graceful degradation" or "anytime computation," and they are all examples of "time-critical computation."

Most of the research to date in time-critical computation for VR focuses on polygon rendering. The prevalent approaches involve approximating the shape of each object with various number of polygons. The rendering algorithm picks the appropriate number of polygons for the current frame to meet performance criteria, e.g., maximizing detail while maintaining a nearly-constant frame rate.

Rendering is an important part of any VR system, but other important tasks can often be at least as expensive computationally. Collision detection, for example, is often left out of a VR system because it is so costly. A time-critical algorithm for this problem involves approximating the surface of each object at various resolutions with sets of spheres. This approach is efficient because collisions between spheres can be found quickly. Time-critical approaches to this and other problems in motion control and animation will become increasingly important as virtual worlds become more complex. These problems are more difficult than rendering because degrading accuracy may lead to cumulative errors whose importance must be understood. Advances in these areas will make essential the problem of coordinating time-critical algorithms for the various tasks of a VR system.

### Randy Pausch

Probably the least understood issue of virtual environments is human factors: how the human's biological system responds to and interacts with the system. This is a complex issue, with many unknown variables. We advise computer scientists to befriend perceptual psychologists, who have the most expertise in understanding these issues. It is probably not practical to attempt to learn enough psychology to address this issue without access to a local psychologist.

The basic argument in favor of virtual reality interfaces is naturalness; by replicating interaction with the real world, we will provide a qualitative improvement in the human-computer interface. We can take advantage of skills humans have evolved and refined. For example, our visual system is tuned to detect relative motion, so being able to walk around objects accesses that ability. By reaching our limbs into the space around us, we can take advantage of our proprioceptive and kinesthetic senses; by the use of grasping we take advantage of our ability to perform three-dimensional manipulations. Most importantly, we make it possible for the human to provide multiple inputs simultaneously, each of which has many degrees of freedom.

In the long run, virtual reality will not succeed unless people are willing to use it. One sociological phenomenon is the aversion of many people to wear the large, heavy equipment currently containing head-mounted displays. Besides being heavy and uncomfortable, the devices (with the exception of the W Industries Visette) were designed for function, not fashion. At the University of Virginia, we have informally observed that approximately 10% of the visitors adamantly decline the opportunity to wear a head-mounted display. By comparison, an earlier, low-cost system we built with Private Eye displays had a very small profile; we mounted the displays on a pair of sunglasses. With that system, we cannot recall ever having a user refuse to wear the display; the difference between sunglasses and a helmet is extremely important for user acceptance.

### Andries van Dam

Immersive virtual reality systems provide a qualitatively different perceptual experience than do conventional desktop systems and impose greater demands on support hardware and software. I will address three software issues for VR applications: interaction models, object-oriented systems, and application development frameworks.

Interaction is the key to a responsive VR environment. In a passive environment, such as an architectural walkthrough or CAD construction, conventional event loops with callbacks may suffice. In general VR environments with multimodal, parallel, high-bandwidth input, however, the situation is more complicated. Decision-making is probabilistic, context-dependent, and hierarchical, in contrast to the deterministic key or mouse button press in a WIMP interface. Another consideration for interaction is that modern UI toolkits are designed to handle user actions (via event-driven callbacks) via user interface (interactor) objects, as opposed to active application domain objects in the environment. For this reason, most current VR systems abandon standard callbacks in favor of (often parallelized) simulation loops, which loop through a list of objects, handling each in turn. This does not solve all problems, however, as a simulation loop will only run as fast as its slowest object, with no provision for preemption. The abstraction of fully concurrent application and interactor objects can be helpful to the programmer, but has to be made efficient at both the operating system and language (or library) level. Finally, there needs to be a tight coupling between the interactor objects and the application objects. In effect, the interactor objects become part of the environment, providing challenges in design and implementation.

Object systems are natural to computer graphics and VR, but traditional object models and systems are not adequate. Objects in VR systems want to share information and communicate in dynamic and changing ways on an object-by-object basis, as the environment and objects change over time. Standard class mechanisms of common object-oriented languages provide only a static, singly polymorphic form of inheritance. This prevents changing the nature of the object without completely recreating it. Furthermore, it is clumsy to provide objects with unique behavior, requiring an entire class definition. What is needed are dynamic, multiply-polymorphic systems that allow objects to collaborate to determine what action to perform.

VR applications force us to look to an ambitious support framework that supports not only geometry primitives, but also time-varying behavior. This support framework should include facilities for time-critical computing and graphics and for direct control over timing and synchronization of multiple, related media. Such a framework should enable the plugging in of modules to implement, for example, physical behavior. The application developer would choose the behavior module appropriate to the application. Designing this framework is a major software challenge.

# Computer Graphics and Economic Transformations

Chair
Walt Bransford, The Premisys Corporation

Panelists
Maury Klein, The University of Rhode Island
Craig Moody, Time Warner Interactive Group
David Reed, Interval Research Corporation
Michael Rothschild, The Bionomics Institute

Computer graphics-based technologies are becoming increasingly intertwined with the patterns of economic change. The technologies of SIGGRAPH are understandable. The economic environment in which they thrive is not. The opportunities of the future are connected to our technological legacy. But forces more biological than mechanical are beginning to shape business and economic methods.

These forces affect the diffusion of computer graphics and other advanced technologies into the commercial landscape. They are radically changing competitive and social environments. Businesses are struggling to find and create markets for a technology with staggering potential. Society is undergoing yet another transformation of communications as well as personal habits and tastes. This panel will try to make sense out of some of the elements that make up this energetic and complex economic arena.

A historian of American technology and business will review the continuum in which invention and innovation continues to flourish. An economic model more suited to the "information age" will be introduced to SIGGRAPH at this panel. Against this background is an entrepreneur's view of turning innovations into economic effect by giving them life in today's market place. Finally, without invention all of this would be meaningless. A researcher's view of the impact of these elements on pre-competitive computer graphics-based products concludes the panel.

A new economic perspective on computer graphics-based technologies is additional way to identify opportunity. These fresh and diverse views will try to establish that perspective.

## Maury Klein

Technology and the market economy are the drivers of growth in modern society. Technology underlies the forces that have transformed the United States from a rural, agricultural society into an urban, industrial world power. In the process it has spawned a complex society of many cultures, without a cohesive center. The new industrialization has transcended ideologies, defied political structures, ignored moral dictums, overturned social orders and unraveled the fabric of tradition. Modern society, which emerged through these dislocations, did so by reorganizing and adapting itself in a new and unexpected matrix: the consumer economy. This economy has become the unifying thread for a culture of diversity by standardizing tastes through consumer products.

SIGGRAPH has created, and continues to invent, computer graphics-based technologies that are introducing cultural advances, opportunities, and dislocations. The transformations resulting from these adaptations must also find a new center within an evolving market economy. Computer graphics and interactive technologies have evolved following a pattern established by mechanized farming, transportation advances and early electricity-based communications. There are lessons to be learned by identifying the connections between modern challenges and those created over a century ago. The adjustments to upheavals in the continuum must be assimilated by society by organizing and formalizing values in new ways.

Continued responsible innovation in computer graphics-based technologies must embody an awareness of its impact and an ability to anticipate the social needs of the future

## Michael Rothschild

Two decades after the microprocessor's invention, the world economy is in the throes of an epochal transformation: from the machine age to the information age. Unfortunately, traditional schools of economic thought offer insufficient insight into the fundamental nature of the emerging information age economy. We are entering uncharted territory.

To meet this challenge, bionomics suggests a new economic paradigm. Where mainstream economics is based on concepts borrowed from classical Newtonian physics, bionomics is derived from the teachings of modern evolutionary biology. Where orthodox thinking describes the economy as a static, predictable engine, bionomics sees the economy as a self-organizing, "chaotic" information ecosystem. Where the traditional view sees organizations as production machines, bionomics sees organizations as intelligent social organisms. Where conventional business strategy focuses on physical capital, bionomics holds that organizational learning is the ultimate source of all profit and growth.

Computer graphics is a technology of feedback. It has redefined the presentation of qualitative and quantitative information. SIGGRAPH discoveries are now being absorbed by a mass market whose social, business and government institutions are undergoing a radical restructuring. This transformation will be more effective and less costly as bionomic principles, based upon feedback and the organized assimilation of information, begin to inform decisions of progress and innovation. The bionomic view also identifies inventive ways to assess the impacts of SIGGRAPH technologies.

## Craig Moody

The future of interactive entertainment, whether location, cartridge, or CD-based, or delivered via interactive television, is looking very promising. Time Warner Interactive is a company committed to making interactive entertainment not only a viable but profitable medium and is taking bold steps toward creating desirable and innovative products.

Business and market models for this industry are rapidly changing and are not yet clearly defined. Interactive technologies emerge from the shifting intersections of many diverse sectors and the creation of products requires the collaboration of creative people from a variety of disciplines. Essential to the success of any company in this new business is understanding the power of the medium and capturing the imagination of the consumer.

These are the challenges that motivate an entrepreneurial group like Time Warner Interactive. Our success as a company depends on providing meaning and value to the products we develop for consumers. Assessing available and new technologies, and the creative application of these technologies, is one of the essential components in development imaginative and appealing products for the interactive consumer market. Time Warner Interactive's products capture the excitement and vision of the future, and are marketed and distributed worldwide today.

### David Reed

SIGGRAPH has staked a position in a stream of innovations that began several hundred years ago. Each advance spawns many others. The refinement of today's products must be balanced by continual innovation of products and services to meet tomorrow's needs. Computer graphics-based technologies are a part of technical contributions driving these innovations.

As automated "information spaces" become more important, computer graphics will play a larger role in visualizing these interactions of information exchange. Computer graphics will continue to take a leading role in the meaningful representation of information, striving to enhance the quality of exchange in order to give depth and meaning to interpersonal encounters.

The emergence of high capacity, low cost, ubiquitous communications, computation and storage will allow very broad application of computer graphics-based technology to communication systems, creating new ways to share information, new approaches to human organization, and new styles of social interaction. Research coupled with entrepreneurial experiments will be needed to establish these opportunities. Computer graphics technology will be coupled to the evolution of technology, economy and culture around new communications patterns, not yet discovered, that are enabled by pervasive synthesis and processing of perceptual space.

### Acknowledgement
Thanks to Clark Dodsworth of Osage Associates for much energy, ideas, and direction in producing this panel.

### References
Cronon, William, *Nature's Metropolis: Chicago and the Great West.* W.W. Norton, 1991.

Jubak, Jim & Lange, Curtis, "How to Make Cybercash," *WORTH.* Vol. 2(7), September, 1993.

Klein, Maury, *Union Pacific vol 1:The Birth of a Railroad.* Doubleday. 1987.

Klein, Maury. *The Life and Legend of Jay Gould.* Johns Hopkins University Press, 1986.

Klein, Maury. *The Flowering of the Third America: the making of an organizational society 1850-1920.* Ivan R. Dee 1993.

Kurtzman, Joel. *The Death of Money.* Simon & Schuster, 1993.

Rothschild, Michael. *Bionomics: Economy as Ecosystem H.* Holt. 1990.

*The Red Herring.* Flipside Communications, Inc, Woodside, CA

*The Wall Street Journal*

*Upside: The Business Magazine for the Technology Elite.* The Upside Publishing Company. Foster City, CA

*Forbes ASAP*: A Quarterly Technology Supplement to Forbes Magazine

# Production for the Long Haul

Chair
John C. Donkin, Lamb & Company

Panelists
Charles Gibson, Rhythm and Hues
Ralph Guggenheim, Pixar
Edward Kummer, Walt Disney Feature Animation
Brad Lewis, Pacific Data Images
Jeff Thingvold, Lamb & Company

Panelists will present and discuss issues related to producing 3D computer animation and digital image synthesis in the context of long format productions. Top producers of feature films, television shows and specials will be the featured speakers.

## Introduction

As digital technology continues its plunge into the film and video production mainstream, more and more demands are being made on production companies to produce large amounts of animation and special effects. It's clear that it's not possible to simply throw more machines and more people at the problem. These demands require that production companies re-think how 3D computer animation is produced.

Perhaps one of the largest challenges faced during long format production is the management and control of resources. In short format animation its often the case that a small production team will work together to meet specific deadlines. If one area of production is falling behind, the small group is able to recover by assigning the task to a member of the team. The communication is simple and the task gets completed. This type of production lends itself well to having each member of the team being a "jack of all trades," in that tasks can be assigned and reassigned to meet the demands of the production.

By contrast, it is more difficult for production of long format animation to prosper using this method. As the team gets larger communication becomes more of an issue. It is also more difficult to equally divide production tasks among production team members. Long format production seems to lend itself better to subdividing the tasks into specific areas which are handled by specialists. Each of the tasks can then be scheduled and assigned to make sure that the production moves along smoothly.

## Production Management

Because longer format animations require many people, large datasets, and huge amounts of computing resources and visual feedback devices, each of these resources must be allocated and controlled to keep the production line running smoothly. If some area of the production line is slowed down, other areas of the production process may be sitting idle wasting valuable time. New project tracking tools and techniques can be developed to help determine which areas of production are running smoothly and which are being slowed down.

## Re-thinking the Design Process

When designing animation for 30-second commercials there is a tendency to produce animation in which each frame is a work of art. The production time spent per frame is huge compared to that in long format animation. To produce the amount of animation necessary for along format piece, animation must be thought of on a per scene basis as opposed to a per frame basis. The design of long format animation must be appropriate for the constraints of the production as a whole

in order to maintain a reasonable workload for the production team.

## Animation Process

The animation process itself can benefit from breakthroughs in technology which can increase the productivity of the animators. The advent of reliable motion capture devices, direct input devices and development of behavioral systems are but a few of the advances that can potentially increase the throughput of animation production.

## Feedback Loop

The feedback that animators require to produce quality animation becomes more of an issue in long format. As scenes are being developed, they must be seen in the context of the surrounding scenes and sequences. This is important to maintain continuity in direction and style. Maintaining a story reel and dailies becomes a large task. Hardware and software developments and the availability of new high-speed data transmission and compression technology may be useful to aid in this process.

## Charles Gibson

The demand for computer graphics and digital techniques in the TV and Film industries will only increase in the future. Many problems, from budget and creative issues to hardware and software issues, will continue to be a challenge for CG producers. The major problem for the near future will be handling a significantly increased production load while maintaining the highest possible quality. The high volume CG studio will need to evolve from the "garage" model into an infrastructure that most closely resembles a feature animation studio. This will ultimately have a profound effect on day to day roles of people in the CG industry as well as CG education.

## Ralph Guggenheim

Pixar is producing the first feature length film made completely with 3D computer graphics. Having only produced short films and television commercials before, we spent a good deal of time planning and designing the process, personnel, and facility needed to carry off a project of this complexity. The complexity of the project is the major issue: some aspects of the work benefit from actual economies of scale while others suffer. For example, most people can keep in mind the 15-20 shots involved in a 30-second commercial without committing a lot of information to paper, but a film with 1,300+ shots requires a different organizational approach altogether!

The process of producing such a large-scale project resembles aspects of conventional animation (scripting, storyboards, storyreels), 3D computer animation (modeling, rendering, film recording), special effects (compositing and approvals) and traditional live action (editorial and post-production). At the same time, when all these disciplines are brought together, they must be revised dramatically to work together as an efficient working unit. Concepts such as work flow and "inventory" must be addressed in detail to ensure that a 2-year production schedule can be met. These are just some of the issues we have confronted and continue to work out as this project moves forward.

### Edward Kummer

Over the last 70 years a definite process has been created to generate high quality animated feature films, taking them from script to the final film. The process defines points that act as natural stages and artistic checks and balances, that ensure the artistic vision gets to the screen with the minimum of rework.

Computer animation has been a part of this process for less than 10 years. As we've grown from doing simple solid objects to fully metamorphosize animating characters, our process too has grown. Unlike other departments that have a singular place in the traditional animation process (like animation or backgrounds), the CGI department lands in many steps along the way, because we may do rough layout, cleanup layout, rough animation, cleanup animation, and painting, or some combination of these.

I'll use the stampeding herd of wildebeests from "The Lion King" to demonstrate how we take a script and a storyboard, design characters, animate them, render them, and merge them with traditional elements. We start with a hand drawn model sheet (this our character design) and from this we build a CGI model of the wildebeest. Then we begin on the rough animation tests. At the same time we began writing the custom software for the herding of the wildebeests, and integration of them into the 2D traditional animation world. Once we had the animation and the model done we did a simple test scene to ensure the marriage of the 2D and CGI animations were working. After the test is OK'd we began animating the scenes and then started taking them through the animation process mentioned above. Our CGI process typically takes a year of pre-production and a year of production.

### Brad Lewis

I would like to discuss the process by which we collaborate with a live-action production company in establishing a strong foundation for producing a long format computer animation project. This will cover the external client relationships and the internal technical and staffing requirements from the perspective of the producer.

Part One - Development of the script and storyboards, bidding, presenting prices, initial creative discussions, re-bidding, developing an internal approach, establishing approval standards, develop relationship with external creatives, develop relationship with internal creatives, managing the internal creative relationships.

Part Two - Live action supervision and internal technical set-up, how to interact on the live action set, what information to gather, internal production pipeline, internal staff set-up (specialists and departments: modeling, motion, lighting, efx, technical direction, rotoscoping and bluescreen, final testing and rendering), initial testing of key sequences.

Part Three - The production process, production flow, working toward approvals, staying on budget and schedule, give and take with client, problem solving, relationship with creatives, CBB's.

Part Four - Final rendering issues, comparing and revising different work completed at different stages of production for continuity, releasing staff appropriately.

### Jeff Thingvold

The ultimate goal of animation software is to reduce the tedium of the animator's job while retaining all the flexibility and creativity the animator needs. However, animators do not work alone, especially on long format projects. Software to support long format projects must address the human organization that accompanies such work.

Throughout the animation process, communication between members of the project is critical to effective, efficient completion of the animation. The challenge is to provide an animation environment that integrates a variety of commercial and proprietary graphics software, while also facilitating the project management and the communication needs of the project members.

The software tools developed for the 1/2 hour special "The Incredible Crash Dummies" have been found to be of immense value to our regular commercial work. Since then, our strategy has been to design all of our software for use in long format projects. It provides a stricter standard by which to develop software and makes better tools for all of our work.

# Approaches to Teaching Introductory Computer Graphics

Chair
Maria M. Larrondo-Petrie, Florida Atlantic University

Panelists
Jack Bresenham, Winthrop University
Cary Laxer, Rose-Hulman Institute of Technology
John Lansdown, Centre for Electronics Arts and Middlesex University, UK
G. Scott Owen, Georgia State University

The panelists will discuss various approaches to teaching an introductory computer graphics course. They represent a wide spectrum of the discipline, offering courses emphasizing systems, engineering, mathematics, science, art design and animation. Sample course syllabi, textbook recommendations, software packages and suggested projects will be available.

This past summer at an Undergraduate Faculty Enhancement Workshop in Computer Graphics sponsored by the NSF and the ACM SIGGRAPH Education Committee, it became apparent that there were widely different viewpoints on the content and methodology for teaching the introductory computer graphics course.

The panelists will discuss various approaches to teaching an introductory computer graphics course. They represent a wide spectrum of the discipline, offering courses emphasizing in systems, engineering, mathematics, science, art design and animation. Included in the discussion will be conventional approaches, beginning with two-dimensional concepts and introducing three-dimensional concepts at the end of the course; an approach that focus on generic graphics pipeline elements and system specification/implementation; a new approach that emphasizes image synthesis based on Physics; and approaches that emphasize art design and animation. Software packages, both commercial and public domain, used to teach computer graphics will be described. The courses described are taught at large public universities as well as small private colleges. The equipment used varies from 8088 personal computers to Sun workstations. Sample course syllabi, textbook recommendations, and suggested projects will be available.

### Jack Bresenham: A "systems" approach
Dr. Bresenham emphasizes a fundamental, systems programmer orientation in teaching introductory computer graphics basics at Winthrop University [Bresenham 92]. His students are expected to understand generic alternative reference models, attribute interactions, transformation concepts, and pixel space post-rastering clipping. His experience as a member of the X3H3.3 graphics standards committee for CGI specification, and more recently as a professor of computer science motivates him to stress understanding of basic principles in an introductory course [Schaller 92].

In convering specific graphics vocabulary, concepts, mathematics, and algorithms, he attempts to emphasize the WHY as much as the HOW. Analysis necessary to assure a consistent, complete architecture for a system specification or implementation is a primary objective [Ajuha, Bresenham 90, Earnshaw 85]. Students should avoid misinterpretations such as incorrect reference point transformations specified in the initial CGI proposed standard (ISO/DP9636) [Bono 88, Bresenham 90]; the final standard issued in 1991 did finally get anisotropic transformations done correctly. Working from basic principles, students are expected to be able to explain apparent anomalies such as why three thick line segments with one end point common will likely be drawn by a PostScript implementation with a quite different visual appearance dependent upon order of drawing sequence.

Students write a small 2-D graphics processing program that interprets geometric, attribute, and control commands then renders pixel by pixel the picture specified. Winthrop University is a 5000 student, state supported, teaching institution. The equipment for past graphics courses has been Leading Edge PC clones with 8088's. For Fall semester 1994, Winthrop should have 80486's in computer science student labs and most faculty offices. With the improved facilities, more compute-intensive graphics applications will become feasible.

### John Lansdown: Teaching and learning computer graphics in art and design
For some years the Centre for Electronic Arts has been involved in teaching artists and designers the use of computers and computer graphics. Most of this work has been at Master's level. However, it is Faculty policy that all undergraduates be computer literate in appropriate application packages and the Centre contributes to teaching these too. As is traditional in skills-based art and design education in the UK, teaching and learning strategies in the Centre rely much more on over-the-shoulder instruction, projects and private study rather than formal lectures. Group working is encouraged (indeed, in most of the Centre's courses, compulsory).

Although we do not formally base our teaching and learning strategies on the van Hiele model of learning (Burger & Shaughnessy 1986), our experience suggests that the ideas underlying that model might have validity in this area. It is, for example, apparent that the levels of learning are sequential and ordered yet continuously connected and that each level has its own terminology and language of discourse. Thus, to ensure student understanding of the concepts of computer use, especially computer graphics programming, it is necessary to provide an environment to enable students incrementally to build up levels of learning. It would be interesting to discuss the forms that this environment might take.

It is clear that current commercial packages (at least of the sort we are able to afford in sufficient numbers for 90 Master's students and 2300 undergraduates) do not always meet the needs of those doing art and design. Our students seem always to want to do things that such packages can't do, especially in means of interacting with images. This is why our longest established Master's courses require students to learn programming. It is a credit to students' motivation and effort that, by this process, they can usually realise their sometimes difficult objectives. We need to examine the means and methods of making such realisation easier.

### Cary Laxer: An "engineering" approach
Rose-Hulman Institute of Technology is a small, predominantly undergraduate, engineering and science college. It attracts some of the brightest students in the country for their college education. Rose-Hulman trains its students to be problem solvers.

The introductory computer graphics course is taught primarily to junior and senior computer science majors and minors, although students studying computer engineering, electrical engineering, mathematics, and physics are frequently enrolled. The prerequisites for the course are courses in algorithm and program design and linear algebra. Hill's *Computer Graphics* is the text for the course. A lab of twenty Sun-3 workstations supports the programming projects. Students program in C, using a locally-developed interface to Xwindows.

The course approach is to have students develop their own library of graphics routines. Students are taught algorithms for drawing lines and curves, clipping, and area filling. They must implement these algorithms and then use them to render an image. Since Rose-Hulman is on the quarter system with ten-week terms, the course focuses heavily on two-dimensional concepts (the students do a two-dimensional ray tracing project) with a brief exposure to three-dimensional concepts during the last week of the term. This background prepares the students well for the Advanced Computer Graphics course, which covers the breadth of three-dimensional computer graphics.

### G. Scott Owen: *A "scientific" approach*

The hardware available for the class has progressed from the Apple II to 80486 based systems with reasonable color raster graphics capabilities. Yet, most instructors still teach Computer Graphics as if they were using Apple IIs. The image synthesis component of Computer Graphics has traditionally been taught as a collection of ad-hoc techniques. Students are taught how to turn on a pixel, draw lines, polygons, two and three dimensional modeling transformations, viewing transformations and finally, perhaps a simple empirical shading model. Most of the course is spent on 2D topics, with a little 3D at the end. There is not underlying theory behind the methods so there is no conceptual framework for the students.

In contrast to this approach, other scientific disciplines, such as chemistry or physics, teach students a basic underlying theory that provides a conceptual framework for the different techniques and approximations. Teaching image synthesis from a physical science viewpoint provides this underlying theory and conceptual framework.

In his current course, Dr. Owen starts from the basic physic of the interaction of light with surfaces and derives simple local (the Phong model) and global illumination (ray tracing) models. The programming assignments are to produce reflection, and texture mapping. After covering this he spends the rest of the time discussing scan line graphics, comparing it with ray tracing. The students do assignments using the Pixar Renderman system. Thus, most of his course is on 3D graphics with only a brief amount of time spent on 2D graphics. As an added benefit, the students are able to produce some very nice images, comparable to what they see in the media.

### References

Ahuja, D. V., "An Algorithm for Generating Spline-like Curves", *IBM Systems Journal*, Vol. 7, No. 3 & 4, 1968, pp. 206-217.

Ahuja, D. V., Coons, S. A., "Geometry for Construction and Display," *IBM Systems Journal*, Vol. 7, No. 3 & 4, 1968, pp. 188-205.

Bono, P. R. and Arnold, D. B., *CGM and CGI: Metafile and Interface Standards for Computer Graphics*. Springer-Verlag, New York, 1988.

Bresenham, Jack, "Computer Graphics & University Curricula," *Jahrestagung Conference Proceedings* (Zurich-Örlikon, Switzerland, July 17, 1992), Swiss Computer Graphics Association and the University of Zurich MultiMedia Laboratory.

Bresenham, Jack, "Attribute Considerations in Raster Graphics," *Computer Graphics Techniques: Theory and Practice*. David Rogers and Rae Earnshaw, eds. Springer-Verlag, New York, 1990, pp. 9-41.

Burger WF and Shaughnessy JM (1986) "Characterising the van Hiele levels of development in geometry," *Journal for Research in Mathematical Education* (17)1, pp 31-48

Earnshaw, Rae, ed. *Fundamental Algorithms for Computer Graphics*. Springer-Verlag, New York, 1985. (paperback printing, 1991).

Owen, G. Scott, "Teaching Image Synthesis as a Physical Science," *Computers & Graphics*, 18:3, March 1994.

Owen, G. Scott, "Teaching Computer Graphics Using Renderman," *Proc. of 23rd SIGCSE Technical Symposium on Computer Science Education*, ACM, March 1992.

Schaller, Nan, panel chair, "Graphics Education for Computer Science," SIGGRAPH '92 Conference Proceedings (Chicago, Illinois, July 26-31, 1992), ACM SIGGRAPH, New York, 1992, pp. 410-411.

Upstill, Steve, *The Renderman Companion*, Addison-Wesley, 1990.

# Exploiting Networks for Visualization and Collaboration: No Network Roadblocks?

Chair
Theresa Marie Rhyne, Martin Marietta/U.S. EPA Scientific Visualization Center

Panelists
George Brett, Clearinghouse for Networked Information Discovery and Retrieval
Don Brutzman, Naval Postgraduate School
Donna J. Cox, National Center for Supercomputing Applications
Adelino Santos, Fraunhofer Institute for Computer Graphics

This panel examines the concepts underlying/supporting visualization and collaboration using high speed networking, multimedia and interactive computer graphics techniques. Efforts among researchers, programmers, and artists (i.e. Renaissance Teams) to use the new National Information Infrastructure (NII) as well as international telecommunication systems are featured. Software tools which support collaborative visualization across heterogenous platforms for research, education and commerical purposes are highlighted.

Collaborative computing involves facilitating information discovery and scientific visualization activities between researchers located at various remote sites. It includes the use of visualization and information retrieval in a high speed networked environment. Computing resources become transparently available to researchers via the networked environment and this results in a metacomputer. Some collaborations involve interdisciplinary teams focused on solving a single problem while others encompass the sharing of different methodologies and resulting solutions to similar problems.

Positive aspects associated with these high speed networked collaborations center on real time visualization and information discovery among geographically remote research or Renaissance Teams. There are also negative impacts or roadblocks associated with metacomputing. Network transmission difficulties and differences in desktop workstation architectures can cloud the actual visualization two collaborating researchers are simultaneously viewing and steering. Setting up and learning to use the metacomputing infrastructure can be all consuming and thus refocus the basic education or scientific discovery process. Various perspectives on these concerns are debated by the panelists.

### Theresa Marie Rhyne

An important initiative of the U.S. EPA High Performance Computing and Communications Program involves research efforts that attempt to examine the multi-dimensional aspects of environmental sciences problems. An example includes the merger of data sets from groundwater, water quality, terrestrial ecology and atmospheric pollution research efforts. Historically, each of these data sets has evolved from research specific to various EPA Research Laboratories. These laboratories are located in geographically dispersed areas of the United States and include Las Vegas, Nevada; Ada, Oklahoma; Gulf Breeze, Florida; Duluth, Minnesota; Athens, Georgia; Narragansett, Rhode Island; Corvallis, Oregon; Cincinnati, Ohio, and Research Triangle Park, North Carolina.

Collaborative computing tools which support real time information discovery and visualization across high speed networks provide the metacomputing infrastructure to support multi-disciplinary environmental sciences research. There are also technical and social concerns associated with implementing these techniques. How do we handle the differences in visual display among the networked heterogenous workstations? Should we provide a controlled user interface so that the remotely located researchers go down the same metacomputing maze for collaborative information

discovery and visualization steering? Will the process of doing collaborative computing overwhelm efforts to conduct actual scientific research, education or policy setting activities? These remain unresolved issues as we move into the realm of multimedia.

### George Brett

Several user-friendly client-server tools have been developed within the last couple of years for locating and retrieving information residing on computers reachable over the Internet. Among them, the Wide Area Information Server (WAIS), the Internet Gopher, archie, and the WorldWide Web (WWW) have become popular. WAIS, archie and Gopher present overviews of where information of interest is likely to reside and then assist the user in locating specific information objects. WWW permits a user to thread a path through the network by selecting tagged hypertext items.

While focused on the particulars of the evolution of wide area information systems like WAIS, The Clearinghouse for Networked Information Discovery and Retrieval (CNIDR) works closely with the developers of other tools toward achieving compatibility and consistency, and, to the extent possible, convergence of the tools. In addition CNIDR works with communities making use of these tools. This enables CNIDR to work as a feedback channel between developers and users.

An example of this process is the Global SchoolHouse (GSH) project where CNIDR will provide technical support. The Global SchoolHouse, funded in part by the National Science Foundation, will use networked information discovery and retrieval (NIDR) tools in conjunction with real-time network applications to do collaborative science projects over a wide geographic area. GSH has been using Cornell's low end desktop video conferencing package (CU SeeMe) and a text based multiuser environment (MUSH). Students will be information providers as well as users with gopher, WorldWide Web, and WAIS. We will demonstrate how NIDR tools combined with real time communications via the internet can serve to enhance a working environment, in this case middle school classrooms.

Questions to be evaluated will include: Is there significant improvement in quality of information when supplemented with real time interactive sessions?? How will networked hypermedia be used? What will be the impact of a publishing environment that includes hypermedia links?

### Don Brutzman

The Multicast Backbone (MBone) gives Internet users live audio, video and whiteboard tools that connect worldwide. A collaborative development community distributes these software tools freely and encourages open participation. Bandwidth constraints are dealt with using multicast networking protocols, software compression, real-time buffering and cooperation. The only cost of admission to use MBone tools is a desire to learn and network connectivity with adequate bandwidth (e.g. a typical campus connection). A distributed approach works both on a human level and a technical level. MBone multicasts complement multimedia tools such as Mosaic, and make conferences such as SIGGRAPH widely available.

The ready availability of MBone, Mosaic and the World Wide Web changes everything you know about the Internet. The network is more than *a* computer, it is *your* computer. Free access to any type of live or archived resource is available for you, your programs, collaborators and even robots. Worldwide collaboration works, both for people and machines. Examples of these kinds of research at the Naval Postgraduate School include distributed simulation, scientific visualization, distributed conferences, live interaction, remote presence and virtual worlds.

## Donna J. Cox

In the past, NCSA has employed interdisciplinary teams involving artists and scientists (Renaissance Teams) who have created a plethora of communication/visualization tools ranging from 'glitzy' computer animations to interactive 'grungy' graphics for scientific data analysis. Now with the advent of high-speed networks, these types of teams may involve individuals and databases that are separated by great geographic distances.

Desktop multimedia software and virtual reality (the CAVE) are being developed at NCSA to provide advanced collaborative tools to allow virtual interaction in cyberspace. Such application tools will allow a future where collaboration among distanced individuals will bring a new level of interaction among various disciplines such as producers, directors, and animators. Will this virtual surrogate really satisfy the needs of humans to interact at a personal level? Will the chism between artists, humanists, and scientists grow greater due to yet another level of indirection in communication and technological mediation?

Donna Cox will present how she and Robert Patterson used network databases provided by Merit Network Inc. to visualize the NSFnet. This visualization is now being used as the icon for the National Information Infrastructure (NII). She will demonstrate how such visualizations and animations are available through Mosaic over the network.

## Adelino Santos

Most of the computer-supported cooperative applications are communication critical — they demand networking technology (machine-machine), interaction concepts (human-computer communication) and know-how about social processes (human-human). Multimedia has also been available for awhile and needs to be applied to demanding applications in science and industry. I think that a mutually advantageous symbiosis can be achieved between these fields. The weak and strong points of these disciplines are complementary: communication demanding vs. communication powerful, latent industrial application vs. enabling technology, and human expressiveness required vs. media expressiveness.

In analyzing the transition from individual work to group work, within different human activities, two pitfalls are often detected if computer support is considered: a) technological communication difficulties, especially if the group is remotely located, associated with a fall in productivity and frequent social inadequacies of the group's computer support; b) the lack of integrated media processing tools available to all the group members. These pitfalls occur specifically in visualization. Visualization groups are, generally, goal-oriented with important tasks and tight deadlines. The group members may be located in the same room or they may be attending an electronic meeting at which not all members are present in the same place or at the same time. Sometimes computer-supported groups are permanent and formal groups; other situations require ad-hoc groups with a finite lifetime and other kinds of properties. The group interaction might be formal or informal, spontaneous or planned, structured or unstructured. Addressing these types of group interactions poses new challenges for evolving the symbiosis of cooperative applications and multimedia.

# Optimization—An Emerging Tool in Computer Graphics

Chair
Joe Marks, Mitsubishi Electric Research Laboratories, Inc.

Panelists
Michael Cohen, Princeton University
J. Thomas Ngo, Interval Research Corp.
Stuart Shieber, Harvard University
John Snyder, Microsoft Corp.

Just a few years ago, all one needed to be a competent researcher or practitioner in computer graphics was a solid background in geometry, algebra, calculus, topology, probability, mechanics, electromagnetism, signal processing, image processing, electrical engineering, mechanical engineering, optics, information theory, structured programming, basic algorithms and data structures, complexity theory, computer architecture, human factors, perceptual psychology, colorimetry, graphic design, industrial design, semiotics, and art! Unfortunately, the list is growing, and one more topic can now be included: optimization. A perusal of the computer-graphics literature reveals a recent trend towards using optimization to solve problems in image rendering, object modeling, animation, and even chart graphics. The techniques used run the gamut from standard function-optimization algorithms that have their roots in continuous mathematics [10], to black-art stochastic techniques that are inspired by natural processes like evolution and annealing [2]. The participants in the panel reflect this diversity in problem domain and optimization approach. Each panelist will list problems in his areas of expertise for which optimization techniques have proven effective, describe the optimization methods that have been most successful for these problems, present a representative example from the panelist's own research of an optimization problem and method, attempt to predict the future impact of optimization on computer graphics, and suggest how engineers and artists might apply optimization techniques to practical problems.

## Michael Cohen: *Lighting, Shape, Animation Design*

Computer graphics technologies have been developed for two very different styles of applications. In the first case, simulation: for example, radiosity for simulating the illumination in a scene to create realistic images; visualization of finite-element analyses, such as a thin plate under some external forces to see bending and other deformation; and physically based simulation of jello cubes, blocks, and linked figures to create realistic animations.

The second type of application is design: for example lighting design for theatre or architecture [6, 12]; shape design for automotive bodies or other man-made objects [18, 8]; and motion design for computer animation of synthetic creatures [19, 9, 17].

The glue that binds these two disparate types of problems together has recently been seen to be optimization techniques. Optimization methods arise naturally, as the question one typically wants to answer can be phrased: "What is the {lighting setup / shape / motion} that gives me the {most visually pleasing or energy-saving illumination / smoothest surface / most visually plausible or energy-saving animation} while also { following the physics of light reflection / passing through these points / satisfying Newton's second law (F=ma) }?"

Common problems that arise in each of these applications are how to deal with nonlinearities, how to take advantage of hierarchy, and how to keep the designer in the optimization loop. Knowledge gained from fields ranging from user-interface design to wavelet decomposition of functions needs to be applied if we are to provide designers with the tools they need.

## J. Thomas Ngo: *Motion Synthesis for Animation*

Much past work in physically based computer graphics is concerned with solving forward problems: computing "what you see" from a complete set of values for the independent variables in an image or animation. By contrast, the human designer's task is usually an inverse problem, i.e., an optimization problem of computing values for the independent variables from "what you want to see" [19, 12, 6]. Witkin and Kass [19], for example, coined the term "Spacetime Constraints" to refer to an important inverse problem in animation, that of synthesizing physically correct motions to satisfy animator-supplied goal criteria.

Experience with inverse problems in physically based animation suggests that local and global optimization techniques may be useful for computer graphics in fundamentally different ways. Local methods, such as gradient-descent approaches to solving Spacetime Constraints problems [19], leave responsibility for generating coarse solutions with the human animator, since the search space is multimodal. More recent algorithms that are capable of global searching [9, 17] can begin to play a creative role in the motion-synthesis process by generating novel, unexpected solutions. We have found that appropriate representation choices are usually critical in making global search possible.

The development of global optimization techniques cannot be separated from related issues such as the quantification of aesthetic criteria, and the development of suitable user interfaces. But with the right combination of global search algorithm, physical model, objective function, and user interface, naive users may soon be able to create Jurassic-Park-like animations interactively.

## Stuart Shieber: *Chart Graphics*

The design of many types of diagrammatic graphics—such as charts, network diagrams, maps, and so forth—and their layout on a screen or page can be thought of as the automating of choices while respecting constraints. For example, the design of a network diagram, with its nodes and links, requires decisions as to what symbology should be used to express the characteristics of the nodes and links, and the relationships among them, and also how nodes should be laid out so as to optimize not only aesthetic criteria (minimizing edge crossings and diagram area, say) but also semantic criteria (such as relationships among nodes to be conveyed by gestalt relationships of grouping or collinearity). From this perspective, automated graphic design is a problem of constrained combinatorial optimization. The constraints result from inherent properties of the graphic type, perceptual abilities of the viewer, aesthetic criteria, and the information to be conveyed [7].

The most interesting optimization problems that arise, and the ones that arguably cause the most grief for designers of presentation graphics, are NP-hard layout problems, which require heuristic solution. In the course of our research, we have explored various heuristic methods for solving the constrained-optimization problems implicit in graphical design problems, and have had especially good results using stochastic optimization methods. To exemplify our general approach, we will briefly describe one particular graphic-design problem, cartographic label placement, and our method of solution, including empirical testing of our and others' algorithms [1].

**John Snyder:** *Geometric Modeling*
With recent advances in the power of computers, optimization methods are becoming increasing useful in the area of geometric modeling. Optimization methods find application in the two major parts of geometric modeling: in shape modeling, or the creation of desired geometry, and in shape analysis, or the computation of properties of the geometry. For shape analysis, the benefits of optimization techniques are immediate (many desired operations are most simply expressed as optimization problems) and have already been used for such operations as collision detection [16], intersecting rays with surfaces [3], interpolation [13], polygonal decimation [5] and approximation/tessellation [4]. For shape modeling, optimization methods may be just as clearly useful, but are harder to apply. How does one create parameterized shapes? What are the constraints on these parameters, and what is to be optimized? What optimization method should be used?

My own research has focused on a symbolic method for the creation of parameterized shapes and the constraints and objective functions involving them, called generative modeling [14]. I have found interval techniques [11, 15] to be effective for many types of optimization problems in geometric modeling. Interval techniques are advantageous because they compute global solutions, and are practical for problems involving small numbers of parameters. At the same time, I have no doubt that other, more standard optimization methods will continue to be used in geometric modeling.

There are several challenges in the use of optimization methods within the design process, whose solution I believe will revolutionize the design of manufactured objects. Clever ways of interactively guiding the optimization will be required so that users do not have to wait as a complex simulation/optimization problem computes. We will need new techniques for the formulation and specification of parameterized shapes, constraints, and objective functions that allow even non-technical users to do high-level design. Essentially, allowing a designer to easily express and manipulate geometry is the "grail" we seek, a grail which will certainly involve optimization methods, but which presents significant research problems for the future.

## References

[1] J. Christensen, J. Marks, and S. Shieber. "Algorithms for cartographic label placement." In *Proc. of the American Congress on Surveying and Mapping* '93, Vol. 1, 75–89, New Orleans, LA, Feb. 1993.

[2] L. Davis. *Genetic Algorithms and Simulated Annealing.* Pitman, London, 1987.

[3] T. Duff. "Interval arithmetic and recursive subdivision for implicit functions and constructive solid geometry." *Computer Graphics*, 26(2):131–138, July 1992.

[4] M. Halstead, M. Kass, and T. DeRose. "Efficient, fair interpolation using Catmull-Clark surfaces." *Computer Graphics*, 27(2):35–44, Aug. 1993.

[5] H. Hoppe, T. DeRose, T. Duchamp, J. McDonald, and W. Stuetzle. "Mesh optimization." *Computer Graphics*, 27(2):19–25, Aug. 1993.

[6] J. K. Kawai, J. S. Painter, and M. F. Cohen. "Radioptimization—goal-based rendering." In SIGGRAPH '93 Conf. Proc., 147–154. Anaheim, CA, Aug. 1993.

[7] C. Kosak, J. Marks, and S. Shieber. "Automating the layout of network diagrams with specified visual organization." *IEEE Trans. on Systems, Man, and Cybernetics*, 24(3), Mar. 1994.

[8] H. P. Moreton and C. H. Sequin. "Functional optimization for fair surface design." *Computer Graphics*, 26(2):167–176, July 1992.

[9] J. T. Ngo and J. Marks. "Spacetime constraints revisited." In SIGGRAPH '93 Conf. Proc., pages 343–350. Anaheim, CA, Aug. 1993.

[10] W. H. Press, S. A. Teukolsky, W. T. Vetterling, and B. P. Flannery. *Numerical Recipes in C. The Art of Scientific Computing.* Cambridge University Press, Cambridge, UK, 2nd edition, 1992.

[11] H. Ratschek and J. Rokne. *New Computer Methods for Global Optimization.* Ellis Horwood Ltd., Chichester, England, 1988.

[12] C. Schoeneman, J. Dorsey, B. Smits, J. Arvo, and D. Greenberg. "Painting with light." In SIGGRAPH '93 Conf. Proc., pages 143–146. Anaheim, CA, Aug. 1993.

[13] T. W. Sederberg and E. Greenwood. "A physically based approach to 2-D shape blending." *Computer Graphics*, 26(2):25–34, July 1992.

[14] J. M. Snyder. *Generative Modeling for Computer Graphics and CAD: Symbolic Shape Design Using Interval Analysis.* Academic Press, Cambridge, MA, July 1992.

[15] J. M. Snyder. "Interval analysis for computer graphics." *Computer Graphics*, 26(2):121–130, July 1992.

[16] J. M. Snyder, A. R. Woodbury, K. Fleischer, B. Currin, and A. H. Barr. "Interval methods for multi-point collisions between time-dependent curved surfaces." *Computer Graphics*, 27(2):321–334, Aug. 1993.

[17] M. van de Panne and E. Fiume. "Sensor-actuator networks." In SIGGRAPH '93 Conf. Proc., 335–342. Anaheim, CA, Aug. 1993.

[18] W. Welch and A. Witkin. "Variational surface modeling." *Computer Graphics*, 26(2):157–166, July 1992.

[19] A. Witkin and M. Kass. "Spacetime constraints." *Computer Graphics*, 22(4):159–168, Aug. 1988.

# Information Visualization: The Next Frontier

Chair
Nahum D. Gershon, The MITRE Corporation

Panelists
Colleen Bushell, National Center for Supercomputing Applications
Jock D. Mackinlay, Xerox Palo Alto Research Center
William A. Ruh, The MITRE Corporation
Anselm Spoerri, Massachusetts Institute of Technology
Joel Tesler, Silicon Graphics

This panel and audience will discuss the use of our experience and knowledge of data visualization methods, software, and hardware in presenting the rather abstract information contained in data bases, digital libraries, and other massive collections of data and information. The panelists and audience will examine and debate how to create effective information visualizations and how to use them effectively in information navigation, retrieval, and access (e.g., in the information highway environment). Bringing this technology to the users, taking their needs into account, may transform business, science, medicine, engineering, and education.

The audience and the public have been encouraged to submit samples of slides and video material illustrating effective and valuable visualizations.

## Information Visualization: The Next Frontier

Increasing amounts of data and information and the availability of fast digital network access (e.g., in the information highway environment) have created a demand for querying, accessing, and retrieving information and data. However, information technology would not transform business, science, medicine, engineering, and education if the users cannot use it easily and efficiently. Technology must come to the users, taking their needs into account. If we do not involve the users, we will develop useless systems.

On the other hand, advances in interactive computer graphics hardware and mass storage have created new possibilities for information navigation, retrieval, and access in which visualization and user interface (UI) could play a central role. The question is how to utilize the advances in graphics technology and experience to lower the cost of navigating through information, finding specific information, and accessing it once found.

Most of recent advances in visualization have occurred in the area of visualization of scientific data. Information spaces are abstract and different from physical data spaces. Thus, information visualization might require modified or different approaches However, since we live and perceive in a physical world it is advantageous to represent information spaces using physical analogs. This panel and the audience will examine and debate these issues and draw a view of a possible future. More specifically:

- How to make information navigation, retrieval, and access cheaper and more efficient from the point of the user?
- How information visualization could transform the traditional methods of information navigation, retrieval, and access beyond the automation of a library process?
- How is information different from plain physical data?
- What are the appropriate ways to visualize information using physical space analogs?
- What are efficient visual abstractions that speed visual perception and understanding?
- How to incorporate use semiautonomous agents with visualization processes to reduce the work load?
- How to maximize the user interaction with the system?
- What are the users' needs?

### Information Spaces and Visualization — Nahum Gershon

To visualize information it is necessary to define an appropriate information space. Generally speaking, this is not a trivial problem. A particular information could be represented in more than one information space. However, the representation of the information within this space could be more flexible than that of physical data. The choice of which information space and which representation should be chosen depends on the kind of information and also on the specific task or goal. Since information is abstract it might not be straightforward to map it to a physical space used in visualization. Another difficulty is that information spaces could be multi-dimensional and 3-D graphics might not be sufficient for all purposes. Dealing with all of these problems makes the field of information visualization more difficult than scientific visualization. However, these problems and the vast number of important potential applications make the field of information visualization both exciting and challenging.

### Colleen Bushell: *Information about the Information*

The application of information design strategies in the area of hypermedia can improve the efficiency and quality of information navigation and consumption. A primary cause for the frustration that often comes from using hypermedia is the inability to grasp an overall understanding of an information space. For example, there is often no method for knowing how much, what media or what kind of information is there except to explore it "frame by frame" - one screen at a time. There is usually no way for the user to know if they have missed something. And often the only way to go back to a previous spot or take another path is to first backtrack frame-by-frame. This method is tedious and inefficient.

With the continued development of global, distributed hypermedia, as well as self-contained hyper documents, the need for unique approaches to interaction design and graphic design are necessary. Scientific visualization, cartography, book design, and other information "containers" provide both qualitative and quantitative representations of an information space. The ability to create and utilize multiple representations of the information space, with methods to directly interact with those representations for navigation, provide a more powerful, useful information environment.

In this presentation, examples of communications with complex data and information which incorporate both visual, qualitative representations, and quantitative data will be discussed (scientific visualization, interface design, cartography, etc.). Visions for navigational features for NCSA Mosaic software (such as quick-scan features, person atlases and knowledge domain maps), and suggestions for the graphic design of "home pages" will be presented.

### Jock D. Mackinlay: *Designing Information Visualizations: A User Interface Perspective*

Scientific visualization has been primarily focused on scientists and their need to understand the fire hose of data that comes from their simulations and instruments. Stuart Card, George Robertson, and I coined the phrase "information visualization" in a set of CHI'91 papers to broaden the concept of scientific visualization to include anyone accessing massive or complex information. Given the national initiative to network the nation, most people will soon find that interesting information will be available to them that is both massive and complex. However, scientific visualization applications may not be appropriate for this commercial mass market. We believe a critical issue for the acceptance of visualization technology is in the area of user interface design.

Most scientific data, for example CAT (Computer-Aided Tomography) scans, tend to be grounded in the physical world, which has an obvious mapping into the virtual world provided by computer graphics machines. Most abstract information found in libraries and offices typically does not have such an obvious spatial mapping. I will describe how we have been designing visualizations for the Information Visualizer (IV), a research prototype based on 3-D graphics and interactive animation. One strategy has been to develop visualizations of different types of information structure. Examples will be shown. Another strategy has been to analyze the "cost structures of information," which we derive from the some task. Finally, I will describe information visualization applications that we are currently building on the IV platform.

**William A. Ruh:** *Dealing with Text Information and Data: Users' View*
Having to deal with seemingly unmanageable and ever increasing amounts of information has been the problem in many areas in the private and the government sectors. To alleviate this problem, methods have been developed for extracting information from large amounts of open source (i.e., publicly available) materials in a system design that is incrementally extensible and applicable across domains.

Users need help in collecting, filtering, and exploiting open source materials for a variety of purposes. A prototype of a realistic user scenario applicable to intelligence and other analysts has been developed to illustrate the following features needed by users of open source systems:

- User profiles or "filtering assistants" can be launched against incoming feeds of heterogeneous information to select items based on user interests.
- Various text analysis tools can identify salient information such as people, geographic locations, organizations, major topics, and chronological events.
- Information collected for a user via profiles or ad hoc retrospective queries is often too voluminous to review. Therefore, graphical presentation techniques such as maps, timelines, histograms, network displays, and spreadsheets give the user insights into the collection.
- These same visualization mechanisms help users discover interesting relationships among the data and point them towards documents worthy of further review.

One of the system's underlying tenets is the automatic enhancement of raw information with meta-data that is efficiently managed and exploited to facilitate interactive assimilation of otherwise overwhelming volumes. Standard Generalized Markup Language (SGML) is used to represent the meta-data as SGML tags, so that they can be processed by tools from other developers or vendors. Examples for generating different levels of (meta-data) tags include statistical approaches for part-of-speech tagging, and linguistics-based heuristics for generating semantic content tags. The prototype also demonstrates the exploitation of video and other media, which are part of the system design.

**Anselm Spoerri:** *A Visual Tool for Information Retrieval*
Information is being generated at a continuously increasing rate and it is becoming available in ever growing quantities as the access possibilities to it proliferate. However, better methods are needed to manage, analyze and visualize these potentially unlimited amounts of information. Many of the visualization problems currently investigated involve continuous, multi-variate fields that vary over space and time. But there exits an even larger class of important data sets that are abstract in nature and do not have explicit spatial properties that can be exploited.

A case in point is a large document space, where it is usually difficult for users to visualize how the documents relate to their interests and how to access the needed information. In particular, the following major problems need to be solved: 1) The currently dominant Boolean or Exact Matching approach, which is used by the major commercial on-line information services, needs to become more user-friendly. General users find it difficult to formulate effective Boolean queries and few have mastered how to fully exploit its expressive power. 2) The competing, but complementary, Exact and Partial Matching approaches need to be combined in a framework that enables users to make effective use of their respective strengths. Recent retrieval experiments have shown that these two approaches are complementary because the sets of relevant documents retrieved by them do not overlap to a great extent.

We will show how information visualization offers ways to develop more effective information retrieval tools. We will describe the InfoCrystal™ that can be used both as a visualization tool and as a visual query language to help users search for information. It enables users to make use of the expressive power of the Exact Matching approach and its broadening/narrowing techniques in an easy-to-use and visual way. Furthermore, we will show how the Partial Matching approach can be visualized in the same visual framework. The InfoCrystal enables users to explore and filter information in a flexible, dynamic and interactive way. There is currently a great need to invent a diverse set of visualization tools designed to enable users to perform complex explorations of abstract and large data sets.

**Joel Tesler:** *Navigating the Information Landscape*
The information landscape is a powerful paradigm for managing large collections of complex multivariate data. Current 2-D tools in the commercial realm are limited by their narrow bandwidth and dimensionality, while newer 3-D visualization techniques are for the most part restricted to representations of objects and phenomena existing in the physical world. Our approach exploits the rich visualization capabilities of 3-D to model data that is primarily a conceptual phenomenon by extending the concept of the 3-D bar chart to the paradigm of the information landscape, in which collections of 3-D bar charts are connected with each other via some structured topology upon an extended landscape plane. I will discuss our experience in applying this paradigm to several different kinds of information navigation problems and review the kinds of user feedback we have received and the challenges we have encountered. The kinds of areas we have modeled in 3-D include the Unix file system, an organizational hierarchy, various kinds of booking and billing sales data, and a mutual fund portfolio. Future directions of research and applications will also be discussed.

Afterword Information technology would not transform business, science, medicine, engineering, and education if the users cannot use it easily and efficiently. Information visualization could help users find and assimilate the information they want and need in environments such as the information highway. Exciting present and future developments hold the potential to fulfill this promise.

### References
Gershon, N.D. and Miller, C.G., "Dealing with the Data Deluge," *IEEE Spectrum*, July 1993, pp. 28-32.

Robertson, G.G., Card, S.K., and Mackinlay, J.D., "Information Visualization Using 3-D Interactive Animation," *Communications of the ACM*, Vol. 36, No. 4, April 1993, pp. 57-71.

Spoerri, A., "InfoCrystal: A Visual Tool for Information Retrieval," *Proceedings* of the IEEE Visualization '93 Conference, IEEE CS Press, Los Alamitos, CA, 1993, pp. 150-157

# Art and Technology: Very Large Scale Integration

Chair
Tom Meyer, Brown University

Panelists
Sally Rosenthal, independent producer
Stephen R. Johnson, director
Mary Lou Jepsen, Brown University
Douglas Davis, artist, author

We must begin to create on the same scale as we can destroy, or else art, and more dangerously
the human spirit and imagination, will be rendered decorative and impotent.
— Kit Galloway & Sherrie Rabinowitz

The panel is made up of artists who create large-scale works using technology. We discuss the future of artistic techniques which incorporate technology, in order to extend the possibilities of human interaction with the machine and with other people.

Technology and artistic creation have always been closely linked, from the invention of painting, through the development of printing, up through the present, which offers new possibilities for people to interact with the technology, with the work, and with each other.

However, much current artistic work is still based on traditional notions of electronic publication: one viewer/reader working with a work of art contained on one computer. Most VR systems are still walk-throughs, with little or no ability to interact with the created environment or with other people. The much-hyped CD-ROMS that are becoming the medium of choice for rock stars still do not provide even the level of intimacy and interaction which a relatively low-tech concert can provide. As social beings, we need shared experience, such as that generated by the spectacular.

But the networked festival, the "digital convergence," is happening. The World Wide Web almost tripled in size between November and December 1993, and more information is being linked into it constantly. On-line communities, such as MUDs and their relations, have become an explosion of creative interaction, and are being used for real-time collaboration, including hypertext creative writing and other art projects — the development of "folk programming." As communication bandwidth becomes cheaper, video teleconferencing and collaboration across cultural boundaries becomes a common occurrence. And the plummeting costs of hardware and networking allow the development of ubiquitous computing, augmenting reality and communication by making the surrounding environment become reactive to its participants.

The members of this panel are each exploring ways to extend human interaction both with technology and with other people, by using the technology as an integral part of their art. Where existing tools are not useful or appropriate, they have extended them or built their own. Their art is art on the large scale, using technology to create artistic endeavors beyond the scale of the individual, to the scale of human communities..

## Sally Rosenthal

Humans are social organisms. We naturally crave interaction with others, to be part of a community, to have fun. The onslaught of personal computers, CD-I, CD-ROM, virtual reality, remote workplaces, and expanded home television services have seen few technology-based experiences which are about leaving the couch and cooperating with other humans. Something magical happens when large groups of people engage in dynamic activities, as evidenced by the Wave, Michael Jackson's Superbowl halftime, and audience participation segments in the SIGGRAPH Electronic Theater. Interactive television has the potential to enable a new genre of group participation. In the same way that computers have given artists and designers new tools to use in new ways, they also give rise to new possibilities for groups of people to interact with each other and with their environment.

## Stephen R. Johnson

The nature of art at its most fundamental level is an attempt to clarify and/or intensify the human experience. Toward the end film art (and other related offsprings) seek to create "realities" that on a sensorial level replace our own. I believe that for the directors of the future being able to remember the taste of a home grown tomato or the smell of an ocean breeze or the look of trusting innocence of a young doe in a damp forest will be just as important as technical virtuosity. Unfortunately VR became a tired cliche that died from the bloated weight of its own PR before it even had time to mature into the marvelously truly immersive and interactive artform that it will no doubt one day become when gigabytes cost pennies.

On another note, the only commercially manufactured systems for showing films involve a relatively small screening room (I think there are five or so test sites now.) Each viewer has a joystick and thus can "vote" their opinion at critical plot points. (The old interruptible movie scam, ho hum.) Apparently audiences do really enjoy themselves and there's a real party atmosphere.

The MoonTV project that Mary Lou Jepsen and myself have been attempting to pull off would not be interactive. It would, however, be a demonstration of massively powerful technology used for a planetary celebration of our shared human-ness. Twenty-five years ago we used out most advanced technology to put footprints on the moon. Today we have the capacity to light up the moon with playful, humanistic, anti-violent, and thought-provoking imagery. Our aim would be to affirm that we are all part of the same race — the human race. Since Mary Lou hold the world-wide patent, we would seek to insure that this is a one-time event. No-one wants out beloved lunar surface to become a billboard eyesore.

Right now, the Internet offers the most potential as the Universal Artistic Nervous system of the planet. If you play music with someone in a hostile country or make art with them or play video games with them, then conflicting belief system walls will rapidly crumble. When we reach the point where simulated environs approach a level of verisimillitude and speed of interactivity that provokes genuine suspension of disbelief, then we will have to face a great many issues regarding the whole nature of reality itself, who pays what to BE whom, and where, when and how such "alternate realities" should be used and what constitutes abuse. It's gonna get fun; and it's gonna get hairy. Control schemes will emerge that will make Machiavelli seem like Geppetto the puppeteer. We'll chat about these and a range of other issues that are soon to be pertinent to our potentially synthetic lives and our artificial interactions.

**Mary Lou Jepsen**

Maybe its a leftover modernist perspective in our so-called post-modern age; but there is a strong rift between art and (science&technology). I've been told that the big difference between art and science is that artists create their own problems to solve and that scientists solve the problems presented to them by others. I don't really buy this, but I suppose that the military-industrial-complex-theory does support the encouragement of even the most creative and technically competent to take well paying jobs where agendas are dictated by others. Yet, how does one invent without passion? I think that the scientists and technologists do solve their own problems; they find a way to dictate their own agendas within the structures in which they find themselves. It's just harder to see.

But today, a new generation of technologically savvy young people is growing up. Certainly this younger generation will show us that technical competence and artistic ability are not mutually exclusive, though that seems to be the current mode of thinking in contemporary Art. Some big big things can happen as we begin to realize that people can be good or even gifted in more than one area and encouraged to explore. It's going to be exciting.

Maybe artists can get away from this "science is bad" motif, and maybe branch into "what reality can I create to change things?" We can find new ways of experiencing the world and learning. High tech art doesn't have to be so boring.

I have recently designed a system (patent pending) which uses the Moon as a gigantic TV screen in the sky. Stephen R. Johnson is directing the *one-time* world-wide broadcast using this system. The system does no damage to the Moon, uses solar energy, and has great potential for raising awareness of global human rights. Yet, some people are scared of the invention; they fear that the Moon will turn into a permanent ad campaign in the sky. I agree about the possibility of even the best laid plans going awry, but we are being extremely careful to prevent any such abominable use of the Moon. The video broadcast system will only be used once.

Anything at all can be used for good or evil, if we want to divide the world like that. However, the option to choose knowledge and exploration over ignorance and staid methodologies is a most fundamental human right. One can not stop people from creating, but with creation comes responsibility. I don't think that we can talk enough about responsibility.

I'm also bored with current VR approaches. I believe that, ultimately, holography is the right way to create temporary group experiences of alternative realities. Holography allows the projection of truly 3-D images into unencumbered immersive environments. No glasses, helmets, or tethers will be necessary.

We seem to be on the cusp of the mass production of such holographic experiences. Several research groups have now created prototype holographic video systems. Film-based holograms are filling larger and larger volumes, as big as even a city block. In fact, holographic images are being projected in all sorts of novel ways in order to move the hologram itself (usually a piece of film) out of the way. The viewers can then interact directly with the 3-D holographic images, which are projected into the "thin air" directly in front of their eyes. In addition, the burgeoning field of digital holographic lens design (so-called "binary optics") is taking off, offering further promise and affordability for some hybrid computer graphic & 3-D imaging techniques. And, I hardly need to say it, but without the maniacal growth of computer graphics in the last decade we would not be creating these new media, which will surely help us to communicate with one another in more ethereal and powerful ways in the future.

**Douglas Davis**

I am far more interested in the state of the art of the intelligence that demands Internet (and all related tools) than the Internet itself. Intelligence is spreading and intensifying at an exponential rate (we need only compare the vast difference in the literacy and education rates in various societies, beginning with Russia and Japan, feudal as this century began, now first and second in literacy). As it does so, as the mind discovers itself, we reach out for delights and means and results rarely available before, at least not in the quality and quantity now available.

Take the sexual dimension of Internet. Perhaps the mind has always been the central agent in coupling, but now it both requires and develops a signifier to represent this truth. The flirting rooms on America On-Line are simply the most banal representation of this point. Then there is the drive for spontaneity in the development of imagery and of ideas. Why does this word and its allies ("intuitive," for example) occur over and over in user interface work, and elsewhere?

The more the mind becomes aware of itself, the more we insist on taking control of nature and ourselves, and the more we learn that our intelligence insists on unplanned, illogical, and essential irrational conclusions. Anecdotal and personal experience teaches us that solutions spring full-figured into the mind, over and over. Desire is often indeed a prompt to these solutions (here chemical tests support anecdotal evidence). Human/artificial/cyborg intelligence is moving us all towards Unreason as a means of coping with the complex and contradictory universe surrounding us.

# Computer Graphics, Are We Forcing People to Evolve?

Chair
Roger E. Wilson, Roger Wilson & Associates

Panelists
Brenda Laurel, Interval Research Corp
Terence McKenna, Author and Explorer
Leonard Shlain, MD, California Pacific Medical Center

We are the one-eyed man handing out eyes in the country of the blind.

The computer graphics industry is changing our world in a massive and basic way, moving from a world in which "written word" communication is our primary method, into a new era of "imagery" communication. This ability to communicate with images is changing how and what people are capable of thinking. There is a conceptual model that says that the language you think in, limits the very ideas that you can think. If you accept the idea that discourse using images is a language; then you may begin to appreciate the change to our culture as large numbers of people increasingly use images to express themselves.

The last time humans communicated graphically (in any major way) was many thousands of years ago. We had communal, non-hierarchical, "partnership" cultures. You communicated with gestures, expressions, smells, and drawings/pictures. As the written word supplanted images as a "stored" method of communicating; our mode of thinking, the very ideas we could think, changed. We developed into "dominator" cultures with a "left-brain", serial, linear, written-word style of communicating. You could say we had become one-sided in our thinking.

Some cultures still retained the use of gestures for dialogue; but as the bulk of our communications became written, we gradually lost the ability to express ourselves with images. There have been a few people who retained that ability, they were called artists (nowadays we call them graphic artists, and sometimes even computer graphic artists.) This raised a problem, because life is not a linear narrow line, it is a wide and constantly unraveling yarn with much texture, strands flying in and out; a gestalt. Today, with television, movies, CD-ROM, and now images over the network, we are bombarded with ever increasing amounts of data both written and graphic. Yet, in the written word, we have both an ineffectual method of processing it, and a limited method of expressing whatever conclusions we come up with after studying the data. The written word that we use is really an agreement to assume that we are discussing the same thing. If I say

"picture an apple", you nod your head yes and we continue the discussion; BUT you were not seeing the same apple that I was thinking about. Now if I show you a picture of a bright red "Granny Smith" , then I know that we are talking about the same apple.

The people who are starting to develop their "graphic language" abilities are running into a new and yet old problem. If you speak French but your friend speaks Dutch, how do you tell her what you just discovered? As people learn new graphic-based ideas, ideas that are untranslatable into words because there are no words to communicate what you have learned visually and experientially, what will you do? While you can describe what a sunset looks like, you can not verbally describe to someone how radiant it looks. The written description pales before the reality. We in the computer graphics industry are providing more than just a new tool for "the masses", we are giving them a long buried language to communicate with. But it is a lonely situation when you are the only "French" speaker in an auditorium of 30,000 Greeks.

Currently, there are graphic packages on MAC's and PC's that allow you to create graphics with an ease that was not available to anyone on any machine 15 years ago. People who might have struggled to write a memo a few years ago are now creating graphics and 3d animations. As more and more people start to use GUI's and VR systems, and as we become proficient in that language of images, we will finds ourselves changing because of the new ideas we come across. We may soon reach a critical mass where our modern societies will change.

Are we prepared to become "graphic language" tutors?

How can we, as computer graphic professionals, assist during this transition?

Do we want to?

Are we prepared to deal with the new ideas that we will find?

Do we even have a choice?

# Computer Graphics for Architecture and Design Presentations: Current Work and Trends Outside the U.S.

Chair
Alonzo C. Addison, University of California at Berkeley


Panelists
Alfredo S. Andia, University of California at Berkeley
Nicolo Ceccarelli, Politecnico di Milano
Gustavo J. Llavaneras, Universidad Central de Venezuela
Makoto Majima, Taisei Corporation
Ken Roger Sawai, Plus One

This panel addresses the growing utilization of advanced computer graphics techniques for design communication and visualization in the Architecture, Engineering, and Construction (AEC) and related design industries. Since there is a great deal of interesting and innovative work being done outside the United States in the area (and with relatively little U.S. exposure), this panel is focused on a few of these international efforts. Architecture is but a small subset of the much larger field of design, and the trends and work being done are in many ways representative of the broader domain. Despite the formal training of all of the panelists in architectural design and the focus of the discussion upon architecture and engineering, the panel should be of interest and value to educators, researchers, software developers, and marketers in the AEC field and those interested in practical and innovative uses of computer graphics presentation techniques outside the U.S.

For years computer-aided design, or "CAD" has been the primary focus of computerization efforts (and funding) among design firms throughout the world. Recently however, as computer graphic visualization and presentation tools have matured, there has been a growing trend to utilize the computer as more than just a drafting tool. Thus, the panel presentations and discussion will steer away from traditional CAD and focus in on rendering, animation, and multimedia in the AEC field. Each panelist will briefly present the current state-of-the-art in their respective country and area and their vision for where their respective fields are heading. The presentations will be followed by a roundtable discussion (and opportunity for audience participation) of how the usage in each region and field parallels or perhaps differs from work in the United States.

The panelists come from a broad slice of the world market. Representing a large AEC firm, a small multimedia house, an architectural presentation service bureau, and research and education, they bring multiple viewpoints, cultures, and perspectives to the discussion. Although each is involved with innovative or unique presentation and visualization work, it is valuable to note that each is also interested and involved with research focusing on moving computer usage in the design profession beyond mere presentation graphics.

## Alfredo S. Andia
The Center for Environmental Design Research at the University of California at Berkeley has, for several years now, been researching the role of computer technology in the AEC industry. Data compiled from numerous interviews of firms throughout the world will be summarized to help set the stage for the presentations by the other panelists. Although the study revealed that computer tools are in limited instances being used in innovative and interesting ways, by and large, it showed that the AEC industry has a long way to go. This should be viewed as both a weakness and an opportunity, as it presents a rare chance for software developers and marketers to tailor their technologies to the needs of the client-base. However, no matter how good presentation tools may become, they are but a stepping stone to much greater benefits offered by computer graphic tools that move beyond the limitations of current paradigms and help designers rethink century-old work processes and met!

## Nicolo Ceccarelli
Despite the increased complexity of the contemporary city, the tools used by designers and planners to visualize and understand it have failed to keep up. Urban planning is a complex process, taking into account multiple people, information, and resources in a variety of formats. Recent developments in computer technology offer improved possibilities to simulate and model the reality and to describe its spatial and dynamic aspects. Secondly, new communicative tools and methodologies offer opportunities for integrating and presenting a wider variety of information. In Italy, work is being done to help designers visualize urban information in new and innovative ways, using relatively inexpensive tools.

As an example, recent work at the Polytechnic of Milan which led to the development of a three-dimensional model of the Italian city of Vicenza will be shown. Developed to help the City Council and public understand and visualize design proposals, the "symbolic" model of the town is detailed enough to allow the populace to compare it with their experiences of the real city, yet simple enough to be flexible and easy to manipulate.

## Gustavo J. Llavaneras
Despite limited technology and funds, computer graphic presentation work in design and urbanism is flourishing in Venezuela and other Latin American nations. Hindered by years of poor construction industry profits and generally weak economies, architect, engineers, and designers in Latin America have learned to make up for the "low-end" technology with "high-end" creativity.

With the exception of oil companies (in oil-based economies like Venezuela) and advertising firms, the majority of Latin American designers and engineers cannot afford to spend large quantities of money on high-end computer tools for graphic design representation. Those that are using computer-based presentation tools tend to have simpler equipment than their U.S. counterparts (much of which would be considered obsolete by North American firms).

For architecture and design representation the trend is to use high-end PCs or Apple Macintoshes. Software ranges from Autocad (for PCs) and FormZ, to MacArchitrion, and the Venezuelan "User's CAD". Adobe Photoshop is used for manipulation and enhancement of low resolution renderings. Some offices work with video animations using mixes of the aforementioned applications along with Autodesk's 3D Studio, MacroMedia's Director, or other low to medium-cost software.

Examples from a variety of users in Latin American countries will help to illustrate these trends and show where the design presentation industry is moving.

## Makoto Majima

Taisei Corporation, one of the world's largest integrated AEC firms, has in the past several years accelerated its usage of high-end 3D graphic technologies. In collaboration with the Japan Broadcasting Corporation (NHK), Taisei has produced animations of several cities and monuments of the ancient world for television (such as its work for the "Treasures of the British Museum" series). Over the past few years as skills and technology has improved, Taisei has accelerated it usage of computer presentation tools and worked to improve the quality of its work as well as its applicability within the organization. Examples of some recent efforts to increase the realism of animations with moving people (both in the form of moving, texture-mapped objects and as overlaid video) will help to illustrate the trend in high-end presentation work in Japan.

The usage and focus on computer graphics in the Japanese AEC field has seen great growth in recent years. Despite the slowdown in the Japanese economy, work is continuing. Although many of the tools used at Taisei are widely available in the United States (such as EDS' GDS, Wavefront Explore, and Matador), a few are primarily limited to the Japanese market (e.g. Links rendering software, Shima Seiki high resolution paint systems, Rembrandt lighting software, etc.). Another difference in Japanese graphic work is the focus upon HDTV. Taisei has rendered several recent works at HDTV resolutions and is continuing research in the area. Despite significant high-end work, the large Japanese AEC firms suffer from limited computer graphic usage among the actual designers and engineers. Although today's tools are much simpler than many of the custom tools firms such as Taisei were using just a few years ago, the industry has a long way to go to simplify this technology to the level of the design team.

## Ken Roger Sawai

Plus One is a small Japanese firm specializing in computer presentations in the AEC industry. As such, it has had to learn how to produce work on much smaller budgets and with less sophisticated tools than the large integrated corporations which dominate the Japanese building industry. With clients ranging from architects such as Shin Takamatsu and Tadao Ando to major AEC firms such as Obayashi Corporation, Plus One has the opportunity to work on a diverse range of project types and sizes.

Architectural animations typically suffer from a lack of realism. Although tools are now available to render with many of the subtleties present in physical buildings, such realism is typically expensive and still lacks the feeling of real world space. People, trees, dirt, and grime are all significant component of buildings, and although not easy or inexpensive to add to animations, their usage can add enormously, as illustrated in Shin Takamatsu's "walk" through one of his designs.

# Why is 3-D Interaction So Hard and What Can We Really Do About It?

Chair
Julian E. Gomez, Apple Computer, Inc.

Panelists
Rikk Carey, Silicon Graphics, Inc.
Tony Fields, IDEO Product Development
Andries van Dam, Brown University
Dan Venolia, Apple Computer, Inc.

What is so hard about 3-D interaction? 2-D interaction is fairly well understood; does the addition of a dimension change the fundamental nature of the problem? What can developers do to decrease the level of complexity for a user to work with a 3-D scene? This panel will cover the role of an Application Program Interface (API) in providing user interaction capabilities, how performance affects the issue, and the concept of "user experience."

Historically, for graphics systems, the API has been the link between the hardware and developer, and the developer has been the link between the hardware and the user. As hardware has grown in power, API's have grown in complexity and power provided to the developer, with a corresponding change presented to the user. Until recently, however, Human Computer Interaction (HCI) has not been an important part of that process. APIs frequently have poor or no support for HCI, and all too frequently developers provide HCI that simply exposes the API to the user. Users are not programmers, however, so the API should support more of an interface than a basic link between user and machine. The question is: just what is it that can be provided?

One approach to the solution would be to provide computing analogs of tools that already exist in the user's discipline. This is not adequate; the existing tools are oftimes anachronistic, having been developed during some prior state of technology and living on through inertia. In addition, physical tools are limited by physical reality; this is not a limitation for computers, where it is frequently useful to work in a mode that can't exist in real life. Thus, the scope of tool development should not be limited by the range of what is already available.

Current practice includes the use of "widgets," which are mechanisms inserted into the 3-D scene that can be directly manipulated by the user to cause some change to the scene and/or the objects within it. Even this process raises some questions, for example, should the widgets be fully participating 3-D objects, casting shadows etc., or should they be some metaphysical tools that are there but not really there? Or, should a widget be multifunctional depending on the context in which it is used?

In addition, there is the issue of how performance affects interaction. In real life, 3-D manipulation is immediate and in fact generally involves some kind of real-time feedback loop ("real time" is used here in its technical rather than its marketing meaning). Many contemporary graphics systems can't provide this kind of throughput, leading to the issue of how and if interaction techniques should be modified in the presence of slower update rates.

The most general issue is one along the lines of: just what is involved in presenting interaction capabilities to the user. Providing widgets allows the user to interact, but shouldn't there be a theme to what the widgets look like and how they behave? It's reasonable for a user to expect consistency in the working environment, therefore it's reasonable for the graphics system to have all aspects of 3-D interaction defined, including colors, modifying widget behavior by manipulating the widget, how widgets present themselves onscreen,

etc. The problem becomes one of not just "user interface" but "user experience," so it addresses not just what pixels to put on the screen, but rather the complete experience of interacting with a 3-D scene.

**Rikk Carey**

3D direct manipulation is late in coming to computer graphics applications. It is rare to see a 3D application make good use of the direct manipulation techniques. Most commercial and academic 3D programs resort to traditional, easier to program 2D widget interfaces. This is mostly due to the technical difficulty and user interface complexity that 3D interaction introduces.

In order to quickly develop 3D interaction interfaces a programmer needs a basic set of 3D tools and utilities. Fast 3D picking that returns accurate intersection information is a fundamental requirement. The picking speed must be extremely fast and not dependent on redrawing. In order to accommodate a variety of 3D interaction "feels," a set of geometry intersection objects, or "projectors," is recommended. These objects provide the intersection and delta intersection information for the various geometry types supported during 3D interaction. These objects are not necessarily rendered; they are used to compute the interaction movement, and may be replaced by surrogate objects during rendering. For example, a sphere projector could be used to compute the interaction computation to rotate a cone. From these basic tools, a set of primitive 3D interaction objects, manipulators, can be created that provide elemental 3D interaction. For example, a "dragPoint" manipulator implements a constrained 3D translation of a point. Primitive manipulators can be combined into compound manipulators such as the "handleBox" which is composed of a cube projector (the faces of the box) providing translation of the box, and eight "dragPoint" manipulators at the corners of the box for scaling. With the set of basic tools and objects, 3D interaction interfaces can be prototyped quickly and provide the real-time performance required for any interaction object.

**Tony Fields**

The creation of three dimensional objects is the primary task of mechanical designers and industrial designers who are developing a product. With both industrial design and mechanical engineering, the design has traditionally been performed on paper or with 2-D CAD systems. In this way, the design is either represented by sketches or by orthogonal projections of the object on a flat plane. When the design process is transferred to three dimensions, the designer is working with a virtual object on the screen, and the user's orientation relative to the geometry is not always obvious. In training new users of 3-D CAD systems, I see the following two issues as the greatest challenge to a new user:

1. Direction and Location Specification. The toughest problem for a new user in my experience is learning to orient oneself in order to perform a creation or modification task. The user must develop an intuitive feel for "where" he or she is in the model, and must

always know exactly what direction a modification or geometry creation command will be done in or about. This is especially true with wire frame and surface modeling systems.

2. Geometry Interaction. New users generally have very little trouble in quickly learning to create a body of some kind. The real difficulty comes in locating that body relative to other bodies, or in modifying that body.

My vision of the ideal 3-D tool for industrial or engineering design work would have the following features:

1. Real Time Rendered Views. The object visualization provided by wire frame or surfaced wire frame systems is vastly inferior to a rendered solid model.

2. Processor Speed. The processor must be sufficiently fast that active rendered rotation of a body or bodies is possible. Body or surface creation and modification must rapid enough that various scenarios may be tried in rapid succession.

3. Freeform Geometry Creation. The current trends in Industrial Design are towards very curvaceous and sculptural forms that can only be represented by complex surfaces. Effective tools must provide many techniques for the creation of freeform surfaces. and they must be rendered accurately on the screen. The accuracy of these surfaces and the nature of the transition between adjacent surfaces is critical, so there must be tools, graphical or otherwise, that can inform the user of the quality of the surface interface (C1 continuity, C2 continuity, etc.).

All of the issues above revolve around correct and rapid feedback of information about the model to the user. In an ideal world, the interaction would be as similar as possible to holding the actual object: it could be viewed from any direction, it can be touched, it can be moved, it can be changed.

### Andries van Dam

Today's applications on workstations and personal computers predominantly use the desktop metaphor and the WIMP (Windows, Icons, Menus, and Pointing) graphical user interface (GUI). This style of GUI was developed at Xerox PARC and then commercialized by Apple's Macintosh and more recently by Microsoft in Windows and the X consortium in Motif. This 20-year old technology is still very useful and will not soon be replaced. I believe, however, that 3D applications, particularly those for Virtual and Augmented Reality, can benefit from interfaces that rely more both on direct manipulation in 3D and on 3D widgets that are part of the environment. Such 3D widgets are like tools in the scene that are built in the same development environment as are the application objects. This is in sharp contrast to 2D widgets for 3D desktop applications, that, like a TV control panel, are outside the 3D environment, and are built with a separate toolkit or interface builder such as Motif. I will discuss examples of 3D widgets implemented at Brown and a visual toolkit for constructing 3D widgets.

### Dan Venolia

To manipulate and create in a 3D scene, the user must first understand shapes and relationships. This understanding comes less from display techniques and more from the user's exploration of and interaction with the scene. The goal of 3D interface is to provide an environment that enables and encourages exploration. The user may explore by looking, by building, by comparing and by evaluating. All these activities must be easy to do and to undo. Two methods, 3D cursor and 3D widgets, provide a foundation for this interaction.

Many of the lessons learned in developing 2D authoring tools are directly applicable to 3D construction. Direct manipulation in 2D is enabled by a 2D cursor and a 2D mouse. Working in 3D is facilitated by a 3D cursor and a 3D pointing device. The present mismatch between the 2D cursor and the 3D task hamstrings an application by requiring highly modal and indirect interaction techniques.

The 3D cursor serves to unify the disparate 3D pointing devices that are available today and in the future. It can be integrated with the 2D cursor so the application developer can choose the most appropriate tools to express the interface, and so the user may move seamlessly between 2D and 3D control.

Just as 2D graphic editors provide "handles" on the selected object, "widgets" can be added to a 3D scene to provide affordances for manipulating the selected shape. Widgets can also represent invisible 3D objects in the scene, such as lights. Widgets represent an interesting design challenge, since they must reside in the 3D scene but not conflict with it.

The 3D cursor allows the user to point and act in the scene. Widgets provide controls to point at and behavior to alter in the scene. Combined with proficient viewpoint control, much of the success that is enjoyed by 2D authoring tools can be extended to 3D.

### References

D. Brookshire Conner, Scott S. Snibbe, Kenneth P. Herndon, Daniel C. Robbins, Robert C. Zeleznik, and Andries van Dam. "Three-Dimensional Widgets," 1992 SIGGRAPH Symposium on Interactive 3D Graphics, March 1992.

Kenneth P. Herndon, Robert C. Zeleznik, Daniel C. Robbins, D. Brookshirt Conner, Scott S. Snibbe, and Andries van Dam. "Interactive Shadows," UIST '92 Proceedings, November 1992.

William M. Hsu and John F. Hughes. "Direct Manipulation of Free-Form Deformations," SIGGRAPH '92 Proceedings, 26(2).

Scott S. Snibbe, Kenneth P. Herndon, Daniel C. Robbins, D. Brookshire Conner, and Andries van Dam. "Using Deformations to Explore 3D Widget Design," SIGGRAPH '92 Proceedings, 26(2).

Paul S. Strauss and Rikk Carey. "An Object-Oriented 3D Graphics Toolkit," SIGGRAPH '92 Proceedings, 26(2).

Dan Venolia. "Facile 3D Direct Manipulation," Proceedings CHI '93, Amsterdam. ACM/SIGCHI, 1993.

Robert C. Zeleznik, D. Brookshire Conner, Matthias M. Wloka, Daniel G. Aliaga, Nathan T. Huang, Philip M. Hubbard, Brian Knep, Henry Kaufman, John F. Hughes, and Andries van Dam. "An Object-Oriented Framework for the Integration of Interactive Animation Techniques," SIGGRAPH '91 Proccedings, 25(4).

Robert C. Zeleznik, Kenneth P. Herndon, Daniel C. Robbins, Nate Huang, Tom Meyer, Noah Parker and John F. Hughes, "An Interactive 3D Toolkit for Constructing 3D Widgets," SIGGRAPH '93 Proceedings, 27(3).

# Computer Technology and the Artistic Process: How the Computer Industry Changes the Form and Function of Art

Chair
Jane Flint DeKoven, Pacific Data Images

Panelists
Tim Binkley, School of Visual Arts
Glenn Entis, Pacific Data Images
Delle Maxwell, Independent Designer
Alvy Ray Smith, Altamira Software

This panel is designed to augment the art show. Its purpose is to create a dialog between artists and engineers, people in the computer graphics industry and those in the field in academia. The panel will discuss the roles that engineers, commercial artists and art academicians play in influencing the development of the process, the content, the product and the context of computer art.

One of the main social functions of art is to understand and communicate the human experience. Because the foundation of understanding is creating relationship and correlation between thoughts, computer technology, with its ability to store many "thoughts," is ideally suited to expanding our base of understanding. And because the nature of communication is connection, computer technology, with its ability to connect the "thoughts" it stores and present a variety of different views and relationships of those thoughts, is a powerful means of elucidating the very process of communication.

However, as Richard Saul Wurman stated several years ago, from his position outside the computer technology arena, "There are only three businesses involved in communication today. The first is the transmission business, all companies starting with tele: television, telephone, telex, etc. The second is the storage business. There, the technology is exploding because of the compression of storage: laser, compact disk, ROM, CD ROM, CDI and all kinds of floppy and hard disks. The third business is the understanding business, and nobody is in it... writers... serve the god of style and the god of accuracy. Graphic designers... and all the universities serve... the god of looking good." If we notice how other high tech communication forms of this century such as film and video have evolved, we can see what Mr. Wurman means. Both media have been influenced greatly by the gods of style and looking good. In addition, because of the high cost of use, mass market saleability has dictated product and the limited accessibility of the media has led to a narrowness of language and a dearth of form. If we do not want the high tech nature of the computer to force the art which it mediates to devolve toward either the banal or the overly precious, and if we desire the growth of the understanding business, we must become aware and make use of the essential changes that the computer has wrought. This awareness is being forged in a number of ways: peoples work and leisure are merging as computer technology becomes a presence in all aspects of living; engineers and artists are becoming collaborators in ways that breed a healthy respect in each for the process of the other; engineers are noticing how people really work and incorporating the unintended use that people make of their tools back in to the tools themselves; artists are rejecting the classic role of standing outside the culture in order to see it and instead infusing themselves into the very heart of the culture... the computer communications industry... and changing it. We are at the crossroads of development of this tool and each of us, by virtue of being a part of this community, can guide that development. Perhaps a bit of hindsight and a bit of projection will illuminate our task: The limits of communication and understanding inherent in how the printing press developed has

lasted for 400 years. In fifty years will the computer have become just another toy, a pastime? Will it have become just another way to do the same things we've always done? Or will we develop it and, in turn, allow it to change us, so that it becomes the most powerful tool we have seen to date, a tool that allows the artist to create with thought itself and for all of us to realize the basic artistic nature of our work? I believe that the crux of these question lays within the institutions of business and academia. If the changes that we see in individuals can begin to trickle upwards into the larger institutions of which we are a part and become incorporated into their processes before they trivialize them or make them too precious we may actually see a whole new culture emerge. If academia could share with industry what it knows about thought, reflection and learning for the sake of learning and help create products that are essential, not frivolous, enduring not throw-away; if industry could share with academia its wealth and what it knows about pragmatic application of knowledge and help connect ideas to realities... perhaps we will create a culture of learning companies and working intellectuals, with more inherent balance than our current culture of excess.

## Panel Goals and Issues

In what ways do the high tech industries that create the tools of computer art contribute to its development? In what ways does it distract? Should software and hardware engineers create tools that consciously serve the artistic process? Should the computer graphics service industry be aware of the images it makes and the language it is creating with them? Do the prevailing academic standards for evaluating the content, product and function of art apply to computer art? Is it the obligation of artists, the art community, the academic art community, collectors, the general public or some other group to decide if computer art is art? Does the restricted accessibility of the tools play a role in how the art form has developed and will develop? What criteria should be used for judging computer art? Historically computer art has been judged as a separate art form. To what extent should we continue to separate it from other art forms? Can we or should we separate the study and understanding of computer art from the study and understanding of the technology that supports it? Does computer art have a social significance that is different from other art forms? Has a unique computer graphics semantic begun to be developed? Is the legitimacy of computer art as an art form well served by the SIGGRAPH Art Show?

## Tim Binkley

The question whether computer art is a fine art may be anachronistic. Fine arts are organized around channels of communication called media. But the computer is not a medium at all, and hence, cannot be comfortably accomodated in the traditional fine art world. The social, cultural and economic institutions that gave rise to "fine art" distiguishing it from craft, decoration, commercial art and advertising, are being supplemented and sometimes challenged by practices heavily imbued with digital technology. These practices are likely to alter many of the ways we interact culturally. Activities taking place through computerized terminals on the information superhighway establish a network of human connectedness that differs radically from the hierarchic relationships in most cultural institutions, from museums to movie theaters. Since computerized communication is increasingly moving towatd interactive multimedia, industry will need the assistance of artists in designing effective formats as well as appealing content. As a society, we will need to make important decisions about who will have access and what kind of information and interactions should be encouraged and supported. As artists, it is incumbent upon us to be aware of new developments in technology and to look for opportunities to use and direct it toward humane and uplifting goals.

## Glenn Entis

There are many levels at which the topic of this panel can be addressed. At the immediate level of the effect of the computer graphics industry on art, I believe that the "industry" is flailing around with a double-edged sword. New tools, hardware, techniques and opportunities are being created for artists, which is great. However, the budgets, business and public attention tend toward mass market visuals with "high production values" (i.e. big budgets and sophisticated technology), which tends to supplant the lone artist's traditional role of visionary, boundary-pusher, and cultural trickster. We don't laugh at Rembrandt's resolution or even Einstien's frame rate, but I've heard a lot of snickers at past SIGGRAPH art shows. Also, what happens when appreciation of aesthetics and technological prowess become inextricably comingled? Will we stop appreciating a piece because it is boring technology, hasn't been updated, etc.? As a firmly entrenched representative of the industry, I really can't say which side of this sword is sharper for artists. In a broader sense, computers can be seen as the continuation of art dilemmas that began in the Industrial Age. Mass production and mass media have challenged traditional notions of artistic craftsmanship and the primacy of "original" art objects. The essential irony of art in an age of mass manufacture was elegantly demonstrated by Marcel Duchamp's gallery display of a signed urinal in 1913, and has been exhaustively debated with the advent of photography as fine art. In this context, computers are the next, albeit more radical, round in an older debate. Broader still is the nature of art and the artistic process. Historically high art has always demanded mastery, and innovation, of a craft. Is computer art and programming just another such craft? The available technology has always molded the art, and the art plus technology has always served to mold humankind's image of itself. For computer images hanging on a wall, these basic issues seem unchanged. However, when art is interactive, collaborative, network-based, etc. these issues do change. The job of the fine art industry is to determine who gets written about, exhibited, sold and collected. I suspect that too many fundamental issues are changing too quickly for many people in that world to have

a clue about what is really going on. I personally accept the view that we are careening wildly out of control and the very best we can do is keep our eyes open.

## Delle Maxwell

Delle Maxwell is the veteran of many cross disciplinary projects, and would like to address the panel's issues from the perpective of that personal experience.

## Alvy Ray Smith

Thinking on the grand scale, it is naive to think that market-driven industry has a responsibility to elevate the computer art form. Nevertheless, industry effectively does so anyhow. We all know, since Adam Smith, the theory of capitalism says private greed serves the public good. For computer graphics companies this translates into: the sheer force of competition causes the generation of finer and finer creative tools and services. Thus the industry's role in the arts is essentially passive (ignoring generous donations from highly prosperous firms which are noble and good events for which there might even be tax breaks). So I do not believe that the computer industry changes the form and function of art. Computer technology, however, certainly does change the form and function of art and the artisitic process. It has extended the notion of art, and it has provided new ways of knowing and judging art. A sure sign of these changes is the difficulty the Art Establishment, or Art Biz, is having with computation. I am not overly concerned with them, however, believing they will come along in time just as they did for abstract expressionism, photography, and video, to name a few previous changes they have managed to sluggishly incorporate. As in these cases, the Establishment has to come to terms with an idea before it can proceed with it. One of the problems is that computation is not easy to categorize. It is not a new style, nor is it a new medium. It is a new tool and a new way of thinking. It affects print art, photographic art, video art and music directly and obviously and other forms, such as sculpture and painting perhaps less obviously. It leads to elevation of what were lesser forms, like collage, and to creation of new forms, like interactive multiply-connected spacetime image and audio sculptures ("multimedia") delivered in the CD-ROM medium. Here are some of the terms of the new vocabulary that computation brings to the visual arts: Graphs structure vs. linear or random structure (cf. multimedia vs. film/video/books). Controlled complexity (cf. simulated evolution of art, chaos, fractals, graftals). Musical terms: syncopation, timbre, attack, dynamics, counterpoint, etc. (music often provides better metaphors than painting for computer art. Process ( often as interesting aesthetically, in the choice and order of techniques, as the end result). And here are some of the new concerns that computation brings to the arts: What to buy (bits or output media?) Private vs. public (is there a public way to present computer art?) Permanence (cf. performance art, 2 inch video, wire recordings, etc.) Credits (cf. music and movies)

# Determinants of Immersivity in Virtual Reality: Graphics vs. Action

Chair
Alan R. Mitchell, Trionix Corporation

Panelists
Stuart Rosen, Whizbang!
William Bricken, In-World Corporation
Ron Martinez, Spectrum HoloByte, Inc.
Brenda Laurel, Interval Research

Psychological immersivity is the most important performance measure of effectiveness for media experiences, from watching a computer generated animation to having an interactive experience in a virtual reality (VR) environment. To offer and foster the best value hardware systems and the most effecive software media, we need to know what determines immersivity: realistic graphics, realistic action , or some sort of balance? The panel will address this critical question with presentations by five experts with varied points of view.

The four key concepts of the panel are Psychological Immersivity, VR, Realistic Action, and Realistic Graphics. Psychological Immersivity is a process in which many of a person's senses are stimulated by an artificial environment, to the point where emotions and intellect follow as though actually in a real-world or other-world event. VR is a computer generated, real time, interactive environment of three-dimensional visual, aural, and other sensed phenomena. Realistic action refers to both the quality of a VR story line or adventure scenario and the fidelity of its dynamic realization, including attributes such as motion, voice generation or recongnition, and virtual character behavior. Realistic graphics refers to visual fidelity attributes, such as resolution, field of view, frame rate, polygon density, and texture map complexity.

The psychologist Mihaly Csikszentmihalyi, writing about years of research into what causes happiness in life's experiences, has identified a state called "flow." Flow is a process characteristic of certain human activities that is akin to what we call psychological immersion for VR experiences. This research supports the contention that psychological immersivity is the most important measure of merit and that interactivity is critical for optimized consumer happiness. But the work does not answer the basic question of whether realistic graphics or realistic action is the greater determinant of immersivity.

The location-based and home entertainment industries are becoming aware that distributed interactive simulation systems developed for Army training (SimNet and Close Combat Tactical Trainer) indicate that VR envrionments can produce a greater depth of immersivity than any other simulation training experience. That evidence from military training is reinforced by reports from consumers of newly emerging location-based and home entertainment VR products. But why is that so? VR graphics are usually inferior to animations due to the need for real time rendering. We also note that VR action can offer a higher level of interactivity because of the four-dimensional, space-time degrees of freedom. Does this mean that realistic action is more important than realistic graphics?

Designers of networked, interactive computer games (MUDs) generally believe that action is much more important than graphics. Players of these text-based adventure games have hours of immersivity. Is this more evidence that realistic action is more important than realistic graphics?

Despite the above evidence, the arcade, the home video, and the home computer game industries are clearly pushing toward vastly improved graphics through CD-ROM multimedia systems, while making realistic action of secondary importance. Consumers are certainly flocking to these products. Is this contrary evidence that realistic graphics are more important than realistic action?

As we address these basic questions, it is important to realize that the interactive VR experience takes place in a "closed, human-in-the-loop system." This realization provides a balanced point of view, an awareness that graphics and action are causally integrated and psychologically interdependent. A graphical object such as a virtual human form with well modeled body dynamics is vusally more pleasing and engrossing in space-time than a still frame image would suggest. This effect becomes more pronounced as the quality of the story line increases. Thus, realistic action enhances the realism of graphics.

Conversely, we also note that virtual characters present action that is much more intriguing and believable when the geometric and texture complexity increases their graphical, still frame fidelity. Thus, realistic graphics enhance the realism of action.

Hence, graphics and action must be modeled in a co-dependent manner that is fitting for the story line, the sophistication of the human participant, and the market's contraints on product cost. And there's the rub! From the point-of-view of the product developer, nothing about VR is more *real* than the market's price constraints and the need to optimize a system design within those constraints. In other words, we must strive to give the greatest value - the deepest level of psychological immersivity - for the dollar paid. When we take this practical, market-driven point of view, the trade between realistic graphics and realistic action suddenly becomes critical, controversial, and esoteric.

The degree of realistic action available in commercial VR products has been at a rather low level due to a dearth of outstanding authors who understand the medium, and immaturity of enabling technologies for authoring tools and real time execution of the dynamic attributes of a story line. Improving realistic action primarily involves software research and development, with potentially high cost and schedule risk if requirements are set too high. Because of these practicalities, most of the promising research in the area of realistic action is occurring in university labs and military system developments. However, this research is being actively published and industry is responding to the opportunities for technology transfer into their product lines.

Despite the risks of pursuing advancements in realistic action, when trading areas for industry R&D and when making production design-to-cost decisions, it often seems that the most cost-effective choice is to achieve more realistic action instead of more realistic graphics. This is true because VR's real time processing requirements can make incremental improvements in graphics much more expensive or even unattainable in terms of hardware throughput and production cost.

It is particularly important to ask, "What could change this cost-effectiveness equation for VR systems that currently favor increasing the realism of action over increasing the realism of graphics?" The answer is that new graphics algorithms, system architectures, and hardware technologies are needed that bring the cost-effectiveness of increasing the realism of graphics in line with the cost-effectiveness of increasing the realism of action.

# Reading the Fine Print: What Benchmarks Don't Tell You

## Chair
Randi J. Rost, Kubota Pacific Computer, Inc.

## Panelists
Jim Bushnell, International Business Machines
David Cooper, Hewlett-Packard Company
Jerry Schneble, Ford Motor Company
Lynn Thorsen-Jensen, Evans & Sutherland

The computer is the most general tool ever developed by mankind. Computers differ from other tools, like cars, in that they can be used in an almost limitless ways. A car has little purpose other than to efficiently move peo- ple and things short distances over smooth terrain. A graphics computer, on the other hand, might be used for a wide variety of complex applications including industrial package design, battle simulation, earth resource analysis, medical diagnosis and surgical planning, genetic research, or virtual reality games.

During the early days of the auto industry, there was little need to provide information to help customers decide which car to buy. Nowadays, manufacturers provide all sorts of specifications to help people make purchasing decisions, including engine size, miles per gallon, time to accelerate from 0 to 50, trunk size, and so on. When combined with the price and the appearance of the car, these specifications and performance metrics can help consumers decide which of the many makes and models of car to buy.

We are in the Model-T stage of developing specifications and performance metrics that help people make computer purchasing decisions. It is clear that the performance of a graphics computer has a large bearing on its ability to solve complex problems, but the problems themselves are of such a wide variety that it is extremely difficult to characterize the machine's performance for all the uses to which it might be put. We have some extremely crude ways to characterize the performance of the pieces that make up a graphics computer. But we have not yet succeeded in developing performance metrics that enable people to easily see whether a graphics computer will have sufficient performance for the problem set that is important to them.

A great deal of energy has been invested in developing ways to quantify graphics performance. Have these efforts helped the industry or have they only served to confuse people even more? This panel takes a look at the attempts that have been made to develop useful measures of graphics performance and how those measurements may be used to compare systems from different vendors. More importantly, the panelists will describe the cave- ats and limitations of various benchmarking metrics and provide some real-world insight into how people might be able to apply published graphics benchmark results to their own needs.

## Background
As a precursor to NCGA's Graphics Performance Characterization (GPC) Committee, the Bay Area SIGGRAPH group laid some groundwork that classified graphics performance measurement efforts into four categories:
- Primitive level (e.g., vectors per second)
- Picture level (draw a picture or a sequence of pictures)
- Systems level (include interactivity considerations: mouse, disk, bus, graphics, CPU)
- Application level (model behavior of a specific application)

After more than five years of forward progress in the graphics industry, these levels still seem to accurately classify our efforts to quantify graphics performance. The panelists will describe how current graphics characterization efforts (Xmark, PLB, viewperf, and the ubiquitous "triangles/sec") fit into the classification levels listed above and how results from each of these benchmarks should be interpreted. Furthermore, we will show how these benchmark results can be misinterpreted. Panelists will each relate some real life anecdotes that show the inadequacies of our current graphics benchmarking techniques. Finally, the panelists will provide some personal advice to people who are trying to sort through the maze of graphics benchmark results in order to make a prod- uct differentiation decision.

### Jim Bushnell
The OpenGL community has made great strides in providing a common window system independent API and a corresponding conformance test suite. Since the OpenGL functionality is now consistent across a variety of implementations, it is obvious that common tools are also required for measuring OpenGL performance.

A group of OpenGL implementors formed early this year to define and develop these tools. The group has been focusing on developing an application/picture level type benchmark and on developing a benchmarking tool to measure primitive level performance. The status, issues and items remaining to be completed will be the focus of this panelist's presentation.

### David Cooper
Ultimately, the end user of a computer system wants to know how fast he/she can get his/her job done. Typically this means the sooner the better. While this could conceivably be boiled down to one number for each computer system, it almost never is done. The number is dependent on the computer, the mix of applications and how the end-user uses the applications. Because this problem is intractable for the computer vendors, they supply a series of computer subsystem numbers which allows the end-user to make an informed decision based on knowledge of their usage patterns.

The benchmarks used by the system vendors are becoming increasingly more sophisticated. These benchmarks take into account a variety of ways real applications make use of the various subsystems of the computer. They replace simple benchmarks of yesteryear which were easily manipulated into giving peak results rarely obtained by any application.

| Benchmark | Performance Measure | Replaces |
|-----------|--------------------|----------|
| SPECint92 | CPU integer | MIPS |
| SPECfp92 | CPU floating point | MFLOPS |
| Xmark93 | Xwindow system | X11perf Overall |
| PLBwire93 | 3D wireframe graphics | 3D vectors/sec |
| PLBsurf93 | 3D shaded surface graphics | 3D polygons/sec |

The above benchmarks are the current industry standard metrics for stating CPU and graphics performance. They were created by the

SPEC and GPC committees both administered by NCGA.

Xmark93 is a weighted geometric mean of 447 separate simple X primitive benchmarks. It is the least application oriented of all the listed benchmarks. The XPC project is working on creating a more application oriented X performance metric by early 1995.

The Picture Level Benchmark (PLB) defines a Benchmark Interchange Format (BIF) and a program which times the display of a BIF file using any arbitrary graphics API. HP supports a Starbase, HP-PHIGS and PEXlib version of the PLB. The PLB can produce a literal or optimized number. The literal number provides an apples-to-apples comparison of different systems and API's doing exactly the same graphics work. The optimzed number produces the same picture as the literal but allows leeway for optimizing to specific API's or platforms.

PLBwire93 is the geometric mean, both literal and optimized, of 3 standardized BIF files taken from real 3D wireframe applications such as EDS/Unigraphics. The benchmarks measure many real world application factors not found in vectors/sec numbers such as, vectors per polyline, color changes, linetypes, etc.

PLBsurf93 is the geometric mean, both literal and optimized, of 4 standardized BIF files taken from real 3D surfaces applications such as Matra Datavision. The files measure lighted and shaded performance of polygons, complex polygons, triangle strips, quad meshes, multiple lights, positional lights, etc.

All of these benchmarks combined give an excellent indication of the potential performance of the workstation in question. Unfortunately there are several factors which may prevent the application user from getting the full potential performance indicated. The application may make extensive use of some part of the system which is not measured, or the application developers may not do the necessary work to get the full potential performance of the hardware. For example, an application compiled without optimizations could see 1/2 to 1/3 the potential performance of the system.

Tuning an application to make efficient use of the graphics subsystem is often required to get the full potential from the workstation. Making use of the full set of system resources and the performance graphics primitives and attributes in an application will assure a high performance port. Once this is done, the graphics benchmarks are an accurate measure of relative graphics performance as seen by the application.

## Randi Rost

What is a vector? Ken Anderson got people together more than five years ago to try and standardize the term "vector" that was used in the "vectors per second" performance claims. The group that was formed became the GPC Committee. More than five years have gone by, and we still don't have complete consensus on the definition of a vector!

There are numerous reasons to take primitive level performance claims with several large grains of NaCL. First, it is usually not stated whether the performance was measured through a supported API or whether the performance claims represent (unrealizable) hardware potential. Second, the conditions of the test are seldom stated. How many pixels were written by each primitive? Were the primitives randomly oriented or horizontally aligned? Did the color change at each vertex? Was lighting enabled? Depth-cueing? In a recent issue of the GPC Quarterly, we published the results of our survey of primitive level performance claims. It turned out that there was actually a large amount of similarity between the vendors reporting primitive level benchmark results. Unfortunately, not all the vendors participated in this "coming out" party.

Another reason that primitive level performance doesn't necessarily correlate well with application level performance is that the primitives drawn in the primitive level tests are very contrived. Applications won't ever generate thousands of primitives that each cover some specific number of pixels on the screen. Chances are,

most applications won't even use the same attribute settings as those used in the primitive level tests. Primitive level benchmarks are typically used by a company to state their graphics performance as positively as possible, so they often look for a definition of primitives that shows their product in the best possible light. A company might define triangles to cover anywhere from 3 to 50 pixels in order to produce the best possible "triangles per second" rate. A company might be tempted to overstate its actual performance by a factor of two by assuming that back face culling will be on, and half of all incoming triangles will be discarded.

All of these add up to the fact that it is very dangerous to use primitive level performance claims for anything more than broad classification of graphics performance. It is quite possible that systems from two different vendors will run your application at the same speed, even though one vendor quotes twice the primitive performance of the other. Investigate primitive level performance claims carefully if you choose to use them at all to make a buying decision.

## Jerry Schneble

Benchmarking graphics systems requires skillful use of good old common sense.

1. Use the NCGA PLB GPC as a starting point to find the fastest possible vendors. Then use price/performance data to pick the "best" vendor.
2. The system cannot update the graphics data any faster than the refresh rate of the graphics monitor. Anyone claiming otherwise is either lying or not displaying all of the data in the frame.
3. Frame rates below one frame/second are useless and should be considered "static" graphics. Anyone falling below this limit, should not be considered for interactive graphics.
4. Use the KISS Principle. The easiest benchmark is to say one thousand and one to yourself mentally and count the number of frames. This is the quickest and most economical benchmark.
5. Some graphics packages have built in frame/sec counters as well as object content/frame dialogues. These can be used for KISS benchmarks also. All software vendors should supply this feature.
6. If you can afford it, use the PLB with your own representative data and representative operations. Use a scalable data set or sets so you can identify system bottlenecks and map the performance range of the "best" system. Use the performance map to specify and purchase the "best" system.
7. Write the performance specifications into the purchase agreement. If the delivered production system does not perform, have a penalty clause that requires the vendor to buy back the system.
8. Buyer Beware !!!

Good Luck!

## Lynn Thorsen-Jensen

The GPC Picture Level Benchmark (PLB) has made excellent inroads toward providing a standard measuring metric for graphics performance. While the PLB is an admirable beginning, it does not provide a comprehensive solution for anyone, end-user or otherwise, who is trying to understand the graphics performance available through the myriad of graphics products from the hardware vendors of today. Some of the limitations that will be addressed during the panel presentation include:

1. Not all graphics hardware vendors publish benchmark results
2. The PLB measurements can be confusing and misleading
3. The current benchmarks do not yet cover the more advanced features and primitives available from many of the hardware vendors
4. There is not an accurate way of correlating PLB numbers to actual graphics performance in an application environment
5. The PLBs can be easily misinterpreted

# Is Visualization REALLY Necessary?
# The Role of Visualization in Science, Engineering, and Medicine

Chair
Nahum D. Gershon, The MITRE Corporation

Panelists
Richard Mark Friedhoff, Visicom Corporation
John Gass, Boeing Computer Services
Robert Langridge, University of California, San Francisco
Hans-Peter Meinzer, German Cancer Center, Heidelberg
Justin D. Pearlman, Beth Israel Hospital, Harvard Medical School

This panel and the audience will discuss if the use of visualization has changed the way scientists, engineers, and physicians conduct their business. The panelists will examine, each in his own field, if it is possible to achieve the same results and effectiveness without using these dazzling visualization tools. In other words: are these just pretty pictures?

Throughout recent history, scientists and engineers used simple or complicated graphs to represent their data visually or just looked at the numbers trying to understand the phenomena they represent. With the advent of computers and modern display technology, it has become possible to represent data visually in two or higher dimensions using color, simulated shading and lighting, texture, and stereo.

"Visualization in Scientific Computing is emerging as a major computer-based field... As a tool for applying computers to science, it offers a way to see the unseen... As a technology, Visualization in Scientific Computing promises radical improvements in the human/computer interface and may make human-in-the-loop problems approachable. ...limited visualization facilities and limited access to visualization facilities are major bottlenecks to progress." This was the "prophecy" of the October 1986 National Science Foundation (NSF)-sponsored meeting [3]. Since then, many scientists, computer scientists, and engineers worked hard to develop new visualization tools and methods and to apply them to science, engineering, medicine, and education.

After 8 years of intense development in the field of visualization, comes the moment of truth. Has this visionary promise been fulfilled, or this dream has not come true? More specifically, "Is Visualization REALLY Necessary?" could mean:

- Has visualization increased productivity in science, medicine, and engineering? Or, has visualization enabled industry, science, medicine, and government to comprehend large amounts of data?
- Has visualization been successful in making complexity more comprehensible?
- Have any breakthroughs been made in science, medicine or engineering using visualization?
- Are research, research and development, and clinical practice today different from the way they were before visualization?
- Is it possible to achieve the same results and effectiveness without using these dazzling tools?
- Are these just pretty pictures? (where is the beef?)
- If they are, what should be done to fulfill the dream?

The audience and the public have been encouraged to submit samples of slides and video material illustrating effective and valuable visualizations.

**Nahum Gershon:** *Introduction and The Role of Visualization in the Earth Sciences*
Visualization has been used extensively by the Earth science and other communities. This use ranges from simple visualizations using 2-D representations to more complex 3-D visualizations using animation. The data sets could be both complex and massive. Some Earth scientists feel that the computer science and engineering communities do not listen to their needs. For example, there are difficulties in dealing with large data sets and with disparate data formats and types (e.g., continuous and disparate data sets). In addition, intuitive representations of data in higher dimensions than 3-D are needed. Finally, at the age of rapid telecommunications and information highways, there is a growing need to collaborate across the network. The Earth science community urgently needs new software systems that allow to perform remote visualizations bridging among disparate visualization packages and user preferences. Progress in all of these areas will make visualization much more useful and effective in the Earth science and other communities.

**John Gass:** *Is Visualization Really Necessary in Industry?*
Visualization is everything. In the aerospace industry, due to the huge scale and complexity of our models and mathematical representations computer aided design and manufacturing are necessities. In support of these activities, visualization of massive scientific data and of gigabytes of design data is a routine operation. Tomorrow's airliner may be explored today in fine detail from every possible angle to plan for assembly, safety, and comfort.

**Robert Langridge:** *The Role of Visualization in Molecular Biology*
The developments in computer graphics hardware which made it such a powerful tool for computational molecular biology were:
1) Interactive, real time, three dimensional rotation (1964).
2) Time sliced (tachistoscopic) stereo (1970).
3) Real time vector color systems (1979).

However, the developments in computer graphics which have gained the most attention in the last ten years have been in the realm of "realistic" representation of objects and scenes, developments which at present only have value in molecular biology research in the production of illustrations for publications or lectures ("realism" in molecular displays often mean realistic displays of plastic models of molecules - models which merely simulate those which can be built on the lab bench and which make minimal use of the freedom which computer graphics provides).

Most day-to-day research demands the ability to manipulate the molecules in three dimensions and in real time (that is the USER'S real-time, not the molecular time being simulated). A system that provides real time, interactive three dimensional ray traced images of arbitrary objects is not here yet. Until it is, the representation of molecules in the classical chemical way as lines for covalent bonds, with clouds of points or meshes as surfaces, meets the needs of the practicing chemist or molecular biologist, though it is often convenient to switch between the real-time (usually vector) interactive display and the shaded "realistic" display.

I emphasize that molecular graphics systems are far from satisfactory for the average user who is more interested in the science to be done than in the computer, an individual who I have described as "aggressively apathetic" about computers. The chemist wants to do chemistry, not computer science. Satisfactory means have yet to be found for the analysis of the dynamics of macromolecular interactions, a problem that will become more acute as the speed of the associated computers increases by orders of magnitude over the next few years. Biochemical complexity is not merely three dimensional, it extends into the time domain.

**Hans-Peter Meinzer:** *The Role of Volume Visualization in Medicine*
For 100 years, two-dimensional Roentgen images have been used for medical diagnosis. Today, several other imaging techniques are available, e.g., Computed Tomography (CT) and Magnetic Resonance Imaging (MRI) producing image slices of the body. There has been a considerable amount of work using series of CT and MRI slices to produce three-dimensional (3-D) views, or volume visualizations. These techniques are still mainly used at the laboratory and are not commonly utilized in clinical routine. Radiologists have been quite hesitant to accept the new 3-D volume visualization, claiming that "We don't need it." Surgeons, on the other hand, are enthusiastic about the possibility of looking into the body before operating on it. They say that these techniques improve their work significantly.

The real problem today is not the visualization but the process of identification and classification of volume elements. We do not completely understand how human beings perceive images and thus we are not able to implement an algorithm and strategies for image understanding. A large amount of research is now devoted to closing the gap between the millions of pixels in an image and the symbolic description of its contents (the signal-to-symbol gap).

**Justin D. Pearlman:** *The Changing Role of Visualization in Medicine*
Medicine has the mandate to save lives and alleviate suffering. This is achieved (or not) by iterations of data collection, interpretation and decision-making. Imaging has played a central role in this process, but until recently the main role of computers in clinical medicine has been data acquisition and management. Modification of the resultant images was minimal. One force for change, driven both by researchers and insurers, is quantitation on computer images. A bigger push forward in computer visualization came from magnetic resonance imaging (MRI). It typically requires data transformation, conversion and reformatting as preparation for effective visualization.

The methods in clir.'cal practice fall into two categories: those performed either automatically or by technician input only, and those that enable interactive visualization by the clinician. An example of the former is the UMS CUBE program that constructs composite angiograms of the coronary arteries with minimal supervision from data obtained noninvasively by MRI. An example of the latter is 3D multislice reformatting by graphics prescription. These and other examples will be presented.

The role of computer-aided visualization in medicine is burgeoning. The demand is driven primarily by MRI but also by other technologies. Reformatting of 3-D and 4-D datasets, selective projection angiography of the coronary arteries and other vessels, and production of parameter maps are good examples. As data collections increase, there will also be a need for automated effective data reduction. Visualization plays an essential role in the rapid recognition of abnormalities and their relation to anatomy. The demand for computer assisted visualization is escalating.

**Richard Mark Friedhoff:** *Problem Solving With and Without Visualization*
Several case studies suggest that visualization can be defined as the substitution of preconscious visual competencies and machine computation for conscious thinking. This definition appears to be useful in most if not all instances in which data is rendered as imagery, including scientific, medical, and design visualization. In each case, visualization replaces ad hoc or improvised, consciously mediated processes with preconscious, hard-wired processes resident in the physiology of the visual system.

Although this distinction between conscious thinking and preconscious visual processing is easy to define qualitatively, and while qualitative distinctions are useful, much remains to be accomplished before we can define this dichotomy more formally and reconcile the perspective of the scientist interested in understanding visualization with that of the visual physiologist or psychophysicist. Vision scientists, more typically utilizing the terminology "preattentive," tend to view vision from the bottom up. Case studies in visualization suggest that this perspective is sometimes opposite that which is useful to the visualization scientist who is obliged to view visual processes from the top down and for whom the molar term "preconscious" may be more suitable.

**Afterword**
Throughout recent history, scientists and engineers used simple or complicated graphs to represent their data visually or just looked at the numbers trying to understand the phenomena they represent. With the advent of computers and modern display technology, it has become possible to represent data visually in two or higher dimensions using color, simulated shading and lighting, texture, and stereo. After years of intense development in the field of visualization, comes the moment of truth: has visualization changed the way scientists, engineers, and physicians conduct their business, or are these just pretty pictures?

**References**
[1] Friedhoff, Richard, Visualization: The Second Computer Revolution, W.H. Freeman and Company, 1991.
[2] Gershon, N.D. and Miller, C.G., "Dealing with the Data Deluge," *IEEE Spectrum*, July 1993, pp. 28-32.
[3] McCormick, B.H, DeFanti, T.A., and Brown, M.D., Visualization in Scientific Computing, *Computer Graphics*, Vol. 21, no. 6, November 1987.

# Conference Committee

## CONFERENCE CHAIR

Dino Schweitzer
(US Air Force Academy)

## CONFERENCE COMMITTEE CHAIRS

Patti Harrison, *Conference Coordinator*
Andrew S. Glassner, *Papers*
 (Xerox PARC)
Mike Keeler, *Panels*
 (Silicon Graphics, Inc.)
Mike Bailey, *Courses*
 (San Diego Supercomputer Center)
Lucy Petrovich, *Electronic Theater*
 (Savannah College of Art and Design)
Kathy Tanaka, *Electronic Theater*
 (independent)
Deanna Morse, *Art and Design Show*
 (Grand Valley State University)
Thomas A. DeFanti, *VROOM*
 (University of Illinois at Chicago)
Maxine D. Brown, *VROOM*
 (University of Illinois at Chicago)
Jacquelyn Ford Morie, *The Edge*
 (University of Central Florida)
Christopher Stapleton, *The Edge*
 (Jack Rouse Associates)
Nancy Ingle, *SIGkids*
 (Orange County Public Schools, Evans High School)
Gray Lorig, *Electronic Media*
 (Barking Trout Productions)
David J. Kasik, *Exhibits*
 (Boeing Commercial Airplane Group)
Brian Blau, *Events Planning*
 (Autodesk, Inc.)
Walt Bransford, *Environmental Space Designer*
 (Premisys Corporation)
Gary Jackemuk, *Student Volunteers*
 (Digital Domain)
Jeff Jortner, *Registration*
 (Sandia National Laboratories)
Mark Hall, *Merchandise*
 (Sun Microsystems, Inc.)
Ralph Orlick, *Computer Systems*
 (University of Illinois at Chicago)
Raoul Buron, *Organization Development*
 (U.S. Air Force Academy)
Carol Byram, *Public Relations*
 (Sony Computer Peripheral Products Company)
Leigh C. Morgan, *Speaker Materials Chair*
 (independent)

Randy Nickel, *Marketing*
 (Technology Marketing Consulting)
John Michael Pierobon, *International Operations*
 (independent)
David Spoelstra, *Audio-Visual and Donations*
 (DFS Consulting)

## CONFERENCE PLANNING COMMITTEE

Maxine D. Brown (University of Illinois at Chicago)
Ray Elliott (independent)
John Fujii (Hewlett-Packard Company)
Patti Harrison (SIGGRAPH 94 Conference Coordinator)
Brian Herzog (Sun Microsystems, Inc.)
Betsy Johnsmiller (SIGGRAPH 95 Conference Coordinator)
Robert L. Judd (Los Alamos National Laboratory)
Peter Meechan (Wavefront Technologies, Inc.)
Molly Morgan-Kuhns (CPC Coordinator)
Adele Newton (Newton Associates, Inc.)
Mark Resch (Luna Imaging, Inc.)
Dino Schweitzer (US Air Force Academy)

## PAPERS COMMITTEE

Andrew S. Glassner (Xerox PARC)
Kurt Akeley (Silicon Graphics, Inc.)
Norman Badler (University of Pennsylvania)
Alan Barr (California Institute of Technology)
James F. Blinn (California Institute of Technology)
Ingrid Carlbom (Digital Equipment Corporation)
Michael F. Cohen (Princeton University)
Rob Cook (Light Source, Inc.)
Alain Fournier (University of British Columbia)
Ned Greene (Apple Computer, Inc.)
Christoph Hoffmann (Purdue University)
John Hughes (Brown University)
James Kajiya (Microsoft Corporation)
Michael Kass (Apple Computer, Inc.)
R. Victor Klassen (Xerox Webster Research Center)
Wolfgang Krueger (German National Research Center for
 Computer Science)
Gary Meyer (University of Oregon)
Greg Nielson (Arizona State University)
Tomoyuki Nishita (Fukuyama University)
Randy Pausch (University of Virginia)
Ken Perlin (New York University)
Przemyslaw Prusinkiewicz (University of Calgary)
Jarek Rossignac (IBM T.J. Watson Research Center)
Robert F. Sproull (Sun Microsystems Computer Corporation)
Ken Torrance (Cornell University)

## PANELS COMMITTEE AND JURY

Mike Keeler (Silicon Graphics, Inc.)
Mark Bolas (Fakespace, Inc.)
Donna Cox (National Center for Supercomputing Applications)
Charles Hansen (Los Alamos National Laboratory)
Leo Hourvitz (Broderbund Software)
F. Kenton Musgrave (The George Washington University)
Vibeke Sorenson (California Institute of the Arts)
Pauline Tso (Rhythm & Hues)

## COURSES COMMITTEE

Mike Bailey (San Diego Supercomputer Center)
Sheldon Applegate (GDE Systems)
Ed Brabant (Megatek Corporation)
Wayne Carlson (The Ohio State University)
Rich Ehlers (Evans & Southerland)
Stephan R. Keith (Sterling Software)
Nan Schaller (Rochester Institute of Technology)
Scott Senften (Shell Development Corporation)

## TECHNICAL SKETCHES JURY

Andrew S. Glassner (Xerox PARC)
Loren Carpenter (Pixar)
Paul Haeberli (Silicon Graphics, Inc.)
Karl Sims (Thinking Machines Corporation)

## INTERNATIONAL COMMITTEE

John Michael Pierobon (independent)
Len Breen
Achameleh Debela (North Carolina Central University)
Masa Inakage (The Media Studio, Inc.)
Myeong Won Lee (Korea Telecom)
Joachim Rix (Fraunhofer Institut für Graphische
Datenverarbeitung (IGD))
Roberto Scopigno (CNUCE, Consiglio Nazionale delle Richerche)
Hung Chuan Teh (National University of Singapore)
Marcelo Knorich Zuffo (Universidade de São Paulo)

## COMPUTER SYSTEMS

Ralph Orlick (University of Illinois at Chicago)
George Konstantinopoulos (University of Illinois at Chicago)
C. J. Murzyn (University of Illinois at Chicago)

## ELECTRONIC MEDIA

Gray Lorig (Barking Trout Productions)
Tim Desley (Cray Research, Inc.)
John Grimes (Illinois Institute of Technology)
John C. Hart (Washington State University)
Stephan R. Keith (Sterling Software)
Jamie Thompson (TIVOLI Systems, Inc.)

## FUNDAMENTALS SEMINAR

Wayne E. Carlson, Chair (The Ohio State University)
Mike Bailey (San Diego Supercomputer Center)
Judith R. Brown (The University of Iowa)

## SIGGRAPH BOWL 2 ORGANIZING COMMITTEE

James F. Blinn (California Institute of Technology)
Kellogg Booth (University of British Columbia)
Nick England (University of North Carolina at Chapel Hill)
Pat Hanrahan (Princeton University)
Paul Heckbert (Carnegie Mellon University)
Rob Pike (AT&T Bell Laboratories)
Thomas Porter (Pixar)

## PUBLICATIONS PRODUCTION

Steve Cunningham, Proceedings and Proceedings CD-ROM
    Production Editor (California State University Stanislaus)
Stephan R. Keith, Course Notes CD-ROM Production Editor
    (Sterling Software)
Stephen Spencer, Proceedings Consulatant
    (The Ohio State University)
Rosalee Wolfe, Slide Sets Production Editor (DePaul University)

## TECHNICAL SLIDE SET JURY

Mike Bailey (San Diego Supercomputer Center)
Andrew S. Glassner (Xerox PARC)
Mike Keeler (Silicon Graphics, Inc.)

## COURSES REVIEWERS

Sheldon Applegate (GDE Systems)
Mike Bailey (San Diego Supercomputer Center)
Ed Brabant (Megatek Corporation)
Wayne Carlson (The Ohio State University)
Rich Ehlers (Evans & Southerland)
Richard Frost (San Diego Supercomputer Center)
Dave Nadeau (San Diego Supercomputer Center)
Nan Schaller (Rochester Institute of Technology)
Scott Senften (Shell Development Corporation)
Jon Steinhart (Jonathon Steinhart Consulting, Inc.)
Warren Wahhenpack (Louisiana State University)

## PAPERS REVIEWERS

| | |
|---|---|
| Jan Allebach | Sheue-Ling Chang |
| John Amanatides | Eric Chen |
| Peter Anderson | Young-il Choo |
| James Arvo | Jung-Hong Chuang |
| Ron Baecker | Charles K. Chui |
| Chandrajit Bajaj | Elaine Cohen |
| Harlyn H. Baker | Brook Conner |
| Thomas Banchoff | Sabine Coquillart |
| Michael Banks | William Cowan |
| Brian A. Barsky | Jim Cremer |
| Richard Bartels | Frank Crow |
| Lyn Bartram | Wolfgang Dahmen |
| Dan Baum | John Danskin |
| Thad Beier | Leila De Floriani |
| Adrian D. Bell | Philippe de Reffye |
| Fausto Bernardini | Michael F. Deering |
| Rama Bindinagavale | Tom DeFanti |
| Gary Bishop | Tony DeRose |
| Avi Bleiweis | Bob Drebin |
| Jules Bloomenthal | Tom Duff |
| Bruce Blumberg | Deba Dutta |
| Harold Boll | Gershon Elber |
| Carlos F. Borges | Conal Elliott |
| Paul Borrel | Steve Ellis |
| Adrian Bowyer | David A. Epstein |
| David Brainard | Brian Evans |
| Mark H. Brown | Rida Farouki |
| Beat D. Bruderlin | Paul Fearing |
| Armin Bruderlin | Steven K. Feiner |
| Pere Brunet | James A. Ferwerda |
| John Buchanan | Dan Field |
| Tom Calvert | Yuval Fisher |
| A. T. Campbell, III | Eugene Fiume |
| Vasilis Capoyleas | Kurt Fleischer |
| Loren Carpenter | Thomas A. Foley |
| Justine Cassell | A. Robin Forrest |
| Ed Catmull | David R. Forsey |
| Indranil Chakravary | Farhad Fouladi |

## PAPERS REVIEWERS (Continued)

F. David Fracchia
Randolph Franklin
Henry Fuchs
George Furnas
Don Fussell
Michel Gangnet
Mark Ganter
Geoffrey Gardner
W. Gates
Guido Gerig
Walter Gish
Michael Gleicher
Ron Goldman
Steven Gortler
David Gossard
Stefan Gottschalk
John Granieri
Chuck Grant
Mark Green
Cindy Grimm
Markus Gross
Brian Guenter
Paul Haeberli
Hans Hagen
Tom Hahn
Eric Haines
Chuck Hains
Roy Hall
Michael Halle
Jim Hanan
Pat Hanrahan
Charles Hansen
Allan Hansen
John C. Hart
Paul Heckbert
Martin Held
James Helman
Mark R. Henderson
Daryl Hepting
Kenneth Herndon
Eric Herrmann
Roger Hersch
Lambertus Hesselink
Deborah Hix
Larry F. Hodges
Jessica Hodgins
Karl-Heinz Hoehne
Michael Hohmeyer
William Hsu
Don Hubbard
Philip Hubbard
John Hughes
Insung Ihm
Masa Inakage
Robert J.K. Jacob
F.W. Jansen
Thomas Jensen
Robert B. Jerard
Peter Jones
Ken Joy
Moon R. Jung
Jaap Kaandorp
Alan Kalvin

Kazufumi Kaneda
Johannes Kasa
Rangachar Kasturi
Arie E. Kaufman
Henry Kaufman
Dave Kirk
Frederick Kitson
Gudrun Klinker
Keith Knox
Hyeongseok Ko
Craig Kolb
James Korein
Thurston Lacalli
James Lackner
Paul Lalonde
Tom Lane
Anselmo Lastra
Maria Laughlin
David Laur
Mark Leather
Jon Leech
Creon Levit
Haim Levkowitz
Marc Levoy
Bob Lewis
Ming Lin
Bruce Lindbloom
James S. Lipscomb
Dani Lischinski
Pete Litwinowicz
Bart Locanthi
Suresh Kumar Lodha
Charles Loop
William E. Lorensen
Maria Loughlin
William Luken
Bruce MacDonald
Christine L. MacKenzie
Jock D. Mackinlay
Bruce Madsen
Pattie Maes
Nadia Magnenat-Thalmann
Tom Malzbender
Dinesh Manocha
Paul Martin
Thomas Marzetta
Nelson Max
Donald Meagher
Barbra Meier
Jai Menon
Dimitri Metaxas
Lee Metrick
Jim Michener
Gavin Miller
Rodney Miller
James R. Miller
Mark Mine
Don Mitchell
Joe Mitchell
Joan Mitchell
Joshua Mittleman
Eric Mjolsness
Steve Molnar

John Montrym
F. Kenton Musgrave
Eihachiro Nakamae
Patrick Naughton
Bruce Naylor
Russell S. Nelson
J. Thomas Ngo
David Nichols
Tom Olson
James Painter
Nicholas M. Patrikalakis
Darwyn Peachey
Catherine Pelachaud
Qunsheng Peng
Sandy Pentland
Alex Pentland
Jorg Peters
Cary Phillips
Tom Piantanida
Steve Platt
Helmut Pottmann
Pierre Poulin
Roger Powell
Dennis Proffitt
Vadakkedathu T. Rajan
Ajay Rajkumar
Ari Rappoport
Bill Reeves
Bruce Reichlen
W. Remphrey
Dan Robbins
George Robertson
Alyn P. Rockwood
Jon Rokne
Chris Romanzin
Remi Ronfard
David S. H. Rosenthal
Holly E. Rushmeier
Takafumi Saito
Georgios Sakas
David H. Salesin
Hanan Samet
Dietmar Saupe
Carla Scaletti
Greg Schechter
Bengt-Olaf Schneider
Peter Schroder
William Schroeder
Thomas W. Sederberg
Mark Segal
Carlo H. Sequin
Nimish Shah
Chris Shaw
Mikio Shinya
Peter Shirley
Ken Shoemake
Francois Sillion
Karl Sims
Alvy Ray Smith
Stuart Smith
Julias Smith
John Snyder
Maureen Stone

Paul S. Strauss
Kokichi Sugihara
Richard Szeliski
Atsushi Takaghi
Tokiichiro Takahashi
Masashi Takaki
Toshimitsu Tanaka
Gabriel Taubin
Joann M. Taylor
Seth Teller
Demetri Terzopoulos
Daniel Thalmann
Larry Thayer
Spencer Thomas
Rich Thomson
Takashi Totsuka
Lloyd Treinish
Jack Tumblin
Greg Turk
Kenneth Turkowski
Joshua U. Turner
Jayaram Udupa
Peter Undrill
Sam Uselton
Michiel van de Panne
Allen Van Gelder
Jarke J. van Wijk
Brad Vander Zanden
George Vanecek
Tomas Varady
Marlon Veal
Luiz Velho
Baba Vemuri
Pamela Vermeer
Marie-Luce Viaud
Doug Voorhies
John Wallace
Gregory J. Ward
Colin Ware
Joe Warren
Keith Waters
Robert E. Webber
Kevin Weiler
William Welch
Stuart Wells
Beth Wenzel
Lee Westover
Scott Whitman
Turner Whitted
Jane Wilhelms
Lance Williams
Jim Winget
Peter Wisskirchen
Andrew Witkin
Ian H. Witten
Hans Jurgen Wolters
Brian Wyvill
Geoff Wyvill
Roni Yagel
David Zeltzer
Xinmin Zhao
Jerry Zhou
Michael J. Zyda

## PROFESSIONAL SUPPORT

### ACM SIGGRAPH Conference Coordinators

Patti Harrison, SIGGRAPH 94
Linda Maher, Deputy Conference Coordinator, SIGGRAPH 94
Betsy Johnsmiller, SIGGRAPH 95

### ACM SIGGRAPH Program Director

Donna Baglio

### Administrative Assistants

Charlotte Smart, Courses
Kathy Mancall, Panels
Chase Garfinkle, Papers

### Audio-Visual Support

*AVW Audio Visual, Inc.*
Ed Goodman
Gary Clark
Jim Costigan

### Conference Accounting

*Smith, Bucklin & Associates, Inc.*
Roger Albert
Nicholas Chibucos
Jesse Del Toro

### Conference Management

*Smith, Bucklin & Associates, Inc.*
Cindy Stark
Jackie Groszek
Peggy Sloyan
Julie Walker

### Conference Travel Agency

*ATI Travel Management, Inc.*
Susan Neal
Laurie Shapiro

### Service Contractor

*GES Exposition Services*
John Patronski
Bob Borsz
John Loveless

### Exhibition Management

*Hall-Erickson, Inc.*
Pete Erickson
Barbara Voss
Mike Weil

### Graphic Design/Editing

*Quorum Incorporated*
Doug Hesseltine
Tom Rieke

### Copy Coordination

*Smith, Bucklin & Associates, Inc.*
Leona Caffey

### Electronic Theater Director

Johnie Hugh Horn (big Research)

### Public Relations/Marketing

*Hi Tech Communications, Inc.*
Gary Thompson
Wendy Moro

# Exhibitors

5D Solutions
Abekas Video Systems
Academic Press
Accom, Inc.
Addison-Wesley Publishing Company
Adobe Systems, Inc.
Advanced Digital Imaging
Advanced Graphics Technology
Advanced Imaging/AVC Presentation
Advanced Visual Systems Inc.
AGFA Division, Miles, Inc.
AK Peters, Ltd.
Alias Research Inc.
Altamira Software Corporation
American Showcase
Ampex Systems Corporation
AmPro Corporation
Anacapa Micro Products, Inc.
Animation Magazine
Apple Computer, Inc.
Apunix Computer Services
Ascension Technology Corporation
ASDG, Incorporated
Association for Computing Machinery (ACM)
AT&T Multimedia Software Solutions
Aurora Systems
auto.des.sys, Inc.
Autodesk, Inc.
Avid Technology, Inc.
AV Video
Barco, Inc.
Biografx Labs
Bit 3 Computer Corporation
Bruvel, Inc.
Byte by Byte Corporation
CAD Institute, Inc.
Cameleon
Cambridge Animation Systems Limited
Canon U.S.A., Inc.
CD Rom World/Virtual Reality World
CELCO
Cine-Byte Imaging Inc.
Ciprico Inc.
CIRAD Unité de Modelisation
Color Publishing
Computer Artist
Computer Design, Inc.
Computer Graphics World
Computer Pictures
Computer Video
Computer Visualizations, Inc.
Coryphaeus Software Inc.
CoSA (The Company of Science & Art)
CrystalGraphics, Inc.

Crystal River Engineering
Cyberware
Cymbolic Sciences International
Data Translation
Depthography Inc.
Desktop Video World
Diaquest, Inc.
Digibotics, Inc.
Digital Connectivity
Digital Equipment Corporation
Digital Processing Systems
Discreet Logic Inc.
Division
DVS GmbH Digital Video Systems
Eastman Kodak Company
Electric Image, Inc.
ElectroGIG USA, Inc.
Electronic Publishing
ENCAD, Inc.
ENEL
Engineering Animation, Inc.
Epson
Eurographics
Evans & Sutherland
Extron Electronics
Falcon Systems, Inc.
FARO Technologies Inc.
Fast Electronic U.S., Inc.
Focus Graphics, Inc.
Folsom Research Inc.
FOR.A Corporation
Forefront Graphics
Fractal Design Corporation
Fraunhofer CRCG, Inc.
Fujitsu Micro Electronics, Inc.
G5G
Genesis Microchip
The Grass Valley Group, Inc.
GW Hannaway & Associates, Inc.
Hash Inc.
Helios Systems
Hewlett-Packard Company
Hotronic, Inc.
IBM Corporation
IEEE Computer Society
Image Resources, Inc.
Imagica Corporation of America
Imagina-INA
Information International Inc. (Triple-I)
Integrated Research
Intelligent Resources Integrated Systems
IRIS Graphics, Inc.
Ithaca Software
ITOCHU Technology, Inc.

JVC Professional Products Company
Kaiser Corporation
Kingston Technology Corporation
Kubota Pacific Computer Inc.
Kurta Corporation
Lasergraphics, Inc.
Legacy Systems International, Inc.
Leitch Incorporated
Lightscape Graphics Software Limited
Lightwave Communications, Inc.
Macromedia
Management Graphics, Inc.
Martin Marietta
Mathematica, Inc.
Matrox Electronic Systems Ltd.
Maximum Strategy, Inc.
Megatek Corporation
Meridian Creative Group
Micron/Green
Minicomputer Exchange
Miranda Technologies Inc.
Mitsubishi Electronics America, Inc.
Mondo 2000
Montpellier LR Technopole
Morgan Kaufmann Publishers
MultiGen Inc.
ND3D
NEC Electronics Inc.
NewGen Systems
NewMedia Magazine
NewTek Inc.
NICOGRAPH
Numerical Algorithms Group, Inc. (NAG)
Odyssey Visual Design
OnLine Magazine
On Production Magazine
Onyx Computing
Open Computing
O'Reilly & Associates, Inc.
Oxberry, Division of Cybernetics Products, Inc.
Pacific Motion
Panasonic Broadcast & Television Systems Company
Parallax Graphics, Inc.
Parallax Software Inc.
PC Graphics & Video
P. E. Photron
PHI Enterprises, Inc.
Pioneer New Media Technologies, Inc.
Pixar
Pixel Magazine/Pixel Vision
PIXIBOX
Polhemus Incorporated
Portable Graphics, Inc.
Post Magazine
Pre-
Prentice Hall PTR
Proxima Corporation
Radiance Software International
Realsoft International
Research Triangle Institute, Electronics & Systems
RFX, Inc.
RGB Spectrum
Roche Image Analysis Systems, Inc.

Ron Scott Inc.
R Squared
Sanyo Fisher (USA) Corporation
Schreiber Instruments, Inc.
Science Accessories Corporation
Scientific Computing & Automation Magazine
Seiko Instruments USA, Inc.
Sense8
Side Effects Software Inc.
SIGGRAPH 95
SIGGRAPH Education Committee
SIGGRAPH Local Groups
SIGGRAPH Video Review
Sigma Electronics, Inc.
Silicon Graphics, Inc.
Silicon Graphics World
Simulation Devices Inc. (SDI Virtual Reality Corporation)
Society of Motion Pictures & Television Engineers
SOFTIMAGE Inc.
Solsource Computers
Sony Electronics Inc.
Springer-Verlag New York, Inc.
StereoGraphics Corporation
Storage Concepts, Inc.
Storage Technology Corporation
Strata Inc.
Sun Microsystems Computer Corporation
Supercomputing '94
Syndesis Corporation
Techexport, Inc.
Tech Images International
Tech-Source Inc.
Tektronix, Inc.
Template Graphics Software, Inc.
Texas Instruments
Texas Memory Systems, Inc.
Texnai, Inc.
Truevision Inc., A RasterOps Company
UNIX Review
VALIS Group
Van Nostrand Reinhold
Vertigo Technology
VIC Hi-Tech Corporation
Videomedia, Inc.
Video Production Systems Company
Video Systems Magazine
Viewpoint Datalabs
Virtuality Entertainment Ltd.
Visionetics International Corporation
Visual Numerics, Inc.
Visual Software
The Vivid Group
Wacom Technology Corporation
Walt Disney Company/Feature Animation
Wasatch Computer Technology, Inc.
Wavefront
Weitek Corporation
John Wiley & Sons
Winsted Corporation
Wired Magazine
Xaos Tools
Yarc Systems Corporation
Zeh Graphics Systems, Inc.

# Index

(Pages marked with * contain panel summaries)

# Cover Image Credits

## Front Cover

"Topiary Dinosaur"
Copyright (C) 1994 Radomír Měch, Przemyslaw Prusinkiewicz, Brian Wyvill (University of Calgary), and Andrew Glassner (Xerox PARC)
A pair of trees are clipped into the shape of a toy dinosaur, defined as an implicit surface. The trees respond to clipping by activating dormant buds and growing new branches. The unpruned trees of the same type are shown in the background. The trees have been modeled using Lindenmayer systems, with an environmentally-sensitive extension to the in-house plant-modeling program pfg. The whole scene was ray-traced using Rayshade, written by Craig Kolb. Special thanks to Mark Hammel for his help with some of the objects. Modeling: Silicon Graphics workstations; rendering: Silicon Graphics and SUN workstations. Reference: "Synthetic topiary," Przemyslaw Prusinkiewicz, Mark James, and Radomír Měch

## Title Page

"Boxes and Bowls"
Copyright (c) 1994, Michael Salisbury, Sean Anderson, Ronen Barzel, and David Salesin, University of Washington
A single scene, drawn in several pen-and-ink illustration styles. Drawing this scene in a variety of styles is recommended as an exercise for illustration students by Henry Pitz in *Ink Drawing Techniques*. The three drawings on top and left are attempts to closely follow examples given in the book, while the lower right is our own stylistic expression. A tone reference for the illustrations was generated using a simple 3D model created with SGI Inventor. Various "stroke textures" were then applied interactively using our pen-and-ink drawing system to create the different illustrations. Finally, the illustrations were output as a PostScript file and printed at 300dpi.
Reference: "Interactive Pen-and-Ink Illustration," Michael P. Salisbury, Sean E. Anderson, Ronen Barzel, David H. Salesin, p. 105

## Back cover, top left

"Sunglasses with a Thin Film Coating"
Copyright 1994, Jay S. Gondek, Gary W. Meyer, and Jonathan G. Newman, University of Oregon
The wavelength-based light scattering function for the lens was characterized by first simulating light incident upon a thin film surface, recording the light scattered in a special data structure, and then using this data structure to render the final image. The texture-mapped environment was created by scanning photographs of a room in Deschutes Hall of the University of Oregon. This image was computed on a Hewlett-Packard 9000/755 workstation.
Reference: "Wavelength Dependent Reflectance Functions," Jay S. Gondek, Gary W. Meyer, and Jonathan G. Newman, p. 218

## Back cover, top right

"Loge with Golden Mask (detail)"
Copyright(c) 1994, Siu C. Hsu and Irene H.H. Lee, Creature House.
A drawing in Skeletal Strokes after the colour lithograph "Loge with Golden Mask" (1894) by Henri de Toulouse-Lautrec (1864-1901). The picture was interactively created from scratch in less than one hour using the Skeletal Draw system on an Intel 80486 PC. Seven types of strokes were used. The whole picture is represented in vector form. Output is in PostScript.
Reference: "Drawing and Animation Using Skeletal Strokes," p. 107

## Back cover, middle left

"Optical Effects Within Water"
Copyright 1994, Tomoyuki Nishita (Fukuyama University) and Eihachiro Nakamae (Hiroshima Prefectural University)
This image was computed on an IRIS Crimson using software by the authors. The image shows optical effects: shafts of light and caustics due to refracted light from waves and the color of water due to scattering/absorption of particles (water molecules and suspensions). Curved surfaces (killer whale) are represented by the improved method of metaballs (or blobs).
Reference: "Method of Displaying Optical Effects within Water using Accumulation Buffer," Tomoyuki Nishita and Eihachiro Nakamae, p. 378

## Back cover, middle right

"Mert with Tarnish"
Shading Reference: Miller, Gavin, "Efficient Algorithms for Local and Global Accessibility Shading", p. 325. Modeling Reference: Williams, Lance, "3D Paint," Proceedings, 1990 Symposium on Interactive 3D Graphics, pp. 225-233. Character design: Bil Maher.

## Back cover, bottom left

"A Sunny Day, High, High Above"
Copyright 1994, Hans K. Pedersen, Carnegie Mellon University.
This image shows a surface that has been displaced along a flow field. It demonstrates that interesting results can be obtained using non-orthogonal displacements. Rendered on an SGI Indigo 2 workstation using software by the author. Thanks to Jakob Gårdsted for his contributions to this image.
Reference: "Displacement Mapping Using Flow Fields," Hans Køhling Pedersen, p. 285

## Back cover, bottom right

"Lilly Library"
Copyright 1994, Architect's Office, Indiana University
Modeled and rendered by Scott Routen and Reuben McFarland using AutoCAD and Radiance
This image shows the existing lighting condition in the main lobby of the Lilly Library on the Bloomington campus of Indiana University. This simulation was prepared to evaluate several solutions to the problem of reflected glare from a large light source overhead. Radiance allows the I.U. Architect's Office to study lighting configurations in detail and to communicate their visual impact with the many individuals involved in making decisions.
Reference: "The RADIANCE Lighting Simulation and Rendering System," Gregory J. Ward, p. 471

# SIGGRAPH Local Groups Active/Forming

## California

*Los Angeles*
Joan Collins
PO Box 90698
Worldway Postal Center
Los Angeles, CA 90009-0698
Phone: +1(310)450-4494
Los_Angeles_SIGGRAPH_Chapter@siggraph.org,

*San Diego*
Mike Amron
2334 Galahad Rd.
San Diego, CA 92123
Phone: +1(619)277-5699

*Silicon Valley*
Dominic Allen
5478 Sharon Lane
San Jose, CA 95124
Phone: +1(408)435-9100x288

## Colorado

*Denver/Boulder*
Dave Miller
PO Box 440785
Aurora, CO 80041
Phone: +1(303)696-6863
Denver/Boulder_SIGGRAPH_Chapter
@siggraph.org

## Georgia

*Atlanta*
Evelyn Hirata
PO Box 250382
Atlanta, GA 30325
Phone: +1(404)785-2911

## Illinois

*Chicago*
Dennis James
P.O. Box 578365
Chicago, IL 60657-8365
Phone: +1(708)387-2149
Chicago_SIGGRAPH_Chapter@siggraph.org

## Massachusetts

*Boston*
Craig J. Mathias
PO Box 194
Bedford, MA 01730
Phone: +1(508)881-6467
New_England_SIGGRAPH_Chapter@siggraph.org

## Minnesota

*Minneapolis/St. Paul*
Stan Bissinger
School of Communication Arts
2526 27th Avenue South
Minneapolis, MN 55406
Phone: +1(612)721-5357
dickm3@aol.com

## New Jersey

*Princeton*
Douglas Dixon
David Sarnoff Research Center
CN 5300
Princeton, NJ 08543-5300
Phone: +1(609)734-3176
Princeton_SIGGRAPH_Chapter@siggraph.org

## New Mexico

*Rio Grande*
David Callahan
Albuquerque, NM, USA
87198-8352
Phone: +1(505)667-1449
Rio_Grande_SIGGRAPH_Chapter@siggraph.org

## New York

*New York*
Deborah Herschmann
SIGMA Imaging
633 3rd Ave
NY, NY 10017
Phone: +1(212)645-0852
New_York_SIGGRAPH_Chapter@siggraph.org

*Rochester*
Karla Kuzawinski
Xerox Business Products
800 Phillips Road
Webster, NY 14580

## North Carolina

*Research Triangle*
Randy Brown
3407 Carriage Trail
Hillsborough, NC 27278
Phone: +1(919)677-8000
Research_Triangle_SIGGRAPH_Chapter@siggraph.org

## Texas

*Dallas*
Wade Smith
PO Box 800691
Dallas, TX, USA 75380-0691
Dallas_SIGGRAPH_Chapter@siggraph.org

*Houston*
Jim Maida
NASA JSC, SP34
Nasa Rd. 1
Houston, TX 77058
Phone: +1(713)483-1113
Houston_Area_SIGGRAPH_Chapter@siggraph.org

## Washington

*Tri Cities Washington*
Don Jones
Battelle Pacific Northwest Labs
Box 999
MS K1-87
Richland, WA 99352
Phone: +1(509)375-2913
Washington_Tri_Cities_Siggraph_Chapter
@siggraph.org

## Washington, D.C.

Washington
P.O. Box 32254
Washington, DC 20007
Phone: +1(703)968-3313
Washington_DC_SIGGRAPH_Chapter@siggraph.org

## Brazil

*Sao Paulo*
Sergio Martinelli
Digital Group
Rua Bairi 294
05059 San Paulo, SP1 Brazil
sigrapsp@lsi.usp.br

## Bulgaria

*Sofia*
Stoyan Maleshkov
Technical Univ of Sofia
Dept of Prog & Computer Appl
1756 Sofia, Bulgaria

## Canada

*Montreal*
Kaveh Kardan
Phone: +1(514)842-6172
kardank@ede.umontreal.ca

*Toronto*
Michael McCool
Deptartment of Computer
Science
University of Toronto
10 King's College Road
Toronto, Ontario M5S 1A4
Phone: +1(416)978-6619
Toronto_SIGGRAPH_Chapter@siggraph.org,

*Vancouver*
Brian D. McMillan
PO Box 33986 Postal Station D
Vancouver, BC, Canada V6J-4L7
Phone: +1(604)822-2466
Vancouver_BC_SIGGRAPH_Chapter@siggraph.org,

## England

*London*
Greg Moore
27 Sinclair House
Sandwish Street
London, WC1H 9PT
Phone: +44(81)362-5000
X7475
London_SIGGRAPH_Chapter@siggraph.org

## France

*Paris*
Alain Chesnais
#2 Rue Henre Matisse
59300 Aulnoy-les-Valenciennes
France
Phone: +33 27-28-42-42
Paris_SIGGRAPH_Chapter@siggraph.org

## Israel

*Central Israel*
Craig Gotsman
Department of Computer
Science
Technion
Haifa 32000
Israel
Central_Israel_SIGGRAPH_Chapter@siggraph.org

## Mexico

*Mexico City*
Arnulfo Zepeda
azepeda@spin.com

## Spain

*Madrid*
Felix Berges Munoz
Postdata
c/ Breton de los Herreros
35 3 Izqda.
Madrid, 28003 Spain
ruy@asterix.fi.upm.es

## Russia

*Moscow*
Yuri Bayakouski
Keldysh Institute of Appl.
Maths
Miusskaya Sq., 4
Moscow, 125047 Russia
Phone: +095 250-7817
Moscow_SIGGRAPH_Chapter@siggraph.org

## Local Groups Steering Committee

Ed Council, Chair
Timberfield Systems
PO Box 2345
Framingham, MA 01701
Phone: +1(508)872-0796

Len Breen
31 Old Gloucester Street
Bloomsbury
London WC1N 3AF
England
Phone: +44 71 242 0551

Alain Chesnais
Wavefront
22 ave Hegesippe Moreau
75018 Paris
France
Phone: +33 1 44 90 11 49

Jeff Jortner, Director for Local
Groups
Sandia National Laboratories
Department 1408, MS 1109
Albuquerque, NM 87185-1109
Phone: +1(505)845-7556

Scott Lang
United Nations Intl. School
24-50 FDR Drive
New York, NY 10010
Phone: +1(212)684-7400x3270

**Mailing to leaders in all
SIGGRAPH local groups:**
localgroupchairs@siggraph.org

**Mailing to members of the
Local Group Steering
Committee:**
lgsc@siggraph.org

**Email contact to get more
information about local groups:**
localgroupinfo@siggraph.org